PROBLEMS AND MATERIALS

PROFESSIONAL RESPONSIBILITY

ELEVENTH EDITION

by

THOMAS D. MORGAN
Oppenheim Professor of Law
The George Washington University

RONALD D. ROTUNDA
The Doy & Dee Henly Chair and
Distinguished Professor of Jurisprudence
Chapman University School of Law

JOHN S. DZIENKOWSKI
Dean John F. Sutton, Jr. Chair
The University of Texas

FOUNDATION PRESS
2011

THOMSON REUTERS

© 1976, 1981, 1984, 1987, 1991, 1995, 2000, 2003 FOUNDATION PRESS

© 2006, 2008 THOMSON REUTERS/FOUNDATION PRESS

© 2011 By THOMSON REUTERS/FOUNDATION PRESS

      1 New York Plaza, 34th Floor

      New York, NY 10004

      Phone Toll Free 1–877–888–1330

      Fax (646) 424–5201

      foundation–press.com

Printed in the United States of America

ISBN 978–1–59941–854–4

Mat #41030148

To Kathryn, Kyndra, and Karla

PREFACE

The three years since the publication of our 10th Edition have seen a transformation in the lives of many American lawyers and students. Over 5,000 lawyers have lost their jobs entirely, many of them partners who thought they had lifetime tenure. Law students who imagined they would enter a highly-compensated, busy profession, now frequently find their entry "deferred" until an often-unspecified future date.

Some of the changes in the realities of practice can be attributed to the current economic recession, but at least part of the transformation may be traced to fundamental changes in the demand for legal services and to alternative ways of providing legal assistance. This book will explore many such changes and examine whether some of the traditional rules regulating lawyer conduct may now lack the moral and practical justification they once had.

This Eleventh Edition tries to acknowledge the profession's changes without losing the qualities that have made the book successful. Problems are still followed by questions designed to provoke discussion. Questions are followed by case and opinion summaries designed to give examples of ways courts and rule makers have approached the issues raised.

As in earlier editions, fundamental questions are presented in black letter and each of those is followed by references relevant to the issues those questions raise. Each problem continues to group its questions under one of four issues, again to more clearly structure student preparation, discussion and understanding. We have not, however, reduced the rigor required to wrestle with the questions raised.

References to the ABA Model Rules of Professional Conduct are to the Model Rules, as amended through 2010. References to the ABA Model Code of Judicial Conduct are to the 2007 version. Restatement references are to the Restatement Third, The Law Governing Lawyers, published by the American Law Institute in 2000.

This edition's three authors thank the authors and publishers cited, in particular the American Bar Association and American Law Institute, for permission to reprint their copyrighted material. We also thank the many professors and practitioners who have offered thoughtful comments and suggestions on our materials. We listen to those comments and we hope you will find the Eleventh Edition an up-to-date and useful successor to its predecessors.

T.D.M.
R.D.R.
J.S.D.

Washington, DC
Orange, CA
Austin, TX

March 2011

SUMMARY OF CONTENTS

DETAILED TABLE OF CONTENTS

TABLE OF CASES

TABLE OF STATUTES

TABLE OF AUTHORITIES

References are to Pages.

PROBLEMS AND MATERIALS

PROFESSIONAL
RESPONSIBILITY

CHAPTER I

THE LEGAL PROFESSION: BACKGROUND AND FUNDAMENTAL ISSUES

A. INTRODUCTION

DOONESBURY   by Garry Trudeau

The Doonesbury humor is still biting after over 35 years, but in this case Garry Trudeau proved a poor prophet. The study of professional responsibility has proved to be more than "just another defunct fad." It has survived and prospered and seems likely to continue to do so. At least three reasons may account for the continuing interest.

First, the subject of the course in professional responsibility is the legal profession itself. Law students may use the substance of their torts course periodically, but they will use the substance of professional responsibility daily. This course is about lawyers as they engage in the practice of law. Whatever the theoretical interest of the subject matter, its practical content is extremely high.

Second, at the time Trudeau produced the Doonesbury cartoon, the ABA Model Code of Professional Responsibility was only five years old. Many people believed that the Code, the product of several years' work by a distinguished commission, had resolved all questions that were worth considering.

Almost as soon as significant numbers of people began to look seriously at the Code, however, they realized it had answered many questions badly

1

and left others unresolved altogether. The work of the ABA Commission on Evaluation of Professional Standards, commonly called the Kutak Commission after its chair, the late Robert J. Kutak, produced the ABA Model Rules of Professional Conduct in 1983 and demonstrated that there were many issues left to debate and discuss. The debate on the appropriate content of the standards, and the work of articulating them in enforceable rules, has continued to this day.

Third, while much of the work in professional responsibility has focused on the legal rules applicable to an attorney's behavior, it has become increasingly clear that the course in "legal ethics" offers an unusually good opportunity to apply the insights of history, sociology, economics, and philosophy to fundamental legal questions.

What such study reveals is that, far from being a unitary profession with a long and consistent tradition grounded in fundamental philosophical ideals, the legal profession is a rich, complex, and often perverse mixture of traditions, roles, and standards. Understanding the insights and distinctions suggested by history and philosophy will not automatically resolve practical problems, but it may help a lawyer better understand the questions presented and better see relationships between issues that otherwise might be obscured.

B. DEVELOPMENT OF THE AMERICAN LEGAL PROFESSION

The United States has about 1,200,000 persons trained as lawyers, of whom about 1,000,000 have law-related jobs.[1] That is over three times the number of lawyers practicing in 1970. Over 40,000 new lawyers are admitted to the bar each year from ABA-accredited schools, while some leave the practice annually due to death, retirement, or because they simply don't like the work.

Not everyone takes a sanguine view of the profession's growth. The rapid growth in the last quarter of the 20th century led Harvard President Derek Bok, for example, to assert:

> The net result of these trends is a massive diversion of exceptional talent into pursuits that often add little to the growth of the economy, the pursuit of culture, or the enhancement of the human spirit. I cannot press this point too strongly. * * * [T]he supply of exceptional people is limited. Yet far too many of these rare individuals are becoming lawyers at a time when the country

---

1. The actual number of lawyers in active practice is surprisingly hard to determine, but U.S. Census Bureau, Statistical Abstract of the United States 2010, Table 603, puts the number of lawyers at 1,014,000, while the American Bar Association says the number with active law licenses in 2008 was 1,180,386. One problem in getting an accurate count is the practical difficulty knowing how many licensed lawyers are still engaged in a law-related activity.

cries out for more talented business executives, more enlightened public servants, more inventive engineers, more able high-school principals and teachers.

* * * A nation's values and problems are mirrored in the ways in which it uses its ablest people. In Japan, a country only half our size, 30 percent more engineers graduate each year than in all the United States. But Japan boasts a total of less than 15,000 lawyers, while American universities graduate 35,000 *every year*. It would be hard to claim that these differences have no practical consequences. As the Japanese put it, "Engineers make the pie grow larger; lawyers only decide how to carve it up."[2]

QUESTIONS

1. Do you agree with President Bok's analysis? Apart from any given lawyer's economic interest in slowing the growth of the legal profession, can one objectively say that there are too many lawyers? What standard would you use to make such an assessment? For example, can you say that all persons with a need for a lawyer now get help at prices they can afford?

2. The average American lawyer earns a little over $125,000 per year.[3] Is such an income level characteristic of a profession that is overcrowded? Does the income data tend to answer President Bok's concerns, or does it tend to reinforce them?

Whatever one's answers to these questions, it is clear that the legal profession and the role of the lawyer in our society is significantly different today than at most times in the nation's history. The following two excerpts help put our present situation into context.

2. Derek Bok, "A Flawed System": Report to the [Harvard] Board of Overseers, 85 HARVARD Magazine 38, 41 (May–June 1983). Ironically, in recent years, 74 new law schools have opened in Japan and the allowed bar exam pass rate has been raised from 3% to 33%. There are still many fewer lawyers per capita in Japan than in the United States, but Japan now recognizes that lawyers have a lot to contribute in business dealings and the Japanese legal profession is starting to look more like that of the United States rather than the other way around. See, e.g., Ronald D. Rotunda, Teaching Professional Responsibility and Ethics, 51 St. Louis U. L.J. 1223, 1230–33 (2007).

3. Bureau of Labor Statistics, 2006 National Occupational Employment and Wage Estimates, http://www.bls.gov/oes/current/oes_nat.htm. This data, although technically accurate, may be misleading. The National Association for Legal Career Professionals (NALP) *Jobs & JDs 2009* report finds that, based on salaries for new lawyers, lawyer income have a bi-modal distribution, i.e., many lawyers earn far less than the median income while another large group earns substantially more.

Richard B. Morris,* The Legal Profession in America on the
Eve of the Revolution, in Harry W. Jones, Ed., Political
Separation and Legal Continuity

4–11, 18–19 (1976).**

If the Revolutionary era was a legal-and constitution-minded age
dominated by lawyers, the period of seventeenth-century settlement was
the miraculous era of law without lawyers, a time when law was shaped by
theologians, politicians, farmers, fishermen, and merchants. This general-
ization applies to all the colonies settled before the Stuart Restoration, but
it is conspicuously appropriate to the Puritan colonies wherein the clergy
played an exceptional role in lawmaking and where laymen universally
acted as judges. Not a single lawyer came to Plymouth on the *Mayflower*.
Massachusetts Bay, settled a decade later, did have some legally-trained
men among its first arrivals, but not one among them had then been
practicing law in England. The first educated attorney venturing to practice in that colony was Thomas Lechford, whose activities dating from 1637
or thereabouts, were limited, since he was disbarred shortly thereafter for
tampering with a jury. While lawyers were not technically prevented from
practice, Article XXVI of the Body of Liberties, the initial law code adopted
in 1641, while permitting attorneys to plead causes other than their own,
disallowed all fees or rewards, thus, for a time at least, withholding
inducements to practice as a respectable means of livelihood. Indeed, many
of John Cotton's fellow Puritans, both in England and in America at that
time, would have agreed with his characterization of lawyers as unconscionable advocates who "bolster out a bad case by quirks of writ and tricks
and quillets of law."

Early hostility to the profession of the law was by no means confined to
reformist New England. It was manifest as well in the tobacco colonies. A
Maryland act of 1674 recited the allegation that the "good people of this
Province are much burthened" by lawyers taking and exacting "excessive
fees." Curbs continued into the eighteenth century. In 1707, Maryland's
legislature set rules for controlling the admission of attorneys on the basis
of the alleged "corruption, ignorance and extortion" of several of them and
set such ceilings on fees that leading attorneys withdrew in protest from
practice for a short time. The limitation on fees continued in force as late
as 1729. In Virginia so deep-seated was anti-lawyer prejudice that a statute
of 1645 virtually disbarred paid attorneys. Its repeal a decade later failed to
end discrimination against the legal profession. In 1657 the court heavily
fined a lawyer for appearing in court on behalf of a client, and the situation
was not stabilized until 1680, when attorneys were permitted to practice
under rigid restrictions and after obtaining a license from the governor.
* * *

---

* At the time this article was written, the author was Gouverneur Morris Professor of History Emeritus at Columbia University.

Whether the low repute of the lawyers stemmed from their relatively obscure social origins in this early period, from their lack of professionalism, or from their tendency to regard law as a minor part of the multiple enterprises in which they were engaged, their early conduct failed to evoke good will. In short, courts dominated by laymen informed by a few basic lawbooks such as Dalton's *Country Justice*, as in the contemporary English county seats, and litigated by attorneys in fact, who were agents with powers of attorney (including among them numerous wives of absent litigants), provided the substance of justice without the benefit of a professional bar. * * *

* * * Somewhere between the Stuart Restoration and that systematic imperial machinery set up following the Glorious Revolution, one finds that the socio-economic structure of the colonies underwent a transformation. In the North a merchant-capitalist system was evolving based upon rapidly expanding transatlantic and intercolonial trade. In the South, a plantation economy emerged, based on the production for export of the great staples, tobacco and rice, and spawning a slave-holding and property-conscious society. That emergent business society was less egalitarian than at the time of settlement and determined to protect its interests against a variety of threats—whether from the constrictive trade laws of Parliament, from challenges to land titles, or from depreciating currencies. Everywhere the propertied class now exerted an influence toward security and stability, while the rapid expansion of business and the utilization of more sophisticated instruments in transatlantic trade necessitated a resort to the more technical legal system of the mother country.

Somewhere, then, around 1690 we find the legal profession establishing a foothold in the colonies. While the roster of trained legal specialists expanded dramatically over the next three decades, nonspecialists without professional training were descending on the courts in hordes. A host of parasitic pettifoggers, encouraged by the practice of filing writs by sheriffs and their deputies, easily outnumbered the trained members of the bar. Shoemakers, wigmakers, and masons procured deputations from the sheriffs and stirred up petty and contemptible litigation. It seems almost incredible that the colonial folk of the eighteenth century would manifest a litigious spirit even more intense than their forbears, but the theologian-statesman Cotton Mather was prompted in 1719 to found, in addition to a variety of organizations for effective lobbying and for suppressing vice, a Society of Peacemakers, which aimed to "divert Law-suits" and promote arbitration. If Mather achieved any success, it was not perceptible to the later generation of lawyers which claimed John Adams. Rather did Adams, whose own town attained such notoriety that "as litigious as Braintree" became proverbial, feel impelled to declaim against "the dirty dabblers in the law" who were taking bread out of the mouths of respectable lawyers.

Efforts to limit the legal profession to qualified attorneys mark the entire pre-Revolutionary era, along with enjoining sheriffs and their deputies from filing writs or giving legal advice. Even earlier, in the first few decades of the eighteenth century we find the legal profession asserting its claims to a monopoly over litigation. In New York a bar association has been unearthed as early as 1710, and one scholar insists that it functioned continuously thereafter, certainly in a rather formal sense by the year 1756. In Massachusetts an embryo bar association can be traced back at least to the year 1759. Even John Adams found its meeting "delightful." Aside from affording their members a chance for sociability, such associations, in effect guilds, were concerned about limiting the number of practitioners, restricting clerkships, barring the disqualified and, in later years, proposing legislative reforms.

To a rising and ambitious lawyer like Adams, the restrictive measures that had been taken by the bar of his province did not seem a sufficient deterrent, and he was led to bemoan the threatening number of his juniors seeking admission to practice. "They swarm and multiply," he complained with characteristic exaggeration. Still, the standards that were drawn up in Massachusetts were rather rigid. The Essex County bar in 1769 prescribed three years of clerking before admission to the inferior courts, another two years of practice in the lower courts before being admitted to the Superior Court as an attorney, and another two years more in practice before the Superior Court as a prerequisite to the status of barrister that they were desperately intent on establishing. Not only did they attempt to transplant those distinctions in the legal profession found in contemporary England, but in 1762 they further introduced the pageantry of the common law courts by requiring judges and lawyers to wear austere judicial gowns and wigs, a practice emulated in New York two years later.

In New York also, the lawyers raised the bars. An agreement entered into in 1756 by the "gentlemen of the Law" provided that they would cease taking any clerks for a period of fourteen years, the only exception being that each subscriber could take one of his own sons. Furthermore, at the end of that period, when clerkships were reopened, the lawyers stipulated that clerks must possess college degrees and that attorneys could take only one clerk at a time. The lawyer was to exact a £200 fee from his clerk, who would be required to serve for a minimum of five years. It was this monopolistic agreement which stood in the way of young John Jay's plans to study law. His father, a prosperous New York merchant, considered sending his son to London or Bristol to clerk in a law office there. He found out that in Bristol a five-year clerkship was required and the payment of a fee of from £200 to £300. If there was no alternative, Jay's father even thought of enrolling his son at the Inns of Court. Fortunately for Jay, in January of 1764 the members of the New York City bar relaxed their rules. Under the new agreement, an attorney could take a second clerk, but only after his first clerk had served for three years, thus insuring that no attorney would have more than two clerks at one time. Benjamin Kissam agreed to take John Jay on under these terms, but in fact Kissam had taken Lindley Murray as his clerk only a year before. Strictly speaking, Kissam should have waited until the end of 1764 before admitting another clerk to his office. Somehow these technicalities were waived; no one seems to have protested, and the first Chief Justice of the United States Supreme Court finally won his chance to climb the ladder of the legal profession.

———

Robert Stevens,* Democracy and the Legal Profession: Cautionary Notes

3 Learning and the Law 18 (No. 3, 1976).**

Law was not a profession [then] open to the masses, and during the 1780s and 1790s in most states an effort was made to keep it as narrow as possible. Each state except for Virginia—and that for peculiar reasons—retained a period of apprenticeship. This period was reduced if the young lawyer attended college, but there were still only half a dozen colleges in the new states. (For instance, Massachusetts had a five-year apprenticeship at that time, but only three years for Harvard or Yale graduates.)

* * * We still don't know what happened to lawyers [from 1820 to 1860] * * *. But what we can say, categorically, is that if the profession was heavily anglicized until 1820, after 1820 the old English notions of the professions slowly collapsed.

The differences between the American and English systems of legal training were made dramatically evident. In America, there was an obvious decline of formal structures; the bar associations had largely evaporated, as had the apprenticeship system. Legal education in the United States had fallen into a decline. The legal profession was "wide open." Such training as there was in law was almost invariably picked up on the job.

What does appear to have emerged from the impact of these forces is that, by the mid-nineteenth century, the lawyer had a different function in America from his counterpart in England. He became the man who greased the wheels of society—what today might be referred to, depending on one's perspective, as the "leading citizen," "hired gun," or "the multi-purpose social science decision maker." Whichever perspective you have, however, there is no question that the concept of the lawyer and the function he served in America after the Civil War bore little resemblance to his English counterparts.

What happened after 1870, both in the society as a whole and in the legal profession, was a process of institutionalization. It followed the years of Civil War, of rapid growth in population and of westward expansion. It was a time when great corporations were born, when great law firms grew and when universities came of age.

Significantly, the development of legal education—or, more accurately, of the resurgence of law schools—preceded that of the legal profession. Dwight at Columbia in the late 1860s, and Langdell, who became dean of

* At the time this article was written, the author was Provost at Tulane University.   ** Copyright © 1976 by the American Bar Association. Reprinted by permission.

Harvard Law School in 1870, were the two who set the pattern for the kind of legal education which we think of today.

What Langdell did was to take the erratic law training as it was being practiced in the law offices and systematize it. Building on the earlier work of Story at Harvard, he completed the process of taking law training out of the law offices and placed it firmly inside the universities. Academic law became respectable, as it never had been under the English system—or during the Jacksonian period. * * *

Langdell had a vision of academic respectability, and he was remarkably successful as a role model. Other universities began developing law schools, as did various private entrepreneurs. At the same time, under pressure from the ABA, states gradually reintroduced a period of apprenticeship.

Indeed, by 1900 most states had returned to the three-year apprenticeship requirement, and bar exams had begun to reappear in the 1890s. Yet legal education still remained voluntary. "The principle of supply and demand works" remarked the Englishman Bryce upon his visit to Harvard during this time. "No one is obliged to attend these courses to obtain admission and the [bar] examinations are generally too lax to require elaborate preparation. But the instruction is found so valuable, so helpful for professional success, that young men throng the lecture halls, willingly spending two or three years in the scientific study of law, which they might have spent in the chambers of a practicing lawyer."

Basically, anyone who wanted to be a lawyer could hang out his shingle, and there were very few requirements for doing so, except limited apprenticeship in some states. So the vast majority of lawyers at the turn of the century—80 to 90 percent—never saw the inside of a university, whether it was a law school or a college. Most of them had to take a bar exam, but, unlike the situation today, the market was the primary determinant of whether they would be successful.

Meanwhile, Harvard Law School continued to grow and to train the elite lawyers—at least those whose parents had money. In 1900 a young man went to Harvard Law School if he wanted to practice with one of the large Boston or New York firms. But in addition, there were a plethora of other law schools—part-time and full-time, one year, two year and three year—while apprenticeship remained the normal method of entry to the profession.

In the last 70 years, we have seen the apprenticeship method go the way of the dodo and formal, institutionalized legal education become compulsory.

What happened was not really the academic lawyer's fault. It was the American Bar Association's. I don't mean to say that the academic lawyer was entirely innocent in the implementation of this retrograde step, but it was the ABA which was the primary mover in making law school compulsory. It wanted to make law school compulsory because it wanted to contribute to "raising standards."

"Raising standards" is purposely vague. What it meant in this case undoubtedly included concern over the large number of illiterate and dishonest lawyers. A significant number of lawyers in 1900 had not finished high school and heretofore the ABA's effort to raise standards was in part a genuine effort to protect the public.

The developments, however, also represented an effort on the part of many practitioners to restrict numbers. The move was, to some extent, an anticompetitive device, and it was also undoubtedly—although I think that some recent studies overstate this—an effort to discriminate against certain groups. It was an effort to keep blacks and immigrant groups—especially Jews—out of the legal profession.

The first state to make law school compulsory was West Virginia which, in 1928, required one year of law school. It was not difficult to see where these pressures were coming from. West Virginia argued the need to inculcate "The Spirit of American Government." A New York delegate to the ABA put it more bluntly: "The need to have lawyers able to read, write and talk the English language—not Bohemian, not Gaelic, not Yiddish, but English." That was the beginning of compulsory legal education and prior college training in the United States—the debates of the House of Delegates in the 1930s and 1940s make it clear that the same sentiment motivated the ABA when it tried to drive out some law schools—and the depression provided a powerful stimulus to "raising standards."

Gradually, between 1929 and 1942 each state, partly for anticompetitive reasons and partly in a genuine effort to raise standards, followed the lead of West Virginia—and the suggestions of the American Bar Association. In 1920 there had still been a certain flexibility: many law schools only had two-year programs and only two or three law schools required an undergraduate degree. Increasingly, lawyers had gone to law school and most of the leading universities had law schools—but not because they were required to. At that time virtually every state allowed, as an alternative, three years of apprenticeship; and the majority of American lawyers had still not been to law school.

By 1950 attendance at law school was compulsory, and during the 1950s law school entrance requirements included two, and later three years of college. It was all part of the movement to "improve standards," although for reasons both good and bad. Moreover, in the post-Second World War years, the number of lawyers who had attended law school for the first time outran the number who had not.

The transition from compulsory apprenticeship to compulsory legal education was accomplished in three steps. First, law schools had become an alternative to apprenticeship; second, they had gradually driven out apprenticeship, and finally, they had become anxious to tighten standards and cut back on the number of accredited schools, thereby further limiting access to a legal education. * * *

The question of access to the legal profession, especially for minorities, is directly tied to the accreditation process. For example, when a new, small, low cost law school opens which has a sizable minority student population, is that school serving a minority group or exploiting it? The line between serving and exploiting is an extremely difficult one, but, in effect, there is always an inherent danger in a self-regulating profession to reproduce itself in the same colors and tones.

C. CHANGES IN THE BAR OVER THE PAST FORTY YEARS

Beginning in 2008, the job market for lawyers changed radically. Lawyers experienced a transformation of expectations and of the work many do. In spite of the seeming swiftness of the changes, however, they did not come all at once. They are the culmination of at least eight important trends over the last 40 years.

First, the legal profession was once self-regulating, i.e., lawyers wrote the rules by which they worked. Not surprisingly, they tended to write them in a way that favored themselves.[4] But that began to change in the mid–1970s. *Goldfarb v. Virginia State Bar*[5] saw the Supreme Court declare a bar association's minimum fee schedule to be a violation of the antitrust laws. *Bates v. State Bar of Arizona*[6] then held that even a state supreme court's prohibition of lawyer advertising violated the free speech guarantee of the U.S. Constitution. Even beyond the substance of those cases, the fact that external law governed lawyers unsettled the quiet life that self-regulation had created.

Second, growth in the number of lawyers over the last 40 years has increased competitive pressure on each of them. It is no wonder that the ability to attract clients has become a primary determinant of a lawyer's success. Indeed, today's law students are having a hard time finding jobs in large part because the nation's demand for new lawyers most closely tracks the rate of increase in the nation's gross domestic product.[7] Every time the economy slows but law schools keep producing the same number of new lawyers, we create a lawyer surplus that does not go away. In 2008–09, for example, law schools produced 4% more lawyers at a time when economic activity contracted almost 6%. In that single year, then, the nation created a large lawyer surplus, but the business model of most law schools makes cutting enrollments almost unthinkable.

Third, the impact of globalization has transformed the reality of many lawyers' practices. Instead of dealing with conflicting state laws, lawyers now can find themselves dealing with entirely different legal systems. Even a will drafter or family lawyer may have to protect the interests of children

---

4. See, e.g., Thomas D. Morgan, The Evolving Concept of Professional Responsibility, 90 Harvard L. Rev. 702 (1977).

5. 421 U.S. 773 (1975).

6. 433 U.S. 350 (1977).

7. See, e.g., Thomas D. Morgan, Economic Reality Facing Twenty–First Century Lawyers, 69 U. Washington L. Rev. 625 (1994); Thomas D. Morgan, Practicing Law in the Interests of Justice in the Twenty–First Century, 70 Fordham L. Rev. 1793 (2002).

in both Indiana and Ireland.[8] The legal complexity created by globalization has contributed to making it nearly impossible to be the kind of generalist we once thought a lawyer could be.

Fourth, the technology revolution of the last 40 years has transformed a lawyer's practice.[9] We are all aware of the changes in legal research and document discovery that e-developments have created. We also know technology has made lawyers' lives more hectic. But most importantly, information technology promises to transform lawyer work that used to be seen as complex, unique, and worthy of substantial fees into a series of commodities: simple, repetitive operations that will be sold to clients by the lowest bidder. Technology available on the simplest personal computer today can allow a lawyer to copy a 500-page document used in one transaction and change the names and terms for use in the next. The result will be a disaster if the document is not equally relevant to the new situation, so the malpractice risk created by easy copying can be enormous, but the benefits of standardizing forms in transactions promises to reduce what lawyers used to think of as creative work.

Likewise, and in some ways even more frustrating for lawyers, is the fact that much of the information lawyers have traditionally sold is now freely available on the Internet. Books about law have been around for years, but technology now makes the information ubiquitous. Free insights may be found in places ranging from Wikipedia to blogs, and the effect has been to make a great deal of formerly exotic legal information broadly accessible. Clearly, lawyers tend to be able to understand and apply such information more quickly and accurately than many clients can, but the breakthrough is that a lawyer's knowledge is no longer a black box that clients cannot penetrate. A client, whether a corporation or individual, can be expected to seek assistance from multiple sources ready to provide publicly-available information rather than buy assistance in a proprietary form created and sold by lawyers alone.

Fifth, and clearly related to the developments we have described, has been the growth of the size of organizations in which lawyers now practice. In 1960, fewer than 20 U.S. law firms employed more than 50 lawyers each, and even by 1968, only 20 firms in the country had over 100 lawyers.[10] Now, Baker & McKenzie and DLA Piper each has over 3,500 lawyers, and at least 20 firms have now crossed the 1,000–lawyer mark. Firms grow for what are often good reasons, but the all-purpose lawyer we remember in stories of Abraham Lincoln, Clarence Darrow, and Atticus Finch is disappearing—and not likely to be seen again.

Sixth, another key development of the last 40 years has been the transformation of what scholars call the "hemispheres" of the bar. Sociolo-

---

8. See, e.g., Laurel S. Terry, The Legal World is Flat: Globalization and Its Effect on Lawyers Practicing in Non–Global Law Firms, 28 Northwestern J. International Law & Business 527 (2008).

9. See, e.g., Richard Susskind, The End of Lawyers?: Rethinking the Nature of Legal Services (2008).

10. Robert L. Nelson, Partners With Power: The Social Transformation of the Large Law Firm 2 (1988).

gist Jerome Carlin reported that in New York in the 1960s, business lawyers made up 45 percent of the bar, while individual-oriented work such as personal injury, criminal, divorce, wills, and real estate made up the other 55 percent.[11] Lawyers tended to work on one side or the other of the individual/business divide, but it was "people" lawyers who represented the public face of the law. Just fifteen years later, Jack Heinz & Edward Laumann documented the individual/ business distinction in the Chicago bar and showed that the lawyers who populated each differed in terms of social class, where they went to law school, how much money they made, their status as leaders of the bar, and the like.[12] They concluded that by 1975, 53 percent of lawyers worked on business issues, while only 40 percent of lawyers still did work for individuals. After another two decades, in 1995, the authors concluded that the proportion of corporate lawyers had increased from 53 percent to 64 percent, while lawyers for individuals had fallen from 40 percent to 29 percent. In short, less than one-third of legal talent in this country now focuses on trying to meet the needs of individual clients.

Seventh, even the growth of law firms and the shift of law practice toward corporate work pale in significance by comparison to the rising power of in-house counsel. Forty years ago, and in many cases much more recently, lawyers in private firms saw their role as providing wise advice to lay officers or employees of corporate clients. That is less true today. The people most lawyers now have to please are other lawyers, this time acting in the role of general counsel to corporations, government agencies, and other organizations. It is the in-house lawyers—who number about 10 percent of all lawyers—that tend to decide what services the client requires and why.[13]

Recruiting in-house lawyers rather than depending exclusively on outside firms began as a way for companies to avoid high law firm billing rates. But a strong internal lawyer staff also helps assure that legal service decisions are made by people who understand the client's business, know the type of legal work that is required, and are able to help managers think about the non-legal issues inherent in important business decisions.

Private law firms are familiar with the practice of hiring contract lawyers, i.e., lawyers hired to do particular tasks when the firm is especially busy on a case or a regulatory filing but who the firm will not need in the long run. Today, private law firms can perhaps best be seen as inside counsel's version of contract lawyers. It hurts for lawyers in private firms to realize that their practice has come to that. The firm they spent their lives building has now become the functional equivalent of a temp agency. And it hurts even more when they are beaten out for commodity work on

11. Jerome E. Carlin, Lawyers' Ethics: A Survey of the New York City Bar (1966).

12. John P. Heinz & Edward O. Laumann, Chicago Lawyers: The Social Structure of the Bar, 319–20 (1982); John P. Heinz, Robert L. Nelson, Rebecca L. Sandefur & Edward O. Laumann, Urban Lawyers: The New Social Structure of the Bar (2005).

13. See, e.g., Robert L. Nelson & Laura Beth Nielsen, Cops, Counsel, and Entrepreneurs: Constructing the Role of Inside Counsel in Large Organizations, 34 Law & Soc. Rev. 457 (2000); Susan Hackett, Inside Out: An Examination of Demographic Trends in the In–House Profession, 44 Arizona L. Rev. 609 (2002).

which they used to train associates but that can be done less expensively by firms in India.

Eighth, the growing significance of corporate counsel managing legal needs and the world-wide availability of help with legal matters has produced a declining need to have an American law license before providing legal services. Later, you will learn about states prohibiting nonlawyers from practicing law, i.e., "unauthorized practice of law" prohibitions. One might think traditional prohibitions of this kind will protect American lawyers' from nonlawyer competition, but changes ranging from who regulates lawyers to the way clients get information are likely to undercut efforts to protect American lawyers against the fundamental transformation of what they do.

Law firms have long used paralegal and other support personnel nominally working under the lawyer supervision that ethical standards require. Now, corporations use non-lawyers to help deliver the total package of services they need done.[14] Negotiating contracts, troubleshooting discrimination claims, and even writing pleadings can all be done by non-lawyers within an organization receiving a level of lawyer supervision and training to which practice rules cannot effectively speak. Current legal ethics rules require a lawyer in a private law firm to supervise and take responsibility for the non-lawyer's work, but that requirement is easily met, and the non-lawyers are often accountants or lobbyists, economists or nurses, statisticians, or business specialists who are more than capable of acting on their own.

In today's world, American lawyers also find themselves in competition with legal service providers all over the globe who operate under different rules. As a result of the Legal Services Act of 2007, for example, British lawyers now can operate in firms with non-lawyers and the attorney-client privilege extends to communication with the non-lawyers. Australian lawyers are now permitted to practice in corporate entities that sell stock to the general public, and the European Union is considering similar changes in lawyer regulation. If American lawyers face direct competitors who play by different rules, they should not be surprised when clients seek the same or better services at lower cost elsewhere.[15]

D.   THE DEVELOPMENT OF STANDARDS OF PROFESSIONAL CONDUCT

For at least 150 years, American lawyers have tried to describe proper professional behavior. The earliest such standards were statements of moral principles that had no legal effect. Throughout most of the 19th century, such principles were developed and published by lawyers who were also teaching law.

---

14. See, e.g., Herbert M. Kritzer, The Future Role of "Law Workers": Rethinking the Forms of Legal Practice and the Scope of Legal Education, 44 Arizona L. Rev. 917 (2002).

15. See Thomas D. Morgan, The Vanishing American Lawyer 89–91 (2010).

In 1836, for example, Baltimore lawyer David Hoffman closed his two-volume *A Course of Legal Study* with "Fifty Resolutions" to which he urged lawyers to adhere. Those resolutions, in turn, became an important influence on the writing of George Sharswood, who published his *A Compend of Lectures on the Aims and Duties of the Profession of the Law* in Philadelphia in 1854.

Sharswood's standards are usually cited as the source of the Code of Ethics adopted by the State of Alabama in 1887. It was the Alabama Code that formed the basis for the American Bar Association's first statement of ethical principles, the Canons of Professional Ethics, published in 1908.

The ABA Canons remained the national professional model for over sixty years, although over that time its original thirty-two Canons were supplemented by fifteen others. You will find the ABA Canons in the Standards Supplement to this book. In many states, however, lawyers were subject to professional discipline for offenses not much more specific than "conduct unbecoming a lawyer."

Thus, in 1969, the ABA adopted its Model Code of Professional Responsibility. That Code, adopted almost universally by state supreme courts around the country, was a set of principles designed to be more specific and more amenable to disciplinary enforcement. The Code became "law" in the same sense that the Rules of Civil Procedure become law when a court adopts them.

The nine "Canons" in the Code were "axiomatic norms," i.e., general propositions serving as little more than chapter headings for the rest of the text. The "Disciplinary Rules" were "mandatory in character," that is, violations would subject the attorney to discipline up to and including disbarment. The Ethical Considerations, in contrast, were "aspirational in character" and were said to be an unenforceable but hopeful statement of the profession's consensus about proper lawyer behavior.

The decade of the 1970s ushered in a period of great ferment in the field of legal ethics. The Supreme Court handed down some important cases and there was vigorous debate about ethical propositions that to that point had been little challenged.

Thus, in 1983, the ABA adopted yet another version of its statement of professional standards. The 1983 ABA Model Rules of Professional Conduct were structured in a "Restatement" format. They had black-letter rules that were followed by explanatory "Comments."

In 2002 and 2003, and again in 2009, the ABA adopted revisions to the 1983 Model Rules of Professional Conduct, although it changed neither the basic format nor the name of the new document. All references to Rule or Comment numbers in these materials are to the ABA Model Rules, as amended.

ABA Model Rules, whenever issued, have only the status of proposed law. They are only a "model," and the ABA must lobby state and federal courts to enact these Rules as positive law. The ABA has been quite successful in its lobbying efforts, but one will find more nonuniform versions of the Model Rules than existed during the heyday of the Model Code. It is important to understand that none of the ABA documents is legally binding on anyone. That is, they are models that must be adopted or rejected by individual state supreme courts before they have any legal effect.

As of July 2010, forty-three jurisdictions had revised their rules to follow the 2002–03 amendments to the Model Rules in substantial part. Most others had formed committees to review the 2002–03 changes and most of the rest of the state supreme courts are likely to adopt many of the changes in due course.[16]

The current ABA Model Rules, the 1983 Model Rules, as amended, the 1970 ABA Model Code of Professional Responsibility, and even the 1908 ABA Canons of Ethics, are reprinted in the Standards Supplement to this book. In this text, we ask primarily how the Model Rules approach the ethical issues lawyers confront. Keep in mind, however, that the "code of ethics" that will be legally binding on you will be the one adopted by the supreme court of the state or states in which you are licensed.[17] It may or may not correspond exactly to the ABA model from which it is derived.[18]

At least four other sources of authority and advice will also be important to your analysis of legal ethics issues. First are court decisions, whether in cases seeking discipline of lawyers, cases seeking malpractice damages, disqualification, contempt proceedings, criminal cases, or the like.

Second, the ABA and state and local bar associations often issue ethics opinions. These are advisory opinions that respond to a specific question or an assumed state of facts. Although these opinions are not formally binding on any lawyer, they are influential with the courts, which often cite them as evidence of the law.

Third, in 2000, the American Law Institute (ALI) finished fourteen years of work on the Restatement Third, The Law Governing Lawyers.[19] Like other ALI Restatements, this one is not legally binding, but courts often cite it as reliably describing the law. The topics addressed in the Restatement go beyond subjects of lawyer discipline to cover issues such as

---

16. The ABA reports changes in state rules at http://www.abanet.org/cpr/pic/ethics_2000_status_chart.pdf. See also, Lucian T. Pera, Grading ABA leadership: State Adoption of the Revised ABA Model Rules of Professional Conduct, 30 Oklahoma City U.L. Rev. 637 (2005).

17. Lawyers licensed in more than one state are subject to discipline in each of them and may face problems of conflicting professional standards. Situations in which disclosure of information is required by some states but prohibited by others can prove particularly difficult. At least in principle, a state supreme court may impose discipline on lawyers it has licensed wherever the conduct

takes place. ABA Model Rule 8.5(b), discussed in Problem 2 *infra*, tries to establish a common choice of law rule with which to deal with this problem.

18. Appendices A, B, & C to the Model Rules in the Standards Supplement consist of charts that map out the important variations among state ethics rules that govern client confidences, lawyer screening, and when fee agreements must be in writing.

19. There is no Restatement, First or Second, of The Law Governing Lawyers. This Restatement is called "Third" because the American Law Institute is now drafting the third wave of Restatements on various subjects. Although we do not normally think of a

the attorney-client privilege, lawyer malpractice, liens to secure legal fees, and the like. These materials will often refer to the Restatement to articulate a particular legal rule, to explain the rationale for a principle of law set forth in the Model Rules, or to suggest the body of tort or agency law on which some provision of the Model Rules is based.[20]

Finally, federal agencies have begun to issue regulations that regulate the work of lawyers who appear before them. They have always had procedural rules, of course, governing practice before the agency, but early in 2003, for example, in response to a series of corporate scandals, the Securities and Exchange Commission issued important new regulations dictating how lawyers for publicly-held companies must respond to possible wrongdoing by or within those companies.[21]

E.   SOME CONTRIBUTIONS FROM MORAL PHILOSOPHY TO THE STUDY OF LEGAL ETHICS

Ethics is a traditional field for philosophers. The dilemma for any course such as this one is how to acknowledge philosophical traditions while recognizing that most questions of modern legal ethics are debated in more traditional legal terms. The most helpful approach seems to be to look at some distinctions that have been important in the philosophical tradition and that can also be useful to us.

1.   THE ETHICS OF DUTY VERSUS THE ETHICS OF ASPIRATION

The task of ethical analysis might be understood as one of (1) defining a minimum standard below which conduct may not fall, (2) establishing standards of ideal behavior toward which individuals should aim but cannot realistically expect to reach, or (3) giving "practical advice" that is somewhere in between. Professor Lon Fuller suggested a distinction between what he called the "morality of duty" and the "morality of aspiration."

Lon Fuller, The Morality of Law
5–6, 9–10 (Rev. Ed. 1969).

The morality of aspiration is most plainly exemplified in Greek philosophy. It is the morality of the Good Life, of excellence, of the fullest

---

"third" unless there is a "first" or "second," there are exceptions. Napoleon III was Emperor of France although there was never a Napoleon II who was Emperor.

20. The Model Rules and Restatement treatment of over two hundred topics are compared in Thomas D. Morgan, Lawyer Law: Comparing the ABA Model Rules of Professional Conduct with the ALI Restatement (Third) of the Law Governing Lawyers (2005).

21. For the SEC regulations, see 17 CFR Part 205, issued Jan. 29, 2003. The IRS has an Office of Professional Responsibility that regulates lawyers, accountants and others who practice in the tax field. E.g., Treasury Department Circular 230, 31 CFR Part 10 (Sept. 26, 2007). The United States Patent & Trademark Office also has ethics regulations that govern lawyers and others who are authorized to practice before it. E.g., 37 CFR Part 11 (Aug. 14, 2008).

realization of human powers. In a morality of aspiration there may be overtones of a notion approaching that of duty. But these overtones are usually muted, as they are in Plato and Aristotle. Those thinkers recognized, of course, that a man might fail to realize his fullest capabilities. As a citizen or as an official, he might be found wanting. But in such a case he was condemned for failure, not for being recreant to duty; for shortcoming, not for wrongdoing. Generally with the Greeks instead of ideas of right and wrong, of moral claim and moral duty, we have rather the conception of proper and fitting conduct, conduct such as beseems a human being functioning at his best.

Where the morality of aspiration starts at the top of human achievement, the morality of duty starts at the bottom. It lays down the basic rules without which an ordered society is impossible, or without which an ordered society directed toward certain specific goals must fail of its mark. It is the morality of the Old Testament and the Ten Commandments. It speaks in terms of "thou shalt not," and, less frequently, of "thou shalt." It does not condemn men for failing to embrace opportunities for the fullest realization of their powers. Instead, it condemns them for failing to respect the basic requirements of social living. * * *

As we consider the whole range of moral issues, we may conveniently imagine a kind of scale or yardstick which begins at the bottom with the most obvious demands of social living and extends upward to the highest reaches of human aspiration. Somewhere along this scale there is an invisible pointer that marks the dividing line where the pressure of duty leaves off and the challenge of excellence begins. The whole field of moral argument is dominated by a great undeclared war over the location of this pointer. There are those who struggle to push it upward; others work to pull it down. Those whom we regard as being unpleasantly—or at least, inconveniently—moralistic are forever trying to inch the pointer upward so as to expand the area of duty. Instead of inviting us to join them in realizing a pattern of life they consider worthy of human nature, they try to bludgeon us into a belief we are duty bound to embrace this pattern. All of us have probably been subjected to some variation of this technique at one time or another. Too long an exposure to it may leave in the victim a lifelong distaste for the whole notion of moral duty.

The ABA Model Code of Professional Responsibility was an explicit attempt to create propositions based on the morality of duty. Its Disciplinary Rules are exactly the kinds of minimum standards that can be enforced in disciplinary proceedings. The ABA Model Rules of Professional Conduct continue that approach. Contrast that with the following provision from the ABA Canons of Professional Ethics, which the Model Code replaced.

ABA Canons of Professional Ethics, Canon 32 (1908)
The Lawyer's Duty in Its Last Analysis

No client, corporate or individual, however powerful, nor any cause, civil or political, however important, is entitled to receive nor should any lawyer render any service or advice involving disloyalty to the law whose ministers we are, or disrespect of the judicial office, which we are bound to uphold, or corruption of any person or persons exercising a public office or private trust, or deception or betrayal of the public. When rendering any such improper service or advice, the lawyer invites and merits stern and just condemnation. Correspondingly, he advances the honor of his profession and the best interests of his client when he renders service or gives advice tending to impress upon the client and his undertaking exact compliance with the strictest principles of moral law. * * * But above all a lawyer will find his highest honor in a deserved reputation for fidelity to private trust and to public duty, as an honest man and as a patriotic and loyal citizen.[21]

QUESTIONS

1. Which approach to ethics seems more appropriate? Could a lawyer ever be prosecuted for violating most of former Canon 32? Does that mean that it was inappropriate to include it in a code of conduct for lawyers? Would lawyers' conduct likely be elevated more by ethical aspirations or by minimum standards?

2. Notice as you look at the ABA Model Code of Professional Responsibility that the Ethical Considerations (ECs) that it contains are nominally aspirational provisions of the sort described by Fuller. Do the ECs qualify as aspirational in any real sense? Could they be rewritten so as to assert principles that elevate a lawyer's thinking about behavior in particular situations?

3. The ABA Model Rules abandoned the use of separate Ethical Considerations. Does that make the Model Rules less aspirational than the Model Code? Could the current ABA and state bar concern about "professionalism" become a new shorthand for an effort to revive aspirational standards? Would restoring such standards be likely to improve lawyer behavior?

---

2. MORAL PEOPLE VERSUS MORAL ACTIONS

Is there a difference between what we want a lawyer to do and the kind of person we want a lawyer to be? Should the law demand only that a

---

21. The sexist language of Canon 32 is jarring to present-day ears, but the terms "he" and "his" did accurately describe the vast majority of members of the bar when Canon 32 was in force.

lawyer comply with applicable rules of professional conduct, or should it be concerned that a lawyer be a person who will seek to act morally in each of life's situations?

Many people assume that personal and professional standards are congruent. That is, if someone has good moral sense, his or her behavior will necessarily comply with professional standards. But professional ethics are not synonymous with moral conduct. It is not "immoral" for a lawyer to form a law partnership with a non-lawyer, for example, but it would violate current professional standards in almost every jurisdiction.

Confusing concepts of personal character and professional conduct has even caused some to assert that legal ethics cannot be taught. If one assumed—and if the assumption were correct—that a law student has largely formed his or her moral character before coming to school, the question would naturally be whether there is anything left to teach in a course such as this one. To the extent one sees differences between personal ethics and professional standards, however, and to the extent that personal moral development continues to occur all through life, there is a lot left to examine in a professional responsibility course.

Furthermore, if the definition of an ethical lawyer consists only of a capacity to follow rules, one might understandably worry about the future of the profession. Real life ethical problems rarely come up in forms that are easily resolvable by simple norms.

Indeed, most important moral choices require a person to make important judgments when no one else is looking. Thus, there must inevitably be a concern for the quality of a lawyer's moral decision making in the countless situations when a lawyer is unlikely to get caught. The source of good decisions in those settings is what we usually call a person's "character."

Psychologist Lawrence Kohlberg is usually credited with identifying six stages of moral development.[22] Adherence to rules such as those imposed on lawyers by state supreme courts is only Kohlberg's first stage and represents no more than the moral development achieved by a small child who knows wrongdoing is associated with punishment.

In the second stage of moral growth, a person basically says "I will be good to you if you are good to me," while in the third stage a person conforms behavior to something he thinks others will approve. Neither is the morality of aspiration, but both forms of moral thought are certainly familiar to lawyers.

Stages four and five of Kohlberg's moral development require conforming acts to what is required by the social order and the social contract respectively. Stage four requires respect for authority, and would be seen in legal ethics as respect for courts and other legal institutions. Stage five

---

22. See, e.g., Lawrence Kohlberg, The Philosophy of Moral Development: Moral Stages and the Idea of Justice 17–19 (1981).

recognizes greater possibilities of change in the social order and is what Kohlberg identifies as the "official" morality of democracy.

Finally, in the sixth and highest stage of moral development, a person looks to "universal ethical principles." These principles ultimately must be self-chosen, but they must appeal to "logical comprehensiveness, universality, and consistency."

In Kohlberg's view, a mature person—certainly a mature lawyer—should be engaged in a lifelong effort to identify and conform behavior to universal ethical principles. As is true when dealing with any field of substantive law, of course, lawyers must also conform their behavior to rules applicable to their conduct. Problems such as the ones in this book should help you analyze how lawyers should decide what constitutes appropriate behavior in concrete and problematic situations. Ideally, you and other lawyers can conform your conduct *both* to law and to "universal ethical principles."

———

3.   ROLE ETHICS VERSUS COMMON ETHICAL STANDARDS

Can a good person be a good lawyer? Can a good lawyer be a good person? Is behavior that would be morally unacceptable for persons in general permitted or even required of persons who have assumed the mantle of attorney? The nature of the debate on these issues is suggested in the following contrasting excerpts:

Richard Wasserstrom, Lawyers as Professionals: Some Moral Issues
5 Human Rights 1 (1975).

[O]ne central feature of the professions in general and of law in particular is that there is a special, complicated relationship between the professional, and the client or patient. For each of the parties in this relationship, but especially for the professional, the behavior that is involved is to a very significant degree, what I call, role-differentiated behavior. And this is significant because it is the nature of role-differentiated behavior that it often makes it both appropriate and desirable for the person in a particular role to put to one side considerations of various sorts—and especially various moral considerations—that would otherwise be relevant if not decisive. Some illustrations will help to make clear what I mean * * *.

Being a parent is, in probably every human culture, to be involved in role-differentiated behavior. In our own culture, and once again in most, if not all, human cultures, as a parent one is entitled, if not obligated, to prefer the interests of one's own children over those of children generally. * * * In short, the role-differentiated character of the situation alters the relevant moral point of view enormously.

A similar situation is presented by the case of the scientist. For a number of years there has been debate and controversy within the scientific community over the question of whether scientists should participate in the development and elaboration of atomic theory, especially as those theoretical advances could then be translated into development of atomic weapons that would become a part of the arsenal of existing nation states. The dominant view, although it was not the unanimous one, in the scientific community was that the role of the scientist was to expand the limits of human knowledge. Atomic power was a force which had previously not been utilizable by human beings. The job of the scientist was, among other things, to develop ways and means by which that could now be done. And it was simply no part of one's role as a scientist to forego inquiry, or divert one's scientific explorations because of the fact that the fruits of the investigation could be or would be put to improper, immoral, or even catastrophic uses. The moral issues concerning whether and when to develop and use nuclear weapons were to be decided by others; by citizens and statesmen; they were not the concern of the scientist *qua* scientist. * * *

All of this is significant just because to be a professional is to be enmeshed in role-differentiated behavior of precisely this sort. One's role as a doctor, psychiatrist, or lawyer, alters one's moral universe in a fashion analogous to that described above. Of special significance here is the fact that the professional *qua* professional has a client or patient whose interests must be represented, attended to, or looked after by the professional. And that means that the role of the professional (like that of the parent) is to prefer in a variety of ways the interests of the client or patient over those of individuals generally.

Gerald Postema, Moral Responsibility in Professional Ethics
55 N.Y.U. L. Rev. 63 (1980).

Maintaining a hermetically sealed professional personality promises to minimize internal conflicts, to shift responsibility for professional "knavery" to broader institutional shoulders, and to enable a person to act consistently within each role he assumes. But for this strategy to succeed, the underlying values and concerns of important professional roles, and the characteristic activities they require, must themselves be easily segregated and compartmentalized. However, since there is good reason to doubt they can be easily segregated, [this] strategy risks a dangerous simplification of moral reality. Furthermore, in compartmentalizing moral responses one blocks the cross-fertilization of moral experience necessary for personal and professional growth. * * * I contend that a sense of responsibility and sound practical judgment depend not only on the quality of one's professional training, but also on one's ability to draw on the resources of a broader moral experience. This, in turn, requires that one seek to achieve a fully integrated moral personality. Because this is not possible under the present conception of the lawyer's role, as exemplified by the Code of Professional Responsibility, that conception must be abandoned, to be replaced by a conception that better allows the lawyer to bring his full moral sensibilities to play in his professional role.

QUESTIONS

1. Are you convinced that a scientist has no moral responsibility for the uses made of his or her discoveries? Why? Can scientist *A* rest comfortably knowing that if she had not learned how to make nuclear weapons someone else would have? Can lawyer *A* make a comparable argument about the work she does?

2. Is Professor Postema correct that role ethics contemplates a "hermetically sealed professional personality"? On the other hand, does Professor Wasserstrom deal with the tough issue of how far from ordinary norms role identity might allow one to stray?

3. In his provocative book, The Practice of Justice: A Theory of Lawyers' Ethics (1998), Professor William Simon argues that much of the anxiety that lawyers experience arises from the fact they are required to do what they know are morally questionable acts (e.g., not revealing information that could help others avoid harm) in order to serve an arguably larger good (e.g., encouraging people to tell their lawyers the truth and get good legal advice). Does that explanation ring true to you?

4. Would you also agree with Professor Simon that an even greater problem for thoughtful lawyers arises when they start to question whether the theoretical long-term future good is in fact worth the significant, concrete, immediate price that must be paid to achieve it?

---

4. CONSEQUENTIAL VERSUS DEONTOLOGICAL STANDARDS

In thinking about universal principles, philosophers sometimes ask whether the ethical analysis is based on achieving a good result (consequentialism) or whether the analysis focuses on absolute values (deontological).

The consequential approach is best illustrated for most lawyers by utilitarianism. The utilitarian asks how particular conduct affects people's happiness and well-being. If more total well-being will be generated by one course of conduct than another, then that course of conduct is morally preferable.

Utilitarianism is not a clearly sound approach; a policy that harmed all African–Americans but benefitted all other racial groups in the United States might be preferred by a utilitarian, for example, because African–Americans constitute a minority of U.S. citizens. Yet lawyers act as utilitarians most of the time in evaluating legal rules. In most substantive fields of law, we ask how a rule seems to "work" and whether people are "better off" as a result of one rule than they would be under some other rule.

Utilitarianism can be divided into two categories—act utilitarianism and rule utilitarianism. The first asks which behavior will lead to more happiness or well being in a particular situation. The second takes the view that there is value in establishing appropriate standards of behavior for particular classes of cases. Thus, one would not ask how best to produce maximum welfare in a unique case, but what principle or course of conduct is most appropriate for a class of similar cases.

Deontological approaches, on the other hand, tend to be based on a set of first principles, such as "responsibility" or "equal rights." Where the first principles come from and how they are justified present problems for deontological theories, but for many people the truths either are revealed by religious faith or are obvious. A deontological approach subordinates goals such as maximizing happiness or welfare to such first principles.

Deontological approaches can also be subdivided into two categories. The first is based on "duty" and says that there are particular general principles of moral responsibility that can be derived logically and applied universally. "Do unto others as you would have others do unto you" might be an example. A moral person acting from this perspective would say that behavior is right or wrong, without regard to particular effects produced by the behavior in a given situation. A person who says it is God's will that he or she behave in a given manner would not be impressed by the argument that the consequence of that behavior in a given case would not serve the utilitarian goal of maximizing happiness in the society.

Another important deontological approach is based on "rights," a term with which lawyers are often more comfortable. This approach would assert, for example, that individuals have certain human rights that lawyers should help preserve and protect. This position sees particular behavior of lawyers as appropriate without regard to what the effect would be on the general happiness or well-being of the rest of society produced by asserting the rights.

Can you comfortably fit your own approach to ethical decision making into one of these general categories? Do you sometimes subordinate your selection of a basis for making ethical decision to your preference for a preconceived outcome?

———

5.   The Ethic of Care

An important alternative line of argument suggests that both adhering to standards of conduct such as those prescribed by the courts and seeking to identify universal moral principles to govern one's behavior may actually reduce the moral quality of a lawyer's actions. Drawing particularly on the insights of feminist writers such as Carol Gilligan,[23] this view stresses enhancing the quality of the *relationship* between the lawyer and "all those affected by a given situation," not on analyzing the inherent propriety of particular conduct of the lawyer.[24]

At a minimum, this represents an important change of perspective on legal ethics and suggests, for example, that neutrality and objectivity are simply not possible for lawyers and clients. Even objectively accurate trial testimony may be impossible because witnesses come from different backgrounds and social settings and express themselves in ways different from those in which lawyers and judges often seek to pigeonhole their answers.

Ultimately, this view holds that the governing ethical concept should be the positive personal relationship the lawyer and client have. There will always be conflicts of interest between lawyers and clients; the task must be to manage them in ways that seem to work for both. Clients are often unsure of what they want and lawyers are often unsure what is possible; thus, one cannot always say that either lawyer or client should "control" the relationship. Issues can be best evaluated by a pragmatic assessment of the concrete contexts out of which they arise.

The basic focus of the ethic of care is on the lawyer's acting as a healer who takes a comprehensive view of her situation and seeks to make everyone—not necessarily just her client—better off. That makes it an attractive alternative for many to the rhetoric of individual rights that pervades so much of legal analysis.

Ask yourself, however, whether such an approach will always be helpful to a lawyer faced with tough issues affecting the interests of many people. Might one need some universal principles—perhaps even some rules—to know what values and interests should best be recognized and advanced? Without such principles, might a lawyer revert to unexamined prejudices or even to the lawyer's own self—interest in formulating approaches to difficult situations?

———

6. PERSONAL VERSUS SOCIAL ETHICS

Up to now, we have largely assumed that ethical issues are limited to choices about personal loyalties and integrity. In a larger sense, however, one should include a sense of the lawyer as a political and social actor within the realm of legal ethics.

It surely is appropriate, for example, to think of Thurgood Marshall's choices of how to invest his professional time and talent as "ethical"

---

23. The key book is Carol Gilligan, In a Different Voice: Psychological Theory and Women's Development (1982). Gilligan criticized Kohlberg, for example, because he primarily used male subjects in his empirical work.

24. Among the best descriptions of this approach is Stephen Ellmann, The Ethic of Care as an Ethic for Lawyers, 81 Georgetown L.J. 2665 (1993).

decisions. Every day, thousands of lawyers make similar ethical choices—for good or ill—about how they try to influence the ways in which legal authority is brought to bear on the allocation of power within society and on political choices the society makes.

Keep these issues in mind as you explore the technical issues of legal ethics. Do ethical rules adequately address who is likely to require legal assistance, obtain it, or both? Are some persons or interests—perhaps those of the poor or powerless—more deserving of legal assistance than others? Should lawyers be compelled to represent persons or interests that would otherwise go unrepresented?

---

7.   The Matter of Professionalism

In 1986, the ABA appointed a "Commission on Professionalism." Its report called for the profession's return to a common set of institutional values based on Roscoe Pound's definition of a profession as "a common calling in the spirit of a public service—no less a public service because it may incidentally be a means of livelihood."[25]

George Bernard Shaw was less glowing in his view of professions, describing them as "conspiracies against the laity."[26] There is some truth to Shaw's cynicism, but just as one can be too naive about professionalism, one can be too dismissive as well. "There is much more to it than rules of ethics. There is a whole atmosphere of life's behavior."[27] And this atmosphere exists whether or not the constable is watching.

In the Middle Ages, it was said that there were four professions: the military, who professed peace; the medical doctors, who professed health; the clergy, who professed God; and lawyers, who professed justice.[28] A risk of labeling the practice of law or other occupations as a "profession" is that this label is then used to justify restraints of trade that would otherwise not be accepted.[29] The most fruitful use of the term "professional" today probably would describe individuals, not groups. Some lawyers act like

---

25. Roscoe Pound, The Lawyer from Antiquity to Modern Times 5 (1953).

26. George Bernard Shaw, Preface to The Doctor's Dilemma 9 (1911), reprinted in, 1 Bernard Shaw, Complete Plays with Prefaces (1962). Shaw made clear that his complaint that the medical profession is "a conspiracy to hide its own shortcomings," is true "of all professions." *Id.* He also complained:

> "The only evidence that can decide a case of malpractice is expert evidence: that is, the evidence of other doctors; and every doctor will allow a colleague to decimate a whole countryside sooner than violate the bond of professional etiquet[te] by giving him away."

Id. at 8.

27. John H. Wigmore, Introduction xxiv, in, Orrin N. Carter, Ethics of the Legal Profession (1915).

28. Roscoe Pound included in the category of "professions," the "callings"—a word that he used—of ministry, medicine, law, and teaching. Roscoe Pound, The Lawyer from Antiquity to Modern Times 5 (1953).

29. See Thomas D. Morgan, The Vanishing American Lawyer (2010); Deborah L. Rhode, Why the ABA Bothers: A Functional Perspective on Professional Codes, 59 Texas L. Rev. 689 (1981); Ted Schneyer, Professionalism as Bar Politics: The Making of the Model Rules of Professional Conduct, 14 Law & Social Inquiry 677 (1989).

professionals, and some do not.[30] But even as applied to individuals, the term has an uncertain meaning.

Society places a dual role on lawyers. Citizens want lawyers to be understanding and socially responsible, but the same people freely admit that, when they have a problem, they want a lawyer who will play hardball.[31] Psychologists are not surprised that these contradictory expectations lead lawyers to be confused and depressed. As one New York Gestalt psychologist explains: "Nobody ever says they want a nice lawyer. They say, 'I want a barracuda. I want a real throat-slitter.' So lawyers have these qualities dumped on them."[32] Lawyers, in short, take on society's distaste for what society's members ask lawyers to do.

While lawyers wax eloquently about professionalism, the general public is not so sure.[33] Artists often capture the public mood. A print in London is titled, *The Law Suit*. In the center is a cow, representing the law suit. On the right is the plaintiff, pulling the cow's head. On the left is the defendant, tugging at the tail. And in the center? In the center is the barrister, milking the law suit for all that it is worth.

Poets as well as artists have their fingers on the public pulse. Carl Sandburg has this to say about lawyers:

> When the lawyers are through
> What is there left, Bob?
> Can a mouse nibble at it
> And find enough to fasten a tooth in?
>
> Why is there always a secret singing
> When a lawyer cashes in?
> Why does a hearse horse snicker
> Hauling a lawyer away?[34]

Sandburg's perception of lawyers is hardly new. Nowadays, ethnic jokes are no longer politically correct, but jokes about lawyers are always in good taste. Needless to say, the jokes are hardly flattering, and they reflect the view of lawyers in the popular culture.[35]

30. ABA Working Group on Civil Justice, Blueprint for Improving the Civil Justice System 12 (ABA 1992):

"Professionalism lies not so much in following certain rules as in the development of personal attitudes and a manner of deportment that leads to appropriate professional relationships and courtesy in manner and creed."

31. William A. Brewer III & John W. Bickel II, Etiquette of the Advocate?, Texas Lawyer, March 21, 1994, at 20, 21 col. 4; James Podgers, Public: "Shyster" OK—If He's on Your Side, 67 A.B.A. J. 695 (1981).

32. Amy Stevens, Why Lawyers Are Depressed, Anxious, Bored Insomniacs, Wall Street J., June 12, 1995, at B1, col. 3 & B6, col. 5 (Midwest ed.).

33. Ronald D. Rotunda, The Legal Profession and the Public Image of Lawyers, 23 Journal of the Legal Profession 51 (1999).

34. Karl Llewellyn, The Bramble Bush: Of Our Law and Its Study 142 (1960), quoting Carl Sandburg, The Lawyers Know Too Much (1951).

35. *E.g.*—Two people searching for grave rubbings were walking in the famous cemetery in the crowded Wall Street area. One noticed a tombstone that read: "Here lies a lawyer and an honest man." He said to his companion, "This cemetery must really be crowded; they're burying them two to a

It is hardly surprising that lawyers would like to be more well-liked. So would mechanics, tax collectors, undertakers, medical doctors, policemen, politicians, cheerleaders, movie stars, grandparents, and just about everyone else. However, lawyers may never be widely loved as long as we are really doing our jobs. Proponents of professionalism sometimes say that lawyers should be less aggressive, nicer to their opponents, and compromise more, but deep in their hearts they also know that if Rosa Parks objects to a law forcing her to sit at the back of the bus, the last thing she needs is a lawyer who will only find her a seat in the middle of the bus.[36]

There is reason for hope. Empirical studies have also shown that people who use lawyers, whether in this country[37] or abroad,[38] have a higher opinion of them than people who have never used them. Familiarity can breed respect.

Several years ago, Justice Harry Blackmun said that if he had his life to live over again, he would like to be a medical doctor. At the time he was a U.S. Supreme Court Justice. One would think that he was at the pinnacle of his career. Why would anyone want to trade that to become a doctor. One person who heard this story suggested, "People often want to be doctors so that they can help people."[39]

But lawyers help people too. Granted, unlike engineers, we construct no bridges. Unlike doctors, we mend no bones. Unlike architects we design no buildings. Unlike artists, we paint no portraits. There is little that we do that the human hand can touch. But—if we are doing our jobs properly—we take on other people's burdens, we relieve stress, and we pursue justice. We enable mankind to live a more peaceful and just life. We take the veneer of civilization and we make it a little thicker.[40]

---

grave." Or, there was the lawyer who was questioned about part of his bill. "What is this $75 charge for?" asked the client. The lawyer replied: "That's when I was walking downtown, saw you on the other side of the street, crossed over to say hello, and found out that it wasn't you."

36. Because lawyers have been instrumental in securing civil liberties for racial minorities, it should be no surprise that in some polls, African–Americans view lawyers more favorably than do whites; 51% of African–Americans say that their overall impression of lawyers is "good," but only 26% of whites come to that conclusion. Randall Samborn, Anti–Lawyer Attitude Up, But NLJ/West Poll Also Shows More People Are Using Attorneys, National Law Journal, Aug. 9, 1993, at 1, col. 1.

37. Barbara Curran, The Legal Needs of the Public: The Final Report of a National Survey 238, *passim* (American Bar Foundation, Chicago, 1977) (surveys showing that people who have used lawyers are more posi-

tive about them than people who have not used lawyers).

38. Sue Farron, Margaret Llewelyn & Kath Middleton, Public Perception of the Legal Profession: Attitudinal Surveys as a Basis for Change, 20 J. Legal Profession 79, 87 (1995–96): ". . . those who have no experience of legal services have a poor perception of them." But, when the "measure of satisfaction was measured for users, the [satisfaction] scores increased."

39. We should not be surprised that medical doctors rate more highly in the public opinion polls than lawyers do, because doctors only "represent" the patient. There is no doctor fighting zealously for the disease. Our legal system gives everyone her day in court, and some litigants are viewed less favorably than ugly diseases. Lawyers are the messengers who are blamed for the bad message.

40. *Cf.* Martin Mayer, The Lawyers 3 (1967).

As you work your way through these materials, ask yourself whether law is still a profession with common core values. Is it united by any more than a set of regulatory provisions? If there are still core values, what do they include? Is the "spirit of a public service" among the values? If not, should the lack of that or other core values be a cause for concern?

F. A WORD ON THE ORGANIZATION OF THIS BOOK

This book is organized as a series of problems. Most are adapted from actual cases collected from ethics opinions, disciplinary proceedings, news articles, and the authors' professional experiences. Of course, all names are hypothetical and facts have been altered to protect the persons involved or to make a question more interesting. Yet most of these problems were faced by real people. They should suggest that an attorney in a concrete situation must sometimes act when no course is wholly satisfactory.

They should also suggest that some situations may present professional dilemmas that are not at first apparent. Professor of psychiatry and law Andrew Watson properly accused law schools of developing analytic barriers to students' reliance on their personal moral reactions to situations.[41] But you will see that lawyers can be disciplined for conduct that may trigger little righteous indignation; developing *sensitivity* to ethical ambiguity is an important objective of these materials.

Each of the problems presented here is designed to require you to think. Initially, many may seem to set you adrift on a sea of ambiguity. To help you stay afloat, each problem begins with an introduction that puts it in context. After presentation of the facts of each problem, the remaining materials present four main topics in legal ethics that the problem raises. Each topic asks a series of black-letter questions that are intended to provide the structure for a logically-ordered discussion. The cases, ethics opinions, and other questions that follow each black-letter question are designed to help you answer the questions and to help you see why some of those questions have puzzled so many lawyers for so long.

As you read the problems in this book, consider questions such as the following:

1. Is the conduct in question a violation of one or more standards of the ABA Model Rules? What should be the penalty, if any, for the misconduct?

2. Is the conduct properly subject to criticism even if not inconsistent with the Model Rules? By what standard do you judge the moral character of the conduct?

3. Should the lawyer have taken particular action even though the failure to take action would not subject the lawyer to discipline?

---

41. Andrew Watson, The Watergate Lawyer Syndrome: An Educational Deficien- cy Disease, 26 J. Legal Ed. 441, 442 (1974).

4.   How could the lawyer have served the client well and still have been professionally responsible?

Another useful way to approach these problems is to recognize that in an important sense, any rules of professional conduct attempt to accommodate at least five interests. The interests are those of (1) the lawyers as individuals, (2) lawyers in their relationships with each other, (3) the lawyers' clients, (4) non-clients with whom the lawyers deal, and (5) institutions of the legal system through which the lawyers work. Look for these interests as they appear and conflict in particular problems. Should the client's interest always be preferred above all others? Do the Model Rules ever give a lawyer's personal interest ethical precedence over legitimate public concerns?

In addition to this book, there is a separate supplement of Selected Standards on Professional Responsibility that is updated annually. That Supplement includes not only the ABA Model Rules of Professional Conduct and its predecessors, but the ABA Model Code of Judicial Conduct (which has also been adopted by many state supreme courts), and other statutes and guides to professional conduct that have proved influential in determining the legal profession's standards. You should begin an analysis of each problem by looking at the ABA Model Rules, but do not assume that they are the only sources of relevant authority.

Finally, be on your guard against two simplistic approaches that initially may be tempting when you read these problems.

First, it will usually not be enough to say, "I would tell the client to get another lawyer." That may, of course, be a part of the answer in some cases, but it is easier for a law student to turn down a hypothetical client than for a practicing lawyer to insult someone who may be a longtime client and a good friend. Save classroom "resignations" for situations in which you believe you would have the courage and necessity to do so in practice. Do not use withdrawal as a substitute for addressing tough questions.

Second, do more than simply decide that you will always stay "well within" ethical boundaries; in some situations the territory between two ethical frontiers may be very narrow. Ethical Consideration 7–1 of the ABA Model Code of Professional Responsibility, for example, said that one of the prime professional obligations of a lawyer was to "represent [a] client *zealously* within the bounds of the law, which includes Disciplinary Rules and enforceable professional regulations." The lawyer cannot always merely decide to forego a certain tactic. The lawyer must serve his or her client *well* and still be professionally responsible.

After you have completed this course you should be in a better position to evaluate the comments expressed at the outset of this Chapter by the Doonesbury characters. Is a course in professional responsibility a naive attempt to teach "right and wrong" to adults with fixed moral views? More cynically, is it only "trendy lip service to our better selves"? Or, do you find that the study of professional responsibility is based on a recognition that (1) ethical issues are as important to a lawyer as any other aspect of his or her professional life; (2) like any other area of law, the law of professional responsibility may be learned; and (3) legal ethics questions present analytic problems as challenging and difficult as any a law student or lawyer will face?

CHAPTER II

REGULATION OF THE LEGAL PROFESSION

As we saw in Chapter I, both entry into the legal profession and the conduct of lawyers once admitted are regulated by the highest court of each state. Most state supreme courts hold that they have *exclusive* power to govern the legal profession, although a few have ceded limited authority over lawyers to their state legislatures.

To exercise their authority, the courts have established admission and disciplinary offices that are often operated as government agencies only loosely related to voluntary bar associations. Some jurisdictions, however, require that lawyers join an official bar organization that is then called an "integrated" or "unified" bar. The responsibilities of such an official bar association may include a role in bar admission and enforcement of conduct standards. Even in states that have no official bar association, courts often turn to lawyers to staff parts of the disciplinary system. Regardless of the system a state uses, courts often fund the disciplinary system by taxing lawyers in the form of mandatory dues and fees.*

State supreme courts regulate the right to practice law even if the lawyer is solely an office counselor and never appears in court. Federal courts separately regulate admission to practice before them, but a lawyer need not be admitted to a federal court unless he or she will be litigating there. Federal courts usually defer to state admission standards, and admission before a federal court is often close to automatic, although lately, some federal courts have been interested in asserting a more active role.

In the problems that follow, consider questions such as:

a. Why do courts regulate admission to the bar and the professional behavior of attorneys? Should they be concerned about specific conduct, discerning a lawyer's moral character, or both?

b. What should be the relative roles of the courts, both state and federal, legislatures, bar associations, individual lawyers, and even lay persons in these processes?

---

* Lathrop v. Donohue, 367 U.S. 820 (1961), with no majority opinion, upheld mandatory bar membership against an attack based on freedom of association. Keller v. State Bar of California, 496 U.S. 1 (1990) considered the uses to which mandatory dues may properly be applied. The Court held that mandatory dues may only be used to finance activities of common benefit to bar members as to which there would be a risk of "free riders" if all lawyers were not required to share the burden. Such activities include recommending bar admission standards, conducting bar discipline, and recommending changes in bar codes of conduct, but they may not include taking positions on broader public questions.

c. What is the range of sanctions that lawyers face for a violation of professional standards? Are public sanctions such as disbarment necessarily of more concern to lawyers than private sanctions such as malpractice liability?

PROBLEM 1

ADMISSION TO THE BAR

Your first "case" as a law graduate will be your application for admission to the bar. In effect, it will be filed as an original action before your state's supreme court. The remedy you seek will be an order placing you on the roll of attorneys licensed to appear before that supreme court and all the state's inferior courts. Typically, the state supreme court will delegate to bar examiners the task of reviewing the applications, the character and fitness reports, and the examination results. The examiners will then submit a list of approved candidates to the court for ratification. Your approval will get you a license that will allow you to give legal advice and engage in whatever other acts the state defines as the practice of law. This problem examines what you will be required to demonstrate to the state supreme court to justify the grant of that license. In particular, it considers the "character and fitness" requirement and your duty of candor in representations that you make in seeking bar admission. Finally, it looks at the education and knowledge required for bar admission and some other standards state and federal courts have imposed on candidates for their bar.

FACTS

You have been in practice for a few years in the city where you went to law school. Gerry Smith, a third year law student, has come to you for help. "I have been accused of cheating on the final exam in my advanced tax class," he tells you. "I did it. I did not have time to study, and I wanted to get a good grade. The exam proctor will testify that he thought he saw me cheat, but I have denied everything. I'm afraid of what this could do to my chances of being admitted to the bar. Please help me."

In addition, Smith has told you, "I changed my name when I was a freshman in college. My name then was Patrick Saville. Under that name, I was convicted of a misdemeanor for possession of marijuana. Do I have to report something like that? Will the bar ever catch me?"

You are an old friend of the law school dean. The dean has offered not to charge Smith and force him to a hearing on the charge of cheating if Smith agrees to accept a failing grade in the course. He can make up the course in summer school (for which he will have to pay tuition), and that will let him graduate in time to take the bar with the rest of his class. The dean also offers to agree not to disclose the incident to the character and fitness committee of the bar. Smith is happy to be able to get off so lightly.

QUESTIONS

A. CHARACTER AND FITNESS FOR ADMISSION TO THE BAR

1. Every American jurisdiction requires that applicants for admission to the bar have the necessary "character and fitness" to practice law. Why should bar admission authorities in your state concern themselves with Smith's character?

a. Restatement Third, The Law Governing Lawyers § 2, Comment *d*, explains the requirement this way:

> "A license to practice law confers great power on lawyers to do good or wrong. Lawyers practice an occupation that is complex and often, particularly to nonlawyers, mysterious. Clients and others are vulnerable to wrongdoing by corrupt lawyers. Hence, as far back as the first bars in medieval England efforts have been made to screen candidates for the bar with respect to their character. * * * The central inquiry concerns the present ability and disposition of the applicant to practice law competently and honestly."

b. Professor Deborah Rhode goes on:

> "The first [purpose] is shielding clients from potential abuses, such as misrepresentation, misappropriation of funds, or betrayal of confidences. * * * A second concern involves safeguarding the administration of justice from those who might subvert it through subornation of perjury, misrepresentation, bribery, or the like.
>
> " * * * [A] less frequently articulated rationale for character screening rests on the bar's own interest in maintaining a professional community and public image. * * * An overriding objective of any organized profession is to enhance its members' social standing, and the bar is scarcely an exception."[1]

2. Does Smith's cheating in law school demonstrate that he lacks "good moral character"?

a. Does cheating involve "dishonesty, fraud, deceit, or misrepresentation" so as to justify disciplining a licensed lawyer for violation of Model Rule 8.4(c)? Should we be as concerned about the subsequent denial of guilt as about the original act of cheating?

---

1. Deborah L. Rhode, Moral Character as a Professional Credential, 94 Yale L.J. 491, 508–10 (1985).

b. Should Smith's earlier drug conviction be conclusive evidence of a lack of "character and fitness"? Would your answer be different if he had been convicted of a drug-related *felony*?[2]

c. Is marijuana possession "a criminal act that reflects adversely on the lawyer's honesty, trustworthiness, or fitness as a lawyer in other respects"? See Model Rule 8.4(b) and Comment 2.

d. In re Hinson–Lyles, 864 So.2d 108 (La.2003) (per curiam), held that a former school teacher's conviction of three felonies involving a sexual relationship with one of her 14–year–old students was sufficient to deny her admission to the bar. Do you agree? Could one argue that there is very little relationship between that crime and situations she would face as a lawyer? How would you make the counterargument?

e. If discipline authorities would not suspend or disbar a practicing lawyer in your state after conviction of marijuana possession, should bar admission authorities necessarily admit Smith to practice? Hallinan v. Committee of Bar Examiners, 421 P.2d 76 (Cal.1966), said the test for discipline and bar admission is the same, namely whether the individual "is a fit and proper person to be permitted to practice law." Most observers agree, however, that, in practice, the bar admissions authorities are more likely to deny a person a license to practice law than discipline authorities are to take it away later for identical conduct.

3. Should dishonesty in the handling of money defeat a person's bar admission?

a. In re Mustafa, 631 A.2d 45 (D.C.1993), involved the chief justice of a law school's moot court program who embezzled over $2000 from the moot court account to pay the emergency expenses of his sister. He repaid the money and the school fully supported his bar admission, but only a year had passed since the misconduct, so the court denied admission. See also, Application of Majorek, 508 N.W.2d 275 (Neb.1993), denying admission of an applicant who embezzled $300 of law student association funds and shoplifted a pack of cigarettes, among other offenses.

b. In re Krule, 741 N.E.2d 259 (Ill.2000), denied admission to a man who had pled guilty to felony theft (insurance fraud) in 1988, several years *before* going to law school. The applicant, while "a mature adult and a licensed [insurance] professional," had organized a group that arranged for excessive or not-performed treatment of accident victims and then submitted their claims to insurance companies. The court said the applicant had not been candid about his criminal history when he applied to law school (he also did not tell the law school about three previous misdemeanor charges resulting in two guilty pleas), and he was still less than forthcoming about it. He had been generous with his volunteer time in recent years, but the court, over the dissent of one justice, found that work insufficient to support a finding that he had the requisite character to be a lawyer.

---

2. Current practice in most states does not automatically deny bar admission to convicted felons. See, e.g., In re Polin, 630 A.2d 1140 (D.C.1993) (applicant admitted to the bar after serving time for conspiracy to distribute cocaine).

c. Should an applicant to the bar be denied admission for borrowing money for his education and then filing for bankruptcy three days before law school graduation? Does such action show a lack of sensitivity to his "moral responsibility to his creditors * * * [and] a lack of the moral values" required of a lawyer? Some states have held that it does, while acknowledging the applicants' legal right to file bankruptcy.[3]

d. Why might financial issues be of particular concern to bar admission authorities? Are lawyers so frequently entrusted with the handling of client funds that honesty in the handling of money should be a significant concern?

4. Should there be a statute of limitations on how long prior incidents can affect current bar admission decisions?

a. Note that some of Smith's problems occurred when he was a freshman in college, years before his graduation from law school. Should that make a difference? Hallinan v. Committee of Bar Examiners, supra, said that "adolescent misbehavior" was not sufficient to disqualify the applicant.[4] Would you want to know how old Smith was at the time of the alleged college incidents before you turned him in? Should you ask, or should you leave seeking such information up to others? Look at ABA Model Rule 8.1.

b. Matter of Prager, 661 N.E.2d 84 (Mass.1996), involved an applicant who was in his late 40s. For about six years in the 1970s, he had headed a "large-scale international marijuana smuggling operation." After indictment for his crimes, he fled the country and lived as a fugitive for several years in England and the Caribbean. He pled guilty in connection with his return to the country, and as a condition of his probation, he provided care in his home to terminal AIDS patients. He also attended the University of Maine law school, served on the law review, and after graduating summa cum laude, clerked for a justice of the Maine Supreme Court. The question was whether he was sufficiently rehabilitated after all that to be permitted to sit for the Massachusetts bar examination. The court held he was not. His flight to avoid prosecution had "undermined the integrity of the judicial process" and his admission without the passage of at least five more years, "would reflect poorly on the integrity of the bar." Do you agree?[5]

---

3. Florida Board of Bar Examiners v. G.W.L., 364 So.2d 454 (Fla.1978) ("he exercised his legal right to be freed of debt by bankruptcy well before the first installments on his debt became due, with absolutely no regard for his moral responsibility to his creditors."); In re C.R.W., 481 S.E.2d 511 (Ga.1997) (applicant must show a good faith effort to meet financial obligations); In re Gahan, 279 N.W.2d 826 (Minn.1979); Application of Taylor, 647 P.2d 462 (Or.1982). But see, Matter of Anonymous, 549 N.E.2d 472 (N.Y.1989).

4. An interesting analogy can be drawn to the problem of an attorney's reinstatement after disbarment. As a general rule, almost no matter how serious the original offense, the attorney may be reinstated upon a showing of rehabilitation and present fitness. See, e.g., In re Hiss, 333 N.E.2d 429 (Mass.1975); In re Wigoda, 395 N.E.2d 571 (Ill.1979).

5. See also, In re Dortch, 860 A.2d 346 (D.C.2004) (same result where applicant had planned and executed a bank robbery in 1974 in which his associate killed a police officer; applicant had been a model prisoner and law-abiding citizen before and during law school).

5. Historically, the principal concern about the character and fitness requirement has been its potential to deny bar admission based on political beliefs rather than character. In the 1950s, for example, it was the principal basis for denying members of the Communist Party admission to the bar.[6] Is there a risk of that misuse of the requirement today?

a.   In re Converse, 602 N.W.2d 500 (Neb.1999), involved an applicant who had engaged in bizarre but non-criminal behavior while in law school. The student wrote to the state supreme court and prominent federal judges to criticize his appellate advocacy teacher. When he got in trouble for displaying a photograph of a "nude female's backside" on his law school carrel, he raised a First Amendment charge. Later, he sold T-shirts with a "nude caricature of [his law school Dean] shown sitting astride * * * a very large hot dog" with a caption "Astride the Peter Principle." The court denied him admission to the bar, saying the "threshold question we must answer is whether conduct arguably protected by the First Amendment can be considered by the Commission during an investigation into an applicant's moral character and fitness to practice law. We answer this question in the affirmative." 602 N.W.2d at 505. The court declared: "abusive, disruptive, hostile, intemperate, intimidating, irresponsible, threatening, or turbulent behavior is a proper basis for the denial of admission to the bar." 602 N.W.2d at 508. Do you agree?

b.   In re Hale, 723 N.E.2d 206 (Ill.1999), cert. denied sub nom. Hale v. Committee on Character and Fitness of the Illinois Bar, 530 U.S. 1261 (2000), involved Matthew Hale, an outspoken white supremacist who founded a "church" to espouse his beliefs. The Illinois character and fitness panel held that, in lawyer regulation, " 'fundamental truths' of equality and nondiscrimination 'must be preferred over the values found in the First Amendment.' " Thus, the panel asserted, if Hale were admitted to the Bar, he would be "on a collision course with the Rules of Professional Conduct." The Illinois Supreme Court refused to review the character and

Frasher v. West Virginia Bd. of Law Examiners, 408 S.E.2d 675 (W.Va.1991), even held that a record of three convictions for driving under the influence, along with other driving offenses, was enough to deny an applicant admission to the bar. The result initially seems harsh, but it represents an important part of a continuing struggle with the problem of lawyer alcoholism and drug abuse that we will see in Problem 2.

6. Important constitutional cases on bar admissions include, Konigsberg v. State Bar, 353 U.S. 252 (1957) (Konigsberg I); Schware v. Board of Bar Examiners, 353 U.S. 232 (1957) (one cannot be denied admission merely because he is a member of the Communist Party); Konigsberg v. State Bar (Konigsberg II), 366 U.S. 36 (1961) (court may refuse admission because applicant obstructs the investigation—e.g., refuses to say whether he is or is not a knowing member of the Communist Party); In re Anastaplo, 366 U.S. 82 (1961); Baird v. State Bar of Arizona, 401 U.S. 1 (1971) (applicant may not be denied bar admission for failure to state whether she has ever been a member of an organization that "advocates overthrow of the United States by force or violence"); Application of Stolar, 401 U.S. 23 (1971); Law Students Civil Rights Research Council, Inc. v. Wadmond, 401 U.S. 154 (1971) (one can be refused admission if, with scienter, he is a knowing member of the Communist Party with intent to further its illegal goals). See generally, 5 Ronald D. Rotunda & John E. Nowak, Treatise on Constitutional Law: Substance and Procedure § 20.44 (4th ed.2008). John E. Nowak & Ronald D. Rotunda, Constitutional Law § 16.44 (8th ed.2010).

fitness panel's opinion, thus affirming its denial of admission. In dissent, Justice Heiple argued: "The Committee seems to hold that it may deny petitioner's application for admission to the bar without finding that petitioner has engaged in any specific conduct that would have violated a disciplinary rule if petitioner were already a lawyer."

c. Do you agree with the results in these cases? Are courts likely to be reliable predictors of which people have sufficient character to be a lawyer? A grand jury later indicted Hale in Chicago for "plotting to kill a federal judge and obstructing justice." Washington Post, Jan. 9, 2003, p. A–2. The jury found him guilty and he is now serving a 40–year sentence. Does that confirm the wisdom of earlier denying him admission to the bar?[7]

B. CANDOR IN THE BAR APPLICATION PROCESS

1. How candid must bar applicants like Smith and their supporters be in the application process?

a. It is often said that an applicant is more likely to be denied admission for covering up his or her past than for what that past contains. In Attorney Grievance Comm'n v. Myers, 635 A.2d 1315 (Md.1994), for example, a lawyer was disbarred for lying on his bar application about the number of traffic tickets he had even though the driving record itself would not have justified denial of admission. Cf. Model Rule 8.1. Is such an approach by admission authorities reasonable? Is it likely to be inevitable?

b. In re Zbiegien, 433 N.W.2d 871 (Minn.1988), rewarded honesty. A bar applicant admitted he had plagiarized several pages of a paper in a products liability seminar, but said that he had been under great stress because of work pressures and injuries that his wife had suffered. Petitioner was given an "F" in the course but permitted to graduate. He reported the incident in his application for admission to the bar, and, while the court held that a single incident of misconduct could be the basis for denial of bar admission, the applicant had been punished for the misconduct and now showed remorse. Thus, the court admitted him to the bar.

c. But candor is not always rewarded. In Application of Taylor, 647 P.2d 462 (Or.1982), the applicant had been arrested for shoplifting but the trial court dismissed the charges when the defendant denied he had intended to steal the item. Before the bar committee, however, the applicant made a clean breast of things and admitted that he really had intended to steal. Rather than commend his current honesty, the committee denied him admission for his misleading testimony in the criminal case. Are you troubled by the result in *Taylor*? Relieved that the dishonesty came out in time? What is its message to bar applicants about how safe it is to volunteer incriminating information?

d. Take a close look at Rule 8.1(b)(2). Is honesty all it demands? What does the rule mean when it requires bar applicants to "correct a misappre-

---

7. Should a lawyer who violated no law but preached racial hatred after bar admission be subject to disbarment? Look at Rule 8.4, Comment 3. Does it address *that* question at all?

hension known by the person to have arisen in the matter"? Assuming you have tried to be completely honest, are you likely in most cases to know whether bar admission authorities have misunderstood what you told them? Should you read communications that you get from those authorities very carefully to be sure to avoid letting misapprehensions go uncorrected?

2.   How much should a state supreme court be able to ask a candidate for bar admission about his or her history of mental illness?

a.   Is such an illness a "disability" within the meaning of the Americans with Disabilities Act? Litigants have filed suits challenging such questions, and the ABA, being concerned that fear of such inquiries may prevent law students from getting mental health assistance, has urged states to limit inquiry to "specific, targeted questions about the applicant's behavior, conduct or any current impairment of the applicant's ability to practice law."

b.   Questions 25, 26, and 27 in the Character and Fitness questionnaire prepared by the National Conference of Bar Examiners now ask:

"25.   Within the past five years, have you been diagnosed with or have you been treated for bi-polar disorder, schizophrenia, paranoia, or any other psychotic disorder?

"If you answered yes, complete Forms 7 and 8. * * *

"26.   A. Do you currently have any condition or impairment (including, but not limited to, substance abuse, alcohol abuse, or a mental, emotional, or nervous disorder or condition) which in any way currently affects, or if untreated could affect, your ability to practice law in a competent and professional manner?

"B.   If your answer to Question 26(A) is yes, are the limitations caused by your mental health condition or substance abuse problem reduced or ameliorated because you receive ongoing treatment (with or without medication) or because you participate in a monitoring program?

"If your answer to Question 26(A) or (B) is yes, complete Forms 7 and 8. * * * As used in Question 26, 'currently' means recently enough so that the condition could reasonably have an impact on your ability to function as a lawyer.

"27.   Within the past five years, have you ever raised the issue of consumption of drugs or alcohol or the issue of a mental, emotional, nervous, or behavioral disorder or condition as a defense, mitigation, or explanation for your actions in the course of any administrative or judicial proceeding or investigation; any inquiry or other proceeding; or any proposed termination by an educational institution, employer, government agency, professional organization, or licensing authority?

"If you answered yes, furnish a thorough explanation * * *."

3. Would you favor a policy of granting only conditional admission to persons who have recently undergone treatment for chemical dependency or mental illness?

a. In February 2008, the ABA House of Delegates approved a model rule for states to use in creating a system of conditional admission for persons "whose rehabilitation or treatment is sufficiently recent that protection of the public requires monitoring of the applicant for a specified period." The rule would only apply to persons whose "chemical dependency, mental or other illness" had previously made the person unable to "meet the functional requirements necessary to practice law." Having the option of conditional admission available would not preclude unconditional admission where rehabilitation had been successful for a sustained period, nor would it preclude outright denial of admission in appropriate cases.

b. If you were part of the bar admission process, what conditions might you consider imposing on a lawyer? If you were a client, would you want to know that your lawyer was only conditionally admitted to the bar? Would letting clients know a lawyer's mental history be too great an invasion of the lawyer's right to privacy? Whether or not to require disclosure proved so controversial that the ABA House of Delegates voted to leave the issue up to each state.

4. If you are Smith's lawyer (or just his friend who happens to be a lawyer), what are your own obligations to the bar admission authorities in connection with Smith's bar application?

a. Look at Model Rule 8.1(b). Must you report what Smith admitted to you about his guilt in the cheating case? Must you report what you know about Smith's change of name and past criminal record?

b. Look at Model Rule 8.1, Comment 3. Why should your responsibilities change when you undertake to represent Smith? Is the public interest in having all the facts before bar admission authorities any less?

5. What should be the obligation of law schools and their deans in cooperating with investigations conducted by bar admission officials?

a. Was it proper for the law school to enter into a "plea bargain" with Smith under which Smith agreed to accept a law school sanction for cheating and the school agreed not to report the matter to the bar? You might want to think about this question after reading about the *Himmel* case in Problem 2.

b. Zielinski v. Schmalbeck, 646 N.E.2d 655 (Ill.App.1995), involved a dean's potential liability for telling the character and fitness committee about a student. The student was accused by another student of sexually harassing her. A professor who knew both students believed the charge and, on his recommendation, the dean informed bar admission authorities. The plaintiff sued the professor and dean under § 1983 of the Civil Rights Act of 1871. The court held that the constitutional right to practice law if bar admission requirements are met does not prohibit character and fitness investigations. The dean's report was subject to absolute immunity from civil liability, and neither the professor nor the dean had acted under color of state law so as to implicate the Civil Rights Act.

c.   Law schools' reluctance to get involved, however, may be partly explained by Rothman v. Emory University, 828 F.Supp. 537 (N.D.Ill.1993). There, a law school dean had submitted a critical letter about an applicant to the Board of Law Examiners reporting the applicant's "chronic hostility" toward other students and the faculty. The applicant was admitted to the Bar, and then sued the law school, alleging that his demeanor was the result of "chronic epilepsy" and that the negative report constituted a violation of the Americans with Disabilities Act. Although the negative report to the Bar was absolutely privileged as a matter of state libel law, the court said that reports to the bar about most students are positive and that such reports are "services" and "privileges" that one may not deny on the basis of an applicant's disability. The court refused to dismiss the ADA claim.

d.   What obligations do you think law schools and individual professors should have in making reports to bar admission authorities? If they fail to be candid, might that damage future clients? Absolute immunity would encourage law school personnel to be candid, but would it also encourage uninformed or idiosyncratic comments?

C.   EDUCATIONAL AND KNOWLEDGE STANDARDS FOR ADMISSION TO THE BAR

1.   Why does almost every jurisdiction require lawyers to graduate from an accredited law school before being able to take the bar examination? Is a formal education the best way to learn what lawyers need to know?

a.   Abraham Lincoln never went to law school. Like many 19th century lawyers, he learned what he needed to know from books and from working in a law office. Other 19th century law students supplemented their experiential learning with lectures given by local practitioners such as David Hoffman in Baltimore and George Sharswood in Philadelphia, both seen as among the definers of modern legal ethics. Even early university law schools such as those at Harvard and Yale were initially staffed primarily by practitioner–lecturers.

b.   Today, it is rare to find a lawyer who has not attended law school. Indeed, one common requirement for bar admission is graduation from a law school accredited by the American Bar Association.[8]

2.   If you were defining the standards for law school accreditation, what standards would you impose? What do you believe are the essential features of a good law school education?

---

8. California is one major state that departs from this requirement, and it separately accredits some law schools that the ABA has not accredited. In addition, it has an additional "baby bar" requirement for students at law schools not accredited either by the ABA or the state. At the end of their first year, students at such schools must pass the special examination or not receive credit for further law study. The requirement has survived a charge that it invidiously discriminates between students at accredited and unaccredited schools. Lupert v. California State Bar, 761 F.2d 1325 (9th Cir.1985).

a.   Would you say that no law school may graduate a student who has not been enrolled in classes totaling 58,000 minutes of instruction time, at least 45,000 minutes of which must be in traditional law school class sessions, for example? ABA Standards for Approval of Law Schools, Standard 304(b).

b.   Would you say that an academic year must contain at least 130 days of regularly-scheduled classes, and that the days must be scheduled to cover parts of at least eight calendar months? ABA Standard 304(a).

c.   Would you say that if a student is employed more than 20 hours per week, the law school may not award the student more than 12 hours credit in the semester? ABA Standard 304(f).

d.   Would you say that a law school must have an "established and announced policy" with respect to faculty academic freedom and tenure in order to be good enough that its graduates may become lawyers? ABA Standard 405(b) makes that a condition of accreditation as well.

3.   Should graduates of schools that take a different approach to legal education be denied the right to sit for the bar examination in their states?

a.   In Massachusetts School of Law at Andover, Inc. v. American Bar Ass'n, 107 F.3d 1026 (3d Cir.1997), the ABA denied accreditation to a new law school, which then sued the ABA on antitrust grounds and asked for a waiver of the accreditation standards. The school asserted that some of the standards had more to do with enhancing faculty salaries and increasing law school tuition than with assuring a quality legal education. The school proposed to offer a less expensive educational program, but—because its students could not take the bar exam in most states—it alleged that the ABA accreditation standards significantly damaged its ability to attract students. The court did not opine on whether requiring ABA accreditation was wise. It held only that the opinions expressed in an ABA inspection report are entitled to First Amendment protection and that any damage the law school suffered arose from the requirement of state law that required bar applicants to have attended an ABA-accredited school. The act of seeking such state action is itself immune from antitrust liability under the *Noerr–Pennington*[9] doctrine, so the court granted summary judgment in favor of the ABA.[10]

---

9.   The Noerr–Pennington doctrine refers to two related cases, Eastern R.R. Presidents Conference v. Noerr Motor Freight, Inc., 365 U.S. 127 (1961), and United Mine Workers of America v. Pennington, 381 U.S. 657 (1965), where the Court held, citing First Amendment concerns, that the Sherman and Clayton Acts do not extend to those who exercise their First Amendment right to petition the government in either a legislative or administrative setting, despite the fact that they are seeking the enactment of laws or regulations with anticompetitive effects.

10.   While this case was pending, the U.S. Justice Department sued the ABA alleging that the gathering of salary data and basing accreditation in part on adequacy of professorial salaries and the share of tuition revenue the law school was allowed to keep constituted violations of the antitrust laws. Rather than conduct the antitrust fight on two fronts, the ABA agreed to change some of its accreditation standards and procedures. See 60 Fed. Reg. 39,421 (1995) (text of consent decree).

b. In re Brooks, 11 S.W.3d 25 (Ky.2000), involved a requirement that a bar applicant graduate from a law school providing an education that is the "substantial equivalent" of one provided by ABA-approved law schools in Kentucky. The applicant had graduated from the Nashville School of Law in Tennessee and the Kentucky bar had sent an inspector to that school to determine what kind of education it provided. The Kentucky court found "no full-time faculty at Nashville [and] no seminars or small class experience." The library was small and there was no "adequate computer facility which would permit students to do legal research." This was not the "substantial equivalent" of a legal education in Kentucky. Dissenting Justice Graves had little good to say about ABA accreditation and said that none of the court's criticism of the law school addressed whether the applicant had learned enough to be a good lawyer.

c. Efforts at accreditation of the Concord Law School of Kaplan University, and applications for bar admission by its graduates, should provide interesting tests of the force of ABA standards. Concord is an Internet-based law school. Students receive video lectures via their home computers, library materials are available online, and students take exams online. This method of study violates ABA standards such as those on hours of class time, numbers of days in which classes are held, and numbers of days in which students are present. There may also be problems of internet security: e.g., how can one be sure that the person who takes the examination is the same person who is enrolled?

d. What do you think of such alternative ways to study law? What important parts of your present law school experience might you miss if you attended law school online or under less than first-class conditions?

4. The requirement of attending an ABA-accredited law school is particularly burdensome on foreign lawyers seeking to practice in the United States. How should states deal with applications from lawyers trained outside the United States?

a. Gail Collins–Bazant was a Canadian citizen who had graduated from the University of Saskatchewan Law School. Pursuant to Canadian practice, she had served a year's clerkship before being admitted to the bar in two provinces. For five years, she was in private practice in Saskatchewan, and for eight more, she was a prosecutor in Newfoundland. In 1997, she moved to Nebraska and applied for admission to the Nebraska bar without examination, even though she had not graduated from an ABA-accredited law school. The court rejected her argument that the North American Free Trade Agreement (NAFTA) required waiver of that requirement. In re Collins, 561 N.W.2d 209 (Neb.1997).

b. The next year, Ms. Collins–Bazant was back in court seeking permission to take the bar examination. The court acknowledged that many states do not create an exception to the requirement of graduation from an ABA-accredited law school for graduates of foreign schools, in part because they cannot evaluate those schools. However, this applicant had studied at a law school giving common law training in English; she had substantial professional experience, and she was making an effort to learn

American law. Thus, while the court recognized that it was making it easier for a Canadian law graduate to get admitted to the bar of Nebraska than for a U.S. graduate of an unaccredited law school, it allowed Ms. Collins–Bazant to sit for the bar exam. In re Collins–Bazant, 578 N.W.2d 38 (Neb.1998).

c.   Osakwe v. Board of Bar Examiners, 858 N.E.2d 1077 (Mass.2006), involved a Nigerian lawyer who had also received training in Trinidad and Tobago. He then had received an LL.M. from the University of Connecticut and passed the New York bar. The court noted that many of the courses he took in Nigeria had the same names, e.g., property, contracts, that U.S. courses have. Even though he took courses in Nigerian law, not U.S. law, and even though his law school in Nigeria almost certainly could not have qualified for ABA accreditation, Mr. Osakwe had "sufficient exposure to the common law tradition" to qualify him for admission in Massachusetts without earning a J.D. at an accredited U.S. school.

d.   In re Application of Singh, 800 N.E.2d 1112 (Ohio 2003), is interesting and potentially problematic in our multicultural society. The Ohio Supreme Court denied Singh's bar application based on his "deficiencies in speaking and writing English and in comprehending the speech and writing of others." Singh was born and educated in India and had practiced law there before coming to the United States. In the course of the board's hearing, Singh had trouble understanding the questions posed and articulating his replies. This language barrier was also reflected in contradictory answers on his bar application, indicating a lack of understanding of the questions. The court reasoned that "the concept of fitness to practice law is not limited to the applicant's moral fitness" because "[c]ommunication skills are essential to the practice of law." The court said that the applicant should study English and refile his application in 18 months.

5.   The principal requirement for successful admission to the bar in most states is passage of a bar examination. Why should applicants be required to pass another examination after they have already received a three-year legal education at an accredited school?

a.   What should the bar exam examine? Could a uniform bar examination be used nationwide? Is the law really so different from state to state that each should use a different test? Development of the Multistate Bar Examination (MBE) has increasingly been a move in the direction of uniformity, but it is often not the only test used by a state and what constitutes a passing score varies from state to state.[11]

---

11. A majority of states also require their lawyers to have passed the Multistate Professional Responsibility Exam (MPRE). For many years, the MPRE only tested issues of legal ethics found in the ABA Model Rules. Now, the MPRE tests "what is widely termed the 'law of lawyering.'" Bar admission standards, malpractice issues, the organization of law firms, formation of the lawyer-client relationship, and so forth are all fair game for the examiners. As a result, *all* of the problems in this book are relevant to the MPRE, not just some of them.

b. Weismueller v. Kosobucki, 571 F.3d 699 (7th Cir.2009), concerned the diploma privilege that Wisconsin affords graduates of in-state law schools. The Wisconsin Supreme Court permits in-state graduates to become a member of the Wisconsin Bar without taking the bar exam. The plaintiffs were graduates of out-of-state law schools not eligible for the privilege. They claimed that the rule violated the commerce clause of the U.S. Constitution because it discriminates against them and other graduates from out-of-state who want to practice in Wisconsin. The district court granted the defendants' motion to dismiss for failure to state a claim, but the Seventh Circuit found that the case had been dismissed prematurely. That court agreed that, although the privilege favors the graduates of Wisconsin law schools, it has only indirect effects on commerce and regulates evenhandedly. The court also acknowledged that a state may regulate the practice of law within its jurisdiction, but the court held that bar admission standards have to be minimally reasonable. As a result of the early dismissal of the case, the court found there was an "evidentiary vacuum" as to benefits and potential burdens of the diploma privilege. There was no evidence concerning whether Wisconsin law schools focused more on Wisconsin law than other schools do, for example.[12]

c. California has long worked on what it calls a "performance test" to supplement traditional bar exam questions. Do you think it will be possible to develop a reliable test of the practical ability to serve a client instead of solely the applicant's legal knowledge?

d. How should the passing score be set for the bar exam? In Amendments to Rules of the Supreme Court Relating to Admissions to the Bar, 843 So.2d 245 (Fla.2003), the Florida Supreme Court raised the pass/fail line from 131 to 136. The opinion struggled with two questions: whether there is any objective minimum level of technical and educational competence necessary to safeguard clients, and whether the increased standard would differentially affect the pass rate of minorities. The court looked at two studies implying that a 131 pass/fail line let applicants pass the exam whom exam readers considered unqualified. The court then noted that the 131 pass/fail line when initially adopted was below the national average. Finally, the court found that if the pass/fail line previously had been set at 136, the pass rate of minorities would not have declined disproportionately. Thus, the Court raised the passing score.

e. Should an applicant have an unlimited number of chances to take the bar examination? Is a failure to provide such opportunities unfair to individuals or groups? Jones v. Board of Comm'rs of Alabama State Bar, 737 F.2d 996 (11th Cir.1984), upheld a limit of five times to take the bar, but there is a thoughtful dissent.

6. The Americans with Disabilities Act (ADA) affects the bar examination process in important ways. How should bar examiners be required to accommodate applicants who have disabilities?

---

12. After remand, the district court held that the plaintiffs' own motion for summary judgment was premature, 667 F.Supp.2d 1001 (W.D. Wis. 2009).

a. D'Amico v. New York State Bd. of Law Examiners, 813 F.Supp. 217 (W.D.N.Y.1993), involved an applicant who was nearsighted and suffered visual fatigue when reading for extended periods. She was given a separate testing room, extra light, a large print exam, and 50% more time than other applicants but she still failed the exam. In this decision, the federal court ordered the state to give her four days to complete the exam that other applicants were required to complete in two days.

b. In Bartlett v. New York State Bd. of Law Examiners, 226 F.3d 69 (2d Cir.2000), the applicant failed the bar exam four times and said it was a result of dyslexia and other learning disabilities. The court upheld a finding that the applicant was disabled by reading difficulties, that her ability to work quickly was impaired, and consequently that she was entitled to extra accommodation in taking the bar exam. Judge Cabranes, in dissent, however, argued that the ADA requires only reasonable accommodations by employers. By extending the ADA to require accommodating disability in taking the bar examination, the majority may make it possible for the applicant to qualify artificially for a license to do a job that she then cannot perform effectively.

c. What approach would you take to cases such as these? How would you try to accommodate genuine disabilities of applicants with equally genuine client needs for high-quality, reliable lawyer performance?

D. OTHER ATTEMPTS AT STATE AND FEDERAL LIMITS ON BAR ADMISSION

1. Should there be anything wrong with a state requiring bar applicants to be United States citizens and state residents?

a. A state may not require a bar applicant to be a U.S. citizen. In re Griffiths, 413 U.S. 717 (1973), held that such a requirement denies aliens the Fourteenth Amendment guarantee of equal protection of the law.

b. The U.S. Supreme Court also struck down states' efforts to limit bar admission to the state's own residents. Supreme Court of New Hampshire v. Piper, 470 U.S. 274 (1985). *Piper* held that the practice of law is a fundamental right that deserves protection under the privileges and immunities clause. Thus, states may not discriminate against nonresidents unless they demonstrate a substantial state purpose and a narrowly drawn restriction to advance that purpose. See also, Supreme Court of Virginia v. Friedman, 487 U.S. 59 (1988) (Virginia may not require nonresident lawyers to take its bar exam but admit its own residents to the bar without doing so); Barnard v. Thorstenn, 489 U.S. 546 (1989) (same result with respect to a one-year residency with an intent-to-remain rule imposed by the Virgin Islands bar).[13]

2. Should federal courts have the right to limit admission of lawyers already certified by a state as qualified to practice law?

---

13. But see, Scariano v. Justices of the Supreme Court of the State of Indiana, 38 F.3d 920 (7th Cir.1994), cert. denied, 515 U.S. 1144 (1995), upholding a rule granting admission only to lawyers who have "practiced predominantly" in Indiana for five years under a conditional license; this rule was said to relate to familiarity with Indiana law and not be a residency requirement per se.

a.   As a practical matter, admission to the highest court of a state will ordinarily be sufficient to qualify for admission to the federal courts of that state. See, e.g., United States District Courts for the Southern and Eastern Districts of New York, Local Civil Rule 1.3, contained in the Standards Supplement.

b.   A federal district court may not require a lawyer seeking admission to practice before it to either reside or maintain an office in the state where the federal court sits. Frazier v. Heebe, 482 U.S. 641 (1987).

c.   However, federal courts may require that litigators appearing before them have more experience than state courts require. Brown v. McGarr, 583 F.Supp. 734 (N.D.Ill.1984), aff'd, 774 F.2d 777 (7th Cir.1985) (upholding special rules for membership in a federal trial bar).

PROBLEM 2

LAWYER DISCIPLINE AND THE DISABLED LAWYER

Admitting an applicant to the bar is only the first time a state supreme court may evaluate that person's conduct. For as long as the lawyer is a member of its bar, the court retains jurisdiction to sanction that lawyer for violations of the court's rules of professional conduct. This problem examines professional discipline in the context of the requirement that a lawyer represent each client competently and diligently. It then considers the serious problem of lawyer disability, primarily in the context of alcohol and drug abuse. Next, it asks which courts have jurisdiction to discipline a lawyer for particular misconduct, and finally, it looks at each lawyer's duty to report the misconduct of other lawyers.

FACTS

Morris Andrews has been watching his peer and good friend Harold Black slowly lose his battle with a drinking problem. Andrews knows from long association that Black was once an able lawyer but that a series of personal crises have stimulated a case of alcoholism that has greatly reduced his effectiveness. In a recent case, Andrews' client had a less-than-even chance of winning, but won easily because Black seemed unable to represent his own client effectively.

Andrews resolved to go to Black and encourage him to withdraw from practice until he had gotten himself together. Black took the suggestion as an officious insult. "I represent my clients better than you do," Black said. "At least I don't take on more work than I can handle. You never finish anything. All your cases are on the back burner and you only appear in court to get continuances. I lay off the bottle when I have a big case, and as for that recent one when you beat me, you were just lucky."

Andrews did not consider Black's outburst wholly responsive to the main issue, but he did have to admit that Black was right about his caseload. Indeed, Andrews made a mental note to settle some of his minor cases so as to spend more time on the rest. But he was still left uncertain about what, if anything, to do about Black.

QUESTIONS

A. CONDUCT THAT CAN SUBJECT A LAWYER TO PROFESSIONAL DISCIPLINE

1. Where does a lawyer look to see what can justify professional discipline?

a. In a state that has adopted the ABA Model Rules, professional discipline is imposed for violations of Rule 8.4. Rule 8.4(a) incorporates by reference the other Model Rules.

b. The remaining parts of Rule 8.4 are what Restatement Third, The Law Governing Lawyers § 5, Comment *c*, calls the "catch all" provisions. Notice that the term "appearance of impropriety" as a ground for discipline does not appear in the Model Rules, although some courts and commentators sometimes still use that phrase in justifying imposing discipline.

2. What should be the purposes and functions of the lawyer discipline process? Should it be only to punish dishonesty or other "serious" wrongdoing? Should the purposes of the process include responding to what clients see to be problems with their lawyers, even if the concerns seem minor to lawyers themselves?

a. Two American Bar Foundation researchers have suggested that the process has three functions: "(1) to identify and remove from the profession all seriously deviant members (the 'cleansing' function), (2) to deter normative deviance and maximize compliance with norms among attorneys (the deterrence function), and (3) to maintain a level of response to deviance sufficient to forestall public dissatisfaction (the public image function)."[1]

b. Restatement Third, The Law Governing Lawyers § 5, Comment *b*, explains that

> "Professional duties defined in lawyer codes are mainly concerned with lawyer functions performed by a lawyer in the course of representing a client and causing harm to the client, to a legal institution such as a court, or to a third person. Those duties extend further, however, and include some lawyer acts that, even if not directly involving the practice of law, draw into question the ability or willingness of the lawyer to abide by professional responsibilities."

c. Do you agree with these analyses and explanations? How many lawyers do you think would have to be disciplined before the bar could

---

1. Eric Steele & Raymond Nimmer, Lawyers, Clients and Professional Regula-tion, 1976 American Bar Foundation Research J. 917, 999–1014.

completely "cleanse" itself of deviant members? Might the effectiveness of "deterrence" depend in part on the likelihood of getting caught?

d.   Would "public image" be improved by highly-publicized discipline in cases that come to public attention but confidential treatment of other instances of lawyer misconduct? Does enhancing lawyers' public image seem to you to be an appropriate *purpose* of professional discipline, as opposed to being a consequence of any effective system?

3.   Applying these ideas to the facts of this problem, does using the discipline process to pursue Andrews and Black seem desirable?

a.   Are Andrews and Black "bad people"? Indeed, is Andrews' problem that too many people have found him to be a good lawyer? As a practical matter, does Andrews have the luxury of determining the amount of work in the office at any one time? Might turning a client away today cause that client (and perhaps a friend of that client) not to come back tomorrow?

b.   Surely, however, representing clients "competently" and "diligently" are among the most important ethical responsibilities of a lawyer. See Model Rules 1.1 and 1.3. Has Andrews violated those rules by taking on more work than he can handle expeditiously and effectively?

c.   Do we have evidence that Andrews has "neglected" his clients' work? ABA Informal Opinion 1273 (Nov. 20, 1973) asserted that:

> "Neglect involves indifference and a consistent failure to carry out the obligations which the lawyer has assumed to his client or a conscious disregard for the responsibility owed to the client. * * * Neglect usually involves more than a single act or omission. Neglect cannot be found if the acts or omissions complained of were inadvertent or the result of an error of judgment made in good faith."

Is the standard set by that definition appropriate for interpreting Model Rule 1.3? Do you suppose clients care how many other cases a lawyer has neglected? May Andrews rely on Opinion 1273 to continue with business as usual? Has Model Rule 1.3 instead effectively overruled Informal Opinion 1273?

d.   Disciplinary authorities have pursued incompetence, negligence and neglect as violations of both Model Rules 1.1 and 1.3. Iowa Supreme Court Bd. of Professional Ethics & Conduct v. Hill, 576 N.W.2d 91 (Iowa 1998), for example, revoked the license of a lawyer who tried to handle an interstate adoption when he knew or should have known he was incompetent to do it. He said that he had "heard of" the interstate compact governing such adoptions but did not know its provisions and did not comply with it. Nor did he know that he had engaged in the unauthorized practice of law in Missouri as part of the adoption process. The Iowa Supreme Court found that a lawyer this incapable of competent practice "does not possess the attributes required of a lawyer licensed to practice in this state."

4. Under Model Rule 8.4(b), what criminal acts should be held to "reflect adversely on the lawyer's honesty, trustworthiness or fitness as a lawyer in other respects"?

a. Some of the conduct sanctioned under that rule borders on the unbelievable. In Attorney Grievance Comm'n v. Protokowicz, 619 A.2d 100 (Md.1993), a divorce lawyer was convicted of helping his former client break into the home of the client's estranged wife. When a feline resident of the home came into the kitchen, the lawyer put it into the microwave oven. You can guess the rest. The Maryland Court of Appeals suspended the lawyer for not less than one year for both breaking into the house and cooking the cat.

b. In People v. Musick, 960 P.2d 89 (Colo.1998), a lawyer was suspended for a year and a day on the basis of three incidents of physical assault on the woman with whom he was living. The hearing board concluded that he was a good lawyer and that his temper was unlikely to affect dealings with his clients, but on review, the Colorado Supreme Court held that even if the assaults were never prosecuted criminally, the conduct was *malum in se* and reflected adversely on his ability to practice law.

c. In The Florida Bar v. Brown, 790 So.2d 1081 (Fla.2001), an attorney assisted his corporate client to make illegal political contributions by soliciting $500 contributions from law firm employees that were to be reimbursed through billing inflated hours in the client's legal matters. The client's officers were convicted of felony violations of state campaign finance laws, but the attorney claimed that he did not know the law banned his conduct. "Our legal system depends on attorneys who appropriately question requests from clients that should arouse suspicion," the court wrote. Even if the lawyer did not purposefully evade the law, his acts assisted a client in conduct the lawyer "should have known was criminal or fraudulent." The court suspended the lawyer for 90 days.

5. Should an attorney be subject to professional discipline for behavior not in his or her capacity as an attorney? What might lead state supreme courts to sanction lawyer misconduct even when the lawyer was not acting as a lawyer at the time?

a. The issues can arise under Model Rule 8.4(b). In re Boudreau, 815 So.2d 76 (La.2002), involved a lawyer importing sexually-explicit child pornography from Europe, a crime for which he served 21 months in prison. The state supreme court disbarred Boudreau even though he had no prior disciplinary record. The court found that even the purchase of magazines constituted participation in the sexual exploitation of children, and analogized the conduct to making unwanted sexual demands on clients. Regardless of revulsion at the content of the magazines, do you agree that buying them reflects adversely on the lawyer's "honesty, trustworthiness or fitness as a lawyer in other respects"?

b. Model Rule 8.4(c) also prohibits a lawyer's engaging "in conduct involving dishonesty, fraud, deceit or misrepresentation," whether or not in a representational setting. In re Fornari, 599 N.Y.S.2d 545 (N.Y.App.Div.

1993), suspended a lawyer for one year for filing fraudulent documents in making a claim with his homeowner's insurer. He submitted bills for work other than that caused by a storm, for example, and altered the figures on other bills, allegedly to speed up payment he legally was due. See also, In re Bikman, 760 N.Y.S.2d 5 (N.Y.App.Div.2003) (attorney moved into her sister's rent-controlled apartment after the sister passed away and forged her sister's signature on rent checks, thus taking advantage of the controlled rent).

c.   In re Scruggs, 475 N.W.2d 160 (Wis.1991), suspended a lawyer for resume fraud. He had taken another student's transcript and inserted his own name and biographical information on it. He also said he had attended American University when he had actually attended American Technological University. Do you agree that these kinds of misrepresentations should cost a lawyer his or her license? Why or why not? See also In re Lamberis, 443 N.E.2d 549 (Ill.1982) (censure imposed for lawyer's plagiarism in work on an LL.M. degree); In re Lamb, 776 P.2d 765 (Cal.1989) (lawyer disbarred for five years for taking the bar exam for her husband).

d.   Matter of Diggs, 544 S.E.2d 628 (S.C.2001), suspended a lawyer for 90 days for filing a form saying he had attended a CLE seminar when, in fact, he arrived near the end of the program. Does this case send an important message to lawyers? You too may find that you don't like some of your CLE courses, but remember that any time you lie to bar regulatory authorities you may be inviting a disciplinary complaint that you will like even less.

6.   What conduct should be sufficient to violate the Model Rule 8.4(d) prohibition of "conduct that is prejudicial to the administration of justice"?

a.   Matter of Karahalis, 706 N.E.2d 655 (Mass.1999), involved a lawyer whose uncle was housed in a federal prison far from his family. Relatives of a congressman told the lawyer that the congressman could get the uncle moved nearer to him if the lawyer paid $12,000 to the congressman, so the lawyer made the payment. He cooperated with the prosecution of the congressman, but the bribery was a serious enough offense that the court suspended the lawyer for four years.[2]

b.   In Iowa Supreme Court Bd. of Professional Ethics & Conduct v. Lane, 642 N.W.2d 296 (Iowa 2002), Lane had represented a client in a federal suit under the Americans with Disabilities Act. He submitted a lengthy post-trial brief to the court, and he certified in his fee application that he had spent 80 hours writing the brief. The district judge noticed style oddities in the brief and made several requests for Lane to submit a list of sources that he used. Lane eventually provided a list of over 200 sources, but failed to call attention to any one. Through independent research, the district judge discovered that over 18 pages of Lane's brief had been copied verbatim, with footnotes, from a treatise on employment

---

2. Cf. The Florida Bar v. Karahalis, 780 So.2d 27 (Fla.2001) (Florida gave the Massachusetts disciplinary findings preclusive effect and disbarred the respondent as well).

discrimination law. The Iowa Supreme Court suspended Lane for six months, finding that billing for plagiarized work and repeated evasion of the court's inquiries constituted a deliberate attempt to perpetrate a fraud upon the court.

c. In Attorney Grievance Comm'n of Maryland v. Sheinbein, 812 A.2d 981 (Md.2002), the attorney's son was wanted for the murder of a neighbor. Attorney Sheinbein assured a police detective that he would contact her once he heard from his son or learned his whereabouts. Instead, Sheinbein encouraged his son to flee the country, drove from Maryland to New York to deliver his son's passport, and purchased his plane ticket to Israel. He never relayed the promised information to the detective. Even though the suspect was his son, the court held, "a lawyer's ensuring that a police investigation is thwarted by sending a main suspect known by him to be the killer in a murder case to a distant country necessarily reflects adversely on that lawyer's trustworthiness." The court disbarred Sheinbein. Two dissenting justices argued that sending one's child abroad before any criminal charges had been filed against him was neither illegal nor unethical. What do you think?

d. If Harold Black were to assert his privilege against self-incrimination in a discipline proceeding against him, should that assertion be deemed "prejudicial to the administration of justice" under Rule 8.4(d)? Spevack v. Klein, 385 U.S. 511 (1967), said no, holding that a state may not disbar an attorney for taking the Fifth Amendment.

B. **AGGRAVATING AND MITIGATING FACTORS IN DISCIPLINE CASES; THE PROBLEM OF ALCOHOL AND DRUG ABUSE, PSYCHOLOGICAL DISORDERS AND MENTAL DISEASE**

1. Think about yourself and your law school colleagues. Are alcoholism and drug abuse serious problems among lawyers?

a. There is evidence suggesting that the problem of lawyers' drug and alcohol abuse is significant. A state of Washington study, for example, reported that 18% of all lawyers and 25% of those in practice over 20 years have a problem with drugs or alcohol. See Wall Street J., Nov. 30, 1991, at B1.

b. A study by the Association of American Law Schools Special Committee on Problems of Substance Abuse in the Law Schools, 44 J. Legal Educ. 35, 41 (1994), found that nearly two-thirds of law students admitted using at least one illegal drug during their lifetime. Over 20% had used marijuana, and nearly 5% had used cocaine during the previous year.

c. Nowadays, we often think of alcoholism as a disease, not a character flaw. Should Harold Black be disciplined for conduct made more likely by a disease over which he possibly lacked full control? Can we justify the discipline as a way to prevent future misconduct arising from such a condition? If that logic were followed to its conclusion, would it follow that all lawyers should have to pass psychological predisposition tests before admission to practice so as to increase the public's protection?[3]

3. Cf. Alan M. Dershowitz, Preventive Disbarment: The Numbers Are Against It, 58 A.B.A.J. 815 (1972).

2.   Should Black's alcoholism be a factor that affects the nature of his discipline?

a.   In re Kelley, 801 P.2d 1126 (Cal.1990), involved a lawyer who was brought into the discipline system after her second conviction for drunken driving. Nominally, this was because she had violated the probation imposed in the first drunken driving case, but it also seems to have been part of California's effort to identify lawyers with an alcohol problem *before* they injure a client. Her professional discipline in this case consisted primarily of three years probation on condition that she abstain from alcohol. Three justices were troubled at what could become an arbitrary use of discipline to coerce behavior that only *might* get worse. Indeed, might sanctions imposed to try to prevent harm rather than punish actual conduct constitute a violation of the Americans with Disabilities Act? Recall the relation of that law to bar admission issues discussed in Problem 1.

b.   Courts have sometimes cited alcoholism as mitigation of the sanction for lawyer misconduct. In Matter of Walker, 254 N.W.2d 452 (S.D. 1977), for example, there was proof that alcoholism had been the causative factor in the lawyer's conduct. Proof the lawyer was now a recovering alcoholic, although not excusing the misconduct, led the court to allow the lawyer to keep his license. Cf. Petition of Johnson, 322 N.W.2d 616 (Minn.1982) (suggests criteria for when proof of recovery should lead to such a result).

c.   Rule 23 of the ABA Model Rules for Lawyer Disciplinary Enforcement (2002) provides for placing lawyers on an indefinite period of "disability inactive status" in case of their mental or physical incapacity. Proceedings are to be conducted in the manner of a discipline case, but they are to be confidential. Provisions are made to notify clients and the public if a lawyer is placed on disability status. Is such a procedure and disposition too severe for a condition such as alcoholism? Is it both necessary for protection of the public and more humane than disbarment? Is it necessary to have the leverage of tough sanctions, if only as a threat to coerce the lawyer into getting help?[4]

3.   Should psychological disorders and mental disease similarly affect a lawyer's level of discipline?

a.   In Conduct of Loew, 642 P.2d 1171 (Or.1982), the lawyer's defense was that he was a victim of "burn-out syndrome." His psychiatrist testified that professionals commonly take on too much work and then psychologically evade it by "procrastination and self-denial." Should this be a good defense? Would recognition of such a defense give adequate protection to clients? This court was sufficiently impressed by the defense that it did not disbar the lawyer, although it did suspend him for 30 days.

---

4.   The impaired attorney has been one of the particular concerns of the American Bar Association in recent years, and Model Rule 8.3 was amended in August 1991 to provide that lawyers need not report to discipline authorities any information they learn as part of a lawyers' assistance program (often called an "L.A.P.") designed to help lawyer-abusers recover from addiction.

b.   People v. Lujan, 890 P.2d 109 (Colo.1995), involved a lawyer who had received a head injury four years earlier that she said had given her a "compulsion to shop." The manifestation of that compulsion was her charging her personal expenses to her firm's credit card and fabricating justifications for the charges. The court accepted her story in mitigation and noted she was on medication for her condition. Because the lawyer was already on disability inactive status, she would have to apply to the court before resuming any active practice of law.

c.   The Florida Bar v. Clement, 662 So.2d 690 (Fla.1995), raised the issue whether the Americans with Disabilities Act (ADA) protects a lawyer with bipolar disorder (often called manic depression) against disbarment. The lawyer engaged in complex financial deals with little attention to whether he was using client funds improperly. The psychiatric testimony was that the disease kept him from knowing right from wrong. The court held that, even if that were true, the ADA did not void the requirement that an impaired individual must be "qualified" to practice his profession. Thus, the ADA did not prevent this lawyer's disbarment.

d.   How would you have treated the lawyers' claims in these cases? Is there any way to find an appropriate accommodation of the lawyer's mental condition and the clients' legitimate expectation that their lawyers will be able to represent them effectively?

C.   INTERSTATE DISCIPLINE: JURISDICTIONS THAT MAY SANCTION AND THE LAW THEY APPLY

1.   What jurisdictions may impose professional discipline on a lawyer?

a.   In our problem, Black and Andrews are practicing in the same jurisdiction. Does the analysis change if Black were admitted in State #1 but lost his case against Andrews in State #2? Assume that Black was admitted in State #2 only for purposes of that particular case. Look at Model Rule 8.5(a). Notice that, basically, any state in which the lawyer is licensed may discipline a lawyer for misconduct wherever it occurs, and even a state to which the lawyer travels for temporary practice may try the lawyer for conduct occurring there.

b.   In the Matter of Spraker, 744 N.E.2d 415 (Ind.2001), shows how Rule 8.5 can work. Discipline was imposed on an Indiana lawyer for conduct that occurred in Illinois but was illegal in both states. Spraker represented clients attempting to obtain permanent residency in the United States. There was evidence that he had failed to properly submit forms to the INS on more than 50 occasions. Indeed, several forms contained misstatements and lies about the clients. However, Spraker's clients all resided in Illinois where the alleged misconduct took place. The Supreme Court of Indiana found it had jurisdiction over Spraker's discipline because of his Indiana license. The court even allowed the hearing to be held in Illinois, given the sensitivity of many of Spraker's former clients to crossing state borders while they were still illegal residents. The court suspended Spraker from practice for two years.

2. Does each jurisdiction simply apply its own standards to evaluate the conduct? If a lawyer is licensed in one state and negotiates a contract in another, which state's rules should govern her professional conduct?

a. Look at Model Rule 8.5(b). Suppose a lawyer licensed in Florida negotiates a commercial transaction with a New Jersey resident and learns that the lawyer's client has lied about certain important facts. New Jersey ethics rules require its lawyers to disclose facts necessary to prevent a fraud and New Jersey clients may have come to expect such conduct from lawyers with whom they deal. Florida ethics law, in contrast, requires its lawyers *not* to disclose such facts. The lawyer's principal office is in Miami but the negotiations occurred in Newark. What is the lawyer to do about disclosure?

b. Must the lawyer assume the risk that a court will later say she followed the rules of the wrong state? How would a lawyer prove he or she had complied with Rule 8.5(b)(2)'s safe harbor for "reasonable belief" that the "predominant effect of the conduct" will be in a particular jurisdiction? Does Model Rule 8.5, Comment 5, provide much help in answering that question?

3. What is the effect of lawyer discipline in one state on a lawyer's status in other states where the lawyer is admitted to practice law?

a. Should whatever sanction is imposed by the first state to discipline a lawyer be binding in all other states? Does Model Rule 8.5, Comment 1, have anything to say about that question?

b. In Matter of Iulo, 766 A.2d 335 (Pa.2001), New Jersey had permanently disbarred the lawyer in 1989 for misapplying client funds. In 1996, Pennsylvania allowed the applicant to sit for the bar, and later admitted him, after being informed of the New Jersey action. In 1999, the Pennsylvania Office of Disciplinary Counsel sought to have the lawyer subjected to reciprocal disbarment based on the New Jersey action. The Pennsylvania Supreme Court said no. Pennsylvania seeks to rehabilitate lawyers, the court said, while New Jersey seeks to exclude them from practice. Principles of reciprocal discipline may require honoring factual findings made elsewhere but they do not require identical sanctions. The court said that "imposition of reciprocal discipline in this instance would be a grave injustice." Do you agree? Pennsylvania has now adopted the 2002 amendment to Model Rule 8.5; would this case be decided differently?

4. Should federal courts create their own disciplinary standards or apply the state disciplinary standards of the state in which they are sitting?

a. United States v. Walsh, 699 F.Supp. 469 (D.N.J.1988), considered New Jersey amendments to Model Rule 1.11 on disqualification of former government lawyers. In practice, many federal courts adopt, as a matter of "dynamic conformity," the ethics rules of the states in which they sit; a few courts adopt their own ethics rules. In this case, the court held that the

Model Rules as adopted by the ABA were controlling in that federal court, not the Rules as adopted by New Jersey, the state in which the court is located.

b. In re Hoare, 155 F.3d 937 (8th Cir.1998), dealt with reciprocal discipline in a federal court based on state discipline. The federal court required that a lawyer disciplined in state court show by clear and convincing evidence that identical discipline should not be imposed by the federal system. The Eighth Circuit upheld that standard and the disbarment of a lawyer for driving while intoxicated, killing another driver in a collision, and refusing a blood alcohol test. See also, In re Kramer, 282 F.3d 721 (9th Cir.2002) (applies the multi-factored test of Selling v. Radford, 243 U.S. 46 (1917), to federal court imposition of reciprocal discipline).

c. Surrick v. Killion, 449 F.3d 520 (3d Cir.2006), addressed whether a lawyer barred from practice in state court may maintain a law office in that state for the purpose of conducting a federal practice. The Pennsylvania Supreme Court had suspended attorney Surrick for five years, but the federal district court before which Surrick was admitted to practice imposed a shorter punishment. Surrick was thus reinstated to practice by the federal court while still suspended by the state. He refrained from opening a law office in Pennsylvania for fear of being prosecuted,[5] but he filed a complaint challenging the state's policy of denying attorneys in his position the right to open an office. The federal district court held that, although a state's disciplinary sanction is entitled to respect, it does not bind the federal courts. Even when a matter of important state concern is involved, if state law conflicts with federal law, the federal law must prevail. Office space is necessary for the "effective representation of [federal-law] clients," the district court noted, so denial of Surrick's right to operate such an office would give the state the power to second-guess a federal court's determination of Surrick's fitness to practice. The Third Circuit affirmed.

D.   THE DUTY TO REPORT ANOTHER LAWYER'S MISCONDUCT; THE DISCIPLINE PROCESS ITSELF

1.   Should the bar discipline a lawyer for failure to report another lawyer?

a. Model Rule 8.3 addresses a lawyer's duty to report misconduct of another lawyer or judge. This requirement tends to be one of the most underenforced rules of professional conduct, although it continues to be the subject of bar association opinions. See, e.g., ABA Formal Opinion 03–431 (Aug. 8, 2003) (duty to report another lawyer suspected of suffering from alcoholism, drug addiction or other mental impairment); ABA Formal Opinion 04–433 (Aug. 25, 2004) (duty to report misconduct that raises a

---

5. Surrick's concern was well based. In Office of Disciplinary Counsel v. Marcone, 855 A.2d 654 (Pa.2004), the court expressly held that an attorney suspended from the practice of law in Pennsylvania may not maintain an office to conduct a federal practice. The court held that while federal courts may regulate practice before them, state courts control who may operate law offices within their states.

substantial question of an admitted but nonpracticing lawyer's honesty, trustworthiness or fitness).

b.   The first case to discipline a lawyer *solely* for the failure to report was In re Himmel, 533 N.E.2d 790 (Ill.1988). Himmel represented Tammy Forsberg, a client who had been injured in a motorcycle accident. Earlier, Forsberg had retained a different lawyer (Casey) to represent her in her personal injury action. Casey had negotiated a settlement of $35,000 on Forsberg's behalf, received the settlement check, endorsed it, and converted the funds. Forsberg then retained Himmel to get her share back. He negotiated an arrangement whereby Casey would pay her $75,000 if she would not report him to the authorities for possible criminal or disciplinary sanction. Casey never paid the $75,000, and "Forsberg told respondent that she simply wanted her money back and specifically instructed respondent to take no other action." Himmel followed Forsberg's direction, recovered a total of $10,400 and took no fee for his work on the case.

The court said that "the client had contacted the [Illinois Attorney Registration and Disciplinary] Commission prior to retaining respondent and, therefore, the Commission did have knowledge of the alleged misconduct." In April 1985, the commission petitioned to suspend Casey from practicing law because of his conversion of client funds and his conduct in matters unrelated to Forsberg's claim. The court subsequently disbarred Casey on November 5, 1985. The commission then pursued Himmel for his failure to report Casey, and the Illinois Supreme Court suspended Himmel from practice for a year. The court asserted:

> "Common sense would dictate that if a lawyer has a duty * * * [to report], the actions of a client would not relieve the attorney of his own duty. * * *

> "As to respondent's argument that he did not report Casey's misconduct because his client directed him not to do so, we again note respondent's failure to suggest any legal support for such a defense. A lawyer, as an officer of the court, is duty-bound to uphold the rules in the Code. * * * A lawyer may not choose to circumvent the rules by simply asserting that his client asked him to do so. * * * "[6]

c.   Is *Himmel* correct that Rule 1.6's confidentiality obligations did not prohibit Himmel from reporting the other lawyer? On the other hand, why should Rule 1.6 give client Forsberg the right to put other clients at risk by telling her lawyer not to disclose Casey's misconduct to the disciplinary commission?

In our problem, might Andrews' knowledge about Black be said to be "confidential" and thereby protected against disclosure by Rule 8.3(c) and Rule 1.6? Would Andrews' client want it known that he won largely because Black was an alcoholic? Is that the kind of information Rule 1.6

---

6.   The court found the information was not protected by the attorney-client privilege because the client's mother and fiancé had been present when the client talked to the lawyer. You will learn more about the attorney-client privilege and protection of confidential information in Problem 7.

was meant to protect? Should the idea of confidentiality be construed broadly or narrowly for this purpose?

d.   Should *Himmel* be limited to its facts? The court acknowledged that, because of his efforts, Forsberg collected an additional $10,400 from Casey. Respondent himself received no fee in the case, but the case arguably involved selling out the public interest for a potentially increased recovery. Did the Illinois Supreme Court seem to place any such limit on its holding?

2.   How soon must the lawyer make a report against a fellow lawyer? How sure should a lawyer be before reporting?

a.   If there is a civil or criminal action pending involving the same conduct, disciplinary authorities often prefer that the lawyer wait until that action is completed. If the information comes in earlier, disciplinary authorities often suspend or abate their own inquiry so as to be able to work with a complete record and avoid duplicative investigation.

b.   How would waiting tend to affect the threat of discipline being used as leverage in the civil case? See ABA Formal Opinion 94–383 (July 5, 1994), expressing a concern that the threat to file a discipline charge might be used to get an advantage in a civil case and urging the postponing of reporting until the conclusion of that case. Do you agree? Might the dynamics work the other way? Would the coercive power of the threatened charge exist *before* reporting and be dissipated thereafter?[7]

c.   Might there be a cost to over-reporting? Might reporting become vindictive or a tactical ploy in litigation? Is that at least part of the message of Rule 8.3, Comment 3? Would it be better to have Black and Andrews call each other's law partners and have their firms impose informal sanctions?

d.   In re Riehlmann, 891 So.2d 1239 (La.2005) (per curiam), discussed a lawyer's duty to report the misconduct of another in a particularly dramatic situation. Riehlmann and his best friend, Deegan, were both former prosecutors. One night Deegan told Riehlmann that he was dying of colon cancer. During the same conversation, Deegan told Riehlmann that he had suppressed exculpatory blood evidence in one of the cases he prosecuted. He did not identify the case. Riehlmann urged Deegan to report what he had done, but Riehlmann did not report Deegan himself.

Five years after Deegan's death, Riehlmann heard about a case in which the crime lab discovered that the perpetrator of a crime had a different blood type than the person now on death row. He realized that this was probably the case to which Deegan had referred, so he told the defendant's attorney of his conversation with Deegan and executed an affidavit attesting to the fact that Deegan had indeed suppressed the exculpatory evidence. The month after signing the affidavit, and five years after Deegan's confession, Riehlmann also reported Deegan's misconduct to the Office of Disciplinary Counsel (ODC). That office's response was to

---

7. Cf. ABA Formal Opinion 94–384 (July 5, 1994), advising that a lawyer who is made the subject of a disciplinary charge filed by the opponent in connection with a pending case is not required to withdraw from representation of the client in that case.

charge Riehlmann with a failure to report earlier, in violation of Louisiana Rule 8.3(a).

The Louisiana Supreme Court found that a reporting requirement is triggered whenever the supporting evidence would allow a "reasonable lawyer under the circumstances" to form a "firm belief that the conduct in question had more likely than not occurred." The court held that the report must be made promptly in order to ensure that someone can investigate the offense and adequately protect the public and the profession against the offending attorney's possible future wrongdoings. In Riehlmann's case, the court found that a reasonable attorney would have formed a firm belief that the misconduct was more likely than not to have occurred at the time of Deegan's confession. Do you agree with the court's analysis? Is ABA Model Rule 8.3(a), Comment 3, nearly that absolute?

What do you think of this result? In *Himmel*, the Illinois disciplinary commission did not seek any discipline against the lawyer who defended Casey in the suit that Forsberg brought. Surely that lawyer also had unprivileged information, such as the allegations in Forsberg's complaint, and the jury verdict finding Casey liable. Should the disciplinary commission have brought an action against Casey's lawyer too? Once we start looking for violators of Model Rule 8.3, will there be any easy place to stop?[8]

3.   If a judge were to observe Black's impaired state or Andrews' inability to keep up with his caseload, would the judge's obligation to report be any different than that of a lawyer?

a.   The Illinois Disciplinary Commission did not seek any discipline against the judge who presided in the case that Forsberg brought against Casey. Should the judge be liable? See ABA Model Code of Judicial Conduct (2007), Rule 2.15(D), which parallels Model Rule 8.3. May a judge assume that an attorney will report all misconduct in a case? Should the lawyers, in turn, rely on the judge?

b.   Are lawyers required to report the misconduct of judges? Look at Model Rule 8.3(b).

4.   If Black or Andrews or one of their clients makes a complaint to a disciplinary agency, what will happen?

a.   A complainant has no personal right to have his or her complaint actively pursued by disciplinary authorities. Doyle v. Oklahoma Bar Ass'n, 998 F.2d 1559 (10th Cir.1993), found the claim of such a right to be frivolous. Do you agree? Was the court acknowledging that so many acts of lawyers could merit professional discipline that disciplinary authorities must exercise substantial discretion and only pursue the most serious offenders?

b.   If a complaint about a lawyer is made to a disciplinary agency, procedures vary from state to state, but those described in Rule 11 of the

---

8. See Ronald D. Rotunda, The Lawyer's Duty To Report Another Lawyer's Un- ethical Violations in the Wake of Himmel, 1988 U. Illinois L. Rev. 977 (1988).

ABA Model Rules for Lawyer Disciplinary Enforcement are representative. A state's "disciplinary counsel," operating under the authority of the jurisdiction's highest court, is required to evaluate all complaints filed by clients or others about a lawyer. If the conduct would not violate the state disciplinary rules even if true, the complaint is dismissed. For example, it is on this basis that disagreements over fees are often dismissed if they do not allege fraud or overreaching.

However, if the facts alleged would constitute a violation of the rules of professional conduct, the disciplinary counsel is required to investigate whether or not the facts are true. Ordinarily, at least by that point, the lawyer is offered a chance to respond to the complaint. If a non-serious violation is found or admitted, the disciplinary counsel may impose a private sanction such as an admonition and the case is closed. However, if the alleged violation is serious, or if the lawyer does not consent to the private sanction, the disciplinary counsel is expected to file a formal charge to which the lawyer must file an answer.

The matter is then set for trial before a hearing panel composed of other lawyers, typically working as volunteers, that either dismisses the matter or recommends a sanction. The lawyer may then appeal the sanction to a review board composed of fellow lawyers. If that board also recommends a sanction, the lawyer may appeal to the licensing court. It is the court decisions in such cases that you will read about throughout this book.

c. The discipline procedures are impressive, but observers are not always impressed by the results. The ABA reports that in 1995 over 116,000 complaints were made to state lawyer discipline agencies; that was about one for every nine lawyers in the country. Of those complaints, however, almost 50,000 were dismissed for failure to allege a violation of the disciplinary rules. Of the 66,000 remaining complaints, 49,000 more were dismissed after investigation. Often in such cases, the complainant was not even told what happened as a result of the complaint.

Indeed, only about 5,700 complaints (under 5%) actually led to formal disciplinary charges, and only about half of those, 2,900, led to convictions after trial. Of lawyers convicted, about 25% were disbarred, 50% suspended, and 25% publicly reprimanded.[9]

---

9. The statistics are taken from ABA Center for Professional Responsibility, Standing Committee on Professional Discipline, 1995 Survey on Lawyer Discipline Systems (1997). We have rounded the data because the ABA data itself is incomplete and to claim more precision than the data justifies would itself be misleading.

Several states have conducted studies of the related question whether discipline is imposed disproportionately on solo practitioners and members of particular racial groups. The reports indicate that racial discrimination does not seem to be present, but being a solo practitioner does increase the chance that a lawyer will face discipline. The reports suggest that many solo practitioners have fewer support systems to help them comply with the rules, e.g. State Bar of California, Investigation and Prosecution of Disciplinary Complaints Against Attorneys in Solo Practice, Small Size Law Firms and Large Size Law Firms (June 2001); Illinois Attorney Registration and Discipline Commission, Annual Report (2003).

d. Should this data be seen as suggesting that lawyers in the discipline process are too forgiving? The ABA Model Rules for Lawyer Disciplinary Enforcement now provide for one-third public members on both the hearing panels and disciplinary board. Do you agree with that approach? Does it represent an undesirable decline in self-regulation by the bar?

e. Another controversial feature of the present discipline process is that, at least until formal charges are filed, the entire process is usually confidential. Potential clients cannot determine, for example, whether a lawyer they are considering retaining has been the subject of numerous complaints, none of which were among the 5% in which charges were filed.

There has been no rush to open the process to the public. Opponents of openness "say their biggest fear is the specter of sensationalist newspaper publicity about a flimsy allegation of misconduct. If the allegation ultimately is disproved, they are convinced, then news of the vindication would be banished to the back pages of the paper, doing little to offset the stigma of the original publicity."

Proponents, however, "say they see no reason for protecting lawyers' privacy in disciplinary proceedings when no similar protective measures exist for laymen charged with crime,"[10] and in 2005, New Jersey became the first state to hold that requiring clients not to reveal the filing of a grievance is unconstitutional.[11]

With which of these positions do you agree?

6. Assuming disciplinary charges were filed, what sanctions should be imposed on Andrews and Black for the conduct discussed in this problem?

a. In 1986, the ABA House of Delegates approved the "Standards for Imposing Lawyer Sanctions." Various courts have referred to these new Standards for guidance. The Standards (as amended in 1992) propose that a court, in imposing a sanction after a finding of lawyer misconduct, should consider four factors:

(a) the duty violated;

(b) the lawyer's mental state;

(c) the actual or potential injury caused by the lawyer's misconduct; and

(d) the existence of aggravating or mitigating factors.

b. If a lawyer "engages in a pattern of neglect with respect to client matters and causes serious or potentially serious injury to a client," the Standards state that disbarment is generally appropriate. Standard 4.41(c). If the lawyer's pattern of neglect causes injury or potential injury that is not serious, the Standards recommend suspension. Standard 4.42(b). If the lawyer is merely negligent, does not act with reasonable diligence, and

---

10. Frank Moya, The Doors Stay Shut on Discipline, National Law Journal, Dec. 8, 1980, at pp. 1, 11 & 12.

11. The case is R.M. v. Supreme Court of New Jersey, 883 A.2d 369 (N.J.2005).

causes injury or potential injury to a client, the Standards recommend only a reprimand. Standard 4.43. If such a lawyer causes little or no actual or potential injury, the Standards recommend admonition. Standard 4.44. A reprimand is a public censure and an admonition is private.[12]

c. In addition to the sanctions of disbarment, suspension, reprimand, admonition, or probation (which allows the lawyer to practice law under specified conditions), the Standards allow "restitution, assessment of costs, limitation upon practice, appointment of a receiver, requirement that the lawyer take the bar examination or professional responsibility examination, requirement that the lawyer attend continuing education courses," or other sanctions that the disciplinary authority may deem appropriate.[13] Standard 2.8.

d. Should the law permit a lawyer to resign from a state bar when charged with a disciplinable offense? Should an admission of guilt be a prerequisite to resignation? Why or why not? Is it important to know how easy it is for an attorney who has resigned to apply for readmission to the bar?[14]

e. Is there any reason to impose professional sanctions only on individual lawyers? Should Black's and Andrews' law firms be subject to sanctions as well? Might imposition of sanctions on law firms create a better incentive for firms to police their own policies and the practices of their individual members?[15]

New York was the first jurisdiction to authorize discipline of a "law firm." Rule 8.4 of the New York Rules of Professional Conduct make a "lawyer or law firm" subject to discipline. While it may be unlikely that a law firm will be "disbarred" pursuant to this rule, lesser sanctions are certainly possible.

7. Should lawyer discipline be considered the equivalent of a criminal sanction and should lawyers be entitled to the constitutional guarantees inherent in a criminal process?

a. People v. Artman, 553 N.W.2d 673 (Mich.App.1996), reasoned that lawyer discipline "is not to punish for wrongdoing, but to protect the public, the courts, and the legal profession." Thus, it found the constitutional prohibition of double jeopardy does not apply. Do you agree?[16]

---

12. A lawyer's physical or mental disability or impairment are to be mitigating factors, while aggravating factors include the lawyer's refusal to acknowledge the wrongful nature of his conduct, the vulnerability of the victim, the lawyer's substantial experience in the practice of law, and his or her indifference to making restitution. Standards 9.22, 9.32.

13. See, e.g., In re Morrell, 859 A.2d 644 (D.C.2004) (denies reinstatement after suspension until lawyer makes restitution to persons injured by his misconduct).

14. Cf. Court Rejects a Nixon Bid to Resign from State Bar, New York Times, Sept. 20, 1975, p. 1.

15. See Ted Schneyer, Professional Discipline for Law Firms, 77 Cornell L. Rev. 1 (1991); Julie Rose O'Sullivan, Professional Discipline for Law Firms? A Response to Professor Schneyer's Proposal, 16 Georgetown J. Legal Ethics 1 (2002).

16. Cases like Department of Revenue of Montana v. Kurth Ranch, 511 U.S. 767 (1994), and United States v. Halper, 490 U.S. 435 (1989), have analyzed double jeopardy issues by asking whether a civil penalty is so

b. In re Conduct of Harris, 49 P.3d 778 (Or.2002), reasoned further that because attorney discipline cases are not traditionally viewed as criminal proceedings, a lawyer charged with a discipline offense has no right to court-appointed counsel to defend him.

c. In re Ruffalo, 390 U.S. 544 (1968), held that discipline proceedings are "quasi-criminal" and thus require fair notice of the charges. A lawyer can be disciplined, however, based on testimony given under a grant of immunity from criminal prosecution. In re Daley, 549 F.2d 469 (7th Cir.1977), cert. denied 434 U.S. 829 (1977).[17]

d. Even a presidential pardon may not eliminate a lawyer's exposure to professional discipline. In re Abrams, 689 A.2d 6 (D.C.1997) (en banc), involved one of President Reagan's aides who had pled guilty to two misdemeanor charges of "unlawfully [withholding] material information" from Congress in the Iran–Contra investigation. Within days after the disciplinary hearing, President Bush (who had lost his bid for reelection) gave Mr. Abrams a full pardon. In a lengthy opinion citing mostly post-Civil War cases, a panel of the D.C. Court of Appeals had held that a pardon makes an offender "as it were, a new man." Thus, the panel held, the president's "act of grace" had rendered it powerless to impose professional discipline for Abrams' acts. 662 A.2d 867 (D.C.1995). On rehearing, however, the full D.C. Court of Appeals reversed the panel by a 5 to 4 vote. Even a presidential pardon cannot wipe out the fact that false testimony was given, the majority said. It can protect the lawyer against criminal prosecution but not from public censure under the lawyer discipline process.

Are you troubled by this result? Should it be significant that Abrams was charged with D.C.'s counterpart to Model Rule 8.4(c), "conduct involving dishonesty, fraud, deceit or misrepresentation," rather than Rule 8.4(b) that requires a "criminal act"?

PROBLEM 3

REGULATING LAWYERS OUTSIDE OF THE FORMAL DISCIPLINARY SYSTEM

We looked at professional discipline in Problem 2. Here, we look at additional sanctions that lawyers may face. Actions for professional malpractice may seek damages against a lawyer for wrongs characterized in at least three ways—as a tort committed by the lawyer against the client, as a breach of the contract the client made for the lawyer's services, or as a

---

severe that later criminal prosecution would create a sanction disproportionate to the offense. United States v. Ursery, 518 U.S. 267 (1996), said that in reviewing a double jeopardy claim, a court must ask whether the civil sanction had a purpose other than punitive.

17. Accord, Anonymous Attorneys v. Bar Ass'n of Erie County, 362 N.E.2d 592 (N.Y.1977); In re Schwarz, 282 N.E.2d 689 (Ill.1972), cert. denied 409 U.S. 1047 (1972).

breach of fiduciary duties that the lawyer owes to the client. Sometimes all of these theories work equally well; sometimes the theory matters, as when the statute of limitations may have run on one or more claims, or when the remedy affects the amount of damages, as when the client may seek punitive damages in tort but not in contract. In this problem, we look first at the standard of care and conduct used in malpractice cases. Next, we examine what goes into determining whether that standard has been violated. Then we consider remedies for professional malpractice and attempts to contract away those remedies. Finally, we look at a range of sanctions other than professional malpractice that a lawyer may face for his or her professional misconduct.

FACTS

Sarah Field is a young lawyer with a great future. She has attracted several clients with a wide range of interests and problems. Her outstanding record before juries is the envy of the local bar. Sometimes, however, she is not as careful as she might be.

Field is active in local politics. At a party picnic, an acquaintance of hers, Mary Moore, took her aside and told Field, "My doctor really messed me up two years ago. He performed supposedly minor surgery but cut the wrong things and now I can never have children." Field put her arm around Moore and said, "That's terrible. I know how to handle doctors like that. Leave everything to me." When Field got back to her office, she wrote a nasty letter to the doctor demanding that he "fully compensate my client." By return mail, she received a settlement offer of $250,000. Moore, the client, said she was delighted and Field was impressed at how intimidated the doctor seemed to be by her letter. Field did not have Moore examined by an independent physician. Had she done so, both would have learned that Moore's injuries were much worse than she believed. Instead, Field recommended that Moore accept the settlement, which she did. Now, Moore has learned the full extent of her injuries, and she realizes how inadequate her settlement really was.

Field does very little tax work. One of her wealthy clients heard that income can be made taxable to her children, instead of herself, by the use of certain trusts. She asked Field to see that the trusts were properly prepared. Field researched the problem as well as her small office library would permit and discussed the issues over coffee with a CPA from down the hall. The client later learned that Field's handiwork was not good enough to accomplish her objectives, and the IRS assessed a large tax deficiency. "Don't blame me," Field said defensively, "If you wanted tax advice you should have called a specialist. I told you I was not positive of the tax consequences."

In yet another incident, this time a criminal trial in which she was appointed counsel, Field had gone on a vacation and failed to appear when the case was called. The case was reset for the following morning. Field's office reached her and she quickly returned. The next day, although she was physically present for the trial, she was not prepared and did a terrible job. The client was convicted and sentenced to a long prison term.

QUESTIONS

A.   THE STANDARD OF CARE AND CONDUCT IN A MALPRACTICE ACTION

1.   By what standard should a lawyer be judged in a malpractice case?

a.   A leading treatise on lawyer malpractice says:

"[T]he essential elements of a cause of action for professional negligence are:

"(1) The employment of the attorney or other basis for imposing a duty;

"(2) the failure of the attorney to exercise ordinary skill and knowledge; and

"(3) that such negligence was the proximate cause of damage to the plaintiff."

1 Ronald E. Mallen & Jeffrey M. Smith, Legal Malpractice § 8.13 (2010 ed.).

b.   Restatement Third, The Law Governing Lawyers § 52(1) is more succinct: "[A] lawyer who owes a duty of care must exercise the competence and diligence normally exercised by lawyers in similar circumstances."

c.   Lawyers sometimes try to comfort themselves by citing Lucas v. Hamm, 364 P.2d 685 (Cal.1961), which said the rule against perpetuities is so difficult that violation of it is not inevitably malpractice. But in reality, *Lucas* is of little help. Horne v. Peckham, 158 Cal.Rptr. 714 (Cal.Ct.App. 1979), made clear that the *Lucas* situation was unusual if not unique. "An attorney's obligation is not satisfied by simply determining that the law on a particular subject is doubtful or debatable [because] an attorney has a duty to *avoid* involving his client in murky areas of law if research reveals alternative courses of conduct. At least he should inform his client of uncertainties and let the client make the decision." 158 Cal.Rptr. at 721.

d.   Biomet Inc. v. Finnegan Henderson LLP, 967 A.2d 662 (D.C. 2009), gave new life to the idea that a litigator's "reasonable judgment" or tactical decision regarding an unsettled point of law may not be the basis for a malpractice claim. The law firm represented the defendant in a patent infringement suit. After a jury verdict in favor of the plaintiff, the district court awarded over $7 million in compensatory damages and $20 million in punitive damages. That was a ratio of punitive to compensatory damages of about 3:1. Because of the low ratio and a jury finding that the defendant's conduct had been reprehensible, the firm decided it might not have a good argument regarding the unconstitutionality of the punitive damages. See BMW of North America, Inc. v. Gore, 517 U.S. 559 (1996). It also thought that, under the case law, it could make such an argument on remand if the compensatory damages were adjusted. The firm thus focused upon the infringement finding, and the Federal Circuit reversed. On remand, compensatory damages were adjusted down to $520 while punitive damages remained the same, producing a new punitive-to-compensatory damage ratio of about 38,000:1.

At that point, the law firm argued that the punitive damages were unconstitutionally excessive, and the district court agreed. But on appeal, the Federal Circuit held the defendant had waived the constitutional argument because it had not raised it in the initial appeal. The client brought a legal malpractice action in the District of Columbia against the firm for failing to preserve the constitutional argument regarding punitive damages. The court granted summary judgment for the firm. Lawyers are not liable for honest mistakes that arise in the course of their professional judgment, the court explained. In light of *BMW*, it was reasonable for the firm to believe that it did not have a strong argument regarding constitutionality of the damages on the initial appeal. The viability of such an argument prior to the reduction of compensatory damages was an unsettled point of law. It is not malpractice for an attorney to make a tactical decision based upon a reasonable reading of unsettled law, even if that reading is proven ultimately to be wrong.

2. Did Sarah Field commit malpractice by recommending the inadequate settlement to the victim of medical malpractice?

a. Traditional doctrine used to say that a client could not sue for malpractice after agreeing to settle a case because she would not have settled unless she were happy with the result. Later cases, however, reason that clients tend to follow their lawyers' advice and do not have independent bases on which to evaluate a settlement. Therefore, recommending an inadequate settlement may indeed constitute malpractice.

b. Woodruff v. Tomlin, 616 F.2d 924 (6th Cir.1980) (en banc), cert. denied, 449 U.S. 888 (1980), relied on the typical rule that there is no malpractice liability for an honest exercise of professional judgment as to whether to call a particular person as a witness. But *Woodruff* said that the rule does not protect a lawyer's decision not to interview a potentially material witness as Field had failed to do in this case. Without interviewing the witness, the lawyer would have no basis on which to make a judgment about the witness' importance, so the failure to interview may indeed be malpractice.

c. Wood v. McGrath, North, Mullin & Kratz, P.C., 589 N.W.2d 103 (Neb.1999), upheld a claim against lawyers who allegedly failed to tell the wife in a divorce action that the law was unsettled but that she might be entitled to a share of her husband's unvested stock options, and capital gain taxes might not have to be deducted from the share to which she was entitled. The lawyers said their overall advice about the merits of the settlement was sound, but the court held the client could not decide whether to settle without adequate information about the particular legal questions presented.

3. Is Field obliged to refer the tax case to a specialist?

a. In Horne v. Peckham, supra, the client had asked Attorney to draft a Clifford trust in order to shelter income from federal taxes. Attorney testified that he told the client: "I had no knowledge of tax matters. I had no expertise in tax matters; that if somebody else could figure out what needed to be done, I could draft the documents." Attorney consulted with the client's accountant and a two-volume set of American Jurisprudence on federal taxation. When the trust failed to qualify for favorable tax treatment, the client sued and the jury awarded damages of $64,983.31. The appellate court affirmed the judgment and upheld a jury instruction that it "is the duty of an attorney who is a general practitioner to refer his client to a specialist or recommend the assistance of a specialist if under the circumstances a reasonably careful and skillful practitioner would do so." If Attorney did not refer the case or seek a specialist's help, it was his duty to have the knowledge and skill possessed and used by specialists in the same locality and under the same circumstances.

b. On the other hand, Battle v. Thornton, 646 A.2d 315 (D.C.1994), held that in a jurisdiction that does not certify specialties, the malpractice standard is the skill of an ordinary lawyer, not persons who concentrate their practice in a given area of the law and usually handle a given kind of case.

c. With which rule do you agree? Does the California rule encourage making legal services more expensive? Should Rule 1.2(c) protect a lawyer who warns a client that he has "no knowledge of tax matters"?

4. Should Field be liable to the criminal defendant whose defense she handled badly?

a. The majority rule on this subject may surprise you. Ordinarily, an element of a suit for lawyer malpractice is that a convicted criminal defendant must prove himself actually innocent of the charges against him, not just that a better lawyer might have obtained a not guilty verdict. Wiley v. County of San Diego, 966 P.2d 983 (Cal.1998), for example, finding that "the clear majority of courts that have considered the question * * * require proof of actual innocence," explained:

> "[A] guilty defendant's conviction and sentence are the direct consequence of his own perfidy. The fact that nonnegligent counsel 'could have done better' may warrant postconviction relief, but it does not translate into civil damages, which are intended to make the plaintiff whole. While a conviction predicated on incompetence may be erroneous, it is not unjust. * * * Only an innocent person wrongly convicted due to inadequate representation has suffered a compensable injury * * *." 966 P.2d at 987.

b.   Restatement Third, The Law Governing Lawyers § 53, Comment *d*, acknowledged cases like *Wiley* but proposed a less restrictive rule, saying:

"Although most jurisdictions addressing the issue have stricter rules, under this Section, it is not necessary to prove that the convicted defendant was in fact innocent. As required by most jurisdictions addressing the issue, it is necessary for a former criminal defendant seeking damages for malpractice causing a conviction to have had that conviction set aside, when process for that relief on the grounds asserted in the malpractice action was available."

Do you agree that courts should be cautious about allowing malpractice actions after criminal cases? Is there a reason to treat criminal and civil clients differently with respect to attorney malpractice? Might it be harder to find lawyers willing to act as criminal defense counsel if the law permitted more such suits?[1]

c.   Even though the majority rule remains intact,[2] courts are chipping away at its edges. Levine v. Kling, 123 F.3d 580 (7th Cir.1997), for example, acknowledged the usual rule but, in dictum, distinguished a situation where a client did the prohibited act but might have a complete legal defense to the criminal charge.

"We used the awkward term 'guilty in law' to distinguish the case in which the defendant is guilty in fact but has a sound legal defense, such as double jeopardy, from a case in which he is both guilty in fact and has no sound legal defense yet might, because of the heavy burden of proof on the prosecution, have obtained an acquittal if he had had a skillful lawyer. Only in the second case is the malpractice suit against the less-than-skillful lawyer barred." 123 F.3d at 582.

d.   In Stichting v. Schreiber, 327 F.3d 173 (2d Cir.2003), a Dutch company, Saybolt International, wanted to buy a parcel of land for its operations in Panama, but its lawyers advised that it would first have to make a $50,000 bribe to a Panamanian official. Allegedly based on the advice of its lawyer, Saybolt believed that it would not violate the Foreign Corrupt Practices Act (FCPA) if it paid the bribe as a Dutch company rather than through its U.S. subsidiary. When the government filed crimi-

---

1. Whether appointed counsel should ever be subject to a malpractice action has been a controversial issue. Dziubak v. Mott, 503 N.W.2d 771 (Minn.1993), held that a public defender is immune from suit; public defenders may not turn down cases, and the public treasury cannot afford to defend malpractice cases. Moreover, immunity may encourage private lawyers to accept court appointments. See also, Polk County v. Dodson, 454 U.S. 312 (1981) (state public defender does not act "under color of state law" so as to be liable for malpractice under 42 U.S.C. § 1983). However, Ferri v. Ackerman, 444 U.S. 193 (1979), said that federal law does not require immunity of appointed counsel in federal cases from state malpractice claim. See also, Mossow v. United States, 987 F.2d 1365 (8th Cir.1993) (government can be sued for malpractice of military lawyer); Rowell v. Holt, 850 So.2d 474 (Fla.2003) (public defender liable where failed to point out that the conduct alleged was not a crime at all).

2. Not all states follow the rule requiring exoneration. Rantz v. Kaufman, 109 P.3d 132 (Colo.2005) rejects the exoneration requirement, although it agrees that denial of post-conviction relief could preclude litigation of some issues in the malpractice case.

nal charges, Saybolt America pled guilty and sued its lawyer for giving advice that the payment would be legal. The district court granted the lawyers' motion for summary judgment, but the Second Circuit disagreed. Because of the lawyers' bad advice, Saybolt had not known its conduct was criminal, so letting Saybolt sue for that bad advice would not allow it to profit from intentionally wrongful conduct. See also, Mrozek v. Intra Financial Corp., 699 N.W.2d 54 (Wis.2005) (guilty plea to securities fraud does not bar malpractice action for bad advice about what disclosures were required).

e. Likewise, in Powell v. Associated Counsel for the Accused, 106 P.3d 271 (Wash.App.2005), a client sued his attorneys for malpractice when he had received a sentence that exceeded the statutory limit. The crime carried a maximum sentence of one year, but the defendant was sentenced to 38.25 months' confinement without objection by his attorneys. When the court discovered its error, it granted Powell's petition for release, but by that time, Powell had been in jail for twenty months. Powell then filed a malpractice case and the court upheld it. Powell had no other way to get compensation for the over eight months of jail time he erroneously served, the court said. Powell had more than paid his debt to society and he was entitled to show that he had been forced to do so by his attorneys' malpractice.

5. May Field be held liable for professional malpractice to persons other than her clients?

a. A lawyer's liability for malpractice to someone who is not her client is a controversial and evolving area of lawyer liability. Restatement Third, The Law Governing Lawyers § 51 suggests four situations in which liability may be found.

b. First, a lawyer may be liable to a prospective client for revealing confidential information communicated to the lawyer or, for example, if the lawyer fails to tell the prospective client that the statute of limitations on his claim will soon run out, e.g., Miller v. Metzinger, 154 Cal.Rptr. 22 (Cal.Ct.App.1979).

c. Second, a lawyer may also be liable to beneficiaries named in a client's will if, due to the lawyer's negligence, the will does not carry out the testator's intention. Blair v. Ing, 21 P.3d 452 (Haw. 2001), for example, found that beneficiaries of a trust had standing to sue the draftsman whose negligence had cost the trust $200,000 in increased taxes. The plaintiffs were the intended beneficiaries of the lawyer-client relationship, the court said, and they could make the lawyer restore the trust corpus to the level it would have been but for the negligence.[3]

d. Third, a lawyer may be liable to a non-client to whom the lawyer expressly assumes an obligation to investigate facts and accurately report

---

3. But see, Miller v. Mooney, 725 N.E.2d 545 (Mass.2000) (will beneficiaries cannot sue lawyer because they were neither clients of the lawyer, nor third-party benefi- ciaries of a contract with the lawyer, nor persons entitled to be told how the testator was leaving her money).

them to the non-client. See, e.g., Greycas, Inc. v. Proud, 826 F.2d 1560 (7th Cir.1987), cert. denied, 484 U.S. 1043 (1988) (lawyer who agreed to investigate state of client's title to property being posted as security for loan held liable to the lender when failed to investigate and inaccurately reported the state of the client's title).[4]

In Paradigm Insurance Co. v. Langerman Law Offices, P.A., 24 P.3d 593 (Ariz.2001), the issue was whether an insurance company that retains a lawyer to defend the insured may sue that lawyer for malpractice. The insurance company had paid a settlement on behalf of the insured doctor after the defendant lawyer had mistakenly concluded the doctor was not covered under the hospital's malpractice insurance. Relying on § 51(3) of the Restatement, the court held that the fact that the lawyer-defendant in this case had earlier represented the doctor (not the doctor's insurance company), did not defeat the insurance company's claims. The court explained that when an insurance company hires a lawyer to represent the insured, the lawyer's obligation to the insured (to defeat the claim) and to the insurer were the same. It would be unjust, the court said, for the lawyer to have no malpractice liability to the insurer that retained him, assigned the case to him, and paid his fees.

e. Fourth, under Restatement § 51(4), and Comment *h*, a lawyer who aids a trustee-like fiduciary to breach an obligation to the intended beneficiary of the fiduciary's duty may be liable to that beneficiary. See, e.g., Fickett v. Superior Court, 558 P.2d 988 (Ariz.App.1976); Reynolds v. Schrock, 107 P.3d 52 (Or.Ct.App.2005).

In Guardianship of Karan, 38 P.3d 396 (Wash.Ct.App.2002), the plaintiff was the successor guardian of a minor, Amanda, who was the beneficiary of her father's life insurance policy. When Amanda's father died, her mother hired the defendant-lawyer to represent the mother in a petition in which she asked to be named the guardian of Amanda's estate. The lawyer obtained an order for Amanda's mother to establish and manage an account in Amanda's name, but he failed to include statutorily-required safeguards requiring the mother to post a bond or to place the funds in a blocked account. By the time the plaintiff was substituted as Amanda's guardian, her mother had spent most of the $50,000 left to Amanda and was judgment-proof. When the plaintiff sued the lawyer for legal malpractice, the lawyer argued that only Amanda's mother, his client, could bring a malpractice claim. The court rejected that defense, pointing to several factors in the case: the lawyer performed the work for Amanda's benefit; it was reasonably foreseeable that a failure to obtain the required safeguards would make depletion of the estate more likely; Amanda suffered harm as a result; the failure to implement the safeguards caused Amanda's injury; if the court refuses to impose a duty on lawyers to act in the interests of the beneficiaries who are minors, similarly situated individuals will be harmed in the future; and imposing such a duty will not create any undue burden

---

4. You will see more about this role of the lawyer as "evaluator" in Problem 21, *infra*.

on lawyers because the beneficiary's interest is not in conflict with any legitimate request of any guardian.

f. In some states, notably New York and Texas, in spite of the cited cases, the theory of liability to non-clients is significantly qualified by the requirement of privity between lawyer and client in order to maintain a malpractice action. The privity limitation is derived from Ultramares v. Touche, 174 N.E. 441 (N.Y.1931), in which Judge Cardozo had feared giving professionals unlimited liability to investors who relied on their opinions. Compare, e.g., Security Pacific Business Credit, Inc. v. Peat Marwick Main & Co., 597 N.E.2d 1080 (N.Y.1992) (continuing to follow *Ultramares*), with Vereins–Und Westbank, AG v. Carter, 691 F.Supp. 704 (S.D.N.Y.1988) (holding lawyer liable on opinion letter). Do you see any good reason to retain the privity requirement today?

B. PROVING A MALPRACTICE CASE

1. How is the trier of fact supposed to know what skill and knowledge a lawyer would ordinarily employ in the circumstances presented in this problem?

a. A plaintiff must ordinarily present expert testimony about the duty of care in a suit for professional malpractice. This rule applies even in a bench trial because the standard of care must be presented on the record with a chance for cross examination rather than left to the subjective standard of the judge.

b. Sometimes the court excuses expert testimony, however, when the issue is so simple or the lack of skill so obvious as to be within the range of ordinary experience of lay people. In Schmitz v. Crotty, 528 N.W.2d 112 (Iowa 1995), for example, while completing death tax returns begun by another lawyer, the successor lawyer did not recognize that the same land was being reported more than once, thus increasing the taxes due. The court found the negligence so obvious that it did not require an expert to explain it to the jury.

2. If a client sues Sarah Field for malpractice, should the state's rules of professional conduct be determinative of the standards of care and conduct?

a. Are violations of professional conduct rules like the violations of law underlying the tort doctrine of negligence per se? For example, if the speed limit is 40 m.p.h., and the driver is traveling at 50 m.p.h, the normal rule is that driver's speeding is negligent. He cannot argue he was not driving too fast; he can only argue causation and damages.

b. Scope ¶ 18 of the 1983 Model Rules disclaimed the use of professional standards in malpractice cases. It said in part: "Violation of a Rule should not give rise to a cause of action nor should it create any presumption that a legal duty has been breached. * * * [N]othing in the Rules should be deemed to augment any substantive legal duty of lawyers or the extra-disciplinary consequences of violating such a duty." What effect do you believe a court should have given to that disclaimer?

c. Most courts have at least allowed expert witnesses to cite the professional rules as evidence of the standards to which most lawyers adhere in the situations they face, e.g., Woodruff v. Tomlin, 616 F.2d 924 (6th Cir.1980) (en banc), cert. denied, 449 U.S. 888 (1980) (Model Code is "some evidence of the standards required of lawyers"); Mirabito v. Liccardo, 5 Cal.Rptr.2d 571 (Ct.App.1992) (disciplinary standards may be the subject of experts' testimony and cited to the jury); Maritrans GP Inc. v. Pepper, Hamilton & Scheetz, 602 A.2d 1277 (Pa.1992) (violation of state disciplinary rule does not *preclude* finding of malpractice; the rule may state a principle of fiduciary duty, for example, that will be enforced in a malpractice case even if the rule is not itself enforced).

However, Hizey v. Carpenter, 830 P.2d 646 (Wash.1992), held that violation of a disciplinary rule is not only not enough to show malpractice, the language of the rule may not even form the basis of a jury instruction. See also, Lazy Seven Coal Sales, Inc. v. Stone & Hinds, P.C., 813 S.W.2d 400 (Tenn.1991); Mergler v. Crystal Properties Associates, Ltd., 583 N.Y.S.2d 229 (App.Div.1992).

d. Restatement Third, The Law Governing Lawyers § 52(2) concluded from the plethora of cases that proof of violation of a professional rule (a) "does not give rise to an implied cause of action" for negligence or breach of fiduciary duty, (b) "does not preclude other proof concerning the duty of care * * * or the fiduciary duty," but (c) "may be considered by a trier of fact as an aid in understanding and applying" the applicable standard of care or conduct.

Does this rule guarantee work for legal ethics experts? What does it mean to say that violation of a professional standard "may be considered by the trier of fact"? Should the jury take the violation seriously or not? Should the judge decide, as a matter of law, what the ethics rules mean, just as the judge decides what other court rules (evidence rules, civil procedure rules) mean?

e. The drafters of the 2002 Model Rules, in what is now Scope ¶ 20, have deleted the earlier disclaimer and substituted: "Nevertheless, since the Rules do establish standards of conduct by lawyers, a lawyer's violation of a Rule may be evidence of breach of the applicable standard of conduct." Now is the relevance of the Rules clear?

3. How should courts deal with the problem of causation? Should a client be able to recover damages if the client would have lost the case no matter what the lawyer had done?

a. The traditional requirement of proof of what a non-negligent lawyer could have obtained for the client is called the "suit-within-a-suit requirement." Restatement Third, The Law Governing Lawyers § 53, Comment *b*, explains:

> "All the issues that would have been litigated in the previous action are litigated between the plaintiff and the plaintiff's former lawyer, with the latter taking the place and bearing the burdens that properly would have fallen on the defendant in the original action.

* * * Similar principles apply when a former civil defendant contends that, but for the misconduct of the defendant's former lawyer, the defendant would have secured a better result at trial."

In Winskunas v. Birnbaum, 23 F.3d 1264 (7th Cir.1994), for example, the court found there was no evidence the plaintiff could have won his suit, so there was no basis for saying that his lawyer's failure to appeal caused his loss. In Pickens, Barnes & Abernathy v. Heasley, 328 N.W.2d 524 (Iowa 1983), the court said the trial court erred in refusing to instruct the jury that any favorable judgment in the original suit might not have been collectible.

b. Applying the suit-within-a-suit requirement to this problem, Field might try to defend against Moore's malpractice claim by showing that Moore did not have a very strong case as to the doctor's negligence, or that Moore herself had been negligent in waiting too long to seek medical help. What do you think of permitting such a defense?

c. Should a lawyer be able to use a client's trust in the lawyer against the client to prove the client's contributory negligence? In Arnav Industries, Inc. Retirement Trust v. Brown, Raysman, Millstein, Felder & Steiner, LLP, 751 N.E.2d 936 (N.Y.2001), the defendant law firm had revised a settlement agreement for the plaintiff client and had represented that the revised version only corrected a typographical error in the original. In fact, the new version also misstated the total amount due, a mistake that was costly to the plaintiff. Given the firm's representation that there was only one change, the plaintiff signed the revised document without reading it. The court held that the plaintiff's failure to read the contract did not defeat a malpractice claim, reasoning that the plaintiff had justifiably relied on its attorney's representations.

d. Other courts have been concerned that a case-within-a-case requirement inadequately explores how a matter would really have proceeded if handled properly by the accused lawyer. In Conklin v. Hannoch Weisman, 678 A.2d 1060 (N.J.1996), for example, the plaintiffs had sold property subject to a purchase money mortgage. They alleged that their lawyer had not sufficiently explained to them the effect of a subordination agreement whereby the defaulting buyer's other creditors got paid but the sellers ultimately did not. The jury had been given a traditional proximate cause instruction and had found the lawyer's advice inadequate but not the cause of the client's loss because the plaintiffs probably would have sold the property anyway. The court reversed and said that, on retrial, the jury should be told that the lawyers' malpractice need only be a "substantial factor" in bringing about the plaintiff's loss. The fact that a client goes ahead with a deal in the face of advice about risks can negate causation, but the fact that the client did not ask about the consequences of the approach the lawyer had chosen did not excuse the lawyers' obligation to tell the client about those consequences.

What do you think of moderating the causation requirement in this way? Does the "substantial factor" test take a more realistic view of the nature of causation? Does it give a jury too much room to speculate about what caused a plaintiff's loss?

C. **MALPRACTICE REMEDIES; ADVANCE WAIVERS OF A LAWYER'S MALPRACTICE**

1. What remedies should be available to redress Sarah Field's professional malpractice?

a. The range of possible remedies is substantial. Typically, the client's damages are what the client would have obtained by way of trial or settlement if the lawyer had handled the matter non-negligently. But malpractice can take other forms; a lawyer who negligently discloses a client's trade secret, for example, might be liable for damage to the client's business resulting from the disclosure. See Restatement Third, The Law Governing Lawyers § 53, Comment *b*.

b. Campagnola v. Mulholland, Minion & Roe, 555 N.E.2d 611 (N.Y. 1990), added a wrinkle to the question of damages. Because the lawyer did not comply with the policy provisions, the client lost her $100,000 uninsured motorist coverage. The lawyer asserted that this sum should be reduced by the portion of the judgment she would have had to pay as the lawyer's contingent fee. In a sharply divided 4 to 3 decision, the New York Court of Appeals said her contract to pay fees to her first lawyer was not part of the measure of what she had lost. Judge Kaye wrote in a concurring opinion that the plaintiff would be required to pay fees to bring this malpractice case, so not deducting fees for the first case from the damage award was necessary to make her whole.

But Horn v. Wooser, 165 P.3d 69 (Wyo.2007), explicitly rejected the result and analysis in *Campagnola*. The Wyoming court said that the plaintiff would have incurred legal fees to collect damages in the underlying case and that an accurate measure of the plaintiff's actual loss must reflect the amount of those fees. Further, Judge Kaye's approach requiring the lawyer malpractice defendant to pay in effect the client's fees for suing the lawyer would be inconsistent with the usual requirement that parties pay their own legal fees. With which decision do you agree?

2. Some cases involving breach of a lawyer's duty to a client involve more than simple negligence. They involve breach of a traditional fiduciary duty such as the duty of loyalty. In the case of a breach of fiduciary duty, might a court properly excuse the client from paying all or part of the lawyer's fee even if the client can show no actual damages?

a. Hendry v. Pelland, 73 F.3d 397 (D.C.Cir.1996), is one of the increasing number of claims for fee forfeiture, even in the absence of economic harm to the client. The law firm had represented all five members of a family selling a parcel of land. All the clients had somewhat different wishes about the terms of sale. While finding no intentional misconduct that would support punitive damages, or even any actual damage suffered by family members, the court found that representation of all five was a conflict of interest. Because a conflict of interest is a breach of fiduciary duty, the court required the law firm to disgorge all fees it had earned in the case.

What do you think of this result? Is there much that lawyers do that cannot be pled as a breach of fiduciary duty? Does the punishment exceed the crime if the court imposes fee forfeiture when the lawyer's action has caused no harm to the client?

b.   Restatement Third, The Law Governing Lawyers § 37, Comment *b*, acknowledges fee forfeiture as a theory of relief but it makes clear:

"Forfeiture of fees * * * is not justified in each instance in which a lawyer violates a legal duty, nor is total forfeiture always appropriate. Some violations are inadvertent or do not significantly harm the client. Some can be adequately dealt with by [other remedies] or by a partial forfeiture. Denying the lawyer all compensation would sometimes be an excessive sanction, giving a windfall to the client. The remedy of this Section should hence be applied with discretion."

c.   Burrow v. Arce, 997 S.W.2d 229 (Tex.1999), agreed with § 37 of the Restatement that the remedy of fee forfeiture does not require proof that a client suffered actual damage from the lawyer's conduct. But, the court went on, the amount of any forfeiture should be set by the trial judge, not the jury.

3.   In the future, in order to reduce her malpractice liability, should Field add a provision to her standard engagement letter providing that the client waives any malpractice claims against Field?

a.   Look at Model Rule 1.8(h)(1). Under what conditions, if any, might Field offer such an option to her client? DR 6–102 of the ABA Model Code of Professional Responsibility would not have allowed such a provision under any circumstances. Do you agree with Rule 1.8(h)(1) that the client should be able to consent to such a provision if he or she is independently represented in doing so?

b.   Why would any client agree to such an arrangement? Suppose that, in return, Field would charge the client less per hour than a specialist. A client has a right to buy a Kia instead of a Mercedes; should the client have the right to buy lower quality legal services?

c.   What client would seek independent legal counsel about whether to sign such a clause? In the case of a corporate client, might such independent advice come from the company's in-house lawyer? Why might a corporate client be willing to sign such a clause?

d.   Are the same concerns raised when a lawyer settles a fee dispute with a client and asks the client for a general release of any malpractice claims the client might assert? Take a look at Rule 1.8(h)(2). State Bar of California, Standing Comm. on Prof'l Responsibility and Conduct, Formal Op. 2009–178 (2009), said that conflict rules are implicated when a fee dispute involves a potential claim for legal malpractice and the proposed release and waiver is broad enough to release the claim. In such a case, an attorney must abide by California Rule 3–400(B) (ABA Model Rule 1.8(h)(2)), which requires that an attorney shall not settle a claim or potential claim a client may have for the attorney's malpractice unless "(1) the client is informed in writing that the client may seek the advice of independent counsel regarding the settlement, and (2) the client is given a reasonable opportunity to seek that advice." When settlement of the fee dispute involves the release of such a claim, the Committee said, the attorney should not continue to represent the client unless he or she provides a written disclosure regarding his or her financial or professional interests surrounding the claim. Further, the attorney should advise the client that he cannot represent the client in connection with the proposed settlement. In determining whether or not to withdraw from the underlying representation, the attorney should evaluate the circumstances motivating the inclusion of the release, the level of antagonism between the attorney and the client, and the degree to which a decision to withdraw would prejudice the client.

e.   Should Rule 1.8(h)(1) be amended to make waivers harder to obtain? Would any such changes in the rule simply make it harder for clients to do something they believe it is in their interest to do?

4.   Does a lawyer have a duty to tell a client about the lawyer's own malpractice in the client's case?

a.   Matter of Tallon, 447 N.Y.S.2d 50 (N.Y.App.Div.1982), held that a lawyer must inform the client, withdraw, and advise the client to get independent legal advice about whether or not to sue. Cf. ABA Model Rule 1.8(h)(2) and California Rules of Professional Conduct Rule 3–400, discussed above.

b.   In re Blackwelder, 615 N.E.2d 106 (Ind.1993), involved a lawyer whose clients had sought to reopen a default judgment entered against them. The lawyer missed the filing deadline for doing so, and he proposed to handle their bankruptcy free in exchange for a release from malpractice liability. The court found that the clients had not been advised in writing to get independent counsel before signing the malpractice release and it publicly reprimanded the lawyer.

c.   New York State Bar Association Committee on Professional Ethics, Opinion 734 (2000) discussed whether a legal aid society is bound by the ethical duty applicable to other attorneys to disclose their lawyer's malpractice to their clients. The opinion states that the society is obliged to keep their clients reasonably informed about their cases and therefore has a duty to disclose any significant error or omission. The society can then continue representing the client only after getting that client's informed consent and a showing that "a disinterested lawyer would believe that the representation of the client would not be adversely affected thereby."

d.   Should a lawyer have any duty to tell a client about the possible malpractice of the client's former lawyer? Suppose the current lawyer learned in the course of representing a client that the previous lawyer had missed a statute of limitations, forfeiting the client's right to sue? Should there be a tacit understanding among lawyers that we will not speak negatively about a fellow professional? May the previous lawyer properly charge the second lawyer with barratry, i.e., stirring up litigation, if the current lawyer mentions the earlier malpractice? Should we take exactly the opposite view?

5.   Should law firms be permitted to shield each of the lawyers from vicarious liability for the malpractice of other lawyers in the firm?

a.   Traditionally, lawyers practiced in general partnerships, and each partner was jointly and severally liable for the torts of the other partners. Now, depending on state statute, the usual vehicle for trying to do that is the limited liability company (LLC) or the limited liability partnership (LLP). Each is a form of law firm organization that limits personal liability to those lawyers who commit the malpractice and those who supervise those lawyers.

b.   ABA Formal Opinion 96–401 (Aug. 2, 1996) ruled that it does not violate the Model Rules for a lawyer to be part of a limited liability partnership. Model Rule 1.8(h)(1) on limiting liability for one's own malpractice does not address vicarious liability, and no other Model Rule requires a lawyer to be liable for his or her partner's malpractice. However, limited liability companies, like other law firms, must comply with Model Rules 5.1 and 5.3 on the duty to supervise and Rule 5.4 on participation of non-lawyers in the organization.

c.   Whether liability is direct or vicarious is a recurring issue in the LLC cases. Sanders, Bruin, Coll & Worley, P.A. v. McKay Oil Corp., 943 P.2d 104 (N.M.1997), involved an LLC whose lawyers voted to terminate representation of a client six weeks before a major arbitration, allegedly because of illness of the partner who was to handle the litigation. The client considered the termination to be malpractice, and the question was whether liability was limited to the firm's assets or could be asserted against each shareholder in the LLC. The court held each lawyer liable. While shareholders in an LLC cannot be held vicariously liable, the court said, in this case the liability was for each shareholder's individual act of voting.

d.   In Gosselin v. Webb, 242 F.3d 412 (1st Cir.2001), a group of lawyers shared office space but were not legally partners. The district court had granted them summary judgment, holding the lawyers could not be vicariously liable for each other's conduct. But the First Circuit remanded for a trial. The lawyers practiced under a common trade name, and the negligent lawyer represented that he was ''with'' a firm. Those acts of holding out as a partnership, the court held, could be found sufficient to make the lawyers vicariously liable for each other's acts.

e.   Do you have any strong feelings about the propriety of lawyers who seek to limit their liability for the malpractice of their partners? Would such limitations reduce partners' efforts to improve the culture of high professional standards in a firm? Does the fact that most law firms carry high levels of malpractice insurance tend to make questions of personal liability of less concern than they would otherwise be?

D. OTHER SIGNIFICANT CONSEQUENCES OF NEGLIGENCE OR MISCONDUCT BY LAWYERS

1. What sanctions should Field expect for missing the first trial date in the criminal case?

a. For a situation such as Field's criminal case, Restatement Third, The Law Governing Lawyers § 6, Comment g, says:

> "[A] lawyer functioning as an advocate in a proceeding may be subject to remedies through contempt orders * * * where necessary and appropriate to * * * prevent significant impairment of the proceedings * * *. Included in such relief may be an appropriate sanction directed toward repairing or punishing harm that the lawyer's contemptuous conduct caused to the lawyer's own client."

b. In re Yengo, 417 A.2d 533 (N.J.1980), cert. denied, 449 U.S. 1124 (1981), involved a trial before a judge who had emphasized to the defense attorneys the need for regular attendance and said that before any tardiness or absence the attorney should secure her prior approval. After an attorney failed to appear for several days of trial, the judge tried to reach the attorney by phone. The judge talked to the attorney's daughter who said that he was in Bermuda on vacation. When the attorney finally appeared before the judge, he explained that he was in Bermuda on business and had no opportunity to obtain the judge's prior approval. The judge summarily held the attorney in contempt and fined him $500. The state supreme court affirmed.[5]

c. In re Aguilar, 97 P.3d 815 (Cal.2004), involved a law firm that represented the appellant in an oral argument scheduled in the California Supreme Court. One week prior to the argument, attorney Kent, who had represented the appellant in prior court proceedings, left the firm. When the time for oral arguments came, neither Kent nor a substitute showed up to argue on behalf of the appellant. The court held that when an attorney willfully fails to appear, the propriety of a contempt finding depends on whether the attorney has an adequate justification for the absence. Kent argued that his departure from the firm, coupled with the fact that the firm, not Kent personally, was the appellant's attorney of record, justified his failure to notify the court of his nonappearance. The court disagreed, finding that Kent had an obligation to appear unless he had arranged for a substitute. The court held Kent in contempt, and fined him $250. Aguilar, the firm's managing partner, received a more severe sanction. The court found that Aguilar had repeatedly lied in both court documents and oral statements when he said that he had no knowledge of the date and time of the oral argument. Aguilar's "contemptuous conduct" led the court to fine

---

5. See also, Matter of Mix, 901 F.2d 1431 (7th Cir.1990) (lawyer censured for seemingly doing as little as he could get away with in appeal on behalf of appointed client).

Aguilar and refer his case to the state bar for investigation and possible disciplinary sanctions.

2.   Even if her client cannot successfully sue for malpractice, should the criminal defendant be able to cite Field's poor representation as a basis of reversing the conviction?

a.   The leading case on "ineffective assistance of counsel" is Strickland v. Washington, 466 U.S. 668 (1984). Even in a death penalty case, the Court held, to justify issuance of a writ of habeas corpus, a court must find that the lawyer's acts or omissions were not only "outside the wide range of professionally competent assistance" but also that the ineffectiveness caused "actual prejudice." "It is not enough for the defendant to show that the errors had some conceivable effect on the outcome of the proceedings." 466 U.S. at 693. "The defendant must show that there is a reasonable probability that, but for counsel's unprofessional errors, the result of the proceeding would have been different. A reasonable probability is a probability sufficient to undermine confidence in the outcome." 466 U.S. at 694.

b.   Cottle v. State, 733 So.2d 963 (Fla.1999), held that it is ineffective assistance of counsel to fail to tell a criminal client about a plea offer from the prosecutor and to fail to give the client the right to decide whether to accept it. The client is not required to show that the trial judge would have confirmed the agreement. See also, People v. Curry, 687 N.E.2d 877 (Ill.1997).

c.   Burdine v. Johnson, 262 F.3d 336 (5th Cir.2001) (en banc), cert. den. sub nom., Cockrell v. Burdine, 535 U.S. 1120 (2002), considered the availability of postconviction relief where the lawyer slept through large parts of the trial for capital murder. The en banc Fifth Circuit granted relief. It found that a lawyer's unconsciousness during critical portions of the trial rendered counsel "in effect, absent" and thus denied effective assistance. The court distinguished an unconscious attorney, who is essentially absent from the proceedings, from a drunk or impaired attorney, who may be capable of giving some assistance. Thus, the court was willing to presume prejudice and overturn the original conviction.

d.   In Wiggins v. Smith, 539 U.S. 510 (2003), Wiggins' counsel never told the jury the horrifying details of Wiggins' life that might have mitigated the murder charge, including that Wiggins' mother was a chronic alcoholic who left him alone for days to eat paint chips and garbage, and to beg for food. His mother and foster mothers abused him physically, and the father in his second foster home repeatedly molested and raped him. In one foster home, the foster mother's sons allegedly gang-raped him on more than one occasion. Under *Strickland*, the Court held that Wiggins was deprived of effective assistance of counsel. The test was whether Wiggins' counsel exercised "reasonable professional judgment," i.e., not whether he should have presented a mitigation case, but rather "whether the investigation supporting counsel's decision not to introduce mitigating evidence of Wiggins' background was itself reasonable." "Counsel's decision not to expand their investigation beyond the PSI and DDS records fell far short of the professional standards that prevailed in Maryland in 1989," a standard that usually involved the preparation of a social history report. Counsel was equipped with funds for such a report, yet chose not to commission one. Finally, the Court said, "In assessing the reasonableness of an attorney's investigation, . . . a court must consider not only the quantum of evidence already known to counsel, but also whether the known evidence would lead a reasonable attorney to investigate further. Even assuming Schlaich and Nethercott [Wiggins' counsel] limited the scope of their investigation for strategic reasons, *Strickland* does not establish that a cursory investigation automatically justifies a tactical decision with respect to sentencing strategy." Justices Thomas and Scalia dissented.[6]

e. Padilla v. Kentucky, 559 U.S. ___, 130 S.Ct. 1473, 176 L.Ed.2d 284 (2010), involved a permanent resident of the United States who pled guilty to transporting a large amount of marijuana in Kentucky. In advising Padilla whether to plead guilty, his lawyer told him he would not need to worry about deportation because he had been in the United States for such a long period of time. That advice was wrong; federal law makes nearly all drug crimes deportable offenses. As a result, Padilla appealed his conviction on the basis that he was denied his Sixth Amendment right to effective assistance of counsel, because if he had received accurate advice, he would not have pled guilty. The Supreme Court of Kentucky denied Padilla relief because it believed erroneous advice about a collateral consequence of his conviction did not fall under Sixth Amendment protection.

The Supreme Court reversed. It noted that, over time, Congress has expanded the number of deportable offenses while reducing the procedures by which convicted aliens may avoid deportation. The Court explained that for noncitizen defendants, deportation may be the most important aspect of the penalty imposed following conviction. Therefore, the Court held that advice regarding deportation is part of the Sixth Amendment right to counsel and Padilla's claim of ineffective assistance of counsel had to be analyzed pursuant to the *Strickland* test. The Court found that the weight of professional norms in the United States supported the view that counsel must advise a defendant regarding the risk of deportation. Thus, when deportation is a clear consequence under the law of a criminal conviction, a lawyer has a duty to give correct advice concerning this consequence. The Court left the second prong of the test, prejudice, to be determined by the Kentucky courts.

Justice Alito's concurring opinion, joined by Chief Justice Roberts, would limit application of *Strickland* to bad advice, not the failure to give advice. They believed the law should not require criminal defense lawyers to provide advice on immigration law, an area often outside their sphere of expertise. Justices Scalia and Thomas dissented, arguing that deportation is a collateral consequence of the criminal conviction, not subject to Sixth

---

6. See also, Rompilla v. Beard, 545 U.S. 374 (2005) (failure to review file in earlier conviction prior to sentencing hearing constituted ineffective assistance); Schriro v. Lan- drigan, 550 U.S. 465 (2007) (not ineffective assistance to follow defendant's instruction not to put on mitigation evidence).

Amendment standards, and they suggested the problems raised in the Court's opinion would be better handled through legislative action.

3.   **When are lawyers the criminal accomplices of their clients?**

a.   It happens more often than lawyers like to think. See, e.g., United States v. Morris, 988 F.2d 1335 (4th Cir.1993), where the government charged a lawyer with conspiracy to distribute drugs based in part on real estate work he did in closing the purchase of a house where crack cocaine was manufactured.

b.   United States v. Cueto, 151 F.3d 620 (7th Cir.1998), affirmed an obstruction of justice conviction against a lawyer who (1) falsely charged an FBI investigator with soliciting a bribe, (2) filed false motions that attacked the operations of the FBI and U.S. attorney, and (3) urged the defendants to file several motions, including one to disqualify the district judge. The National Association of Criminal Defense Lawyers filed a brief on behalf of the defendant who said he was just doing his job and only committed, if anything, a victimless crime, but the court disagreed. "We refuse to accept the notion that lawyers may do anything, including violating the law, to zealously advocate their clients' interests and then avoid criminal prosecution by claiming that they were 'just doing their job'." 151 F.3d at 634.

c.   Durie v. State, 751 So.2d 685 (Fla.App.2000), illustrates that a too-clever lawyer can be charged criminally. Durie's two clients were hurt in a bar fight. They sued the bar and collected for their injuries. Medicaid had paid the medical expenses of one of them and placed a lien on the proceeds of the lawsuit. So Durie had the settlement paid primarily to the victim not subject to the lien, and that client then made a "gift" to the other client. A jury called this Medicaid fraud and convicted the lawyer of grand theft. The court affirmed, holding that "while an attorney must do the best job he can for his client, he cannot engage in dishonest or fraudulent conduct." It is one thing to minimize lien claims and quite another to affirmatively misrepresent what the settlement arrangement was.

d.   In United States v. Sattar, 314 F.Supp.2d 279 (S.D.N.Y.2004), the government alleged that attorney Lynne Stewart had facilitated communication between her client, alleged terrorist Sheikh Abdel Rahman, and Sattar, his alleged surrogate in Egypt. Stewart argued that lawyers should be exempt from charges of alleged conspiracy to commit terrorism, at least as they relate to communications with their clients. The court rejected any such "roving commission to flout the criminal law with immunity," and Stewart was convicted.

4.   **What other kinds of remedies and sanctions for improper conduct do lawyers face?**

a.   While professional malpractice is the most common civil claim against a lawyer, it is far from the only one. Disqualification of the lawyer from participation in a case is another common remedy that we will see primarily in Chapter 4. Indeed, Restatement Third, The Law Governing

Lawyers § 6 lists thirteen remedies available to a client or non-client to redress a lawyer's conduct.

b.   A court may void transactions made in violation of the lawyer's professional obligations, for example. See, e.g., Abstract & Title Corp. of Florida v. Cochran, 414 So.2d 284 (Fla.App.1982) (lawyer's right of first refusal on client's property set aside); Spaulding v. Zimmerman, 116 N.W.2d 704 (Minn.1962) (tort settlement with minor set aside where lawyer for defendant did not disclose what he knew of the seriousness of plaintiff's injury).

c.   Shartzer v. Israels, 59 Cal.Rptr.2d 296 (Ct.App.1996), opinion modified, 67 Cal.Rptr.2d 42 (Ct.App.1997), found a lawyer liable to a witness for the other side for invasion of privacy. In a sexual battery prosecution, the defense counsel subpoenaed the complaining witness' confidential mental health records as California law permits. The doctor was supposed to send the records to the court to be reviewed for relevance before defense counsel received them. However, the records were sent directly to the defense counsel who did not send them to the court. He read them, gave them to the defense expert, and used them in cross-examining the witness before the jury. The court held that the mere reading of the confidential records under these circumstances rendered the lawyer liable to the complainant and there was no litigation privilege defense. See also, Bakker v. McKinnon, 152 F.3d 1007 (8th Cir.1998) (patients' lawyer requested credit reports about dentist and his adult daughters from a local credit bureau when federal law allows only persons with a legitimate "business need" to request such reports; actual and punitive damages assessed).

d.   In Heintz v. Jenkins, 514 U.S. 291 (1995), a unanimous Supreme Court held that lawyers who collect consumer debts through litigation may be sued under the Fair Debt Collection Practices Act for engaging in abusive and unfair practices. Depending on the nature of their practice, lawyers can come within the statutory description of persons who "regularly collect or attempt to collect [consumer] debts," and there is no basis to exclude them from the Act's coverage.

Jerman v. Carlisle, McNellie, Rini, Kramer & Ulrich LPA, 559 U.S. ___, 130 S.Ct. 1605, 176 L.Ed.2d 519 (2010), held that the "bona fide error" defense against civil liability for violations of the Fair Debt Collection Practices Act does not include mistaken interpretations of law. The Court found that a lawyer and law firm violated the Act by requiring an individual to dispute a debt in writing. There was a division of authority as to whether a debt collector could require a written expression of dispute. Although the district court found that the lawyer and firm violated the Act, it granted them summary judgment on the basis of § 1692k(c) of the Act, which relieves a debt collector from liability if the violation was the result of a bona fide error. The lower courts found that that provision included mistakes of law, but in an opinion by Justice Sotomayor, the Supreme Court disagreed.

The statutory text states that "[a] debt collector may not be held liable in any action brought under [the FDCPA] if the debt collector shows by a preponderance of evidence that the violation was not intentional and resulted from a bona fide error * * *." The Court explained that Congress uses more specific language when it intends to include a mistake of law defense in a statute. Congress used the term "intentional" in the FDCPA rather than "willful," whereas the latter is typically used when a statute is intended to cover mistakes of law. The Court dismissed concerns raised by the respondents and dissenting justices that its holding would open the floodgates for litigation under the Act for mistaken interpretations of law. Justices Kennedy and Alito dissented.

      f.   The bottom line of the cases in this problem is that being a lawyer is a risky business. The issues you will see in the remainder of this book raise not only questions about potential disciplinary sanctions, but also questions of civil liability and even whether you will be able to stay out of jail. Ethical issues raise important questions of right and wrong, but the law governing lawyers also has teeth.

CHAPTER III

FUNDAMENTALS OF THE LAWYER–CLIENT RELATIONSHIP

A good lawyer-client relationship works on many levels. Ideally, a lawyer and client like each other and trust that each will communicate with candor and act with integrity. Ideally, the lawyer acts as a client's friend, telling the hard truth when necessary but consistently providing reliable support. Ultimately, however, the relationship between lawyer and client is based on law. Many of the legal elements of the relationship seem *sui generis*, but they are made up of familiar elements—agency law, contracts, and requirements of the ABA Model Rules.

The lawyer-client legal relationship can best be seen as a mixture of status and contract. That is, some elements of the relationship are the subject of a contract between lawyer and client that is basically like any other service contract. Other obligations, however, are inherent in the status of a lawyer as a fiduciary and are not entirely subject to amendment by lawyer and client.

Throughout this chapter, ask yourself which obligations justify an absolute requirement or prohibition and which should be controlled by informed consent of the client. Think about questions such as the following:

a. How is the lawyer-client relationship formed? At what point do preliminary discussions produce enforceable obligations? What does it mean to call the lawyer's relationship with a client a "fiduciary" relationship?

b. What is a lawyer required/authorized to do on behalf of a client? May lawyer and client define and limit the scope and objectives of the representation? What are the lawyer's rights and obligations if they fail to do so?

c. What legal protection is afforded to communications between lawyer and client? What obligations does that protection impose on the lawyer?

d. What is the impact of the financial relation between lawyer and client on the lawyer's obligations? May a lawyer refuse to provide legal services until the fee is paid, for example? Should the lawyer's obligation to protect confidential information of the client be suspended in a fee dispute?

e. What are the lawyer's obligations to protect client property in the lawyer's possession? Should failure to keep accurate financial records be grounds for the lawyer's disbarment?

PROBLEM 4

UNDERTAKING TO REPRESENT A CLIENT

If you join a large law firm, you will find, at first, that work for existing clients appears as if by magic on your desk. Each of the firm's clients, however, was once a prospective client, and the client and firm each had to decide whether to commit to the relationship. Obviously, a firm cannot turn down all prospective clients and remain in operation, but neither is the decision to take on a client automatic. Once representation begins, a lawyer assumes duties not easily shed and cases sometimes assume a life of their own. This problem puts you first in the role of dealing with a prospective client. Then, you will make the decision whether to undertake a representation and work through the matter of documenting that relationship. Finally, you will consider decision making within the lawyer-client relationship.

FACTS

You are a lawyer in a private firm. Not long ago, Morris Cannell, an elderly man whom you had never met before, came to you complaining about the handling of his investment account by a local broker. Cannell told you that the broker invested over $200,000 of Cannell's pension money in speculative stocks and the account's value has now been reduced to less than $20,000. Cannell claimed that the broker not only took excessive risks with his money, he also bought and sold the stocks frequently, with the result that the broker made a lot in commissions while the client's retirement savings almost vanished.

As Cannell talked, he became more animated and more candid. "I knew what he was doing," he said, "and I suppose I could have stopped him at any time. But I guess I got greedy and wanted to turn my nest egg into millions just like I thought all my friends were doing." Cannell was very bitter and told you in no uncertain terms, "I want you to throw the book at my broker. He showed me no mercy and I don't want you to show any to him."

In researching the problem before deciding whether to take the case, you concluded that your best arguments would be that the broker engaged in illegal churning (excessive buying and selling), and that he violated federal rules relating to an investor's suitability (what stocks are suitable to meet a given investor's objectives, here safety and income). With respect to both arguments you planned to allude to Cannell's age and relative lack of sophistication.

When you told Cannell the results of your analysis, however, he was angry and wanted you to do more. "He must have a license," Cannell said. "Do everything you can to get him suspended. See what you can do to tie up his bank accounts. If you won't do it, show me what to do and I'll do it myself."

The statute of limitations was about to run on all state and federal claims, and you told Cannell you would only represent him if he agreed to raise no more than the churning and suitability issues. You refused to seek suspension of the broker's license or to try to harass him financially, and you refused to give Cannell the behind-the-scenes help to take those steps himself. Cannell reluctantly agreed to your terms and signed your engagement letter. You entered an appearance as Cannell's attorney and filed suit on his behalf.

After extensive discovery, the broker's lawyer made what to you seemed a fair settlement offer. Knowing that your client was still angry, you did not want to have him throw away the opportunity to conclude the case and you accepted the offer on the spot.

QUESTIONS

A. THE LAWYER'S DUTIES TO A PROSPECTIVE CLIENT

1. Before you had agreed to represent Mr. Cannell, did you have any obligations to him?

a. Lawyers often like to think that until they agree to represent a client, they owe no duties to the person across their desk. However, that simply is not true. Until the adoption of Model Rule 1.18, no professional rule described the relationship in detail, but as Restatement Third, The Law Governing Lawyers § 15 reports, the law has long been clear on at least three points:

(1) Communications from a prospective client are legally privileged and protected by the lawyer's duty of confidentiality as if they were communications from an actual client;

(2) If the lawyer takes possession of documents or other property of a prospective client, the lawyer must protect those items as if they were documents or property of a client; and

(3) If the lawyer gives advice to a prospective client, for example, by saying "you have no claim and it is not worth your while to retain a lawyer," the lawyer may be responsible to the prospective client for malpractice if that advice is wrong.

b. ABA Model Rule 1.18 confirms these principles; see especially, Comments 3 & 9. The term used to describe Mr. Cannell, both in Restatement § 15 and Model Rule 1.18, is "prospective client." As you see, such persons are legally far from strangers.

2. Suppose that shortly after Mr. Cannell left your office, you learned that someone else in your firm had already agreed to represent Mr. Cannell's broker in the matter. May you or your firm continue to represent the broker?

a.   As you will learn from Model Rule 1.7, you clearly would have to decline to represent Mr. Cannell, because a law firm may not represent both sides in the same litigated case. As you will also learn in later problems, the fact that a lawyer has learned confidential information from an *actual* client typically means that neither that lawyer—nor anyone else in that lawyer's firm—may oppose that client in the same or a substantially related matter. See Model Rules 1.9 and 1.10.

b.   You will also have no doubt after reading Model Rule 1.18(b), (c) & (d), that ordinarily you personally could have no involvement whatsoever in the broker's defense. Do you suppose that on the facts in this problem, Mr. Cannell would be likely to consent to your involvement?

c.   Under what conditions may others in your firm be involved in the broker's representation? What does it mean to have avoided "exposure to more disqualifying information than was reasonably necessary to determine whether to represent the prospective client?" Model Rule 1.18, Comments 4 & 5, may be helpful in suggesting ways to conduct an initial interview so as to minimize the likelihood of later disqualification. See also, ABA Formal Opinion 90–358 (Sept. 13, 1990).

d.   Model Rule 1.18(d)(2)(i) would also require that you be "timely screened" from participation in the broker's defense. You will see screening possibilities in later problems as well. You will find "screened" defined in Model Rule 1.0(k) and Comments 8–10. See also, Model Rule 1.18, Comment 7.

Why are you required to notify Mr. Cannell about the fact you have been screened? Is he likely to be pleased to hear from you? What does "timely" notice require? Look at Model Rule 1.18, Comment 8. Is the notice required to be given before the time Mr. Cannell would normally learn what firm is going to represent the broker?

e.   Clark Capital Management Group, Inc. v. Annuity Investors Life Insurance Co., 149 F.Supp.2d 193 (E.D.Pa.2001), a pre-Rule 1.18 opinion, roughly illustrates how the Rule 1.18(d)(2) process might work. The defendant in a trademark infringement suit sought to disqualify plaintiff's counsel based on telephone conversations between the defendant's attorney and attorney Biemer, a member of plaintiff's law firm, during which the defendant's attorney had discussed possibly retaining that firm to act as co-counsel for the defendant. The calls occurred prior to the time the plaintiff retained the law firm. The attorneys never reached any agreement concerning representation, but the defendant's attorney said that he revealed confidential client information to Biemer that he had a reasonable expectation that Biemer would keep confidential. The court found, however, that the expectation of confidentiality was unreasonable. Both the defendant's lawyer and Biemer had recognized Biemer's need to perform a conflict check before consenting to represent him. Furthermore, Biemer was not currently working on the case because the firm had already screened him from any involvement with it, and the likelihood that confidential information would reach the trial attorneys was minimal.

3. Imagine that, instead of meeting Mr. Cannell in your office, you had talked to him during the pro bono work that you do at a local legal services agency. Suppose that Mr. Cannell did not want to hire you; he simply wanted to be given some basic advice and told how to file a claim against the broker himself. Under those circumstances, would Mr. Cannell have been a prospective client or an actual client?

a. Would you have been permitted to provide advice to Mr. Cannell in that context without your usual conflicts review? Look at Model Rule 6.5 and Comment 1.

b. Suppose that when you get back to your office, you find that—although you did not know it earlier—your firm represents the broker. Has your discussion with Mr. Cannell in the legal services context disqualified your firm from continuing that representation? Look at Model Rule 6.5, Comments 3 & 4.

c. Does Model Rule 6.5 even prevent you from representing the broker yourself? At what time is the lawyer's "knowledge" of a conflict disqualifying under Model Rule 6.5(a)(1)? Whatever your answer to that question, does anything in Model Rule 6.5 require that you be screened from future involvement in the matter?

d. Are you satisfied that legal services clients are adequately protected by Model Rule 6.5? Is the Rule structured as it is to help assure that private lawyers will be available to staff "hot line" services? Should we be concerned that if we insist on giving middle class and poor clients "first class" service, we may deny them needed legal help altogether? Should we be more concerned that if we insist on giving such clients "second class" service, we may discourage them from seeking legal help at all?

4. Now imagine that your discussion with Mr. Cannell occurred online in a chat room for people interested in investing. Would you be comfortable that you knew how your obligations to Mr. Cannell would later be characterized? Are lawyers wise to "fish" for clients in such places?

a. D.C. Bar Association Opinion 316 (2002) deals with chat rooms where lawyers give real-time, online advice and invite inquirers to contact the lawyers for further help.[1] After reviewing the possible ineffectiveness of disclaimers that no lawyer-client relationship is formed with such inquirers, the opinion recognizes a tension between the desirability of educating the public about their legal rights and the danger of inviting reliance on a lawyer-client relationship that the lawyer wants to avoid. The opinion advises lawyers to make clear from the outset that they are providing only legal "information," not legal advice. It also suggests running a conflicts check before agreeing to consider client-specific information. However, the opinion does not condemn chat rooms and notes that they someday may become useful ways to deliver legal services to poor and middle class persons who today often go unserved.

---

1. We will explore the "solicitation" implications of doing so in Problem 31.

b.   ABA Formal Opinion 10–457 (Aug. 5, 2010) focused its attention on law firm websites. The opinion approves a website's including biographical information about firm lawyers and describing the firm's areas of practice. The website may even provide legal information that is general in nature if it warns site visitors not to rely on it as legal advice.

Rule 1.18 issues can arise, however, when visitors respond to a website's invitation to contact the firm about legal advice or representation. Rule 1.18, Comment 2, recognizes that a "unilateral" communication to a lawyer "without any reasonable expectation that the lawyer is willing to discuss the possibility of forming a client-lawyer relationship" does not make someone a prospective client. But if a website invites a visitor to submit confidential information about a proposed representation, such a submission will likely be entitled to all Rule 1.18 protections, including the requirement of timely screening all lawyers who received the confidential information. To avoid such consequences, a firm must use warnings or disclaimers on the site that are "reasonably understandable" and "conspicuously placed to assure that the reader is likely to see [the disclaimers] before proceeding."

B.   The decision to represent a client

1.   Did you have an obligation to accept Cannell as your client?

a.   ABA Model Code of Professional Responsibility, EC 2–26, stated the traditional view that:

> "A lawyer is under no obligation to act as advisor or advocate for every person who may wish to become his client; but in furtherance of the objective of the bar to make legal services fully available, a lawyer should not lightly decline proffered employment. The fulfillment of this objective requires acceptance by a lawyer of his share of tendered employment which may be unattractive both to him and the bar generally."

b.   The Model Rules contain no comparable statement; the nearest analogue is Model Rule 6.2, Comment 1, dealing with the duty to accept court appointments to represent indigent clients.

2.   Is it fair to say that a lawyer makes an implicit moral decision every time the lawyer undertakes to use his or her talent and training in support of a cause?

a.   Given the fact that every client's right to have a lawyer does not necessarily translate into a personal obligation on every lawyer to undertake every proffered representation, Professor Monroe Freedman says:

> "[A] lawyer's decision to represent a client may commit that lawyer to zealously furthering the interests of one whom the lawyer or others in the community believe to be morally repugnant. For that reason, the question of whether to represent a particular client can present the lawyer with an important moral decision—a decision for

which the lawyer can properly be held morally accountable, in the sense of being under a burden of public justification.

"That would not be so if each lawyer were ethically bound to represent every client seeking the lawyer's services. If there were no choice, there would be no responsibility. Under both rule and practice, however, lawyers have always been free to choose whether to represent particular clients. * * * [Indeed,] the Comment to Rule 6.2 of the ABA Model Rules of Professional Conduct says * * * that a lawyer ordinarily is 'not obliged to accept a client whose character or cause the lawyer regards as repugnant.' ''[2]

b. Do you agree with Professor Freedman's conclusion? Does that make Model Rule 1.2(b) disingenuous when it says that in accepting a representation, a lawyer does not "endorse" the "client's political, economic, social or moral views or activities"?

3. Even assuming that there is no obligation to accept every client, are there legal limits that restrain a lawyer's right to reject a case?

a. Until recently, the lawyer's right to decline a case for any reason—or no reason—has been virtually absolute, except perhaps when appointed by a court.

In Stropnicky v. Nathanson, 19 M.D.L.R. 39 (M.C.A.D.1997), however, the Massachusetts Commission Against Discrimination found that a law firm that specialized in representing women in divorce cases violated the state's antidiscrimination law by refusing to represent a man in such a case. The firm was known as having obtained large awards for women who had put their husbands through professional school, and the prospective male client had done the same thing for his wife.

Is *Stropnicky* correctly decided? Should lawyers be permitted to devote their time and talent to representing only women? Is that different from electing to represent only corporations? Suppose the law firm wanted to represent only abused women with children? Would your answer be different if the lawyers wanted to represent only *white* women? Only men? What is the basis for the distinctions you would draw?

b. Wishnatsky v. Rovner, 433 F.3d 608 (8th Cir.2006), is another example of a limit on a lawyer's freedom to reject a case. The clinic at the University of North Dakota School of Law rejected a prospective client, Martin Wishnatsky, who had earlier objected to the fact that the clinic had filed a suit challenging public display of the Ten Commandments. Now, Wishnatsky wanted the clinic to file a suit on his behalf challenging the county's display of a statue of the goddess Themis on top of the county courthouse. The clinic declined his request for representation, and Wishnatsky filed this action *pro se* asserting that the clinic's refusal to represent him violated the First Amendment. The district court dismissed the com-

---

2. Monroe Freedman, Must You Be the Devil's Advocate?, Legal Times, Aug. 23,   1993, p. 19.

plaint, but the Eighth Circuit reversed. The First Amendment requires that a public law school clinic not deny representation to someone "simply because he has engaged in protected speech that the director of the program finds disagreeable," the Eighth Circuit said. "[W]hich cases and clients to accept in an academic environment should be entitled to substantial deference," but the reasons the clinic rejected this case raised questions of fact that the judge should not resolve on a motion to dismiss. The clinic had implicitly argued that "it may exclude persons from the program solely on the basis of their viewpoint," but the Eighth Circuit said no.

Do you agree? Was this a unique case? Should every law school clinic director potentially have to explain to a federal court each decision about whom the clinic chooses to represent?

4. Should you have given greater weight to your client's anger at the broker in deciding whether to take the case?

a. Suppose you believed that your client's claim had modest merit, but that the main reason the client wanted to sue was to make the broker's life miserable. Is your time and effort something you are willing to sell simply to help a client settle a grudge? Remember that Cannell has admitted to you privately that "I knew what he was doing and I could have stopped him at any time, but I guess I got greedy."

b. Cannell has already shown himself willing to sue one professional—the broker. Are you worried that he would choose to sue you next if he becomes unhappy with the result in the case against the broker? Is that appropriate to think about as you decide whether to represent Cannell?

C. DOCUMENTING THE DECISION TO UNDERTAKE A REPRESENTATION

1. When did Mr. Cannell become your client?

a. The magic moment when someone becomes your client is an important issue in many cases seeking to define your obligations. Restatement Third, The Law Governing Lawyers § 14 says:

"A relationship of client and lawyer arises when:

"(1) a person manifests to a lawyer the person's intent that the lawyer provide legal services for the person; and either

"(a) the lawyer manifests to the person consent to do so; or

"(b) the lawyer fails to manifest lack of consent to do so, and the lawyer knows or reasonably should know that the person reasonably relies on the lawyer to provide the services * * *."

b. ABA Formal Opinion 07–448 (Oct. 20, 2007) considered the obligations a court-appointed lawyer owes to a "client" who rejects the lawyer's representation. Once informally called the "Guantanamo question," the opinion notes that some states require that defendants have lawyers in some criminal cases but the defendant insists on representing himself. The lawyer may be required by the court to attend the proceedings and to be available as a stand-by, the opinion notes, but a "lawyer whose would-be client has never accepted the client-lawyer relationship * * * has no such relationship." There is thus no obligation of confidentiality or to avoid conflicts of interests with the purported client, the opinion asserts. "The lawyer's ethical duties are limited to complying with the Rules defining a lawyer's obligations to persons other than a client."

Do you agree that an appointed but unwanted lawyer's obligations should be this limited? What good could such a lawyer be expected to be, for example, if she had a conflict of interest that would otherwise bar her participation in the matter?

2. Who should bear the risk of ambiguity about whether the lawyer-client relationship has been formed?

a. In Togstad v. Vesely, Otto, Miller & Keefe, 291 N.W.2d 686 (Minn.1980), Mrs. Togstad consulted an attorney about a possible medical malpractice claim. The attorney said he did not believe she had a case but that he would "discuss this with his partner." The attorney did not send a bill and Mrs. Togstad waited a full year before talking to another attorney. By then, the statute of limitations had run. The court held the first law firm liable to the Togstads for $649,500, the amount the jury found she would have won if the lawyers had timely filed the medical malpractice case. The informal advice the lawyer had given Mrs. Togstad about her lack of a case was both inaccurate and inadequate. At a minimum, the lawyer should have told Mrs. Togstad about the statute of limitations.

b. In DeVaux v. American Home Assurance Co., 444 N.E.2d 355 (Mass.1983), a prospective client had called the attorney's firm asking for legal help in connection with an accident at a store. The lawyer's secretary advised her to write a letter to the store and arranged a medical examination by the store's insurance company. Finally, the secretary asked the potential client to write to the attorney requesting legal assistance. The client did so but the secretary misfiled it when it arrived so the lawyer never saw it until after the statute of limitations had expired. The law firm asked for summary judgment but the court denied it, concluding that a jury could reasonably find that an attorney-client relationship had been formed. Does that help clarify whether the test is whether the lawyer believed the relation had been formed or whether a reasonable client would so conclude?

3. What matters will you want to address in any engagement letter with your client?

a. At the outset of any representation, a lawyer should prepare an "engagement letter" that will be transmitted to, and typically countersigned by, the client. At least the following items should typically appear in a good engagement letter.[3]

(1) Who the client is (and sometimes who the client is *not*). This is particularly important in the case of a corporation with multiple subsidiar-

---

3. We will take up the substantive content of various of these items in later prob- lems.

ies, but it can also be important where, for example, the law firm agrees to represent a husband in drafting a will but will not be representing the wife.

(2) The scope of the representation, i.e., what the lawyer is undertaking to do and not to do. See Model Rules 1.2(c) and 1.5(b). This problem illustrates the negotiation of such matters with a prospective client, but the point is important in any case both to avoid malpractice liability for matters the firm never thought it was supposed to undertake and to establish what work is covered by the fee.

(3) The fee for the representation, or the basis of the fee, and an outline of expenses for which the client will be responsible. See Model Rule 1.5(b) & (c). It is also helpful to specify when bills will be rendered, how promptly they must be paid, and whether interest will be charged for late payments.

(4) Conflicts of interest the lawyer may have and sufficient information to let the client give informed consent if it is willing to waive the conflicts. See Model Rule 1.7 and 1.9.

(5) Any departures from the usual assumptions about handling confidential information, such as a possible agreement not to share information between spouses who come in for joint estate planning. See Model Rule 1.6.

(6) Undertakings the client will be asked to make in connection with the representation, such as an agreement to be candid with the lawyer about the relevant facts.[4]

b.   If a lawyer decides not to represent a client, a wise lawyer will send a letter documenting that fact so as to avoid a later claim that the prospective client reasonably believed the lawyer had undertaken the representation.

4.   Why might you want to limit the scope of your representation of a client?

a.   Few issues are more basic to the lawyer-client relationship that what the client has retained the lawyer to do. Does the client with $50,000 in assets want the lawyer to do the same kind of estate planning the lawyer would do for a client worth $100 million? If the client is leaving for a trip later in the afternoon, does the client expect more than a form will today to address the client's current testamentary wishes, with more work to be done later? Does a litigation client want the lawyer to research causes of action under the law of 50 states, or is the case one in which getting on file based on one cause of action is the current objective? In every representation, questions such as these help define the scope of the lawyer's work. What do Model Rule 1.2(c), and Comments 6–8 say about when limitations on the scope of representation are appropriate?

b.   Amendments To Rules Regulating the Florida Bar * * * (Unbundled Legal Services), 860 So.2d 394 (Fla.2003), represents a developing approach to practice (and obligations assumed to clients) whereby a lawyer

---

4. More suggestions for engagement letters, file control, and the like, may be found in Ronald E. Mallen & Jeffrey M. Smith, Legal Malpractice, Ch. 2 (2010 ed.).

does not undertake complete representation of a client, but rather contracts to provide specific "unbundled" services. Pursuant to this new rule, for example, the lawyer could provide forms to a limited-service client, but not accompany the client to court. The Florida Supreme Court believes that such limited services may make the legal system more accessible to persons who now proceed *pro se*. These developments are spreading;[5] see, e.g., proposed Virginia Rule 1.2(c): "A lawyer may assist in the preparation of pleadings or other filings in court on behalf of an unrepresented person."

c. The lawyer may not treat limitations on the scope of representation as self-evident. A client may later file a malpractice charge against a lawyer who fails to secure consent to such a limitation. In Nichols v. Keller, 19 Cal.Rptr.2d 601 (Cal.Ct.App.1993), the client was a construction worker who had been hit in the head by a piece of steel while on the job. He signed a retainer asking the lawyer to file a worker's compensation claim on his behalf. Later, Nichols learned he could have filed a third-party claim as well, and he sued the lawyer for not telling him. The court held that when a lawyer takes on a case, the client may not know the range of remedies that is possible. It is not enough to present a retainer agreement for the worker's compensation case without discussing with the client what other remedies may be possible and either bringing those actions as well or advising the client that he may get other counsel to do so.[6]

d. Is it wise to reach an agreement to limit the issues you will assert at the outset of the representation, as opposed to later? Typically, an agreement between lawyer and client made after representation has begun may be avoided by the client unless both the substance of the agreement and the manner of reaching it are shown by the lawyer to have been fair and reasonable to the client. Terzis v. Estate of Whalen, 489 A.2d 608 (N.H.1985) (attempt to revise fee agreement); Restatement Third, The Law Governing Lawyers § 18(1)(a).

D. DECISION MAKING DURING REPRESENTATION—ISSUES THE LAWYER IS TO DECIDE AND ISSUES RESERVED TO THE CLIENT

1. Should you have to get permission from your client to say what you plan to say in the pleading about his lack of financial sophistication?

a. Look at Model Rules 1.4 and 1.6. Is your client reasonably entitled to be interested in what you say about him in a public document?

b. Assume that you explain the pleading to Cannell and he says, "I'm paying you to represent me; I don't want you to say that." Your firm has a reputation as a tough litigator, and you are reluctant to abandon your best

---

5. See, e.g., Rachel Brill & Rochelle Sparko, Limited Legal Services and Conflicts of Interest: Unbundling in the Public Interest, 16 Georgetown J. Legal Ethics 553 (2003).

6. See also, AmBase Corp. v. Davis Polk & Wardwell, 866 N.E.2d 1033 (N.Y.2007) (firm that undertook only to resolve tax issues with the IRS not guilty of malpractice for failing also to recommend allocating tax burden to another corporation).

argument. May you, notwithstanding client objection, make the argument? Are Model Rule 1.2(a), and its Comments 1 & 2, helpful on this issue?

2.   May the client require you to make an argument that, although not frivolous, seems to you to be a loser that will weaken the case?

a.   Suppose Mr. Cannell has a theory that the broker's firm had registered its name incorrectly, for example. You explain the weakness of that argument, but the client insists that you use it anyway and you have to admit that doing so would not violate Model Rule 3.1. If you may make the argument, must you do so?[7]

b.   Is making such an argument a matter of "objectives" or "means" as those terms are used in Model Rule 1.2? Does Rule 1.2, Comment 2, provide much help about how such disagreements are to be resolved?

c.   Notice that Rule 1.2 expects that the "communication" required by Rule 1.4 will ordinarily be sufficient for the lawyer and client to reach agreement about most important issues. Look at Rule 1.4(a)(2) and Comment 3. What is the lawyer supposed to do if the disagreement about use of the argument cannot be resolved?

3.   May a lawyer accept what the lawyer thinks is a good settlement of a civil case?

a.   Look at Model Rule 1.2(a). Who has the authority to decide whether or not to settle a civil case? Should the client be bound by a settlement that the lawyer was not authorized by the client to make? Put another way, may a lawyer assume the lawyer for the other side has authority to make the settlement being proposed?

b.   The law's answer may surprise you. Restatement § 27, Comment *d*, says:

> "Generally, a client is not bound by a settlement that the client has not authorized a lawyer to make by express, implied, or apparent authority (and that is not validated by later ratification under § 26(3)). * * * When a lawyer purports to enter a settlement binding on the client but lacks authority to do so, the burden of inconvenience resulting if the client repudiates the settlement is properly with the opposing party, who should know that settlements are normally subject to approval by the client and who has no manifested contrary indication from the client. The opposing party can protect itself by obtaining clarification of the lawyer's authority."

7.   We will see this issue in Problem 29 when we consider possible limits on the proper zeal of a prosecutor. Cf. Bill Johnson's Restaurants, Inc. v. NLRB, 461 U.S. 731, 742–43 (1983) (In light of "the First Amendment right of access to the courts," the "filing and prosecution of a well-founded lawsuit may not be enjoined as an unfair labor practice, even if it would not have been commenced but for plaintiff's desire to retaliate against the defendant for exercising rights protected by the [National Labor Relations] Act.").

See also Restatement Third, The Law Governing Lawyers § 22 (authority reserved to client); § 26 (lawyer's actual authority); § 30(3) (lawyer's liability to third person for [unauthorized] conduct on behalf of client).

c. In Luethke v. Suhr, 650 N.W.2d 220 (Neb.2002), the parties' lawyers thought they had reached a settlement agreement, but when the defendants tried to enforce it, the plaintiff said he had not authorized his lawyer to settle. The plaintiff was developmentally disabled, and his lawyer had not been able to reach him before agreeing to the settlement. The defense lawyer knew of those circumstances but had been assured by the plaintiff's lawyer that there would be no problem getting the plaintiff's agreement. In affirming a finding that the plaintiff's lawyer could not bind her client, the court said, "The ordinary employment or retainer of a lawyer * * * does not of itself give the lawyer the implied or apparent authority to bind the client by a settlement or compromise of the claim; and, in the absence of express authority, knowledge, or consent, the lawyer cannot do so." 650 N.W.2d at 221.[8]

d. In Makins v. District of Columbia, 861 A.2d 590 (D.C 2004) (en banc), Makins had hired attorney Harrison to represent her in a Title VII sex discrimination and retaliatory firing case against her employer, the D.C. Department of Corrections (District). At a pre-trial conference, the judge referred the case to a magistrate for settlement purposes. The judge ordered the District to send someone "with full settlement authority" to each settlement meeting, but failed to say the same thing to Makins and Harrison. At the settlement conference, Harrison negotiated a deal with the District, then left the room, ostensibly to call Makins. He returned, shook hands with opposing counsel, and reduced the deal to writing. However, when Harrison gave Makins a copy to sign, she refused. The District filed a motion to enforce the settlement, and, represented by new counsel, Makins testified that she did not give Harrison the authority to settle the case on the terms Harrison had accepted. The trial court found for the District on an alternative ground that Harrison was acting under apparent authority to bind Makins in settlement negotiations. Makins appealed.

The D.C. Court of Appeals said first that apparent authority may be found only when the principal places her agent "in a position which causes a third person to reasonably believe the principal has consented to the exercise of authority the agent purports to hold." Under agency law, it is the principal's conduct—not that of the attorney—that must be examined to determine whether the third party reasonably believed the principal consented to the agent's authority. Relying on both D.C. Rule of Professional Conduct 1.2(a) and Restatement Third, The Law Governing Lawyers §§ 22 & 27, the court acknowledged the well-accepted principle that "the

8. A lawyer who affirmatively misrepresents his or her settlement authority to a non-client is subject to liability for damages proximately caused by that misrepresentation. Restatement Third, The Law Governing Lawyers § 30. Many of these issues are also discussed in a useful report of the ABA Section of Litigation, Ethical Guidelines for Settlement Negotiations (2002).

decision to settle belongs to the client," not the attorney. The District's evidence was replete with instances where Harrison manifested his authority to bind Makins, but it did not contain a single instance where Makins' conduct should have led the District's attorneys to believe she had given Harrison authority to finalize a settlement agreement on her behalf. Settlement talks were properly in Harrison's domain, but the court held that absent representations made by Makins, the District was unreasonable in believing that Harrison had the authority to execute the settlement.

4. Is Model Rule 1.2(a) wise to give the client exclusive authority to decide what plea to enter in a criminal case?

a. Giving a criminal defendant authority analogous to the right to settle a civil case seemed questionable in People v. Bloom, 774 P.2d 698 (Cal.1989). By the time of the penalty phase of his murder trial, Bloom demanded to address the jury directly and ask that they sentence him to death. Both the trial judge and the defense counsel tried to talk Bloom out of his decision, but he insisted and the jury gave him his wish. Ultimately, so did the Supreme Court of California, which said:

> "Given the importance which the decisions of both this court and the United States Supreme Court have attached to an accused's ability to control his or her own destiny and to make fundamental decisions affecting trial of the action, and given this court's recognition that it is not irrational to prefer the death penalty to life imprisonment without parole, it would be incongruous to hold that a trial court lacked power to grant a mid-trial motion for self-representation in a capital case merely because the accused stated an intention to seek a death verdict. While we do not suggest that trial courts must or even should grant such mid-trial motions, we do not find the trial court's ruling on the motion in this case to be violative of defendant's rights or contrary to any fundamental public policy."

Do you agree? Does this decision take deference to client wishes beyond all reasonable limits? Is it allowing the client to choose death with what to him may seem relative dignity?

b. Should the law require a court to ignore efforts of lawyers to prevent the defendant's attempt to commit suicide? Did the court in *Bloom* simply conclude that a defendant must be bound by what he has elected to do so that he cannot later rely upon his own bad judgment as a basis for a new trial?

5. What values are at stake in the question of who controls the litigation?

a. Do you agree with the commentator who argued: "Unless the client chooses to delegate decision-making authority to the lawyer, the client should be presumed to have control over all aspects of his case. [Client control increases] the moral force and acceptability of the decisions made by the system, in that each party has had the opportunity 'to choose his strategy, plot his fate, and rise or fall by his own choices.' * * * When the lawyer, as a representative, acts without authority, he violates the client's integrity by presenting the client falsely to others."[9] If all key decisions have to be made by the client, what is the professional role of the lawyer?

b. Does it follow that the client should be able to control decisions about trial strategy? How about decisions to show common courtesy? Suppose that after you file the complaint, defense counsel asks you for a short delay to allow him extra time to file an answer. May the client forbid you to grant any delays on the ground that he is anxious to move the case along? Look at the last sentence of Rule 1.3, Comment 3: "A lawyer's duty to act with reasonable promptness * * * does not preclude the lawyer from agreeing to a reasonable request for a postponement that will not prejudice the client." Who gets to decide what will "prejudice" the client? Suppose the client is simply so angry at the broker that he does not want to give any quarter?

c. Restatement Third, The Law Governing Lawyers § 23 identifies only two matters that are beyond the reach of client direction. The lawyer may alone decide "to refuse to * * * [act in a way] that the lawyer reasonably believes to be unlawful," and "to take actions * * * that the lawyer reasonably believes to be required by law or an order of a tribunal." Do you agree that lawyers require no more inherent discretion than that?

d. Model Rule 1.2(a) seems to give the client control over objectives of a representation and the lawyer control over the means of reaching those objectives. However, Rule 1.2, Comment 2, recognizes that the lawyer and client may disagree about means to be used: "Because of the varied nature of the matters about which a lawyer and client might disagree and because the actions in question may implicate the interests of a tribunal or other persons, this Rule does not prescribe how such disagreements are to be resolved." What should a lawyer do when such disagreements arise?

e. Suppose Mr. Cannell had been investing the $200,000 as trustee for his grandchildren. Would that change your obligation to follow the client's directions? Suppose a trustee asked you to settle a case on terms that would enrich himself, but not benefit the trust?

The point is that a client's authority to direct a lawyer depends in part on restrictions the law imposes on the client's conduct. If in your own practice, you knowingly accept a direction the client does not have legal authority to give, you may be liable to the party to whom the client owed duties. As you will see later in Problem 22, many lawyers paid substantial sums in damages to the receiver of their savings and loan clients for accepting direction from officers of those clients to do things the officers were not authorized by law to have the clients do.

———

9. Mark Spiegel, Lawyering and Client Decision–Making: Informed Consent and the Legal Profession, 128 U. Pennsylvania L. Rev. 41, 73–76 (1979).

PROBLEM 5

BILLING FOR LEGAL SERVICES

Noble as it might seem to pretend otherwise, the ability to earn a substantial fee is a major part of many lawyers' decisions to take some cases and reject others. How lawyers charge for their work, however, has varied over the years. For a long time, lawyers charged fixed fees for routine work. Indeed, not that many years ago, local bar associations published schedules of minimum fees for particular services and lawyers in that area adhered to them.

Goldfarb v. Virginia State Bar, 421 U.S. 773 (1975), however, changed all that. The Supreme Court of the United States intervened in the world of the previously state-regulated legal profession and held that such "minimum fee schedules" violate federal antitrust laws. Since *Goldfarb,* other bases for setting fees have assumed more importance. Fees based on hourly rates, for example, have dominated life in most firms in recent years, while contingent fees continue to predominate in personal injury cases. This problem first asks when a fee agreement must be reached, then what limit the law imposes on the size of a lawyer's fee. It then considers specialized rules applicable to contingent fees, and problems surrounding hourly rate fees as well.

FACTS

A well-known local psychiatrist has a contract claim for about $100,000 against a local company. The matter appears to be of average complexity. She has brought her case to attorney Paul T. Novak. "I'll take your case," Novak says. "My fee will be only 44 per cent of the amount recovered." Shocked, the psychiatrist says that she has never heard of even psychiatrists charging such high fees. "One-third is average," Novak tells her. "I am giving you a bargain. I am only charging you one-third more than the going rate and I am at least twice as good as the average lawyer."

Novak also has agreed to represent a plaintiff in a personal injury suit for a "discount" contingent fee of one-third of the amount recovered. The other side has offered, before Novak begins work, to pay his client $15,000. Based on what he knows about the case, Novak believes the actual damages that a jury would award would be more like $60,000, but it would take him about 200 hours of work to recover that amount, and, of course, the client might not recover anything at all. Novak has concluded that it is best to recommend to the client that he accept the $15,000 immediately so that Novak can pocket a $5,000 fee with little effort and go on to the next case.

When a prospective client asked Novak about his willingness to charge a fee on an hourly-rate basis, Novak simply laughed and said he would never agree to charge fees on any basis other than one that let him share in any good result. Novak added that other lawyers charge hourly fees and the prospective client could always go there.

QUESTIONS

A. THE FEE AGREEMENT BETWEEN LAWYER AND CLIENT

1. Must a lawyer's fee agreement be in writing?

a. Notice that Model Rule 1.5(c) requires a written agreement in the case of a contingent fee but Model Rule 1.5(b) declares only that a written agreement is "preferable." Does that distinction make sense to you?

Starkey, Kelly, Blaney & White v. Estate of Nicolaysen, 796 A.2d 238 (N.J.2002), dealt with the Rule 1.5(c) requirement that a contingent fee agreement be in writing. The law firm represented an elderly couple who were attempting to sell their farm. The firm had represented the couple over several years, and the parties initially entered into an oral contingent fee agreement that entitled the attorney to 30% of any purchase price obtained in excess of the price in an earlier contract. The firm did not reduce the agreement to writing for two-and-a-half years, however, and when it did, the percentage was reduced to 20%. The couple died, and when the attorneys sought payment from the couple's estate, the beneficiaries refused to recognize the fee agreement. They argued it was invalid because the attorneys had waited too long to formalize it. The Supreme Court of New Jersey agreed, and refused to uphold the contract. The court found, however, that the attorneys satisfied the requirements for *quantum meruit* recovery by showing (1) that legal services had been performed in good faith, and (2) that the clients had accepted the services, (3) with expectation of payment for the services, (4) and the value of the services could be ascertained.[1]

b. Should the law require all fee agreements to be in writing? D.C. Rule of Professional Conduct 1.5(b), for example, requires a writing in all cases where the lawyer has not regularly represented the client before.

c. Should the requirement turn instead on how large the bill is likely to be? California Business & Professions Code § 6148 requires a writing when it is "reasonably foreseeable" that fees and expenses in a matter will exceed $1000.

d. Quite apart from any formal requirement, would you be wise to rely on an oral agreement to be paid an hourly fee? Would you want to put the agreement in writing for your own protection and possible use in later efforts to collect the fee?

---

1. See also, Mullens v. Hansel–Henderson, 65 P.3d 992 (Colo.2002) ("When an attorney completes the legal services for which he was retained, the fact that the underlying fee agreement was unenforceable does not itself preclude the attorney from being paid the reasonable value of his services. When a contract fails, equity steps in to prevent one party from taking advantage of the other.")

2. The 2002 revision of Model Rule 1.5(b) added a require-ment that the lawyer communicate to the client, "preferably in writing," the expenses for which the client will be responsible. Why is it important to spell out responsibility for those expenses?

a. Would it shock you to know that some lawyers view their copy machine as a profit center in their practice, charging 50 cents or more per page copied? One lawyer once called the firm's photocopy machine a "silent partner." Should a firm be able to charge the client $2 per page faxed, even for local calls? Can you think of other ways in which a client might feel cheated if not told in advance how a lawyer planned to bill expenses?

b. Does this requirement in Model Rule 1.5(a) now make it potential-ly unreasonable for a lawyer to fly first class? Assuming that the bill to the client accurately lists all expenses, is it inherently unreasonable for a lawyer to order an expensive wine with dinner?

In short, what constitutes an "unreasonable amount for expenses" in violation of Model Rule 1.5(a)? Do the eight factors listed in Model Rule 1.5(a) help you answer that question? Those factors were originally intend-ed to define what constitutes an unreasonable fee; one can argue they are not of much help with respect to expenses.

c. Columbus Bar Association v. Brooks, 721 N.E.2d 23 (Ohio 1999), suspended a lawyer for two years, all but six months stayed, for various violations, including collecting a one-third contingent fee but then also charging an hourly rate for the lawyer's secretary and paralegal as addi-tional expenses. The court found that, unless clearly agreed otherwise in writing, secretarial and legal assistant expenses are general overhead, not separately billable: "by collecting for secretarial and law clerk expenses, in addition to filing fees, deposition fees, and his thirty-three percent of the settlement, respondent did not adhere to his written contract with the Jacksons and thereby charged a clearly excessive fee in violation of DR 2–106(A)."

d. Does Rule 1.5, Comment 1, give more help in understanding what costs are reasonable? Does it limit the lawyer to simply passing through out-of-pocket costs? Should it be limited in that way? ABA Formal Opinion 00–420 (Nov. 29, 2000) considered whether a firm may add a surcharge in billing for the services of a contract attorney that it hires to work on a case. Absent a separate agreement, the opinion says, if the firm treats the work as an expense item (over and above its fee), the firm must bill only what it actually paid for the contract lawyer's services. However, if the contract lawyer is billed as just another lawyer whose work makes up the fee for the matter, the firm may bill any reasonable rate for the services just as it does for one of its associates.

3. Should a lawyer be permitted to charge a client a "nonre-fundable retainer"? That is, may the lawyer say that her entire fee is payable before any work is begun and is not refundable even if the work turns out to take little time or if the client later fires the lawyer?

a. Matter of Cooperman, 633 N.E.2d 1069 (N.Y.1994), said that many nonrefundable fees are invalid. Cooperman in effect told his clients, "Once I enter an appearance in this case, even if you fire me, I will not have to return any part of the fee." In at least three cases, the clients fired him before he did much work. Nonrefundable fees violate the fiduciary relationship between lawyer and client, the New York Court of Appeals said; they inhibit the client's right to terminate the lawyer. Thus, the court affirmed the lawyer's two-year suspension from practice.[2] But the court said: "Minimum fee arrangements and general retainers that provide for fees, not laden with the nonrefundability impediment irrespective of any services, will continue to be valid and not subject in and of themselves to professional discipline."

b. Do you agree that the issue is that simple? Suppose a lawyer incurs real opportunity costs by taking a case? What if the client tells the lawyer he wants her to set aside the month of May to try a matter. She agrees to do so for a "nonrefundable" fee of $25,000, her typical monthly billing, and turns down work she would otherwise do in May. On April 30, the client fires the lawyer. Is it clear the lawyer should not be able to keep all or most of the fee?

c. Consider Raymark Industries, Inc. v. Butera, Beausang, Cohen & Brennan, 1997 WL 746125 (E.D.Pa.1997), aff'd, 193 F.3d 210 (3d Cir.1999), where a client adopted an aggressive strategy for defense of asbestos cases against it, including filing suits against opposing counsel. To control overall costs, it retained firms at fixed fees of $1 million each, nonrefundable, plus extra fees based on days of trial and the like. When ten weeks into work for the client, the law firm demanded time to investigate before filing a suit accusing another law firm of wrongdoing, the client fired the firm and demanded its million dollars back. The court said the firm could keep it. The fee agreement had been proposed by a sophisticated client, and while that client can terminate the relationship at any time, the law firm had performed properly and may keep its fee.[3]

d. In Federal Savings & Loan Ins. Corp. v. Angell, Holmes & Lea, 838 F.2d 395 (9th Cir.1988), cert. denied sub nom. Van Voorhis & Skaggs v. FSLIC, 488 U.S. 848 (1988), the savings and loan paid its counsel a large fee that purported to be nonrefundable. Three weeks later, the client went into receivership. The FSLIC fired the lawyer and asked for return of the retainer. Because a client is always free to fire its lawyer, the firm had to

---

2. Kelly v. MD Buyline, Inc., 2 F.Supp.2d 420 (S.D.N.Y.1998), distinguished *Cooperman* as only involving single-case, or "special" retainers; a non-refundability retainer is permissible if it is for a fixed amount to be available for a defined period. "[G]eneral retainer agreements provide that the attorney will be available for a period of time, whereas in 'special' retainer agreements the attorney is hired to handle a specific case or matter." The court concluded that a three-year retainer agreement was a *general* retainer agreement and thus was enforceable.

3. See also, In re Gastineau, 857 P.2d 136 (Or.1993) (nonrefundable flat fee not per se improper, but results in a prohibited unreasonable fee where the lawyer did not do the necessary legal work); In re Hirschfeld, 960 P.2d 640 (Ariz.1998) (failure to return unearned portions of nonrefundable retainers rendered fees unreasonable).

return all but a reasonable fee for work done before termination.[4] Put into that context, where the lawyer has incurred no significant opportunity cost, does the rule against nonrefundable fees make more sense?[5]

4. Should a lawyer be able to increase her fees during the course of the representation?

a. Severson & Werson v. Bolinger, 1 Cal.Rptr.2d 531 (Cal.Ct.App. 1991), says the issue turns on the understanding of a reasonable client. The firm's standard contract said the client would pay the firm's "regular hourly rates" and the client had been told orally what those rates were. The court held that under these circumstances, the firm could not increase the rates it charged the client "without notice."

b. The court left open the option of giving notice of an increase and then imposing it if the client did not object. But what if the client objects? Should a client have a right to insist that a lawyer's rates be frozen for the many years it may take to complete a matter? Remember that, as discussed in Problem 4, a lawyer and a client may revise their agreement as to scope of work and fees after the representation has begun, but at that point the lawyer assumes a greater burden of showing the agreement to be fair and reasonable to the client. See Restatement Third, The Law Governing Lawyers § 18(1)(a).

B. THE REQUIREMENT THAT A LAWYER CHARGE ONLY A "REASONABLE" FEE

1. Is the fee Novak proposes to charge the psychiatrist unreasonable? Should all fees negotiated at arm's length between the lawyer and a competent adult be held to be reasonable?

a. Is the case likely to take extraordinary skill? Has the doctor set unusual time limitations on the lawyer's work? Do Novak's reputation and experience justify a higher-than-normal fee?

b. Should the rules say that any fee is inherently reasonable if a sophisticated client has agreed to it? Rule 4–200(B)(11) of the Rules of Professional Conduct of the State Bar of California provides that, among the factors that may be considered in determining the reasonableness of the fee is the "informed consent of the client to the fee." Should that factor be added to the ABA Model Rules as well?

c. King v. Fox, 851 N.E.2d 1184 (N.Y.2006), was a case where the plaintiff alleged that a lawyer's charging a musician a share of future royalties constituted an unconscionable fee. The Second Circuit certified to

---

4. But cf., National Credit Union Admin. Bd. v. Johnson, 133 F.3d 1097 (8th Cir.1998) (lawyer not necessarily required to refund a nonrefundable retainer paid by a credit union right before it was taken over by the government).

5. In re Sather, 3 P.3d 403 (Colo.2000), asked how a lawyer must account for a nonrefundable retainer. This lawyer did not put the retainer into his trust account, arguing it had been fully earned upon accepting the retainer. The court held that a lawyer is entitled to a fee only after doing work to earn it. "Engagement retainers" may be justified if the lawyer turns down other work or otherwise benefits the client, but even flat fees must be put into a trust account, the court said, because nonrefundable retainers will deter the client from discharging the lawyer. We consider lawyer accounting more fully in Problem 6.

the New York Court of Appeals the question whether an unconscionable fee could be rendered valid and enforceable by the client's ratification of the fee. The New York court said yes. While it will be a "rare case," the court said, if "a fully informed client with equal bargaining power knowingly and voluntarily affirms" a fee arrangement otherwise voidable as unconscionable, the ratification should be given effect.

d.   In re Fordham, 668 N.E.2d 816 (Mass.1996), involved a prominent lawyer who charged a client $50,000 to defend the client's son's drunk driving case. The evidence showed that other lawyers would have taken the case for between $3,000 and $10,000, but this lawyer billed at his large firm's regular hourly rates. The son was acquitted, but the father balked at paying such a large amount. The court found the hours the firm spent on the case were disproportionate to its difficulty, and it publicly embarrassed the lawyer by the imposing a public censure.

e.   Do all fee arrangements present an inherent conflict of interest because they create a way for a lawyer to put his or her interest ahead of the client's? Should we consider the process of agreeing upon a fee itself inherently "unethical" because it is a time in the lawyer-client relationship that the lawyer and client are adversaries? Could lawyers ever get paid if we took that view?

2.   Are there situations in which it is important to limit freedom of contract between lawyer and client?

a.   In American Home Assurance Co. v. Golomb, 606 N.E.2d 793 (Ill.App.1992), a lawyer in a medical malpractice case had his clients sign an agreement purporting to pay a contingent fee of 40% and to "hold the lawyer harmless" from any reduction of fees required by an Illinois statute limiting fees in such cases. The court held the fee contract void for encouraging an illegal act and it denied the lawyer all fees for the representation, even on a *quantum meruit* basis.

b.   In Matter of Hanna, 362 S.E.2d 632 (S.C.1987), the lawyer charged 40% to collect the no-fault benefits under a client's auto policy. The benefits were "no-fault," so there really was no contingency. The court found the fee excessive, publicly reprimanded the lawyer, and required him to make restitution.

c.   White v. McBride, 937 S.W.2d 796 (Tenn.1996), involved a contract to charge a one-third contingent fee to help a surviving spouse collect what was due to him from his wife's estate. The client had an inventory of the wife's assets and there was very little to do. The court held that the lawyer's continuing effort to collect the unreasonable fee showed his conduct was not inadvertent, and he thus lost his right to collect a fee on a *quantum meruit* basis as well.

d.   In re Green, 11 P.3d 1078 (Colo.2000), found a fee excessive when it was based on time the *lawyer* spent faxing documents, calling the clerk's office, and other tasks that would usually be done by an assistant. "There is no reason or excuse for charging a client," the court said, "for one's own inefficiencies."

3.   May a local bar association simply adopt a schedule of fees that lawyers must charge for particular services?

a.   As discussed in the introduction to this problem, Goldfarb v. Virginia State Bar, 421 U.S. 773 (1975), established that such a fee schedule would violate the antitrust law. The *Goldfarb* plaintiffs needed a title examination to secure title insurance and only a member of the Virginia State Bar could legally perform that service. Their lawyer "quoted them the precise fee suggested in a minimum fee schedule published by respondent Fairfax County Bar Association," and no other lawyer would charge them less than that rate. The bar association was "a purely voluntary association of attorneys" with "no formal enforcement powers." In principle, the state disciplinary agency could have charged lawyers with improperly soliciting clients if they regularly charged less than the prescribed fee, but it had never done so. Petitioners argued that the use of such a minimum fee schedule constituted price fixing in violation of § 1 of the Sherman Act, and the Supreme Court unanimously agreed.

The County Bar had argued that lawyers were members of a "learned profession," not engaged in "trade or commerce," and thus not subject to the Sherman Act. But the Court answered that the "public service aspect of professional practice [is not] controlling in determining whether § 1 includes professions. * * * Whatever else it may be, the examination of a land title is a service; the exchange of such a service for money is 'commerce' in the most common usage of that word. It is no disparagement of the practice of law as a profession to acknowledge that it has this business aspect * * *." 421 U.S. at 787–88.

The Court acknowledged that a "purely advisory fee schedule issued to provide guidelines, or an exchange of price information without a showing of an actual restraint on trade, would present us with a different question," but in this case there was a "desire of attorneys to comply with announced professional norms; the motivation to conform was reinforced by the assurance that other lawyers would not compete by underbidding." 421 U.S. at 781–82.

b.   Should *Goldfarb* also prohibit lawyers from agreeing to maximum fees? For example, might a local voluntary bar association, in an effort to deal with complaints that lawyers make too much money, publish a schedule of maximum fees in routine cases? See, e.g., Arizona v. Maricopa County Med. Soc'y, 457 U.S. 332 (1982) (schedule of doctors' maximum rates to be reimbursed by insurance companies held per se illegal).

c.   After *Goldfarb*, could lawyers seek to take advantage of the antitrust "state action" exemption by lobbying their state supreme court or legislature to enact into law the minimum fee schedule that *Goldfarb* held violated the Sherman Act?[6] Lawyers did not respond to *Goldfarb* in that way. Why would lawyers be reluctant to do so?

---

6. The *Goldfarb* Court distinguished situations in which a state agency sets the prices for services:

"In Parker v. Brown, 317 U.S. 341 (1943), the Court held that an anticompetitive marketing program 'which de-

4. May a lawyer properly consider the client's ability to pay in setting a "reasonable" fee? Assume the lawyer would be charging some clients more than others for the same kind of work. Should that be improper?

a. Look at Model Rule 1.5, Comment 5. What does the Comment mean when it says that "it is proper to define the extent of services in light of the client's ability to pay?" Does it shock you to think that a lawyer might agree to do less for a poor client than she would for a more prosperous one? In any event, must that Comment be read in light of Model Rule 1.1 that requires a lawyer to deliver at least "competent" representation in any case?

b. May wealthy clients be charged an otherwise "unreasonable" fee in order to subsidize work done without compensation? Even if we do not explicitly tolerate such overcharging, is that the practical effect of charging some clients more than others for the same kind of work?

5. At what point in the case should one judge the reasonableness of a fee?

a. If a case turns out to be resolved more easily than expected, should a client be able to have a large fee reduced? Restatement Third, The Law Governing Lawyers § 34, Comment *c*, says:

> "Although reasonableness is usually assessed as of the time the contract was entered into, later events might be relevant. * * * [E]vents not known or contemplated when the contract was made can render the contract unreasonably favorable to the lawyer or, occasionally, to the client. Compare Restatement Second, Contracts §§ 152–154 and 261–265 (doctrines of mistake, supervening impracticality, supervening frustration). To determine what events client and lawyer contemplated, their contract must be construed in light of its goals and circumstances and in light of the possibilities discussed with the client * * *. Events within [the contemplated] range of risks, such as a high recovery, do not make unreasonable a contract that was reasonable when made."

Do you agree that this standard captures the proper considerations for evaluating a fee after the work is done? Do you believe the standard will be easy to apply in concrete cases?

b. In Holmes v. Loveless, 94 P.3d 338 (Wash.Ct.App.2004), the client was still making payments to the attorneys thirty years after the fee agreement had been executed. In 1972, attorneys Holmes and Kruger agreed to provide legal services to Loveless and Barclay, two real estate developers, to develop a shopping mall. The fee agreement provided that

---

rived its authority and efficacy from the legislative command of the state' was not a violation of the Sherman Act because the Act was intended to regulate private practices and not to prohibit a State from imposing a restraint as an act of government. * * * [But h]ere we need not inquire further into the state action question because it cannot fairly be said that the State of Virginia through its Supreme Court Rules required the anticompetitive activities of either respondent." 421 U.S. at 788–90.

the firm would provide discounted legal services for two-and-a-half years, but after that fees would be paid in full. In exchange for the initial reduced rates, the developers agreed to pay the attorneys' firm 5% of cash distributions produced by the shopping mall. The mall turned out to be a success, and by 2001, the developers had paid over $380,000 to the law firm, whereas the discounted value of legal services rendered in the 1970s had been about $8,000. The developers argued that the fee agreement violated Rule 1.8(a) as an unreasonable business transaction with a client and Rule 1.5 as an unreasonable fee. The attorneys argued that the fee was reasonable, but the court agreed with the developers. A fee agreement is not a typical "business transaction" with a client, the court said, but it found that this one was directly linked to the success of the shopping mall. Consistent with Restatement § 34, the court said that a seemingly fair agreement at the time of its execution must be reevaluated "when subsequent events alter the circumstances of the relationship." Given the combination of a limited initial period of fee discount, the payments already made, and the lack of any end date, the court held that the fee agreement was unreasonable and therefore no longer enforceable.

c. In Lawrence v. Miller, 901 N.E.2d 1268 (N.Y. Ct. App. 2008), the law firm represented a client in settlement of her husband's estate. After the firm had already billed $18 million and was billing almost $1 million per quarter, the client asked for a new deal. The firm offered a billing method, which the client accepted, of $300,000 per quarter and a 40% share of the gross recovery, less sums already paid. Five months later, the firm settled the case for $104.8 million, apparently generating an attorney's fee in excess of $40 million. In addition to the issue whether the client understood the revised agreement, the N.Y. Court of Appeals held the fee should be examined for unconscionability—both at the time it was made and at the end of the case.

C. SPECIAL RULES APPLICABLE TO CONTINGENT FEES

1. In England, the contingent fee was traditionally considered inherently unethical as a violation of the rule against champerty that prohibited financially supporting a lawsuit in exchange for a share in the expected recovery.[7] Should the same be true in this country?

a. The contingent fee is sometimes called a "poor person's fee." Should a contingent fee be improper if the client can afford to pay an hourly rate? Why would a corporation or wealthy individual prefer a contingent fee in some cases?

b. The Chicago Council of Lawyers has suggested "that the contingent fee 'problem' is a symptom, rather than a cause of a much wider problem—the unequal access to the courts for the poor and near poor."[8]

---

7. England no longer prohibits all contingent fees, although their use is still less frequent than in the United States.

8. Chicago Council of Lawyers, Report on Code of Professional Responsibility 20 (1972).

Thus, the Council favors dealing with that "wider problem." Do you agree? In what ways could a system of prepaid legal insurance, for example, radically change the calculation as to the proper time to charge a contingent fee? Would that be a change for the better? Should that affect the bar's position on prepaid insurance?[9]

c. Should a lawyer have to advise a client that he or she may choose between a contingent fee and a non-contingent fee? What is now Model Rule 1.5, Comment 5, used to say:

> "When there is doubt whether a contingent fee is consistent with the client's best interest, the lawyer should offer the client alternative bases for the fee and explain their implications."

The 2002 revisions deleted that sentence. Does that mean that lawyers may insist on contingent fees even if they are not in their client's best interests? Would a lawyer who did so be breaching his or her fiduciary obligations to the client?

d. Drafters of the change were told that some lawyers—like Novak in our problem—only charge contingent fees. Does that justify the deletion? In such a situation, would it simply make sense for the lawyer to say, "In this circumstance, where there is strict liability and only a minor dispute over damages, it may make more sense for you to pay a lawyer an hourly fee. I only work for contingent fees, but I can recommend others who charge hourly or fixed fees."

2. May Novak claim a $5,000 fee in the personal injury suit if the case is settled before he begins work?

a. What if Novak says that the reason the defendant quickly offered to settle is because he knew that Novak now represented the plaintiff? Is it enough to say that Novak needs to make a few easy fees, as here, to make up for the losing cases on which he works long hours but realizes nothing? Judge John Grady takes that argument head on:[10]

> "I propose to analyze the typical automobile accident case * * * [that] accounts for the vast majority of personal injury claims. * * * I think it should take a competent lawyer no more than 15 hours to prepare this type of case for trial. * * * The trial itself should not take more than * * * about ten hours in court and five hours spent before and after court sessions at the office, including any time required for post-trial motions. * * *
>
> "Let us assume that the lawyer has taken the case on a one-third contingent basis, which is typical. If plaintiff's injury was not very serious—assume he sustained soft tissue injuries with modest special damages—we might have a verdict of $4,500. This would certainly be in the low range of cases that would be thought worth trying to a jury

9. Issues relating to prepaid legal insurance will be taken up in Problem 34 of these materials.

10. John F. Grady, Some Ethical Questions About Percentage Fees, 2 Litigation 20 (Summer, 1976). Copyright 1976 by the American Bar Association. Used with permission.

verdict. On such a verdict, the lawyer would receive a fee of $1,500, which, divided by his 30 hours of effort, results in compensation at the rate of $50 per hour. * * *

"What causes me to question the propriety of the ever-increasing fee in proportion to the size of the verdict is this: there is little, if any, relationship between the efforts of the lawyer and the size of the verdict, once we assume a verdict in favor of the plaintiff. The size of the verdict is determined by the nature and extent of the plaintiff's injury and resulting damages. Conceding that some lawyers are more brilliant and more eloquent than others, we flatter ourselves unduly if we think the performance of counsel is a large factor in the size of the verdict. * * * To illustrate the point, the identical collision can cause a whiplash injury or result in an amputation of a leg. * * * But even though the same amount of work is involved, the whiplash verdict might be $4,500, for a fee of $50 per hour, while the amputation verdict might be $200,000, providing a fee of more than $6,000 per hour. * * *

"Another fortuitous circumstance affecting the fee is the number of claimants the lawyer represents in a particular case. Assume that a father, mother and two children are struck at an intersection and all of them sustain injuries. The liability evidence is the same for all. Frequently, they will have the same doctor, who simply brings four sets of records to court instead of one. His testimony takes longer, and I admit that there is some additional work required of the lawyer. However, in the typical case of four plaintiffs, the additional work is not at all proportionate to the additional fees the lawyer will realize when he charges each of the plaintiffs the same percentage, which— make no mistake about it—is what he ordinarily does. * * *

"Thus far, I have been raising questions about the propriety of the fees charged in cases tried to verdict. As we all know, however, * * * [r]oughly 90 percent of the cases filed are settled before trial commences. * * * The ethical questions presented in the settled cases are, I think, even more serious than those presented by the cases which are tried. In the case of the $45,000 settlement, for example, how can a $15,000 fee be justified? Such a fee amounts to $1,000 an hour, assuming the lawyer has completed his trial preparation and settles just as the trial is about to start. But it might not happen that way. The case may be settled before suit is even filed, or shortly after it is filed, or midway through discovery. In any of those situations (and, again, confining ourselves to the simple automobile accident case), the lawyer will spend less than 15 hours. * * *

" * * * Surely there is much to be said for providing a means to permit indigent persons to engage counsel to press meritorious suits. * * * [But t]he problem, it seems to me, is that we have regarded the 'one-third contingent fee' arrangement as applicable to all cases involving personal injuries, without paying enough attention to the facts of the particular case and the needs of the particular client. * * *

"One sometimes hears the argument that the attorney is entitled to collect his 'third' in easy cases to make up for all the 'losers' he handles. This explanation does not withstand analysis. Putting aside for a moment the question of whether one client can properly be surcharged to compensate for the deficiencies in another client's case, the fact of the matter is that there just are not very many 'losers.' As we have seen, at least 95 percent of the total claims handled by lawyers are settled before trial, and many of these settlements involve very little work on the part of the lawyer. * * *

"I think we must start determining our fee charges in personal injury cases on the same basis we determine fees in any other kind of litigation. * * * Specifically, I think the lawyer must consider at least these three questions in each case:

"1.   Is there a genuine and substantial question on liability, or is the only real question the amount of damages?

"2.   Is the case likely to be settled or tried to verdict?

"3.   Is the amount of the recovery likely to be small or large—for example, is it a soft tissue injury or does it involve the death of the family breadwinner?

"Until the lawyer knows the answers to these questions, he has insufficient basis for determining whether a percentage fee is proper and, if proper, what percentage would be fair."

b.   Do you agree with Judge Grady?[11] Should clients simply shop around for the best lawyer at the lowest price? When we discuss advertising of legal services in Problem 31, you will see that it is easier to shop around now than when Judge Grady wrote his article. Based on what you have observed about law practice, however, do you think clients are likely to be offered a wide range of contingent fee percentages?

c.   Judge Grady also says, "there is little, if any, relationship between the efforts of the lawyer and the size of the verdict, once we assume a verdict in favor of the plaintiff." Is that an heroic assumption? When the client has a 90% chance of winning, he doesn't get 10 throws of the dice with the jury, only one. Is Judge Grady's point that most cases are settled and never get to the jury, so that genuinely injured plaintiffs can reasonably assume they will recover at least something?

d.   One court has established and enforced a schedule of maximum fees in medical malpractice cases. The schedule provides for 30% on the first $250,000 recovered, 25% on the next $250,000; 20% on the next $500,000, 15% on the next $250,000, and 10% thereafter. An attorney's fee at or below these sums is conclusively deemed "reasonable." Any sum in

11. The ABA Standing Committee on Ethics and Professional Responsibility has said only that "the charging of a contingent fee * * * does not violate ethical standards as long as the fee is appropriate in the circum- stances and reasonable in amount, and as long as the client has been fully advised of the availability of alternative fee arrange- ments." ABA Formal Opinion 94–389 (Dec. 5, 1994).

excess of these figures is by definition "unconscionable" unless approved by the court.[12] Would you favor such an approach?

e.   Levine v. Bayne, Snell & Krause, Ltd., 40 S.W.3d 92 (Tex.2001), decided how a contingent fee should be calculated when the lawyer drafts a vague contract. The Levines had agreed to pay a fee of one-third of "any amount received" from the Smiths for defects in their house. Because of the defects, the Levines had stopped making contract payments to the Smiths, so the Smiths filed a counterclaim. At the end of the day, the Levines recovered about $240,000 and the Smiths about $160,000, leaving a net to the Levines of about $80,000. The question became whether the Levines owed a contingent fee based on $240,000 or $80,000. The court agreed that the Levines had received $240,000 worth of benefit because they now owned the house free of the mortgage, but the better interpretation of the words "any amount received" would be to base the fee on the net, or $80,000. The court put the burden on lawyers to write their contracts more clearly if they intended any other result.

f.   Note that Novak wanted to recommend the prompt settlement offer of $15,000 before he had really begun work on the case. Was that proper? Suppose the law required personal injury lawyers to ask the defendant to make an offer of settlement very early. If the offer were accepted, the plaintiff's lawyer would have to bill based on hours worked and the total fee could be no more than 10% of the recovery. If the initial offer were rejected, the contingent fee could be charged on only so much of the ultimate recovery as exceeded the initial offer.

Would you favor such a plan? What would it do to the dynamics of settlement negotiations? Would it tend to reduce the number of lawyers who would serve injured clients? Would it tend to reduce the amount of lawyer advertising as the expected return to the lawyer from getting each new client in the office decreased? See Lester Brickman, Michael Horowitz & Jeffrey O'Connell, Rethinking Contingency Fees (1994).[13]

3.   Are there kinds of cases in which a contingent fee should not be proper?

a.   May a lawyer charge a contingent fee in a domestic relations case? Look at Model Rule 1.5(d)(1). What is the basis for such a prohibition? Is Model Rule 1.5, Comment 6, helpful in explaining the rationale?

---

12.   N.Y. Judicial Law § 474a (McKinney 1983). Cf. California Business & Professions Code § 6146 (maximum percentage fees in cases against health care providers) and § 6147.5 (maximum fees in recovery of claims between merchants).

13.   In this connection, see Committee on Legal Ethics of the W. Va. State Bar v. Gallaher, 376 S.E.2d 346 (W.Va.1988). The court found that a 50% contingent fee was excessive for recovering personal injury damages where the lawyer advised acceptance of the first real offer the insurance company made: "If an attorney's fee is grossly disproportionate to the services rendered and is charged to a client who lacks full information about all of the relevant circumstances, the fee is 'clearly excessive' within the meaning of Disciplinary Rule 2–106(A), even though the client has consented to such fee." The court ordered restitution to the personal injury plaintiff of an amount sufficient to reduce the fee to one-third.

Connecticut Bar Ethics Opinion 87–17 (1988) takes the position that a lawyer may charge a contingent fee in an action to partition ownership of a house owned by an unmarried couple. The court said that the rule against charging a contingent fee in domestic relations matters does not apply where the couple is not married. Do you agree with the distinction? In a time when unmarried relationships are common, might one ask whether the policies behind the rule, e.g., not discouraging parties from reconciling, should apply to such cases too?

b.   Should the law allow a contingent fee in a criminal case?[14] Look at Rule 1.5(d)(2). What reasons support such a prohibition? What kinds of clients would benefit from allowing contingent fees in criminal cases?

Winkler v. Keane, 7 F.3d 304 (2d Cir.1993), considered whether a defense lawyer's charge of a contingent fee in a criminal case should be per se grounds for reversal of the conviction. The state accused the defendant of killing his father. The fee agreement provided that if the lawyer secured an acquittal so that the defendant could inherit from his father, the lawyer would get an extra $25,000. The New York Court of Appeals accepted the defendant's contention that allowing contingent fees in criminal cases may discourage the lawyer from working out a guilty plea in an appropriate case, seeking a charge on a lesser included offense, or the like. That court had held, however, that while charging the contingent fee is grounds for professional discipline of the lawyer, it was not per se grounds for reversing the criminal conviction. For that, the defendant must show actual prejudice, and, in this case, the Second Circuit found none.

4.   Should the law prohibit contingent fees in other kinds of cases?

a.   Should the ethics rules ban contingent fees for defense counsel in civil cases?

Wunschel Law Firm, P. C. v. Clabaugh, 291 N.W.2d 331 (Iowa 1980), was a defamation action. The defendant agreed with defense counsel that the law firm would defend him for a fee that would be one-third of the difference between the prayer in the petition and the amount actually awarded. Defendant was offered the alternative of paying a fee of $50 per hour. The court held that such a contingent defense fee is void and unenforceable as a matter of public policy. The court reasoned that such a fee would be based on "pure speculation" because "it provides for determination of the fee by factors having no logical relationship to the value of the services." Do you agree?

ABA Formal Opinion 93–373 (Apr. 16, 1993), expressly rejected that view and held that contingent fees for defense counsel in civil cases do not violate the Model Rules provided that the amount saved is "reasonably ascertainable," the total amount of the fee is reasonable, and the client's consent to the arrangement was "fully informed." See also, D.C. Bar

---

14.   See, e.g., Pamela S. Karlan, Contingent Fees and Criminal Cases, 93 Columbia L. Rev. 595 (1993) (examining the effect of contingent fees in criminal cases on the right of defendants to obtain an experienced advocate).

Opinion 347 (Mar. 2009), adopting the conclusion of Formal Opinion 93–373, when the lawyer is dealing with a sophisticated client and when the lawyer describes, preferably in writing, the base from which savings will be calculated and the percentage to be applied to the savings.

b.   Should lawyers in takeover fights receive a "premium" if they successfully pursue or defeat the takeover attempt? Would expanding the use of contingency fees bring lawyers dangerously close to engaging in "business"? Is that something about which we should be concerned? Does the practice sound better if a lawyer calls it "value billing" and consistently sets the fee on the basis of how much the client has benefited from the lawyer's efforts? See, e.g., ABA Commission on Billable Hours Report (2002).

D.   THE ALTERNATIVE OF THE HOURLY-RATE FEE

1.   At least a generation of lawyers has experienced the hourly rate fee as dominant in the life at most large firms, and many smaller firms as well. Does hourly rate billing harmonize the interests of lawyers and clients?

a.   What abuses are inherent in hourly billing? Does hourly billing give firms the wrong incentives, such as the incentive to use more hours than if they were billing on a contingent fee basis? For example, does hourly billing encourage a firm to file every possible motion, and to have their associates research tangential legal theories?

b.   In re Myers, 127 P.3d 325 (Kan.2006), involved attorney Myers who charged a client for 43.5 hours of work in closing an estate. In all but one instance, he billed services in one hour increments, i.e., not six-minute or even quarter-hour units. Myers freely acknowledged that if he had spent only 45 minutes on a project, he billed it as a whole hour, although he insisted that if he worked on something for less than 15 minutes, he usually would not bill at all. The Kansas Supreme Court agreed with its hearing panel that "billing in one-hour increments when one-hour is not spent working on a matter is an improper billing practice and is in violation of [Rule] 1.5." It publicly censured Mr. Myers.

c.   What about billing twice for the same time if the lawyer is doing two different things? Suppose a lawyer has to fly to a meeting for Client A, but works on the airplane on a matter for Client B. May the lawyer bill the same hour twice, once to each client? ABA Formal Opinion 93–379 (Dec. 6, 1993) addressed the issue as follows:

> " * * * [I]t is helpful to consider these questions, not from the perspective of what a client could be forced to pay, but rather from the perspective of what the lawyer actually earned. A lawyer who spends four hours of time on behalf of three clients has not earned twelve billable hours. A lawyer who flies for six hours for one client, while working for five hours on behalf of another, has not earned eleven billable hours. A lawyer who is able to reuse old work product has not re-earned the hours previously billed and

compensated when the work product was first generated. * * * [If] it turns out that the lawyer is particularly efficient in accomplishing a given result, it nonetheless will not be permissible to charge the client for more hours than were actually expended on the matter. * * * [T]he economies associated with the result must inure to the benefit of the client, not give rise to an opportunity to bill a client for phantom hours."

Not all lawyers and firms have taken the ABA's directions to heart. See Lisa G. Lerman, Lying to Clients, 138 U. Pennsylvania L. Rev. 659 (1990), and Lisa G. Lerman, Unethical Billing Practices, 50 Rutgers L. Rev. 2151 (1998).

d.   Clients are increasingly hiring independent specialists to "audit" their lawyers' bills. In Glenn K. Jackson Inc. v. Roe, 273 F.3d 1192 (9th Cir.2001), for example, the plaintiff law firm was hired by an insurance company to represent its insureds against workers' compensation claims. In its engagement letter, the firm had agreed to let the insurer hire a legal auditor to verify the firm's bills. The auditor found that over $200,000 of the nearly $800,000 charged should be disallowed, and the law firm filed this action against the auditors for breach of fiduciary duty, interference with contract, fraud, deceit, defamation, unfair competition, and false advertising. The district court dismissed all of the plaintiff's claims and the Ninth Circuit agreed, finding that the audit firm owed no duty to the law firm. The law firm was a sophisticated party that agreed to be audited, and if auditing firms were held liable to third parties, it would encourage the auditors to be less candid in rendering opinions. Quite apart from the result itself, however, the case illustrates how much "fat" auditors can often find in the bills of even reputable law firms.

2.   What collateral effects may charging hourly fees have had on the practice of law? Should those effects concern you?

a.   Judge Patrick J. Schiltz reports:

"Conventional wisdom just a few decades ago was that lawyers could not reasonably expect to charge for more than 1200 to 1500 hours per year. Thirty years ago, most partners billed between 1200 and 1400 hours per year and most associates between 1400 and 1600 hours. As late as the mid–1980s, even associates in large New York firms were often not expected to bill more that 1800 hours annually. Today, many firms would consider these ranges acceptable only for partners or associates who had died midway through the year."

b.   It may seem that lawyers of an earlier day just did not know how to work hard, but Judge Schiltz points out that:

"you will end up billing only about two hours for every three hours that you spend at 'work.' And thus, to bill 2000 hours per year, you will have to spend about sixty hours per week at the office, and take no more than two weeks of vacation/sick time/personal leave. If it takes you, say, forty-five minutes to get to work, and another forty-five minutes to get home, billing 2000 hours per year will mean leaving home at 7:45 a.m., working at the office from 8:30 a.m. until 6:30 p.m., and then arriving home at 7:15 p.m.—and doing this six days per week, every week. That makes for long days, and for long weeks. And you will have to work these hours not just for a month or two, but year after year after year.''[15]

c. Professor Deborah L. Rhode, Chair of the ABA Commission on Women and the Legal Profession, writes that women have been particularly disadvantaged by some law firm expectations.

''[I]ncreasing billable hour quotas have pushed working hours to new and often excessive limits. Lawyers remain perpetually on call— tethered to the workplace through cell phones, emails, faxes, and beepers. 'Face time' is taken as a proxy for commitment, ambition, and reliability under pressure. The result is a 'rat race equilibrium' in which most lawyers feel that they would be better off with shorter or more flexible schedules, but find themselves within institutional structures that offer no such alternatives. * * * Particularly in large firms, unmarried associates report finding it 'difficult to have a cat, much less a family.' As one lawyer responded to a bar survey on quality of life: 'This is not a life.' ''[16]

3.   Are there alternatives to hourly rate and contingent fees that would better align the lawyer's incentives with client's interests and also produce an appropriate return for the lawyer's efforts?

a.   The ABA Commission on Billable Hours Report (2002) found a move toward fixed fees for recurring, routine tasks (sometimes called ''commodity'' work) because clients want the burden of doing the work efficiently placed entirely on the law firm. Billable Hours Report at 25. Can you see any collateral effects to such a development?

b.   The report also suggests that lawyer productivity might be measured in terms of revenue generated for the firm, in whatever form, and not on hours worked. Billable Hours Report at 28. Would you prefer to work under such a system?

c.   Fixed fees make it easier for corporate counsel to conduct auctions in which firms compete to offer the lowest prices for the right to do defined packages of work, say defense of sets of 100 personal injury cases. Billable Hours Report at 33. Does that represent a move in a direction you would favor?

d.   Does the move toward fixed fees seem appropriate for services that are not routine and that require work by experienced experts? Are fees ultimately likely to be set at some combination of fixed fee for routine services, hourly rate where complexity of the case is hard to predict, and a

15. Patrick J. Schiltz, On Being a Happy, Healthy, and Ethical Member of an Unhappy, Unhealthy, and Unethical Profession, 52 Vanderbilt L. Rev. 871 (1999).

16. Deborah L. Rhode, Gender and the Profession: The No–Problem Problem, 30 Hofstra L. Rev. 1001 (2002).

contingent element where intensity of the lawyer's efforts may make a difference?[17]

———

PROBLEM 6

HANDLING CLIENT PROPERTY AND WITHDRAWING FROM REPRESENTATION

Issues of the relationship between lawyer and client are in some ways best seen when the going gets tough. The client may be unhappy because things are going more slowly or less well than hoped. The lawyer may be unhappy because the client demands more services than expected and pays less promptly than promised. Some clients are "high maintenance." This problem examines some of the issues that can arise in such contexts. It first considers the lawyer's duty to protect and account for a client's property. It then examines the circumstances under which a lawyer may withdraw from representing the client. Then, it considers how lawyers should deal with clients who fail to pay the lawyer's fee. Finally, it considers the lawyer's possible right to a lien on client property and papers.

FACTS

In a recent suit to recover a valuable ring that the defendant had wrongfully withheld, a jury awarded Elizabeth Jackson's client the ring and $100,000 punitive damages. The fee contract between Jackson and her client provided that Jackson would get 40% of all punitive damages. "That was because we thought the punitive damages would be low," the client complained after the verdict was announced. "On a big recovery such as this, 40% is unfair," the client said. "I'll pay you 25% and not a penny more." The defendant satisfied the judgment by giving Jackson the ring and a check for $100,000 payable to Jackson and the client. Jackson promptly deposited the full amount of the check into her client trust account and put the ring on her finger. She told the client, "Until we get this fee dispute worked out, I'm not giving you a nickel."

Jackson is a well-known and very busy litigator and she doesn't have time for difficult clients. When one client told her that she was not returning his phone calls quickly enough, she told him to get another lawyer, filed a notice of withdrawal with the court before which the matter was pending, and did no more work on the matter.

In another case, Jackson represented a local business person in a dispute over title to real estate. She anticipated a hard time

---

17. See, e.g., Ronald D. Rotunda, Moving from Billable Hours to Fixed–Fees: Task– Based Fees and Legal Ethics, 47 U. Kansas L. Rev. 819 (1999).

collecting her fee, so she took a security interest in the real estate that was the subject of the suit. When the case was over and the client was slow to pay, Jackson filed suit to collect her fee out of the proceeds of an involuntary sale of the real estate. She also refused to send her client a copy of the judgment entered in the underlying case that the client needed to reassure his bank that the suit was indeed over.

QUESTIONS

A. Handling client property

1. Why is it important that lawyers pay attention to their handling of client property?

a. A lawyer has a fiduciary relationship with a client. "Fiduciary" is a title also applied to trustees and guardians, i.e., people who manage the property of others. In that sense, the trustworthy management of a client's property is one of the most fundamental duties of a lawyer.

b. Violation of fiduciary standards with respect to client property is also one of the most certain ways for a lawyer to be disbarred. That is only partly because of the seriousness of the offense. It is also in part because proof of a violation of accounting rules is typically much more straightforward than proof of a failure to be forthcoming in disclosing information, proof of less-than-competent representation of a client, or even proof of a conflict of interest. Disciplinary authorities have limited resources and tend to use them in cases where the results will be most certain.

c. It is thus critically important that you as a lawyer know the rules for management of client property. Large firms will have a whole staff devoted to preserving and accounting for such property, but ultimately the ones with their licenses on the line will be the lawyers for whom the staff work. Those lawyers need to know the rules as well.

Recent ethics opinions have considered the kind of client property a lawyer must keep and what the lawyer may destroy. Association of the Bar of the City of New York Committee on Professional and Judicial Ethics Formal Opinion 2008–1 (July 2008), for example, said that a lawyer must retain all emails and other electronic versions of client files and must turn them over to client when asked. The lawyer may, however, charge the client the cost of doing so.

Arizona State Bar Opinion 08–02 (Dec. 2008), said that a client is entitled to most of the contents of its closed file and the lawyer must retain such files. A lawyer may adopt a file retention policy that destroys files after a given period, but the lawyer must tell the client the lawyer's policy at the outset of the relationship and act only in accordance with it. If the lawyer has no policy, the lawyer ordinarily must notify the client before destruction of a client's file.

Advisory Comm. of the Supreme Court of Missouri Formal Opinion 127 (2009) said that after the conclusion of a representation, a law firm may destroy the paper copy of a client's file without the client's consent if the firm maintains a scanned, electronic copy. Only items with intrinsic value, and wills and documents with legal significance, the Committee said, must be kept in paper form. The electronic storage media, however, must be of archive quality integrity for the entire maintenance period. In this regard, the firm may need to periodically transfer the data to new forms of media to protect its integrity. The firm must maintain the proper hardware and software to be able to access the file, and this may require the lawyer or firm to stay abreast of technological developments, and perhaps consult with individuals with technological expertise.

2.   Was it proper for Jackson to wear the client's ring while it was in her possession?

a.   Restatement Third, The Law Governing Lawyers § 44, Comment *e*, makes clear:

> "This Section requires a lawyer to use reasonable measures for safe-keeping such objects, for example, by placing them in a safe-deposit box or office safe. The reasonableness of measures depends on the circumstances, including the market value of the property, its special value to the client * * *, and special difficulties that would be required to replace it if known to the lawyer * * *."

b.   The Florida Bar v. Grosso, 760 So.2d 940 (Fla.2000) (per curiam), illustrates how a lawyer failed to protect client property. When the court sentenced the lawyer's client to probation, it provided that he could not have a gun. The lawyer agreed to keep the client's gun collection for him and put the guns in his garage. Florida weather being humid, when the lawyer returned the guns a year later, they were rusty, pitted, and parts were missing. The court suspended the lawyer for 90 days for not adequately caring for the client's guns.

3.   How must an attorney keep his or her office accounts?

a.   A lawyer need not deposit each client's funds into a separate account, but the lawyer must keep individual records of each client's funds. In August 2010, the ABA House of Delegates adopted the Model Rules for Client Trust Account Records. They are not officially part of the Model Rules of Professional Conduct, but they may be influential in the states. These detailed rules require a lawyer to maintain records for at least five years of (a) all deposits to and withdrawals from client trust accounts, "as well as the date, payee and purpose of each disbursement;" (b) ledger records that show, for each beneficiary, the source and disbursement of all funds, (c) copies or all retainer and compensation agreements with clients, (d) copies of all accountings made to clients, (e) copies of all bills for fees and expenses, (f) copies of all records showing disbursements on behalf of clients, and (g) "physical or electronic equivalents of all checkbook registers, bank statements, records of deposit, pre-numbered cancelled checks, and substitute checks provided by a financial institution."

b.   In re Mance, 980 A.2d 1196 (D.C. 2009), illustrates the difficulty of characterizing when a fee payment becomes the property of the lawyer. When a father retained a lawyer to defend his son, a homicide suspect, the fee agreement provided that the father would pay a flat fee of $7500 up front. Upon receiving the $7500, the lawyer placed $6010 of it in his client trust account, but placed the remainder into his office operating account. After a while, the father felt the lawyer was not doing enough to help represent the son, so he ended the representation. The lawyer agreed to refund the $7500, but he was unable to do so for several months because the funds were not readily available. The court agreed with the bar counsel that payment of a flat fee paid is at the outset an advance of unearned fees. The lawyer must hold these funds in a client trust account until they are earned. The funds are considered the property of the client unless the client consents to an alternate arrangement. The court distinguished a flat fee from a payment to ensure the lawyer's availability for representation. The latter kind of payment immediately becomes the property of the lawyer. The court explained that in the flat fee case, the lawyer was obligated to return at least a portion of the fee because he had not yet performed all of the services for which the fee was expected to pay. The court limited the sanction, however, to a public censure.

c.   Columbus Bar Association v. Zauderer, 687 N.E.2d 410 (Ohio 1997), involved a lawyer who collected a lot of money for his clients. His problem arose when he started to allocate expenses of the cases. Without prior agreement with his clients, he accrued many of his litigation-related expenses in a "general" category and then created a formula to assign them to individual cases. Some claimants complained, and the bar charged him with failure to keep adequate records. The Ohio Supreme Court agreed and suspended Zauderer for a year.

d.   The Florida Bar v. Bailey, 803 So.2d 683 (Fla.2001), shows that even living legends are not immune from trouble under these rules. The accusations against F. Lee Bailey, a celebrated criminal defense lawyer, arose out of his representation of an alleged drug smuggler. Bailey arranged a plea agreement by which his client pled guilty and forfeited all of his assets to the U.S. Government in the hopes of receiving a lighter sentence. The defendant was French and owned a significant amount of property in France. To maintain the properties and cover the expenses of their liquidation, Bailey took control of a block of stock owned by the defendant. After selling the stock, Bailey was to return the proceeds to the government; the higher the amount Bailey was able to remit to the government, the less the defendant's sentence would be. The Florida Bar charged Bailey with commingling the defendant's assets with his own during the liquidation process. The evidence showed that he had borrowed against his client's money to fund his own investments and used the client's money for his own profit instead of remitting the maximum amount to the government as would have been in his client's best interest. Although the court acknowledged that Bailey had been a member of the bar in two states for over 40 years and was admitted to practice before several federal courts, it found that his acts warranted his permanent disbarment in Florida.[1]

4. Did Jackson violate Model Rule 1.15 by depositing the $100,000 settlement check into her trust account?

a. A lawyer may sign the lawyer's own name on a settlement check made out to the lawyer, but the lawyer may sign the client's name on a settlement check only if she has actual authority to do so. Sometimes such authority is given, but too often the need for such authority is overlooked. A lawyer who, without such authority, signs the client's name on a check may not only commit a disciplinary violation, but also the crime of conversion. See, e.g., Sampson v. State Bar, 524 P.2d 139 (Cal.1974) (endorsement of clients' names to checks without authorization of clients, accepting false acknowledgments and failing to secure clients' authorization for payment of settlement funds to doctor may properly be the subject of disciplinary action).

b. In the Matter of Advisory Committee on Professional Ethics Docket No. 22–95, 677 A.2d 1100 (N.J.1996), a lawyer doing debt collection work for an institutional creditor was permitted to accept the creditor's suggestion that the lawyer endorse checks as they arrive, deduct the lawyer's contingent fee, and transmit the balance to the creditor. The court found that it was reasonable for the client to give this authority because debt collection is a big business with many small transactions; any other system would be unnecessarily complex.

c. Bazinet v. Kluge, 764 N.Y.S.2d 320 (N.Y.Sup.Ct.2003), presented a lawyer's worst nightmare. Lawyer Reiser received an escrow deposit of 10% of the value of Kluge's property in connection with its sale. When the initial contract failed to close, Reiser received another 10% escrow deposit related to a second contract. The combined deposits totaled $2.73 million, which Reiser deposited in a small bank. When the second sales transaction closed, and his client sought the money, Reiser learned that the FDIC had closed the bank and was now the receiver. The FDIC only insured each account up to $100,000, so the other $2.53 million was apparently lost. In a claim for malpractice, the court said: "an attorney is not held to the rule of infallibility and is not liable for an honest mistake of judgment where the proper course is open to reasonable doubt." But the client had raised a sufficient claim of negligence to withstand the motion to dismiss.

5. When the client asked for his money, should lawyer Jackson have paid over the full $75,000 that the client thought was due? Would it have been proper for Jackson to pay the client only what Jackson thought was due?

---

1. The sad Bailey saga goes on. Bailey was disbarred in Massachusetts as well for the Florida events. In re Bailey, 786 N.E.2d 337 (Mass.2003). United States v. McCorkle, 321 F.3d 1292 (11th Cir.2003), found that he had been paid a fee from laundered funds, and that matter too was referred to The Florida Bar for potential disciplinary action. But see, United States v. Bailey, 419 F.3d 1208 (11th Cir.2005) (Bailey held not guilty of conversion or civil theft).

a. Look at Model Rule 1.15(d). How much is Jackson required to pay over to the client?

b. What should she do with the portion of the fee that the client agrees Jackson is due? May she keep it in the trust account? Would that be consistent with Model Rule 1.15(a) and (b)?

c. What must she do with the amount of the fee that remains in dispute?

d. Suppose a creditor of the client asserts a lien on the client's share of the judgment. May the lawyer ignore that lien? Take a look at Model Rule 1.15(e). A lawyer who pays settlement proceeds over to the client in knowing disregard of a creditor's lien may become directly liable to the lienholder and basically required to pay twice. Kaiser Foundation Health Plan, Inc. v. Aguiluz, 54 Cal.Rptr.2d 665 (Cal.Ct.App.1996).

6. Should the bar subject a lawyer to discipline for the dishonesty of her office staff or associated lawyers? Have no doubt; it happens.

a. In Office of Disciplinary Counsel v. Ball, 618 N.E.2d 159 (Ohio 1993), a lawyer gave responsibility for most of his probate practice to his secretary. She took in money and wrote checks on his trust accounts. Ultimately, she diverted funds from some accounts to others. The lawyer said he knew nothing about this. Even if that were true, the court said, the lawyer failed in his duty of supervision, see Model Rule 5.3, and the court suspended him from practice for six months. If a lawyer adequately supervises a secretary, but the secretary steals client money anyway, should the lawyer be subject to discipline? Should the lawyer be liable to the clients to repay the money?

b. Duggins v. Guardianship of Washington Through Huntley, 632 So.2d 420 (Miss.1993), involved a lawyer retained to pursue a medical malpractice action on behalf of a child. He associated himself with a second lawyer who was to try the case. The second lawyer ultimately settled the case without telling the client or Duggins, and ran off with most of the money. The question was Duggins' tort liability to the clients. The court held that under these circumstances, the lawyers were partners or joint venturers with respect to the case. Thus, Duggins was liable for all damage caused by the second lawyer, plus punitive damages, even though he had no moral culpability for what had occurred.[2]

c. Is there good reason for taking this kind of strict liability approach to the problem? The *Duggins* court asserted that "an agreement, preferably in writing, with the client concerning the division of legal representation may prevent the liability of one attorney for any errors committed by the other," but if "the division of responsibility is not clearly spelled out, the client's consent to the association does not prevent vicarious liability between or among counsel when the attorneys share the representation

2. Notice that the case dealt only with tort liability, not professional discipline. Do Model Rules 5.1, 5.2, and 5.3 apply to these facts?

and legal fees." Does that make strict liability in the absence of an agreement more palatable?

7. Should a lawyer's trust account be subject to random audits by disciplinary authorities? Should lawyers collectively have to reimburse clients victimized by the acts of other lawyers?

a.   Traditional doctrine requires that there be no audit unless there is probable cause to believe that the accounts have not been properly maintained. In February 1992, the ABA House of Delegates approved proposals for disciplinary reform that called for random audits, but states do not yet seem to have adopted the proposals. Proponents believe that such audits would catch some lawyers who commingle funds and deter others from doing so.

b.   Some lawyers have tried to resist audit of their trust accounts, citing attorney-client privilege or their own expectation of privacy. Those defenses have generally not prevailed, e.g., In re Kennedy, 442 A.2d 79 (Del.1982) (spot check system), cert. denied, 467 U.S. 1205 (1984); Doyle v. State Bar of California, 648 P.2d 942 (Cal.1982) (subpoena system).

c.   Even where the audit determines that the lawyer has stolen from his or her law firm instead of from a client, disbarment of the lawyer may follow. See, e.g., In re Busby, 855 P.2d 156 (Or.1993) (lawyer suspended for four months for lying to his firm about the fees he was paid and pocketing the difference).

d.   Suppose the lawyer who converted client funds is now judgment-proof. What remedies, if any, should you pursue on the client's behalf? Most states have established a client security fund to reimburse clients victimized by their attorneys.[3] Should all members of the bar be assessed to provide the corpus of such a fund? Should the existence of the fund be kept quiet so as to prevent the lawyers' assessments from becoming as high as doctors' malpractice premiums?

B.   LAWYER WITHDRAWAL WITHOUT CONSENT OF THE CLIENT

1.   Should a lawyer ever be *required* to terminate a representation?

a.   Model Rule 1.16(a)(1) requires withdrawal if the lawyer's continued representation will violate another Model Rule. As you go through this course, watch for situations that might trigger such a requirement. Conflicts of interest create such situations, for example. Also watch for situations involving uncorrected client fraud.

b.   Model Rule 1.16(a)(2) makes withdrawal mandatory where "the lawyer's physical or mental condition materially impairs the lawyer's

---

3. See, e.g., Murray T. Bloom, The Trouble With Lawyers 1–35 (1969). Beard v. North Carolina State Bar, 357 S.E.2d 694 (N.C.1987), upheld a system by which the state supreme court requires each lawyer to pay $50 each year into the client security fund. See also, Clients' Security Fund of State v. Grandeau, 526 N.E.2d 270 (N.Y. 1988) (upholds suit by New York Fund against the partner of defaulting lawyer on a theory of vicarious liability).

ability to represent the client.'' How should that rule apply to aging lawyers? Where should we draw the line between ''he's not what he once was'' and a situation requiring mandatory withdrawal?

c.   Model Rule 1.16(a)(3) requires withdrawal when the client discharges the lawyer. Ordinarily the client may discharge the lawyer at any time and for any reason, having an obligation only to pay for work done up to that time. Restatement Third, The Law Governing Lawyers § 32(1), Comment *b*, says bluntly: ''A client may always discharge a lawyer, regardless of cause and regardless of any agreement between them.'' Why should a client have more right than a lawyer to walk away from what is otherwise a binding contract between them? Are Model Rule 1.16, Comments 4–6, at all helpful in answering that question?[4]

2.   We know a lawyer has significant discretion whether to undertake representation of a client, but once having done so, does the lawyer have less ability to terminate that representation over the client's objection?

a.   Model Rule 1.16(b)(1) authorizes a lawyer to withdraw from representation at any time if the withdrawal affects no material interests of the client adversely. If the client does not want the lawyer to withdraw, are the client's material interests *always* adversely affected?

b.   Is withdrawal a breach of the lawyer's duty of loyalty to the client unless the lawyer has a reason for withdrawal other than being tired of the client's personality? If the lawyer does withdraw, who should pay for the cost of bringing a new lawyer up to speed?

c.   In Gilles v. Wiley, Malehorn & Sirota, 783 A.2d 756 (N.J.Super.App.Div.2001), the lawyer had agreed to represent the plaintiff in a medical malpractice case. The first medical expert consulted by the lawyer said that the plaintiff's doctor had not acted negligently, but a later expert gave an opinion more favorable to the plaintiff. After getting the second opinion, the lawyer held the case for six more months and only about three weeks before the statute of limitations expired, he sent his client (the plaintiff in this case) a letter terminating the representation. In the letter, the lawyer explained that his firm had moved away from medical malpractice claims because they were not very profitable, and he advised the plaintiff to find another lawyer because her claim faced a two-year statute of limitations. The plaintiff ultimately did not find another lawyer until after the statute of limitations had expired and thus sued the first lawyer for malpractice. The court refused to grant summary judgment for the defendant. The lawyer's late withdrawal had a material adverse effect on the plaintiff's interests, and the lawyer did not take reasonable measures to protect those interests. At the very least, the lawyer could have prepared a

---

4. Kolschefsky v. Harris, 72 P.3d 1144 (Wyo.2003), presented an unexpected case of client discharge. The trial court held that ''their voluntary bankruptcy petition constituted an anticipatory breach or repudiation of the contingent fee arrangement with their attorney, discharging him from any further performance as their attorney.'' The Wyoming Supreme Court affirmed.

pro se complaint for the plaintiff to file while she sought representation elsewhere.

3. Should a lawyer be permitted to withdraw under Model Rule 1.16(b)(4) whenever the client insists on taking action "with which the lawyer has a fundamental disagreement"?

a. Is it the lawyer or the client who has authority to define the objectives of representation under Model Rule 1.2(a)? Can that authority be real if a lawyer who disagrees with client decisions may simply resign?

b. The "fundamental disagreement" language replaced a standard permitting a lawyer to withdraw in the face of any decision the lawyer found "imprudent." Was that ground even more favorable to lawyer withdrawal?

c. Is the answer that Model Rule 1.16(d) requires a lawyer to take "reasonably practicable" steps "to protect a client's interest"? Are you satisfied that such a cautionary requirement overcomes the consequences of a lawyer's election to withdraw?

4. Should a lawyer be permitted to withdraw from a case that has become financially unprofitable for the lawyer to pursue?

a. In Smith v. R.J. Reynolds, 630 A.2d 820 (N.J.Super.App.Div.1993), a firm had agreed to charge a contingent fee to represent a smoker in a damage claim against R.J. Reynolds. As discovery went on, however, the firm had expended over $1 million in out-of-pocket costs and $5 million in lawyer time. The prospect of much more expense remained before the case would come to trial, but the plaintiffs wanted to go to trial to establish a "principle." The lawyers responded that "there comes a time when we can't afford to operate on the fuel of just principle * * * when the finances are such that it becomes an unreasonable burden." 630 A.2d at 825.

Should the court let the lawyers off the hook? In this case, the appellate division concluded that if the litigation had been paid for at hourly rates, all would agree the time had come to call it quits. Because a contingent fee contract gives the client no incentive to drop the matter, the court ordered the trial judge to determine the likelihood of success in the case, the likely recovery, if any, and then make the assessment that new Model Rule 1.16(b)(6) contemplates. But see Haines v. Liggett Group, 814 F.Supp. 414 (D.N.J.1993), a related case in which the court said the firm had made a deal with the client and had to live with it.

b. Restatement Third, The Law Governing Lawyers § 32 identifies no ground comparable to Model Rule 1.16(b)(6). Should courts permit withdrawal on financial grounds? Would failure to do so harm future clients by making it hard to get lawyers to take cases with uncertain costs and outcomes? See, e.g., Fidelity Nat'l Title Ins. Co. v. Intercounty Nat'l Title Ins. Co., 310 F.3d 537 (7th Cir.2002) (business firms "have no right to free legal aid in civil suits").

5. What role should courts play in reviewing attempted withdrawal?

a. If a matter from which the lawyer seeks to withdraw is pending before a tribunal, the rules of that tribunal will ordinarily require the tribunal's permission to withdraw. See Model Rule 1.16(c).

b. Can you imagine circumstances in which a court will not permit a lawyer to withdraw even where withdrawal would be required under Model Rule 1.16(a)? Keep that question in mind when you look at Problem 27, for example, on what to do when a client lies in court testimony.

c. As an alternative to withdrawal, should Jackson be able to turn to the court for help in seeing that the client pays the fee in advance? Journalist Martin Mayer writes that:

> " * * * criminal practice is the one branch of the law where lawyers collect their fees in advance. Not long ago, an older New York lawyer with little experience in the criminal courts had a client who had been picked up in another county for drunk driving, and for whom a conviction at precisely this moment would be extremely inconvenient. He wanted a postponement, but knew of no excuse a judge would have to accept, so he consulted with the young assistant district attorney who would be on duty that day. The DA heard the reason for the postponement, which was a good one, and said. 'That's all right. You just tell the judge that you haven't been able to get hold of your witness, Mr. Green.'

> " 'But I don't have any witness, Mr. Green.'

> "The DA looked incredulously at the older lawyer's white hairs and said, 'Don't you *know*? It means you haven't been paid. Any judge will give you an adjournment on that.'

> "In Washington, D.C., these matters are handled with greater formality: a lawyer still waiting for his fee comes into court and demands an adjournment 'pursuant to Rule I of this Court.' "[5]

Should a judge assist an attorney to collect a fee in this way? Is it only professional courtesy to do so? Is there anything else the judge could do to assist the lawyer other than grant a delay? What is the professionally responsible way for both lawyer and judge to handle this situation?

C. LIMITATIONS ON A LAWYER'S EFFORTS TO COLLECT A FEE

1. Should the ethics rules permit a lawyer to sue a client to collect a fee?

a. ABA Formal Opinion 250 (1943) upheld suits against clients, but without enthusiasm. Do you agree with the committee's view that "ours is a learned profession, not a mere money-getting trade"? ABA Model Code of Professional Responsibility, EC 2–23 provided that "suits to collect fees should be avoided."

b. Any legal prohibition on suits to collect legal fees is now ancient history, see Restatement Third, The Law Governing Lawyers § 42(1),

---

5. Martin Mayer, The Lawyers 161–62 (1967) (emphasis in original).

although such suits often backfire against lawyers when clients use them as an occasion to file a counterclaim alleging professional malpractice.

2. Should a lawyer be bound by the obligation to preserve client confidences and secrets in establishing the elements of the lawyer's claim?

a. As you will see in later problems, a lawyer's duty to keep information about a client confidential is very strict. However, look at Model Rule 1.6(b)(5). What principle, if any, would justify sacrificing the client's interest in confidentiality in favor of furthering the lawyer's interest in getting paid?[6]

b. Model Rule 1.6(b)(1) creates an exception to the obligation of confidentiality when disclosure is required to avoid "reasonably certain death or substantial bodily harm." However, until 2003, when the ABA House of Delegates amended Rule 1.6 after the Enron scandals, the lawyer had no option to disclose to prevent third parties from being victims of securities fraud. Why should the law allow disclosure to be sure the lawyer gets paid, but not to protect innocent victims of the client's fraud in aid of which the lawyer's services had been used?

c. Restatement Third, The Law Governing Lawyers § 65, Comment *b*, argues:

> "Without this exception, a lawyer could be deprived of important evidence to prove a rightful claim. Clients would thus sometimes be immune from honest claims for legal fees. Moreover, at least some disclosures necessary to establish a fee will not involve information that a client would find embarrassing or prejudicial, other than in defeating the client's position in the dispute."

Are you convinced by this argument? By failing to pay the lawyer's fee, has the client breached the contract that underlies the lawyer's confidentiality obligation?[7]

3. In order to "encourage" the client's payment, may the lawyer threaten to reveal more client confidences than necessary to prove the lawyer's case?

a. In re Disciplinary Proceeding Against Boelter, 985 P.2d 328 (Wash. 1999), suspended a lawyer for six months for his threats to reveal confidential client information in order to collect a fee. The lawyer had told the

---

6. Lawyers' claims of a right to do so are not new. ABA Opinion 250 (1943) concluded that Canon 4 of the former ABA Model Code of Professional Responsibility did not prevent a lawyer from disclosing confidential information in order to attach the client's property to collect his fee. See also, Nakasian v. Incontrade, Inc., 409 F.Supp. 1220, 1224 (S.D.N.Y.1976) (in order to collect fee, lawyer may attach the funds of his clients, even where the attachment is facilitated by confidential information possessed by the lawyer).

7. D.C. Bar Legal Ethics Committee, Opinion No. 298 (2000) says that a lawyer may use a collection agency to collect legal fees as long as the ethical standards of the agency is consistent with the lawyer's ethical standards and the lawyer only discloses the minimal information about the representation necessary to collect the fee. The opinion advised that the ethics rules prohibit the outright sale of client accounts receivable to a collection agency.

client that failure to pay means "you forego the attorney-client privilege and I would be forced to reveal that you lied on your statements to the IRS and to the bank as to your financial condition. This would entail disclosure of the tapes of our conversations about your hidden assets. There is a federal statute, 18 U.S.C. § 1001, which provides for up to one year in jail for such perjury. The choice is yours." Fair warning about the firm's limited ability to disclose confidential information is permissible, the court said, but the "tape" was a fabrication and the fees being claimed were excessive. The threats justified the lawyer's six-month suspension.

b.   In State ex rel. Counsel for Discipline of Nebraska Supreme Court v. Lopez Wilson, 634 N.W.2d 467 (Neb.2001), the lawyer represented a client in obtaining a visa and in divorce proceedings. However, when the lawyer learned that the client was engaged in an intimate relationship with the lawyer's ex-wife, he withdrew and threatened both to tell the INS that the client's job status had changed and to reopen the prior divorce proceedings unless the client paid him for services that the lawyer had theretofore provided free of charge. In upholding a two-year suspension, the court stated that Canon 4 of the Model Code of Professional Responsibility allowed limited disclosure of client confidences in a suit to collect a legal fee, but it did not permit "violent threats" to disclose such information more generally.

c.   Are these cases consistent with the Model Rules? Look at Model Rule 1.6, Comment 14.

4.   Should a fee dispute between attorney and client be subject to mandatory arbitration at the request of the client?

a.   Several states require fee arbitration if the client wants it. Anderson v. Elliott, 555 A.2d 1042 (Me.1989), cert. denied, 493 U.S. 978 (1989), upheld the Maine requirement. The lawyer argued that arbitration denied him his constitutional right to a jury trial, but the court held that the right must be read in the context of the court's supervisory power over attorneys.

b.   In Guralnick v. Supreme Court of New Jersey, 747 F.Supp. 1109 (D.N.J.1990), aff'd, 961 F.2d 209 (3d Cir.1992), lawyers argued that a New Jersey system of fee arbitration that only a client may initiate unconstitutionally denied them due process, violated their Thirteenth Amendment rights and violated the antitrust laws as well. In a thoughtful opinion, the court rejected all such challenges.

c.   A. Fred Miller, P.C. v. Purvis, 921 P.2d 610 (Alaska 1996), held that the lack of judicial review of an arbitration award did not deny due process. The court agreed that judicial review on the merits is desirable in an arbitration process, but part of the purpose of arbitration is to achieve a quick, binding review of a dispute. Judicial review would put a burden on clients that the Constitution does not require. See also, Nodvin v. State Bar of Georgia, 544 S.E.2d 142 (Ga.2001) (upholds fee arbitration procedure).

5. Should a lawyer's engagement letter be able to specify that non-fee complaints the client has about the lawyer must be submitted to arbitration as well?

a. A lawyer's suit for unpaid fees will often trigger a malpractice claim from the client who hopes to reach a compromise of the fee amount. As you may remember, Model Rule 1.8(h) forbids limiting the lawyer's liability for malpractice or settling a malpractice claim without advising the client of the need for independent counsel. The question thus is whether an arbitration requirement in a lawyer's engagement letter violates either or both prohibitions.

b. ABA Formal Opinion 02–425 (Feb. 20, 2002) said that an arbitration clause, by itself, does not violate Rule 1.8(h). The opinion acknowledged that an attorney has a fiduciary duty under Rule 1.4(b) "to advise clients of the possible adverse consequences as well as the benefits that may arise from the execution of an agreement," and because a client potentially waives significant rights by agreeing to mandatory arbitration, the attorney has a duty to explain the potential consequences of that "to the extent reasonably necessary to permit the client to make [an] informed decision about the contract." However, the opinion reasoned that because the arbitration clause only defines the forum in which the disgruntled client must proceed, it does not limit the lawyer's liability for malpractice.

6. In the absence of agreement, what rights should a lawyer have if the client terminates the relationship the day before trial, or under other circumstances where significant time has been invested but no results achieved on which to calculate a contingent or percentage fee?

a. The usual rule permits the lawyer a *quantum meruit* recovery. In the case of a contingent fee, the first lawyer can usually recover only if the second lawyer wins the case, i.e., if the plaintiff ultimately prevails, e.g., Plaza Shoe Store, Inc. v. Hermel, Inc., 636 S.W.2d 53 (Mo.1982) (en banc).

b. Gagne v. Vaccaro, 766 A.2d 416 (Conn.2001), involved a lawyer who had not entered into a written contingent fee agreement with his client. Then, a second lawyer, who replaced the first one, successfully pursued the matter and collected a contingent fee. Now, the first lawyer wanted a fair share of the fee earned. The court held he could get a *quantum meruit* payment. The lack of a written agreement was not enough to deny him all fees, and where he had acted loyally and his work had contributed to the final outcome, *quantum meruit* recovery was appropriate.

7. May a lawyer charge interest or a "late payment penalty" on overdue accounts? May a lawyer accept MasterCard in payment of his fees and simply leave all collection problems up to the credit card company?

a. These used to be serious questions, but the ABA upheld both charging interest and accepting credit cards in ABA Formal Opinion 338

(Nov. 16, 1974) and reconfirmed that result in ABA Formal Opinion 00–420 (Nov. 29, 2000).

b.   Lustig v. Horn, 732 N.E.2d 613 (Ill.App.2000), however, refused to allow a firm's charge of 1% of its fee for late payment, plus additional attorney's fees if the fee had to be collected in court. The charges put the firm in a position of "prosecuting" its own client, and they could be used "to silence a client" who wanted to protest an improper fee.

c.   D.C. Bar Legal Ethics Committee Opinion No. 310 (2001) also re-examined when a lawyer may charge interest on past due fees. It said that even where the original fee agreement makes no provision for interest, if the client gets behind in payments, the lawyer may condition further representation on the client's willingness to pay interest in the future. The opinion acknowledges that any such situation involves a conflict of interest between lawyer and client, but it says that every fee arrangement creates such a conflict. Any such change in the fee arrangement will be subject to "strict scrutiny," the opinion says, but it is not absolutely prohibited.

D.   ATTORNEYS' LIENS AND OTHER SECURITY INTERESTS

1.   Should a lawyer be permitted to retain a client's property and papers until the lawyer's fee is paid?

a.   In Sage Realty Corp. v. Proskauer Rose Goetz & Mendelsohn L.L.P., 689 N.E.2d 879 (N.Y.1997), a client who had paid over a million dollars in fees in a large financing transaction decided to switch lawyers. It asked the firm for its file, now totaling so many volumes that the index alone ran 58 pages. The firm turned over the closing documents, client-supplied papers and correspondence with third parties, but not its own internal work product. Citing what is now § 43 of the Restatement Third, The Law Governing Lawyers, the New York Court of Appeals held that the client is presumptively entitled to all its papers, save for documents that might violate the firm's duty of nondisclosure owed to a third party, duties otherwise imposed by law, and firm documents intended for internal law office review and use (such as "documents containing a firm attorney's general or other assessment of the client, or tentative preliminary impressions of the legal or factual issues presented in the representation, recorded primarily for the purpose of giving internal direction to facilitate performance of the legal services entailed in that representation."). The court said that the firm may ordinarily charge the client for the function of assembling and delivering the documents to the client.

b.   In many states (California is a major exception), an attorney has a "retaining lien" that gives the lawyer a possessory interest in the client's papers and funds in the attorney's possession.[8] But the Restatement Third,

---

8.   The retaining lien does not apply to property simply given to the lawyer for safekeeping. See Akers v. Akers, 46 N.W.2d 87 (Minn.1951) (evidence sustained finding that property was originally left with attorney for purpose of placing it beyond reach of defendant Akers and not for security for payment of attorney's fees). Similarly, a lawyer may not take excess funds deposited by the client for payment of court reporter charges and apply them to payment of the lawyer's unpaid fees. See State ex rel. Oklahoma Bar Ass'n v. Cummings, 863 P.2d 1164 (Okl. 1993).

The Law Governing Lawyers § 43, rejected the general availability of such a lien on the ground that "[a] broad retaining lien could impose pressure on a client disproportionate to the size or validity of the lawyer's fee claim." Do you think lawyers should have a right to assert a retaining lien?

c. The significance of the retaining lien is greatest when the client really needs the papers, for example, where new counsel needs the files to prepare for trial. Pomerantz v. Schandler, 704 F.2d 681 (2d Cir.1983) (per curiam), found an exception to the attorney's retaining lien when the client had an urgent need for papers to defend a criminal case and lacked the means to pay the lawyer's fee.

d. However, that exception is not broad. The whole purpose of a retaining lien is to put pressure on the client to pay the lawyer's bill. An "attorney's lien cannot otherwise be disregarded merely because the pressure it is supposed to exert becomes effective." 704 F.2d 681, 683.

e. Thus, even the Restatement recognizes that "[a] client who fails to pay for the lawyer's work in preparing particular documents * * * ordinarily is not entitled to receive those documents." Restatement Third, The Law Governing Lawyers § 43, Comment c.

2. In order to guarantee payment of a lawyer's fee, should the lawyer be able to assert a lien on sums recovered on behalf of the client?

a. Most states give the attorney a right to assert a "charging lien" that gives the lawyer a right to apply the recovery in a case to payment of his or her fees. Restatement Third, The Law Governing Lawyers § 43, Comment d, explains that many states "recognize a charging lien without a contract" between the lawyer and client, but Restatement § 43(2) provides that there should be a written contract in order to safeguard the client. See also, Fletcher v. Davis, 90 P.3d 1216 (Cal.2004), that refuses to enforce an oral charging lien.

b. The attorney must give notice to the person paying the judgment or settlement. Once such notice is given, the person paying the judgment or settlement is liable for the attorney's fees if that person pays the entire judgment or settlement directly to the attorney's client. See Restatement Third, The Law Governing Lawyers § 43, Comment e.

c. People v. Philip Morris, Inc., 759 N.E.2d 906 (Ill.2001), shows that huge sums can turn on the application of these principles. This case arose out of several states' lawsuits against the tobacco industry. The Illinois attorney general selected an Illinois Special Counsel (ISC) and agreed that its compensation would be 10% of the total recovery to the state of Illinois. Subsequently, the state and the tobacco defendants entered into the Master Settlement Agreement (MSA) pursuant to which Illinois would receive an estimated $9 billion, i.e., $360 million annually for 25 years from the tobacco defendants. Section 17 of the MSA also created an arbitration panel to award attorneys' fees. That panel awarded the ISC $121 million (about

1.3% of the recovery), also to be paid over 25 years. The ISC (which was not precluded by the panel from seeking additional fees) then served notice of its attorney's lien of 10%, based on the fee agreement with the attorney general. The circuit court ordered that 10% of all settlement payments be deposited into an escrow account pending a decision on the merits of the lien petition, and the Illinois Supreme Court held that, pursuant to the Attorneys Lien Act, a lawyer may assert a lien if the lawyer was hired by a client to assert a claim and the lawyer serves notice, in writing, upon the party against whom the client has the claim. Further, the court held that an attorneys' lien proceeding is not a claim against the state and thus need not be asserted before the state's court of claims. The funds recovered are not "state funds" until after "ISC's attorney fees are paid and the funds go into the state treasury."

d. In Schneider, Kleinick, Weitz, et al. v. City of New York, 754 N.Y.S.2d 220 (N.Y.App.Div.2002), the plaintiff law firm had been discharged without cause by its client in a case that was subsequently settled. The law firm unsuccessfully attempted to recover its share of the fee from the counsel that replaced it. The issue then became whether the fee could be recovered from the defendants in the underlying matter. The court held that it could. After its discharge, the law firm gave formal notice of its charging lien to the defendant, the city of New York. Once the settlement occurred, the law firm moved to restrain the city from disbursing the attorneys' fees until its own fees were determined. However, the city paid the full amount of attorney's fees to the replacement firm. When the city did this, "it did so at the risk of being sued by the Schneider firm for its share of the award." The court held that " 'a defendant who has knowledge of a plaintiff's attorney's lien is under an affirmative duty to protect the lien, and if he fails to do so, he is liable for the reasonable value of that attorney's services to his client.' " 754 N.Y. S.2d at 225–26.

3. May the engagement letter with a client give the lawyer a security interest in the property that is the subject matter of the litigation?

a. Look at Model Rule 1.8(i). Why might such a security interest be suspect? Restatement Third, The Law Governing Lawyers § 36, Comment *b*, traces the prohibition to common law fears of champerty and maintenance, i.e., that wealthy lawyers would buy claims and clog the courts with litigation. If that were the only rationale, would you favor repeal of Model Rule 1.8(i)?

b. However, the same Comment continues:

"The justification for the rule in its present form is that a lawyer's ownership gives the lawyer an economic basis for claiming to control the prosecution and settlement of the claim and provides an incentive for the lawyer to relegate the client to a subordinate position. * * * The rule also prevents a lawyer from disguising an unreasonably large fee, violative of § 34, by buying part of the claim for a low price."

Does that give you more confidence that Model Rule 1.8(i) has a place in modern law?[9]

4. Is Model Rule 1.8(i) the only Rule governing the lawyer taking an interest in the client's property?

a. Hawk v. State Bar of California, 754 P.2d 1096 (Cal.1988), says that when a lawyer takes any interest in property of the client as security for payment of the lawyer's fee, the arrangement is a business transaction with the client subject to the California equivalent of Model Rule 1.8(a). The court implies that in some cases the arrangement could properly be entered into as a way of helping the client afford necessary legal services. If the lawyer ignores the conflict of interest concerns and does not comply with the safeguards of the cited rules, however, he or she will be subject to discipline. In this case, the court suspended attorney Hawk for six months and put him on probation for four years.

b. ABA Formal Opinion 02–427 (May 31, 2002) also said that "there is nothing inherently unethical in a lawyer asking a client to provide security for payment of fees." Such a transaction is subject to the standards in Model Rule 1.8(a), however, and if the lawyer takes possession of the security, the lawyer must safeguard it as provided in Model Rule 1.15(a). Further, if property is transferred to the lawyer as payment of the fee, the lawyer may retain only so much of the proceeds as represents a reasonable fee. Any excess value must be treated as property belonging to the client.

PROBLEM 7

THE DUTY OF CONFIDENTIALITY

The ability to talk freely and confidentially is one of the central elements defining the relationship between lawyer and client. What lawyers can find confusing, however, is the fact that their confidentiality obligation is made up of three quite different bodies of law:

1. The attorney-client privilege is part of the law of evidence and allows a lawyer and client to refuse to testify about communications between them, made in confidence, for the purpose of giving or receiving legal advice.

---

9. The Comment continues: "The prohibition * * * is limited to matters in litigation. Thus, * * * a lawyer may acquire an ownership or other proprietary interest in a client's patent when retained to file a patent application, while * * * the lawyer could not acquire such an interest if retained to bring a patent-infringement suit. The difference in treatment is largely historical." In other words, in litigation, the lawyer cannot use the contingent fee to become part owner of the property such that he can prevent settlement. Assuming the fee is otherwise reasonable, he can become a 10% owner of a patent as a charge for filing the patent. If there is litigation, as long as the lawyer is not an owner of the patent, he can charge 10% of the value of the patent as his contingent fee, but he cannot become a 10% owner of the patent because that would make him a co-plaintiff.

2. Work product immunity, which arises out of the law of civil procedure, protects a lawyer's work done in anticipation of litigation from otherwise applicable requirements to turn over relevant information, typically during pre-trial discovery.

3. The professional duty of confidentiality, on the other hand, found in Model Rule 1.6, broadly forbids a lawyer from using of revealing information relating to the representation other than for the client's benefit. This duty grows out of fiduciary obligations of trustees and agents.

The first three topics in this problem try to help you keep those concepts straight. You will see that the scope and character of each of the protections can vary considerably in a given case. The fourth topic examines how privilege and confidentiality protection might be lost and suggests the care a lawyer must take against that eventuality.

FACTS

Your longtime client, John Carter, recently came to your office to tell you that he expects to be sued by the person who bought his house. When expressly asked by his prospective buyer prior to the sale, he told the buyer that the house had a dry basement. He has admitted to you, however, that although the basement had never flooded in the five years he had lived there, Carter had been warned by a prior owner that the basement regularly flooded after a heavy rain. There was such a rain this year, and some of the buyer's expensive electronic equipment suffered major damage.

Shortly before his death, you were able to interview the prior owner of the house, who confirmed to you what he had told Carter about the tendency to flood. You have notes of that interview in which you comment on the former owner's likely credibility at trial. Later, at a party at a friend's home, Carter's banker let slip that Carter is in bad financial condition. You mentally filed that away as important to your settlement posture in case Carter were sued.

The buyer has now filed suit against Carter. The buyer has subpoenaed your notes of your interview with the prior owner. Someone else has asked you informally if the rumors that Carter has suffered financial reverses are true.

QUESTIONS

A. INFORMATION PROTECTED BY THE ATTORNEY-CLIENT PRIVILEGE

1. Protecting information covered by the attorney-client privilege is one of a lawyer's most basic obligations. How will you know such information when you see it?

a. Restatement Third, The Law Governing Lawyers § 68 says that the attorney-client privilege protects "(1) a communication, (2) made between privileged persons,[1] (3) in confidence, (4) for the purpose of obtaining or providing legal assistance for the client.''

b. Proposed Federal Rule 503[2] goes into more detail about when the privilege protects or does not protect:

"*(a) Definitions.* As used in this rule:

"(1) A 'client' is a person, public officer, or corporation, association, or other organization or entity, either public or private, who is rendered professional legal services by a lawyer, or who consults a lawyer with a view to obtaining professional legal services from him.

"(2) A 'lawyer' is a person authorized, or reasonably believed by the client to be authorized, to practice law in any state or nation.

"(3) A 'representative of the lawyer' is one employed to assist the lawyer in the rendition of professional legal services.

"(4) A communication is 'confidential' if not intended to be disclosed to third persons other than those to whom disclosure is in furtherance of the rendition of professional legal services to the client or those reasonably necessary for the transmission of the communication.

"*(b) General Rule of Privilege.* A client has a privilege to refuse to disclose and to prevent any other person from disclosing confidential communications made for the purpose of facilitating the rendition of professional legal services to the client, (1) between himself or his representative and his lawyer or his lawyer's representative, or (2) between his lawyer and the lawyer's representative, or (3) by him or his lawyer to a lawyer representing another in a matter of common interest, or (4) between representatives of the client or between the client and a representative of the client, or (5) between lawyers representing the client.

"*(c) Who May Claim the Privilege.* The privilege may be claimed by the client, his guardian or conservator, the personal representative of a deceased client, or the successor, trustee, or similar representative of a corporation, association, or other organization, whether or not in existence. The person who was the lawyer at the time of the communication may claim the privilege but only on behalf of the client. His authority to do so is presumed in the absence of evidence to the contrary.

---

1. "Privileged persons" are "the client (including a prospective client), the client's lawyer, agents of either who facilitate communication between them, and agents of the lawyer who facilitate the representation." Restatement Third, The Law Governing Lawyers § 70.

2. When the Federal Rules of Evidence were approved by Congress, none of the 13 rules dealing with privileges, including Proposed Rule 503 were enacted, see Fed. Rules of Evidence, Pub.L. 93–595 (Jan. 2, 1975). The reasons for non-enactment did not reflect on the merits of Proposed Rule 503, which is, in general, a fair summary of the law of most states.

"(d) Exceptions. There is no privilege under this rule:

"(1) Furtherance of crime or fraud. If the services of the lawyer were sought or obtained to enable or aid anyone to commit or plan to commit what the client knew or reasonably should have known to be a crime or fraud; or

"(2) Claimants through same deceased client. As to a communication relevant to an issue between parties who claim through the same deceased client, regardless of whether the claims are by testate or intestate succession or by *inter vivos* transactions; or

"(3) Breach of duty by lawyer or client. As to a communication relevant to an issue of breach of duty by the lawyer to his client or by the client to his lawyer; or

"(4) Document attested by lawyer. As to a communication relevant to an issue concerning an attested document to which the lawyer is an attesting witness; or

"(5) Joint clients. As to a communication relevant to a matter of common interest between two or more clients if the communication was made by any of them to a lawyer retained or consulted in common, when offered in an action between any of the clients.''

2.   Because the privilege applies only to certain communications, there is substantial litigation over when it may be asserted. Should the privilege be held to apply in the following situations?

a.   In Commonwealth v. Mrozek, 657 A.2d 997 (Pa.Super.Ct.1995), a potential client called the lawyer's office to ask the receptionist for an appointment because "I've just committed a homicide." The court held that statement to the receptionist (a non-lawyer) was privileged because she was an employee of the lawyer whose job it was to communicate with clients and potential clients.

b.   In D'Alessio v. Gilberg, 617 N.Y.S.2d 484 (N.Y.App.Div.1994), the question was the privileged character of the client's identity. A client who had caused a hit-and-run accident consulted a lawyer about the accident. The victim wanted to sue the client but did not know his name. The identity of a client is normally not privileged; it is the first thing the lawyer discloses when entering an appearance in a case. But, in this situation, no appearance had been entered and revealing the client's identity could cause the client both to be prosecuted criminally and to be sued. Thus, the court held the identity privileged.

c.   In re Grand Jury Subpoenas Dated March 9, 2001, 179 F.Supp.2d 270 (S.D.N.Y.2001), sought production of documents related to the effort by lawyers for Marc Rich and Pincus Green to get them a presidential pardon. Since 1983, Rich and Green were living abroad and refused to come to the United States to face criminal charges. Prosecutors in the Southern District of New York refused to drop the charges, so the defendants' lawyers developed a network of contacts with then-President Clinton who pardoned the two men in early 2001. In this case, the Justice Department sought production of documents as part of its investigation of circumstances surrounding the pardon. The court held that materials related to procuring Rich's pardon were not privileged because the attorneys were acting as lobbyists, not lawyers, once the decision to seek a pardon was made. Because lobbying could legally be done by non-lawyers, the lawyers' communications were not for the purpose of rendering legal assistance to Rich. Do you agree? Needless to say, this opinion has worried many lawyers who do things for clients, e.g., lobbying, that non-lawyers could also legally do.

d. Al Odah v. United States, 346 F.Supp.2d 1 (D.D.C.2004), considered the scope of the privilege for communications between Guantanamo Bay detainees and lawyers working on their habeas corpus petitions. Pursuant to the September 14, 2001, Joint Resolution of Congress authorizing the president to use "all means necessary" to defeat terrorism, the FBI promulgated a set of monitoring procedures for "designated detainees" held at Guantanamo Bay. Under these procedures, a "privilege team" from the FBI—one or more agents or Department of Defense attorneys screened from other aspects of the detainees' cases—would "monitor [and record] oral communications in real time between counsel and the detainee during any meetings," and conduct a "classification review" of all written materials brought in or out of any such meetings, including the attorney's notes. The petitioner, one of three "designated detainees" held at Guantanamo Bay, challenged the procedures as an impermissible infringement on the attorney-client privilege. The court recognized that the government had significant national security concerns with respect to certain detainees. In order to balance these concerns with the confidentiality required by the privilege, the court had previously required detainees' counsel to obtain the necessary security clearances for access to the information the government believes that the detainee may have. Thereafter, information the attorney received from the detainee in confidence would fall under the protection of the privilege, but if the detainee disclosed information "involving future events that threaten national security or involve immediate violence," the attorney would be *required* to disclose the information. The government's attempt at more extensive monitoring, however, "fl[ies] in the face" of the principles behind the attorney-client privilege, so the court did not allow real-time monitoring of attorney-client meetings.

e. In Stengart v. Loving Care Agency, Inc., 973 A.2d 390 (N.J. Super. Ct. App. Div. 2009), a company executive resigned her position and sued the company for violating anti-discrimination laws. Prior to resigning, the plaintiff had communicated via email with her attorney regarding her case. The emails were sent from her personal email account that she had accessed from a company-owned laptop. After her resignation, the company's counsel made a copy of the laptop hard drive and discovered the emails. The plaintiff objected, but the trial court refused to treat the communications as privileged, because the company had a policy giving it the right to intercept and monitor email. The appellate division agreed that employer handbooks can create unilateral contracts with employees, but it said the policies have to be construed according to the reasonable expectations of employees and must be reasonable to be enforceable. The court found that the policy did not support the company's claim of ownership of the personal communications. Citing Thyroff v. Nationwide Mut. Ins. Co., 864 N.E.2d 1272 (N.Y. 2007), the court found that a company computer used to send personal emails is analogous to a filing cabinet; property rights are offended when an employer searches and claims ownership of an employee's private papers or communications. In an electronic age it can be difficult to segregate company from personal business, and employees have a reasonable expectation of privacy in their personal emails regarding attorney-client matters. Therefore a policy where the company claims to own all personal communications because they own the computer on which they were sent does *not* serve a "legitimate business interest."

3. With all this in mind, go back to the facts in our problem. May the other lawyer force you, Carter's lawyer, to testify that your client, John Carter, admitted to you that he had lied to the buyer of his home about the tendency of the basement to flood?

a. Why should the law protect against disclosure, communications with a lawyer that were solely designed to help the client avoid the consequences of his wrongful conduct? Professor Wigmore says:

> "In order to promote freedom of consultation of legal advisers by clients, the apprehension of compelled disclosure by the legal advisers must be removed; hence the law must prohibit such disclosure except on the client's consent." 8 Wigmore, Evidence § 2291 at 545 (McNaughton rev. 1961).

Are you convinced?

b. Because the exercise of the attorney-client privilege so clearly conflicts with the search for truth, commentators and courts have long held that the privilege "ought to be strictly confined within the narrowest possible limits consistent with the logic of its principle." 8 Wigmore, supra § 2291, at 554. Thus:

> (1) While Carter cannot be forced to testify about the content of his conversation with you, the fact that he talked to you about what he knew will not prevent Carter himself from being forced to testify as to the underlying facts about his knowledge of the tendency to flood.

> (2) The attorney-client privilege will not prevent you from being compelled to produce your notes of the statement by the former owner. Do you see why?[3]

> (3) Likewise, the privilege will not protect against your being forced to reveal what you heard about your client from the banker. When you look at the factors required before a statement is protected

---

3. The work product immunity doctrine may protect the notes against disclosure, but the attorney-client privilege will not. Because the attorney-client privilege provides absolute protection while the work product immunity is subject to a necessity exception, the distinction is important to understand.

by the attorney-client privilege, you should see several reasons why this is so.

(4) If Carter told you that he planned to lie to the buyer *before* he did so, is that statement privileged? Look at the crime-fraud exception in Proposed Federal Rule of Evidence 503(d)(1), supra.

c.   The point of this discussion is that lawyers often glibly cite the "privilege" when it either doesn't apply or when they are relying on some other doctrine. The attorney-client privilege would protect only one kind of material in this problem against testimony from the lawyer. If the lawyer is not to reveal other facts in the problem, it must be on the basis of some other principles.

B.   INFORMATION PROTECTED BY WORK PRODUCT IMMUNITY

1.   What constitutes a lawyer's "work product" and what are the consequences of so designating it?

a.   Restatement Third, The Law Governing Lawyers § 87 says:

"(1) Work product consists of tangible material or its intangible equivalent in unwritten or oral form, other than underlying facts, prepared by a lawyer for litigation then in progress or in reasonable anticipation of future litigation.

"(2) Opinion work product consists of the opinions or mental impressions of a lawyer; all other work product is ordinary work product.

"(3) Except for material which by applicable law is not so protected, work product is immune from discovery or other compelled disclosure * * *."

b.   Work product immunity is the legacy of Hickman v. Taylor, 329 U.S. 495 (1947). Construing the proper scope of discovery, the Court wrote: "Not even the most liberal of discovery theories can justify unwarranted inquiries into the files and the mental impressions of an attorney." The Court went on to say that where one side had information other than mental impressions that was "essential to the preparation of [the other side's] case," it could be discovered "and production might be justified where the witnesses are no longer available or can be reached only with difficulty." The doctrine is now embodied in Federal Rules of Civil Procedure, Rule 26(b)(3).

c.   In re Cendant Corp. Securities Litigation, 343 F.3d 658 (3d Cir. 2003), involved "Dr. Phil" McGraw in the role in which Oprah found him, that of a trial consultant who helped lawyers and witnesses prepare a master plan for their case. In deposition, a lawyer asked one of the witnesses how often Dr. Phil met with him and what they discussed. The Third Circuit sustained a claim that the information constituted protected work product. Work product protects an attorney's mental processes and tactical planning, the court said, and that includes the mental processes of the attorney's agents and consultants whose work was in anticipation of litigation, as Dr. Phil's work clearly was. Moreover, the information constituted opinion work product, which would require exceptional circumstances before the court would order discovery. See also, In re Grand Jury Subpoenas, 265 F.Supp.2d 321 (S.D.N.Y.2003) (grants work product protection to suggestions of public relations consultant hired by lawyers for a potential criminal defendant).[4]

d. In re Sealed Case, 146 F.3d 881 (D.C.Cir.1998), involved materials prepared in anticipation of litigation that had not yet been filed. The Republican National Committee (RNC) had founded a think tank and lent it $2.5 million. The *Washington Post* raised a question whether federal election laws applied to the RNC, and the Democratic National Committee filed suit alleging that they did. In between the news story and the lawsuit, lawyers prepared various memoranda and the question was whether work product protection applied to them. The court held that it did. The test is whether litigation could reasonably have been anticipated; the lack of a specific case at the time the documents were prepared did not deny the protection.

e. In United States v. Adlman, 134 F.3d 1194 (2d Cir.1998), a tax lawyer asked a CPA to prepare a report predicting how the IRS would view a proposed transaction. The court held that the report qualified as prepared "in anticipation of litigation." A document prepared "because of" the prospect of litigation would tend to show legal strategy expected to be employed and would be exactly the kind of document *Hickman* intended to protect.[5] Do you agree? Was Judge Kearse right in her dissent that planning lawyers will now claim work product immunity for a wide variety of documents, saying that litigation about the validity of the transaction was always a possibility?

2. Is any of the information in this problem protected by work product immunity?

a. What about the interview with the former owner? Did you interview him in anticipation of litigation? Does it matter whether the anticipated litigation was this particular lawsuit?

b. Should the fact that the former owner is now dead mean that the notes you took will be discoverable? A witness' death does not itself affect the character of the notes as work product. However, under Federal Rule 26(b)(3), a "party seeking discovery [may show it] has substantial need of the materials in preparation of the party's case and that the party is unable without undue hardship to obtain the substantial equivalent of the material by other means."

---

4. In 2010, the Supreme Court approved a modification to Federal Rule of Civil Procedure Rule 26(b)(4) that expands work product protection of drafts of expert reports and communications between counsel and the expert. Discovery of communications relating to expert compensation, assumptions provided to and relied upon by the expert, and facts the expert has considered will, however, continue to be discoverable.

5. Note that the work product issue is only presented because a lawyer asked the CPA to prepare the report. If the client had asked a CPA to prepare the report, there would have been no work product protection.

3. Does it matter whether the notes of the discussion with the now-deceased former owner are considered ordinary or opinion work product?

a.   Look at the language of Hickman v. Taylor quoted above; "ordinary" work product may be obtained in discovery upon a showing of "substantial need." However, according to Restatement Third, The Law Governing Lawyers § 89:

> "[O]pinion work product is immune from discovery or other compelled disclosure unless * * * extraordinary circumstances justify disclosure."

b.   Should the fact that the former owner is now dead constitute such "extraordinary circumstances" that compelled disclosure is justified? Restatement § 89, Comment *d*, says that "the concept of 'extraordinary circumstances' has never been intelligibly defined. It apparently signifies unwillingness on the part of tribunals to put the work-product immunity on quite the same footing as the attorney-client privilege."

c.   In re Green Grand Jury Proceedings, 492 F.3d 976 (8th Cir.2007), drew another important distinction between ordinary and opinion work product. The defendant had given his lawyer a benign account of his plans but then used the lawyer's advice and documents to engage in illegal conduct. The government moved to compel the lawyer to testify before the grand jury and bring relevant documents, urging that the crime-fraud exception to work product immunity applied. The court held that the client's illegal conduct indeed denied the client the right to assert work product protection for 36 of the documents. The court held, however, that because the lawyer did not know the client's true plans, the lawyer had independent work product protection for the lawyer's opinion work product contained in the documents, and that protection was not tainted by the client's crime or fraud.

d.   How should work product immunity apply in this problem? If you make sure to comment in your notes about the witness' credibility, should the notes be absolutely immune from discovery?

C.   THE LAWYER'S PROFESSIONAL OBLIGATION OF CONFIDENTIALITY

1. May you respond to the informal inquiry about your client's financial situation? Is the chance information learned at a party something the lawyer must keep confidential unless ordered by a court to disclose it?

a.   Is the information about your client's financial situation covered by either the attorney-client privilege or work product immunity? Why or why not?

b.   Look at Model Rule 1.6(a). Does the information you received from the banker qualify as "relating to the representation"? Remember, you have said to yourself that the information may affect your settlement posture.

c. Look at ABA Model Code of Professional Responsibility, DR 4–101(A). Is the information learned at the party a "confidence" of the client as defined there? Is it a "secret"? Would it tend to embarrass the client? Was it learned as part of the "professional relationship"?

2. What does it mean to say that the information is protected against disclosure by these rules? Does it mean any more than that the lawyer may not volunteer the information to others?

a. In Matter of Goebel, 703 N.E.2d 1045 (Ind.1998), the lawyer represented a criminal defendant while the lawyer's partner was handling an unrelated guardianship. By chance, the husband of the guardianship client was to be a prosecution witness in the criminal case. The criminal client asked the guardianship client's address. To prove he didn't know, the lawyer showed the criminal client an envelope returned because it had the wrong address. However, even the wrong address was enough to help the criminal client find the prosecution witness and kill him. The court said that the incorrect address was "information relating to the representation" of the guardianship client. Thus the court publicly reprimanded and admonished the lawyer for revealing it.

b. Iowa Sup. Ct. Attorney Disciplinary Bd. v. Marzen, 779 N.W.2d 757 (Iowa 2010), found that a lawyer breached the duty of confidentiality even though the information was publicly available. A lawyer had been appointed to represent a woman in a hospitalization commitment proceeding. He later agreed to represent her in other matters, including a dispute with her mother and a child-custody proceeding. During an interview with a television news reporter, the lawyer revealed the fact that the woman had previously sued and received a settlement from a parole officer whom she claimed had engaged in sexual misconduct. The lawyer argued he had done nothing wrong because information about the prior suit was available from public sources, but the court disagreed. The ethical requirement of maintaining client confidentiality is broader than information protected by the attorney-client privilege. The lawyer's comments were intended to defame his own client and justified suspension from practice. Notice that the information was available but not "generally known," the standard used in Rule 1.9(c)(1). If a lawyer may only disclose information that is generally known about a *former* client, surely a lawyer may not disclose more about a *current* client.

c. If you were called to testify about what you heard at the party about Carter's financial situation, would you be required to reveal the information? It is important to see that one of the important distinctions between information that is "privileged" and information that is protected only by the obligation of "confidentiality" is that a lawyer may be required to testify about the latter. See Model Rule 1.6(b)(6); Restatement Third, The Law Governing Lawyers § 63.

3. How much affirmative effort must a lawyer undertake to preserve the confidentiality of communications with clients and others?

a. It is important that lawyers carefully maintain the confidentiality of their oral and written communications with clients. See Restatement Third, The Law Governing Lawyers § 60(1)(b): "[T]he lawyer must take steps reasonable in the circumstances to protect confidential client information against impermissible use or disclosure." See also, Model Rule 1.6, Comment 2.

b. ABA Formal Opinion 99–413 (Mar. 10, 1999) discussed sending unencrypted email and concluded that a failure to use encryption neither violates the duty of confidentiality nor waives the privilege unless the client insists on, or unusual circumstances require, heightened security. Email communications are legally protected against interception, the opinion said, so lawyer and client have a reasonable expectation of privacy. Further, the risk of interception is no greater than that inherent in landline phones. Several state bar opinions come to the same conclusion. Could lawyers effectively carry on their practice in modern times if the rule were different? See ABA Model Rule 1.6, Comment 17: a lawyer need not "use special security measures if the method of communication affords a reasonable expectation of privacy."

c. New York State Bar Opinion 782 (Dec. 8, 2004) looked at a lawyer's duty to protect against sending metadata in documents transmitted electronically. Metadata is hidden text generated and saved in computer-prepared documents that may contain privileged information, legal strategies, information embarrassing to clients, legal advice, and other protected information. The opinion first declared that New York law imposes a duty to use reasonable care to prevent inadvertent disclosures of client confidences and secrets, even those in documents transmitted over the Internet. Because computer technologies differ, the opinion could not lay down absolute rules, but it said that what constitutes reasonable care depends on the circumstances. Lawyers need to keep up to date on changing technologies, and in determining reasonable precautions they should consider (1) the document's subject matter; (2) whether the document was created from a template used in other clients' cases; (3) whether there have been multiple drafts of the document with comments from multiple sources; (4) whether the document contains client confidences; and (5) the identity of the intended recipients of the document. See also, ABA Formal Opinion 06–442 (Aug. 5, 2006) (describes ways to remove metadata from documents but imposes no duty to do so). We return to metadata issues in Problem 24, *infra*.

d. Ill. State Bar Ass'n Advisory Op. 10–01 (2009) advised that it is permissible for a lawyer or law firm to hire an off-site network administrator to manage its computer network, monitor the server, and respond to problems. Because access to the computer system would be required, the third-party administrator could potentially have access to confidential client information. The opinion acknowledged that such an arrangement would implicate Rule 1.6(a) on confidentiality of client information and Rule 5.3 on the responsibilities of supervising non-lawyer assistants. The opinion cited ABA Opinion 95–398 (Oct. 27, 1995) and ABA Opinion 08–451

(Aug. 5, 2008), which take the position that such arrangements are permissible in light of rapidly changing technology but the lawyer must make reasonable efforts to prevent the disclosure of any confidential information. The opinion further noted that if the third-party administrator breaches confidentiality, the lawyer may be obligated to disclose the breach to the client if it is likely to affect the client's case. The opinion stressed the need for reasonable efforts to protect confidential information, including consulting with the third-party administrator about the nature of the information, ensuring that it will only be accessed when necessary for technical purposes, and trying to assure that the administrator will maintain the confidentiality of all information.

e.   Many law firms have placed their client files on servers accessible remotely by lawyers and clients. The storage of confidential client information on computer networks exposes those files to theft or destruction by cyber thieves and hackers. Arizona Bar Opinion 05–04 requires that lawyers take "competent and reasonable steps" to secure the client information from theft or destruction. Such steps may include the use of firewall, password, and encryption technology to prevent unauthorized access to the network. The constantly changing threats from cyber criminals require constant attention from lawyers to protect client information. See also, N.Y. State Bar Ass'n Comm. on Professional Ethics, Opinion 842 (2010) (lawyer may store information in an online "cloud" computer system that the lawyer has taken reasonable care to assure is secure).

D.   How legal protection against disclosure can be lost

1.   Should disclosure of privileged information outside the confidential relationship forfeit the attorney-client privilege?

a.   If the client, by mistake or otherwise, tells an outsider—even a trusted friend—the content of your confidential conversations with him, the attorney-client privilege as to those conversations will be lost for all time. Restatement Third, The Law Governing Lawyers § 79. And if some privileged information is revealed, the privilege often will be lost at least for all information needed to put the privileged material into context. Indeed, the waiver may be construed even more broadly. See Restatement Third, The Law Governing Lawyers § 79, Comment *f* (subject matter waiver).

b.   Suppose your revelation of privileged information is made in settlement negotiations, i.e., you say "I have told my client to be willing to accept $50,000." Typically, such a revelation—whether by lawyer or client—will result in waiver of the privilege. See, e.g., United States v. Martin, 773 F.2d 579 (4th Cir.1985) (attempt to settle tax case).

c.   Would revelation in a settlement discussion ordinarily violate your professional obligation of confidentiality? Look at Model Rule 1.6(a). A lawyer may make disclosures that are "impliedly authorized to carry out the representation." The point is that the fact that disclosure does not violate the obligation of confidentiality has no effect on whether it forfeits the attorney-client privilege.

d.   If a lawyer is ordered to testify about confidential information that the lawyer believes is protected by the attorney-client privilege or work product immunity, does the lawyer have to resist the order to testify? Is a lawyer required to go to jail for contempt of court rather than provide the testimony? Take a look at Model Rule 1.6, Comment 13. Does the approach outlined there make sense to you?

e.   A criminal defense client's assertion that his lawyer provided constitutionally ineffective assistance of counsel ordinarily waives the attorney-client privilege with respect to communications relevant to that contention. Restatement Third, The Law Governing Lawyers § 80(1)(b), Comment c. But does that waiver extend to the lawyer's Rule 1.6 obligation not to disclose information relating to the representation? ABA Formal Opinion 10–456 (July 14, 2010) said no. If asked by the prosecutor for the defendant's file, defense counsel must raise all non-frivolous defenses to disclosure. The lawyer may be required by a court to testify in response to the defendant's charges, but until ordered to do so, the lawyer must remain silent. Some might believe that a claim of ineffective assistance falls within the "self-defense" exception of Rule 1.6(b)(5), the opinion said, but that exception only applies where a response from the lawyer is objectively *necessary*. "[I]t will be extremely difficult for defense counsel to conclude that there is a reasonable need in self-defense to disclose client confidences to the prosecutor outside any court-supervised setting."

f.   Mohawk Industries, Inc. v. Carpenter, 558 U.S. ___, 130 S.Ct. 599, 175 L.Ed.2d 458 (2009), decided the important practical question whether a party may take an interlocutory appeal of an order requiring disclosure of a communication arguably protected by the attorney-client privilege. A former company employee had sued a company claiming he was fired for reporting to the company that it was employing illegal immigrants. After his initial report to the company, the employee claimed to have met with company lawyers, who allegedly coerced him to recant his statements. When he refused, he claimed the company fired him. At the same time, in a class action filed against the company for allegedly driving down wages by hiring illegal immigrants, the plaintiffs moved for an evidentiary hearing regarding the employee's allegations. The company responded by claiming the employee had fabricated the allegations, and that in fact the employee was fired because he attempted to have the company hire an illegal immigrant in violation of federal law. The employee moved to compel the company to produce information about his meeting with the company's attorney and its decision to fire him. The district court held that information privileged, but also held the company had waived the privilege by its representations in the class action suit. It ordered the company to produce the requested information. The Eleventh Circuit dismissed an appeal from the order because it was not an immediately reviewable collateral order, and it refused to issue a writ of mandamus.

The Supreme Court held that an order is only immediately reviewable under the collateral order doctrine if it "(1) conclusively determines the disputed question; (2) resolves an important issue completely separate from the merits of the action; and (3) is effectively unreviewable on appeal from a final judgment," citing Cohen v. Beneficial Industrial Loan Corp., 337 U.S. 541 (1949). This test focuses on the entire class of claims, and not the individualized order in a particular case. Under the test, the third prong was not met because orders that are adverse to the attorney-client privilege can be reviewed following a final judgment. On appeal, a court could find an order regarding the privilege erroneous, vacate the judgment, and remand for a new trial where the "privileged material and its fruits" are excluded.

The Court asserted that the risk that a trial court may order disclosure probably will not reduce the incentives for lawyers and clients to communicate fully under the anticipated benefit of a broad attorney-client privilege. A litigant facing an injurious or novel privilege ruling may seek certification of the order for interlocutory appeal, seek a writ of mandamus, or refuse to comply, thereby having the trial court impose sanctions or hold the party in contempt so as to seek post-judgment review of the order. Even if the damage done to some litigants was "only imperfectly reparable" upon review of a final judgment, the Court said, it is inappropriate to make disclosure orders immediately appealable as of right. Do you agree?

2. What should happen if a lawyer or client inadvertently reveals confidential client information? Suppose, for example, the lawyer's secretary mistakenly faxes a highly confidential memo to opposing counsel instead of to the client?

a. Restatement Third, The Law Governing Lawyers § 79, Comment *h*, says that a privilege "waiver does not result if the client or other disclosing person took precautions reasonable in the circumstances to guard against such disclosure." See, e.g., In re Reorganization of Electric Mutual Liability Ins. Co. (Bermuda), 681 N.E.2d 838 (Mass.1997) (if the client could show that adequate protective steps were taken to preserve the confidentiality of the information, the disclosure would be presumed not to have been voluntary).

b. However, the courts have often found waiver of the privilege or work product where a lawyer was insufficiently attentive to guarding information against disclosure. United States v. Gangi, 1 F.Supp.2d 256 (S.D.N.Y.1998), involved a government strategy memorandum in a securities and bank fraud case that was mistakenly handed to a magistrate judge in open court in Arizona in the belief it was a copy of the indictment. In fact, however, it contained highly confidential wiretap material and information about witnesses. It bore the legend "This Document Contains Grand Jury Material" but it was not otherwise marked confidential or privileged. The judge turned the document over to defense counsel, it got into the hands of other corporate officers, and for three weeks it was in the public court file. Only when the case was moved to New York did the government realize the mistake and ask that all copies of the document be returned. Under these circumstances, Judge Chin held the privilege was waived, although he did permit redacting a limited amount of sensitive information. See also, S.E.C. v. Cassano, 189 F.R.D. 83 (S.D.N.Y.1999) (erroneously disclosed 100–page trial memo cannot regain its character as attorney-client privileged and protected as work product).

c.   In Amgen v. Hoechst Marion Roussel, Inc., 190 F.R.D. 287 (D.Mass. 2000), the defense counsel inadvertently produced a box of over 3200 pages of privileged material among boxes with 70,000 pages of unprivileged material. The opinion distinguishes three ways courts have approached such situations—the "never waived" rule that requires giving the documents back, the "strict accountability" rule that treats all such situations as waivers, and a third or middle ground that looks at (1) reasonableness of precautions taken, (2) time taken to discover the error, (3) scope of the production, (4) extent of the disclosure, and (5) the interests of fairness in the situation. In this case, the defendant didn't realize what had happened until the plaintiff called the situation to its attention and little could be done to avoid damage. The court treated the privilege as waived, saying it would be unjust to reward counsel's "gross negligence."

d.   To try to minimize some of these consequences, especially in the context of high volume electronic discovery, Federal Rule of Civil Procedure 26(f) now provides for putting a "clawback" provision in a discovery plan pursuant to which the parties may assert privileges as to documents even after they have been initially turned over. The effect of such agreements on the documents' privileged character in later state cases, however, remains to be determined.[6]

3.   What if you, the lawyer, want ethics advice from a lawyer in another firm about your own obligations in a particular matter? May you discuss the issues in the matter with the other lawyer without violating your duty of confidentiality and forfeiting the privilege?

a.   ABA Formal Opinion 98–411 (Aug. 30, 1998) acknowledged that such consultations, made typically without fee and without intending to create an additional lawyer-client relationship, are often useful and in the interest of the client. However, the opinion tells the lawyer to: (1) do so in hypothetical terms, (2) get permission from the client if the consultation might put the client at risk, (3) not consult a lawyer who might represent the adverse party, and (4) obtain assurances of confidentiality for the information.

b.   The ethics opinion does not resolve the issue of waiver of the attorney-client privilege, of course, although the exclusive use of hypothetical facts in the consultation should be helpful. Cf. Model Rule 1.6, Comment 4.

c.   Notice that the Model Rules now specifically allow a lawyer to use confidential information as reasonably necessary to seek legal advice about

---

6. Further, the question for the *recipient* of the information is how to know whether the privilege has been lost. Look at Model Rule 4.4(b) and Comment 2: "Whether the lawyer is required to * * * [return a] document is a matter of law beyond the scope of these Rules, as is the question of whether the privileged status of a document has been waived." We return to the recipient's duties in Problem 24, *infra*.

the lawyer's compliance with ethics requirements. See Model Rule 1.6(b)(4) & Comment 9.

4.   Should the attorney-client privilege, work product immunity, or the lawyer's duty of confidentiality be lost by the passage of time or by the client's death?

a.   Restatement Third, The Law Governing Lawyers § 77, after noting that lawyers may sometimes testify to privileged conversations in order to explain the terms of a will or otherwise carry out the wishes of the deceased client, says in Comment *d*:

> "It would be desirable that a tribunal be empowered to withhold the privilege of a person then deceased as to a communication that bears on a litigated issue of pivotal significance. The tribunal could balance the interest in confidentiality against any exceptional need for the communication. The tribunal also could consider limiting the proof or sealing the record to limit disclosure. Permitting such disclosure would do little to inhibit clients from confiding in their lawyers."

Do you agree with this attempt to balance the competing interests in cases where the confidential communications could help do justice in a pending matter? Do you agree that such a rule would have little effect on the willingness of clients to entrust information to their lawyers?

b.   Matter of John Doe Grand Jury Investigation, 562 N.E.2d 69 (Mass.1990), gave the usual answer on some tough facts. The case involved whether the late Charles Stuart had been responsible for the deaths of Carol and Christopher Stuart. Charles Stuart had talked with his lawyer for two hours on the day before his suicide, and the prosecutor guessed that he had admitted the crime to the lawyer. If so, the state could both stop looking for a suspect for the murders and be sure not to charge someone else for them. The court held, however, that the privilege did not end with Charles' death and no amount of interest in knowing the truth could justify making the lawyer testify. Do you agree? If the prosecutor gave Stuart criminal immunity, he could have been forced to testify. Now, Stuart was dead. Should the court treat that as the functional equivalent of immunity in order to find the truth?

c.   What rule would you apply in a case like State v. Macumber, 544 P.2d 1084 (Ariz.1976)? The defendant had been convicted of two murders and was serving a life term. At trial, his lawyer tried to call two other lawyers who were prepared to testify that their now-deceased client had confessed to them that he, not Macumber, had committed the murders. The court excluded the testimony. Communications with a lawyer are privileged, the court said, and that privilege does not end with death. Is the Restatement wrong to suggest that sometimes the need to do justice to the living should prevail over the interests of the dead?[7]

---

7. We will see this issue later when we get to Problem 30, *infra*. At least part of the   problem in *Macumber* may have been doubts about the truth of such confessions. One can

d. Swidler & Berlin v. United States, 524 U.S. 399 (1998), was the celebrated case testing whether the Office of Independent Counsel could obtain notes of conversations between Vincent Foster (a White House lawyer) and his lawyer shortly before Mr. Foster's suicide. The D.C. Circuit had found that, while cases often say the attorney-client privilege survives death, it is usually said in the context of finding an exception to the rule to assist in construction of a will, the so-called testamentary exception. Thus, the court said, it is reasonable to make another exception for communications significant to a criminal prosecution since the client's own criminal liability obviously expires when he does. Further, the court held, post-death reputation is not sufficiently important to most people to make them not be candid with their lawyer even if the privilege would not survive them. See In re Sealed Case, 124 F.3d 230 (D.C.Cir.1997).

The U.S. Supreme Court reversed by a vote of 6 to 3. Writing for the Court and upholding survival of the privilege, Chief Justice Rehnquist said:

> "While the arguments against the survival of the privilege are by no means frivolous, they are based in large part on speculation—thoughtful speculation, but speculation nonetheless—as to whether posthumous termination of the privilege would diminish a client's willingness to confide in an attorney. In an area where empirical information would be useful, it is scant and inconclusive." 524 U.S. at 410.

Do you agree that the problem is a lack of empirical evidence? Commentators dispute whether there is solid evidence demonstrating the value of the attorney-client privilege in the first place. Do you base your views about the privilege on empirical studies, or on instinctive ideas of what justice requires?

e. In Wesp v. Everson, 33 P.3d 191 (Colo.2001), Wesp sought tort damages against her mother and stepfather, Cheryl and Frank Brewer, based on charges that Frank had sexually abused her. After criminal charges were filed against Frank, both Brewers wrote letters to family and friends and committed suicide. Wesp sought to depose Brewer's defense attorney in the criminal action to find out what Brewer had told him. She argued that the suicide letters mentioned a joint meeting between Cheryl and Frank Brewer and Frank's defense attorney and constituted a waiver of the privilege with respect to the subject matter of all meetings with the lawyer. The court agreed that the meeting with both Brewers was not privileged because Cheryl, who was not represented by that lawyer, was present. However, the fact of that meeting could not operate as a waiver of the privilege as to private meetings that Frank had with his lawyer. The court relied on *Swidler* to hold that the privilege survives the death of the client and declined either to create a "manifest injustice" basis to invade

give a relatively costless gift to a friend by making a deathbed confession to a crime the friend committed.

the privilege or to expand the "testamentary exception" to tort cases such as this one. Do you agree with this result?

PROBLEM 8

CONFIDENTIALITY AND THE ORGANIZATION AS A CLIENT

A corporation is not a "person" that has a privilege against self-incrimination.[1] One can therefore argue that a corporation should also not have an attorney-client privilege. However, the law has not developed that way. Business corporations and other organization clients have the protection of the attorney-client privilege, work product immunity, and the lawyer's professional duty of confidentiality. Yet the fact that a client is an organization rather than an individual raises some additional important issues that are considered in this problem. The problem closes with some critically important issues of limits on the duty of confidentiality when it collides with important interests of third parties.

FACTS

Your client, the Western Chemical Company, produces some of the country's best known chemical fertilizers. The availability of those fertilizers is among the reasons American agriculture is the world's most productive. But fertilizers are composed of materials that are highly toxic. If even small quantities of those materials seep into a region's drinking water, for example, deaths from cancer over a ten-year period can be expected to rise by at least 5%. Thus, companies like Western Chemical are required to file detailed reports to the EPA about the quantities of such materials they have on hand, when and how they are converted into fertilizer, and the disposition of any unused materials. Filing an intentionally inaccurate report is a federal crime.

An employee in one of Western Chemical Company's regional offices sent a letter to company management claiming that, when a plant manager recently found he could not account for 10,000 pounds of a phosphate compound, the manager falsely reported the material had been sold to another company at a large profit. Western Chemical asked your firm to interview employees of its regional offices to determine whether the incident occurred and whether it was part of a larger pattern of deception.

As a result of your investigation, you concluded that the incident reported to the company probably happened. Indeed, you learned that a former assistant general counsel of Western Chemical had written a confidential memorandum authorizing the plant

---

1. McPhaul v. United States, 364 U.S. 372 (1960).

manager to file inaccurate reports "if you think you won't get caught." You also learned that the company's auditors did not discover that the purported sale of the compound was erroneous. Thus, they certified a report of company earnings that exceeded analysts' estimates and earned large bonuses for company managers.

Recently, International Chemicals offered to purchase Western Chemical. International's own general counsel has asked you for a copy of the report of your investigation, but the former officers of Western Chemical have refused to permit you to turn it over. Of course, the EPA would also like to see—but has not subpoenaed—a copy of your report and any supporting documentation, which would include the memorandum that purported to authorize deceptive reporting.

QUESTIONS

A. **PRIVILEGE AND CONFIDENTIALITY RULES WHEN THE CLIENT IS AN ORGANIZA-TION**

1. Will the results of your internal investigation be protected by the attorney-client privilege, the work product immunity, or both?

a. By far the leading case on the corporate attorney-client privilege is still Upjohn Co. v. United States, 449 U.S. 383 (1981).

Upjohn makes and sells pharmaceuticals all over the world. In January 1976, accountants doing an audit of one of Upjohn's foreign subsidiaries found that the subsidiary made payments to or for the benefit of foreign government officials in order to secure government business. Such payments were very likely a violation of U.S. law, and Upjohn's general counsel launched an investigation. Upjohn managers were directed to treat the situation as highly confidential and to cooperate fully in the investigation. Some received questionnaires that they returned to the general counsel; others were interviewed in person by inside or outside counsel.

In March 1976, the company voluntarily submitted a preliminary report to the Securities and Exchange Commission on Form 8–K disclosing certain questionable payments. A copy of the report was simultaneously submitted to the Internal Revenue Service, which immediately began an investigation to determine the tax consequences of the payments. Agents conducting the investigation were given lists by Upjohn of all those interviewed and all who had responded to the questionnaire, but in November 1976, the Service issued a summons to Upjohn demanding all of its internal files relating to the general counsel's investigation. Upjohn said those files and reports were protected both by the attorney-client privilege and as work product.

The Court of Appeals ordered disclosure, finding that the investigation ranged far beyond senior management officials, that only interviews with the corporate "control group" could be protected by the attorney-client privilege, and that work product immunity did not protect corporations at all. The Supreme Court reversed, saying:

"The attorney-client privilege is the oldest of the privileges for confidential communications known to the common law. Its purpose is to encourage full and frank communication between attorneys and their clients and thereby promote broader public interests in the observance of law and administration of justice. The privilege recognizes that sound legal advice or advocacy serves public ends and that such advice or advocacy depends upon the lawyer's being fully informed by the client. * * *

" * * * [Limiting protection to communications from a control group] overlooks the fact that the privilege exists to protect not only the giving of professional advice to those who can act on it but also the giving of information to the lawyer to enable him to give sound and informed advice. The first step in the resolution of any legal problem is ascertaining the factual background and sifting through the facts with an eye to the legally relevant. * * *

" * * * Middle-level—and indeed lower-level—employees can, by actions within the scope of their employment, embroil the corporation in serious legal difficulties, and it is only natural that these employees would have the relevant information needed by corporate counsel if he is adequately to advise the client with respect to such actual or potential difficulties. * * *

"The narrow scope given the attorney-client privilege by the court below not only makes it difficult for corporate attorneys to formulate sound advice when their client is faced with a specific legal problem but also threatens to limit the valuable efforts of corporate counsel to ensure their client's compliance with the law. * * *

"The communications at issue were made by Upjohn employees to counsel for Upjohn acting as such, at the direction of corporate superiors in order to secure legal advice from counsel. * * * Information, not available from upper-echelon management, was needed to supply a basis for legal advice concerning compliance with securities and tax laws, foreign laws, currency regulations, duties to shareholders, and potential litigation in each of these areas. The communications concerned matters within the scope of the employees' corporate duties, and the employees themselves were sufficiently aware that they were being questioned in order that the corporation could obtain legal advice. * * * Consistent with the underlying purposes of the attorney-client privilege, these communications must be protected against compelled disclosure.

" * * * Here the Government was free to question the employees who communicated with Thomas and outside counsel. * * * While it would probably be more convenient for the Government to secure the results of petitioner's internal investigation by simply subpoenaing the questionnaires and notes taken by petitioner's attorneys, such considerations of convenience do not overcome the policies served by the attorney-client privilege. * * * "[2]

b. *Upjohn* is also still the leading case on lawyer work product in the corporate setting.

"The Government concedes, wisely, that the Court of Appeals erred and that the work-product doctrine does apply to IRS summonses. This doctrine was announced by the Court over 30 years ago in Hickman v. Taylor, 329 U.S. 495 (1947). * * * The 'strong public policy' underlying the work-product doctrine * * * has been substantially incorporated in Federal Rule of Civil Procedure 26(b)(3).

" * * * While conceding the applicability of the work-product doctrine, the Government asserts that it has made a sufficient showing of necessity to overcome its protections. * * *

"The Government stresses that interviewees are scattered across the globe and that Upjohn has forbidden its employees to answer questions it considers irrelevant. * * * [However,] forcing an attorney to disclose notes and memoranda of witnesses' oral statements is particularly disfavored because it tends to reveal the attorney's mental processes.

"Rule 26 * * * permits disclosure of documents and tangible things constituting attorney work product upon a showing of substantial need and inability to obtain the equivalent without undue hardship. * * * Rule 26 goes on, however, to state that '[i]n ordering discovery of such materials when the required showing has been made, the court shall protect against disclosure of mental impressions, conclusions, opinions or legal theories of an attorney or other representative of a party concerning the litigation.' Although this language does not specifically refer to memoranda based on oral statements of witnesses, the *Hickman* court stressed the danger that compelled disclosure of such memoranda would reveal the attorney's mental processes. It is clear that this is the sort of material the draftsmen of the Rule had in mind as deserving special protection.

"While we are not prepared at this juncture to say that such material is always protected by the work-product rule, we think a far stronger showing of necessity and unavailability by other means than was made by the Government or applied by the Magistrate in this case would be necessary to compel disclosure. * * * "

c. However, the Supreme Court's embrace of the corporate privilege has been significantly qualified by the highest court in Europe. In Australian Mining & Smelting Europe, Ltd. v. European Commission, [1982] 2 C.M.L.R. 264, 1982 WL 221208, the European Court of Justice held that in-house counsel are not sufficiently "independent" of their corporate col-

---

2. Chief Justice Burger filed an opinion concurring in part and concurring in the judgment.

leagues to make communications with them legally privileged. The opinion was reaffirmed in Akzo Nobel Chemicals Ltd. v. European Commission, Case C–550/07 P, Celex No. 607J0550, 2010 ECJ EUR–Lex Lexis 807, 23–24 (ECJ EUR–Lex 2010). The European Court of Justice reasoned:

"45.   * * * An in-house lawyer, despite his enrolment[sic] with a Bar or Law Society and the professional ethical obligations to which he is, as a result, subject, does not enjoy the same degree of independence from his employer as a lawyer working in an external law firm does in relation to his client. Consequently, an in-house lawyer is less able to deal effectively with any conflicts between his professional obligations and the aims of his client.

"48.   * * * [U]nder the terms of his contract of employment, an in-house lawyer may be required to carry out other tasks, namely, as in the present case, the task of competition law coordinator, which may have an effect on the commercial policy of the undertaking. Such functions cannot but reinforce the close ties between the lawyer and his employer."

Do you agree that the corporate privilege should only apply to communications with outside counsel who are licensed in Europe? Lest you think such European decisions will have no effect on your practice, think about how conflicting approaches to privilege questions will affect internal investigations at multinational companies, for example, or how you as a U.S. lawyer give advice to a U.S. company's European subsidiary.

2. We know that *Upjohn* rejected the "control group" test. Does that mean there are no limits on which individuals' communications within a corporation should be protected?

a. In Samaritan Foundation v. Goodfarb, 862 P.2d 870 (Ariz.1993), a paralegal had interviewed operating room personnel in preparation for defense of a medical malpractice case, and the plaintiff wanted summaries of the interviews. The court asked whether the interviews were conducted "to assist the lawyer in assessing or responding to the legal consequences of [the employee's own] conduct for the corporate client." The court ordered the notes disclosed because, although the personnel were witnesses to acts alleged to be negligent, their own acts were not alleged to be negligent.

b. Payton v. New Jersey Turnpike Authority, 691 A.2d 321 (N.J. 1997), examined application of the privilege to an investigation of alleged sexual harassment. Federal law requires an employer to conduct a prompt, thorough investigation of such charges, and the plaintiff wanted to see what the investigation turned up. Both lawyers and non-lawyers had participated in the investigation, and the court acknowledged that assuring confidentiality is an important way to encourage complete and accurate reporting. But it allowed the plaintiff access to some of what the defendant had discovered. The presence of lawyers among the investigators did not privilege all documents, the court said. Indeed, the defendant, by asserting the investigation as a defense to the plaintiff's claim, waived its privilege except as to documents giving what could fairly be called legal advice or conclusions. The court thus ordered the trial judge to conduct a document-by-document review of the materials and to redact privileged material if possible, rather than denying access to a document altogether.

c.   Pritchard v. County of Erie, 473 F.3d 413 (2d Cir.2007), involved an attempt to discover emails and other documents sent between an assistant county attorney and county officials who were accused of having subjected a class of plaintiffs to unconstitutional strip searches. The court reaffirmed that government entities such as this county have attorney-client privilege protection. Further, the privilege extends to issues of county policy as long as the primary purpose of the communication is seeking or giving legal advice. Lawyers often do and should go beyond narrow legal questions, the court said, and communication about those issues are also privileged. The court held that mandamus was appropriate to review the trial court, and then reversed the trial court and held that the attorney-client privilege protects the emails.

d.   Satcom Int'l Group, PLC v. Orbcomm Int'l Partners, L.P., 1999 WL 76847 (S.D.N.Y.1999), however, held that the entire meeting of a corporation's executive committee was privileged because its general counsel was present. The meeting had been called solely to discuss termination of a contract with the plaintiff, so legal issues were central to the discussions. The fact that the participants also discussed possible business consequences of the action did not render the meeting unprivileged.

e.   Does the complexity of many modern corporate organizations mean that, without protection of the privilege, it would be impossible for management to identify instances of non-compliance with the law as *Upjohn* tried to do? Or, it is more likely that corporations would conduct compliance audits whether or not they were privileged simply because failing to comply with the law would potentially subject them to massive liability?[3]

3.   Suppose that another, or even the principal, target of the investigation is a leading figure in the organization. How should these rules apply when the organizational setting is the government, for example, and one possible client is a prominent government official?

a.   In re Grand Jury Subpoena Duces Tecum, 112 F.3d 910 (8th Cir.1997), cert. denied sub nom. Office of the President v. Office of Independent Counsel, 521 U.S. 1105 (1997), involved the grand jury assisting Independent Counsel Kenneth Starr. It had subpoenaed "all documents created during meetings attended by any attorney from the Office of Counsel to the President and Hillary Rodham Clinton (regardless whether any other person was present)." The White House said nine sets of notes met that description but refused to produce them, citing the attorney-client

---

3.   Some courts have recognized a related "self-evaluative" privilege protecting internal reports done by non-lawyers. See, e.g., Bredice v. Doctors Hospital, Inc., 50 F.R.D. 249 (D.D.C.1970), aff'd, 479 F.2d 920 (D.C.Cir.1973). But as suggested in Federal Trade Commission v. TRW, Inc., 628 F.2d 207 (D.C.Cir.1980), the concept has met with limited success in the courts.

privilege and work product immunity. The court permitted Ms. Clinton to intervene.

Citing Restatement Third, The Law Governing Lawyers, § 74, the court held that the government but not Ms. Clinton could assert an attorney-client privilege. It said United States v. Nixon, 418 U.S. 683 (1974), makes clear that the White House cannot easily resist a subpoena, particularly one from a federal grand jury. If a government official wants advice about possible criminal liability for past acts, the court said, he or she should get it from a private lawyer, not a government employee. Further, although White House lawyers attended meetings that Ms. Clinton had with her personal lawyer, the court found no common interest that would extend the privilege to notes that the government attorneys took. The fact that Ms. Clinton's problems had political ramifications did not create a cognizable governmental interest in having White House lawyers there, because their duties were to the government. While Ms. Clinton might herself face litigation in Whitewater-related matters, there was no reason to believe the White House had the same problem because the Office of the White House cannot be indicted. Thus, the government lawyers' notes did not have work product immunity either.[4]

b.   In re Lindsey, 158 F.3d 1263 (D.C.Cir.1998), involved a deputy White House counsel talking to President Clinton and outside counsel for the president in connection with a grand jury investigation of the president's alleged criminal conduct. The attorney-client privilege for White House counsel communications, the court said, ran only to the government. The government had no legitimate interest in covering up criminal conduct, and government lawyers are not hired "to protect wrongdoers from public exposure." Even the possibility Congress might use the lawyer's testimony against the president in an impeachment was not enough to make it privileged, the court said. The president can retain a personal lawyer. He did, and to the extent the White House lawyer was used as an "intermediary" between the president and his private counsel, the privilege did apply. Judge Tatel, dissenting in part, agreed that personal legal advice that Mr. Lindsey gave to President Clinton was not privileged, but he argued that official legal advice that any White House counsel gave a sitting president should be privileged, lest no president know what would later be considered confidential.

c.   In re Witness Before Special Grand Jury 2000–2, 288 F.3d 289 (7th Cir.2002), involved conversations between Roger Bickel, then chief legal

4.   While part of the White House resistance was based on Ms. Clinton's alleged status as a White House official, albeit an unpaid one, that argument cut both ways. The Eighth Circuit held that lawyers in the White House do not have a governmental attorney-client privilege to withhold relevant information from the independent counsel (who stands in the shoes of the attorney general), in light of 28 U.S.C.A. § 535(b), which provides:

"Any information, allegation, or complaint received in a department or agency of the executive branch of the Government relating to violations of Title 18 involving Government officers and employees shall be expeditiously reported to the Attorney General by the head of the department or agency."

counsel to Illinois Secretary of State George Ryan, and Mr. Ryan. Secretary Ryan consulted with Bickel on both official and non-official matters, then and later when Ryan was governor of Illinois. Meanwhile, federal prosecutors had begun investigating the secretary of state's office for evidence of an alleged bribery scheme, and the grand jury hearing the bribery case subpoenaed Bickel. Bickel and Governor Ryan resisted the subpoena, arguing that Bickel's conversations in the secretary of state's office were privileged, but the Seventh Circuit ordered Bickel to testify. The court did more than say that a state official does not enjoy a personal attorney-client privilege with a state-employed attorney. It said that federal courts recognize no attorney-client privilege at all for government officials in a criminal case, even if the officials and the lawyers had been discussing official state business. A government lawyer has an overarching duty to act in the public interest, the court said, and thus is unlike a lawyer for an individual or corporation. In addition, the government lawyer's client, the state, may not be held criminally liable for its actions. Thus, the law recognizes that the attorney-client privilege in this context is not necessary to foster open communications. No attorney-client privilege exists for federal government officials in such cases (citing cases like *Lindsey*), and the court declined to create such a privilege for state officials.

d.   In re Grand Jury Investigation, 399 F.3d 527 (2d Cir.2005), however, seemed to reject holdings that government officials may not rely on the attorney-client privilege to protect discussions of personal legal problems with government lawyers. The case involved former Connecticut Governor John Rowland who became the target of a federal investigation into bribery charges. When a grand jury subpoenaed Rowland's former chief legal counsel, Anne George, to compel her testimony, she admitted to having numerous conversations with Rowland on the topic of bribery, but invoked the attorney-client privilege as to the content of the discussions. The district court entered an order compelling George's testimony. In doing so, it distinguished the government attorney-client privilege in the grand jury context, stating that "unlike a private lawyer's duty of loyalty to an individual client, a government lawyer's duty" lies with both the client and the public. The Office of the Governor and Rowland appealed. A unanimous panel of the Second Circuit rejected the Seventh, Eighth, and D.C. Circuit's position in such cases. It rejected the government's assertion that George's loyalty to the governor "must yield to her loyalty to the public, to whom she owes ultimate allegiance." Citing a Connecticut statute which specifically recognizes the government attorney-client privilege in any legal proceeding, the court said that the statute highlights the fact that "the public interest is not nearly as obvious as the government suggests." In upholding George's privilege claim, the court reasoned that "the traditional rationale for the privilege applies with special force in the government context," where there is a vital public interest for high state officials "to receive and act upon the best possible legal advice."

4.   Is a law firm an organization that may assert an attorney-client privilege of its own?

a. United States v. Rowe, 96 F.3d 1294 (9th Cir.1996) involved a law firm that assigned associates to investigate how one of the law firm's lawyers handled client funds. A grand jury investigating that lawyer issued a subpoena to require the associates to testify about their report to the firm's senior partner. The district court held that the associates were not in a lawyer-client relationship with the senior partner and that the fact finding did not qualify as "professional legal services." The Ninth Circuit disagreed on both counts. The associates were effectively in-house counsel and fact finding is an important part of lawyering, the court said. Hence, the district court could not force the associates to testify.

b. Nesse v. Shaw Pittman, 206 F.R.D. 325 (D.D.C.2002), involved a malpractice case against a firm from which the plaintiff sought notes made by the firm's general counsel in his internal investigation of the conduct of firm members. Citing *Upjohn*, the court held such notes privileged and said they do not lose their protection when the general counsel discusses the findings with firm management. Notes taken by another member of the management committee in separate discussions with some of the same people, however, were held not privileged. The firm management committee is composed of lawyers, of course, but the court says that when they act as managers of the firm, the primary purpose of their activity is not legal representation. Thus, neither privilege nor work product protects the documents from discovery. Clearly, the case is likely to cause well-advised firms to have internal investigations conducted only by duly-appointed "counsel" to the firm.[5]

c. But Thelen Reid & Priest LLP v. Marland, 2007 WL 578989 (N.D.Cal.2007), shows that having a law firm general counsel does not guarantee privilege protection when firm lawyers discuss possible claims against the firm by a current client. Basically, the Thelen firm had represented Marland, who was trying to get paid by the California Department of Insurance (CDOI) for telling the CDOI of fraud in an auction CDOI had conducted. When CDOI failed to offer acceptable compensation, Thelen, on behalf of Marland, filed his own *qui tam* lawsuit on behalf of the state of California and CDOI. Then, CDOI asked Thelen to also represent it in a similar lawsuit, with Marland and his European counsel sharing a portion of Thelen's legal fees if it succeeded in the litigation. Thelen claimed that it had informed Marland of CDOI's proposal and potential conflicts between CDOI's lawsuit and Marland's own *qui tam* lawsuit. Marland disputed that. In this discovery dispute, Marland wanted to see all records of Thelen's discussion of its ethical duties. The court held law firms should be able to get privileged advice about their ethical duties, but once the Thelen firm knew there was a likely basis for a claim against it, it had a duty to notify Marland. "While consultation with an in-house ethics adviser is confidential, once the law firm learns that a client may have a claim against the firm or that the firm needs client consent in order to commence

---

5. The development is discussed in Symposium, Why Do Lawyers Need a General Counsel? The Changing Structure of American Law Firms, 53 Kansas L. Rev. 795 (2005).

or continue another client representation, then the firm should disclose to the client the firm's conclusions with respect to those ethical issues." In these circumstances, internal firm discussions about the nature and extent of the possible violation, potential liability, and the like, were not privileged.[6]

e. ABA Formal Opinion 08–453 (Oct. 17, 2008) focused on law firm members' right to turn to a law firm's "ethics counsel" for advice on how to proceed in a matter. The opinion says that such consultations clearly do not violate a client's rights under Rule 1.6 because disclosure is entirely within the firm. Nor is consultation a per se conflict of interest with the client under Rule 1.7. Rule 1.4 does not require the lawyer to tell the client about the consultation unless the answer is that the lawyer may not proceed in the way the client expects. Rule 1.13 may require the ethics counsel or the firm itself to report misconduct to a corporation if the lawyer does not, but ordinarily, Rule 8.3 makes the duty of such ethics counsel to turn in firm member for misconduct no greater than that an outside lawyer for the law firm member would have.

B. CONTROL OF WAIVER OF PRIVILEGE AND CONFIDENTIALITY PROTECTION

1. In this problem, the former managers of Western Chemical—the ones who hired you to conduct the internal investigation—do not want you to turn your report over to new management. Who should control the privilege in a case like this one?

a. An individual client to whom you owe a duty of confidentiality is typically the only one who can tell you when the protection should be waived. When the client is an organization, ordinarily whomever is in charge of the organization at the moment controls the waiver. Thus, the basic rule is that neither the privilege nor the duty of confidentiality prevents successor corporate management from learning the content of discussions of former management with corporate counsel.

b. A trustee in bankruptcy may waive the privilege in the face of former management's opposition to revelation of their discussions with counsel. Commodity Futures Trading Commission v. Weintraub, 471 U.S. 343 (1985).

2. Suppose the client is a trustee, a person with fiduciary obligations to others? Is the trust an "organization" like those we have been considering in this problem? Even if it is for some purposes, who controls waiver of the privilege? For example, should a beneficiary of the trust be entitled to know what transpired in the discussion between lawyer and trustee?

a. ABA Formal Opinion 94–380 (May 9, 1994) says that ordinarily the answer is no; a trustee or other fiduciary is entitled to consult a lawyer,

---

6. See also, In re Sunrise Securities Litigation, 130 F.R.D. 560 (E.D.Pa.1989); Bank Brussels Lambert v. Credit Lyonnaise (Suisse), S.A., 220 F.Supp.2d 283 (S.D.N.Y. 2002); Koen Book Distributors v. Powell, Trachtman, Logan, Carrle, Bowman & Lombardo, P.C., 212 F.R.D. 283 (E.D.Pa.2002); Elizabeth Chambliss, The Scope of In–Firm Privilege, 80 Notre Dame L. Rev. 1721 (2005).

and Rule 1.6 has no exception where persons with fiduciary duties are involved. See, e.g., Wells Fargo Bank v. Superior Court (Boltwood), 990 P.2d 591 (Cal.2000) (trust beneficiaries have no right to see trustee-attorney communications about administration of the trust; trustee may have duties to the beneficiaries, but the lawyer does not).

b.   Restatement Third, The Law Governing Lawyers § 84, notes an important exception. The beneficiary can get access to communications between a trustee and a lawyer where (1) the trustee is charged with a breach of fiduciary duty, (2) the communication is relevant to the claimed breach, and (3) the lawyer was retained to advise the trustee concerning the administration of the trust (as opposed to being hired later to defend the trustee).[7]

c.   In Wachtel v. Health Net, Inc., 482 F.3d 225 (3d Cir.2007), Health Net provided health insurance programs and benefit plans for a number of employers. It was a fiduciary with respect to employer plans covered by the federal ERISA law. In a class action by beneficiaries, the plaintiffs asserted that a "fiduciary exception" to the attorney-client privilege discussed in Restatement § 84 entitled them to see all communications with Health Net's lawyers. Wrong, the court said. The exception relates to fiduciaries taking advantage of identified beneficiaries. In the case of ERISA fiduciaries, we have corporate fiduciaries trying to live within a complex regulatory scheme. Companies such as Health Net need competent counsel and may have privileged communications with them.

3.   Should the attorney-client privilege and work product immunity be lost as to later private litigation if a company voluntarily turns documents over to a government agency in an effort to demonstrate there has been no violation of law?

a.   The leading case recognizing the doctrine known as limited or selective waiver was once Diversified Industries v. Meredith, 572 F.2d 596 (8th Cir.1977) (en banc). Pursuant to subpoena, the company had given the SEC documents underlying an independent investigation in a "non-public SEC investigation." The privilege was waived as to the SEC, of course, but the waiver was held to be "limited" and the documents remained privileged in later private litigation.

b.   In re Columbia/HCA Healthcare Corporation Billing Practices Litigation, 293 F.3d 289 (6th Cir.2002), is more representative of current law. The defendant had turned over privileged matter to the Justice Department and the Health Care Finance Administration pursuant to an agreement that the disclosure did not "constitute a waiver of any applicable privilege or claim under the work product doctrine." The court acknowledged that recognizing confidentiality even after such a turnover would

---

7. An analogous issue is presented when shareholders seek access to attorney-corporate communications in order to prosecute a derivative suit, i.e., a suit brought in the name of the corporation. The leading case authorizing their access is Garner v. Wolfin- barger, 430 F.2d 1093 (5th Cir.1970), cert. denied sub nom. Garner v. First American Life Ins. Co., 401 U.S. 974 (1971). See Restatement Third, The Law Governing Lawyers § 85.

tend to make it easier for the government to obtain needed information. It concluded, however, that the same principle of practicality would permit confidential turnover of information in a private case, and that is clearly not the law. Thus, the court affirmed a holding that disclosure to the government constituted a waiver of both the attorney-client privilege and work product protection in a later private action. See also, In re Qwest Communications International Inc., 450 F.3d 1179 (10th Cir.2006).

c. Limited waiver is of great current interest because of its relevance to the Department of Justice's "Filip Guidelines" as to when the DOJ will give "cooperation" credit to possible corporate criminal defendants. In earlier forms, variously called the Holder, Thompson and McNulty Memoranda, the DOJ promised to be more lenient with corporations that waived their attorney-client privilege as to important documents. The DOJ especially wanted to see the reports produced after internal investigations by outside counsel. The incentive to release the report was the promise that either the investigation would end or at least that the company would get credit for cooperation when it negotiates a sanction. Now, as a result of intense ABA lobbying and interest from Senators Leahy and Spector, the Filip Guidelines purport not to make privilege waiver a factor in negotiations about corporate criminal charges.[8]

d. One principal argument in favor of the ABA position was that, as a practical matter, turning over the report constituted an involuntary waiver of the attorney-client privilege of corporate employees interviewed for—and possibly implicated in the report of—the internal investigation. Cf. United States v. Stein, 435 F.Supp.2d 330 (S.D.N.Y.2006) (failure to advance employees' legal fees).

Did corporate release of internal investigation records violate employee privilege and confidentiality rights? Is an employee's interview with a company lawyer privileged as to the employee at all? To the extent the company disclosed the information to the government, was it waiving any rights but its own? Regardless of the law's answer to those questions, defending the alleged rights of the corporate employees seemed a substantially stronger rhetorical position for the ABA and its allies than defending the rights of the corporation might have been.

4. Should the attorney-client privilege and work product immunity be lost in later litigation as to documents a company turns over to its outside accounting firm as part of the company's annual audit?

---

8. At the same time as the discussions with the Department of Justice, a committee revising the Federal Rules of Evidence was considering putting a selective waiver provision into Rule 502. The ABA and its allies defeated such a provision, believing that it might undercut their political position that corporations should not have to share the results of an internal investigation with the government at all. Thus, new Federal Rule of Evidence 502 now says that intentional corporate disclosure of information to the government will be deemed to waive the attorney-client privilege and work product protection, thus also making the information available to private parties in possible future litigation.

Merrill Lynch & Co. v. Allegheny Energy, Inc., 229 F.R.D. 441 (S.D.N.Y.2004), drew a distinction between the attorney-client privilege and work product protection as they relate to such information. Allegheny Energy, Inc. (Allegheny) acquired Merrill Lynch's energy-commodities trading business, Global Energy Markets (GEM). After the purchase agreement was finalized, Allegheny learned that GEM had financial problems and had engaged in a number of "sham" energy trades with Enron. Allegheny refused to honor part of the purchase agreement, and Merrill Lynch sued to enforce it. During discovery, Allegheny sought documents Merrill Lynch's internal auditor had given the company's independent auditor "to iden-tif[y] any potential internal control, accounting or audit issues of which [the investigator] was not already aware based on [his] routine and regular prior discussions with Merrill Lynch during the course of the audit." Both the internal auditor and the independent auditor said they understood that the documents were meant to be kept confidential and were not to be further disclosed. Merrill Lynch conceded that the turnover waived the attorney-client privilege, but it claimed that the documents were still protected work product because they contained mental impressions and opinions of the lawyers for Merrill Lynch. The court held that turning the documents over to the auditors did not cause them to lose their work product status. The test is "whether [an independent auditor] should be conceived of as an adversary or a conduit to a potential adversary." Auditors are often "gatekeepers" and, in that sense, they work for the public, not the company. On the other hand, "[a] business and its auditor can and should be aligned insofar as they both seek to prevent, detect, and root out corporate fraud." In a case like this, disclosure to the auditors was part of the company's internal review, and the "obligations of [the independent auditor] under the applicable accounting standards simply do not make out a waiver."[9]

C.   The common interest privilege among multiple organizations

1. What effect is there on assertion of the attorney-client privilege when organizations or individuals take a "we're all in this together" approach to the use of counsel?

a. Remember from Problem 7 that, ordinarily, if your client talks with a lawyer in a setting where a third party is present, the discussion is not privileged at all.

b. Suppose the EPA has begun an investigation of several area fertilizer producers. You have been asked to represent Western Chemical in discussions with lawyers for Colorado Chemical, a nearby producer, about data each company has and possible positions to take during the investigation. Should the EPA be able to treat those discussions as unprivileged and question all participants in common-interest discussions about the content of their talks?

---

9. See also, United States v. Deloitte LLP, 610 F.3d 129 (D.C.Cir.2010) (work product protection not waived by disclosure to independent auditor).

c. Ordinarily, defendants with a common interest may hold joint discussions at which they and the various lawyers talk freely with each other about matters relevant to their common interest. Any client who is part of that discussion or similar information exchange may assert the privilege just as it could if the client had been talking to its lawyer alone. See Restatement Third, The Law Governing Lawyers § 76; Hanover Insurance Co. v. Rapo & Jepsen Insurance Services, Inc., 870 N.E.2d 1105 (Mass.2007) (adopting common interest doctrine and citing Restatement § 76).

2. What happens when the former friends have a falling out? If International Chemical wants to take confidential minutes of the talks with Western Chemical to the EPA, may it freely do so?

a. Ordinarily, the answer is no. International Chemical may waive the common interest privilege and disclose what it and its attorney discussed, but the privilege continues to apply to what you and your client, Western Chemical, said.

b. In Hunydee v. United States, 355 F.2d 183 (9th Cir.1965), for example, at a joint conference attended by two defendants (husband and wife) and their separate attorneys, the husband agreed to plead guilty of income tax evasion and "take the blame." But he went to trial, and the government, over objection, had the wife and her attorney testify to what was said at this joint conference. The court held that it was error to admit the testimony. The joint conference was privileged to the extent it concerned a common issue and was intended to facilitate representation in possible subsequent proceedings.

c. If International Chemical learns in the course of the discussions that Western Chemical has polluted International Chemical's land, it may file a suit for damages and use against Western whatever may have been disclosed. Unless the parties have agreed otherwise in advance, the common interest privilege does not protect information disclosed by the participants in "subsequent adverse proceedings" between them. See Restatement Third, The Law Governing Lawyers § 76, Comment f.

d. In re Regents of University of California, 101 F.3d 1386 (Fed.Cir. 1996), cert. denied, 520 U.S. 1193 (1997), involved patent litigation between Genetech, Eli Lilly and the University of California at Berkeley concerning recombinant DNA technology. Genetech and Lilly settled the claims between them, and Genetech then wanted to depose Lilly lawyers about discussions concerning prior art that the Lilly lawyers had with university officials earlier in the proceeding. The university had patented the process that the Lilly lawyers helped Lilly license. Both Lilly and the university had an interest in having the patent upheld, the Court reasoned, and the prior art discussions could affect the patent's validity. Because the university could assert a common interest privilege with respect to those discussions, Genetech could not discover them.

3. If a single lawyer represents more than one defendant, she is likely to get confidential information from each. Does informa-

tion from multiple defendants constitute "privileged" or "confidential" information of all of the client(s)?

a. Assume now that you represent *both* Western Chemical and International Chemical. Each has told you things they would not tell the EPA. Do you need permission before you use the information to try to get a better deal for both clients? Is a secret still a secret once it is told to others?[10]

b. McCormick on Evidence states the principle as:

"When two or more persons, each having an interest in some problem or situation, jointly consult an attorney, their confidential communications with the attorney, though known to each other, will of course be privileged in a controversy of either or both of the clients with the outside world, that is, with parties claiming adversely to both or either of those within the original charmed circle. But it will often happen that the two original clients will fall out among themselves and become engaged in a controversy in which the communications at their joint consultation with the lawyer may be vitally material. In such a controversy it is clear that the privilege is inapplicable."[11]

c. Furthermore, if one client tells the common lawyer something relevant to the other client[s] in the joint representation, under traditional doctrine, unless the clients have agreed otherwise, the lawyer must disclose that information to the other clients even if the disclosing client would prefer that it be kept confidential. See Restatement Third, The Law Governing Lawyers § 60, Comment *l*: "Sharing of information among the co-clients with respect to the matter involved in the representation is normal and typically expected."

d. ABA Formal Opinion 08–450 (Apr. 9, 2008) has now weighed in, saying that issues of dealing with co-clients' confidential information arise first at the outset of the representation "when both the scope of the representation and the clients' intentions concerning the lawyer's duty with respect to confidentiality can best be clarified for each client." The opinion advises that an "advance waiver from the carrier or employer, permitting the lawyer to continue representing the insured in the event conflicts arise, may well be appropriate." Absent such an express agreement, the opinion says, "whenever information related to the representation may be harmful to the client in the hands of another client or a third person, the lawyer is prohibited by Rule 1.6 from revealing that information to any person, including the other client and the third person, unless disclosure is permitted under an exception to Rule 1.6." The opinion argues that consent to disclosure cannot reasonably be implied in such a situation and "implied authority" to share information among co-clients also cannot

---

10. See Restatement Third, The Law Governing Lawyers § 75.

11. McCormick on Evidence § 91, at 219 (E. Cleary, 3d ed. 1984) (footnote omitted).

be inferred. "Each client is entitled to the benefit of Rule 1.6 with respect to information relating to that client's representation, and a lawyer * * * is bound to protect the information of each client from disclosure, [even] to other clients * * *." The opinion says that if the lawyer cannot share information relating to the representation with each co-client, then the lawyer must withdraw from one of more of the representations pursuant to Rule 1.7.

The opinion is not the ABA Committee's best work. Model Rule 1.4 requires a lawyer to share information relating to the representation with each co-client lest the client left in the dark be disadvantaged. Rule 1.7, Comment 18, "Informed Consent," warns the lawyer that when she represents "multiple clients in a single matter," she must inform the clients of the "implications of the common representation, including possible effects on loyalty, confidentiality and the attorney-client privilege and the advantages and risks involved." If the multiple clients do not consent to the necessary disclosures, the lawyer cannot undertake the representation. See Comment 19. One would think the ABA Formal Opinion would have addressed or distinguished these sections before reaching its conclusions.

e. The net effect of all this is to suggest that the decision of multiple defendants to adopt a common defense is not risk-free. The Commentary to Proposed Rule 503 of the Federal Rules of Evidence, discussed in Problem 7, was also cautious. It said that in the "joint defense" or "pooled information" situation, the "better view" is not that one of the various clients "could prevent another from disclosing what the other had himself said," but rather that "if all resist disclosure, none will occur."

D. LIMITS OF CONFIDENTIALITY IN CASES OF RISK TO THIRD PARTIES

1. Does either the attorney-client privilege or work product immunity protect the memorandum from the former assistant general counsel that purports to authorize false reporting?

a. You may remember from Problem 7 that the privilege does not extend to discussions in furtherance of an intended, unlawful end. The traditional common law view required that the communication be in furtherance of a crime or fraud before the privilege was lost. See Proposed Federal Rule of Evidence 503(d)(1).

b. Restatement Third, The Law Governing Lawyers § 82 states the rule this way:

"The attorney-client privilege does not apply to a communication occurring when a client:

"(a) consults a lawyer for the purpose, later accomplished, of obtaining assistance to engage in a crime or fraud or aiding a third person to do so, or

"(b) regardless of the client's purpose at the time of consultation, uses the lawyer's advice or other services to engage in or assist a crime or fraud."[12]

c.   In re BankAmerica Corp. Securities Litigation, 270 F.3d 639 (8th Cir.2001), cert. denied, 535 U.S. 970 (2002), summarizes what a party must show to rely on the crime-fraud exception. Under United States v. Zolin, 491 U.S. 554 (1989), the party must make a threshold showing that "the legal advice was obtained in furtherance of the fraudulent activity and was closely related to it." To do this, it must make a specific showing that a given communication was made in furtherance of the client's alleged crime or fraud. Indeed, the party seeking discovery must make this showing separately for each document or communication. If the threshold is met, the district court has discretion to conduct an *in camera* review of the allegedly privileged documents.

d.   In re Richard Roe, Inc., 68 F.3d 38 (2d Cir.1995), involved a subpoena for legal records that the government argued "collectively have the real potential of being relevant evidence of activity in furtherance of a crime." The court quashed the subpoena. The claim was much too general and a "relevant evidence" test would leave virtually nothing protected. The crime-fraud exception "applies only when the court determines that the client communication or attorney work product in question was *itself* in furtherance of the crime or fraud." Further, there must be "probable cause to believe that the particular communication with counsel * * * was intended in some way to facilitate or to conceal the criminal activity." 68 F.3d at 40.

e.   In re Sealed Case, 107 F.3d 46 (D.C.Cir.1997), involved a corporation that allegedly had made an illegal campaign contribution even after its lawyers had briefed its officers and given them a legal memorandum explaining what the election laws do not permit. The D.C. Circuit held that the fact a client violates the law after talking with a lawyer does not place the communication within the crime-fraud exception and thus subject to disclosure. The crime-fraud exception for work product immunity also did not apply to a memorandum that the general counsel wrote concerning a vice president's violation of campaign finance law. Otherwise, the court said, corporations could not freely consult "a lawyer for the purpose of achieving law compliance." While the memorandum might show client *scienter*, it did not show that the *lawyer* had assisted the client in committing the alleged crime.

2.   Putting aside attorney-client privilege and work product issues, would your duty of confidentiality under Model Rule 1.6 prevent you from voluntarily turning the memorandum over to the EPA?

a.   Remember that your report and the memorandum clearly show that the company does not account for its chemicals well, but they do not show what has happened to the chemicals. Yet, if the chemicals really have

---

12. The corresponding work product exception is § 93: "Work-product immunity does not apply to materials prepared when a client consults a lawyer for the purpose, later accomplished, of obtaining assistance to engage in a crime or fraud or to aid a third person to do so or uses the materials for such a purpose."

been illegally dumped and in fact get into the region's drinking water, the effects over the next decade could be catastrophic.

b. Before the 2002 amendments, Model Rule 1.6(b)(1) only permitted a lawyer to disclose "to prevent the client from committing a criminal act that the lawyer believes is likely to result in imminent death or substantial bodily harm." In this problem, even if you assume the worst, is your client *about to* commit a crime, or has it already done so? Are any deaths resulting from the client's acts "imminent," or simply made more likely to occur in the future?[13]

c. To what extent does Model Rule 1.6(b)(1), after 2002, increase your authority to disclose?[14] Does the new rule require that what you are disclosing must be an act of the client? Is your authority to disclose limited to criminal acts? Must the conduct occur in the future or only have future effects? Does the new rule require that the adverse effects occur within any particular time period? Model Rule 1.6, Comment 6, makes clear that the drafters clearly intended these changes.[15]

3. When International Chemicals proposed to buy Western Chemical and wanted to see the report of your investigation of the company, would any privilege or other obligation prevent your disclosing it to International if Western would prefer that you not do so?

a. As you remember, the crime-fraud exception to the attorney-client privilege and work product immunity applies to fraud as well as crime. Non-disclosure may not always be fraudulent, but when it is, neither the privilege nor work product immunity will bar disclosure. Indeed, take a look at Model Rule 4.1(b). Does that provision mandate disclosure in a case like the one in this problem? Would such disclosure be "prohibited by Rule 1.6"?

b. Do you find an exception permitting disclosure in Model Rule 1.6(b)? Until 2003, the ABA House of Delegates had consistently rejected any proposed authority of a lawyer to reveal information to prevent or rectify a fraudulent act of the client, even an act "that the lawyer reasonably believes is likely to result * * * in substantial injury to the financial interests or property of another." The ABA did not adopt Model Rules 1.6(b)(2) & (b)(3) until the controversy created by the Enron and WorldCom collapses made some action inevitable.

13. Model Rule 1.6(b)(1), prior to its 2002 amendments, did not really state the law applicable in most jurisdictions. Many states permitted—or even required—a lawyer to make disclosure in a situation like the one in this problem.

14. Current Model Rule 1.6(b)(1) is taken directly from Restatement Third, The Law Governing Lawyers § 66(1) "A lawyer may use or disclose confidential client information when the lawyer reasonably believes such use

or disclosure is necessary to prevent reasonably certain death or serious bodily harm to a person."

15. In 2004, California adopted its Rule 3–100. It is slightly less broad than Model Rule 1.6(b)(1), but it allows an attorney to disclose confidential client information if "necessary to prevent a criminal act that the member reasonably believes is likely to result in death of, or substantial bodily harm to, an individual."

c. Even before 2003, Restatement Third, The Law Governing Lawyers § 67(1)(d), had said that lawyers already had the authority to disclose in such cases, at least if "the client has employed or is employing the lawyer's services in the matter in which the crime or fraud is committed." See also, state rules on this issue in Appendix A, "Ethics Rules on Client Confidences," that comes after the Model Rules in the Standards Supplement.

d. Until 2003, the Model Rules had limited lawyers to "noisy withdrawal" in such cases. The idea was that, pursuant to Model Rule 1.16(b) & (c), a lawyer should withdraw and then send a notice of withdrawal to others with whom the lawyer had dealt in the matter saying something like "I have withdrawn from this matter for ethical reasons." Some lawyers objected that this withdrawal was "flying a red flag" and thus prejudiced their client's interests. However, the pre-2003 Comments specifically approved of noisy withdrawal, and the present Rules still refer to it.[16]

4. Do you welcome this clearer authority to disclose? Are lawyers often more comfortable trying to avoid the issue of harm to third parties by saying to them, in effect: "I am too ethical to ever protect you against the evil my client may do?"

a. Assuming that you want to disclose the report and memorandum to the EPA voluntarily, is there anything you must to do before disclosure? Look at Model Rule 1.6, Comment 14. Do you agree that "Where practicable, the lawyer should first seek to persuade the client to take suitable action to obviate the need for disclosure"?[17]

b. Why does Rule 1.6 add this caveat? If the lawyer discusses the issue with the client and gets him focused on the problem, might that obviate the need for disclosure? Does this caveat tell us that it is better that the client do the right thing than for its lawyer to tattle on the client?

c. Does Model Rule 1.6(b) provide other authority for disclosure? Suppose the EPA asserts that you knew about the false reporting before the reports were filed and adds you as a defendant. Would that allow you to reveal your report? Take a look at Model Rule 1.6(b)(5). To what other situations might the lawyer's "self-protection" exception apply?

d. Should the lawyer be subject to discipline—or liability—for a failure to disclose what Rule 1.6(b)(1) merely *permits* the lawyer to disclose? What does Model Rule 1.6, Comment 15, say about that? The counterpart to Comment 15 is Restatement Third, The Law Governing Lawyers § 66(3), which provides: "A lawyer who takes action or decides not to take action permitted under this Section is not, solely by reason of such action or inaction, subject to professional discipline, liable for damages to the lawyer's client or any third person, or barred from recovery against a client or third person."

---

16. Provisions that now allude to a notice of withdrawal are in Model Rule 1.2, Comment 10 and Model Rule 4.1, Comment 3.

17. This comes directly from Restatement Third, The Law Governing Lawyers § 66(2).

What is the rationale for this protection against civil liability? Is it that it is difficult in many cases for a lawyer to assess the risks correctly before the harm occurs and then impossible later for the lawyer to explain the ambiguity to a jury that is looking for deep pockets? Is that a complicated way of saying that the purpose of this rule against civil liability is to protect the lawyer's self-interest?[18]

18. We will revisit the issue of a lawyer's possible civil liability to investors in   Problem 22.

CHAPTER IV

THE REQUIREMENT OF LOYALTY TO THE CLIENT

The biblical injunction against serving inconsistent masters has long been a fundamental principle of fiduciary duty. Because lawyers have a fiduciary relationship with their clients, the principle applies with full force in the Model Rules. For a lawyer, interests possibly conflicting with the client's interest may be the interest of another client, a former client, a third party, or even the lawyer's own self-interest.

Each client of a lawyer expects full loyalty, yet it is as usual for a lawyer to represent many clients as for a doctor to treat many patients. Indeed, in some cases, several clients may believe they want a common attorney. Moreover, the lawyer's partners will all have clients, thus extending the possible conflicts, because the Model Rules typically impute the conflicts of one lawyer to others in the same firm.

Lawyers are usually not happy to discover a conflict of interest; they face economic pressures that discourage them from turning away business. But the law of legal ethics sets limits beyond which lawyers may not go without client consent. Those limits are the subject of this chapter, and you are likely to find that the questions you examine here will be the ethical issues that most frequently arise in your practice. In the problems that follow, consider questions such as:

a. How can a lawyer recognize, anticipate, and avoid conflicts of interest?

b. When will your personal interests, as opposed to those of your other clients, raise questions about the zealousness of your representation?

c. Do rules about conflicts of interest ever serve to increase, unnecessarily, the cost of legal services? Might they prevent clients from legitimately choosing to save the cost of the extra lawyer?

d. If a lawyer determines that he or she is in a conflict situation, how should the lawyer deal with it? Is it enough to obtain consent of all the affected persons? When must the lawyer refuse to take the case? When must she withdraw?

e. To what extent do conflict of interest rules represent ends in themselves, and to what extent do they further other objectives such as the obligation to preserve client confidences?

PROBLEM 9

REPRESENTING MULTIPLE PARTIES
DEALING WITH EACH OTHER

Probably the most basic kind of conflict of interest is that between two clients, simultaneously represented by a single lawyer, when everything gained by one of them will be at the other's expense. It might seem never appropriate to have a single lawyer represent both parties to such a "zero-sum game," but many real-life situations make such representation tempting, and starting our analysis of conflicts of interest there is helpful in identifying the factors that will be important throughout this chapter.

FACTS

Mr. and Mrs. Wilson have been married for 12 years. They have children ages 10, 8, and 6. They both realize that their marriage has not been going well for the past four years, and while they consider each other friends, they no longer wish to remain married. They have come to attorney Wayne Green's office and have asked Green to help them secure a divorce.

The Wilsons tell Green they have agreed that Mr. Wilson will be the custodial parent of the 8–year–old son and Mrs. Wilson will be custodial parent of the two daughters. Each will have liberal rights of contact with the children living with the other. Mrs. Wilson wants $1000 a month child support, and Mr. Wilson considers that a bargain.

Neither of the Wilsons wants a separate attorney called into the case because of the added expense. "We both trust you," they say. "Why create problems when there aren't any now?"

QUESTIONS

A.   DETERMINING WHETHER A LAWYER HAS A CONFLICT OF INTEREST

1.   Will the simultaneous representation of both Wilsons involve attorney Green in a conflict of interest?

a.   The Wilsons have told Green that they have worked everything out. Do you agree that they have done so? Are there practical problems Green should foresee in helping two people achieve even an amicable dissolution of an unwanted legal relationship? What might be some of those practical problems?

b.   Restatement Third, The Law Governing Lawyers § 121 describes the basic rule prohibiting a lawyer's conflict of interest.

"Unless all affected [persons give informed consent] * * *, a lawyer may not represent a client if the representation would involve a conflict of interest. A conflict of interest is involved if there is substantial risk that the lawyer's representation of the client would be materially and adversely affected by the lawyer's own interests or by the lawyer's duties to another current client, a former client, or a third person."

c.   The most nearly corresponding provision in the ABA Model Rules is Model Rule 1.7(a):

"Except [with informed consent] * * *, a lawyer shall not represent a client if the representation involves a concurrent conflict of interest. A concurrent conflict of interest exists if:

"(1) the representation of one client will be *directly adverse* to another client; or

"(2) there is a significant risk that the representation of one or more clients will be *materially limited* by the lawyer's responsibilities to another client, a former client or a third person or by a personal interest of the lawyer." [emphasis added]

d.   Under these definitions, are the representations of Mr. Wilson and Mrs. Wilson each "directly adverse" to the other? The lawsuit for divorce will be called *Wilson v. Wilson*. The lawyer cannot be on both sides of that lawsuit. Does "direct" only cover that example? Right now, they may only be asking the lawyer to advise them what to do and how to draw up the papers. Does that mean the representation is not "directly adverse," at least not yet?

e.   What "material limits" on the representation of Mr. or Mrs. Wilson is Green likely to experience? Is "materially limited" a subjective test or an objective one? Is the problem that Green personally may have a subjective inability to diligently pursue the interest of each client? Or, is it that no reasonable lawyer could be expected to argue for more child support for Mrs. Wilson while also arguing for less if Mr. Wilson prefers that?

2.   What concerns underlie the rules governing conflicts of interest?

a.   Model Rule 1.7, Comments 6 and 8, provide a start toward answering the question. Is the inability of Wayne Green to push hard for one client at the expense of the other a serious problem? If Mr. Wilson is willing to pay only $1000 a month, for example, may Green, on behalf of Mrs. Wilson, ask for $1500?

b.   Both the Restatement and Model Rule provisions replaced ABA Model Code of Professional Responsibility DR 5–105(A) that provided:

"A lawyer shall decline proffered employment if the exercise of his independent professional judgment in behalf of a client will be or is likely to be adversely affected by the acceptance of the proffered employment, or if it would be likely to involve him in representing differing interests * * *."

c.   Was the concept of "independent professional judgment" in DR 5–105(A) a useful one for defining the fundamental concern underlying conflict of interest regulation? On the other hand, is the effect on lawyer "judgment" the real concern?

3. Should Green be able to avoid the conflict problem by representing Mr. Wilson himself while having his law partner represent Mrs. Wilson?

a. It is important to understand that ABA Model Rule 1.10(a) usually "imputes" a single lawyer's conflicts to all other lawyers in the firm. That would be true even if Mrs. Wilson were to consult Green's partner who worked out of an office in another city. It would be true even if the two lawyers never talk to each other except with their clients present. It would be true even if Mr. and Mrs. Wilson have no material secrets to keep from each other about this matter.

b. What concerns or assumptions about attorney behavior underlie such imputation? Do you agree with those assumptions? Does it follow that the imputation should be automatic?

c. Whatever your view of imputation, it represents well-settled law that you should presume applies throughout most of the issues in the chapter. We will explore the most important implications of the concept later, primarily in Problem 15.

B. WAIVER OF A CONFLICT OF INTEREST; THE REQUIREMENT OF INFORMED CONSENT

1. Is the short answer to conflicts issues that clients may waive the conflicts whenever the rules get in the way of what the clients want to do?

a. A moment's reflection reveals that the conclusion that a conflict exists does not mean Green is prohibited from undertaking the common representation. It simply means that whether he may do so is for the Wilsons to decide, not for Green alone.

b. Restatement Third, The Law Governing Lawyers § 122(1) says:

"A lawyer may represent a client notwithstanding a conflict of interest prohibited by § 121 if each affected client or former client gives informed consent to the lawyer's representation. Informed consent requires that the client or former client have reasonably adequate information about the material risks of such representation to that client or former client."

The corresponding provision in the ABA Model Rules is Rule 1.7(b)(4).

2. What kind of information should Green provide the Wilsons about the "material risks" of his representing them both?

a. Does Model Rule 1.7, Comment 18, give a complete answer to that question? As you can see from that Comment, even discussion of the effects of the conflict on "loyalty, confidentiality and the attorney-client privilege and the advantages and risks involved" includes quite a list of topics.

b.   Also look at Model Rule 1.0 on Terminology. The need for "informed consent" appears throughout the Model Rules, so a definition is provided in Model Rule 1.0(e) and lengthy Comments 6 & 7 provide more guidance than you will find in Rule 1.7 itself.

c.   What disadvantages should Green mention? May he contrast them with the potential cost saving if he represents them both? Do you suppose Green will be telling the Wilsons something they do not already know? If they already know or should know, for example, that Green will not keep any of Mr. Wilson's secrets from Mrs. Wilson, is Green's reminder still useful?

3.   Should the Model Rules require that any client consent to a conflict be in writing?

a.   California Rule of Professional Conduct 3–310 imposes such a requirement. Model Rule 1.7, prior to 2002, did not.

b.   Look at the requirement now imposed by Model Rule 1.7(b)(4). What does it mean to have consent "confirmed in writing"?

c.   Model Rule 1.7, Comment 20, provides the answer. Do you agree that it should be sufficient to send a client a letter that the client does not need to acknowledge? Will a failure to challenge the accuracy of the representations that the lawyer makes about consent constitute agreement with the representations?

d.   As a matter of prudence, of course, most lawyers will discuss conflicts in the engagement letter that they will have the client countersign. If they have fully recorded the advice they gave about the advantages and disadvantages of waiving the conflict, any subsequent dispute will more likely be resolved in their favor. Of course, any advice they forget to mention in the letter may seem never to have been said.

4.   For how long should a conflict waiver be effective? Suppose that in the course of the representation, the lawyer learns facts that make the conflict more severe than first appeared. Must she secure a new waiver?

a.   In re Cohen, 853 P.2d 286 (Or.1993), illustrates how a relatively simple situation can quickly get out of hand. Wife accused Husband of beating their daughter. Husband faced criminal charges and both parents faced the possibility that the child would be taken from them. The lawyer agreed to represent Husband in the criminal case and to represent both parents in the custody matter. Later, Wife called the lawyer and told him that Husband was not going to counseling. A presentence report agreed and also said that Wife was often calling the police about Husband. Wife said she still wanted lawyer to represent them jointly so they could "act as a team." In imposing discipline on the lawyer, the court found that he had neither adequately explained the potential conflict at the outset nor dealt with the actual conflict later.

b.   In re Houston, 985 P.2d 752 (N.M.1999), was another case of the lawyer going too far trying to represent everyone in a family. The wife went to the lawyer, who advised her to report to police that her husband had beaten her and molested her daughter. The lawyer then defended the husband against the wife's charges; the wife consented to this but the lawyer did not tell her that she would have to testify at the trial. He also represented both husband and wife in a divorce and secured a court decree giving the husband unsupervised visitation rights that the wife found unsatisfactory. For this web of conflicts, the court required the lawyer to submit to 18 months of supervised probation.

5.   Should a client be permitted to revoke consent and then require that the lawyer not represent either of the clients?

a.   Look at Model Rule 1.7, Comment 21. Clearly, either of the clients may terminate his or her own representation for any (or no) reason. The subject of this Comment is whether the client can thereby preclude the lawyer from representing the other client.

b.   Comment 21 is derived from Restatement Third, The Law Governing Lawyers § 122, Comment *f.* Two examples that the Restatement offers illustrate the distinction. Illustration 4 says:

> "Client A and Client B validly consent to be represented by Lawyer in operating a restaurant in a city. After a period of amicable and profitable collaboration, Client A reasonably concludes that Lawyer has begun to take positions against Client A and consistently favoring the interests of Client B in the business. Reasonably concerned that Lawyer is no longer properly serving the interests of both Clients, Client A withdraws consent. Withdrawal of consent is effective and justified. Lawyer may not thereafter continue representing either Client A or Client B in a matter adverse to the other and substantially related to Lawyer's former representation of the clients."

Contrast Illustration 6:

> "Clients A and B validly consent to Lawyer representing them jointly as co-defendants in a breach-of-contract action. On the eve of trial and after months of pretrial discovery on the part of all parties, Client A withdraws consent to the joint representation for reasons not justified by the conduct of Lawyer or Client B and insists that Lawyer cease representing Client B. At this point it would be difficult and expensive for Client B to find separate representation for the impending trial. Client A's withdrawal of consent is ineffective to prevent the continuing representation of B in the absence of compelling considerations such as harmful disloyalty by Lawyer."

c.   Could a lawyer eliminate this issue by drafting the consent more carefully? For example, could the clients' consent provide that either Client A or Client B may revoke consent at any time, for any reason, but that if either A or B does that, the Lawyer may continue to represent the other client? Are there fiduciary obligations inherent in such situations that should override such private agreements?[1]

---

1.   We will return to an issue much like this, the issue of advance consent, in Problem 10.

C. CONFLICTS FOR WHICH CONSENT IS NOT EFFECTIVE

1. Should there be some conflicts that a client may not waive?

a. Restatement Third, The Law Governing Lawyers § 122(2) says:

"(2) Notwithstanding the informed consent of each affected client or former client, a lawyer may not represent a client if:

"(a) the representation is prohibited by law;

"(b) one client will assert a claim against the other in the same litigation; or

"(c) in the circumstances, it is not reasonably likely that the lawyer will be able to provide adequate representation to one or more of the clients."

The corresponding Model Rule provisions are Model Rules 1.7(b)(1)–(b)(3).

b. The first two Restatement subsections are easy enough to understand. What about the third? When should the law provide that competent and fully-informed adults should not be able to waive a conflict?

c. Is the rule really trying to identify situations in which a reasonable party would not grant consent if he or she were fully informed? Does the rule instead assume that sometimes the system of justice has an interest in the way parties are represented that makes some conflicts not subject to waiver?

2. When should Rule 1.7 not allow a client to waive a conflict?

a. Matter of Michelman, 616 N.Y.S.2d 409 (N.Y.App.Div.1994), leave to appeal denied 84 N.Y.2d 811 (1994), considered the problem of representing both a biological mother and adoptive parents in a private adoption. The adoptive parents were already the lawyer's clients and a medical doctor referred the biological mother to the lawyer, who prepared the necessary papers and explained the process to her. Assuming that all the participants consented to the common representation, do you see any problem with it? What about a biological mother's possible right to revoke consent to the adoption? Because it is easy to foresee that an effort to revoke consent might occur, ABA Informal Opinion 87–1523 (1987) concluded that the situation presented a nonconsentable conflict. This court agreed, and under the circumstances of the case, suspended the lawyer for three years.

b. In Fiandaca v. Cunningham, 827 F.2d 825 (1st Cir.1987), New Hampshire Legal Assistance (NHLA) represented women prison inmates who claimed that their prison facilities were overcrowded. The state offered to move some of the female inmates to another facility that mentally retarded patients currently used as a hospital. The NHLA, which represented these patients in another case challenging conditions at that facility, rejected the state's offer because it would adversely affect the mentally retarded clients if the hospital were converted into a women's prison. The court held that it was error for the trial court to certify NHLA as class counsel. When a lawyer must decline a settlement offer in one case in order to benefit the lawyer's clients in another case, there is a fatal conflict of interest requiring NHLA's disqualification from continuing to act for the prisoners.

c.   Baldasarre v. Butler, 625 A.2d 458 (N.J.1993), involved a lawyer who represented the sellers in a real estate transaction, while knowing that the buyer, his other client, had arranged immediately to sell the property to someone else at a large profit. Needless to say, the sellers believed their lawyer should have told them that the ultimate buyer wanted the property and should have helped them get the higher price. The New Jersey Supreme Court said there was no way the lawyer could have acted loyally to both clients in such a situation and held that a lawyer may not represent both buyer and seller in a commercial real estate deal, even with the consent of each.

Do you agree with this result? Is this simply a case where no valid consent could be obtained because the lawyer could not fully inform the original sellers of the buyer's plans?

d.   Association of the Bar of the City of New York Committee on Professional and Judicial Ethics, Formal Opinion 2001–2 (Apr. 2001), was more sympathetic to joint representation. It concluded that, particularly if the lawyer regularly represents each of the parties, each client has an almost fundamental right not to be required to get new counsel. In short, a single law firm could even represent two clients negotiating a major merger. The key issue in each case should be whether a "disinterested lawyer" would conclude that the lawyer cannot adequately represent each client. That, in turn, will require a focus on the nature of the conflicts, the ability to preserve confidential information of each client, the ability of the lawyer to explain and the client to understand the reasonably foreseeable risks of the conflict, and whether the lawyer has a closer or longer-standing relationship with one of the clients than the other.

e.   Are Comments 15–17 of Model Rule 1.7 helpful in determining whether the clients may waive a conflict? Do they persuade you whether all of the above cases and opinions are correct?

3.   Should courts and disciplinary authorities treat Green's representation of Mr. and Mrs. Wilson as a nonconsentable conflict?

a.   Even an uncontested divorce is filed in most states in the form of litigation between the husband and wife. May a lawyer represent both the plaintiff and defendant in a litigated case? Does the fact that the court will have to approve the Wilsons' divorce mean that there could be no harm from Green's representing them both?

b.   The Reporter's Note to Restatement Third, The Law Governing Lawyers § 128, Comment *c* says:

> "The question of representing opposing clients in hearings on uncontested marital dissolution has arisen frequently. Some courts have permitted use of only one lawyer in some of those situations.

While the divorce proceeding is still a nominally contested litigation in most jurisdictions, in some remedial contexts, courts will confirm a negotiated property settlement where both parties consented to the simultaneous representation and the settlement appears fair. See, e.g., Klemm v. Superior Court, 142 Cal.Rptr. 509 (Cal.Ct.App.1977) (while parties may not waive conflict in contested litigation, they may do so in an uncontested dissolution); * * *. [However, s]everal jurisdictions treat joint representation of spouses in a dissolution action as a nonconsentable conflict in all instances."

c. Might Green handle the representation jointly through negotiation of the property settlement, but have the Wilsons hire another lawyer to represent one of the parties at the divorce hearing while Mr. Green represents the other? Is there any public interest in requiring that the process be bifurcated in that way? If Mr. Green represents one of the parties, how will he choose which one? If a new lawyer represents the other party, is that lawyer required to accept the property settlement as given, or should he or she independently evaluate it?

4. Should consent be more likely to be possible in business planning matters and other nonlitigation settings that are less contentious than a divorce?

a. Assume, for example, that the parties who have come to Green are three individuals who wish to set up a close corporation. Green has met none of them before. Is it possible that he can represent them all effectively?

b. Before the ABA House of Delegates deleted Model Rule 2.2 in the 2002 revisions, that Rule addressed this situation, calling the lawyer an "intermediary between clients." It permitted the lawyer to undertake such representation if:

"(1) the lawyer consults with each client concerning the implications of the common representation, including the advantages and risks involved, and the effect on the attorney-client privileges, and obtains each client's consent to the common representation;

"(2) the lawyer reasonably believes that the matter can be resolved on terms compatible with the clients' best interests, that each client will be able to make adequately informed decisions in the matter and that there is little risk of material prejudice to the interest of any of the clients if the contemplated resolution is unsuccessful; and

"(3) the lawyer reasonably believes that the common representation can be undertaken impartially and without improper effect on other responsibilities the lawyer has to any of the clients."

c. At the time the ABA Commission revised the Model Rules in 2002, the drafters concluded that these principles were already inherent in Model Rule 1.7. Do you agree?

d. Although the ABA has repealed Model Rule 2.2, some of its ideas are reflected in Rule 1.7, Comments 28–33. What would you conclude from those Comments about the ability of the parties to consent to using a single lawyer in establishing a business?

5.   Could Green represent both Mr. and Mrs. Wilson if, instead of seeking a divorce, they came to Green for estate planning advice?

a.   An ABA report analyzed the issue as follows:

"From an ethical standpoint, the risk is that, in counseling the couple as a unit for tax and planning purposes, neither individual will receive the representation a single individual might receive under the same circumstances. Yet family needs, tax incentives, and the very nature of marriage often make separate counseling unnecessary, and indeed, inappropriate."[2]

b.   Under that analysis, should a lawyer normally obtain a conflicts waiver before beginning estate planning for the couple? May the lawyer properly "view the couple as unified in goals and interests until shown otherwise"?[3]

c.   Restatement Third, The Law Governing Lawyers § 130, Comment *c*, cautions: "A lawyer is not required to suggest or assume discord where none exists, but when a conflict is reasonably apparent or foreseeable, the lawyer may proceed with multiple representation only after all affected clients have consented as provided in § 122." Do you agree with the Restatement approach?

6.   What are Green's obligations to Mr. Wilson if, during estate planning, Mrs. Wilson privately discloses confidential information to Green but not to her spouse?

a.   Confronted with the choice between both hiring the same lawyer or each hiring a lawyer from separate law firms, which option do you believe most couples would choose, at least when they were together in a lawyer's office? However, what should Green do if, the day after both wills are signed, Mrs. Wilson comes back to the lawyer's office and says, "I want to change my will and don't want my husband to know"? Does your answer depend on whether Mr. Wilson is leaving all his property to his wife in the expectation that she is doing the same for him?

b.   A v. B. v. Hill Wallack, 726 A.2d 924 (N.J.1999), presented a very similar question. Husband and Wife sought estate planning advice from Hill Wallack. Because of a mistake in conflicts checking, Hill Wallack did not discover until later that it had already accepted another woman's paternity action against Husband. Husband did not object to Hill Wallack's handling that case against him, and DNA tests showed he was the father of the woman's child. At that point, Hill Wallack wanted to tell Wife that, because she was leaving the residue of her estate to Husband, part of that

---

2. Report of the Special Study Committee on Professional Responsibility, Comments and Recommendations on the Lawyer's Duties in Representing Husband and Wife, 28 Real Property, Probate & Trust Journal 765, 770 (1994).

3. Id. at 779.

estate could wind up going to his illegitimate child. Husband did not want the firm to tell Wife that he had fathered the child, and this action sought to prevent that disclosure. The court said that a lawyer for co-clients should reach an agreement *in advance* with co-clients about how confidential information of each will be handled. Citing an earlier version of what is now Restatement Third, The Law Governing Lawyers § 60, Comment *l*, however, the court held that, in the absence of such an agreement, the lawyer has the "discretion" to tell each client the secrets of the other that may adversely affect that client's interest. It authorized the firm to tell Wife the existence but not the identity of the child.

c.   What does "discretion to tell" mean? The Restatement section on which the *Wallack* court relied makes clear that "[s]haring of information among the co-clients with respect to the matter involved in the representation is normal and typically expected. * * * Moreover, the common lawyer is required to keep each of the co-clients informed of all information reasonably necessary for the co-client to make decisions in connection with the matter." When the lawyer gets information that one client wants to keep secret from the other, however, there is a conflict of interest between the clients that the lawyer cannot ignore. That is the context of the Restatement passage that the *Wallack* court quotes: "In the course of withdrawal [because of the conflict], the lawyer has discretion to warn the affected co-client that a matter seriously and adversely affecting that person's interests has come to light, which the other co-client refuses to permit the lawyer to disclose."

d.   D.C. Bar Legal Ethics Opinion 296 (2000) concluded that a lawyer may *not* reveal a secret of one joint client to another but must withdraw from the representation of both. A lawyer who undertakes dual representation has a duty to clarify, at the outset of the representation, "the impact of joint representation on the lawyer's duty to maintain client confidences and to keep each client reasonably informed, and obtain each client's informed consent to the arrangement." In the absence of such an agreement, when one joint client discloses confidential information that a lawyer would have a duty to disclose to the other in order to keep that client reasonably informed, the lawyer must seek consent to disclose such information from the disclosing client. According to the opinion, if the lawyer is unable to obtain consent, a conflict of interest arises and the lawyer must withdraw from the case. After withdrawal, the lawyer may not represent either client in the matter without the consent of the other.

e.   The Model Rules now address this issue in Rule 1.7, Comments 30 & 31. How do they direct Green to proceed? How should the lawyer have proceeded in the *Wallack* case?

f.   If the lawyer knows, before undertaking the representation, that one of the clients is withholding relevant information from the other, may the lawyer take the case at all? Look at Model Rule 1.7, Comment 19. Might he take the case with the informed consent of the other client? Does the inability to make full disclosure render informed consent impossible?

7. Are the Model Rules too quick to find conflicts and prohibit consent?

a. In spite of the obvious problems associated with Mr. and Mrs. Wilson using the same lawyer for their divorce, might it nonetheless be reasonable for them to desire that arrangement? Is their desire for noncontentious resolution of the matter a legitimate concern? Should the ethics rules require two lawyers if one will do?

b. Do you agree with the following view?

> "[H]aving more than one lawyer to accomplish the parties' objectives may be an unnecessary and wasteful luxury. Individuals entering upon a contractual relationship, for example, might find it significantly less expensive and less disruptive to hire a single lawyer to draft a contract incorporating the business consensus of both sides than to have two lawyers, each trying to exact the marginal pound of flesh for his client. So, too, in many cases of uncontested divorce, the presence of combatant lawyers may re-open wounds better left closed and exacerbate problems rather than solve them.

> "The response to this argument from many lawyers is that a situation which appears nonlitigious at the moment may develop into a contested situation in the future. This is not an unreasonable concern * * *. But having two lawyers from the outset in every case is expensive insurance against the unknown. Moreover, in many situations where things go badly, both sides can simply bring in separate counsel. The only person hurt by such a procedure would be the first lawyer who will now represent neither party. That the lawyer might not like this result is understandable. That his unhappiness should rise to the level of an ethical precept is less clear."[4]

c. ABA Formal Opinion 07–447 (Aug. 9, 2007) addresses the growing practice of using collaborative lawyering in lieu of adversarial litigation in divorce. The opinion acknowledges the value of reaching agreement with minimal adversarial complications. A "collaborative law process" involves lawyers seeking to focus on the interests of both clients and to find a mutually acceptable divorce settlement, for example, that the parties jointly can submit to a court for approval. The parties must consent in advance to such a process, the opinion said, and if no agreement is reached, both lawyers must withdraw and have new lawyers prepare the matter for trial. But the opinion rejected the idea that a "limited scope" representation is not consentable, and although the collaborative process at issue involved a separate lawyer for each party, it might not be a long step from there to permitting a single lawyer to broker the agreement.

---

4. Thomas D. Morgan, The Evolving Concept of Professional Responsibility, 90 Harvard L. Rev. 702, 727–28 (1977). Copyright © 1977 by the Harvard Law Review Association.

D.   REMEDIES OTHER THAN PROFESSIONAL DISCIPLINE FOR A CONFLICT OF INTEREST VIOLATION

1.   Should a judge enforce the rule against representing conflicting interests by ordering the representation terminated, or should judges leave enforcement to the lawyer discipline process?

a.   In litigated matters, a court faced with a conflict of interest will most often order the lawyer disqualified from representing any or all of the clients in the matter. Restatement Third, The Law Governing Lawyers § 6, Comment *i* explains:

> "Disqualification draws on the inherent power of courts to regulate the conduct of lawyers * * * as well as the related inherent power of judges to regulate the course of proceedings before them * * *. Disqualification, where appropriate, ensures that the case is well presented in court, that confidential information of present or former clients is not misused, and that a client's substantial interest in a lawyer's loyalty is protected."[5]

b.   In nonlitigation matters, some courts will issue an injunction against the continued representation and thereby achieve the practical effect of a disqualification. See Maritrans GP Inc. v. Pepper, Hamilton & Scheetz, 602 A.2d 1277 (Pa.1992).

c.   Yet, as Panduit Corp. v. All States Plastic Mfg. Co., Inc., 744 F.2d 1564, 1576–77 (Fed.Cir.1984), warns: "Judges must exercise caution not to paint with a broad brush under the misguided belief that coming down on the side of disqualification raises the standard of legal ethics and the public's respect. The opposite effects are just as likely—encouragement of vexatious tactics and increased cynicism by the public."

d.   If a judge concludes that failing to disqualify would make a trial unfair, should the judge refuse to disqualify because the moving party seems to have bad motives? The 2002 revisions to the Model Rules eliminated former Comment 15 of Rule 1.7, which said that opposing counsel may "properly raise the question" of disqualification if the "conflict is such as clearly to call in question the fair or efficient administration of justice," but such an objection "should be viewed with caution," because "it can be misused as a technique of harassment."

---

5.   In federal courts, the denial of a disqualification motion in a civil case is *not* appealable as a final order under 28 U.S.C.A. § 1291. Firestone Tire & Rubber Co. v. Risjord, 449 U.S. 368 (1981). Similarly, the grant of a disqualification is not immediately appealable. Richardson–Merrell, Inc. v. Koller, 472 U.S. 424 (1985). The same rule applies in criminal cases. Flanagan v. United States, 465 U.S. 259 (1984) (granting disqualification motion not immediately appealable); United States v. White, 743 F.2d 488 (7th Cir.1984) (the denial of a motion to disqualify in a criminal case).

However, a few courts of appeal have agreed to review lower court decisions when the losing party has sought a writ of mandamus, e.g., In re American Airlines, Inc., 972 F.2d 605 (5th Cir.1992); Matter of Sandahl, 980 F.2d 1118 (7th Cir.1992). The Seventh Circuit has concluded that mandamus is appropriate if the trial judge applied an incorrect legal rule; it continues to defer to the trial judge on questions of fact. Do you think the law/fact distinction is likely to be applied easily in disqualification cases?

Do you agree with the sentiment of the former Comment? Should a court grant a disqualification motion that will protect the trial process, because doing so will encourage parties to bring an important issue to the attention of the court? Should the moving party's subjective motive be relevant at all, if the motion is not frivolous?

e.   Throughout this chapter, watch for this tension between rigorous enforcement of professional standards and the desire to prevent opportunistic efforts by the parties to impose additional costs on each other by seeking to disqualify their lawyers.

2.   What other remedies should be available to sanction a lawyer who represented conflicting interests?

a.   If either of the clients has been disadvantaged by the conflict, a malpractice remedy is often available. See, e.g., Hughes v. Consol–Pennsylvania Coal Co., 945 F.2d 594, 617 & n.3 (3d Cir.1991) (client called for advice whether transaction was fair; lawyer did not disclose he represented the other side; trial court erred by failing to uphold the jury verdict on malpractice); Milbank, Tweed, Hadley & McCloy v. Boon, 13 F.3d 537 (2d Cir.1994) ($2 million in damages awarded for acting adversely to client in same transaction).

b.   Even in the absence of economic harm to the clients, some courts deny lawyers part or all of their fees as a sanction for the breach of fiduciary duty inherent in a lawyer's conflict of interest.

In Hendry v. Pelland, 73 F.3d 397 (D.C.Cir.1996), for example, the law firm represented all five members of a family selling a parcel of land. Each of the clients had somewhat different views about acceptable terms for the sale. While finding no intentional misconduct that would support punitive damages, or even any actual damage suffered by family members, the court ruled that representation of all five family members was a conflict of interest that required the law firm to disgorge all fees it had earned in the case. See also, Burrow v. Arce, 997 S.W.2d 229, 240 (Tex.1999): "a client need not prove actual damages in order to obtain forfeiture of an attorney's fee for the attorney's breach of fiduciary duty to the client."

c.   United States v. Gellene, 182 F.3d 578 (7th Cir.1999), held that failure to disclose a conflict of interest can sometimes be a crime. Gellene, a partner in the New York firm Milbank, Tweed, Hadley & McCloy, represented the debtor in a Chapter 11 bankruptcy. He signed a sworn declaration identifying the firm's connection to all other parties in interest, but he failed to disclose that the firm also represented the senior secured creditor. He admitted bad judgment but denied a fraudulent intent. The jury found otherwise. The court sentenced Gellene to 15 months in the penitentiary and imposed a $15,000 fine. The court said it increased the sentence because Gellene, as a lawyer, abused a "position of trust."[6]

---

6.   This case is the subject of an absorbing book by Professor Milton C. Regan, Jr., Eat What You Kill: The Fall of a Wall Street Lawyer (2006).

e. Should each of these remedies be exclusive, or should all be available simultaneously in appropriate cases?

———

PROBLEM 10

THE DUTY OF LOYALTY

Problem 9 involved representation of clients with opposing positions in the same case. More commonly, a lawyer is asked to represent one client against another client whom the lawyer represents in a different case. Literally any of the clients that a lawyer represents in any matter might coincidentally become the opponent of another of the lawyer's clients. The growth of multistate and multinational law firms with hundreds of lawyers, each of whose conflicts is imputed to the other, means the possibility that one of a law firm's clients will oppose another is enormous. This problem explores how firms deal with the problem of "direct adversity;" how one determines who is "currently" a client of a law firm; whether the firm may simply terminate a client so as to eliminate the conflict; and how lawyers are to deal with situations in which two clients, in two factually unrelated cases, differ on how they believe a court should rule on a point of law.

FACTS

You represent the First National Bank in its commercial lending work. The bank had made a large mortgage loan to International Bolts Co., a parts manufacturer, for construction of a new plant. The loan has now gone into default, and the bank has directed you to commence foreclosure proceedings.

International Bolts has occasionally hired you over the last few years to write opinion letters on labor law matters. You do not now happen to be drafting any opinion for that company. You have never represented International Bolts in connection with this loan, but when you mention to the president of International Bolts that you will soon be handling the foreclosure of his plant, he is personally offended. "I really would not like you to be the one that does that to us," he says, "after all we've been through together."

Meanwhile, a neighbor has consulted you with respect to a "prepayment penalty" in the residential mortgage loan he has with the Second National Bank. Second National is not one of your clients, and you agree with the neighbor that prepayment penalties seem not to be in consumers' best interests. Thus, as a favor to your neighbor, you have agreed to file a declaratory judgment action challenging the validity of such agreements under state and federal law.

You have informed the Second National Bank of the impending suit, and you later receive a call from the president of your client, the First National Bank, who says: "I've heard about your proposed law suit against the Second National Bank. We do not want the law of prepayment penalties changed." Then the president tells you: "You owe it to us to withdraw from representing the plaintiff in the pending suit." First National Bank has nothing to do with the proposed lawsuit against Second National Bank, which has never been your client, but First National Bank is concerned about the holding that may emerge from your prospective lawsuit.

QUESTIONS

A. TAKING A CASE AGAINST A CURRENT CLIENT

1. Is International Bolts' demand that you not represent the First National Bank in the foreclosure proceeding more than simply a question of keeping good relations with a sometimes client? Does International Bolts have a legal right to keep you out of the case?

a. Look at Model Rule 1.7(a)(1). Must you take International Bolts' objection seriously?[1] As a matter of good business, you may not want to offend International Bolts, but would you be acting "unethically" if you were willing to do so?

b. What is the purpose of Model Rule 1.7(a)(1)? Does the concern about protecting clients' confidences help justify it? Remember that in many instances, like the one in this problem, there will be no substantive factual or legal relationship between the cases at all and thus no significant likelihood of misuse of any confidential information.

2. Does the overarching concern go to the lawyer's loyalty to the client rather than protection of the client's confidences?

a. Early cases like Grievance Committee v. Rottner, 203 A.2d 82 (Conn.1964), focused on loyalty. A law firm aggressively pursued an assault and battery case for O'Brien against Twible. When that case began, the firm was representing Twible in a collection matter against a third party. The cases were not at all related but the court explained:

> "When a client engages the services of a lawyer in a given piece of business he is entitled to feel that, until that business is finally disposed of in some manner, he has the undivided loyalty of the one upon whom he looks as his advocate and his champion. If, as in this case, he is sued and his home attached by his own attorney, who is representing him in another matter, all feeling of loyalty is necessarily destroyed, and the profession is exposed to the charge that it is interested only in money." 203 A.2d at 84.

---

1. In re Dresser Industries, Inc., 972 F.2d 540 (5th Cir.1992), holds that the principle against filing suit for one client against another current client is a national standard that federal courts must use in ruling on disqualification motions, even in the face of contrary state law.

b.   Cinema 5, Ltd. v. Cinerama, Inc., 528 F.2d 1384 (2d Cir.1976), applied this principle where attorney Fleischmann was a partner in two different law firms, one in New York City and one in Buffalo. Cinerama hired the Buffalo firm to represent it in an antitrust action that upstate New York theater operators filed. Later, several plaintiffs retained the New York City firm to sue several companies, including Cinerama, for alleged attempts to take over theater companies in New York City. Thus, one law firm was suing Cinerama while the other law firm was defending Cinerama. Because Fleischmann was the common partner in the two firms, the court treated the situation as a single law firm representing its client in one case while suing it in a different case.

The firm appealed the district court disqualification, saying that two different cases in completely different markets were involved. The Second Circuit assumed the two lawsuits were not related and responded:

"The 'substantial relationship' test is indeed the one that we have customarily applied in determining whether a lawyer may accept employment against a former client. * * * However, in this case, suit is not against a former client, but an existing one. One firm in which attorney Fleischmann is a partner is suing an actively represented client of another firm in which attorney Fleischmann is a partner. The propriety of this conduct must be measured not so much against the similarities in litigation, as against the duty of undivided loyalty which an attorney owes to each of his clients.

"A lawyer's duty to his client is that of a fiduciary or trustee. * * * When Cinerama retained Mr. Fleischmann as its attorney in the Western District litigation, it was entitled to feel that at least until that litigation was at an end, it had his undivided loyalty as its advocate and champion, * * * and could rely upon his 'undivided allegiance and faithful, devoted service.' * * * Because 'no man can serve two masters', Matthew 6:24; * * * it had the right to expect also that he would 'accept no retainer to do anything that might be adverse to his client's interests.' * * * Needless to say, when Mr. Fleischmann and his New York City partners undertook to represent Cinema 5, Ltd., they owed it the same fiduciary duty of undivided loyalty and allegiance. * * * "

"Whether such adverse representation, without more, requires disqualification in every case, is a matter we need not now decide. We do hold, however, that the 'substantial relationship' test does not set a sufficiently high standard by which the necessity for disqualification should be determined. That test may properly be applied only where the representation of a former client has been terminated and the parameters of such relationship have been fixed. Where the relationship is a continuing one, adverse representation is prima facie improper, * * * and the attorney must be prepared to show, at the very least, that there will be no actual or *apparent* conflict in loyalties or diminution in the vigor of his representation. We think that appellants have failed to meet this heavy burden * * *. [T]he record shows that after learning of the conflict which had developed, the Jaeckle firm, through Mr. Fleischmann, offered to withdraw its representation of Cinerama in the Western District actions. However, that offer was not accepted, and Mr. Fleischmann continued, albeit reluctantly, to have one foot in each camp." 528 F.2d at 1386–87.

Thus, the court affirmed the disqualification order.

3. In addition to the issue of loyalty, should there be a concern that the lawyer might represent Client A less vigorously so as not to offend Client B?

a. In Zuck v. Alabama, 588 F.2d 436 (5th Cir.1979), a law firm represented a defendant in a criminal case while also representing the prosecutor sued in his personal capacity in an unrelated civil matter. The prosecutor was not the real party in interest in the criminal case: he was not the state. Yet, "the defense attorneys were subject to the encumbrance that the prosecutor might take umbrage at a vigorous defense of Zuck and dispense with the services of their firm." In other words, the defense lawyer might be cautious about offending the prosecutor, his civil client, such as by charging prosecutorial misconduct. This constituted an actual conflict of interest rendering the criminal trial unfair in the absence of the criminal defendant's knowing and intelligent waiver. The court also said that although a witness apparently informed the defendant that his attorneys were also representing the prosecutor, that did not establish that the defendant waived his right to conflict-free representation absent a showing that the defendant was aware of the consequences of proceeding to trial with such counsel or that he knew that he had a right to have other counsel. See Rule 1.0(e) ("informed consent") and Rule 1.7, Comments 6 & 18.

b. ABA Formal Opinion 97–406 (Apr. 19, 1997) considered the case where one lawyer (Lawyer 1) represents another lawyer (Lawyer 2). For example, Lawyer 2 might be a defendant in a malpractice case. At the same time, Lawyer 1 simultaneously represents clients who oppose parties who are represented by Lawyer 2 in different, unrelated cases. The opinion said that the issue should be analyzed under what is now Model Rule 1.7(a)(2), not 1.7(a)(1). The opinion advised that there is a conflict if there is reason to believe that one or the other of the representations "may be materially limited" by duties the lawyer owes the other client. In the view of the opinion, six issues affect the determination of this issue: (1) the relative importance of the matters to the represented lawyer, (2) the relative sizes of the fees expected by the representing lawyer, (3) the relative importance of the clients' matters to each lawyer and client, (4) the sensitivity of each matter, (5) the similarity of the subject matter of the cases, and (6) the nature of the relationship of the lawyers with each other and with their clients. If the lawyer concludes that her representation would not be affected by the relationship with the other lawyer, she may seek client consent to her continued representation. However, if a reasonably objective observer would conclude that her representation would be adversely affected, she may not even ask for client consent.[2]

4.   Should the concern about lawyer loyalty extend to more than instances of filing suit against another client?

a.   The ABA Standing Committee on Ethics and Professional Responsibility has explored the suit against a present client issue in several other contexts. For example, ABA Formal Opinion 97–407 (May 13, 1997) asked whether a lawyer who serves as an expert witness in a matter has a lawyer-client relationship with the party for whom he or she testifies so as to prevent that lawyer from acting contrary to the interest of that party in another matter. The opinion said "no" if the lawyer is only testifying on the party's behalf, but "yes" if the lawyer is also consulting with lawyers for that party. However, if the lawyer's duty of confidentiality to other clients would be affected, consent of those other clients would be required before the lawyer could act as an expert at all.

b.   May a lawyer cross-examine an opponent's expert witness whom the lawyer concurrently represents in unrelated matters? ABA Formal Opinion 92–367 (Oct. 16, 1992) concluded that the cross-examination would "ordinarily" present a conflict under what is now Rule 1.7(a)(1). The opinion reasoned that vigorous cross-examination would violate the lawyer's duty of loyalty to one client, the expert, while failure to cross-examine vigorously would violate the duty to zealously represent the lawyer's other client. Furthermore, the lawyer might know confidential information about the expert that would be relevant to the cross-examination but that the lawyer would be forbidden to use. The opinion suggests that a lawyer from another firm could be retained to conduct the cross-examination, and that the first lawyer could continue to conduct the rest of the defense. Do you agree that such a solution should suffice? Cf. Rule 1.7, Comment 8.

c.   Is a lawyer who is also a public official (a member of the county council) liable for breach of fiduciary duty to a client because he voted in a way that was adverse to that client? Joe v. Two Thirty Nine Joint Venture, 145 S.W.3d 150 (Tex.2004), involved the firm of Jenkens & Gilchrist, which represented 239 Joint Venture in its sale of a tract of land designated for apartments. Prior to the sale's closing, the county council voted to place a moratorium on apartment construction in the county. Joe, who was both a partner in Jenkens & Gilchrist and a member of the county council, voted

---

2. Association of the Bar of the City of New York Formal Opinion 1996–3 (Apr. 2, 1996) says that the concerns about letting one firm [Firm A] represent another law firm [Firm B] as a client when Firm B represents clients in other cases that Firm A opposes are that (1) Firm A will learn things about Firm B that can be used adversely to Firm B's clients in the other matters, and (2) Firm A will tend to pull its punches in the unrelated matters so as to preserve the good will of Firm B. The opinion concludes that no bright line test can be formulated as to when the representation represents a conflict of interest. If a lawyer in a big firm closes a residential real estate transaction for a lawyer in another firm whose out-of-state office is litigating against a different office of the first firm, there may be no conflict at all. If a solo practitioner represents a small firm lawyer in a divorce case, taking even unrelated cases against each other might be a nonconsentable conflict. Somewhere between those extremes, the clients in the unrelated matters should be notified and be given the chance to consent or get other counsel.

in favor of the moratorium. 239 Joint Venture sued Joe and Jenkens & Gilchrist claiming that Joe's vote constituted a breach of fiduciary duty to the client. The Texas Supreme Court held that official immunity shielded Joe from any conflict of interest arising from Joe's legitimate legislative functions. The court found that Joe's actions "involved personal deliberation, decision, and judgment characteristic of a discretionary act that was delegated to him as a public official."

d.   Rule 1.7(a)(1) speaks of a conflict if the lawyer's representation of one client is "directly adverse" to another client. What makes a representation "directly adverse," as opposed to "materially limited," which is the standard in Rule 1.7(a)(2)? "Directly adverse" suggests that the lawyer is permitted to be "indirectly adverse," so long as no "material limitation" is involved.

ABA Formal Opinion 05–434 (Dec. 8, 2004) said there is no "direct adversity" when a lawyer represents a testator who seeks to disinherit a person who is also one of the lawyer's clients. Obviously, no potential beneficiary wants to be disinherited, but such a person has only an expectancy interest—not a legal right—to a bequest. Therefore, unless the testator has contractual or quasi-contractual obligations to leave property to the person, the lawyer is not representing a client "directly adverse" to another client, under Rule 1.7(a)(1). Turning to the "materially limited representation" standard of Rule 1.7(a)(2), the opinion advised that, in most cases, preparing an instrument to disinherit a beneficiary is a "simple, straightforward, almost ministerial task." However, if the lawyer provides *advice* as to whether to disinherit one of the lawyer's other clients or drafts documents in violation of "previously agreed-upon family estate planning objectives," there is a "heightened risk" that representing a testator trying to disinherit one of the lawyer's other clients will be materially limited by the lawyer's obligations to the beneficiary.

ABA Formal Opinion 05–435 (Dec. 8, 2004) involved a lawyer who represents a liability insurer in various matters and also represents a client who seeks to sue someone covered by a policy issued by that insurer. The opinion concludes that the lawyer in that case is not normally "directly adverse" to the insurer unless the lawyer names the liability insurer as a defendant or the attorney takes discovery of the insurer's representatives. However, the lawyer's representation of the plaintiff seeking recovery may have a "material limitation" conflict. The opinion says the critical issues are the "likelihood that a difference in interests will occur" and whether such differences "will materially interfere with the lawyer's independent professional judgment in considering alternatives or foreclose courses of action that reasonably should be pursued on behalf of the client." For example, if the lawyer learned information in connection with the representation of the liability insurer that would materially help the new client's case *against* the insured defendant, a conflict of interest would exist under Rule 1.7(a)(2).

5.   May a lawyer avoid conflicts by limiting the scope of the representation?

a. In Sumitomo Corp v. J.P. Morgan & Co., Inc., 2000 WL 145747 (S.D.N.Y.2000), the Paul Weiss firm represented Sumitomo in investigating an employee who was responsible for losses from copper trading. Later, various banks demanded payments from Sumitomo with respect to transactions of which it was unaware. Paul Weiss realized that it represented some of those banks and told Sumitomo it could not evaluate or litigate the bank claims on Sumitomo's behalf. Paul Weiss represented Sumitomo in filing suit against J.P. Morgan, but Chase Manhattan, a Paul Weiss client in other matters, refused to waive the conflict, so Sumitomo had another firm represent it in filing suit against Chase. Hence, Chase was not a party to the litigation where Paul Weiss was representing Sumitomo. However, the judge then consolidated the two cases for pretrial discovery, and Chase then moved to disqualify Paul Weiss from suing J.P. Morgan. The court refused. "Chase is a huge financial institution," the court said. It is not an individual that would feel a betrayal of trust. The two cases became consolidated for discovery purposes only because the court granted Chase's motion to do that. Chase's lawyers acknowledged that there were no issue involving the use of confidences.

b. Association of the Bar of the City of New York Committee on Professional and Judicial Ethics, Formal Opinion 2001–3 (2001), also addressed this issue. The opinion approved of having another firm bring the case against the client the principal firm cannot sue, and referred to negotiations in multiparty business deals where the technique might also be used. The practice may not be used as a sham in which the otherwise conflicted firm becomes a behind-the-scenes manager of the matter that it has undertaken not to pursue. The firm also may not take actions that hurt the firm's other client. With those caveats, however, the presence of one or two avoided areas of conflict does not mean the lawyer is disqualified altogether.

c. Does this approach make sense to you? Can you think of other situations where the lawyer can use Rule 1.2(c) to limit the scope of representation so that the lawyer will avoid violating Model Rule 1.7(a)(1)?

6. Can concern about loyalty to the lawyer's current clients be so excessive that it leads to injustice to clients who are trying to find a capable lawyer to represent them?

a. In Flatt v. Superior Court (Daniel), 885 P.2d 950 (Cal.1994), a prospective client asked a law firm to sue his former lawyer. The prospective client disclosed confidential information to a lawyer in this new firm who told him that he "definitely" had a good malpractice claim. A week later, the firm called the prospective client back and declined the representation because it was representing the prior lawyer in an unrelated matter. The firm did not tell the prospective client about the statute of limitations for his claim or recommend that he retain other counsel. The California Supreme Court declared that this handling of the conflict was proper because giving the prospective client information about protecting his interests would have been disloyal to the existing client. Do you agree?

b. What is the relevance of Model Rule 4.3 to the situation presented in *Flatt?* Rule 4.3 says: "The lawyer shall not give legal advice to an unrepresented person, other than the advice to secure counsel, if the lawyer knows or should reasonably should know that the interests of such a person are or have a reasonable possibility of being in conflict with the interests of the client." Is a prospective client just like any other unrepresented person in terms of the application of Rule 4.3?

B. ASCERTAINING WHO IS A CURRENT CLIENT

1. Assume it is well established that a lawyer may not represent someone in litigation against a current client without both parties' consent. Is International Bolts a current client? At this moment you are not doing any work for International Bolts, and the company may never call again.

a. In IBM Corp. v. Levin, 579 F.2d 271 (3d Cir.1978), IBM sought to disqualify a law firm, CBM, for representing a client in a suit against IBM. The trial court disqualified CBM and the court of appeals affirmed. The trial court "found as a fact that at all relevant times CBM had an on-going attorney-client relationship with both IBM and the plaintiffs. This assessment of the relationship seems entirely reasonable to us. Although CBM had no specific assignment from IBM on hand on the day that [CBM filed] the antitrust complaint [against IBM] and even though CBM performed services for IBM on a fee-for-services basis rather than pursuant to a retainer arrangement, the pattern of repeated retainers, both before and after the filing of the complaint, supports the finding of a continuous relationship." 579 F.2d at 281.

b. Should a law firm be able to avoid the inference of continued representation by writing a letter to each client terminating the relationship at the end of a given matter? Why do you suppose firms are loath to do that? Is the approach in IBM v. Levin simply recognizing a relationship the firm hopes the client believes still exists?

c. Are some apparent clients not really clients for purposes of Model Rule 1.7(a)(1)? In Commercial Union Ins. Co. v. Marco International Corp., 75 F.Supp.2d 108 (S.D.N.Y.1999), Commercial Union retained a law firm to file suit to determine the coverage of one of its insurance policies written on behalf of Marco International. Marco moved to disqualify Commercial's counsel because that law firm nominally represented Marco in an unrelated subrogation suit arising out of Commercial's payment to Marco with respect to a different loss. (After an insurance company pays its insured for a loss caused by a wrongdoer, the insurance company files a subrogation action in the name of the insured but really to get the insurance company's money back from the wrongdoer.) The issue in this case thus was whether filing case A in the name of the insured (but in the interest of the insurance company) should disqualify a law firm from representing the insurance company in case B, which was unrelated coverage litigation with the insured. The court took what it called a "flexible" approach and refused to disqualify the firm. Marco had no "material pecuniary or other interest" in the other case, it paid no fees, and it had no control over the prosecution or settlement of that action. There would be no reason "beyond empty formalism" to treat the present action as a prohibited suit against a current client.[3]

2. Should every division and wholly-owned subsidiary of a current client be considered to be a client of the lawyer for conflict purposes?

a.   A division within one corporation typically is treated as part of the client itself. In Image Technical Services, Inc. v. Eastman Kodak Co., 820 F.Supp. 1212 (N.D.Cal.1993), for example, the law firm prepared plaintiffs' briefs in a Supreme Court antitrust case against Kodak. At the same time, the firm's Hong Kong office represented a division of Kodak that was doing completely unrelated work in China and other international markets. The law firm obtained oral consent from the division representative with whom the firm worked, but it did not seek consent from the Kodak general counsel. The court disqualified the law firm from all further participation in the case. Later, when the plaintiff (using different counsel) won the case on remand to the trial court, the first law firm applied for statutory attorneys' fees due the prevailing plaintiff under the Clayton Act. The Ninth Circuit held the law firm could not get attorney fees for its representation of plaintiff prior to its disqualification. Image Technical Service v. Eastman Kodak Co., 136 F.3d 1354 (9th Cir.1998).

b.   ABA Formal Opinion 95–390 (Jan. 25, 1995), broadly analyzed conflicts of interest in the corporate family context. The opinion said that corporate family relationships are too varied to adopt a bright-line rule forbidding a law firm that represents a parent corporation, for example, from bringing suit against the parent's subsidiary. The lawyer must ask whether (1) the subsidiary and parent are in effect operated as one entity, (2) there has been an agreement to treat the whole corporate family as the client, or (3) the lawyer's obligations to the parent will materially limit pursuit of the claim against the subsidiary.[4] See also, Model Rule 1.7, Comment 34 & 35 ("Organizational Clients"); Association of the Bar of the City of New York Committee on Professional and Judicial Ethics, Formal Opinion 2007–3 (Sept. 2007) (consider law firm dealings with the affiliate during work for the current client, confidential information the firm may have learned, and any significant risk of material limitation on the firm's ability to act for either the current or adverse client).

c.   GSI Commerce Solutions, Inc. v. Babycenter, LLC, 618 F.3d 204 (2d Cir. 2010), relied on ABA Formal Opinion 95–390 and Model Rule 1.7, Comment 34, when it upheld the trial court's disqualification of a law firm. The law firm simultaneously represented a parent company (Johnson &

---

3. For more about the history of the rule and the desirability of tempering its application with a rule of reason as illustrated by *Marco*, see Thomas D. Morgan, Suing a Current Client, 9 Georgetown J. Legal Ethics 1157 (1996).

4. See, e.g., Ronald D. Rotunda, Conflicts Problems When Representing Members of Corporate Families, 72 Notre Dame L. Rev. 655 (1997); Robert C. Hacker & Ronald D. Rotunda, Representing the Corporate Client and the Proposed Rules of Professional Conduct, 6 Corporation L. Rev. 269 (1983).

Johnson) on various matters, while representing a party adverse to one of Johnson & Johnson's wholly-owned subsidiaries. The litigation involved a matter unrelated to the law firm's representation of Johnson & Johnson. The Second Circuit held that the district court did not abuse its discretion in granting the disqualification motion that the subsidiary filed because the operational relationship between the two companies was close and thus the representation reasonably could diminish "the level of confidence and trust in counsel" held by Johnson & Johnson. In determining whether the parent company and its subsidiary are effectively one entity for conflict-of-interest purposes, the court looked at (1) the entities' financial interdependence and (2) the operational commonality across multiple departments (e.g. accounting, audit, cash management, employee benefits, finance, human resources, information technology, insurance, payroll, and travel services and systems). The court emphasized that both entities relied on the same in-house legal department to handle their legal affairs. This counsel was involved in the underlying dispute since it first arose, including mediation efforts and obtaining outside counsel for the subsidiary. This combination of these factors called for disqualification of the firm.[5]

d.   ABA Formal Opinion 97–405 (Apr. 19, 1997) found it "fairly clear" that, under Model Rule 1.7(a)(1), a lawyer who currently represents a government entity in some kinds of work may not represent a private client against that entity, even in an unrelated matter. The question then became whether the lawyer for one government entity, say a school board, may represent a private client against a different government entity in the same jurisdiction, say the city government. The opinion said that the identity of a government client is "to some extent a matter of common sense and sensibility," and is a matter of functional considerations of how the government works. If the same city attorney represents both entities, for example, they would be more likely considered a single client for purposes of Rule 1.7(a)(1). Ideally, lawyer and governmental client will reach agreement on that issue at the outset of the representation of the government entity.[6] See Model Rule 1.13, Comment 9 (Government Agency).

e.   Association of the Bar of the City of New York, Formal Opinion 2008–2 (Sept. 2008), examined when in-house counsel may represent both a

---

5. See also, Discotrade Ltd. v. Wyeth–Ayerst Int'l Inc., 200 F.Supp.2d 355 (S.D.N.Y. 2002) (Dorsey & Whitney disqualified from representing plaintiff because it also represented the defendant's sister corporation in unrelated matters. All of the directors of the sister companies were the same, they shared the same president, computer system, and financial management, and the same in-house legal department served them all.) Cases such as these are discussed in Ronald D. Rotunda, Conflict Problems When Representing Members of Corporate Families, 72 Notre Dame L. Rev. 655 (1997).

6. A particularly difficult form of conflict can arise in the patent field where a law firm has two clients seeking related patents. Under the rules of the Patent and Trademark Office, 37 C.F.R. § 1.56, a lawyer for an applicant must disclose all "prior art" in the applicant's field. At the time of consideration of the applications, however, they are each confidential and Rule 1.6 would protect information about each. Although the court acknowledged the impossible situation the law firm found itself in, it ruled that failure to disclose the application of one client in the application of the other was "inequitable conduct" that rendered the issued patent invalid and unenforceable. Molins PLC v. Textron, Inc., 48 F.3d 1172 (Fed.Cir.1995).

parent and its corporate affiliates where the interests of the units are not identical, e.g, when the parent does not wholly own the subsidiary. Inside counsel must do the same kinds of conflicts checks that outside firms do, and sometimes handling the conflicts incorrectly may disqualify the whole legal department. Two ways that in-house counsel may deal with this issue are by seeking advance waivers or limiting the scope of representation.

3.   Should a lawyer for a business partnership or trade association be treated as the lawyer for each of the individual members?

a.   Most courts hold that it depends on the facts. Courts will ordinarily enforce a specific undertaking to represent the partnership and not to represent its individual members, whether the partnership (for purposes of state partnership law) is an "entity" or an "aggregate" of the individual partners. See, e.g., Greate Bay Hotel & Casino, Inc. v. Atlantic City, 624 A.2d 102 (N.J.Super.L.1993) (a lawyer for a business trust represents the trust as an "entity" and thus is not barred from suing a member of the trust in an unrelated matter); Responsible Citizens v. Superior Court (Askins), 20 Cal.Rptr.2d 756 (Cal.Ct.App.1993) (lawyer who represents partnership may sue individual partner in unrelated proceeding).

Fassihi v. Sommers, Schwartz, Silver, Schwarts & Tyler, P.C., 309 N.W.2d 645 (Mich. App. 1981), held that the lawyer for a professional medical corporation did not have an attorney-client relationship with the 50% physician shareholder. Thus, when the president-physician asks the lawyer to revoke the medical privileges of the vice president-physician so as to terminate the Professional Corporation, the lawyer may take such action. However, the court held that the lawyer may have had a fiduciary duty to inform the vice president-physician of the president's request.

b.   ABA Formal Opinion 91–361 (July 12, 1991) concludes that the Model Rules treat partnerships as entities and that Rule 1.13 governs their representation. One or more individual members of a partnership may separately retain the partnership lawyer, as provided in Rule 1.13(e), but representation of an individual partner is not automatic. The opinion concludes that lawyers should make clear to the individual partners at the outset of the representation whom the lawyers represent so as to avoid misunderstandings later. See Model Rule 1.7, Comment 34 and Model Rule 1.13, Comments 7 and 8.

c.   In Westinghouse Electric Corp. v. Kerr–McGee Corp., 580 F.2d 1311 (7th Cir.1978), cert. denied 439 U.S. 955 (1978), Kirkland & Ellis filed an antitrust action on behalf of its client, Westinghouse, against various corporations alleging price fixing violations in the uranium industry. Meanwhile the American Petroleum Institute (AmPI) retained Kirkland to oppose legislative proposals introduced in Congress to cause energy companies to divest uranium companies that they owned. On the same day that Kirkland's Chicago office filed the antitrust suit, Kirkland's Washington, D.C. office, representing AmPI, released a report that developed the opposite thesis and took an affirmative position on the subject of competition in the oil-uranium industry. AmPI was not a defendant in the antitrust suit, but three AmPI *members* were defendants.

Individual members of AmPI had given Kirkland & Ellis' Washington office confidential information on their uranium assets in order to aid the firm in opposing the threatened legislation. Moreover, the general counsel of AmPI and Kirkland & Ellis promised the members that this information would be held confidential. The Seventh Circuit held that AmPI members "each entertained a reasonable belief that it was submitting confidential information regarding its involvement in the uranium industry to a law firm which had solicited the information upon a representation that the firm was acting in the undivided interest of each company." 580 F.2d at 1321. Hence, it disqualified Kirkland.

Do you agree? Should *Westinghouse* be read to say any more than that when information is supplied on a promise of confidentiality, a court will see that the promise is honored? Could the lawyers have avoided this problem if they had not promised confidentiality and had clarified their role? Model Rule 1.13, Comment 10. Or, is the court saying that when a law firm is representing a trade association it is also representing each individual member of that association?

d. D.C. Bar Legal Ethics Opinion 305 (2001), concludes that representation of a trade association as an entity does not create an attorney-client relationship between the lawyer and members of the association. However, there are circumstances where representing a client adverse to a member of the association can create a conflict of interest. If the member reasonably believes that it is being individually represented by the lawyer, the member is, regardless of an express agreement, a *de facto* client of the lawyer. Factors to look include whether the member disclosed confidential information to the association's lawyer, whether the member has separate representation, whether the lawyer had ever previously represented the member individually, and whether the member relied on the lawyer's representation of his individual interest.

See also, ABA Formal Opinion 92–365 (July 6, 1992) (law firm that represents a trade association ordinarily may file an unrelated action against a member of the association with whom the lawyer has formed no attorney-client relationship unless the representation would impair the lawyer's representation of the association itself).

Do these opinions reject *Westinghouse* or apply it?

e. Jesse v. Danforth, 485 N.W.2d 63 (Wis. 1992), adopted a "retroactive entity" theory when a number of individuals hired a lawyer to form an entity. Under this theory, when the entity is formed, the court presumes that the only client of the lawyer is the entity and not the individuals. Hence, the court treated the lawyer's preincorporation involvement with the individuals as representation of the entity, not the various individuals. In *Jesse*, a law firm formed an entity for a group of 23 physicians. Later, a spouse of one of the physicians asked the law firm to represent her in a divorce. The physician moved to disqualify the law firm, but the court refused. The law firm had never had an attorney-client relationship with the individual physicians. Thus, no conflict arose and the law firm could represent the spouse.

Only a minority of jurisdictions apply this retroactive entity theory. Do you agree with the analysis in *Jesse*? Would your answer change if the law firm had met with the physicians and obtained significant and relevant confidential information from them in forming the entity?

C. FIRING A CURRENT CLIENT; THE HOT POTATO RULE

1. If you find that a conflict develops between two clients, may you avoid the problem by "firing" one of the clients and continuing to represent the other?

a. At the end of *Cinema 5*, supra, the Second Circuit noted that attorney Fleischmann offered to withdraw from representation of Cinerama in the Western District actions, but Cinerama refused and pressed forward on its disqualification motion. The court did not treat Cinerama's refusal to permit withdrawal as a waiver of its conflict claim. Why not? We know that at least part of the justification for disqualification is the breach of fiduciary duty of loyalty inherent in a conflict of interest. If Fleischmann were permitted to withdraw from further representation of Cinerama without penalty, would he be seeking to profit from his breach of loyalty?

b. Unified Sewerage Agency of Washington County, Oregon v. Jelco Inc., 646 F.2d 1339, 1345 n.4 (9th Cir.1981), recognized the problem of choosing to represent one client against another and noted that a challenged attorney may not convert a *current* client governed by Rule 1.7 into a *former* client governed by Rule 1.9 merely "by choosing when to cease to represent the disfavored client."

c. In Picker International, Inc. v. Varian Associates, Inc., 670 F.Supp. 1363 (N.D.Ohio 1987), aff'd, 869 F.2d 578 (Fed.Cir.1989), a large national law firm merged with a firm in another city, and when the client lists were compared, it turned out that the merging firms represented clients who were opponents in current litigation. The merged firm was suing *B* on behalf of *A* (a longtime client of the acquiring firm), while representing *B* (the acquired firm's client) on various other matters. The firm sought to withdraw from representation of *B*, and to continue to represent the longtime client of the big firm. The court held that the firm could not do that without consent of all affected clients. Failing consent, the new firm must withdraw from *all* representation of all parties in the case of *A v. B*. The court said: "A firm may not drop a client like a hot potato, especially if it is in order to keep a far more lucrative client." 670 F.Supp. at 1365. In the case law, this principle is often called the "hot potato" rule. The law of conflicts develops from a metaphor of the kitchen.

2. Should the "hot potato" rule recognize exceptions?

a. The law of ethics does not have the certainty of Euclidian geometry, and courts do not always apply the hot potato rule inflexibly. In Pennwalt Corp. v. Plough, Inc., 85 F.R.D. 264 (D.Del.1980), the law firm represented Pennwalt for decades. In 1978, the firm began to defend Scholl against antitrust charges. In April 1979, Schering–Plough acquired Scholl as a wholly owned subsidiary. Because Plough was already a wholly owned subsidiary of Schering–Plough, Scholl and Plough became sister corporations. In May 1979, the law firm filed suit against Plough on behalf of its longtime client Pennwalt. Upon learning a week or two later that it represented Scholl in one case and simultaneously represented Pennwalt against Scholl's "sister," the firm sought to withdraw from representing Scholl. After the court granted that motion, Plough moved to disqualify the firm from the case against Plough. The court agreed that counsel may not eliminate a conflict "merely by choosing to represent the more favored client and withdrawing its representation of the other." However, in this case the firm's conflict was inadvertent: the merger activities of the client created the problem. "Scholl is a corporate entity distinct from Plough and Schering–Plough," and it was highly unlikely that as of the date of the law firm's representation there was any misuse of confidential information or adverse effect on its exercise of independent judgment. Thus, the court did not mandate disqualification. See Rule 1.7, Comment 5, which takes this case into account.

b. In Gould, Inc. v. Mitsui Mining & Smelting Co., 738 F.Supp. 1121 (N.D.Ohio 1990), the Jones Day law firm was representing Gould in suing various defendants who allegedly misappropriated Gould trade secrets. One of these defendants was Pechiney. In 1989, Pechiney acquired IG Technologies (IGT), a company that Jones Day represented in an unrelated matter. Thus, Jones Day found itself in a conflict between Gould and IGT's parent. In response to a motion to disqualify Jones Day from representing Gould against Pechiney, the court reasoned that, because of the "explosion of merger activity by corporations during the past fifteen years" it is appropriate to adopt a "less mechanical approach" and "balanc[e] the various interests." In this case, there was "no demonstration that Pechiney has been prejudiced by the law firm's representation of Gould." Further, disqualification would cost Gould a great deal of time and money, and significantly delay progress in this case. Moreover, "the conflict was created by Pechiney's acquisition of IGT several years after the instant case was commenced, not by an affirmative act of Jones Day." However, the court held, the conflict "must not endure." Hence, the law firm must discontinue its representation of either Gould or IGT, and erect a "screen" around the lawyers who had worked for the party that the firm dropped.[7]

c. In Pioneer–Standard Electronics, Inc. v. Cap Gemini America, Inc., 2002 WL 553460 (N.D.Ohio 2002), plaintiff Pioneer–Standard, moved to disqualify defendant's counsel, Shearman & Sterling, arguing that the firm currently represented it. Shearman & Sterling's relationship with Pioneer–Standard began when Shearman merged with a German firm that had been handling Pioneer–Standard regulatory matters before the European Commission. After the merger, Shearman & Sterling billed approximately ten hours to Pioneer–Standard on those matters, but after Pioneer–Standard refused to waive the conflict, Shearman & Sterling withdrew from the European representation. Although the court found that Pioneer–Standard was a current client of Shearman & Sterling, it refused to disqualify. It

---

7. You will see more about "screening" in Problems 15 & 16, *infra.*

acknowledged the hot potato rule but found that there should be no disqualification if the matters "were unrelated and posed no likelihood of passing confidential information." The European regulatory matters did not generate confidential information that could be used against Pioneer–Standard in this case; there was no other prejudice to Pioneer–Standard from the continued representation; the foreign matter was limited to registering a commercial transaction of plaintiff; it consumed few hours of counsel's time; and the case was wholly unrelated to the instant litigation.

The court refused to apply the hot potato rule but offered no bright-line test to replace it. Instead, it said the court would not disqualify a law firm "if the attorney can show that he can represent adverse clients concurrently with equal vigor, without conflict of loyalties and without using confidential information to the detriment of either client." Does the case simply acknowledge that a rule of reason is appropriate in a world of complex legal relationships? Or, does a vague rule give a competitive advantage to the least ethical firms—the ones most willing to test the limits of ethical conduct?

3. What about waivers of possible future conflicts? Should clients be able to agree at the outset of the representation that, if a conflict later arises, the lawyer may represent one of the clients against the other? Should law firms make an advance waiver of conflicts part of the boilerplate in their retainer agreements?

a. Restatement (Third) The Law Governing Lawyers § 122, Comment *d*, says:

> "A client's open-ended agreement to consent to all conflicts normally should be ineffective unless the client possesses sophistication in the matter in question and has had the opportunity to receive independent legal advice about the consent. * * *

> "On the other hand, particularly in a continuing client-lawyer relationship in which the lawyer is expected to act on behalf of the client without a new engagement for each matter, the gains to both lawyer and client from a system of advance consent to defined future conflicts might be substantial. A client might, for example, give informed consent in advance to types of conflicts that are familiar to the client. Such an agreement could effectively protect the client's interest while assuring that the lawyer did not undertake a potentially disqualifying representation."

b. General Cigar Holdings, Inc. v. Altadis, S.A., 144 F.Supp.2d 1334 (S.D.Fla.2001), honored a broad advance waiver. Latham & Watkins, counsel to General Cigar in an antitrust suit against Altadis, continued to represent General Cigar, Altadis, and other tobacco companies in an action to challenge state advertising restrictions in Massachusetts. When the firm accepted the Massachusetts engagement, it secured a signed waiver from each client waiving any objection to current or future representation of one against the other in some other matter. None of the lawyers handling the antitrust suit had worked on the Massachusetts case, nor did firm members have access to other confidential information about Altadis. The court concluded that Altadis' advance consent was valid. It was made by informed and sophisticated parties who knew of the firm's standing relationship with General Cigar, even though they did not know of the planned antitrust litigation. The court also found that the antitrust/trademark claims in this suit were not substantially related to the free speech/advertising claims in the other case. The court concluded that representation of the plaintiff in this case would not impair the firm's substantive representation of Altadis in any other matter.

c.   Worldspan, L.P. v. Sabre Group Holdings, Inc., 5 F.Supp.2d 1356 (N.D.Ga.1998), however, was less friendly to advance waivers. The law firm was counsel to Worldspan in state tax matters in Georgia and Tennessee. In this case, it agreed to represent the defendants in an unrelated suit that Worldspan had filed. The firm relied on its standard engagement letter that Worldspan signed six years earlier on the advice of experienced, independent counsel. The letter stated that "we will not be precluded from representing clients who may have interests adverse to Worldspan" that are not substantially related and do not involve the use of adverse information. The court held that this six-year-old waiver did not constitute an informed prospective consent to the current representation; its language was not specific enough to cover representing an adverse party in a lawsuit filed by Worldspan, even where the letter expressly named that adverse party as an existing client of the law firm. The court also found the tax work was more closely related to the current litigation than the law firm had believed.

d.   ABA Formal Opinion 05–436 (May 11, 2005) advises that general and open-ended prospective consent is more likely to be valid when the client is an experienced user of legal services, "particularly if, for example, the client is independently represented by other counsel in giving consent and the consent is limited to future conflicts unrelated to the subject of the representation." The intent of the 2002 amendments to Rule 1.7 is to permit "a lawyer to obtain effective informed consent to a wider range of future conflicts than would have been possible under the Model Rules prior to their amendment." This opinion specifically withdrew (i.e., overruled) Formal Opinion 93–372 (Apr. 16, 1993) (Waiver of Future Conflicts of Interest). Now, there is a new Comment 22, which specifically authorizes prospective consents to future conflicts. The term "waiver" in Comment 22, means "the same thing as the term 'informed consent,' as used in Rule 1.7 and elsewhere in the Comments."

This opinion concludes that if a conflict is not consentable at all, it is not subject to advance consent. Further, the client's consent must be confirmed in writing, Rule 1.7(b)(4). Also, "a client's informed consent to a future conflict, without more, does not constitute the client's informed consent to the disclosure or use of the client's confidential information against the client." Finally, the advance consent does not eliminate the lawyer's need to secure informed consent from the client the lawyer wants to represent in the later matter.

See also, D.C. Bar Legal Ethics Opinion 309 (2001); Association of the Bar of the City of New York, Committee on Professional and Judicial Ethics, Formal Op. 2006–1 (Feb. 17, 2006) (advance waivers permissible where given by sophisticated clients who have advice of counsel and where no confidential information of one client will be used to advantage another).

D.   THE PROBLEM OF POSITIONAL CONFLICTS

1.   What duty of loyalty, if any, do you have not to take a legal position on prepayment penalties that is inconsistent with the interest of a regular client like the First National Bank? Is there a technical conflict of interest that would obligate you not to take this case?

a.   Should a lawyer be permitted to assert a legal position in one case that—if accepted by the court—may conflict with the legal position of another client in a different case that another lawyer in the same firm advances? We know that lawyers often take inconsistent legal positions in the *same* case. A lawyer for an alleged debtor pleads, for example, "My client did not borrow the money (it was a gift), but even if he did borrow it, he already has repaid the debt." Is the problem of inconsistency *between* cases different?

b.   Does the permissibility of positional conflicts depend on whether interpretations of fact or of law are involved? Might you represent Client Y in one case arguing that facts justify a finding of negligence, but defend Client Z in another case on identical facts saying that the conduct showed due care? Should the propriety of the conduct be different if, as in this problem, you plan to try to change a controlling legal standard?

2.   Should it matter whether your inconsistent positions are taken before the same court? What if your law firm takes inconsistent positions in different forums?

a.   Before the 2002 amendments, Model Rule 1.7, Comment 9, said:

"[I]t is ordinarily not improper to assert such [inconsistent] positions in cases pending in different trial courts, but it may be improper to do so in cases pending at the same time in an appellate court."

Do you agree that the trial-appellate and different appellate court distinctions are useful ways to decide when a positional conflict is proper or improper?

b.   ABA Formal Opinion 93–377 (Oct. 16, 1993) cast doubt on the trial-appellate court distinction. It analyzed the so-called "positional conflicts" issue as follows:

"[I]f the two matters are being litigated in the same jurisdiction, and there is a substantial risk that the law firm's representation of one client will create a legal precedent, even if not binding, which is likely materially to undercut the legal position being urged on behalf of the other client, the lawyer should either refuse to accept the second representation or (if otherwise permissible) withdraw from the first, unless both clients consent after full disclosure of the potential ramifications of the lawyer continuing to handle both matters. * * *

"[Even if the matters are being litigated in different jurisdictions,] if the lawyer concludes that the issue is of such importance and that its determination in one case is likely to have a significant impact on its determination in the second case, thus impairing the lawyer's effectiveness—or if the lawyer concludes that, because of the dual representation, there will be an inclination by the firm either to 'soft pedal' the issue or to alter the firm's arguments on behalf of one or both clients, thus again impairing the lawyer's effectiveness—the lawyer should not accept the second representation."

c. Model Rule 1.7, Comment 24, takes a different approach to positional conflicts. The Comment suggests looking at various factors, such as whether the issue is procedural or substantive, where the cases are pending, the clients' "reasonable expectations," the "temporal relationship between the matters," and the importance of the issue to the short-and long-term interests of the clients. It posits two examples: First, advocating Client A's position that "*might* create precedent adverse to the interests" of Client B whom the lawyer represents in an unrelated matter is not a conflict. Second, if the lawyer has successfully advanced Client A's position, and the resulting decision "*will create* a precedent *likely* to seriously weaken the position" taken on behalf of Client B, the Comment advises that this does present a conflict of interest. Is this clear?

d. Does Model Rule 1.7 provide good guidance to lawyers trying to conduct a complex practice in a manner consistent with appropriate professional standards? Is it too vague? Association of the Bar of the City of New York Committee on Professional and Judicial Ethics, Formal Opinion 2003–03 discussed how modern firms should run conflicts checks. Firms must keep written or electronic records and maintain them in a form that allows them to be quickly and accurately searched. New York records must go back at least to 1996 when the rule first required these records. They must include client names, adverse party names, and a brief description of each engagement, and each office must consult those records before undertaking any new matter. Firms need not keep detailed lists of all corporate family relationships except for those they regularly represent. Would even such records let a law firm check for positional conflicts?

3. Would Model Rule 6.3 impose different obligations if you were a member of a legal service organization's board of directors that wanted to take a position contrary to one of your paying clients?

a. When the president appointed John Erlenborn, a former member of Congress, to the board of the Legal Services Corporation (LSC), he was also a partner in a major law firm that represented growers in disputes over farm workers' conditions; the farm workers were often represented by LSC-funded lawyers. The American Farm Bureau Federation, a private lobbying group representing agricultural interests, began a campaign to persuade the firm's agricultural clients (the Farm Bureau was not one of the firm's clients) to object to what the Farm Bureau characterized as Erlenborn's conflict of interest, i.e., he took positions as an LSC board member that the Farm Bureau claimed were harmful to farm interests.

Erlenborn offered to recuse himself from any decisions of the LSC board that directly involved reform legislation that the Farm Bureau supported, or that involved agricultural activities that could have an impact on his firm's clients, but the Farm Bureau's objections (including its objection to Erlenborn's proposed congressional testimony on the reform legislation) continued until Erlenborn resigned from the LSC board. The ABA president-elect said that there was no conflict of interest that required Erlenborn's resignation.[8] Do you agree? Did the Rules require Erlenborn to resign from the LSC board, or was he simply bending over backwards to please some firm clients?

b.   Suppose that the legal services agency agrees with your bank client and opposes regulations prohibiting prepayment penalties because it believes such regulations will raise the cost of credit to unacceptable levels. May you lobby on the agency's behalf against the regulatory proposals? Must you inform the agency that you also represent the First National Bank who will be pleased by the agency's position? Look at Model Rule 6.4.

c.   Assume that you fully inform the legal services agency and the bank of your representation of each. Does either Rule 3.9 or Rule 6.4 require you to voluntarily disclose to the regulatory body that in appearing on behalf of the legal services agency you also further the interests of the First National Bank?

4.   Even if the ethics rules allow you to represent the consumer against the bank, are there other problems you might face?

a.   Could your banking client force you out of the case indirectly? Could it insist that, although it is not now a party, it wants you to file an amicus brief on its behalf? If you agreed and withdrew from representing your neighbor, could your neighbor force you to withdraw from the case altogether? Of course you could ask your regular client, the First National Bank, to relieve you of any further obligations to represent it in paying matters, but that would make your pro bono activities on behalf of your neighbor a lot more costly.

b.   If you want to take this case and in fact do so, must you warn your neighbor that one of your best clients is a bank that is opposed to your attacking the prepayment penalty? Even if no technical conflict of interest exists, would the neighbor consider this information relevant? Remember that your consumer-client is not a repeat litigator, but the bank is.[9] In

8. Anne Kornhauser, Sowing Client Discord, Reaping Political Fallout, 13 Legal Times of Washington 1, 15–16 (June 25, 1990).

9. For further analysis, see John S. Dzienkowski, Positional Conflicts of Interest, 71 Texas L. Rev. 457 (1993).

other words, the banks constantly face challenges to prepayment penalties and the issue may be worth millions of dollars to them over a twenty year time period. Should that affect your answer.

c. Now, assure that the bank belongs to an industry banking group that has confidential guidelines on how to oppose challenges to the prepayment penalties. If you had access to those guidelines it would help you craft the neighbor's attack on prepayment penalties because you would know the bank's "playbook," i.e., its general approach to settlement, litigation strategy, strengths, weaknesses, and attitudes. Should you be disqualified if you have access to that information even if you do not in fact look at it?

PROBLEM 11

CONFLICTS OF INTEREST IN CRIMINAL LITIGATION

Criminal cases present some of the most interesting conflicts of interest questions. We require that a client's decision to waive a conflict be informed and unconstrained, yet criminal defendants often make that decision in a setting where they view their consent to common representation as a sign of loyalty to fellow defendants or as an unwillingness to make a deal with prosecutors. In most cases, we assume there is little public stake in a decision whether to consent to a conflict of interest. In criminal cases, however, courts have a duty to protect defendants' constitutional right to a fair trial. Criminal cases can sometimes make or break the careers of prosecutors and defense counsel. They can create personal incentives for those lawyers to represent their clients differently than they might in another setting. All those issues are presented in this problem.

FACTS

Barbara Bentley regularly represents Bitter Creek, Inc., the defendant in a case charging price fixing, a criminal violation of the federal antitrust laws. Chuck Carson, manager of the widget division at Bitter Creek, is accused of conspiring with Mary Morton, his counterpart at Widgetech, Inc., a major competitor. In Bentley's first interview with Carson, Carson told Bentley he was unrepresented and asked her to represent him. Carson told Bentley that Mary Morton also needed a lawyer and thought it would be best if Bentley would represent her as well. Widgetech, Inc., has in-house counsel and Bentley already has been meeting with him to share information and develop a joint defense.

Bentley confirmed Morton's interest in retaining her and she has now entered an appearance on behalf of Bitter Creek, Carson and Morton. The United States attorney is interested in demonstrating his commitment to consumers because he plans to run for governor next year. Thus, he is determined to obtain convictions, although he does not care who takes the fall. He proposes to Bentley that she get Carson and Morton to plead guilty to charges for which he will recommend no jail time. In exchange, he will drop the felony charge against Bitter Creek. Because this will reduce the chance of subsequent treble damage actions against the corporation, Bentley finds the proposal attractive. She recommends that Carson and Morton accept it, accurately telling them that if they were found guilty after a trial, their sentences could be more severe.

Bentley sees herself as an extraordinary lawyer, and she plans to write an article about her handling of the Bitter Creek case under the title, "There's Nothing I Won't Do to See That at Least One of My Clients Goes Free."

QUESTIONS

A.   LIMITS ON ONE LAWYER'S REPRESENTING CO-DEFENDANTS IN A CRIMINAL CASE

1.   Why should courts warn criminal defendants about possible conflicts of interest?

a.   For federal criminal cases like the one in this problem, Rule 44(c), Federal Rules of Criminal Procedure provides:

"(c) JOINT REPRESENTATION. Whenever two or more defendants have been jointly charged pursuant to Rule 8(b) or have been joined for trial pursuant to Rule 13, and are represented by the same retained or assigned counsel or by retained or assigned counsel who are associated in the practice of law, the court shall promptly inquire with respect to such joint representation and shall personally advise each defendant of his right to the effective assistance of counsel, including separate representation. Unless it appears that there is good cause to believe no conflict of interest is likely to arise, the court shall take such measures as may be appropriate to protect each defendant's right to counsel."

b.   Holloway v. Arkansas, 435 U.S. 475 (1978), raised the question of a lawyer's conflicts of interest to a constitutional dimension. It said that a state criminal conviction must be reversed if a trial judge requires joint representation in a criminal case after a defendant's timely objection. The joint representation is presumed prejudicial. "Joint representation of conflicting interests is suspect because of what it tends to prevent the attorney from doing." 435 U.S. at 489–90.

c.   *Holloway* illustrated some of the problems inherent in joint representation. In that case, the conflict may have precluded defense counsel "from exploring possible plea negotiations and the possibility of an agreement to testify for the prosecution, provided a lesser charge or a favorable sentencing recommendation would be acceptable. Generally speaking, a conflict may also prevent an attorney from challenging the admission of evidence prejudicial to one client but perhaps favorable to another, or from arguing at the sentencing hearing the relative involvement and culpability of his clients in order to minimize the culpability of one by emphasizing that of another." 435 U.S. at 490.

2.   How does the concern about conflicts relate to the constitutional guarantee of effective assistance of counsel?

a.   The constitutional concern about lawyer conflicts of interest is linked directly to the Sixth Amendment concern for the effective assistance of counsel. *Holloway* was so based, and it, in turn, must be read in light of later cases. However, a criminal defendant has a constitutional right to represent himself in a state or federal trial when he voluntarily and intelligently elects to do so. Faretta v. California, 422 U.S. 806 (1975). The government may not force a lawyer on a competent defendant even if there is no conflict.

b.   Cuyler v. Sullivan, 446 U.S. 335 (1980), dealt with the situation in which no party lodges an objection to multiple representation and later the defendant seeks to overturn the conviction based on a possible conflict. If there is no objection and absent special circumstances, the trial court may assume that multiple representations do not result in a conflict or that the clients knowingly accept such risk of a conflict. However, if the court knows or reasonably should know that a particular conflict of interest exists, it must initiate an inquiry into the propriety of multiple representation. If the court does not know of the conflict, the lack of an inquiry is not constitutionally significant. In order to establish a Sixth Amendment violation based on multiple representation when the defendant did not object at trial, it is not enough for the defendant to show a "possibility of a conflict of interest arising from multiple representation;" instead, the defendant must prove there was an "actual conflict of interest that adversely affected" the lawyer's performance.

c.   The leading case dealing with claims of ineffective assistance of counsel in general is Strickland v. Washington, 466 U.S. 668 (1984). *Strickland* created a high hurdle for the criminal defendant. To justify a reversal, the defendant must show that (1) the lawyer's acts or omissions were "outside the wide range of professionally competent assistance," 466 U.S. at 690, and (2) the lawyer's "deficient performance prejudiced the defense." In other words, the lawyer made errors "so serious as to deprive the defendant of a fair trial, a trial whose result is reliable." Defendant must do more than "show that the errors had some conceivable effect on the outcome of the proceedings." 466 U.S. at 693.

d.   *Strickland* then explained why conflicts of interest are so bad:

"In *Cuyler v. Sullivan*, the Court held that prejudice is presumed when counsel is burdened by an actual conflict of interest. In those circumstances, counsel breaches the duty of loyalty, perhaps the most basic of counsel's duties. Moreover, it is difficult to measure the precise effect on the defense of representation corrupted by conflicting interests. Given the obligation of counsel to avoid conflicts of interest and the ability of trial courts to make early inquiry in certain situations likely to give rise to conflicts, it is reasonable for the criminal justice system to maintain a fairly rigid rule of presumed prejudice for conflicts of interest. Even so, * * * [p]rejudice is presumed only if the defendant demonstrates that counsel 'actively represented conflicting interests' and that 'an actual conflict of interest adversely affected his lawyer's performance.' " 466 U.S. at 692.

e.   In Burger v. Kemp, 483 U.S. 776 (1987), one lawyer represented one defendant while the lawyer's partner represented the co-defendant in a separate proceeding. After conviction, the first defendant complained of a conflict of interest. The Court (5 to 4) explained that *Holloway* rejected a per se approach and required the defendant to show that any conflict adversely effected the lawyer's performance. The two partners in *Burger* did talk about trial strategy, but there were separate trials, reducing any incentive of one lawyer to change tactics for the benefit of the other client. There was no argument that any conflict prevented counsel from negotiating a plea bargain because the prosecutor refused to bargain. If there was any conflict of interest because one defense lawyer was a partner with the lawyer representing his client's coindictee, that did not affect attorney's advocacy. Any error was harmless. There was no support in the record for the defendant's argument that a truly independent attorney would have negotiated a plea agreement

f.   In Mickens v. Taylor, 535 U.S. 162 (2002), after Mickens was sentenced to death for murder, he discovered that his court-appointed attorney had been representing the victim on other criminal charges at the time the victim was murdered. His lawyer did not disclose his other representation to the defendant. The trial court judge, who had appointed the lawyer in both instances, apparently failed to realize what had happened and did not inquire whether the situation presented a conflict of interest. Following *Cuyler*, the Supreme Court upheld Mickens' conviction and sentence.

Writing for the five-person majority, Justice Scalia emphasized that *Cuyler* only presumes prejudice to the defendant if the conflict has an effect on the representation. Justice Kennedy, concurring, said the particular facts of the case indicated that Mickens' attorney did not believe he had a continuing duty to his former client, the murder victim, and the lawyer in question did not pursue an unreasonable trial strategy. The four dissenters disputed that defense counsel would have handled the case the same without this conflict. Justice Stevens said Mickens' attorney passed up several opportunities to present negative character evidence about the victim. Justice Souter read *Cuyler* and *Holloway* to impose a duty to inquire into a possible conflict of interest in such cases, and argued that the trial judge had a duty to inquire in this case, because the same judge appointed counsel for both killer and victim.[1]

United States v. Stevens, 978 F.2d 565 (10th Cir. 1992), did not find per se ineffective assistance when the defendant's appointed lawyer was disbarred a week before trial, but neither the defendant, nor the lawyer, nor the court, nor the government knew that before the trial. In that case, the lawyer at least fulfilled the substantive requirements for admission to the bar. United States v. Mouzin, 785 F.2d 682, 696–98 (9th Cir.), cert. denied, 479 U.S. 985 (1986), also held that there is no per se ineffective assistance of counsel because the defense lawyer was disbarred during trial, for conduct not related to the case. The trial judge did not commit error by allowing the lawyer to continue representation to end of case. Even the failure of trial judge to inform defendant of his lawyer's disbarment during trial did not render the defendant's conviction invalid, where the lawyer retained the ability to render effective assistance of counsel at trial.[2]

3. Was Bentley's independent judgment on behalf of each client likely to have been compromised in this case?

a. Notice that the Federal Rules of Criminal Procedure require the court to "take such measures as may be appropriate to protect each defendant's right to counsel." What kind of inquiry should the judge conduct to assure the effective assistance of counsel for Carson and Morton?

b. In Lettley v. State, 746 A.2d 392 (Md.2000), a client told trial counsel in a murder case that he and not the current defendant committed the crime. The lawyer asked to withdraw, reasoning that she could neither reveal this confession nor effectively represent the current client without using the information, such as by seeking to show that the other person looked like the defendant. The trial judge refused to let the lawyer withdraw because no new lawyer would have known the information and so would not have provided better representation. The Maryland Court of Appeals reversed because of divided loyalties. Defense counsel would feel constrained in such things as cross-examination; the conflict was serious enough to constitute ineffective assistance of counsel requiring that the defendant receive a new trial.

c. In Thomas v. State, 551 S.E.2d 254 (S.C.2001), a lawyer represented both petitioner and her husband after both were arrested and indicted for drug trafficking. Each client waived the possible conflict of interest. The prosecutor then offered a plea bargain to the couple's attorney that would allow husband and wife to each accept responsibility for half of the drugs seized and serve a reduced jail sentence, or one spouse to accept responsibility for all of the drugs and serve the 25–year statutory minimum

---

1. See also, State ex rel. S.G., 791 A.2d 285 (N.J.Super.Ct.,App.Div.2002) (refusing to disqualify retained defense counsel in a murder trial who previously represented the victim in unrelated incidents).

2. In contrast, United States v. Bergman, 599 F.3d 1142 (10th Cir. 2010), in- volved a purported lawyer (in reality an ex- convict who had never taken the bar, never attended law school, and never graduated from college) who represented the criminal defendant. In those circumstances, there was per se ineffective assistance of counsel be- cause there was no trained counsel at all.

sentence. The attorney advised both clients to accept some responsibility in order to obtain the lesser sentence, but the wife took responsibility for the entire amount. There was no direct appeal, but the court granted the wife post-conviction relief on the grounds that she did not have effective assistance of counsel. Once the state offered the plea agreement, the initial conflicts waiver was insufficient to let the lawyer represent both clients, because any action in either spouse's best interest would unavoidably harm the other. This unusual plea bargain was unexpected, and neither client knowingly waived a conflict of the type they actually faced.

d.   United States v. Schwarz, 283 F.3d 76 (2d Cir.2002), involved a police officer (Schwarz) convicted of brutally assaulting Abner Louima while he was in police custody. The Policeman's Benevolent Association (PBA) retained a lawyer named Worth to represent Schwarz at trial. The district court sentenced Schwarz to over 15 years in prison for the crime. Before the trial, the PBA retained Worth's firm at $5 million per year to represent its members in all disciplinary and criminal proceedings. Louima also filed a civil suit against the PBA. The government objected to Worth representing Schwarz while Worth's firm represented co-defendants as well as the PBA itself. After the trial court gave Schwarz careful and specific warnings of the risks of such multiple representation, Schwarz waived the conflict and the trial went ahead. The Second Circuit reversed Schwarz's conviction, finding that the client could not waive this conflict. For example, a lawyer with no loyalties to PBA might have blamed the assault on one of the other officers, but that strategy would have hurt the civil case where the lawyer's law firm was representing the PBA. That also may have explained the lawyer's failure to present exculpatory evidence that could have changed the outcome at trial.[3] What the case makes abundantly clear is that a trial judge cannot take a conflict waiver as the last word on who will represent a criminal defendant.

e.   In United States v. Infante, 404 F.3d 376 (5th Cir.2005), Infante was convicted of three drug-related offenses. Foster, Infante's attorney, recently represented two witnesses who actually testified against Infante. Although Foster denied learning confidential information about Infante's case from the other two clients, the facts of the cases were remarkably similar. All three cases occurred within a short period of time, and Foster had not clearly terminated his representation of the witnesses. In fact, Foster had announced his intent to seek sentencing relief for the two witnesses in exchange for their testimony *against* Infante. The Fifth Circuit vacated Infante's conviction and remanded his ineffective assistance claim to determine whether Foster's conflict of interest actually had an adverse affect on his performance.

4.   Should it be a conflict of interest for a lawyer to defend a client when the lawyer is personally and simultaneously facing charges filed by the same prosecutor?

3. See also, United States v. Newell, 315 F.3d 510 (5th Cir.2002) (attorney pitted one client against the other by defending Raley at Newell's expense; district court failed to take action when the actual conflict became clear at trial; conviction reversed because there was no knowing and intelligent waiver of right to a conflict-free trial).

a.   In Government of Virgin Islands v. Zepp, 748 F.2d 125 (3d Cir. 1984), defense counsel not only faced potential criminal liability on the same charges for which defendant was tried; he was also a potential prosecution witness. The defendant was convicted for possession of cocaine and destruction of evidence. Defense counsel, in order to avoid being called as a witness and thereby being disqualified, stipulated that he (who was alone with the defendant in her house at a time when the toilet was heard to flush several times) did *not* personally flush any toilets. Later, the police discovered the cocaine in the house's septic tank, giving rise to the client's prosecution. The Third Circuit reversed the conviction and concluded: "Trial counsel's interest in testifying [via the stipulation] on his own behalf impaired the exercise of independent professional judgment on behalf of the client," because "[p]lastic bags of cocaine do not fall off of trees into septic tanks."

b.   In Campbell v. Rice, 265 F.3d 878 (9th Cir.2001), the jury convicted appellant on several counts of burglary. He sought habeas corpus and argued that his lawyer had an impermissible conflict because the same office that was prosecuting the lawyer on drug charges also was prosecuting the appellant. The prosecutor had brought the situation to the attention of the trial judge, and the judge allowed the trial to continue. The Ninth Circuit ruled that habeas relief was appropriate. The lawyer might have felt pressure to refrain from antagonizing the prosecutor (e.g., by filing a motion alleging prosecutorial misconduct), even when it might be in the best interest of her client to do so. Furthermore, the trial court's inquiry into the conflict was "insufficiently searching and specific." The trial court neither asked the attorney whether she could effectively continue the representation, nor sufficiently determined that appellant understood and waived the conflict.

c.   In United States v. Fulton, 5 F.3d 605 (2d Cir.1993), a prosecution for importing heroin, one lawyer represented four co-defendants. One of the defendants told the DEA that the lawyer was himself personally involved in the heroin sales. The United States Attorney informed the court, and the Second Circuit held that where a defense lawyer is accused of being involved in the same or closely related criminal conduct, the conflict is per se unwaivable. Continued representation constitutes ineffective assistance of counsel.

d.   Rubin v. Gee, 292 F.3d 396 (4th Cir.2002), also involved conduct that justified habeas corpus relief. Rubin was convicted of first degree murder. When she called her lawyers after the crime, they admitted to a hospital under a false name and then helped her escape detection while she withdrew $105,000 to pay their fee. The lawyers' desire to collect their fee, "caused them to counsel Rubin to act in an unnecessarily suspicious fashion when they caused her to delay her surrender to the police for 24 hours." They also hid the evidence of the crime at their law office and only then turned the client over to the police. Other lawyers acted for Rubin at trial, but the original lawyers continued to represent her. The Fourth Circuit found this conduct rendered the lawyers "almost accessories after the fact," and their efforts to help Rubin escape detection allowed the prosecutors to refute her claim of self-defense. The lawyers' desire to collect a large fee undercut their efforts to defend their client, the court found. They did not even testify at trial to help Rubin explain why her conduct was not inconsistent with a plea of self-defense. This conflict denied Rubin effective assistance of counsel. The dissent agreed that the lawyers acted badly but argued that they were not the counsel at trial whose conduct is the test of ineffectiveness.

B.   THE PUBLIC INTEREST IN OBJECTING TO MULTIPLE REPRESENTATION

1.   Should a court ever grant a prosecution motion to require that defendants have separate counsel?

a.   Deputy Assistant Attorney General Joe Sims announced that the Department of Justice Antitrust Division would aggressively seek to stop multiple representation by seeking relief from the court having supervisory power over the grand jury. "[T]hese conflicts—where both the corporation and potentially culpable employees are represented by a single counsel—are so inherently serious that there should be a presumption against such multiple representation during a criminal investigation." He continued:

> "[T]he target corporation all too often sees its best interest served by keeping witnesses in 'friendly' hands and limiting the cooperation of its employees. Such an attitude will inevitably lead to bad advice for the individual if he does not have independent counsel. [M]erely informing the employee of the existence of the potential conflict and seeking a waiver from him [does not] satisfactorily deal with this problem. For example, it is frequently in the interest of one or more low level employees in a corporation to seek immunity by offering evidence against higher level employees or the corporation itself. In this situation, even if there has been a waiver, it is impossible for a single lawyer to give each of his clients effective legal representation."[4]

b.   Do you agree with Mr. Sims? What if it is in fact in the best interests of all defendants to keep each other in "friendly" hands rather than risk the chance that one of the parties will plead guilty and implicate the others? Do public policy and professional responsibility forbid, or require, the attorney to seek knowing waivers of the conflicts and participate in a "we're all in this together" arrangement? See ABA Standards Relating to the Defense Function, § 4–3.5(c), in the Standards Supplement, advising that, except for preliminary matters such as applications for bail, the "potential for conflict of interest in representing multiple defendants is so grave" that lawyers should not do it. And, if they do, they should secure informed consent on the record after questioning by the judge.

4. Bureau of National Affairs, Antitrust & Trade Reg.Rptr., No. 819, June 23, 1977,   at p. A–13.

c.   Wheat v. United States, 486 U.S. 153 (1988), held (5 to 4) that the district court was within its discretion in rejecting defendant's waiver of his right to conflict-free counsel and in refusing to permit defendant's proposed substitution of attorneys. Two days before trial, defendant asked to be represented by the lawyer who was representing others charged in a series of cases against an alleged drug conspiracy. The government objected on the grounds that defendants in some cases would be witnesses in others. If the same lawyer represented them all, he would be restricted in his cross-examination of his clients when they were witnesses and would lay the predicate for a later claim of ineffective assistance of counsel.[5]

The Court upheld the district court's power to limit the joint represen-tation: "Federal courts have an independent interest in ensuring that criminal trials are conducted within the ethical standards of the profession and that legal proceedings appear fair to all who observe them. Both the American Bar Association's Model Code of Professional Responsibility and its Model Rules of Professional Conduct * * * impose limitations on multiple representation of clients * * *. DR 5–105(C); Rule 1.7. * * * Not only the interest of a criminal defendant but the institutional interest in the rendition of just verdicts in criminal cases may be jeopardized by unregulated multiple representation. * * * The District Court must recog-nize a presumption in favor of petitioner's counsel of choice, but that presumption may be overcome not only by a demonstration of actual conflict but by a showing of a serious potential for conflict." 486 U.S. at 160. The trial judges have substantial latitude in refusing waivers of conflicts because, even if the defendant waives any conflicts, experience shows that the defendant will later still claim ineffective assistance of counsel.

2.   Does the government have the power to disqualify counsel to "protect the interest" of the accused and make it easier for the government to get a conviction? What should be the standard for overriding the defendant's choice of counsel?

a.   United States v. Locascio, 6 F.3d 924 (2d Cir.1993), cert. denied, 511 U.S. 1070 (1994), involved the prosecution of alleged mob boss John Gotti. Bruce Cutler had very effectively represented Gotti in previous criminal trials. The government did not want him to do so again. This time, the Government caught him on tapes of conversations with Gotti. The government intended to introduce these tapes at trial to show the planning of illegal acts. Thus, even if Cutler would not testify, he was in a position analogous to an "unsworn witness" who would be forced to defend his own conduct before the jury. Further, Cutler had once represented a Gotti associate, Michael Coiro, who would be government witness. Therefore, Cutler would be impaired in cross-examining Coiro. Over Gotti's objection,

---

5.   See also, Burden v. Zant, 510 U.S. 132 (1994) (remanding for factual findings to see if pretrial counsel's representation of a prosecution witness who had been granted immunity created an actual conflict affecting the result). On remand, the court held that an actual conflict affected counsel's perform-ance entitling defendant to habeas relief. 24 F.3d 1298 (11th Cir. 1994).

the court intervened to "protect" Gotti from Mr. Cutler's conflicts. The Second Circuit affirmed. Do you suppose the late Mr. Gotti was pleased by the court's concern for his welfare? Was the Second Circuit right?

b.   United States v. Gonzalez–Lopez, 548 U.S. 140 (2006), involved a trial court's erroneous refusal to grant *pro hac vice* status to the defendant's first choice of counsel. Justice Scalia, for the Court, held (5 to 4) that the right to counsel of choice "commands, not that a trial be fair, but that a particular guarantee of fairness be provided—to wit, that the accused be defended by the counsel he believes to be best." The trial court did not violate the defendant's right to a fair trial, but it denied the defendant his counsel of choice and "No additional showing of prejudice is required to make the violation 'complete.'" The Court advised that "the right to counsel of choice does not extend to defendants who require counsel to be appointed for them. Nor may a defendant insist on representation by a person who is not a member of the bar, or demand that a court honor his waiver of conflict-free representation." However, there also is no "harmless error" test when counsel of choice is denied, for the error is "structural." In contrast, "a violation of the Sixth Amendment right to *effective* representation is not 'complete' until the defendant is prejudiced." (emphasis in original, citing *Strickland*). Justice Alito filed a dissenting opinion, in which Chief Justice Roberts and Justices Kennedy and Thomas joined.

C.   CONFLICTS OF INTEREST FACED BY PROSECUTORS

1.   Of what relevance is it that the prosecutor in this problem is highly motivated to get convictions that will tend to further his political ambitions? Could a prosecutor's personal motives ever constitute a conflict of interest with his or her duties as a public prosecutor?

a.   People v. Superior Court (Greer), 561 P.2d 1164 (Cal.1977), upheld the trial court's decision to disqualify the district attorney from prosecuting a murder case. The unusual conflict was based on the fact that the victim's mother was employed in the prosecutor's office. Moreover, the mother was scheduled to be a material witness for the prosecution, and if the defendant were convicted, the mother would stand to gain custody of her grandchild. Evidence surrounding the arrest of the criminal defendant suggested that the arrest had been used to aid the victim's mother in gaining such custody. The court concluded that a district attorney may prosecute vigorously, "but both the accused and the public have a legitimate expectation that his zeal, as reflected in his tactics at trial, will be born of objective and impartial consideration of each individual case." 561 P.2d at 1172.[6] See Model Rule 1.7(a)(2) ("personal interest of the lawyer").

---

6. For discussion of the subsequent California statute modifying the standard for prosecutor disqualification see People v. Conner, 666 P.2d 5 (Cal.1983): " 'The motion [to recuse] shall not be granted unless it is shown by the evidence that a conflict of interest exists such as would render it unlikely that the defendant would receive a fair trial.' This standard differs from that enunciated by us in *Greer*." 666 P.2d at 8 (Cal.1983).

b. In re Complaint of Rook, 556 P.2d 1351 (Or.1976) (per curiam), involved a state district attorney accused of refusing to plea bargain with 15 criminal defendants on the same basis as previously offered to another criminal defendant so long as the 15 were represented by either of two attorneys. After the two attorneys withdrew as counsel and another attorney represented the 15, the district attorney allowed the 15 to accept the plea bargain that he earlier offered another defendant. When the district attorney was asked to explain his position, he is reported to have said that one of the unacceptable defense attorneys was involved in "organized crime" and that he was upset with the other for saying "bad things" about him. The state Supreme Court publicly reprimanded the district attorney. The court found a violation of DR 1–102(A)(5), based on a state statute which provided, inter alia, that "[s]imilarly situated defendants should be afforded equal plea bargaining opportunities." It also found that the district attorney was motivated in his conduct not only by frustration but also by "animosity and a desire to punish" that supported the finding of a violation of DR 7–102(A)(1) as well.

c. In Lewis v. Superior Court, 62 Cal.Rptr.2d 331 (Cal.Ct.App.1997), the defendant was the auditor-controller of Orange County whose alleged negligent supervision of the county treasurer's investment of county funds contributed to the county's need to seek bankruptcy protection. The bankruptcy resulted in drastic budget cuts in the prosecutor's office, deletion of staff lines, cancellation of pay raises, and the like. In short, the prosecutor apparently took the case personally and even called a county supervisor to try to persuade him not to vote to pay for the auditor-controller's defense. The court ordered the entire county prosecutor's office disqualified from handling the case.

2. Would conflicts problems be created if the prosecution function were "privatized"?

a. In People ex rel. Clancy v. Superior Court (Ebel), 705 P.2d 347 (Cal.1985), cert. denied sub nom., City of Corona v. Superior Court, 475 U.S. 1121 (1986), a city hired a private attorney to bring abatement proceedings against an adult book store. The fee arrangement with the lawyer provided that his fee would double if he won the case. The court pointed to the "prosecutor's duty of neutrality," which stems from the fact that "he is a representative of the sovereign" and "has the vast power of the government available to him." Giving a prosecutor a contingent fee compromises his duty of fairness and neutrality inherent in the role of prosecutor. Hence the court disqualified the private attorney.

Later, in County of Santa Clara v. Superior Court, 235 P.3d 21 (Cal. 2010), various counties and other public entities brought a representative public nuisance action against lead paint manufacturers, seeking abatement as the sole remedy. The manufacturers moved to bar the public entities from compensating private counsel (who were representing these entities) by contingent fees. The California Supreme Court held that there was no absolute bar to public entities from hiring private lawyers to represent their interest on a contingent fee basis in assist in civil public nuisance actions. To protect the public, "contractual provisions must provide explicitly that all critical discretionary decisions will be made by public attorneys-most notably, any decision regarding the ultimate disposition of the case." In contrast, in criminal cases, "giving a public prosecutor a direct pecuniary interest in the outcome of a case that he or she is prosecuting 'would render it unlikely that the defendant would receive a fair trial.' "

Do you agree with these results? Should Model Rule 1.5(d)(2) be revised so that it is not limited to the case of "a contingent fee for representing a *defendant* in a criminal case"? (emphasis added).

b. In Young v. United States ex rel. Vuitton et Fils S.A., 481 U.S. 787 (1987), the trial judge enjoined violation of Vuitton's trademark. When Vuitton learned that defendants were violating its trademark, the judge appointed Vuitton's counsel as special prosecutor to bring a charge of criminal contempt against defendants. The Supreme Court reversed the contempt conviction, because there is an actual conflict of interest: the special prosecutor also represented the private party who would be the beneficiary of the court order allegedly violated. While the trial court has inherent authority to appoint someone to enforce its order, the matter must be referred first to the public prosecutor. If he refuses to prosecute, the court should appoint someone not connected to the civil plaintiff. Only in that way can the court avoid the "potential for private interest to influence the discharge of public duty."[7] The Court rejected the claim that the trial judge's supervision of a contempt prosecution would avoid the conflict. The prosecutor (unlike Vuitton's lawyer) must be disinterested.

c. People v. Eubanks, 927 P.2d 310 (Cal.1996), involved defendants who were charged with stealing trade secrets in the computer industry. When Borland International went through one of its executive's email, it found he had sent confidential messages to an executive of Symantec, a competitor. This situation was significant to Borland but possibly less so to the local district attorney, so Borland offered to contribute up to $10,000 to pay for the work of experts necessary to build the criminal case. The district attorney hired the expert who sent his bill to that office, but the D.A. accepted reimbursement from Borland, justifying his actions by explaining that victims often cooperate with prosecutors in the preparation of cases. The California Supreme Court disagreed. Even though the prosecutor was not lining his own pockets, no private citizen may direct the exercise of prosecutorial discretion, and such private contributions will

---

7. Federal Trade Commission v. American Nat'l Cellular, 868 F.2d 315 (9th Cir. 1989), considered what effect *Vuitton* should have on the FTC practice of having its attorneys act as special prosecutors to punish TRO violations in cases it has won. The court found *Vuitton* not controlling where a government lawyer rather than a private attorney is acting as a special prosecutor. But the court said that appearances are important. The U.S. attorney's office should be in control of the contempt matter, although it may then delegate prosecution to the agency attorney.

See also, Crowe v. Smith, 151 F.3d 217, 231–33 (5th Cir.1998) (improper to appoint opposing counsel in RICO case to prosecute attorney sanction matters). But see, Wilson v. Wilson, 984 S.W.2d 898 (Tenn.1998) (not inherently improper to have beneficiary of order prosecute charge of contempt).

inevitably influence the decision whether to prosecute the defendants. The court affirmed the trial court's order forcing recusal of the entire D.A.'s office.

d.   Hambarian v. Superior Court, 44 P.3d 102 (Cal.2002), involved the audit of a local trash collection business in the city of Orange, California. The city was suspicious that Hambarian artificially inflated its costs in an effort to overcharge the city millions of dollars in excess trash fees. The Orange police department launched an investigation, but transferred the case to the major fraud unit of the county district attorney's office because it lacked the expertise to handle a complex accounting matter. The district attorney retained a private certified public accountant, Franzen, to review Hambarian's books. Over the course of two years, the city paid Franzen over $450,000 to conduct his investigation. Citing *Eubanks*, Hambarian argued that the court should disqualify the prosecutor because it accepted the efforts of an expert witness who was compensated by the victim, in this case the city. The California Supreme Court disagreed and distinguished *Eubanks* on various grounds. The city investigated as part of a civil suit against Hambarian. Further, the victim was a public agency; the prosecutor and the victim/city had a common interest to represent the citizens of Orange and obtain refunds from the defendant. Franzen, the accountant, did not have a supervisory role in the investigation and cross-examination could easily reveal any bias.[8]

D.   CONFLICTS OF INTEREST OF DEFENSE COUNSEL; PUBLICATION RIGHTS

1.   Assume that the Bitter Creek case becomes high profile litigation. May Bentley write an article about her representation of Bitter Creek? To what extent may a defense lawyer personally and financially benefit from the publicity surrounding a major trial? May a criminal lawyer write a book about her trials, or a particular case that she defended?

a.   Look at Model Rule 1.8(d). What purpose does the rule serve? Does Model Rule 1.8, Comment 9, help provide an answer?

b.   People v. Corona, 145 Cal.Rptr. 894 (Cal.Ct.App.1978), held that by entering into a literary rights contract with the accused prior to trial, he "was forced to choose between his own pocketbook and the best interests of his client, the accused." The lawyer's financial stake in the literary rights encouraged him to insist on a lengthy and sensational trial, rather than invoke various defenses that might abort or change the nature of the trial.[9]

---

8. See also, Commonwealth v. Ellis, 708 N.E.2d 644 (Mass.1999) (upholds funding criminal insurance fraud prosecutions out of fund into which insurance companies paid; "A prosecutor's discretionary choices must be unaffected by private interests," the court held, but "routine cooperation from a victim of crime is * * * often necessary and should be encouraged." Id. at 649. The fund was industry-wide and spent on cases prosecutors independently determined had merit; individual companies could not influence how prosecutorial resources would be employed).

9. Compare United States v. Hearst, 638 F.2d 1190 (9th Cir.1980), ordering a hearing in which Patty Hearst would be required to show that the conflict in fact affected her lawyer's judgment whether to seek a continuance and a change of venue, and whether to have the defendant testify. It

c.   Beets v. Scott, 65 F.3d 1258 (5th Cir.1995) (en banc), reversed an earlier decision that found ineffective assistance of counsel where the defendant had given media rights to the son of his lawyer as payment of attorney's fee. The lawyer thought giving the rights to the son would avoid the Rule 1.8(d) problem. The court rejected that trick out of hand, and then decided whether to reverse the conviction. Over a vigorous dissent, it held that the *Strickland* "actual prejudice" test of ineffective assistance applied, not *Cuyler v. Sullivan's* willingness to reverse in cases of attorney breach of loyalty. Beets received a fair trial, the court said; enforcement of state ethics rules was up to the state.

d.   Rule 1.8(d) appears to apply only to defense counsel. Why? Should there be similar limits on prosecutors writing their memoirs?

2.   Should a client be able to waive the protection of Rule 1.8(d)? Is this rule only to protect the defendant's private interest or is there a public interest involved?

a.   Maxwell v. Superior Court, 639 P.2d 248 (Cal.1982), allowed a waiver by relying on a California provision, Rule 5–101, which allows lawyers to enter into business relations adverse to a client if the client consents. The defendant, charged with capital crimes, signed a contract with his attorneys in which the attorneys promised to act competently but also warned the defendant of the possible conflicts and prejudice which the publication agreement would create: "It declares that counsel may wish to (1) create damaging publicity to enhance exploitation value, (2) avoid mental defenses because, if successful, they might suggest petitioner's incapacity to make the contract, and (3) see him convicted and even sentenced to death for publicity value." The defendant filed a mandamus action against the trial judge for relying on the rule to disqualify his defense lawyer and the California Supreme Court ordered the disqualification overturned.

Do you agree with this result? Is there a systemic interest (an interest in the interest of justice) in seeing that defendants get a fair trial? If the latter interest is relevant, should it be improper for a court to accept the defendant's "waiver" of the conflict?

b.   May a criminal defense lawyer secure literary rights *after* the conclusion of the legal matter? Why should we draw this distinction? Should publication of a lawyer's memoirs waive the attorney-client privilege of the clients regardless of when the contract is made? See, e.g., In re von Bülow, 828 F.2d 94 (2d Cir.1987), where von Bülow acquiesced in his lawyer's publication of the book regarding details of the prior representation. He even joined with his lawyer in actively promoting sales of book. The court held that the client waived the privilege as to matters specifically

would not be necessary, however, for her to   result in the case.
show that the conflict actually changed the

revealed in the book, but there was no broader subject matter waiver as to undisclosed communications not mentioned in the book.[10]

PROBLEM 12

CONFLICTS BETWEEN CLIENT INTERESTS AND THE LAWYER'S PERSONAL INTEREST

A lawyer who represents a client must put the client's interest ahead of the lawyer's own. That is easy to say, harder to assure, and proving that the requirement has been met can be harder still. This problem presents some situations in which a lawyer might profit as a result of a professional relationship in ways that go beyond collecting normal legal fees. We first ask under what conditions a lawyer may properly collect a fee in a form that makes the lawyer a business associate of the client. Next, we ask whether a lawyer may use confidential client information to engage in business transactions with third parties. Then we look at whether a lawyer may accept a client's gift, and at what happens when the lawyer and client fall in love.

FACTS

Attorney Joan Doe went to high school with James Johnson, a local engineer. Johnson asked Doe to help him set up a small business. He had very little money, and the capital he had raised from a few local investors was not enough to pay much of a legal fee. Johnson asked if he could pay the fee over an extended period of time, with interest. Instead, Doe suggested that Johnson pay her by giving her 10 percent of the stock in the new corporation as payment for all the work necessary to establish it and carry it through the first year. Doe thought the business looked like a good, relatively cheap investment opportunity, and after Johnson agreed to the arrangement, Doe drafted the articles of incorporation, bylaws and a shareholders' agreement.

Johnson's company is doing very well. Doe has learned from him that the company will be building a new plant in an industrial park near town. The plans for the industrial park are a secret to all but a few people, and Doe realizes that property in proximity to the park is likely to increase in value. She knows of such a nearby parcel that is for sale, and, after concluding that Johnson probably does not plan to buy it, she has now done so.

---

10. In that case, the state prosecuted Count von Bülow for attempting to kill his wife, Martha "Sunny" by allegedly injecting her with insulin causing her to lapse into an irreversible coma. He was convicted and sentenced to 30 years. Professor Alan Dershow- itz represented him on appeal and secured a reversal. Von Bülow was acquitted at the second trial. That led to a movie, Reversal of Fortune (1990), adapted from Dershowitz's book, Reversal of Fortune: Inside the von Bülow Case (1985).

After his company had made its first million dollars, Johnson was thrilled. "Joan," he said, "you have been my lawyer these three years and I could not have succeeded without you. Please draw up the papers to transfer the title to my year-old Mercedes Benz to yourself." The car is worth $75,000. Doe was stunned and does not know how to reply to Johnson's generous direction.

Now, Doe and Johnson have fallen in love. Marriage seems in their future, but meanwhile, they are together whenever they are not both at work.

QUESTIONS

A. ACCEPTING PAYMENT IN THE FORM OF STOCK; BUSINESS TRANSACTIONS WITH A CLIENT

1. Does the law prohibit lawyers from taking all or part of their fee in the form of stock in the client's business?

a. Historically, lawyers have entered into business transactions with clients. For example, oil and gas lawyers have purchased interests in their client's oil wells and real estate lawyers have purchased client properties as investments. In some of those cases, the lawyers exchanged legal services for the investments. However, prior to 2000, lawyers generally did not invest in the stock of corporate clients. The notable exception to this was in California's Silicon Valley, where law firms took advantage of the more liberal California conflicts rules and often invested in client equity. With the dot.com boom of the late 1990s, law firms all over the United States sought to participate in the wealth generated through initial public offerings of client stock. These efforts led to a series of ethics opinions approving, with certain limitations, such investments and trading legal services for equity. Proponents of such arrangements argued that (1) clients wanted lawyers to take equity positions as a way of showing lawyer confidence in the client's business model, (2) lawyers' equity positions reduced the clients' need for capital and aligned the interests of lawyers and clients, (3) paying lawyers with equity made legal fees lower than they otherwise would have been, (4) law firm equity investments created a compensation structure that allowed firms to retain lawyers and promoted innovative client fee structures, and (5) equity investments tended to keep the client loyal to the law firm and thus retain the client for future business.

b. ABA Formal Opinion 00–418 (July 7, 2000) makes clear that Model Rule 1.8(a) treats fees paid in the form of stock as business transactions with a client. Such a fee is also subject to Rule 1.5(a)'s requirement that the total fee be reasonable. The stock should be valued at the time it is acquired, and its reasonableness should be determined at that time. The opinion also notes other conflicts that can arise, e.g., problems under Rule 1.8(i) if the company's only asset is a cause of action, and under Rule 1.7(a)(2) if the stock is a major asset of the lawyer.

c. Utah State Bar Advisory Opinion 98–13 (1998) agrees that Rules 1.5, 1.7(a)(2), and 1.8(a) are all implicated when a lawyer takes stock in payment of a fee. The lawyer should be especially concerned if the stock will be publicly traded or if the client might want restrictions on its trading. Both will affect determination of the stock's value and the latter could constitute a conflict of interest. In any event, Rule 1.8(a) requires that the terms of a stock transaction be fair and reasonable and disclosed in writing to the client. The value of the stock must also be reasonable as required by Rule 1.5.[1]

d. The law firm of Wilson Sonsini has held equity investments in clients since the 1950s and has adopted several policies to minimize potential conflicts of interest. The firm never trades services for stock; it charges normal attorneys' fees and purchases stock with cash, not to exceed an investment of $100,000. The stock is held in a law firm investment partnership separate from the law firm, and the partners in the firm are partners in the investment vehicle. Decisions to invest are made by the management committee of the investment partnership. Stock is held long term, and the partnership never votes stock to break a tie.[2]

It is important to note that many law firms still refuse to invest in client equity because of the risks that such investments entail. Suppose Enron's outside law firm had invested in Enron stock and provided advice regarding the company's reporting obligations, for example?

2. Why do the courts view business dealings with clients with suspicion? What are the ways in which the lawyer might take advantage of the client?

a. In re Hibner, 897 N.Y.S.2d 489 (N.Y.App.Div. 2010), is a good example of overreaching a poor couple. The lawyer represented a couple in child neglect proceedings in family court. During the representation, lenders prepared to foreclose on the clients' home. To help avoid foreclosure, the lawyer advised the clients to deed the property to him—apparently in an attempt to defraud creditors. Then the lawyer paid the balance of the mortgage to the lender. The lawyer then leased the house back to the clients, who then missed several rent payments. So the lawyer, while still representing the clients in the child neglect proceedings, sued his current clients and obtained a judgment for eviction. The clients sued the lawyer to vacate the deed and enjoin the eviction. That suit was ultimately settled.

As a result of his actions, the Grievance Committee brought disciplinary charges against the lawyer. He had permitted his own interests to affect his professional judgment in the course of the representation. He entered into a business transaction with clients where they had differing interests without adequately disclosing the terms and obtaining the clients'

---

1. Two more opinions providing helpful analysis of these issues are D.C. Bar Legal Ethics Opinion 300 (July 25, 2000), and Association of the Bar of the City of New York, Committee on Professional and Judicial Ethics, Formal Opinion 2000–3 (2000).

2. John S. Dzienkowski & Robert J. Peroni, The Decline in Lawyer Independence: Lawyer Equity Investments in Clients, 81 Texas L. Rev. 405, 416 n.39 (2002).

informed consent to the transaction and conflict of interest, and he intentionally damaged the clients' during the course of the representation by attempting to evict them. The court sustained all charges and concluded that the appropriate sanction was a suspension of four years.

b.   Cotton v. Kronenberg, 44 P.3d 878 (Wash.App.2002), involved the defense of Cotton against serious charges of child rape. Cotton signed two fee agreements with lawyer Kronenberg. The first provided that Cotton would pay Kronenberg an hourly fee of $140. The second, signed three days later, required Cotton to pay for the services upfront and estimated the cost at between $10,000 and $30,000. In satisfaction of the fee, Cotton deeded real property to Kronenberg, but before the trial even began, the court disqualified Kronenberg because he had improperly contacted some of the prosecution's witnesses. Nevertheless, Kronenberg kept Cotton's land, and eventually sold it for about $42,000. Cotton sought a full refund, arguing that the fee agreement was void because Kronenberg breached his fiduciary duty to Cotton. The court agreed. Taking the land in payment was a business transaction with the client under Rule 1.8(a), and the land-for-services transaction was not fair and reasonable to the client. The lawyer breached his fiduciary duty, which justified forfeiture of his entire fee.

c.   In Medina County Bar Ass'n v. Carlson, 797 N.E.2d 55 (Ohio 2003) (per curiam), the health department ordered a mentally ill client to clean up his property. Carlson represented the client, who offered to sell the land to the lawyer for $52,500 the day before another buyer offered $470,000 for the property. Carlson had the client sign a statement that gave the appearance that he fully understood the deal with Carlson, the conflict of interest that it presented, and that he had consulted independent counsel (who gave no substantive advice). When the client was about to go to discipline authorities, Carlson offered to unwind the deal, but the Ohio Supreme Court suspended Carlson for two years.

3.   Are all business transactions with clients suspect? Is Model Rule 1.8(a) a trap for the unwary?

a.   In Passante v. McWilliam, 62 Cal.Rptr.2d 298 (Cal.Ct.App.1997), a client invented baseball cards imprinted with a hologram to prevent counterfeiting. The company flourished, but early in its history it lacked $100,000 to buy an order of paper without which it would have failed. The lawyer stepped up to the plate and went to bat for the client, lending it the desperately-needed $100,000. In gratitude, the company orally promised to give him 3% of the common stock. The lawyer never sought repayment of the $100,000 loan, but when the 3% share became worth $33 million, he asked for the shares. The court, however, said he could not have them. If they were a gift from the company, he had no contractual right to the shares. Further, as a business deal, he had not complied with the professional rules. His apparent home run became simply a long out.

b.   In re Kirsh, 973 F.2d 1454 (9th Cir.1992), involved a lawyer who lent money to his client, a close friend. The lawyer knew the friend was in financial trouble, lent him $40,000, and took some real property as security. He took the client's word that the title was good. It was not, the client filed for bankruptcy, and the lawyer alleged that his client had defrauded him, and thus that the court should not discharge the debt. The court disagreed. While lawyers ordinarily should not engage in business transactions with clients, the court said, the purpose of that rule is to protect clients against overreaching. In this case, the terms of the loan were fair to the client, and the lawyer was the victim. The Rules of Professional Conduct "were not intended as a protection for clients who wrong their lawyers." Nonetheless, because of his specialized knowledge and experience, this lawyer did not reasonably rely on his client's knowingly false representation about that title within the meaning of the bankruptcy law. Hence the court discharged the client's debt.

c.   In Committee on Professional Ethics v. Mershon, 316 N.W.2d 895 (Iowa 1982), a farmer owned 100 acres of farmland adjacent to a country club near the city. He was interested in developing the land for residential purposes and hired an engineer to prepare a preliminary plat and market study. The farmer and engineer then came to the lawyer for advice, telling the lawyer that the farmer did not have enough cash to pay for the engineering and legal work. The lawyer (Mershon) advised the farmer to convey the land to a corporation. Then Mershon advised that, based on the value of the land and the usual cost of the professional work, the farmer should receive 40% of the stock, the engineer should receive 40%, and Mershon should receive 20%. Because none of the three individuals was willing to give a personal guarantee of a loan needed to develop the parcel, the bank would not lend the money and the project never went forward. Mershon, the lawyer, believed that this meant that he and the engineer must turn in their stock. Mershon did so, but the engineer did not, and after the farmer's death, his children litigated their rights with the engineer.

The question in the case, however, was whether these facts revealed a violation of what is now Model Rule 1.8(a). The Iowa Supreme Court found that they did.

"* * * Miller [the farmer and land owner] and Mershon plainly had differing interests in at least two aspects of the transaction. One was the issue of giving respondent [Mershon] a present interest in the corporation in anticipation of future legal services. * * * Because respondent's fee was tied to the amount of his stock in the corporation, he and Miller [the farmer] had differing interests concerning the extent of respondent's stock ownership. Another differing interest involved making respondent a debtor of the corporation to assure that the services would be performed. Because Miller's interest was aligned wholly with the corporation, he and respondent had differing interests with respect to respondent's promissory note. * * *

"The fighting issue * * * was whether respondent made full disclosure to Miller within the meaning of the [ethics rule] before Miller entered the transaction. If full disclosure means only that respondent made Miller fully aware of the nature and terms of the transaction, this requirement was satisfied. * * * Full disclosure, however, means more than this.

"Because of the fiduciary relationship which exists, the attorney has the burden of showing that the transaction 'was in all respects fairly and equitably conducted; that he fully and faithfully discharged all his duties to his client * * * by active diligence to see that his client was fully informed of the nature and effect of the transaction proposed and of his own rights and interests in the subject matter involved, and by seeing to it that his client either has independent advice in the matter or else receives from the attorney such advice as the latter would have been expected to give had the transaction been one between his client and a stranger.' * * * " 316 N.W.2d at 899.

Even though the court found that Mershon had been "forthright and honest and gained no profit from the transaction," it concluded that he had violated what is now Model Rule 1.8(a) and reprimanded him.

d.   Do you agree with the results in these cases? Should the law allow the lawyer a complete defense if the transaction is fair? Restatement Third, The Law Governing Lawyers § 126, Comment *b*, says the rationale for the strict rule is that "[p]roving fraud or actual overreaching might be difficult." Do you agree? Might the law deal with that difficulty by putting the burden of proving fairness on the lawyer?

4.   Must a lawyer comply with the terms of Model Rule 1.8(a) when she buys a car from her car dealer client? Does a lawyer who owns a restaurant have to abide by Model Rule 1.8(a) whenever a client comes in for a meal?

a.   Look at Comment 1 to Model Rule 1.8. Does it resolve both questions? Restatement § 126 also makes clear that Rule 1.8(a) does not prohibit "standard commercial transactions in the regular course of business of the client, involving a product or service as to which the lawyer does not render legal services." Comment *c* explains that these are transactions "regularly entered into between the [lawyer or] client and the general public, typically in which the terms and conditions are the same for all customers."

b.   Comment *c* warns, however, that "where a lawyer engages in the sale of goods or services ancillary to the practice of law, for example, the sale of title insurance, the requirements of this Section do apply." Do you see a good reason for such an exception to the rule? Rule 5.7 deals with lawyers providing "law-related services," a topic considered in Problem 37.

c.   Comment *a* to Restatement § 126 says that "ordinary client-lawyer fee agreements providing, for example, for hourly, lump-sum, or contingent fees" are not business transactions with the client. Is that statement literally true? Does it make more sense to conclude that fee agreements are business transactions that are found in almost every lawyer-client relationship, and that Model Rule 1.5 separately addresses that particular issue?

B.   USING CONFIDENTIAL CLIENT INFORMATION TO MAKE PRIVATE INVESTMENTS

1.   May Doe, without Johnson's consent, invest in the parcel near the industrial park? As we have posed the problem, Johnson does not want to buy the property himself.

a.   ABA Canons of Professional Ethics (1908), Canon 11, made clear that: "The lawyer should refrain from any action whereby for his personal benefit or gain he abuses or takes advantage of the confidence reposed in him by his client." This provision was held to prohibit a lawyer from using confidential client information for the lawyer's benefit, even if the lawyer did not reveal the information to third parties and even if the client did not suffer detriment. See, e.g., Healy v. Gray, 168 N.W. 222 (Iowa 1918).

b.   Model Code of Professional Responsibility DR 4–101(B)(3) was equally definitive that, absent informed client consent, a lawyer may not "knowingly * * * [u]se a confidence or secret of his client for the advantage *of himself* or of a third person." (emphasis added).

c.   Model Rule 1.8(b) instead says that, without the client's informed consent, a lawyer "shall not use information relating to representation of a client *to the disadvantage of the client*" unless the client consents. (emphasis added).

2.   Do you agree with the Model Rules' limitation of the prohibition? Is possible disadvantage of the client the only concern that underlies the rule?

a.   The source of the earlier ethics rule is agency law. A lawyer is an agent of the client; the client is the principal. The typical agency rule is that an agent (whether a lawyer, or other agent) may not use secret information of a principal without securing the principal's consent. The remedy in agency law is for the agent to disgorge the profit to the principal. See Restatement Second, Agency § 388, Comment *c*:

> "[If] a corporation has decided to operate an enterprise at a place where land values will be increased because of such operation, a corporate officer who takes advantage of his special knowledge to buy land in the vicinity is accountable for the profits he makes, even though such purchases have no adverse effect upon the enterprise."

b.   One draft of Restatement Third, The Law Governing Lawyers, Tentative Draft No. 3 (1990), followed Model Rule 1.8(b). However, following the law of agency, the final Restatement provides in § 60 that, unless the client consents, "a lawyer who uses confidential information of a client for the lawyer's pecuniary gain other than in the practice of law must account to the client for any profits made."

c.   Comment *j* to this section of the Restatement explains that this duty exists "regardless of lack of risk of prejudice to the affected client." The Comment goes on to say that the

> "sole remedy of the client for breach of duty is restitutionary relief in the form of disgorgement of profit (see Restatement, Second, Agency § 388, Comment *c*). The lawyer codes differ over whether such self-enriching use or disclosure constitutes a disciplinary violation in the absence of prejudice to the client."

3. Do you agree that the only remedy for a violation of this principle should be a suit for disgorgement? Why should professional discipline not be a possible sanction?

a. Look at ABA Model Rule 1.8, Comment 5. Does it give a satisfactory explanation of why discipline for use of the information should be unavailable? Indeed, does it attempt to give any explanation at all?

b. United States v. O'Hagan, 521 U.S. 642 (1997), addressed the securities law consequences of insider trading in securities of a client. Grand Metropolitan PLC (Grand Met), a London corporation, retained Dorsey & Whitney in Minneapolis, in an effort to acquire Pillsbury, a large publicly-traded company. O'Hagan, a Dorsey & Whitney partner not working on the matter, purchased call option contracts and shares of Pillsbury stock on the open market. When Grand Met announced its takeover plans, Pillsbury stock rose from $39 to $60 and O'Hagan made over $4.3 million. The SEC prosecuted him criminally for securities fraud under the so-called "misappropriation theory," i.e., it said he defrauded both his law firm and its client, persons to whom he owed a fiduciary duty, by taking their information and using it to benefit himself. Writing for a six-person majority, Justice Ginsburg sustained the application of the misappropriation theory to Rule 10b–5 cases. Use of the information is inherently "deceptive," the Court said, and the fraud is "consummated" when the confidential information is used "in connection with the purchase or sale of [a] security."

c. Where does that ruling leave the lawyer for purposes of professional discipline? If a lawyer engages in illegal insider trading in a client's stock, but the trading does not directly injure the client, is the lawyer immune from professional discipline? Should Model Rule 8.4(b) trump Rule 1.8(b) in such a case?

C. ACCEPTING UNSOLICITED GIFTS FROM HAPPY CLIENTS

1. May Doe follow Johnson's direction to prepare the documents necessary to give herself title to the Mercedes Benz?

a. Does your answer turn on fact that a Mercedes Benz is more valuable than a Hyundai? What does Model Rule 1.8(c) tell you are the relevant issues for Doe to consider?[3]

b. Would all ethical questions vanish if Johnson had simply thrown Doe the keys to the car and no paperwork were involved? Of course, the car title has to be transferred for the gift to be effective, so Johnson cannot avoid the language of Rule 1.8(c) referring to an instrument. But why

---

3. In re Barrick, 429 N.E.2d 842 (Ill. 1981), decided before the prohibitory language of Model Rule 1.8(c), upheld a gift by an elderly widow to her lawyer. The widow was said to have been "adamant" that she did not want to consult independent counsel. The state supreme court said: "[A]lthough undue influence might [be] presumed, the evidence established that there was none. There was no overreaching by the respondent. On the contrary, he urged his client to employ another attorney until she would hear no more about it. Exactly how far to press the point was a matter of judgment, and we will not snipe at the respondent's." 429 N.E.2d at 846. Do not rely on this case. Rule 1.8(c) does not embrace it.

should preparation of an instrument be relevant? Does it make sense that a gift without an instrument would present fewer ethical issues?

c. Restatement Third, The Law Governing Lawyers § 127(2), tells lawyers that they "may not *accept*" (emphasis added) a substantial gift from a client, whether or not preparation of an instrument is required. The different statement of the rule may be explained by Model Rule 1.8, Comment 6, which says that a lawyer may accept a substantial gift, but the gift "may be voidable by the client under the doctrine of undue influence, which treats client gifts as presumptively fraudulent." In short, the Restatement is addressing a variety of sources of law, while the lawyer will only be disciplined if preparation of an instrument was involved.

d. Attorney Grievance Commission of Maryland v. Stein, 819 A.2d 372 (Md.2003), held that the attorney violated Maryland's Rule 1.8(c) when he drafted a will for his client providing a substantial gift to himself. The issue was the appropriate sanction. The court imposed an indefinite suspension upon Stein, because "[w]e consider a violation of Rule 1.8(c) to be most serious." However, the majority refused to require the lawyer to renounce any interest in his deceased client's estate as a condition of reinstatement. The majority believed there was no precedent for such a sanction. It acknowledged that there may be the potential for a "cost/benefit analysis" leading to a lawyer's violation of the rule, but it found no evidence that Stein had engaged in such an analysis. The dissent was obviously troubled by the failure to implement "the one sanction that, more than any other, will assure that the Rule is followed." 819 A.2d at 381. "If lawyers know that a violation of the Rule will bring them no financial gain, they will have no incentive to violate the Rule, and that, above all else, is what will protect the public." 819 A.2d at 382. Given the Restatement treatment of gifts to clients, did the majority view the appropriate sanction too narrowly?

2. Would it be proper for Doe to admire the car and let Johnson know she would like to have it?

a. Before the 2002 amendments, Model Rule 1.8(c) did not prohibit Doe from "soliciting" a substantial gift. Do you agree the change to prohibit such solicitation was an improvement? Does Model Rule 1.8, Comment 6, supply a persuasive explanation of why solicitation of a substantial gift from a client should subject a lawyer to discipline?

b. Morrissey v. Virginia State Bar, 448 S.E.2d 615 (Va.1994), helps illustrate the concern, albeit in an very unusual situation. As part of a plea agreement in a rape case, the defendant agreed to pay the victim $25,000 damages and to give a $25,000 gift to charities selected by the prosecutor. (The prosecutor originally wanted the $25,000 to fund a "prosecutor's corner" show on a local TV station.) The prosecutor did not disclose the charitable gift portion of the agreement to the victim or the court. The court found that, in soliciting this arrangement, the prosecutor had misled the victim of the crime into accepting this resolution of the case and had concealed the terms of the gift from the court, both in violation of what are now Model Rules 8.4(c) and (d). The court suspended the prosecutor from practice for six months.

3.   Why does Model Rule 1.8(c) have an exception for gifts to relatives and others in a "familial relationship" with the lawyer?

a.   Is the exception self-evident? Would any other rule mean that if the lawyer's spouse is also a client, the spouse could never throw the lawyer a birthday party?

b.   On the other hand, is it really a good idea for lawyers to represent their relatives as this rule clearly tolerates? What problems can you see if you draft your mother's will, for example, and she gives you a gift that is larger than the one she gives your sister? Restatement Third, The Law Governing Lawyers § 127(1) provides that the lawyer may not prepare an instrument effecting a gift unless the lawyer is a relative or in a similar position *and* the "gift is not significantly disproportionate to those given other donees similarly related to the donor." Do you think this is a more appropriate statement of the rule than that found in Model Rule 1.8(c)?

4.   Is a lawyer's appointment as a compensated executor of a client's estate, or to a similar fiduciary position, a "gift" from the client within the meaning of Model Rule 1.8(c)?

a.   The executor of an estate collects the decedent's assets and, after payment of bills owed by the estate, distributes the assets to the beneficiaries designated in the decedent's will. Being an executor takes work, and the executor typically may be paid a fee. Sometimes, the fee is specified by statute; sometimes, it must be approved by a court. In either case, the fee can be significant. A family member who is designated executor, on the other hand, will often waive the fee and leave more to distribute to the beneficiaries.

b.   In addition, an executor ordinarily consults a lawyer who receives a fee as well. Law firms have been accused of trying to be appointed executor, lawyer for the executor, or both, of their clients' estates. Should the lawyer or law firm that drafts the will be able to accept such an appointment? Is an appointment the equivalent of receiving a substantial bequest from a client? Why or why not?

c.   Comment 8 to Model Rule 1.8 tries to give an authoritative answer to such questions. The first sentence is definitive. On the other hand, does the remainder of Comment 8 give adequate guidance to a lawyer about what the lawyer must tell a client about the client's options? Could a lawyer's appointment as executor ever *not* create a conflict of interest for the lawyer that requires her to secure client consent under Model Rule 1.7(b)? When does the possibility of a "lucrative fiduciary position" ever not "materially limit" the lawyer's likely advice?

d.   ABA Formal Opinion 02–426 (May 31, 2002) advises that the lawyer/fiduciary's law firm may represent the lawyer in administration of the estate, but the combined fee for acting as fiduciary and as lawyer must be reasonable under Model Rule 1.5(a). Now is your mind at ease? If the fee is "reasonable" under Model Rule 1.5(a), do the other ethics issues go away?

5. Suppose that in our problem, before Johnson gives any gift to lawyer Doe, he seeks the advice of a different lawyer as Model Rule 1.8, Comment 7 advises. What should that new lawyer advise Johnson?

a. The new lawyer should obviously be concerned that Doe is not exercising any coercion or undue influence. Is there anything else? Should the recommendations of Comment 7 be lifted into the Rule, so that substantial gifts under Rule 1.8(c) are treated the same as business transactions under Rule 1.8(a)(2)?

b. Consider Restatement Third, The Law Governing Lawyers § 127, Comment *g*. It advises that even if outside counsel is involved in reviewing a gift, the gift "remains subject to invalidation if the circumstances warrant under the law of fraud, duress, undue influence, or mistake." Do you agree that a court should always be able to look behind a gift if it is challenged on these grounds?

D. INTIMATE RELATIONSHIPS BETWEEN LAWYERS AND CLIENTS

1. Should Doe's license to practice be put at risk if Doe and Johnson enter into a consensual relationship involving physical intimacy? Why might we be concerned about such a relationship between lawyer and client?

a. ABA Formal Opinion 92–364 (July 6, 1992) wrestled with this issue, concentrating on (1) potential abuse of the fiduciary relationship between the lawyer and a vulnerable client, (2) loss of emotional distance from the client required for good professional judgment, (3) potential conflicts of interest between lawyer and client, and (4) confusion between which communications were made in a professional relationship and which were personal. The opinion concluded:

> "[B]ecause of the danger of impairment to the lawyer's repre-sentation associated with a sexual relationship between lawyer and client, the lawyer would be well advised to refrain from such a relationship. If such a sexual relationship occurs and the impair-ment is not avoided, the lawyer will have violated ethical obli-gations to the client. * * *

> "The client's consent to sexual relations alone will rarely be sufficient to eliminate this danger. In many cases, the client's ability to give meaningful consent is vitiated by the lawyer's potential undue influence and/or the emotional vulnerability of the client."

b. How do those considerations apply to the facts of this problem? Look at Rule 1.8(j). Is James Johnson, the client, likely weak or vulnerable, for example? On the other hand, are Joan Doe's possible loss of emotional distance, potential conflicts of interest, and possible compromise of confi-dentiality all likely to be legitimate concerns?

2. Did ethical standards prior to the adoption of Model Rule 1.8(j) prohibit sexual relationships between lawyers and clients?

a. Many reported cases involved sex with clients. The ABA adopted new Model Rule 1.8(j) in large part because, in some cases, lawyers were exonerated because of the lack of specific prohibition in the Model Rules, even though lawyers are fiduciaries who are required not to overreach their clients. Some cases have seen the problem as one of lawyers who appear to take advantage of their clients; other cases have been less concerned about the seriousness of the issue.

b. Suppressed v. Suppressed, 565 N.E.2d 101 (Ill.App.Ct.1990), for example, involved a divorce client who testified that her lawyer had twice taken her to an apartment where he had her inhale something that disoriented her and then had sexual relations with her. She filed a charge with the Illinois Attorney Registration and Disciplinary Commission, but it dismissed the matter. A malpractice action alleging breach of fiduciary duty was also dismissed. This Illinois appellate court said that a lawyer's only fiduciary obligation to a client is not to make sex a quid pro quo for legal services. The client felt coerced into sex, the court acknowledged, but that alone was not enough. Further, the client only suffered emotional harm, not "quantifiable" injury. Are you shocked by this result?[4]

c. Drucker's Case, 577 A.2d 1198 (N.H.1990), in contrast to *Suppressed*, involved a lawyer who knew his divorce client was under psychiatric care and emotionally fragile. The lawyer initiated, then ended their affair, but the client had fallen in love with him and her husband found her diary describing her feelings, thus prejudicing her in the divorce case. In spite of the lack of a specific prohibition of the relationship, the court found that the lawyer had taken advantage of his client and suspended him for two years.

d. In Lawyer Disciplinary Bd. v. Artimez, 540 S.E.2d 156 (W.Va. 2000), a lawyer for the victim of an auto accident started a sexual relationship with the client's wife. She later left her husband and, at that point, the lawyer asked his partner to represent the husband in the accident case. Of course, he lied to both the client and his partner about the reason why. After the husband discovered the sexual relationship, he sued the lawyer for malpractice and threatened to file ethics charges against him. The lawyer agreed to take a lesser legal fee in exchange for the client's agreement not to tell the disciplinary authorities, but ultimately, the client went to the authorities anyway. The investigative panel found the sexual

---

4. In re Rinella, 677 N.E.2d 909 (Ill. 1997), later agreed that such charges are serious even in Illinois. Even without a disciplinary rule specifically on pressuring a client into a sexual relationship, the Illinois Supreme Court held that it constituted a conflict of interest in that the women believed they had to submit to get quality legal representation. The conduct was also prejudicial to the administration of justice, and the court ruled that the lawyer should be suspended for three years. Doe v. Roe, 681 N.E.2d 640 (Ill.App.Ct.1997), appeal denied, 686 N.E.2d 1160 (Ill.1997), went even farther. Rejecting much of the analysis in *Suppressed*, the court held that a lawyer in a divorce case who coerces the client into a sexual relationship breaches a fiduciary duty to the client and emotional distress may be considered as an element of damages.

relationship violated Rule 1.7(b), while lying about it violated Rule 8.4(c). The West Virginia Supreme Court, however, found that no ethics rule specifically forbids a sexual relationship with the wife of a client, so the conduct could not lead to discipline. The court further concluded that the lawyer's initial lie about his inappropriate sexual relationship concerned a matter that did not constitute an ethical violation per se, and, thus, "we are hard-pressed to find that his failure to be forthcoming with his law partner about this matter violated Rule 8.4(c)." The court "appreciate[d] his recognition of his irreconcilable conflicting personal interests" in asking his partner to take over the case. Only the effort to get the husband not to file ethics charges resulted in discipline for the lawyer, and the court limited that discipline to a public reprimand.

e.   Gaspard v. Beadle, 36 S.W.3d 229 (Tex.App.2001), involved a lawyer who undertook a real estate matter for a couple. The wife then filed for divorce and began a sexual relationship with the lawyer. The lawyer also represented her individually in a matter collateral to the divorce. He did not bill her while the relationship continued, but after it ended, he sent a bill for all the work done. A jury found him guilty of fraud and intentional infliction of emotional distress for his conduct, but this court reversed. A man giving the impression that he loves a woman is not actionable fraud, the court said. Further, failing to send a legal bill until a sexual relationship with a client ended amounted only to the kind of "occasional malicious and abusive" conduct that society must tolerate, not the "extreme and outrageous conduct" that could give rise to a cause of action.

Is it any wonder that the ABA thought a specific regulatory rule was required?

3.   Does Model Rule 1.8(j) deal adequately with the issues that sexual relationships present?

a.   Does Model Rule 1.8(j) reach relationships with clients' spouses of the kind found in *Artimez*, for example? In Hernandez v. State, 750 So.2d 50 (Fla.Ct.App.1999) (motion on rehearing en banc), a lawyer had an affair with his criminal defense client's wife. A panel of the court originally concluded this was per se ineffective assistance of counsel; the lawyer could not truly have wanted the defendant acquitted so as to return home. The full court, however, saw the case differently. The conflict of interest was only "potential," not actual, the court said. Suggestion of an effect on the defense was simply "informed speculation;" indeed, the defendant was acquitted of the most serious charge against him.[5] Do you agree? Should such conduct be prohibited? Do Comments 17–19 to Model Rule 1.8 explain the rule sufficiently and suggest appropriate areas of caution?

---

5. The defendant's unqualified endorsement of the results achieved by the same lawyer in a concurrent federal prosecution also undercut the defendant's argument. See also, Hernandez v. Spears, 2002 WL 1205058 (S.D.Fla.2002), denying habeas corpus and saying it would be possible for a lawyer to provide an effective defense even though his success would let the defendant possibly bring an end to the affair.

b.   Should the ethics rules only prohibit intercourse with a client? In re Heilprin, 482 N.W.2d 908 (Wis.1992), for example, disbarred the lawyer for asking women clients "sexually explicit and suggestive * * * questions." The court had earlier suspended the lawyer after he had been exposing himself to clients. Should acts that fall short of intimate physical contact raise discipline issues? Should the court discipline a lawyer who makes explicit and suggestive remarks to his secretary or another person who is not a client or client's spouse?

c.   Is it important to create an exception for preexisting sexual relationships? Is that exception necessary so that a lawyer may represent his or her spouse? Should the rule not allow the exception because the spouse or paramour probably should have a different lawyer anyway? Note that even if the lawyer complies with Rule 1.8(j), Rule 1.7(a)(2) is still relevant. See Model Rule 1.8, Comment 18.

d.   Should the prohibition extend to relationships between lawyers and officials of the lawyers' corporate clients? Look at Model Rule 1.8, Comment 19. Are such relationships likely to present the same problems as those with individual clients? Does Comment 19 take the prohibition too far?

e.   If one lawyer in a firm enters into a sexual relationship with a client, should the lawyer be able to refer the client to another lawyer in the firm? Notice that Model Rule 1.8(k), confirmed in Comment 20, expressly does not impute the Model Rule 1.8(j) prohibition throughout a law firm. Can you see any good reason for not doing so?

f.   In United States v. Dyess, 231 F.Supp.2d 493 (S.D.W.Va.2002), the court disqualified the entire U.S. attorney's office for the Southern District of West Virginia. The court found that Ursala, the then-wife of defendant Dyess, was involved in a "personal/sexual relationship" with the lead DEA Task Force agent investigating Dyess. The criminal defendants claimed drug investigators shared the proceeds of drug transactions with Ursala, and may have engaged in other improprieties, while the appeal was pending. At least one lawyer in the U.S. attorney's office might be required to testify about some of the facts. "The allegations involve the personal and sexual relationship of an agent of the United States with a key 'prosecuting' witness who received lenient treatment as a Defendant when sentenced; alleged misallocation of substantial amounts of money; possible coerced testimony and perjury; and perhaps, other wrongdoings." 231 F.Supp.2d at 498. The court found that what happened adversely affected the reputation of the office, and the appearance of impropriety was so great that it required disqualification. Do you agree?[6]

----

6. See also, Commonwealth v. Croken, 733 N.E.2d 1005 (Mass.2000) (investigation ordered into adequacy of defense where appointed defense counsel had a "close relationship" with an assistant district attorney who later became his wife; defense counsel should have disclosed relationship to his client and obtained informed consent.) Do you agree? If

PROBLEM 13

REPRESENTING THE INSURED AND THE INSURER

In a simple model of lawyer-client relations, the client pays the lawyer's fees. However, things do not always work out that way. Sometimes, a third party pays the fee; indeed, the lawyer might look to that third party for fees in multiple cases. Such a situation arises when a company pays its employees' legal fees in matters arising out of their work, or a parent pays the legal fees of a child who gets into trouble. It arises most often when insurance companies pay lawyers pursuant to contractual obligations to pay the legal fees of policyholders who face liability claims. In such cases, the lawyers typically never expect to see the policyholders again, but they devoutly hope that the insurance company will repeatedly retain them. That arrangement may create an incentive to serve, not the client, but the source of the fee. In this problem, we explore the nature of a lawyer's relationship with an insurance company and its insured, the duty to protect confidential information of the insured, the right of the insurer to approve a settlement, and whether the insurance company may impose limits on efforts to be made in defense of the client's case.

FACTS

Terry Tenant is the son-in-law of Larry Landlord. Tenant rented an apartment in one of Landlord's apartment complexes. Landlord has a liability insurance policy with the All–Mutual Company covering all accidents in the apartment complex up to $100,000. One cold evening in January 1993, Tenant injured himself when he slipped on some ice just outside the main entrance. Landlord saw the accident and rushed to help Tenant, but Tenant said that he would "be all right." Thus, Landlord did not report the accident to All–Mutual. Unknown to Landlord, Tenant took several weeks off from work claiming back injuries. In June 1993, Tenant sued Landlord, his father-in-law, for $175,000 for his alleged pain and suffering and expenses in connection with the resulting back injury.

All–Mutual's liability insurance policy has several standard clauses. First, a "Notice of Accident" clause requires the insured to notify the carrier promptly of any accident for which it will expect coverage; failure to so notify is said to be a waiver of coverage. Second, the policy requires All–Mutual to provide and pay for a lawyer to defend the insured from any claim arising under the policy and to pay any claim within the monetary limits of the policy. Third, the policy requires the insured to cooperate with All–Mutual in defending against any claims.

there is no actual conflict of interest, why   her social life to a client?.
should defense counsel have to disclose his or

After Tenant filed suit, Landlord notified All–Mutual, and All–Mutual retained Sara Henderson to investigate and prepare the defense. All–Mutual also wrote Landlord that it "was not waiving any defenses under the policy." Henderson interviewed Landlord and Tenant but was unable to find any other witnesses who had a clear recollection of the accident. Landlord's and Tenant's version of the events were almost identical and very favorable to Tenant. Henderson, on the other hand, has wondered how Tenant could be so careful and suffer such severe injuries, and yet have an immediate reaction that he would "be all right." Moreover, because Landlord and his son-in-law seem to be on good terms, she has wondered why Tenant neither told Landlord of the alleged "serious complications" nor, at least prior to filing, that Tenant was going to bring a lawsuit.

Tenant has offered to settle for $50,000, and Landlord has told Henderson that he would prefer All–Mutual's agreeing to that amount rather than going to trial and placing Landlord at risk for the $75,000 in excess of policy coverage.

Henderson believes that Landlord's failure to notify All–Mutual about the accident at the time it happened has so hampered factual development of the case that All–Mutual should deny coverage under its prompt notice clause. She has not told either Landlord or All–Mutual of her opinion. She also believes that Landlord is not cooperating, although she also has not said this to Landlord or All–Mutual either. During one interview Landlord told Henderson: "Just between you and me, my son-in-law and I remain the best of friends, but I wouldn't want All–Mutual to know that."

Henderson has sent Tenant's settlement offer to Landlord and All–Mutual. All–Mutual has asked for her advice on whether it should accept the offer.

QUESTIONS

A.   A LAWYER'S CLIENT(S) WHEN RETAINED BY AN INSURER TO REPRESENT AN INSURED

1.   Whom does Sara Henderson represent when she is retained by an insurance company under circumstances like the one in this problem?

a.   You might be surprised to learn that whether Henderson represents only Landlord, the insured, or whether she also represents All–Mutual, the insurance company, is a hotly-disputed issue. Henderson clearly represents Landlord. He is the named defendant in the case and the person for whom Henderson will enter her appearance as defense counsel. However, insurance companies typically argue that they, too, are clients of the lawyers they retain on behalf of their policyholders.

b. Initially, it might seem important to identify whom Henderson represents in order to determine whether this is a third-party payer situation to which Model Rule 1.8(f) applies. Furthermore, if All–Mutual is also Henderson's client, Rule 1.7(a) would come into play because Henderson would be representing two clients in the same matter.

However, even if All–Mutual were held to be Henderson's client, Rule 1.8(f) would still apply because Henderson would still be "accept[ing] compensation for representing a client [Landlord] from one other than the client." Alternatively, even if All–Mutual is not Henderson's client, the concerns of Model Rule 1.7(a)(2) are clearly still present.

c. For reasons such as these, Restatement Third, The Law Governing Lawyers § 134, Comment *a*, takes the position that whether the lawyer has one client or two is a matter of insurance law, not the law governing lawyers. Comment *f* then goes on to say that "it is clear in an insurance situation that a lawyer designated to defend the insured has a client-lawyer relationship with the insured. The insurer is not, simply by the fact that it designates the lawyer, a client of the lawyer."[1]

2. Are the problems of obtaining consent different depending on whether the insurance company is characterized as a client?

a. Look at Model Rule 1.8(f). To get informed consent under that provision, must Sara Henderson explain to Landlord the advantages and disadvantages of having her be Landlord's lawyer? What disadvantages should she be required to mention? Should she be required to tell the client the amount of all payments she received or anticipated from All–Mutual over the past year as an indication of her financial dependence on the company?

b. Suppose the law said that there are two clients and thus that Model Rule 1.7(a)(2) governs the situation. Would Henderson have to get informed consent from All–Mutual as well? Would the fact that All–Mutual retained Henderson constitute consent to the joint representation? Do we say in any other situation that the fact of retention alone constitutes consent to a conflict of interest?

c. May the lawyer assume that the insurance policy, which both parties signed when insurance was obtained, constitutes whatever consent is necessary to waive whatever conflicts of interest may be presented? Would the usual conversation between insurance agent and the insured guarantee the kind of informed consent the Model Rules demand?

3. You remember from Problem 10 that a lawyer ordinarily must secure client consent to file suit against a current client. Would Henderson be barred from representing a client in an unrelated case suing the insurance company that retains her in other cases to represent its policyholders?

---

1. For a further development of these issues, see Thomas D. Morgan, Whose Lawyer Are You Anyway?, 23 Wm. Mitchell L. Rev. 11 (1997).

a.   In re Anonymous Member of South Carolina Bar, 432 S.E.2d 467 (S.C.1993), said that Model Rule 1.7(a)(1) forbids a lawyer to help a client collect under the uninsured motorist coverage of his own policy if the lawyer is retained by the insurance company to represent its policyholders in other cases. Do you agree that this result is required?

b.   In Nevada Yellow Cab Corp. v. Eighth Judicial District Court, 152 P.3d 737 (Nev.2007), Insurance Company of the West (ICW) retained the Vannah firm to represent Yellow Cab in a tort case that was settled for more than policy limits so that Yellow Cab had to pay the excess. Yellow Cab then retained the Vannah firm to sue ICW for bad faith refusal to settle earlier, a claim that would require ICW to pay the full amount. The Nevada Supreme Court held that ICW should be treated as a co-client with Yellow Cab in the first case. It held the later bad faith case was substantially related to the underlying tort action, so it disqualified the Vannah firm.

c.   Regardless of the answer under Rule 1.7(a)(1) or 1.9(a), if one analyzes the situation under Rule 1.7(a)(2), is it not clear that representation of the client may be affected by the lawyer's own financial interests, i.e., her desire that the insurance company continue to refer cases to her? Remember that Rule 1.7(a)(2) contemplates that a third person (not just another client) can create the disqualifying interest. In other words, does the analysis come to the same conclusion whether or not the insurance company is also a "client"?

4.   Suppose that, when Landlord gets on the witness stand, he tells a story more favorable to Tenant than he had told Henderson earlier. May Henderson seek to impeach Landlord's story and thus help reduce the amount the insurance company will have to pay?

a.   Restatement Third, The Law Governing Lawyers § 134, Comment *f*, says:

> "With respect to events or information that create a conflict of interest between insured and insurer, the lawyer must proceed in the best interests of the insured, consistent with the lawyer's duty not to assist client fraud (see § 94) * * *. If the designated lawyer finds it impossible so to proceed, the lawyer must withdraw from representation of both clients * * *."

Is withdrawal a practical alternative when the surprise testimony occurs in the middle of a trial?

b.   In Montanez v. Irizarry–Rodriguez, 641 A.2d 1079 (N.J.Super.Ct. App.Div.1994), Wife sued Husband for injuries suffered in an auto accident. In pretrial interviews Husband told his lawyer (appointed by the insurer to represent him) that he had been driving safely but a tire had blown out. On the witness stand, however, Husband said that the blowout occurred after the accident and that he had not driven safely. The defense lawyer then demanded the right to treat his client as a "hostile witness" to try to minimize the sum the insurer would have to pay Wife. The court held that impeachment of one's own client was improper. If the insurer later wanted to sue the client for noncooperation, it could do so, but the lawyer represented the insured, not the insurer, in the action before the court.[2]

B.   A LAWYER'S OBLIGATION TO PROTECT CONFIDENTIAL INFORMATION OF THE INSURED

1.   What must a lawyer do when he or she learns embarrassing or incriminating information about the insured that the insurance company would want to know?

a.   A leading case on defense counsel handling of confidential information is Parsons v. Continental National American Group, 550 P.2d 94 (Ariz.1976). Fourteen-year-old Michael Smithey had brutally assaulted a neighbor. A CNA claims representative investigated the incident and wrote a detailed letter to his company on his investigation of Michael's background. The letter concluded:

> "In view of this information gathered and in discussion with the boy's father's attorney, Mr. Howard Watts, and with the boy's parents, I am reasonably convinced that the boy was not in control of his senses at the time of this incident. It is, therefore, my suggestion that, and unless instructed otherwise, I will proceed to commence settlement negotiations with the claimant's attorney so that this matter may be disposed of as soon as possible."

However, the lawyer that CNA retained to defend Michael told CNA:

> "I have secured a rather complete and confidential file on the minor insured who is now in the Paso Robles School for Boys, a maximum-security institution with facilities for psychiatric treatment, and he will be kept there indefinitely and certainly for at least six months * * *. The * * * file shows that the boy is fully aware of his acts and that he knew what he was doing was wrong. It follows, therefore, that the assault he committed on claimants can only be a deliberate act on his part."

This information was important because the insurance policy specifically excluded liability for intentional acts. After receiving the lawyer's report, CNA sent a reservation of rights letter to the boy's parents saying that it would investigate and defend the case, but that it did not waive this possible defense against payment of any judgment.

b.   Later, in preparing for trial, the defense attorney interviewed Michael and wrote to CNA: "His own story makes it obvious that his acts were willful and criminal." At trial, the lawyer offered no defense, and the court entered a $50,000 judgment against Michael. When the plaintiffs asked the trial court to order CNA to pay them the amount of its policy, CNA, at trial, successfully claimed that the intentional act exclusion applied. The lawyer who handled CNA's defense was the same one who had previously represented the insured in the underlying action.

---

2. Lurking within this question is an issue we discuss in Problem 27: what a law-yer must do when a client wants to give perjured testimony.

c. Did the defense attorney act properly? Where did he go wrong, if at all? What should be the consequence of the attorney's conduct?

d. The Arizona Supreme Court held that CNA was estopped to deny coverage and thus had to pay the judgment. The court found that CNA "took advantage of the fiduciary relationship between its agent (the attorney) and Michael Smithey." The court explained:

> "The attorneys, retained by CNA, represented Michael Smithey at the personal liability trial, and, as a result, obtained privileged and confidential information from Michael's confidential file at the Paso Robles School for Boys * * * [because of] the attorney-client relationship. Both the A.B.A. Committee on Ethics and Professional Responsibility and the State Bar of Arizona * * * have held that an attorney that represented the insured at the request of the insurer owes undivided fidelity to the insured, and, therefore, may not reveal any information or conclusions derived therefrom to the insurer that may be detrimental to the insured in any subsequent action. * * *

> "The attorney in the instant case should have notified CNA that he could no longer represent them when he obtained any information (as a result of his attorney-client relationship with Michael) that could possibly be detrimental to Michael's interests under the coverage of the policy. * * *

> "The attorney in the present case continued to act as Michael's attorney while he was actively working against Michael's interests. When an attorney who is an insurance company's agent uses the confidential relationship between an attorney and a client to gather information so as to deny the insured coverage under the policy in the garnishment proceeding we hold that such conduct constitutes a waiver of any policy defense, and is so contrary to public policy that the insurance company is estopped as a matter of law from disclaiming liability under an exclusionary clause in the policy." 550 P.2d at 97–99.

2. Given the authority of *Parsons*, what should Henderson tell All–Mutual with respect to the prompt notice clause?

a. Would it constitute disloyalty to the insured to report to the company that five months had passed between the accident and the insured's report? Would that information be obvious to the company if it looked at dates in the insured's own report of the accident?

b. Remember that all information "relating to the representation" is protected by Model Rule 1.6. Most insurance policies, however, give the insured a contractual duty to cooperate with the insurer in preparing the defense. Should there be a distinction between a lawyer's disclosure of "innocent" information given under the duty of cooperation and the disclosure of more sensitive information that the lawyer learns in the course of preparing the defense?

c. Rhode Island Ethics Opinion 98–10 (Apr. 1998) declared that an insured has the right to see all communications from the lawyer to the insurance company about the progress of the case. Does that approach protect all relevant interests? Remember that such reports might, for example, include the lawyer's assessment of how credible a witness the client would be. That is something the lawyer and company might not want the insured to see, but it might be very relevant to the company as it decides how much liability exposure the case presents.

3. Where would telling the company about the "I wouldn't want All–Mutual to know" comment fit into this analysis? Would such a report constitute a breach of Henderson's duty of confidentiality?

a. Are you at all troubled by the suggestion that Henderson could not tell All–Mutual about the possibility of collusion between Landlord and Tenant here? Would a failure to report it constitute participation by Henderson in a possible fraud by the insured?

b. Restatement Third, The Law Governing Lawyers § 134, Comment *f*, advises that when there is a question of the insured's right to policy coverage, the lawyer for the insured "may not reveal adverse confidential client information of the insured to the insurer concerning that question without explicit informed consent of the insured. That follows whether or not the lawyer also represents the insurer as co-client and whether or not the insurer has asserted a 'reservation of rights' with respect to its defense of the insured." The Comment continues that the lawyer must proceed in the insured's best interest, "consistent with the lawyer's duty not to assist client fraud," and if that is impossible, "the lawyer must withdraw from representation of both clients * * *." Note that the Restatement, at this point, assumes that the lawyer may have two clients.

c. If Henderson obtains "sensitive" information about the insured's coverage, should she withdraw from the representation under Rule 1.16? Could she do so without signaling to the company that there was a possible policy or coverage defense? Is this signaling appropriate? Compare Model Rule 1.2, Comment 10, which refers to a "notice of the fact of withdrawal," with Rule 4.1, Comment 3, which also refers to a "notice of the fact of withdrawal."

d. ABA Formal Opinion 08–450 (Apr. 9, 2008) considered the situation where the insurance company hires the lawyer to defend both an insured employer and its employee for whom the employer may vicariously be liable. In the course of interviewing the employee, the lawyer learns that the employee may have acted outside the scope of his employment. Under the insurance contract, the employee may not be entitled to the protection of the employer's insurance. The employee reasonably believes this conversation was confidential. The lawyer also learned similar information when interviewing another witness. The lawyer believes that the insurance company may have a contractual right to deny protection to the employee based on these facts. And, the employer could invoke scope-of-employment principles to defend against its own liability to the plaintiff. The opinion advised that in "the situation of insurer-engaged counsel, the scope of the representation normally is understood by the insurer to be limited to defending the action under the policy, and not to include representing the carrier or the insured in any coverage or other dispute between the two." If continuing to represent a client would cause the lawyer to participate in any fraud, "withdrawal from that representation will be required."

4. The problem says that All–Mutual is defending the insured under a "reservation of rights" of the kind in *Parsons*. Does that in itself create a conflict of interest for a lawyer?

a. The reservation of rights is a statement that the insurance company is not waiving any policy defenses it may have against bearing the ultimate liability. Traditionally, the insurer's duty to defend and its duty to pay a damage award are separate duties. That is, a policy may provide coverage of defense costs even though the company would have a valid defense against paying the ultimate judgment. Thus, defense of the plaintiff's claim and the gathering of evidence as to policy coverage tend to go on simultaneously for some period.

b. The point at which a reservation of rights is asserted is usually seen as a time when the insured and the insurer have a conflict of interest. The usual rule is that two different lawyers must be involved, i.e., one to give the insurer an opinion on policy defenses or policy coverage and one to defend the insured.

c. In Allstate Ins. Co. v. Keller, 149 N.E.2d 482 (Ill.App.Ct.1958), for example, the attorneys assigned to represent the insured deposed the insured to gather evidence that he was not the driver of the vehicle at the time of the accident. They did not explain to the insured that the purpose of the deposition was to strengthen the insurer's claim of lack of coverage. The court agreed that the insured's initial false statements that he was the driver were a breach of the cooperation clause, but it held the defense was waived. After the insured's assigned attorneys "became aware of a conflict of interest between their client, the defendant [insured], and their employer, the plaintiff [insurer]," they had to disclose this information and its significance to the insured. Failure to deal with this conflict in a way that assured the insured had loyal, independent representation, resulted in loss of the policy defense.

d. Similarly, in Employers Cas. Co. v. Tilley, 496 S.W.2d 552 (Tex. 1973), the insured had claimed that his failure to report an accident promptly, as the policy required, was because he had not known about it until he was sued. A lawyer was assigned to defend him, pursuant to a reservation of the company's rights. All the while he was preparing the defense, however, the lawyer was apparently also gathering evidence of just when Tilley or his employees first knew of the accident. The court held that "[a]n attorney employed by an insurer to represent the insured simply cannot take up the cudgels of the insurer against the insured." 496 S.W.2d at 560. The lawyer's dual role prejudiced the insured, so the court estopped the insurer "as a matter of law" from asserting its policy defense.

e.   No matter what the courts say about who the client is in situations like this, is it realistic to presume that the attorney faces no conflict of loyalties? Concern about this conflict has led some courts to say an insured himself must be entitled to select the lawyer who will represent him (at the insurer's expense) on the liability issues when the insurer has raised a policy defense. See, e.g., CHI of Alaska, Inc. v. Employers Reinsurance Corp., 844 P.2d 1113 (Alaska 1993). In any event, a case like this may be one in which Henderson must treat possible policy defenses as someone else's problem.

5.   Move the questions to a context other than insurance company cases. If parents pay a lawyer to represent their child accused of a hit-and-run accident, for example, must the lawyer secure the child's consent before disclosing information to the parents?

a.   The answer is almost surely yes, and because the parents may not understand that, the lawyer should make it clear at the outset of the representation.

b.   Illinois State Bar Association Advisory Opinion on Professional Conduct, Opinion 00–02 (2000) advised that a lawyer may not release a psychiatric report of his mentally disabled adult client to the adult client's parents. Because the mentally disabled adult is the lawyer's client, not the parent, even under Model Rule 1.14 such disclosure would violate a lawyer's duty to preserve his client's confidential information.

c.   Might a lawyer paid by a legal aid office to represent an indigent client face issues very similar to those in this problem? What should the lawyer do about verifying the client's eligibility for free assistance, for example? Should the legal aid lawyer and the insurance defense lawyer resolve such questions in exactly the same way? What differences might there be?

d.   Cincinnati Bar Ass'n v. Lukey, 851 N.E.2d 493 (Ohio 2006), is a vivid illustration of the problem of third-party payment in a non-insurance situation. Lukey was a sole practitioner who had been retained by the grandparents of a 13–year–old boy whom they had adopted years before. The child had been charged with aggravated arson (for burning paper towels in a school bathroom). A public defender represented the child while Lukey represented the grandparents, who were afraid of losing custody for their own acts of mistreatment. Without meeting the child or investigating the facts or the boy's general behavior, Lukey plea bargained with the prosecutor for a lesser but still felony charge for the boy. When the public defender appeared for trial, the prosecutor told him that Lukey was the child's private lawyer, which Lukey confirmed. Lukey reconfirmed his representation of the boy with the magistrate at the hearing to confirm the plea. At that hearing, a social worker failed to report that the child had been removed from the grandparents' home because of mistreatment, and Lukey did not bring that out on the boy's behalf. For his conflicted representation, and what the court found as prejudice to the administration of justice, the court suspended Lukey for two years, 18 months of which to be served on probation with another lawyer assigned to oversee his practice.

C. A LAWYER'S DUTY AT THE TIME OF A SETTLEMENT OFFER IN A THIRD-PARTY PAYMENT CASE

1. How should Henderson react to the settlement offer? Does Rule 1.8(f) offer concrete guidance on the question?

a. Do you see the conflict of interest? The insured would normally want to settle any case at a figure within policy limits because that would assure he will not have to bear liability in excess of those limits; the insurer, on the other hand, faced with an offer for the full amount of the policy, has relatively little to lose by going to trial.

b. In such cases, as a matter of substantive law in many states, if the insurance company rejects a reasonable offer within policy limits, it must bear any sum—even in excess of policy limits—that the court ultimately awards, e.g., Crisci v. Security Ins. Co., 426 P.2d 173, 176 (Cal.1967) ("when 'there is great risk of a recovery beyond the policy limits so that the most reasonable manner of disposing of the claim is a settlement which can be made within those limits, a consideration in good faith of the insured's interest requires the insurer to settle the claim.' ").

c. Under these circumstances, can there be any doubt that the lawyer must at least tell the insurance company of the settlement offer? Restatement Third, The Law Governing Lawyers § 134, Comment *f*, advises that if the lawyer tells the company of the offer, he or she has not breached any duty to the insured.

2. What is the lawyer to do if the insurer wants to settle the case but the insured does not?

a. You remember that Model Rule 1.2(a) gives the "client," i.e., the insured, the absolute right to decide whether to settle a matter. On the other hand, it is standard insurance law and often a part of the standard insurance contract that an "insurance company is free to exercise its own judgment as to whether to enter into a settlement. It can, therefore, absent an express policy provision to the contrary, settle a case despite the insured's request that it not do so."[3]

b. Professional malpractice policies, however, are sometimes written differently than the garden variety liability policy. The professional may want to protect her reputation and avoid any implication that she was incompetent. Thus the insured may want the insurer to fight, not settle. Consequently "[p]rofessional liability policies usually contain a *settlement clause* permitting the insured to refuse to consent to a settlement, and expressly limiting the insurer's liability in the event of a subsequent excess

---

3. Allan D. Windt, Insurance Claims and Disputes; Representation of Insurance Companies and Insureds 191 (1982). See also, Mitchum v. Hudgens, 533 So.2d 194 (Ala. 1988) (insurance contract may give the insurance company the right to settle a case within the policy limits, even over the objection of the insured); Feliberty v. Damon, 527 N.E.2d 261 (N.Y.1988).

judgment."[4] What should the lawyer do with a settlement offer when representing a professional under such an arrangement?

3. Suppose there is no clause reserving the right of the insured to settle the case; must the lawyer nevertheless obtain the insured's permission to settle? Must the lawyer inform the insured about the offer of settlement even if the insured legally has no veto power?

a.   The Illinois Supreme Court said yes to both questions in Rogers v. Robson, Masters, Ryan, Brumund & Belom, 407 N.E.2d 47 (Ill.1980). Plaintiff was a doctor who had an insurance policy that provided that the insurer did *not* have to secure the written consent of the insured before the insurer made a settlement of any claim or suit. The doctor was sued for medical malpractice and the lawyers assigned by the insurer to defend the case negotiated a settlement with the victim. The insurer accepted the settlement, paid $1250, and the lawyers effected dismissal of the action. The doctor had "repeatedly informed" one of the law partners that he would not consent to settlement and the doctor was never advised that the insurer intended to settle. The Illinois Supreme Court held that these facts gave rise to a cause of action. The court said that the doctor and the insurance company were both the lawyers' clients, and the doctor—

> "was entitled to a full disclosure of the intent to settle the litigation without his consent and contrary to his express instructions. Defendants' duty to make such disclosure stemmed from their attorney-client relationship with plaintiff and was not affected by the extent of the insurer's authority to settle without plaintiff's consent. * * * Nor need we reach the question whether plaintiff can prove damages which are the proximate result of the breach of the duty to make a full disclosure of the conflict between the defendants' two clients." 407 N.E.2d at 49.

Do you agree with this analysis? What is the "conflict between the defendants' two clients" in a case like this? What should the lawyer do if the insured does not want to settle? Should the lawyer advise the insured that, if he forbids the insurance company to make the settlement, a court may conclude that he breached the policy terms and will have to pay the legal fees and final judgment himself? May the lawyer advise the doctor that he can waive the policy, reject the insurance company's aid, and fight the suit as he thinks proper?

b.   Lysick v. Walcom, 65 Cal.Rptr. 406 (Cal.Ct.App.1968), also illustrates the importance of these issues. The insurer was prepared to concede liability and initially authorized the lawyer to settle for up to $9500, policy limits being $10,000. The plaintiff proposed to settle for $12,500, and the estate of the insured had expressed a willingness to contribute $2,500 over the policy limits. However, because the lawyer lacked the authority to pay full policy limits and was hesitant about seeking more authority from the insurer, he failed to tell the insured's estate about the offer. Nor did he tell

4.   Windt, *supra* Note 3, at 191 n.22.

the insured's estate when he rejected the offer on its behalf. The action went to trial and resulted in a judgment in favor of plaintiff for $225,000. The court held:

> "[When the attorney for the insured] became aware of a conflict of interest between his two clients concerning the settlement offer made by plaintiffs[,] [h]e could have then terminated his relationship to the estate, but chose to continue to act as attorney for both clients. Accordingly, by so continuing to act, he impliedly agreed to use such skill, prudence and diligence in the representation of the estate as lawyers of ordinary skill and capacity commonly possess in the performance of like tasks. Moreover, since he was representing two parties with divergent interests, insofar as the settlement of the case was concerned, defendant labored under the duty of disclosing all facts and circumstances which, in the judgment of a lawyer of ordinary skill and capacity, were necessary to enable each of his clients to make free and intelligent decisions regarding the subject matter of the representation. * * *
>
> " * * * By continuing to act as counsel for the estate, while entertaining the belief that his primary obligation in the matter of settlement was to the insurer, defendant violated the legal and ethical concepts which delineated his duties to the estate." 65 Cal.Rptr. at 416.

The court concluded that, assuming proximate cause, the attorney would be personally liable for the amount of the judgment in excess of policy limits.

c. Is the implication, then, that Henderson should advise acceptance of the settlement in this problem? Will that protect her against personal liability? Does she inevitably have a personal stake in whatever she recommends that itself creates a conflict of interest under Model Rule 1.7(a)(2)?

d. ABA Formal Opinion 96–403 (Aug. 2, 1996) tried to straighten out the seeming conflict between ethics law and insurance law that a lawyer faces when the insurance contract has given the insurance company the right to control the defense and settlement of a case. The ABA opinion refused to take sides in the debate as to whether the lawyer has one client or two, but it made clear that the lawyer must communicate with the insured to inform him or her about the limited nature of the representation and the lawyer's intent to take direction from the insurance company. The opinion says that the lawyer does not need formal consent from the insured before the lawyer may take direction from the company, but if the insured objects and wants to control the defense—thereby assuming the risk of a loss of insurance coverage—the lawyer must honor that demand.

D. DEFINING THE APPROPRIATE LEVEL OF EFFORT WHEN AN INSURER PAYS FOR THE DEFENSE

1. Suppose the insurance company faces a maximum liability of $10,000 under the policy. Litigation costs could well be that

much or more, in addition to the amount of the liability. In order to reduce the cost of litigation, may the insurer direct the lawyer to take no more than, say, two depositions in the case?

a.   Look at Model Rule 1.8(f). Does it forbid the lawyer to honor such a direction by the insurer? Is a prohibition against accepting direction by others something that is generally in the interest of clients? Might it be in the interest of lawyers? Does such a prohibition serve the interest of policyholders in cases such as the one in this problem?

b.   Utah State Bar Ethics Advisory Committee Opinion 02–03 (2002), found that an attorney's agreement to abide by an insurer's case management guidelines is not per se unethical. Instead, it required evaluation of such agreements on a case-by-case basis, finding that they were illegal only if the agreement in fact caused the attorney to act contrary to the interest of his client, the insured. The opinion emphasized that an attorney may not contract around general ethical obligations under the state rules of professional conduct and suggested that the attorney tell the insured any restrictions on the representation, how the case would be handled especially regarding settlement, the insured's responsibility for adverse verdicts in excess of the policy coverage, and the insured's other rights. Further, the opinion says, within the defined terms of the representation, the attorney must continue to exercise independent professional judgment on behalf of the insured client.

c.   Is the concern in such cases the same one people have about the incentives of their HMOs? That is, should we be afraid insurance companies will put a concern about profits ahead of protection of their policyholders? Don't accept the analogy too quickly. An HMO will not get sick if care is inadequate. If foreseeable liability is within policy limits in an automobile accident case, on the other hand, and the company will pay the whole award, is there any reason the insurance company should not be permitted to make a tradeoff between the cost and value of specific litigation tactics? If the company were willing to pay the full amount of the claim, could it decide to put on no defense at all? However, does the *Rogers* case, above, suggest that lawyers can never be wholly confident they can ignore the insured's noneconomic interest in vigorously fighting a claim?

d.   Restatement Third, The Law Governing Lawyers § 134, Comment *f*, advises that the lawyer "may not follow directions of the insurer if doing so would put the insured at significantly increased risk of liability in excess of the policy coverage." The illustration to the Comment says that the lawyer may accept the insurer's direction not to double the number of depositions at a cost of $5,000 even if taking them would "somewhat increase" the insured's chances of winning. In this illustration, the claims against the insured are within the policy coverage, the insurance contract "confers authority on Insurer to make such decisions," and the lawyer believes that he can forgo these depositions "without violating the duty of competent representation" that he owes the insured.

2.   How should a lawyer respond to an insurance company's demand that it show its files to an "auditor" retained by the

insurance company to review the lawyer's compliance with insurance company guidelines?

a.   State ethics committees, unsurprisingly, express the view that to give auditors that information would be to expose confidential client information and interfere with the lawyer's professional judgment. Alabama State Bar Formal Opinion RO–98–02 (1998), for example, says that lawyers should not turn over information to such a reviewer if by doing so they will compromise privilege or work product protection, or waive the protection of confidential client information. Maryland Ethics Docket 99–7 (1999) reaches the same result, and cites opinions from Florida, South Carolina, Louisiana, Washington, and Kentucky to the same effect.

b.   Do you agree with these opinions? Of course, enforcing these ethical dictates in a world in which the insurance company will refuse to refer cases to lawyers who decline to cooperate is likely to prove more difficult than asserting the principles involved. Restatement § 134, Comment *f*, concludes that referral of progress reports, case evaluations, and settlement offers to the insurer should not cause them to lose their privileged character even if the insurer is not treated as a client. Does that make it easier to justify letting the insurance company auditor see such documents?

c.   ABA Formal Opinion 01–421 (Feb. 16, 2001) is the probable culmination of opinions on acceding to demands that lawyers submit their records to outside auditors. A lawyer may disclose information to the insurance company itself, the opinion says, if the lawyer reasonably believes it will advance the interest of the insured, i.e., by helping the company decide when to settle, assuring the company that all is being handled properly, etc. However, the lawyer may not disclose information that may reveal the client's motives or other sensitive insights, nor disclose information to third-party auditors, without the insured's consent. In seeking consent, the lawyer may have to explain to the insured that a failure to consent could result in denial of insurance coverage and that disclosure to an auditor could result in loss of the attorney-client privilege. The opinion concludes that a lawyer may only comply with insurance company litigation guidelines where they do not materially impair the lawyer's own independent professional judgment on behalf of the client.

d.   United States v. Legal Services for New York City, 100 F.Supp.2d 42 (D.D.C.2000), enforced a subpoena from the inspector general's office of the Legal Services Corporation (LSC) for similar information from local legal aid organizations. The LSC was concerned that organizations were overstating the number of cases handled, so it required data by case number, subject matter, and client names. The court rejected a blanket assertion of privilege, saying client names were typically not privileged. In addition, it held that the LSC's statutory authority to audit trumped Rule 1.6's requirement of confidentiality.

3.   If states try to enforce restrictions on directions to lawyers that insurance companies retain to represent their insureds, are the companies likely to respond by having their own in-house

lawyers represent the policyholders? Should the law permit that response?

a.   Gardner v. North Carolina State Bar, 341 S.E.2d 517 (N.C.1986), said insurance companies may not move to such a practice. Nor may an insurance company's in-house attorney appear as counsel of record for the insured in the prosecution of a subrogation claim for property damage. North Carolina law (like the law of many states) bans corporations (although typically not professional legal corporations) from performing legal services for another. "Since a corporation cannot practice law directly, it cannot do so indirectly by employing lawyers to practice for it." 341 S.E.2d at 521.[5]

b.   In re Allstate Ins. Co., 722 S.W.2d 947 (Mo.1987) (en banc), however, went the other way. It specifically refused to follow *Gardner* and concluded that the insurance company may either hire independent lawyers or use its own employee-lawyers instead. "An insurer has a very substantial interest in litigation involving its insured, and is entitled to retain counsel of its own choosing to protect its interest." 722 S.W.2d at 950. If the insurer can hire an independent contractor it can act through its employee. Any danger of conflict of interest is minimized because the insurance company uses its employee-lawyers "only when there is no question of coverage, and when the claim is within policy limits."

c.   In re Petition of Youngblood, 895 S.W.2d 322 (Tenn.1995), involved review of an ethics opinion that had opposed an insurance company's using an in-house lawyer to represent the insured. The court agreed that an insurance company may not tell the insured that the in-house lawyer is practicing independently, and the lawyer's loyalty in any given defense must be to the insured alone. However, the court ruled that it was proper for the insurance company to use employed attorneys as an economical way to assure experienced counsel for policyholders.[6]

d.   ABA Formal Opinion 03–430 (July 9, 2003), addressed two issues regarding an insurance company's use of in-house counsel to represent its policyholders.

First, the opinion said that staff attorneys could represent both the insurance company and the insured so long as the lawyers: (1) inform all insureds whom they represent that the lawyers are employees of the insurance company, and (2) exercise independent professional judgment in advising or otherwise representing the insureds. In the majority of cases, the insurance company and the insured have a common interest, and thus there is no inherent conflict of interest. The opinion also says, however, that in cases where a conflict exists, the lawyer must either secure the permission of the insured to continue the representation or terminate his representation of the insured. Model Rule 5.4(c) requires the attorney to

---

5.   We will look at the unauthorized practice implications of a corporation practicing law when we get to Problem 37, *infra.*

6.   But see, American Ins. Ass'n v. Kentucky Bar Ass'n, 917 S.W.2d 568 (Ky.1996)

(forbids use of in-house lawyers, citing the ancient maxim for rule construction: "If it ain't broke, don't fix it").

exercise independent judgment in representation, thus safeguarding the interests of the insured. Model Rule 1.8(f) also requires an insurance company staff attorney to disclose his relationship with the insurance company to the insured at the earliest possible opportunity. With these safeguards in place, the possibility of undue influence should be low, and dual representation would normally be permissible.

Second, the opinion concluded that insurance staff counsel may practice under a trade name or under the names of one or more of the practicing lawyers, if the lawyers function as a law firm and disclose their affiliation with the insurance company to the insureds whom they represent. This opinion noted that often staff attorneys are physically and organizationally different from the rest of the insurance company, have their own staff, and act as a "firm." Thus, the staff attorneys could refer to themselves as a "firm" and could name the "firm" after one or more of the staff attorneys. The firm could call itself, "Able & Baker," instead of "State Farm Law Office." This "firm" must comply with Model Rule 7.1 ("Communications Concerning a Lawyer's Service") and not give any misleading information about the nature of the firm or the services that it offers. The opinion said that the firm must disclose its affiliation with the insurance company to any *insured clients*, but need *not* add other public disclaimers, nor inform *nonclients* of their affiliation.

4. Should the lawyer be concerned about potential malpractice liability to the insurer, the insured, or both, if the lawyer accedes to the company's limited-effort demand?

a. Might the lawyer simply ask the insurer and insured to waive in advance any right to sue for any malpractice that results from adhering to the insurance company's direction? Be careful! What about Rule 1.8(h)? Does Rule 1.2(c) save the day for the lawyer? Which "client's" consent must the lawyer secure?

b. Should the insurance company be liable for malpractice committed by the lawyer it retains to defend the insured? Should it matter how much direction the company exercised over the lawyer? State Farm Mut. Auto. Ins. Co. v. Traver, 980 S.W.2d 625 (Tex.1998), said there could be no vicarious liability. The lawyer is an independent contractor retained to defend the insured who is the lawyer's client, not an agent of the insurer. However, if the insured claims the insurance company intruded on the lawyer-client relationship, failed to defend in good faith, or undermined the defense, that would constitute a direct action against the insurance company that could proceed.

c. May the insurance company sue the lawyer for malpractice, even if the insurer is not treated as a client of the lawyer? Cases have split as to that question.

Atlanta Int'l Ins. Co. v. Bell, 475 N.W.2d 294 (Mich.1991), used a doctrine of equitable subrogation to permit it to do so. Unigard Ins. Group v. O'Flaherty & Belgum, 45 Cal.Rptr.2d 565 (Cal.Ct.App.1995), found the insurer and insured were both the lawyer's clients in order to reach the same result.

However, Jones Lang Wootton USA v. LeBoeuf, Lamb, Greene & MacRae, 674 N.Y.S.2d 280 (N.Y.App.Div.1998), said no. Under New York law, the insurer could not sue its insured for being required to pay the judgment, so the insurer may not stand in the client's shoes to pursue the claim. See also, Fireman's Fund Ins. Co. v. McDonald, Hecht & Solberg, 36 Cal.Rptr.2d 424 (Cal.Ct.App.1994) (California law does not recognize equitable subrogation).

d. Restatement Third, The Law Governing Lawyers, says that the insurance company may sue the lawyer. "Because and to the extent that the insurer is directly concerned in the matter financially, the insurer should be accorded standing to assert a claim for appropriate relief from the lawyer" if the lawyer's professional negligence or other wrongful act caused the damage. Restatement § 134, Comment *f.* Do you agree that such an analysis of the relationship between the insurance company and the lawyer is accurate?

––––––––

PROBLEM 14

THE LAWYER AND HER FORMER CLIENT

So far, we have seen problems involving conflicts among prospective clients, current clients, conflicts with the lawyer's own interest, and conflicts created by the involvement of a third party. Now, we look at how the lawyer's duties to a former client might be affected by a current representation and present a threat to the former client, the current client, or both. Lawyers and law firms often have long lives. That means they have a great many former clients, and it would impossibly limit the choice of counsel available to current clients to say that lawyers are as prohibited from opposing a former client as they are from opposing a current one. We will ask, then, how broadly the prohibition of opposing a former client extends, what makes matters the same or substantially related, whether nonlawyers face similar prohibitions, and what may be done with the work product of a lawyer who is not permitted to continue in a case.

FACTS

Martha Heath has a wide reputation for her success in handling medical malpractice cases for plaintiffs. She is in great demand and is rightfully feared by doctor defendants.

Recently, Linda Parker came to Heath with a claim against Dr. Charles Abraham. Heath investigated the facts, found they seemed sound, and proceeded to go to work on the matter. Until she had worked on the case for about 90 days, Heath had not recalled that about five years earlier she had represented Dr. Abraham in the routine adoption of his wife's children.

Heath might have forgotten Dr. Abraham but he had not forgotten her. "How could you of all people—my own lawyer—sue me?" he said. More to the point, he had his malpractice defense counsel move to disqualify Martha Heath from handling Parker's claim.

QUESTIONS

A. MATTERS AS TO WHICH DISQUALIFICATION IS REQUIRED

1. Does a lawyer owe the same duty of loyalty to a former client as to a current one? What standard defines when a lawyer may undertake a matter that is contrary to the interest of a former client?

a. Judge Weinfeld developed the basic standard limiting such representation in the leading case of T. C. Theatre Corp. v. Warner Bros. Pictures, Inc., 113 F.Supp. 265, 268–69 (S.D.N.Y.1953):

"* * * I hold that the former client need show no more than that matters embraced within the pending suit wherein his former attorney appears on behalf of his adversary are *substantially related* to the matters or cause of action wherein the attorney previously represented him, the former client. The Court will assume that during the course of the former representation confidences were disclosed to the attorney bearing on the subject matter of the representation. It will not inquire into their nature and extent. Only in this manner can the lawyer's duty of absolute fidelity be enforced and the spirit of the rule relating to privileged communications be maintained." (emphasis added.)

b. The Model Rules now incorporate Judge Weinfeld's test in ABA Model Rule 1.9(a). Lawyers look to Rule 1.9, not Rule 1.7(a), to determine their obligations to a former client.[1]

c. Restatement Third, The Law Governing Lawyers § 132, Comment *b*, says that the former client rule:

"accommodates four policies. First, absent the rule, a lawyer's incentive to serve a present client might cause the lawyer to compromise the lawyer's continuing duties to the former client. Specifically, the lawyer might use confidential information of the former client contrary to that client's interest * * *. The second policy consideration is the converse of the first. The lawyer's obligations to the former client might constrain the lawyer in representing the present client effectively, for example, by limiting the questions the lawyer could ask the former

---

1. You will see a reference to "former client" in Model Rule 1.7(a)(2). That refers to the effect of the lawyer's obligations under Model Rule 1.9 to a former client on the interest of the lawyer's current client.

client in testimony. Third, at the time the lawyer represented the former client, the lawyer should have no incentive to lay the basis for subsequent representation against that client, such as by drafting provisions in a contract that could later be construed against the former client. Fourth, and pointing the other way, because much law practice is transactional, clients often retain lawyers for services only on specific cases or issues. A rule that would transform each engagement into a lifetime commitment would make lawyers reluctant to take new, relatively modest matters."

Would those policies help a judge in deciding Dr. Abraham's motion to disqualify Martha Heath?

2. Does the term "matter" refer only to litigated cases?

a. Notice that Judge Weinfeld makes clear that "matters" are not limited to "causes of action." Model Rule 1.9, Comment 2 also makes clear that the term "matter" covers more than lawsuits. For example, should a lawyer be barred from seeking to rescind a contract drafted for a former client? Is the rationale offered by the Restatement convincing in explaining why the rule might extend that far?

b. In Berry v. Saline Memorial Hospital, 907 S.W.2d 736 (Ark.1995), a lawyer in the plaintiff's firm had been a director of the defendant hospital. He did not know confidential information about this case; but he knew generally the hospital's policies and practices that were at issue in this matter. Because the lawyer-director owed a continuing duty of loyalty to the hospital, the court disqualified his firm from taking the case.[2]

c. In Townsend v. Townsend, 474 S.E.2d 424 (S.C.1996), a lawyer tried to represent a father who was trying to reduce his child support payments. Earlier, the lawyer had served as guardian ad litem for the child. The court conceded that a guardian ad litem is an officer of the court and does not technically represent the child. However, as guardian, the lawyer needed to have the confidence of the child and the family and may have received confidential information that would justify invoking Rule 1.9's bar.

d. Fields–D'Arpino v. Restaurant Associates, Inc., 39 F.Supp.2d 412 (S.D.N.Y.1999), asked whether an act of "informal mediation" constituted a "matter" for purposes of Rule 1.9. The plaintiff complained that the defendant was discriminating against her because of her pregnancy. A lawyer from the outside law firm representing the defendant held a meeting of the parties to try to resolve the dispute short of litigation. Even after the filing of an administrative complaint, the lawyer tried to mediate the dispute, and now the question was whether the firm could represent the defendant in the subsequent litigation. The court held it could not. All parties to a mediation must have the assurance it will be confidential. That could not be assured if the mediator's firm now represented one of the parties, so the court required disqualification.[3]

2. Conflicts created by a lawyer's "fiduciary or other legal obligation to a nonclient" are the subject of Restatement Third, The Law Governing Lawyers § 135.

3. See also, McKenzie Constr. v. St. Croix Storage Corp., 961 F.Supp. 857 (D.Virgin Islands 1997), holding that a lawyer who had been an unsuccessful mediator in a case

B. DETERMINING WHEN MATTERS ARE THE "SAME OR SUBSTANTIALLY RELATED"

1. In the middle of her representation of Dr. Abraham in the adoption matter, could Heath withdraw and take the side of Mrs. Abraham's former husband in seeking to resist the doctor's adoption of his and his former wife's children?

a.   Something as blatant as a lawyer switching sides in the *same* case rarely arises in practice. Far more often, what happens is that Heath would resign from one firm and move to a new firm that has been representing Mrs. Abraham's former husband. Remember, under Rule 1.10(a), if a lawyer is disqualified and then changes law firms, her disqualification is normally imputed to everyone at the new firm (unless she is screened, an issue we discuss in Problem 15).

b.   The harder problem for lawyers is deciding when two matters are "substantially related" within the meaning of Model Rule 1.9. Restatement Third, The Law Governing Lawyers § 132 says:

"* * * The current matter is substantially related to the earlier matter if:

"(1) the current matter involves the work the lawyer performed for the former client; or

"(2) there is a substantial risk that representation of the present client will involve the use of information acquired in the course of representing the former client, unless that information has become generally known."

Comment 3 to Model Rule 1.9 expands on this definition and provides examples. Can you begin to identify some recurring types of issues lawyers will face?

c.   One type of substantially related matter consists of later developments in an earlier matter. In Damron v. Herzog, 67 F.3d 211 (9th Cir.1995), cert. denied, 516 U.S. 1117 (1996), Lawyer had represented Seller in sale of his business. Nine years later, Lawyer represented Buyer and told him to stop making payments for the company because Seller had not complied with the terms of the deal. The court held that such advice breached Lawyer's continuing "ethical duty of loyalty to his former client" and constituted a basis for a malpractice action even though there was no showing that the lawyer used or disclosed confidential information of the former client.

Sullivan County Regional Refuse Disposal Dist. v. Town of Acworth, 686 A.2d 755 (N.H.1996), involved a lawyer who had previously helped set up a multi-town garbage disposal district. The court prohibited the lawyer from helping one of the member towns to withdraw from that agreement. If

could not become of counsel to the firm representing one of the parties without disqualifying that firm from work on the case. The court cited Poly Software Int'l, Inc. v. Su, 880 F.Supp. 1487 (D.Utah 1995), and Cho v. Superior Court, 45 Cal.Rptr.2d 863 (Cal.Ct.App. 1995). We focus more directly on limitations on former mediators in Problem 16.

there is a violation of Rule 1.9(a) the court will disqualify. No confidential information of the district was at issue, and the agreement was a public document, but the case involved construction of language drafted while the lawyer was principal counsel for the district. If the lawyer now advocated a particular interpretation of the agreement, that would be contrary to his duty of loyalty to the rest of the towns in the district. Even "in the absence of any confidences, an attorney owes a duty of loyalty to a former client that prevents that attorney from attacking, or interpreting, work she performed, or supervised, for the former client."

Contrast Oasis West Realty, LLC v. Goldman, 182 Cal.App.4th 688 (Cal. Ct. App. 2010), where the lawyer was no longer representing a new client but simply advocating his personal views. Plaintiff was attempting to redevelop real estate it owned in Beverly Hills. The defendants were a law firm and a partner at the firm. Plaintiff had hired this particular partner (lawyer) because he was heavily involved in Beverly Hills politics and homeowners' matters, and the plaintiff believed he could assist in getting the project approved. Defendants represented the plaintiff for a little over a year, and then the representation ended.

Two years later, some Beverly Hills citizens opposed this project and sought a referendum on it. The lawyer and his wife signed the petition and solicited signatures from neighbors. The lawyer also sent two emails to city council in his capacity as president of a local homeowners' association urging it to not approve the project until certain traffic issues were resolved. The plaintiff sued the lawyer and his law firm for breach of fiduciary duty, breach of contract, and professional negligence. The defendants argued that the partner had engaged in protected activity as a private citizen pursuant to his rights of petition and free speech. The trial court ruled for plaintiff, but the appellate court reversed. The acts of the lawyer were protected free speech in these circumstances. The lawyer never undertook a subsequent representation or employment; he was acting as a private citizen. He also never revealed confidential information during his activities, or even hinted at the possibility that his positions on the development were influenced by confidential information. There was no violation of the common law duty of loyalty to the plaintiff. A lawyer may take personal positions adverse to a former client, provided that a current representation is not compromised. In this case, the plaintiff was a former client, so there was no current representation.

d.   Some cases find a substantial relationship if the legal issues in the two cases are likely to be the same, even though the facts differ. See, e.g., Government of India v. Cook Industries, Inc., 569 F.2d 737 (2d Cir.1978) (cases substantially related because both involved short-weight shipping of grain, albeit in different factual settings); State v. Barnett, 965 P.2d 323 (N.M.App.1998) (defendant in a burglary recognized prosecutor as former public defender who represented him when he pled guilty to charges of a different burglary three years earlier).

2. Should the current medical malpractice case and the former adoption proceeding discussed in this problem be held to be "substantially related" matters?

a. The touchstone in most cases is whether the lawyer received relevant confidential information in the prior representation. If use of confidential information is the key issue, of course, courts and lawyers have an inevitable dilemma. Restatement Third, The Law Governing Lawyers § 132, Comment *d(iii)*, explains:

> "A concern to protect a former client's confidential information would be self-defeating if, in order to obtain its protection, the former client were required to reveal in a public proceeding the particular communication or other confidential information that could be used in the subsequent representation. The interests of subsequent clients also militate against extensive inquiry into the precise nature of the lawyer's representation of the subsequent client and the nature of exchanges between them.

> "The substantial-relationship test avoids requiring disclosure of confidential information by focusing upon the general features of the matters involved and inferences as to the likelihood that confidences were imparted by the former client that could be used to adverse effect in the subsequent representation. The inquiry into the issues involved in the prior representation should be as specific as possible without thereby revealing the confidential client information itself or confidential information concerning the second client. When the prior matter involved litigation, it will be conclusively presumed that the lawyer obtained confidential information about the issues involved in the litigation. When the prior matter did not involve litigation, its scope is assessed by reference to the work that the lawyer undertook and the array of information that a lawyer ordinarily would have obtained to carry out that work. The information obtained by the lawyer might also be proved by inferences from redacted documents, for example."

b. In making the substantial relationship determination, courts often apply factors such as those articulated in H.F. Ahmanson & Co. v. Salomon Bros., Inc., 280 Cal.Rptr. 614 (Cal.Ct.App.1991): (1) the factual similarity of the cases, (2) their legal similarity, and (3) the extent of the lawyers' involvement in the cases. The fact that firm members testify they do not presently remember anything about the prior representation is ordinarily *not* a relevant factor.

c. Other courts use a two-step inquiry: (1) are the matters related, and if so, (2) did the law firm learn confidential information that would help the client in the second matter. Some states place a burden on the law firm to prove that it does not possess confidential information from the prior representation.

In Analytica, Inc. v. NPD Research, Inc., 708 F.2d 1263 (7th Cir. 1983), the Seventh Circuit asked whether, from an objective perspective, it was likely that the firm learned confidential information that would be helpful in the second case. But the court refused to inquire into what actual information was learned, lest the information thereby lose its confidential character. The Fifth Circuit, however, in In re American Airlines, 972 F.2d 605 (5th Cir.1992), read the substantial relationship test to focus more on law firm loyalty to former clients rather than on confidential information alone. Which approach do you believe is more consistent with the principles underlying Model Rule 1.9?

d. National Medical Enterprises, Inc. v. Godbey, 924 S.W.2d 123 (Tex.1996), disqualified a law firm in a damage suit against a chain of psychiatric hospitals because one of its lateral hires had previously represented one of the hospitals' administrators in a criminal case arising out of the same facts. The lawyer in question had never represented the hospital itself, but he had expressly promised to keep confidential the corporate information he had learned while representing the administrator. In addition, the information turned up by the firm in the tort case could lead to the filing of new criminal charges against the administrator who was clearly a former client.

e. Cardona v. General Motors Corp., 939 F.Supp. 351 and 942 F.Supp. 968 (D.N.J.1996), involved firms who specialized in so-called "lemon law" cases involving allegedly defective cars. The small firm that represented hundreds of lemon law plaintiffs hired a lawyer who had defended hundreds of lemon law cases on behalf of General Motors (GM). To GM, that disloyalty violated Rule 1.9 even though the plaintiffs in the cases the lawyer would work on now were all different from the parties in the cases he had defended. The court agreed that while every car and every "lemon" was different, there was a factual nexus running through the cases that made it very likely confidential knowledge of GM's approach to the cases would be important in the lawyer's new job. The court held that the cases were substantially related and ordered disqualification.

3. Suppose Heath knows no crucial secrets (e.g., that Abraham operates while intoxicated), but she does have general impressions of Abraham's personality and specific knowledge of his financial situation. Could that make the cases "substantially related"?

a. In Chugach Electric Ass'n v. United States Dist. Court, 370 F.2d 441 (9th Cir.1966), cert.denied, 389 U.S. 820 (1967), the attorney was general counsel and later a consultant to Chugach. The board of directors of the company was divided on many issues and when a minority of the board gained control and became a majority, the attorney resigned. The attorney later represented the trustee in bankruptcy of a coal company and sued Chugach, claiming an antitrust conspiracy because of alleged agreements and overt acts occurring after the attorney severed any connection with Chugach. The court disqualified the attorney. "The problem here is not limited to the question whether [the attorney] was connected with petitioner as its counsel at the time agreements were reached and overt acts taken, but includes the question whether, as attorney, he was in a position to acquire knowledge casting light on the purpose of later acts and agreements. * * * A likelihood here exists which cannot be disregarded that [the attorney's] knowledge of private matters gained in confidence would provide him with greater insight and understanding of the significance of subsequent events in an antitrust context and offer a promising source of discovery." 370 F.2d at 443.

b. In Franzoni v. Hart Schaffner & Marx, 726 N.E.2d 719 (Ill.App.Ct. 2000), plaintiff's counsel in an age discrimination and retaliatory discharge case had served for 14 years as the defendant's in-house counsel. Some years earlier, on behalf of the company, the lawyer had negotiated a settlement with the plaintiff in another case and had worked on over 580 employment-related matters for all divisions of the company. The court found the lawyer was "privy to the secrets and confidences of [the company]" as it related to cases like the current one. Further, executives he might be required to depose or cross-examine were persons with whom he had worked while at the company. Thus, the lawyer was disqualified.

c. In Mitchell v. Metropolitan Life Ins. Co., 2002 WL 441194 (S.D.N.Y.2002), plaintiffs sued their former employer for gender-based employment discrimination. Fleishman, a partner at one of two firms hired by the plaintiffs, had previously worked at a different firm and defended MetLife in a variety of products liability suits over a period of several years. The court disqualified Fleishman's current firm. First, the scope of Fleishman's prior representation of MetLife exposed her to matters that would be at issue in the instant case. For instance, Fleishman defended MetLife against claims for unfair selling practices and interviewed several employees in the company's sales division. The plaintiffs in this case worked in that division and lodged their discrimination complaints against supervisors whom Fleishman had interviewed. Thus, the matters were substantially related even though the legal issues were much different. Fleishman learned "confidential" information that is "substantially related to disputed factual issues material to the resolution of the present action."

d. State ex rel. Wal–Mart Stores v. Kortum, 559 N.W.2d 496 (Neb. 1997), was a suit for damages from a fall in the store's parking lot. The lawyer had previously defended the store in a claim for a fall inside the store and in so doing had received access to Wal–Mart's policies and general defense strategy. The court said the fact the pleadings in the two cases were similar was not controlling. Similarly, the Wal–Mart procedures were common knowledge and the policies manuals were discoverable. Thus, neither represented truly confidential information. The court concluded that the cases were not substantially related. See also, ABA Formal Opinion 99–415 (Sept. 8, 1999) ("general knowledge of the strategies, policies, or personnel of the former employer" is not sufficient to justify disqualification. Otherwise, a lawyer could never sue a former client).

4. Should cases be considered "substantially related" if the factual issues in two or more cases are closely related, but there is no confidentiality?

a. Allegaert v. Perot, 565 F.2d 246 (2d Cir.1977), was a bankruptcy case. Law Firm earlier represented a joint venture consisting of Company A and Company B. Company B was now bankrupt. Law Firm wanted to represent Company A in the bankruptcy proceeding but the trustee for Company B objected. Law Firm was obviously closely involved with the factual issues relating to the joint venture, the court held, but Company B had no reasonable expectation that the facts it learned would be kept confidential from Company A. Thus the "substantial relation" test was not met. "[B]efore the substantial relationship test is even implicated, it must be shown that the attorney was in a position where he could have received information which his former client might reasonably have assumed the attorney would withhold from his present client." 565 F.2d at 250 (emphasis in original).

b. Restatement Third, The Law Governing Lawyers § 132, Comment *i*, created the concept of an "accommodation client" to deal with cases where the lawyer clearly represented one client but agreed to act for the benefit of another in a setting in which the clients did not expect to keep any confidences from each other. There is an "accommodation client" when the lawyer, as an accommodation to the existing client, will represent another client "typically for a limited purpose in order to avoid duplication of services and consequent higher fees." When the interests of the two later differ, the Comment says, the lawyer may not continue to represent both, but she may continue to represent the original client even contrary to the interest of the client that had been "accommodated." The typical circumstances that warrant the inference that the "accommodation client" understood and at least impliedly consented to the lawyer's continuing to represent the regular client are that "the lawyer has represented the regular client for a long period of time before undertaking representation of the other client, that the representation was to be of limited scope and duration, and that the lawyer was not expected to keep confidential from the regular client any information provided to the lawyer by the other client."

c. In re Rite Aid Corp. Securities Litigation, 139 F.Supp.2d 649 (E.D.Pa.2001), applied the accommodation client principle in a securities action filed against the Rite Aid Corporation and some of its directors and officers. Ballard Spahr, long-time company counsel, represented all of the defendants, including Grass, the former CEO, from the time the suit commenced. Grass then resigned from Rite–Aid, and other director-defendants retained other lawyers to represent them, but Ballard Spahr continued to represent the corporation. When new corporate management directed the firm to attempt to settle with the plaintiffs, a settlement agreement was reached under which the plaintiffs preserved their claims against Grass. In this motion, Grass sought to disqualify Ballard Spahr from settling with the rest of the defendants, arguing that the firm had taken a position adverse to his interests as a client without obtaining consent. The court denied the motion. First, the court said, from the beginning, the corporation had been the primary client and Grass's interests were secondary. Furthermore, Grass left the company after the litigation had started; the conflict of interest was created by his act. Next, the court held that representing Grass was simply an accommodation and that Ballard Spahr had agreed with Rite–Aid that, if a conflict arose between Rite–Aid and Grass, it would continue to represent Rite–Aid. The court held that by using the corporation's counsel at all, Grass effectively consented to this provision of the engagement.

C.   OTHER SITUATIONS WHERE MODEL RULE 1.9 MAY REQUIRE DISQUALIFICATION

1.   Assume that Martha Heath had not represented Dr. Abraham in any earlier malpractice case, but she had represented a co-defendant in such a case. Should that bar her from taking the current case against Dr. Abraham?

a.   Does Rule 1.9 apply to the co-defendant situation? See Wilson P. Abraham Const. Corp. v. Armco Steel Corp., 559 F.2d 250 (5th Cir.1977), and Kevlik v. Goldstein, 724 F.2d 844 (1st Cir.1984), holding that, absent the consent of both clients, the lawyer must be disqualified because confidences are shared in such a common defense.

b.   In GTE North, Inc. v. Apache Products Co., 914 F.Supp. 1575 (N.D.Ill.1996), there had been a "joint investigation agreement" (JIA) under which separately represented firms shared the costs of determining responsibility for waste at a Superfund site. Later, counsel for one potential defendant undertook representation of a claimant suing a different defendant who had been part of the JIA for the same site. The court found that each JIA member was an "implied client" of the firm and consequently ordered disqualification.

c.   ABA Ethics Opinion 95–395 (July 24, 1995) asked whether a lawyer who had once represented one member of a joint insurance-defense consortium might take on a related case against one of the other insurer-members. Relevant confidential information learned from the prior client clearly could not be disclosed, the opinion said, and the lawyer could not act contrary to the interest of his own former client. If the lawyer knows no relevant confidences, and if the new case is not contrary to the interests of the prior client, or if the prior client waives its rights, there is no per se prohibition. But the new client should know these limitations and be told of any implications they may have for the lawyer's role in the present case.

d.   Colorpix Systems of America v. Broan Mfg. Co., 131 F.Supp.2d 331 (D.Conn.2001), applied a similar analysis to determine when representation of a parent company in a prior case would bar later representation against a subsidiary. The plaintiffs alleged that two fires were caused by defective bathroom exhaust fans made by Broan. The plaintiff's law firm had represented Broan's parent company, Nortek, in an earlier case of the same kind. First, the court noted that Broan shared the same legal department with Nortek, and Broan and Nortek had developed a common strategy for defending cases such as these. Then, in order to determine whether Broan had been a "vicarious client" of the plaintiff's law firm in the prior case (and thus could be said to be a former client in this case), the court asked (1) whether the current litigation will have a financial impact on the former client, Nortek, (2) the importance that the former client has attached to the current litigation against its subsidiary in terms of supervision, and (3) whether the affiliated companies share an "identity of interest." In this case, Broan accounted for a substantial share of Nortek's business, Nortek's general counsel had supervised Broan's defense in the present action, and Broan and Nortek shared an "identity of interest" because they shared a legal department and business philosophy. Thus, disqualification was required.

2. Suppose that, while doing discovery in her earlier representation of Dr. Abraham's co-defendant, Heath had learned something about a different patient of that doctor—the patient's tendency to alcoholism, for example. Could Heath use that information in a suit against that other patient on behalf of a current client?

a. Look at Model Rule 1.9(c). Notice that, quite apart from whether two matters are the same or substantially related, a lawyer may not use or reveal information acquired in a prior representation contrary to the interest of the former client unless the information has become generally known.

b. The former client—the doctor—has a duty to protect the confidentiality of his patients' medical information. While defending him, Martha Heath learned information about his prior cases subject to that confidentiality obligation. Thus, it would be contrary to the interest and obligation of the former client to have the information used by Heath in a current case.

c. Restatement Third, The Law Governing Lawyers § 132, Comment *g(ii)*, Illustration 7 explains:

> "Lawyer has represented Hospital in several medical-malpractice cases. In the course of preparing to defend one such case, Lawyer reviewed the confidential medical file of Patient who was not a party in the action. From the file, Lawyer learned that Patient had been convicted of a narcotics offense in another jurisdiction. Patient is now a material witness for the defense in an unrelated case that Lawyer has filed on behalf of Plaintiff. Adequate representation of Plaintiff would require Lawyer to cross-examine Patient about the narcotics conviction in an effort to undermine Patient's credibility. Lawyer may not reveal information about Patient that Hospital has an obligation to keep confidential. That limitation in turn may preclude effective representation of Plaintiff in the pending case."

Does recognition of this obligation make sense to you?

3. Suppose Heath recently settled a class action on behalf of all the residents of her city against a local department store for systematically overcharging interest on past due accounts. Is Heath now prohibited from representing the department store suing a customer who happened to be a member of the former class for failure to pay a department store bill?

a. Because of the many members of a represented class and the lack of confidential information acquired by the class action lawyer about any one of them, typically a lawyer is not barred from proceeding in a later action against such a former class member. See ABA Model Rule 1.7, Comment 25.

b. Fuchs v. Schick, 2002 WL 538842 (S.D.N.Y.2002), was an exception to that principle because the class action lawyer conferred confidentially with a particular member of the class. Fuchs sued Schick for selling partnership units in a Marriott hotel venture at a price that exceeded the market value for the units. The lawyer for Fuchs previously represented Schick when Schick was a plaintiff in a similar class action suit against Marriott. In that suit, Schick served as the head of a committee of plaintiffs and, as such, had conversations with lawyers for the class regarding the purchase and sale of the partnership units. Schick's prior relationship with those lawyers led the court to reject the motion of Fuchs' lawyer to be admitted pro hac vice. Because Schick had not been a *passive* class member, it was fair to say that his former lawyer secured secret information from Schick in that earlier case and would now be appearing against him in a substantially related matter.

4. Suppose that the lawyer does not change firms, but the lawyer's nonlawyer assistant, e.g., a secretary or paralegal, does. Does Model Rule 1.9 have anything to say about that situation?

a. Rule 1.9 only talks of lawyers, but Model Rule 1.10, Comment 4, says that law firms ordinarily must screen people like paralegals. The leading case on the issue is Herron v. Jones, 637 S.W.2d 569 (Ark.1982), requiring disqualification of the new firm unless the secretary is screened from work on the case for the new firm.[4]

b. In re Complex Asbestos Litigation, 283 Cal.Rptr. 732 (Cal.Ct.App. 1991), upheld the disqualification of a law firm representing plaintiffs in asbestos claims because it had hired a paralegal who had worked for one of the defense firms on similar cases. The danger of misuse of defense confidences was too great given the failure to screen the paralegal from participation in asbestos matters.

c. In re American Home Products, 985 S.W.2d 68 (Tex.1998), concerned disqualification of a law firm that hired a legal assistant. This assistant earlier had worked for a lawyer representing one of the defendants in the Norplant litigation. She billed 72.5 hours interviewing potential witnesses, meeting with counsel, investigating plaintiffs, and writing memoranda about witnesses. Then, the lawyers for the plaintiffs hired her, and the defendant moved to disqualify that firm. The Texas Supreme Court ordered disqualification. It was not improper to hire an opposing firm's legal assistant, but in this case it was improper not to screen her. Indeed, the court must disqualify because her new law firm assigned to work on the

4. Although requirements that someone be "screened" are usually applied to lawyers, and the ABA Model Rules' definition of "screened" speaks of the isolation of a "law- yer," the requirements for such a "screen" described in new ABA Model Rule 1.0(k) and Comments 8–10 would presumably apply to the screening of nonlawyers as well.

very case she had researched for the other side. The court did not automatically disqualify plaintiffs' co-counsel, but it might have done so if co-counsel had jointly prepared the case for trial or otherwise could be presumed to have shared the legal assistant's tainted information. Compare, Phoenix Founders, Inc. v. Marshall, 887 S.W.2d 831 (Tex.1994) (firm not disqualified where paralegal worked only 0.6 hours looking for a pleading and the new law firm screened her).

d.   However, Zimmerman v. Mahaska Bottling Co., 19 P.3d 784 (Kan. 2001), rejected the usual rule that a secretary that moves from one law firm to another may be screened at all. In this case, the secretary had not worked for anyone connected with the case, although lawyers at the former firm had talked about it in front of her. The court concluded that the secretary acquired material and confidential information regarding the personal injury suit while working for plaintiff's lawyers, and thus the court disqualified the defendants' firm where the secretary began working after leaving plaintiff's firm. If the secretary had been a lawyer moving from one firm to the other, she would have been disqualified in spite of screening, the court said, and there was no reason to treat nonlawyers differently. The court observed: "a majority of courts have rejected screening because of the uncertainty regarding the effectiveness of the screen, the monetary incentive involved in breaching the screen, the fear of disclosing privileged information in the course of proving an effective screen, and the possibility of accidental disclosures." 19 P.3d at 793.[5]

5.   Bring the facts closer to home. Suppose you, a law student, worked on a case for Firm A between your first and second years in law school but work for opposing counsel, Firm B, the next summer. Should that disqualify Firm B from continuing in the case? Must you be screened from participation in the matter that you worked on at Firm A?

a.   Allen v. Academic Games Leagues of America, Inc., 831 F.Supp. 785 (C.D.Cal.1993), was a suit for trademark and copyright infringement that a maker of educational games filed. Wright (now the lawyer for the defendant) had worked with the plaintiff when he was a law student. Wright also had served on the plaintiff's advisory committee, and had even tried to help settle this lawsuit. Once he became a lawyer, he went to work for the firm that represented the defendant and participated actively in that defense. Because Wright had been a law student at the earlier time, the plaintiff was not his "former client." Wright had a duty to protect the plaintiff's confidential information, however, because Wright was the common law agent of the plaintiff and assumed a fiduciary duty. To prevent a violation of that duty, the court disqualified Wright and his law firm from continuing to represent the defendant.

5. See also, First Miami Securities, Inc. v. Sylvia, 780 So.2d 250 (Fla.App.2001) (holding that screening is not a valid alternative if the legal secretary has "actual knowledge" of material confidences instead of merely being "exposed" to this information, and then remanding for a hearing).

b. In Actel Corp. v. Quicklogic Corp., 1996 WL 297045 (N.D.Cal. 1996), an associate in the firm representing the plaintiff had worked a split-summer for the firm defending a case while he was in law school. When interviewed by the plaintiff's firm, he said he had no memory of working on the case. Later he said that he remembered nothing substantive about the case, but his time records showed he spent two hours working on a memorandum and "reading the case file." The court found these facts raised a presumption that the student, now a lawyer, had received and shared confidential information. Given that his new firm neither screened the lawyer nor overcame the presumption of shared confidential information, the court disqualified the plaintiff's firm.

c. Do these cases give you pause? Why should law firms be able to screen law students and lawyers who obtained their disqualifying information before becoming lawyers? Notice that Model Rule 1.10, Comment 4, expressly adopts this rule.

Restatement Third, The Law Governing Lawyers § 123, Comment *f*, says that law clerks "typically have limited responsibilities and thus might acquire little sensitive information. Absent special circumstances, they should be considered nonlawyer employees for the purposes" of imputing their knowledge to others in the law firm. On the other hand, "[p]ersons who have completed their legal education and are awaiting admission to practice at the time of providing services to a client of a law firm typically have duties comparable to admitted lawyers and accordingly should ordinarily be treated as lawyers for purposes of imputation."

d. Do you agree with this approach to law student conflicts? Would any other rule make it too risky for firms, particularly large firms, to hire students during law school? Should placement concerns be relevant where issues of ethical conduct are at stake?

6. What about "lawyer-temporaries" engaged by a law firm for a limited period of time, either directly or through a placement agency? Should they be treated as any other lawyers for purposes of imputing disqualification?

a. Functionally, a "temp" looks a lot like a law student or other nonlawyer. Temps may work on a single matter or on several different matters. Sometimes, they may simultaneously work on different matters for two or more firms. Firms typically hire temporaries to meet short-term staffing needs or to supply special expertise on a particular matter. On the other hand, they are not nonlawyers; they are licensed to practice law.

b. ABA Formal Opinion 88–356 (Dec. 16, 1988) said that Model Rules 1.7 and 1.9 govern such lawyers. For example, under Rule 1.7, a temporary lawyer may not personally work simultaneously on matters for clients of different firms if the work for each is directly adverse to the other.

c. Are temporary lawyers "associated" with a firm for purposes of the *imputed* disqualification sections of Rule 1.10? ABA Opinion 88–356 concluded that the answer must be determined by a functional analysis of the facts and circumstances involved.

"Ultimately, whether a temporary lawyer is treated as being 'associated with a firm' while working on a matter for the firm depends on whether the nature of the relationship is such that the temporary lawyer has access to information relating to the representation of firm clients other than the client on whose matters the lawyer is working and the consequent risk of improper disclosure or misuse of information relating to representation of other clients of the firm."

d.   D.C. Bar Association Ethics Opinion 352 (2010) came to a similar conclusion. Law Firm A hires a temporary lawyer (TL) to work on Case #1. Law Firm B represents the adverse party in Case #1. That case continues but TL has left Firm A. Now, Law Firm B wants to hire TL to work on unrelated matters in Case #2. Does TL have a conflict imputed to Law Firm B?

The D.C. Opinion advised that a fact-specific analysis governs whether to impute the conflict. TL's conflicts will not be imputed to Firm B if TL's new work would be for a limited duration, TL would work either at a separate location or at a segregated area in the firm's offices, and TL's access to confidential information would be limited to the issue upon which TL was working.

By contrast, TL is "associated" with the Firm B (and the conflict imputed) if TL works in the Firm B's offices on multiple matters simultaneously, is listed on Firm B's website or materials (thus leaving the impression that he has full association with the law firm), and has access to Firm B's files and email. In short, Law Firm B should screen TL who still has an ethical obligation to preserve client confidences learned while employed by Firm A.

e.   What do these examples suggest to you about the general duty of a law firm to supervise the handling of confidential information by its professional and support employees? Look at Model Rules 5.1 and 5.3.

D.   ACCESS TO THE WORK PRODUCT OF DISQUALIFIED COUNSEL

1.   If Dr. Abraham's motion were granted and Heath were disqualified, should substituted counsel have access to Heath's work product?

a.   Should the answer depend on why the lawyer was disqualified? For example, if the court disqualifies the lawyer because the lawyer knew material confidences, and transferring the work product would transfer the confidences, then the rule should bar the transfer. But if the work product was not tainted by the confidential information, why should the new counsel not be entitled to it?

b.   In First Wisconsin Mortgage Trust v. First Wisconsin Corp., 584 F.2d 201 (7th Cir.1978) (en banc), the majority held that there is no per se rule against subsequent counsel's use of work product developed by disqualified counsel. Thus, unless there is evidence of "improper advantage" having been secured, "such as the use of confidential information," it is an abuse of discretion for the trial court to prevent turning over of the work product. The work product at issue in that case was an analysis of loan files conducted by a team of 15 lawyers for more than a year prior to the ultimate disqualification of the firm. The majority thought the loan file summaries were "the result of routine lawyer work of a type which any competent lawyer, by spending the substantial time which would be required, could accomplish just as well as did [the disqualified counsel]." 584 F.2d at 204. Accord, IBM Corp. v. Levin, 579 F.2d 271 (3d Cir.1978).

c. In re EPIC Holdings, Inc., 28 S.W.3d 511 (Tex.2000), was a case in which the court had earlier disqualified the plaintiff's first firm. Some of that firm's members had been at the firm that had incorporated the defendant company and thus they could have received relevant confidential information. Now, the disqualified firm sought to prevent plaintiff's new counsel from using the former counsel's work product. The firm was afraid that defendant could later accuse it of turning over confidential information and wanted to assure it had a defense to that charge. The Texas Supreme Court refused to prohibit use of all such work product. First, "when an attorney is disqualified, successor counsel is presumptively entitled to obtain the pleadings, discovery, correspondence and all other materials in the public record or exchanged by the parties." 28 S.W.3d at 514. As for other material, the court created a rebuttable presumption that the work product contained confidential information. There were three dissents.

2. How can the new lawyer demonstrate that no confidential information is included in the material being used?

a. Is the theoretical ability to use the work product merely a mirage? The dissent in *First Wisconsin* accused the majority of "attempting to draw fine ethical lines based upon the specific content of the objectionable material," an approach "which has been repeatedly condemned. * * * [T]he majority further compounds its error by intimating that once the defendants have disclaimed the use of confidential information, the former client is the one who must point to the confidences used in the work." *In camera* inspection of the work product, the dissenters argued, would be "both unworkable and a dangerous departure from long-accepted ethical guidelines." 584 F.2d at 211–13.

b. Similar arguments were made by the dissenters in *EPIC Holdings*. The majority, however, outlined standards for determining whether the material contained or reflected confidential information of the defendant. The subject matter of the work product is relevant, e.g., factual information or legal research, the court said. So is its nature, i.e., lawyer notes or deposition transcripts. The trial judge should inspect the materials *in camera* if the answer is not obvious.

c. Who has the better of the argument on this issue? The right to such work product will not be worth fighting about if the litigation costs outweigh the cost of redoing the work. Thus, the client may wind up paying twice for discovery of the information.

———

PROBLEM 15

IMPUTED DISQUALIFICATION

Ever since Problem 9, we have assumed that if one lawyer in a law firm has a conflict of interest, every lawyer in the firm is treated as having such a conflict. Thus, if one lawyer in a firm formerly represented the plaintiff in a lawsuit, another lawyer in the firm may not now represent the defendant even if the respective lawyers worked in offices in different cities. Not all conflicts are imputed,[1] but many are, and that obviously creates a very important limit on the operation of law firms. In this problem we look at particular issues that arise in administration of the principle. We first ask how the principle applies in firms and organizations other than traditional firms. Next, we ask to how many firms in any single case the reach of the rule might extend. We then ask whether the same principle should impute conflicts among family members who practice law in different firms, and whether "screening" the conflicted lawyer should be sufficient to overcome the force of the rule.

FACTS

Charles & Burls (C & B) is a prestigious, 200–person Wall Street firm with a national clientele. It represents World Wide Container Corp. (World Wide) in many matters, one of which is a suit by National Gasket Co. against World Wide for contribution in a products liability case. The case is to be tried in New Orleans, and C & B is cooperating with Willis & Xeres (W & X), the law firm that World Wide uses as local counsel in New Orleans.

Willis of W & X is the only lawyer in that firm actively working on the case. His only role is to file papers, motions, and other pleadings forwarded to him by C & B. National Gasket has now moved to disqualify both C & B and W & X from acting as World Wide's lawyers because Xeres (while he had been in a solo practice before forming W & X) had represented National Gasket in various product liability matters arising out of the same facts that led to the present suit. Xeres learned confidential information that, if disclosed, would be useful to World Wide's defense of the present suit. C & B has never represented National Gasket.

---

1. Note that the general imputation rule, Rule 1.10(a), imputes only Rules 1.7 and 1.9. Rule 1.8(k) makes clear that all of that Rule is imputed except Rule 1.8(j), dealing with sexual relations with a client. Rule 3.7(b) makes clear that the provisions of Rule 3.7(a) are not imputed unless the lawyer is also covered under Rules 1.7 or 1.9. And Rule 1.10(d) recognizes that Rule 1.11 has special rules for imputation involving former government lawyers.

QUESTIONS

A.   IMPUTATION OF CONFLICTS THROUGHOUT A LAW FIRM

1.   May Willis continue to act as local counsel for World Wide?

a.   Look at Model Rule 1.10(a). We know from Problem 14 that Xeres could not represent World Wide because of his previous representation of National Gasket in a matter substantially related to the present matter. What reasons justify a sweeping disqualification of everyone in Xeres' firm?

b.   Should disqualification turn on whether Willis has learned any relevant confidential information from Xeres? Could Xeres properly disclose any such information to Willis, whether or not the firm was involved in this lawsuit? Remember that Xeres learned the information while working somewhere else. Why shouldn't the law simply assume that Xeres will comply with his duties of loyalty and confidentiality and let the other W & X lawyers work on the case?

c.   W.E. Bassett Co. v. H.C. Cook Co., 201 F.Supp. 821 (D.Conn.1961), aff'd per curiam, 302 F.2d 268 (2d Cir.1962), was one of the early cases establishing the clear and sweeping imputation rule. Lawyer X had represented the plaintiff in a lengthy case. X then joined a firm—one member of which had once represented and advised a corporate defendant on some important issues in the same controversy. The lawyers in X's new firm agreed that X would continue to represent the plaintiff corporation in the matter, but without any participation by X's new partners in either the work or the fees. But when the district court learned of this plan, it *sua sponte* held a hearing on the disqualification of X. The court found X's partners and X "made every effort to comply with Canons 6 and 37 [of the 1908 ABA Canons of Ethics as amended] as they honestly interpreted them," but the circumstances "will inevitably lead to suspicion and distrust in them in the minds of the defendants and the opportunity for misunderstanding on the part of the public. * * * " 201 F.Supp. at 825. Thus, the court required X to cease all further participation in the case.

2.   Should conflicts that are "personal" to one lawyer be imputed throughout a firm?

a.   Look at ABA Model Rule 1.10(a) and Comment 3. Note that, ordinarily, the Rules do not impute "personal" interest conflicts. Assume that Lawyer A in a criminal defense firm objects to defending persons charged with rape because of strongly held moral or political beliefs. His objection is such that he could not do a competent job. Clearly, Lawyer A may not take that case because to do so would violate Rule 1.1. But if the law firm excuses Lawyer A from working on such cases, should Lawyer A's disqualification be imputed to other members of the firm? If lawyer L, in the firm of A & B, is unable to represent fur companies because she is a member of PETA and objects strongly to wearing animal fur, should the entire law firm of A & B be disqualified?

b.   Restatement Third, The Law Governing Lawyers § 123 and § 125, Comment *g*, were written when Model Rule 1.10(a) did not have the "personal interest" exception. Thus, they restated the law as imputing such conflicts but suggested that the rule should not apply where "the personal interest conflict [of Lawyer A] was not known to the [other] lawyer handling the matter and could not have been determined by use of a reasonable conflict-checking system." Comment *g* also says that one should not impute "idiosyncratic" personal interests. For example, if Lawyer A has "strong philosophical or political aversion" to the objectives of Landlord, Lawyer B in the same firm can represent Landlord "as long as Lawyer A has no part in the representation and no supervisory or other control over Lawyer B * * *." Restatement § 125, Comment *g*, Illustration 7.

c.   Should personal interest conflicts be imputed to others in the firm? How do you define a personal conflict of interest? Why should the law treat personal conflicts differently from law firm business conflicts? Should it matter whether the lawyer with the strong beliefs is a new associate or the firm's influential senior partner?

3.   How should courts approach the question of imputation outside the traditional law firm setting?

a.   How should one define a "firm" for purposes of Rule 1.10? See Rule 1.10, Comment 1, and Rule 1.0(c). For example, should strict imputation be required if opposing parties are both clients of a legal aid office? That is, if one legal aid lawyer represents the plaintiff, may another represent the defendant? See Rule 1.10, Comment 1. Some argue that, unlike a private law firm, a "government-financed organization of lawyers does not receive any compensation directly from its clients; therefore, a legal aid attorney has no economic interest in a client represented by a colleague in the same office." Lawyers "in a legal aid service are not associated for the practice of law in the same sense that private law firm members are associated. Legal aid operates solely as a nonprofit, public benefit organization."[2]

b.   Should that distinction be controlling? What problems are raised if the legal aid lawyers are part of a single office? Flores v. Flores, 598 P.2d 893 (Alaska 1979), said that a state must supply private counsel to one party where the legal services agency's internal procedures were inadequate to guarantee confidentiality to both. Restatement Third, The Law Governing Lawyers § 123, Comment *d(v)*, agrees.

Compare, In re Charlisse C., 194 P.3d 330 (Cal. 2008), the Juvenile Dependency Court appointed the L.A. Children's Law Center to represent Charlisse C, a minor, in a case to protect her from abuse due to mental health problems of her mother. Her mother moved to disqualify the Law Center because it had represented her in the past. The Law Center is a single agency, but it was organized into three units with separate offices and no contact with each other. The purpose of this organization was precisely to deal with such conflicts. The California Supreme Court held that, in a former client case, the question is not loyalty but rather

---

2. Donald E. Woody, Note, Professional Responsibility—Conflicts of Interest Between   Legal Aid Lawyers, 37 Missouri L. Rev. 346, 349 (1972).

protection of the former client's confidential information through screening and structural safeguards. The court would disqualify the Law Center unless it could prove that it would protect the mother's confidences

c. Does the same analysis apply to dual representation by a public defender's office? A state's chief public defender asked for an ABA ethics opinion as to whether the public defender department could represent two criminal defendants in the same case if the defendants had conflicting interests. The public defender office in City 1 had 16 lawyers and public defender office in City 2 had five lawyers. The opinion ruled that if one public defender in City 1 is disqualified, all those in the City 1 office are disqualified, and because all offices of the public defender department are "subject to the common control" of the chief public defender, all the lawyers in the City 2 office are disqualified as well. The ethics committee offered no reason and merely cited DR 5–105(D). ABA Informal Opinion 1418 (1978). Accord, Commonwealth v. Westbrook, 400 A.2d 160 (Pa.1979) (members of public defender's office are members of the "same firm" for conflict of interest purposes); Duvall v. State, 923 A.2d 81 (Md.2007) (actual prejudice to defense is presumed when the defendant's lawyer would be trying to try to pin crime on another client of the public defender's office within a particular judicial district); State v. Veale, 919 A.2d 794 (N.H.2007) (state appellate defender has a conflict of interest in a case requiring it to argue that a local public defender provided inadequate assistance of counsel).

d. In United States v. Reynoso, 6 F.Supp.2d 269 (S.D.N.Y.1998), the Federal Defender Division of the Legal Aid Society assigned Lawyer 1 to represent Reynoso. Four years earlier, Lawyer 2, while in private practice but now also in the Federal Defender Division, had represented Vasquez in another trial. Vasquez was now a potential government witness against Reynoso. The government argued that Lawyer 2 would be disqualified from cross-examining his former client about the matter that was the subject of the former representation, and the court agreed. The government then argued that Lawyer 2's disqualification should be imputed to Lawyer 1, but the court disagreed and refused to impute disqualification within the Federal Defender Division. The lawyers had no common financial interest in the cases, they did not talk about the cases, and the files in the earlier case had been sent to storage. The Federal Defender Division should not be treated as a private law firm.

Do you agree? Are there costs to imputing the disqualification of one public defender to other lawyers in the organization? How great are the costs of failing to do so?

4. Should there be imputation among private lawyers who share office space but not fees?

a. In Great Britain, chambers of barristers are not partnerships. Each barrister is an independent lawyer, and it is possible for one barrister in the chambers to be prosecuting a case that another is defending. America has not copied the barrister model, but there are many instances of lawyers who are not partners but who share offices, share a library, and even share secretarial staff. If one lawyer is disqualified, should another lawyer in the same office suite be disqualified, even though they are not partners?

b. ABA Informal Opinion 1486 (1982) says it all depends. There should be no imputation if the lawyers "exercise reasonable care" to protect confidences of the clients. See also, Rule 1.0, Comment 2. Restatement Third, The Law Governing Lawyers § 123, Comment *e*, is to the same effect.

c. How would you organize such an office to assure that confidential information is appropriately protected? How should lawyers make clear to the world that they are not in the same firm, only in the same office?

B.   PERSONS AND FIRMS TO WHICH IMPUTATION WILL EXTEND

1.   If the court disqualifies the firm of W & X and all of its partners and associates, may C & B simply get new local counsel? Will the disqualification of W & X require that C & B be disqualified as well?

a. What reasons would justify such a result? Willis is presumed to know what Xeres knows, so should that presumption extend to C & B, the firm with which Willis regularly talks?

b. Is that result required by Model Rule 1.10(a), Comment 1? Should W & X and C & B be considered one firm for purposes of the imputation rules? Rule 1.0, Comment 3 recognizes that some corporations are "affiliated" with other corporations. Should a law firm ever be treated as "affiliated" with another firm?

c. ABA Formal Opinion 94–388 (Dec. 5, 1994) issued some useful warnings as it considered issues of "affiliations" between firms that are initiated and advertised to give a national scope to relatively small local firms. The opinion notes that when firms suggest they are affiliated, they risk misleading a client into believing a small firm has more resources at its disposal than it really has. In addition, if two firms hold themselves out as a single firm, e.g., use a common name, they have long been held to be one for conflict purposes. While the opinion refused to draw bright lines as to when relationships would require firms to be treated as one, it said it should be relevant whether the law firms have a "close and regular, continuing and semi-permanent" relationship. See also, Mustang Enterprises, Inc. v. Plug–In Storage Systems, Inc., 874 F.Supp. 881 (N.D.Ill.1995) (firms in different cities who hold themselves out as "affiliated" will be held to be one firm for conflicts purposes).

d. Traditionally, lawyers who are "of counsel" to a firm also have their conflicts imputed to others in the firm. An "of counsel" designation is normally used to indicate that the person will assist in the legal matter but is not a partner or an associate in the firm. ABA Formal Opinion 90–357 (May 10, 1990) said that the title "of counsel" on letterheads, law lists, professional cards, notices, office signs and the like is "a holding out to the world at large about some general and continuing relationship between the lawyers and the law firms in question. A different use of the same term occurs when a lawyer (or firm) is designated as of counsel in filings in a particular case: in such circumstances there is no general holding out as to a continuing relationship, or as to a relationship that applies to anything but the individual case." A lawyer may be "of counsel" to more than one firm, and a firm may be "of counsel" to another firm. The opinion concluded:

> "There can be no doubt that an of counsel lawyer (or firm) is 'associated in' and has an 'association with' the firm (or firms) to which the lawyer is of counsel, for purposes of both the general imputation of disqualification pursuant to Rule 1.10 of the Model Rules and the imputation of disqualifications resulting from former government service under Rules 1.11(a) and 1.12(c); and is a lawyer *in* the firm for purposes of Rule 3.7(b), regarding the circumstances in which, when a lawyer is to be a witness in a proceeding, the lawyer's colleague may nonetheless represent the client in that proceeding."

But see, Hempstead Video, Inc. v. Incorporated Village of Valley Stream, 409 F.3d 127 (2d Cir.2005) (where a lawyer was of counsel to firm for some purposes but a solo practitioner for others, the lawyer should be allowed to rebut the presumption that he had shared confidential information with the firm).

2. If Xeres' confidential knowledge about National Gasket is imputed to Sandra Jones, an associate at W & X, and then Jones leaves to join a second firm, what does Model Rule 1.9(b) say about whether her new firm will also be disqualified?

a.   American Can Co. v. Citrus Feed Co., 436 F.2d 1125 (5th Cir.1971), is the leading case on the point. The Fifth Circuit noted that: "All authorities agree that all members of a partnership are barred from participating in a case from which one partner is disqualified. * * * [O]nce a partner is thus vicariously disqualified for a particular case, the subsequent dissolution of the partnership cannot cure his ineligibility to act as counsel in that case. * * * However, new partners of a vicariously disqualified partner, to whom knowledge has been imputed during a former partnership, are not necessarily disqualified: they need show only that the vicariously disqualified partner's knowledge was imputed, not actual." The court was concerned that "imputation and consequent disqualification could continue *ad infinitum*," and that such a result is not needed "to maintain public confidence in the bar." 436 F.2d at 1128–29.

Do you agree with this analysis? Is it consistent with Model Rule 1.9(b)? Dicta in *American Can* says that the subsequent dissolution of the partnership cannot cure the conflict of the *vicariously* disqualified lawyer. Does Rule 1.9(b) reject that conclusion? The Rules now impute a lawyer's knowledge, but do they impute the lawyer's imputed knowledge, making him or her a Typhoid Mary? Does Rule 1.9 reject "double imputation"?

b.   Essex Chemical Corp. v. Hartford Accident and Indemnity Co., 993 F.Supp. 241 (D.N.J.1998), involved an action filed by Essex seeking a declaration of insurance coverage for certain environmental claims. In

1988, Essex had retained Skadden Arps to fight off a takeover, and in that work, Skadden had learned confidential information about Essex. In this case, filed in 1993, Skadden appeared for Home Insurance, one of the defendants. The court found the confidences previously acquired were sufficient to disqualify Skadden, and in an earlier opinion, 975 F.Supp. 650 (D.N.J.1997), the magistrate judge had also disqualified the firms representing all the other defendants who were party to a joint defense agreement in the case. But the district court found the last step went too far. Citing *American Can*, it said the court should not presume that the law firm was sharing confidences with other firms; it ordered a hearing on the real nature of the joint defense work.

c.   Adams v. Aerojet–General Corp., 104 Cal.Rptr.2d 116 (Cal.Ct.App. 2001), confirms that California law reaches the same result as Model Rule 1.9(b). Plaintiff's lawyer in an environmental case had formerly been at a firm that represented the defendant on environmental issues. The trial court disqualified the lawyer, presuming that he had learned the confidential information the firm had received. The Court of Appeals rejected such an automatic rule: a firm-switching attorney is not automatically disqualified, on the basis of imputed knowledge, from a case involving a client of a former law firm. The court remanded and concluded that the lawyer whose disqualification is sought should carry the burden of proving that he had no exposure to confidential information relevant to the current action while he was a member of the former firm. The trial court must review the lawyer's billing records or other evidence of what information he may have received.

3.   Now suppose Xeres resigns from the firm of W & X. Will Willis still be disqualified from representing World Wide?

a.   What factual determination does Rule 1.10(b) require be made? Who should have the burden of proof on the question of what information was disclosed by Xeres before he left the firm? Would a hearing on that question ever consist of more than testimony about who told what to whom at W & X, testimony that the other side could neither challenge nor rebut?

b.   Should the extent of imputation depend in part on how large a part the disqualified lawyer played in the earlier matter? In Silver Chrysler Plymouth, Inc. v. Chrysler Motors Corp., 518 F.2d 751 (2d Cir.1975), the court considered whether an attorney was disqualified from representing an automobile dealer by reason of once having been an associate in the firm that represented the manufacturer. At that firm, he conceded he had worked on Chrysler matters. The court concluded, however, that the "cases and the Canons on which they are based are intended to protect the confidences of former clients when an attorney has been in a position to learn them." The court held that the attorney had rebutted the presumption that he had received significant confidential material when he was associated with the 80–member firm. The attorney's involvement—

> "was, at most, limited to brief, informal discussions on a procedural matter or research on a specific point of law. * * * [W]e do not believe that there is any basis for distinguishing between partners and associates on the basis of title alone—both are members of the bar and

bound by the same Code of Professional Responsibility. But there is reason to differentiate for disqualification purposes between lawyers who become heavily involved in the facts of a particular matter and those who enter briefly on the periphery for a limited and specific purpose related solely to legal questions. In large firms at least, the former are normally the more seasoned lawyers and the latter the more junior." Id. at 756–57.

While purporting not to make a distinction between partners and associates, is the *Silver* case in effect making such a distinction? While neither the Model Rules nor the Model Code distinguish between partners and associates, should they? Would a bright line test be appropriate?

c. These issues are further illustrated by Novo Terapeutisk Laboratorium A/S v. Baxter Travenol Laboratories, Inc., 607 F.2d 186 (7th Cir.1979) (en banc). During July 1976, while at the Hume law firm, Attorney Cook spent 2 1/4 hours reviewing legal authorities and conferring with Baxter attorneys, during which time he received confidential information relating to a patent infringement matter. In December 1976, Cook left the Hume firm and took the Baxter account with him. In February 1977, plaintiff Novo filed a patent infringement action (substantially related to the July conference) against Baxter, and in August 1977, the Hume firm filed an appearance on behalf of Novo. The court readily agreed that on these facts Cook could not represent Novo, but that was not the issue; Cook was at a new firm and was still counsel for Baxter. The question was whether Cook's disqualification should be imputed to the other members of the Hume firm. "It is reasonable to presume that members of a law firm freely share their client's confidences with one another," but the circumstances of this case demonstrated that such a presumption need not be irrebuttable. Since Cook received the confidences, "he is in a position to know exactly what confidences he may have shared with others in his firm." 607 F.2d at 196. He said he did not share any and the remaining members of the Hume firm submitted affidavits confirming that they did not receive any confidential information from Cook. The court thus refused to disqualify the Hume firm.

4. In deciding these cases, should courts give weight to the fact that lawyers' movement from one position to another is very common these days?

a. City of Cleveland v. Cleveland Elec. Illuminating Co., 440 F.Supp. 193, 211 (N.D.Ohio 1976), aff'd without published opinion, 573 F.2d 1310 (6th Cir.1977), noted: "Imputing to an attorney in the private practice all confidential information obtained, or presumed to have been obtained, by other members of his law firm may severely limit the scope of the private attorney's future career and the effective operation of his firm, as well as the individual's right to legal counsel of choice." 440 F.Supp. at 211.[3]

---

3. The court also asserted a narrow, but now rarely followed test. "The * * * rule in the private practice of law should there- fore limit the imputation of confidential disclosures, actual or presumed, to only those lawyers practicing in the attorney's area of

b. Court of Appeals opinions following *Silver Chrysler Plymouth* include Gas–A–Tron of Arizona v. Union Oil Co. of California, 534 F.2d 1322 (9th Cir.1976) (per curiam), cert. denied, 429 U.S. 861 (1976), and Schloetter v. Railoc of Indiana, Inc., 546 F.2d 706 (7th Cir.1976). In the latter, the court suggested:

> "a different result in *Gas–A–Tron* or *Silver Chrysler* might have severely restricted mobility within the legal profession. For law firms would be understandably reluctant to hire a young lawyer who had previously worked at a large firm if it were to mean full automatic disqualification from any case involving a party represented by the young lawyer's former employer." 546 F.2d at 712 n. 11.

c. What role do you think facilitation of lawyer mobility should play in conflicts analysis? Do you agree with Reardon v. Marlayne, 416 A.2d 852, 860 (N.J.1980), that "problems of the job market and mobility are not solved by loosening ethical standards required of the profession"?

C. IMPUTATION WITHIN LAWYERS' FAMILIES

1. Assuming that Willis & Xeres may not represent World Wide in the case brought by National Gasket, may W & X suggest that World Wide go to the firm across the street in which Xeres' wife practices?

a. Why might there be reason for concern if Xeres' wife represents a client that her husband was prohibited from representing? If we presume that lawyers in a firm share confidential information, for example, should we presume the same about lawyers in a marriage?

b. ABA Formal Opinion 340 (Sept. 23, 1975) addressed such questions and concluded:

> "It is not necessarily improper for husband-and-wife lawyers who are practicing in different offices or firms to represent differing interests. No disciplinary rule expressly requires a lawyer to decline employment if a husband, wife, son, daughter, brother, father, or other close relative represents the opposing party in negotiation or litigation. Likewise, it is not necessarily improper for a law firm having a married partner or associate to represent clients whose interests are opposed to those of other clients represented by another law firm with which the married lawyer's spouse is associated as a lawyer.

> " * * * We cannot assume that a lawyer who is married to another lawyer necessarily will violate any particular disciplinary rule, such as those that protect a client's confidences, that proscribe neglect of a client's interest, and that forbid representation of differing interests. Yet it also must be recognized that the relationship of husband and

concentration. Absent direct proof to the contrary, the attorney would not be deemed to have shared confidential information relating to matters and services exclusively within the sphere of representation of another department or section of his firm. This * * * rule is more acutely dramatized in the large, departmentalized law firm characteristically more prevalent in an era of evolving legal specialization." 440 F.Supp. at 211. Should modern courts apply this rule?

wife is so close that the possibility of an inadvertent breach of a confidence or the unavoidable receipt of information concerning the client by the spouse other than the one who represents the client (for example, information contained in a telephoned message left for the lawyer at home) is substantial. * * *

" * * * [T]he possibility of a violation of DR 5–101, in particular, is real and must be carefully considered in each instance. If the interest of one of the marriage partners as attorney for an opposing party creates a financial or personal interest that reasonably might affect the ability of a lawyer to represent fully his or her client with undivided loyalty and free exercise of professional judgment, the employment must be declined. We cannot assume, however, that certain facts, such as a fee being contingent or varying according to results obtained, necessarily will involve a violation of DR 5–101(A). * * *

"In any event, * * * the lawyer should advise the client of all circumstances that might cause one to question the undivided loyalty of the law firm and let the client make the decision as to its employment. If the client prefers not to employ a law firm containing a lawyer whose spouse is associated with a firm representing an opposing party, that decision should be respected."

c. Do you agree with the analysis in this opinion? If the representation is not inherently improper, why does the opinion require disclosure to, and consent by, the client? Note that the end of this opinion says that "the lawyer should advise the client," who can then decide whether it wants to "employ a law firm containing a lawyer whose spouse is associated with a firm representing an opposing party." Do the Rules now contain such a requirement? Look at Model Rule 1.7, Comment 11.

2. Should we presume that Xeres' wife would share whatever relevant information she learned from Xeres with others in her firm?

a. Why should we assume she will treat this information differently from other relevant information she learns? If we assume such sharing as to all other information and thus disqualify law firms under Model Rule 1.10(a), why shouldn't all lawyers in the wife's firm be disqualified as well?

b. Model Rule 1.7, Comment 11, says the conflict is "personal," and thus "ordinarily is not imputed." Restatement § 123, Comment *g*, agrees that "in general, the law does not impute conflicts" because of family relationships, but the husband and wife may not "personally represent" clients adverse to each other. If there is any logic to the analogy between imputation within a family and imputation within a law firm, is there a good reason not to say that the law firms of the wife and husband are disqualified as well?

c. Is the problem one of knowing where we can arbitrarily terminate the logic of imputation? Should it be relevant that there are many two-lawyer marriages today and that without some limit on imputation, most couples could not get jobs in the same geographic area? See Restatement

Third, The Law Governing Lawyers § 123, Comment *g*, offering this rationale for the failure to require broader imputation.

3. Does the concern that spouses might intentionally or inadvertently share confidential information apply with the same force to other relationships?

a. Are persons in familial relationships other than marriage likely to get each other's phone messages or share fees earned in a matter? How about a brother and a sister sharing an apartment? Or a child taking a phone message and leaving it with the wrong parent?

b. What has caused the rules to lump all such relationships into the same rule? Are we concerned that a parent might pull her punches so as not to embarrass her child (an adult daughter) who is representing the other side? Does that same concern arise if siblings are opposing lawyers?

c. Note that Model Rule 1.7, Comment 11, like the case law, refers to lawyers related by "blood or marriage." What if lawyers are living together but not joined by benefit of clergy? Does Model Rule 1.7(a)(2) ("a personal interest of the lawyer") clearly cover that situation? Suppose that, instead of being married, the opposing lawyers had gone to dinner together several times? Is it fair to have a strict rule governing those who marry and no rule for the rest?

d. Restatement Third, The Law Governing Lawyers § 123, Comment *g*, says: "Conflicts arising out of relationships in which financial resources are pooled and living quarters shared in circumstances closely approximating marriage should be treated in the same way as spousal conflicts." Do you agree? Should lawyers in such relationships be required to inform their clients of their relationship and to obtain informed consent to continued representation of the parties? How much privacy should lawyers have to give up to avoid a charge of conflict of interest?

e. State Bar of Arizona Opinion 2001–10 (2001), says that cohabiting couples who opposed each other in a criminal case should be subject to the same rules as married couples. The same problem of inadvertently getting confidential information can arise, the opinion says, as can the same loss of professional distance. Thus, where a prosecutor and public defender live together, the opinion holds, they may not work on cases against each other without the consent of their respective clients.[4]

D. USING "SCREENING" TO AVOID IMPUTATION

1. Does ABA Model Rule 1.10 recognize the availability of screening to avoid imputation in the case of lawyers like Xeres who have moved from one private firm to another?

---

4. See also, People v. Jackson, 213 Cal. Rptr. 521 (Cal.Ct.App.1985) (defendant's conviction set aside because neither the prosecutor nor the appointed defense counsel disclosed that they were dating each other be- fore the trial and that they continued to meet on a "regular basis" for movie and dinner dates throughout duration of the criminal proceedings against the defendant).

a. For many years, the ABA Model Rules rejected screening when lawyers moved from one private firm to another. Yet the Rules certainly recognize screening in other contexts. Rule 1.11 provides for screening the former government lawyer, Rule 1.12 permits screening of former judges and law clerks, and Rule 1.18 allows screening of the lawyer who talked to a prospective client. Proponents of modifying the imputation rules have argued that recognition of widespread lateral movement of lawyers from firm to firm today required that screening should be more widely available.

b. Even before the recent amendment to Model Rule 1.10(a), some courts recognized screening as effective in a limited number of cases.

Nemours Foundation v. Gilbane, Aetna, Federal Ins. Co., 632 F.Supp. 418 (D.Del.1986), upheld screening Lawyer, formerly an associate at Firm A, even though the ethics rule did not authorize a screen. Firm A represented Client. At the direction of lead counsel, Lawyer prepared books of documents to use in a "mini-trial," used as a part of settlement negotiations. After the mini-trial, Firm B (the firm that represented Opponent in the litigation) hired Lawyer to work on completely different matters. Firm B "screened" Lawyer from the ongoing litigation between Client and Opponent. No one at Firm B could talk to Lawyer about the case, and Lawyer had no access to Opponent's files. Because of what the court called the policies underlying Rule 1.6, it held that the "cone of silence" that Firm B created around Lawyer was sufficient to avoid disqualification. In addition, Lawyer had been an associate at Firm A and was not intimately involved in the case. The court refused to adopt a per se rule, arguing that, "Attorney mobility, especially among young associates, would be severely restricted if a per se rule against a 'cone of silence' were adopted." 632 F.Supp. at 430.

In Cromley v. Board of Educ. of Lockport Tp. High School Dist. 205, 17 F.3d 1059 (7th Cir.1994), the law firm represented a teacher who said that she was improperly denied administrative positions. A lawyer in that firm moved to the law firm representing the school board. The court ruled that the same matter was involved and (citing *Schiessle v. Stephens*), it found that the law firm had established an effective screening procedure that promptly went into effect when the firm hired this lawyer. The screen denied the lawyer access to the relevant files (which were kept in a different city), instructed the lawyer not to discuss the case, and denied him any share in the fees derived from the case.[5]

5. Other cases were more restrictive. State ex rel. Freezer Services, Inc. v. Mullen, 458 N.W.2d 245 (Neb.1990), for example, involved a merger of the law firm representing the plaintiff with the firm representing the defendant. The new firm wished to continue to represent the defendant and to screen the lawyer who had handled the plaintiff's case. The court held the firm must be disqualified. When a lawyer who has been "intimately involved" with one side of a case joins the firm on the other side, no amount of screen-ing can give the first client a secure feeling that its confidential information will be safe. Courts have also rejected screening as a remedy in Lansing–Delaware Water Dist. v. Oak Lane Park, Inc., 808 P.2d 1369 (Kan.1991); United States v. Davis, 780 F.Supp. 21 (D.D.C.1991); and Henriksen v. Great Am. Savings & Loan, 14 Cal.Rptr.2d 184 (Cal.Ct. App.1992). See also, Kala v. Aluminum Smelting & Refining Co., 688 N.E.2d 258 (Ohio 1998) (screening imposed when lawyer arrived at firm, but lawyer's job negotiations

c. Restatement Third, The Law Governing Lawyers § 124(2), completed in 2000, rejected screening in most cases, but left the door open slightly. Even if a lawyer in a law firm has confidential information about a former client, the Restatement does not require the firm's disqualification when—

" * * * there is no substantial risk that confidential information of the former client will be used with material adverse effect on the former client because:

"(a) any confidential client information * * * is unlikely to be significant in the subsequent matter;

"(b) the personally prohibited lawyer is subject to screening measures adequate to eliminate participation by that lawyer in the representation; and

"(c) timely and adequate notice of the screening has been provided to all affected clients."

d. What do you think of the Restatement approach? Do the standards appropriately balance the competing interests? Do they unwisely capitulate to the interests of large law firms who want to be able to take on more cases? How should a court determine if the information is "unlikely to be significant" in the later case without requiring the moving party to reveal its confidential information in open court?

e. Proponents of change finally succeeded in 2008 when the ABA amended Rule 1.10(a). Now, pursuant to Rule 1.10(a)(2), if a lawyer is disqualified because of his association with a prior law firm, the new law firm can avoid disqualification by screening the disqualified lawyer. Many states now approve some form of screening. They are identified in Appendix B, "Chart on Lawyer Screening," found in the Standards Supplement.

2. When should a court decide that the screen is sufficiently opaque and not translucent?

a. Model Rule 1.0(k) defines screening by saying that to be " 'screened' denotes the isolation of a lawyer from any participation in a matter through the timely imposition of procedures within a firm that are reasonably adequate under the circumstances to protect information that the isolated lawyer is obligated to protect under these Rules or other law."

b. Even before the change in Model Rule 1.10(a)(2), some courts considered what kind of screening would be sufficient. Schiessle v. Stephens, 717 F.2d 417 (7th Cir.1983), required that a "specific institutional mechanism" must be implemented to insulate effectively against confidential information flowing from the "infected" lawyer to any other member of his present firm.

"Such a determination can be based on objective and verifiable evidence presented to the trial court and must be made on a case-

with opposing counsel at the same time he was representing the client were not so egre- giously disloyal, so that the screen will avoid the new firm's disqualification).

by-case basis. Factors appropriate for consideration by the trial court might include, but are not limited to, the size and structural divisions of the law firm involved, the likelihood of contact between the 'infected' attorney and the specific attorneys responsible for the present representation, the existence of rules which prevent the 'infected' attorney from access to the present litigation or which prevent him from sharing in the fees derived from such litigation." Id. at 421.

c. In Manning v. Waring, Cox, James, Sklar & Allen, 849 F.2d 222 (6th Cir.1988), the court remanded for factual findings but held that the law firm can avoid imputed disqualification if it proves that there is an effective screen by "objective and verifiable evidence." The lower court should consider factors such as the "size and structural divisions" of the firm, rules that prevent the "infected" lawyer from having access to case files, and rules preventing the infected lawyer from sharing fees from the case.

d. In Burgess–Lester v. Ford Motor Co., 643 F.Supp.2d 811 (N.D. W.Va. 2008), a lawyer who had been representing Ford Motor in this very case moved to the law firm representing plaintiff. The new firm said it restricted the lawyer's access to any computer files relating to the case, stored all case files in a location where the lawyer had no access, told the firm employees not to talk to the lawyer about it, and provided that the lawyer would share no fees in the case. However, the lawyer himself said he did "not know the precise details of the barrier," and the firm size was relatively small. Therefore, the court disqualified the firm.

e. Kirk v. First American Title Ins. Co., 108 Cal. Rptr. 3d 620 (Cal. Ct. App. 2010), articulated what law firms must do to make the screen truly opaque (quoting an earlier California case):

"The typical elements of an ethical wall are: [1] physical, geographic, and departmental separation of attorneys; [2] prohibitions against and sanctions for discussing confidential matters; [3] established rules and procedures preventing access to confidential information and files; [4] procedures preventing a disqualified attorney from sharing in the profits from the representation; and [5] continuing education in professional responsibility."

3. Should the Model Rules allow for more screening, or less?

a. Was amending Rule 1.10(a)(2) a good idea? Should the Model Rules reject screening? One commentator has argued that imputed disqualification based on an irrebuttable presumption of shared confidential information "is required by three realities of life in the modern law firm."

"First is the relative informality of information exchange within most law firms [because] people tend to specialize their work within firms and tend to consult others in the firm who can give them necessary help on areas outside their expertise.

"Second is the powerful economic incentive to use information that will help the firm win a case on behalf of a current client.

* * * Indeed, a highly-regarded American Bar Foundation study of Chicago lawyers suggests that the fear of losing clients creates the single most important pressure to engage in less-than-clearly ethical behavior today.

"Third and perhaps most important is the fact that no one outside a firm—indeed often leadership inside a firm—can ever be sure what has transpired behind the law firm's closed doors."

The proper question, therefore, is "not whether one can screen the disqualified lawyer from contact with others in the firm—but whether the lawyer realistically should be said to have received enough of the former client's information that the court's protection is required."[6]

b. The Ad Hoc Committee on Ethics 2000 of the ABA Section of Business Law unsuccessfully urged the ABA to allow screening for conflicts arising under Rule 1.7 and not simply Rule 1.9. Thus, one lawyer in a law firm could represent Client A in one matter while another lawyer in the same law firm could simultaneously represent Client B in a matter adverse to Client A. The Committee urged the ABA to allow such representation if (1) screening is in place, (2) the matters are not related, (3) each affected client is notified (but need not consent), and (4) there is no significant risk of diminution of the loyalty owed by any lawyer in the firm to its clients. The Committee argued that the law should not assume that lawyers would engage in improper conduct. As you see, the ABA ultimately did not recognize this type of screening in the current client situation.

c. While Rule 1.10(a)(2), as now written, limits disciplinary exposure when a personally conflicted lawyer is properly screened, should it prevent a court from disqualifying the firm from continuing to represent the client? Notice that Rule 1.10, Comment 7, expressly warns that courts might impose disqualification. If courts refuse to recognize the change to Rule 1.10 in disqualification cases, will the large firms who advocated the change have won a pyrrhic victory?

PROBLEM 16

CONFLICT OF INTEREST ISSUES FOR GOVERNMENT LAWYERS AND JUDGES

Federal, state, and local governmental entities employ lawyers to represent them in various legal tasks including criminal and civil litigation, investigations, drafting and interpreting laws and regulations, and adjudicating disputes. Some of these lawyers spend their careers in government practice, but many lawyers, including at the highest levels of government practice, come from private practice and subsequently return there. The

---

6. Thomas D. Morgan, Screening the Disqualified Lawyer: The Wrong Solution to the Wrong Problem, 10 U. Arkansas Little Rock L. J.37, 48 (1987–88).

rules of professional responsibility apply to all lawyers, but the role of the lawyer in representing a government client presents special issues. Government lawyers have long been seen to have responsibilities beyond those of lawyers in private practice. Some have worried, for example, that the lawyers might be tempted to use their public position to benefit a future private employer. Others fear that former private clients might get special treatment—whether favorable or unfavorable—from their former lawyer. Concerns such as these have produced the conflicts of interest rules governing government lawyers that this problem explores. First, we look at the limits on the conduct of former government lawyers under the Model Rules and the corresponding federal criminal statute. Then, we examine limits on the practice of former private lawyers while in government. Third, we consider the special screening rules applicable to government lawyers, and finally we look at the rules applicable to former judges, arbitrators, mediators, and analogous third-party neutrals.

FACTS

Harold Smithers was a commissioner with the Federal Trade Commission for several years until 10 months ago when his term expired. Prior to his appointment as a commissioner he had spent about 15 years—over half of his professional·life—on the staff of the FTC.

Smithers retired from the government at the end of his term and became a partner in the well-respected firm of Able & Baker in Washington, D.C. Smithers became familiar with Able & Baker because it engages in a great deal of FTC work and has a reputation for excellence. In fact, for the last year, the firm has been representing the subject of a major investigation before the FTC. Although Smithers disagreed with the strategy that Able & Baker was using in that case, he carefully avoided discussing that case while he was quietly negotiating with Able & Baker about his future employment at the firm.

Now that Smithers has moved to Able & Baker, P. D. Quick, chief executive officer of Quick, Inc., has come from California to seek Able & Baker's help. The Commission staff has threatened to file an action in United States District Court seeking a preliminary injunction pending institution of a proceeding before the Commission alleging consumer fraud by Quick, Inc. The fraud is minor, but Quick is personally worried about it and wants to end the matter as soon as possible.

Neither Quick nor Quick, Inc., had ever before consulted with Able & Baker about this matter. P. D. Quick, during his initial conference with Smithers, mentioned in passing that the reason he decided to come to Able & Baker was because Smithers was there and a recent article about Smithers in *Forbes* (published as he was leaving the FTC) said that Smithers had been one of the most influential and hardworking members in the history of the Commission. The article quoted one FTC staff member who said that "even today when Smithers calls me on the phone, I instinctively straighten my tie and call him 'Sir!'"

The actual drafting of papers to be filed with the Commission staff will be handled by another partner of Able & Baker, but Smithers has been asked by the client and the active partner to give "a topside look" at the client's problems and to sign the important papers that will be filed with the Commission. Smithers also has agreed to call several staff members and a current commissioner or two who "owe their jobs to me." This last remark was made in an offhand way in the presence of P. D. Quick who appeared pleased.

QUESTIONS

A.   THE RULES APPLICABLE TO FORMER GOVERNMENT LAWYERS

1.   What legal standards govern Smithers' return to private life?

a.   Because Smithers is a lawyer, he is subject to ABA Model Rule 1.11, even though he was not acting as a lawyer when he was a Commissioner. He is not subject to Model Rule 1.9, except as Model Rule 1.11(a)(1) expressly subjects him to Model Rule 1.9(c).[1]

b.   The content of Model Rule 1.11 derives from ABA Formal Opinion 342 (Nov. 24, 1975), which interpreted ABA Model Code of Professional Responsibility DR 9–101(B). This Opinion is old, but its rationale is still valid.

"The policy considerations underlying DR 9–101(B) have been thought to be the following: the treachery of switching sides; the safeguarding of confidential governmental information from future use against the government; the need to discourage government lawyers from handling particular assignments in such a way as to encourage their own future employment in regard to those particular matters after leaving government service; and the professional benefit derived from avoiding the appearance of evil.

"There are, however, weighty policy considerations in support of the view that a special disciplinary rule relating only to former government lawyers should not broadly limit the lawyer's employment after he leaves government service. Some of the underlying considerations

---

1. Before the 2002 revisions of the Model Rules, there was some precedent for applying both Model Rules 1.9 and 1.11 to former government lawyers, e.g., Violet v. Brown, 9 Vet.App. 530 (Ct.Vet.App.1996). ABA Formal Opinion 97–409 (Aug. 2, 1997), on the other hand, said that Rule 1.11, not Rule 1.9, governs the conflict of interest obligations of a former government lawyer. Because Rule 1.9(c), prohibiting use and disclosure of a former client's confidential information, has no counterpart in Rule 1.11, however, the ABA Opinion said it was applicable to a former government lawyer as well. Now, Model Rule 1.11 alone is intended to govern the conduct of former government lawyers. See Comment 1 to Model Rule 1.9.

favoring a construction of the rule in a manner not to restrict unduly the lawyer's future employment are the following: the ability of government to recruit young professionals and competent lawyers should not be interfered with by imposition of harsh restraints upon future practice nor should too great a sacrifice be demanded of the lawyers willing to enter government service; the rule serves no worthwhile public interest if it becomes a mere tool enabling a litigant to improve his prospects by depriving his opponent of competent counsel; and the rule should not be permitted to interfere needlessly with the right of litigants to obtain competent counsel of their own choosing, particularly in specialized areas requiring special, technical training and experience. * * *

"As used in DR 9–101(B), 'substantial responsibility' envisages a much closer and more direct relationship than that of a mere perfunctory approval or disapproval of the matter in question. It contemplates a responsibility requiring the official to become personally involved to an important, material degree, in the investigative or deliberative processes regarding the transactions or facts in question. Thus, being the chief official in some vast office or organization does not *ipso facto* give that government official or employee the 'substantial responsibility' contemplated by the rule in regard to all the minutiae of facts lodged within that office. Yet it is not necessary that the public employee or official shall have personally and in a substantial manner investigated or passed upon the particular matter, for it is sufficient that he had such a heavy responsibility for the matter in question that it is unlikely he did not become personally and substantially involved in the investigative or deliberate processes regarding that matter. * * *

"The extension by DR 5–105(D) of disqualification to all affiliated lawyers is to prevent circumvention by a lawyer of the Disciplinary Rules. Past government employment creates an unusual situation in which inflexible application of DR 5–105(D) would actually thwart the policy considerations underlying DR 9–101(B). * * *

" * * * The purposes of limiting the mandate to matters in which the former public employee had a substantial responsibility are to inhibit government recruitment as little as possible and enhance the opportunity for all litigants to obtain competent counsel of their own choosing, particularly in specialized areas. An inflexible extension of disqualification throughout an entire firm would thwart those purposes. So long as the individual lawyer is held to be disqualified and is screened from any direct or indirect participation in the matter, the problem of his switching sides is not present; by contrast, an inflexible extension of disqualification throughout the firm often would result in real hardship to a client if complete withdrawal of representation was mandated, because substantial work may have been completed regarding specific litigation prior to the time the government employee joined the partnership, or the client may have relied in the past on representation by the firm.''

2. How do these rules apply in concrete cases like Smithers'?

a. In re Sofaer, 728 A.2d 625 (D.C.1999), was a case where the disciplinary authorities accused a well-known lawyer, Abraham Sofaer, of violating Rule 1.11(a). While serving as legal advisor (functionally the general counsel) to the State Department, he took part in ''legal activities flowing from the government's efforts to address'' the Pan Am 103 bombing incident that the Libyan government had ordered. After leaving the State Department, Libya retained Sofaer at a fee of $250,000 per month to represent it in connection with civil and criminal litigation arising out of that incident. When charged with a violation of Rule 1.11(a), Sofaer responded that his involvement in the matter at the State Department had not been ''personal and substantial.'' Indeed, while he was in the government, most of the suspicion focused on other possible perpetrators. Amici curiae added that if Sofaer were found guilty, no lawyer could safely move in and out of government. However, the court found that there was a clear violation of Rule 1.11 and ordered an informal admonition.

b. D.C. Bar Legal Ethics Opinion 297 (2000) explored whether a former government lawyer may represent a private party in a negotiated rulemaking in which the lawyer had participated while in government. A special statute authorizes a negotiated rulemaking committee, which is ''an advisory committee established by an agency'' in order ''to consider and discuss issues for the purpose of reaching a consensus in the development of a proposed rule.'' 5 U.S.C.A. § 562(7). The D.C. opinion said that there is no violation of Rule 1.11 because negotiated rulemaking does not involve specific participants. Instead, it deals with formation of general policy and thus is not the kind of ''matter'' involving particular parties to which conflicts rules apply.

c. Outdoor Advertising Ass'n of Ga., Inc. v. Garden Club of Ga., Inc., 527 S.E.2d 856 (Ga.2000), involved a former state attorney general's subsequent employment. The client wanted to trim trees to make billboards easier to see from the highway. Earlier, Michael Bowers was Georgia attorney general while his office was counsel of record for the state Department of Transportation. The deputy attorney general who handled the litigation never consulted with Bowers, who made no court appearances. However, his office issued a legal opinion about some of the relevant legal issues. The court would not disqualify Bowers because he had no ''substantial responsibility'' for the earlier matters. Otherwise, he would be disqualified from all 16,000 cases that were in his office while he was attorney general.

d. In E.E.O.C. v. Exxon Corp., 202 F.3d 755 (5th Cir.2000), the EEOC alleged that Exxon violated the Americans with Disabilities Act because it would not allow alcoholics to pilot oil tankers. Part of Exxon's defense was that its policy grew out of a requirement that the federal government placed on it as part of settling criminal charges arising out of a massive oil spill involving the Exxon Valdez, an oil tanker. In that earlier suit the government had charged that Exxon's failure to monitor an employee's alcoholism contributed to the accident. For its defense, Exxon hired two former Justice Department lawyers, now in private practice, as expert witnesses to testify about the events leading up to the earlier settlement. The Justice Department asserted that their testimony would violate federal ethics standards, but the court permitted the testimony insofar as it was limited to publicly-known information. Being an expert witness is not the same as representing a party, the court said, so it is not forbidden by the ABA Model Rules. For the same reasons, there was also no violation of the Texas Ethics Rules (the jurisdiction where this action arose) or the D.C. Bar Rules (the jurisdiction in which the lawyers were admitted).

e. United States v. Philip Morris Inc., 312 F.Supp.2d 27 (D.D.C.2004), involved *confidential* government information. The court disqualified a former Justice Department lawyer and his law firm from defending certain cases involving tobacco companies. The lawyer had worked for the Justice Department for 28 years. He also worked on an FDA rulemaking that asserted the FDA's right to regulate tobacco; he worked on the litigation seeking to defend that rule; he worked on an analysis of the Master Settlement Agreement between the tobacco industry and the states; and he wrote a memorandum on obtaining access to internal tobacco company documents. After his retirement, Shearman & Sterling had hired him. In this motion to disqualify Shearman & Sterling, the court found that the work the lawyer did on the earlier FDA cases constituted a "matter" and that work done on the rulemaking was closely related to it. It concluded the lawyer learned confidential government information that could be relevant to the current litigation and ordered Shearman & Sterling disqualified because it had not created a screen.

3. ABA Model Rule 1.9 only prohibits representation that is "materially adverse" to the former client. Is Rule 1.11 so limited?

a. Why should the ethics rules forbid a lawyer who has left government from taking a case that *furthers* the government's objectives? Does it seem that government lawyers are likely to be in a position to bring cases while in government whose results they could later exploit? Do you agree that government lawyers have access to information that private lawyers would not have or could not obtain through discovery?

b. ABA Model Rule 1.11(a) and Comment 3 are derived from General Motors Corp. v. City of New York, 501 F.2d 639 (2d Cir.1974). While a lawyer for the U.S. Government in 1956, the lawyer had filed and signed an antitrust complaint against General Motors. Subsequently, in 1972 while he was in private practice, he agreed to represent New York City in another, similar antitrust claim on a contingent fee basis.[2] The court disqualified the lawyer. It concluded that his prior responsibility for the

---

2. There is no statute of limitations on the bar to subsequent representation of a private party in such a case. For example, if Smithers had personally worked on a case 15 years ago (early in his career at the FTC),

one might think that he should now be free to work on that matter in private practice. As the *General Motors* case shows, however, that is not the law.

case was "substantial;" that his contingent fee arrangement with the city constituted private employment; that the city's antitrust suit was sufficiently similar to the federal case so as to constitute the same "matter" for purposes of DR 9–101(B); that it was irrelevant that the lawyer had not "switched sides" but had continued to litigate against General Motors; and that the lawyer's representation of the City would constitute the "appearance of impropriety." Do you think the court reached the right result?

c. Suppose that while working at the FTC, Smithers learned some shocking information about the business practices of several companies. May he represent persons who were injured by the companies whose practices he had studied? Take a look at ABA Model Rule 1.11(c). Why should the law prevent Smithers from working *on behalf of* companies whose injuries he is especially well suited to redress? Does Rule 1.11, Comment 4 explain the underlying policies to your satisfaction? Does the rule prohibiting Smithers' use of confidential government information give too much protection to wrongdoers whom the agency may lack the resources to pursue?

d. Iowa Supreme Court Attorney Disciplinary Board v. Johnson, 728 N.W.2d 199 (Iowa 2007), is a poignant reminder that this aspect of Rule 1.11 can be a trap for the unwary. Johnson was an assistant county attorney responsible for emergency removal and child-in-need petitions. She signed several such petitions and appeared in several such cases. Later, she became executive director of the Youth Law Center, an organization that employs lawyers who are appointed guardians ad litem for children. She intended to screen herself from cases in which she had appeared earlier for the state, but eventually she made some mistakes. Even though she was clearly trying to act in the best interests of the children in both the earlier and later roles, the court said, Rule 1.11 bars later involvement in any matter in which the lawyer had personal and substantial responsibility while in government. Seeing the big picture, however, the court limited its sanction to a public reprimand.

4. Is Smithers barred from all activity within his own law firm in the case involving Quick, Inc.? May Smithers talk to Quick, for example, about what the FTC is likely to do? May he give tactical advice to his partners who are handling the Quick matter?

a. ABA Formal Opinion 342 (Nov. 24, 1975), quoted above, said that application of the usual rules of imputation of disqualification within a firm would "actually thwart the policy considerations underlying [Model Rule 1.11]." ABA Model Rule 1.11(b) accepts that view and provides that the law firm can avoid imputation by timely "screening" the former government lawyer.[3]

b. Problem 15 discussed the debates over whether to permit screening when a lawyer moves from one private firm to another. Are there any different risks (either in degree or in kind) with screening in cases involv-

---

3. Remember, the requirements for an effective screen are set forth in ABA Model Rule 1.0(k) and Model Rule 1.0, Comments 8–10.

ing former government lawyers? Is it easier to keep track of cases on which a former SEC employee may not work, than to do so in the case of a private litigator whose cases may have involved many different clients? On the other hand, what dangers of intentional or inadvertent "breaches in the wall" can you see? Are there any different incentives to violate the screen?

5. In addition to Model Rule 1.11, statutes often govern the "revolving door" between government and private sector employment. Because Smithers is a former *federal* employee, he is also subject to 18 U.S.C.A. § 207. Does the federal statute apply different standards than Rule 1.11?

a. 18 U.S.C.A. § 207(a)(1):

"Any person who is an officer or employee * * * of the executive branch of the United States * * * and who, after the termination of his or her service or employment * * * makes, with the intent to influence, any communication to or appearance before any officer or employee of * * * the United States * * * in connection with a particular matter—

"(A) in which the United States * * * is a party or has a direct and substantial interest,

"(B) in which the person participated personally and substantially as such officer or employee, and

"(C) which involved a specific party or specific parties at the time of such participation, shall be punished [by up to 5 years imprisonment, a $50,000 fine, or both]."

b. Section 207 is a complicated statute. Notice first that the federal statute (i) applies to nonlawyers as well as lawyers, and (ii) applies to representation consistent with the former employee's work while in government as well as representation adverse to the government's position. One of the other important differences, of course, is that 18 U.S.C. § 207 is a *criminal* provision whose violation exposes the former federal employee to five years in prison, a fine, or both.

b. Question 4 asked if Rule 11 bars Smithers from all activity within his own law firm in the case involving Quick, Inc.? Does § 207 impute its restrictions? Under § 207, may Smithers talk to Quick about what the FTC is likely to do? May he give tactical advice to his partners who are handling the Quick matter? Why does the federal statute only forbid Smithers from talking with current agency officials? The legislative history of § 207 shows that Congress meant to have questions about imputation within a law firm, and any right of the government to waive the disqualification, governed by the bar's own rules of ethics, not federal statutes.[4] So, why does the statute allow Smithers to talk to his partners? Is the federal government more concerned about abuse of personal relationships within federal agencies than about exchange of information within law firms?

---

4. See Thomas D. Morgan, Appropriate Limits on Participation by a Former Agency Official in Matters Before an Agency, 1980 Duke L.J. 1, 11.

6. If a matter came to the Commission the week *after* Smithers left the agency, does ABA Model Rule 1.11 limit Smithers' ability to contact his friends back at the agency? Remember that Smithers, under the new assumption, was not personally and substantially involved with work on the matter.

a. Look at 18 U.S.C.A. § 207(c) in the Standards Supplement. Notice that it requires one year of no contact with certain high-ranking employees' former agencies, sometimes called a "cooling-off" period, regardless whether the employee was personally and substantially involved with a matter. Does this provision reinforce the view that the policy concerns underlying 18 U.S.C. § 207 are different than those underlying Model Rule 1.11?

b. United States v. Nofziger, 878 F.2d 442 (D.C.Cir.1989), reversed the conviction of President Reagan's assistant, Lynn Nofziger, who was convicted for violating this "cooling-off" provision, 18 U.S.C.A. § 207(c). On behalf of clients of his lobbying firm, Nofziger sent a letter to Edwin Meese, then counselor to the President, urging that the Army give a contract to Wedtech, a minority-owned firm in the South Bronx. He also sent a copy of a letter to a Meese deputy urging use of civilian crews on noncombatant Navy ships, and he met with National Security Council staff members to urge continued production on the A–10 aircraft for which Congress had cut off funds. Nofziger argued that the government had not proved that he knew these were issues where the agencies he had contacted already had a "direct and substantial interest." Judges Buckley and Williams found a knowledge requirement arguably in the statute and concluded that if there is ambiguity in a *criminal* statute the defendant should prevail. Judge Edwards dissent found no ambiguity. Because 18 U.S.C. § 207 is a criminal statute, should the courts interpret it more narrowly than Model Rule 1.11?

B. THE FORMER PRIVATE LAWYER WHO ENTERS GOVERNMENT SERVICE

1. Consider the other direction of the revolving door. What must a lawyer consider when he or she enters government service?

a. Must a government official recuse herself every time something comes up involving a former private client? Does the lawyer continue to owe the former client duties under ABA Model Rules 1.6 and 1.9(a)? In what ways does ABA Model Rule 1.11(d) differ from Rule 1.9(a)?

b. ABA Model Rule 1.11(d) is also based on ABA Formal Opinion 342, supra, which said:

> "When the Disciplinary Rules of Canons 4 and 5 mandate the disqualification of a government lawyer who has come from private practice, his governmental department or division cannot practicably be rendered incapable of handling even the specific matter. Clearly, if DR 5–105(D) were so construed, the government's ability to function would be unreasonably impaired. * * * The relationships among lawyers within a government agency are different from those among partners and associates of a law firm. The salaried government employ-

ee does not have the financial interest in the success of departmental representation that is inherent in private practice. * * * The channeling of advocacy toward a just result as opposed to vindication of a particular claim [also] lessens the temptation to circumvent the disciplinary rules through the action of associates. Accordingly, we construe DR 5–105(D) to be inapplicable to other government lawyers associated with a particular government lawyer who is himself disqualified * * *. Although vicarious disqualification of a government department is not necessary or wise, the individual lawyer should be screened from any direct or indirect participation in the matter, and discussion with his colleagues concerning the relevant transaction or set of transactions is prohibited by those rules."

c. In analyzing these issues, D.C. Bar Legal Ethics Opinion 308 (2001), concluded that the lawyer's first constraint stems from the duty of confidentiality. Rule 1.6 says that (1) the lawyer must be vigilant not to reveal any protected information obtained from the former client, and (2) the lawyer may not knowingly "use" protected information "to the disadvantage of the client." Thus, even though not all uses of a former client's confidences involve revealing them to others, the second part of Rule 1.6 does not allow use either.

The second constraint stems from Rule 1.9. The test to determine if a lawyer may work on a matter while in government, the opinion says, is "whether the lawyer was so involved in the matter that the subsequent representation can be justly regarded as a changing of sides in the matter in question." If the answer is yes, the lawyer may not continue without written consent from both sides. If written consent is not obtained, the lawyer may not work for the government in the matter.

d. For the reasons stated in ABA Formal Opinion 342, the principles of imputed disqualification do not apply to lawyers who practice in a government agency with the lawyer who is disqualified. However, D.C. Opinion 308, supra, says that voluntary screening measures in the agency should be considered. See also, ABA Model Rule 1.11, Comment 2.

2.   Should disqualification be imputed within a prosecutor's office when a prosecutor is hired from private practice?

a. Restatement Third, The Law Governing Lawyers § 123, Comment *d(iii)*, concludes that imputation should not be inevitable "if the [prosecutor's] office is operated so as to avoid material risk that confidential information will be inadequately safeguarded."

b. State ex rel. Romley v. Superior Court In and For the County of Maricopa, 908 P.2d 37 (Ariz.App.1995), held that if the disqualified prosecutor is screened from participation in a matter, the court need not disqualify the whole Maricopa County prosecutor's office. Are courts justifiably concerned that states not wind up in a situation in which no persons will be available to prosecute criminal defendants if courts impose strict imputation?

c. In City & County of San Francisco v. Cobra Solutions, Inc., 135 P.3d 20 (Cal.2006), however, the California Supreme Court (5 to 2) disqualified the whole San Francisco city attorney's office because the elected city attorney had formerly represented a company that the city was now charging with fraud in its dealings with the city. The city attorney had not assisted the client with the alleged fraudulent transactions, but he had worked on substantially related matters. Further, when the fraud investigation began, the city attorney did not know it would lead to his former client, but when it did, he was immediately screened from involvement in the matter. The court recognized that Model Rule 1.11(d)(2) would allow a prosecutor's office to continue to handle the case, but "California has not adopted the ABA Model Rules," although "they may serve as guidelines absent on-point California authority or a conflicting state public policy." In this case, the court was concerned that a city attorney has policymaking and supervisory duties that make it hard for staff in the office not to be affected by what they think even a screened city attorney would want done. For individual attorneys coming into the office, screening should be enough; for supervisory attorneys, a factual investigation should be conducted. But to protect public confidence in the city's decisions, even screening could not avoid imputing the city attorney's own conflicts to others in the office.

3. What conflicts might exist if a government lawyer advises multiple agency clients?

a. State Bar of California Formal Opinion No. 2001–156 (2001), discusses when a conflict of interest arises under California Rule 3–310(C) where a city attorney offers legal advice to different constituent sub-entities or to officials of a city whose positions differ on a subject.

The opinion recognizes that application of the Rules of Professional Conduct must consider factors peculiar to the governmental context. It says the courts have developed a two-part test to determine potential conflicts of interest arising from an attorney advising different bodies or officials within a city government: (1) An attorney for a governmental entity such as a city usually has only one client, the entity itself, and (2) A constituent sub-entity or official may become an independent client of the entity's attorney only if the sub-entity or official possesses authority to act independently of the main entity and if the entity's attorney is asked to represent the constituent sub-entity or official in its independent capacity.

Therefore, no conflict of interest arises when there is a disagreement between a government entity and its subordinate constituents, or between subordinate constituents of the entity. However, a conflict of interest may arise if a constituent or official has an independent right of action that would require the attorney to choose between conflicting duties. In the case of a city council and a mayor seeking legal advice from the city attorney, but taking different positions, no conflict of interest exists because the attorney represents neither the city council nor the mayor; the lawyer represents only the municipal corporation as an indivisible unit. Further, because neither of these sub-entities of the municipal corporation can function independently, the attorney may not represent either in its independent capacity. See ABA Model Rule 1.13, Comment 9.

b.   Military legal offices regularly also represent multiple clients and multiple interests. Except in cases of military necessity, the ABA Standing Committee on Ethics and Professional Responsibility says, "representation of opposing sides by lawyers working in the same military office and sharing common secretarial and filing facilities should be avoided." ABA Informal Opinion 1474 (1982) (citing Formal Opinion 343 and Informal Opinion 1309).

4.   Should legislative branch officials be subject to limits such as those imposed on officials in the executive branch?

a.   Assume Smithers had been a member of Congress instead of an FTC commissioner. What limitations on his law practice would Smithers face when he retired from Congress? Suppose Smithers had been chairman of a subcommittee charged with oversight of the FTC, and P. D. Quick wants Smithers to persuade his old subcommittee to approve a proposed law that would permit a practice being investigated by the FTC. Would former-Congressman Smithers be under the same ethical restraints as ex-Commissioner Smithers?

b.   Take a look at 18 U.S.C.A. § 207(e)(1) in the Standards Supplement. Why should the scope and duration of the rules differ depending on the branch of government in which the former official served?

c.   Assume that the chief counsel of the House subcommittee joins Able & Baker. Is the chief counsel subject to the same limitations as former–Congressman Smithers? See 18 U.S.C.A. § 207(e)(3).

d.   Assume that Smithers, a practicing lawyer, is elected to Congress. Because Smithers is familiar with the problems of the First Savings Bank, which is owned by some of his constituents, he decides that he will introduce a bill in Congress to cut back the powers of the Federal Reserve Board and other federal agencies to investigate alleged inappropriate credit behavior of banks. Is there anything wrong with introducing such a bill if the lawyer does not charge First Savings Bank for this service?

e.   Office of Disciplinary Counsel v. Eilberg, 441 A.2d 1193 (Pa.1982), suspended a lawyer/congressman from the practice of law for violating 18 U.S.C.A. § 203(a), which prohibits a member of Congress from receiving compensation for representing a client before a federal agency. The lawyer had set up a "dual practice," i.e., the lawyer's law partners set up a separate entity to receive compensation for representing clients before federal agencies. But the lawyer/congressman encouraged prospective clients to hire the "other" firm to represent the clients, and, in one case the lawyer/congressman (apparently because of an accounting error) received a portion of the profits from the representation before a federal agency. The court said that it need not rule on the ethics of the "dual practice" law firm, but said it is ethically "dubious," even though it did not technically violate section 18 U.S.C.A. § 203(a).

C. NEGOTIATING FOR POST-GOVERNMENT EMPLOYMENT WHILE STILL IN GOVERNMENT

1. Did Smithers do anything wrong when he was negotiating for employment prior to his retirement from the FTC? How may a lawyer in government service look for a job on the outside?

a. May the government lawyer seeking employment contact firms that regularly deal with the lawyer's agency? Look at ABA Model Rule 1.11(d)(2)(ii). Are those firms the ones most likely to find the lawyer's experience valuable?

b. Federal employees are also subject to 18 U.S.C. § 208(a) that provides:

> "[W]hoever, being an officer or employee of the executive branch of the United States Government * * * participates personally and substantially as a Government officer or employee * * * in a * * * particular matter in which to his knowledge, * * * any person or organization with whom he is negotiating or has any arrangement concerning prospective employment, has a financial interest [may be imprisoned up to 5 years, pay a $50,000 fine, or both]."

c. Section 208 creates an exception where the government employee makes a full advance disclosure of all relevant facts to the "Government official responsible for appointment to his or her position" and receives a written determination "that the interest is not so substantial as to be likely to affect the integrity of the services" that the employee will render in the matter.

To whom would Smithers write such a letter? Do you suppose the President of the United States spends a lot of time making the determinations required by such notifications?

2. Smithers told P.D. Quick that several commissioners "owe their jobs to me." Is there anything wrong with saying that? How about saying it to law firms with whom he is negotiating employment?

a. Assuming that this statement is factually correct and well known, what is the comment trying to imply? Does the comment violate Model Rule 8.4(e)? Consider P.D. Quick's view of the situation. If Smithers cannot work on the matter, why should Quick travel all the way from California to hire Smithers when there are plenty of good lawyers in California? Does Model Rule 8.4(e) have any effect on what Smithers can say about his ability to help Quick?

b. Is it be unrealistic to require people like Smithers never to use the access they obtained while working for the government? President Truman—

> "had strong feelings about using one's official position, *past or present*, for gain. He was extremely fond of General Omar Bradley, the fellow Missourian who at one time during Mr. Truman's administration was Chief of Staff. After Bradley retired, he took a

job as chairman of the board of the Bulova Watch Company, and one day in discussing General Bradley Mr. Truman said, 'I hold it against him, taking that job. They weren't hiring him; what they thought they were doing was buying some influence in the Pentagon, and I don't care at all for that sort of thing, and I can't understand how General Bradley could bring himself to do it.' Being an admirer of General Bradley, I said, no doubt apologetically, 'He probably felt he needed the money.' And Mr. Truman said, 'Nobody ever needs money that bad.' "[5]

c.   When President Kennedy appointed Arthur Goldberg to the cabinet as secretary of labor, Goldberg promised never to practice labor law again, although that field of law had been his specialty. Goldberg always kept that promise. Would such a prophylactic rule—preventing a former government employee from using the benefits of his former position while in private practice—tend to discourage many good persons from entering government service?

D.   CONFLICTS OF THE FORMER JUDGE OR THIRD PARTY NEUTRAL

1.   Where does one find the limits on the activities of a former judge?

a.   Notice that former government officials who have served as judges are subject, not to ABA Model Rule 1.11, but to Model Rule 1.12. That rule also governs judges' law clerks, private arbitrators, mediators and other third-party neutrals.

b.   What values are we trying to protect by imposing limits on later private work by judges and other neutrals? None of the former adjudicators governed by Model Rule 1.12(a) "represented" anyone in their prior role. None of them has any duty of "loyalty" to the parties who appeared before them. Nor is information that comes out at trial "confidential" in any meaningful sense. What, if anything, is left to worry about?

c.   Model Rule 1.12, Comment 1, says that Model Rule 1.12 generally parallels Model Rule 1.11, as well as corresponding provisions in the ABA Model Code of Judicial Conduct. Look at Comment 3. Does it provide an independent rationale for the rule?

d.   In James v. Mississippi Bar, 962 So.2d 528 (Miss.2007), when James was a judge, she had presided in a case alleging that Husband had abused his wife and child. She had ordered that Husband not have unsupervised visitation of the child. Now, James sought to represent Wife in a proceeding to modify the child custody provisions of the couple's divorce decree that had been entered by a different judge. The court acknowledged that the abuse case and the current one were not the same, but both involved the "same party or parties." Further, the allegations of physical abuse were at the heart of both proceedings, and James had earlier

5. Merle Miller, Plain Speaking: An   n. † (1974) (emphasis added).
Oral Biography of Harry S. Truman 201–02,

ruled on an issue of child custody. Thus, the court found a violation of Rule 1.12, but limited the sanction to a public reprimand.

e. Comparato v. Schait, 848 A.2d 770 (N.J.2004), is one of the relatively few cases that deals with the disqualification of a judge's former law clerk and her firm. While Priscilla Miller was working as a law clerk for Judge Convery, a divorce case was before that judge. A few months before her clerkship ended, Miller interviewed for a position with the firm representing Schait, the defendant in the case. She took the position, informed the judge that she had done so, and began working at the firm shortly after her clerkship ended. At the law firm, Miller worked on defendant Schait's case. She reviewed the plaintiff's motion for leave to appeal, drafted an appellate brief for defendant Schait, and met with Schait. When plaintiff's counsel became aware that Miller had been Judge Convery's law clerk while the case was before him, the counsel moved to disqualify defendant's law firm in the case. The New Jersey Supreme Court noted that N.J. Rule 1.12(a) forbids an attorney from representing a client where the lawyer "participated personally and substantially as a . . . law clerk" in connection with a matter involving that client unless all parties consent to the representation after full disclosure. The court warned that a law clerk's involvement could be "personal and substantial" if the clerk's role was substantive, such as recommending a certain disposition to the judge. However, while Miller was a clerk, any contact she may have had was non-substantive: she certified that her responsibilities had consisted mainly of calendaring motions filed during her tenure and performing other related ministerial tasks. Furthermore, she was not privy to confidential information regarding the case. Thus, Miller's involvement in the case was not sufficient to require disqualification. As a precautionary matter, however, Miller's firm screened her from further participation in the case, and the court made screening a part of its order.

2. What does Model Rule 1.12(b) tell us about how judges should accomplish a transition back to practice?

a. Isn't it likely that almost *all* the major firms in a given area are likely to be counsel, or potentially counsel, in cases before the judge while she is looking for post-judicial employment? Does Model Rule 1.12(b) mean that the judge may not talk to any of them?

b. Comment 3 to Model Rule 1.11 states that Model Rule 1.11(d)(2) is designed to "prevent a lawyer from exploiting public office for the advantage of another client." That is not literally applicable to the judge, but does the same concern underlie Model Rule 1.12(b)?

c. Boumediene v. Bush, 476 F.3d 934 (D.C.Cir.2006), asked how former judges may describe themselves in litigation. A group of former federal judges had sought leave to file an amicus brief in a case challenging the Military Commissions Act of 2006. The court denied the motion for the sole reason that the former judges had all used the title "judge" to describe themselves in their brief. The court cited Advisory Opinion No. 72 of the Committee on Codes of Conduct of the U.S. Judicial Conference: "Judges should insure that the title 'judge' is not used in the courtroom or in papers involved in litigation before them to designate a former judge, unless the designation is necessary to describe accurately a person's status at a time pertinent to the lawsuit." As the opinion noted, there used to be very few former federal judges. Now there are many, and they are more active in litigation. The opinion said that it is unfair for a party to have to oppose persons who can call themselves "judge" while other lawyers are not able to do so. Do you agree?

3. If the judge does not comply with the requirements of Model Rule 1.12, what remedies or sanctions should the judge expect?

a.   *Pepsico, Inc. v. McMillen,* 764 F.2d 458 (7th Cir.1985), involved a judge who had become eligible to take senior status. He contacted a "head hunter" who agreed to contact Chicago firms to see if any would want the judge to become affiliated with them. Inadvertently, and contrary to the judge's instructions, the head hunter contacted firms representing both the plaintiff and defendant in a pending antitrust case. Neither expressed an interest in hiring the judge, although the plaintiff's firm left the matter a bit more open than did the other. The judge did not go to work for either firm. Defendants sought a writ of mandamus to disqualify the judge. The Court of Appeals was careful to stress that there was no intentional impropriety committed in the case, but it ordered the judge recused to avoid any "appearance of partiality" in the matter before him. See Model Rule 1.12(b).

b.   *Kentucky Bar Ass'n v. Bates,* 26 S.W.3d 788 (Ky.2000), is part of the "what was he thinking" line of cases. A part-time judge also practiced law as permitted by the state's code of judicial conduct. On behalf of one of his private divorce clients, he filed a petition seeking a divorce; five days later, he filed another petition, also on behalf of this client, seeking an emergency protective order against the wife, alleging an immediate danger of domestic violence. Purportedly because no other judge was handy, the lawyer not only drafted the order on behalf of his client but signed it in his capacity as a judge. The next day, another judge signed the protective order. The court found a violation of Rule 1.12(a) because the lawyer had acted as counsel in a matter on which he had acted as a judge. It issued a public reprimand.

4.   Are the rationales for Model Rules 1.12(a) and 1.12(b) the same?

a.   One can readily understand why under Model Rule 1.12(b) a judge may not negotiate for employment with law firms representing parties whose cases have not yet been decided; the opportunity for bribery is obvious.

b.   Does a similar opportunity for dishonesty exist where a former judge, who decided a case long ago, represents the winner in seeking to get the loser to comply with the earlier order? Model Rule 1.12(a) clearly prohibits that representation. Why? Is it realistic to expect that the other party would consent to such representation? Why should the other party be concerned about the former judge's involvement?

c. Does the screening authorized by Model Rule 1.12(c) provide adequate protection for the values implicit in Model Rule 1.12? If one is concerned that a party might reward a judge who grants a favorable verdict by later hiring the law firm where the judge now works, does the prohibition on the judge's directly collecting a fee for the matter remove all concern?

5. Is it wise to try to deal with all forms of third-party neutrals in a single rule? For example, is our concern about later involvement by a mediator different than our concern about a former arbitrator or judge?

a. Mediators often necessarily learn each side's bargaining positions that would never come out at a trial, for example. See ABA Model Code of Judicial Conduct (2007), Rule 2.9(A)(4). Should the rule at least treat persons who have obtained such confidential information differently from those who have not?

b. Cho v. Superior Court, 45 Cal.Rptr.2d 863 (Cal.Ct.App.1995), involved a judge who had presided over settlement discussions in a case and then left the bench and joined the defendant's law firm while the case was still pending. The court ordered the former judge's entire firm disqualified: "[A]lthough mediators function in some ways as neutral coordinators of dispute resolution, they also assume the role of a confidant, and it is that aspect of their role that distinguishes them from adjudicators." 45 Cal. Rptr. at 868.

c. *Cho* said that screening under Model Rule 1.12 is proper for former adjudicators who only see what each side shows the other, but in the case of judges acting as mediators, disqualification of the entire firm is required. Do you agree? Does the current version of Model Rule 1.12 draw this distinction? Should it do so?

CHAPTER V

ADVISING CLIENTS

A news story reported a class discussion in a business school:

"What should your role as a manager be when a subordinate comes to you reporting a product safety defect?" [Professor James Wilson of the University of Pittsburgh] asks. "Is your primary motivation to make a good widget or a good profit?"

"I'd get another opinion," ventures one candidate for a master's in business administration.*

The lawyer for this widget producer should not be surprised if the manager comes to her for the other opinion. What should the lawyer say?

Lawyers usually spend more time counseling and trying to stay out of court than they do trying cases. At least two different kinds of issues arise in trying to help clients solve their own problems rather than leaving the solution up to courts. First, how are you expected to interact with your client and react to his or her assessment of the problem? Second, how are you to deal with others on behalf of your client in settings such as negotiation or investigation? More specifically, consider questions such as these:

a. What is the standard for determining the best interest of the client? Is the client by definition the best judge of his or her interest? Does the lawyer have a right—an obligation—to offer an opinion about what course of action would be in the client's best interest? Should a lawyer ever try to pressure a client into taking one course of action rather than another?

b. What special questions are presented when the client is not an individual, e.g., when the client is a partnership or a corporation? When the client is a corporation, who really speaks for the client? Is it the board of directors? The managers? The common stockholders? If the client is the fictional corporate entity, what does that mean when the flesh and blood persons are at odds and the lawyer is in the middle?

c. Does a lawyer ever owe obligations to persons or entities other than the client? Does the lawyer owe the same obligation to a third party that the client owes to that party? Are there circumstances when the lawyer voluntarily assumes an obligation to report accurate information on which third parties may rely? Why would a lawyer assume that obligation

---

* Victor Zonana, Bribery & Slush Spur Ethics Courses at Business Schools: Would You Have Gone Along With Equity Funding Deal? Many Students Say Yes, Wall Street J., July 8, 1975, p. 1, col. 4.

even where the report does not reflect entirely favorably on the lawyer's client?

d.   Does a lawyer have a right—an obligation—to warn third parties about potential wrongdoing by the lawyer's client? On what theory would such a right or obligation rest? Should the lawyer with knowledge of potential wrongdoing have a different right or obligation of disclosure than a nonlawyer would have?

————

PROBLEM 17

THE LAWYER FOR AN INDIVIDUAL CLIENT

Clients have the almost infinite range of characteristics human beings can have. Some seek to protect their wealth, others hope to expand their influence, still others want to avoid being hurt by someone else. As we introduce you to the lawyer's advisor role, we focus on how you deal with your own client. Your new client is confused and frustrated by a legal system that she believes has not served her or her family well. This problem first asks the difference between a lawyer's acting as an advisor and acting as an advocate; indeed, it asks whether a lawyer may have both roles in the same matter. Then, it explores what limits there are on the advice a lawyer may give and the projects a lawyer may assist. Next, it examines how the lawyer's role differs if the lawyer concludes that the client lacks normal mental ability. Finally, it asks the lawyer's options if the client's conduct seems likely to endanger others.

FACTS

Marilyn Anderson came to you for legal help. "They have taken away my children," she told you bitterly. "I have a right to them, don't I? I am a good mother, but the welfare department has put my babies in a foster home."

You were moved by Anderson's sincerity and agreed to take the case. In the course of your subsequent investigation, however, you discovered that Anderson had not told you all the facts. The children, Mary, age 7, and Billy, age 3, were removed from the home based on a finding of both neglect and abuse. Social workers at Mary's school became suspicious when the little girl appeared bruised and malnourished after several days' absence. The social workers' questioning of Mary revealed that Anderson sometimes hit the children and sent them to bed hungry. Anderson also often left the home for hours at a time leaving no adult to care for them.

But that was only the beginning of the story. Anderson herself told you that her husband, John, has frequent violent episodes during which Anderson sometimes leaves the house and the children because she literally fears for her life. John has a job, but he is paid in cash and the family cannot rely on how much will be left in the pay envelope after he gets home. Anderson had been employed as a hospital aide before Mary was born, but she has enjoyed staying home with her children.

The problem of Anderson's mother has been a particular irritant in the Andersons' relationship. She is alert and lives in her own house, but she is lonely. Anderson wants to invite her to come to live with the family, but whenever she suggests it, John flies into a violent rage.

You wonder whether or not Marilyn Anderson should win the upcoming custody hearing. Although you sympathize with her situation, you hesitate to use all the skill and resources at your command to overwhelm the overworked counsel for the Department of Children and Family Services. If you do restore custody to Anderson, you worry about the children's future.[1]

QUESTIONS

A.   The difference between advice and advocacy

1. In this problem, is Marilyn Anderson asking you only to advocate for the return of her children? Is she also seeking your experience and judgment about how to deal with her situation?

a. In 1952, the ABA and the Association of American Law Schools established a Joint Conference on Professional Responsibility. Among its conclusions were:

> "The most effective realization of the law's aims often takes place in the attorney's office, where litigation is forestalled by anticipating its outcome, where the lawyer's quiet counsel takes the place of public force. Contrary to popular belief, the compliance with the law thus brought about is not generally lip serving and narrow, for by reminding him of its long-run costs the lawyer often deters his client from a course of conduct technically permissible under existing law, though inconsistent with its underlying spirit and purpose.

> "Although the lawyer serves the administration of justice indispensably both as an advocate and as office counselor, the demands imposed on him by these two roles must be sharply distinguished. * * * [R]esolution of doubts in one direction [in favor of the client] becomes inappropriate when the lawyer acts as counselor. * * *"[2]

b. Later, Model Code of Professional Responsibility Ethical Consideration 7–3 picked up that theme, saying:

---

1. This problem is adapted with permission from one discussed in Murray Teigh Bloom (ed.), Lawyers, Clients & Ethics 1–5 (Council on Legal Education for Professional Responsibility, Inc. 1974).

2. Professional Responsibility: Report of the Joint Conference, 44 A.B.A.J. 1159, 1161 (1958).

"A lawyer may serve simultaneously as both advocate and adviser, but the two roles are essentially different. In asserting a position on behalf of his client, an advocate for the most part deals with past conduct and must take the facts as he finds them. By contrast, a lawyer serving as adviser primarily assists his client in determining the course of future conduct and relationships. While serving as advocate, a lawyer should resolve in favor of his client doubts as to the bounds of the law. In serving a client as adviser, a lawyer in appropriate circumstances should give his professional opinion as to what the ultimate decisions of the courts would likely be as to the applicable law."

c. Is this distinction between advice and advocacy self-righteous and naive? Is a client always entitled to a lawyer who makes a pit bull seem docile? What does Model Rule 2.1 tell you about your duty to Anderson? Is the distinction instead capturing an important reality about how lawyers best serve their clients' interests?

d. Is there a difference between Anderson's short-term and long-term interests? Which should be more important as you decide how to proceed yourself and what to advise her to do? Does the answer to that question vary from client to client?

2. Are you confident that you know what the dynamics of this family really are? Are you obliged to accept what your client tells you as true? Should you assume that most clients will lie about things that embarrass them, at least until they come to trust you?

a. Professor Naomi Cahn suggests that almost all events are likely to come to the lawyer in the form of "inconsistent stories."

"A woman, Darlene Adams, has come into my office, saying that she wants to leave the man she has been living with because he has beaten her up. In the initial interview, she states that the most recent time this happened was yesterday, when she was leaving the apartment with a female friend to go out to the movies. Mr. Ponds pleaded with her not to go; when she refused, he called her a whore and threatened to call Child Protective Services. He then slapped her face and pulled out a clump of hair. Her face stung for several hours, and her scalp still hurt when she came to see me. * * * She wants Mr. Ponds to leave the apartment and to stay away from her; she also wants custody of their child.

"At the interview, I take a picture of the bald spot on her head. Ms. Adams then tells me that the friend with whom she was going to the movies came with her to my office and would be happy to talk to me about what happened. When I interview the friend, Ms. Campbell, she tells me that she and Ms. Adams had talked to each other earlier in the day, and that Ms. Adams had told her that the situation at home was tense. When Ms. Campbell came over, the two of them decided to go to a movie, taking along young Ben. As they were leaving, Ms. Adams walked past Mr. Ponds, who then reached out towards her head. After Ms. Adams pulled away from him, he was left holding some hair. The friend did not see Mr. Ponds slap Ms. Adams. * * * I begin to prepare the papers and I ask Ms. Adams to return in two days, so that she can review and sign them.

"Two days later, Ms. Adams calls to say that she has decided not to go through with any legal action. Mr. Ponds has told her that he loves her, and has been especially nice to her. * * * She says that he really has not hurt her all that much * * *. * * *

"I have recognized, after reflection on these experiences * * * the following layers of inconsistent stories: the two different stories my client tells on different days, the discrepancies between my client's perceptions and those of her witness, the differences between what my client wants and what I think she needs, and the variation between my client's desire to stay and the oft-asked question, 'Why doesn't she leave?' Underlying these different stories include the stories my client tells me and what she tells herself. Once we file the papers, there will be another set of inconsistent stories: differences between my client's language and 'courtroom' language, dissimilarities between my client's story and her desired remedies, which differ from the judge's story and stock of remedies, which further differ from the definitions of what her 'case' actually is.

"The issues of whose story is told and of how the story will be related are complex. A lawyer envisions several tellings of the story; the client envisions several tellings as well. Each has (in)complete information about what will happen within the legal system, and about what 'actually happened.' Different approaches by lawyers and clients and a more fluid ethical system will allow for some better attorney-client relationships and some better retellings. Some stories will also 'seem' truer than others. But the conflicts will remain, conflicts between stories within the same 'case,' conflicts over what constitutes the 'case,' and conflicts between and within outsider groups seeking to tell their own stories. * * * So long as we have a legal system that values consistent stories, we must confront, and challenge, the possibility of constructing a true story of a case. Examining how inconsistent stories are left out of traditional legal ethics makes visible their presence and their significance, and provides an opportunity to accept and use them."[3]

b.   Bring these insights to bear on our problem. How do you know that Mary, the young daughter, told the social workers the truth about her mother's hitting her? How do you know the social workers accurately reported what Mary said? How do you know that Anderson's account of her husband's conduct is reliable? How should you as a lawyer go about determining the facts you need to know?

3.   Do you have sufficient skills to handle this case effectively?

3.   Naomi R. Cahn, Inconsistent Stories,   permission.
81 Georgetown L.J. 2475 (1993). Used with

a. Is your law school training preparing you to be a social worker? Are you confident of your skills as a family therapist? May you simply say that you will limit your practice to giving legal advice and not worry about the context in which the client's legal problem arises?

b. Is that a cop-out? Can you deal effectively with the legal problems without addressing the context? Should you get a restraining order against John Anderson's domestic violence? Should you get an order requiring that a regular part of his pay to be sent to a bank account to which only Mary would have access?

c. In short, rather than being overwhelmed by what you don't know and can't fix, should you concentrate your efforts on steps that only deal with some of the problem but that are steps that only a lawyer knows how to take?

4. What "styles" of client counseling should you adopt in your dealings with Anderson?

a. Any categorization of counseling styles is obviously arbitrary, but that has not stopped commentators from trying to do it. Professors David Binder and Susan Price, for example, are identified with "client-centered" counseling in which the lawyer's primary role is to help the client understand what the client wants and how to achieve it.[4]

b. By contrast, Professor William Simon suggests taking a more directive view that urges lawyers to move clients toward results that are just, not simply favorable to one's own clients.[5]

c. Professors Thomas Shaffer and Robert Cochran advocate a counseling of moral discourse and treating the client as one would treat a good friend, being supportive but willing to urge moral considerations as well as merely legal advice.[6]

d. Does any one of those approaches seem intuitively better to you than the others? Whatever your initial view, keep these kinds of alternatives in mind as you think about what you would do in counseling Anderson and other clients you will meet in this chapter.

B. LIMITS ON THE ADVICE A LAWYER MAY GIVE

1. Look at Model Rule 1.2(d) and Comments 9 & 10. Do you agree that there should be no exceptions to the rule that a lawyer may not "counsel or assist" a client to commit a crime or fraud?

a. People v. Chappell, 927 P.2d 829 (Colo.1996), was a discipline case in which the lawyer represented the wife in a custody dispute. Court orders forbade both parents to take the child out of state. When the lawyer for the

---

4. Their leading book on the subject is David Binder & Susan Price, Legal Interviewing and Counseling: A Client–Centered Approach (1977).

5. See, e.g., William Simon, The Practice of Justice: A Theory of Lawyers' Ethics (1998). See also, Deborah L. Rhode, In the Interests of Justice: Reforming the Legal Profession (2000).

6. See, e.g., Thomas Shaffer & Robert F. Cochran, Jr., Lawyers, Clients and Moral Responsibility (1994). See also, Thomas D. Morgan, Thinking About Lawyers as Counselors, 42 Florida L. Rev. 429 (1990).

mother learned that the court-appointed evaluator was going to recommend giving the father custody of both her living and her unborn child, the lawyer "advised her [the client] as an attorney to stay, but as a mother to run" and told her of a network of safe houses that would take her in. At the lawyer's request, a friend of the client came into the client's home and moved her belongings into a storage locker to which the lawyer kept the key. When the lawyer came to the next hearing and the court asked where her client was, the lawyer told the court that the client's location was privileged. Only at a later hearing did the lawyer admit the client had fled the state. The court ruled that the lawyer violated Rule 1.2(d) by counseling the client to commit a crime, and what is now Rule 3.3(b) by not revealing the client's action to the trial judge. The court disbarred the lawyer.

b. Iowa Supreme Court Bd. of Professional Ethics & Conduct v. Hughes, 557 N.W.2d 890 (Iowa 1996), imposed a public reprimand on a lawyer who advised his client to ignore a court order to undergo substance abuse testing at the client's expense. The lawyer believed such an order was beyond the authority of the court. The client disregarded the advice and underwent the testing, but the trial judge referred the lawyer's conduct to the disciplinary committee. The Iowa Supreme Court assumed, without deciding, that a lawyer could counsel a client to ignore a void order, i.e., the order of a court with no jurisdiction over the matter, but in a case like this one, when the client's interests "conflict with a lawful court order, the lawyer's duty to uphold the law is paramount." 557 N.W.2d at 894.

c. Do you agree with the results in these cases? Can you imagine ever counseling a client to flee the jurisdiction or violate a court order? What if you believed your client's life would be in danger if she did not flee? What if violation of a court order is the only way to make the order ripe for appellate review?

2. Is it obvious what it means to "counsel or assist" wrongdoing?

a. Would you be "counseling" wrongdoing if you gave the client honest information about whether it was likely that the state was likely to prosecute a particular violation of law? Does Model Rule 1.2, Comment 9, answer that question?

b. Would you be "assisting" wrongdoing if a client charged with murder asked you which South American countries have no extradition treaties with the United States? Look at Model Rule 1.2, Comments 9 & 10.

c. In Morganroth & Morganroth v. Norris, McLaughlin & Marcus, 331 F.3d 406 (3d Cir.2003), plaintiffs sued the Norris McLaughlin law firm for assisting a client's fraudulent conveyances that sought to evade a writ of execution to enforce plaintiffs' claim against the client. The firm's involvement consisted of the preparation of a deed purporting to confirm the conveyance of an interest in land, the creation of a purported life lease on certain land, and facilitation of delivering shares the client owned in a

Nevada corporation into his brother's control. Plaintiffs alleged that these transfers were made with the intent to hinder, delay, and defraud the plaintiffs. The court found that plaintiffs "have alleged facts that, if proven, would establish that defendants went beyond the bounds of permissible advocacy; they allege that defendants were active participants and planners in the scheme to obstruct the plaintiffs' efforts to execute on their judgment." 331 F.3d at 412.

d.   Should a lawyer in such cases offer such information and assistance as a way of providing the client full service? Must the lawyer refuse to answer questions that a dishonest client could use to avoid the consequences of past misconduct or plan future misdeeds? Must the lawyer ask a client for his passport and hold it lest the client try to flee?

3.   Assume that Anderson's mother owns her own house and a few stocks but has no other source of income. If she were to become ill, the house could be seized to reimburse Medicaid authorities for her care. What would you think of encouraging her to give her house to Anderson as a way of avoiding that result?

a.   Assume that, as long as she did not make clear she had given her house to a relative, Anderson's mother could also qualify for welfare because she would be without assets and unable to work. She could even pay part of her benefits to Anderson as "rent."

b.   Would it be appropriate for you to suggest this approach to Anderson's mother and offer to draft the documents necessary to transfer the property to Anderson?[7] Would it be important for you to have Anderson promise to care for her mother or otherwise show some consideration for the transfer?

c.   Section 217 of the 1996 Health Insurance Portability and Accountability Act, 42 U.S.C.A. § 1320a–7b, purported to deal with the practice described in this question by making it a crime to dispose of assets to qualify for Medicaid. Thus, the law was nicknamed the "Granny Goes to Jail Act." The provision was then briefly reinforced by § 4734 of the Balanced Budget Act of 1997 that also made it a crime to take a fee for counseling someone how to manipulate assets in prohibited ways.[8]

d.   An analogous issue is presented by the Bankruptcy Abuse Prevention and Consumer Protection Act of 2005, a section of which prohibits any "debt relief agency" from advising clients "to incur more debt in contemplation" of filing for bankruptcy. Lawyers argued that it would be unconsti-

---

7.   Lest you think this proposal is hypothetical, the ethics of "asset management" of elderly clients is an everyday issue faced by "elder law" attorneys around the nation. See, e.g., Steven H. Hobbs & Fay Wilson Hobbs, The Ethical Management of Assets for Elder Clients: A Context, Role, and Law Approach, 62 Fordham L. Rev. 1411 (1994).

8.   New York State Bar Ass'n v. Reno, 999 F.Supp. 710 (N.D.N.Y.1998), was a suit to enjoin the attorney general's enforcement of the prohibition. The Justice Department had already notified Congress it would not enforce the provision and said an injunction was not necessary, but the court found that even the existence of the statutory prohibition was enough to cause self-censorship by lawyers who had taken an oath to abide by the law. Because the court found the plaintiffs were likely to succeed on the merits, it granted a preliminary injunction.

tutional to allow the provision to prevent them from giving truthful legal advice. Milavetz, Gallop & Milavetz, P.A. v. United States, 559 U.S. ___, 130 S.Ct. 1324, 176 L.Ed.2d 79 (2010) read the law narrowly to avoid that constitutional problem. It held that lawyers are "debt relief agencies" but the law only prohibits them from "advising an assisted person to incur more debt when the impelling reason for the advice is the anticipation of bankruptcy." 130 S.Ct. at 1338. For example, a lawyer may advise a client to buy a car on credit when doing so will let the client work, even if the debtor later files for bankruptcy, because it was the hope of enhanced financial prospects, not the anticipated filing, that was the impelling cause of incurring further debt.

e. Given the relative freedom these decisions suggest lawyers have to give advice, if you fail to give such asset-management advice, will you be violating Model Rule 1.1's obligation to act "competently"? Will you be committing malpractice? If you *do* give the advice, will you be violating Model Rule 1.2(d)? Which rule should control?

4. Would you be uncomfortable about helping a wealthy client buy an expensive house in Florida or set up a trust in the Cook Islands that would exempt those assets from being seized by creditors if the client ever went bankrupt?

a. Would you justify the conduct by saying that the wealthy are such deep-pocket targets of frivolous litigation that any action is justified to defend them against such injustice? Do you think that some lawyers may become moralistic about poor people cheating the system while vigorously defending the rights of their own clients to do something quite similar?

b. Are no moral issues presented if a technically-defensible interpretation of the law permits a course of conduct? Do you suppose that lawyers for companies accused of misleading investors about their financial condition can rest easy that the public will be comfortable with that answer?[9]

C. THE CLIENT SUFFERING FROM DIMINISHED CAPACITY

1. Would you still follow Anderson's directions if you concluded that she had less than normal intelligence and was immature for her age?

a. Look at Model Rule 1.14 and Restatement Third, The Law Governing Lawyers § 24, which advised, in part:

"(1) When a client's capacity to make adequately considered decisions in connection with the representation is diminished, whether because of minority, physical illness, mental disability, or other cause, the lawyer must, as far as reasonably possible, maintain a normal client-lawyer relationship with the client and act in the best interests of the client as stated in Subsection (2).

---

9. We return to questions of counseling in the corporate context in Problems 18, 21, and 22, *infra*.

"(2) A lawyer representing a client with diminished capacity as described in Subsection (1) and for whom no guardian or other representative is available to act, must, with respect to a matter within the scope of the representation, pursue the lawyer's reasonable view of the client's objectives or interests as the client would define them if able to make adequately considered decisions on the matter, even if the client expresses no wishes or gives contrary instructions."

When should you conclude that your client has "diminished capacity"? Are you competent to tell? Does Model Rule 1.14, Comment 6 give you helpful guidance? Should you be found guilty of malpractice if you treat your client as sovereign when she really is impaired?

b. If your client was not legally competent, did she have the capacity to retain you? Can she consent to your continuing to act as counsel? Does such a client have the capacity to fire you? Look at Model Rule 1.16, Comment 6. Many such clients have the capacity to make decisions to retain and terminate a lawyer without having the realistic capacity to make all decisions about the objectives and conduct of the representation.

2. May or must you ever seek to have a guardian appointed to act on an apparently incompetent client's behalf? What if the client objects to having a guardian?

a. Look at Model Rule 1.14, Comments 7 and 8. May you testify at the client's competency hearing? In doing so, should you be permitted to reveal what the client told you in confidence? What if the incoherence of those confidential conversations is your best evidence of the client's need of a guardian's assistance?

b. ABA Formal Opinion 96–404 (Aug. 2, 1996) acknowledges that if a client's "ability to communicate, to comprehend and assess information, and to make reasoned decisions is partially or completely diminished," Rule 1.14's admonition to "maintain a normal lawyer-client relationship" with the client "may be difficult or impossible." Indeed, in some states, the agency relationship between lawyer and client may be dissolved by the principal-client's incompetence, but lawyer withdrawal may be impossible without significant adverse effect on the client's interests. The opinion counsels a lawyer to take the "least restrictive action under the circumstances;" a guardianship should be sought only "if other, less drastic, solutions are [not] available." Further, even if a guardian is needed for some purposes, the lawyer should seek something less than a general guardianship if possible. While the lawyer may file the petition for guardianship, it must be because the lawyer concludes it is necessary, not because someone else (such as a family member) requests it. If the lawyer recommends a guardian, the lawyer must disclose any expectation of future employment by the guardian to the appointing court, as well as any preference the client may have expressed about who should be appointed guardian.

c.   Matter of M.R., 638 A.2d 1274 (N.J.1994), involved a moderately-retarded 21–year–old woman with Down syndrome who was said to be "generally incompetent" and in need of a guardian. The question before the court was whether M.R. could decide whether she wanted her father or her mother to be that guardian. Part of the court's analysis involved whether appointed counsel should advocate M.R.'s preference to have her father as guardian or should make an independent report to the court about M.R.'s best interest. The court drew a distinction between a court-appointed lawyer and a court-appointed guardian ad litem. The latter is to make an investigation and report. Citing Model Rule 1.14, however, the court said that counsel appointed to represent M.R. must try to maintain "a normal client-lawyer relationship" with her. The lawyer must advocate what the client wants, short of things "patently absurd or that pose an undue risk of harm to the client." 638 A.2d at 1285. Do you agree?

3.   Should special rules apply if immediate action must be taken on behalf of a person—typically not a current client of the lawyer—who seems to lack the ability to make the necessary decisions to provide for his or her own welfare?

a.   In response to ABA Formal Opinion 96–404, supra, the ABA House of Delegates amended the Comments to Rule 1.14 in February 1997 to add what are now Comments 9 & 10 on "Emergency Legal Assistance." The core idea of Comment 9 is that "where the health, safety or a financial interest of a person with seriously diminished capacity is threatened with imminent and irreparable harm, a lawyer may take legal action on behalf of such a person even though the person is unable to establish a client-lawyer relationship or make or express considered judgments about the matter, when the person or another acting in good faith on that person's behalf has consulted with the lawyer."

b.   Comment 10 goes on to say that the lawyer should protect the confidences of the person with seriously diminished capacity, should not provide assistance if the person has another lawyer, and normally should not charge a fee for the services rendered.

c.   How would you exercise the authority and responsibility given by these Comments? Should you seek to find and involve family members of the person? Should you see if she belongs to a church or other religious or social community whose members could help her? Might the lack of such a support network help explain why this person is now in crisis?

4.   If there were grounds to believe that your client were about to make a fatal mistake, would you have an obligation to disregard the client's expressed preference and substitute your own judgment of what was best for the client?

a.   Convicted killer Gary Gilmore said that he "had to" die for a crime he had committed two centuries ago in England, and that he would still be in existence after his death. His attorneys thought that Gilmore's references to eighteenth century England would have made a difference to psychiatrists if they had heard it. The lawyers said, "we feel duty bound to go ahead with the appeal." Gilmore sent a letter to the attorneys saying: "butt out" and "you're fired." The attorneys then filed a notice of appeal in their own names saying that it was "in the best interest" of Gilmore, who was eventually executed.[10]

Were the lawyers right to ignore the client's call for his own death? One commentator has argued: "If the client expresses ends which, due to imprudence or excessive moralism, seem self-destructive, * * * [i]t is the lawyer's job to question the client's competence where it may need questioning * * *. When, on the other hand, the client is able to make his or her ends plausible to the lawyer, the check which he means to provide must give way."[11]

Do you agree? Should the client have to convince the lawyer before the lawyer has to give the client his own way?

b. Massachusetts Bar Association Opinion 01–2 (2001) discusses whether the lawyer should reveal a client's intention to commit suicide. Because neither suicide nor attempted suicide is a crime in Massachusetts, its Rule 1.6 did not authorize disclosure. The opinion focused on Rule 1.14. It says that if a lawyer reasonably believes the client's suicide threat is real and that the client is suffering from a mental disorder or disability that prevents him from making a rational decision about whether to continue living, the lawyer may notify family members, adult protective agencies, the police, or the client's doctors in an attempt to prevent the suicide. The opinion does not give the lawyer a blanket authority to disclose the client's wish to die. The opinion suggests that if the client were in great pain from a terminal disease, but not mentally depressed or otherwise mentally impaired, Rule 1.14 would not authorize the lawyer to disclose the client's plans.

Do you agree? Under Restatement, § 24, supra, or the Massachusetts Opinion, what should you do if the client told you that she intended to take her own life?

D. THE CLIENT WHO IS LIKELY TO ENDANGER OTHERS

1. Should the interest of your client be the only interest relevant to you? Should a lawyer properly consider the interests of others, including the public interest, in rendering advice to a client?

a. In his address at the laying of the cornerstone of the American Bar Center in 1954, Justice Robert Jackson said:

"We believe in an independent Bar, free not only from government control, but intellectually independent of client control. In the client-and-attorney relation the client is not a master, the lawyer is not a mere hired hand—he is an officer of the court, with a duty of independent judgment in

---

10. Norman Mailer, The Executioner's Song 490, 513–14 (1979).

11. David Luban, Paternalism and the Legal Profession, 1981 Wisconsin L. Rev. 454, 493.

the performance of his professional service and under a duty to serve all sorts and conditions of men."[12]

b.   Do you agree? Should lawyers be "intellectually independent of client control"? If a lawyer acts with "independence," is the client getting what the client properly thinks he or she is paying for? Putting aside his rhetorical excess, is Justice Jackson really saying that no client is an island and no client's act should be seen as without consequences that a lawyer must consider in giving sound advice?

2.   May a lawyer properly refuse to pursue a legally sound but unjust cause?

a.   The question of pursuing an unjust cause often seems not to trouble lawyers today. Our instincts seem to be to look to positive law, not natural law or "justice" in some other sense. But to many, the problem of what causes to champion has been one of the fundamental moral issues facing the legal profession.

b.   David Hoffman, the Baltimore lawyer who in 1836 was one of the first to organize and espouse legal ethics principles, looked down upon a client who owes a just debt, but relies on the Statute of Limitations to bar suit. His conclusion would surprise many modern lawyers.

> "I will never plead the Statute of Limitations, when based on the *mere efflux of time;* for if my client is conscious he owes the debt; and has no other defence than the *legal bar*, he shall never make me a partner in his knavery."[13]

Is that idea archaic? Would a lawyer who lived out his own morality in this way have to answer in malpractice to his client?

c.   Or consider George Sharswood, whose lectures laid the groundwork for the Alabama Code of Ethics of 1887, and in 1908, for the American Bar Association Canons of Ethics:

> "Counsel * * * have an undoubted right, and are duty bound, to refuse to be concerned for a plaintiff in the legal pursuit of a demand which offends his sense of what is just and right. The courts are open to the party in person to prosecute his own claim, and plead his own cause; and although * * * he ought to examine and be well satisfied before he refuses to a suitor the benefit of his professional skill and learning, yet * * * it would be on his part an immoral act to afford that assistance, when his conscience told him that the client was aiming to perpetrate a wrong through the means of some advantage the law may have afforded him."[14]

12.   Robert H. Jackson, The American Bar Center: A Testimony to Our Faith in the Rule of Law, 40 A.B.A.J. 19, 21 (1954).

13.   David Hoffman, A Course of Legal Study 754 (2d ed.1846).

14.   George Sharswood, Professional Ethics 33–35 (1854).

Is that shocking to you? Does a lawyer bear a moral responsibility for accepting an unjust cause?[15] Is Sharswood right that it is only plaintiffs' cases to which that responsibility attaches (because defendants don't have a choice whether or not to be sued)? Does Model Rule 1.2(b) contradict this view of the lawyer's role?

d. In an even earlier time, James Boswell once reported that Dr. Johnson's solution to supporting a cause he knew to be bad was:

> "Sir, you do not know it to be good or bad till the Judge determines it. I have said that you are to state facts fairly; so that your thinking, or what you call knowing, a cause to be bad, must be from reasoning, must be from supposing your arguments to be weak and inclusive. But, Sir, that is not enough. An argument which does not convince yourself, may convince the Judge to whom you urge it: and if it does convince him, why, then, Sir, you are wrong and he is right."[16]

Do you agree with Dr. Johnson, or was Johnson engaged in ethical sophistry?

3.   How do these considerations apply when a lawyer knows about child abuse?

a. Association of the Bar of the City of New York, Formal Opinion 1997–2, 52 Record of the Association of the Bar of the City of New York 430 (1997), written in the context of a lawyer for a social services agency, acknowledges that children ordinarily have the right to have their communications with a lawyer kept confidential. The opinion even suggests that a lawyer may not be required to disclose some intentions of the child to kill or maim himself. If the lawyer observes physical evidence of child abuse, however, the visual observations are not privileged. Indeed, even the child's communications may be disclosed if: (1) disclosure is "required by law," (2) necessary to save the life of the child, or (3) the child is too young to have the capacity to make decisions.

b. Utah Bar Opinion 97–12 (Jan.1998) addressed the situation where a client tells his lawyer that he is a child abuser. The opinion says that state law requiring "any person" who suspects child abuse to report it does not apply to such cases. Under Rule 1.6(b)(1), the lawyer may disclose the client's intent to commit *future* abuse, but a client's confession to a lawyer about past conduct is privileged and the lawyer may not disclose it.

c. L.A. County Bar Association, Formal Opinion 504 (2000) discusses an attorney's duty with regard to confidential information of a minor client's being a victim of ongoing sexual abuse. The opinion says the attorney has a duty to keep such information confidential if, after discussing the matter with the minor, the attorney reasonably believes that the client is competent to make a decision on the matter. What the attorney thinks is in the best interest of the client is not controlling. Indeed, even if

---

15. You may remember that this was an important question in Problem 4, *supra.*

16. James Boswell, 2 The Life of Johnson 47 (Hill Ed. 1887).

the attorney feels that the minor is not competent to make such a decision, the attorney may not substitute her own decision for that of the client but may seek other appropriate measures such as having a guardian ad litem appointed and disclosing the information to that guardian.

4.   Is your duty different now that you have taken the case than it would have been had you not yet decided to represent Anderson?

a.   In re Pressly, 628 A.2d 927 (Vt.1993), involved a client who had obtained a restraining order against her husband and had custody of the children, subject to the husband's visitation rights. Later, she told the lawyer she wanted the husband to have only supervised visitation. When asked why, she said she thought he had sexually abused their daughter but she explicitly told the lawyer not to tell her husband of her suspicions. When the lawyer told opposing counsel the wife wanted supervised visitation, however, opposing counsel asked if it was because of suspected sexual abuse. The lawyer confirmed that abuse was suspected and asked opposing counsel not to tell the husband. Opposing counsel did tell the husband, and the wife was shocked and furious at her lawyer. The Vermont Supreme Court said the confirmation that abuse was suspected—contrary to the client's express direction not to reveal it—justified a public reprimand of the lawyer.

b.   How would you have responded to opposing counsel's question in *Pressly*? Was the lawyer's mistake accepting the client's original direction without discussion or qualification? A client can always fire her lawyer, of course, so the client necessarily has the last word. Should the lawyer take the client's direction as the beginning of a conversation with the client, rather than as an order to be carried out blindly?

5.   What creative ways can you see to deal with Anderson's situation?

a.   Think back to Anderson's mother. What would you think of having Anderson and the children move in with her? Anderson's mother could watch the children while Anderson went back to work. In exchange, Anderson would make sure her mother was in good health. She could start proceedings to divorce John and request child support. Do you have some better ideas?

b.   Suppose that at the custody hearing the social worker from the Department of Children and Family Services appears without counsel. You still represent Anderson, but no one represents Anderson's children. May you suggest that counsel be appointed for the children even though you surmise that, if that suggestion is implemented, your chances of winning will be substantially lessened?

c.   Do you have an ethical obligation to Anderson to oppose appointment of such counsel? Does Model Rule 4.3 provide a good analogy that helps you decide what to do?[17] If the court appoints counsel, does that

---

17.   D.C. Bar Legal Ethics Committee Opinion 326 (2004) expressly affirms that it is not a conflict of interest for a lawyer to help even an unrepresented opposing party get legal counsel. It follows that it would be proper to assist the child to get counsel in the circumstances described.

lessen your own ethical burden and allow you to use all the tricks in your bag on Anderson's behalf?

———

PROBLEM 18

ADVISING THE BUSINESS CORPORATION

This is a second problem that focuses on your duty to give candid advice to a client. It is one thing to advise an individual whom the lawyer can address face to face. When the client is a business corporation, however, the lawyer can only counsel the client's agents. Those agents, in turn, are likely to believe themselves limited by the authority of others, so the lawyer's task of giving wise counsel becomes immeasurably more complex. This problem explores who the lawyer's ultimate client is when the lawyer represents an organization and from whom the lawyer is to accept direction. Next, it asks when a lawyer may or must disclose wrongdoing either inside or outside the organization. It then examines whether a lawyer may personally be liable to persons hurt by client conduct that the lawyer did not prevent, and finally, it considers whether the role of inside counsel as to these issues differs from that of a lawyer in an outside firm.

FACTS

You have long been outside counsel to Sleepware, Inc., a clothing manufacturer. The company makes a line of children's pajamas that is a big seller. Recent tests have shown, however, that the pajama fabric can catch fire if a match is held against it for a few seconds.

Sleepware's vice president for pajamas wants to keep selling the pajamas. Regulations of the Consumer Product Safety Commission (CPSC) prohibit sale of products known to cause burns to children, but the vice president believes that the CPSC is unlikely to recognize the potential injuries the pajamas could cause.

Further, the vice president points out that, although children wearing pajamas sometimes play with matches, experts he has consulted say that not more than one in 50,000 children would hold the matches on their pajamas long enough for it to catch fire. The experts admit that if the pajamas burn, the child's injuries could be expected to be severe, but a management consulting firm has estimated that civil damages would not exceed $250,000 per victim. Sleepware sells 200,000 of these pajamas each year, the vice president tells you proudly, and it makes a profit of $4,000,000 on this product. Thus, even under a worst-case scenario, he has calculated that it will be $3 million more profitable to sell the pajamas than not to sell them.

You have not been asked for advice about whether to market this product; you only learned about the flammability while working on an unrelated matter. Indeed, the vice president is annoyed that you have raised the issue with him. "The president will retire soon," he tells you, "and I am his natural successor. My enemies in the company would love to embarrass me with this."

QUESTIONS

A.   THE CLIENT TO WHOM A CORPORATE LAWYER OWES PRIMARY LOYALTY

1.   Is your client in this problem Sleepware's vice president for pajamas?

a.   Describing the corporate lawyer's client has proved harder for lawyers than for rule drafters. It is tempting to think that the "clients" are the individual human beings to whom the lawyer gives her advice and from whom she receives confidential information. Other lawyers sometimes think of their clients as shareholders generally, or perhaps the largest shareholder—the one who influences decisions the corporate managers will make.

b.   To try to deal with this issue, Model Code of Professional Responsibility, Ethical Consideration 5–18 simply said:

> "A lawyer employed or retained by a corporation or similar entity owes his allegiance to the entity and not to a stockholder, director, officer, employee, representative, or other person connected with the entity."

c.   That statement of the rule was and is accurate, but to point out that corporations and other organizations only act through living people, Model Rule 1.13(a) now says:

> "A lawyer employed or retained by an organization represents the organization acting through its duly authorized constituents."

d.   The Restatement Third, The Law Governing Lawyers § 96(1)(a) refines this principle:

> "When a lawyer is employed or retained to represent an organization, the lawyer represents the interests of the organization as defined by its responsible agents acting pursuant to the organization's decision making procedures."

2.   How do these definitions apply in real life? Do they all point the same way in particular cases?

a.   Is the interest of the entity always self-evident? For example, the employees may want higher pay and secure jobs, while some shareholders may want to change the company's direction in search of faster growth, while the bondholders may oppose adding more debt.

b. Is it best to treat the board of directors as having the last word on defining the goals of a corporate client? Is it realistic to believe they represent all affected constituencies in the corporation? Is it enough that the law places them at the top of the corporate decision-making pyramid?

c. Should a lawyer mentally stand outside the corporation and see the "entity" as the objectives and purposes that are shared by most of the people who have invested in and managed the corporation? Those people will each have many different private interests, of course, but the lawyer for the corporation would not represent those private interests and should see that they are subordinated to the purposes they have in common.

d. Look at the first two sentences of Model Rule 1.13, Comment 3. Do they eliminate such an affirmative role for the corporate lawyer, except in matters serious enough to require action under Model Rule 1.13(b)? Do you think the line between poor business decisions and illegal conduct is always as clear as the Comment suggests?

3. If you are Sleepware's counsel, may you also become a director of Sleepware? Are the duties of corporate counsel and director both duties to the corporate entity and thus sufficiently close that the roles would be compatible?

a. ABA Formal Opinion 98–410 (Feb. 27, 1998) concluded that the dual relationship is not per se improper, but problems of conflicts of interest and preservation of privilege often arise. First, the opinion says, at the outset of the dual relationship, the lawyer should advise the company— preferably in writing—of both kinds of problems, and should independently satisfy herself that problems are unlikely to become serious. At least four types of conflicts may arise in such situations: (1) acting as counsel as to a decision the lawyer opposed as a director, (2) opining on past board action in which the lawyer participated as a director, (3) voting on corporate action affecting the lawyer's firm, and (4) representing the corporation in litigation that may involve a conflict of interest. Further, when the client seeks legal advice as opposed to business judgment, the lawyer should take precautions to make a record as to what kind of advice is being given so as to be sure the privilege is preserved.

b. A longtime corporate lawyer further explained the concerns:

"The most difficult situation arises when an attorney is himself a witness to events involving a corporation in which he has a financial interest as a stockholder-director as well as being counsel. His questioning is continually interrupted by assertions of privilege because of the attorney-client relationship. Once again all parties must wade through a morass to determine whether the privilege is being misused.

"Another set of problems exists when an attorney is called upon to advise a client as to the client's exercise of his privilege against self-incrimination. Sometimes it is apparent that the business dealings of the attorney involved were perhaps more incriminating than the acts of his client involving the same set of circumstances. How can such an attorney be expected to impartially advise his client as to the wisdom of the exercise of the privilege against self-incrimination, when the attorney's own incrimination may possibly be involved? * * *

"The attorney in such position potentially may be involved in the conflict of interest that may emerge within his mind when he weighs advice. For that task, he wears two hats. He is a businessman quite often with a personal business stake in the decisions of the company. However, he is more than likely to be called on for legal advice by the company. Can it not be said that determinations made by such an attorney, when asked for legal advice, are necessarily colored by the personal interest which he has as a substantial stockholder, option-owner, salaried official, or otherwise? To put it more simply, the question is whether we should permit the continuing growth of such conflicts in the practice of law by which the lawyer-confidant merges with the interested businessman."[1]

c. Does Model Rule 1.7, Comment 35, adequately describe the potential concerns about a lawyer also serving as a director of a client? Does it give inadequate recognition to the benefits of having a lawyer who is also a director?

4. Today, of course, large corporations are often composed of several divisions and subsidiaries. They also get into financial trouble. Who is the lawyer's client in those situations?

a. Assume that Sleepware produces hats through an existing subsidiary. It wants to acquire a new firm in the same industry, but to do so it must divest itself of the present subsidiary. Is it clear whose interests Sleepware's corporate counsel must represent in structuring the sale of the subsidiary firm? Would it matter to you whether the subsidiary was wholly owned or whether it still had other shareholders as well? See, e.g., FTC v. Exxon Corp., 636 F.2d 1336 (D.C.Cir.1980) (separate counsel required for divested subsidiary because former parent might structure sale so as to see that it did not survive as a viable competitor).

b. What if the corporate subsidiary is a regulated entity that has duties to interests other than those of the parent? Lincoln Savings was a wholly-owned subsidiary of ACC, the holding company that its principal shareholder, Charles Keating, used to make other investments. Keating eventually pled guilty to bankruptcy fraud. The Federal Deposit Insurance Corporation (FDIC) sued the law firm representing Lincoln Savings for not preventing that fraud. It argued that, because the FDIC must make good the losses of an insured savings and loan, once Lincoln Savings was in financial trouble, the law firm could not properly accept direction from ACC's officers; it had to consider the interest of Lincoln Savings' insurer, the FDIC, as well. In re American Continental Corp./Lincoln Sav. & Loan

---

1. Hon. Louis J. Lefkowitz, The Attorney–Client Relationship and the Corporation, 26 Record of the Association of the Bar of the City of New York 697 (Nov.1971).

Sec. Litigation, 794 F.Supp. 1424 (D.Ariz.1992), held that this theory supported claims against Lincoln Savings' attorneys.

c. In re JTS Corp. (Decker v. Mitchell), 305 B.R. 529 (Bankr.N.D.Cal. 2003), involved a law firm whom the client retained to close sales of company real estate. It did that job properly and well. What it did not do is tell the company's board that the sales were at a price below the appraised value of the property. Because the company was in serious financial trouble, the so-called "trust fund" doctrine required the company to be run for the benefit of creditors. Because the sales may have damaged the creditors, the court found that the bankruptcy trustee had a cause of action against the law firm. Once again, the case reminds lawyers that they must focus on the interests of the "entity" rather than the direction of current managers because they can never know who will be asserting the entity's interest in the future.

**B.   REPORTING CORPORATE MISCONDUCT WITHIN AND OUTSIDE THE CLIENT OR-
       GANIZATION**

**1.   What steps are you required to take in the situation pre-
sented in our problem? Is the vice president's instruction to drop
the matter something you must or may accept as final? When does
a lawyer's obligation shift from taking orders to taking action?**

a.   Look at Model Rule 1.13(b). It explains how the lawyer goes up the corporate ladder (or exhausts his or her internal remedies) to determine what the "entity" really wants. How do you apply Rules 1.13(b) to the present problem? Is the sale of the pajamas "a violation of a legal obligation to the organization"? Is it "a violation of law that reasonably might be imputed to the organization"? Is it "likely to result in substantial injury to the organization"?

b.   Is it relevant that the corporation did not ask you for advice on this matter and you only learned of it while working on an unrelated matter? Does Model Rule 1.13(b) make your obligation turn on the relation of the information to the question on which you are working? Do Comments 3–6 give you an answer?

c.   On the "substantial injury" issue, is the vice president's judgment the only relevant one? Are his "experts'" estimates of the rate of injury and the management consultant's estimate of the likely jury award convincing? Indeed, is reevaluation of critical factual assumptions such as these one of the services a lawyer should perform for a client?

**2.   If you conclude that the conditions specified in Model Rule
1.13(b) are met, are you required to take action? What action?**

a.   What does it mean to "proceed as is reasonably necessary in the best interest of the organization"? Is that requirement appropriately flexible or only maddeningly vague?

b.   Does Model Rule 1.13(b) describe any more about what the lawyer is to do? Can you imagine situations serious enough to require action under

Model Rule 1.13(b) but not serious enough to refer to "higher authority in the organization"?

c. Assuming that you take the matter "up the ladder" to the president of Sleepware, if the president supports the vice president and tells you to take the issue no further, may you accept that as binding? Would your inaction be "warranted by the circumstances"? Can you answer that question without knowing the reasons for the president's direction?

d. If you take the matter to Sleepware's board of directors, what will be your appropriate role? Must you be an advocate against the continued sale of the product? Is such advocacy an appropriate role for the lawyer? Whatever happened to the idea that the client is the principal and the lawyer only the agent?

e. If your advice to discontinue sales of the pajamas is ignored by the board of directors, may you report the situation to the shareholders? Shareholders ordinarily do not have authority to "act on behalf of" a corporation. Nor may they ordinarily countermand decisions of the board of directors. Is it likely that Model Rule 1.13(b) ordinarily would let the lawyer tell the shareholders what is going on?

3. May you report the dangerous product to a public enforcement agency such as the Consumer Product Safety Commission?

a. Look at Model Rule 1.13(c), adopted in 2003 at the time of the changes seen earlier in Model Rule 1.6. Do you now have a basis for disclosure outside the corporation if the board of directors refuses to act?

b. Are the conditions for such outside disclosure the same as for disclosure within the corporation under Model Rule 1.13(b)? What additional conditions must be met under Rule 1.13(c) before you may make an outside disclosure? How would you distinguish something that is "clearly a violation of law" (Rule 1.13(c)(1)) from simply a "violation of law" (Rule 1.13(b))?

c. Do you agree that Model Rule 1.13(d) should *forbid* a lawyer who has investigated internal corporate wrongdoing from making a Model Rule 1.13(c) disclosure? Why or why not? Do you feel the same way about a lawyer retained to defend a case against the client? Does the rationale offered in Comment 7 persuade you that those situations are the same?

4. If you are fired because the vice president does not want you to pursue the flammable pajama issue, what will you be required to do?

a. What kind of action would you normally believe is "necessary to assure that the organization's highest authority is informed of the lawyer's discharge or withdrawal"? Could you write a letter to the chairman of the board and be confident he or she would receive it? Suppose you tried to make an appointment with one or more board members but they refused to see you. Does Comment 8 offer any more guidance than what Model Rule 1.13(e) already provides?

b.   Notice that the obligation to inform the highest authority in the organization also applies if you "withdraw under circumstances that require or permit [you] to take action" under either Model Rule 1.13(b) or (c). Is this provision a trap for the unwary lawyer who thinks simple withdrawal is enough?

5.   Does a corporate lawyer have to look to Model Rule 1.13(c) to find authority to disclose the dangerous character of the product? How about looking to Model Rule 1.6(b)(1)?

a.   Remember from Problem 8 that Model Rule 1.6(b)(1) has been amended to permit a lawyer to make disclosure whenever "the lawyer reasonably believes necessary to prevent reasonably certain death or substantial bodily harm." That standard no longer requires criminal conduct. Nor does it require that the death or injury be "imminent."

b.   Do Model Rules 1.13(b) and (c) preempt Model Rule 1.6(b) in the case of a corporate client? Look at Model Rule 1.13, Comment 6. Does it leave any doubt about the answer when a dangerous product is involved? See also, Restatement Third, The Law Governing Lawyers § 66.

C.   LAWYER LIABILITY FOR FAILURE TO TAKE APPROPRIATE ACTION

1.   If you assume that disclosure of the danger to children is permitted in this case, could you be held liable to anyone for a failure to disclose?

a.   Model Rule 1.6, Comment 5 advises: "A lawyer's decision not to disclose as permitted by paragraph (b) does not violate this Rule."

b.   Restatement § 66(3) says:

"A lawyer who takes action or decides not to take action permitted under this Section is not, solely by reason of such action or inaction, subject to professional discipline, liable for damages to the lawyer's client or any third person, or barred from recovery against a client or third person."

c.   Is that the end of the matter? Is there any information a lawyer should be *required* to disclose?

In State v. Hansen, 862 P.2d 117 (Wash.1993), a lawyer received a call from a prospective client, recently out of prison, who said of the participants in his criminal trial, "I am going to get a gun and blow them all away, the prosecutor, the judge and the public defender." The lawyer did not take the case but he did call the prosecutor and the judge. The police arrested Hansen, the prospective client, who was convicted of intimidating a judge. He claimed that his threats were privileged. Not surprisingly, the court found that the comments were within the crime-fraud exception, and the court went on to say that "attorneys, as officers of the court, have a duty to warn of true threats to harm members of the judiciary communicated to them by clients or by third parties." 862 P.2d at 122.

Do you agree? Is the "duty" in this passage only a rhetorical flourish?

2. If you are liable to anyone for a failure to disclose, is one possible plaintiff your client, the corporation itself?

a. May the corporation claim that you failed in your obligation to protect it from the wrongdoing of its management and directors? The failures of a number of savings & loan associations in the 1990s led to a series of law suits against law firms for not taking sufficiently tough steps to prevent the failure of their savings and loan clients. The lawyer's "client" is not the current manager but the corporation as an "entity."

b. In FDIC v. Mmahat, 907 F.2d 546 (5th Cir.1990), cert. denied, 499 U.S. 936 (1991), a lawyer was general counsel of a savings and loan association for over 20 years. Indeed, he served as chairman of the board of directors of the institution for six of those years. When the Garn–St Germain Act of 1982 allowed savings and loan associations to lend more freely, his association did so. Even if a loan would violate the Federal Home Loan Bank Board's "loans to one borrower" regulations, the lawyer did not seek to prevent its making the loan. The FDIC sued and recovered $35 million against the lawyer.[2]

c. In FDIC v. O'Melveny & Myers, 969 F.2d 744 (9th Cir.1992), rev'd on other grounds sub nom. O'Melveny & Myers v. FDIC, 512 U.S. 79 (1994), the FDIC sued the law firm that helped a bank create real estate syndications that it sold to large investors. The firm wrote much of the private placement memorandum and purported to do a due diligence review of the relevant facts. Much of the success of the deal depended on the financial health of the bank. The bank's auditors concluded the bank had little or no net worth, but the law firm apparently did not talk to them. The FDIC paid the defrauded investors and then sued, as the bank's receiver, to recover funds it had to refund. The law firm argued that the client had deceived it and that the firm did not have to protect the client against its own wrong. The court rejected such a bright line test. "It is an attorney's duty to protect the client in every possible way," the court said. "No California cases advise us of an exception to the general rule that a lawyer has to act competently to avoid public harm when he learns that his is a dishonest client." 969 F.2d at 748. It reversed summary judgment for the law firm.[3]

d. FDIC v. Clark, 978 F.2d 1541 (10th Cir.1992), gave lawyers more reason for concern. The law firm represented the bank in many matters since its opening. Unknown to the law firm, several bank officers initiated a "heist money scheme" in which they used $2 million in bank money to

---

2. As usual in such cases, even though Mmahat was the only lawyer in the firm involved, all lawyers in the firm were liable for his acts. To the chagrin of the lawyers, however, because the court found that the cause of the losses was Mmahat's dishonesty, the firm's malpractice carrier was excused from liability by the terms of its policy. The lawyers apparently had to come up with the money themselves.

3. The Supreme Court found no duty under federal law, and remanded. 512 U.S. 79 (1994). The 9th Circuit then said that this duty exists under state corporate law and reached the same result expressly relying on California law. FDIC v. O'Melveny & Myers, 61 F.3d 17 (9th Cir.1995).

buy $9 million in stolen money. To implement this scheme, they created loan files for nonexistent borrowers and forged checks on nonexistent accounts. Ultimately, they were caught, but the FDIC argued that the lawyers were too slow to act when they first heard the charges. The bank officers had told the lawyers that it was all a misunderstanding and not to worry about it. The law firm so advised the bank's board without making its own investigation. The court, citing *O'Melveny & Myers*, upheld a jury verdict that inaction under these circumstances was a sufficient basis for imposing liability. A lawyer may not necessarily rely on the client's officers' assertions about their lack of wrongdoing.[4]

e. These cases were more about a failure to inquire than a failure to disclose. Nonetheless, would you feel comfortable doing nothing after your lunch with the research director and your conversation with the engineer?

3. Can the shareholders of the corporation sue you directly for a decline in the value of their stock?

a. Waggoner v. Snow, Becker, Kroll, Klaris & Krauss, 991 F.2d 1501 (9th Cir.1993), dealt with corporate counsel's dealings with the major shareholder. When the company was in financial trouble, Waggoner, the CEO and major shareholder, agreed to sign guarantees in exchange for voting control of the corporation while his guarantees were in effect. Corporate counsel said that could be arranged, drew up the papers, which Waggoner signed. Later, the board fired Waggoner, and he tried to remove them using what he thought was his voting control. It turned out, however, that corporate counsel's work had not successfully delivered control to Waggoner, so Waggoner both lost his job and remained liable on the guarantees. He sued the corporate counsel for malpractice. The court found that corporate counsel had made clear he represented only the corporation and had not assumed any personal duties to Waggoner. It affirmed summary judgment for the lawyer.

b. The same principle often applies to partnerships, i.e., a lawyer who purports only to represent the partnership often has civil liability only to the partnership as an entity. Hopper v. Frank, 16 F.3d 92 (5th Cir.1994) reached that result and quoted with approval, ABA Formal Opinion 91–361 (July 12, 1991):

> "[A] lawyer who represents a partnership represents the entity rather than the individual partners unless the specific circumstances show otherwise. * * * This analysis may include such factors as whether the lawyer affirmatively assumed a duty of representation to the individual partner, whether the partner was separately represented by other counsel when the partnership was created or in connection

4. But see, FDIC v. Ferguson, 982 F.2d 404 (10th Cir.1991), holding that the proportion of the loss for which the lawyer can be held liable can be reduced by extent of the contributory acts of the bank client's officials. Cf. Reves v. Ernst & Young, 507 U.S. 170 (1993), holding that for purposes of RICO liability, professionals such as lawyers may not be sued unless they actually took part in the management of the client. See also, Kansas Public Employees Retirement System v. Kutak Rock, 44 P.3d 407 (Kan.2002) (law firm does not have duty to warn client about doubtful financial wisdom of a transaction).

with its affairs, whether the lawyer had represented an individual partner before undertaking to represent the partnership, and whether there was evidence of reliance by the individual partner on the lawyer as his or her separate counsel * * *." 16 F.3d at 95–96.

c.   In some states, a "partnership" is an "aggregate" under partnership law (a group of individuals); in other states, it is an "entity" (a legal creature distinct from its individual members). Does it matter, for purposes of ethics law, whether the partnership is an aggregate or entity?

4.   Are you liable for civil damages to consumers hurt by the flammable pajamas?

a.   Consider Tarasoff v. Regents of the University of California, 551 P.2d 334 (Cal.1976), vacating 529 P.2d 553 (Cal.1974). The court held that a psychotherapist who knew of a planned murder and did not warn the victim was liable in tort to the victim. The court said:

> "When a therapist determines, or pursuant to the standards of his profession should determine, that his patient presents a serious danger of violence to another, he incurs an obligation to use reasonable care to protect the intended victim against such danger. The discharge of this duty may require the therapist to take one or more of various steps, depending upon the nature of the case. Thus it may call for him to warn the intended victim or others likely to apprise the victim of the danger, to notify the police, or to take whatever other steps are reasonably necessary under the circumstances." 551 P.2d at 340.

b.   Should the *Tarasoff* rule extend to lawyers? Restatement Third, The Law Governing Lawyers § 66, Comment *g*, warns:

> "Critical facts may be unclear, emotions may be high, and little time may be available in which the lawyer must decide on an appropriate course of action. Subsequent re-examination of the reasonableness of a lawyer's action in the light of later developments would be unwarranted; reasonableness of the lawyer's belief at the time and in the circumstances in which the lawyer acts is alone controlling."

Are you convinced? Could you have made the same argument for the therapist in *Tarasoff*?

c.   Crawford & Lewis v. Boatmen's Trust Co. of Arkansas, Inc., 1 S.W.3d 417 (Ark.1999), illustrates a similar question of liability arising in the context of trust administration. There were two trustees, a bank and an individual trustee who was also the residuary beneficiary. The individual trustee wanted to use trust assets to help himself buy a house. The bank resisted that move as self-dealing but the individual went ahead with the purchase and the lawyer for the trust represented him at the closing. Later, the individual sold the house to someone who filed for bankruptcy protection before he finished paying what he owed for the house. When the law firm filed a petition for fees, the court held that its assistance in a breach of the trustee's fiduciary duty justified denying additional fees and disgorgement of the fees already paid. Most of the firm's efforts were on behalf of the individual trustee, not the trust itself, and the law does not require the trust to pay for those efforts.[5]

D. SOME SPECIAL PROBLEMS OF COUNSEL EMPLOYED BY THE CORPORATION

1. Would you expect to see the number of lawyers employed by corporations to be increasing or decreasing?

a. Corporate counsel, sometimes known as in-house or inside counsel, represent one of the fastest growing segments of the bar. In 1980, for example, the number of lawyers employed as such by private industry was 54,626, or just over 10% of the 542,205 lawyers in the country. That was a 40% increase from 39,000 such lawyers in 1970.[6] In 2002, the number was reported to be 65,086.[7]

b. This trend may well continue, in part because outside counsel are very expensive. For example, the chairman of the board of IBM once said that its general counsel "is the only department head to whom we've given an unlimited budget—and he's already exceeded it." Many corporations, in an effort to cut costs, as well as to have lawyers who intimately know the client's business, increasingly rely on their inside corporate legal staff. The average hourly cost of work of inside counsel has been estimated to be approximately half that of outside counsel.[8]

2. Is the trend to increase the work done by inside corporate counsel desirable?

a. Several years ago, a commentator wrote that a lawyer sometimes chooses the life of "salaried employment" in a corporate law department because he may be "just happier in a job where someone else has the ultimate responsibility." And—unlike a private practice—the salaried lawyer's job has "aspects of dependence."[9]

b. Another observer, however, defended the independence of in-house counsel and contended that "a lawyer is a lawyer whether he charges fees or receives a salary. A salary corrupts no more than does a fee. * * * "[10]

---

5. See also, Restatement Third, The Law Governing Lawyers § 51(4) (liability to nonclient for client's breach of fiduciary duty); Wolf v. Mitchell, Silberberg & Knupp, 90 Cal.Rptr.2d 792 (Cal.Ct.App.1999) (residuary beneficiary of trust permitted to sue the trustee's lawyer for assisting the trustee to use trust assets to pay his gambling debts and otherwise engage in self-dealing). But see, ABA Formal Opinion 94–380 (May 9, 1994) (lawyer's duties run only to fiduciary, not the beneficiary); Model Rule 1.7, Comment 27 (lawyers should make clear to whom the lawyer owes duties when representing fiduciary).

6. See Barbara A. Curran, et al., The Lawyer Statistical Report 19–21 (1985), and the 1988 supplement thereto, published in 1991. No reliable statistics are available to bring these numbers up to date for the 21st century.

7. Susan Hackett, ACCA's Revealing Trends, Legal Times, June 17, 2002, p. 20.

8. John Ryan, Costly Counsel, Wall Street J., Apr. 13, 1978, at 1, col. 1. (midwest ed.); Wall Street J., Apr. 26, 1984, at 1, col. 6 (midwest ed.) (major bank's outside legal costs up to 250% more than inside legal costs).

9. William L. Hanaway, Corporate Law Departments—A New Look, 17 Business Lawyer 595, 599 (Apr. 1962).

10. Stephen E. Davis, Corporate Law Departments—A New Look at the "New Look," 18 Business Lawyer 569, 570 (Jan. 1963).

c. Who is correct? Do you think it is true that corporate counsel lack "ultimate responsibility" and "independence"? Whatever the answer might once have been, the Sarbanes–Oxley Act of 2002, passed in the wake of the Enron and WorldCom financial scandals, imposes significant personal liability on high-level officers if they fail to comply with heightened corporate reporting requirements. These officers expect the company's general counsel's office to monitor the company's compliance. The days are gone when corporate counsel could expect to live a quiet life. Problem 22 focuses on issues related to Sarbanes–Oxley and securities fraud.

3. One of the major functions of the corporate general counsel is the selection and supervision of outside counsel. How does that affect the freedom of outside counsel to tell the officers of the corporation what they might not want to hear?

a. If outside counsel knows that the corporate general counsel can find other firms who will provide answers management wants, might that affect the willingness of outside counsel to provide the advice that management ought to hear?

b. Are inside counsel likely to have an even greater fear of the consequences of pointing out embarrassing problems? Should such lawyers have whistleblower protection when they bring such issues to the attention of the general counsel and corporate management? When we return to this question in Problem 33, we will see that the law gives whistleblowers more protection than they once had, but far from perfect protection.

c. In connection with the possible differences in pressures bearing on inside and outside counsel consider the following:

> "One should not overdraw the differences between outside and inside counsel. The associate of a law firm is also subject to similar pressures because disagreement with the ethical judgment of his partners means he must withdraw from the firm. The Code does not provide in such instances for a discreet withdrawal from a particular matter any more than it provides for discreet withdrawal on the part of in-house counsel. Even a large firm may be under economic pressures because a large percentage of its business may come from a very few corporate clients. Although this line, which distinguishes the differing pressures on in-house and outside counsel may not be a bright one, it still provides a useful starting point."[11]

4. Should judicial concerns about the perceived lack of independence of corporate counsel affect whom corporate management must consult and whether the consultation is privileged?

a. In re Oracle Securities Litigation, 829 F.Supp. 1176 (N.D.Cal. 1993), found that a company's directors lack the requisite independence to settle a corporate derivative action without the advice of independent

---

11. Ronald D. Rotunda, Law, Lawyers, and Managers, in C. Walton, ed., The Ethics of Corporate Conduct 127, 136 (American Assembly 1977).

counsel. In-house lawyers gave legal advice about the settlement, but those in-house lawyers have to live with management, and thus they "are inevitably subservient to the interests of the defendant directors and officers whom they serve." The court said:

> "Although some courts have gone so far as to appoint corporate counsel in derivative actions, it seems more appropriate here to defer to the independent directors on the selection of corporate counsel. '[N]ew counsel will recognize their duty to represent solely the interests of the corporate entit[y]. And should difficulties arise, the parties or counsel may apply to the court for additional relief.' [I]f the investigation of independent counsel confirms derivative plaintiffs' case to be as weak as the parties have so far presented it, then termination of the derivative suit would seem the most sensible course to take." 829 F.Supp. at 1190.

Do you think the court's assessment of in-house counsel is fair? Does it make sense to always require expensive outside assessments of what will sometimes be meritless suits?

b. In contrast, Bell Atlantic Corp. v. Bolger, 2 F.3d 1304 (3d Cir. 1993), approved settlement of a derivative action where a single law firm represented both the corporation and the directors. The action alleged the directors were guilty of mismanagement, but not fraud. There was a convergence of individual and corporate interests in this case, the court found. It takes allegations of intentional wrongdoing or self-dealing, the court suggested, to make separate representation mandatory. Model Rule 1.13, Comments 13 & 14 attempt to summarize the current law in this area.

c. As discussed in Problem 8, concerns about the lack of "independence" of inside counsel have led the highest court in Europe, the European Court of Justice, to say that communications between corporate officials and their inside counsel are not protected by the attorney-client privilege. Akzo Nobel Chemicals Ltd. v. European Commission, Case C–550/07 P, Celex No. 607J0550, 2010 ECJ EUR–Lex Lexis 807, 23–24 (ECJ EUR–Lex 2010). The Court had reached the same result almost 30 years earlier in Australian Mining & Smelting Europe, Ltd. v. Commission, [1982] C.M.L.R. 264, and in spite of the pleas of several European governments and many lawyer organizations such as the International Bar Association, the Court refused to change its view.

Do you agree that in-house counsel so lack independence that corporate officials should have to consult outside counsel every time they want to have a privileged conversation? If the privilege is limited to communications with outside counsel, are we likely to see fewer in-house counsel in Europe? Is there good reason to drive practice in that direction?

———

PROBLEM 19

CONTACT WITH REPRESENTED AND
UNREPRESENTED PERSONS

Lawyers frequently contact others on behalf of clients, often to obtain or deliver information, or to suggest solutions to contentious problems. It might initially seem odd that the law regulates these contacts, but concerns that lawyers might mislead an opposing party or interfere with that party's relationship with its own lawyer have carried the day. This problem first considers the regulation of such contacts in general. Next, it applies the rule to contacts with corporate employees. Then, it explores the standards governing contacts with officers and employees of the lawyer's own client. Finally, it considers the rule in a criminal context, asking whether police who are questioning suspects should be considered agents of the prosecuting attorney and whether national ethical rules should govern federal prosecutors rather than state standards in the states that issued the prosecutors' law licenses.

FACTS

Speedy Corp. has a fleet of trucks and couriers to deliver packages throughout the city. The company has made a standing offer to return the shipper's fee for any package not delivered within one hour. There is reason to believe that this policy causes Speedy's drivers and couriers to take dangerous chances.

One rainy Tuesday, President Mary Speedy was standing across the street from the company headquarters. Barry Winters, an employee in the accounting department of Speedy Corp., happened to be standing beside her. Just then, a Speedy delivery truck came out of the headquarters building at a high rate of speed. It hit an elderly man, causing him serious injuries.

Before filing the complaint, Louis Shabazz, lawyer for the injured man, interviewed Barry Winters and the truck driver and took their statements about how the accident happened. Barbara Bentley, lawyer for Speedy Corp., was not told of those interviews or invited to be present. Now, Shabazz has called Mary Speedy and asked to interview her as well; Speedy, in turn, has called Bentley who has told Speedy to decline to be interviewed in any setting other than a formal deposition.

Bentley herself now wants to investigate to find out what the facts surrounding the accident are. She wants to prepare for litigation and to formulate recommendations for possible changes of the one-hour guarantee. Indeed, she fears a grand jury may be convened to determine whether Speedy's guarantee of one-hour service can support a charge of criminal negligence. Bentley wants to talk to present and former employees of Speedy, both officers and nonofficers, who might know how the policy has affected safety. Shabazz, of course, would like to talk to the same people.

QUESTIONS

A. CONTACT WITH A REPRESENTED OPPONENT IN GENERAL

1. Attorney Shabazz just wants to question witnesses to an accident without the formality and expense of deposing them. What rules regulate his questioning?

a. ABA Model Rule 4.2 is the principal authority:

"In representing a client, a lawyer shall not communicate about the subject matter of the representation with a person the lawyer knows to be represented by another lawyer in the matter, unless the lawyer has the consent of the other lawyer or is authorized to do so by law or court order."

Read that rule again; every part of it is significant.

b. ABA Formal Opinion 95–396 (July 28, 1995) says that the ban on contact applies (1) in both criminal and civil cases, (2) to represented persons and not just parties, (3) less clearly in the investigation phase of criminal cases prior to an arrest or charge, (4) only when the lawyer should know the other person is represented, (5) only to contacts related to the subject matter of the case, (6) even though the represented person initiates the contact, (7) until the representation of the person is in fact terminated, and (8) to contacts made by a lawyer's investigators, not just the lawyer personally.

c. Restatement Third, The Law Governing Lawyers § 99 provides:

"(1) A lawyer representing a client in a matter may not communicate about the subject of the representation with a nonclient whom the lawyer knows to be represented in the matter by another lawyer or with a representative of an organizational nonclient so represented as defined in § 100, unless:

"(a) the communication is with a public officer or agency to the extent stated in § 101;

"(b) the lawyer is a party and represents no other client in the matter;

"(c) the communication is authorized by law;

"(d) the communication reasonably responds to an emergency; or

"(e) the other lawyer consents.

"(2) Subsection (1) does not prohibit the lawyer from assisting the client in otherwise proper communication by the lawyer's client with a represented nonclient."

d.   Formal Opinion 2009–1 of the Association of the Bar of the City of New York Committee on Professional and Judicial Ethics, 2009 WL 399764, concludes that a lawyer may not send a communication simultaneously to opposing counsel and to the opposing party, unless the opposing lawyer consents. However, citing Restatement § 99, it says that a course of dealing between the lawyers may constitute implied consent. For example, regular use of the "reply all" function in email communication may imply such consent.

2.   Does the rule against ex parte contact with a represented person make sense to you? Whom does the rule seek to protect? Is the concern that a persuasive lawyer will cause the represented person to take action disadvantageous to himself without understanding what is going on?

a.   In Attorney Grievance Comm'n v. Kent, 653 A.2d 909 (Md.1995), a criminal defendant (Accomplice), represented by counsel, pled guilty and agreed to testify against Kent's client in exchange for a reduced sentence. Then, Lawyer Kent persuaded Accomplice to fire his separate counsel, deny responsibility for the crime, and let Kent take over his case. The jury then acquitted Kent's original client. However, because of Accomplice's refusal to cooperate after he had pled guilty, the court sentenced Accomplice to two life terms. Kent asserted that all he had done was zealously defend his original client, but the court found his conduct violated both Rules 1.7 and 4.2. The court disbarred Kent for his role in contacting and misleading Accomplice.[1]

b.   Parker v. Pepsi–Cola General Bottlers, Inc., 249 F.Supp.2d 1006 (N.D.Ill.2003), involved Robert Gena, who was represented by counsel in a suit against Pepsi for employment discrimination. Pepsi subpoenaed Gena for a deposition in a related discrimination case. Pepsi's counsel served Gena personally with the subpoena and did not send a copy to Gena's attorney. When Gena arrived at the deposition and informed Pepsi counsel that he had not told his attorney about it, Pepsi's counsel nevertheless asked Gena questions pertaining to Gena's suit against Pepsi. The court held that Pepsi and its lawyers violated Illinois' version of Model Rule 4.2. The court barred Pepsi from using Gena's deposition testimony or any evidence obtained from it, required Pepsi to destroy all copies, summaries, and analyses of the testimony, and granted Gena attorney's fees for the motion.

c.   In State v. Harper, 995 P.2d 1143 (Okla.2000), an insurance defense lawyer dealt only with the plaintiff's lawyer until the plaintiff told the company she was going to fire her lawyer that very day. The defense lawyer then took a statement directly from her, telling her she could have an lawyer present if she wished. Later, it turned out that she had not fired her first lawyer after all. The court found no evidence the defense lawyer

---

1. See also, Matter of Alcantara, 676 A.2d 1030 (N.J.1995), reprimanding a lawyer for asking represented co-defendants not to testify against his client, and United States v. Santiago–Lugo, 162 F.R.D. 11 (D.P.R.1995), censuring a lawyer and barring use of any notes made while interviewing the client's co-defendants ex parte.

knew the true facts and held that, in the absence of such knowledge, there is no violation of Rule 4.2.[2] Rule 4.2, Comment 8 supports this result.

d. Utah State Bar Ethics Advisory Opinion 98–07 (1998) examined whether a lawyer for the plaintiff in an accident may contact the adjuster for the defendant's insurance company directly. The opinion said that, in the period before the case is referred to a lawyer for defense, the answer is clearly yes. However, after the insurance company has hired a lawyer for the defendant, the question is whether the insurance company is also a represented party. If it is, the rule prohibits the lawyer from contacting it except through counsel. The opinion said that at a minimum, the insurance company has a "direct interest in the results of any litigation or settlement." Thus, the opinion concluded, the plaintiff's lawyer may only contact the insurance company through its counsel unless the plaintiff's lawyer knows that the insurance company does not consider itself to be represented by counsel in the matter.[3]

Does this rule make sense to you? How would the lawyer know what the insurance company intended? If the defense lawyer files an appearance for the insured and not the insurance company, should that be enough to tell the lawyer what the insurance company thinks?[4]

e. May a lawyer contact the in-house counsel of an opponent that is represented by outside counsel? ABA Formal Opinion 06–443 (Aug. 5, 2006) says yes. Model Rule 4.2 presumes clients are unsophisticated, but lawyers will be unlikely to be able to take advantage of inside counsel. However, the Opinion adds, if a corporation tells the opposing lawyer to contact only outside counsel, the lawyer's failure to comply might violate Rule 4.4(a), but Model Rule 4.2 would not prohibit the contact.

3. Are any reasons for the anticontact rule lawyer-centered instead of client-centered? Might some lawyers want to control their clients, so that the clients will not settle disputes without their lawyer's help? Might some lawyers want to spend more billable hours being involved in the pretrial process?

a. ABA Formal Opinion 92–362 (July 6, 1992) says that a lawyer who communicated an offer to opposing counsel may neither call the opposing party to see if the offer has been communicated nor send the opposing party a copy of the offer. Is such a rule likely to be in the interest of the opposing party? Is it likely to be primarily in the interest of the opposing party's lawyer?

---

2. Oregon State Bar Opinion, Formal Opinion 2001–164 (2001) reaches what may be an obvious conclusion that a lawyer may visit the web site of a represented person so long as there is no interaction with the site, such as sending a message with the expectation of receiving a personal response. A lawyer may visit a company's website, for example, and read what is publicly posted without violating Rule 4.2.

3. See also, Association of the Bar of the City of New York Committee on Professional and Judicial Ethics, Formal Opinion 2005–4 (same conclusion).

4. Arons v. Jutkowitz, 9 N.Y.3d 393 (N.Y.2007) (once plaintiff raises issue of his or her medical condition, defense lawyer may interview plaintiff's treating physician).

b.   Cleveland Bar Ass'n v. Rossi, 690 N.E.2d 501 (Ohio 1998), illustrates how strictly some courts apply Rule 4.2. A claimant under a will hired Lawyer to see if the inventory compiled by the executor was undervalued. Lawyer could not reach the executor's lawyer because he had changed offices and his phone was disconnected. Time to object to the inventory was running, so the claimant's Lawyer called the executor directly and determined that the estate did indeed have more assets than previously thought. For that contact, the court imposed a public reprimand on him. Two dissenting justices would have suspended him, saying that the lawyer could do no more than ask the executor to have his attorney call the Lawyer.

4.   May represented clients talk to each other without going through their lawyers?

a.   State Bar of California, Formal Opinion 1993–131 (1993) gives the standard answer that the clients *may* talk; indeed, it says that failure to encourage such talks may forfeit opportunities to terminate disputes short of trial. The lawyers for each client may advise the clients before they get together, but, the opinion says, the communications must be those of the clients, not the clients acting out the lawyers' "scripts" for them. What does no "scripts" mean? Aren't lawyers supposed to advise clients about how to act in all kinds of situations?

b.   Association of the Bar of the City of New York Committee on Professional and Judicial Ethics, Formal Opinion 2002–3, on the other hand, concludes that a lawyer may advise a client what to say in the meeting between the clients. Opposing such coaching is "at odds with modern authority," the opinion says, citing both Restatement Third, The Law Governing Lawyers § 99, Comment *k*, and Model Rule 4.2, Comment 4.[5]

c.   In Holdren v. General Motors Corp., 13 F.Supp.2d 1192 (D.Kan. 1998), plaintiff's counsel urged his client to talk about the case with other GM employees, including managers, who might offer favorable testimony at trial, and to get affidavits from them. The court recognized that clients may talk to each other without violating Rule 4.2, but it said plaintiff's counsel "circumvented" Rule 4.2 in violation of Rule 8.4(a) by "encouraging" his client to obtain the affidavits. The court acknowledged that there was "no evidence" that the lawyer "knowingly or deliberately" violated the no-contact rule, but it enjoined further efforts to secure affidavits and required the plaintiff to turn over names of persons contacted and any evidence obtained in this way, so the court could determine which persons were protected against contact under the rule.

Do you agree with this result? Did the plaintiff's counsel "circumvent" the Rule or apply it? Look at Model Rule 4.2, Comment 4, which cites Rule 8.4(a) (lawyer may not using another to do what the lawyer cannot do), but

5. See also ABA Formal Opinion 92–362 (July 6, 1992) (lawyer for client making a settlement offer may advise client that the other attorney may not have communicated the offer and suggest that the client convey the information to the opposing party directly).

says that parties may communicate directly with each other and that lawyers may so advise them.

5.   If a lawyer is a party to the litigation, should Model Rule 4.2 bar that lawyer's contact with the opposing party?

a.   D.C. Bar Ethics Opinion 258 (Sept. 20, 1995) says that a lawyer's ability to overreach is no less because he is a party. Thus, the no-contact rule controls, and a lawyer appearing pro se may not contact the other side directly if the opposing party is represented by counsel, even though a *pro se* layperson could do so. See also, Runsvold v. Idaho State Bar, 925 P.2d 1118 (Idaho 1996) (upholds private reprimand to *pro se* lawyer for writing and sending court papers directly to represented ex-wife instead of to her lawyer).

b.   Restatement Third, The Law Governing Lawyers § 99, Comment *e*, on the other hand, says that a "lawyer representing his or her own interests *pro se* may communicate with an opposing represented nonclient on the same basis as other principals. * * * [But a] lawyer representing both a client and the lawyer's own interests in the same matter is subject to the anti-contact rule * * *."

c.   Which of those positions makes more sense to you? In re Knappenberger, 108 P.3d 1161 (Or.2005) (per curiam), involved two employees who sued their employer-lawyer on an employment related issue. Shortly after he received the papers, the lawyer confronted one employee-plaintiff in a one-minute or shorter conversation at the office. The next day, he confronted his other employee-plaintiff, who "told the accused to direct his questions to her lawyer, but the accused said that he had a right to speak with her directly. Finally, when [she] threatened to leave the room if the accused did not discuss work-related matters, he gave her some papers to file and left." This second conversation lasted for 5 to 20 minutes. The employees alleged a violation of DR 7–104(A)(1) [Model Rule 4.2]. The Oregon Supreme Court agreed that the lawyer-defendant intentionally violated his duty to "not communicate * * * on the subject of the representation or on directly related subjects" with a person the lawyer knew to be represented by another lawyer. The court went on to hold that the fact that the lawyer was also a party to the case did not save him; the rule is designed to prevent overreaching by lawyers and offers no exception for *pro se* litigants. Do you agree with this result?

B.   SPECIAL ISSUES WHEN DEALING WITH OFFICERS AND EMPLOYEES OF AN ORGANIZATION

1.   After considering all the above issues, does Shabazz yet have an answer about his right to interview Mary Speedy, Barry Winters and the truck driver? You can assume that none of them has yet hired personal counsel to represent them in connection with the accident.

a.   It is relatively easy to proscribe contacts with individuals. When the opposing "person" is a corporation or other organization, however, the question becomes when contact with particular living people will be considered prohibited contact with the organization. One might imagine a rule that said that because all employees are agents of the corporation, each of them is off limits to contact. On the other hand, such a rule would be broader than necessary to protect the interests the rule is legitimately designed to protect and would impose increased costs on litigation because expensive depositions would replace many informal interviews.

b. In Niesig v. Team I, 558 N.E.2d 1030 (N.Y.1990), a personal injury lawyer for a plaintiff wished to interview a corporate defendant's employees who had witnessed an accident that occurred at a construction site. This corporation was a party to a lawsuit. "The issue therefore distills to which corporate employees should be deemed parties for purposes of DR 7–104(A)(1), and that choice is one of policy. The broader the definition of 'party' in the interests of fairness to the corporation, the greater the cost in terms of foreclosing vital informal access to facts." 558 N.E.2d at 1033. The court noted that public policy favors reducing litigation costs by allowing plaintiffs to use informal, off the record, private interviews rather than costly depositions or interviews attended by the adversary counsel, and the corporation has ample opportunity to interview its own employees, gather facts, and counsel them so that they do not make improvident disclosures. The court concluded that "parties" for purposes of New York DR 7–104(A)(1) should include only "corporate employees whose acts or omissions in the matter under inquiry are binding on the corporation (in effect, the corporation's 'alter egos') or imputed to the corporation for purposes of its liability, or employees implementing the advice of counsel." The opposing party may informally interview all other employees.

c. Both Model Rule 4.2, Comment 7, and Restatement Third, The Law Governing Lawyers § 100(2) are consistent with *Niesig*. The Restatement says that opposing counsel may *not* contact current corporate employees and agents without the other lawyer's permission:

"(a) if the employee or other agent supervises, directs, or regularly consults with the lawyer concerning the matter or if the agent has power to compromise or settle the matter;

"(b) if the acts or omissions of the employee or other agent may be imputed to the organization for purposes of civil or criminal liability in the matter; or

"(c) if a statement of the employee or other agent, under applicable rules of evidence, would have the effect of binding the organization with respect to proof of the matter."

Do these standards help you decide whom Shabazz may interview without asking Bentley?

d. In Messing, Rudavsky & Weliky, P.C. v. President and Fellows of Harvard College, 764 N.E.2d 825 (Mass.2002), a law firm represented a former employee in her sex discrimination suit against Harvard College. While investigating its client's claim, the firm conducted informal interviews with five of the client's co-workers in the Harvard University police department, and the Superior Court granted Harvard's motion to sanction the firm for violating Rule 4.2. The Massachusetts Supreme Court, however, citing *Niesig* and the Restatement, held that Rule 4.2 only prohibits lawyers from contacting "employees who exercise managerial responsibility in the matter, who are alleged to have committed the wrongful acts at issue in the litigation, or who have authority on behalf of the corporation to make decisions about the course of the litigation." 764 N.E. 2d at 833. Thus, the court denied Harvard's motion for sanctions, finding that the employees interviewed did not have "supervisory authority over the events at issue in the litigation." 764 N.E. 2d at 836.

2. Should the prohibition against contacting corporate employees apply to former employees? Are they still part of the "person" that opposing counsel is forbidden to contact? Would the same concerns that underlie Rule 4.2 apply to contact with former employees as well?

a. Restatement Third, The Law Governing Lawyers § 100, Comment *g*, says:

> "Contact with a former employee or agent ordinarily is permitted, even if the person had formerly been within a category of those with whom contact is prohibited. * * * [However,] a former employee who, as the lawyer knows, continues regularly to consult about the matter with the lawyer for the ex-employer [may not be contacted] * * *."

b. In Camden v. Maryland, 910 F.Supp. 1115 (D.Md.1996), the plaintiff filed a discrimination case against a university; the university's affirmative action officer was a nonlawyer who later left the school with some bad feelings and subsequently talked to the plaintiff's lawyer about the case. The court recognized that lawyers may contact most former employees of a represented firm, but said that lawyers may not contact former employees who had "been extensively exposed to relevant trade secrets, confidential client information, or similar confidential information of another party interested in the matter." 910 F.Supp. at 1122. The defendant's former in-house manager of the case was someone the plaintiff's lawyer could not interview ex parte. See Rule 4.2, Comment 7. As a remedy for this misconduct, the court disqualified the lawyer.

c. G–I Holdings, Inc. v. Baron & Budd, 199 F.R.D. 529 (S.D.N.Y. 2001), involved former employees of the defendant whose work had exposed them to privileged information and whom plaintiff's investigators wanted to interview. Because both the interviewers and former employees were lay persons who might inadvertently disclose the privileged information, the court issued a protective order so that the interviews could only continue if the lawyer either (1) gave notice and the right of defendants' counsel to be present, or (2) conducted the interviews in the presence of a special master who would make sure that no privileged information would be disclosed.

d. Muriel Siebert & Co. v. Intuit Inc., 868 N.E.2d 208 (N.Y.2007), declined to disqualify Intuit's counsel for interviewing a former Siebert official that the lawyer knew had substantial privileged and confidential information. The court made clear that "the right to conduct ex parte interviews is [not] a license for adversary counsel to elicit privileged or confidential information from an opponent's former employee." In this case, however, Intuit counsel expressly told the former employee who they were and their role in the litigation, told him not to disclose privileged or confidential information, and told him not to answer any questions that might lead to disclosure of such information. Those warnings were sufficient to make the questioning proper.

3. Should different considerations apply the lawyer contacts officers or employees of a government agency?

a. Restatement Third, The Law Governing Lawyers § 101, says that (1) the fact that the government agency has a general counsel's office does not ordinarily bar contact with employees or officials of that agency, (2) the no-contact rule applies to negotiation or litigation of a specific claim against the agency, but (3) the rule does not bar lawyer contact with agency officials with respect to issues of general policy.

b. ABA Formal Opinion 97–408 (Aug. 2, 1997) advised that Model Rule 4.2 applies to a lawyer for a private party who has a dispute with a government agency. But then it added a caveat—Rule 4.2 has "an important exception based on the constitutional right to petition and the derivative public policy of ensuring a citizen's right of access to government decision makers." Rule 4.2 "permits a lawyer representing a private party in a controversy with the government to communicate about the matter with government officials who have authority to take or recommend action in the matter, provided that the sole purpose of the lawyer's communication is to address a policy issue, including settling the controversy." In such cases, the opinion announced, "the lawyer must give government counsel reasonable advance notice of his intent to communicate with such officials in order to afford them an opportunity to seek advice of counsel before deciding whether to entertain the communication."

c. Do you see anything in Model Rule 4.2 that supports this requirement of advance notice to government counsel? Does Model Rule 4.2, Comment 5 offer any textual basis for the requirement? The ABA Committee argued that the requirement is necessary to allow the government official to consult counsel and learn where the boundary is between policy discussions and talk about the merits of the litigated case. That may be a good idea, but is it the most natural reading of the Rule?

C. INTERVIEWING CLIENT EMPLOYEES AND OTHER UNREPRESENTED PERSONS

1. Now turn your attention to Barbara Bentley and her defense of Speedy Corp. Should we be concerned that she could overreach in her interviews of unrepresented persons like Winters and the truck driver?

a. *The Florida Bar v. Buckle*, 771 So.2d 1131 (Fla.2000), involved a criminal defense lawyer's telephone calls and letter to an unrepresented complaining witness. In an attempt to get her to drop the criminal complaint, he called her at home and sent her religious materials that the discipline referee found "objectively humiliating and intimidating." The court found that the letter "essentially threatens to take away her job, her children and to expose her to ridicule, contempt, and hatred." The lawyer even threatened to raise questions about a prior murder in the complainant's family. This kind of intimidation, the court found, is "patently unfair and prejudicial to the administration of justice," but the only sanction it imposed was a public reprimand.

b. How should professional rules be drafted to guard against such overreaching? Before the 2002 amendments, ABA Model Rule 4.3 said only:

> "In dealing on behalf of a client with a person who is not represented by counsel, a lawyer shall not state that the lawyer is disinterested. When the lawyer knows or reasonably should know that the unrepresented person misunderstands the lawyer's role in the matter, the lawyer shall make reasonable efforts to correct the misunderstanding."

Model Code of Professional Responsibility DR 7–104(A)(2) said that a lawyer may not "give advice to a person who is not represented by a lawyer, other than the advice to secure counsel, if the interests of such person are or have a reasonable possibility of being in conflict with the interests of his client."

In 2002, the ABA moved that Model Code language from where it had been in Rule 4.3, Comment 1, into the black letter of Rule 4.3. Was that an important change? Compare Restatement Third, The Law Governing Lawyers § 103.

c. In re Lawrence, 98 P.3d 366 (Or.2004) (en banc) (per curiam), illustrates the significance of the language in a state with rules still based on the Model Code. Lawrence was part of a six-person law firm appointed to represent Warren Battle, a man accused of domestic violence. Lawrence became aware that the victim, Patricia Battle, wanted to drop the charges against her husband, but the district attorney's office refused her request. Lawrence told the victim about a novel theory of constitutional law that Lawrence had developed under which the victim would charge the district attorney with violating her state constitutional right to drop the charges against her husband. Lawrence drafted an affidavit for the victim to this effect, without advising her to seek her own counsel. She also advised her what to say at a later hearing.

The Oregon Supreme Court held that in domestic violence cases, the "interests of an alleged batterer and the batterer's victim are inherently adverse," therefore triggering DR 7–104(A)(2) [Model Rule 4.3]. Although the rules do not define "advice," the court concluded that Lawrence's actions undoubtedly were "advice." Therefore, it violated what is now Rule 4.3 for Lawrence to give advice to an unrepresented person who had interests in conflict with Lawrence's client. Do you agree? Did Lawrence's efforts likely impede or assist the victim, Ms. Battle, in achieving the result she wished?

2.   How should Bentley handle the interviews with her client's officers and employees?

a.   Should she take a "we're all in this together" approach? Should she instead advise the truck driver to obtain independent counsel? How about the vice president in charge of the truck maintenance facility? The board members who approved the on-time delivery guarantee? Look beyond Model Rule 4.3; does Model Rule 1.13(f) provide important direction as well?

b.   Should Bentley become the lawyer for each of the corporate officers, directors and employees personally? At minimum, that would make them all "represented persons" and the corporation could invoke the protection of Rule 4.2. Model Rule 1.13(g) would seem to permit such representation, but what problems would arise if Bentley chose that course?

c.   In United States v. Ruehle, 583 F.3d 600 (9th Cir. 2009), the Government prosecuted the chief financial officer (CFO) of Broadcom and other defendants for charges arising from the corporation's stock option granting practices. The law firm of Irell & Manella represented Broadcom. William Ruehle, Broadcom's CFO, was clearly a possible target of the investigation. Irell concurrently represented Ruehle personally in a different matter, and in this one, they interviewed Ruehle about Broadcom's stock option practices. According to the trial judge, without Ruehle's knowledge or consent, the Irell lawyers gave Broadcom a copy of the report of their Ruehle interview. Broadcom, in turn, instructed Irell to give a copy of this report to the FBI in order to show the Government that Broadcom was cooperative. Ruehle, in response, asserted that his attorney-client privilege protected his interviews. The trial court found that the apparent candor with which the Irell lawyers discussed the case with Ruehle reasonably led him to believe that the Irell lawyers represented him in this case as well. There was no evidence that the lawyers gave Ruehle an oral warning to the contrary, so the trial court concluded that the Irell lawyers breached their duty of loyalty to Ruehle. In addition to suppressing government use of the Ruehle statements, the court referred the Irell lawyers to the State Bar of California for discipline.

The Government filed an interlocutory appeal and Ninth Circuit reversed. The Court of Appeals concluded that CFO's statements to the lawyer were made for the purpose of disclosure to outside auditors and thus were not made in confidence. The CFO admitted he understood the fruits of attorneys' inquiries would be disclosed to accounting firm in order to convince independent auditors of the integrity of corporation's financial statements or to take appropriate accounting measures to rectify any misleading reports. The court noted that Ruehle asserted that "clear breaches of professional duties warrant suppression in a criminal prosecution. We disagree and reject this novel argument, which stands apart from the attorney-client privilege determination." Do you agree?

d.   Look also at Rule 3.4(f), which allows Bentley to advise even employees who are not her clients not to talk to the other side if they will "not be adversely affected" by the refusal. Is that a better way for Bentley to proceed?

3. If Bentley is interviewing a witness who is an employee of her corporate client—but who is not her client—and the witness starts giving incriminating information that is helpful to Bentley's corporate client, must Bentley give *Miranda*-like warnings?

a. Restatement Third, The Law Governing Lawyers § 103, Comment *e* discusses the dilemma the situation presents:

> "Failing to clarify the lawyer's role and the client's interests may redound to the disadvantage of the organization if the lawyer, even if unwittingly, thereby undertakes concurrent representation of both the organization and the constituent. * * * Among other consequences, the lawyer may be required to withdraw from representing both clients because of the conflict. * * * [However, t]he absence of a warning in such a situation will often be in the interests of the client organization in assuring that the flow of information and decisionmaking is not impaired by needless warnings to constituents with important responsibilities or information. * * * "

b. W.T. Grant Co. v. Haines, 531 F.2d 671 (2d Cir.1976), involved a corporation's antitrust action against one of its former employees and others. The employee moved to disqualify the corporation's law firm, alleging it violated what is now Model Rule 4.3 when corporate attorneys had earlier interviewed the employee. When this interview took place, counsel correctly identified the character and nature of their representation, but he did *not* disclose that earlier that morning the corporation sued this employee. The court found no violation of the Rule. The employee had expressed a desire to be interviewed to help "clear the air." He was said to be sophisticated, "neither a callow youth nor a befuddled widow." As for whether the lawyer gave advice to unrepresented persons with interests opposed to the client's, the court said that the question was "close," but that even assuming a violation, there was no "taint" of the trial. Disqualification of counsel was inappropriate and would unduly delay the proceedings. This is an old case; do you think a court should be as restrained about enforcing Rule 4.3 today?

c. ABA Standards Relating to the Administration of Criminal Justice, The Defense Function, Standard 4–4.3(c) says: "It is not necessary for defense counsel or defense counsel's investigator, in interviewing a prospective witness, to caution the witness concerning possible self-incrimination and the need for counsel."

Do you agree? Does a lawyer's duty of loyalty to her client require that she take advantage of the ignorance of the employee she is interviewing?

d. How does Model Rule 1.13(f) deal with the issue? Does it give the lawyer any latitude to take advantage of such ignorance? Are Comments 10 and 11 to Model Rule 1.13 less absolute in their direction? See also Model Rule 1.13(g).

D. THE POSSIBILITY THAT SPECIAL RULES APPLY TO FEDERAL PROSECUTORS

1. Now suppose the police want to interview the same group of company employees. Must they refrain from such interviews without permission of Bentley, the corporate counsel?

a. Look at ABA Prosecution Function Standard 3–2.7:

"(a) The prosecutor should provide legal advice to the police concerning police functions and duties in criminal matters.

"(b) The prosecutor should cooperate with police in providing the services of the prosecutor's staff to aid in training police in the performance of their function in accordance with law."

Does this provision in effect make police the agents of the prosecuting attorney for purposes of Model Rule 4.2 when they conduct questioning?[6]

b. Consider United States v. Thomas, 474 F.2d 110 (10th Cir.1973), cert. denied, 412 U.S. 932 (1973), where the court held that, even though the defendant had waived his *Miranda* rights:

"[O]nce a criminal defendant has either retained an attorney or had an attorney appointed for him by the court, any statement obtained by interview from such defendant may not be offered in evidence unless the accused's attorney was notified of the interview which produced the statement and was given a reasonable opportunity to be present. To hold otherwise we think would be to overlook conduct which violated both the letter and the spirit of the canons of ethics. This is obviously not something which the defendant alone can waive.

"A violation of the canon of ethics as here concerned need not be remedied by a reversal of the case wherein it is violated. This does not necessarily present a constitutional question, but this is an ethical and administrative one relating to attorneys practicing before the United States courts. * * * The enforcement officials are agents of the prosecuting party, and in the event use is made of information secured by interviews of the nature which here took place, short of its introduction in evidence, the problem will be dealt with in the proper case." 474 F.2d at 112.

Should the *Thomas* analysis be applied in a typical state system where the state's attorney, usually a county officer, has no direct control over the police, typically a city agency? In any event, is it a good idea to enforce an ethics rule by excluding testimony that violates no Constitutional guarantee?

c. In State v. Miller, 600 N.W.2d 457 (Minn.1999), prosecutors coordinated a surprise search of a corporation's offices. During this search, law enforcement personnel told the employees that they were not under arrest and that law enforcement officials were "simply gathering information."

---

6. Long before adoption of Model Rule 4.2, in Formal Opinion 95 (May 3, 1933), the ABA Ethics Committee said: "It would be unavailing to contend that the police officers or detectives are not under the supervision and control of the law officer * * *."

When the police served a search warrant, Miller faxed it to his lawyer, so investigators knew he had counsel. Indeed, the lawyer appeared at the office and demanded that the police detective terminate his interview. The detective called the prosecutor who told him that he did not need to terminate the interview or allow lawyer on the premises unless the defendant "requested his presence." The court concluded that the prosecutors had ratified police detective's conduct by refusing to terminate the interview with the defendant at the request of defendant's attorney and by preventing that attorney from being present during the interview. The Minnesota Supreme Court made clear that Rule 4.2 provides more protection than *Miranda* rights. Even assuming that the interview was not unconstitutional, the court held that the prosecutor's involvement in keeping the lawyer out of the interview room violated Rule 4.2, and the appropriate sanction for that violation was suppression of the statement.

2. How should this principle apply when the lawyers involved are U.S. attorneys supervising FBI and other federal agents in drug and antiterrorism investigations?

a. United States v. Ryans, 903 F.2d 731 (10th Cir.1990), involved the government's use of an informant to initiate and record conversations with a suspect before the suspect's indictment but after he had retained a lawyer. The court reported that "it is now well settled that [Model Rule 4.2] applies to criminal as well as civil litigation," and that it applies to agents of public prosecutors " 'when they act as the alter ego of the government prosecutor.' " 903 F.2d at 735. The court acknowledged that courts have differed on whether what is now Rule 4.2 applies to pre-indictment interviews when the defendant is in custody, and whether an appropriate remedy is exclusion of the defendant's statements from evidence. This court then concluded that what is now Model Rule 4.2 does *not* apply "before the initiation of criminal proceedings."

Does that make sense to you? Notice that Rule 4.2, Comment 5, now says that the Rule applies to "the accused in a criminal matter." Does experience with the conflict of interest rules suggest that making Rule 4.2 into an exclusionary rule would make a disciplinary rule into a trial diversion?

b. Should the court enforce Rule 4.2 only when its violation taints the veracity of the fact-finding process? For example, should the court exclude evidence that a lawyer obtained in violation of rules protecting client confidences?

In United States v. Ofshe, 817 F.2d 1508 (11th Cir.1987), the defendant faced drug charges. He retained one lawyer (Black) to prepare for trial and another (Glass) to negotiate with the government about a plea. Glass later found himself accused in Chicago's "Operation Greylord" corruption cases and wanted to do what he could to win favorable treatment for himself. Chicago Assistant U.S. Attorney (and well-known author) Scott Turow arranged for attorney Glass to wear a body bug to his meeting with Ofshe, his Florida client. Agents monitoring the tape "were given very strict guidelines to instruct Glass not to violate any attorney-client privilege;" instead, Ofshe and Glass discussed other criminal plans. Ofshe argued that the government's use of his defense counsel as an informer justified dismissing the indictment against him. The court held that, absent prejudice, the remedy is not warranted. The government obtained no useful information developed from the bug, and the Chicago U.S. attorney's office gave none of it to the Florida U.S. attorney's office. Finally, although Glass did not provide effective assistance of counsel to Ofshe, his co-counsel did, so Ofshe suffered no prejudice.

What do you think of this analysis? Should a prosecutor ever be able to use a suspect's lawyer as an informant? Does such a practice make Barbara Bentley look like a model of ethical virtue by comparison?

3. Does the federal government have a legitimate interest in having its lawyers not be subject to the strictures of Model Rule 4.2 at all?

a. Following the lead of former Attorney General Richard Thornburgh, Attorney General Janet Reno promulgated what was called the Reno Memorandum. See Communications with Represented Persons, 28 C.F.R. Part 77 (1994). In the comments accompanying this rule, the attorney general emphasized that the Department of Justice "has long maintained, and continues to maintain, that it has authority to exempt its attorneys from the application of DR 7–104 and Model Rule 4.2 and their state counterparts." 59 Fed. Reg. 39910–11 (Aug. 4, 1994).

b. The Reno Memorandum listed various exceptions to the no-contact rule. For example, there was an exception for discovery by legal process (such as during a grand jury testimony); or when the "represented party initiates the communication directly with the attorney for the government or through an intermediary" and the party knowingly waives his or her right and a federal judge or magistrate concludes that the waiver is knowing and voluntary; or when there is a waiver of *Miranda* rights at the time of arrest; or when there is an investigation of "additional, different or ongoing crimes or civil violations," including "undercover or covert" operations; or when the government attorney believes in "good faith" that the communication is necessary to prevent the "risk of injury or death" to any person.

c. United States v. Lopez, 4 F.3d 1455 (9th Cir.1993), was a particularly interesting example of these issues. Lopez, charged with a drug offense, feared his children were being abused while he was incarcerated and awaiting trial. He wanted to discuss cooperation with the government in order to secure an earlier release. However, Lopez's lawyer told him that "his general policy not to negotiate a plea with the government in exchange for cooperation." Thus, Lopez tried to deal with the government through the lawyer for a co-defendant and, after obtaining permission of a magistrate judge, the U.S. attorney's office negotiated a deal with him—later rejected by both defendants—through that lawyer. When Lopez' lawyer heard about the negotiations behind his back, Lopez' lawyer withdrew, and substitute counsel moved to dismiss the indictment based on government misconduct. The district court ruled that—even where the defendant initiated the contact—it was improper for the U.S. attorney's office to meet with him in the absence of his lawyer. Then, the judge dismissed the indictment. The Ninth Circuit opinion overruled and held that the trial court abused its discretion. The Ninth Circuit was contemptuous of the Justice Department position that it was exempt from California Rule 2–100 (Model Rule 4.2) and equally critical of the U.S. attorney's claim that the contact with Lopez was "authorized by law," but it concluded that dismissing the indictment went too far. In a concurring opinion, Judge Betty Fletcher opined that both defense counsel's unwillingness to negotiate on Lopez' behalf and the magistrate judge's failure to apprehend the complete picture of what was going on were big parts of the problem and there was plenty of blame to go around.

d. How would you have decided the *Lopez* case? Do criminal defendants sometimes need protection from their own lawyers? What if the drug kingpin hired the counsel that shows up to represent the drug runner; in that case, should it be improper for a prosecutor to talk with a defendant who voluntarily seeks such a meeting? The "or court order" language that the ABA added to Model Rule 4.2 in 2002 is intended to make clear that in cases like *Lopez*, both state and federal prosecutors may take the defendant before a magistrate judge who can evaluate the sincerity of the defendant's wish to talk to the prosecutors and authorize such discussions in appropriate cases. Do the *Lopez* facts suggest, however, that magistrate judges may not always make decisions in such cases that reviewing courts will conclude were appropriate?

4. As a matter of policy, should the attorney general be able to exempt federal prosecutors from the operation of Model Rule 4.2 as it applies in the states that have licensed the prosecutors?

a. United States v. Colorado Supreme Court, 87 F.3d 1161 (10th Cir.1996), was one of the first direct Justice Department challenges to the applying state ethics rules to federal prosecutors. The rule at issue was what is now Model Rule 3.8(e), which forbids a prosecutor from requiring a lawyer to testify before a grand jury or in any other setting if the prosecutor could obtain the evidence from another source. The district court held that, because the state had not disciplined any federal prosecutor, there was no case or controversy, but the Tenth Circuit rejected that holding: the mere threat of discipline is enough to give jurisdiction. The Rule 3.8 prohibition also raised a threat to the grand jury process sufficient to require a hearing in the district court. The court then remanded for further proceedings.

b. Earlier, in United States v. Williams, 504 U.S. 36 (1992), Justice Scalia (5 to 4) held that grand juries were independent of the judicial branch and traditional judicial regulation did not apply to their operation. Thus, usual court rules do not apply and federal prosecutors need not present exculpatory evidence to a grand jury. In light of *Williams*, on remand, the district court held that Rule 3.8(e) was invalid as applied to federal prosecutors practicing before a grand jury, but valid in other settings. United States v. Colorado Supreme Court, 988 F.Supp. 1368 (D.Colo.1998). The 10th Circuit affirmed, 189 F.3d 1281 (10th Cir.1999).

c. Matter of Howes, 940 P.2d 159 (N.M.1997) (per curiam), was the first state case to impose discipline on a federal prosecutor who complied with the Justice Department regulations on *ex parte* contact. When Howes was an assistant U.S. attorney (AUSA) in the District of Columbia, he was a member of only the New Mexico bar. Following office policy, Howes permitted a D.C. police detective to talk to a represented criminal defendant in the absence of his appointed counsel as long as the defendant initiated the contact. Howes knew such conversations were being held and did not notify the defendant's lawyer, who moved to dismiss the indictment for prosecutorial misconduct. The court denied the motion but sent the matter to the D.C. Board of Professional Responsibility, which said its rules did not apply to an AUSA not admitted in the District of Columbia. Therefore, New Mexico took up the case. The New Mexico Supreme Court upheld a sanction of public censure, holding that neither a superior's direction nor office policy can excuse a lawyer's violation of clear ethical standards. The court also said that no statute authorizes the Reno Memorandum, and the supremacy clause did not independently protect a federal prosecutor from state professional discipline for his official acts.

d. Congress has now resolved this issue by enacting a law that expressly makes federal lawyers subject to state ethics rules. Called the McDade Act, the law took effect in April 1999 and is found at 28 U.S.C.A. § 530B. Do you agree with this resolution of the issue?

PROBLEM 20

THE ETHICS OF NEGOTIATION

Negotiation may be the quintessential activity of a lawyer and the best example of the lawyer's contact with a third party on the client's behalf. Reaching agreement on a sale of an asset or formation of a contractual relationship can provide protection for and benefits to the lawyer's client. Indeed, year in and year out, even where relationships sour and litigation results, over 90% of the parties to filed cases resolve their differences by negotiation before trial. Is negotiation an ethical wasteland where the lawyer has no standards of conduct? Is it a world where literally anything goes? This problem suggests that the answer is no. It considers first where the lawyer gets authority to negotiate and the boundaries of that authority. Next, it looks at the duty to tell the truth in negotiations and any limits to that duty. Then, it asks whether lawyers ever have to volunteer information in order to avoid a misapprehension by the other side. Finally, it examines limits on what negotiated results parties and their lawyers may reach.

FACTS

James Young, age 19, was in a traffic accident. The driver of the other car suffered personal injuries and has paid medical bills of $18,000. There was $7,000 in property damage to the other car. Young was unhurt, but his car suffered $5,000 damage.

At the scene of the accident, the investigating officer charged Young with drunken driving. Young denied it and told the officer that he had nothing alcoholic to drink the entire day. He told you, however, that he had three large drinks within an hour of the accident. By chance, the arresting officer failed to bring along his kit to test for blood alcohol, so there is no scientific evidence on that issue.

Young's criminal trial is coming up next week. Conviction of drunk driving would probably mean that Young would pay a large fine and lose his driving privileges for a year. You have plea negotiations scheduled with the prosecutor this afternoon. Settlement discussions about the potential civil claims are also expected soon.

You have not talked at all with Young about what kind of plea he might enter, but you have authority from his insurance company to pay up to a total of $20,000 for the combined personal injuries suffered by the other driver and the property damage incurred by the owner of the other car.

QUESTIONS

A. AUTHORITY TO PARTICIPATE IN AND CONSUMMATE NEGOTIATIONS

1. What gives you the authority to conduct negotiations on behalf of James Young? Is the authority to negotiate inherent in a lawyer's role as a client's representative?

a. Restatement Third, The Law Governing Lawyers § 21, Comment *e*, says:

"A lawyer has authority to take any lawful measure within the scope of representation that is reasonably calculated to advance a client's objectives as defined by the client, unless there is a contrary agreement or instruction and unless a decision is reserved [by law] to the client."

b. Thoughtful lawyers acknowledge, however, that they have only as much authority to conduct negotiations as their client gives them. Remember what Model Rule 1.2(a) says about who ultimately has the legal authority to settle a matter?[1]

---

1. The fact that a client is not bound by a settlement negotiated by the client's lawyer without the client's authority is discussed in Problem 4, Issue D.

c. Restatement Third, The Law Governing Lawyers § 22 reinforces Rule 1.2(a):

"(1) As between client and lawyer, * * * the following and comparable decisions are reserved to the client except when the client has validly authorized the lawyer to make the particular decision: whether and on what terms to settle a claim; how a criminal defendant should plead; * * *

"(3) Regardless of any contrary contract with a lawyer, a client may revoke a lawyer's authority to make the decisions described in Subsection (1)."

2. Why is even the commencement of negotiations something the lawyer should not take lightly?

a. Is even starting to negotiate something the lawyer must discuss with the client pursuant to Model Rule 1.4? Is talking about settlement of a case a "means by which the client's objectives are to be accomplished" within the meaning of Model Rule 1.4(a)(2)?

b. Can a lawyer intelligently even make a first offer or respond to one from the other side without knowing what the client is currently prepared to accept? Negotiators often talk about trying to find ways to "create value," i.e., to identify ways to engage in sufficient "trade" of issues that both parties feel themselves better off as a result of the negotiations. In short, most negotiations involve a range of potential outcomes and the optimal result will vary with the personal values placed on them by the parties.

c. Is obtaining authority to negotiate and determining the range of acceptable settlement terms a one-time event? Does Model Rule 1.4 create a continuing obligation on the lawyer? Is negotiation often an evolving process in which settlement authority that seemed reasonable at one time may require revision as new opportunities for agreement open up while others seem less likely?

3. Do lawyers in a criminal case have an obligation to consider plea bargaining?

a. ABA Standards Relating to the Administration of Criminal Justice, The Prosecution Function, Standard 3–4.1(a) says:

"The prosecutor should have and make known a general policy or willingness to consult with defense counsel concerning disposition of charges by plea."

b. ABA Standards Relating to the Administration of Criminal Justice, The Defense Function, Standard 4–6.1(b), says in turn:

"Defense counsel may engage in plea discussions with the prosecutor. Under no circumstances should defense counsel recommend to a defendant acceptance of a plea unless appropriate investigation and study of the case has been completed, including an analysis of controlling law and the evidence likely to be introduced at trial."

c. In re Stanton, 682 A.2d 655 (D.C.1996), is an interesting case of a lawyer whose license was suspended and whose reinstatement was delayed for several years because he refused to assist clients to plea bargain. He believes "attorney-assisted guilty pleas are unconstitutional." The lawyer argued that, under Rule 1.2(c), he and his client could agree in advance to limit the scope of his representation, and he would plan to do so if readmitted. He would also only represent clients who truly wanted to plead guilty, as opposed to those whose plea he negotiates as part of a settlement package. The court ruled that this attitude reflects an "inability to draw workable distinctions between his philosophical beliefs and his ethical obligations," and thus sufficiently draws into question his willingness to "seek a client's lawful objectives" as to deny readmission.

The dissenting justice suggested that the plea bargaining process is indeed broken and that a lawyer's personal philosophical views should not be held to support a finding of a lack of character. Do you agree?

d. Imagine that in this problem the prosecutor is willing to forego most sanctions if Young will plead guilty to some misdemeanor. Young, in turn, would accept almost any offense that will not involve jail time or a fine in excess of $1,000. May you negotiate competently on your client's behalf without knowing the relative importance of such alternatives to your client? Can you know those objectives without communicating with your client as Model Rule 1.4 requires?

4. Should a lawyer be required to tell the client about all settlement offers received from the other side?

a. Restatement § 20, Comment *e*, says:

"A lawyer must ordinarily report promptly to the client a settlement offer in a civil action or a proposed plea bargain in a criminal prosecution."

b. Model Rule 1.4, Comment 2, goes on:

"[A] lawyer who receives from opposing counsel an offer of settlement in a civil controversy or a proffered plea bargain in a criminal case must promptly inform the client of its substance unless the client has previously indicated that the proposal will be acceptable or unacceptable or has authorized the lawyer to accept or reject the offer."

c. Is this requirement realistic? May a lawyer ever say: "That offer is so bad I would not dignify it by taking it back to my client"? Do we want lawyers to make such statements without having learned what kinds of settlement offers are acceptable to the client?

d. Think back to Problem 19. Is requiring a lawyer to convey all offers to his or her client a necessary corollary to Rule 4.2's prohibition of the other side's direct contact with that lawyer's client?

B. THE DUTY OF HONESTY IN NEGOTIATIONS

1. When you start to discuss this case with the prosecutor, or the opposing counsel in the civil case, may you assert that Young had nothing alcoholic to drink on the day of the accident?

a. Remember that Young has told that story to everyone but you, and if you fail to take that position, you may undercut Young's credibility.

b. As you will see in Problem 27, you clearly cannot encourage Young to testify falsely in the upcoming criminal trial that he did not drink any alcoholic beverage. Does Model Rules 4.1 and 8.4(c) support any distinction between perjury in a trial and deception in negotiation? Should there be a distinction? Should the answer that governs the trial setting be controlling in a negotiation setting as well?

c. May your negotiating position in the civil and criminal cases be that, whether or not your client drank anything alcoholic before the accident, he was not intoxicated at the time the accident occurred? Is that a different question than what he had to drink? Is it a representation you in fact *know* is untrue?

d. Instead, may you claim that neither the police nor the plaintiff can prove that Young was intoxicated? Are statements about facts and statements about strength of the evidence different as a practical matter? Are they—should they be—different as a matter of ethics?

e. May you tell the opposing lawyer that your client will testify that the other car was traveling at an excessive rate of speed and "came out of nowhere" to cause the accident? May you say that if you know that your client will not say that, because you know that he does not really remember the accident very well, but you hope that the other side will factor into its estimate of the worth of the case the risk that your client would tell such a story?

2. Are all lies created equal? Are some lies tolerated, some even encouraged, while other lies are forbidden?

a. In Office of Disciplinary Counsel v. DiAngelus, 907 A.2d 452 (Pa.2006), during the course of plea bargaining a relatively serious motor vehicle violation down to a lesser one, DiAngelus told the prosecutor that the arresting officer had agreed to a reduction of the charges. Later, however, the arresting officer denied that he said that and he could prove he had been elsewhere when DiAngelus said the conversation had occurred. The court found the lawyer's misrepresentation was dishonest, violated Rule 8.4(c), and materially affected the outcome of the case in violation of Rule 8.4(d). DiAngelus was suspended for 5 years.

b. Rule 4.1(a) prohibits making a false statement of "material" fact or law. Does Rule 8.4(c) incorporate that restriction when it prohibits "dishonesty"? Now, look at Model Rule 4.1, Comment 2:

> "Under generally accepted conventions in negotiation, certain types of statements ordinarily are not taken as statements of material fact. Estimates of price or value placed on the subject of a transaction and a party's intentions as to an acceptable settlement of a claim are ordinarily in this category * * *."

What about misrepresenting one's attitude? Is it proper to fake anger during negotiations? May a lawyer lie about the client's alternatives? Is it proper to delay making or responding to an offer so as not to let the other side get the sense that your client is in a hurry to dispose of the case by settlement?

c.   ABA Formal Opinion 06–439 (Apr. 12, 2006) acknowledges that it is not unusual for negotiators to make statements that are "less than entirely forthcoming." So long as the statements are of a kind "upon which parties to a negotiation ordinarily would not be expected justifiably to rely," they are acceptable of a form of "posturing" or "puffing," the opinion says. Negotiators may not, however, make false statements of material fact. Thus, even though a client has authorized a $100 settlement figure, a lawyer may say the client does not wish to settle for more than $50; what the lawyer may not say is that the client has not authorized a settlement for more than $50. Do you agree? Is the ABA Committee too willing to split ethical hairs?

d.   The late Federal Judge Alvin B. Rubin took a strong stand on the issue of honesty in negotiations:

> " * * * Most lawyers say it would be improper to prepare a false document to deceive an adversary or to make a factual statement known to be untrue with the intention of deceiving him. * * *
>
> "Interesting answers are obtained [, however,] if lawyers are asked whether it is proper to make false statements that concern negotiating strategy rather than the facts in litigation. Counsel for a plaintiff appears quite comfortable in stating, when representing a plaintiff, 'My client won't take a penny less than $25,000,' when in fact he knows that the client will happily settle for less; counsel for the defendant appears to have no qualms in representing that he has no authority to settle, or that a given figure exceeds his authority, when these are untrue statements. Many say that, as a matter of strategy, when they attend a pre-trial conference with a judge known to press settlements, they disclaim any settlement authority both to the judge and adversary although in fact they do have settlement instructions; estimable members of the bar support the thesis that a lawyer may not misrepresent a fact in controversy but may misrepresent matters that pertain to his authority or negotiating strategy because this is expected by the adversary.
>
> "To most practitioners it appears that anything sanctioned by the rules of the game is appropriate. From this point of view, negotiations are merely, as the social scientists have viewed it, a form of game; observance of the expected rules, not professional ethics, is the guiding precept. But gamesmanship is not ethics."[2]

2. Alvin B. Rubin, A Causerie on Law-   Rev. 577, 585–86 (1975).
yers' Ethics in Negotiation, 35 Louisiana L.

e. Consider a largely opposing view. Professor James J. White writes of the "paradoxical nature of the negotiator's responsibility":

> "On the one hand the negotiator must be fair and truthful; on the other he must mislead his opponent. Like the poker player, a negotiator hopes that his opponent will overestimate the value of his hand. Like the poker player, in a variety of ways he must facilitate his opponent's inaccurate assessment. The critical difference between those who are successful negotiators and those who are not lies in this capacity both to mislead and not to be misled."[3]

Do you agree with Professor White or with Judge Rubin? Can both be right?

3. Do lawyers have a higher obligation to be truthful than nonlawyers?

a. Look closely at Model Rule 4.1 and its Comments. Does it prohibit anything more than "false" statements of "material" fact? May the lawyer lie about where James was going on the day of the accident? May he say James was going to church services when he really was going to shoot pool? Is the issue of where he was going "material" to the legal issues in the case? Would it be disloyal to the client to suggest that he is other than a choir boy?

b. If a nonlawyer knowingly made a false statement of material fact, wouldn't the nonlawyer be guilty of fraud? Does Model Rule 4.1 demand any more of lawyers? Put another way, if a statement would not constitute the tort of fraud or intentional misrepresentation, would it violate Model Rule 4.1? Look especially at Comment 2. Is there any statement that would subject a lawyer to professional discipline but not to liability for damages?

c. Fire Ins. Exchange v. Bell by Bell, 643 N.E.2d 310 (Ind.1994), involved a lawyer's client who had been burned in a fire at his grandfather's home. The homeowner's insurer retained one of the state's most prominent law firms. The insurer offered to pay policy limits, which the law firm represented to be $100,000. Although the injuries would have justified a higher verdict against the plaintiff's grandfather, the plaintiff's lawyer recommended taking the settlement as the only money the plaintiff would be likely to collect. Only later did the lawyer learn that the policy limits were in fact $300,000, not $100,000. Plaintiff then sued the defense lawyers for misrepresentation. The lawyers basically argued that no one can reasonably rely on what a lawyer says in "adversarial settlement negotiations." But the court answered: "[t]he reliability and trustworthiness of attorney representations constitute an important component of the efficient administration of justice." 643 N.E.2d at 312. Even though the plaintiff's counsel could have gotten discovery of the policy and learned the policy limits himself, he was entitled to rely on what opposing counsel told

---

3. James J. White, Machiavelli and the Bar: Ethical Limits on Lying in Negotiation, 1980 American Bar Foundation Research J. 926, 927.

him about this material matter. Hence, plaintiff could seek damages for fraudulent misrepresentation.[4] The law firm may not lie.

d. Restatement Third, The Law Governing Lawyers § 98, Comment *c*, suggests that Model Rule 4.1 has two functions. First, it shows that lawyers at least have the same obligations of truthfulness as do persons generally, i.e., lawyers are not specially privileged to make material misstatements of fact. Second, to prove a violation of Model Rule 4.1, it is not necessary to show either reliance on the misstatement or actual damages as a tort suit would require.

e. Should the law require lawyers to be more honest than it requires nonlawyers to be? Because people are more on their guard when dealing with a lawyer, should the lawyer's obligation to tell the truth be less?

4. Is deception and withholding of information inevitably good negotiating strategy?

a. Is negotiation inevitably a zero-sum game in which anything one side receives is at the expense of the other? Assume Ann has a candy bar and Bill has a pen. Ann needs something with which to write and Bill is hungry. Will Ann and Bill each be better off trying to figure out how to trick the other out of what the other has? Will the lot of both of them improve once they acknowledge the possibility of a fair trade?

b. Some students of negotiating strategy have used computer simulations to explore approaches to negotiation and have evaluated them in terms of benefits to each negotiator. One successful strategy is known as tit-for-tat.[5] A wise negotiator breaks the process down into a series of small deals, not just one large one. For the first deal, you begin by being open and honest in your negotiating. If your opposing number responds in the same way, you reward her by continuing to be open and honest. If your opponent deceives you or takes advantage of your honesty, however, you punish her by noncooperative behavior as to the next issue. The point is that neither side needs to trust the other or sacrifice its own interests. It simply will turn out to be better for all sides to make honesty and cooperation pay.

c. However, is every negotiating situation one that has multiple steps? Is every situation one that both sides can win? Even negotiations that ''increase the size of the pie'' have a stage in which the pie gets divided. At that stage, what would good negotiators do? Should they agree on a solution that mimics the situation in which one party cuts the pie and the other chooses the first piece?[6]

---

4. See also, Shafer v. Berger, Kahn, Shafton, Moss, Figler, Simon & Gladstone, 131 Cal.Rptr.2d 777 (Cal.Ct.App.2003) (false assertion that claim not covered by insurance); Siegel v. Williams, 818 N.E.2d 510 (Ind.Ct.App.2004) (false assertion that paying more than $25,000 would force lawyer into bankruptcy).

5. See Robert Axelrod, The Evolution of Cooperation (1984).

6. Many observers remain unconvinced that honesty is the best policy if the only measure is to be ''profit and effectiveness.'' See, e.g., Gerald B. Wetlaufer, The Ethics of Lying in Negotiations, 75 Iowa L. Rev. 1219, 1230 (1990): ''In those bargaining situations which are at least in part distributive, a category which includes virtually all negotiations, lying is a coherent and often effective strategy.'' Professor Wetlaufer argues that

5. Is it a mistake to think of negotiation as a single type of phenomenon?

a.   Consider the argument of Professor White:

"One who conceives of negotiation as an alternative to a lawsuit has only scratched the surface. Negotiation is also the process by which one deals with the opposing side in war, with terrorists, with labor or management in a labor agreement, with buyers and sellers of goods, services, and real estate, with lessors, with governmental agencies, and with one's clients, acquaintances, and family. * * * Surely society would tolerate and indeed expect different forms of behavior on the one hand from one assigned to negotiate with terrorists and on the other from one who is negotiating with the citizens on behalf of a government agency. * * * Performance that is standard in one negotiating arena may be gauche, conceivably unethical, in another."[7]

b.   Do you agree with Professor White? Would you have a right to mislead management in a labor negotiation about your union client's willingness to strike?

c.   Do you have a *duty* to mislead a hostage-taker about whether he will be granted amnesty if he lets his hostages go? What ethical values lead to your conclusions?

C.   THE DUTY TO VOLUNTEER INFORMATION OR CORRECT A MISAPPREHENSION

1.   Should the law require a lawyer to disclose affirmatively adverse facts in a negotiation? Is it instead the duty of the adverse side to ask direct questions to the opposing lawyer to confirm its assumptions, and not that lawyer's obligation to volunteer harmful facts?

a.   Virzi v. Grand Trunk Warehouse & Cold Storage Co., 571 F.Supp. 507 (E.D.Mich.1983), raises this question in a particularly interesting form. The plaintiff in a personal injury case died from causes unrelated to the lawsuit prior to a pretrial conference and settlement negotiation. Plaintiff's lawyer did not inform either opposing lawyer or the court of the plaintiff's death throughout negotiations. But defendant's lawyer at no time specifically asked plaintiff's lawyer if plaintiff was still alive and available for trial. The opposing lawyer did not lie, but he did fail to volunteer his client's death. When the probate appointed a personal representative to administer the plaintiff's estate, the plaintiff's lawyer did not move to substitute parties. When the defendant later learned what had happened, it moved to set aside the settlement. The court relied, inter alia, on what is now Model Rules 3.3 and 4.1, and on Judge Rubin's article, to grant that relief, saying that zealous representation

"lying in negotiations is instrumentally effective and that most such lies are ethically impermissible." Id. at 1221.

7.   James J. White, Machiavelli and the Bar: Ethical Limits on Lying in Negotiation, 1980 American Bar Foundation Research J. 926, 927.

"does not justify a withholding of essential information, such as the death of the client, when the settlement of the case is based largely upon the defense attorney's assessment of the impact the plaintiff would make upon a jury because of his appearance at depositions. Plaintiff's attorney clearly had a duty to disclose the death of his client both to the Court and to opposing counsel prior to negotiating the final agreement." 571 F.Supp. at 512.

b. ABA Formal Opinion 95–397 (Sept. 18, 1995) addressed the same question and explained why the lawyer must voluntarily disclose her client's death while the law does not normally require the lawyer to volunteer adverse facts in negotiation. The client's death is special because that death automatically terminates the agency relationship and the lawyer has no client. The failure to disclose is "tantamount to making a 'false statement of material fact' " to the opponent and to any tribunal. The lawyer "must inform her adversary of the death of her client in the first communication with the adversary after she has learned of that fact."

c. Most cases are consistent with this result. In Kentucky Bar Ass'n v. Geisler, 938 S.W.2d 578 (Ky.1997), the client was a pedestrian hit by a car. The lawyer told the defense lawyer that the client was too ill to be deposed. After the client's death, she wrote to defense counsel and asked for an offer of settlement. The defense first learned of the client's death when the plaintiff's administrator endorsed the settlement check. Citing ABA Opinion 95–397 and *Virzi*, the court condemned her silence about the client's death in the letter opening settlement talks and ordered a public reprimand.[8]

2. Should each round of settlement discussions have to begin with questions by each side designed to trigger disclosure of unfavorable facts? Would a general obligation on lawyers to disclose relevant changes in circumstances be preferable? Can you see problems with such an approach?

a. State v. Mark Marks, P.A., 698 So.2d 533 (Fla.1997), involved a Florida criminal statute that prohibited filing "incomplete" claims with insurance companies in an attempt to obtain payment. It expressly forbade lawyers from helping clients file such claims, apparently out of concern about insurance fraud. The court found the term "incomplete" unconstitutionally vague as applied to lawyers who had failed to include medical records that cast doubt on their clients' injuries in claims that they filed. The state argued that the law only forbade withholding information with an "intent" to defraud, but the court held that even the intent requirement did not cure the vagueness. Lawyers often are required to withhold unfavorable information, the court said, and this statute did not clearly tell them what they were required to disclose.

---

8. See also, Matter of Forrest, 730 A.2d 340 (N.J.1999) (discussing settlement while saying a deceased client was "unavailable" for an arbitration hearing and delaying court-ordered medical examination justified lawyer's six-month suspension); In re Warner, 851 So.2d 1029 (La.2003) (lawyer suspended for assisting client's daughter to negotiate settlement and forge her father's name after client's death).

b. ABA Formal Opinion 314 (Apr. 27, 1965) considered the lawyer's obligation in settling a tax claim with the IRS:

> "Negotiation and settlement procedures of the tax system do not carry with them the guarantee that a correct tax result necessarily occurs. The latter happens, if at all, solely by reason of chance in settlement of tax controversies just as it might happen with regard to other civil disputes. In the absence of either judicial determination or of a hypothetical exchange of files by adversaries, counsel will always urge in aid of settlement of a controversy the strong points of his case and minimize the weak; this is in keeping with Canon 15 [of the ABA Canons of Ethics of 1908, as amended], which does require 'warm zeal' on behalf of the client. Nor does the absolute duty not to make false assertions of fact require the disclosure of weaknesses in the client's case and in no event does it require the disclosure of his confidences, unless the facts in the attorney's possession indicate beyond reasonable doubt that a crime will be committed. A wrong, or indeed sometimes an unjust, tax result in the settlement of a controversy is not a crime."

Do you agree? Are these insights peculiar to negotiations with the IRS? Do they represent a realistic understanding of many kinds of negotiations?

c. ABA Formal Opinion 94–387 (Sept. 26, 1994) narrowly interpreted the duty to disclose. It ruled that "where the lawyer knows that her client's claim may not be susceptible of judicial enforcement because the statute of limitations has run, * * * the ethics rules do not preclude a lawyer's nonetheless negotiating over the claim without informing the opposing party of this potentially fatal defect." However, the lawyer must "be careful not to make any affirmative misrepresentations about the facts showing that the claim is time-barred, or suggest that she plans to do something to enforce the claim (e.g., file suit) that she has no intention of doing. See Rule 4.1." According to the opinion, there is also no violation of Rule 3.1 (frivolous suits) or Rule 3.3 (candor to tribunal) to file a time-barred claim in court "so long as this does not violate the law of the relevant jurisdiction," such as would be the case if the limitations defect were jurisdictional. Normally, the opinion noted, the statute of limitations is an affirmative defense that the opposing party must assert. Finally, there is no basis in the ethical rules to hold a government lawyer to a higher or different standard.

Committee member Richard McFarlain filed a dissent. He regarded this opinion much "as Julia Child would regard a fly in her soup;" it is "unneeded, unwanted, and too much to swallow." In his view, Rule 8.4(c), prohibiting deceit, prohibits lawyers from engaging in this activity.

d. With which of these views do you agree? If the opposing lawyer objects to your statute of limitations defense in his negotiations, but does not know of recent authority that helps his case by creating a laches defense to prevent the limitations from barring your client, do you have any obligation to volunteer that case to him? If you were in court and writing a brief on the issue, would you have to volunteer the case to the judge? Compare Rule 3.3(a)(2) with Rule 4.1(a).

3. Should the rules about negotiation be different in criminal cases? How candid must a prosecutor be about the strength of the evidence?

a. In People v. Jones, 375 N.E.2d 41 (N.Y.1978), cert. denied, 439 U.S. 846 (1978), the court held that there was no due process violation when the district attorney did not disclose, during plea negotiations, that the complaining witness had died. Under Brady v. Maryland, 373 U.S. 83 (1963), the prosecutor is under a constitutional duty to respond to defendant's request that he disclose material evidence favorable to the accused, either as to guilt or punishment. The death of the state's critical witness did not fit within *Brady,* the court reasoned, because while it affected the prosecutor's practical ability to prove the case, it did not cast doubt on the defendant's guilt.

b. Do you agree? Should either Model Rule 3.8(d) or ABA Standard Relating to the Prosecution Function 3–3.11(c) change the result in this case? Do the cited provisions merely incorporate the *Brady* rule?

Kyles v. Whitley, 514 U.S. 419, 437 (1995), said: "*Brady* requires less of the prosecution than the ABA Standards for Criminal Justice, which call generally for prosecutorial disclosures of any evidence tending to exculpate or mitigate. See [also], ABA Model Rule of Professional Conduct 3.8(d) (1984) ('The prosecutor in a criminal case shall . . . make timely disclosure to the defense of all evidence or information known to the prosecutor that tends to negate the guilt of the accused or mitigates the offense')."

c. United States v. Ruiz, 536 U.S. 622 (2002), made clear that, under *Brady,* in negotiating a plea bargain, the government need not tell a criminal defendant about impeachment information relevant to its witnesses even though it would have to disclose that information if the case went to trial. After immigration agents found 30 kilos of marijuana in Ruiz' luggage, the government offered a "fast track" plea bargain if Ruiz would waive trial in exchange for a two-level sentence reduction. The government agreed to tell Ruiz of any exculpatory information it had if she waived receiving exculpatory information about informants or information supporting affirmative defenses she might raise. The Ninth Circuit held that defendants are entitled to such information before entering a plea and the required waiver was thus unconstitutional, but the Supreme Court reversed. Justice Breyer, for the Court, said that this "impeachment" information might affect the fairness of a trial but not affect a guilty plea. Full disclosure of matters such as informant identity "could seriously interfere with the Government's interest in securing those guilty pleas that are factually justified, desired by defendants, and help to secure the efficient administration of justice." 536 U.S. at 631. Does Model Rule 3.8(d) require more?

4. In the plea bargaining negotiations with the prosecutor, may criminal defense counsel assert that he or she "knows" the

client is innocent? Is the case for stretching the truth stronger in criminal defense work?

a. Why? Is it because potential sanctions are more severe than in most civil litigation? Is it because "everyone expects" counsel for criminal defendants to be dishonest?

b. Timothy McVeigh was tried and convicted of the bombing of an Oklahoma City federal building, a bombing described as one of the worst terrorist acts in the country's history. Shortly before the trial, the media obtained what was described as McVeigh's "confession" to his lawyer. One of McVeigh's lawyers, Stephen Jones, explained the "confession" by saying that it was an intentionally false document prepared by the defense to show to potential witnesses to see if they would stick to their stories. Is it consistent with Rule 4.1 to "lie" to potential witnesses to see if they are telling the truth?

c. Is there a difference between lying to deceive someone into changing their position and lying to see how they would honestly react to a set of facts? Should this distinction justify sending "testers" of different races, none of whom really wants to buy a house, to a real estate agency to see if they receive discriminatory treatment? Or, should we say that a lie is a lie, and Rule 4.1 should condemn them all?[9]

d. Should a lawyer have a duty of candor when making representations to a federal regulatory agency on behalf of a financial institution client? Matter of Peter M. Fishbein * * * and Kaye, Scholer, Fierman, Hays & Handler, 1992 WL 560939 (1992) attracted lawyers' attention. Lincoln Savings' semiannual routine regulatory examination in 1986 turned up signs that the institution was in trouble. The regulators wanted more information, and Charles Keating allegedly knew the future of his organization was at stake. He hired the Kaye Scholer firm to protect him from the regulators and Peter Fishbein, a litigator, took over the defense. Fishbein allegedly treated the situation as adversary litigation, resisted document requests, and did not volunteer negative information. The Office of Thrift Supervision (OTS), in response, charged that Kaye Scholer had thus become the alter ego of the client. Lincoln was obliged to make information available, OTS argued, so the law firm could not assume that the secrecy that would be proper in litigation was proper in this situation. The regulations required disclosure to protect third parties such as the depositors. If Lincoln Savings had to disclose this information pursuant to regulation, Lincoln's lawyers had no right to refuse to disclose. After a "freeze" of the law firm's assets, Kaye Scholer agreed to pay the government $42 million. What would you have done if you were in Mr. Fishbein's position? At the very least, can we say that lawyers should not assume they

---

9. You will also see this issue in Problem 24. A leading case on the issue is In re Conduct of Gatti, 8 P.3d 966 (Ore.2000) (court reprimands lawyer who misrepresented that he was a doctor interested in working for a company in order to conduct his "private sting" against that company, which he was planning to sue).

can do things for their clients that the clients could not legally do for themselves?[10]

D. POSSIBLE LIMITS ON THE RESULTS THAT CAN BE REACHED IN NEGOTIATIONS

1. Should there be any limit on what parties to a negotiation may agree? May a lawyer agree, for example, that in exchange for a generous financial payment to the lawyer's client, neither the lawyer nor the client will file criminal charges against the opposing party for conduct that would justify such charges?

a. ABA Model Code of Professional Responsibility, DR 7–105(A) seemed to say "no" when it asserted:

> "A lawyer shall not present, participate in presenting, or threaten to present criminal charges solely to obtain an advantage in a civil matter."

See also, California State Bar Rule 5–100(A):

> "A member shall not threaten to present criminal, administrative, or disciplinary charges to obtain an advantage in a civil action."

b. You will not find a comparable provision in the ABA Model Rules, and ABA Formal Opinion 92–363 (July 6, 1992) found that a lawyer *may* use the possibility of bringing criminal charges in negotiations in a civil case if both the civil case and criminal violation are well founded in fact and law, the lawyer does not suggest improper influence over the criminal process, and the threat would not constitute extortion under state law. The lawyer may even agree not to file criminal charges as an element of settling a civil claim if that agreement would not violate a provision of law that required reporting of crimes.

Do you agree with this result? Is the ABA getting more realistic? Does the opinion simply represent a further decline in lawyers' ethical standards?

c. Should the Rules permit a lawyer to agree to refuse to file disciplinary charges against an opposing lawyer in order to induce settlement of a civil case? Recall that In re Himmel, 533 N.E.2d 790 (Ill.1988), cited in Problem 2, held that a lawyer may not bargain away a duty to report a lawyer's disciplinary violation in order to secure a better settlement for a client. ABA Formal Opinion 94–383 (July 5, 1994) also says that a lawyer may not agree to fail to report anything that Model Rule 8.3(a) requires the lawyer to report. Even as to matters sufficiently minor as to not require reporting, a threat to report may be "prejudicial to the administration of justice" because it may introduce extraneous calculations into the decision to settle. Do you agree?

2. In the course of defending James Young, you have discovered that the city often has problems with its alcohol detection kits.

---

10. The ABA's formal opinion commenting on these issues is 93–375 (Aug. 6, 1993).

That is information the city would prefer be kept quiet. Assume the city proposes to drop all charges against Young in exchange for your agreement never to defend another drunken driving case. Do the Model Rules permit you to get Young off the hook on that basis?

a.   Look at Model Rule 5.6(b). What rationale justifies that rule? Why should a rule require a lawyer to sacrifice the interests of a current client, Young, to protect the interests of a hypothetical future drunken driving defendant?

b.   ABA Formal Opinion 93–371 (Apr. 16, 1993) addressed only proposed "global settlements" on behalf of both present and future claimants, but it is relevant to this problem because it identified three important policies underlying Model Rule 5.6(b):

> "First, permitting such agreements restricts the access of the public to lawyers who, by virtue of their background and experience, might be the very best available talent to represent these individuals. Second, the use of such agreements may provide clients with rewards that bear less relationship to the merits of their claims than they do to the desire of the defendant to 'buy off' plaintiff's counsel. Third, the offering of such restrictive agreements places the plaintiff's lawyer in a situation where there is conflict between the interests of present clients and those of future clients. While the Model Rules generally require that the client's interests be put first, forcing a lawyer to give up future representations may be asking too much, particularly in light of the strong countervailing policy favoring the public's unfettered choice of counsel."

c.   Feldman v. Minars, 658 N.Y.S.2d 614 (N.Y.App.Div.1997), enforced an agreement like the one in this question even though the court conceded that the agreement violates New York DR 2–108(B) [and Model Rule 5.6(b)]. The court acknowledged that many courts in other jurisdictions have held such agreements nonenforceable for violating public policy, but it asserted that the rule makes no sense because, if the legal claim is legitimate, the market will supply another lawyer to take the next case. Thus, it directed the trial court to disqualify the lawyer from acting in violation of his agreement.

Do you agree with the court? Are lawyers fungible? If the fact that future clients could not have you on their side meant nothing to the defendant, would it have bothered to bargain and pay for that result in the first place?

d.   Florida Bar v. St. Louis, 967 So.2d 108 (Fla.2007) (per curiam), disciplined lawyer St. Louis. He filed 20 cases alleging crop damage from a DuPont fungicide called Benlate, which led to settlement negotiations. DuPont demanded that St. Louis agree not to file such cases in the future. Both sides knew that Rule 5.6 forbade such an agreement, so DuPont offered to hire St. Louis. DuPont agreed to pay St. Louis a $6.445 million retainer to give it unspecified advice in future Benlate cases. Although the documents recited that the retainer had nothing to do with the settlement of the 20 cases, the court found otherwise. It said that the future retainer created a conflict with St. Louis' efforts to get extra money in the original cases. The court concluded that Rule 5.6 was not ambiguous, was not unconstitutional, and forbids DuPont from hiring its adversary/lawyer, Mr. St. Louis. Then the court ordered disbarment for St. Louis and forfeiture of the $6.445 million retainer to the state's Client Security Fund. Note that DuPont got exactly what it wanted (St. Louis can bring no more cases involving Benlate) because the court disbarred Mr. St. Louis. The court also found St. Louis engaged in "acts of dishonesty such as lying to a judge and the Bar regarding the secret engagement agreement." Should the court, instead, have ordered DuPont to forfeit the retainer to the clients of Mr. St. Louis?

The court emphasized that there was a "secret engagement agreement" that the lawyer "arranged directly with DuPont while still representing its Benlate clients." Assume that St. Louis did not keep any information secret from his clients, and DuPont did not negotiate the retainer with St. Louis until after the case was over. Then, should there be a violation of Rule 5.6?

3. Suppose that in investigating Young's case you learn that his car had a serious steering defect that could have involved him in an even more serious accident. You realize that thousands of other drivers have cars with the same defect that the manufacturer has not acknowledged. May you negotiate a handsome settlement for Young that includes a provision that you will keep quiet about what you know and not use it on behalf of any future client?

a.   Do you see why people are troubled by such "secret settlements"? While their secrecy makes it difficult to determine how great a social problem they present, a pattern of such settlements could allow dangerous conditions to go uncorrected for years.[11]

b.   It has been difficult to reach an understanding that secret settlements should be prohibited. Judges tend to see such settlements, if at all, in the context of resolution of particular cases whose significance they may not appreciate. Defendants argue, in turn, that the settlements are an important way to protect trade secrets that liberal discovery rules put at risk, so the public interest favors protecting confidentiality though such settlements.[12]

c.   ABA Formal Opinion 00–417 (Apr. 7, 2000) considered settlements containing the condition that a lawyer not use any information learned against the defendant in the future. A settlement term that prohibits a lawyer from, e.g., using the same expert witness or subpoenaing certain records on behalf of the new client that the lawyer had previously subpoe-

---

11. This issue is discussed in Richard Zitrin & Carol M. Langford, The Moral Compass of the American Lawyer, Ch. 9 (1999).

12. Such agreements are defended vigorously in Arthur R. Miller, Confidentiality, Protective Orders, and Public Access to the Courts, 105 Harvard L. Rev. 427 (1991).

naed on behalf of the former client would, "[a]s a practical matter" effectively bar the lawyer from future representations, and that would violate Rule 5.6(b), because the lawyer's inability to use that information would materially limit her representation of a future client. "On the other hand," the opinion noted, "it is generally accepted that offering or agreeing to a bar on the lawyer's disclosure of particular information is not a violation of the Rule 5.6(b) proscription." The information is "information relating to the representation" and protected by Rule 1.6. Thus, if the client agrees to a restriction on the lawyer's use of the information, for the lawyer to abide by that agreement violates no ethical standard.

4.   **In this problem, the insurance company has authorized you to pay $20,000 to settle a total of $25,000 in claims. May counsel for Young's opponents negotiate a settlement that would pay the other driver $18,000 for his personal injuries and then tell his other client, the car owner, that there is only $2,000 left to pay for the property damage?**

a.   If the driver and owner were represented by separate counsel, how would the settlement talks have proceeded? Would they be likely to have involved a race to settle, i.e, for one or the other plaintiffs to have sought to settle first for a disproportionate share of the sum offered?

b.   Take a look at ABA Model Rule 1.8(g). Why should the result be different when a single lawyer represents both plaintiffs? Should a lawyer who represents two clients be able to settle on behalf of the most deserving first, without giving the less deserving a right to veto that settlement?

c.   Restatement Third, The Law Governing Lawyers § 128, Comment *d(i)*, suggests that any such situation presents a conflict of interest and that Model Rule 1.8(g) should be seen as a requirement of informed consent that simply takes a particular form in the context of an aggregate settlement. See also, Model Rule 1.8, Comment 13. Does that make sense to you? What is the justification for requiring a "writing signed by the client" in this context while consent "confirmed in writing" is sufficient for most conflicts?

d.   ABA Formal Opinion 06–438 (Feb. 10, 2006) considered these issues and said two problems with "aggregate settlements" are that the lawyer might be tempted not to investigate the cases individually and might be tempted to close the cases too early. What Rule 1.8(g) requires is that the lawyer disclose to all the clients the entire deal, what each plaintiff will be getting, the total fee paid to the lawyer, how costs are to be allocated, and the like. The Rule also requires consent in writing from each of the clients. Because making that kind of disclosure could violate the Rule 1.6 interests of the individual clients, however, lawyers should get a waiver of such Rule 1.6 protection from each of the clients prior to undertaking the representation. If the lawyer cannot secure the waivers, she should not be representing all the clients in the first place.

———

PROBLEM 21

THE LAWYER AS EVALUATOR

A lawyer has duties of confidentiality and loyalty to a client's interest. The lawyer also has a duty of honesty in negotiations. The lawyer's role as an evaluator involves each of those obligations. When the lawyer acts as an evaluator, the lawyer undertakes to vouch for facts or legal conclusions in an effort to assist the client to complete a transaction or resolve a disagreement. This problem looks first at the traditional legal opinion a lawyer addresses to a client. It then examines what, if anything, changes when the opinion is designed to give comfort to a third party to whom the lawyer does not otherwise owe duties. Next, it looks at reports the lawyer makes to a client's auditor, and then it asks what consequences flow from an inaccurate opinion.

FACTS

Luther Klose is president of the Klose Corporation, a privately-held family enterprise. All of the stockholders are also officers of the corporation and receive benefits from the corporation both in the form of dividends and in the form of salary. In order to keep the overall tax liability at a minimum, the shareholders would prefer that as much money as possible be paid as salary that is deductible to the corporation, rather than as dividends that are not. Mr. Klose would like you, the corporation's outside attorney, to write him an opinion letter explaining that a new salary schedule to be inaugurated by the company properly represents greater responsibilities of the shareholder officers and thus is bona fide and not adopted with intent to circumvent the tax laws.

Klose Corporation is also seeking a large loan from the local bank. Given the Klose Corporation's local reputation for taking aggressive tax positions, the bank wants to be aware of any foreseen tax difficulties that could materially affect the Klose Corporation's ability to repay its loan. Mr. Klose, at the suggestion of the bank, has asked you to write a letter to the bank giving your legal opinion that all of the major tax deductions that the Klose Corporation took in the last three years are reasonable under the tax laws and that, if the Internal Revenue Service disallows any of these major deductions, the taxpayer is likely to prevail in litigation.

Now, the company's auditor has asked for information on "all actual or potential legal problems that might materially affect the Klose Corporation." You know that Klose Corporation has sold a large stock of defective goods, but no customer has yet discovered the defects. When the defects are discovered it may be difficult to trace them back to your client, but if the tracing is made, the company may be liable for up to half its net worth in damages.

QUESTIONS

A.   DUTIES TO A CLIENT WHO ASKS FOR A LEGAL OPINION

1.   Does Mr. Klose have a right to "purchase" the opinion letter he wants from you concerning the reasonableness of his salary?

a.   Think back to Model Rule 2.1. What obligation do you have to tell a client something the client does not want to hear? To what extent, if any, must you "audit" the client to assure yourself that the duties of the officers are in fact as your opinion will assume them to be?

b.   To whom does your duty run in this situation? Even when your client is a privately-held corporation, does your professional duty of loyalty run solely to Mr. Klose? Remember Model Rule 1.13(a).

2.   Would you let a client purchase your ratification of its officials' socially beneficial objectives in the guise of a legal opinion?

a.   Suppose the president of the corporate client wants the company to make a significant charitable contribution to engender goodwill or for other positive reasons, but also wants to nip in the bud a shareholder suit second-guessing the president's judgment.

b.   May you tell the client that certain legal considerations make it proper to make the contribution when your real reason for the conclusion is based on nonlegal considerations? Assume that the legal justification is at least arguable but that you need to be less than candid about the client's primary motivation. Medical doctors, some people claim, are sometimes justified in lying to their patients. May juris doctors ever lie to the clients for the clients' own good? How about to make the lawyer feel good?

3.   Does the fact that this problem involves a tax opinion increase or decrease the lawyer's responsibilities? Can one say that anything is fair where avoiding taxes is concerned?

a.   ABA Formal Opinion 314 (Apr. 27, 1965), concerning the lawyer's duty of candor in dealing with the IRS, said:

> "The Internal Revenue Service is neither a true tribunal, nor even a quasi-judicial institution. * * * [F]ew will contend that the service provides any truly dispassionate and unbiased consideration to the taxpayer. * * *

> "It by no means follows that a lawyer is relieved of all ethical responsibility when he practices before this agency. * * *

> "[A] lawyer who is asked to advise his client in the course of the preparation of the client's tax returns may freely urge the statement of positions most favorable to the client just as long as there is reasonable basis for those positions. Thus where the lawyer believes there is a reasonable basis for a position that a particular transaction does not result in taxable income, or that certain expenditures are properly deductible as expenses, the lawyer has no duty to advise that riders be

attached to the client's tax return explaining the circumstances surrounding the transaction or the expenditures."

b. However, in Formal Opinion 85–352 (July 7, 1985), the ABA modified Opinion 314. The ABA Standing Committee on Ethics and Professional Responsibility reported that it learned that many lawyers interpreted "reasonable basis" to mean they could they could use "any colorable claim on a tax return to justify exploitation of the lottery of the tax return audit selection process." To correct the record, the Standing Committee offered this guidance:

> "[A] lawyer may advise reporting a position on a return even where the lawyer believes the position probably will not prevail, there is no 'substantial authority' in support of the position, and there will be no disclosure of the position in the return. However, the position to be asserted must be one which the lawyer in good faith believes is warranted in existing law or can be supported by a good faith argument for an extension, modification or reversal of existing law. This requires that there is some realistic possibility of success if the matter is litigated. In addition, in his role as advisor, the lawyer should refer to potential penalties and other legal consequences should the client take the position advised."

Does that help? Now is your responsibility clear?

c. Shortly after the ABA released Opinion 85–352, the ABA Section on Taxation published a Report of the Special Task Force on Formal Opinion 85–352, 39 Tax Lawyer 635, 638–39 (1985). This Report stated:

> "More important to differentiating between 'reasonable basis' and the standard articulated by Opinion 85–352 is that the new standard requires not only that there be some possibility of success, if litigated, rather than merely a construction that can be argued or that seems reasonable, but also that there be more than just any possibility of success. The possibility of success, if litigated, must be 'realistic.' A possibility of success cannot be 'realistic' if it is only theoretical or impracticable. This clearly implies that there must be a substantial possibility of success, which when taken together with the assumption that the matter will be litigated, measurably elevates what had come to be widely known as the minimum ethical standard.
>
> "A position having only a 5% or 10% likelihood of success, if litigated, should not meet the new standard. A position having a likelihood of success closely approaching one-third should meet the standard. * * * "

Does this report clarify the lawyer's obligation?

4. Suppose you conclude and say in your opinion that the ultimate tax liability will depend to a great extent on the intent of the taxpayer. May you help Klose "manufacture" intent? Does your answer depend on whether you personally believe that Klose has the proper legal intent and you are merely helping him preserve and articulate it?

a.   How may you properly counsel creation of proof of intent? May you prepare minutes of meetings that never occurred in which the participants recite their intent? Does it matter whether these minutes are eventually approved ("ratified") by the participants?

b.   One might argue that the lawyer is not justified in "drawing a misleading minute" in order to develop intent for tax consideration, but that "having made the decision in his own mind that the action the client proposes is justified under the law, he is entitled to set out in the minutes the considerations that led him to that conclusion, and when he has done that he probably has gone as far as he can."[1] Do you agree?

B.   DUTIES IN PREPARATION OF A LEGAL OPINION FOR DELIVERY TO A THIRD PARTY

1.   Look at Model Rule 2.3. Did it add something not in the Model Code? Was it an important addition? Do you suppose lawyers were "evaluators" even before adoption of the Rule?

a.   Restatement Third, The Law Governing Lawyers § 95, Comment *b,* suggests that the role is familiar and reasonable.

> "For example, a lawyer for a corporation entering into a contract with a third person may address an opinion letter to the third person as to the authority of the officers of the corporate client to bind the corporation to the contract. In a real-estate transaction, a title opinion rendered by the lawyer for the seller may be addressed to the purchaser or a financial institution lending funds to the purchaser to be secured by the property. In such instances, the * * * client's interest is advanced by making it possible for the third person to proceed with the transaction on the basis of the evaluation."

b.   In connection with the bank loan described in this problem, what does Rule 2.3 require of you? Why must you "consult" with the client before agreeing to give the opinion? Why isn't the fact the client asked you to prepare the evaluation enough?

2.   What circumstances would ever make you conclude that an evaluation was incompatible with other aspects of your relationship with the client?

a.   Does the attorney-client privilege apply when one is conducting an internal investigation, the results of which may be available to others? Look again at Upjohn Co. v. United States, 449 U.S. 383 (1981), in Problem 8. The protection that will be granted to communications with inside and outside corporate counsel is broad in cases where no public disclosure is planned, but the result may be different where the lawyer's conclusions are intended to be made available outside of the corporation. See also, Model Rule 2.3(c).

---

1. Business Planning and Professional Responsibility—Problem 1, 8 The Practical   Lawyer 18, 33 (1962).

b. Suppose you learn something in the course of your investigation that is harmful to your client, e.g., that its factory is too close to the property line under applicable zoning regulations. Might it be more prudent for the client not to seek the loan rather than publicly to reveal its problem?

c. Both such possibilities should suggest to you that, while rendering third-party opinions is a significant part of many transactional lawyers' work, a lawyer should not routinely decide that it is wise to render such an opinion.

3. May you cover up or ignore embarrassing facts in your opinion? What relationship do you assume vis-a-vis the nonclients to whom your opinion will be addressed?

a. Restatement Third, The Law Governing Lawyers § 95, Comment *c*, says:

> " * * *Unless otherwise required or permitted by the terms under which the evaluation is given, the lawyer's duty is to provide a fair and objective opinion. * * * By statements in the evaluation, the lawyer may undertake to exercise a higher or lesser standard of care. * * *

> " * * * [However, t]he third-person recipient of a lawyer's evaluation does not thereby become the client of the lawyer, and the lawyer does not thereby undertake all duties owed to a client, such as confidentiality or avoidance of conflicting interests * * *."

b. Is your obligation of factual accuracy greater, less, or the same as one you would assume in giving an opinion to your own client? Restatement § 95, Comment *c*, continues:

> "In all events, unless stated or agreed otherwise, a lawyer's evaluation does not entail a guarantee by the lawyer that facts stated in it are accurate. In some circumstances, such as when the lawyer purports to be making a report of a factual investigation undertaken by the lawyer, a reasonable reader of the report would assume that the lawyer is reporting facts known by the lawyer to be accurate. A lawyer normally may rely on facts provided by corporate officers and other agents of a client that the lawyer reasonably believes to be appropriate sources for such facts without further investigation or specific disclosure, unless the recipient of the opinion objects or the version of the facts provided or other circumstances indicate that further verification is required."

c. May you simply base your opinion on an *assumed* set of facts? Comment *c* responds:

> "A lawyer may not without express disclosure rely for purposes of a legal opinion or other evaluation report on a fact or factual assumption that the lawyer knows to be inaccurate or, in the case of a factual representation, to have been provided under circumstances making reliance unwarranted."

d.   In 1998, the ABA Business Law Section's Committee on Legal Opinions published its own "Legal Opinion Principles" that summarize the emerging consensus in this area. Among the principles declared are:

(i) "The matters usually addressed in opinion letters, the meaning of the language normally used, and the scope and nature of the work counsel is expected to perform are based (whether or not so stated) on the customary practice of lawyers who regularly give * * * opinions of the kind involved." An opinion giver may vary any of the customary practice, but must do so expressly.

(ii) "The opinions contained in an opinion letter are expressions of professional judgment regarding the legal matters addressed and not guarantees that a court will reach any particular result."

(iii) " * * *[A]n opinion recipient ordinarily need not take any action to verify the opinions it contains."

(iv) Opinions may and customarily do "specify the jurisdiction(s) whose law they are intended to cover and sometimes limit their coverage to specified * * * [laws] of the named jurisdiction(s)."

(v) "Customary practice permits [an opinion author to rely 'in large measure on factual information obtained from others, particularly company officials'] * * * unless the factual information * * * appears irregular on its face or has been provided by an inappropriate source."

(vi) "An opinion should not be based on a factual representation that is tantamount to the legal conclusion being expressed."

(vii) "An opinion letter speaks as of its date. An opinion giver has no obligation to update an opinion letter for subsequent events or legal developments."[2]

e.   Because these so-called "third-party opinions," i.e., opinions to be relied upon by persons other than the lawyer's client, have become such a central part of commercial dealing, several groups have developed standard definitions for the usual representations that lawyers make.[3]

C.   SPECIAL PROBLEMS RESPONDING TO AN AUDITOR'S REQUEST FOR INFORMATION

1.   What are your responsibilities in replying to the independent auditors of the Klose Corporation who have required the company to get a letter from you evaluating various legal claims that have been or are likely to be asserted against the company?

a.   Such letters are routinely required at the time of any corporation's certified audit. Auditors want to be confident there will be no surprises that

---

2. For background and more detail about these principles, see Donald W. Glazer, It's Time to Streamline Opinion Letters, Business Lawyer Today, Nov/Dec 1999, at pp. 32, 35.

3. These definitions are collected and analyzed in Scott FitzGibbon & Donald W. Glazer, Legal Opinions: What Opinions in Financial Transactions Say and What They Mean (1992).

will render their conclusions misleading, and—to be realistic—they want someone at whom to point a finger if surprises do arise.

b. As courts began to hold accountants liable in damage actions if they did not maintain independence from and verify the representations of the corporate clients whose books were being audited, the auditors sought "comfort" from the corporation's lawyers. The auditors asked the lawyers to verify the corporation's contingent liabilities. The company's lawyers were reluctant to candidly assess future or current litigation because that would benefit the litigation adversaries. But the accountants regarded the lawyers' failure to respond a limitation on the scope of their audit, which would not please investors.

"That, in turn, had a serious impact on the client—which often was required to pay its auditors and its attorneys to debate the question—since it was required to file audited financial statements under the 1934 Act or, in the case of any new registration of securities, the 1933 Act." Lawyers had several concerns. First, they had to preserve the confidentiality of client information. Clients could waive confidentiality, but they could later claim that their consent was coerced and invalid, "particularly when—as was usually the case—the client was not fully cognizant that such disclosure might destroy the confidentiality privilege for all purposes." In addition, lawyers feared being liable for failing to "recognize the full consequences of facts coming to the attention of their lawyers in a context other than request by the client for advice. For example, a lawyer involved in litigating one case might easily become aware, through discovery, of facts that could constitute the basis for another action by a different party against the client." And, significantly, "disclosure of a contingent liability could often lead to removal of its contingent aspect." A publicly held company could "properly be required to disclose some potential liabilities to existing or potential shareholders, the analysis of whether or not disclosure was, in fact, required could often be a close question of judgment. Since it was obviously not in the interest of all shareholders to increase the claim's potential by disclosure, lawyers were understandably reluctant to substitute their judgment for that of their clients."[4]

c. Thus, the legal and accounting professions a formal agreement—through the ABA and the American Institute of Certified Public Accountants—reached a compromise and both groups issued coordinated statements.[5] This Statement is often called the "ABA/AICPA treaty." The treaty

4. Simon Lorne, The Corporate and Securities Adviser, The Public Interest, and Professional Ethics, 76 Michigan L. Rev. 425, 448–49 (1978) (footnote omitted).

5. The American Institute of Certified Public Accountants (AICPA), which is the principal organization of practicing accountants, issued Statement on Auditing Standards (SAS) No. 12, Inquiry of a Client's Lawyer Concerning Litigation, Claims and Assessments (1976), which coordinates with the ABA Statement of Policy Regarding Lawyers' Responses to Auditors' Requests for Information * * * [an edited version of which] is reprinted here. The text of each statement may be found in 31 Business Lawyer 1709 (1976).

While Chairman of the Securities and Exchange Commission, Roderick M. Hills called this ABA/AICPA agreement "a major step forward," others have seen the compromise "as resting, in the final analysis, upon a mutual abdication of purported responsibili-

distinguishes between litigation that is "pending or which a third party has manifested to the client a present intention to commence," and "other contingencies of a legal nature or having legal aspects."

As to the first category (pending and threatened litigation), the lawyer representing the client in that litigation matter "may be the best source for a description of the claim or claims asserted, the client's position (e.g., denial, contest, etc.) and the client's possible exposure in the litigation." However, for the second category (possible but not threatened litigation), the Statement says that "it is not in the public interest for the lawyer to be required to respond to general inquiries from auditors concerning possible claims."

Paragraph (3) of the Statement stated that the lawyer's response to the auditors request for disclosure of the loss contingencies of the client may be limited "to items which are considered individually or collectively material to the presentation of the client's financial statements."

Paragraph (5) then provides:

"(5) *Loss Contingencies. When properly requested by the client,*[6] it is appropriate for the lawyer to furnish to the auditor information concerning the following matters if the lawyer has been engaged by the client to represent or advise the client professionally with respect thereto and he has devoted substantive attention to them in the form of legal representation or consultation:

"(a) overtly threatened or pending litigation, whether or not specified by the client;

"(b) *a contractually assumed obligation* which the client has specifically identified and upon which the client has specifically requested, in the inquiry letter or a supplement thereto, comment to the auditor;

"(c) *an unasserted possible claim or assessment* which the client has specifically identified and upon which the client has specifically requested, in the inquiry letter or a supplement thereto, comment to the auditor.

Clause (a)—overtly threatened litigation—means that a potential claimant has indicated "to the client an awareness of and present intention to assert a possible claim or assessment unless the likelihood of litigation

---

ties. As such it is only a matter of time before its frailty is exposed." Lorne, *supra*, at 449–50. For a frail document, the agreement has remained in force for a long time.

The Sarbanes–Oxley Act of 2002 created both a Financial Accounting Standards Board (FASB) and a Public Company Accounting Oversight Board (PCAOB) to create new accounting rules to regulate auditor conduct. In 2008, the PCAOB adopted an interim posi-

tion that affirms that auditors and lawyers may rely on the "ABA/AICPA treaty." At the same time, the FASB has been considering new accounting standards for contingent liabilities and loss contingencies that might one day affect the "treaty." But as of the end of 2010, the FASB has not approved any such changes.

6. Emphasis added.

(or of settlement when litigation would normally be avoided) is considered remote."

Clause (c)—unasserted claims—means the client should ask the lawyer to furnish information to the auditor "only if the client has determined that it is probable that a possible claim will be asserted, that there is a reasonable possibility that the outcome (assuming such assertion) will be unfavorable, and that the resulting liability would be material to the financial condition of the client." Examples of clause c could include: "(i) a catastrophe, accident or other similar physical occurrence in which the client's involvement is open and notorious, or (ii) an investigation by a government agency where enforcement proceedings have been instituted or where the likelihood that they will not be instituted is remote, under circumstances where assertion of one or more private claims for redress would normally be expected, or (iii) a public disclosure by the client acknowledging (and thus focusing attention upon) the existence of one or more probable claims arising out of an event or circumstance."

In all these situations, the lawyers may disclose to the auditors an identification of the proceedings or matter, the stage of proceedings, the claims asserted, and the position taken by the client. However—

"In view of the inherent uncertainties the lawyer should normally refrain from expressing judgments as to outcome except in those relatively few clear cases where it appears to the lawyer that an unfavorable outcome is either 'probable' or 'remote;' for purposes of any such judgment it is appropriate to use the following meanings:

"(i) **probable**—an unfavorable outcome for the client is probable if the prospects of the claimant not succeeding are judged to be extremely doubtful and the prospects for success by the client in its defense are judged to be slight.

"(ii) **remote**—an unfavorable outcome is remote if the prospects for the client not succeeding in its defense are judged to be extremely doubtful and the prospects of success by the claimant are judged to be slight. * * * No inference should be drawn, from the absence of such a judgment, that the client will not prevail.

"The lawyer also may be asked to estimate, in dollar terms, the potential amount of loss or range of loss in the event that an unfavorable outcome is not viewed to be 'remote.' In such a case, the amount or range of potential loss will normally be inherently impossible to ascertain, with any degree of certainty, as the outcome of the litigation. Therefore, it is appropriate for the lawyer to provide an estimate of the amount or range of potential loss (if the outcome should be unfavorable) only if he believes that the probability of inaccuracy of the estimate of the amount or range of potential loss is slight. * * * The lawyer should not be asked, nor need the lawyer undertake, to furnish information to the auditor concerning loss contingencies except as contemplated by this Paragraph 5."

Paragraph (6) provides that the lawyer may not "knowingly" participate in any violation by his client "of the disclosure requirements of the securities laws" and that "[i]ndependent of the scope of his response to the auditor's request for information" the "lawyer also may be required under the Code of Professional Responsibility to resign his engagement if his advice concerning disclosures is disregarded by the client." While the lawyer is under a duty to consult with the client concerning the question of disclosure, there is no requirement that the lawyer inform the auditor.

2. How do these standards apply to Mr. Klose and the Klose Corporation?

a. If the IRS challenges the accounting treatment of the Klose Corporation's salaries, are you required to disclose that to the auditors? Look at Paragraph 5(a) of the Statement of Policy. The challenge would almost certainly constitute "overtly threatened or pending litigation."

b. How would you describe the client's chance of successfully resisting the IRS claim? Do the terms "probable" and "remote" used in the Statement of Policy leave a large range of possibilities as to which neither term accurately applies?

c. Must you disclose, in your letter to the auditor, the possible litigation regarding the product defect? Would the Statement of Policy call that an "unasserted possible claim or assessment"? Would you expect your client to "specifically identify" and request you to comment on that heretofore undiscovered risk?

3. What should a lawyer do if an auditor demands more information than the Statement of Policy contemplates?

a. It is not uncommon in today's environment of multimillion dollar suits against accounting firms for auditors to demand that companies ask their lawyers to disclose more information than the Statement of Policy would authorize.

b. What exposure would your law firm incur trying to respond to a demand for "all actual or potential legal problems that might materially affect the Klose Corporation"? Could you ever respond to that question in a way that would assure you would not be later surprised by a claim that you had not anticipated? Would answering such a question tend to turn your firm into an insurer of the client's financial health?

c. Think back to Problem 8. What will happen to the attorney-client privileged character of information that you turn over to the auditors? Remember that your turn-over may also waive the privilege as to everything related to the subject matter of the information.

d. Should the lawyer resist the auditor's demands? Should the lawyer seek to negotiate a more limited scope of disclosure? Would such an effort imply that the company has something to hide? Needless to say, these are the kinds of concerns that cause Rules 1.4 and 2.3 to require consultation between lawyer and client before the lawyer gives any response to the auditors.

e. Can the state disciplinary authority sanction you for providing inadequate information in response to an auditor's inquiry? The stakes are very high for both lawyer and client. Section 303 of the Sarbanes–Oxley Act of 2002, discussed in Problem 22, makes it unlawful "to fraudulently influence, coerce, manipulate or mislead any independent public or certified accountant" engaged in an audit of most publicly-traded companies. Whether disclosure limited to the ABA/AICPA treaty could violate Section 303 remains an open and potentially very expensive question.

D. LAWYER LIABILITY FOR AN INACCURATE OPINION

1. Mr. Klose wants you to write him a letter that will make him feel good about his decision to raise the salaries of his family members. Might you be liable to your client, the Klose Corporation, for the opinion that Mr. Klose wanted you to render but that turned out to be inaccurate?

a. It is tempting for lawyers to tell their clients what they want to hear. In a world in which clients can fire lawyers at will and a dozen new lawyers stand ready to pursue the client's business, a naive person might assume that lawyers could not behave otherwise. Remember, however, that the lawyer's corporate client is not Mr. Klose; it is the Klose Corporation. If the company should be sold or go into bankruptcy, do you suppose the bankruptcy trustee or the new owner will be impressed that your opinion was solicited by Mr. Klose rather than based on your independent professional judgment?

b. If the law firm did not use reasonable care in rendering an opinion, even one solicited by the client's management, the client will very likely have a malpractice claim against the lawyer. See, e.g., FDIC v. O'Melveny & Myers, 969 F.2d 744 (9th Cir.1992), rev'd on other grounds, 512 U.S. 79 (1994), aff'd on remand, 61 F.3d 17 (9th Cir.1995) (firm held liable for failing to discover that its client was in poor financial health); FDIC v. Clark, 978 F.2d 1541 (10th Cir.1992) (firm failed to discover that bank officers were diverting bank funds to their own use), both discussed in Problem 18.

2. If you write an opinion for your client, knowing that it will give your opinion to the bank, will you be liable to the bank (a non-client) if your report is inaccurate or misleading?

a. Restatement Third, The Law Governing Lawyers § 51(2) makes clear that lawyers may be held liable to a nonclient "when and to the extent that: (a) the lawyer or (with the lawyer's acquiescence) the lawyer's client invites the nonclient to rely on the lawyer's opinion or provision of other legal services, and the nonclient so relies * * *." Numerous cases confirm that basis for lawyer liability.

b. In Greycas, Inc. v. Proud, 826 F.2d 1560 (7th Cir.1987), cert. denied, 484 U.S. 1043 (1988), a borrower sought to raise money from a finance company on the strength of a security interest in certain farm machinery. The lender, Greycas, agreed to put up the money if the borrower would supply the borrower's lawyer's opinion that there were no prior liens on the assets. Lawyer Proud, who was the borrower's brother-in-law, wrote a letter saying that he had "conducted a U.C.C., tax, and judgment search" and that Greycas had the only perfected security interest. In fact, Proud made no such inquiry, the assets were encumbered, and when the borrower defaulted, Greycas was left with no security.

Under these circumstances, the court held, the lawyer was liable to Greycas for the amount of the loan. The lawyer argued that he owed no duty to someone not his client. The court agreed with that general proposition, and indeed called it "an undesirable novelty to hold that every bit of sharp dealing by a lawyer gives rise to prima facie tort liability to the opposing party in the lawsuit or negotiation." 826 F.2d at 1563. The court also assumed that Greycas could not be said to have become Proud's client. However, the court said that Proud supplied information to Greycas knowing that it was to be relied upon by Greycas. Whether the suit was treated as one for negligent misrepresentation or professional malpractice, it stated a cause of action and the lawyer was liable.[7]

c. In Rubin & Cohen v. Schottenstein, Zox & Dunn, 143 F.3d 263 (6th Cir.1998) (en banc), a group of potential investors met with company officials about putting money into the company in exchange for bonds and stock. The officials told the investors to call the company's lawyers for confirmation of the company's financial soundness and its relationship with its bank lender. The lawyers told the investors all was well and that there was no need to call the bank as part of their due diligence. However, the investment constituted a default under the company's financing agreement with the bank, the bank froze all company funds, the company filed for bankruptcy and the investors lost their money. A panel of the Sixth Circuit had held that the lawyers could not be held liable to persons not their clients, but this en banc opinion reversed. It held that, under both the securities laws [Rule 10b–5] and the common law, while a lawyer does not have an "independent duty to volunteer information about the financial condition of the client, he assumes a duty to provide complete and non misleading information with respect to subjects on which he undertakes to speak." 143 F.3d at 268.

d. In Orshoski v. Krieger, 2001 WL 1388037 (Ohio App.2001), a couple built a prefabricated home in violation of a subdivision covenant. Before building, they asked their real estate agent whether their plans would violate the covenant. The real estate agent asked the developer who then asked the lawyer who had drafted the covenant. The lawyer said the house would not be in violation. A court later held the covenant indeed was violated, and the issue became whether a third party, not the client of the lawyer, could recover economic damages resulting from such a negligent misrepresentation. The court held, based on § 552 of the Restatement Third of Torts, that in limited situations a third party may bring suit for

---

7. Accord, Vanguard Production, Inc. v. Martin, 894 F.2d 375 (10th Cir.1990) (title opinion used in selling oil and gas leases); Vereins–Und Westbank, AG v. Carter, 691 F.Supp. 704 (S.D.N.Y.1988) (lawyer's letter to support issuance of surety bond).

negligent misrepresentation against a lawyer (as opposed to an action for legal malpractice). The plaintiff in such an action must show, "that the defendant [attorney] knew that its report or opinion is intended to be used for a particular purpose, that the plaintiff relied on that statement in furtherance of the purpose, that the defendant understands the reliance, that the report of opinion contains a misrepresentation, and the plaintiff suffers damage as a result of reliance on the misrepresentation." In this case, the court found all of these requirements well pleaded and reinstated the complaint.

e. In Vega v. Jones, Day, Reavis & Pogue, 17 Cal.Rptr.3d 26 (Cal.Ct. App.2004), a shareholder in an acquired corporation sued the acquiring corporation's lawyers, Jones Day, for fraud. The acquirer provided a disclosure schedule to the lawyers for the company being sold; the schedule indicated that the $10 million price for the deal would be raised through third-party financing. Both Jones Day and the acquiring corporation knew the financing included "toxic" stock, i.e., restricted stock that seriously dilutes the value of all the company's shares. Plaintiff alleged that Jones Day knew that "toxic" stock financing is a "desperate and last resort of financing for a struggling company," and 95% of companies who engage in such financing end up in bankruptcy. Jones Day prepared the disclosure schedule; it properly characterized the transaction but gave it only to their client; they gave a sanitized version to acquired company's lawyers and it made no mention of "toxic" stock and called the financing "standard." The plaintiff shareholder learned the true nature of the financing eight months after the deal closed and after losing nearly $3.5 million. Jones, Day responded that it had not made affirmative misstatements and had no duty to disclose the terms of the third party investment to an adverse party in the merger transaction. The court held that the complaint stated a fraud claim based on nondisclosure. "The complaint alleged the law firm, while expressly undertaking to disclose the financing transaction, provided disclosure schedules that did not include material terms of the transaction."

The California Court of Appeals agreed that a lawyer ordinarily owes a professional duty of care only to his client and intended beneficiaries of his work, but fraud claims are different: a lawyer may be liable to a nonclient if he knowingly makes false statements of material fact. The fact that Jones, Day filed documents revealing the true nature of the financing across the country in Delaware before the closing was no defense. The court found that in writing the disclosure schedule, telling a "half-truth calculated to deceive" was the equivalent of "active concealment or suppression of facts." A half-truth is a whole lie. Jones Day had a duty not to engage in fraudulent activity, "even if ... negotiating at arm's length," so the court allowed the case to go to trial.

3. Are you likely to be liable to investors if your advice about the likely success of a tax shelter turns out to be erroneous?

a. United States v. Sidley Austin Brown & Wood LLP, 2004 WL 905930 (N.D.Ill.2004), enforced an IRS subpoena requiring the law firm to turn over names of its tax shelter clients. Sidley & Austin allegedly marketed tax shelters that earned them very high fees and also sold opinion letters reassuring the clients that the shelters would work. The IRS believed the schemes were unlawful and ineffective, but without the lists, it could not know who used them.

b. As one indication of what is at stake in such cases, on May 14, 2004, a court gave preliminary approval to a settlement with investors in one such shelter. The amount of the settlement was reported to be $75 million, making it one of the largest malpractice settlements ever reached. See Denney v. Jenkens & Gilchrist, P.C., 340 F.Supp.2d 338 (S.D.N.Y. 2004), for an earlier opinion that explains some of the allegations in the cases.[8]

c. In partial response to cases like these, the IRS has issued standards regarding tax shelter opinions. IRS Circular 230, 31 CFR Part 10 (Dec. 20, 2004), at http://www.irs.gov/pub/irs-utl/circular_230.pdf (published Sept.26, 2007), deals with "covered opinions," i.e., opinions that address transactions or issues that have a significant purpose of avoiding or evading taxes. An opinion then becomes a "reliance opinion" if it expresses more than 50% confidence that the effort to reduce taxes would be resolved in the taxpayer's favor. A "marketed opinion" is one the lawyer knows will be used to sell a plan to one or more taxpayers.

Practitioners must use "reasonable efforts" to identify and ascertain all relevant facts regarding the transactions. They may not rely on facts, assumptions, or statements they know or should know are unreasonable, and each opinion must contain a section that details all factual assumptions, representations, statements, or findings relied upon. Opinions must relate applicable law to the relevant facts in the case and must evaluate all significant federal tax issues, giving reasoned conclusions and the likelihood of success on the merits. If a practitioner cannot reach such a conclusion, the opinion must clearly say the evaluation could not be made.

Any opinion must "prominently disclose[]" any referral or compensation arrangements between the practitioner and any promoter, marketer, or anyone else who referred the matter to the attorney, and practitioners may not give advice "contrary to or inconsistent with the required disclosure." To ensure proper implementation, the IRS requires practitioners to take "reasonable steps" to guarantee their firm has "adequate procedures" in place for associates, employees, and other firm members to comply with new requirements. Practitioners who fail to take such steps or who themselves fail to comply with the rules through willfulness, recklessness, or "gross incompetence" may be censured, suspended, or disbarred from practice before the IRS.

----

8. Largely as a result of this litigation and the settlements it had to pay, the firm of Jenkens & Gilchrist permanently closed its doors in 2007.

PROBLEM 22

OBLIGATIONS WHEN THE CLIENT
MAY BE ENGAGED IN FRAUD

A series of financial collapses at major companies greeted the 21st century. Each of the companies that collapsed had many lawyers, and at first glance, each of the companies engaged in transactions and practices that many people said the lawyers could have prevented. On the other hand, circumstances may not be as they initially appear. To the lawyers, individual steps in the company's decline might have seemed innocent, even mundane. As you work through this problem, ask yourself when a client has crossed the line from risk taking to dishonesty, from brash optimism to fraud. We look at the lawyer's general duty not to assist a client's crime or fraud, and then at the special world of securities lawyers. We also examine special duties that the SEC has imposed on lawyers for publicly traded companies. Finally, we consider analogous issues faced by government employees.

FACTS

International Energy, Inc., a publicly held company listed on the New York Stock Exchange, has done most of its recent financing through bank loans. It is about to sell a new issue of securities. The company, to induce the bank to lend and the public to invest, has written a glowing account of its prospects.

The strength of the company has been based on its reputation for vigorous research, which thus far has resulted in a series of patents for energy-saving devices. The new product, production of which will be financed by the loan, will be another patented device. All of the company reports suggest glowing prospects for its performance. The company's auditors have declared International Energy to be in outstanding financial health. The current draft of your firm's opinion letter indicates no knowledge of material facts inconsistent with that optimism.

You had lunch today with your good friend, the director of research and development at International Energy, Inc. "A great company is in real trouble," he told you. "When our former president retired, a sense of integrity retired as well." Your friend and his scientist colleagues have great concern that the device described in the documents given investors has not been sufficiently tested and that its reliability and performance have been overrated.

In addition, the engineer told you that the production facility for the new product was recently purchased from a shell corporation owned by the company's new president. He said the price paid by the company was outrageously high. The auditors did not catch the problem and thus their audit did not footnote the fact that the purchase was from a corporate officer. As a result, the balance sheet of the corporation looks significantly better than it would if the facility were carried at its true value.

QUESTIONS

A. DISCLOSURE OF A CLIENT'S INTENDED CRIME OR FRAUD

1. Has your lunch given you indigestion? What will you do with the information you now have?

a. May your firm's opinion letter that will accompany the new issue of securities reflect what the director of research and development has told you? Must it do so?

b. How sure are you that what your friend has told you is true? Do you really *know* that the new product is unreliable? Perhaps your friend, the engineer, is simply depressed. Is that possibility enough to let you ignore what he has told you?

c. How will you go about finding out what is really going on at International Energy, Inc.? Will you ask questions in any event as part of your due diligence before completing your opinion letter?

d. What kinds of questions will you now ask? If your client's officers are dishonest, will you be confident they will give you reliable answers? Could you tell the client's auditors the information you have received and rely on them to ask the necessary questions?

2. What is the legal status of what you have learned from the director of research and development? What legal right or obligation do you have to reveal it to others?

a. Is the information protected by the attorney-client privilege? If so, whose privilege would it be? Was the information communicated in confidence? Was it communicated for the purpose of seeking legal advice? Did it involve the client's possible crime or fraud?

b. Does the information "relate to the representation" within the meaning of ABA Model Rule 1.6(a)? Would disclosure of the information to other members of corporate management violate Model Rule 1.6(b)? Does Model Rule 1.13(b) require the disclosure?

c. May you disclose the information to persons or entities outside the corporation? Look at Model Rules 1.6(b)(2) & (3) and 1.13(c).[1] Do any of them permit disclosure outside the corporation in a situation like the one in this problem?

3. Is confidentiality the only relevant issue that you face? What other obligations do you have under the Model Rules that you need to take into account?

---

1. See also, Restatement Third, The Law Governing Lawyers § 67. It was the source for most of the ideas incorporated into Model Rules 1.6(b)(2) & (3).

a. Take a look at ABA Model Rule 1.2(d): "A lawyer shall not counsel a client to engage, or assist a client, in conduct that the lawyer knows is criminal or fraudulent."

b. Model Rule 4.1(b) continues: "In the course of representing a client a lawyer shall not knowingly fail to disclose a material fact when disclosure is necessary to avoid assisting a criminal or fraudulent act by a client, unless disclosure is prohibited by Rule 1.6."

c. Where does this combination of obligations leave you? Remember Model Rule 1.16(a): "[A] lawyer shall not represent a client or, where representation has commenced, shall withdraw from the representation of a client if: (1) the representation will result in violation of the rules of professional conduct or other law."

4. What is the significance of the fact that the information you have relates in part to the security of bank loans the company has already received? Are a lawyer's rights and responsibilities different when dealing with a client's (and perhaps the lawyer's) past statements?

a. Think of the opinions your firm has rendered that have been transmitted to the bank. In them, you have opined that the appropriate corporate resolutions were adopted and powers granted. You may even have opined that you know of no material facts that have been misstated or omitted from the documents that the bank has received. If preparing those opinions was part of your role, what should you do now that you have had your lunch with the chief engineer?

b. ABA Formal Opinion 92–366 (Aug. 8, 1992) assumes that a lawyer for a small manufacturing firm has given an opinion that its client's accounts receivable represent legal obligations of the purchasers of the goods. Later, the lawyer finds that many of the accounts are fictional and that the client is in financial trouble. The opinion says that under Model Rule 1.6, the lawyer must withdraw from all future dealings involving this loan, and may or, in some cases, must disavow the prior opinion. Otherwise, the lawyer would be "assisting" the client to get future extensions of credit. That opinion was written before the 2002 and 2003 revisions to the Model Rules; those revisions eliminated the "notice of withdrawal" provisions of Rule 1.6 and replaced them with the permissive disclosure of Rule 1.6(b).

c. ABA Formal Opinion 92–366 was controversial, and there was a vigorous dissent, but Model Rule 1.2, Comment 10 now provides:

"* * * A lawyer may not continue assisting a client in conduct that the lawyer originally supposed was legally proper but then discovers is criminal or fraudulent. The lawyer must, therefore, withdraw from the representation of the client in the matter. See Rule 1.16(a). In some cases, withdrawal alone might be insufficient. It may be necessary for the lawyer to give notice of the fact of withdrawal and to disaffirm any opinion, document, affirmation or the like. See Rule 4.1."

d.   Suppose, instead, that you gave advice to the company about how to structure the financing transaction but did not render an opinion to any third parties. May you assume that therefore the bank will not rely on anything you did? Does it mean you need do nothing to correct misstatements that you now believe were made?

e.   Is withdrawal the best approach to the situation you face? Even if withdrawal were to get you off the hook, will it help either your corporate client or its past lenders and potential investors?

5.   Should a lawyer have the same duties in a nonfinancial context? Does a lawyer's right or obligation to withdraw or disclose depend on the kind of matter involved and the lawyer's role in the matter?

a.   Suppose your firm is doing work with the Department of Energy (DOE) to get the client's new device approved for sale. Suppose further that if the DOE had the device tested at an independent laboratory it would be likely to find the device unreliable and thus ruin the likelihood of the loan being made. May you argue to DOE officials that it should not require such outside testing?

b.   Look at Model Rule 3.9, "Advocate in Nonadjudicative Proceedings." Does it require representations to the DOE to have the same level of integrity and candor as representations to a court? Does it mean only that you may not help the company invent records of nonexistent outside tests to persuade the DOE to approve the product?

c.   What is the significance of Model Rule 3.9, Comment 3, which says that the Rule does not "apply to the representation of a client in connection with an investigation or examination of the client's affairs"? If the rule does not apply in that setting, to what matters does it apply?

d.   In re American Continental Corp./Lincoln Savings and Loan Securities Litigation, 794 F.Supp. 1424, 1450–52 (D.Ariz.1992), involved a regulatory investigation of a savings and loan association in which the court, refusing to grant summary judgment approving the conduct of the law firm, observed:

> "During the regulatory compliance audit * * * the law firm found multiple regulatory violations. There is evidence that Jones Day knew that Lincoln had backdated files, destroyed appraisals, removed appraisals from files, told appraisers not to issue written reports when their oral valuations were too low, and violated affiliated transaction regulations. * * *

> "There is evidence that Jones Day instructed ACC in how to rectify deficiencies so that they would not be apparent to FHLBB examiners. * * *

> * * *

> "Jones Day contends that it may not be held liable for counseling its client. The line between maintaining a client's confidence and violating the securities law is brighter than Jones Day suggests,

[handwritten margin note: Comment 1. No, unless the engineer is involved]

however. Attorneys must inform a client in a clear and direct manner when its conduct violates the law. If the client continues the objectionable activity, the lawyer must withdraw 'if the representation will result in violation of the rules of professional conduct or other law.' Ethical Rule 1.16. * * * An attorney may not continue to provide services to corporate clients when the attorney knows the client is engaged in a course of conduct designed to deceive others, and where it is obvious that the attorney's compliant legal services may be a substantial factor in permitting the deceit to continue. * * * "

e. ABA Formal Opinion 93–375 (Aug. 6, 1993) was the ABA's reflection on a lawyer's duty to disclose adverse information in the context of a bank examination. The opinion says that while the lawyer may not lie to the examiners, the lawyer is not affirmatively obliged to warn about problems at the bank or otherwise reveal confidential client information. The bank itself may have disclosure obligations, however, and if the lawyer reasonably believes the bank is engaged in fraud, the lawyer *must* take steps to avoid assisting it to do so, including, in some cases, withdrawing from the representation.

B. THE SPECIAL OBLIGATIONS OF A SECURITIES LAWYER

1. What changes when the lawyer represents an issuer of publicly traded securities? What kind of inquiry about the relevant facts must the lawyer make?

a. While he was an SEC commissioner, A.A. Sommer argued:

"[T]he registration statement has always been a lawyer's document and with very, very rare exceptions the attorney has been the field marshal who coordinated the activities of others engaged in the registration process, wrote (or at least rewrote) most of the statement, made the judgments with regard to the inclusion or exclusion of information on the grounds of materiality, compliance with registration form requirements, necessities of avoiding omission of disclosure necessary to make those matters stated not misleading. * * *

"[T]he professional judgment of the attorney is often the 'passkey' to securities transactions. * * * If he judges that certain information must be included in a registration statement, it gets included (unless the client seeks other counsel or the attorney crumbles under the weight of client pressure); if he concludes it need not be included, it doesn't get included. * * *

"I would suggest that in securities matters (other than those where advocacy is clearly proper) the attorney will have to function in a manner more akin to that of the auditor than to that of the advocate. * * * "[2]

---

2. A.A. Sommer, Emerging Responsibilities of the Securities Lawyer, [1973–1974 Transfer Binder] Fed.Sec.L.Rep. ¶ 79,631 (Jan. 1974).

b. Do you agree with Mr. Sommer that—at least as to documents the lawyer bears primary responsibility for preparing for disclosure to third parties—the lawyer should act as an auditor rather than an advocate? Indeed, is that the underlying assumption about opinions issued pursuant to Model Rule 2.3? Should the fact that, unlike in the usual Rule 2.3 opinion situation, the lawyer does not know the individual recipients of disclosure documents make the lawyer less obliged to make complete and accurate disclosure? Should it increase the lawyer's obligation to be thorough and candid?

2. May the securities lawyer accept her client's representations about matters to be disclosed? Must the lawyer independently investigate the client?

a. ABA Formal Opinion 335 (Feb. 2, 1974) addressed that issue in the context of a securities lawyer certifying that the conditions exist in which it is proper to sell unregistered securities. The opinion says:

"It is, of course, important that the lawyer competently and carefully consider what facts are relevant to the giving of the requested opinion and make a reasonable inquiry to obtain such of those facts as are not within his personal knowledge. Depending upon the circumstances, the lawyer may or may not need to go beyond directing questions to his client and checking the answers by reviewing such appropriate documents as are available. * * *

"[T]he lawyer should, in the first instance, make inquiry of his client as to the relevant facts and receive answers. If any of the alleged facts, or the alleged facts taken as a whole, are incomplete in a material respect; or are suspect; or are inconsistent; or either on their face or on the basis of other known facts are open to question, the lawyer should make further inquiry. The extent of this inquiry will depend in each case upon the circumstances; for example, it would be less where the lawyer's past relationship with the client is sufficient to give him a basis for trusting the client's probity than where the client has recently engaged the lawyer, and less where the lawyer's inquiries are answered fully than when there appears a reluctance to disclose information.

"Where the lawyer concludes that further inquiry of a reasonable nature would not give him sufficient confidence as to all the relevant facts, or for any other reason he does not make the appropriate further inquiries, he should refuse to give an opinion. However, assuming that the alleged facts are not incomplete in a material respect, or suspect, or in any way inherently inconsistent, or on their face or on the basis of other known facts open to question, the lawyer may properly assume that the facts as related to him by his client, and checked by him by reviewing such appropriate documents as are available, are accurate. * * *

"If the lawyer has some reason to believe that one or more of the statements of fact furnished him as a basis for the opinion may not be correct, he should make a determination as to whether to refuse to give an opinion or whether to attempt to verify one or more of the relevant facts. * * *

"A properly drafted opinion will recite clearly the sources of the attorney's knowledge of the facts. Where verification is otherwise called for, an attorney should make appropriate verification and should not rely on the use of such phrases as 'based upon the facts as you have given them to me' or 'apart from what you have told me, I have not inquired as to the facts.'

"The essence of this opinion * * * is that, while a lawyer should make adequate preparation including inquiry into the relevant facts that is consistent with the above guidelines, and while he should not accept as true that which he should not reasonably believe to be true, he does not have the responsibility to 'audit' the affairs of his client or to assume, without reasonable cause, that a client's statement of the facts cannot be relied upon."

Does this opinion impose a higher standard on attorneys than do the Model Rules? Does it provide good counsel to *any* attorney asked to sign an opinion?

b.   Describing the lawyer's duties in connection with a related kind of issue—the lawyer's declaration that a promoter's tax shelter is likely to receive favorable treatment by the IRS—ABA Formal Opinion 346 (Jan. 29, 1982) said bluntly:

"The lawyer who accepts as true the facts which the promoter tells him, when the lawyer should know that a further inquiry would disclose that these facts are untrue, * * * gives a false opinion. * * * [L]awyers cannot 'escape criminal liability on a plea of ignorance when they have shut their eyes to what was plainly to be seen.' United States v. Benjamin * * *. Recklessly and consciously disregarding information strongly indicating that material facts expressed in the tax shelter opinion are false or misleading involves dishonesty. * * * We equate the minimum extent of the knowledge required for the lawyer's conduct to have violated these disciplinary rules with the knowledge required to sustain a Rule 10b–5 recovery, see Ernst & Ernst v. Hochfelder, 425 U.S. 185 (1976), rather than the lesser negligence standard.

"But even if the lawyer lacks the knowledge required to sustain a recovery under the *Hochfelder* standard, the lawyer's conduct never-theless may involve gross incompetence, or indifference, inadequate preparation under the circumstances, and consistent failure to perform obligations to the client. If so, the lawyer will have violated DR 6–101(A). ABA Informal Opinion 1273 (1973)."

c.   In SEC v. Frank, 388 F.2d 486 (2d Cir.1968), the defendant, an attorney, appealed from a district court's temporary injunction ordering him to refrain from "drafting or causing to be drafted any offering circular, prospectus or other document or writing containing any untrue statements of material facts, or omissions to state material facts necessary in order to make the statements made in the light of the circumstances under which they were made, not misleading, concerning Nylo–Thane Plastics Corp.'s principal product * * *." 388 F.2d at 487. The court, per Judge Friendly, while reversing and ordering an evidentiary hearing, stated:

> "Although Frank makes much of this being the first instance in which the Commission has obtained an injunction against an attorney for participation in the preparation of an allegedly misleading offering circular or prospectus, we find this unimpressive. As this court said in United States v. Benjamin, 328 F.2d 854, 863 (2 Cir.), cert. denied, 377 U.S. 953 (1964), 'In our complex society the accountant's certificate and the lawyer's opinion can be instruments for inflicting pecuniary loss more potent than the chisel or the crowbar.' A lawyer has no privilege to assist in circulating a statement with regard to securities which he knows to be false simply because his client has furnished it to him. At the other extreme it would be unreasonable to hold a lawyer who was putting his client's description of a chemical process into understandable English to be guilty of fraud simply because of his failure to detect discrepancies between their description and technical reports available to him in a physical sense but beyond his ability to understand. The instant case lies between these extremes. * * * [A] lawyer, no more than others, can escape liability for fraud by closing his eyes to what he saw and could readily understand. Whether the fraud sections of the securities laws go beyond this and require a lawyer passing on an offering circular to run down possible infirmities in his client's story of which he has been put on notice, and if so what efforts are required of him, is a closer question on which it is important that the court be seized of the precise facts, including the extent, as the SEC claimed with respect to Frank, to which his role went beyond a lawyer's normal one * * *." 388 F.2d at 488–89.

d. In United States v. Flores, 454 F.3d 149 (3d Cir.2006), the lawyer (Flores) helped a South American client set up several U.S. corporations and bank accounts through which the client laundered money. Flores was charged with the same offenses, but he described himself as the unwitting victim of his client's acts. In affirming Flores' conviction, the court relied on the idea of "selective blindness." The client initially used false social security numbers, for example, and rejected efforts to get him valid ones. Nevertheless, Flores set himself up as president of the client's companies and signed blank checks for the client to use in a series of financial transactions with no clear business purpose. Flores also met with banks that said the transactions the client engaged in looked so much like money laundering that they closed the accounts. Flores then simply assisted the client to open accounts at new banks at which Flores had contacts. The court rejected the claim that Flores must know the exact source of the funds to be guilty of money laundering. He was willfully blind to the fact that the source was illegal and that was enough to sustain the convictions.

3. Should the SEC have authority to discipline lawyers whose conduct results in inadequate disclosures or other violations of the securities laws?

a. Remember that, up to now, we have largely assumed that lawyers were regulated by the state supreme courts that license them. Normally, a lawyer does not need a license to practice before the SEC. Even if everyone would agree that an SEC administrative law judge may regulate the conduct of lawyers at a hearing, does it follow that the SEC should be able to sanction lawyers who draft registration materials issued by regulated companies?

b. In SEC v. Universal Major Industries Corp., 546 F.2d 1044 (2d Cir.1976), cert. denied, 434 U.S. 834 (1977), the agency pursued a lawyer it believed violated Section 5 of the Securities Act of 1933, 15 U.S.C.A. § 77e, by aiding and abetting his client's selling over three million shares of unregistered stock. The lawyer advised UMI that the stock could be sold as a private offering exempt from registration only under certain conditions. When UMI failed to comply with the conditions, the lawyer instructed the client to register the securities. UMI hired a second lawyer to process the registration, but he never did. Later, the company's stock transfer agent required an opinion letter from the first lawyer stating that various stock transfers were legal. The first lawyer sent a letter stating that he had no opinion, but "I rely on the opinion of [the second lawyer] * * *." He enclosed that opinion that said that because the first sales was illegal, resales would not compound the problem. The opinion was wrong, and the district court rejected the first lawyer's "obvious attempt to avoid a personal commitment in [his own] letters." The district court enjoined the lawyer from "doing business while he is in violation of SEC rules," and the Court of Appeals affirmed.

c. Then, SEC v. National Student Marketing Corp., 457 F.Supp. 682 (D.D.C.1978), sought an injunction against lawyers at Lord, Bissel & Brook and others involved in a merger of National Student Marketing Corp. (NMSC) with Interstate National Corporation and the immediate sale of newly-acquired NSMC stock by former Interstate principals. The court explained:

> "These transactions are alleged to have occurred despite the prior receipt by the defendants of information which revealed that NSMC's interim financial statements, used in securing shareholder approval of the merger and available to the public generally, were grossly inaccurate and failed to show the true condition of the corporation. The information was included in a comfort letter prepared by NSMC's accountants." 457 F.Supp. at 687.

The court concluded that the defendant-attorneys aided and abetted violations of the securities laws by going ahead with the closing in the face of this information. When information is "obvious[ly]" material:

> "the attorneys' responsibilities to their corporate client required them to take steps to ensure that the information should be disclosed to the

shareholders. * * * [A]t the very least, they [the lawyers] were required to speak out at the closing concerning the obvious materiality of the information and the concomitant requirement that the merger not be closed until the adjustments were disclosed and approval of the merger was again obtained from the Interstate shareholders. Their silence was not only a breach of this duty to speak, but in addition lent the appearance of legitimacy to the closing. The combination of these factors clearly provided substantial assistance to the closing of the merger." 457 F.Supp. at 713.

However, in spite of the finding of clear illegality, the court denied the SEC's request for injunctive relief because "the Court is confident that [the defendants] will take appropriate steps to ensure that their professional conduct in the future comports with the law." 457 F.Supp at 717.

d.   Later, In re Carter & Johnson, Exchange Act Release No. 17,597 (1981), involved lawyers who represented a telephone leasing company from 1973 until it went out of business in 1975. During 1974, the company concealed its cash flow problems from the public by drawing down its line of credit. The lawyers knew of the problems, but prepared a press release and materials filed with the SEC that said nothing of the impending end of its access to credit and its need to end business operations. The company's president failed to heed the lawyers' advice to disclose, but the lawyers themselves did not disclose. Rather than sanction the lawyers, however, in a legal environment in which the norms governing securities lawyers had not been "firmly and unambiguously established," the Commission simply announced that in the future—

> "When a lawyer with significant responsibilities in the effectuation of a company's compliance with the disclosure requirements of the federal securities laws becomes aware that his client is engaged in substantial and continuing failure to satisfy those disclosure requirements, his continued participation violates professional standards unless he takes prompt steps to end the client's noncompliance."

e.   The current version of the SEC disciplinary standard is 17 CFR 201.102(e). In part because of a running dispute with the ABA about whether federal agencies may discipline lawyers, for a long time the SEC did not bring any Rule 102(e) complaints against lawyers after *Carter & Johnson*, although In re Gutfreund, Exchange Act Release No. 31 (1992), reiterated the Commission's belief that the duties set out in *Carter & Johnson* remained in force and could even be construed to require disclosure of client misconduct "to [state] regulatory authorities."[3]

---

3. Checkosky & Aldrich v. S.E.C., 139 F.3d 221 (D.C.Cir.1998), involved accountants but dealt with the same "improper professional conduct" provision of SEC Rule 102(e) that applies to lawyers. The decision, which came after earlier SEC efforts to articulate and defend the Rule, held the Commission offered "no clear and coherent standard" for what would constitute a violation of Rule 102(e) and thus dismissed the charges against the defendants.

4. If the client will not disclose what the lawyer believes should be disclosed, is the lawyer limited to withdrawing from the representation? May the lawyer do more?

a.   In Meyerhofer v. Empire Fire & Marine Ins. Co., 497 F.2d 1190 (2d Cir.1974), cert. denied, 419 U.S. 998 (1974), lawyer Goldberg was working on a registration statement and expressed concern to the partners in his firm that the company had failed to disclose adequately certain features of the compensation arrangements between the company and the law firm, as well as other matters. Goldberg insisted on a full and complete disclosure but the partners disagreed, so he resigned from the firm. That same day he appeared before the SEC and gave it the relevant information on the nondisclosure.

Later, another law firm sued on behalf of the purchasers of the common stock alleging that the registration statement and prospectus were materially false and misleading. One of the named defendants was Goldberg. After consulting his own attorney and a special counsel to the SEC's Division of Enforcement, Goldberg, in an attempt to avoid the charges, gave the plaintiffs' firm a copy of the affidavit with exhibits that he had earlier given to the SEC. The other defendants, relying on Canons 4 and 9, moved to disqualify the plaintiffs' lawyers and to enjoin Goldberg from disclosing any confidential information.

The district court granted the motions but the Second Circuit reversed.

> "There is no proof—not even a suggestion—that Goldberg had revealed any information, confidential or otherwise, that might have caused the instigation of the suit. To the contrary, it was not until after the suit was commenced that Goldberg learned that he was in jeopardy. * * * The cost in money of simply defending such an action might be very substantial. The damage to his professional reputation which might be occasioned by the mere pendency of such a charge was an even greater cause for concern. Under these circumstances Goldberg had the right to make appropriate disclosure with respect to his role in the public offering [citing DR 4–101(C)(4)]." 139 F.2d at 1194–95.

b.   Do you agree that Model Rule 1.6 would permit disclosure in a case like *Meyerhofer* today? Look at Model Rule 1.6(b)(5).

C.   Specific ABA and SEC responses to a series of corporate failures

1.   Should the SEC and other federal agencies be obliged to adopt requirements that are congruent with those in the Model Rules? Why should the desire to protect the public against securities fraud require different ethical standards for lawyers than the desire to protect the public against any other crime or fraud?

a.   Whatever the theoretical answers to those questions, the collapse of Enron and the accounting "corrections" at WorldCom and other high-profile companies led Congress to adopt the Sarbanes–Oxley Act of 2002, Pub. L. 107–204. Section 307 of that act required the SEC to:

"establish rules, in the public interest, setting forth minimum standards of professional conduct for attorneys appearing and practicing before the Commission in any way in the representation of public companies, including a rule requiring an attorney to report evidence of a material violation of securities law or breach of fiduciary duty or similar violation by the company or any agent thereof to the chief legal counsel or the chief executive officer of the company (or the equivalent thereof), and if the counsel or officer does not appropriately respond to the evidence (adopting, as necessary, appropriate remedial measures or sanctions with respect to the violation), requiring the attorney to report the evidence to the audit committee of the board of directors or to another committee of the board of directors comprised solely of directors not employed directly or indirectly by the company, or to the board of directors."

b. On January 29, 2003, the SEC issued the Final Rule mandated by Section 307. It is 17 CFR Part 205, found in the Standards Supplement to this book.

2. How do the SEC regulations define when a lawyer has a duty to act?

a. The SEC regulations apply to lawyers "appearing and practicing before the Commission," which the SEC defines to include anyone "providing advice * * * regarding any document that the attorney has notice will be filed with * * the Commission" or even providing advice that information need not be filed with the Commission. 17 CFR §§ 205.2(a). Does this definition only reach lawyers who would self-identify as securities lawyers?

b. The attorney's duty to act is triggered when he or she "becomes aware" of "evidence" of a client's "material violation" of federal or state securities law, a material breach of fiduciary duty by an officer or agent of the client, or a "similar" violation of any other federal or state law. 17 CFR §§ 205.2(i). Is that the same class of cases as to which action is required by Model Rule 1.13(b)? Is the class larger or smaller than Model Rule 1.13(b) requires?

c. The "evidence" required is "credible evidence, based upon which it would be unreasonable, under the circumstances, for a prudent and competent attorney not to conclude that it is reasonably likely that a material violation has occurred, is ongoing, or is about to occur." 17 CFR §§ 205.2(e). Why does the definition use a double negative? Is that formulation likely to broaden or narrow the number of reports required?

3. If the lawyer must act at all, what must the lawyer do?

a. The attorney who becomes aware of "evidence of a material violation" must "report such evidence to the [client's] chief legal officer" (CLO). If you are a "subordinate attorney," i.e., one who works "under the supervision or direction of another attorney," it is sufficient to report the evidence to your superior. It then becomes the supervisor's responsibility to report the information to the client's CLO. 17 CFR §§ 205.3(b)(1), 205.4 & 205.5.

b. Upon getting the report, the CLO must "cause such inquiry into the evidence of a material violation as he or she reasonably believes is appropriate to determine" whether there has been or will be such a violation. Whether the CLO concludes that no such violation has or will occur, or concludes that the reporting attorney was right and takes steps to correct the violation, the CLO must report the conclusion back to the reporting attorney "and advise the reporting attorney of the basis for such determination." 17 CFR § 205.3(b)(2).

c. Unless the reporting attorney "reasonably believes" that the [CLO] has provided an appropriate response within a reasonable time, the attorney must report the evidence of a material violation to the "audit committee of the [client's] board of directors," a different committee composed solely of independent directors, or the full board of directors. 17 CFR § 205.3(b)(3).

d. Alternatively, if the client has established a qualified legal compliance committee (QLCC) composed solely of independent directors and given authority to investigate and report to the full board about evidence of the client's possible material violations of the law, the attorney may make the initial report directly to that QLCC and have no further obligation to evaluate what they do to investigate or correct the situation. 17 CFR § 205.3(c).

e. Is this process clear and logical? How, if at all, does it differ from the procedure contemplated in Model Rule 1.13(b)? Which approach do you prefer to protect the corporate client? Have the Sarbanes–Oxley regulations increased the level of protection for corporate clients? Have they instead primarily created inflexible procedures that may increase costs for clients but provide little more protection?[4]

f. Van Asdale v. International Game Technology, 577 F.3d 989 (9th Cir. 2009), involved a married couple who worked as in-house intellectual property lawyers for a casino gaming machine manufacturer. They sued and alleged retaliatory discharge under the Sarbanes–Oxley Act. The court held that state ethics rules cannot bar lawyers from bringing a whistleblower claim under the Sarbanes–Oxley Act. In enacting Sarbanes–Oxley, Congress expected that lawyers would play a role in uncovering fraud. The company argued that the couple would use attorney-client privileged information in their lawsuit. However, the trial court has many equitable measures at its disposal "to minimize the possibility of harmful disclosures" without dismissing the suit. The court then concluded that the couple established a prima facie case and remanded for further proceedings.

4. When, if ever, should the law *require* a lawyer to disclose the wrongdoing to persons or agencies outside the client organization?

---

4. These issues are explored in Thomas D. Morgan, Sarbanes–Oxley: A Complication, Not a Contribution in the Effort to Improve Corporate Lawyers' Professional Conduct, 17 Georgetown J. Legal Ethics 1 (2003).

a.   A draft report of the ABA Task Force that ultimately produced the 2003 changes in Model Rules 1.6 and 1.13 proposed making disclosure outside the corporation, not just permitted, but mandatory—

"in order to prevent client conduct known to the lawyer to involve a crime, including violations of federal securities laws and regulations, in furtherance of which the client has used or is using the lawyer's services, and which is reasonably certain to result in substantial injury to the financial interests or property of another."

b.   Would you favor that requirement? Is it better that disclosure is discretionary, provided that if the discretion is exercised unreasonably the lawyer may be subject to discipline? Would it be best to say that, whether or not the lawyer discloses, the lawyer should not be able to be second-guessed?

c.   At the same time it published the regulations that the Sarbanes–Oxley Act required, the SEC issued a proposed rule that would provide that, if the response from the CLO is insufficient or not received within a reasonable time, the lawyer must withdraw from the representation and inform the SEC of that action. Under one alternative, the rule would require the client, not the lawyer, to notify the SEC of the lawyer's action.[5] The report would then presumably trigger an SEC investigation and would likely be disclosed to the securities markets.

d.   Would this obligation give lawyers leverage with which to require clients to do what the lawyers believe they should do? If lawyers were required to withdraw and report that withdrawal to the SEC, do you suppose most clients would change their conduct so as to avoid reaching that point?

5.   Should you be liable to investors in an offering of securities if your investigation is inadequate or if you fail to prevent fraudulent conduct by your client?

a.   Central Bank of Denver, N.A. v. First Interstate Bank of Denver, N.A., 511 U.S. 164 (1994), is the leading securities case limiting lawyers' financial exposure under § 10(b) of the Securities Exchange Act of 1934. In 1986, the city issued municipal bonds to finance public improvements related to a residential and commercial project near Colorado Springs. The bonds required that the appraised value of the land exceed 160% of the amount of the bonds. Central Bank, the indenture trustee, delayed getting an independent 1988 appraisal, allegedly because it might show land values had been declining. When the bonds went into default, plaintiff-investors sued the issuer and underwriter claiming that they were primarily liable under § 10(b), and that Central Bank was secondarily liable for aiding and abetting the violation. The Supreme Court held that there is no "aiding and abetting" liability under § 10(b). Before this decision, many securities

---

5.   Release No. 33–8186 (Jan. 29, 2003), proposing addition of a 17 CFR § 205.3(d). Because of the personal hardship of withdrawal on a lawyer who works as inside counsel, the proposed rule would require inside counsel to tell the CLO that the response was insufficient, but it would not require inside counsel to resign from the company.

plaintiffs sued lawyers, accountants, and other professionals under an "aiding and abetting" theory. Does this rule give lawyers more protection than they deserve?

b. In re Enron Corp. Securities, Derivative & ERISA Litigation, 235 F.Supp.2d 549 (S.D.Tex.2002), held that "professionals, including lawyers and accountants, when they take the affirmative step of speaking out, whether individually or as essentially an author or co-author in a statement or report, whether identified or not, about their client's financial condition, do have a duty to third parties not in privity not to knowingly or with severe recklessness issue materially misleading statements on which they intend or have reason to expect that those third parties will rely." 235 F.Supp.2d at 610. The court worried, however, about "opening the professional liability floodgates to any and every potential investor or foreseeable user of the allegedly misleading information who might obtain and rely on the statement." Thus, the court limited the class of plaintiffs to persons "the attorneys or accountants allegedly intended, or might reasonably have expected, to rely on their material misrepresentations." 235 F.Supp.2d at 610–11.

In considering potential liability of the Vinson & Elkins law firm, the court found that the pending "complaint goes into great detail to demonstrate that Vinson & Elkins did not remain silent, but chose not once, but frequently, to make statements to the public about Enron's business and financial situation. * * * Moreover in light of its alleged voluntary, essential, material, and deep involvement as a primary violator in the ongoing Ponzi scheme, Vinson & Elkins was not merely a drafter, but essentially a co-author of the documents it created for public consumption concealing its own and other participants' actions." 235 F.Supp.2d at 705.[6]

c. The Supreme Court revisited these issues in Stoneridge Investment Partners v. Scientific–Atlanta, Inc., 552 U.S. 148 (2008). Investors in Charter Communications, Inc., filed suit against vendors and customers that had entered into sham or mislabeled transactions with Charter. Those transactions allowed Charter to issue financial statements showing its condition to be much better than it really was. The Court held (5 to 3) that the allegations against the vendors and customers were charges of aiding and abetting and thus not actionable under *Central Bank*. The vendors and customers dealt with Charter "in the marketplace for goods and services, not in the investment sphere," so they could not be held liable as primary

---

6. The National Law Journal, June 5, 2006, p. 3, col. 1, reported that Vinson & Elkins agreed to pay $30 million in settlement of claims against it arising out of its representation of Enron, although the firm continues to maintain that it did nothing wrong. Later, in In re Enron Corporation Securities, Derivative and "ERISA" Litigation, 2007 WL 209923 (S.D.Tex.2007), Judge Harmon approved the dismissal of class action plaintiffs' claims against Vinson & Elkins and the Enron directors. The opinion acknowledges: "Defendants have argued that by dismissing those most directly responsible for Enron's business and instead pursuing secondary-actor banks, Lead Plaintiff is 'taking the Enron out of Enron.'" But the court based its decision on the Lead Plaintiff's statement that the dismissal was "based on [V & E's] relative financial status, not on the merits of the claims against them," and the fact that, at least in theory, class members could pursue individual claims against the lawyers and directors.

actors under § 10(b). Congress had the chance to reverse *Central Bank*, the Court said, and it expressly did not do so.

d.   Pacific Inv. Mgmt. Co. v. Mayer Brown LLP, 603 F.3d 144 (2d Cir. 2010), held that secondary actors (such as lawyers) are not liable for false statements in securities offerings in private actions brought under § 10(b) of the Securities Exchange Act, unless the secondary actor made the statement. The Offering Memorandum and the IPO Registration Statement noted that Mayer Brown represented Refco in connection with those transactions, but none "of the documents specifically attribute any of th[is] information" to the law firm or individual lawyer. The defendants in the case were the primary outside counsel to the now-bankrupt brokerage firm Refco Inc. In the late 1990s customers of Refco were unable to pay back millions of dollars worth of margin loans that Refco extended to them. Refco, with the assistance of the law firm, engaged in a series of sham loan transactions to hide the losses suffered by the company. Later, the law firm allegedly helped to draft bond and initial public offering statements for Refco that contained false or misleading statements concerning Refco's financial condition. The plaintiffs purchased securities from Refco. They sued the defendants for violations of securities laws concerning the fraudulent statements, under § 10(b) and § 20(a) of the Securities Exchange Act and SEC Rule 10b–5. The district court dismissed for failure to state a claim, and the plaintiffs appealed.

Relying on *Stoneridge Investment Partners*, the court affirmed. The plaintiffs, along with the SEC as *amicus curiae*, urged the court to adopt a "creator standard" that would make a party liable if either "he or she creates a false or misleading statement or allows a false statement to be attributed to him or her." The court rejected that. Plaintiffs must meet an "attribution" test in order for a secondary actor to be primarily liable for private damages under § 10(b) and Rule 10b–5. But "secondary actors can be liable in a private action under Rule 10b–5 for only those statements that are explicitly attributed to them. The mere identification of a secondary actor as being involved in a transaction, or the public's understanding that a secondary actor 'is at work behind the scenes' are alone insufficient." 603 F.3d at 155. Attribution is necessary to satisfy the reliance element of a private damages action under Rule 10b–5 under *Stoneridge*. Otherwise, the secondary actor would simply be aiding and abetting the fraud for which there is not a private cause of action under § 10(b) and Rule 10b–5.

e.   However, even if the lawyers are not liable under federal law, they may be liable under state law. In Mehaffy, Rider, Windholz & Wilson v. Central Bank Denver, N.A., 892 P.2d 230 (Colo.1995), a lawsuit challenged the validity of bonds that the town development authority had issued. The lawsuit made Central Bank unwilling to buy the bonds unless a lawyer's opinion concluded that the lawsuit had no merit. Therefore, the law firm, on behalf of the authority, issued that opinion to induce potential purchasers to buy the bonds. Ultimately, the court found the lawsuit was meritorious, and the bonds went into default. The case makes clear that a lawyer who renders an opinion that the lawyer knows will be used to induce a nonclient to purchase bonds is liable to those nonclients for any negligent, material misstatements of fact. However, the court said, the lawyer would not be liable to nonclients for legal malpractice.

D.   SPECIAL ISSUES OF DISCLOSURE BY A GOVERNMENT LAWYER

1.   Are the issues of "whistleblowing" by a government lawyer comparable to those we see in a corporate context?

a.   Should the client of a government lawyer be said to be the "public"? Would that mean that a government lawyer has no enforceable duty of confidentiality comparable to that owed to a private client? Does Model Rule 1.6 give any indication that it does not protect confidential information of government agency clients?

b.   Further, lest there be any doubt, Restatement Third, The Law Governing Lawyers § 74 provides: "Unless applicable law otherwise provides, the attorney-client privilege extends to a communication of a governmental organization * * *."

c.   Are government agencies "organization" clients? Look at Rule 1.13, Comment 9. Do you agree that "a different balance may be appropriate between maintaining confidentiality and assuring that the wrongful act is prevented or rectified, for public business is involved"?

2.   To whom should the government lawyer turn with information about what he or she believe is improper behavior in government?

a.   Crandon v. State, 897 P.2d 92 (Kan.1995), cert. denied, 516 U.S. 1113 (1996), upheld a state agency firing its general counsel. The general counsel reported to the Federal Deposit Insurance Corporation that she believed that the deputy commissioner of the state banking commission had received loans from banks she regulated. If true, that would violate both state and federal law. However, the general counsel did not take her concerns to the state banking commissioner, because she thought that he knew of the issue from other sources and believed there was no violation. In fact, the commissioner only learned from the FDIC about the general counsel's reports of illegality. The court ruled that the agency dismissed the general counsel, an "at will" employee, because she had gone behind the commissioner's back. "[A]lthough plaintiff may have acted in utmost good faith, she used poor judgment and did not take steps available to her that a reasonably prudent attorney would have taken prior to reporting" her concerns outside the agency. 897 P.2d at 103.

b.   Consider In re Conduct of Lackey, 37 P.3d 172 (Or.2002). Respondent (Lackey) worked as the full-time judge advocate for the Oregon National Guard. In 1991, Lackey objected that the appointment of his new superior was illegal because that appointee was only a reservist. Lackey refused to follow that reservist's orders and complained about the "illegal" appointment to senior officers and oversight committees. A later investigation determined that Lackey's position was technically correct, but it still recommended his termination as full-time judge advocate. An arrangement was reached whereby Lackey resigned and kept his retirement rights. Shortly thereafter, Lackey disclosed to local reporters that a recent internal audit revealed that senior Oregon National Guardsmen had erroneously received over $38,000 in overpayments. In connection with that overpayment, Lackey recommended that certain officers be sanctioned for negligence, but Lackey's superiors decided to impose a less severe sanction. Lackey argued that a public policy exception to Rule 1.6 allowed lawyers to expose illegal actions by public officials. The Oregon Supreme Court found that Lackey's leak to the news media about the audit and a second personnel matter revealed client confidences and secrets and was primarily an act of revenge, so it suspended Lackey for one year.

c.   Do you agree with the results in these cases? Do they make going through channels more important than reaching the right result? Do they illustrate that whistleblowing may have complex motives? Can you come up with an approach that would protect legitimate concerns about confidentiality of government information without inhibiting appropriate disclosure of wrongdoing by government officials?

CHAPTER VI

ETHICAL PROBLEMS IN LITIGATION

The classic role of the lawyer is to act as an advocate. Our legal system embraces the model of an impartial judge presiding over two parties represented by lawyers who present their clients' cases to the judge and jury. Canon 7 of the 1969 Model Code imposed upon all lawyers a duty of zealous representation within the bounds of the law. The Model Rules no longer use the term "zeal" within any rule, but the preamble does note that: "As advocate, a lawyer zealously asserts the client's position under the rules of the adversary system."

Civil and criminal litigation present dramatic problems of legal ethics that have attracted a great deal of public attention. The lawyers who face these issues do not always think of themselves as litigators. Because the issues that any lawyer confronts ultimately may be resolved in a courtroom, a lawyer may face many problems presented in this chapter no matter what the nature of her practice. As you think about these problems, ask yourself such questions as:

a. How far may an attorney go to suppress the truth in representing a client in litigation? How far *must* he or she go? For example, may or must the lawyer refrain from disclosing relevant information to the trier of fact? May or must she allow her client to offer perjured testimony to further the client's interest?

b. To what extent may or must a lawyer adopt the client's values and objectives? Is the lawyer solely the client's advocate and never a judge of the client's position?

c. How is the role of the lawyer as litigator different from the role of the lawyer as counselor? May a lawyer defend what she could not recommend?

Remember as well that the reputation of a lawyer is his or her most important asset. A litigator may appear before the same judge or agency with some frequency. If hindsight shows that she was too clever by half in one case, she may develop a reputation that will haunt her and her clients in other cases. The extent to which a lawyer should take into consideration the effect on her future clients of the way she represents the present client is a recurring issue of professional responsibility.

PROBLEM 23

THE DECISION TO FILE A CIVIL SUIT

It may seem that the decision to file a civil suit is an easy one. Your client feels wronged and knows that the courts are available to vindicate him. A moment's reflection, however, suggests how simplistic that view is. Litigation is expensive; although one side may prevail on paper, there may be no real winner. Sometimes, parties may use litigation as a tactic, perhaps a delaying tactic, rather than an instrument for reaching a particular result. This problem looks first at the minimum standards governing the filing of a civil action. Next, it examines the tactical use of litigation as an instrument of delay. It then considers a possible obligation to counsel the client about alternative forms of dispute resolution, and finally, it asks what the sanctions might be for abusive use of the litigation process.

FACTS

Your client is a producer of a large assortment of California wines. Many of its wines do not "travel well" from California to their destination and have a short bottle life. In order to enable the wines to travel better and maintain their quality for a longer period of time, your client uses a unique process that places a small amount of a chemical substance into each bottle. Recent testing of that substance suggests that when large amounts of the substance are consumed by rats, a statistically significant number of rats contract cancer of the throat. Assume that under an applicable provision of the Food and Drug Act, if the Food and Drug Administration (FDA) determines that any substance consumed in any amount by man or animal causes cancer, the FDA must ban the substance.

Some reputable scientists fully support the very conservative approach taken by the Food and Drug Act; others do not. Your client tells you that it is imperative that the FDA delay banning his wines, because he believes he would likely go bankrupt if he could not sell the thousands of cases he has already shipped out. The food and drug laws do not provide for any compensation for your client, and the chances of Congress passing a private bill for your client are remote. Moreover, he tells you that the shelf life of his wine is only six months (that is, within six months, over 95% of the wine he has shipped will have been sold to consumers by the liquor stores and removed from the shelves). The new wines that he is producing will not contain substances that have been found to be carcinogenic.

You plan to file suit attacking the factual basis for the FDA order in this case and the constitutionality of the Food and Drug Act provision. You know that court dockets are so crowded that such a suit is likely to delay the effectiveness of the FDA's order banning the wines. Several years ago, however, your circuit upheld the law against just such a constitutional attack.

QUESTIONS

A. ETHICAL STANDARDS GOVERNING THE FILING OF A CIVIL ACTION

1.   Do the Model Rules tell you whether or not you may file suit in this case? Is the fact that the delay obtained by such a suit might serve to save the client from bankruptcy the only relevant concern?

a.   Look at Model Rule 3.1. Is there any proposition of law that cannot be the subject of a good faith proposal for at least a change in the law?

b.   In re Capoccia, 709 N.Y.S.2d 640 (N.Y.App.Div.2000) (per curiam), involved a lawyer who represented debtors in consumer collection cases. The lawyer had assembled a list of defenses and counterclaims that courts in over 70 prior cases had uniformly rejected, but the lawyer continued to assert them anyway. "A common finding in many of these decisions sanctioning or warning respondent was that he had intentionally engaged in a course of conduct whereby he barraged the court system with meritless and 'canned' defenses and counterclaims as a tactic to force settlements," the court said. The court found, first, that the determinations of courts in prior actions that the lawyer had engaged in frivolous conduct had a collateral estoppel effect, and second, that the lawyer's conduct violated various disciplinary rules, including "knowingly advancing a claim or defense that is unwarranted under existing law which could not be supported by a good-faith argument for an extension, modification or reversal of existing law."

Does *Cappocia* confirm for you that Model Rule 3.1 has teeth? Does it suggest instead that it takes so much to violate the rule that it is not a significant deterrent to frivolous law suits?

c.   Why should anyone care that a lawyer files frivolous litigation? Is the burden imposed on the court to consider and reject the frivolous claim a complete justification for the prohibition? Does the cost of defense involuntarily imposed on the defendant provide a sufficient explanation? Is frivolous litigation a form of economic mugging? See Restatement Third, The Law Governing Lawyers § 110 (frivolous advocacy).

d.   Then why shouldn't the law prohibit even some nonfrivolous filings? Why should a lawyer be permitted to file a claim that has been rejected in another case by the court before which the new case will be heard? Is the answer that if one could not file suit seeking legal change, there never would have been a *Brown v. Board of Education*?

2.   What other rules might impose discipline for the filing of frivolous litigation?

a.   In federal court, Rule 11 of the Federal Rules of Civil Procedure has a much greater impact on the filing of civil actions than does Model Rule 3.1. Many states have adopted a similar rule to govern state proceedings.

b.   Rule 11, as amended in 1993, is not a traditional standard of professional discipline because courts enforce it in the course of litigation, while disciplinary authorities enforce their state versions of Model Rule 3.1. Federal Rule 11 certainly offers the most important practical sanction if a lawyer fails to verify the factual basis of a representation made to a federal court. Rule 11 provides:

Rule 11. Signing of Pleadings, Motions, and Other Papers; Representations to Court; Sanctions

(a) Signature. Every pleading, written motion, and other paper shall be signed by at least one attorney of record in the attorney's individual name, or, if the party is not represented by an attorney, shall be signed by the party. * * *

(b) Representations to Court. By presenting to the court (whether by signing, filing, submitting, or later advocating) a pleading, written motion or other paper, an attorney or unrepresented party is certifying that to the best of the person's knowledge, information, and belief, formed after an inquiry reasonable under the circumstances,—

(1) it is not being presented for any improper purpose, such as to harass or to cause unnecessary delay or needless increase in the cost of litigation;

(2) the claims, defenses, and other legal contentions therein are warranted by existing law or by a nonfrivolous argument for the extension, modification, or reversal of existing law or the establishment of new law;

(3) the allegations and other factual contentions have evidentiary support or, if specifically so identified, are likely to have evidentiary support after a reasonable opportunity for further investigation or discovery; and

(4) the denials of factual contentions are warranted on the evidence or, if specifically so identified, are reasonably based on a lack of information or belief.

(c) Sanctions. If, after notice and a reasonable opportunity to respond, the court determines that subdivision (b) has been violated, the court may, subject to the conditions stated below, impose an appropriate sanction upon the attorneys, law firms, or parties that have violated subdivision (b) or are responsible for the violation.

(1) How Initiated.

(A) By Motion. A motion for sanctions under this rule * * * shall not be filed with or presented to the court unless, within 21 days after service of the motion * * *, the challenged paper, claim, defense, contention, allegation, or denial is not withdrawn or appropriately corrected. If warranted, the court may award to the party prevailing on the motion the reasonable expenses and attorney's fees incurred in presenting or opposing the motion. Absent exceptional circumstances, a law firm shall be held jointly responsible for violations committed by its partners, associates, and employees.

(B) On Court's Initiative. On its own initiative, the court may enter an order describing the specific conduct that appears to violate subdivision (b) and directing an attorney, law firm, or party to show cause why it has not violated subdivision (b) with respect thereto.

(2) Nature of sanction: Limitations. A sanction imposed for violation of this rule shall be limited to what is sufficient to deter repetition of such conduct or comparable conduct by others similarly situated. Subject to the limitations in subparagraphs (A) and (B), the sanction may consist of, or include, directives of a nonmonetary nature, an order to pay a penalty into court, or, if imposed on motion and warranted for effective deterrence, an order directing payment to the movant of some or all of the reasonable attorneys' fees and other expenses incurred as a direct result of the violation.[1]

c. Before its amendment in 1993, Rule 11 had a Procrustean quality that neither gave lawyers a chance to correct a pleading prior to sanctions being imposed nor gave the trial court discretion to reject sanctions. Cross & Cross Props., Ltd. v. Everett Allied Co., 886 F.2d 497 (2d Cir.1989), for example, imposed Rule 11 sanctions for a single improper count in a complaint, although all other counts in the complaint were well pleaded. Cooter & Gell v. Hartmarx Corp., 496 U.S. 384 (1990), imposed sanctions even though the plaintiff had withdrawn the offending complaint.

d. Some lawyers report that judges suggest or threaten them with Rule 11 sanctions as a way to affect conduct without creating an appealable issue. For example, the judge might say, with respect to a motion, "If I rule against you, I may decide to impose Rule 11 sanctions." The lawyer then may withdraw the motion. There is no appeal because judge decided

---

1. Consider also, 28 U.S.C.A. § 1927, which provides:

"Any attorney or other person * * * who so multiplies the proceedings in any case unreasonably and vexatiously may be required by the court to satisfy personally the excess costs, expenses, and attorneys' fees reasonably incurred because of such conduct."

California Bar Formal Opinion 1997–151 (July 1997), considered whether a motion for sanctions filed against both lawyer and client created a conflict of interest between them. The opinion says that a conflict clearly is presented if they plan to file different answers to the charges, i.e., blame each other for the misconduct. Ordinarily, however, the lawyer will defend the client and herself without a problem. Who pays sanctions, in turn, should be addressed in the retainer agreement and applied accordingly unless the court orders one or the other to bear them alone.

nothing, but he affected the proceeding in a way that the appeals process cannot alter. Is that fair? Is it a good way for judges to manage unruly lawyers?

3.   Does the current version of Rule 11 appropriately balance the interests of forcing lawyers to do their homework before they file a document against the danger of turning sanctions issues into collateral litigation that ultimately delays justice in the case?

a.   Examine the language of Rule 11(b). A lawyer is required to certify to four aspects of each filing after an "inquiry reasonable under the circumstances." This language imposes upon a lawyer a duty to investigate before filing a complaint, answer, or other motion with the court. It may be reasonable to require a lawyer to investigate the law so as not to file a frivolous legal claim, but is it always equally easy to investigate the facts? Suppose that the statute of limitations is about to expire in two days. What steps should a lawyer take before filing the case with the tribunal? What is the lawyer to do when the information is possessed by the adversary? Does this rule unfairly punish plaintiffs' lawyers?

b.   In re Keegan Mgmt. Co., Securities Litigation, 78 F.3d 431 (9th Cir.1996), the plaintiffs alleged that sellers of Nutri/System weight loss centers had not disclosed gall bladder problems that the system could cause. Ultimately, the district court found insufficient connection between weight loss and gall bladder damage and granted summary judgment for the defendant. At the same time, on its own motion, the court imposed Rule 11 sanctions on the plaintiff's lawyers for failure to do adequate inquiry into the facts. In evaluating the lawyers' conduct, the district court considered only what they knew when they filed their complaint, not the confirming evidence learned afterwards. The Ninth Circuit reversed and said that, if the facts turn out to be nonfrivolous, there is no Rule 11 violation, regardless of the quality of the lawyer's original investigation. It held that a court cannot sanction a lawyer for filing a well-founded complaint solely because of the lawyer's failure to conduct a reasonable inquiry.

c.   Whitehead v. Food Max of Mississippi, Inc., 332 F.3d 796 (5th Cir.2003) (en banc), affirmed a Rule 11 sanction for attorney Minor's behavior in trying to execute a judgment against Kmart. After getting a $3.4 million judgment, Minor invited the media to accompany him to a local Kmart store where he attempted to execute the judgment by seizing currency in the cash registers and vault. News reports about the execution of the writ included "Minor's extremely hyperbolic, intemperate, and misleading comments." 332 F.3d at 800. The Fifth Circuit upheld sanctions because Minor violated Rule 11(b)(1) ("improper purpose" in obtaining writ of execution). His improper purposes in obtaining the writ were "to embarrass Kmart and advance his personal position." 332 F.3d at 808.[2]

---

2. In Cunningham v. Hamilton County, Ohio, 527 U.S. 198 (1999), the Court unanimously held that an order imposing sanctions on a lawyer for discovery abuse pursuant to the Federal Rule of Civil Procedure is not a "final" decision and not immediately appeal-

d. U.S. Bank Nat'l Ass'n v. Sullivan–Moore, 406 F.3d 465 (7th Cir. 2005), is yet another warning that courts will not take sloppy practice lightly. The Fisher & Fisher law firm, acting on behalf of U.S. Bank National Association in a mortgage foreclosure case, sent notification to the wrong address, obtained a default order and a judgment of foreclosure, and then purchased the wrong property. Although one set of attorneys knew or should have known of the error, a second set of Fisher & Fisher attorneys moved for an order approving the sale and an order for possession. Ultimately, Sullivan–Moore was evicted. It was at the hearing on the motion for a renewed order of possession that the district court learned that the Fisher & Fisher attorneys had never served Sullivan–Moore. The court held that, while the initial mistake as to Sullivan–Moore's address "was an honest one," the firm's actions after it learned of the mistake were sanctionable. It ordered the firm to pay Sullivan–Moore's lawyers' expenses, and it required all Fisher & Fisher lawyers to attend a 16–hour course in civil procedure. On appeal, Seventh Circuit found no abuse of discretion. The firm claimed the second set of attorneys did not know of the error, to which the court responded "an empty head but a pure heart is no defense." The Seventh Circuit noted that the trial court has wide latitude to determine what sanctions should be imposed and may, when appropriate, impose non-monetary sanctions to deter repetition of an offense. The court held that the requirement to view or attend a 16–hour course in civil procedure was neither excessive nor overly burdensome.[3]

e. The Private Securities Litigation Reform Act, 15 U.S.C.A. § 78u–4(c)(1), requires that district judges in securities fraud cases make "specific findings regarding compliance by each party and each attorney * * * with each requirement of Rule 11(b) of the Federal Rules of Civil Procedure as to any complaint, responsive pleading, or dispositive motion." Ledford v. Peeples, 605 F.3d 871, 919 (11th Cir.2010). The court in Ledford details how district judges are to comply with the statute by examining every party's legal and factual claims alleged in the litigation. If a Rule 11 violation is found, the court must impose sanctions on the offending attorneys, law firms, or parties.

4. Are the same answers about what is frivolous appropriate when one is selecting issues to raise on appeal? Should it matter whether the appeal involves a criminal conviction instead of a verdict in a civil case?

able under either the final judgment rule or the collateral order doctrine, even if the court has disqualified the lawyer from representing the party in the case. The Court noted that if an immediate appeal were permitted, that would undermine the purpose of Rule 37(a), Federal Rules of Civil Procedure, which was designed to protect courts and opposing parties from delaying or harassing tactics during discovery. On the other hand, one could just as well argue that, if the sanctioned lawyer's conduct were that bad, an immediate appeal would not take the appellate court much time.

3. Use of a sanction other than attorneys' fees is not unprecedented. For example, in EIU Group, Inc. v. Gulf Insurance Co., 489 F.3d 405 (1st Cir.2007), the court upheld a requirement that the offending lawyer perform ten hours of pro bono service.

a.   Anders v. California, 386 U.S. 738 (1967), held that appointed counsel in a criminal case may not withdraw a nonfrivolous appeal. The Court required counsel appointed in appeals of criminal cases of indigents to file what is now called an *Anders* brief. If the appointed lawyer, after conscientious examination, finds the criminal defendant's case to be wholly frivolous, the lawyer should advise the court and request permission to withdraw. However, the lawyer must then supply a brief referring to anything in the record that may arguably support an appeal. The lawyer should furnish the defendant with a copy of the brief with enough time to raise any points that the defendant chooses. Then, the court (not counsel) should proceed, after full examination of all proceedings, to decide whether the case is wholly frivolous, grant the lawyer's request to withdraw if it finds the claims to be frivolous, and afford assistance of counsel to argue the appeal for the indigent if it finds some legal issues to be nonfrivolous.

b.   Later, Jones v. Barnes, 463 U.S. 745 (1983), held that an indigent defendant has no constitutional right to compel appointed counsel to press all nonfrivolous issues requested by the client "if counsel, as a matter of professional judgment, decides not to present those points." Both the Court and the dissent in *Barnes* cited Model Rule 1.2(a) and Defense Function Standard 4–5.2.[4] Who has the better argument? Is a client usually competent to specify errors worthy of appeal? Is giving the client the sense that he or she is in control as important as the inherent force of the arguments raised? If a client who can afford a lawyer can insist on focusing on a particular nonfrivolous issue (although it may not be wise to do so), should an indigent defendant have fewer rights?[5]

c.   Smith v. Robbins, 528 U.S. 259 (2000), considered how much appointed counsel must do to comply with *Anders*. Robbins defended himself at trial. On appeal, his appointed counsel filed a no-merits brief, which briefly outlined the facts surrounding the trial and presented no possible grounds for appeal. Robbins then filed a brief of his own, which the California courts rejected. In a federal habeas corpus proceeding, the district court held that, in these circumstances, the *Anders* brief amounted to ineffective assistance of counsel. The Court of Appeals affirmed, but the U.S. Supreme Court reversed (5 to 4), holding that the California procedure adequately protects a defendant's rights. Justice Thomas, writing for the Court, said that although California's procedure does not comply in all respects with *Anders*, under the procedure, appellate counsel allows the defendant to file a supplemental brief and the lawyer remains available to brief any issue requested by the appellate court. The *Anders* reference to the lawyer's noting any points that might support an appeal was an

---

4. Each Circuit is required to have a "criminal justice plan" for providing counsel to indigent defendants. The Fourth Circuit plan required counsel to file petitions for certiorari on behalf of indigent defendants regardless of whether there were any nonfrivolous claims to raise. In Austin v. United States, 513 U.S. 5 (1994), the Supreme Court required that the plan be amended to not require filing frivolous claims.

5. On sanctions for a frivolous civil appeal, see Cooter & Gell v. Hartmarx Corp., 496 U.S. 384 (1990), and Hilmon Co. (V.I.) Inc. v. Hyatt International, 899 F.2d 250 (3d Cir.1990).

example of acceptable procedure, the Court said, not the minimum procedure tolerable. The California procedure allows "adequate and effective" appellate review, and the Supreme Court should not impose a single procedure on the states.

Justices Stevens, Souter, Ginsburg, and Breyer dissented, arguing that the Court had effectively overruled *Anders* and that, while frivolous litigation is a problem, denying defendants an appeal by a "committed representative" who will engage in a "partisan scrutiny of the record" is much more serious. "Without the assurance that assigned counsel has done his best as a partisan, his substantial equality to a lawyer retained at a defendant's expense cannot be assumed."[6] Do you agree with the dissenters? Can *Anders* and *Robbins* both be right?

5. States also have counterparts to Federal Rule 11. Should Model Rule 3.1 be changed to incorporate any Rule 11 elements?

a. In Jandrt ex rel. Brueggeman v. Jerome Foods, Inc., 597 N.W.2d 744 (Wis.1999), several employees of a company bore children with birth defects. A law firm noted the coincidence and filed suit on behalf of a client, alleging a causal connection. However, when the law firm later interviewed experts in birth defects, the experts said the medical science was inconclusive and an epidemiologist's study would be needed to provide proof of causation. The law firm decided the study would be too expensive and voluntarily dismissed the case. A sharply divided Wisconsin Supreme Court concluded that the law firm had done sufficient scientific research to justify filing the case, particularly because a law was about to take effect limiting such suits, but it waited too long to dismiss the case. The court remanded to determine the attorney's fees for the extra time before dismissal.

b. In Seltzer v. Morton, 154 P.3d 561 (Mont.2007), an art authenticator had opined that a painting was the work of a lesser artist than the one the owner hoped. The owner's law firm, Gibson, Dunn & Crutcher (GDC), filed suit trying to get the authenticator to recant his opinion and engaged in discovery abuse to make it costly for him to continue the litigation. Ultimately, the authenticator sued GDC for malicious prosecution and abuse of process. A jury assessed $1.1 million in compensatory damages and $20 million in punitive damages against GDC. The trial court reduced the punitive damages to $9.9 million and the Montana Supreme Court affirmed in all respects. The court said, "Here, GDC's conduct represents the antithesis of the pursuit of truth. * * * [T]he price of dishonesty must be made unbearable to thwart the inevitable temptation that zealous advocacy inspires." 154 P.3d at 608–09.

---

6. In Hughes v. Booker, 220 F.3d 346 (5th Cir.2000), appointed appellate counsel had followed Mississippi procedure and found "no [substantial] issue evidencing reversible error." The defendant had a right to file a brief of his own, and counsel had asked the Mississippi Supreme Court to review the record itself. Nevertheless, the Fifth Circuit found this procedure insufficient even under *Robbins*. In California, the court reasoned, the state court *must* independently review the record; in this case it had only been asked to do so. Perhaps that is a persuasive distinction, but it may also suggest that some courts of appeal are uncomfortable with the *Robbins* holding.

c. What do you think about these cases? Do they properly create a remedy that protects litigants against harassment? Do they give a sense that sanctions litigation can itself become a problem?

d. Givens v. Mullikin ex rel. Estate of McElwaney, 75 S.W.3d 383 (Tenn.2002), explored who besides the lawyer may be liable under state law for sanctions for a lawyer's conduct. Givens' suit stemmed from a car accident. Allstate, Mullikin's insurer, hired a lawyer to defend Mullikin. Now, Givens sought to hold Allstate liable for that lawyer's alleged misconduct during the course of the lawyer's representation of Mullikin. Specifically, Givens said that the defendant's lawyer harassed her by requiring an exorbitant number of interrogatories and deposing her more than necessary. The court recognized that the lawyer was an independent contractor, not an agent of the insurer. Nonetheless, it allowed the claim to proceed against Allstate, holding that both the insurer and the insured face liability for misconduct of an attorney when they have control over and direct his actions. Although Allstate had no legal right to control the representation of the insured, it had hired the attorney. Furthermore, Allstate hired the offending attorney after another firm had already completed discovery, giving rise to the inference that Allstate wanted the new firm to harass Givens. However, the court found that the insured himself was not liable, because he had no personal input into directing the defense.

Couldn't Givens' lawyer have sought sanctions against Mullikin's lawyer earlier, asserting that the lawyer asked too many interrogatories or deposed her more than necessary? What is the advantage of creating a separate remedy against the insurance company that retained the lawyer to represent the insured?

B.   THE ETHICAL STATUS OF DELAY AS A LITIGATION TACTIC

1. Does Model Rule 3.2 establish a different ethical standard for the use of litigation to resolve differences? Its key principle is that a lawyer must "expedite" resolution of the dispute. Why should a lawyer be required to do that? Is the Rule focused only on the inefficient use of court time that delay engenders?

a. What does Rule 3.2 mean when it says that a lawyer need only expedite litigation when "consistent with the interests of the client"? Look at the last sentence of the Comment. If one cannot use delay to "realize financial or other benefit," what other "interests of the client" would justify it? If the reason for a delay is "nonfrivolous" and thus not subject to Rule 11 sanctions, does that mean the lawyer has complied with the requirements of Model Rule 3.2? Should the drafters of the Model Rules have put the prohibition on realizing financial benefit in the rule itself rather than in the Comment?

b. Must a motion be justified only in terms of its probability of success? May one never consider the benefits of delay that arise from filing the motion? May the benefits of delay be considered if there is *some* possibility of success, i.e., the motion is not filed *solely* for purposes of delay? Because the Comment refers to "otherwise improper delay," may the lawyer file a nonfrivolous motion with delay as its dominant purpose? Is it significant that in the Model Rules revisions of 2002, the ABA removed from Rule 3.1, Comment 2, the statement that an action is frivolous if the "client desires to have the action taken primarily for the purpose of harassing or maliciously injuring a person"?

c. If your motion is not baseless, and if your client desires delay, *must* you file a motion that will delay resolution of the matter? In short, are you required to use every tool in your bag to further your client's interest? Suppose you conclude that if you pull your punches in this case, the FDA may be pleased and more likely to give the benefit of the doubt to your *other* clients, and to this one on other cases?

d. One manual of trial practice states that the "duty of supporting the client's cause is sometimes so forcefully stated as to support the argument that as a trial lawyer you are obliged to assert every legal claim or defense available, except those you reject on tactical grounds relating to the immediate case. But the aim of the trial system to achieve justice, the interests of future clients, and your legitimate interest in your own reputation and future effectiveness at the bar compel moderation of that extreme view." Robert Keeton, Trial Tactics and Methods § 1.3 (2d ed. 1973). See also, Ronald D. Rotunda, Book Review, 89 Harvard L. Rev. 622, 628–29 (1976). Do you agree?

2. What obligation do you have to make witnesses available for trial and for deposition by the opposing party?

a. Assume that prior to any FDA hearing to determine whether or not to issue a ban against your client's wine additive, you knew that the first and most important witness that the FDA would seek to call would be the chief research chemist for your client. The chemist prefers not to testify because his testimony would greatly damage his employer, your client. Would it be proper for you to recommend that the chemist be hospitalized for tests and possible surgery on his recently discovered knee injury that, while not life-threatening nor terribly painful, limits his workday? Would you be let off the ethical hook if the company doctor initiated the suggestion that the knee needs treatment? Is it a rationalization to think that creating delay eliminates the possibility that the zealously loyal chemist might commit perjury?

b. May you advise a witness who is not your client not to talk to the other party? Suppose that the witness does not want to "become involved." Look at Model Rules 3.4(a) and (f).

In People v. Kenelly, 648 P.2d 1065 (Colo.1982), the Colorado courts suspended an attorney because he drew up a contract under which his client settled a civil case against *X,* and, in exchange, agreed to evade a subpoena in *X*'s upcoming criminal trial. Accord, In the Matter of Lutz, 607 P.2d 1078 (Idaho 1980).[7]

---

7. See also, Snyder v. State Bar, 555 P.2d 1104 (Cal.1976) (attorney disbarred, in-ter alia, for advising clients not to be available for depositions); Florida Bar v. Machin,

c.   To cope with the knee problem, should you simply ask the FDA staff for a delay in the hearings? Remember, in six months the case will be moot as far as your client is concerned, although it would still be a real issue to the FDA and possibly other wine producers. Is the only ethical issue your motive for delaying the expected testimony of the research chemist?

d.   In Chevron Chemical Co. v. Deloitte & Touche, 501 N.W.2d 15 (Wis.1993), the lawyer represented that a witness would be unavailable for six weeks due to surgery; in fact, he had hernia surgery and would be available in two days. For this and other misconduct, the court granted a judgment against the defendant notwithstanding the verdict and remanded the case to assess damages. The court said, "The unprofessional misconduct of counsel in using misleading, if not outright false, statements to the circuit court and in the presence of the jury is conduct that this court will not tolerate." Do you agree that this misconduct justified such a severe sanction? Could the professional discipline process produce a sanction that was nearly this quick and sure?

e.   Should the appropriateness of delay in litigation vary depending on the type of legal proceeding involved? Consider Ronald D. Rotunda, Law, Lawyers, and Managers, in Clarence Walton, ed., The Ethics of Corporate Conduct 142–43 (1977):

> "[D]elay is a knife that cuts both ways. Some corporate lawyers have charged that environmentalists and other public-interest litigants have used delay to bog down the regulatory system, to prevent needed rate increases, to prohibit or delay power plant expansion, to obstruct programs for highway construction, and to delay or modify housing developments."

Is delay permissible when invoked in service of the public interest?

f.   What about delay in criminal cases? Should filing appeals and habeas corpus petitions for purposes of delay be a permissible strategy in a death penalty case, for example? Is it often the *only* strategy?

3.   In the dispute with the FDA, are you representing your client in your capacity as a lawyer giving advice in litigation or your capacity as a lawyer advising a client more generally?

a.   Look at Model Rule 2.1 governing the lawyer as advisor. Now look again at Model Rule 3.1. If the lawyer may advance any nonfrivolous claim without being likely to suffer professional discipline, does if follow that the lawyer acting under Rule 2.1 should advise the client to take any position that is not utterly frivolous?

b.   Does it trouble you that, under the assumptions in this problem, your delay will allow tainted wine to be sold *in the future?* That is, what

635 So.2d 938 (Fla.1994) (lawyer suspended for offering to establish a trust fund for the child of a murder victim if the victim's family agreed not to testify at the client's sentencing hearing). Cf. Taylor v. Commonwealth, 233

S.W. 895 (Ky.1921) (attorney disbarred when he was party to an arrangement under which a witness was paid to leave the jurisdiction and not return).

you do here may expose consumers to the risk of getting cancer, not simply help allocate losses after an event has occurred.

c.   Will selling the wine expose your client to unwanted publicity or litigation if the additive in the wine becomes public knowledge? Would you then be liable to your client for a failure to warn it about the adverse consequences of pressing its litigation right to the limit? See, e.g., Restatement Third, The Law Governing Lawyers § 94 (Advising and Assisting a Client—In General).

d.   Rather than seek delay, should you suggest that your client—before the FDA's expected order becomes effective—immediately sell his stock of tainted wine to a foreign wholesaler, assuming foreign law and scientific understanding are different and that the wine can be resold abroad? Will you sleep better knowing that only people you are unlikely to meet will have their cancer risk increased?

C.   OTHER SANCTIONS FOR LITIGATION MISCONDUCT

1.   Do courts have authority to sanction lawyers beyond Rule 11 and its state-law equivalents?

a.   Earlier in this problem, we saw that lawyers may be sanctioned for violations of Model Rule 3.1 and Rule 11 of the Federal Rules of Civil Procedure. Other sources of sanction authority are available as well.

b.   Chambers v. NASCO, Inc., 501 U.S. 32 (1991), held that a federal court has inherent power to award attorneys' fees to a party whom the court concludes has engaged in harassing litigation. Chambers had agreed to sell his television station to NASCO, but then changed his mind. The Court found that he tried to prevent the sale by fraudulently trying to deprive the federal court of jurisdiction and by other tactics of "delay, oppression and harassment." Rule 11 would have allowed sanctions for frivolous pleadings, of which there were several, but not for the other wrongs. The Supreme Court held that a district judge has inherent power to manage the proceedings and may award attorneys' fees to sanction bad faith and oppressive conduct, even if it is not covered by Rule 11.

Chief Justice Rehnquist and Justices Kennedy, Scalia, and Souter dissented, suggesting the Court had granted *carte blanche* to judges to sanction lawyers. Are you equally concerned?

c.   United States v. Eisen, 974 F.2d 246 (2d Cir.1992), found lawyers guilty of criminal and tortious conduct—here, mail fraud and RICO violations—for acts in their role as lawyers. The government convicted the lawyers of conspiring with private investigators and others in a scheme of contriving phony traffic accidents and then filing claims with insurance companies. The opinion looked at several issues. For example, it held that the "fortuity" that a witness' testimony as "influenced turned out to be truthful" is not a defense to the bribery of the witness because: "The essence of bribery is the intent to influence improperly the conduct of another by bestowing a benefit, [so] there is no requirement that the intended result be accomplished." 974 F.2d at 256. The lawyers' "misrepresentations in pleadings and pretrial submissions were made in the hope of fraudulently inducing a settlement before trial. And in cases that went to trial, fraudulent representations concerning the claims were directed at the civil defendants and their insurers in an effort to induce settlement before verdict. In fact, several of the lawsuits listed in the indictment were settled. Even in cases decided by a jury, defendants' misconduct was intended to defraud their adversaries." 974 F.2d at 253.

d.   Zamos v. Stroud, 87 P.3d 802 (Cal.2004), held that the tort of malicious prosecution covers situations where a lawyer who had probable cause to initiate a lawsuit continues to prosecute the case after discovering that the probable cause no longer exists. Citing the Restatement of Torts § 674 and "every other state that has addressed the question," the California Supreme Court held the traditional standard—that malicious prosecution is actionable in instances where "any reasonable attorney" would find the claims are "totally and completely without merit"—applies to both initiation and continuation of a suit. Extending the tort to continuation of the lawsuit improves the efficiency of the court system by encouraging early dismissals, and serves the clients' best interests by saving them from unnecessary legal fees. The bottom line is that Rule 11 and the Model Rules may be the least of a lawyer's worries in some cases.

2.   Should courts have the power to sanction a lawyer for filing a lawsuit that is nonfrivolous, but would not have been filed but for the plaintiff's desire to hurt or somehow impose costs on the defendant? Should litigants have a Constitutional right to impose burdens on their enemies?

a.   Dove Audio, Inc. v. Rosenfeld, Meyer & Susman, 54 Cal.Rptr.2d 830 (Cal.Ct.App.1996), involved statements that Audrey Hepburn's lawyer made in a letter seeking to get celebrities to join in a complaint against a recording company that had allegedly reneged on its promises to make gifts to the celebrities' favorite charities. The recording company sued the lawyer's firm for defamation, but the court dismissed the suit, finding that statements relating to litigation were privileged against a defamation charge. More interesting, the court held that the lawyer had his own claim for damages (over $27,000) from the recording company filing the action. California has an anti-SLAPP (strategic lawsuit against public participation) statute that permits the award of attorney's fees against someone who uses litigation to try to prevent someone else from asserting First Amendment rights.

b.   These SLAPP statutes can raise their own First Amendment problems. The First Amendment guarantees a right to petition the government for redress of grievances. A lawsuit is a classic petition, and if it is not frivolous, i.e., not "baseless," ordinarily it would be protected conduct. The plaintiff may harbor ill will towards the defendant, but the law does not require litigants to like each other; indeed, they often grow to dislike each other immensely.[8]

8. See, e.g., Bill Johnson's Restaurants, Inc. v. N.L.R.B., 461 U.S. 731, 742–43 (1983), where the Court said that, in light of "the First Amendment right of access to the

c. The First Amendment protection even applies if the lawsuits are ultimately unsuccessful. In BE & K Constr. Co. v. National Labor Relations Board, 536 U.S. 516 (2002), unions had lobbied and filed health and safety charges against a nonunion contractor who had secured a large contract. The contractor retaliated by filing secondary boycott and antitrust claims against the unions; all of the claims were either dismissed or voluntarily withdrawn with prejudice. Then, the unions complained to the National Labor Relations Board (NLRB), which found that the contractor's suits were "unmeritorious" and the employer had a bad motive: it had filed the suits in order to retaliate against union members who were engaged in conduct that the National Labor Relations Act protects. The NLRB and the Sixth Circuit agreed that the employer had engaged in an unfair labor practice, but the Supreme Court reversed.

Justice O'Connor wrote for the Court that lawsuits could not constitute an unfair labor practice unless they were "sham litigation," that is, both (1) subjectively brought with a bad motive and (2) "objectively baseless," which these were not. The NLRB may not "burden an unsuccessful but reasonably based suit" even though it "was brought with a retaliatory purpose." Mere ill will is not enough because "ill will is not uncommon in litigation." The right to petition, said the Court, is one of "the most precious of the liberties safeguarded by the Bill of Rights,"and the "right of access to the courts" is "one aspect of the right of petition. * * * As long as a plaintiff's *purpose* is to stop conduct he reasonably believes is illegal, petitioning is genuine both objectively and subjectively." 536 U.S. at 534 (emphasis added). The Court made clear, however, that it was not undercutting the right of lower courts to impose "common litigation sanctions," e.g., Rule 11.

Justice Breyer, joined by Justices Stevens, Souter, and Ginsburg, concurring in part and in the judgment, read the majority's ruling narrowly, as covering only cases where the NLRB "rests its finding of 'retaliatory motive' almost exclusively upon the simple fact that the employer filed a reasonably based but unsuccessful lawsuit and the employer did not like the union. The Court expressly leaves open other circumstances in which the evidence of 'retaliation' or antiunion motive might be stronger or different, showing, for example, an employer, indifferent to outcome, who intends the reasonably based but unsuccessful lawsuit simply to impose litigation costs on the union." 536 U.S. at 539.

3. Should there be a remedy against the government for a wrongful or vexatious criminal prosecution?

a. United States v. Gilbert, 198 F.3d 1293 (11th Cir.1999), considered the criminal law counterpart to Rule 11. The jury convicted Gilbert of fraudulently concealing assets in bankruptcy, but the court reversed his

---

courts," the "filing and prosecution of a well-founded lawsuit may not be enjoined as an unfair labor practice, even if it would not have been commenced but for plaintiff's de-

sire to retaliate against the defendant for exercising rights protected by the [National Labor Relations] Act."

conviction because the statute of limitations had run. The defendant then sued for attorneys' fees under the 1997 Hyde Amendment, 18 U.S.C. § 3006A, which allows such fees if the prosecution was "vexatious, frivolous or in bad faith." The court determined that the decision as to when the statute of limitations began to run had been a matter of first impression in the circuit and that the government was entitled to take the position it did. Thus, the statute did not justify any fee award.

b.   United States v. Adkinson, 247 F.3d 1289 (11th Cir.2001), on the other hand, found that the government, with full knowledge, asserted a position that recent and controlling precedent had foreclosed. That conduct constituted "vexatious," "frivolous," and "bad faith" prosecution that entitled the defendant to Hyde Amendment fees.

c.   Should the fact the government fails to prove its case be enough to demonstrate that the proceeding was vexatious? In United States v. Sherburne, 249 F.3d 1121 (9th Cir.2001), the government had prosecuted thirteen defendants for alleged abuses in the funding and construction of a housing development. The prosecution charged over fifty offenses, and the court failed to convict on any of them. In a subsequent related hearing the trial court awarded attorney's fees pursuant to the Hyde Amendment to some, but not all, of the defendants. The Ninth Circuit found that the use of a solely objective standard to measure "vexatiousness" was incorrect, and that the correct standard involved both subjective and objective characteristics. The test should be whether "the prosecution was unwarranted because it was intended to harass and [was] without sufficient foundation." The court stated that to use a solely objective standard would put too much of a burden on the prosecution and would lead to judicial second-guessing. Do you agree?

D.   CONSIDERATION OF **ADR** ALTERNATIVES

1.   What is your obligation to propose nonlitigation alternatives to your client, the wine producer?

a.   The buzzword in modern times is Alternative Dispute Resolution, or ADR. In the 2002 revisions to the Model Rules of Professional Conduct, the ABA added a sentence to Model Rule 2.1, Comment 5, that now provides: "[W]hen a matter is likely to involve litigation, it may be necessary under Rule 1.4 to inform the client of forms of dispute resolution that might constitute reasonable alternatives to litigation." What alternatives to litigation does the Comment have in mind? Is negotiation an alternative to litigation, or is negotiation always done in the shadow of litigation, i.e., whether or not litigation is actually filed, does the right to litigate make the alternative of negotiation more compelling?

b.   Many federal and state courts require that parties mediate their cases before a trial date will be set.[9] Litigators may face the reality of the

---

9.   See, e.g., Ettie Ward, Mandatory Court Annexed Alternative Dispute Resolution in the United States Federal Courts: Panacea or Pandemic?, 81 St. John's L. Rev. 77 (2007).

vanishing trial as the risks and cost of litigation as well as the mandatory use of ADR techniques has had a significant effect on the number of cases that go to trial. Many federal and state agencies have established mediation procedures to settle adjudicative disputes involving a government agency and a private party.

c. The Model Rules explicitly give their approval to ADR in particular instances. Rule 1.5, Comment 9, for example, requires lawyers to comply with any system of mandatory arbitration or mediation of fee disputes. Another clause in that same sentence urges lawyers to submit to arbitration or mediation "even when it is voluntary." Further, if the lawyer and client have a dispute as who owns funds in the lawyer's trust fund account, Rule 1.15, Comment 3, advises the lawyer to suggest means, "such as arbitration," for resolving the dispute promptly.

2. Why are there special rules restricting lawyers who act as third party neutrals that do not apply to nonlawyers who occupy the same role?

a. In the 2002 amendments, the ABA added a new provision dealing specifically with ADR. Model Rule 2.4, "Lawyer Serving as Third–Party Neutral," defines a "third-party neutral" as a person who acts as a "mediator, arbitrator, conciliator or evaluator," to assist two or more persons who are not the lawyer's clients. See Model Rule 2.4(a) and Comment 1.

b. At the same time the ABA created Model Rule 2.4, it eliminated Model Rule 2.2, which had governed the lawyer as "intermediary." Model Rule 2.2 had defined an intermediary as a lawyer who represented two or more clients with "potentially conflicting interests," typically a dispute between them. In contrast, under Rule 2.4, the lawyer explicitly does not represent any clients.

c. Model Rule 2.4 does not, of course, regulate the conduct of third-party neutrals who are not lawyers. Why are people who use a third-party neutral more likely to be confused by the neutral's role if the neutral is a lawyer? Look at Model Rule 2.4, Comment 3. Are you convinced?

d. Should Rule 2.4(b) require more than an explanation that the lawyer does not represent either of the disputing parties? Does the suggestion in Comment 3 that the lawyer tell parties that the attorney-client privilege is inapplicable sound suspiciously like the giving of legal advice? Is anything wrong with that? The ABA Ethics 2000 Commission rejected a proposal that would have prohibited third-party neutrals from giving legal advice to the parties.[10] Does that mean the third-party neutral should be permitted to help the parties draft a settlement agreement, for example?

e. Should the ABA leave the rules governing third-party neutrals to standards-setting bodies more focused on current thinking about ADR

---

10. Margaret Colgate Love, The Revised ABA Model Rules of Professional Conduct: Summary of the Work of Ethics 2000, 15 Georgetown J. Legal Ethics 441, 462 (2002).

processes? Model Rule 2.4, Comment 2 suggests that a great deal of regulation of ADR neutrals will come from such other sources.

3. Does it seem likely that you can help your client, the wine producer, in this case by suggesting the use of a third-party neutral?

a. Many states today require or make available the alternative of mediation. A mediator who has the confidence of both sides may determine the relative intensity of their preferences for items in dispute—immediate cash vs. particular assets, for example—and propose trades that will make both sides feel better off. Further, in some contexts, some outcomes may be possible as a result of mediation—e.g., specification of the future religious training made available to children after a divorce—that would be more difficult to get a court to order.

b. Arbitration is yet another form of ADR. When is it most effectively employed? The relative lack of discovery in many arbitration settings, and the limited rights to appeal an arbitration ruling to a court help account for the reputation of arbitration as a relatively quick way to get a decision in a matter.

c. Might arbitration work especially well when the subject matter of the dispute is complex and specialized? If the question is whether a medical technician has the skills to do a particular job, for example, is it better to get an answer directly from a panel of doctors than from a lay jury who hears from doctor-witnesses with opposing views?

d. Will mediation or arbitration work in the case of the wine producer? At least to date, the alternative seems unlikely. In disputes with the government, the FDA and similar agencies do not have a reputation of favoring mediation or arbitration over litigation, although there is some evidence that policy could be changing.

4. If a lawyer has been a third-party neutral in a matter, may that lawyer or one of his partners later represent a client in a related matter?

a. Assume that after the FDA required the recall of wine from retailers' shelves, one of the retailers wanted your client to reimburse it for its loss. Alpha was the arbitrator who decided that dispute. Now, your client has another dispute with the retailer that is tangentially related to the earlier one. In the new dispute, the retailer has hired Beta, who has recently become Alpha's law partner. Your client did not give any information to Alpha during the arbitration that you expected he would keep secret from the retailer. Do you have any grounds to object to Beta's representing the wine retailer in the controversy?

b. Look at Model Rule 1.12 (a) and (c). How related should two disputes be before Rule 1.12(a) would prohibit Alpha's own representation of the retailer in the second dispute? Remember that Alpha did not represent either party to the arbitration so Model Rules 1.9 and 1.10 are not controlling. What is the rationale for excluding Alpha from involvement in later stages of the same "matter"? What will the Alpha Beta firm have to do to screen Alpha so that Beta may continue to represent the retailer even if Alpha is disqualified?

c. If Beta had represented the retailer on various other matters over the years, although not this one, should Alpha (Beta's partner) be ineligible to serve as arbitrator? Does either Rule 1.12 or Comment 4 to Rule 2.4, authoritatively answer the question? How would you answer it? How would you explain your answer?

d. Rule 1.12(d) expressly permits a partisan arbitrator on a multi-member panel to represent the party in subsequent matters. Parties to domestic and international agreements often use the tripartite method of selecting a three member panel for the arbitration of disputes. Each party selects a partisan arbitrator and the two select a third neutral arbitrator. Notice that the limitations of Rule 1.12 do not apply to partisan arbitrators.

————

PROBLEM 24

LITIGATION TACTICS

Some of the public's favorite stories involve lawyers uncovering deception or acting as deceivers in order to uncover deception. Early television lawyer Perry Mason was adept at goading the guilty party into confessing in open court (with Mason sometimes suggesting that he knew more than he did) just before Mason's client was about to be bound over for trial at the end of each episode. This problem explores when we should admire a lawyer's imagination and when we should condemn it. We first look at the line between creative lawyering and deception, wonder if the line is bright or equivocal, and then explore the role of deception in the search for truth. Next, we ask when a lawyer may use confidential information inadvertently disclosed by an opponent, and whether and how judges should enforce standards of civility among litigators.

FACTS

Hugh Martin, one of the most famous insurance defense lawyers in San Francisco, defends clients of many of the largest insurance companies in the United States. His firm's office overlooks the bay and occupies an entire floor of the Transamerica building. Yet despite his luxurious office and income to match, Martin cuts a different figure in court. He dresses in baggy tweed jackets with elbow patches, his shirts have badly frayed sleeves, and his unpolished shoes have very worn heels and soles. While he is a dapper figure outside of the courtroom with his custom suits and handmade cigars, he justifies his shabby attire and country lawyer act in the halls of justice as an effort to win sympathy from the juries while helping insurance companies avoid large tort judgments.

Martin confides to his young associates that they should avoid choosing younger jurors because of their "social worker, do-gooder mentality." He also advises: "Try to pick a jury with racial and class differences; by exploiting and encouraging dissension you create disunity; a disunified jury rarely grants large awards."

In one lecture to new associates in his firm he explained:

"You have to use your ingenuity and use all the tricks of the trade to win for the defense in a large tort claim. If you see that you can exploit an opposing witness' emotional weakness to make him seem uncertain about a fact, don't hesitate to do so even if the fact is true. The client doesn't pay for justice. It pays for victory."

Martin also trains his associates to impose costs upon opposing parties and counsel. "Be sure to schedule depositions at the most unfavorable times and in remote places. We can teach opponents a lesson that we will go to all ends to prevail in litigation."

In a case that Martin likes to brag about, he defended a manufacturing concern charged with the negligent death of the wife of a middle-aged worker. All during the trial Martin had his attractive secretary sit in the courtroom. Then, according to plan, Martin had this secretary—just before closing arguments, during a short break in the proceedings when the plaintiff's lawyer's back was turned—ask the plaintiff-widower the time; she smiled at his response, patted him on the head, and then left. The three older members of the jury looked with icy stares at the plaintiff and five hours later the jury returned a verdict for the defense. One or more of the jurors mistakenly assumed that Martin's secretary was the plaintiff's new wife.

Martin justifies these and similar practices (he calls them "tricks") as necessary to counteract what he considers the unfair advantage of the plaintiff's lawyer in winning verdicts because of sympathy and other reasons not connected with the merits of the case.[1]

QUESTIONS

A.   THE AMBIGUOUS LINE BETWEEN CREATIVE LAWYERING AND DECEPTION

1. Which of Hugh Martin's litigating "tricks" are proper, if any? Are some in a gray area? Should Martin be subject to criticism for wearing different clothes in court than he wears to the office, for example?

[1] This problem is adapted, with permission, from the discussion of a somewhat analogous situation in Ending Insult to Injury: No–Fault Insurance for Products and Services 4–6 (Univ. of Illinois Press 1975) by Professor Jeffrey O'Connell.

a.   Should regulation of Martin's wardrobe be the responsibility of the judges before whom he appears? Courts sometimes do try to regulate the clothing of lawyers who appear before them. In State v. Cherryhomes, 840 P.2d 1261 (N.M.App.1992), for example, the lawyer appeared in a dress shirt with a bandanna at his neck. A local court rule required that he wear a necktie. He argued that a bandanna was a form of tie, but he was fined for contempt. The Court of Appeals affirmed. A lawyer's dress is not a form of "speech," the court ruled, and the judge's interpretation of the local rule controlled. Do you agree?

b.   In Berner v. Delahanty, 129 F.3d 20 (1st Cir.1997), a court required a lawyer to take off a political advocacy button when he was in the courtroom. The button said "No on 1" and referred to an upcoming referendum issue. The First Circuit held that the prohibition of all advocacy buttons did not discriminate on the basis of content and was appropriate to preserving an atmosphere of impartiality in the courtroom.

2.   Is there anything improper about Martin's approach to jury selection? When, if ever, does a lawyer have a duty to the justice system to pick only jurors who will be fair to both sides?

a.   Georgia v. McCollum, 505 U.S. 42 (1992), held that it is unconstitutional for either prosecutor or defense counsel to exercise peremptory challenges based on race. J.E.B. v. Alabama ex rel. T.B., 511 U.S. 127 (1994), reached the same result as to sex-based challenges; Edmonson v. Leesville Concrete Co., Inc., 500 U.S. 614 (1991), came to the same conclusion in a civil case involving only private litigants.

b.   United States v. Omoruyi, 7 F.3d 880 (9th Cir.1993), held that a prosecutor's statement indicating that he exercised peremptory challenges against two unmarried female prospective jurors because he was concerned they would be attracted to a "good-looking" male defendant was an admission of purposeful sex discrimination in violation of the defendant's right to equal protection.

c.   What should the result be in a medical malpractice case if the defense lawyer exercises a peremptory challenge against a potential juror (a Jehovah's Witness or a Christian Scientist) for religious reasons? Assume that the lawyer believes that the juror may be prejudiced against the defendant medical doctor. See State v. Davis, 504 N.W.2d 767 (Minn.1993) (religiously-motivated peremptory challenge against Jehovah's Witness is not unconstitutional).

d.   Given this authority, why do the Model Rules include the following sentence in Model Rule 8.4, Comment 3: "A trial judge's finding that peremptory challenges were exercised on a discriminatory basis does not alone establish a violation of this rule"? Should unconstitutional conduct by a litigator constitute virtually a per se violation of Model Rule 8.4(d)?

e.   In Virgin Islands v. Weatherwax, 77 F.3d 1425 (3d Cir.1996), the white defendant was accused of killing a black man. Black persons made up a majority of potential jurors, and the jury selected had nine blacks and three whites. One day during the trial, defense counsel saw that a white juror had taken a newspaper with a story prejudicial to the defendant into the jury room in violation of a court order. Counsel failed to call it to the judge's attention, however, because he did not want a white juror dismissed. Ultimately, the jury convicted the defendant of second degree murder and he appealed his lawyer's failure to challenge the juror misconduct. By a 2–1 vote, the Third Circuit refused to second guess the lawyer's decision. This was a tactical matter within the "exclusive province of the lawyer," the court held, and the failure to act did not constitute ineffective assistance of counsel. Do you agree? Is taking race into account in this circumstance consistent with *McCollum*?

3. When Martin cross examines a truthful witness, may he properly try to get that witness to express uncertainty about something that Martin knows to be true?

a. Read Model Rule 3.3(a)(1). If a lawyer may not "make a false statement of fact or law to a tribunal," why should Martin be permitted to try to impeach the reliability of testimony that he knows to be accurate? What understanding of "justice" would warrant Martin's approach? Is Martin right that the client is not paying for justice? Should that end the ethical discussion?

b. Read Model Rule 4.4(a). What seems to be its primary concern? Should the proper issue for a lawyer be whether the witness is "embarrassed" or "humiliated unnecessarily"? Should the issue instead be whether the lawyer is misleading the trier of fact?

c. Consider In re Zawada, 92 P.3d 862 (Ariz.2004) (en banc). It stemmed from a murder case where the defendant, Alex Hughes, presented an insanity defense. Six psychiatric experts, including the state's experts, concluded that Hughes was mentally ill. Prosecutor Zawada, however, tried to discredit the experts. For example, during cross-examination he accused the witnesses, without any basis, of fabricating their testimony. He "accused the psychiatrist of indecision and of reaching a conclusion of insanity only *after* he was hired by the defense and paid for his services. Zawada knew there was no evidentiary basis for the accusation, nor did he offer one. He continued the attack in closing argument, suggesting, still without evidence, that defense counsel paid money to the mental health expert to fabricate a diagnosis of insanity for the defendant." (emphasis in original) He also sought to discredit the mental health profession as a whole by arguing that they "create excuses for criminals," and he appealed to the jurors' fear during closing arguments to prejudice the defendant. Despite strong evidence of Hughes' insanity, the jury found him guilty of murder and other felonies. The state supreme court later overturned Hughes' conviction because of Zawada's repeated prejudicial conduct, and the trial judge later barred retrial because of double jeopardy.

The Arizona Bar then filed a complaint against Zawada, alleging violation of Rules 3.1, 3.4(c), 3.4(e), and 8.4(d), and the Arizona Supreme Court agreed. While a prosecutor is entitled to his own opinion regarding the persuasiveness of psychiatric testimony, the court held that "a prosecutor cannot attack the expert with non-evidence, using irrelevant, insulting cross-examination and baseless argument designed to mislead the jury...." In considering the sanction, the court noted that Zawada had engaged in misconduct in a number of cases, making him "single-handedly responsible for much of the law in Arizona on the consequences of extreme prosecutorial misconduct." His misconduct caused serious injury and he refused to acknowledge that it was wrongful. The court imposed a six-month plus one-day suspension, a subsequent one-year probation, referral to the Members Assistance Program, and continuing education on the use of mental health testimony. The court also ordered Zawada to pay the costs and expenses of the disciplinary proceedings.

d. How would you draft a rule that prohibits vigorous cross-examination of a truthful witness and yet preserves the essence of the adversary system? If the lawyer had to go easy on witnesses who were telling the truth, would that send the jury too clear a signal about whom they should believe? Would that be a bad thing? Are there times when the adversary system is too adversarial for its own good?

e. Restatement Third, The Law Governing Lawyers § 106, Comment *c*, defends the present rule by arguing:

"A particularly difficult problem is presented when a lawyer has an opportunity to cross-examine a witness with respect to testimony that the lawyer knows to be truthful, including harsh implied criticism of the witness's testimony, character, or capacity for truth-telling. Even if legally permissible, a lawyer would presumably do so only where that would not cause the lawyer to lose credibility with the tribunal or alienate the factfinder. Moreover, a lawyer is never required to conduct such examination, and the lawyer may withdraw if the lawyer's client insists on such a course of action in a setting in which the lawyer considers it imprudent or repugnant."

Is a lawyer "never required to conduct such examination" when the best hope for the client is to persuade the jury that the nervous witness with bad eyesight is wrong, even though the lawyer knows that the witness is accurate in this instance?

4. Do any of Martin's other "tricks" raise ethical issues?

a. Would it be proper for Martin to have a low-income employee sit at the counsel table instead of a company manager to make the company appear nearly broke? Look at Model Rule 3.4(e).

b. Were you offended by the incident where Martin's secretary implied that she had a relationship with the plaintiff? What, if anything, made the incident ethically improper? Should we worry about trial tactics at all? Is the point of the adversary system that a lawyer may rely on opposing counsel's guile to counterbalance his or her own?

c. In deciding which of Martin's "tricks" are unethical, should the test be a bright line or should it vary depending on whether a case is before a jury, for example? Would one argue that wearing shabby clothes during a settlement conference is improper? Is the test whether the lawyer's *motive* was to mislead? Is the test whether in a given case a juror or lawyer was in fact misled?

B.   USING DECEPTION IN THE SEARCH FOR TRUTH

1.   May a lawyer ever use deception as a way of bringing out the truth in court?

a.   Model Rule 3.3(a)(1) provides that a lawyer shall not knowingly "make a false statement of fact or law to a tribunal." Model Rule 4.1(a), the rule as applied to third persons (not tribunals), is similar, except that it adds the word "material."

b.   Does "never" mean "never"? Is there a place for deception in the search for truth? What if the purpose of the deception is to uncover an honest, but significant, mistake in identification? Commentators tell us that some of the most persuasive testimony is eyewitness identification, but sometimes that testimony is simply mistaken. Witnesses "tend to incorporate post-identification feedback into their recollections of events," and "witnesses to a crime in which the perpetrator displays a weapon tend to focus their attention on the weapon, not the perpetrator."[2]

c.   Consider the lawyer's strategy in United States v. Thoreen, 653 F.2d 1332 (9th Cir.1981), cert. denied, 455 U.S. 938 (1982). The court tells us:

"In February 1980, Thoreen represented Sibbett, a commercial fisher, during Sibbett's nonjury trial * * * for criminal contempt for three violations of a preliminary injunction against salmon fishing. In preparing for trial, Thoreen hoped that the government agent who had cited Sibbett could not identify him. He decided to test the witness's identification.

"He placed next to him at counsel table Clark Mason, who resembled Sibbett and had Mason dressed in outdoor clothing—denims, heavy shoes, a plaid shirt, and a jacket-vest.

"Sibbett wore a business suit, large round glasses, and sat behind the rail in a row normally reserved for the press.

"Thoreen neither asked the court's permission for, nor notified it or government counsel of, the substitution.

"On Thoreen's motion at the start of the trial, the court ordered all witnesses excluded from the courtroom. Mason remained at the counsel table.

2.   Mark Hansen, Expertise on Trial: Testimony on Reliability of Eyewitness Identification Stalls on General Acceptance, ABA Journal, Dec. 2002, at 22.

Furthermore, what one remembers may not be true. For example, there were no television pictures of the first airplane hitting the World Trade Center on September 11, 2001, yet 77% of New Yorkers surveyed, and 73% of people nationwide recall that they saw such coverage. Memories "suffused with emotion are barely more likely to be true than memories of last Tuesday's lunch." The September 11 memory studies "confirm that eyewitness recall is fallible." Sharon Begley, The Memory of September 11 Is Seared in Your Mind: But Is It Really True?, Wall Street J., Sept. 13, 2002, at B1, col. 1.

"Throughout the trial, Thoreen made and allowed to go uncorrected numerous misrepresentations. He gestured to Mason as though he was his client and gave Mason a yellow legal pad on which to take notes. The two conferred. Thoreen did not correct the court when it expressly referred to Mason as the defendant and caused the record to show identification of Mason as Sibbett.

"Because of the conduct, two government witnesses misidentified Mason as Sibbett. Following the government's case, Thoreen called Mason as a witness and disclosed the substitution. * * *

[The court let the government recall the government agent who then made the proper identification. Sibbett was convicted, and the Judge held Thoreen in contempt.]

"Thoreen's principal defense is that his conduct was a good faith tactic in aid of cross-examination and falls within the protected realm of zealous advocacy. He argues that as defense counsel he has no obligation to ascertain or present the truth and may seek to confuse witnesses with misleading questions, gestures, or appearances. * * *

"While we agree that defense counsel should represent his client vigorously, regardless of counsel's view of guilt or innocence, we conclude that Thoreen's conduct falls outside this protected behavior.

"Vigorous advocacy by defense counsel may properly entail impeaching or confusing a witness, even if counsel thinks the witness is truthful, and refraining from presenting evidence even if he knows the truth. When we review this conduct and find that the line between vigorous advocacy and actual obstruction is close, our doubts should be resolved in favor of the former. * * *

"Thoreen's view of appropriate cross-examination, which encompasses his substitution, crossed over the line from zealous advocacy to actual obstruction because, as we discuss later, it impeded the court's search for truth, resulted in delays, and violated a court custom and rule. Moreover, this conduct harms rather than enhances an attorney's effectiveness as an advocate.

" 'It is fundamental that in relations with the court, defense counsel must be scrupulously candid and truthful in representation of any matter before the court. This is not only a basic ethical requirement, but it is essential if the lawyer is to be effective in the role of advocate, for if the lawyer's reputation for veracity is suspect, he or she will lack the confidence of the court when it is needed most to the serve the client.'[3] * * *

"The record shows that Sibbett's identification was not an issue, contradicting the need to attack credibility."

3. The court was quoting American Bar Association Standards for Criminal Justice, The Defense Function 4.9 (1980).

The court upheld the finding of contempt but did not indicate what sanction was imposed.[4]

d. Do you agree that Thoreen's conduct crossed the line and was impermissible deception? How else was he to establish reasonable doubt about the government's identification? In a later portion of the opinion, the court suggests:

> "If identification is at issue, an attorney could test a witness's credibility by notifying the court and counsel that it is [at issue] and by seeking the court's permission to (1) seat two or more persons at counsel table without identifying the defendant * * *; (2) have no one at counsel table; (3) hold an in-court lineup."

Would you as defense counsel have chosen any of those alternatives? Is our problem with Thoreen's conduct that it was designed to mislead the trier of fact, not aid the search for truth? What if Thoreen did not trust the judge and did not seek the court's permission for that reason? Would that change the behavior we should expect of him?

e. May the lawyer pretend to be reading from a document, or pretend to have one, when he does not? See Model Rule 8.4(c). Consider Cincinnati Bar Ass'n v. Statzer, 800 N.E.2d 1117 (Ohio 2003), which sanctioned a lawyer for conduct during a deposition. In a hearing on allegations that the lawyer had induced her former legal assistant to execute a false affidavit and provide false testimony, Statzer deposed the legal assistant. During the deposition, Statzer conspicuously placed nine audio cassette tapes in front of her former legal assistant. "By suggestively labeling the tapes and referring to them during questioning, respondent implied that she had recorded conversations with the legal assistant that could impeach and personally embarrass the legal assistant." The cassettes were actually blank or irrelevant and never introduced into evidence. Statzer contended that the tactic she employed was necessary "to draw honest testimony from a theretofore untrustworthy witness." The Ohio Supreme Court acknowledged the importance of latitude in the discovery process, but that does not include "subterfuge that intimidates a witness." While this kind of "deception may induce truthful testimony, it is just as likely to elicit lies if a witness believes that lies will offer security from the false threat. Respondent's deceitful tactic intimidated her witness by creating the false impres-

---

4. By a 4 to 3 vote, the Illinois Supreme Court followed *Thoreen* on similar facts. People v. Simac, 641 N.E.2d 416 (Ill.1994), as did the Massachusetts Supreme Judicial Court in Matter of Gross, 759 N.E.2d 288 (Mass.2001). Attorney Gross represented a woman on drunk driving charges. Even though his client had admitted at the accident scene that she had been driving the car, Gross chose to present an alibi witness to testify that the defendant had been at home watching television. Upon discovering that the alibi witness also looked like the defendant, and believing that the accident victim could probably not identify the driver, Gross had the alibi witness impersonate the defendant in court. A police investigator present in the courtroom realized that the alibi witness was not the real defendant and that the defendant was present as a spectator. Even after the court questioned Gross as to the identity of the woman he had presented as the defendant, Gross continued to contend that she was his client. The district attorney reported this conduct to the state Board of Bar Overseers, and the Massachusetts Supreme Judicial Court upheld an 18–month suspension of Gross.

sion that respondent possessed compromising personal information that she could offer as evidence." The court imposed a six-month suspension, stayed on the condition that Statzer employ no further "fraud, deceit, dishonesty, or misrepresentation."

2. May a lawyer use deception as part of law enforcement or other investigatory functions?

a. A different use of deception in a search for truth is found in In re Gatti, 8 P.3d 966 (Or.2000). Lawyer Gatti knew that a company, CMR, did reviews for State Farm Insurance of how badly hurt claimants were. He believed State Farm had CMR deny benefits using a formula rather than relying on doctors' professional judgment of the injuries. State Farm denied the claim of Gatti's client, and the lawyer suspected that State Farm based its denial on a CMR report. The lawyer then called both the doctor who had conducted the review for CMR and the director of operations for CMR. He said—or at least wanted them to believe—that he was a chiropractor who wanted to work as a claim reviewer for CMR. He asked them detailed questions about their protocols and guidelines, hoping in fact to develop facts to support a lawsuit, which he later filed, alleging fraud by CMR and State Farm.

The Oregon Supreme Court found that lawyer Gatti violated DR 1–102(A)(3) and DR 7–102(A)(5) [Model Rules 8.4(c) and 4.1]. "A misrepresentation may be a lie, a half-truth, or even silence," the court said, and a "material fact consists of information that, if disclosed, would have influenced the recipient's conduct." This lawyer's conduct clearly met that definition. The court, in this attorney discipline case, imposed a public reprimand.

The lawyer defended his conduct by saying that government lawyers use deception all the time in undercover operations that seek to "root out evil." He, too, was trying to root out evil in the insurance industry. Even the U.S. attorney intervened in the case to assert the importance of the government's ability to do undercover work, as did the Oregon Fair Housing Council and other groups that use testers to develop discrimination cases. However, the court held that there were no exceptions (not even a law enforcement exception) to the rule against misrepresentation. Until the Rules are formally amended, it said, the prohibition applies to all lawyers in all cases. As you might imagine, this case joined Rule 4.2 as Exhibit A in the Justice Department's campaign against its lawyers being subject to state ethics rules while engaged in customary law enforcement operations.

What do you think of Gatti's defense? Is Model Rule 4.1(a) too absolute? Gatti was, after all, trying to get people to talk honestly who would not have talked at all if he had told them the truth.

b. In response to the public reaction to *Gatti*, the Oregon Supreme Court amended its Code of Professional Responsibility DR 1–102 to add a (D) that says:

"Notwithstanding DR 1–102(A)(1), (A)(3) and (A)(4) and DR 7–102(A)(5), it shall not be professional misconduct for a lawyer to advise clients or others about or to supervise lawful covert activity in the investigation of violations of civil or criminal law or constitutional rights, provided the lawyer's conduct is otherwise in compliance with these disciplinary rules. 'Covert activity,' as used in this rule, means an effort to obtain information on unlawful activity through the use of misrepresentations or other subterfuge. 'Covert activity' may be commenced by a lawyer or involve a lawyer as an adviser or supervisor only when the lawyer in good faith believes there is a reasonable possibility that unlawful activity has taken place, is taking place or will take place in the foreseeable future."

c. Oregon Formal Opinion 2003–173, 2003 WL 22397289, discusses three hypotheticals dealing with a lawyer's covert investigation under the Oregon rule.

First, assume a client is injured on her employer's property and the sole witness refuses to testify. The lawyer advises her client to have a friend approach the witness pretending to be an employee with the personnel office seeking information about the accident. Because a worker's compensation case raises no issue of "civil or criminal law or constitutional rights," the lawyer's activity does not fall within the safe harbor under Oregon's DR 1–102(D).

Second, assume that a lawyer (who thinks a doctor falsified his client's injury report) calls the doctor pretending to be another patient to talk the doctor into revealing that he falsified the report. The issue presented by this hypothetical is whether a lawyer himself can engage in covert activity. Both public and private lawyers may "commence" a covert activity "by initiating the contact with a client or by conceiving the concept of a covert activity," but the lawyer may not "speak the deceptive words, take deceptive action, or undertake an 'undercover' identity in the course of that activity." The new rule permits "advice and supervision regarding covert activity but not direct participation in that activity."[5]

Third, assume that police officers believe that illegal drug activity is occurring based on increased foot traffic to a house. A deputy district attorney advises a police officer to act as a drug customer and go to the house to purchase drugs. The Ethics Commission found that, as long as the lawyer has a subjective good faith belief that criminal activity is occurring, he meets the standard set forth by the new Rule.

What do you think of the Oregon rule?

5. Earlier, In re Ositis, 40 P.3d 500 (Or.2002), had reaffirmed *Gatti* and reprimanded a lawyer who advised an investigator to pose as a journalist to interview an alleged animal rights advocate who might "raid" his client's medical research breeding business. The court expressly reserved comment on whether the conduct would violate its newly amended rule. Oregon Opinion 2003–173 [now renumbered as 2005–173] concluded that *Ositis* should come out differently: "the conduct in In re Ositis would now be permissible" under the new Oregon rule.

d. D.C. Ethics Opinion 323 (Mar. 29, 2004) discussed "whether attorneys who are employed by a national intelligence agency violate the Rules of Professional Conduct if they engage in fraud, deceit, or misrepresentation in the course of their non-representational official duties." The opinion acknowledged that the law sometimes requires intelligence officers acting in their official capacity to act deceitfully. For example, a lawyer working for the CIA in a clandestine capacity might be required to offer false information about her identity or employment. The opinion concludes that Rule 8.4 addresses deceitful conduct that "calls into question a lawyer's suitability to practice law." Understood in this light, "the category of conduct proscribed by the Rule does not include misrepresentations made in the course of official conduct as an employee of an agency of the United States if the attorney reasonably believes that the conduct in question is authorized by law."

e. One prominent case on deception never made it into the case reports. Hewlett–Packard paid $14.5 million to settle civil charges stemming from a probe of what members of its board were leaking sensitive company information to the press. The company allegedly hired investigators to engage in pretexting, i.e., pretending to be board members so as to get those individuals' phone records. Hewlett–Packard did not admit wrongdoing under its settlement with the California attorney general, and criminal charges are possible against former Hewlett–Packard officials involved in the investigation. The executives all pled not guilty. Christopher Lawton, H–P Settles Civil Charges in "Pretexting" Scandal, Wall Street J., Dec. 8, 2006, at A3.[6]

f. What about befriending a witness or opposing party on the social networks, Myspace or Facebook, to discover "public information" about the person? Philadelphia Bar Ass'n Professional Guidance Committee Opinion 2009–02 (Mar. 2009) held that a lawyer could not use an agent to befriend a target in order to find out information on the personal page because such conduct involved deception under Rule 8.4(c). The opinion found that even when the agent used a real name, the purpose for contacting the target was not for friendship, but for gaining access to personal information.

g. New York County Lawyers' Ass'n Ethics Opinion 289 (May 2007) concluded that lawyers may supervise nonlawyer investigators that use "dissemblance," defined as "misstatements as to identity and purpose made solely for gathering evidence," but only if four conditions are present. First, the investigation must involve civil rights violations or intellectual property rights or must be authorized by law. Second, the evidence may not be readily available by other means. Third, the conduct may not otherwise

6. Since the publicity surrounding the Hewlett–Packard case, Congress enacted a statute that makes it a federal crime to obtain an individual's phone records without his or her approval. About a dozen states had already prohibited pretexting, but there was no clear federal prohibition related to telephone records until now. In 1999, Congress prohibited pretexting to obtain financial records. David Rogers & Robert Guy Matthews, Congress Approves Bill To Criminalize "Pretexting", Wall Street J., Dec. 11, 2006, at p. A6.

violate ethical standards, and fourth, the dissemblance must not unlawfully or unethically violate the rights of third persons.

Now are you clear what you may and may not do? How would you resolve the conflicting concerns inherent in the use of deception in the search for truth?

3.   May a lawyer use deception to help catch a criminal?

a.   In re Pautler, 47 P.3d 1175 (Colo.2002), is a dramatic case about the place of deception in seeking an important objective. A man named William Neal, who had already brutally murdered several people, attacked and kidnapped a woman and then told her to tell the police how to contact him. On the phone, Neal described his gruesome crimes in detail for over three-and-a-half hours, but the police did not know where he was and he demanded to talk to a defense lawyer before turning himself in.

Chief Deputy District Attorney Mark Pautler, who was with the police, spoke to Neal on the phone and posed as a public defender. Pautler did not advise Neal about his rights, but he promised to meet Neal when he turned himself in. Later, when the real public defender met Neal and listened to a tape recording of the earlier conversation, he recognized Pautler's voice and realized that Pautler had impersonated someone other than a prosecutor. The court convicted Neal and imposed the death penalty.

b.   Would you have given Pautler a medal for saving Colorado from a serial killer or would you have considered him deceitful and an embarrassment to the bar?

The Colorado Supreme Court took the latter view, suspending him from practice for three months, which was stayed for twelve months of probation. The court acknowledged that Pautler was motivated by a strong desire to protect other potential victims, but it said that no imminent public harm exception existed to Model Rule 8.4(c)'s prohibition of deceptive conduct. Further, Paulter had violated Rule 4.3, which provides that, in dealing on behalf of a client with a person not represented by counsel, the attorney is required to state that he is representing a client and could not state or imply that he was disinterested. The court also emphasized that Pautler did not attempt to contact a real public defender after failing to reach Neal's preferred attorney and that he showed no "remorse" for his use of deceit to help get a violent killer off the streets.

Are you impressed by the court's adherence to principle? Or, do you wonder if some people lose all common sense when they put on a black robe?

C.   USING AN OPPONENT'S INADVERTENTLY DISCLOSED CONFIDENTIAL INFORMATION

1.   May a lawyer take advantage of a confidential fax that her adversary inadvertently sent to her?

a.   Remember from Problem 7 that, under the rules of evidence, some courts hold that the inadvertent disclosure of confidential information forfeits the attorney-client evidentiary privilege, even if the lawyer acted "reasonably." Other courts are more forgiving, finding that inadvertent disclosure (whether reasonable or not) does not necessarily result in loss of the evidentiary privilege. The question remains what a litigator who *receives* such documents should do with them. If the law of evidence says that the privilege is waived when the lawyer sends a misdirected fax, does the lawyer *receiving* the fax have any ethical obligation in Model Rule 1.6 to refrain from using the document? May she use the misdirected fax (or misdirected email) to argue that the opposing lawyer has "waived" the privilege? *Must* she use, or try to use, the information as part of her duty to fight zealously for her client? Should the recipient of the information let her opponent off the hook while thinking, "there but for the grace of God go I," or should she press the advantage on behalf of her own client?

b. ABA Formal Opinion 92–368 (Nov. 10, 1992), came down in favor of letting the lawyer who made the mistake off the hook. It held that as a matter of ethical responsibility, a lawyer who gets misdirected material from an opponent [a fax, an email] should refrain from reading it, notify the sending lawyer, and either return or destroy the material as the sending lawyer directs.

c. But the Model Rules of Professional Conduct were silent on these issues until 2002 when the ABA House of Delegates added subsection (b) to Model Rule 4.4. This Rule requires a lawyer who receives an inadvertently sent document to "promptly notify the sender" but does not require the receiving lawyer to avoid reading or using the document. Faced with this change in law and policy, the ABA Standing Committee on Ethics and Professional Responsibility withdrew Formal Opinion 92–368. See ABA Formal Opinion 05–437 (Oct. 1, 2005).

d. Look at Model Rule 4.4, Comment 2. What "protective measures" should the sender seek? May the receiving lawyer ask a court to approve the lawyer's use of the document, hoping that the rules of evidence in that jurisdiction say that misdirecting the fax serves to waive the privilege?

Now look at Comment 3. What "professional judgment" is involved in deciding whether to return the document unread? Is the citation in Comment 3 to Model Rules 1.2 and 1.4 an implicit acknowledgment that what to do is tell the client: "Using the document is very helpful to us, and the rules of evidence in this jurisdiction conclude that their mistake serves to waive the privilege. So, you tell me what to do." If so, why does Comment 3 seem to say just the reverse?

e. The California Supreme Court has taken its own approach to these issues. In Rico v. Mitsubishi Motors Corp., 171 P.3d 1092 (Cal.2007), the defense lawyer had made notes of a meeting with defense experts discussing litigation strategy and vulnerabilities. Later, the defense lawyer deposed the plaintiff's experts and left the notes in his briefcase while he went to the restroom. Somehow, the plaintiff's lawyer got the defense notes; the court could only say that it was "through inadvertence." Thereafter, the plaintiff's lawyer made copies of the notes and used them to impeach the defense experts at their deposition. When the defense realized what had happened, it moved to disqualify the plaintiff's lawyer and experts.

The court agreed. The notes were attorney work product and absolutely protected against discovery, the court held. Where a lawyer "receives materials that obviously appear to be * * * confidential and privileged and where it is reasonably apparent that the materials were provided or made available through inadvertence, the lawyer receiving the materials should refrain from examining the materials any more than is essential to ascertain if the materials are privileged, and shall immediately notify the sender that he or she possesses material that appears to be privileged. The parties may then proceed to resolve the situation by agreement or may resort to the court for guidance * * *." The plaintiff's lawyer admitted that he had soon known the document was confidential and that he had not notified the defense, so the court affirmed the order of disqualification.

2. May (must) the lawyer use the information that a whistle-blower from the opposing party *intentionally* sent?

a. ABA Formal Opinion 94–382 (July 5, 1994) dealt not with the misdirected fax but with documents that the sender intended to send to the lawyer but the sender had no authority to send. The sender might be a whistleblower, a disgruntled employee (whether or not the discontent is justified), or someone seeking to rectify what he or she considered to be improper or unjust conduct, for example, the failure to disclose documents pursuant to a valid subpoena.

The ABA opinion first discussed the case of In re Shell Oil Refinery, 143 F.R.D. 105 (E.D.La.1992). That case required that the party receiving the materials not make use of them. The person was said to be required to identify and return the materials and have no further contact with the disclosing persons. The opinion noted (but did not find convincing) a number of state ethics opinions that concluded that "the receiving lawyer has no obligation to disclose to a court or an adverse party that she possesses the adverse party's privileged or confidential information and that the receiving lawyer may use such materials." The opinion rejected an "absolute rule that would prohibit a receiving lawyer from reviewing or using such materials under all circumstances;" the receiving lawyer, for example, may have a legitimate claim that the documents should have been produced during discovery, or the person sending the documents may be acting under the authority of a whistleblowing statute. The opinion recommended that the lawyer's actions include:

"(a) refraining from reviewing materials which are probably privileged or confidential, any further than is necessary to determine how appropriately to proceed; (b) notifying the adverse party or the party's lawyer that the receiving lawyer possesses the documents, (c) following the instructions of the adverse party's lawyer, or (d), in the case of a dispute, refraining from using the materials until a definitive resolution of the proper disposition of the materials is obtained from a court."

Does this advice make sense to you?[7]

b. It made sense to the court in Maldonado v. State, 225 F.R.D. 120 (D.N.J.2004). Maldonado sued for employment discrimination, a hostile work environment, and retaliation. Someone unknown sent Maldonado a copy of a letter that his employers addressed to their lawyer containing their impressions as to the credibility of certain prospective witnesses. Maldonado turned the document over to his lawyers, who incorporated the information into their amended complaint. The lawyers did not, however, notify opposing lawyers that they had possession of the letter. Defense counsel realized that the plaintiff had the letter when they received the amended complaint, so they asked the lawyers to return it. When Maldonado's lawyers refused, defense counsel sought a protective order. After a hearing, the trial judge ruled that the document was privileged and that defendants were not "careless in their handling of the letter." Defense counsel moved to dismiss the case or to disqualify plaintiff's lawyers based on the substantial prejudice their knowledge would have on the defendants' case at trial. The judge refused to dismiss the case, but, relying on ABA Formal Opinion 94–382, he decided that the plaintiff's lawyers, after their reading showed that the information was privileged, should have notified opposing counsel and returned the document. Because plaintiff's lawyers were wrongly privy to what was "[e]ssentially ... a blue print to [the] merits" of his case, their continued representation would have a "substantial taint" on future proceedings. So the court disqualified the lawyers.[8]

c. Do these "stolen papers" cases present different issues than those raised by the "inadvertent disclosure" cases? Does Model Rule 4.4(b)'s approach work in both situations?

3. If the other side's word processing program leaves metadata in documents turned over in discovery, may a lawyer receiving the documents use that metadata to learn how the document was created?

a. Some word processing programs such as Microsoft Word have a feature that allows someone who receives an electronic version of the document to see when the document was created, what changes were made in the document during its preparation, and similar information that can be very helpful in determining authenticity of the document and alternatives the preparers considered and rejected. Most lawyers would not want their opponents to have that information, and yet the information can be retrieved relatively simply. The information can be "scrubbed" and rendered unavailable by creating a PDF version of the document, but not everyone remembers to transmit only scrubbed versions.

---

7. ABA Formal Opinion 06–440 (May 13, 2006) withdrew Opinion 94–382, not because the analysis was wrong, but because the Model Rules as amended in 2002 seemed not to answer the question.

8. See also Lipin v. Bender, 644 N.E.2d 1300 (N.Y.1994) (plaintiff took privileged documents belonging to defense counsel that she found in a conference room while the lawyers were engaged in a heated exchange; court dismissed the plaintiff's complaint with prejudice).

b. ABA Formal Opinion 06–422 (Aug. 2006) considered whether a lawyer receiving an unscrubbed document could properly access the metadata and concluded somewhat controversially that if Rule 4.4(b) had meant the ability to retrieve metadata is to be treated as inadvertent disclosure it would have said so. Therefore, the opinion placed no limitation on a recipient's retrieving and using the concealed information and said that anyone who does not want an opponent to use such information must negotiate a special agreement to that effect, send the document in hard copy only, or send only a version in which the metadata is not retrievable.

c. What do you think of the result reached in Opinion 06–422?[9] Does the ABA need to amend the Model Rules every time a new technology presents the inadvertent disclosure problem in a new form? Should we want to encourage scrubbing metadata out of documents? If a document has forensic value, won't scrubbing improperly alter the evidence?

D. JUDICIAL EFFORTS TO ENFORCE CIVILITY

1. Should courts attempt to require "civility" of litigators who appear before them? May a state bar discipline Martin for his "rambo" litigation tactics designed to impose costs on the opponent and to teach them a lesson?

a. "Civility" is a modern buzzword in litigation, with efforts to require civility both frequent and increasing. Dondi Properties Corp. v. Commerce Savings & Loan Ass'n, 121 F.R.D. 284 (N.D.Tex.1988) (en banc), promulgated a code of civility for civil litigation, for example. The Texas Code was designed to end "unnecessary contention and sharp practices between lawyers." See also the Northampton County Bar Association Guide to Conduct and Etiquette at the Bar contained in the Standards Supplement. Are civility standards "trendy lip service to our better selves" or are they more than that?

b. Do civility standards add anything not already in the ABA Model Rules? Are such standards unnecessary or even counterproductive? Look at Model Rule 3.5(d). Some conduct is already disallowed as "conduct intended to disrupt a tribunal." Do modern civility codes give proper notice to lawyers about the range of conduct that is prohibited?

2. What should courts do, if anything, to impose or encourage civility?

a. Cook v. American Steamship Co., 134 F.3d 771 (6th Cir.1998), involved a lawyer who physically assaulted opposing counsel, resulting in the court declaring a mistrial. Relying on the right to sanction a lawyer who "multiplies the proceedings * * * vexatiously," the court affirmed a sanction that required the lawyer to pay his opponent's costs of conducting the additional trial. Of course, a physical assault is already a crime. Should the court have simply referred the case to the local prosecutor?

---

9. Some state ethics opinion have come out the other way. See, e.g., New York State Bar Ethics Opinion 749 (Dec. 14, 2001); Alabama State Bar Opinion 2007–2 (Mar.14, 2007).

b. In Lee v. American Eagle Airlines, 93 F.Supp.2d 1322 (S.D.Fla. 2000), the court cut plaintiff's counsel's fee award as a sanction for lack of civility in the courtroom. "Let's kick some ass," counsel called out as the trial for employment discrimination got underway. In another incident, counsel told a defense lawyer she had only been assigned to work on the case because she was African–American. On another occasion, counsel said to the court reporter, "What are you here for, just to look pretty?" In addition, counsel accused the judge of bias and laughed and looked up at the ceiling in response to rulings. Ultimately, the court halved the lawyers' rates for pretrial work and gave them nothing for their time in trial. It also sent a copy of the order to the Florida Bar for possible disciplinary action.

c. In Florida Bar v. Martocci, 791 So.2d 1074 (Fla.2001), during a divorce proceeding, the lawyer had harassed the opposing side, repeatedly telling the opposing client that she was "crazy" and a "nut case," telling opposing counsel that she should "go back to Puerto Rico," and threatening to beat up the opponent's father in open court. The court found the lawyer's conduct crossed the line from "zealous advocacy" to "unethical misconduct." The court ordered that the lawyer be publicly reprimanded, put on probation for two years, and evaluated for possible anger management assistance.

d. In Pounders v. Watson, 521 U.S. 982 (1997), the trial court held the lawyer in summary contempt for failing to obey the trial court's order not to tell the jury the possible sentence the defendant faced. The Ninth Circuit reversed, saying a lawyer could not be sentenced for summary contempt without a hearing to determine whether the violation was willful. But the U.S. Supreme Court agreed with the trial court, holding that where the contempt occurs in open court and prompt action is required to avoid "demoralization of the court's authority," summary action is proper even if the conduct is not inherently disruptive of the proceeding. Justices Stevens and Breyer dissented.

3. What should a judge do if abusive conduct occurs in depositions, outside the presence of the judge, who is therefore unable to correct any misconduct immediately?

a. In Paramount Communications Inc. v. QVC Network Inc., 637 A.2d 34 (Del.1994), the Delaware Supreme Court *sua sponte* criticized remarks of Texas lawyer Joseph Jamail towards opposing counsel during a deposition. At one point in the record, Mr. Jamail instructed his witness not to answer a question and then said: "He's not going to answer that. Certify it. I'm going to shut it down if you don't go to your next question." The other lawyer said, "No. Joe, Joe." Mr. Jamail responded, "Don't 'Joe' me, a_____. You can ask some questions, but get off of that. I'm tired of you. You could gag a maggot off a meat wagon." The court did not discipline Mr. Jamail, who did not otherwise appear in the case, was not a member of the Delaware bar, and was not admitted *pro hac vice*. However, the court said that his conduct "relates to a serious issue of professionalism involving deposition practices in Delaware trial courts." Do you agree?

b. In re Estiverne, 741 So.2d 649 (La.1999), involved even wilder conduct. After Lawyer A accused Lawyer B of misconduct during a deposition, Lawyer B suggested "stepping outside and settling the matter man to man." After the deposition, Lawyer A stepped out, returned with a gun and threatened to kill Lawyer B. Lawyer A explained that Lawyer B held a black belt in karate while Lawyer A was less physically fit. The court found threatening a legal colleague with a gun was less egregious than killing him, but it still suspended Lawyer A for a year and a day—a sanction that required the lawyer to file a petition for readmission.

c. Matter of Golden, 496 S.E.2d 619 (S.C.1998), imposed a public reprimand on a lawyer whose deposition conduct involved "sarcasm and maliciousness," "unnecessary combativeness," "gratuitous threatening and intimidation," and "unequivocal bad manners." At one point in the deposition, for example, he called the female opposing party a "meanspirited, vicious witch" and said he wanted to be "locked in a room naked with you with a sharp knife," explaining that he wanted to kill the woman.

d. Do these examples of conduct by members of our learned profession help explain why Model Rule 3.5 now has Comment 5?

4. What should a court do about other disruptive conduct that occurs out of the courtroom setting?

a. In Hirschfeld v. Superior Court In and For County of Maricopa, 908 P.2d 22 (Ariz.Ct.App.1995), the lawyer who represented the father in a child custody dispute believed the mother was not living up to a joint custody agreement. During an overnight recess in the proceedings, the lawyer followed the mother and kept calling out and asking her in a loud voice to tell him where she had hidden the child. The judge's office had to summon help from the sheriff to protect the mother from further harassment. This court affirmed holding the lawyer in contempt: "the court has the right and the duty to protect litigants, witnesses, attorneys and jurors from misbehavior and harassment while they are in or near the courtroom, whether they are arriving, waiting, or departing."

b. In United States v. Wunsch, 84 F.3d 1110 (9th Cir.1996), a male criminal defense lawyer wrote a letter to the female assistant U.S. attorney with an attachment stating in large, bold type: "MALE LAWYERS PLAY BY THE RULES, DISCOVER TRUTH AND RESTORE ORDER. FEMALE LAWYERS ARE OUTSIDE THE LAW, CLOUD TRUTH AND DESTROY ORDER." The trial court ordered the lawyer to apologize, but the Ninth Circuit reversed. Although the court acknowledged cases in which a *pattern* of sexist speech was sanctioned, it found that this single incident neither impugned the "integrity of the court" nor interfered with the "administration of justice." The court held that California Business & Professions Code § 6068(f)—requiring an attorney to "abstain from all offensive personality"—was unconstitutionally vague. The court expressed concern about the First Amendment problems in sanctioning lawyer for speech, even uncouth speech.

c.   Redwood v. Dobson, 476 F.3d 462 (7th Cir.2007), involved what Judge Easterbrook, writing for the court, called a "grudge match." One of the lawyers, clearly trying to provoke the witness, asked about his driving violations, his mental health, and whether he was part of a "homosexual clique." The lawyer defending the deposition instructed his client not to answer those questions. Later, the witness (who was himself a lawyer) answered "I don't know" or "I don't remember" to simple questions whose answers the witness likely knew. The court said the tactics of both sides were improper; a witness may not refuse to answer except based on privilege. The proper course for the harassed witness is to adjourn the deposition and seek a protective order, not give back in kind. "It is precisely when animosity runs high that playing by the rules is vital." The court issued a censure against three of the lawyers, one of them the evasive witness, for their "conduct unbecoming a member of the bar."[10]

d.   In Brewer & Bickel, Etiquette of the Advocate?, Texas Lawyer 20, 21 (Mar. 21, 1994), litigators argue that the courts' efforts to encourage loose and nondefinable concepts as "civility" will be counterproductive and will chill lawyers's legitimate behavior. Clients "are bound to be adversely affected as they witness their lawyers tiptoeing toward compromise with opposing counsel as 'cooperatively' as possible." Do you agree? Do you believe effective advocacy demands boorish behavior by lawyers? Is "speech" simply the use of words or can it constitute intimidation? Should lawyers be more disposed to win on the merits than to make their opponents' lives hellish?

e.   Do courts already have so much to do so that, on a scale of evil, "boorishness" does not rank terribly high? Should lawyers have to learn to live with crude and callous conduct, or does failing to sanction such conduct tend to encourage more of it in the future? Judges sometimes make callous or gratuitous remarks about lawyers in their opinions. Should judges be reluctant to cast the first stone when they are not always without fault themselves?

PROBLEM 25

DISCLOSURE OF LAW OR FACTS FAVORABLE TO THE OTHER SIDE

Confidentiality is the watchword for much of what a lawyer does. Litigators in particular assert work product immunity, as well as the attorney-client privilege and their ethical duty of confidentiality, as bases for nondisclosure. Some advocates are surprised to learn that the confidentiality obligation has important exceptions. Indeed, in some situations, the

---

10. Professor Steven Lubet's column in The American Lawyer, May 1, 2007, p. 226, suggests that the court's requirement of run-ning to the court for relief is unrealistic in a real-time deposition context. Do you agree?

law requires lawyers to volunteer information they prefer to keep undisclosed. This problem begins by discussing the duty to reveal adverse legal authority. It then examines when factual information must be disclosed. Next, it explores the lawyer's duty when discovery responses have been incomplete or inaccurate, and it examines the lawyer's duty where the court's mistake about publicly-available information favors the lawyer's client.

FACTS

You have prepared your case fully, and you consider it a sure winner on the motion for summary judgment. However, hours before the argument on that motion, you discovered several cases with dicta directly against you. Two of the cases have holdings that by analogy are against you. You have concluded that the likelihood is great that the judge would rule against your client on the summary judgment motion if she knew of the cases you have discovered. Your opponent (perhaps because he is less prepared than you) has not referred to these cases.

Now, you have come across a witness who can supply a *factual* piece of evidence harmful to your client's case. You conclude that if you make a motion for summary judgment you would win because opposing counsel has not been able to present an affidavit on a vital point. However your secretly-discovered witness could supply the essential link in the opposition's evidentiary chain. The opposing party has not contacted this witness, and you assume no one else knows of his existence.

You are in the midst of discovery. Your client has been asked to produce emails and documents pertaining to the litigation and the client has several mainframe computers full of information. Your client also automatically deletes emails daily that are over three months old. You are concerned that such data may be part of the discovery request. But as a lawyer you are not computer savvy and will simply do your best to comply.

As you are reviewing the deposition testimony that you have attached to your motion for summary judgment, you realize that one of your best witnesses testified about a fact important to your case in a way that you know is false. You don't know whether she was lying or simply mistaken, and the other side clearly has not discovered the inaccuracy.

In another case, you represent a convicted client who stands before the judge to be sentenced. The court clerk indicates to the court that the defendant has no record. The court thereupon says to the defendant—who stands silent—"Since you have no criminal record, I will only put you on probation." You know, either by independent investigation or from what your client has told you, that he in fact has a criminal record and the clerk's information is incorrect. The judge turns to you and says, "Anything to add, counsel?"

QUESTIONS

A.   CANDOR ABOUT ADVERSE LEGAL AUTHORITY

1.   Must you cite all relevant cases to the court, even those not favorable to your position? What are the limits, if any, on that obligation?

a.   Look at Model Rule 3.3(a)(2). What does this rule imply the courts expect of a lawyer? May you simply put contrary cases in a footnote in your brief without in any way explaining their relevance? Do you have to highlight the contrary authority?

b.   In Katris v. Immigration and Naturalization Service, 562 F.2d 866 (2d Cir.1977), the attorney for petitioner failed to cite a particular Second Circuit case and several cases from other circuits because, he said "these decisions were adverse to his position here and that he did not agree with them." The attorney had represented one of the parties in the adverse Second Circuit case. The court concluded the lawyer had misled the court and taxed costs against the attorney personally.

c.   ABA Informal Opinion 84–1505 (Mar. 5, 1984) reaffirmed the disclosure obligation. A plaintiff's lawyer had successfully beaten the defendant's motion to dismiss in a case of first impression interpreting a recently enacted statute. Based on earlier analogous cases, the trial court's ruling had been correct. Later, however, during the pendency of the action, plaintiff's lawyer learned that an appellate court elsewhere in the state had recently interpreted the statute in a way that was arguably contrary to the trial court's ruling. He asked the ABA Standing Committee on Ethics and Professional Responsibility whether he was obliged to disclose the new appellate opinion to the trial court. Even though one could have interpreted the appellate ruling in a way not "directly adverse to the position of the client," another reading was clearly adverse. The trial court would certainly be benefitted in this case of first impression by having information about the appellate decision, so the ABA Committee concluded that the plaintiff's lawyer had a duty to reveal the information to the court.

d.   In re Thonert, 733 N.E.2d 932 (Ind.2000), involved a client who wanted to withdraw his guilty plea. The lawyer argued that the trial judge had a duty to ask whether the client understood his rights at the time of the plea, in spite of the fact the client had seen a videotape explaining those rights. The lawyer's position was directly contrary to a decision by the same Indiana Supreme Court a year earlier in a case argued by the same lawyer. He neither cited that decision nor argued that the result should be changed or distinguished. For the failure to do so—and for taking a fee from the client without disclosing what a long shot the argument was—the court formally admonished the lawyer.

e. In Tyler v. State of Alaska, 47 P.3d 1095 (Alaska App.2001), Tyler, the defendant, appealed his felony DWI conviction by asserting that one of his two prior convictions had been invalid. Although Tyler had conceded his guilt in the instant case, he contended that invalidation of the prior offenses would make felony prosecution inappropriate. Tyler's attorney, Cyrus, however, failed to cite a case of the Alaska Supreme Court that had decided against Tyler's theory in a felony DWI case. The court fined Cyrus $250 for violating his ethical duty to cite directly adverse authority. First, the court found that Cyrus was aware of the prior case, because he had participated in it as defense counsel. Although Cyrus argued that he did not cite the case because he believed it was distinguishable, the court stated that the attorney was under a duty to cite any case that would reasonably be considered to "cast substantial doubt" on the argument being made and thus be important to the judge hearing the case. It was irrelevant, the court said, whether the omitted case would completely control the decision.

f. In Precision Specialty Metals, Inc. v. United States, 315 F.3d 1346 (Fed.Cir.2003), the court issued a formal reprimand against a Justice Department attorney named Walser for selectively quoting passages from precedents, which had the effect of changing the meaning of quotes. The department had filed a motion for extension of time, which the court denied. Its order required the government to file its response "forthwith." The government did not file its response for 12 days, which the court considered untimely. In the motion for reconsideration, attorney Walser argued that there was no uniform definition of the term "forthwith." Quoting from other cases, she argued that the term meant "reasonable under the circumstances." However, she omitted from her quotations sentences and citations referencing an opinion harmful to her case—an opinion stating that "forthwith" is sometimes defined as within twenty-four hours. She also italicized certain words in her quotations, without saying "emphasis added." By omitting, from one of her quotations, the words "as it is used in the SAA [Suits in Admiralty Act]," after "forth-with," she made the opinion seem broader than it really was. The court of appeals affirmed the reprimand and added the following: "While the court did not err in formally reprimanding Walser, that reprimand should not be seen as in any way detracting from the department's own responsibility to establish high standards for its lawyers and to provide adequate training and supervision, so that episodes such as this are not repeated." 315 F.3d at 1358.

2. Do these cases make sense to you? What is the rationale underlying the obligation to cite adverse authority? Does the rule simply serve to penalize a lawyer who engages in more effort to uncover the relevant case law? Why should one lawyer have the obligation to do her opponent's homework?

a. One statement of the rationale is found in Model Rule 3.3, Comment 4. It says: "A lawyer is not required to make a disinterested exposition of the law, but must recognize the existence of pertinent legal authorities. * * * The underlying concept is that legal argument is a discussion seeking to determine the legal premises properly applicable to the case."

b.   Restatement Third, The Law Governing Lawyers § 111, Comment *c*, says that failure to disclose adverse legal authority—

"may have the same effect as a misstatement of the law. It deprives the court of useful information and serves no interest of the client other than obtaining a result not provided for by the law. It is sometimes argued that the rule requires the advocate to act against the client's interest * * *. However, the advocate's role is to present the client's case within the framework of the law, which requires common terms of legal reference with the court and opposing counsel."

c.   Another analyst put the explanation this way:

"[T]here is no obligation to the client to withhold knowledge of the applicable law. The obligation is to present the applicable law to the court. This, of course, is not to say that the lawyer need not do his best to distinguish, or even obtain an overruling of the prior law. The obligation is to represent the client fully in obtaining a determination of the law, but to extend it to a concealment of the law would be to distort our judicial process which relies upon stare decisis as a corner-stone. An allied question is whether or not the advocate is required to advance new theories, which may be controlling, on behalf of the other party to the lawsuit, as an aid to the court. I agree with those who say 'no'. This inaction does not mislead the court in deciding disputed points of law which are before the court. A contrary position involves an abandonment of the adversary system in regard to the decisional process."[1]

d.   Do these explanations put to rest any reservations you have about the rule? Are most briefs and oral arguments you have observed simply a "discussion seeking to determine the legal premises properly applicable to the case"? Is the law so clear that "common terms of legal reference" will inevitably be found if all cases are cited to the court?

e.   Does a conclusion about what constitutes "legal authority that is directly adverse" require the lawyer to develop a theory of the case that competes with the lawyer's own? Might the result of that effort be to suggest to the opponent a theory about the case that it had not earlier realized? In short, does this rule require a lawyer to do the other side's work for it?

B.   CANDOR ABOUT ADVERSE FACTS

1.   Why do the Rules treat disclosure of newly discovered facts differently from the disclosure of adverse legal authority?

---

1. E. Wayne Thode, The Ethical Standard for the Advocate, 29 Ins. Counsel J. 33,   39–40 (1962) (footnotes omitted).

a.   Must a lawyer reveal a witness when opposing counsel has neither sought the witness nor asked questions in discovery that would lead to the witness? Must the lawyer reveal the witness to the court in order to further the search for truth? *May* a lawyer reveal the witness to the court? Listen to Samuel Williston:

> "The case was tried before Chief Justice Knowlton. I opened the case at some length and I also made the preliminary part of the final argument. The Chief Justice decided promptly in favor of [my client,] the defendant, and since the decision was upon the facts, there was no opportunity for the plaintiffs to carry the case further. The handsomely bound volumes of interrogatories were only useful as waste paper. The plaintiffs either did not have so full a file of their correspondence with the defendant as we did, or it had not been so carefully examined by their counsel, for we had letters in our file that would have been useful to them. They did not demand their production and we did not feel bound to disclose them. In the course of his remarks the Chief Justice stated as one reason for his decision a supposed fact which I knew to be unfounded. I had in front of me a letter that showed his error. Though I have no doubt of the propriety of my behavior in keeping silent, I was somewhat uncomfortable at the time.

> "One of the troublesome ethical questions which a young trial lawyer is confronted with is the extent to which he is bound to disclose to the court facts which are injurious to his client's case. The answer is not doubtful. The lawyer must decide when he takes a case whether it is a suitable one for him to undertake and after this decision is made, he is not justified in turning against his client by exposing injurious evidence entrusted to him."[2]

Professor Williston reports that he was "uncomfortable at the time" with his ethical decision. Are you satisfied that he was being "professional" in suppressing his discomfort?

b.   People v. Cassas, 646 N.E.2d 449 (N.Y.1995), makes clear that a lawyer does not have a right to make a unilateral decision not to protect the client's rights. The defendant shot his wife to death at their home. The next morning, the lawyer brought the defendant to the nearest police precinct, said the defendant had committed the crime, and told the police where to find the body and the gun. The state introduced those statements to the jury. The court found the defendant had not authorized those statements, so they had been erroneously admitted into evidence. The court ordered a new trial.

2.   Should the law impose a higher standard than Professor Williston followed?

2. Samuel Williston, Life and Law: An Autobiography 271–72 (1940). In a similar case, New York County Lawyers' Association Opinion No. 309 (1933) ruled, without discussion, that it is "not professionally improper" for the attorney not to volunteer this witness to the court.

a. Federal Rule of Civil Procedure 26, as amended in 2000, for example, provides that:

Rule 26. Duty to Disclose; General Provisions Governing Discovery
* * *

(a) Required disclosures. (1) Initial Disclosure.

(A) In General. Except as * * * otherwise stipulated or ordered by the court, a party must, without awaiting a discovery request, provide to the other parties: (i) the name and, if known, the address and telephone number of each individual likely to have discoverable information—along with the subjects of that information—that the disclosing party may use to support its claims or defenses, unless the use would be solely for impeachment; (ii) a copy—or a description by category and location—of all documents, electronically stored information, and tangible things that the disclosing party has in its possession, custody, or control and may use to support its claims or defenses, unless the use would be solely for impeachment; (iii) a computation of each category of damages claimed by the disclosing party * * *; and (iv) * * * any insurance agreement * * * [available] to satisfy all or part of a possible judgment in the action or to indemnify or reimburse for payments made to satisfy the judgment.

* * *

(e) Supplementing Disclosures and Responses. (1) In General. A party who has made a disclosure under Rule 26(a)—or who has responded to an interrogatory, request for production, or request for admission—must supplement or correct its disclosure or response: (A) in a timely manner if the party learns that in some material respect the disclosure or response is incomplete or incorrect, and if the additional or corrective information has not otherwise been made known to the other parties during the discovery process or in writing; or (B) as ordered by the court.

b. If Federal Rule 26 were applicable in the circumstances of this problem, what would it compel you to do about disclosure of the newly-discovered adverse witness?

3. What should the sanction be if a court concludes that a lawyer deceived it by not volunteering factual information?

a. In Toledo Bar Ass'n v. Fell, 364 N.E.2d 872 (Ohio 1977) (per curiam), the lawyer had filed a workers' compensation claim for permanent disability of his client, but his client died before the hearing on the claim. The attorney did not volunteer this information to the Industrial Commission because he knew it routinely denied permanent disability claims in such cases. Assuming the claim was originally filed in good faith, what discipline, if any, is justified by this nondisclosure? The Ohio Supreme Court indefinitely suspended the attorney. Would you have done the same?[3]

b.   The court in *Fell* relied on several provisions then in the Model Code of Professional Responsibility, the predecessor of the present Model Rules of Professional Conduct. One rule, DR 7–102(A), said simply that a lawyer shall not "conceal or knowingly fail to disclose that which he is required by law to reveal." What provision in the present Model Rules comes closest to saying the same thing? Is it Model Rule 3.3(a)(1)? When the lawyer's client dies, under the law of agency, the lawyer no longer has a client; the agency is terminated by death. Is it easy to see that the lawyer should have told the court that he no longer had a client in the case?

c.   If the lawyer must volunteer this adverse fact, what other facts must the lawyer volunteer? Should the lawyer have to volunteer that one of his major witnesses is ill and may not be able to testify, thereby undercutting the settlement value of his case?

d.   Virgin Islands Housing Authority v. David, 823 F.2d 764 (3d Cir.1987), reminds lawyers that they must state accurately what happened below when they make an argument on appeal. Tenant had clearly lost in the territorial court on the issue whether an administrative hearing had been denied the tenant before his eviction. The housing authority had not appeared at the hearing before the district court, however, and so was not in a position to correct the record when the tenant's lawyer flatly denied that any finding on the issue had been made below. Thus, the trial court had mistakenly reversed the judgment of eviction. The Third Circuit reversed the district court and then directed it to consider imposing sanctions on the tenant's lawyer for lying about the events in the territorial court.

4.   What sanction should a lawyer expect if a court concludes that the lawyer has deceived it by affirmatively misrepresenting facts?

a.   Matter of Jeffers, 3 Cal. State Bar Ct. Rptr. 211, 1994 WL 715918 (Cal.Bar Ct.1994), imposed a two-year probation on an attorney who, among other things, affirmatively made misstatements to the court about his client's death. The lawyer told the court at a September 1990 mandatory settlement conference that he had last communicated with his client just before this conference and that the client had indicated that he was not responsible for the accident and wanted the matter to go to trial. The lawyer did not tell the court that the client had died on June 21. The lawyer then said that he could not presently communicate with client because the "client's brain was not functioning," but he presented no medical verification of this fact. The court asked the lawyer how he could personally know of his client's brain incapacity if there had been no medical verification. "After a long pause," the lawyer admitted to the court that his client had died months earlier.

---

3.   If this result sounds familiar, it may be because we looked at a similar answer in Problem 20 to the question of the duty to disclose adverse facts in negotiation.

b.   In Office of Disciplinary Counsel v. Hazelkorn, 480 N.E.2d 1116 (Ohio 1985), the defendant, whose real name was Foster, gave his name as Frantz when he was arrested. The lawyer knew that his client had given a false identity but represented him in the bond hearing as if his name were Frantz. If defendant had used his real name, the prosecutor and court would have realized that he had an extensive record; instead, they accepted a no-contest plea and sentenced him to a fine. When he failed to pay the fine, a contempt citation and then an arrest warrant were issued. He was arrested, and the judge learned of the original misinformation. When the court determined that the lawyer had known all along about his client's deception to the court, the court indefinitely suspended the lawyer from practice.

c.   State v. Casby, 348 N.W.2d 736 (Minn.1984), upheld a misdemeanor criminal conviction of an attorney for misleading the court. The state prosecuted the lawyer's client for speeding and littering. It did not know that he had been driving after revocation of his license, because he identified himself using his brother's name when the police arrested him. At his arraignment and pretrial hearing, the client continued the deception. Later he pled guilty, still using the name of his brother. There was an issue whether the attorney knew the real name of her client, but the court found that she did. The lawyer asserted that, even if she knew the client's name, she was required by the attorney-client privilege and the professional obligation to keep the client's secrets not to disclose the deception he was perpetrating on the court. The court held that the lawyer had gone far beyond *passively* protecting confidential information. She had undertaken plea negotiations and written letters in which she referred to her client using the brother's name. At minimum, she should have withdrawn, but the court went on to say that it believed she could and should properly have revealed her client's true identity. Do you agree? Does the present version of Rule 3.3(a)(3) support this result?

5.   Do different rules of candor apply to a lawyer's application for a temporary restraining order (TRO)? Why do the Model Rules draw this distinction?

a.   Assume that your recently discovered witness has evidence adverse to your position at the ex parte hearing on your application for a TRO. Must you ask the witness the questions that will put the disadvantageous testimony before the court?

b.   Take a look at Model Rule 3.3(d). Why do the Rules create this distinct obligation for ex parte matters? Does Model Rule 3.3, Comment 14, answer the question to your satisfaction?

c.   What should qualify as an ex parte matter for purpose of applying Rule 3.3(d)? Should a prosecutor's appearance before a grand jury be subject to its requirements, for example? You can imagine that prosecutors and defense counsel differ as to the degree of candor a prosecutor should be required to express to a grand jury. At the moment, prevailing thought is that grand jury processes are *sui generis* and that Rule 3.3(d) may *not* apply to them. United States v. Williams, 504 U.S. 36 (1992). Do you agree with the wisdom of that conclusion?

6. If a *pro se* litigant asks a lawyer to draft or review documents the litigant will submit, does the lawyer have an obligation to inform the court that the litigant had such assistance?

a. ABA Model Code of Judicial Conduct, Rule 2.2, Comment 4 provides: "It is not a violation [of the duty of impartiality and fairness] * * * for a judge to make reasonable accommodations to ensure pro se litigants the opportunity to have their matters fairly heard." Would a failure to reveal the lawyer's role mislead the court into giving latitude where none is required?

b.   There is considerable disagreement among courts and bar authorities as to the propriety of a lawyer "ghostwriting" legal documents for a pro se litigant. Some authorities require that the lawyers specifically identify themselves and provide information about their role to the court to avoid misleading the tribunal. See, e.g., Colorado Ethics Bar Association, Ethics Opinion 101 (Jan. 1998). One court viewed disclosure as necessary because courts often treat pro se litigants with leniency. See Duran v. Carris, 238 F.3d 1268, 1272 (10th Cir. 2001). Some authorities require that the ghostwriting lawyers simply indicate that a lawyer was involved by noting on the document "Prepared with the Assistance of Counsel," but do not need to identify their names or role. See, e.g., Kansas Bar Association, Legal Ethics Opinion 09–01 (Nov. 2009). Other authorities do not require the lawyers to disclose anything. This is the view adopted by the ABA in ABA Formal Opinion 07–446 (May 5, 2007), which concludes that "there is no reasonable concern that a litigant appearing pro se will receive an unfair benefit from a tribunal as a result of behind-the-scenes legal assistance." If that is so, why are lawyers and their apparently *pro se* clients often reluctant to admit the lawyers' involvement?

C. CANDOR ABOUT INCOMPLETE OR INACCURATE DISCOVERY RESPONSES

1. What obligations do you have to comply with discovery requests by the opposing party?

a.   Model Rule 3.4(d) requires that a lawyer make a "reasonably diligent effort to comply with a legally proper discovery request." Of course, this brings into consideration the entire body of discovery law and procedure. Modern discovery was implemented in the 1970s through Federal Rule of Civil Procedure 26 and included depositions, written interrogatories, document production, physical examinations, and requests for admissions. The concept of discovery was a broad search reasonably calculated to lead to the discovery of admissible evidence. In the 1980s, judges began to use discovery conferences to manage discovery issues and abuse. In 1983, the rules were amended to provide for protective orders to limit discovery and for imposing some standards on lawyers to ensure that they only engage in legitimate discovery requests.

b. Historically, lawyers treated discovery as a poker match. If the opposing party did not ask the question, no obligation existed to disclose adverse information. Skilled advocates were trained to ask questions in depositions and in interrogatories that would produce the facts necessary to present their best case. Over the years, scholars and judges have sought to move the gaming of discovery to a more open and cooperative system. In the 1990s, the federal rules and several federal courts even moved to a system of open discovery, in which both parties were obligated to share opening all information relating to the claims and defenses presented by the parties. Open discovery presented interesting ethical issues as lawyers were asked to self-disclose information they believed to be relevant to the other side's case. Some questioned how such discovery methods could co-exist with the concept of the adversary system.

c. Modern storage of data in computer files instead of file cabinets requires discovery rules that recognize electronic data as a major source of discoverable information necessary for litigation. What must a client do with electronic files and data when a lawsuit is filed? What are the lawyer's obligations in asking a client to preserve such information? If the client's information technology department claims such information is too costly to provide, may the client refuse to cooperate in discovery? And, if the lawyers and clients delay in preserving such information, what should a court do when such data is destroyed or altered?

In a prominent series of decisions that largely created the modern world of e-discovery, Judge Shira Scheindlin addressed the application of traditional discovery rules to electronic data in the context of a gender discrimination lawsuit against UBS Warburg. Zubulake v. UBS Warburg, LLC, 217 F.R.D. 309 (S.D.N.Y. 2003) (*Zubulake I*), held that a plaintiff has a right to electronically stored emails as documents within the scope of proper discovery.

When the defendant refused to provide the plaintiff with access to data on backup tapes because of the cost of making such data accessible, Judge Scheindlin crafted a multifactor test to determine how the costs should be shared between the parties. With respect to accessible data in a computer readable format, the producing party must bear the costs of production. But with respect to restoring inaccessible data, the court must balance factors of need, the amounts at stake in the litigation, the importance of the issues in the case, and the benefit to the parties of obtaining the information. In *Zubulake III*, the judge held that the plaintiff should pay 25% of the costs of restoring the data. Zubulake v. UBS Warburg, 216 F.R.D. 280, 292 (S.D.N.Y. 2003).[4]

UBS Warburg was unable to produce some of the data because it had been destroyed, and Judge Scheindlin found that parties who reasonably

---

4. Zubulake v. UBS Warburg, LLC, 230 F.R.D. 290 (S.D.N.Y.2003) (Zubulake II) involved the plaintiff's request to disclose the transcript of a UBS Manager's deposition to the SEC because it revealed that UBS had failed to follow SEC document retention policies. The court denied the motion because it found that the plaintiff had no duty to disclose such information to the SEC.

anticipate litigation must suspend their document destruction programs and implement a "litigation hold." Zubulake v. UBS Warburg, 220 F.R.D., 212 (2003) (*Zubulake IV*), although in this decision, no sanctions were imposed because the value of the lost information was not proven.

But when subsequent depositions of the UBS Warburg witnesses disclosed that additional emails had been destroyed after receiving instructions from counsel to retain all emails, in *Zubulake V*, Judge Scheindlin found willful destruction of discoverable evidence and ordered an adverse inference instruction to the jury. Zubulake v. UBS Warburg, 229 F.R.D. 422 (S.D.N.Y. 2004). A jury awarded Ms. Zubulake $29 million at trial, and taken together, this series of decisions illustrated the need for lawyers to preserve electronic data and to instruct clients on the obligations under the discovery rules.

d. In 2006, the Federal Rules of Civil Procedure were amended to specifically address e-discovery. Under Rule 34, a party may request electronic data as part of its discovery request. Such information must be produced in an accessible format. Parties may object to production of electronic data on the grounds of its cost or undue burden. See Fed.R.Civ.P. 26(b)(2)(B). Under Rule 26(c), a judge may limit or condition disclosure of electronic information after considering a series of factors. Rule 37 provides a safe harbor for electronic data that is lost "as a result of the routine, good-faith operation of an electronic information system."

e. What does the average litigator know about electronically stored information in a client database? Given that likely lack of knowledge, how can a lawyer comply with discovery rules? At a minimum, lawyers need to inform their clients about the litigation hold and duty to provide accessible data. But should lawyers have a duty to physically monitor compliance with these electronic discovery rules? Should litigation law firms have a computer specialist on staff to ensure client compliance with these rules?

2. What sanctions should the courts impose for failure to comply with discovery requests?

a. Should stonewalling by a plaintiff in the face of defendant's discovery requests justify dismissal of the case? It did in Penthouse International, Ltd. v. Playboy Enterprises, Inc., 86 F.R.D. 396, 406–07 (S.D.N.Y.1980), aff'd 663 F.2d 371 (2d Cir.1981). On appeal the Second Circuit noted: "Penthouse deliberately disobeyed Judge Griesa's March 22, 1978, order to produce in full all of its financial statements for the relevant periods relating to gross income, net income and circulation revenue, including its balance sheets, and profit and loss statements, as had been requested by Playboy's Rule 34 demand * * *. The fact that the March 22 order was oral rather than written, and that it was not entered pursuant to a formal written Rule 37(a) motion, does not deprive it of any of its binding force and effect."

b. Pumphrey v. K.W. Thompson Tool Co., 62 F.3d 1128 (9th Cir. 1995), cert. denied, 516 U.S. 1158 (1996), was a wrongful death case. The decedent dropped a handgun, which went off and killed him. The defendant gun manufacturer introduced videotaped evidence showing that guns dropped from various heights and in various ways did not fire. However, the court later learned that the defendant had not produced in discovery a video showing times that the gun *did* fire. The court set aside the verdict because the failure to produce the other video was a fraud on the court.[5]

c.   In Qualcomm Inc. v. Broadcom Corp., 2008 WL 66932 (S.D. Cal. 2008), Qualcomm was assessed an $8.5 million sanction for failing to comply with a discovery request that would have shown its participation in a standards setting project called the Joint Video Team (JVT). In the course of preparing a witness to testify at trial, Qualcomm's outside counsel discovered email that Qualcomm had not produced in discovery showing that Qualcomm had indeed been involved in the JVT. Counsel did not produce the email as it was required to do, however, nor did it look for more electronic evidence that Qualcomm would have been required to produce. The court concluded that its "review of Qualcomm's declarations, the attorneys' declarations, and Judge Brewster's orders leads this Court to the inevitable conclusion that Qualcomm intentionally withheld tens of thousands of decisive documents from its opponent in an effort to win this case and gain a strategic business advantage over Broadcom. Qualcomm could not have achieved this goal without some type of assistance or deliberate ignorance from its retained attorneys."

In addition to the financial sanction against Qualcomm, the opinion lists all the lawyers involved by name and law school attended and refers them to the State Bar of California for possible discipline.

3. Should judges direct sanctions at counsel rather than simply punish the client when counsel is part of the failure to turn over evidence?

a.   In Litton Systems, Inc. v. AT & T, 700 F.2d 785 (2d Cir.1983), the court upheld the jury verdict for Litton but also upheld the trial court's finding that Litton's attorneys had engaged in a "pattern of intentional concealment of evidence" relating to certain documents. Thus, the Second Circuit upheld the trial court's decision to deny Litton recovery of all costs and attorneys' fees to which it would otherwise be entitled. These fees had been expected to run "well into the eight figure range." Litton Systems, Inc. v. AT & T, 91 F.R.D. 574, 578 (S.D.N.Y.1981).

b.   In The Florida Bar v. Burkich–Burrell, 659 So.2d 1082 (Fla.1995), the lawyer represented her husband, the plaintiff, in a suit for personal injuries suffered in an auto accident. One of the interrogatories asked if the plaintiff had been injured before, and if so, for the names of doctors who had treated him. He had been previously injured but did not disclose the requested information. The lawyer tried to blame the omission on a

---

5. But see, Washington State Physicians Ins. Exch. & Association v. Fisons Corp., 858 P.2d 1054 (Wash.1993), discussed in Stuart Taylor, Jr., Sleazy in Seattle, The American Lawyer, Apr. 1994, p. 5 (describing the trial court's failure to impose sanctions on a firm that withheld a "smoking gun" document in spite of its representation that it had produced all relevant documents).

paralegal working in her office, but the court did not buy it. The court suspended the lawyer for 30 days.

c.   In Cleveland Hair Clinic, Inc. v. Puig, 200 F.3d 1063 (7th Cir.2000), the plaintiff wanted to get out of federal court and file in state court instead. The defendant wanted to remain in federal court, so the plaintiff's plan was to make it appear that another lawyer had filed a different case in the state system. The lawyer told the federal judge that he was not involved in the state matter, when in fact he had worked closely with the other lawyer: "Tinaglia claims he did not literally lie to the court when he told Judge Shadur that he was not representing Haenschen because he says he meant that he was not representing Haenschen in the *instant federal* case. Such hairsplitting may be appropriate for a transplant surgeon, but not for an attorney." (emphasis in original) Ultimately, the trial judge imposed sanctions and attorney's fees exceeding $250,000! The Court of Appeals said that the high amount "strikes us as a bit much" but refused to set it aside as an abuse of discretion: the lawyer's objection to the sanction as excessive was also seen as "tardy."

d.   Should litigation sanctions ever be imposed on government lawyers, who often make salaries far below those paid to private counsel, and who are presumably working for the public interest? Is it relevant that there is authority that holding the government itself liable for sanctions would violate principles of sovereign immunity, so that if anyone on the government side can be sanctioned, it will likely be the lawyer? See, e.g., United States v. Horn, 29 F.3d 754 (1st Cir.1994).

In Chilcutt v. United States, 4 F.3d 1313 (5th Cir.1993), cert. denied sub nom. Means v. Wortham, 513 U.S. 979 (1994), the court imposed sanctions on government counsel for his discovery abuse. The lawyer argued that it violated separation of powers for a federal judge to discipline an executive branch official, but the court held that the Federal Rules of Civil Procedure override Justice Department regulations governing lawyers. The court even forbade him from seeking reimbursement from the U.S. Government for sanctions that the court imposed on the lawyer personally. "There is no question but that a court can forbid a private attorney from seeking reimbursement from clients or employers," and the court can impose that rule on government lawyers too.

4.   What should a lawyer do if, as in this problem, she discovers that the client or a material witness has given false testimony in a deposition?

a.   Look at Rule 3.3(a)(1) and Rule 3.3(a)(3). Must a lawyer reveal the truth if doing so will injure the client? ABA Formal Opinion 93–376 (Aug. 6, 1993) made clear that a lie in response to a deposition question or a discovery request is "perjury" and the requirement of current Model Rule 3.3(a)(3) controls. As provided in Model Rule 3.3, Comment 1, the lawyer has an obligation to correct the record in spite of the usual operation of Model Rule 1.6.

b. Jones v. Clinton, 36 F.Supp.2d 1118 (E.D.Ark.1999), confirms the client's duty not to dissemble in a deposition. Judge Wright held President Clinton in contempt for providing misleading answers in his deposition in a case filed by Paula Jones, an Arkansas state employee, alleging sexual harassment. Judge Wright noted she had ruled that Ms. Jones, in discovery, was entitled to "information regarding any individuals with whom the President had sexual relations * * * and who were during the relevant time frame state or federal employees." In spite of those rulings, Judge Wright found that "the President responded to plaintiff's questions by giving false, misleading and evasive answers that were designed to obstruct the judicial process." The two answers that Judge Wright found no reasonable person could believe were truthful were whether the president had ever been alone with Monica Lewinsky and whether he had ever had sexual relations with her. Judge Wright also referred the matter to the Arkansas Supreme Court for possible disciplinary action because President Clinton, the deponent, was also a lawyer. The Arkansas court suspended President Clinton from practice for five years and fined him $25,000.[6]

c. Feld's Case, 815 A.2d 383 (N.H.2002), suspended attorney Feld for one year for violating Rules 3.4 and 8.4 during discovery. Feld's clients, who recently purchased a piece of property, filed an eviction claim against Bussiere. Prior to the purchase, Bussiere notified the clients that he had a leasehold interest and enclosed supporting documentation. When questioned during discovery, however, Feld's clients denied knowledge of Bussiere's documentation. Feld was found to have " 'orchestrated, assisted, counseled and tolerated the formulation of inaccurate and incomplete sworn responses that he knew were inaccurate' in violation of New Hampshire Rules of Professional Conduct 3.4 and 8.4." Feld was also present during his client's deposition where she gave numerous evasive answers. "Given the importance placed by Bussiere upon this line of inquiry, and Feld's repeated involvement with false answers, the record does not support Feld's claim that his assistance with the response to the request for admission was inadvertent." 815 A.2d 383. In another incident, the client answered evasively on the nature of his involvement with the financing of the property. "A pattern of evasive or non-responsive conduct, such as that demonstrated in the responses to the interrogatory," the court held, "demonstrates a lawyer's failure 'to make reasonably diligent effort to comply with a legally proper discovery request made by an opposing party.' " 815 A.2d at 388. The one year suspension imposed by the court was equivalent to similar sanctions it had imposed for intentional deceit during trial.

6. Neal v. Clinton, 2001 WL 34355768 (Ark.Cir.2001). The United States Supreme Court suspended Mr. Clinton from practice before it and issued a rule to show cause, returnable in 40 days, why he should not be disbarred. In re Discipline of Clinton, 534 U.S. 806 (2001). On the 40th day, Mr. Clinton resigned from membership in the Supreme Court bar.

The president's counsel, Robert Bennett, later notified Judge Wright that he had, unknowingly, submitted false evidence during the course of the president's deposition. See 36 F.Supp.2d at 1130 n. 15.

D.   Candor about Factual Matters that are not easily verifiable

1. Is the third item not disclosed to the court in this problem—the prior criminal record of your client—a factual matter or a legal matter, i.e., is it more analogous to the situation in Part A or Part B of the problem?

a. Is a conviction legal authority? Is it the duty of defense counsel to correct the court clerk who mistakenly informed the judge that the client had no previous record? In ABA Formal Opinion 287 (June 27, 1953), the ethics committee ruling on this question split three ways. The committee included Henry S. Drinker, later author of *Legal Ethics*, and William B. Jones, later a district judge in the District of Columbia. The majority concluded:

> "If the court asks the lawyer whether the clerk's statement is correct, the lawyer is not bound by fidelity to the client to tell the court what he knows to be an untruth, and should ask the court to excuse him from answering the question, and retire from the case, though this would doubtless put the court on further inquiry as to the truth.

> "Even, however, if the court does not directly ask the lawyer this question, such an inquiry may well be implied from the circumstances, including the lawyer's previous relations with the court. The situation is analogous to that discussed in our Opinion 280 where counsel knows of an essential decision not cited by his opponent and where his silence might reasonably be regarded by the Court as an implied representation by him that he knew of no such authority. If, under all the circumstances, the lawyer believes that the court relies on him as corroborating the correctness of the statement by the clerk or by the client that the client has no criminal record, the lawyer's duty of candor and fairness to the court requires him, in our opinion, to advise the court not to rely on counsel's personal knowledge as to the facts of the client's record. * * * The indignation of the court * * * on learning that the lawyer had deliberately permitted him, where no privileged communication is involved, to rely on what the lawyer knew to be a misapprehension of the true facts, would be something that the lawyer could not appease on the basis of loyalty to the client. No client may demand or expect of his lawyer, in the furtherance of his cause, disloyalty to the law whose minister he is (Canon 32) or 'any manner of fraud or chicane' (Canon 15).

> "If the lawyer is quite clear that the court does not rely on him as corroborating, by his silence, the statement of the clerk or of his client, the lawyer is not, in our opinion, bound to speak out."

The dissenting opinion argued that the lawyer may in no event "stand idly by in open court and permit the court to be deceived at a time when the lawyer knows that the court is relying upon an untrue statement."[7]

b. What is the law today, under Rule 3.3, if the court clerk mistakenly tells the court that the defendant has no criminal record? The lawyer did not make a false statement about the client's previous record; the client made no statement; the lawyer called no witness who misled. Will the lawyer be confirming a false statement (that the client has no criminal record) if she simply stands silent?

The ABA Committee on Ethics and Professional Responsibility revisited this issue after adoption of the Model Rules and concluded that, on the assumption that the client has engaged in no fraud or perjury, the ABA Committee "could offer no better guidance under the Model Rules" than that offered by the authors of Formal Opinion 287. ABA Formal Opinion 87–353 (Apr. 20, 1987). California Formal Opinion 1986–87 (undated) is to the same effect. Do you agree with this analysis? Is the proposed course of conduct workable? If the judge turns to you and asks, "Anything to add, counsel?" what do you say? Do you just hem and haw?

c. In re Seelig, 850 A.2d 477 (N.J.2004), involved a criminal case in which attorney Seelig had represented defendant Poje, who was charged with felonies arising out of the death of two people in an automobile collision. Poje also received motor vehicle summonses for reckless driving, leaving the scene of an accident, and failing to report an accident. Each citation indicated that the accident involved either personal injury or property damage. A prosecutor handled the arraignment on the felony charges before Judge Lake, and a different prosecutor handled the citations before the same judge. Seelig informed the prosecutor handling the motor vehicle citations that Poje would plead guilty to the charges. He did not mention the felony cases. Judge Lake, who did not remember Poje from earlier in the day, called the motor vehicle citations after the prosecutor had left the courtroom and Seelig entered guilty pleas on Poje's behalf. When Judge Lake asked whether the accident had involved injuries or property damage, Seelig said simply "[i]njuries." Judge Lake did not ask about the extent of the injuries, and Seelig did not educate him. Thus, unaware of the serious indictable offenses, Judge Lake accepted Poje's guilty plea. Poje's pleas to the motor vehicles charges ordinarily would have forced the prosecutor to dismiss the felony charges because of double jeopardy, but the court granted the prosecution motion to vacate Poje's guilty pleas on the grounds of "substantial defects in the proceeding that resulted in manifest injustice," so Seelig's ploy was ultimately unsuccessful.

Seelig's failure to notify the court of Poje's indictable offenses, however, raised the question whether he violated New Jersey Rules 1.6(b)(2), 3.3(a)(1), 3.3(a)(5), and 8.4(c). Seelig argued that he had responded to all questions truthfully, albeit without elaboration. The court disagreed, relying on New Jersey Rule of Professional Conduct 3.3(a)(5), which stated: "A lawyer shall not knowingly fail to disclose to the tribunal a material fact

---

7. ABA Formal Opinion 287 also considered what the lawyer should do if the lawyer knows that the client will lie about his or her previous record, or the lawyer discovers later that the client had lied. These issues are considered in Problem 27, *infra*.

with knowledge that the tribunal *may tend to be misled* by such failure." (emphasis added) Acknowledging that the ABA Model Rules did not go that far, the court found that 3.3(a)(5) imposes a "heightened duty of candor towards the tribunal." The New Jersey rule required defense counsel to disclose to the municipal court that two deaths had occurred and that indictable charges were also pending against his client so that the court would not be misled as to double jeopardy implications that the client's guilty plea would have on the more serious pending charges. The court also rejected Seelig's claim that his client's Sixth Amendment right to counsel trumped duties in the Rules of Professional Conduct. Although Seelig made no affirmative misrepresentations to the tribunal, his failure to take "numerous opportunities for open and forthright responses ... about the indictable offenses" violated Rule 3.3(a)(5). The court refused to discipline him, however, finding that he had a good faith view of his obligations under Rule 3.5(a)(5). Because the issue raised in the case was novel, the court held, the ruling should only apply prospectively.

2. In determining what to say about the criminal record, is it helpful to analyze the distinction drawn between candor regarding adverse law and nondisclosure of adverse facts?

a. Is the distinction best grounded in the law of confidential client information? That is, while one may correctly view disclosure of contrary legal authority as detrimental to the client, is it properly thought of as the client's confidential information? Is all "information relating to the representation" properly viewed as confidential? Cf., Model Rule 1.9, Comment 8 (information that is "generally known" may be used in a later case on behalf of another client).

b. ABA Formal Opinion 93–370 (Feb. 5, 1993) addressed whether a court should be able to ask a lawyer to be candid about the limits of the lawyer's settlement authority. The opinion recognized that settlement discussions are an important part of modern trial management but concluded that a lawyer should not tell a judge the extent of settlement authority the client has given. Further, because such authority would be a material fact about which the lawyer could not lie if asked, a judge should not inquire into the authority.

Is asking about the client's criminal record the same as asking about the lawyer's settlement authority? If asked either question, should a lawyer tell the judge, "Don't ask me about that?" Or, "I am not permitted to answer that question?" Is there any way to deflect a judge's question gracefully?

c. ABA Formal Opinion 98–412 (Sept. 9, 1998) dealt with the obligation of a lawyer who learns that his client has violated a court order prohibiting the transfer of assets. The opinion says that the lawyer must disclose the fact to the court (1) if necessary to avoid or correct a misrepresentation made by the lawyer to the court, or (2) to avoid assisting the client in a fraud upon the court. If the lawyer has made misstatements to the court, the correction is required by Rule 3.3(a)(1). If the client made the misstatement, what is now Rule 3.3(a)(3) requires the correction. If no misrepresentation has been made, the opinion says, the lawyer is not required to report a violation of a court order if the violation is unlikely to have a material effect on the resolution of the case. However, if failure to report the violation would imply that all was well, a lawyer must correct that misapprehension.[8]

Are the governing principles all becoming clear to you? How, for example, is the lawyer supposed to know if failure to report the violation implies that all is well?

PROBLEM 26

HANDLING PHYSICAL EVIDENCE

Information "relating to the representation" comes in a variety of forms. The lawyer is required by Model Rule 1.6(a) to hold most of it in confidence. Yet some kinds of confidential material *may* be disclosed, while others are the subject of required disclosure. In this problem, we first examine the name of the client, normally something a lawyer discloses to anyone with whom the lawyer deals. Next, we look at physical evidence of a crime that has come into the lawyer's possession. Then, we ask whether there is a difference between concealing information and simply not disclosing it. Finally, we consider how a lawyer may advise a client on whether and when he or she may or should destroy documents or other potential evidence of misconduct.

FACTS

Neil Hammer, a person whom you have never advised before, has come into your office, set a gun and a bag of money on your desk, and said, "I have just used this gun to rob a bank, and I killed a guard in the process. Help me; I don't want to get caught. What should I do?"

Only yesterday, J.B. Wallace, president of the Wallace Corporation, came into your office. The *Wall Street Journal* had reported that the Justice Department is investigating a firm in Wallace's industry for possible price fixing. A *Wall Street Journal* reporter had asked for an interview with Mr. Wallace about industry pricing practices, and Mr. Wallace asked you to help him prepare for the interview. He told you that in order to help you evaluate any allegation involving him and price fixing, you could listen to the secret tape recordings of all discussions in his office for the last

----

8. ABA Formal Opinion 98–412 also says that if the client discharges the lawyer before the client engages in misconduct, but the lawyer knows that the misconduct is planned, the lawyer has neither the duty nor the right to disclose those plans, even to successor counsel, without the client's consent. Is that advice consistent with the present version of Model Rule 3.3(b)?

three years. He keeps these tapes at his home and plans to use them to help write his memoirs. You have learned that the department is about to file a criminal antitrust action against the corporation and perhaps Mr. Wallace personally.

The local police have contacted you about reports that a man with a gun was seen entering your office. You are thinking about how to respond.

QUESTIONS

A.   Confidentiality of a client's identity

1.   What will you say when the police ask you who came to your office at the time a witness saw Hammer enter? Are the names of your clients confidential? How about the names of your prospective clients?

a.   Client identity is not normally confidential; it is something the lawyer is "impliedly authorized" to disclose. After all, if lawyers did not tell courts and other lawyers whom they represented, the lawyers could get little done for those clients. However, a client may ask an attorney to keep the client's identity confidential from third persons. A lawyer may act as a agent for an undisclosed principal in purchasing real estate. Or a lawyer may represent several confidential investors putting together a bid for a race track. The ethical duty of confidentiality governs the analysis of these questions.

Suppose the lawyer is called before the grand jury to disclose information about the client? The usual evidentiary rule is also that the identity of the client, the amount of the fee, the identification of payment by case file name, and the general purpose of the work performed are not protected from disclosure by the attorney-client privilege, because such information ordinarily reveals no confidential professional communications between attorney and client.

On the other hand, what if there are situations in which the fact one had consulted a lawyer is itself incriminating or embarrassing? Suppose you are a divorce lawyer. During an Internal Revenue Service audit of your tax records, the investigator discovers a $25,000 cash deposit that you made into your client trust account marked "retainer." The client has not yet told his wife he is considering a divorce. If the investigator asks you whose money it is, may you reply without asking the client's permission to do so? In such cases, disclosing the identity of the husband may disclose that he is considering a divorce from his wife.

b.   Baird v. Koerner, 279 F.2d 623 (9th Cir.1960), is the leading case on the attorney-client privilege and client identity. The clients consulted a lawyer for legal advice as to what to do about unpaid taxes. Paying the taxes stops the accrual of interest, and there are clients who would like to clear their consciences by paying the money owed, but do not want to confess to tax fraud. The lawyer, on behalf of the undisclosed clients, paid the additional income tax. The IRS wanted to know the clients' identity, but the court concluded that the attorney-client privilege protected their identity against disclosure.

If the unidentified clients in *Baird* had hired a nonlawyer to deliver the money to the IRS, would there be any evidentiary privilege protecting the nonlawyer from disclosing the identity of the payer? Why should the fact that the money was transmitted by a lawyer change that result?

c. Restatement Third, The Law Governing Lawyers § 69, Comment *g*, concludes that the privileged character of client identity cannot be determined categorically but should be decided based on the extent to which the information sought would, "directly or by reasonable inference, reveal the *content* of a privileged communication" (emphasis added). The evidentiary privilege, the Restatement continues, does not protect clients or lawyers "against revealing a lawyer's knowledge about a client solely on the grounds that doing so would incriminate the client or otherwise prejudice the client's interests."

d. In a criminal setting, some cases have called the *Baird* rule the "last link" doctrine: if the fact of consultation would itself be sufficient to tie the client to a crime, the lawyer should not have to disclose the client's identity. See, e.g., In re Grand Jury Proceedings 88–9, Cherney, 899 F.2d 1039, 1043 (11th Cir.1990):

> "the 'last link' doctrine is only applicable to rare situations 'where the disclosure of fee information would give the identity of a previously undisclosed client/suspect.' In essence, the last link doctrine extends the protection of the attorney-client privilege to nonprivileged information—the identity of the client—when 'disclosure of that identity would disclose *other*, privileged communications (e.g., motive or strategy) and when the incriminating nature of the privileged communications has created in the client a reasonable expectation that the information would be kept confidential.' "

2. Would you have ruled the client identity privileged in the following cases?

a. Baltes v. Doe I, 57 U.S.L.W. 2268 (Fla.Cir.Ct.1988) (No. CL–88–1145–AD), was a celebrated case where a client told a lawyer that he had been the driver in a highly publicized hit-and-run accident. Without disclosing the client's identity, the lawyer tried to plea bargain on his behalf. The victim's survivors filed a civil action against the unknown driver and tried to compel the lawyer to disclose his identity. The trial court held that, under these circumstances, the client's identity was privileged. The client ultimately turned himself in before a higher court heard the appeal.

b. Matter of Nackson, 555 A.2d 1101 (N.J.1989), considered whether an attorney may refuse to disclose the whereabouts of a client who jumped bail and consulted the lawyer about a fugitive warrant for his arrest. The client wanted to return to the jurisdiction only if his lawyer could work out a plea agreement in advance. Citing *Baltes*, the court held that the privilege can protect against disclosure of client whereabouts; it offered as an example, matrimonial cases where the attorney need not disclose the whereabouts of a wife who feared injury from her husband. The privilege is not absolute, the court said, but prosecutors must first use all other reasonable ways of learning the defendant's whereabouts. Even then, before ordering disclosure, the lower court must "balance" the need to know against the client's right to confidentiality. However, the court did not calibrate the scales and tell us how to weigh the competing interests. The court made no reference to the last link doctrine.

Should the court have denied the applicability of the privilege on the ground that the purpose of keeping the client's whereabouts secret was to assist the client to avoid lawful process in a proceeding pending at the time the lawyer gave his advice? See In re Doe, 456 N.Y.S.2d 312 (1982) (bail jumper's counsel required to reveal his client's whereabouts to a grand jury).

c. In re Grand Jury Subpoena, 204 F.3d 516 (4th Cir.2000), was another effort to get a lawyer to reveal his client's identity. The government filed a petition for forfeiture of property used as an open-air drug market. The property was titled in the name "Daniel C. Quispehuman," a name likely to be a straw owner. The lawyer said that he would be representing the owner of the property whom he said was not Quispehuman, but he refused to reveal the client's real name because, he argued, its disclosure would reveal the client's confidential communication—his motive or purpose for seeking legal advice. The court agreed that a lawyer sometimes may avoid identifying a client who has not sought to get involved in a matter, but once the client authorized the attorney to disclose the client's motives or purposes in retaining the attorney (to deal with the allegations of drug-trafficking on his property), those motives or purposes were no longer confidential, and thus the client's identity was not within the attorney-client evidentiary privilege. The court specifically rejected the "last link" doctrine as giving too much protection to clients.

3. Must you appeal a court order making you reveal your client's identity?

a. Suppose you refuse to disclose the client's identity to the investigator. The IRS, in turn, asserts a claim against you for back taxes on the $25,000, asserting that it is unreported income. Are you still obliged not to disclose the name of the client? Look at Model Rule 1.6(b)(5).[1]

b. Suppose, in order to test a lower court order, you must appeal it. Must you go to jail before revealing the client's identity? Does Model Rule 1.6(b)(6) adopt the position of two judges in People v. Kor, 277 P.2d 94 (Cal.Ct.App.1954), who stated that the attorney, rather than having testi-

---

1. 26 U.S.C.A. § 6050I, adopted as part of the war on drugs, requires cash transactions in excess of $10,000 to be reported to the Internal Revenue Service on its Form 8300. On its face, the requirement applies to everyone, but lawyers have argued that transactions with them should be exempt from the requirement. The IRS considers lawyers subject to the law, but criminal defense lawyers complain that reporting will render Baird v. Koerner a nullity. This issue is discussed further in Problem 29, *infra*.

fied, "should have chosen to go to jail and take his chances of release by a higher court"? 277 P.2d at 101. Is such self-sacrifice necessary or realistic?

c. These cases deal with the evidentiary privilege. The confidentiality protection of Model Rule 1.6 is broader. Assume that the court rules that the name of the client who owns property in your trust account is unprivileged and orders you to disclose the name to the grand jury. You do so. Then, you leave the grand jury room and a reporter asks you, "Did you disclose the name of your client?" You respond that you obeyed the court order. The reporter then says, "What is the name?" Can you answer that question, knowing that the court held that the evidentiary privilege did not to apply to the information and that you earlier disclosed the name to the grand jury?

B. TAKING POSSESSION OF PHYSICAL EVIDENCE FOR TESTING OR SAFEKEEPING

1. May you take Hammer's gun for safekeeping? Is the gun privileged against discovery if Hammer turns it over to you?

a. The leading case on that issue is In re Richard R. Ryder, 263 F.Supp. 360 (E.D.Va.) (per curiam), aff'd per curiam, 381 F.2d 713 (4th Cir.1967). The issue before the district court was whether to remove Richard R. Ryder, a former assistant U.S. attorney, from practice before that court.

"On August 24, 1966 a man armed with a sawed-off shotgun robbed the Varina Branch of the Bank of Virginia of $7,583. Included in the currency taken were $10 bills known as 'bait money,' the serial numbers of which had been recorded.

"On August 26, 1966, [after a bank robbery], Charles Richard Cook rented safety deposit box 14 at a branch of the Richmond National Bank. Later in the day Cook was interviewed at his home by agents of the Federal Bureau of Investigation, who obtained $348 from him. Cook telephoned Ryder, who had represented him in civil litigation. * * *

"Later that afternoon Ryder telephoned one of the agents and asked whether any of the bills obtained from Cook had been identified as a part of the money taken in the bank robbery. The agent told him that some bills had been identified. * * *

"The next morning, * * * Ryder conferred with Cook again. He urged Cook to tell the truth, and Cook answered that a man, whose name he would not divulge, offered him $500 on the day of the robbery to put a package in a bank lockbox. Ryder did not believe this story. Ryder told Cook that if the government could trace the money in the box to him, it would be almost conclusive evidence of his guilt. He knew that Cook was under surveillance and he suspected that Cook might try to dispose of the money.

"That afternoon Ryder telephoned a former officer of the Richmond Bar Association to discuss his course of action. * * *

"The lawyers discussed and rejected alternatives, including having a third party get the money. At the conclusion of the conversation Ryder was advised 'Don't do it surreptitiously and do be sure that you let your client know that it is going back to the rightful owners.' * * *

"Ryder did not follow the advice he had received on Saturday. He did not let his client know the money was going back to the rightful owners. He testified about his omission:

'I prepared [the power of attorney] myself and told Mr. Cook to sign it. In the power of attorney, I did not specifically say that Mr. Cook authorized me to deliver that money to the appropriate authorities at any time because for a number of reasons. One, in representing a man under these circumstances, you've got to keep the man's confidence, but I also put in that power of attorney that Mr. Cook authorized me to dispose of that money as I saw fit, and the reason for that being that I was going to turn the money over to the proper authorities at whatever time I deemed that it wouldn't hurt Mr. Cook.'

"Ryder took the power of attorney which Cook had signed to the Richmond National Bank. He rented box 13 in his name with his office address, presented the power of attorney, entered Cook's box, took both boxes into a booth, where he found a bag of money and a sawed-off shotgun in Cook's box. * * * He transferred the contents of Cook's box to his own and returned the boxes to the vault. He left the bank, and neither he nor Cook returned.

" * * * Within a half-hour after he left the bank, he talked to a retired judge and distinguished professor of law. * * * Ryder testified that he told about the shotgun. The judge also testified that Ryder certainly would not have been under the impression that he—the judge—thought that [Ryder] was guilty of unethical conduct. That same day Ryder talked with other prominent persons [and] was advised that a lawyer could not receive the property and if he had received it he could not retain possession of it. * * *

"On September 12, 1966, F.B.I. agents procured search warrants for Cook's and Ryder's safety deposit boxes in the Richmond National Bank. They found Cook's box empty. In Ryder's box they discovered $5,920 of the $7,583 taken in the bank robbery and the sawed-off shotgun used in the robbery. * * *

"We reject the argument that Ryder's conduct was no more than the exercise of the attorney-client privilege. * * *

"It was Ryder, not his client, who took the initiative in transferring the incriminating possession of the stolen money and the shotgun from Cook. Ryder's conduct went far beyond the receipt and retention of a confidential communication from his client. * * *

"The money in Cook's box belonged to the Bank of Virginia. The law did not authorize Cook to conceal this money or withhold it from the bank. His larceny was a continuing offense. Cook had no title or property interest in the money that he lawfully could pass to Ryder. * * * No canon of ethics or law permitted Ryder to conceal from the Bank of Virginia its money to gain his client's acquittal.

"Cook's possession of the sawed-off shotgun was illegal. Ryder could not lawfully receive the gun from Cook to assist Cook to avoid conviction of robbery. Cook had never mentioned the shotgun to Ryder. When Ryder discovered it in Cook's box, he took possession of it to hinder the government in the prosecution of its case, and he intended not to reveal it pending trial unless the government discovered it and a court compelled its production. No statute or canon of ethics authorized Ryder to take possession of the gun for this purpose. * * *

"Ryder's action is not justified because he thought he was acting in the best interests of his client. To allow the individual lawyer's belief to determine the standards of professional conduct will in time reduce the ethics of the profession to the practices of the most unscrupulous. Moreover, Ryder knew that the law against concealing stolen property and the law forbidding receipt and possession of a sawed-off shotgun contain no exemptions for a lawyer who takes possession with the intent of protecting a criminal from the consequences of his crime. * * *

"[However,] Ryder intended to return the bank's money after his client was tried. He consulted reputable persons before and after he placed the property in his lockbox, although he did not precisely follow their advice. Were it not for these facts, we would deem proper his permanent exclusion from practice before this court. In view of the mitigating circumstances, he will be suspended from practice in this court for eighteen months * * *."

The Fourth Circuit affirmed and called the suspension "lenient in the circumstances." It then "suspend[ed] Ryder from practice before * * * [the Court of Appeals] for the duration of his suspension from the District Court."

Are you equally incensed by Mr. Ryder's conduct? What is it about his behavior that most troubles you?

b. Compare State ex rel. Sowers v. Olwell, 394 P.2d 681 (Wash.1964). Olwell was a lawyer who refused to honor a coroner's subpoena for the knife allegedly used by his client in a murder. He asserted both the attorney-client privilege and the client's privilege against self-incrimination. The court held him in contempt and he appealed. The court held:

"The attorney should not be a depository for criminal evidence (such as a knife, other weapons, stolen property, etc.), which in itself has little, if any material value for the purposes of aiding counsel in the preparation of the defense of his client's case. Such evidence given the attorney during legal consultation for information purposes and used by the attorney in preparing the defense of his client's case, whether or not the case ever goes to trial, could clearly be withheld for a reasonable period of time. It follows that the attorney, after a reasonable period of time, should, as an officer of the court, on his own motion turn the same over to the prosecution.

" * * * [T]he state [in order to protect the attorney-client privilege], when attempting to introduce such evidence at the trial, should take extreme precautions to make certain that the source of the evidence is not disclosed in the presence of the jury and prejudicial error is not committed." 394 P.2d at 684–85.

The court also found the self-incrimination privilege inapplicable because it must be asserted by the client alone. Is the decision consistent with *Ryder*? Does the procedure suggested by the court protect all the relevant interests?

2. May you hold the bag of money for safekeeping? What if you are concerned that the client will spend the money instead of returning it to its rightful owners?

a.   The money belongs to the bank, while the gun presumably belongs to Hammer. In *Ryder*, the court noted that Ryder "knew that Cook was under surveillance and he suspected that Cook might try to dispose of the money." Does that make it more or less reprehensible for Ryder to hold the money? Compare Rule 1.4, Comment 7, with Rule 3.4, Comment 2.

b.   Consider In re January 1976 Grand Jury, 534 F.2d 719 (7th Cir.1976). The attorney refused to comply with a grand jury's subpoena *duces tecum* to turn over money received by him from clients suspected of bank robbery. The Court of Appeals affirmed the contempt order, and Judge Tone, joined by Judge Bauer, argued:

"We must assume for purposes of this appeal that shortly after robbing a savings and loan association, the robbers delivered money stolen in the robbery to appellant. If that occurred, the money was delivered either for safekeeping, with or without appellant's knowledge that it was stolen, or as an attorney's fee.

"If it was the latter, the robbers voluntarily relinquished the money and with it any arguable claim that might have arisen from their possession or constructive possession. As Judge Pell points out, the payment of a fee is not a privileged communication. The money itself is non-testimonial and no plausible argument is left for resisting the subpoena.

"If the money was not given as a fee but for safekeeping, the delivery of the money was an act in furtherance of the crime, regardless of whether appellant knew it was stolen. The delivery of the money was not assertive conduct and therefore was not a privileged communication, and, as we just observed, the money itself is non-testimonial. The attorney is simply a witness to a criminal act. The fact that he is also a participant in the act, presumably without knowledge of its criminal quality, is irrelevant since he is not asserting his own privilege against self incrimination. There is no authority or reason, based on any constitutional provision or the attorney-client privilege, for shielding from judicial inquiry either the fruits of the robbery or the fact of the later criminal act of turning over the money to appellant. Accordingly, it is immaterial that in responding to the subpoena appellant will be making an assertion about who turned over the money and when.

"Finally, the proceedings have not yet reached the point at which we must decide whether, when the robbers have chosen to make appellant a witness to their crime, they may invoke the Sixth Amendment [right to effective assistance of counsel] to bar his eyewitness testimony at trial, although, for me, to ask that question is almost to answer it." 534 F.2d at 730–31 (concurring opinion).

3. What principles can you derive from these cases? Is a client's statement to the lawyer linking the gun to the crime a privileged communication?

a. Morrell v. State, 575 P.2d 1200 (Alaska 1978), upheld the decision of the trial court to admit incriminating evidence of a kidnapping plan that the defendant had allegedly written. A friend of the defendant had turned the plan over to defense counsel, who then aided the friend in turning the evidence over to the police. Defense counsel then withdrew from the case. After examining the cases discussed in the text, the Alaska Supreme Court held, at 575 P.2d at 1210–12:

"From the foregoing cases emerges the rule that a criminal defense attorney must turn over to the prosecution real evidence that the attorney obtains from his client. Further, if the evidence is obtained from a non-client third party who is not acting for the client, then the privilege to refuse to testify concerning the manner in which the evidence was obtained is inapplicable. * * *

"We believe that [defense counsel] would have been obligated to see that the evidence reached the prosecutor in this case even if he had obtained the evidence from Morrell. His obligation was even clearer because he acquired the evidence from [a third party], who made the decision to turn the evidence over to [defense counsel] without consulting Morrell and therefore was not acting as Morrell's agent.

"[Defense counsel] could have properly turned the evidence over to the police himself and would have been obliged to do so if [the third party] had refused to accept the return of the evidence.

"[Finally, while] statutes which address the concealing of evidence are generally construed to require an affirmative act of concealment in addition to the failure to disclose information to the authorities, taking possession of evidence from a non-client third party and holding the evidence in a place not accessible to investigating authorities would seem to fall within the statute's ambit. Thus, we have concluded that [defense counsel] breached no ethical obligation to his client which may have rendered his legal services to Morrell ineffective."

Do the earlier cases in this problem support the court's conclusion?

b.   Consider People v. Meredith, 631 P.2d 46 (Cal.1981). The defendant told his lawyer the location of the robbery-murder victim's wallet. The lawyer then had his investigator remove it. The court held that the client's disclosure was privileged and telling the investigator the location did not destroy the privilege. On the other hand, removing the wallet did destroy it. When defense counsel removes or alters evidence, he necessarily deprives the prosecution of the opportunity to observe that evidence in its original condition or location. The lawyer's decision to remove evidence is therefore tactical; if he leaves the evidence where he discovered it, his observations derived from privileged communications are insulated from revelation. If he removes the evidence to examine or test it, "the original location and condition of that evidence loses the protection of the privilege." 631 P.2d at 54. Do you agree that it makes sense to put defense counsel to such a choice?[2]

c.   Restatement Third, The Law Governing Lawyers, tries to sum up these cases in § 119, which says that with respect to physical evidence of a client crime, a lawyer

"(1) may, when reasonably necessary for purposes of the representation, take possession of the evidence and retain it for the time reasonably necessary to examine it and subject it to tests that do not alter or destroy material characteristics of the evidence; but

"(2) following possession under Subsection (1), the lawyer must notify prosecuting authorities of the lawyer's possession of the evidence or turn the evidence over to them."

Comment *a* to § 119 then provides that the rules on turning over physical evidence of client crime apply to "contraband, weapons, and similar implements used in an offense. It also includes such materials as documents and material in electronically retrievable form used by the client to plan the offense, documents used in the course of a mail-fraud violation, or transaction documents evidencing a crime."

d.   Model Rule 3.4, Comment 2, also summarizes these principles. Do you agree that courts should sometimes require defense counsel to turn over evidence that will help convict their clients?

---

2. See also, Commonwealth v. Stenhach, 514 A.2d 114 (Pa.Super.Ct.1986), leave to appeal denied 534 A.2d 769 (Pa.1987), where the court affirmed the rule that physical evidence of a crime in possession of criminal defense attorneys who acquired the evidence at client's direction was not protected against disclosure by the attorney-client privilege. The court reversed the criminal conviction of the lawyers for failure to turn over the physical evidence, however, on the ground that the statutes prohibiting hindering prosecution and tampering with evidence were unconstitutionally vague or overbroad as applied to lawyers engaged in representation of criminal defendants.

The good faith of an attorney who advises his client to invoke the Fifth Amendment in response to a subpoena in a civil case protects the lawyer from being held in contempt. Maness v. Meyers, 419 U.S. 449, 468 (1975). Should the same principle apply here?

C. NONDISCLOSURE OF PHYSICAL EVIDENCE

1. Is failure to disclose facts different from affirmatively concealing them? Are there times a lawyer simply must keep quiet about information others would consider significant to them?

a. A news story, highly publicized at the time, reported what became known as the "buried bodies" case:

> "An Onondaga County grand jury this afternoon [February 7, 1975] cleared a lawyer, Frank H. Armani, of criminal wrongdoing in failing to disclose that his client in a murder case had told him where he had hidden two bodies. * * *

> "Mr. [Francois] Belge and Mr. Armani were lawyers for Robert Garrow, who was found guilty of murder after a trial in Hamilton County last summer.

> "During the trial Mr. Belge revealed that he and Mr. Armani had discovered the two bodies after having been told of their whereabouts by Mr. Garrow, but that they did not tell authorities. * * *

> "Mr. Armani's attorney, Elliot A. Taikoff of New York City, said later that his client had been 'very troubled' over his role in the matter and had received advice from a 'very high-ranking judge in this state.' He refused to name the judge, but said he had testified before the grand jury."[3]

Was the grand jury's decision consistent with that of the *Ryder* court? Were the situations analytically different?

b. In considering the *Belge* case, N.Y. State Bar Comm. on Prof'l Ethics Opinion No. 479 (Mar. 6, 1978), advised: "the lawyer was under an injunction not to disclose to the authorities his knowledge of the two prior murders, and was duty-bound not to reveal to the authorities the location of the bodies." The opinion also concluded that the attorney acted properly by using the information, with his client's consent, in engaging in plea bargaining and in destroying photographs the lawyer took of the bodies and records the lawyer made of his conversation with the client.

Do you agree with the opinion's analysis? Were the photographs Belge took of the bodies privileged information? Were Belge's duties affected by the fact that he had moved some of the body parts to get a better picture? Could Belge have told the police about the location of the bodies—so that they could receive a decent burial—by calling the police anonymously and not revealing either his name or the name of his client?

c. In Clutchette v. Rushen, 770 F.2d 1469 (9th Cir.1985), cert. denied, 475 U.S. 1088 (1986), the government accused the defendant of shooting a man in the defendant's car. The police were having a hard time proving their case until the defendant's wife voluntarily turned over some receipts

---

3. New York Times, Feb. 8, 1975, p. 54, col. 5. See also, People v. Belge, 372 N.Y.S.2d 798, 803 (Co.Ct.1975) (indictment on same facts dismissed on "grounds of a privileged communication and in the interests of justice * * *").

to them. She had been acting as an investigator for her husband's defense lawyer, and the lawyer had sent her to Los Angeles to get (and arguably to destroy) the receipts that showed that her husband had arranged for the car to be reupholstered shortly after the murder. With the help of the receipts, the police found the former seat covers and matched the blood type to the victim's. The court held that the wife's surrender of the receipts was not a violation of the defendant's attorney-client privilege. If the attorney had not done anything to retrieve the receipts, he would not have had to tell the police about them. Having the wife-investigator take possession of the receipts, however, made them fair game for police discovery.

2. Suppose you, like Belge, have a client who claims that he killed several women and buried their bodies in a secluded place. This time, however, when you check out his story, one of the victims is not yet dead. May you tell the police her location?

a. Look at Model Rule 1.6(b)(1), a provision that was not in effect at the time of the *Belge* case. Do you agree with the disclosure authority given to you by that rule? Should you disguise your voice when you disclose the information about the victims to the police so they cannot connect you to your client?

b. Under the auspices of the Roscoe Pound–American Trial Lawyers Foundation, a special commission prepared its own proposed ethics rules called The American Lawyer's Code of Conduct.[4] The commission applied its proposed Code to this hypothetical as follows:

"[S]he is seriously injured and unable to help herself or to get help. The lawyer calls an ambulance for her, but takes care not to be personally identified. The lawyer has *committed a disciplinary violation* * * *."[5]

Do you agree that loyalty to the client requires this result? What logic would lead otherwise sensible lawyers to such a conclusion?

c. Such cases do arise in real life. In McClure v. Thompson, 323 F.3d 1233 (9th Cir.2003), McClure had clubbed Jones to death with the butt of a gun, then murdered her two children and hid them in the woods. He was convicted of all three murders. In discussions with his original defense attorney, Mecca, days after the murder, McClure drew Mecca a map indicating where the children were located. McClure did not say whether the children were dead or alive, but he did say that Satan had killed Jones, while Jesus had saved the children. Mecca tried to bargain with the prosecutor for a lesser charge once he had the map, but the prosecutor refused, so Mecca arranged for his secretary to anonymously call the police,

4. The proposal was intended to compete with the ABA Model Rules. It provides interesting contrast to the Model Rules on several issues, but no state has yet adopted it and it has not proved to be influential.

5. The American Lawyer's Code of Conduct, Illustrative Case 1(g) (Revised Draft, 1982) (emphasis added).

telling them the location of the child victims in the belief that they might be alive. He then withdrew from the case.

McClure argued that Mecca had not provided the "effective assistance of counsel" in that he (1) failed to obtain McClure's informed consent before disclosing what McClure had told him, and (2) failed to verify whether disclosure was necessary to prevent the children's deaths. McClure argued that Mecca's concern for the victims was a conflict of interest that rendered Mecca's representation constitutionally ineffective. The court found Mecca's disclosure permissible because of his reasonable belief that it was necessary to prevent imminent deaths. Mecca's attempt to negotiate with the prosecution and his concern that McClure's kidnaping charges would be aggravated to murder if the children were found dead were sufficient evidence of his overall loyalty to the client, and the court denied habeas relief because McClure could not "demonstrate that his counsel 'actively represented a conflicting interest.' " 323 F.3d at 1248. Do you agree with the court's analysis?

d. Henderson v. State, 962 S.W.2d 544 (Tex.Ct.Crim.App. 1997), cert. denied, 525 U.S. 978 (1998), addressed the issue of whether a lawyer must disclose a client-drawn map of where the client had allegedly buried the body of an infant. A public defender witnessed the client draw the map in prison and subsequently sent it to the client's criminal defense lawyer. A prosecutor filed a motion to compel production of the map. The trial court ordered production of the map on the theory that it was not privileged because the client had not intended to keep the map confidential at the time it was drawn. There was some discussion that the client may wish to cooperate with the police. The appellate court affirmed the production of the map but on a different theory that "authorities had reason to believe that the baby might still be alive.... Even if authorities believed that the chance of the maps leading to a live baby was remote, they were entitled to pursue that remote possibility."

D. DESTROYING, OR FAILING TO RETAIN, PHYSICAL OR DOCUMENTARY EVIDENCE

1. If Hammer's fingerprints were on the gun that he put on your desk, may you advise him to wipe off the fingerprints?

a. Does Hammer's right not to incriminate himself allow him to wipe the gun clean? Would you, his lawyer, have a right to do it for him? Does even the privilege against self-incrimination give a client authority to try to cover up evidence of a crime?

b. If Hammer does not wipe off his fingerprints, should you tell him the consequences of leaving his prints undisturbed? Should you send the gun to the police with the fingerprints on it?

c. Cases have routinely held that a party may be charged with a "conspiracy to obstruct the due administration of justice in a proceeding which [is not pending but which] becomes pending in the future. * * * "[6]

---

6. United States v. Perlstein, 126 F.2d 789, 796 (3d Cir.1942), cert. denied, 316 U.S. 678 (1942). See also, e.g., In re Williams, 23 N.W.2d 4, 9 (Minn.1946) (per curiam).

In general, it is an obstruction of justice "to stifle, suppress or destroy evidence knowing that it *may* be wanted in a judicial proceeding or is being sought by investigating officers. * * * "[7] How should that construction of the law affect the lawyer's ethical responsibilities in a case like this? See also Rule 3.4, Comment 2.

2. Turning to your second client, Mr. Wallace, may you properly counsel him to destroy the incriminating tape recordings? Does it matter whether or not suit has already been filed?[8]

a. No law compelled Wallace to make the tape recordings. Will Wallace be obstructing justice if he destroys these tapes so that they are not later subpoenaed?

b. Assume that the Justice Department is not yet involved but that Wallace is afraid the *Wall Street Journal* reporter may come across information that indicates the secret taping device has been set up in the office. May you advise Wallace to destroy the tapes, using as your reason the embarrassment that would be caused if his business associates knew he had secretly taped and retained tapes of private conversations?[9] Look at Rule 3.4(a) and Comment 2.

3. After Wallace has told you of his taping system and you have listened to the relevant conversations, should you tell Wallace that the tapes are damaging and are likely to be subpoenaed by the government?

a. May you tell Wallace this bad news if you privately expect him to destroy the incriminating material which has not yet been subpoenaed? Can you do anything about that? How does Model Rule 1.2(d) require you to act? How about Model Rule 3.4(a)?

---

7. Rollin M. Perkins, Criminal Law 499 (2d ed.1969) (emphasis added).

8. There is an important question presented whether you represent the corporation as an entity, the president of the corporation, or both, and whether or not representing both the president and the corporation would be a conflict of interest. For now, assume that you just represent Wallace, because that is the focus of this question.

9. Cf. Wall Street J., Apr. 7, 1975, at 7, col. 1–2 ("Official at ITT Unit Destroyed Letters After Journal Questioned Some Practices"):

"A retired official of International Telephone & Telegraph Corp. subsidiary disclosed in testimony before a Senate subcommittee that last summer, while he was still with the company, he destroyed certain letters in his file after the Wall Street Journal began questioning the unit's competitive practices.

" 'I was scared,' John James told the Senate subcommittee on Antitrust and Monopoly, which is investigating the effectiveness of voluntary industry standards. 'I have been associated with code and standard-making activities for many years, and this was the first time in all of that experience that I had anybody question the propriety of the way I conducted myself in connection with this type of work,' he said. * * *

"After reviewing the testimony, an arm of the [American Society of Mechanical Engineers] came up with a conclusion that appears in the current issue of Mechanical Engineering. It commends Mr. James on this testimony and says the society's Professional Practice Committee 'finds no improper or unethical conduct in his action.' "

Would this conclusion have been the same if a lawyer had been the one who destroyed the letters?

b. Could the attorney in *Belge*, supra, ethically have destroyed the photographs of the dead girls' bodies if his client had taken them? If the attorney had kept them for safekeeping? If they were subject to subpoena? Does the work product immunity protect them from disclosure in any event?

c. To prevent Wallace from destroying the evidence, may you refuse to tell him that the material in the files is damaging? May you refuse to return the materials to him if you believe that he will then destroy them? Remember Rule 1.4, and Comment 7. Would you do this to protect Mr. Wallace? Would you do it to protect yourself?

4. May you tell Mr. Wallace that if he destroys only the tapes, he may well be involved in an obstruction of justice but that the next time he engages in a regular housecleaning of his files he should destroy the tapes and any transcripts of them?

a. Must a client keep all incriminating material even though businesses routinely dispose of countless other documents every day?

b. If you suspect that the government may soon subpoena materials, may you send an email to your client's employees advising them that if there is no business reason to keep the materials, they should destroy them? If the Wallace Corporation has a document retention policy but has not followed it (e.g., the policy says to destroy documents after they are four years old if no one has accessed them for two years, but the company just keeps the documents around), may you advise them to destroy the documents now that the newspapers report that the government may want to subpoena them?

c. In 2002, when the Enron Corporation fell into bankruptcy after its stock collapsed amid charges of fraud, attention turned to Enron's auditors, Arthur Andersen. After an Andersen lawyer emailed Andersen employees reminding them of a policy that, after an audit, they should not keep documents that were not necessary to back up the audit, the employees engaged in extensive shredding of documents. Later, the federal government indicted Arthur Andersen for obstruction of justice. On June 15, 2002, the jury found Arthur Andersen guilty. "Soon afterward, Andersen informed the government that it would cease auditing public companies as soon as the end of August, effectively ending the life of the 89–year–old firm."[10]

d. Did the lawyer serve her client well? The stakes associated with decisions to destroy potential evidence were increased by Congress in the

---

10. Kurt Eichenwald, Andersen Guilty in Effort to Block Inquiry on Enron, New York Times, June 16, 2002 at § 1, pp. 1, 22. The story went on: "The jury verdict, reached in the 10th day of deliberations, reflected a narrow reading of the events last fall that led to Andersen's indictment. In interviews, jurors said that they reached their decision because an Andersen lawyer had ordered critical deletions to an internal memorandum, rather than because of the firm's wholesale destruction of Enron-related documents. At bottom, then, the guilty verdict against Andersen—on a charge brought because of the shredding of thousands of records and deletion of tens of thousands of email messages—was ultimately reached because of the removal of a few words from a single memorandum." Id.

wake of the Arthur Andersen scandal by passage of § 802 of the Sarbanes–Oxley Act of 2002, 18 U.S.C.A. § 1519. That provision increases to twenty years in prison and a fine of up to $10 million, the sanction for obstruction of justice by destruction of corporate and financial records.

e.   Ironically, after the public outcry and adoption of the new statute, in Arthur Andersen LLP v. United States, 544 U.S. 696 (2005), the Supreme Court unanimously reversed the firm's obstruction of justice conviction. The federal statute, 18 U.S.C.A. § 1512, requires the defendant to have acted "corruptly." Telling people to follow a records destruction policy is not inevitably corrupt, the Court said. " 'Document retention policies,' which are created in part to keep certain information from getting into the hands of others, including the Government, are common in business." So, it is "not wrongful for a manager to instruct his employees to comply with a valid document retention policy under ordinary circumstances." 544 U.S. at 704. Moreover, the trial judge told the jury too little about both the mental state required for a conviction and the nexus between the destruction and the particular government case thereby prejudiced. A knowingly corrupt persuader "cannot be someone who persuades others to shred documents under a document retention policy when he does not have in contemplation any particular official proceeding in which those documents might be material."

Arthur Andersen LLP was ultimately acquitted of wrongdoing, but the damage had already been done. And you thought practicing law was going to be easy!

PROBLEM 27

THE CLIENT WHO INTENDS TO COMMIT PERJURY

Now we turn to perhaps the classic, most-mooted problem in legal ethics. Surely every law student has been asked, "How can you defend someone you know is guilty?" It is one thing to answer that the prosecution must be put to its proof, but your client may present an affirmative defense. Indeed, he may want to take the witness stand to deny his guilt even though you and he knows he is guilty. This problem initially explores what it means to "know" a client plans to lie. What is a lawyer's duty when the client offers to produce a witness who will be willing to lie on the client's behalf? Does the criminal defendant have a right to testify in his or her own defense? Then, the problem asks what the lawyer is to do when the defendant actually gives false testimony.

FACTS

William Smith is a defendant in a robbery prosecution. Smith is also one of the many criminal defendants represented by M. Maynard Hawley. Smith said to Hawley that he would like to be called as a witness in order to present an alibi defense. After Hawley reminded him that he had never mentioned an alibi defense before, Smith said that his friend had now agreed to testify that he was at her house at the time of the robbery. Smith told Hawley that he would like to take the stand to confirm his friend's story.

Hawley told Smith, "I cannot be a party to perjured testimony." Smith retorted that he had a right to take the stand and testify, but Hawley was reluctant to let Smith do so. Smith assured Hawley: "The last thing I would want you to do is to be unethical. Put me on the stand; I will tell the truth."

Hawley put Smith on the stand. Contrary to Smith's pledge, he lied.

QUESTIONS

A. KNOWING WHEN A LAWYER KNOWS SOMETHING

1. How does an attorney ever really "know" that a witness will commit perjury?

a. When the Model Rules talk about "knowing," do they mean "know pragmatically" or "know absolutely"? How does Model Rule 1.0(f) define what it means to "know" something? If you think that you only "reasonably believe"—Rule 1.0(i)—something, is there a risk that a disciplinary panel, or a judge or jury in a later malpractice case, will decide that you really did "know" the information?

b. At some point, the lawyer cannot close her eyes to what she "knows." The client may confide in the lawyer that he intends to lie. Or, the lawyer may know because the client's testimony keeps changing in order to accommodate new evidence. The lawyer may know that the client seeks to deny the existence of a document that the lawyer (but not the opposing side) knows exists. At some point, in short, the lawyer does not "suspect" or "infer" but "knows" within the meaning of Rule 1.0(f). Rule 3.3, Comment 8, states "although a lawyer should resolve doubts about the veracity of testimony or other evidence in favor of the client, the lawyer cannot ignore an obvious falsehood."

c. In Patsy's Brand, Inc. v. I.O.B. Realty, 2002 WL 59434 (S.D.N.Y. 2002), the court introduced its opinion by stating this case "arises from this Court's *sua sponte* issuance of an order requiring Pennie & Edmonds, the attorneys for the principal defendants, to show cause why it should not be sanctioned for permitting its client to submit a false affidavit." The court did "not dispute counsel's assertion that they acted with subjective good faith." But the court concluded that, "rather than risk offending and possibly losing a client, counsel simply closed their eyes to the overwhelming evidence that statements in the client's affidavit were not true."

The underlying dispute centered around the trademark rights to use of the name "Patsy's" in marketing spaghetti sauce. A principal of the defendant in an infringement suit submitted an affidavit stating that he had created the Patsy's name before the plaintiff registered its mark. The man further stated that he had taken the mark to a printer at that time and submitted a sample jar label to the court. The plaintiff, however, showed that the label the defendant submitted was created long after the defendant asserted, based on a bar code on the label and the printer's own records. Defense counsel then withdrew from representation and was replaced by Pennie & Edmonds, a firm specializing in trademark law. Although the plaintiff had already proven the falsity of the defendant's affidavit in court, Pennie & Edmonds allowed its client to submit a new affidavit that contained substantially the same statements as the first. The firm argued that it was required to rely on its clients' assertions about the date the mark was created. The court, however, found that no reasonable attorney ("a lawyer of even modest intelligence"), much less one knowledgeable in trademark law, could believe the statements in the affidavits.[1]

2.   In preparing Smith's testimony, if Smith tells Hawley a story that appears untruthful, may Hawley explain to him the weaknesses that the prosecutor would see in his story?

a.   What, if anything, should give Hawley pause about engaging in such coaching? If Smith then revises his story to eliminate the weaknesses Hawley saw, may Hawley counsel him as to whether the new story is more plausible? May Hawley advise him that the new story would be even more plausible if Smith would change it slightly again? Might Hawley simply be helping Smith tell a true story more convincingly? At some point, might Hawley be suborning perjury? See Rule 1.2(d).

b.   In Resolution Trust Corp. v. Bright, 6 F.3d 336 (5th Cir.1993), the district judge disbarred two lawyers from practice in his court for trying to get a witness to sign an affidavit that described how certain events had occurred. The witness had said she had no knowledge about some of the things they wanted her to say and she refused to sign the affidavit. The Fifth Circuit reversed the disbarments and described the conduct as follows:

> "With respect to some of the statements in the affidavit, the attorneys were not content to accept Erhart's initial refusal to revise her changes. In an effort to have Erhart see things their way, Lovato and Graber described their understanding of how certain events transpired at Bright Banc, presented Erhart with

---

1. Ultimately, the court adopted what many consider to be a light sanction: "Given Pennie & Edmonds' reputation and its candor in these proceedings, the Court is persuaded that little sanction beyond the publication of this Opinion is required to prevent repetition of similar conduct. Thus all that the Court will require is that a partner of the firm submit to the Court an affidavit stating that a copy of this Opinion has been delivered to each of the lawyers in the firm with a memorandum that states that it is firm policy that its partners and associates adhere to the highest ethical standards and that if a lawyer's adherence to those standards results in the loss of a client, large or small, the lawyer will not suffer any adverse consequence."

independent evidence to support this interpretation of events, and aggressively challenged some of Erhart's assumptions about Bright and Reeder. After making their case for further revisions, Lovato and Graber asked Erhart whether she believed them and whether she was now convinced that their version of certain events was correct. Erhart, unconvinced, declined to alter the initial changes she had made to the draft affidavit. When it was clear to the attorneys that Erhart would not sign a statement agreeing with the attorneys' version of some of the disputed events at Bright Banc, they incorporated Erhart's handwritten changes into a new draft affidavit. Erhart read this draft and made a few changes which were then included in a third draft. Erhart read and approved this version of the affidavit, signed it and left the offices of Hopkins & Sutter."

The witness, Erhart, initially described the lawyers' conduct as "almost like browbeating me" but later said that the lawyers "were doing their job, just like everybody else." The Fifth Circuit rejected the District Court's conclusion that the lawyers were "making or urging the making of 'false' statements," and concluded: "The attorneys' sometimes laborious interviews with Erhart were conducted with the goal of eliciting an accurate and favorable affidavit from a key witness in the underlying case."

Are you convinced that account accurately describes what the lawyers were doing?

c. State ex rel. Abner v. Elliott, 706 N.E.2d 765 (Ohio 1999) (per curiam), involved asbestos workers who had been given instructions about the answers to give in their depositions. Plaintiffs said the instructions were helpful advice; defendants said they were improper "coaching." The trial court found that a particular deposition preparation document constituted evidence of improper coaching of prospective deponents.

The document, entitled "Preparing For Your Deposition," started off by telling plaintiffs what they will need to say to make the defendant "want to offer you a settlement." The document stated: "try to remember how close you were [to these products at the place where you worked]. The more often you were around [them], the better for your case." This witness preparation statement advised that the defendants and their attorneys "have NO RECORDS to tell them what products were used on a particular job." And, "never mention" the existence of this witness preparation document. It also instructed: "You will be asked if you ever saw any WARNING labels on containers of asbestos. It is important to maintain that you NEVER saw any labels on asbestos products that said WARNING or DANGER."[2] The court upheld the trial court's order that plaintiffs turn

2. Lester Brickman & Ronald D. Rotunda, When Witnesses Are Told What to Say, Washington Post, Jan. 13, 1998, at A–15. See also, G–I Holdings, Inc. v. Baron & Budd, 179 F.Supp.2d 233, 242 (S.D.N.Y.2001), which said that: "Baron & Budd conducted regular in-house training sessions concerning the giving of misleading and false deposition testimony and issued various memoranda instructing employees how to prepare clients for giving testimony without regard to its truth."

the "advice" documents over to the defendants in discovery or face adverse jury instructions about them.

d.   In re Foley, 787 N.E.2d 561 (Mass.2003), involved an undercover FBI agent who posed as a client and sought Foley's assistance after the agent caused himself to be arrested for driving under the influence of alcohol and possession of a handgun. Foley concocted a false story for the "client," denying ownership and knowledge of the gun in the automobile. The FBI "client" expressed concerns about perjury, but Foley encouraged the fabrication to secure success at trial. All the while, the agent was tape recording the conversations. A single justice suspended Foley for 18 months for assisting and encouraging his "client" in preparing a fabricated defense. Foley argued that this suspension was too long; the full court increased it to three years. Client perjury on the witness stand is serious, but Foley's conduct was found to be worse because trial conduct concerns "the actions of lawyers in the heat of proceedings and without the planning, the premeditation, and the level of manipulation present in [Foley's] conduct. Their conduct can fairly be categorized as serious errors of judgment, rather than calculated corruption. The respondent's conduct is the latter." 787 N.E.2d at 571–572.

B.   THE DECISION TO CALL A WITNESS WHO MAY TESTIFY FALSELY

1.   Must the lawyer refuse to call Smith's friend if he knows she will commit perjury on his client's behalf?

a.   The general rule is clear: Lawyers, like anyone else, have a duty not to aid and abet perjury, which is a criminal offense. See, e.g., Model Rule 3.3(a)(3), and Comments 5–8; Harris v. New York, 401 U.S. 222 (1971) (a criminal defendant's privilege to testify in his own behalf does not include a right to commit perjury). Complying with this rule, however, has been difficult for some litigators.

b.   In Louisiana State Bar Ass'n v. Thierry, 366 So.2d 1305 (La.1978), a grand jury indicted Thierry (a lawyer) for having Henry Joshua testify falsely as an alibi witness for Thierry's client in a robbery prosecution. Thierry was found guilty of suborning the perjury of Joshua and sentenced to three years. Thierry's main defense "appears to be that in his enthusiasm he acted zealously in the interest of his client as well as out of naivete or ignorance * * *." He argued that "a more experienced lawyer would perhaps have considered the impropriety of his conduct and 'have seen [it] as a stop sign,' but respondent demonstrated a 'lack of caution.'" The state supreme court ordered Thierry disbarred. "So basic to the criminal justice system of this country is the sanctity of the oath of witnesses and the integrity of lawyers that these principles cannot be unknown to or violated by, the least learned or experienced in the profession of law." 366 So.2d at 1307.

c.   In Breezevale Ltd. v. Dickinson, 759 A.2d 627 (D.C.2000), the night before a deposition in which Client's records custodian was going to be asked about key documents, the witness told the lawyer the documents had been forged. She said she didn't want to lie, and the lawyer told her to tell the truth. Before her deposition testimony reached those issues, Client demanded that the lawyer and witness walk away from the deposition, but the lawyer said he had no basis for doing so. Thus, the fact of the forgery came out at the deposition, and the case consequently settled for a much lower amount. At that point, Client sued the firm for malpractice, arguing that the employee was lying and that the documents were real. The jury in the malpractice case found that the documents were indeed forged but that it was malpractice to have let the witness testify truthfully without at least vigorously trying to prevent her from testifying at all.

The trial judge set aside the malpractice verdict, saying that if the documents were forged (as he too found they were), the plaintiff could not use the failure to introduce forged documents as the basis for the underlying claim. Thus, the lawyer's conduct could not have caused the plaintiff's loss. The trial judge also ordered plaintiff to pay defendant's attorneys fees in the malpractice case, finding that plaintiff filed the case in bad faith and in knowing reliance on the forged documents. The D.C. Court of Appeals reversed, arguing that the jury could have found that the firm did not do enough to try to protect its dishonest client. The jury could have found that the law firm's failure to postpone the deposition of the employee and to settle the case before the defendants caught on to the fraud were the cause of the plaintiff's loss.

The en banc court of appeals then vacated that opinion, reheard the case, and reaffirmed the original appellate ruling. The en banc court said, 783 A.2d 573 (D.C.2001), that the former client's forging of documents in an attempt to bolster its underlying suit for breach of contract, did *not* bar Client from bringing a malpractice action against the lawyers, where Client's wrongdoing was not "central[ ]" to the damages it was seeking. The court was "unable to agree with the sweeping nature of an assertion that regardless of malpractice, a client who engages in wrongdoing in connection with any aspect of litigation thereby as a matter of law forfeits all rights of recovery against the attorney." The court still left the question of "sanctions in the discretionary hands of the trial court upon remand."

On remand, the trial court assessed Client a total of over $4 million in attorneys' fees and costs, and $1 million in punitive damages, and dismissed the cause of action for legal malpractice (thus vacating a jury verdict of nearly $3.4 million), after finding by clear and convincing evidence that Client knowingly brought the malpractice litigation primarily relying on documents that it knew to be forgeries. The Court of Appeals sustained the dismissal and the award of attorneys' fees. However, it vacated the separate $1 million award of punitive damages as excessive given that the attorneys' fees and dismissal also bore punitive elements.

d.   In United States v. Lamplugh, 334 F.3d 294 (3d Cir.2003), a client fabricated documents that she wanted to use in defense of her prosecution for willfully failing to file tax returns. Her lawyer turned the documents over to the prosecution, not knowing that they were false but without fully investigating their authenticity. The district court found ineffective assistance of counsel because of the lawyer's failure to conduct an adequate examination of the documents and warn his client of the consequences of producing fabricated documents.

The Third Circuit reversed, holding that clients "forfeited" their right to effective assistance of counsel by certain "extremely serious misconduct." The client's conduct here met the "extremely serious misconduct" standard. Granting relief to a dishonest client would allow her "to manipulate the justice system by knowingly presenting fabricated written documents to her counsel in an attempt to deceive the court, the jury, and the Government into accepting her theory of defense." 334 F.3d at 300.

Do you agree? Is a lawyer ever authorized to facilitate a client's fraudulent conduct?

2.   What do the Model Rules tell a lawyer to do when the client wants to call an alibi witness whom the lawyer knows will lie on the stand?

a.   Look at Model Rule 3.3(a)(3) and (c). Look also at Rule 3.3, Comments 5–13. How should the lawyer proceed?

b.   The Model Rules build on some of the prior case law. People v. Schultheis, 638 P.2d 8 (Colo.1981), examined the procedures a lawyer should follow when confronted with a client who insists that the lawyer call an alibi witness who will testify perjuriously. The court declared:

> "A lawyer who presents a witness knowing that the witness intends to commit perjury thereby engages in the subornation of perjury. We will not permit the truth-finding process to be deflected by the presentation of false evidence by an officer of the court. Therefore, we hold that a lawyer may not offer testimony of a witness which he knows is false, fraudulent, or perjured." 638 P.2d at 11.

The court said further that if the lawyer cannot persuade the client to stop insisting that the lawyer offer false testimony, the lawyer should request permission to withdraw based on an irreconcilable conflict. The motion should not elaborate further. If the trial court denies the motion to withdraw, the lawyer must continue to represent the defendant but still not offer the false testimony of the witness. Because of the possibility of postconviction challenges, the lawyer "should proceed with a request for a record out of the presence of the trial judge and the prosecutor if the court denies the motion to withdraw." 638 P.2d at 14.

c.   In Tibbs v. United States, 628 A.2d 638 (D.C.1993), the defendant was convicted of armed robbery. He said the victim had identified the wrong man. At his first trial (which ended in a hung jury), his wife provided him with an alibi. At the second trial, his lawyer did not call her: the wife had told the lawyer before the second trial that she would not testify because "her testimony [at the first trial] was not true and [the defendant] knew this." The defendant said that the lawyer's failure to call her was ineffective assistance of counsel, but the court held that a lawyer may not call a witness who would testify falsely and thus, "as a matter of law," the failure to do so cannot be ineffective assistance.

3. What if the lawyer discovers that the witness lied under oath, but the lawyer has an argument that the factual misrepresentation is not "material"?

a. May the lawyer refuse to disclose a lie to the court if it is likely that the factual matter is not "material"? What if it is merely arguable that the matter is not "material"?

b. Model Rule 3.3(a)(1) used to say that the lawyer shall not knowingly make "a false statement of material fact. . . ." The 2002 revisions deleted the word "material." Now, Rule 3.3(a)(3) prohibits the lawyer from offering any evidence that the lawyer "knows" to be false. There is no requirement of materiality. Yet the next sentence requires the lawyer to take remedial measures only if the lawyer learns that the witness has offered "material evidence" that is false. Why does Model Rule 3.3 draw this distinction?

c. In *United States v. Shaffer Equipment Co.*, 11 F.3d 450 (4th Cir.1993), the Environmental Protection Agency (EPA) on-site coordinator lied to the court about his academic and professional record. When the government lawyers discovered this inconvenient fact, they did not tell the court. When the trial court found out about it, the court dismissed the case as a sanction. The Fourth Circuit remanded so the trial court could determine if a lesser sanction was appropriate. In the meantime, the government lawyers argued that the falsity (the witness, for example, falsely claimed to have a college degree) was not "material." The Fourth Circuit rejected that argument: "the significance of impeaching the principal EPA witness, who was largely responsible for developing the record, renders impeachment information material." 11 F.3d at 460–61.

d. *Florida Bar v. Cox*, 794 So.2d 1278 (Fla.2001), suspended a prosecutor for a year for having an informant use a false name during trial. The state charged the defendant with solicitation of a minor to engage in a sexual act. The U.S. Customs Service had used an informant to pose as a 13–year–old girl on the Internet. Before trial, the magistrate ordered the prosecution to provide the informant's real name to the defense, but instead, it gave her pseudonym and used it during the trial. Midway through the trial, it came out that the informant had a previous criminal history. Because the prosecution's strategy had prevented the defense from discrediting the witness or even seeking a mistrial, the court found that the prosecutor's failure to give the defendant the informant's real name was intentional misconduct. The referee in the disciplinary proceedings recommended that the lawyer receive a public reprimand and be placed on probation, but the court found the presumptive sanction should have been disbarment. The court said that prosecutors have heightened responsibilities to assure that justice is served. However, because this was apparently an isolated incident by a prosecutor with an otherwise good record, the court suspended her with the requirement that rehabilitation be proven prior to reinstatement.

4. Is there any justification for using perjury if the lie comes from government witnesses and its purpose is to trap criminals?

a. In re Friedman, 392 N.E.2d 1333 (Ill.1979), was a lawyer discipline case that arose because the government introduced false testimony to catch a lawyer who was suborning perjury. The respondent, an attorney in the criminal division of the Cook County State's Attorney office, learned that the defense lawyer had solicited a police officer to commit perjury. The respondent instructed the officer to agree in order to apprehend the briber. After the officer testified falsely under oath that a witness was unavailable, the defense lawyer gave the officer $50, and the state indicted the defense lawyer for bribery. Although the assistant state's attorney allowed the false testimony to be introduced solely for the purpose of developing evidence to be used in a subsequent prosecution, a disciplinary action was brought against him.

Two justices found a violation of Illinois DR 7–102(A)(4), (6), and DR 7–109(B), which correspond to Model Rule 3.3(a)(3). They said: "The integrity of the courtroom is so vital to the health of our legal system that no violation of that integrity, no matter what its motivation, can be condoned or ignored." 392 N.E.2d at 1335. These justices refused to impose any sanctions, however, because respondent had acted without the guidance of settled opinion, and because of the belief of many lawyers that respondent's conduct in the circumstances of this case was proper. Two justices went further and found the respondent guilty of prejudicing the administration of justice. Two justices found that the respondent did not violate any ethical proscriptions at all.

What do you think? How else could the prosecutor have trapped the crooked lawyer? If the police officer had not testified falsely pursuant to the deal, the prosecutor might not have been able to convict the lawyer, who would simply have denied that he had offered a bribe. Should Rule 3.3, Comment 5 (lawyer may offer evidence "for the purpose of establishing its falsity") change the result in *Friedman*?

b. What if the prosecutor wants to run a "sting" operation against a judge or group of judges and file contrived cases? Not long after *Friedman*, a federal effort to prosecute Chicago state court corruption began in what was called "Operation Greylord." In some of these cases, lawyers filed contrived disputes to see if judges would accept bribes to help assure particular results. In several of the cases resulting from Operation Greylord, defendant judges relied on *Friedman* for the proposition that "before injecting a contrived case into the court system and thereby conducting its undercover project in the Illinois courts, the government was required to notify appropriate court officials."

In United States v. Murphy, 768 F.2d 1518, 1528–29 (7th Cir.1985), the court answered:

> "Bribery, like a wholesale transaction in drugs, is a secret act. * * * Because the crime leaves no complaining witness, active participation by the agents may be necessary to establish an effective case. * * * In the pursuit of crime the Government is not confined to behavior suitable for the drawing room. It may use decoys, and provide the essential tools of the offense. * * * The FBI and the prosecutors

behaved honorably in establishing and running Operation Greylord. They assure us that they notified the Presiding Judge of the Circuit Court's Criminal Division, the State's Attorney of Cook County, the Attorney General of Illinois, and the Governor of Illinois. Such notice may not be necessary, and certainly a criminal defendant is in no position to complain of the absence of such notice (for he has no personal right to protect the dignity of the Cook County courts) * * *.''

Do exceptional circumstances require exceptions from the rule against using testimony that is objectively untrue? What if the prosecutors reasonably believed that notifying the courts would result in a leak of the information to potential targets?

c.   After *Murphy*, federal courts did not suppress such testimony, but should the state courts discipline lawyers (e.g., FBI agents who were lawyers) who "lied" to the judge by pretending that they were filing real cases or not disclosing that they were not offering a bribe in a real case? At the time of Operation Greylord, there were those who argued that these federal investigators should be disciplined but the matter was never tested in the courts.

C.   THE DECISION TO CALL THE DEFENDANT WHO MAY COMMIT PERJURY

1.   May a lawyer decide whether or not a client in a criminal case will take the witness stand to testify in his or her own defense?

a.   Look at Model Rule 1.2(a). Is there any question who has the right to make that decision? See also, Restatement Third, The Law Governing Lawyers § 22, to the same effect.

b.   That right of the client has a constitutional dimension. Rock v. Arkansas, 483 U.S. 44 (1987), held that criminal defendants have a right to testify as a result of the due process clause of the Fourteenth Amendment, the compulsory process clause of the Sixth Amendment, and the Fifth Amendment's privilege against self-incrimination. This right to present relevant evidence has limitations, the Court said, but any restrictions must not be "arbitrary or disproportionate." Thus, the Court ruled (5 to 4) that Arkansas' per se rule excluding all hypnotically refreshed testimony impermissibly infringed on the criminal defendant's right to testify on her own behalf.

c.   Nichols v. Butler, 953 F.2d 1550 (11th Cir.1992) (en banc), is a good example of how not to proceed. The court found ineffective assistance of counsel where the lawyer threatened to withdraw in the middle of trial if the defendant elected to testify. The facts of the case did not relate to any claim that the defendant would testify falsely. In addition, the majority noted that there was substantial evidence that the defendant was not guilty, that defendant's trial lawyer was simply concerned that defendant's "prior felony record and serious drug problem might be exposed to the jury and severely damage him." The lawyer told defendant that if he chose to testify, counsel would seek to withdraw from his case. The counsel did not inform defendant that he had a right to testify and that "even if counsel sought to withdraw from the case after the first day of trial, the trial court could have refused the request."

d. On the other hand, many courts do not grant defendants new trials simply because their lawyers decided to keep them off the witness stand, sometimes without regard to whether the defendant understood that the decision whether or not to testify was his to make. See, e.g., United States v. Edwards, 897 F.2d 445 (9th Cir.1990) (defendant's silence at trial effectively waived his right to testify on his own behalf, despite the defendant's contention that his attorney refused to allow him to testify and that the defendant was unaware that he had right to testify; the defense lawyer "testified that he made the decision not to call Edwards [the defendant] without consulting Edwards, and that he conveyed the decision to the trial judge in chambers, out of the presence of Edwards"); Brown v. Artuz, 124 F.3d 73 (2d Cir.1997) (the lawyer did not tell the client of his right to testify, but this failure was harmless error, so the court affirmed the conviction).

Do you agree with the results in these cases? Is the lawyer's duty to explain the client's normal right to take the witness stand inherent in the lawyer's obligation under Model Rule 1.4? How else can the client make the decision that Model Rule 1.2(a) reserves to the client? Are the cases simply saying that, even if the lawyer has not complied with her professional obligations, that failure does not determine the constitutional issue of effective assistance of counsel?

2. Must the lawyer sit by, allow the criminal defendant to testify falsely under oath, and then argue to the jury as if the client's perjury is truthful?

a. The most definitive word from the Supreme Court about whether a criminal defendant has a right to lie on the witness stand, or a right to seek the aid of his lawyer in lying, is Nix v. Whiteside, 475 U.S. 157 (1986). In 1977, Whiteside went to Calvin Love's apartment to buy marijuana. Love was in bed and an argument arose during which Whiteside stabbed Love to death. Whiteside told his lawyer, Gary Robinson, that he had seen Love reach under his pillow, apparently to grab a gun.

> "Until shortly before trial, Whiteside consistently stated to Robinson that he had not actually seen a gun, but that he was convinced that Love had a gun in his hand. About a week before trial, during preparation for direct examination, Whiteside for the first time told Robinson and his associate Donna Paulsen that he had seen something 'metallic' in Love's hand. When asked about this, Whiteside responded that
>
> > " '[I]n Howard Cook's case there was a gun. If I don't say I saw a gun I'm dead.'
>
> "Robinson told Whiteside that such testimony would be perjury and repeated that it was not necessary to prove that a gun was available but only that Whiteside reasonably believed that he was in

danger. On Whiteside's insisting that he would testify that he saw 'something metallic' Robinson told him, according to Robinson's testimony,

> '[W]e could not allow him to [testify falsely] because that would be perjury, and as officers of the court we would be suborning perjury if we allowed him to do it; * * * I advised him that if he did do that it would be my duty to advise the Court of what he was doing and that I felt he was committing perjury; also, that I probably would be allowed to attempt to impeach that particular testimony.'

"Robinson also indicated he would seek to withdraw from the representation if Whiteside insisted on committing perjury.

"Whiteside testified in his own defense at trial and stated that he 'knew' that Love had a gun and that he believed Love was reaching for a gun and he had acted swiftly in self defense. On cross examination, he admitted that he had not actually seen a gun in Love's hand. Robinson presented evidence that Love had been seen with a sawed-off shotgun on other occasions, that the police search of the apartment may have been careless, and that the victim's family had removed everything from the apartment shortly after the crime. Robinson presented this evidence to show a basis for Whiteside's asserted fear that Love had a gun." 475 U.S. at 160–62.

The jury convicted Whiteside of second-degree murder. Whiteside moved for a new trial, claiming he had been denied effective assistance of counsel by Robinson's advice not to add to his testimony the claim that he had actually seen a gun in Love's hand. The trial court denied the motion, and the Iowa Supreme Court affirmed Whiteside's conviction.

Whiteside applied for a writ of habeas corpus, which the district court denied but the Eighth Circuit granted. The Eighth Circuit accepted the finding that Whiteside intended to perjure himself on the witness stand, but "the court reasoned that an intent to commit perjury, communicated to counsel, does not alter a defendant's right to effective assistance of counsel and that Robinson's admonition to Whiteside that he would inform the court of Whiteside's perjury constituted a threat to violate the attorney's duty to preserve client confidences."

The Supreme Court reversed, with several opinions but no dissent. Chief Justice Burger wrote for the Court, joined by Justices White, Powell, Rehnquist, and O'Connor. The Court began by noting that the "right of an accused to testify is of relatively recent origin." By the end of the 19th century, statutes had abolished the rule that the accused was disqualified by virtue of his or her interest as a party to the case. Then the Court turned to the merits:

> "[We have] recognized counsel's duty of loyalty and his 'overarching duty to advocate the defendant's cause.' Plainly, that duty is limited to legitimate, lawful conduct compatible with the very nature of a trial as a search for truth. Although counsel must take all reasonable

lawful means to attain the objectives of the client, counsel is precluded from taking steps or in any way assisting the client in presenting false evidence or otherwise violating the law. * * *

"Both the Model Code of Professional Conduct and the Model Rules of Professional Conduct also adopt the specific exception from the attorney-client privilege for disclosure of perjury that his client intends to commit or has committed. DR 4–101(C)(3) (intention of client to commit a crime); Rule 3.3 (lawyer has duty to disclose falsity of evidence even if disclosure compromises client confidences). Indeed, both the Model Code and the Model Rules do not merely *authorize* disclosure by counsel of client perjury; they *require* such disclosure. See Rule 3.3(a)(4); DR 7–102(B)(1).

"These standards confirm that the legal profession has accepted that an attorney's ethical duty to advance the interests of his client is limited by an equally solemn duty to comply with the law and standards of professional conduct; it specifically ensures that the client may not use false evidence. This special duty of an attorney to prevent and disclose frauds upon the court derives from the recognition that perjury is as much a crime as tampering with witnesses or jurors by way of promises and threats, and undermines the administration of justice. * * *

"It is universally agreed that at a minimum the attorney's first duty when confronted with a proposal for perjurious testimony is to attempt to dissuade the client from the unlawful course of conduct. * * *. The Commentary [to the Model Rules] * * * also suggests that an attorney's revelation of his client's perjury to the court is a professionally responsible and acceptable response to the conduct of a client who has actually given perjured testimony. Similarly, the Model Rules and the commentary, as well as the Code of Professional Responsibility adopted in Iowa expressly permit withdrawal from representation as an appropriate response of an attorney when the client threatens to commit perjury. Model Rules of Professional Conduct, Rule 1.16(a)(1), Rule 1.6, Comment 14, 15 (1983); Code of Professional Responsibility, DR 2–110(B), (C) (1980). Withdrawal of counsel when this situation arises at trial gives rise to many difficult questions including possible mistrial and claims of double jeopardy.

"The essence of the brief *amicus* of the American Bar Association reviewing practices long accepted by ethical lawyers, is that under no circumstance may a lawyer either advocate or passively tolerate a client's giving false testimony. This, of course, is consistent with the governance of trial conduct in what we have long called 'a search for truth.' The suggestion sometimes made that 'a lawyer must believe his client not judge him' in no sense means a lawyer can honorably be a party to or in any way give aid to presenting known perjury.

"Considering Robinson's representation of respondent in light of these accepted norms of professional conduct, we discern no failure to adhere to reasonable professional standards that would in any sense make out a deprivation of the Sixth Amendment right to counsel. Whether Robinson's conduct is seen as a successful attempt to dissuade his client from committing the crime of perjury, or whether seen as a 'threat' to withdraw from representation and disclose the illegal scheme, Robinson's representation of Whiteside falls well within accepted standards of professional conduct and the range of reasonable professional conduct acceptable under *Strickland*. * * *

"Whatever the scope of a constitutional right to testify, it is elementary that such a right does not extend to testifying *falsely*. * * * In Harris [v. New York,] we held the defendant could be impeached by prior contrary statements which had been ruled inadmissible under Miranda v. Arizona, 384 U.S. 436 (1966). *Harris* and other cases make it crystal clear that there is no right whatever—constitutional or otherwise—for a defendant to use false evidence. * * *

"Robinson's admonitions to his client can in no sense be said to have forced respondent into an *impermissible* choice between his right to counsel and his right to testify as he proposed for there was no *permissible* choice to testify falsely. * * * The crime of perjury in this setting is indistinguishable in substance from the crime of threatening or tampering with a witness or a juror. A defendant who informed his counsel that he was arranging to bribe or threaten witnesses or members of the jury would have no 'right' to insist on counsel's assistance or silence. Counsel would not be limited to advising against that conduct. * * * We hold that, as a matter of law, counsel's conduct complained of here cannot establish the prejudice required for relief under the second strand of the *Strickland* inquiry. * * * If a 'conflict' between a client's proposal and counsel's ethical obligation gives rise to a presumption that counsel's assistance was prejudicially ineffective, every guilty criminal's conviction would be suspect if the defendant had sought to obtain an acquittal by illegal means. Can anyone doubt what practices and problems would be spawned by such a rule and what volumes of litigation it would generate?" 475 U.S. at 166–76.

b.   Justice Blackmun, joined by Justices Brennan, Marshall, and Stevens, concurred in the judgment:

"How a defense attorney ought to act when faced with a client who intends to commit perjury at trial has long been a controversial issue. But I do not believe that a federal habeas corpus case challenging a state criminal conviction is an appropriate vehicle for attempting to resolve this thorny problem. When a defendant argues that he was denied effective assistance of counsel because his lawyer dissuaded him from committing perjury, the only question properly presented to this Court is whether the lawyer's actions deprived the defendant of the fair trial which the Sixth Amendment is meant to guarantee. Since I believe that the respondent in this case suffered no injury justifying federal habeas relief, I concur in the Court's judgment. * * *

* * *

" * * * [T]he American Bar Association's implicit suggestion in its *amicus curiae* brief that the Court find that the Association's Model Rules of Professional Conduct should govern an attorney's responsibilities is addressed to the wrong audience. It is for the States to decide how attorneys should conduct themselves in state criminal proceedings, and this Court's responsibility extends only to ensuring that the restrictions a State enacts do not infringe a defendant's federal constitutional rights. * * *[4]

c. What would have happened on remand in the *Nix* case if the Eighth Circuit ruling had prevailed? If the client lied at the new trial, could the prosecutor call the first lawyer as a witness to impeach his former client? The client's disclosure to his former lawyer ("call me so I can testify perjuriously") is a conversation in furtherance of a crime and likely not protected by the attorney-client evidentiary privilege.

3. If the lawyer knows the client wants to testify falsely, how should the lawyer proceed? Given *Nix v. Whiteside*, how should the lawyer advise the client pursuant to Model Rules 1.4 and 2.1?

a. In United States v. Teague, 953 F.2d 1525 (11th Cir.1992) (en banc), the defense lawyer advised the client not to testify and the client took the advice. Then he argued that this advice violated his constitutional right. The court was unwilling to go that far. It agreed that the decision whether or not to testify is for the defendant to make, but the lawyer's professional advice on the question is a part of the effective assistance of counsel, not a denial of it.

b. United States v. Scott, 909 F.2d 488 (11th Cir.1990), showed how a trial court should *not* proceed. When the lawyer moved to withdraw, the judge told the defendant that if he were to have counsel, he would have to agree not to testify; otherwise, he would have to proceed *pro se*. He chose the *pro se* alternative, and the Court of Appeals reversed the conviction. It recognized that the proper way of dealing with client perjury was unclear, but it relied on an alleged lack of evidence that the defendant would have lied if he were represented. Basically, it said the trial judge's approach of requiring the defendant to act *pro se* from the outset prematurely dealt with a problem that might not have arisen.

c. In United States v. Litchfield, 959 F.2d 1514 (10th Cir.1992), on the other hand, defense counsel held an ex parte conference with the judge during the trial. He told the judge that he had advised the client he should testify but the lawyer now feared the client would not be truthful. The judge told the lawyer it was for the jury to decide what was true and untrue, so the trial went on normally, the defendant took the stand, and he

4. Justice Brennan, concurring in the judgment and joined by no other justice, argued that the "Court's essay regarding what constitutes the correct response to a criminal defendant's suggestion that he will perjure himself is pure discourse without force of law." He advised: "Lawyers, judges, bar associations, students and others should understand that the problem has not now been 'decided.' " 475 U.S. at 176–77. Justice Stevens also filed an opinion concurring in the judgment, and said that, in his view, the "much more difficult question" is what must or may the lawyer do if "his client has given testimony that the lawyer does not believe."

was convicted. The Court of Appeals held that the lawyer's alerting the judge about his concerns, by itself, did not deny the defendant effective assistance of counsel. Under the Model Rules, is it correct to conclude that a lawyer has to alert the judge about his concerns if the client insists on testifying falsely?

d. State v. Berrysmith, 944 P.2d 397 (Wash.Ct.App.1997), involved a lawyer who believed his client was about to commit perjury, so he sought and received permission to withdraw. The case was then continued beyond the Speedy Trial Act date to let the new lawyer prepare. The client was convicted and then argued that he was denied a speedy trial because the judge did not have sufficient evidence to permit the first lawyer to withdraw. The court found that the client had significantly changed the story he had told his lawyer and that this gave rise to a reasonable belief the client intended to lie. Thus, the request to withdraw was proper, as was the delay to give new counsel time to prepare.

e. In United States v. Midgett, 342 F.3d 321 (4th Cir.2003), the defendant repeatedly told his lawyer that he had not committed the crimes and wanted to testify that a third person with him on the night in question had committed them. The lawyer refused to put Midgett on the stand, and in a private conference with the judge, the lawyer moved to withdraw. The court reported this to the defendant and gave him two choices: testify and proceed without counsel or not testify and keep his lawyer. Midgett said that he could not proceed without a lawyer, so he chose not to testify and was convicted of the crimes. On these facts, the Fourth Circuit reversed the convictions. Midgett never told his lawyer he was guilty; indeed, he always asserted his innocence. It was not for counsel to decide whether a client should testify based on his own beliefs about the defendant's truthfulness, nor was it proper for the district court to give the defendant an ultimatum that required him to choose between two constitutionally protected rights— the right to counsel and the right to testify.

4. Should the lawyer advise a client who wants to testify falsely that he must give his testimony in the form of a narrative?

a. Rule 3.3(b) of the D.C. Rules of Professional Conduct provides that a lawyer for an accused in a criminal case who plans to lie should first "make a good faith effort to dissuade the client from presenting the false evidence." If unsuccessful, "the lawyer shall seek leave of the tribunal to withdraw." However, if withdrawal is not permitted: "the lawyer may put the client on the stand to testify in a narrative fashion, but the lawyer shall not examine the client in such manner as to elicit testimony which the lawyer knows to be false, and shall not argue the probative value of the client's testimony in closing argument."

What do you think about the narrative approach? It was once the heart of Proposed Standard 4–7.7 of the ABA Standards Relating to the Defense Function, but no longer. Nor does the ABA embrace the "narrative approach" in Model Rule 3.3.[5]

5. Likewise, Florida Bar Rule 4–3.3(4) prohibits all false testimony, whether or not in narrative form.

b. In a footnote, the majority opinion in Nix v. Whiteside expressly acknowledged the debate about the narrative approach:

"In the evolution of the contemporary standards promulgated by the American Bar Association, an early draft reflects a compromise suggesting that when the disclosure of intended perjury is made during the course of trial, when withdrawal of counsel would raise difficult questions of a mistrial holding, counsel had the option to let the defendant take the stand but decline to affirmatively assist the presentation of perjury by traditional direct examination. Instead, counsel would stand mute while the defendant undertook to present the false version in narrative form in his own words unaided by any direct examination. This conduct was thought to be a signal at least to the presiding judge that the attorney considered the testimony to be false and was seeking to disassociate himself from that course. Additionally, counsel would not be permitted to discuss the known false testimony in closing arguments. * * * Most courts treating the subject rejected this approach and insisted on a more rigorous standard, [but t]he Eighth Circuit in this case and the Ninth Circuit have expressed approval of the 'free narrative' standards." * * * 475 U.S. at 170 n.6.

The court was alluding to Lowery v. Cardwell, 575 F.2d 727 (9th Cir.1978), which approved narrative testimony in principle but found it inappropriate in a trial where the judge is the fact finder. In the midst of a trial, the court went on, if defense counsel is surprised by a client's perjury, counsel need not withdraw because that course is not feasible. Instead, the lawyer should not "advance" the perjury. Judge Hufstedler, concurring, said: "No matter how commendable may have been counsel's motives, his interest in saving himself from potential violation of the canons was adverse to his client, and the end product was his abandonment of a diligent defense." 575 F.2d at 732.

c. State v. McDowell, 681 N.W.2d 500 (Wis.2004), held that defense counsel may not substitute narrative questioning for the traditional question-and-answer format unless counsel first knows that the client intends to testify falsely. "Absent the most extraordinary circumstances, such knowledge must be based on the client's expressed admission of intent to testify untruthfully." The court added that the lawyer must advise the client, opposing counsel, and the trial court of the change of questioning style prior to using the narrative. In this case, during a confidential interview, defendant said that he might testify falsely at trial. Defense counsel warned him that he would then have to use narrative questioning. Later, the defendant said that he would testify truthfully, so his counsel said he would use the traditional question-and-answer format. However, when the defendant took the stand, his lawyer employed narrative questioning without telling the defendant beforehand. In this case, the defense counsel's performance was defective for two reasons: (1) he failed to inform the defendant of his intentions to use narrative questioning beforehand;

and (2) he employed the narrative questioning technique despite believing that the defendant intended to testify truthfully. Still, the court affirmed the conviction after finding that the defendant was not prejudiced by defense counsel's actions.

d.   Contrast People v. Andrades, 828 N.E.2d 599 (N.Y.2005), where the defense attorney sought relief from representing the defendant during the course of a murder trial, citing an ethical conflict upon which he could not elaborate. The trial court inferred that the defendant intended to perjure himself. It concluded that the attorney could continue to represent the defendant effectively and that he had complied with his ethical responsibilities. At a hearing on a motion to suppress the defendant's confession, the defendant testified mainly in narrative format and his attorney offered no closing argument. At trial, the defendant primarily defended himself and was convicted of second-degree murder.

On appeal, the New York Court of Appeals agreed that the lawyer must balance zealous representation of a client with the "truth-seeking function of the justice system." Yet, it made clear that counsel must refrain from participating in a client's committing perjury or presenting false evidence. It expressly rejected the idea that counsel should remain silent to protect a defendant who commits perjury because such an approach was incompatible with counsel's role as an officer of the court. The court said that a client's intent to commit the crime of perjury is not protected as attorney-client privilege and that counsel's ethical obligations are the same regardless whether a judge or jury is the fact-finder. Because defense counsel properly balanced his duties to his client and the court and did not breach any recognized professional duty, the court held that the defendant had a fair trial and the effective assistance of counsel.

e.   Should we be more troubled than some courts have been by the use of narrative testimony? What should the court do if the opposing counsel makes the obvious evidentiary objection? A lawyer is supposed to ask nonleading questions to which the other lawyer may object; the lawyer is not supposed to say, "tell us your side of the story."

D.   WHAT TO DO WHEN THE CLIENT DOES GIVE FALSE TESTIMONY

1.   When Smith takes the stand and breaks his promise to be truthful, what should Hawley do? Should Hawley try to withdraw from the representation in the middle of the trial?

a.   If the client knows that the lawyer will urge him not to testify if he plans to testify falsely, we can expect savvy, street-smart defendants (who are ready to lie under oath) to lie to their lawyers when they are not under oath.

b.   Did the ABA Model Code of Professional Responsibility provide helpful guidance on this point? Look at DR 7–102(B)(1), for example:

"A lawyer who receives information clearly establishing that [h]is client has, in the course of the representation, perpetrated a fraud upon a person or tribunal shall promptly call upon his client to rectify the same, and if his client refuses or is unable to do so, he shall reveal the fraud to the affected person or tribunal, except when the information is protected as a privileged communication."

Did that rule give the lawyer clear guidance? Did it instead create as many questions as answers for the lawyer? Is a client's admission to past perjury privileged, for example? What may the lawyer do if the client has not admitted anything, but the lawyer knows testimony was perjured based on earlier privileged discussions the lawyer had with the client?

   c.   After the adoption of the Model Rules and the Supreme Court's decision in Nix v. Whiteside, the ABA Standing Comm. on Ethics and Prof'l Responsibility issued Formal Opinion 87–353 (Apr. 20, 1987). The opinion reviewed and superseded Formal Opinion 287 (June 27, 1953) (discussed in Problem 25), and Formal Opinion 341 (Sept. 30, 1975). The committee wrote: "It is now mandatory * * * for a lawyer, who knows the client has committed perjury, to disclose this knowledge to the tribunal if the lawyer cannot persuade the client to rectify the perjury."

   In 2002, the ABA amended Rule 3.3 to make the mandate clearer. What do Model Rules 3.3(a)(3) and 3.3(b) mean by the term "reasonable remedial measures"? Do Model Rule 3.3, Comments 10, 11, and 15, help you answer that question?[6]

   e.   Torres v. Donnelly, 554 F.3d 322 (2nd Cir. 2009), involved the propriety of a criminal defense counsel's correction of a witness' testimony. A witness present at the time of the robbery had identified the defendant out of photo array presented by the police. At trial, she testified to that fact but stated that six months later she could not identify the defendant in a second police photo array. When the defense attorney later realized that this second identification had taken place at his office and not at the police station, he sought to correct this false testimony of the witness. The attorney agreed to a stipulation that the jury be instructed that the witness had identified the defendant in the only police array that she was shown. On appeal after a conviction, the defendant argued that his lawyer's stipulation created a conflict of interest and prejudiced his representation. The Second Circuit rejected both arguments, finding no conflict and no prejudice. Should the attorney have allowed the witness to take the stand again and the prosecutor to cross examine her testimony?

   2.   Could someone responsibly argue that the Model Rules approach to client perjury is wrong, i.e., that the right to testify is meaningless if the defendant cannot tell the story he wants to tell, even if that story is false?

   a.   Professor Monroe Freedman has been a prime advocate of the argument that the lawyer's duty is to call the client, ask the relevant questions, let the client tell his own story even if the story is fabricated,

---

   6. See also, Restatement Third, The   and i.
Law Governing Lawyers § 120, Comments h

and then rely on the client's story in his summation to the jury. He says that any other approach ignores what he calls the lawyer's "trilemma":[7]

"[T]he attorney functions in an adversary system of justice which imposes three conflicting obligations upon the advocate. The difficulties presented by these obligations are particularly acute in the criminal defense area because of the presumption of innocence, the burden on the state to prove its case beyond reasonable doubt, and the right to put the prosecution to its proof.

"First, the ABA Standards Relating to the Defense Function requires the lawyer to determine all relevant facts known to the accused * * *. The lawyer who is ignorant of any potentially relevant fact 'incapacitates himself to serve his client effectively,' because 'an adequate defense cannot be framed if the lawyer does not know what is likely to develop at trial.'

"Second, the lawyer must hold in strictest confidence the disclosures made by the client in the course of the professional relationship. * * * [C]ounsel is required to establish a relationship of trust and confidence, to explain the necessity of full disclosure of all facts, and to explain to the client the obligation of confidentiality which makes privileged the accused's disclosures.

"Third, * * * the lawyer is an officer of the court, and his or her conduct before the court 'should be characterized by candor.'

"As soon as one begins to think about those responsibilities, it becomes apparent that the conscientious attorney is faced with what we may call a trilemma—that is, the lawyer is required to know everything, to keep it in confidence, and to reveal it to the court. * * *

"In my opinion, the attorney's obligation [when the client wants to lie] would be to advise the client that the proposed testimony is unlawful, but to proceed in the normal fashion in presenting the testimony and arguing the case to the jury if the client makes the decision to go forward. Any other course would be a betrayal of the assurances of confidentiality given by the attorney to induce the client to reveal everything, however damaging it might appear.

"A frequent objection to the position that the attorney must go along with the client's decision to commit perjury is that the lawyer would be guilty of subornation of perjury. Subornation, however, consists of willfully procuring perjury, which is not the case when the attorney indicates to the client that the client's proposed course of conduct would be unlawful, but then accepts the client's decision. Beyond that, there is a point of view which has been expressed to me by a number of experienced attorneys, that the criminal defendant has a 'right to tell his story.' What that suggests is that it is simply too much to expect of a human being, caught up in the criminal process

---

7. The version of the argument quoted here comes from Monroe H. Freedman, Per-   jury: The Lawyer's Trilemma, 1 Litigation 26 (Winter 1975).

and facing loss of liberty and the horrors of imprisonment, not to attempt to lie to avoid that penalty. * * *

"I agree that * * * the case involving collateral witnesses is not at all as clear as that involving the client alone. [However,] * * * a spouse or parent would be acting under the same human compulsion as a defendant, and I find it difficult to imagine myself denouncing my client's spouse or parent as a perjurer, and, thereby, denouncing my client as well. I do not know, however, how much wider that circle of close identity might be drawn."

b.   What do you think of Professor Freedman's position? Is any other position consistent with the desire to leave a convicted defendant with the sense that he had a fair trial? Is giving the defendant a sense that he did everything he could more important than giving the jury only honest evidence upon which to base its verdict?

c.   The implications of Professor Freedman's position are provocative. Professor Freedman was one of the reporters for the Proposed American Lawyer's Code of Conduct (Rev.Draft, 1982), prepared under the auspices of the Roscoe Pound–American Trial Lawyers Foundation. That Code proposed to solve the problem of client perjury by protecting client confidences completely. Consider some of its illustrative cases:

Illustrative Case 1(j). "A lawyer learns from a client during the trial of a civil or criminal case that the client intends to give testimony that the lawyer knows to be false. The lawyer reasonably believes that a request for leave to withdraw would be denied and/or would be understood by the judge and by opposing counsel as an indication that the testimony is false. The lawyer does not seek leave to withdraw, presents the client's testimony in the ordinary manner, and refers to it in summation as evidence of the case. The lawyer has not committed a disciplinary violation."

Illustrative Case 3(e). "A lawyer is conducting the defense of a criminal prosecution. The judge calls the lawyer to the bench and asks her whether the defendant is guilty. The lawyer knows that the defendant is guilty, and reasonably believes that an equivocal answer will be taken by the judge as an admission of guilt. The lawyer assures the judge that the defendant is innocent. The lawyer has not committed a disciplinary violation."

Illustrative Case 3(f): "The same facts as in 3(e), but the lawyer replies to the judge, 'I'm sorry, your Honor, but it would be improper for me to answer that question.' The lawyer has committed a disciplinary violation."

What do you think? Would you want to try cases in a system that was tolerant of the fact that defendants' testimony is untrue? What do you think juries believe about such testimony today?

d.   Does the use of narrative testimony avoid the "trilemma" about which Professor Freedman writes? Professor Freedman writes:

"It is difficult to imagine a more unprofessional and irresponsible proposal. * * *

"[E]xperienced trial attorneys have often noted that jurors assume that the defendant's lawyer knows the truth about the case, and that the jury will frequently judge the defendant by drawing inferences from the attorney's conduct in the case. There is, of course, only one inference that can be drawn if the defendant's own attorney turns his or her back on the defendant at the most critical point in the trial, and then, in closing argument, sums up the case with no reference whatsoever to the fact that the defendant has testified or to the evidence presented in that testimony. Ironically, the Standards reject any solution that would involve informing the judge, but then propose a solution that, as a practical matter, succeeds in informing not only the judge but the jury as well."

e. Does Professor Freedman convince you that the Supreme Court was wrong in *Nix*? Do you agree that a defendant's rights include the choice of what to say from the witness stand? Does the fact that a lawyer would be aiding and abetting perjury if he or she knowingly elicited false testimony from the client ultimately make the Freedman argument unsatisfying?

PROBLEM 28

THE VERDICT THAT MAY BE TAINTED

Lawyers don't like to lose, and win or lose, they like to know how jurors reacted to their presentation. Lawyers often ask jurors, after the verdict, why they voted the way they did. Jurors have no obligation to respond but they often do, and in this and other settings, lawyers sometimes want to preserve an accurate record of what was said. Hence, this problem first explores the propriety of a lawyer contacting jurors after trial to find out where a lawyer went wrong. It then moves to the rules restricting the contact of jurors before or during trial, and the restrictions relating to the payment of experts and fact witnesses. Following that, the problem explores the ethics of the lawyer secretly tape recording a conversation, and, finally, it looks at the rules governing when a lawyer may testify about what she has heard and observed.

FACTS

Marian Talley represented the defendant in a products liability case in which the jury returned an unexpectedly large verdict against her client. After the verdict, Talley sought to determine what had gone wrong. She asked a juror to come to her office and he did so. He was completely cooperative and said, "Most of the jurors initially voted to find no liability, or at least to set a much lower damage figure. One juror held out, however, and we finally came around to his position. That juror later confided to me, after the foreman announced the verdict, that he worked for a competitor of your client and would be paid handsomely for making the verdict come out as it did. It was too late to do anything, and I don't want to get involved, but it is good to get this off my chest."

Talley was angered by this explanation of the verdict and she asked the former juror to put the story in an affidavit. The juror said that he would prefer not to do so, but he told Talley where the supposed payoff was to be made. The juror threatened to deny everything if he were ever asked about the incident in court. At that point Talley activated a secret tape recording device that she always carried with her for occasions in which she needed to preserve what was said in a conversation. Talley skillfully got the former juror to repeat most of the story, and Talley left satisfied that she had gotten the information on the tape.

Using the information supplied by the former juror, Talley went to the place established for the payoff and saw a fat envelope handed to the allegedly dishonest juror by an executive of the juror's employer. She has moved for a new trial and plans to authenticate the tape recording of the former juror's disclosures and testify about her own observations of the payoff at the hearing on her motion. She had asked one of the firm's investigators to accompany her, but he never showed up (it turns out he got sick), so she is the only witness to the transfer of the envelope.

QUESTIONS

A.   THE ETHICS OF CONTACTING JURORS AFTER TRIAL

1. Was it proper for Talley to talk to the juror and investigate the jury's deliberative process?

a. Consider one report of how juries really work:

"In an unusual post-trial move, the lawyer for Eric Menendez invited seven sympathetic female jurors to her office where they told reporters on Saturday that a battle between men and women on Mr. Menendez's jury doomed the chances for a verdict.[1] * * *

" 'It was hostile in there,' said one juror * * *. 'There were insults, sexual comments. * * *

"Another juror * * * said, 'We were called ignorant asses and empty headed and those women.' " We had one juror who would

---

1. The state prosecuted Eric and Lyle Menendez for killing their parents in order to inherit a substantial fortune. They ultimately admitted the killing but claimed self-defense, asserting that they had been molested by their father for many years and were afraid he would kill them to prevent them from disclosing his acts.

put on his sunglasses and be balancing his checkbook and cutting out coupons when the women were talking.' * * *

"A vote on the first day of deliberations indicated the jury was split, the female jurors said, with six women for manslaughter convictions and six men for first-degree murder. Ultimately, five men voted for first-degree murder, one for second-degree. The women voted for voluntary manslaughter."[2]

b.   Look at Model Rule 3.5. Are you surprised by any of the restrictions placed on contacting jurors? Do you think they unduly restrict lawyers' ability to get the kind of information Talley was seeking? Did the juror's reluctance to put the facts in an affidavit indicate a desire not to communicate with Talley?

c.   Rapp v. Disciplinary Bd. of Hawaii Supreme Court, 916 F.Supp. 1525 (D.Haw.1996), held that restrictions on post-trial contact with jurors violate free speech rights of the lawyers, the litigants and the jurors. Rapp, a lawyer, had been a *pro se* plaintiff in a state case. The jurors voted in his favor and he wanted to thank the jurors and learn how they had reacted to aspects of his advocacy. Alleging a fear of discipline if he contacted jurors, he filed this federal court action to have Rule 3.5 held unconstitutional. The court held that by allowing only contact with jurors that was "permitted by law," Rule 3.5(c) placed a vague and overbroad limitation on First Amendment rights. Do you agree with this decision? Does the court seem to have been "solving" a nonexistent problem?

d.   In Commission for Lawyer Discipline v. Benton, 980 S.W.2d 425 (Tex.1998), the plaintiff's lawyer in a personal injury action in which the jury had awarded no damages wrote to all the jurors: "I was so angry with your verdict that I could not talk with you after the trial. I could not believe that 12 allegedly good people from Cameron County, who swore to return a verdict based on the evidence, could find [as you did]. * * * Your cold and unfair conduct does not matter now. Judge Hester * * * decided that your verdict was obviously unjust and granted * * * a new trial." The Texas Commission for Lawyer Discipline found that by sending this letter, the lawyer had violated the Texas version of Rule 3.5. It put the lawyer on probation. The Court of Appeals reversed, finding the Rule itself unconstitutional, but a badly split Texas Supreme Court found the Rule did not violate the lawyer's right of free speech, was not unconstitutionally overbroad, and was not unconstitutionally vague in prohibiting communications calculated to influence a juror's actions in future jury service. The court remanded for a new hearing.

Does the lawyer's letter in *Benton* violate Model Rule 3.5(c)(3)? If a lawyer wrote such a letter to the judge after a trial, could the judge hold the lawyer in contempt of court?

e.   The ethics rules regulate lawyers, not representatives of the press. Yet, some people believe that the risk that the news media will harass jurors is no less serious than the concern that lawyers will harass them.

2.   New York Times, Jan. 13, 1994, sec. A. p. 13, col. 1.

Others object that some jurors try to sell stories about their deliberations to the highest bidder.[3] Would greater constitutional issues be raised if a court tried to impose restrictions such as those in Model Rule 3.5 on reporters?

2. Now that Talley believes that a juror violated his oath, what should she do?

a. Rule 606(b) of the Federal Rules of Evidence provides that "a juror may testify on the question whether extraneous prejudicial information was improperly brought to the jury's attention or whether any outside influence was improperly brought to bear upon any juror." Many state laws similarly make it possible to impeach a jury's verdict by showing that one or more of the jurors has been corrupted and that the integrity of the verdict is in doubt. Does that possibility, in turn, create a duty on a lawyer to bring the issue to the attention of the court?

b. Do the Model Rules give Talley such a professional obligation? Look at Rule 3.3(b) and Comment 12. Do you have any doubt about what Talley is required to do?

c. Talley is undoubtedly glad she did not learn it was her client who had tried to bribe a juror. Suppose it had been her client who committed that crime. What would Talley's obligation be? Is she required to reveal information that clearly relates to the representation and thus that would be confidential under Model Rule 1.6(a)? Look at Model Rule 3.3(c).

B. CONTACTING JURORS BEFORE TRIAL; COMPENSATION OF WITNESSES

1. Was it unethical for Talley's opponent to try to bribe one or more of the jurors before the trial?

a. Do not ponder long whether or not a lawyer may bribe a juror. That is clearly illegal under the law of all jurisdictions.

b. Do the Model Rules also prohibit this conduct? Look at Rule 3.5(a). Remember also Rules 8.4(b), 8.4(c), and 8.4(d). Everywhere Talley's opponent turns, it is clear that he or she is in big trouble.

2. Does the complex mix of people in a modern society mean that the trial lawyer should investigate the characteristics of individual members of the jury pool?

a. Would Talley or any other lawyer be violating the Model Rules if she interviewed members of the jury pool before the trial outside the presence of the judge? Should a lawyer be permitted to have private investigators do background checks on potential jurors? Should prosecutors have the information as well as defense counsel? Should they be able to use police officers to investigate the jurors?

b. Given the Supreme Court's limitations on the use of peremptory challenges to strike jurors based on general categories of race and sex,[4] do

---

3. See, e.g., Mark Hansen, Post–Trial Interview Limits Criticized, ABA J., Apr. 1994, at p. 26 (limits imposed on interviews of "Crazy Eddie" fraud trial jurors).

4. Georgia v. McCollum, 505 U.S. 42 (1992) (unconstitutional for either prosecutor or defense counsel to exercise peremptory challenges based on racial stereotypes);

lawyers need more freedom to investigate so as to be able to challenge for cause and to defend their peremptory strikes? Should judges give lawyers less information in order to limit the lawyers' ability to exclude jurors for reasons that do not relate to their impartiality?

3. If there is to be a prohibition on pretrial communication or contact with jurors, how broadly should the rule be drafted?

a. Restatement Third, The Law Governing Lawyers § 115(1) says that, "except as allowed by law," a lawyer may not "communicate with * * * a person known by the lawyer to be a member of a jury pool from which the jury will be drawn." Comment *b* to § 115 explains: "The rules concerning jury trial undertake to ensure that no juror will have a predisposition toward either party. Prohibition of pre-trial communication with prospective jurors both prevents improper influence and avoids the necessity of inquiry concerning such contacts."

Are you convinced that the entire jury pool should be off-limits to lawyer contact? Would a prohibition directed at any smaller group of jurors adequately protect the interest in seeing that none of the jurors is tainted?

b. Is the desire to protect the privacy of jurors part of the justification for restrictions on pre-trial contact? In the O.J. Simpson murder case, the court forced prospective jurors to answer a court questionnaire over 50 pages in length about their religion, political attitudes, and life experiences. Should we be concerned about lawyers intruding into the jurors' personal lives and not worry about the court's intrusion?

4. Is it proper for the lawyer to pay a witness for the time it takes to prepare and give testimony?

a. Look at Model Rule 3.4(b) and Comment 3. A lawyer clearly may not pay a witness for the content of his or her testimony, i.e., only pay the witness if he or she testifies in a particular way.[5] It is routine, however, to pay expert witnesses for the time they spend preparing and testifying in a case.[6]

b. In re Hingle, 717 So.2d 636 (La.1998), disbarred a lawyer for arranging to have his clients assume debts owed by an employee in exchange for the employee's favorable testimony. The lawyer told the

---

J.E.B. v. Alabama ex rel. T.B., 511 U.S. 127 (1994) (same result regarding sex-based challenges). These issues were discussed earlier in Problem 24.

5. E.g., Florida Bar v. Wohl, 842 So.2d 811 (Fla.2003). Wohl represented Bruce Winston, son of jeweler Harry Winston, in a dispute with his brother over his mother's estate. Wohl solicited the help of Kerr, a former employee of the Winston jewelry business, and offered compensation of $25,000 for her first 50 hours of service, and up to a one million dollar "bonus" depending on the "usefulness" of the information. The Florida Supreme Court held that this agreement violated Rule 3.4(b), because it was an unlawful inducement to a witness. The court suspended Wohl for 90 days, imposed one year probation, and required that he successfully complete a practice and professional enhancement program.

6. However, expert witnesses may not be paid fees contingent on their testimony or the success of the client in the matters. See, e.g., Person v. Association of the Bar of the City of New York, 554 F.2d 534 (2d Cir.), cert. denied, 434 U.S. 924 (1977), discussed in Problem 36, *infra*.

district attorney "[i]f you as prosecutors can offer immunity to a witness to get him to cooperate, why can't I offer him money?" Are you persuaded by the lawyer's analogy?[7]

c.   Should it be proper for Martin to pay a fact witness (not an expert) for his time when he testifies and prepares for the testimony? ABA Formal Opinion 96–402 (Aug. 2, 1996) concluded that it is indeed proper to pay fact witnesses who have to devote substantial time to a case. Comment 3 to Model Rule 3.4 does not literally permit such payments, the opinion conceded, but ABA Model Code of Professional Responsibility DR 7–109 did allow paying fact witnesses for the "loss of time in attending or testifying." The amount of any compensation paid must be reasonable, the opinion says, so as not to suggest payment for the content of the testimony. But even retired people who do not forego salary while they are testifying may be paid for the value of their time, not just in testifying but in preparing for testimony as well.

What do you think of this opinion? Do you think the distinction between paying for time and paying for testimony will be easily maintained? On the other hand, could a company pay a current employee her regular salary for time spent working on and testifying in the case? Is the payment to a former employee or other outside witness significantly different?

d.   In re Bruno, 956 So.2d 577 (La.2007), arose out of a class action involving an explosion at a Shell refinery. Zewe, a longtime Shell employee, contacted Bruno, a member of the plaintiffs' coordinating committee, and proposed to bring Bruno evidence that Shell was trying to get its employees to lie. Bruno agreed to pay Zewe $5,000 for his information as an "expert witness." In fact, the money was paid about three months after the agreement. Ultimately, when Shell learned it had a mole in its midst, Russ Herman, another member of the plaintiffs' committee, denied that Zewe had been paid money and Bruno did not correct him. After the case settled, the U.S. attorney started an investigation. The local federal courts suspended Bruno from practice for one year. In this opinion, the Louisiana Supreme Court suspended him for three years with 18 months deferred because Bruno previously had a clean record.

C.   SECRET TAPE RECORDING

1.   Was it professionally responsible for Talley to tape record the conversation when it became clear that the juror would not commit his testimony to paper or repeat it to any other person?

---

7.   We will look at prosecutors' practice of granting immunity in Problem 29. Note that statutes authorize the immunity, the courts technically grant it on application of the prosecutor, and the court fully discloses to the jury that the prosecutor's witness has immunity from prosecution. ABA Standards Relating to the Administration of Justice, The Prosecution Function, Standard 3–3.2(b) states explicitly that there must be "no attempt to conceal the fact of reimbursement." The court said in Kastigar v. United States, 406 U.S. 441, 446 (1972): "many offenses are of such a character that the only persons capable of giving useful testimony are those implicated in the crime."

How should Talley be able to preserve accurate evidence of what was said?

a.   Talley's secret recording may or may not be a violation of state civil or criminal law. However, it is not a violation of federal law. Section 2511 of the Omnibus Crime Control and Safe Streets Act of 1968, 18 U.S.C.A. § 2511(2)(d), reads: "It shall not be unlawful under this Chapter for a person not acting under color of law to intercept a wire or oral communication where such person is a party to the communication * * * unless such communication is intercepted for the purpose of committing any criminal or tortious act * * *."[8]

b.   Federal Communications Commission (FCC) regulations are applicable only if telephones are used; these require that there be an automatic tone warning device furnished, installed, and maintained by the telephone company before telephone conversations may be recorded. Failure of a person to use this device is not criminal, although it can subject one to loss of phone service. The law of evidence has been held not to prohibit the introduction of tapes obtained in violation of these FCC tariffs. Battaglia v. United States, 349 F.2d 556 (9th Cir.1965), cert. denied, 382 U.S. 955 (1965).

c.   State laws vary, but some states allow what is called "consensual" recording, i.e., one party to the conversation knows that it is being taped and does not object.

2.   If Talley's tape recording did violate state law, would her conduct also make her subject to professional discipline or other remedies?

a.   Whatever the answer where the recording is legal, what if the recording is not legal? Look at Model Rule 4.4(a). In this context, is tape recording a method of "obtaining evidence that violate[s] the legal rights" of the person being recorded?

b.   Nissan Motor Co., Ltd. v. Nissan Computer Corp., 180 F.Supp.2d 1089 (C.D.Cal.2002), involved a dispute over whether defense counsel could tape record conversations it had with plaintiff's counsel. Defense counsel allegedly believed the plaintiff's lawyers misrepresented what they had said in phone conversations and threatened to record those calls. Plaintiff's counsel objected to such recording, and the court said that taping conversations with opposing counsel without consent violated California state law against wiretapping. More broadly, the court found that threatening to tape record conversations between counsel would violate Federal Rule of Civil Procedure 1, which mandates the "just, speedy, and inexpensive determination of every action." The court explained that inhibiting the ability of attorneys to freely communicate over the telephone would impair the progress of litigation by forcing the parties to put everything in writing, resulting in inevitable delays and complications. The court did not address the argument that using recording to reduce disagreement about what was

---

8. See also, United States v. White, 401 U.S. 745 (1971) (Sections 2510–2520 of the Omnibus Crime Control Act permit a participant to record a conversation secretly).

actually said over the telephone might actually tend to reduce disputation and delay.

c. Whether or not a crime has been committed, however, there may be a violation of Model Rule 8.4(c) if circumstances indicate the lawyer deceived the person into believing there would be no taping. For example, in Committee on Professional Ethics and Conduct of the Iowa State Bar Ass'n v. Mollman, 488 N.W.2d 168 (Iowa 1992), the lawyer had agreed to wear a concealed microphone to a meeting with his drug client in exchange for leniency in his own prosecution for drug possession. The court held that for the lawyer to mislead his client in this way justified a 30–day suspension.

3.   Should the ethical principle be that it is always unprofessional for a lawyer to engage in tape recording, whether of a client or a third party?

a. This is more than a theoretical inquiry. ABA Formal Opinion 337 (Aug. 10, 1974), advised lawyers:

> "With the exception noted in the last paragraph, the Committee concludes that no lawyer should record any conversation whether by tapes or other electronic device, without the consent or prior knowledge of all parties to the conversation.

> "There may be extraordinary circumstances in which the Attorney General of the United States or the principal prosecuting attorney of a state or local government or law enforcement attorneys or officers acting under the direction of the Attorney General or such principal prosecuting attorneys might ethically make and use secret recordings if acting within strict statutory limitations conforming to constitutional requirements. This opinion does not address such exceptions which would necessarily require examination on a case by case basis. It should be stressed, however, that the mere fact that secret recordation in a particular instance is not illegal will not necessarily render the conduct of a public law enforcement officer in making such a recording ethical."

b. Was the ABA Committee too sweeping in its conclusion? Does our society have a common moral revulsion against secret tape recording? Notice the date of the opinion. It was written the same year that President Nixon (a lawyer) resigned from the presidency. During the Watergate investigation it became public knowledge that he had secretly taped conversations to which he was a party. Many people objected to the secret taping along with a lot of other things President Nixon had done.

c. Parrott v. Wilson, 707 F.2d 1262 (11th Cir.1983), cert. denied, 464 U.S. 936 (1983), denied work product protection for clandestine tape recordings of witnesses, citing the view that secret taping violated an attorney's ethical standards even though neither federal nor the relevant state law prohibited taping. Thus, the tapes had to be produced in discovery.

d. Should private attorneys in criminal cases be placed under stricter ethical standards than the prosecutor? Should it be unethical for prosecutors to engage in secret tape recordings as well? Opinion 337 did not bless such secret recordings; it said: "the mere fact that secret recordation in a particular instance is not illegal will not necessarily render the conduct of a public law enforcement officer in making such a recording ethical."

4. Is the Opinion 337 position on tape recording now outdated?

a. Does the text of the Model Rules justify the ABA opinion? The rules at the time, and the rules today, forbid deceitful conduct. Is it deceitful to secretly tape a conversation to which you are a party, if you do not make any representation about whether or not it is being taped?

b. Opinion No. 80–95 (1982) of the Association of the Bar of the City of New York partly rejected ABA Formal Opinion No. 337 and held that, because prosecutors may surreptitiously record a conversation by placing a tape recorder on one of the parties to the conversation with only the consent of that party, criminal defense lawyers should be able to record their conversations with witnesses as well. Recording of conversations with the lawyer's own clients and recording in commercial or civil contexts remained prohibited.

c. In Opinion No. 515 (1979), the New York State Bar Association added that a lawyer should be able to respond to a question initiated by a client and advise that client that the client himself may surreptitiously record a conversation where that recording is lawful. Counsel, however, may not do the recording. See also, Texas Prof'l Ethics Comm. Opinion No. 514 (Dec. 27, 1995), to the same effect.

Does that distinction make sense to you?

d. Restatement Third, The Law Governing Lawyers § 106, Comment *b*, says:

> "When secret recording is not prohibited by law, doing so is permissible for lawyers conducting investigations on behalf of their clients, but should be done only when a compelling need exists to obtain evidence otherwise unavailable in an equally reliable form. Such a need may exist more readily in a criminal-defense representation."

Do you agree that there should be a "compelling need" requirement to engage in secret tape recording? Do criminal defense lawyers have a greater such need than other lawyers?

e. The ABA explicitly overruled ABA Formal Opinion 337 in ABA Formal Opinion 01–422 (June 24, 2001). The new opinion preserves the prohibition of recording in violation of state law. Nor may a lawyer falsely represent that a conversation is not being recorded. However, the opinion concluded: (1) that it is no longer universally accepted that nonconsensual taping of conversations is inherently deceitful, (2) that there are circumstances in which disclosure would defeat a legitimate and necessary activity, and (3) that Opinion 337 is no longer consistent with the Model Rules.

However, the opinion said that it is inadvisable for a lawyer to record a conversation with his own client concerning the subject matter of the representation without the client's knowledge.

Has the opinion touched on all the relevant issues to your satisfaction?

D.   THE LAWYER AS A WITNESS AT THE CLIENT'S TRIAL

1.   Is any ethical problem presented if Talley testifies at the hearing on her motion for a new trial? Does Talley's testimony fall within any recognized exceptions?

a.   Look at Model Rule 3.7(a). For whose protection were the restrictions on the lawyer's acting as a witness intended? The court? The opposing party? The client?

b.   Do you think that a jury is not able to distinguish between a lawyer's argument and her testimony? Does that mean the rule should not apply when the advocate testifies in a bench trial? A hearing on a motion for new trial? A *pro se* litigant may both represent himself and testify even if he has a law license, so how can one argue that the two roles are inherently inconsistent?

c.   Lawyers may become witnesses for a client in many different ways. Transactional lawyers are present when documents are drafted and when parties negotiate agreements. Wills and estates lawyers may be asked to witness a testamentary document for a client. And criminal defense lawyers may be present at police lineups and other interrogations. When lawyers work in a large firm, litigation and nonlitigation functions are often separated into different departments, so the advocate-witness rule may not affect current practice. However, in small law firms and smaller communities, the advocate-witness rule may more severely impact law firm practice.

d.   The prohibition against a lawyer acting as an advocate and a witness does not apply if the testimony involves (1) an uncontested issue, (2) a dispute over the value of legal services in the case, or (3) if the disqualification of the lawyer would impose substantial hardship on the client. Rule 3.7(a). Would Talley's testimony fall within any of these exceptions? The first two exceptions do not involve situations that would confuse the finder of fact about the lawyer's role in the matter. The third exception must be narrowly interpreted, lest it simply eradicate the rule. The substantial hardship exception does give a lawyer grounds for a motion to stay the case when the lawyer becomes a necessary witness just days before the trial is scheduled to begin.

e.   In Zurich Insurance Co. v. Knotts, 52 S.W.3d 555 (Ky.2001), the plaintiff sued an insurance company to obtain payment of a personal injury award against the insured. Plaintiff's lawyer had handled the claim throughout initial settlement negotiations and jury trial, and the plaintiff now says the insurance company acted in bad faith by not acting reasonably and promptly during the course of negotiations. The plaintiff's attorney filed a personal affidavit attesting to some of the practices of the defense counsel, although the attorney indicated no intention to actually testify at trial. The court held that filing the affidavit did not disqualify the attorney from continuing to represent the plaintiff. The court found it would be unduly prejudicial to disqualify counsel and any potential prejudice to the defendant could be mitigated by effective cross-examination. Disqualification is an extreme measure, and factors such as the attorney's level of expertise, familiarity with the claim, and the level of trust and confidence of the client in the attorney were all relevant considerations.

Do you agree with this result? Is it consistent with Model Rule 3.7(a) and (b)?

2. Should a party be able to "waive" the protections of Model Rule 3.7?

a. If the lawyer's testimony were expected to be adverse to the client, the situation would present a conflict of interest under Model Rule 1.7(a) that would itself disqualify the lawyer. Unless prohibited by Model Rule 1.7(b), however, this conflict would be one the client could waive.

b. On the other hand, notice that Model Rule 3.7 does not provide for a waiver. Why not? Is the purpose of the rule to protect the parties or to protect the court and the fact-finding process?

c. California does allow the client to "waive" the disqualification. The rule grew out of the decision in Comden v. Superior Court, 576 P.2d 971 (Cal.1978), cert. denied, 439 U.S. 981 (1978). Plaintiff argued that disqualification of the firm created a "substantial hardship" because of the distinctive value of the services of the law firm. The lawyer argued that, although some of his work product could be transferred to new counsel, his "impressions and rapport with the people involved" could not be transferred. The court rejected these arguments and held that loss of expertise, interviews, research, and preliminary discussions of trial strategy do not constitute enough to support the substantial hardship exception also found in Model Rule 3.7(a)(3).

California responded to *Comden* by amending its Rule [now Rule 5–210] to allow a lawyer to let the client decide how to balance the need for the lawyer against the possible problems created by the dual role. A lawyer could be both advocate and witness if the lawyer secures the "informed, written consent of the client" after fully advising the client and after giving the client a reasonable opportunity to seek the advice of independent counsel.

Do you agree with the California approach? Is this a case in which, where California leads, the nation should follow?

3. When is the lawyer required to be disqualified? Is it at the moment the lawyer is put on a witness list? Is it at some earlier time?

a. In Comden v. Superior Court, supra, the California Supreme Court upheld a trial court decision disqualifying a lawyer who could testify as to what was said in certain meetings involving the litigants. The plaintiffs argued that the disqualification order was premature because later discovery might make the attorney's testimony unnecessary. However, the court concluded that withdrawal is required whenever the attorney "ought" to testify. Contra, e.g., Connell v. Clairol, Inc., 440 F.Supp. 17, 19 n.1 (N.D.Ga.1977) (the attorney's testimony must be "in fact, genuinely needed"). Which rule do you think is better?

b. Chappell v. Cosgrove, 916 P.2d 836 (N.M.1996), involved a lawyer who had been one of five persons at a meeting where the defendants allegedly agreed to construct a park. The plaintiff residents moved to disqualify him, alleging he was a potential witness. The court said that the test for disqualification is materiality of the testimony, the need for the lawyer to give it, and the prejudice if the lawyer does testify. Because there were several people at the meeting, the court concluded that the lawyer's testimony would be cumulative, not necessary, and therefore it did not order disqualification.

c. Restatement Third, The Law Governing Lawyers § 108, Comment *e*, however, says that the advocate-witness prohibition "is not affected by the character of the testimony as cumulative." Even cumulative testimony may be important, the Comment says, so the issue is whether "a reasonable lawyer, viewing the circumstances objectively, would conclude that failure of the lawyer to testify would have a substantially adverse affect on the client's cause."

d. If an attorney is disqualified from representing a client because the attorney will be a witness and the client then hires another law firm to handle the litigation, may the lawyer/witness help prepare the new lawyers? Why or why not, given the rationale that animates the Rule?

4. If the lawyer-witness is not herself the trial lawyer, are there any justifications for imputing the advocate-witness rules to other members of her firm who are trial counsel?

a. Look at ABA Model Rule 3.7(b) and Comments 1 and 5 that discuss the rationale for the Rule. The ABA Model Code of Professional Responsibility drew no distinction between trial counsel and other members of the lawyer's firm acting as witnesses. It imputed disqualification of the advocate-witness to all lawyers in the same firm.

b. Does Model Rule 3.7(b) represent more realism or simply a decline in ethical standards? If Talley's investigator in this problem had not gotten sick at the last minute, could Talley have avoided the problem by having the investigator act as the witness? If so, why should there be any question about allowing other lawyers in the same law firm to conduct the trial while Talley is the one who testifies?

c. Rule 3.7(b) notes that a law firm may not be able to represent the client because of obligations under Rule 1.7 or 1.9. How may these two rules come into play when a lawyer in the firm is likely to be a necessary witness? One possible scenario involves a lawyer who will testify adversely to the client's position. That would create a concurrent conflict of interest. Another possible situation arises when a lawyer in the firm committed potential malpractice and those acts are now subject of this litigation. The conflict between the firm's interests and the client's interests may prevent the law firm from representing the client when a lawyer in the firm may be a witness.

5. What should be defense counsel's response if the prosecutor in a criminal case tries to testify against the defendant? How can the prosecutor avoid the problem if it becomes necessary for her to testify?

a. People v. Donaldson, 113 Cal.Rptr.2d 548 (Cal.Ct.App.2001), granted a new trial based on ineffective assistance of counsel in a case of child endangerment. The prosecution had only one witness to the defendant's alleged acts; that witness testified at the preliminary hearing that she had actually seen the defendant holding a pillow over the defendant's daughter's face, but at trial, the witness seemed confused and said that she had never actually seen anything occur. The witness also said that the prosecutor had intimidated her and made her feel as though if she did not testify, she would be put under arrest. Then, the prosecutor called herself as a witness to impeach the credibility of this key prosecution witness by giving a narrative account of the conversations she had with the witness before the witness testified. The court held that by calling herself as a witness, she violated the professional conduct rule generally prohibiting a lawyer from acting as both advocate and witness. The defense counsel thus rendered ineffective assistance by failing to object when the prosecutor took the witness stand.

b. Did the prosecutor in *Donaldson* violate any other rules? Look at Model Rule 3.4(e). Did the prosecutor "state a personal opinion as to * * * the credibility of a witness," for example? The court found that in her closing argument, the prosecutor indeed had improperly expressed personal belief in defendant's guilt.

PROBLEM 29

THE CRUSADING PROSECUTOR

The prosecutor, as a representative of the state, is a lawyer with special authority and special responsibilities. It should not be surprising, then, that some ethical standards of prosecutors are also *sui generis*. This problem first considers the use of the media and other publicity as a tool in modern litigation in the context of a prosecutor's work. Next, it looks at the prosecutor's decision what to charge. Third, it asks when a prosecutor may subpoena the files or otherwise investigate a criminal defense lawyer. The problem then examines restrictions on the leverage available to a modern prosecutor and broader questions about the ethical responsibilities of government lawyers.

FACTS

"Clean Gene" White is the crusading young state's attorney of Springfield County, the home of the state legislature. He says he sees a public interest (and his detractors say a personal political benefit) in uncovering what he publicly has called a "lot of skeletons under the beds of some state legislators." Gene has started a "special prosecutions" branch of his office that is charged with discovering the misdeeds of legislators. Each week, on Monday, Gene holds a press conference to assert his belief in ethics, report on indictments just issued, allude to possible indictments, and answer questions put to him by the reporters covering his office.

Newspapers have begun to report rumors and rumors of rumors as to which persons are likely to be indicted; Gene has denied publicly that he or anyone in his office is responsible for the leaks and has said that he "denounces the rumor mill."

The special unit is responsible thus far for successfully prosecuting three cases: one consisting of forty-six unpaid parking tickets received by the chairman of the motor vehicle committee (a "callous breach of the public trust," according to Gene); a second for failure to report a sale of race track stock on a legislator's ethics form; and a third against a House committee chairman for taking a $5,000 bribe to kill a bill.

Though his office normally exercises discretion not to prosecute persons found with minor amounts of marijuana, the office recently indicted a state official found with one marijuana cigarette in his car. This particular legislator is widely suspected of being in league with organized crime, although no admissible evidence has ever been found to support such a charge. Gene privately told one of his assistants to follow this legislator in an effort to uncover some wrongdoing. When the assistant reported the discovery of the marijuana cigarette, Gene said: "Prosecute. I know we normally don't in such cases, but I want to make it hot for this fellow."

QUESTIONS

A. MEDIA RELATIONS IN MODERN LITIGATION

1. Why do the Model Rules place limits on White's use of press conferences and other public statements to tell the public about his office's work?

a. ABA Model Rule 3.8(f) imposes specific trial publicity rules on the prosecutor, while Model Rule 3.6 imposes other publicity restrictions equally on both prosecutors and private lawyers. The history of the development of the modern day rules reflect the ABA responses to Supreme Court rulings in both free speech and fair trial cases. Canon 20 of the Canons of Professional Ethics (1908), in the Standards Supplement, provided:

> "Newspaper publications by a lawyer as to a pending or anticipated litigation * * * [g]enerally * * * are to be condemned. * * * An ex parte reference to the facts should not go beyond quotation from the records and papers on file in the court; but even in extreme cases it is better to avoid any ex parte statement."

b. Sheppard v. Maxwell, 384 U.S. 333 (1966), made clear that excessive pretrial and trial publicity could constitute a denial of due process of law. Marilyn Sheppard, wife of prominent Dr. Samuel Sheppard, was bludgeoned to death in their home. Dr. Sheppard was accused of the crime, although he said there had been an intruder in the home. From shortly after the murder, repeated news stories criticized Dr. Sheppard's alleged failure to cooperate with the police and accused prosecutors of letting Sheppard "get away with murder." The stories continued through jury selection and the trial, and the jurors saw much of it. With only Justice Black dissenting, the Court put primary blame for the "carnival atmosphere" on the trial judge. It said "the trial court might well have proscribed extrajudicial statements by any lawyer, party, witness, or court official which divulged prejudicial matters." 384 U.S. at 361.

c. It was in the context of the *Sheppard* case that the ABA adopted DR 7–107 of the Model Code of Professional Responsibility. Take a look at it in the Standards Supplement. It permitted more pretrial publicity than Canon 20 had, but it was quite specific about what lawyers could and could not say. Was the greater liberality of DR 7–107 a move in the right direction? A start down the slippery slope of declining professional standards? Was DR 7–107 too restrictive, in light of the First Amendment?

d. The Seventh Circuit held the latter was true. In Chicago Council of Lawyers v. Bauer, 522 F.2d 242, 249 (7th Cir.1975), cert. denied sub nom. Cunningham v. Chicago Council of Lawyers, 427 U.S. 912 (1976), the court said:

> "We are of the view that the rubric used in the rules under consideration, that lawyers' comments about pending or imminent litigation must be proscribed 'if there is a reasonable likelihood that such dissemination will interfere with a fair trial or otherwise prejudice the due administration of justice' is overbroad and therefore does not meet constitutional standards. Instead, we think a narrower and more restrictive standard * * * should apply: Only those comments that pose a 'serious and imminent threat' of interference with the fair administration of justice can be constitutionally proscribed."[1]

---

1. The court also ruled that comments during the period between completion of trial and sentencing could "never be deemed a serious and imminent threat of interference with the fair administration of justice" and thus that the prohibition of comments "reasonably likely to affect the imposition of sentence" was invalid.

e.   Later, the Fourth Circuit, in Hirschkop v. Snead, 594 F.2d 356 (4th Cir.1979) (per curiam), went even further. It upheld the constitutionality of Virginia DR 7–107 as applied to *criminal jury* trials, but invalidated it as applied to all other litigation, such as bench trials, presentencing hearings, disciplinary proceedings before a judge, civil cases, and matters pending before administrative agencies.

2.   Is the current version of Model Rule 3.6 consistent with the First Amendment?

a.   Gentile v. Nevada State Bar, 501 U.S. 1030 (1991), was the first Supreme Court case in many years to test the rules on pretrial statements to the press. In *Gentile,* drug evidence had disappeared from a safe deposit box that undercover police officers had rented. The state charged Gentile's client with taking the drugs. Gentile held a press conference on the day of the arraignment at which he said that a police officer had likely taken them and that the police were using his client as a scapegoat. The jury later acquitted his client and then the Nevada State Bar sought to discipline Gentile for creating a "substantial likelihood of material prejudice" by influencing the potential jury pool against the state. The Nevada Supreme Court affirmed a private reprimand.

The U.S. Supreme Court reversed in two separate opinions authored by Chief Justice Rehnquist and Justice Kennedy. The Chief Justice persuaded a slim majority (Justices White, O'Connor, Scalia, and Souter) that lawyers' speech may be regulated by less than a "clear and present danger" standard, and that the "substantial likelihood of material prejudice" standard used by Nevada balanced relevant interests permissibly. However, Justice Kennedy persuaded an equally slim majority (Justices Marshall, Blackmun, Stevens, and O'Connor) that the specific Nevada rule was void for vagueness. The rule permitted a lawyer to announce the "general nature of the defense" but only to do so "without elaboration." That, said the Kennedy majority, was too vague to let Gentile know what he could and could not say. Instead of creating a safe harbor, Rule 3.6(c) created a "trap for the wary as well as the unwary." The ABA amended Rule 3.6 in response to *Gentile.*

b.   In United States v. Bingham, 769 F.Supp. 1039 (N.D.Ill.1991), a district judge ordered the U.S. attorney to consider prosecuting defense counsel who, on the eve of jury selection in a case involving street gangs, gave television interviews criticizing the judge, among other things, for planning to empanel an "anonymous jury," i.e., not reporting their names. The judge considered this statement to be a serious and imminent threat to the administration of justice and subject to discipline in spite of *Gentile.*

Do you agree with the judge's response? If the lawyer had objected to the anonymous jury in open court, could he then have repeated the objection to the media? See Model Rule 3.6(b)(2) ("state * * * information contained in a public record"). The *Bingham* opinion, at 769 F.Supp. at 1041, even quotes from a court rule that specifically says "the United States Attorney, or lawyer or law firm may quote from or refer without comment to public records of the court in the case." Do you agree that it is different to report something already said in court than to have the judge read your views for the first time in the newspaper?

c. In re Morrissey, 168 F.3d 134 (4th Cir.1999), involved criminal defense counsel Morrissey who used the media as part of his effort to help his client fight drug charges. For example, Morrissey obtained a list of witnesses who testified before the state grand jury and interviewed one on videotape recanting his grand jury testimony. Morrissey knew that person would be called as a government witness in the federal case, and he said he was releasing the tape to send a message to other witnesses. Later, he said the prosecution was vindictive and the charges would have been laughed out of court if he had filed them when he was a prosecutor. The district judge, in a bench trial, convicted the attorney for criminal contempt for violating the local version of Rule 3.6. The judge sentenced Morrissey to ninety days imprisonment and three years probation and also suspended him from practicing law in the Eastern District of Virginia for two years. The Fourth Circuit affirmed and rejected the First Amendment challenge to the rule, which required a "reasonable likelihood" of material prejudice to a fair trial or the administration of justice.

d. In Attorney Grievance Comm'n of Maryland v. Gansler, 835 A.2d 548 (Md.2003), the respondent was the state's attorney for one of Maryland's largest counties. He held press conferences about highly publicized cases; reported evidentiary details, prior criminal records, and alleged confessions; and offered plea deals. The Maryland Supreme Court agreed with Gansler that "information contained in a public record" includes all information made public from any source, including the media. Thus, publicly revealing a defendant's criminal record is permissible, even if prejudicial to the defendant, if the speaker can show that a private citizen could discover the record from public documents. Confessions, however, could not be so discovered, nor could information about plea discussions, so Gansler's reference to them was improper. The fact Gansler was a public official was important, because "Prosecutors are held to even higher standards of conduct than other attorneys due to their unique role as both advocate and minister of justice." In addition, "a prosecutor's opinion of guilt is much more likely to create prejudice, given that his or her words carry the authority of government and are especially persuasive in the public eye." 835 A.2d at 572. The court concluded that a formal reprimand, issued publicly, would adequately deter future violations of professional standards.

e. Maldonado v. Ford Company, 719 N.W.2d 809 (Mich.2006), upheld the dismissal of a sexual harassment case because of the plaintiff's lawyer's release of pretrial publicity. A Ford employee had previously been convicted of sexual harassment, and the conviction had later been expunged. The trial judge ruled the fact of the conviction could not be admitted in the current case, so plaintiff's counsel went to the media to disclose both the conviction and the judge's ruling. When later rulings similarly would have kept information from the jury that the lawyer wanted them to know, he went to the media "definitely over ten" times to be sure the jury pool would be informed. After several such incidents, the trial judge dismissed the case and the Michigan Supreme Court affirmed, two judges dissenting. "The trial court has a gate-keeping obligation," the court said, "when such misconduct occurs, to impose sanctions that will not only deter the misconduct but also serve as a deterrent to other litigants."

3.   Assuming that some restrictions on pretrial comment are constitutional, on whom should such restrictions be imposed?

a.   Were you struck by the fact that in most of the above cases it was defense counsel, not prosecutors, who were accused of prejudicial publicity? Do you suppose the incidence of excessive publicity is as one-sided as these numbers suggest?

A notable exception, of course, was the disciplinary proceeding brought against Durham, North Carolina, district attorney Mike Nifong in connection with his prosecution of members of the Duke lacrosse team.[2] One of the key issues was Nifong's going on television to announce on several occasions that Duke lacrosse players were guilty of raping an exotic dancer at a team party, a charge later found to be baseless.

Robert Shapiro, a well known criminal defense attorney, has argued that prosecutors have a significant advantage in the publicity battle.[3] The media reports details about the crime and the arrest. Police officers often calm the public with statements such as "We have found the person responsible for these crimes." Shapiro argues that if a defense attorney refuses to comment, that very fact sends a message to the potential jury pool that the defendant must be guilty. Thus, Shapiro believes that defense attorneys have a duty to monitor press accounts and respond appropriately.

b.   Is the public interest often served by news stories about lawsuits? Think about suits filed by public interest groups, for example? Are some lawsuits filed more for the publicity they will generate than for the actual result expected at trial? Should that practice be discouraged? Should Federal Rule 11, discussed earlier in Problem 23, be relevant?

c.   Do the Model Rules recognize an important public disclosure interest in cases involving alleged public corruption?

When Archibald Cox, the first Watergate special prosecutor, moved to prevent the Senate Watergate Committee from granting testimonial immunity from prosecution to John Dean and Jeb Stuart Magruder on the grounds that their testimony in public would create prejudicial pretrial publicity, Judge Sirica denied the motion and stated, inter alia:

> "It is apparent as well that a committee's legislative purpose may legitimately include the publication of information."[4]

2. See Robert P. Mosteller, The Duke Lacrosse Case, Innocence and False Identifications: A Fundamental Failure to "Do Justice," 76 Fordham L. Rev. 1337 (2007).

3. See Robert L. Shapiro, Using the Media to Your Advantage, Champion Magazine, Jan.–Feb. 1993, at 6 (Journal of the National Association of Criminal Defense Lawyers).

4. In re Application of United States Senate Select Comm. on Presidential Campaign Activities, 361 F.Supp. 1270, 1281–82 (D.D.C.1973).

It was the official position of the Senate Watergate Committee that:

"the public had a right to know. * * * The full import of the hearings could only be achieved by observing the witnesses and hearing their testimony. * * * The committee believes that its position has proven correct and its public hearings awakened the public to the perils posed by the Watergate affair to the integrity of the electoral process and our democratic form of government.

"Perhaps proof of the impact of the committee's hearings is found in the unprecedented public response to the firing of Special Prosecutor Cox on October 20, 1973. On that weekend alone, a half million telegrams came to the Congress. Hundreds of thousands of telegrams flowed in during the following days. The overwhelming sentiment of these telegrams was in opposition to the President's action. It is doubtful that public sentiment would have been so aroused by the President's action had the public not been sensitized to the issues involved through the committee's hearings."[5]

d. In re Sealed Case No. 99–3091 (Office of Independent Counsel Contempt Proceeding), 192 F.3d 995 (D.C.Cir.1999) (per curiam), involved alleged leaks of grand jury information from Independent Counsel Kenneth Starr's office. In an opinion not as widely publicized as the original charge, the D.C. Circuit expressly found that the OIC had engaged in no illegal leaking, and there was no prima facie violation of the grand jury secrecy rule, Rule 6(e), Federal Rules of Criminal Procedure. The Justice Department supported the Office of Independent Counsel on this matter and argued that Rule 6(e) was not violated if a prosecutor made a statement of opinion about someone's potential liability, even if some evidence supporting that conclusion was also presented to a grand jury. "[P]rosecutors often have a legitimate interest in revealing aspects of their investigations 'to inform the public that the investigation is underway, to describe the general scope of the investigation, to obtain assistance in the apprehension of a suspect, to warn the public of any dangers, or otherwise aid in the investigation.' "[6]

4. Did "Clean Gene" White violate Rule 3.6? If so, when?

a. Did White violate Rule 3.6 when he said that there are "a lot of skeletons under the beds of some state legislators"? When he held press

---

5. The Final Report of the Select Comm. on Presidential Campaign Activities, United States Senate, Report No. 93–981, 93d Cong., 2d Sess. (June, 1974) at xxxi–xxxii.

That a committee claims a need for publicity does not mean that types of publicity may not be distinguished. The Select Committee ruled for its public sessions:

"The committee followed a practice not typical of certain congressional hearings. It refrained from calling a witness in

public session that it knew would refuse to testify on the assertion of the Fifth Amendment privilege against self-incrimination. * * * This policy was instituted * * * on the belief that no legislative purpose would be served by public exhibition of witnesses who claimed the privilege." Id. at xxxi.

6. The case is discussed in Ronald D. Rotunda, Independent Counsel and the Charges of Leaking: A Brief Case Study, 68 Fordham L. Rev. 869 (1999).

conferences to report on indictments just issued? When he alluded to possible indictments? Should White not give any press conferences but let his press secretary perform that function? Look at Model Rule 3.6(d). Would it help if his press secretary were not a lawyer? See Model Rule 3.8(f).

b.   Would White violate Rule 3.6 if he truthfully stated, "We have just filed a motion to force Judge Smith to recuse himself, because, as our motion states, 'the judge's actions in this case show that he is soft on public corruption' "? Why or why not? Cf. Model Rule 8.2(a).

c.   Would White violate Rule 3.6 if he truthfully said, "We have just indicted Kyle Jones, who often calls himself 'Kyle the Killer.' He was last seen heading south on Route 66. If you see him, call police, but do not try to apprehend, for he is considered armed and dangerous"? Should prosecutors have the latitude to make such statements?

d.   Was Gene White acting properly in denouncing "the rumor mill"? If a commentator claims that a trial court once ruled in an unpublished opinion that one of White's assistants is "an overzealous prosecutor," may White respond truthfully, "The commentator is simply repeating a false charge that one of the suspects has made several times. The suspect is lying; the commentator should check his facts before he opens his mouth." Does Model Rule 3.6(c) protect such responses from prosecutors or only the responses of defense counsel?

5.   Should the fact that Rule 3.6 allows certain kinds of trial publicity preclude other remedies against lawyers if they say that which Rule 3.6 allows?

a.   In Buckley v. Fitzsimmons, 509 U.S. 259 (1993), plaintiff filed a damage suit against a prosecutor for allegedly fabricating evidence of defendant's guilt and for announcing the defendant's arrest at a press conference that may have prejudiced the later trial. The defendant spent about three years in jail and went through one mistrial before a third party confessed to the crime and the defendant was released. The Seventh Circuit held the conduct of the prosecutor subject to an absolute privilege because it was all part of normal preparation of a case. The Supreme Court reversed and instead applied a "functional test" looking to the function being performed rather than the role of the actor. "Comments to the media have no functional tie to the judicial process," the Court said. In some cases, such comments may serve an important public function, but that is not enough to cloak them in the absolute immunity that applies to statements made in the course of a trial. Do you agree?

b.   In Seidl v. Greentree Mortgage Co., 30 F.Supp.2d 1292 (D.Colo. 1998), plaintiff's counsel in a suit charging Internet "spamming" (i.e., bulk email advertising) issued a press release about the case and published it on her web page. She argued that an attorney's absolute privilege against defamation liability for statements connected with the case protected her against the defendant's claim of libel. The court disagreed. It is one thing to say a lawyer cannot be sued for libel for what is in a complaint, but in this case the recipients of the press release had nothing to do with the case, so the release did not bear "some relation to the proceeding" and was not privileged.

c.   Kennedy v. Zimmermann, 601 N.W.2d 61 (Iowa 1999), shows that compliance with ethical standards may protect the lawyer from professional discipline, but not from liability under other law. Lawyer Kennedy represented Richmond, who was an inmate, in a child custody matter. Kennedy was dating a different inmate at the same penitentiary. Richmond complained to Kennedy about her representation of him, and shortly thereafter, Kennedy's boyfriend assaulted Richmond. Richmond then hired Zimmermann to sue Kennedy, claiming she told her boyfriend what Richmond had said to her in confidence. The case attracted some media attention, and a reporter called Zimmermann about it. Zimmermann reported the allegations already published in the complaint, saying that Richardson claimed that "Kennedy's alleged actions were a 'breach of her ethical duties and negligent.' "

Kennedy then sued Zimmermann for defamation. Zimmermann claimed that what a lawyer says in the course of a judicial proceeding is absolutely privileged against a defamation claim. The court disagreed. The absolute privilege only applies to communications made in a judicial proceeding; it does not apply to interviews with reporters. The fact that the state's counterpart to Model Rule 3.6(b)(2) did not prohibit the statement did not change the defamation law.[7]

6.   Suppose White prosecutes the state legislator with a marijuana cigarette in his car. If publicity will help the legislator beat the charge, may the legislator's lawyer advise him of that? Does it make any difference whether the state legislator is a lawyer?

a.   Does Rule 3.6(c) provide defense counsel with a necessary defense against statements or leaks from prosecutors and police officers? Why is Model Rule 3.8(f) not sufficient protection? Do Model Rules 3.6(c) and 3.8(f) threaten to turn pretrial proceedings into successive rounds of public statements by defense counsel and motions for sanctions against prosecutors? Or, does this Rule merely reflect the axiom that one should fight fire with fire?

b.   May the legislator himself call a press conference to give his side of the story? Cf. Rule 8.4(a). If the legislator does give a press conference, may his lawyer answer questions that reporters pose and that relate to the upcoming trial?

c.   In the background of all of these cases is the reluctance of state and federal courts to allow discovery of print and broadcast media. United States v. Cutler, 6 F.3d 67 (2d Cir.1993), involved John Gotti's lawyer,

7. See also Bochetto v. Gibson, 860 A.2d 67 (Pa.2004) (lawyer transmittal of complaint to freelance reporter was extrajudicial act that did not provide absolute immunity in a defamation action). For more on a lawyer's privilege against defamation for statements made in litigation, see Restatement Third, The Law Governing Lawyers § 57, Comment c.

Bruce Cutler, who was quoted in several news stories commenting on the lack of merit of the government's case, all in apparent violation of a gag order imposed by the trial judge. When charged with a violation of the order, Cutler sought the notes of all the reporters who had quoted him, including their notes of statements made by others than Cutler. The court held that Cutler was entitled to notes relating to his own statements, including portions of televised interviews that were not used, but that he was not entitled to notes of the reporters' conversations with government officials or others. Later, United States v. Cutler, 58 F.3d 825 (2d Cir.1995), affirmed the lower court, holding that Cutler willfully violated the trial court's valid gag order and that his statements were reasonably likely to prejudice prospective jurors in the case. The court upheld Cutler's three-year suspension from practice in the Eastern District of New York.[8]

d. Also lurking in all of these cases are state and federal constitutional restrictions on the breadth of gag orders. Twohig v. Blackmer, 918 P.2d 332 (N.M.1996), for example, vacated a gag order at the request of defense counsel for a Native American charged with vehicular homicide in the deaths of an Anglo mother and her three daughters. The case got unprecedented media attention, most of it favorable to the prosecution. Two trials ended in hung juries, but the prosecutor promised to try again. Defense counsel appeared on radio talk shows and wrote a newspaper article saying enough was enough. At that point the trial judge imposed the gag order, but the state supreme court vacated the order because it did not lay out a factual foundation for finding "substantial likelihood of prejudice or clear and present danger to fair and impartial trial." It contained no analysis of facts supporting the trial court's conclusion that a gag order was necessary, and it did not indicate that the court considered alternatives less restrictive of free speech than an outright ban on all communication with the media.

B. Standards governing a prosecutor's decision whether and what to charge

1. May a prosecutor file a charge that he or she does not believe can be proved beyond a reasonable doubt? Suppose overcharging would help encourage the defendant to enter a plea to an offense the defendant clearly committed?

a. Look at Model Rule 3.8(a). Is a probable cause standard too restrictive on prosecutors? Not restrictive enough? Compare this requirement to Model Rule 3.1's obligation placed upon lawyers who file civil cases. Does such a standard belong in a code of professional standards rather than simply in a code of criminal procedure? If the grand jury is willing to indict, has the prosecutor necessarily complied with Rule 3.8(a)?

---

8. Matter of Cutler, 650 N.Y.S.2d 85 (N.Y.App.Div.1996), was another round in the Cutler saga in which the state court suspended his New York license for six months for committing the federal criminal offense (which was reduced by the three months he was under federal house arrest and thus unable to practice). Effective June 12, 1997, the state court, without opinion, reinstated Mr. Cutler as a lawyer. Application of Cutler, 658 N.Y.S.2d 835 (N.Y.App.Div. 1997).

b.   In United States v. Goodwin, 457 U.S. 368 (1982), the government originally filed several misdemeanor charges against the defendant, but after he asked for a jury trial, the government obtained an indictment that included a felony count. The defendant alleged prosecutorial vindictiveness and retaliatory intent that he argued should void the conviction. The Supreme Court disagreed. "Just as a prosecutor may forego legitimate charges * * *, a prosecutor may file additional charges if an initial expectation that a defendant would plead guilty to lesser charges proves unfounded." Thus, a presumption of vindictiveness was inappropriate and it found no actual vindictiveness in the circumstances of the case. See also, Bordenkircher v. Hayes, 434 U.S. 357 (1978) (prosecutor, without violating due process, may threaten defendant with more severe charges to which he is plainly subject, if defendant does not plead guilty to lesser charges).

2.   Do any of the Model Rules require the prosecutor to give exculpatory information to the grand jury when seeking an indictment?

a.   In United States v. Williams, 504 U.S. 36 (1992), the government had charged the defendant with giving willfully false financial statements to a bank in order to get a large loan. At the time the prosecutor obtained the indictment, he allegedly had exculpatory information in his possession that he did not reveal to the grand jury. The Supreme Court rejected a claim that therefore it should dismiss the indictment. A grand jury sits to determine whether there is enough evidence to charge, Justice Scalia wrote for the Court; it does not sit to weigh conflicting evidence. Justices Stevens, Blackmun, O'Connor, and Thomas dissented.

b.   Even assuming that the Constitution does not require disclosure at the pre-indictment stage, what should the prosecutor's ethical duty be? If the prosecutor has a lot of exculpatory evidence, can the prosecutor still have probable cause to charge within the meaning of Model Rule 3.8(a)? Can the prosecutor properly ignore portions of the evidence in his or her possession in making that determination?

c.   Is it wise for the prosecutor to withhold exculpatory information from the grand jury? If the grand jury believes that the information significantly undercuts the prosecution's case, does it make more sense for the prosecutor to know that before the trial? Will Model Rule 3.8(d) necessarily mandate its eventual disclosure to the defense?

3.   What should the state's attorney's obligation be when she believes the police are lying?

a.   In People v. Berrios, 270 N.E.2d 709 (N.Y.1971), the New York County district attorney joined the defense in an effort to have the New York Court of Appeals shift the burden of proof to the state when the police alleged—in reply to a motion to suppress contraband drugs—that the defendant had abandoned the drugs. The district attorney had become very concerned that the police seemed to have a consistent story that the drugs had been abandoned. The New York court rejected the joint request, quoting then-Judge Warren Burger in Bush v. United States, 375 F.2d 602,

604 (D.C.Cir.1967): "[I]t would be a dismal reflection on society to say that when the guardians of its security are called to testify in court under oath, their testimony must be viewed with suspicion."

Do you agree that the prosecutor should rely on Judge Burger's analysis and put the problem out of mind?

b. Zahrey v. Coffey, 221 F.3d 342 (2d Cir.2000), was a civil case charging an assistant U.S. attorney with coercing or bribing witnesses into offering false evidence against the plaintiff, a police officer. The prosecutor allegedly agreed to drop serious charges, for example, if a defendant would testify against the officer. The trial judge dismissed the case, citing a prosecutor's immunity for official acts. The Second Circuit held that a prosecutor has only qualified immunity for acts in an investigative role. The plaintiff has a constitutional right "not to be deprived of liberty as a result of the fabrication of evidence by a government officer acting in an investigative capacity," the court said, and reinstated the case.

c. Idaho State Bar v. Warrick, 44 P.3d 1141 (Idaho 2002), explored the duty of a prosecutor to correct erroneous testimony of a government witness. Warrick served as the lead prosecutor in a drug trial. An assistant prosecutor in Warrick's office negotiated a plea bargain with one of the defendant's associates under which the individual received a substantially reduced sentence in exchange for his testimony in the trial. Warrick knew the agreement had been struck, although not the leniency of the sentence recommendation. During both direct and cross examination, the witness denied having a plea arrangement with the state and Warrick did not correct the witness. Later that day, the same judge presided over the witness's arraignment, and quickly realized that the witness had testified falsely earlier. Warrick met with the witness that evening and stated that he intended to recall the witness the next day to cure any defects in the testimony. However, the Professional Conduct Board, which initiated discipline, "found that he knew [the witness'] testimony was false at the time it was presented * * *." Warrick, the court said, "knew it was false when the testimony was presented, and at that time he did not take any action to correct the testimony. Waiting until after the district judge and defense counsel learned the testimony was false was not reasonable," citing Rule 3.3(a)(3). The Professional Conduct Board imposed a 30–day suspension for this and another offense, and the state supreme court upheld the suspension.

d. In re Peasley, 90 P.3d 764 (Ariz.2004), involved a prosecutor who deliberately presented false testimony from the lead investigator in two capital murder cases. To determine the appropriate sanction, the court looked to the ABA Standards for Imposing Lawyer Sanctions (1992). Under the Standards, the court evaluated four factors: "(1) the duty violated; (2) the lawyer's mental state; (3) the actual or potential injury caused by the misconduct; and (4) the existence of aggravating or mitigating factors." The presentation of false testimony "could not have been more harmful to the justice system," especially because the perjury occurred in capital cases. Because of the severity of the aggravating circumstances—Peasley's multiple offenses and dishonest motive (obtaining a conviction at any cost)—the court found that disbarment was the only appropriate sanction.

4. May a prosecutor let a criminal defendant go free in exchange for testimony against someone the prosecutor believes poses a greater danger to society? Should anyone have a basis to complain about such conduct?

a. United States v. Singleton, 165 F.3d 1297 (10th Cir.1999) (en banc), cert. denied, 527 U.S. 1024 (1999), reversed an earlier panel decision that garnered a great deal of national publicity when it prohibited the government in a criminal case from offering immunity and leniency to a witness in exchange for his or her testimony. The three-judge panel had ruled that this exchange constituted payment for testimony, i.e., bribery. The en banc Tenth Circuit rejected that result because the antibribery statute refers to an individual offering the bribe. By contrast, an assistant United States attorney who offers a plea bargain is acting as the United States, not as an individual. Moreover, the court, not the prosecutor, actually grants the immunity. The statute cannot be meant to restrict the sovereign's prosecutorial powers and to prohibit that which other federal statutes authorize, the court said. Further, to so hold would upset generations of prosecutorial practice. Congress acts against a background of such practice; the statute could not have the meaning the panel found. Judges Kelly, Seymour, and Ebel dissented, saying the statute is simple and means what it says. United States v. Lowery, 166 F.3d 1119 (11th Cir.1999), disagreed with the panel decision in *Singleton* and agreed with the en banc majority.

b. Asking the court to grant immunity to a witness in exchange for testimony is not done in the dark of night. It occurs in court and requires the judge's approval. On the other hand, in In re Disciplinary Proceedings Against Charles O. Bonet, 29 P.3d 1242 (Wash.2001), the agreement was not so open. The respondent had prosecuted a defendant on drug-related charges. One of the defendant's co-conspirators had been named to testify on his behalf at trial, though he had made conflicting statements as to whether or not he actually planned to testify. The respondent allegedly told the potential witness that he would dismiss the criminal charges against him if he agreed to assert the Fifth Amendment and refrain from testifying for the defense. When the court asked whether the respondent had made any such agreement, the respondent denied it, but the court found that the respondent had done so, and in so doing had offered an improper inducement to persuade a witness not to testify. The court found a violation of Rules 3.4(b) and 8.4(d): "a public or private attorney may not offer an inducement to a witness in order to influence that person to not testify at a trial * * * regardless of whether the offer or inducement influenced the witness's decision to testify or not testify." The witness' prior subjective intent not to testify was irrelevant because the inducement itself was improper.[9]

---

9. Cf. North Carolina State Bar v. Graves, 274 S.E.2d 396 (N.C.Ct.App.1981), disciplining a lawyer who attempted to influence a witness (not his client) to not testify

c. May the prosecutor accept a plea to a reduced charge when she believes the defendant is guilty of a more serious charge, but that the jury might acquit on that charge, thus hurting the prosecutor's batting average?[10]

May a prosecutor negotiate the defendant's agreement to perform charitable work for a certain time in exchange for dropping all charges if the negotiated disposition conforms to rough justice?[11]

d. If an assistant prosecutor personally believes that the defendant is innocent and does not want to prosecute the case, may the chief prosecutor (who believes the defendant is guilty) order her to prosecute anyway? How does Model Rule 5.2 affect your answer?

C. LIMITS ON PROSECUTORS INVESTIGATING DEFENSE ATTORNEYS

1. Should a prosecutor be permitted to subpoena office records of lawyers known to do criminal defense work? May prosecutors require defense counsel to appear before a grand jury? What if there is a reasonable concern that the defense lawyer may also be involved in the criminal conduct?

a. On October 1, 1985, the Massachusetts Supreme Judicial Court adopted a new disciplinary rule, Prosecution Function 15, which stated:

> "It is unprofessional conduct for a prosecutor to subpoena an attorney to a grand jury without prior judicial approval in circumstances where the prosecutor seeks to compel the attorney-witness to provide evidence concerning a person who is represented by the attorney-witness."

United States v. Klubock, 639 F.Supp. 117 (D.Mass.1986), affirmed by an equally divided court 832 F.2d 664 (1st Cir.1987) (en banc), rejected a supremacy clause challenge to this Massachusetts rule as applied to federal prosecutors. Whitehouse v. U.S. District Court for Dist. of Rhode Island, 53 F.3d 1349 (1st Cir.1995), also upheld a rule requiring federal prosecutors to get advance judicial approval before issuing a subpoena to a lawyer. Model Rule 3.8(e) is the ABA version of the Massachusetts rule.

b. Is Rule 3.8(e) really a rule of procedure dressed up to look like an ethics rule? Critics of such rules often argue that the ABA and organized

---

or to plead the Fifth Amendment. The witness could plead the Fifth, but it is still a criminal act for someone "with corrupt motive to induce a witness to exercise that privilege."

10. For a discussion of the prosecutor and selective prosecution, prejudgment of credibility, and conflict of interest in the light of the ABA Standards Relating to the Prosecution Function, see H. Richard Uviller, The Virtuous Prosecutor in Quest of an Ethical Standard: Guidance from the ABA, 71 Michigan L. Rev. 1145 (1973). For a different view,

see Monroe H. Freedman, The Professional Responsibility of the Prosecuting Attorney, 55 Georgetown L.J. 1030 (1967).

11. Iowa Supreme Court Disciplinary Board v. Barry, 762 N.W.2d 129 (Iowa 2009), suspended a prosecutor for various ethical lapses, including a practice of reducing criminal charges or excusing public service elements of sentences if the defendants would contribute to the sheriff's "drug fund." The court found that this practice gave the "appearance to the public that justice was for sale," and was prejudicial to the administration of justice.

bars of defense lawyers have little success in getting courts to adopt particular evidence rules so they dress them up as rules governing lawyers. But see, Stern v. Supreme Judicial Court, 184 F.R.D. 10 (D.Mass.1999), holding that the Massachusetts federal court had the power to adopt what is now Rule 3.8(e).

2. Should lawyers have any more right than nonlawyers to resist a subpoena to produce records or appear for questioning?[12]

a. Two lawyers who specialize in the defense of white collar criminal cases have argued that government subpoenas of attorneys are a serious interference with the attorney-client relationship and should not be issued without prior judicial approval:

> "Regardless of the type of information sought, * * * an attorney-subpoena has an obvious, unavoidable, and substantial impact on the attorney-client relationship. The fragile relationship of trust, built upon the understanding that what is said to the attorney is confidential and that the attorney's sole function is to serve as a zealous advocate for the client within the bounds of the law, is seriously strained whenever the government even attempts to have the attorney act as a witness against his client. As a practical matter, most clients simply do not understand the fine distinctions the courts have drawn between what is a privileged communication and what is not. [A client may] hold back critical information for fear that a future subpoena might be enforced. Nor can the client be absolutely sure that the attorney has actually invoked the privilege in response to all of the substantive questions asked in the secrecy of the grand jury room. The attorney, too, may decide to skimp on eliciting certain information from the client for fear he may have to divulge it in the future. * * * [O]nce the subpoena is served on the attorney, the attorney's own philosophical, emotional and financial concerns may color his professional judgment. Any advice he gives in this situation, whether it be to fight, to comply, or to compromise, may reasonably be seen by the client, or by others, as having been affected by those concerns. The resulting peril to the attorney-client relationship, and to the adversary system, is apparent. * * *

> "Finally, and perhaps most importantly, by using the subpoena the prosecutor can effectively exercise a veto power over the defendant's choice of counsel. Disciplinary Rule 5–102(B) of the Code of Professional Responsibility requires that an attorney withdraw from a case if 'it is apparent that [the attorney's] testimony is or may be prejudicial to his client.' The unrestrained power to

---

12. Lawyers should understand that, contrary to the wishful thinking of some, neither the work product doctrine, the attorney-client privilege, nor the Constitution absolutely prohibits a police search of a lawyer's office if there is probable cause to believe that the lawyer may be aiding in commission of a crime. See, e.g., Law Offices of Bernard D. Morley, P. C. v. MacFarlane, 647 P.2d 1215 (Colo.1982); Lackland H. Bloom, Jr., The Law Office Search: An Emerging Problem and Some Suggested Solutions, 69 Georgetown L.J. 1 (1980).

issue a grand jury or trial subpoena, therefore, may substantially skew the adversary system—defendant's counsel serves at the pleasure of the prosecution. * * * "

David S. Rudolph & Thomas K. Maher, The Attorney Subpoena: You Are Hereby Commanded to Betray Your Client, 1 Crim. Justice 15 (Spring 1986).

b. In re Grand Jury Subpoena Served Upon Doe, 781 F.2d 238 (2d Cir.1986) (en banc), cert. denied sub nom. Roe v. United States, 475 U.S. 1108 (1986), involved a defendant who asserted that if the government required his attorney to testify before the grand jury, the attorney would be disqualified from representing him in the later criminal case. The government was investigating the "Colombo organized crime family and a faction of that enterprise known as the 'Anthony Colombo crew.' " The grand jury sought "to determine whether Colombo paid for, or otherwise arranged for, the legal representation of members of his crew. Evidence of such benefactor payments made to [Attorney] Slotnick might establish Colombo as the head of 'an enterprise' as that term is defined in the Racketeer Influenced and Corrupt Organizations Act (RICO)," 18 U.S.C.A. § 1961(4). The government had not attempted to show a compelling or reasonable "need" for the lawyer's information. In fact, it expressly asserted that there was no requirement that it demonstrate need, i.e., that it could not obtain the information from alternative sources.

The en banc court agreed and held that in the "preindictment context" a requirement of such a showing of need "would unjustifiably impede the grand jury process." The possibility that the lawyer's testimony would disqualify him from later representing the defendant under the lawyer/witness rule was not sufficient to change the result. The majority said: "Before disqualification can ever be contemplated, the attorney's testimony must incriminate his client; the grand jury must indict; the government must go forward with the prosecution of the indictment; and ultimately, the attorney must be advised that he will be called as a trial witness against his client." After all, the attorney's grand jury testimony "may be exculpatory or neutral," or be otherwise inadmissible, or come within one of the exceptions to DR 5–102(B) or Model Rule 3.7. "The pretrial stage, not the grand jury stage, is the appropriate time to balance Colombo's interest in his right to counsel against the public interest in obtaining benefactor payment information, should the issue of disqualification arise."

c. In 1990, the ABA amended Rule 3.8(e) to require prosecutors to obtain prior judicial approval before subpoenaing defense counsel. In 1995, the ABA again amended Rule 3.8(e) so that it no longer requires prior judicial approval of subpoenas directed to lawyers but does place some roadblocks in a prosecutor's path. Is the current version of the rule likely to reduce the concerns raised by defendants and defense counsel?[13]

13. Cf. United States v. Mittelman, 999 F.2d 440 (9th Cir.1993), that involved a motion to suppress evidence seized in the search of a lawyer's office. The affidavit for the search warrant said the office was believed to contain evidence of conspiracy to commit

3. How should defense counsel respond to such a subpoena?

a. ABA Formal Opinion 94–385 (July 5, 1994) advised lawyers to resist such subpoenas, if issued. If the client whose files are subpoenaed by a government agency does not consent to disclosure, the lawyer must seek to limit the subpoena and resist disclosure "on any legitimate available grounds." However, such grounds are often unavailable.

b. In re Grand Jury Proceedings, 13 F.3d 1293 (9th Cir.1994), was a proceeding to force a lawyer to testify before a grand jury about what fees he had been paid by a particular client, the amount of any trust funds held by the lawyer for that client, and what the lawyer knew about the client's lifestyle, spending habits, and sources of income. When the lawyer refused to talk, the court upheld the finding of contempt. The lawyer's Fifth Amendment rights were not at issue, it said, the facts did not relate to privileged information, and any Sixth Amendment challenge was premature.

c. In re Subpoena to Testify Before Grand Jury (Alexiou v. U.S.), 39 F.3d 973 (9th Cir.1994), cert. denied, 514 U.S. 1097 (1995), held that a lawyer must tell the court which client paid him with a counterfeit bill. The government had not accused the client of counterfeiting and the client may have received the bill from someone else. The court held that the name was not privileged and it required disclosure.

d. Conn v. Gabbert, 526 U.S. 286 (1999), considered a challenge to a prosecutor's execution of a search warrant on a defense lawyer who represented Traci Baker, a former girlfriend of Lyle Menendez, one of two brothers who were murder defendants. The prosecutors learned that Menendez may have written Baker a letter asking her to testify falsely at the brothers' first trial. The grand jury subpoenaed Baker and any letters that Menendez had sent her. She told investigators earlier that she had given them to her lawyer (Gabbert), so when she and her lawyer arrived for the grand jury appearance, the prosecutors executed a search warrant on Gabbert as well. It turned up two pages of a three-page letter from Menendez to Baker. Gabbert sued the prosecutors under 42 U.S.C.A. § 1983 (creating a private right of action for violation of constitutional rights). The Ninth Circuit held that the prosecutors had no qualified immunity because it is "common sense" that the search warrant violated Gabbert's constitutional rights. Gabbert v. Conn, 131 F.3d 793 (9th Cir. 1997). The Supreme Court unanimously reversed. The lawyer's brief interruption as a result of legal process did not violate his liberty interest, nor was his client prejudiced by having her lawyer respond to the subpoena rather than assisting her to answer grand jury questions because a grand jury witness has no constitutional right to have counsel present during the grand jury proceeding.

---

bankruptcy fraud. The lawyer was subsequently charged with that crime along with the client. The court found the search had exceeded the terms of the warrant, but said only evidence seized in "flagrant disregard" of those terms would be suppressed.

e. In People v. Superior Court (Laff), 23 P.3d 563 (Cal.2001), prosecutors suspected two attorneys of possible automobile insurance fraud and, armed with a search warrant, seized documents from their homes and law offices even though the grand jury had not yet returned an indictment against the attorneys. The attorneys claimed that they had a right to a hearing to determine whether any of the documents were privileged. The court agreed that a lawyer who is a suspect—like any other lawyer—has a duty to protect confidential files. The trial court was ordered to examine the seized documents, rule upon the claims of privilege, and prohibit disclosure of documents that it found to be privileged.

4. How should a lawyer respond if the government serves notice that his or her retainer may be subject to forfeiture because the money was generated by the client's illegal activities (e.g., drug dealing)?

a. Significant issues for criminal defense lawyers arise from issues relating to their fees. With the enactment of the Comprehensive Forfeiture Act of 1984, amending the Continuing Criminal Enterprise Statute (CCE), 21 U.S.C.A. §§ 848–853, and the Racketeer Influenced and Corrupt Organization Act (RICO), 18 U.S.C.A. §§ 1961–1968, title to income or property derived directly or indirectly from various criminal activities is subject to government forfeiture at the time the defendant committed the illegal acts. This "relation back" doctrine lets the government argue that even property that is now in the hands of a third party can be seized by the government.

b. Some commentators argue that applying RICO and CCE forfeiture provisions to moneys paid to a defendant's retained counsel violate constitutional and ethical commands. Public defenders are "overwhelmed" and often have neither the staff nor experience necessary to handle a complex RICO or drug case. The forfeiture potential, it has also been argued, creates a prohibited contingency fee—see Model Rule 1.5(d)(2)—in that the lawyer only gets paid if the client avoids conviction of an offense subject to the forfeiture rule, but the "compelling objection" is that to "hold that a defendant may be deprived of the assets necessary to defend himself against criminal charges before those charges are proved is obnoxious to basic notions of due process as well as to the presumption of innocence."[14]

c. Others have supported the forfeiture statutes. The purpose of forfeiture is "to separate convicted criminals from the economic power bases essential to continuation of their unlawful activities." The defendant who is indigent has only a right to appointed counsel, not to retained counsel of his choice; defendants whose assets are subject to forfeiture are no worse off. "An attorney's decision not to represent a defendant whose assets are threatened with forfeiture seems constitutionally indistinguishable from his decision not to represent a defendant whose assets have been seized as contraband or subjected to an IRS levy, or a defendant who has no

14. William W. Taylor & Richard G. Strafer, Attorney Fee Forfeiture: Can It Be Justified?, 1 Crim. Justice 9, 43 (Spring 1986).

assets at all." The lawyer has no ethical duty "to preserve forfeitable assets as a fee," though he does have a duty to "serve his client loyally."[15]

Another commentator noted: "[S]uppose a defendant is accused of stealing a car and pays a lawyer to defend against that charge by giving the car to the lawyer. Few would argue that the lawyer has a worthy claim to the car if the defendant is convicted and the jury finds that the car the lawyer received is the one that was stolen. Even fewer would champion the lawyer's right to keep the car if the lawyer had reason to know it was stolen. Suggest, however, that a lawyer who receives money generated by drug dealing or racketeering, is not entitled to keep that money for defending the drug dealer or racketeer, and an acrimonious debate ensues." Lawyers claim that they "must be immune from the hazards that others face when transacting business with drug dealers and racketeers."[16]

d.   Lower courts had split on this issue. Most had interpreted the statutes to exempt attorneys' fees, assuming that the payment was not a fraud or sham designed to protect illegal activities of the client. The Supreme Court resolved the issue in United States v. Monsanto, 491 U.S. 600 (1989). The Second Circuit had said that a pretrial order may not freeze the defendant's assets intended to be paid as attorneys' fees, but by a 5 to 4 vote, the Supreme Court reversed. Writing for the majority, Justice White found first that the statutory language was "clear and unambiguous." All property of a defendant was subject to forfeiture; the statute did not say "crime does not pay, except for attorney's fees."

e.   Caplin & Drysdale v. United States, 491 U.S. 617 (1989), then considered whether forfeiture of the defendant's assets under such a statute was constitutional. The same majority (Justices White, Rehnquist, O'Connor, Scalia, and Kennedy) held that it was. The Sixth Amendment does not give "impecunious defendants" the right to "choose their own counsel;" it only gives them the right to be "adequately represented by attorneys appointed by the courts." Further, the government has a valid interest in getting the forfeited assets back to their rightful owners or having them go into a fund for law enforcement use. Any Fifth Amendment due process concern must await an instance of actual deprivation, e.g., a plea to a nonforfeiture offense induced by a lawyer interested only in preserving his fee.

Justice Blackmun, for himself and Justices Brennan, Marshall and Stevens, found no express statutory language requiring forfeiture of attorneys' fees and urged a reading that would permit district courts latitude not to order it. On the constitutional issues, the dissenters asserted, "When the Government insists upon the right to choose the defendant's counsel

---

15. Kathleen F. Brickey, Forfeiture of Attorneys' Fees: The Impact of RICO and CCE Forfeitures on the Right to Counsel, 72 Virginia L. Rev. 493 (1986). In addition, Professor Brickey notes that the Justice Department's internal guidelines require the government to describe with particularity the specific assets subject to forfeiture before

they are transferred. Id. at 537–38. See U.S. Atty. Manual, § 9–111.530, reprinted in 38 Criminal L.Rep. 3001, 3006 (Oct. 2, 1985).

16. William J. Landers, Attorney Fee Forfeiture: Can It Be Justified? Yes, 1 Crim. Justice 8, 10 (Spring 1986).

for him * * * counsel is too readily perceived as the Government's agent rather than his own." 491 U.S. at 645. The effectiveness of our "equal and adversarial" system is thus at risk because the power to seek disclosure gives the prosecutor a powerful club. This will, the dissenters predict, "decimate the private criminal-defense bar." They called on Congress to rewrite the statute and reverse the Court's construction of it. Congress has not done so.

f.   United States v. Velez, 586 F.3d 875 (11th Cir. 2009), dealt with the issue of whether defendants could be prosecuted for money laundering when the funds were used to secure legal representation. One of the defendants, a prominent Miami lawyer, was retained by the defense team of an accused Colombian drug lord to review and ascertain the source of funds that were to be used to pay for the drug lord's criminal defense in the United States. The lawyer retained two other persons, a Colombian attorney and an accountant, to assist him in the work. The three, who were the defendants in this case, concluded that the proceeds were not criminally derived, and they transferred the money, approximately $5.3 million, to the drug lord's defense team. The federal government then charged the defendants with money laundering under 18 U.S.C. §§ 1956(h) and 1957, alleging that documents had been falsified to conceal the criminal source of the funds. The defendants moved to dismiss the money laundering charge, arguing that they fell under a statutory exemption covering "any transaction necessary to preserve a person's right to representation as guaranteed by the sixth amendment to the Constitution." (quoting 18 U.S.C. § 1957(f)(1)). The district court granted the motion to dismiss and the government appealed. The Eleventh Circuit affirmed dismissal of the charges. The court found that the plain meaning of the statute was to exempt from prosecution transactions that involved criminally derived proceeds when the purpose of the transactions was to secure representation for a criminal defendant.

5.   The Internal Revenue Code, 26 U.S.C.A. § 6050I, requires lawyers to report the source of cash payments in excess of $10,000 even when the payments are made by clients. Should that information be held to be privileged?

a.   One purpose of this law, of course, is to see that taxes are paid on the money. Another broader purpose may be to find out who is trying to conceal the fact they have hired lawyers. Cf. Baird v. Koerner, 279 F.2d 623 (9th Cir.1960), discussed in Problem 26. And, the government may also be concerned that large cash payments may serve to launder ill-gotten goods. The IRS has announced that it will prosecute lawyers' failures to file this form.

b.   In United States v. Ritchie, 15 F.3d 592 (6th Cir.1994), the lawyer moved to quash subpoenas asking the names of clients who had made cash payments to the law firm in excess of $10,000. The lawyer had reported the three payments but not the name of the client or the nature of the legal services. The lawyer said that he gave the IRS enough information to determine his own tax liability, and nothing else was relevant to legitimate

IRS concerns. Consistent with the majority of cases on the issues, however, the court refused to quash the subpoena and found no violation of the Fifth or Sixth amendments, the attorney-client privilege, or due process. See also Gerald B. Lefcourt P.C. v. United States, 125 F.3d 79 (2d Cir.1997).

c. In United States v. Sindel, 53 F.3d 874 (8th Cir.1995), however, Judge Arnold held that the common law privilege could, when sufficiently strong, overcome the mandate of § 6050I. Thus, one client's identity remained protected from disclosure on Form 8300, but another client's identity was not so protected. Ralls v. United States, 52 F.3d 223 (9th Cir.1995), also held that if the question of who paid the lawyer's fee is so inextricably intertwined with the client's privileged communications, then the lawyer may not be forced to tell who paid that fee on the client's behalf.

d. See also, Office of Disciplinary Counsel v. Massey, 687 N.E.2d 734 (Ohio 1998) (lawyer suspended for six months for having a client pay in several units of cash, each less than $10,000, to try to evade the IRS reporting requirement); DeGuerin v. United States, 214 F.Supp.2d 726 (S.D.Tex.2002) (genuine issue of fact presented as to whether the clients' names were privileged).

D. Prosecutorial obligations to defendants (including efforts to get "cooperation" of corporate defendants)

1. What are the obligations of a prosecutor to provide favorable evidence to the defense? Should a prosecutor disclose all favorable evidence to the defense or just material exculpatory evidence? May a prosecutor ask a defendant to waive the rights provided by Rule 3.8(d)?

a. The Supreme Court in Brady v. Maryland, 373 U.S. 83 (1963), held that prosecutors were constitutionally required to disclose material exculpatory evidence relating to the question of guilt or punishment to the defendant. United States v. Bagley, 473 U.S. 667 (1985) linked the definition of materiality to a Strickland v. Washington standard: The information only needs to be disclosed "if there is a reasonable probability that, had the evidence been disclosed to the defense, the result of the proceeding would have been different." The narrow definition of material exculpatory evidence and the practices of prosecutors to delay disclosure until the last possible moment raised questions about the relationship between Rule 3.8(d) and the constitutional requirement under *Brady*.

b. Read Rule 3.8(d). Does this rule incorporate the constitutional requirement described above in *Brady* and *Bagley*? Or does it propose a broader standard of conduct for prosecutors?

c. ABA Formal Opinion 09–454 (July 2009), analyzed the scope of the Model Rule 3.8(d) through a hypothetical involving a purse-snatching where the victim and a bystander had identified the defendant, but the prosecutor was aware that two other bystanders had not identified the defendant in a line-up, and a confidential informant had named another suspect. The prosecutor had pursued these alternate leads and found that they were not credible. The questions posed were whether the prosecutor must disclose this information, when the prosecutor must disclose it, and whether the defendant could consent to the prosecutor's non-disclosure.

The Committee first traced the history of Rule 3.8(d) and determined that it created an ethical obligation to disclose that is independent from the constitutional requirement established in Brady v. Maryland, 373 U.S. 83 (1963). The constitutional standard requires the disclosure of favorable information that is "material," or likely to lead to acquittal. The Committee said the materiality element was not incorporated into Rule 3.8(d). Therefore, the scope of Rule 3.8(d) is more demanding than the constitutional standard, and a prosecutor must disclose all favorable evidence and let the defendant determine its utility. The information includes all that tends to negate guilt or mitigate the offense. It also includes information that is favorable when viewed independently or when viewed in conjunction with other information or evidence. Information or evidence does not need to be admissible at trial for disclosure to be required, and there is no *de minimis* exception to the duty. Therefore, under the hypothetical, the Committee determined that the prosecutor would be obligated under Rule 3.8(d) to disclose the information about the alternate identifications to the defendant.

A prosecutor only needs to disclose information or evidence of which he has knowledge. A prosecutor need not conduct independent investigations for exculpatory evidence, unless the prosecutor was willfully ignoring the likely existence of such evidence. The prosecutor also need not search a voluminous case file or police report, unless the prosecutor knows that or it is obvious that the file or report contains exculpatory information.

As for the requirement that the disclosure be timely, the Committee defined timely as "early enough that the information can be used effectively." The disclosure should be early enough to allow the defendant to use the information to conduct investigations, decide whether to plead guilty, decide whether to raise an affirmative defense, or to determine trial strategy. The Committee recommended that a prosecutor seek a protective order from the court if he believes disclosure would jeopardize a witness or undermine an investigation.[17]

d. Federal judges have taken federal prosecutors to task for failing to disclose evidence. The corruption conviction of the late Alaska Senator Ted Stevens, for example, was overturned because the government did not disclose exculpatory evidence. See Evan Perez, Judge Orders Probe of

---

17. The Committee also addressed whether a defendant could consent to non-disclosure and answered that question in the negative. Allowing a defendant to consent to non-disclosure would impede a defense attorney's ability to advise and defend the defendant. It would also undermine the "public's interest in the fairness and reliability of the criminal justice system."

The Committee also explained that the disclosure duty is slightly different in the context of sentencing. The prosecutor must disclose mitigating information that could lead to a lesser sentence, and the prosecutor must disclose the information to the tribunal as well as the defendant. When a defendant pleads guilty, mitigating information that normally would be disclosed in the course of a trial otherwise might not come to the court's attention.

Prosecutors, Wall Street J., Apr. 8, 2009. And in Massachusetts, Chief District Judge Wolf, "listed at least nine major cases he presided over during the last two decades in which prosecutors . . . withheld important evidence." Jonathan Saltzman, Judge Chastises Federal Attorney: Says Prosecutor Failed to Disclose Crucial Evidence, Boston Globe, Jan. 27, 2009.

2. Should it be improper for a prosecutor to reduce the sanction on a corporate defendant in exchange for assistance in prosecuting culpable officers or employees of the corporation?

a. The conviction of Arthur Andersen—at the time one of America's largest and most respected accounting firms—for obstruction of justice made it unable to continue in practice (see Problem 26). As a result, thousands of innocent partners and employees suffered.

b. In response, many suggested that prosecutors concentrate their efforts on individual dishonest corporate officials rather than on entities themselves. The result was the so-called Thompson Memorandum, issued by Deputy Attorney General Larry Thompson to U.S. attorneys around the country. The memorandum encouraged prosecutors to give corporations the opportunity to "cooperate" with the government in convicting the employees responsible for illegal actions and to give credit for the cooperation in making charging decisions against those corporations.[18] What do you think of that policy in general? What might make it plausible to believe that corporate officials were acting on their own rather than in furtherance of the corporation's policy?

c. The most controversial aspect of the Thompson Memorandum for those interested in legal ethics was Part VI that asserted a "general principle" that a "prosecutor may consider the corporation's willingness to identify the culprits within the corporation, including senior executives; to make witnesses available; to disclose the complete results of its internal investigation; and to *waive attorney-client and work product protection.*" (emphasis added)

d. Why might prosecutors believe they need privilege waivers? Deputy Attorney General Thompson answered in part:

"Such waivers permit the government to obtain statements of possible witnesses, subjects, and targets, without having to negotiate individual cooperation or immunity agreements. In addition, they are often critical in enabling the government to evaluate the completeness of a corporation's voluntary disclosure and cooperation."

Are you convinced by either or both of these arguments? Do either or both of them seem to constitute overreaching?

e. If the government waits for a corporation's own investigators to interview company employees and then receive the results of that investiga-

---

18. http://www.usdoj.gov/dag/cftf/ business_organizations.pdf. In large part, the Thompson Memorandum continued policies issued by Deputy Attorney General Eric Holder in the Clinton Administration.

tion, must the investigators give the employees a *Miranda* warning? If the employees lie to the corporate investigators, could they be accused of violating 18 U.S.C. § 1001 (prohibiting lying to a government investigator)?

3. Should government policies pressure corporations and other entities to turn over individual wrongdoers for criminal prosecution?

a. In response to concern expressed by the ABA, the Association of Corporate Counsel, and several other organizations, the Thompson Memorandum was later replaced by the McNulty Memorandum in 2006 that required approval by central DOJ officials before a U.S. attorney may demand privilege waiver. The McNulty memorandum did not, however, repudiate the claim that such demands are appropriate.

b. The McNulty Memorandum provided guidelines for prosecutors to limit waivers only to those situations presenting a legitimate need. It offered four factors to balance in the determination of the legitimate need: (1) the benefit of the information to the government, (2) whether other means to conduct the investigation were available, (3) the extent of the voluntary disclosure by the company, and (4) the consequences of the waiver to the company. The Memorandum also classified information into two categories and established procedures for obtaining permission to ask for the information included within each category. Despite these specific rules that seemed to restrict the routine requests for broad waiver of corporate attorney-client privilege, the ABA and others still complained that federal prosecutors could ask for voluntary waivers without going through the requirements of the McNulty Memorandum.

c. Attorney General Mark Filip in 2008 authored the Filip Memorandum that refocused the federal efforts from a waiver of privileged information to the provision of relevant facts and documents, whether privileged or not. The Filip guidelines define cooperation for the purposes of lenient sentencing on the company's cooperation to provide relevant facts. The guidelines also require high level approval for waiver of the privilege. Also, companies that participate in joint defense agreements or reimbursement of employee attorneys' fees are not per se failing to cooperate with the Justice Department. Note that all of these Memorandums only apply to the Department of Justice and not other agencies such as the SEC.

4. May the government encourage corporations not to advance attorneys' fees to company officials so as to pressure the officials to confess wrongdoing?

a. The Thompson Memorandum provided that "a corporation's promise of support to culpable employees and agents, either through the advancing of attorneys' fees, through retaining the employees without sanction for their misconduct, or through providing information to the employees about the government's investigation pursuant to a joint defense agreement, may be considered by the prosecutor in weighing the extent and value of a corporation's cooperation." Do you agree that all three kinds of employee "support" are equally culpable?

b.   United States v. Stein is said to be the largest criminal tax case in the nation's history. Nineteen employees of the accounting firm KPMG stood accused of creating illegal tax shelters for wealthy clients. KPMG itself desperately wanted to avoid the fate of Arthur Andersen, so it departed from its usual policy and refused to advance the employees' legal fees, at least in part to get the promised cooperation credit. District Judge Lewis Kaplan ruled that the company's action—done with the government's encouragement—violated the defendants' Fifth and Sixth Amendment rights. United States v. Stein, 435 F.Supp.2d 330 (S.D.N.Y.2006). Judge Kaplan then asserted ancillary jurisdiction over KPMG to order it to advance the fees, an act the Second Circuit held exceeded the district court's authority, Stein v. KPMG, LLP, 486 F.3d 753 (2d Cir.2007). In response, Judge Kaplan dismissed the charges against all but four of the defendants, United States v. Stein, 495 F.Supp.2d 390 (S.D.N.Y.2007). The Second Circuit upheld the dismissal because KPMG followed an earlier version of the Department of Justice Guidelines that forbade paying attorneys' fees of company constituents. The court found that the failure to reimburse the attorneys' fees was the product of government action and a denial of due process.

c.   The Filip Memorandum prohibits the government from requesting that a company refuse to pay its constituent's attorneys' fee.

5.   Should government lawyers have greater ethical obligations to do justice than lawyers in general have?

a.   Model Rule 3.8 places special rules on government lawyers who are prosecutors. What about other government lawyers, who represent the government in civil cases? Do the Model Rules place any stricter obligations on them than on lawyers who represent private clients in civil cases?

b.   Freeport–McMoRan Oil & Gas Co. v. F.E.R.C., 962 F.2d 45 (D.C.Cir.1992) argued that government lawyers have a special duty to be fair in *civil* litigation. The government knew certain orders had been superseded, but instead of conceding the point, it made the plaintiff challenge them in court.

Do you agree that courts should condemn such conduct? Do you believe that the government should press every advantage? If private lawyers, instead of government lawyers, had refused to concede the obvious point, would that not have been just as wrong? If so, does that suggest that the government lawyers in civil cases do not have a special duty, but have the same duty as private lawyers?

———

PROBLEM 30

THE DUTY TO SEE JUSTICE DONE

We often refer to lawyers as "officers of the court" and as having public duties as well as duties to their clients. This problem examines how those assertions play out in the context of a case in which the lawyer believes someone has been wrongly imprisoned. Deciding what the lawyer should do proves harder than it might first appear. The problem asks us to think about the nature of the lawyer's legal obligations to various people where the lawyer sees that an injustice may have occurred. Is it plausible for lawyers to believe that the criminal process may have convicted the wrong person? Do lawyers have a moral obligation to respond to a likely injustice, and if so, how do they satisfy that obligation in a variety of difficult circumstances?

FACTS

Hamilton York was hired by a workers' compensation insurance carrier in the defense of a compensation claim brought by a woman who had been assaulted in the course of her duties as a hotel night clerk. As a direct result of the assault, the woman suffered severe psychological shock that disabled her and prevented her from obtaining and holding gainful employment.

In the course of defending the substantial claim for compensation, the attorney was furnished psychological reports indicating that the claimant said she had been assaulted by "a black man." The psychologist concluded that, as a result of her experience, whenever she encountered an African–American male, she became extremely fearful and withdrew into herself. Indeed, her psychological problems were such that if she even encountered a dark-skinned man walking down the street, she became terrified and would turn around and run. Further, she was unable to distinguish one African–American man from another. She considered all such men to be her attacker and this psychological situation had existed since the time of the attack.

In connection with the investigation of the facts underlying this compensation claim, York also learned that the victim had identified the first African–American male she had seen in the lineup. At his criminal trial, the defendant, James Brooks, asserted an alibi that had been supported by two corroborating witnesses. However, the testimony of the victim had been so compelling that the jury apparently believed her. Brooks was convicted and sentenced to a life term in the penitentiary.

Some of this information, at least as to the general nature of the victim's disability, was available to both the prosecution and defense at the time of the criminal trial, but not to the extent it was developed later in the course of the workers' compensation negotiations. The psychologists' reports were furnished by the claimant's attorney to York with an explicit demand that their contents be revealed only to persons involved in settling the claim. The claim will soon be settled without a trial and the reports will not become a matter of public record.

York has never handled a criminal case in his professional career, and the facts he finds himself facing in this instance are the closest he has ever come to the criminal justice system. He believes an innocent man may be in the penitentiary for the rest of his life unless he acts, but Brooks is not his client and he does not know how to proceed.

QUESTIONS

A.   DUTIES OF A LAWYER WHO LEARNS AN INJUSTICE MAY HAVE BEEN DONE

1.   To whom does York, the workers' compensation attorney, owe duties in this situation? What kinds of duties?

a.   Does York owe a duty of confidentiality and a duty of loyalty to the hotel where the incident occurred and the insurance company that retained him? Does Model Rule 1.6(a) impose such a duty? How about Model Rule 1.9(c)? Must York secure the consent of either the hotel or the insurer before he may reveal what makes him believe there was an unjust conviction in the criminal case?

b.   If the hotel or the insurance company will not consent, perhaps out of fear that it will upset settlement negotiations in the workers' compensation case, should that end all analysis of York's obligations? Are there some client decisions that a lawyer simply must take as final?

2.   Does York have a duty to the rape victim not to make her psychiatric studies public?

a.   What would be the source of York's obligation, if any, to the victim? Restatement Third, The Law Governing Lawyers § 132, Comment *g(ii)*, for example, says that a "lawyer might have obligations to persons who were not the lawyer's clients but about whom information was revealed to the lawyer under circumstances obligating the lawyer not to use or disclose the information." Does this sound like the kind of case to which such a principle should apply?

b.   Does Model Rule 4.4(a) apply to this situation? Would the victim's lawyer's demand that the reports not be shown to others mean that York could say no more? Should York feel a moral if not a legal obligation not to further injure a person who has been severely traumatized?

3.   Does York have any duty to the court that tried the case or to the man he believes is wrongly convicted?

a.   Look at Model Rule 3.3. Is its requirement limited to revealing false evidence and fraud in the case York is now handling? Was the identification in this problem "dishonest" at all? The cited rules are disciplinary provisions, of course, but do they suggest a moral obligation to the court to disclose information necessary to overturn an unjust result?

b.   Does York have any legal duty to Brooks, the man York believes was wrongly convicted? Does any provision of the Model Rules come close to creating such a duty? But does the absence of any affirmative duty to him suggest there is anything wrong with York's *assuming* an obligation to help? Put another way, should lawyers see discipline rules as *floors* on their conduct rather than as *ceilings*?

B. Concerns about the reliability of results in our legal system

1. Can York rest easy in the knowledge that our justice system is highly reliable and that if there were reason to doubt the defendant's guilt, the jury most likely would have been told about it?

 a. Since 1989, when DNA evidence first served as the basis for the exoneration of an innocent convicted criminal defendant, the American courts have exonerated 259 wrongfully convicted individuals.[1] A study of the first 225 DNA exoneration cases has produced the following data about the wrongful convictions: "77 percent had eyewitness misidentification; 52 percent had improper forensic evidence; 23 percent had false confessions or admissions; and 16 percent had informants or snitches standing to gain from their testimony."[2] Do these exonerations prove that, at least in some cases, the system can be self-correcting? Furthermore, honest mistakes will slip into any system of justice.

 b. However, cases abound in which prosecutors have been found to have suppressed materially exculpatory evidence, knowingly used false evidence at trial, or both. In some cases, such conduct has put the defendants on death row. See, e.g., Guerra v. Collins, 916 F.Supp. 620 (S.D.Tex.1995); People v. Jimerson, 652 N.E.2d 278 (Ill.1995); United States v. Boyd, 833 F.Supp. 1277 (N.D.Ill.1993); Bowen v. Maynard, 799 F.2d 593 (10th Cir.1986).[3]

 c. Furthermore, the misconduct is not limited to the prosecutor. In some cases, courts find that police officers or crime lab personnel have falsified the evidence, requiring that verdicts be set aside. See, e.g., Matter of W.Va. State Police Crime Lab., Serology Division, 438 S.E.2d 501 (W.Va.1993), finding that the chief of the serology division of the crime lab had a "long history of falsifying evidence in criminal prosecutions."

1. See www.innocenceproject.org for more information about the 259 exoneration cases noted as of October 17, 2010.

2. Contributing Factors in Wrongful Convictions, 37 Florida Bar News 1 (Oct. 1, 2010).

3. See also, Ken Armstrong & Maurice Possley, Trial & Error: How Prosecutors Sacrifice Justice to Win, Chicago Tribune, Jan. 10–14, 1999 (five-part series concluding that prosecutors are rewarded for convictions, not doing justice, and that even when they have been caught using false evidence or failing to disclose exculpatory information, they tend to get promoted to judgeships rather than being subjected to discipline). Following the series, Illinois Chief Justice Charles Freeman asked that prosecutors who commit misconduct be named in court opinions and that the facts be referred to the Attorney Registration and Disciplinary Commission for action. See Ken Armstrong and Maurice Possley, Illinois Courts May End Secrecy, Chicago Tribune, Feb. 3,1999. See also, John Gibeaut, "Yes, I'm Sure That's Him": Eyewitness Reliability Under Question By Experts, Courts, 85 A.B.A. Journal 26 (Oct. 1999). In January, 2002, Illinois's outgoing Republican Gov. George Ryan commuted the death sentences of 167 people to life in prison after concluding that the capital punishment system was "haunted by the demon of error." Robert E. Pierre & Kari Lydersen, Illinois Death Row Emptied: Citing "Demon of Error," Ryan Commutes Sentences, Washington Post, Jan. 12, 2003, at A1.

d. Or, sometimes scientific tests thought to be foolproof turn out to be unreliable. See, e.g., John Solomon, FBI Forensic Test Full of Holes, Washington Post, Nov. 18, 2007, p. A–1, col. 2 (reporting that bullet-lead analysis done by the FBI lab and used to convict approximately 2500 defendants had no reliable scientific basis).

2. Does a criminal defendant's right to counsel assure that counsel will leave no stone unturned in providing a thorough defense?

a. Unfortunately, sometimes the defendant's problem is not false evidence but defense counsel who does an inadequate job of discovering and presenting available information about the defendant's innocence. Then, when the result is later challenged in a petition for a writ of habeas corpus, it is hard for the defendants to secure reversal of convictions unless they can show that they were negatively prejudiced by that ineffective assistance of counsel.

b. As discussed in Problem 11, the standard used by the Supreme Court requires that the criminal defendant must show that the lawyer acted "outside the wide range of professionally competent assistance" and that the result was "actual prejudice" to the defendant. Strickland v. Washington, 466 U.S. 668 (1984). In *Strickland*, the Court held that (1) the defense counsel's strategy at the sentencing hearing was reasonable, so the defendant was not denied effective assistance of counsel; and (2) even assuming the challenged conduct of counsel was unreasonable, the defendant suffered insufficient prejudice to warrant setting aside his death sentence.[4] See, e.g., Stephen Bright, Counsel for the Poor: The Death Sentence Not for the Worst Crime But for the Worst Lawyer, 103 Yale L.J. 1835 (1994).

c. Court challenges to the adequacy of representation illustrate that the problem of inadequate counsel is concrete and substantial. In State v. Peart, 621 So.2d 780 (La.1993), for example, the state supreme court found that the funding of public defenders was so poor in some parts of the state that it ruled that defendants had a rebuttable presumption that they had received inadequate assistance of counsel.[5]

d. In other cases, public defender programs have become so overwhelmed with clients that many say they cannot represent any of them effectively. See, e.g., In re Public Defender's Certification of Conflict and Motion to Withdraw Due to Excessive Caseload, 709 So.2d 101 (Fla.1998) (backlog in preparing appellate cases presents "a significant problem of constitutional magnitude"; courts ordered to appoint private lawyers and legislature encouraged to "examine the structure and funding of indigent

4. Justice O'Connor wrote the opinion for the Court. Justice Brennan concurred in part and dissented in part, and Justice Marshall dissented.

5. Cases rejecting such claims have usually only done so on jurisdictional grounds. See, e.g., Kennedy v. Carlson, 544 N.W.2d 1 (Minn.1996) (public defenders lack standing to assert interests of their future clients); Luckey v. Miller, 976 F.2d 673 (11th Cir.1992) (upholds federal court abstention from case that sought to reform the Georgia system of providing indigent defense).

representation in criminal cases"); United States ex rel. Green v. Washington, 917 F.Supp. 1238 (N.D.Ill.1996) (delay in appellate defender's filing of briefs on appeal violated due process and justified issuance of conditional writs of habeas corpus).

3. Is there a deeper issue than individual justice? Should it be relevant to York that the innocent man is an African-American?

a. Do you think our jury system may be more likely to believe the testimony of a white victim than an African-American accused? Is the convicted man likely to have fewer persons coming to his defense than he would if he were white?[6] Should that reinforce York's resolve to pursue justice in the man's case?

b. DNA tests led to the dismissal, in December of 2002, of five males who each served between 5 and 13 years in prison for rape and beating of a jogger in New York City's Central Park. This crime "exposed New York City's racial tensions and made national headlines." In 2001, a serial rapist said he alone attacked the 28-year-old woman as she jogged in Central Park on April 19, 1989. The prosecutor reinvestigated and DNA testing showed that semen samples from the scene belonged to Matias Reyes, the serial rapist, and "new forensic tests, more precise than those used a decade ago, failed to link the five convicted men to the rape." District Attorney Robert Morgenthau relied on that evidence "in recommending all convictions in the case be dropped. Prosecutors have said that they have no plans to retry any of the five." The primary evidence that had been used to convict the five defendants "had been confessions that the five, all black and Hispanic boys ranging in age from 14 to 16 at the time, had made to detectives."[7]

c. Must our only response to such realities be that no system can be perfect? Is there any possible way to reduce the likelihood that such injustices will happen again?

C. THE OBLIGATION, IF ANY, TO RESPOND TO CONCERNS ABOUT AN INJUSTICE

1. Does anyone have an obligation to listen to York? Would the former defense counsel have such an obligation, for example? How about the trial judge?

a. How long does the "zealous representation" obligation of the former criminal defense counsel continue? Look at Standard 4–8.5 of the ABA Standards Relating to the Defense Function? Does it suggest that former counsel, either trial or appellate, would have a duty to act?

b. Does the trial judge have a duty higher than the responsibility of the defense counsel? Does the judge have any duty at all?

6. For further background on these issues, see, e.g., Cornel West, Race Matters (1993); Paul Butler, Racially–Based Jury Nullification: Black Power in the Criminal Justice System, 105 Yale L.J. 677 (1995); Norval Morris, Race & Crime: What Evidence Is There That Race Influences Results in the Criminal Justice System, 72 Judicature 111 (1988).

7. Associated Press, Judge Vacates Rape Verdicts In Central Park Jogger Case, Wall Street J., Dec. 19, 2002.

c. Lest you think that courts are always open to newly discovered evidence that an innocent person has been wrongly convicted, look at Herrera v. Collins, 506 U.S. 390 (1993), holding that even a defendant on death row has no automatic right to federal habeas corpus relief based on a claim of newly discovered evidence of actual innocence. In that case, the original conviction included two eyewitness identifications, numerous pieces of circumstantial evidence, and petitioner Herrera's handwritten letter impliedly admitting his guilt. Ten years after his conviction, he submitted affidavits tending to show that his now-dead brother had committed the murders.[8]

d. The case of Alton Logan provides a heartbreaking illustration of lawyers who were faced with a decision of disclosing knowledge of a conviction of an innocent man. Over 25 years ago, Dale Coventry and Jamie Kunz were Cook County public defenders who represented Andrew Wilson. At that time, Wilson disclosed to his lawyers that he had committed the murder at a McDonalds restaurant for which Alton Logan was being tried. Wilson was already facing a death penalty for other crimes and his lawyers decided that a disclosure of his involvement in the McDonalds crime would enhance his risk of a severe sentence for his current crimes. Coventry and Kunz concluded that they could disclose their client's involvement in the crime if Alton Logan was sentenced to death, but instead he received a long prison sentence. They asked their client, Wilson, if they could disclose his involvement in the crime after his death and he agreed. For 26 years, they kept silent until January 2008 when Wilson died. At that time, Coventry and Kunz disclosed an affidavit signed by Andrew Wilson admitting to the McDonalds murder. With this information and other evidence, Alton Logan secured post-conviction relief and was released from prison in September 2008.

Regardless what the law was 26 years ago, what do the Model Rules now say about such a situation? Is lengthy imprisonment "substantial bodily" harm? Examine Restatement § 66, Comment c "Serious bodily harm * * * includes * * * the consequences of events such as imprisonment for a substantial period * * *."

Could and should Coventry and Kunz have asked Wilson for permission to use the information to try to secure a prosecutor's agreement not to seek the death penalty? Would the prosecutor be likely to have agreed? Remember what happened to Armani and Belge when they tried a similar ploy on behalf of Robert Garrow in Problem 24. Might these two lawyers have asked their client directly to disclose the information and suffer the consequences?

---

8. Courts are sometimes especially suspicious of a defense based on an alleged confession of someone who cannot himself be convicted of a crime. See, e.g., Valdez v. Winans, 738 F.2d 1087 (10th Cir.1984) (confession of crime A by defendant in case B is not a basis for setting aside conviction of defendant in case A); State v. Macumber, 544 P.2d 1084 (Ariz.1976) (attorney-client privilege precludes use of confession by now-deceased person in trial of person accused of crime). But see People v. Burrows, 665 N.E.2d 1319 (Ill.1996) (conviction set aside when co-defendant admits she acted alone).

2.   Should the former or current prosecuting attorney have an obligation to take another look at the case?

a.   Do the obligations of Model Rule 3.8 extend beyond the end of a case? ABA Standard Relating to the Prosecution Function 3–1.2(c) says only what many cases say, that the "duty of the prosecutor is to seek justice, not merely to convict." Should that platitude be given meaning?

b.   Imbler v. Pachtman, 424 U.S. 409 (1976), was a damages action under 42 U.S.C. § 1983 against a prosecutor who had allegedly knowingly suppressed favorable evidence and knowingly used false evidence against a defendant. The facts leading to the defendant's release had been turned up by and reported to the governor after the conviction by the prosecutor who was now being sued. In upholding an absolute privilege against liability for a prosecutor's acts in the "judicial process," the Supreme Court said it did not want to discourage a prosecutor from reporting evidence of an unjust conviction. "[A]fter a conviction," the Court said, "the prosecutor is * * * bound by the ethics of his office to inform the appropriate authorities of after-acquired or other information that casts doubt upon the correctness of the conviction." 424 U.S. at 427 n. 25.

c.   In 2008, the ABA House of Delegates added new paragraphs (g) and (h) to Model Rule 3.8. They require that when "a prosecutor knows of new, credible and material evidence creating a reasonable likelihood that a convicted defendant did not commit an offense of which the defendant was convicted," the prosecutor must tell the defendant of the evidence and begin an investigation to determine whether the defendant had been wrongly convicted.[9] The rule goes on: "When a prosecutor knows of clear and convincing evidence establishing that a defendant in the prosecutor's jurisdiction was convicted of an offense that the defendant did not commit, the prosecutor shall seek to remedy the conviction." Are you convinced that defendants can now be confident that any mistakes made in the criminal justice system will be corrected promptly?

d.   As of September 2010, only two states (Delaware and Idaho) have adopted Rule 3.8(g) and (h) and two states (Colorado and Wisconsin) have modified the ABA language to soften the duty on prosecutors in light of limited resources to investigate allegations of erroneous convictions in closed cases. Does this amendment place too high a burden on prosecutors to investigate closed cases? Is this instead a burden that society *must* bear in light of the numbers of wrongfully convicted defendants?

3.   Suppose no one would listen to York. Should he try to interest "60 Minutes"? Oprah? Nancy Grace?

a.   The news media's ability to raise questions and stimulate change has made it a serious venue for many accused and convicted people. The news media has often become the "court of last resort" in the United States today.

---

9.   See, e.g., Fred C. Zacharias, The Role of Prosecutors in Serving Justice After Con-   victions, 58 Vanderbilt L. Rev. 171 (2005).

b. Is that a positive development? Would a televised account of this story likely protect the assault victim, for example? Remember that she did not intentionally lie about what happened and her welfare and privacy are surely appropriate for the lawyer's moral concern.

D. OTHER CONFLICTS BETWEEN PROFESSIONAL OBLIGATIONS AND DOING JUSTICE

1. Suppose you learned that, in spite of the fact that you recently defeated a pollution charge against your client, it did indeed sometimes discharge toxic chemicals into a stream from which a nearby city gets its water supply.

a. Suppose an employee of the client admits, after the trial and after the time for any appeal has passed, that he lied at the trial. Do you have any obligations under Rule 3.3(c)?

b. Suppose you learn that the company no longer discharges the waste, but the toxic waste that was earlier discharged is still there and it will slowly harm people unless it is cleaned up? The company accidentally discharged the waste, and it is confident that it will not do it again, but it does not want to admit what it did.

c. May you disclose this information if you believe that the toxic discharge will eventually, but inevitably, cause substantial bodily harm, even though accidental discharge is not a crime? Would Model Rule 1.6(b)(1) now apply to the situation? How about Model Rule 1.13(b)? Would you go to the EPA if the company refused to make all necessary changes? Would you go back to court and confess error?

2. What actions would you take if you learned that the plaintiff suing your client had a life-threatening condition of which that person was unaware?

a. That was the situation presented in the well-known case of Spaulding v. Zimmerman, 116 N.W.2d 704 (Minn. 1962). David Spaulding, a teenaged boy, sustained injuries in an automobile accident. His injuries were diagnosed by his family physician, Dr. Cain, as

> "a severe crushing injury of the chest with multiple rib fractures; a severe cerebral concussion, probably with petechial hemorrhages of the brain; and bilateral fractures of the clavicles. At Dr. Cain's suggestion, on January 3, 1957, David was examined by * * * an orthopedic specialist, who made X-ray studies of his chest. * * * Nothing in [that] report indicated the aorta aneurysm with which David was then suffering."

In the meantime, defense counsel also had a physical examination performed on David. The report from that doctor read as follows:

> " 'The one feature of the case which bothers me more than any other part of the case is the fact that this boy of 20 years of age has an aneurysm, which means a dilatation of the aorta and the arch of the aorta. Whether this came out of this accident I cannot say with any degree of certainty and I have discussed it with the Roentgenologist

and a couple of Internists. * * * Of course an aneurysm or dilatation of the aorta in a boy of this age is a serious matter as far as his life. This aneurysm may dilate further and it might rupture with further dilatation and this would cause his death.'

" 'It would be interesting also to know whether the X-ray of his lungs, taken immediately following the accident, shows this dilatation or not. If it was not present immediately following the accident and is now present, then we could be sure that it came out of the accident.' "

The day after the court called the case for trial, the parties settled for $6,500. David and his father did not know, and defense counsel did not tell them, how serious his injury really was. Two years later, David underwent a physical examination required for army reserve service. That exam fortuitously revealed the aneurysm, and after immediate surgery, David was cured.

Once David was no longer a minor, he filed suit to set aside the earlier settlement and seek additional damages for the aneurysm. In its opinion upholding reopening of the case, the court said:

" * * * The seriousness of this disability is indicated by [the defense doctor's] report indicating the imminent danger of death therefrom. This was known by counsel for both defendants but was not disclosed to the court at the time it was petitioned to approve the settlement. While no canon of ethics or legal obligation may have required them to inform the plaintiff or his counsel with respect thereto, or to advise the court therein, it did become obvious to them at the time that the settlement then made did not contemplate or take into consideration the disability described. * * * "

b. Are you struck by the court's simultaneous findings of (1) nondisclosure sufficient to reopen the settlement and (2) a lack of "ethical or legal obligation" to reveal the plaintiff's life-threatening condition to him? Are those findings consistent?

c. If David had died, do you think the defense lawyers would have borne any legal or moral responsibility for his death? Why or why not?

d. What would you have done if you were the defense lawyer in *Spaulding*? Would you have asked the driver for permission to tell the other side about David's life threatening medical condition? Would the insurance company normally have a right to control this decision? Is this a decision that the lawyer may make without informing the client?

e. Might you instead try to work out an agreement to disclose the condition so long as the information could not be used against your client? Would that realistically be possible in the context of negotiating a settlement? If you had been counsel for David and defense counsel had promised "life-saving information" in exchange for a waiver of some of his rights, would you have accepted the offer? Is genuine concern for the welfare of a nonclient so rare among lawyers today that you would have suspected a trick?

f. In some jurisdictions, medical reports of all consulting physicians are automatically shared with both sides. In other states, the opposing party must ask for them specifically. If the plaintiff's lawyer did not ask for the report, could the defendant's lawyer share this information with David? May a law firm have a policy of sharing medical reports in all cases even if the plaintiff's lawyer forgets to ask for them?

g. The 1983 Model Rules permitted disclosure only to prevent a client crime involving imminent death or substantial bodily harm. Was there a crime in *Spaulding* that would justify disclosure? In 2002, the ABA changed Model Rule 1.6(b)(1) to its current form. May a lawyer now disclose the life-saving information to David Spaulding?

h. Does a physician have an independent duty to inform David about the aneurysm? Physicians take a Hippocratic Oath to save the lives of their patients, but in this case the doctor was hired as an expert and not a treating physician. At the time of this case, consulting physicians did not have a duty to disclose information to the subject of the medical examination, but recent cases are beginning to recognize that a consulting physician who is aware of a life threatening condition of which the subject is not aware has a duty to inform the patient in a timely manner.[10]

3. Suppose you have learned that the client whom you have just helped to defeat a charge of child molestation is indeed a pedophile and you have inadvertently helped put him back on the streets. May you ethically do anything?

a. What if you learn that he has just become a camp director and that he disclosed neither the earlier charge nor the reality of his condition. Massachusetts Bar Ass'n Ethics Opinion 90–2 (June 15, 1990) concluded that, in this circumstance, the lawyer may disclose the necessary information to the authorities "if the lawyer believes that the client's proclivities rise to the level where he is reasonably likely to commit a crime again against the children currently under his care."

b. Would you welcome the authorization this opinion gives you to report your former client? How certain do you have to be to "believe" that the client is "reasonably likely" to return to his old ways?

c. If you had been the lawyer in this problem, or the lawyer for the pedophile, would you just try to forget what you now know and reason that trials are never perfect? Would you see whether there are any openings in medical school or seek some other career confronting you with less stress-producing questions?

---

10. See, e.g., Reed v. Bojarski, 764 A.2d 433 (2001) (in a pre-employment physical exam paid for by the prospective employer, the physician has a duty to inform patient of findings that pose an imminent danger to the examinee); AMA Ethics Opinion 10.03 (Patient–Physician Relationship in the Context of Work–Related and Independent Examinations requires physician to inform the examinee of "important health information or abnormalities."). See also, Roger C. Cramton & Lori P. Knowles, Professional Secrecy and Its Exceptions: Spaulding v. Zimmerman Revisited, 83 Minnesota L. Rev. 63, 98 n.121 (1998).

CHAPTER VII

THE DELIVERY OF LEGAL SERVICES

As discussed in Chapter I, the world of practicing lawyers has changed dramatically over the last thirty years. The changes profoundly impact the delivery of legal services in the United States and around the world. This chapter considers many of those changes.

Before 1977, for example, ethics rules said that making legal services broadly available to people who need them was the essence of professional activity. Yet those same rules prohibited lawyers from advertising or seeking clients through other communications. Today, all lawyers and law firms are concerned with getting their names before a desired group of prospective clients. Lawyers talk openly and aggressively about "marketing" services, stimulating client demand for those services, and seeking to take away clients currently served by other lawyers.

Over the same forty years, law firms, corporate legal departments, and government legal offices have become important institutions for training and supervising lawyers. It is no longer sufficient to require that each lawyer follow the rules of ethics. Partners who profit from their organization and supervisory lawyers who direct and monitor groups of lawyers and nonlawyers each must play an important role in the implementation of ethical standards. These problems are accentuated as today's lawyers often switch firms or employers several times during their careers.

Changes in the manner in which legal services are offered to clients continue to challenge the development of ethical standards. Referrals from one law firm to another are commonplace today. And, traditional litigation has given way to class actions and other complex litigation to provide clients with redress. As litigation has become more complex and expensive, lawyers continue to look for new ways of funding and securing their fees.

The complexity of laws in today's society also means a continued need for legal services that cannot be met by the market. Many citizens cannot afford to hire lawyers to represent them in criminal and civil cases. As law becomes more of a business, the tradition of providing pro bono legal service to the poor and middle class presents an important challenge for the legal profession.

In the most recent two decades, the legal profession has also faced challenges to its monopoly of the delivery of legal services and receiving legal fees. American lawyers have resisted efforts to allow nonlawyer investors to own all of part of law firms. We have resisted accounting firms' attempts to introduce multidisciplinary practices. However, pressures from different rules in the United Kingdom, Australia, and elsewhere have pushed the American legal profession to consider alternative forms of practice. Lawyers talk of making their firms into "one-stop shopping" resources for both legal services and ancillary activities such as accounting, business consulting, investment banking, lobbying and real estate development. In a global economy with instant telecommunications, international pressures become more real when clients can use law firms and non-lawyer services outside the United States to serve their global needs.

This chapter provides several such windows on current issues in the delivery of legal services. As you examine the materials in this chapter, ask yourself such questions as:

a. Has law become a "commercial" activity? Is that inevitable? Desirable for lawyers? Desirable for clients? Does such a change make law less of a "profession"? Is there a difference between practicing a "profession" and working in a "trade or business"?

b. What role are the federal courts—as distinguished from state supreme courts—playing in transforming the profession? At whose expense are the rules being changed?

c. What is the nature of a law firm today? How does it come into being? How does it break up? What are the duties of its members to each other?

d. How can legal services be made more widely available? Should the law require lawyers to volunteer their services to persons unable to pay for assistance? Should the law give lawyers an incentive to bring cases in the public interest by requiring defendants to pay the plaintiffs' legal fees?

e. Do alternatives to traditional law firms better provide legal services to persons not now receiving them? To what standards of conduct should those providers be expected to adhere?

———

PROBLEM 31

MARKETING PROFESSIONAL SERVICES

Most lawyers enjoy practicing law and obtaining good results for their clients. However, for many lawyers, the problem is finding clients to consult them in the first place. A lawyer without clients finds it hard to pay the bills, but for many years the organized bar, and state courts in their regulation of lawyers, forbade lawyer advertising. Canon 27 of the ABA Canons of Professional Ethics (1937) said simply: "It is unprofessional to solicit professional employment by circulars, advertisements, through touters or by personal communications or interviews not warranted by personal relations."[1] Much has changed since the 1977 Supreme Court decision in

---

1. The 1908 Canons originally permitted lawyer advertising, but a 1937 revision imposed substantial restrictions on lawyer efforts to communicate with prospective clients. See ABA Formal Opinion 276 (Sept. 20, 1947)

Bates v. State Bar of Arizona, 433 U.S. 350, 97 S.Ct. 2691, 53 L.Ed.2d 810 (1977), found such state bar efforts unconstitutional under the First Amendment. Advertising is everywhere, and skill at "marketing" is now a requirement for promotion to partner at many law firms. This problem first traces the constitutional analysis that led to the current rules about lawyer advertising. Next, it considers the distinction between advertising and in-person solicitation, and then it looks at what limits may or should be imposed on both advertising and solicitation.

Facts

Jerry Harrold has just moved to a new community. He has published the following quarter-page advertisement in the local newspaper:

Introducing

JERRY HARROLD

Doctor of Law

Hi—

I'm Jerry Harrold, and I'm a lawyer. I'm 34 years old and a native of this state. I was born in Rushville and have practiced law for the past six years in Capital City. I went to State Law School, was a member of the moot court team, and served my country for three years as a Judge Advocate in the Army. My doctor's degree in law is the professional degree a lawyer normally earns. I don't claim to be the best lawyer in the state, but some of my former clients have agreed to act as references. I'll be glad to supply their names to you so that you can check me out yourself.

I am unusual in one respect. I charge clients a flat rate of $95 per hour, win or lose, big case or small. That lets me cover my expenses and have a decent income, but most of my clients have found that it saves them a great deal in legal fees, particularly in routine matters like real estate and probate for which many lawyers charge a percentage of the sum involved in the transaction.

I look forward to meeting you soon.

Jerry

425 Center Street
Suite 518
Lewistown, Michigan 40608
332–4816

[C2593]

After practicing for a year, Jerry personally made a phone call to each of his current or former clients who was over 50 years of age. He said, "Everyone is worried about how they are going to pay for their retirement and provide for their loved ones after they're gone. Lawyers can help with some of those issues. Why don't you stop by soon and have a routine legal checkup. I will only charge you for a one-hour consultation, and it will help to put your mind at ease." If they expressed interest, he signed them up for an appointment. If they said they were not interested, he respected that decision.

At the end of last week, an airplane crash near Lewistown killed 45 people and badly injured 15 others. At least half of the victims lived near Lewistown, and Jerry plans to send a personal note to each of them or their survivors that expresses his deep personal sympathy for what the airline's negligence has forced them to bear. He plans to follow up with a personal visit where he plans to say, "It's up to you to decide whether to retain me, but if you wish to do so, I will be there for you."

QUESTIONS

A.   THE CONSTITUTIONAL CONTEXT OF THE REGULATION OF LAWYER MARKETING

1.   What makes state-regulated lawyer advertising a matter of federal court concern?

a. The legal profession takes pride in regulating itself, but even lawyers live under the authority of the Constitution. For many years, the Constitution carefully protected political speech, but "commercial speech" was thought to be fair game for regulation. The leading case was Valentine v. Chrestensen, 316 U.S. 52 (1942), which held that New York could regulate distribution of leaflets advertising a tour of a submarine even though regulating the distribution of political leaflets would have raised constitutional concerns.

b. By the mid–1970s, however, that distinction was breaking down. In Bigelow v. Virginia, 421 U.S. 809 (1975), the Supreme Court said that Virginia could not punish a newspaper that published an advertisement for a New York abortion referral service. Similarly, Virginia Pharmacy Bd. v. Virginia Citizens Consumer Council, 425 U.S. 748 (1976), held that a pharmacist's advertising of prescription drug prices was entitled to First Amendment protection, in part because of consumers' interest in receiving the information.

c. Thus, when John Bates and Van O'Steen left the Maricopa County Legal Aid Society to open what they called a "legal clinic" and sought to advertise their "very reasonable fees," the time was right for the Court to say that prohibition of such advertising violated constitutional standards. A low cost legal clinic needed a high volume of clients to survive, so Bates and

O'Steen believed they had no choice but to place a newspaper ad listing their services and fees. In Bates v. State Bar of Arizona, 433 U.S. 350 (1977), Justice Blackmun, writing for the Court, expressed doubt about the alleged state interest in maintenance of the prohibition:

" * * * [W]e find the postulated connection between advertising and the erosion of true professionalism to be severely strained. At its core, the argument presumes that attorneys must conceal from themselves and from their clients the real-life fact that lawyers earn their livelihood at the bar. We suspect that few attorneys engage in such self-deception. And rare is the client, moreover, even one of modest means, who enlists the aid of an attorney with the expectation that his services will be rendered free of charge. * * * If the commercial basis of the relationship is to be promptly disclosed on ethical grounds, once the client is in the office, it seems inconsistent to condemn the candid revelation of the same information before he arrives at that office.

"Moreover, the assertion that advertising will diminish the attorney's reputation in the community is open to question. Bankers and engineers advertise, and yet these professions are not regarded as undignified. In fact, * * * [s]tudies reveal that many persons do not obtain counsel even when they perceive a need because of the feared price of services or because of an inability to locate a competent attorney. Indeed, cynicism with regard to the profession may be created by the fact that it long has publicly eschewed advertising, while condoning the actions of the attorney who structures his social or civic associations so as to provide contacts with potential clients. * * *

"We are not persuaded that restrained professional advertising by lawyers inevitably will be misleading. Although many services performed by attorneys are indeed unique, it is doubtful that any attorney would or could advertise fixed prices for services of that type. The only services that lend themselves to advertising are the routine ones: the uncontested divorce, the simple adoption, the uncontested personal bankruptcy, the change of name, and the like—the very services advertised by appellants. * * *

" * * * Advertising [also] does not provide a complete foundation on which to select an attorney. But it seems peculiar to deny the consumer, on the ground that the information is incomplete, at least some of the relevant information needed to reach an informed decision. * * * Although, of course, the bar retains the power to correct omissions that have the effect of presenting an inaccurate picture, the preferred remedy is more disclosure, rather than less. If the naiveté of the public will cause advertising by attorneys to be misleading, then it is the bar's role to assure that the populace is sufficiently informed as to enable it to place advertising in its proper perspective. * * *

" * * * The ban on advertising serves to increase the difficulty of discovering the lowest-cost seller of acceptable ability. As a result, to this extent attorneys are isolated from competition, and the incentive to price competitively is reduced. * * *

" * * * In the absence of advertising, an attorney must rely on his contacts with the community to generate a flow of business. In view of the time necessary to develop such contacts, the ban * * * serves to perpetuate the market position of established attorneys. Consideration of entry-barrier problems would urge that advertising be allowed so as to aid the new competitor in penetrating the market. * * *

* * *

"In holding that advertising by attorneys may not be subjected to blanket suppression, and that the advertisement at issue is protected, we, of course, do not hold that advertising by attorneys may not be regulated in any way. We mention some of the clearly permissible limitations on advertising not foreclosed by our holding.

"Advertising that is false, deceptive, or misleading of course is subject to restraint. * * * In fact, because the public lacks sophistication concerning legal services, misstatements that might be overlooked or deemed unimportant in other advertising may be found quite inappropriate in legal advertising. For example, advertising claims as to the quality of services—a matter we do not address today—are not susceptible to measurement or verification; accordingly, such claims may be so likely to be misleading as to warrant restriction. Similar objections might justify restraints on in-person solicitation. We do not foreclose the possibility that some limited supplementation, by way of warning or disclaimer or the like, might be required of even an advertisement of the kind ruled upon today so as to assure that the consumer is not mislead. In sum, we recognize that many of the problems in defining the boundary between deceptive and nondeceptive advertising remain to be resolved, and we expect that the bar will have a special role to play in assuring that advertising by attorneys flows both freely and cleanly.

"As with other varieties of speech, it follows as well that there may be reasonable restrictions on the time, place, and manner of advertising. * * * And the special problems of advertising on the electronic broadcast media will warrant special consideration. * * *

"The constitutional issue in this case is only whether the State may prevent the publication in a newspaper of appellants' truthful advertisement concerning the availability and terms of routine legal services. We rule simply that the flow of such information may not be restrained, and we therefore hold the present application of the disciplinary rule against appellants to be violative of the First Amendment."[2]

---

2. The decision was 5 to 4. Justice Powell, a former ABA President, wrote the principal dissent; he believed the threat to professionalism from lawyer advertising was substantial. In a separate dissent, Chief Justice Burger predicted that disciplinary authorities would be ill-equipped to regulate lawyer advertising as contemplated by the Court. Justice Rehnquist, in his dissent, said he thought *Valentine* had been decided correctly and he would not depart from it.

2.   What do lawyers have an inherent constitutional right to say in an advertisement after *Bates*? Does Jerry Harrold's ad deal with any subjects that could constitutionally be limited?

a.   After *Bates* the ABA extensively revised DR 2–101 (A) of the Model Code to prohibit any "false, fraudulent, misleading, deceptive, self-laudatory or unfair statement or claim." However, DR 2–101(B) identified 25 safe harbors, i.e., specific things lawyers could say about themselves and their practice without violating DR 2–101(A). Today, Model Rules 7.1 through 7.5 represent a significant departure from the detailed guidelines of the Model Code.

b.   Would Harrold have been subject to discipline for violating DR 2–101? Can you find the statements in his letter that fail to fit within the safe harbors of DR 2–101(B)? Now look at Model Rules 7.1 and 7.2. How do they differ in approach from that taken in the Model Code? Do they differ in substance too?

c.   Does Harrold's letter comply with the requirements of the Model Rules? For example, could the state discipline Harrold for saying that he charges "$95 per hour, win or lose, big case or small"? Could the state require him to add a disclaimer or say more about his charges, such as the fact that the client will also have to pay filing fees and other costs associated with the representation? The Supreme Court's decision in Zauderer v. Office of Disciplinary Counsel, 471 U.S. 626 (1985), upheld state bar discipline for failing to note in a newspaper advertisement that clients would be responsible for paying court filing costs regardless of the outcome of the case.

3.   Did the Supreme Court accurately predict the nature and extent of lawyer advertising?

a.   Data reported shortly after *Bates* tended to confirm that advertising led to reduced fees for legal services. For example, the Bates & O'Steen clinic charged $195 for an uncontested divorce; a year later, clients could get such a divorce in Phoenix for as little as $125.[3]

b.   Does most of the lawyer advertising you see on television facilitate the kind of price competition that the Court thought would follow from its decision? Indeed, at least on television, do you often see anything at all about lawyers' fees except for statements like: "No fee unless you recover"?

c.   Go to the Internet and see what lawyer advertising you can find. If you were looking for a lawyer in another city to represent one of your family members, would you be satisfied that you were getting the type of information needed to choose a lawyer?

d.   Do you agree with the Supreme Court's statement that advertising has no effect on lawyer professionalism? How about on the public perception of professionalism? A major empirical study found that lawyers'

---

3. Jesse Choper, Consequences of Supreme Court Decisions Upholding Individual Constitutional Rights, 83 Michigan L. Rev. 1, 167 (1984). See also, Timothy Muris & Fred S. McChesney, Advertising and the Price and Quality of Legal Services: The Case for Legal Clinics, 1979 American Bar Foundation Research J. 179.

advertisements actually have had little effect on the general public's view of lawyers. ABA Commission on Advertising, Lawyer Advertising at the Crossroads: Professional Policy Considerations (1995).[4]

4.   Are all lawyer communications considered advertising? If a newspaper reporter interviews Jerry Harrold about the rights of plaintiffs in an airplane crash, will his statements be subject to the advertising rules? Can Jerry develop a law firm website tailored to the legal questions of prospective clients involved in an airplane crash?

a.   Not all lawyer communications to the outside world are subject to Model Rules 7.1 through 7.5. Lawyers are permitted to write scholarly articles even though prospective clients may approach them because they discuss the legal issues in an area of the law. Similarly, lawyers may respond to questions from reporters even though those who see the statements about a current case may get the impression that the lawyer can achieve similar results.

b.   Lawyers who deliver presentations at legal conferences or in educational settings also are not normally said to be engaged in advertising their services. The test is whether a main purpose of the communication is to attract clients to the lawyer's services. See N.Y. State Bar Ass'n, Comm. on Prof'l Ethics Opinion 830 (2009).

c.   Model Rule 7.1's prohibition against false and misleading statements directly applies to a lawyer's communications about the lawyer or the lawyer's services. This rule clearly covers lawyer statements on law firm websites. ABA Formal Opinion 10–457 (Aug. 5, 2010) offers guidelines as to what a lawyer may include on the firm website to comply with Model Rule 7.1. Websites may include information about the lawyers, their practice areas, and the identity of their present or former clients who have given informed consent for website listing. Such information must be regularly updated so as to avoid becoming false or misleading. Websites may also include information about the law, but should avoid providing legal advice. Information about the law similarly may not be false or misleading. Therefore, it needs to be current, accurate, and not raise false expectations about the results a client can achieve. To avoid misleading clients who may rely on legal information as advice, a lawyer should consider including a disclaimer that such information can never substitute for the personal advice provided by a lawyer.

B.   WHEN LAWYER ADVERTISING BECOMES IN-PERSON SOLICITATION

1.   Is all lawyer marketing treated the same way? What is the distinction between lawyer advertising and in-person solicitation?

a.   Although the ABA sets out principles applicable to all lawyer marketing in Model Rule 7.1, it draws a sharp distinction between lawyer

---

4. The ABA report is discussed and evaluated in Ronald D. Rotunda, Professionalism, Legal Advertising, and Free Speech in the Wake of Florida Bar v. Went For It, Inc., 49 Arkansas L. Rev. 703 (1997).

advertising (Model Rule 7.2) and in-person solicitation (Model Rule 7.3). That distinction has its own important history.

b. After the Court decided *Bates* in 1977, many lawyers worried there would be few practical limits on what lawyers could do to solicit clients. The next year, the Supreme Court considered the case of a lawyer, Albert Ohralik, whose conduct the Court concluded justified discipline. The case was Ohralik v. Ohio State Bar Association, 436 U.S. 447 (1978).

One day when Ohralik was picking up his mail at the post office, he heard about an auto accident in which Carol McClintock, an 18–year–old woman, had been injured. He called Carol's parents, who said their daughter was in the hospital. They told him that Carol had been driving the family car when she was hit by an uninsured motorist. Both Carol and her passenger, Wanda Holbert, were hospitalized. When Ohralik suggested to the McClintocks that they hire a lawyer, Mrs. McClintock said that such a decision would be up to Carol.

Then, Ohralik went to the hospital, where he found Carol lying in traction. After a brief conversation about her condition, Ohralik told Carol he would represent her and asked her to sign an agreement. Carol said she would have to discuss the matter with her parents. By the time he got to her parents' home, however, they said Carol had called to say Ohralik should "go ahead" with the representation. Two days later, Ohralik returned to Carol's hospital room to have her sign a contract that provided he would receive one-third of her recovery.

In the meantime, Ohralik found Wanda Holbert's address and showed up at her home uninvited. He carried a concealed tape recorder and told Wanda that he had a "little tip" for her; the McClintocks' insurance policy contained an uninsured motorist clause which might net her a recovery of up to $12,500. He offered to represent her, as well as Carol, for a contingent fee of one-third of any recovery, and Wanda said "O.K."

Wanda's mother attempted to repudiate her daughter's oral assent the following day. She said that if they decided to sue they would consult their own lawyer, but Ohralik insisted that Wanda had entered into a binding contract. A month later Wanda ordered Ohralik to notify the insurance company that he was not her lawyer, because the company would not release a check to her until he did so. Carol also eventually fired Ohralik. Although another lawyer represented Carol in working out a settlement with the insurance company, she paid Ohralik one-third of her $12,500 recovery in settlement of his suit against her for breach of contract.

Both Carol and Wanda filed complaints with the lawyer discipline commission. The Ohio Supreme Court found that Ohralik's conduct was not constitutionally protected, and it increased the recommended sanction of a public reprimand to indefinite suspension.

Justice Powell, who was the principal dissenter the preceding year in *Bates*, wrote the Court's opinion in *Ohralik*:

"Appellant contends that his solicitation of the two young women as clients is indistinguishable, for purposes of constitutional analysis, from the advertisement in *Bates*. * * * But in-person solicitation of professional employment by a lawyer does not stand on a par with truthful advertising about the availability and terms of routine legal services, let alone with forms of speech more traditionally within the concern of the First Amendment. * * *

"In-person solicitation by a lawyer of remunerative employment is a business transaction in which speech is an essential but subordinate component. While this does not remove the speech from the protection of the First Amendment, as was held in *Bates* and *Virginia Pharmacy*, it lowers the level of appropriate judicial scrutiny.

" * * * Unlike a public advertisement, which simply provides information and leaves the recipient free to act upon it or not, in-person solicitation may exert pressure and often demands an immediate response, without providing an opportunity for comparison or reflection. The aim and effect of in-person solicitation may be to provide a one-sided presentation and to encourage speedy and perhaps uninformed decision making; there is no opportunity for intervention or counter-education by agencies of the Bar, supervisory authorities, or persons close to the solicited individual. The admonition that 'the fitting remedy for evil counsels is good ones' is of little value when the circumstances provide no opportunity for any remedy at all. * * *

" * * * [N]either of the disciplinary rules here at issue prohibited appellant from communicating information to these young women about their legal rights and the prospects of obtaining a monetary recovery, or from recommending that they obtain counsel. [They] merely prohibited him from using the information as bait with which to obtain an agreement to represent them for a fee. * * *

" * * * While entitled to some constitutional protection, appellant's conduct is subject to regulation in furtherance of important state interests. * * *

* * *

"The substantive evils of solicitation have been stated over the years in sweeping terms: stirring up litigation, assertion of fraudulent claims, debasing the legal profession, and potential harm to the solicited client in the form of overreaching, overcharging, underrepresentation, and misrepresentation. * * *

"We need not discuss or evaluate each of these interests in detail as appellant has conceded that the State has a legitimate and indeed 'compelling' interest in preventing those aspects of solicitation that involve fraud, undue influence, intimidation, overreaching, and other forms of 'vexatious conduct.' * * *

" * * * But appellant errs in assuming that the constitutional validity of the judgment below depends on proof that his conduct constituted actual overreaching or inflicted some specific injury on Wanda Holbert or Carol McClintock. * * * the rules prohibiting solicitation are prophylactic measures whose objective is the prevention of harm before it occurs. * * *

"The State's perception of the potential for harm in circumstances such as those presented in this case is well-founded. The detrimental aspects of face-to-face selling even of ordinary consumer products have been recognized and addressed by the Federal Trade Commission, and it hardly need be said that the potential for overreaching is significantly greater when a lawyer, a professional trained in the art of persuasion, personally solicits an unsophisticated, injured, or distressed lay person. * * * Although it is argued that personal solicitation is valuable because it may apprise a victim of misfortune of his or her legal rights, the very plight of that person not only makes him or her more vulnerable to influence but also may make advice all the more intrusive. Thus, under these adverse conditions the overtures of an uninvited lawyer may distress the solicited individual simply because of their obtrusiveness and the invasion of the individual's privacy, even when no other harm materializes. Under such circumstances, it is not unreasonable for the State to presume that in-person solicitation by lawyers more often than not will be injurious to the person solicited.

"The efficacy of the State's effort to prevent such harm to prospective clients would be substantially diminished if, having proved a solicitation in circumstances like those of this case, the State were required in addition to prove actual injury. * * * It therefore is not unreasonable, or violative of the Constitution, for a State to respond with what in effect is a prophylactic rule."[5]

c.   Justice Powell also wrote for the Court in a companion case, In re Primus, 436 U.S. 412 (1978). *Primus* gave constitutional protection to the conduct of a lawyer who first addressed a gathering of women about their legal rights resulting from their having been sterilized as a condition of receiving public medical assistance, and who then sent one of them a letter advising them that the ACLU was offering free legal assistance to women who had been involuntarily sterilized. The Court distinguished *Primus* from *Ohralik* on several grounds. First, it was important that the personal solicitation was in writing, which gave the recipient time for reflection. Second, the case had a political character and was a form of expression because it sought to redress an injustice done to many women. Third, the practicing lawyer who sent the letter was cooperating with the local branch of a nonprofit organization. The Court thus had two extreme cases. In one, it protected in-person contact; in the other, it did not. It left open where other cases would fall along this continuum.

---

5. The opinion was for a six-member majority. Justice Marshall concurred in the judgment, but said that even unsolicited contact from a lawyer can often provide important information and help to an accident victim whom the defendant or its insurer is already free to contact and with whom they may negotiate a settlement. Justice Rehnquist, also concurring in the judgment, continued to say that lawyer marketing was not constitutionally protected. Justice Brennan did not participate.

d.   Examine the modern-day ABA Model Rule 7.3. What you see is the product of a long series of changes, most of which responded to litigation that invalidated various restrictions that the ABA tried to impose on advertising and solicitation, first in the Model Code and later in the Model Rules. Model Rule 7.3 now limits "direct contact" with prospective clients only when pecuniary gain is a "significant motive," but the definition of direct contact now extends to "in-person, live telephone or real-time electronic contact."

2.   Do Jerry Harrold's phone calls proposing a "legal check-up" present issues under Model Rule 7.3(a)?

a.   Should the fact the calls are all to clients or former clients make the contact less problematic or more so?[6] If, in another month or so, Jerry calls back those who turned him down the first time, would his conduct violate Model Rule 7.3(b)?

b.   Is it proper for a lawyer to print color brochures extolling the law firm's virtues? Is there any question the lawyer's motive would be to bring more business to the law firm? Must the words "Advertising Material" appear on the brochure itself? Why does Model Rule 7.3(c) require that such a legend be printed on any envelope in which the lawyer mails a brochure, but not on the brochure the lawyer passes out at the local Rotary Club?

c.   May a lawyer hold seminars or make public speeches about the law and legal problems? Before the decision in Bates v. State Bar of Arizona, many states prohibited lawyers from delivering speeches to the general public unless they were sponsored by a bar association. N.Y. State Bar Ass'n, Comm. on Prof'l Ethics Opinion 830 (2009) considered whether a lawyer now may contact a lay organization to inform them about the lawyer's availability to speak on a legal topic. The opinion noted that speeches to the public should not normally be considered advertising because they are designed to educate and inform, but if the lawyer's purpose in delivering the speech is to encourage participants to retain the lawyer or the law firm, the communications must meet the requirements of Rules 7.1 and 7.3. May a lawyer represent a person who comes for advice after attending one of the programs? Would you be troubled if the lawyer distributed his or her business card at the events?

3.   When does permitted lawyer advertising become prohibited in-person solicitation? May Jerry Harrold send his proposed personal note to each of the victims of the plane crash?

a.   Contact with persons believed to have a specific current need for legal service is called "targeted direct mail." Should targeted mail be seen as more like advertising protected by *Bates* or subject to the greater regulation of in-person solicitation?

6. A 1958 study of the ABA Special Committee on the Economics of Law Practice recommended trying to get all one's clients back to the office periodically for a "routine legal checkup" as a way of raising lawyers' incomes more nearly to the incomes of doctors. Should such a concern for the lawyer's income be improper in evaluating advertising for, and solicitation of, clients? Can such issues ever be wholly ignored?

b.   Matter of Von Wiegen, 470 N.E.2d 838 (N.Y.1984), saw targeted mailing as advertising. In-person solicitation "permits the exertion of subtle pressure and often demands an immediate response," the court said, while targeted direct mail gives the recipient time to reflect about—or indeed ignore—the offer of services and "the process of decision-making may actually be aided by information contained in the mailing." 470 N.E.2d at 841.

c.   Not all states agreed, and the Court resolved the issue by invalidating a state rule that banned targeted direct mail. In Shapero v. Kentucky Bar Association, 486 U.S. 466 (1988), Mr. Shapero had applied to the state attorney general's advertising commission for approval of a letter he planned to send to persons against whom he believed foreclosure suits had been filed. The commission did not find the letter false or misleading, but it cited a Kentucky Supreme Court rule that prohibited sending letters "precipitated by a specific event or occurrence involving or related to the addressee" rather than to the public generally.

The Supreme Court held that such a blanket ban was unconstitutional. The lawyer clearly could have published his truthful letter in a newspaper or mailed it in bulk throughout the community, the Court said. There is nothing about the constitutionality of advertising that requires that the method of distribution be inefficient. As for *Ohralik*'s concerns about "overwhelming" the targets of the letters, the Court said that whether or not letters are overwhelming has nothing to do with how randomly they are sent. Furthermore, no form of written communication presents the dangers of overreaching that *Ohralik* illustrated. "A letter, like a printed advertisement (but unlike a lawyer), can readily be put in a drawer to be considered later, ignored, or discarded." 486 U.S. at 475–76. The fact that some targeted direct mail might be abusive did not justify banning all such mail.[7]

4.   How do Internet communications fit into this analysis? If a lawyer surfs the web looking for chat rooms, for example, and then seeks to get participants to consult the lawyer for legal services, how does Model Rule 7.3(a) apply?

a.   Does "real-time electronic contact" present the same concerns about solicitation that face-to-face contact presents? Consider a lawyer's activity in (1) typing messages to prospective clients in a chat room, (2) texting a prospective client whose cell number was listed on the internet, (3) posting information about a legal issue likely to attract prospective clients in a high profile blog, or (4) creating a Facebook or Myspace profile and posting notes likely to be noticed by prospective clients. The lawyer providing truthful information in an electronic "chat room" is engaged in "real-time" contact, but no one has to respond. Quietly leaving a chat room is not considered as impolite as abruptly hanging up a phone. If anyone in a

---

7.   Justice O'Connor, joined in dissent by Chief Justice Rehnquist and Justice Scalia, was willing to reconsider all of the attorney advertising cases. Justice O'Connor said that the cases were "built on defective prem- ises and flawed reasoning." The entire ana- lytical framework, she argued, "should be reexamined." She implicitly did so in Florida Bar v. Went For It, Inc., *infra*.

chat room says he does not want to be solicited, Rule 7.3(b)(1) requires the lawyer to stop.

Should the Rules seek to ban solicitation of prospective clients through this medium? Is "real-time electronic contact" more like a letter that one can throw away, like a prerecorded telephone call, or like a live telephone call that Rule 7.3 has long treated as direct contact?

b. Philadelphia Bar Ass'n Prof. Guidance Comm. Opinion 2010–6 (June 2010) examined lawyer involvement in blogging, email, and chat room posts. It concluded that each of these forms of communication could occur in real-time, but the important test was whether the prospective client could "turn off" the lawyer's communications by not responding or logging off. Thus, blogging, email, and posts in chat rooms were not within the area of prohibited solicitations. The opinion warned lawyers not to participate in real-time voice conversations in chat rooms and to abide by the prohibitions against false and misleading statements.

c. D.C. Bar Legal Ethics Opinion No. 316 (July 2002) discussed a variety of ways lawyers operate in chat rooms. It reports one chat room in which inquirers write questions and lawyers visiting the site write answers. The lawyers often invite the questioner to call for a brief, initially free, consultation. The opinion recommends that lawyers give "legal information" on such web sites, but not "legal advice." The former "involves a discussion of legal principles, trends and considerations [such as] * * * one might give in a speech or newspaper article." The latter "involves offering recommendations tailored to the unique facts of a particular person's circumstances." Giving advice, the opinion warns, may involve the lawyer in an attorney-client relationship with someone the lawyer does not know and create obligations greater than the lawyer means to assume. Do you agree?

d. California State Bar Opinion 2004–166 stated that chat room contact with prospective fee-paying clients did not necessarily constitute improper solicitation under California Rule 1–400. The lawyer in question was a personal injury attorney who entered a chat room created for the purpose of providing emotional support for the victims and families of a recent disaster. The lawyer had conceded that she had hoped to enlist clients. The lawyer's conduct was a "communication," because she entered the chat room and identified herself as an attorney to show her "availability for professional employment," and the lawyer's pecuniary gain was a significant motive. But, the opinion said, the conduct was not a "solicitation" for purposes of Rule 1–400(B) because chat room communications occur via a computer, and thus are not "in person."

The opinion found, however, that the communication was presumptively impermissible under 1–400(D)(5), which prohibits communications transmitted in a manner involving "intrusion, coercion, duress, compulsion, intimidation, threats, or vexatious or harassing conduct." The purpose of this chat room was to support disaster victims, the opinion noted, and a lawyer should know that disaster victims are likely to be relatively less able to make careful judgments about hiring a lawyer.

C. CONTINUING ISSUES IN THE FIELD OF LAWYER ADVERTISING

1. Is it proper for a state to regulate advertising out of concern that it will increase litigation by encouraging people to bring suit who otherwise would not do so?

a. The Court gave added content to the constitutional standards in *Bates* when it decided in Zauderer v. Office of Disciplinary Counsel, 471 U.S. 626 (1985). Philip Zauderer put an advertisement in 36 Ohio newspapers offering to represent women injured by use of the Dalkon Shield Intrauterine Device (IUD). The ad included a drawing of the device and a question "Did you use this IUD?" Zauderer's ad said that his firm was representing other women in such cases and that the cases "are handled on a contingent fee basis of the amount recovered. If there is no recovery, no legal fees are owed by our clients."

b. Ohio disciplinary counsel raised concern that such advertising constituted "stirring up litigation," but the Supreme Court answered:

"That our citizens have access to their civil courts is not an evil to be regretted; rather, it is an attribute of our system of justice in which we ought to take pride. The State is not entitled to interfere with that access by denying its citizens accurate information about their legal rights. Accordingly, it is not sufficient justification for the discipline imposed on appellant that his truthful and nondeceptive advertising had a tendency to or did in fact encourage others to file lawsuits." 471 U.S. at 643.

2. Do illustrations in a lawyer's advertisement have the same constitutional protection as the text message? May the state regulate illustrations if they are "undignified"?

a. The *Zauderer* Court held the illustrations were protected speech.

"The use of illustrations or pictures in advertisements serves important communicative functions: it attracts the attention of the audience to the advertiser's message, and it may also serve to impart information directly. Accordingly, commercial illustrations are entitled to the First Amendment protections afforded verbal commercial speech: restrictions on the use of visual media of expression in advertising must survive scrutiny under the *Central Hudson* test."[8] 471 U.S. at 647.

b. It also found that the state has no valid regulatory interest in preserving the dignity of the legal profession's image.

"[A]lthough the State undoubtedly has a substantial interest in ensuring that its attorneys behave with dignity and decorum in the courtroom, we are unsure that the State's desire that attorneys maintain their dignity in their communications with the public is an

---

8. The Court's reference was to Central Hudson Gas & Elec. Corp. v. Public Service Comm'n of New York, 447 U.S. 557 (1980), which held that commercial speech could only be regulated in pursuit of a substantial government interest and by means narrowly tailored to protect that interest.

interest substantial enough to justify the abridgment of their First Amendment rights. * * * [T]he mere possibility that some members of the population might find advertising embarrassing or offensive cannot justify suppressing it. The same must hold true for advertising that some members of the bar might find beneath their dignity. * * * " 471 U.S. at 647–48.

3. Should a lawyer be entitled to make claims as to her quality? Her won-lost record? How about publishing client testimonials?

a.   In Matter of Zang, 741 P.2d 267 (Ariz.1987), cert. denied, 484 U.S. 1067 (1988), two lawyers claimed to have "a personal injury law firm" with the capability to discover facts "essential to victory in the courtroom." Each of their advertisements emphasized their thorough preparation and use of investigators. The television ads showed Mr. Zang arguing before a jury. In fact, Mr. Zang had very little trial experience and "scrupulously avoided" taking a case to trial. If a trial were ever necessary, he would refer the case to another firm. He personally had never tried a personal injury case, and he conceded in the discipline proceeding that he did not feel competent to try one. He argued that the advertisements did not say that the lawyers were good at trial; they only said the lawyers were good at *preparing for* trial. The court rejected the distinction and suspended the lawyers for 30 days. The court found the advertisement "flattering beyond the point of deception."

b.   In re Keller, 792 N.E.2d 865 (Ind.2003), involved a lawyer whose television commercial showed insurance adjusters planning to delay payments to an accident victim. One of them asks who is representing the defendant, and when he is told it is Keller & Keller, he says, "Let's settle this one." Actor Robert Vaughn then appears and says, "The insurance companies know the name Keller & Keller." The Indiana Supreme Court held that this advertisement and others that the firm used falsely implied that Keller & Keller usually obtained a favorable outcome for their clients. The court imposed a public reprimand.

c.   In re Anonymous Member of the S.C. Bar, 684 S.E.2d 560 (S.C. 2009), involved a disciplinary proceeding against a lawyer who practiced primarily in the area of personal injury and worker's compensation. In 2003, he produced and began airing a television commercial to promote his practice. The commercial said:

> "It's not your fault you were hurt on the job, but I know you're afraid to file a job injury claim. You're afraid your boss won't believe you're really hurt—or worse, that you'll be fired. We'll protect you against these threats—these accusations—and work to protect your job. I'm not an actor, I'm a lawyer. I'm [Anonymous]. Call me and we'll get you the benefits you deserve. The [Law] Firm."

The Supreme Court of South Carolina held that the Office of Disciplinary Counsel failed to prove a violation of the state version of Model Rule

7.1. First, no evidence showed that a member of the public was misled by the ad. Further, the text of the advertisement did not contain material misrepresentations and did not create any unjustified expectations. The respondent attorney truthfully said that he would work to protect the client's job, and that the statement simply demonstrated his intention to act as an advocate for the client and utilize all means to protect the job, including statutory provisions which provide liability for employers who retaliate against employees who file worker's compensation claims.

d.   Comment 3 to Model Rule 7.1 notes that accurate statements about a lawyer's successes for other clients "may be misleading if presented so as to lead a reasonable person to form an unjustified expectation that the same results could be obtained for other clients in similar matters without reference to the specific factual and legal circumstances of each client's case." May a lawyer report a 75% acquittal rate for criminal cases that go to a jury trial? May a plaintiff's lawyer report that she has won jury verdicts of $1 million in over 90% of her cases that have gone to trial? What is potentially misleading about these statements? What problem would a lawyer encounter with an advertisement presenting a client testimonial?

4.   Would requiring a disclaimer excessively "chill" protected speech?

a.   The Court in *Zauderer* distinguished requiring disclaimers from prohibiting speech altogether. It said:

> "[There are] material differences between disclosure requirements and outright prohibitions on speech. In requiring attorneys who advertise their willingness to represent clients on a contingent-fee basis to state that the client may have to bear certain expenses even if he loses, Ohio has not attempted to prevent attorneys from conveying information to the public; it has only required them to provide somewhat more information than they might otherwise be inclined to present. * * *

> "We do not suggest that disclosure requirements do not implicate the advertiser's First Amendment rights at all. We recognize that unjustified or unduly burdensome disclosure requirements might offend the First Amendment by chilling protected commercial speech. But we hold that an advertiser's rights are adequately protected as long as disclosure requirements are reasonably related to the State's interest in preventing deception of consumers."471 U.S. at 650–51.

b.   Tillman v. Miller, 133 F.3d 1402 (11th Cir.1998), held the Georgia Workers' Compensation Truth in Advertising Act of 1995 unconstitutional. The Act required all lawyers and others involved in filing workers' compensation claims to put a large legend in their television ads saying that "willfully making a false * * * representation to obtain * * * benefits is a crime * * *." The court acknowledged that *Zauderer* permits a state to require disclaimers necessary to render an advertisement not false or misleading, but these ads were truthful. A state may not impose on a lawyer "the burden of the cost of educating the public about the criminal penalties for filing fraudulent claims." 133 F.3d at 1403–04.

c. In Mason v. The Florida Bar, 208 F.3d 952 (11th Cir.2000), the state bar sought to discipline a lawyer who publicly advertised his rating in the Martindale–Hubbell Legal Directory. The bar notified Mason that his advertisement must include a full explanation as to the meaning of the Martindale–Hubbell ratings and how the publication chooses the participating attorneys. This explanation must state "that the ratings and participation are based 'exclusively on * * * opinions expressed by * * * confidential sources' and that these publications do not undertake to rate all Florida attorneys." The lawyer's advertisement said that he was " 'AV' Rated, the Highest Rating Martindale–Hubbell National Law Directory." Specifically, the bar objected to the phrase, "highest rating." The court held that the bar was not able to prove that the public would be misled by Mason's truthful advertisement. Moreover, "the Bar is not relieved of its burden to identify a genuine threat of danger simply because it requires a disclaimer, rather than a complete ban on Mason's speech."

d. In many states, magazine publishers have seized upon the idea of publishing the ratings of the best lawyers in the locality by legal specialty. The lawyers then use such designations in their own advertising. In 2006, New Jersey Supreme Court Committee on Lawyer Advertising Opinion 39 (2006), examined the use of the designation "Super Lawyer" or "Best Lawyers in America" and found that, in contrast to Martindale–Hubbell ratings, the "Super" and "Best" designations are directed at the public and convey misleading comparative information. The publisher allegedly grants the designations after a minimal system of peer review, and the program makes its money by firms buying ads in the publication congratulating lawyers who have received the designation.

Do you agree that states should be able to prohibit use of the "Super Lawyer" designation? Do you believe the apparently insatiable public desire for comparative information can be effectively suppressed? In 2008, the New Jersey Supreme Court vacated Opinion 39 and adopted twelve standards for determining whether lawyers may advertise such designations. In re Opinion 39 of the Committee on Attorney Advertising, 961 A.2d 722 (N.J. 2008).

In 2009, the New Jersey Supreme Court amended its version of Model Rule 7.1 to make clear that lawyers may advertise information listing the designation of a "Super Lawyer" or "Best Lawyers in America." See Supreme Court of New Jersey, Notice to the Bar: Supreme Court Adopts Amendments and Official Comment to RPC 7.1 (Nov. 2, 2009). The new rule requires that "(i) the name of the comparing organization is stated, (ii) the basis for the comparison can be substantiated, and (iii) the communication includes the following disclaimer in a readily discernable manner: 'No aspect of this advertisement has been approved by the Supreme Court of New Jersey'." Does the required disclaimer go too far by casting doubt on the validity of the designation? Is the disclaimer needed to inform potential lay clients about the source of the rating authority?

5. May a lawyer use a memorable trade name or Internet web address such as "The Winning Team" or "www.suethebums.com"?

Under what circumstances may a firm name be false or misleading?

a. DR 2–102(B) of the ABA Model Code of Professional Responsibility provided:

> "A lawyer in private practice shall not practice under a trade name * * * or a name containing names other than those of one or more of the lawyers [currently or formerly] in the firm * * *."

What justification does Model Rule 7.5, Comment 1, offer for elimination of the broad prohibition? What should be the relevant concerns with respect to the names law firms use? Do you agree that even firms whose names are those of former partners in effect are using a trade name?

b. Model Rule 7.5 is largely an elaboration of Model Rule 7.1's prohibition against false and misleading statements as applied to firm names and letterhead. For example, a law firm that used the name Official Texas Child Support Enforcement Firm might confuse potential users that in some way they were contacting the division of the State Attorney General's Office that handles child support enforcement.

c. Now that lawyers can form law firms as general partnerships, limited liability partnerships, and professional corporations, all references to the firm must accurately describe the organizational status. Similarly, when a law firm creates business cards or letterhead with the names of individual lawyers, the presumption is that all lawyers are licensed to practice in the jurisdiction listed. If some lawyers are not, the business card or letterhead must so indicate in order to avoid the false and misleading prohibition. When a firm lawyer accepts a government position, the firm must stop using the lawyer's name during any period where the person is not "actively and regularly practicing with the firm." Model Rule 7.5(c).

d. Although Model Rule 7.5 is titled, "Firm Names and Letterhead," it covers all professional designations of a law firm including internet domain names. Thus, under Maryland State Bar Ethics Opinion 2004–15 (Apr. 15, 2004), the internet domain, www.marylandadoptions.us, would imply a connection with a governmental entity and thus be false and misleading. Would it be appropriate to prohibit domain names like the ones suggested in this question?

6.   Does television advertising justify special regulation?

a. Remember that *Bates* itself acknowledged that "the special problems of advertising on the electronic broadcast media will warrant special consideration." The issue became significant after Committee on Professional Ethics and Conduct of Iowa State Bar Ass'n v. Humphrey, 377 N.W.2d 643 (Iowa 1985). The Iowa Supreme Court had adopted strict limits on television advertising. The Iowa rules forbade background, visible displays, more than a single nondramatic voice, and any self-laudatory statements. The U.S. Supreme Court remanded *Humphrey* to see if Iowa believed its rules could still stand in light of *Zauderer*, and on remand, the Iowa Supreme Court again said that they could. The problems with television advertising, the Iowa court believed, are that:

"Both sight and sound are immediate and can be elusive because, for the listener or viewer at least, in a flash they are gone without a trace. Lost is the opportunity accorded to the reader of printed advertisements to pause, to restudy, and to thoughtfully consider." 377 N.W.2d at 646.

Once again there was an appeal to the U.S. Supreme Court, which surprised almost everyone by dismissing the appeal for lack of a substantial federal question, 475 U.S. 1114 (1986). Do you agree that no substantial question was presented?[9] Had the Iowa court simply articulated concerns the U.S. Supreme Court had raised as early as *Bates* and *Ohralik*?

b. Should Jerry Harrold be permitted to hire someone from the cast of *Law and Order* to say they wished they had someone like Jerry on their team? Should a lawyer buy an ad on reruns of *Boston Legal* if she wanted to emphasize her sophisticated, tough trial style, or on *Entertainment Tonight* if she wanted to imply that she had high-profile celebrity clients? The court in *Humphrey* did not think so, saying: "Electronically conveyed image-building was not a part of the information package which has been described [by the U.S. Supreme Court] as needed by the public." 377 N.W.2d at 647. Is that correct? Are most lawyer ads that you see any more than image building?

c. Office of Disciplinary Counsel v. Shane, 692 N.E.2d 571 (Ohio 1998), publicly reprimanded lawyers who used "not inaccurate" but self-laudatory claims of success in their television advertising. Former clients of the lawyers appeared before the camera saying such things as: "They really fought for me. * * * I never expected the large settlement they won for me," and "They fought for me and got me a very good judgment. * * * Take my word for it, they're the best." Do such testimonials "create unjustified expectations of similar outcomes in the future"?

d. In 2009, the New York Court of Appeals implemented a revision of its code of ethics that included several restrictions on the content of lawyer advertising. The amendments prohibited portrayals of judges, portrayals of fictitious law firms, testimonials from clients concerning still pending matters, "attention-getting techniques" that were not related to lawyer competence, and trade names or nicknames that imply an ability to get results.

Alexander v. Cahill, 598 F.3d 79 (2d Cir. 2010), involved a challenge to the New York advertising rules. The Second Circuit relied on the four-part test for constitutionality of restrictions on commercial speech in Central Hudson Gas & Elec. Corp. v. Public Serv. Comm'n of N.Y., 447 U.S. 557, 564–66 (1980). Under the test's first prong, the court found that portraying fictitious law firms was inherently misleading and thus that its restriction did not raise First Amendment concern. The rest of the content-based amendments did have First Amendment protection, so the other prongs

9. The Court was divided on this issue. Justices White, Blackmun, and Stevens would have set the case for oral argument.

had to be analyzed to determine whether the other restrictions were constitutional. The court found that the second prong was satisfied, because preventing misleading or deceptive advertising, as well protecting the image and reputation of the legal profession, are substantial state interests. Under the third prong, the regulations had to materially advance the state's stated interests, and the court found that the "rote invocation of the words 'potentially misleading' " was insufficient to meet the state's burden under this prong. The state had failed to provide evidence that the stated interests were materially advanced by the rules. The court likewise found that the content-based amendments would fail under the fourth prong, as they were blanket bans and not narrowly tailored. The court thus held that, except for the fictitious law firm prohibition, the content-based amendments were unconstitutional.

e.   Do you think it was similarly wrong for Jerry Harrold to offer to give potential clients the names of some of his past clients who can give personal testimonials about his services? What differences do you see between actually talking with a former client and seeing one on television?

D.   CONTINUING ISSUES OF IN-PERSON SOLICITATION BY LAWYERS

1.   Now, turn to the plane crash and Jerry's response to it. Is the concern that Jerry is too assertive in this context? Is the concern that a lawyer will make potential clients do something they would rather not do?

a.   Some Supreme Court authority on solicitation of clients by professionals involved accountants. In Edenfield v. Fane, 507 U.S. 761 (1993), Florida had tried to regulate CPAs' personal solicitation of business clients. The plaintiff sued for the right to make unsolicited calls to such clients and to arrange appointments to explain his expertise and lower fees. The state said that the rule against such contacts was designed both to protect consumers of accounting services against overreaching and to assure the independence of financial audits. Justice Kennedy, speaking for the Court, found the state interests "substantial in the abstract" but concluded that business clients were able to protect themselves against overreaching. In addition, the concern about a lack of audit independence is greater if businesses *cannot* turn to newcomers like Fane because then the incumbent firm could get too close to management.

b.   The state expressly relied on *Ohralik*, and the Court expressly distinguished it. The *Ohralik* "holding was narrow and depended upon certain 'unique features of in-person solicitation by lawyers' that were present in the circumstances of that case." CPAs, the Court observed, are not "trained in the art of persuasion" and clients being solicited for accounting work "are sophisticated and experienced business executives who understand well the services that a CPA offers." 507 U.S. at 774–75.

c.   Do you agree with the Court's concern that lawyers have qualities of intimidation against which clients need protection? Do you consider yourself intimidating? Are there any of your classmates against whom you think potential clients need protection?

2.   May a law firm send "investigators" to the victims' homes to leave the attorney's business cards and encourage the signing of retainers?[10]

a.   In Falanga v. State Bar of Georgia, 150 F.3d 1333 (11th Cir.1998), two lawyers challenged state restrictions on in-person, uninvited solicitation of professional employment. The lawyers tended to represent poor, uneducated persons in personal injury cases. The lawyers obtained names of potential clients by having law firm "public relations agents" contact doctors and chiropractors while other employees sifted through police reports. The lawyers then visited the potential clients and tried to persuade them to sign a retainer. The court found this conduct much more like that in *Ohralik* than that in *Edenfield*. The conduct fell "squarely within [the] category of 'ambulance chasing,'" and the bar had anecdotal evidence the public did not like unsolicited, intrusive contact from these lawyers. Thus, the court held the state had sufficiently justified its prohibitions on in-person solicitation, at least as applied to lawyers who approach "unsophisticated, injured, or distressed lay person[s]." 150 F.3d at 1347 (quoting both *Ohralik* and *Edenfield*).

b.   Under Model Rule 8.4(a), a lawyer may not violate the advertising and solicitation rules through the acts of another. May a lawyer hire a nonlawyer to hand out leaflets as relatives arrive in an airport following a mass disaster? May the nonlawyer verbally inform the arriving relatives as the leaflets are handed out that the lawyer is available for free consultations in the airport hotel?

c.   Should your law firm be permitted to write to real estate agents asking the agents to recommend your law firm to their customers? The New York Court of Appeals affirmed a finding of discipline, because the lawyer might have an incentive to find good title to assure that the referring agent received his fee. Greene v. Grievance Comm. for Ninth Judicial Dist., 429 N.E.2d 390, 395 (N.Y.1981). Do you agree? Is it the letter that should be the subject of discipline? Would the later conflict of interest be so hard to prove that the court must have a broad prophylactic rule?

d.   ABA Model Rule 7.2(b)(4) now permits lawyers to refer clients to particular real estate agents pursuant to an understanding that the real estate agents will refer customers to the lawyers, so long as the agreement is not exclusive and the lawyers fully disclose the details of the agreement to the client. If such reciprocal referral arrangements are permitted, why should lawyers not be able to ask real estate agents to make the referrals unilaterally? Note that such agreements may only be made with another lawyer or nonlawyer professional. Could a lawyer make a reciprocal referral agreement with a tow truck driver?

10.   Several courts have suspended attorneys who used such nonlawyer agents. Koden v. United States Department of Justice, 564 F.2d 228 (7th Cir.1977), and Goldman v. State Bar, 570 P.2d 463 (Cal.1977) (both decided before *Ohralik* and *Primus*), and In re Arnoff, 586 P.2d 960 (Cal.1978), and In re Teichner, 387 N.E.2d 265 (Ill.1979) (both decided later).

3.   Other circumstances in which lawyers engage in face-to-face solicitation of accident victims continue to amaze, but are all of them equally appropriate for discipline?

a.   In The Florida Bar v. Weinstein, 624 So.2d 261 (Fla.1993), the lawyer tried to solicit a brain injury victim who was still in the hospital. In Texas State Bar v. Kilpatrick, 874 S.W.2d 656 (Tex.1994), the lawyer waited until the brain-damaged victim had been transported to a nursing home, but otherwise the solicitation—and the disbarment sanction—were the same.

b.   In Norris v. Alabama State Bar, 582 So.2d 1034 (Ala.1991), a young child died after being left in a closed van in the hot sun by a day care center. Someone called the lawyer's office and told the receptionist that the family was "broke" and too poor to buy flowers for the funeral. The lawyer sent a wreath to the funeral home with his firm brochure attached and a letter inviting the family to contact him if he could be of any help. The story of his gesture got into the news and a disciplinary hearing followed. The Alabama Supreme Court acknowledged that DR 2–103 of its Code of Professional Responsibility did not precisely cover this situation, but said that Norris showed "indifference to the purpose and spirit of the rule." The court rejected Norris' reliance on *Shapero* (the flowers did not go through the mail) and suspended him for two years. Does Model Rule 7.3 require this result?

c.   Matter of Ravich, Koster, Tobin, Oleckna, Reitman & Greenstein, 715 A.2d 216 (N.J.1998), reprimanded members of a law firm a/k/a TEAM-LAW who showed up outside a Red Cross shelter on the morning after at a gas line explosion that displaced many apartment residents. TEAMLAW rented an RV, taped copies of their newspaper ad to the RV's windows, and distributed toiletries to the victims after they were interviewed by the lawyers. The New Jersey Committee on Attorney Advertising said this conduct went too far. The New Jersey Supreme Court agreed. That close to the time of the explosion, victims were "in a state of mind not conducive to making reasoned judgment about such a weighty matter as legal representation." 715 A.2d at 221. The court recognized that insurance agents were not similarly prevented from contacting the victims while they were confused and distraught, but it said the lawyers should have contented themselves with warning victims not to sign away their rights and not gone on to solicit future employment. 715 A.2d at 222.

d.   In Kentucky Bar Ass'n v. Mandello, 32 S.W.3d 763 (Ky.2000), a lawyer had written a letter recommending that a woman call for legal help. The woman's husband had died while in the hospital and some nurses, in a social setting, had told the lawyer facts suggesting that the death was due to gross negligence. The court found the lawyer's letter misleading because she did not volunteer that she was young and had no experience in medical malpractice cases. The letter also was a form of "advertising" and, the court said, the lawyer should have submitted it to the state's attorneys advertising commission for prior review. The court suspended the lawyer for six months for these mistakes.

Are potential clients better off as a result of decisions such as this? Do lawyers perform a public service by telling potential clients about the negligence of doctors and hospitals? Is the requirement that the lawyer submit an advertisement to a state agency for prior review an unconstitutional prior restraint? Do the ABA Model Rules require prior review of lawyer advertising?

4. The ABA responded to *Shapero* by revising Model Rule 7.3. In contrast, Florida prohibits lawyers for potential plaintiffs from sending any targeted direct mail within 30 days of an accident. Does the Florida rule go too far? Is it constitutional?

a. The U.S. Supreme Court considered the Florida rule in Florida Bar v. Went For It, Inc., 515 U.S. 618 (1995). The rule prohibited plaintiffs' lawyers from using targeted direct mail to contact victims and their families within 30 days following an accident or disaster, but it did not regulate similar contact by defense lawyers or insurance adjusters. The lawyers challenging the regulation relied on *Shapero*, but Justice O'Connor, the longtime dissenter in lawyer advertising cases, spoke for the Court and upheld the Florida rule. Chief Justice Rehnquist, and Justices Scalia, Thomas and Breyer joined her opinion.

First, in this case, the state's "substantial interest" justifying the regulation was "the protection of potential clients' privacy." Second, the state showed that its regulation advanced that interest "in a direct and material way" by citing a collection of newspaper editorials and a survey the bar commissioned to study citizen attitudes. "Significantly, 27% of direct-mail recipients reported that their regard for the legal profession and for the judicial process as a whole was 'lower' as a result of receiving the direct mail." 515 U.S. at 627. The Court concluded that this factual basis justified regulation of post-accident contact.

The Court distinguished *Shapero* as a case that dealt with a broad ban on targeted direct mail. That case did not justify striking down a narrower ban directed at protecting the privacy of persons who have recently suffered a traumatic event. It was not sufficient to respond that recipients of mailings could just dispose of them because mailings sent to bereaved persons inflict their pain when they were first seen, i.e., before recipients could throw them away. The majority also argued that the Florida regulation was a "reasonable fit" for the problem that the bar had identified. It was "narrowly tailored to achieve the desired objective," even if not the "least restrictive means" of addressing the concern. Other ways remain for lawyers to make themselves known to potential clients, e.g., television, newspapers, billboards, the Yellow Pages, or even non-targeted direct mail. 515 U.S. at 633–34.

b. Justice Kennedy led Justices Stevens, Souter and Ginsburg in an indignant dissent. The fact that advertising is "offensive" or "undignified" has not been enough before to justify state regulation, the dissent noted, so to say that this result followed the earlier precedents was disingenuous. The dissenters found the bar's "proof" that a problem existed to be methodologically flawed and largely anecdotal. Finally, they found the "flat ban" on direct mail contact too broad because it applied no matter how serious the accident or disaster. They found the bar's regulation self-serving and the Court's decision a "retreat" from constitutional guarantees. "[T]he State is doing nothing more * * * than manipulating the public's opinion [of lawyers] by suppressing speech that informs us how the legal system works. * * * This, of course, is censorship pure and simple." 515 U.S. at 639–40.

c.   With which opinion do you agree? Note that the ABA has not added the Florida restriction to the Model Rules. Do you think it should do so?[11]

PROBLEM 32

THE ETHICS OF REFERRAL TO A SPECIALIST

Your directory listing will say "lawyer." Your business card will call you a "member of the bar" of one or more jurisdictions. You will know, however, that you cannot competently provide all of the services that those titles suggest. No lawyer and few law firms stand ready to practice all the substantive areas of law that the modern world demands. Indeed, as a practical matter, most lawyers find it a full time job to keep their skills honed in enough areas to be able to sustain a satisfying practice. This problem asks you to think about how lawyers should be able to describe the fields in which they practice and their level of expertise in those fields. It also explores when lawyers may take a case in some other field, and how they may distribute the financial rewards from the cases that come into their office so as to provide incentives to refer cases, when necessary, to practitioners better able to handle an unfamiliar matter.

FACTS

Hector Ramirez has represented the Peron family for several years in minor matters for which he has charged minimal fees. Young Joseph Peron was recently seriously injured when a telephone company truck went out of control and into a schoolyard. The Peron family wants to file suit and has come to Ramirez for help.

Ramirez realizes that he is a competent attorney and could handle this case without obvious errors. However, he also knows that he is not experienced in personal injury work, that the medical evidence necessary to prove the case correctly will be

---

11. The New York Rules of Professional Conduct (2009) do include the Florida 30–day limit. It was upheld in Alexander v. Cahill, 598 F.3d 79 (2d Cir. 2010). The Second Circuit found that, while contact with potential clients was protected speech, the state had a substantial interest in protecting the privacy and tranquility of accident victims and their families. A 30–day prohibition of contact with victims materially advanced this interest in a narrowly tailored way, so the moratorium was a constitutionally-permissible restriction on commercial speech.

complex and that he may not be able to cross-examine the defense doctors effectively. Ramirez can see, on the other hand, that the fee this case would justify would be the largest he has ever earned and would support him while he did other, less remunerative work.

Ramirez also knows that Joe Castro is a very successful "Certified Trial Specialist." He is experienced at handling personal injury cases and will take the Peron case very seriously. Best of all, Castro has offered to pay Ramirez one-third of his own one-third fee, or $10,000, whichever is less, as a "finder's fee" for sending the case to him. If Ramirez prefers, he and Castro will "jointly" handle the case on the same financial basis. Ramirez also has met another personal injury lawyer who might do an even better job than Castro but who is so ethical that he would be shocked at being asked to share his fee with Ramirez.

QUESTIONS

A. A LAWYER'S DUTY WHEN A MATTER REQUIRES NEW SKILLS OR RAISES UNFAMILIAR ISSUES

1. Does Ramirez have an ethical obligation not to handle this case entirely by himself?

a. What are the elements of "competence" identified in ABA Model Rule of Professional Conduct 1.1? Assume that Ramirez will work hard on the matter and prepare to the best of his ability. Does Model Rule 1.1 require any more?

b. Look at Model Rule 1.1, Comments 1–4. Do they help you understand the level of legal knowledge and skill Ramirez must have before he decides not to send the Peron family to a different lawyer? Is the discussion in those Comments sufficient to guide the lawyer to an appropriate decision?

c. What distinction is Comment 1 drawing between a case in which "the required proficiency is that of a general practitioner" and one in which "expertise in a particular field of law may be required?" On which side of that line does this case fall?

2. If Ramirez believes that he can perform well enough that it is unlikely he could be successfully sued for malpractice, should that be the end of the issue of his "competence" to take on the matter?

a. There is no doubt under Rule 1.1, Comment 2, that a lawyer may take a case "of a type with which the lawyer is unfamiliar." Indeed, the rule could not be otherwise. Everyone has a "first case" of any particular type. If one could not take cases with which he or she were initially unfamiliar, how could any lawyer ever get experience?

b.   Yet in our problem, Ramirez is clearly not at ease with the freedom that minimum compliance with Model Rule 1.1 seems to give him. How would you feel in his shoes? Would you be satisfied that you would be giving your longtime clients, the Peron family, the kind of legal service they need and deserve?

B.   CALLING A LAWYER A "SPECIALIST" IN ONE OR MORE FIELDS OF PRACTICE

1.   Should the law be concerned about lawyers calling themselves specialists? Is there any question that good lawyers like Ramirez—or like you—will limit their practices primarily to litigation or to particular substantive fields?

a.   Virtually all lawyers specialize, of course, in the sense of concentrating their practice in particular areas of law. The principal question about specialization, then, is what a lawyer may tell the public about the nature of his or her practice. For many years, the answer was that the lawyer could say little or nothing, unless he or she was licensed to practice patent law or was a recognized proctor-in-admiralty, fields that had become de facto specialties because of special licensing requirements or accidents of history. See ABA Model Rule 7.4.

b.   Why is there any concern about using the term "specialist"? What does the word "specialist" convey? Would many clients assume the term has the meaning that it has in the medical profession, i.e., someone who has had additional training and separate certification by his or her professional peers?

2.   Do you agree that the term "specialist" or "specialty" is misleading? In the belief that the term "specialist" suggests special expertise, states long forbade use of that designation unless lawyers had indeed met special conditions. What conditions should a state require?

a.   For many years, states most often imitated California's plan that was put into operation in 1973.[1] Today, to become a certified specialist, California requires that a lawyer:

(1) Have practiced in the specialty field for at least 25% of the lawyer's professional time during the preceding three years;

(2) Have performed designated tasks in the specialty field during the preceding five years;

---

1. Initially, states adopted one of two types of specialization plans: (1) board-certification of lawyer specialties, and (2) individual lawyer self-designation. The California plan and most others are board-certified specializations plans. A state bar board implements the certification process by administering the exam, examining the lawyer's application and references, and awarding the certification. Individual lawyer self-designation plans allowed lawyers to designate themselves a specialist if the lawyer met some objective criteria on years of practice in a field. Board-certification plans sought to assess and raise the level of competence of practitioners, while self-designation plans allowed those who focused in an area to refer to themselves as specialists. Today, most plans are based upon the board-certified model.

(3) Have completed at least 45 hours of approved education in the specialty field during the preceding three years;

(4) Pass an independent examination in the specialty field; and

(5) Submit references who can attest to the lawyer's proficiency in the field.

Recertification is required every five years and comparable criteria are applied in the recertification decision.[2]

b. Peel v. Attorney Registration and Disciplinary Commission, 496 U.S. 91 (1990), rejected the argument that *only* state agencies can certify a lawyer. Gary Peel's letterhead said that he had been "certified as a civil trial specialist by the National Board of Trial Advocacy (NBTA)," a bona fide group of judges, academics, and practitioners established after Chief Justice Burger had complained about the general quality of U.S. trial practice. Standards required for certification included "specified experience as lead counsel in both jury and nonjury trials, participation in approved programs of continuing legal education, a demonstration of writing skills, and the successful completion of a day-long examination. Certification expires in five years unless the lawyer again demonstrates his or her continuing qualification."

Illinois censured Peel for noting his NBTA certification on two grounds. First, it said the letterhead constituted an implied claim "as to the quality of [petitioner's] legal services." Second, the state feared that potential clients might think that the NBTA was a state agency and that Peel's claim of specialty had state endorsement. The U.S. Supreme Court reversed the Illinois court. Although it could not agree on a majority opinion, five justices agreed that completely prohibiting Peel's reference to his certification was unconstitutional.

Justice Stevens, joined by Brennan, Blackmun and Kennedy, found that Peel's claim of specialty certification was "true and verifiable" and there was no evidence anyone had been deceived by the claim. The idea of an implied claim of special quality, Justice Stevens said, "confuses the distinction between statements of opinion of quality and statements of objective facts that may support an inference of quality. A lawyer's certification by NBTA is a verifiable fact, as are the predicate requirements for that certification. * * * In this case, there is no evidence that a claim of NBTA certification suggests any greater degree of professional qualification than reasonably may be inferred from an evaluation of its rigorous requirements. Much like a trademark, the strength of a certification is measured by the quality of the organization for which it stands." 496 U.S. at 101–02. Similarly, "there has been no finding that any person has associated certification with governmental action—state or federal—and there is no basis for belief that petitioner's representation generally would be so construed." 496 U.S. at 102–03.

---

2. The standards may be found at www.californiaspecialist.org

Justices Marshall and Brennan concurred in the judgment but found Peel's claim at least potentially misleading and thus subject to reasonable regulation short of the total ban that Illinois had imposed. Justice White, dissenting, agreed the claim was potentially misleading and would have required Peel to put explanations or disclaimers on his letterhead and with any other use of the specialty designation.

Dissenting Justices O'Connor, Scalia, and Chief Justice Rehnquist saw the case as "yet another example of the difficulties raised by rote application of the commercial speech doctrine in the context of state regulation of professional standards for attorneys." 496 U.S. at 119. They found Peel's claims incapable of verification by "the ordinary consumer of legal services." Even disclaimers would not be sufficient, these dissenting justices wrote, because review of their adequacy would impose an excessive regulatory burden on the states.

c.   In light of the *Peel* case, consider the present version of Model Rule 7.4(d)? Is the unstated assumption that the ABA will "accredit" all private organizations like the NBTA that should be authorized to grant certification? Is there a certain arrogance in the ABA's assumption that the Supreme Court will conclude that the ABA will always make accreditation decisions correctly?

d.   Hayes v. Elmore, 2010 WL 1407997 (W.D.N.Y.2010), involved a challenge to New York's requirement that all advertisements of a specialization by a private group, such as the NBTA, needed to be accompanied by a "prominently made" disclaimer: "The [NBTA] is not affiliated with any governmental authority. Certification is not a requirement for the practice of law in the State of New York and does not necessarily indicate greater competence than other attorneys experienced in this field of law." The plaintiff, a personal injury lawyer, argued that the "prominently made" requirement was unconstitutionally vague. The court granted the bar's motion for a summary judgment based upon a theory that this phrase was sufficiently clear to allow a person of "ordinary intelligence" to understand the requirements of the rule. Do these disclaimers effectively make certain types of advertisements impractical to use? For example, does this requirement discourage advertisements of specializations on a billboard or radio advertisement?

3. May lawyers with a specialty designation affirmatively claim that they will perform at a higher level of skill than would the average lawyer?

a.   Does a lawyer have a First Amendment right to say that she is better than other lawyers? Look back at Model Rule 7.1 and particularly Comment 3. Is a designation as a specialist a factual substantiation of a comparison with others?

b.   Is the ability to claim special skill an unmixed blessing? If the state allows a lawyer to claim that he or she is a specialist in a particular area of law, courts might impose a higher standard of performance for determining malpractice liability. See Wright v. Williams, 121 Cal.Rptr. 194, 199 (Cal.Ct.

App.1975) ("[A] lawyer holding himself out to the public and the profession as specializing in an area of the law must exercise the skill, prudence and diligence exercised by other specialists of ordinary skill and capacity specializing in the same field.").

4. Should only complex areas of law—e.g., bankruptcy and tax—be recognized as specialties, or should every area of law practice be a potential candidate?

a. The bar has never resolved that question in an entirely satisfactory way. In some states, the primary question surrounding specialty designation seems to be whether significant numbers of lawyers actually tend to limit their activities to the area. For example, trial practice is often a specialty so defined.

b. At least three kinds of collateral meanings have been given to specialization.

(i) *"Certifying"* specialists simply refers to designating certain people as having special skills and experience in an area.

(ii) *"Licensing"* specialists typically means that *only* a specialist may legally practice in an area. In such a system, if trial practice were a "licensed" specialty, Ramirez would have no choice but to refer the Peron case to a trial specialist.

(iii) *"Limiting"* specialists would say that specialists may practice *only* their specialty. In such a system, a trial specialist like Castro could not, for example, prepare a trust for his accident client to help assure proper management of the proceeds of a settlement.

c. Do you favor one of those versions of specialization over the others? Do some of them work better for more populous specialties like trial practice while others might work better for narrower fields such as international partnership taxation?

5. What other descriptions of a lawyer's areas of practice do the Model Rules allow?

a. Shortly after *Bates v. State Bar of Arizona*, the lawyer advertising case discussed in Problem 31, some states tried to limit disclosure of fields of practice to very precise categories, e.g., permitting "property law" but not "real estate." A unanimous Supreme Court held such efforts unconstitutional because they furthered no substantial public purpose. In re R.M.J., 455 U.S. 191 (1982).

b. If a lawyer is presented with an award by a bona fide bar organization (e.g., the "Crystal Gavel" awarded by the State Bar Civil Practice Section for "outstanding contributions to the law of Civil Practice in 2005") should the lawyer be permitted to advertise that fact? If a lawyer belongs to the American Law Institute, or some other bona fide, prestigious private lawyers' group, may the lawyer note that on a business card? May the lawyer so distinguish herself from other lawyers even though the state does not recognize or certify specialties?

c. May a lawyer say that she is "experienced" in a field of law, or has "15 years' experience"? Is that a surreptitious claim of specialty forbidden even if the lawyer in fact has 15 years of experience in the particular field of law? Is it an impermissible comparison with other lawyers? What should the claim of "experience" require in this context? See, e.g., N.Y. State Bar Ass'n Comm. on Professional Ethics Opinion 487 (July 15, 1978), asserting that a representation of "experience" without "further qualification implies that the lawyer's experience over the stated period has been frequent rather than merely occasional, and substantial as distinguished from casual." Does such a claim of "experience" provide useful information to potential clients?

d. In re Appeal of Hughes & Coleman, 60 S.W.3d 540 (Ky.2001), reviewed the Kentucky Bar Association's disapproval of respondents' television advertisement that contained their claim to be "injury lawyers." The Kentucky Supreme Court reversed, finding the disapproval was arbitrary because other lawyers had been allowed to call themselves "international lawyers" or even "a full-service business law firm." The bar association had argued that the respondents' ads implied the lawyers were specialists in the field of personal injury law, but the court found that the designation did not necessarily carry that implication and gave potential clients an accurate sense of the kinds of cases the firm handled.

C. PAYMENT OF A "REFERRAL FEE" IN A CASE SUCH AS THIS

1. Do you suppose it is an accident that this problem describes solo practitioners and small firm lawyers? If Ramirez were a partner in a large firm, how would he be likely to handle the Peron family's case?

a. If Ramirez were in a law firm, don't you think he would probably go down the hall to the litigation department for the help he needed? All fees earned in the matter would stay in the firm, and "credit" for compensation purposes would be awarded within the firm on bases that are completely outside the scope of professional regulation. In most firms, Ramirez would get credit for "originating" the matter.

b. The propriety of paying or receiving a referral fee—what Model Rule 1.5(e) calls a "division of a fee between lawyers who are not in the same firm"—should be seen in this context. Indeed, as you look at Model Rule 1.5(e), you will see an acceptance of practices acknowledged as appropriate within law firms, e.g., securing access to specialists and rewards for bringing in business, something that "rainmakers" in the big firms do without thinking. Look also, however, at ways in which the relation of partners within a law firm may be different from that between solo practitioners like Ramirez and Castro in our problem.

2. What has traditionally concerned lawyers about the payment of referral fees?

a. In a rebuttal to an American Trial Lawyers Association proposal defending use of above-the-table referral fees, the editors of a legal newspaper argued that the proposal "amounts to saying that a lawyer should be bribed to act ethically. For it happens to be the unambiguous rule * * * that lawyers not competent to handle cases should not handle them." The editorial continued, "if a lawyer can afford to forgo some percentage of his fee in favor of a lawyer who does no work on the case, then that lawyer * * * is charging too much." National Law Journal, Feb. 5, 1979, p. 18, col. 1. Can you suggest any responses to these arguments? Note that a minority of jurisdictions permit *pure* forwarding fees by eliminating a requirement of proportionality or joint responsibility.

b. Even if prohibiting referral payments would discourage less experienced lawyers from sending clients to more experienced ones, does allowing referral payments tend to corrupt the judgment of the referring lawyer as to who the best qualified person is to handle the case? Do some lawyers simply refer cases to the highest bidder?

c. The fee arrangement in Ohio State Bar Ass'n v. Kanter, 715 N.E.2d 1140 (Ohio 1999), illustrates a stark form of some of the concerns. Outside counsel for Glidden Company made regular payments of 30% of his legal fees to the inside counsel who referred the matters to him. "Kickbacks undermine the lawyer-client relationship and the relationship between in-house and outside counsel as well as the integrity and reputation of legal professionals," the court noted. 715 N.E.2d at 1141. "[K]ickbacks turn the careful selection of professionals into secret bidding contests and prevent attorneys from competing for legal employment in a fair and corruption-free environment." 715 N.E.2d at 1142. Do you agree with the court's assessment of the arrangement in *Kanter*? Does it follow that all referral fee arrangements are subject to similar condemnation?

d. If referral fees were unregulated, would some lawyers use television advertising to attract clients for the purpose of referring them to others instead of representing the clients themselves? Should that be a cause for concern? If a law firm refers the vast majority of its cases to outside lawyers, should it be required to disclose this fact in advertisements?

e. Would you be equally troubled if Ramirez acted as an "agent" for the Peron family in finding a lawyer? Would it be proper for Ramirez to interview tort lawyers, get "bids" on their taking the Peron child's case, and help the family decide which lawyer to retain? If so, why should it matter whether the Peron family paid Ramirez' fee or whether the winning lawyer paid it? Would Ramirez have to be a member of the bar in order to provide this service to the Perons?

3. Look at Model Rule 1.5(e)(1) and Rule 1.5, Comment 7. What does it mean to require the lawyer to "assume joint responsibility for the representation"?

a. Does assumption of joint responsibility imply assumption of malpractice liability? Why is that thought to be an important requirement?

Does it put the referral arrangement more nearly on terms equivalent to what happens in a law firm?[3]

b.   In Elane v. St. Bernard Hospital, 672 N.E.2d 820 (Ill.Ct.App.1996), a lawyer took "legal responsibility" for a referred case "as though he were the other lawyer's partner." The lawyer referred four cases to another lawyer, and then the referring lawyer became a judge. The lawyer to whom the cases were referred said that he no longer had any obligation to pay the referral fee because, as a judge, the referring lawyer was now prohibited from practicing law and could not help in any way with prosecution of the cases. Thus, it arguably would be improper to pay her the 45% of the ultimate fee that the referral agreement required. The court held that the Illinois counterpart to Model Rule 1.5(e) required only that the judge remain liable for the new lawyer's malpractice and that the Rule did not constitute a barrier to collection of the referral fee.[4]

c.   In Morris & Doherty, P.C. v. Lockwood, 672 N.W.2d 884 (Mich. App.2003), the referring lawyer became a law professor and placed her bar membership on inactive status. The law firm argued that she therefore was ineligible to receive part of an active lawyer's fee. The Michigan Court of Appeals agreed. A lawyer on inactive status is a nonlawyer for purposes of Rules 1.5(e) and 5.4(a), the court said. Forwarding a case to another lawyer constitutes engaging in "law business," something inactive lawyers may not do. Thus, the fee-sharing contract was void and unenforceable as a matter of public policy. The referring lawyer was entitled to nothing.[5]

d.   New York State Bar Ass'n Comm. on Prof'l Ethics Opinion 745 (July 18, 2001) considered whether a lawyer who is disqualified from a matter because of a conflict of interest may collect a referral fee. It advised that under New York Disciplinary Rule 2–107, each lawyer must assume joint responsibility for the representation. When a lawyer is disqualified due to a conflict of interest, he may not assume responsibility for the representation and so may not collect a fee. However, the opinion says, if the client had consented to the conflict of interest, the lawyer could collect the referral fee.

4.   In order to make the referral proper, must the lawyers tell the client what percentage of the fee the referring lawyer will receive?

a.   Model Rule 1.5, prior to 2002, did not require such disclosures. Was the former approach parallel to what a client would know in dealing with a

---

3.   Note that Rule 1.5(e) is not radical. It hearkens back to an earlier era. Canon 34 of the ABA Canons of Professional Ethics, in the Standards Supplement stated simply: "No division of fees for legal services is proper, except with another lawyer, based upon a division of services *or* responsibility." (emphasis added)

4.   The *Elane* case is criticized in Ronald D. Rotunda, Judges as Ambulance Chasers, 8 The Professional Lawyer 14 (1997).

5.   In language that should humble the many authors of state ethics opinions, the court added that: "defendant's discussion of, and comparison to, various state bar ethical opinions is not persuasive with regard to the issues presented in the present case." Ethical opinions "clearly are not binding on this Court and provide little, if any, precedential value," the court added. 672 N.W.2d at 896.

private firm? Does a law firm client usually know the intra-firm division of the fee?

b.   Restatement Third, The Law Governing Lawyers § 47(2) came out the other way and said that clients must consent to "the terms of the [fee] division." The present version of Model Rule 1.5(e)(2) now also requires that the client agree to "the share each lawyer will receive." What might be the reason for this change? Do you agree with the additional requirement?

5.   Should the provisions of Model Rule 1.5(e) be controlling in a civil suit by one lawyer against the other?

a.   Kaplan v. Pavalon & Gifford, 12 F.3d 87 (7th Cir.1993), held that an agreement to divide fees was unenforceable unless it was made in accord with the state's version of Rule 1.5(e). Even though that rule only purports to create a disciplinary standard, the court said, it also articulates the state's policy about the need for consent and a writing before such contracts will be deemed proper. Thus, a lawyer who orally promised to pay a referral fee could avoid a contract that did not comply with the rule.

Do you agree? Were the requirements of Rule 1.5(e) drafted primarily for the protection of clients? Why, then, should lawyers be able to claim the protection of those provisions? If you had been trying to protect lawyers from each other, would you have drafted Rule 1.5(e) the same way? By refusing to enforce oral agreements, is the court making sure that agreements are put in writing so that the courts can better police them?

b.   In Chambers v. Kay, 56 P.3d 645 (Cal.2002), Chambers acted as co-counsel with Kay in a sexual harassment case on behalf of Kay's client. When the lawyers had a disagreement, Kay removed Chambers from the case but promised to pay him a portion of the recovery. Neither lawyer, however, told the client about the fee arrangement or received her written consent to the referral as required by California Rule 2–200(A)(1). "Chambers, in effect seeks the aid of this court in dividing the fees of a client without satisfaction of the rule's written consent requirement," the court said. "We decline such aid." 56 P.3d at 654. The court concluded that both lawyers had violated Rule 2–200(A)(1) and Chambers did not deserve the aid of the court in avoiding a problem he had created for himself. Do you agree?[6]

D.   ALTERNATIVES TO REFERRAL FEES DESIGNED TO ACHIEVE SIMILAR BENEFITS

1.   Could Ramirez avoid the referral issue by "associating" with Castro in handling the case, i.e., by creating a joint venture in which each lawyer would contribute some services?

a.   Would Ramirez retain significant obligations in an association that he could avoid by referral? May the fee allocation in an association relationship be different in amount than a traditional "finder's fee"?

---

6. Later, Huskinson & Brown, LLP v. Wolf, 84 P.3d 379 (Cal.2004), held that the California ethics rule requiring a written fee sharing agreement and client consent did not bar recovery by the lawyer in *quantum meruit*.

b.   Would such an arrangement inevitably be a sham? To the contrary, could Ramirez serve an important function by remaining involved in the case as an active co-counsel or even by acting as lead counsel and hiring help for the trial itself? Do we sometimes overemphasize trial experience, given that only 5% or so of cases go to trial? May the Peron family's confidence in Ramirez and his own desire to see them well served be among the most important factors in assuring that the Perons will get a satisfactory resolution of their case?

2.   Could Ramirez avoid all referral fee problems by saying to Castro, for example, "I'll send you this big case if you'll refer some good clients my way"?

a.   New Jersey Supreme Court Advisory Opinion No. 681 (July 17, 1995), considered a proposed affiliation between a New Jersey and a London firm whereby each would refer clients to the other and share fees in those cases. The opinion condemned the arrangement. Even though it made business sense and might help clients of each firm find qualified counsel in the other country, the opinion said it would violate what is now Model Rule 7.2(b). Do you agree that the arrangement would be "giving * * * value to a person for recommending the lawyer's services"? Do you see any other reasonable objections to such an arrangement?

b.   Look at ABA Model Rule 7.2(b)(4) and Comment 8. This new provision is designed to allow informal "networks" among solo practitioners and small firms. Is the development of such networks a positive one for both lawyers and clients? Is it likely to allow lawyers to deliver "full service" to their clients without being absorbed into a larger law firm? How should bar authorities interpret the requirement that such referral agreements not be exclusive? Should this hinge on whether the lawyers offer clients more than one referral option or should we examine whether all business referrals flow exclusively between two firms?

3.   May lawyers make payments analogous to referral fees to nonlawyers, assuming that the client does not object? Would such arrangements always be corrupt or can you see ways where they are another way to deliver a range of services to clients?

a.   In Florida Bar v. Barrett, 897 So.2d 1269 (Fla.2005), attorney Barrett hired Cooper, an ordained pastor, to find clients for Barrett. To secure Cooper's access to hospital emergency rooms, Barrett paid for his training as a hospital chaplain. In one instance, Cooper dressed in pastoral clothing and "counseled" a family whose son was in intensive care to retain Barrett. For such referrals, Barrett paid Cooper large bonuses said to be for "pastoral services" to clients. The court acknowledged that solicitation cases often no longer result in significant sanctions, but this case involved both solicitation and lying to hospital staff. The court disbarred Barrett. Does this case help you understand the bar's traditional condemnation of such practices?

b.   In re Cohn, 139 N.E.2d 301 (Ill.1956), concerned a lawyer's "investigator" who would find out about accidents, call upon the injured person, and recommend retaining the respondent. The Illinois Supreme Court found acceptance of cases from this source "reprehensible" and said it "deserves nothing but contempt in the eyes of judges, lawyers and the public generally." 139 N.E.2d at 303.

In his opinion specially concurring, however, Justice Bristow was unwilling to be wholly critical, saying: "Today, * * * [i]t is a veritable scramble between the claim agent and the 'chaser' to see which one can reach an injured claimant first. The net result of a timely arrival of the solicitor is that the claimant will eventually receive an amount that a court and jury deems adequate and just. * * * [S]olicitation of personal injury cases is the natural reflex or defensive response to the unfair methods of claim adjusters, just as naturally as the human organism elaborates its own antibodies to combat disease." 139 N.E.2d at 305–06.

With which opinion do you agree?

c.   Illinois State Bar Ass'n Comm. on Prof'l Ethics Opinion 01–05 (2002) asked whether a law firm could create a subsidiary to handle only mediation cases and use it to pay referral fees to nonlawyers. The law firm both rendered traditional legal services and conducted mediations. It proposed to form a subsidiary that would be owned by most or all of the law firm shareholders, share the same facilities and staff as the law firm, but generate profits only through lawyers' mediation activities. That second firm would then accept clients, some referred by an accounting firm, in return for a 20% referral fee. The committee found that creation of a mediation subsidiary controlled entirely by lawyers was a "sham designed only to circumvent the applicable rules." The committee found that state rules against fee sharing with nonlawyers applied, and it prohibited the proposed arrangement.

Do you agree that the issue is that simple? Is there reason to prohibit payment to a financial planner who refers a client to the lawyer to implement provisions of the client's financial plan? Are referrals among professionals, each trying to meet part of a client's needs, different from payments to hospital staff to distribute a lawyer's cards to victims of traffic accidents?

d.   In "We the People" Paralegal Services, L.L.C. v. Watley, 766 So.2d 744 (La.App.2000), a firm of paralegals orally contracted with a law firm to perform paralegal services for a percentage of any legal fee recovered in the cases. When the law firm accepted the services but refused to pay, the paralegals sued. The court held that a contract to share fees with a nonlawyer is null and void, but the services performed in this case were not those of a "runner" or someone engaged in unauthorized practice. Thus, the court permitted the paralegals to proceed on a theory of unjust enrichment, not for a percentage of the fees, but for the fair value of their services.

If a law firm employs the paralegals instead of the paralegals being part of a different firm composed entirely of nonlawyers, does Model Rule 5.4(a) allow the lawyers to share fees with them? Model Rule 5.4(a)(3) permits law firms to include its nonlawyer employees in a compensation plan based on profit sharing. Is there any reason to treat fee sharing and profit sharing differently in this context?

4.   Should sharing legal fees with a recognized lawyer referral service be prohibited? Or, is it a reasonable way to meet client needs?

a.   In ACLU/Eastern Missouri Fund v. Miller, 803 S.W.2d 592 (Mo. 1991), an ACLU staff attorney had agreed that any attorney's fees recovered in actions he filed would be turned over to the ACLU. On behalf of two clients, Miller and a volunteer lawyer pursued and won a civil rights action against the city of St. Louis. The court awarded the client fees totaling $8,090 for the work done by Miller, who by this time had resigned from the ACLU. The defendant paid the fees to Miller, who then refused to turn the fee over to the ACLU, asserting that to do so would violate the Missouri version of Model Rule 5.4(a). The court agreed with Miller, although there was a strong dissent arguing that Miller had been paid by the ACLU for his work and was now getting paid twice.

Do you agree with the court that the ACLU is the functional equivalent of an ambulance driver who puts a lawyer's card on a stretcher and wants to be paid for doing so? Would any significant principle of ethical conduct be violated by requiring Miller to keep the promise he made to the ACLU? The ABA Standing Committee on Ethics and Professional Responsibility did not believe any such principle existed and rejected this reading of Model Rule 5.4(a) in ABA Formal Opinion 93–374 (June 7, 1993).

b.   Richards v. SSM Health Care, 724 N.E.2d 975 (Ill.App.2000), involved sharing fees with a bar-sponsored nonprofit lawyer referral service. The West Suburban Bar Association near Chicago charges potential clients $25 for a referral to a lawyer but demands that lawyers remit to it up to 25% of the fee they receive from referred clients. Lawyer Dahlgren refused to pay, citing the Illinois versions of Model Rules 1.5(e) and 5.4(a), and noting that the referral service did not agree to assume joint responsibility for the matter. The court rejected the argument. The controlling rule was what is now Model Rule 7.2(b)(2). Some 117 state and local bar associations are supported by percentage referral fees, the court noted. Referral services help potential clients make informed decisions, the court said, and public policy favors continuing financial support of their existence.

c.   Examine Model Rule 5.4(a)(4). The ABA has clearly come down in favor of sharing fees with the organizations involved in the cases described in the two previous notes. Do you agree that approach is the wisest one to take?

d.   If a law firm may share court-awarded legal fees with a nonprofit organization, why do the rules prohibit sharing a percentage of the fees with a for-profit firm of nonlawyers? Do lawyers usually view making a profit as a bad thing?

PROBLEM 33

ROLES AND RESPONSIBILITIES IN A MODERN LAW FIRM

Although a majority of American lawyers do not work for large law firms, in popular culture and the minds of many students, such firms define where high-quality lawyering is done. Working at a major firm is often seen as both a way to learn how the best lawyers practice and a way to pay off student loans. Increasingly, however, lawyers are coming to question both ideas. This problem examines some issues about practice in modern firms. First, it considers the obligations of supervisory lawyers and those that they supervise. Next, it examines the rights of a lawyer who reports an ethical violation of someone else in the practice organization. Third, it asks whether lawyers are entitled to the same statutory and other legal rights to fair treatment in employment as are employees generally. Finally, it considers concerns expressed about life in many large law firms and some ideas about overcoming those concerns.

FACTS

Smart & Howe is one of the most successful new firms in its region of the country. It regularly reports one of the highest earnings per partner among firms under 300 lawyers in *The American Lawyer*'s annual surveys, and its starting salary of $150,000 per year is among the region's highest. So is its minimum annual billing requirement for associates of 2,500 hours per year.

Sarah Smart is co-managing partner of Smart & Howe, and she is in charge of the firm's real estate group. Smart assigns work to the sixteen associates who work with her, evaluates their work, and signs all legal opinions and other documents prepared by her group in the name of the firm.

One of her associates, Arnie Able, has billed over 3,500 hours in each of his first two years, over 30% more than any other associate in the real estate group. Smart was surprised that Able could report such billings, because he seemed to leave at five o'clock most days and did not appear in the office on weekends. Clients had not complained, however, and Smart had appreciated the boost in her own compensation she got because she supervised such a productive associate. Indeed, when a middle-aged partner, Ted Truthful, confronted Smart with concrete evidence that Able was billing fictitious hours, Smart's only response was to try to force Truthful to retire and to deny him a promised pension.

Recently, Smart & Howe has noticed that associates stay with the firm an average of 2.8 years and then most move to less stressful work environments. Andy Howe, the other co-managing partner, has proposed creation of a part-time program under which associates could elect to be paid 80% of a normal salary for those of their age and experience, but would have a minimum annual billing requirement of only 2,000 hours per year. Sarah Smart resists that idea, believing few associates would choose that alternative and saying, "We don't want to retain the kind of lawyer who will not give client needs the top priority in his or her life."

QUESTIONS

A. THE OBLIGATIONS OF SUPERVISORY LAWYERS AND THOSE THEY SUPERVISE

1. Is there any doubt that Arnie Able is subject to discipline for billing hours he never worked?

a. How would you characterize his conduct for purposes of imposing discipline? Is billing more than on the basis agreed per se "unreasonable" under Model Rule 1.5(a)? Does it constitute "dishonesty" under Model Rule 8.4(c)?

b. In Matter of Disciplinary Proceeding Against Haskell, 962 P.2d 813 (Wash.1998), the evidence showed that a lawyer had billed at his own hourly rate for work done by lower paid associates. He traveled first class in violation of his client's direction and billed for the higher fares, but he had his travel agent give him bills showing the tickets were for coach class. Finally, while he was having a cabin built for himself in Idaho, he had his secretary "bury" phone and blueprint charges for the work in bills sent to clients. The court suspended the lawyer for two years.

2. What was Smart's responsibility to assure that Able did not engage in dishonest billing?

a. Did Smart meet her responsibilities under Model Rule 5.1 in this case? Do her responsibilities flow from her role as co-managing partner or as head of the real estate group? Are her duties as a "supervisor" different from those she has as a firm manager? As far as we know, Smart did not "order" the overbilling or even "ratify" it, but does that mean she is off the hook? Did she "know of the conduct at a time when its consequences [could] be avoided" but fail "to take reasonable remedial action"? Should she be deemed to have known of the overbilling even if she asserts now that she lacked actual knowledge of it? What remedial action should she take? Is it ever too late to return overbilled fees to a present or former client?

b. Attorney Grievance Comm. of Maryland v. Ficker, 706 A.2d 1045 (Md.1998), imposed an indefinite suspension on a lawyer, in part for a failure to supervise associates. The respondent had a high-volume practice—750 to 850 cases per year—including many serious drunk driving cases. He had virtually no case management system and associates rarely stayed with him long enough to have any experience in his field of practice. The court found that he regularly assigned cases to associates the day before trial. The lawyers typically would not have met the clients and they often had not even read the file. "Ficker essentially operated his practice like a taxicab company," the court found. "What he apparently, and inexcusably, failed to realize is that * * * legal services cannot routinely be dispensed on that basis with an acceptable degree of competence." 706 A.2d at 1054. The court found violations of the state version of Model Rules 1.1, 5.1, 5.3 and 8.4(d). The facts are extreme, but they show that the duty to supervise can have teeth.

c.   In re Cohen, 847 A.2d 1162 (D.C.2004), suspended Cohen for 30 days for his failure to supervise an associate who ended up representing conflicting interests. The firm was retained to register a trademark for a client. In the course of events, the two individuals interested in obtaining the registration had disagreements; the firm (which ended up representing both) "took actions favoring one without notifying the other or safeguarding his interests." This happened because Cohen had failed to supervise the work of an associate in the firm (who happened to be his son).

d.   Notice that Model Rule 5.3 imposes similar obligations on all lawyers—potentially even new lawyers—who supervise nonlawyer assistants. In re Bailey, 821 A.2d 851 (Del.2003) (per curiam), suspended Bailey, the managing partner of Bailey & Wetzel, for six months and one day. He was the partner responsible for maintaining firm books and records and paying taxes. When an auditor for the Lawyers' Fund for Client Protection audited the firm's books and records, he discovered, inter alia, that the firm had taken money from client trust accounts to pay personal debts, failed to timely file and pay certain taxes, and overdrawn firm accounts. Bailey conceded that these acts violated Rules 1.15 and 8.4, but he testified that the firm's bookkeeper had made the transfers without Bailey's consent or knowledge. Bailey expressed remorse, but the court held that Bailey, as managing partner, had a duty to properly supervise his employees, including his bookkeeper. "A lawyer who accepts responsibility for the administrative operations of a law firm stands in a position of trust vis-à-vis other lawyers and employees of the firm. The managing partner must discharge those responsibilities faithfully and diligently." 821 A.2d at 864–65. Bailey breached this duty by failing to exercise "even a modicum of diligence."

e.   In re Wilkinson, 805 So.2d 142 (La.2002), involved Wilkinson's employment of a law school graduate, Paul Stewart, who had taken the bar examination but had not yet been admitted. When a client approached Wilkinson about handling an estate matter, Wilkinson referred her to Stewart. He explained that Stewart was not yet licensed, but said he could handle preliminary aspects of the case before he was admitted to the bar. Wilkinson also instructed Stewart not to give any legal advice to the client, but when the client needed to know what to do, Stewart offered legal advice that resulted in significant losses to the estate. Moreover, when Stewart left the firm, Wilkinson did not even look at the file for several months. The court held that Wilkinson had violated both Rules 5.1(b) and 5.3(b) as a result of his lack of supervision of Stewart. He received a 60–day suspension from practice as a result of that inattention.

3.   Is Andy Howe, Sarah Smart's co-managing partner, equally responsible for Able's overbilling?

a. What does Model Rule 5.1(a) mean when it requires each partner in a law firm—and each lawyer with "comparable managerial authority"—to "make reasonable efforts to ensure that the firm has in effect measures giving reasonable assurance" that each lawyer in the firm is living up to applicable professional standards. Are law firms required to hire "time sheet police" to prevent what Able did?

b. In re Fonte, 905 N.Y.S.2d 173 (N.Y.App.Div.2010), relied upon Rule 5.1 to suspend a partner for three years for failing to discover and prevent another partner's fraud that resulted in a theft of over $17 million from firm accounts. The grievance committee charged the partner with (1) failing to supervise the accounts and failing to discover the fraud at a time when the loss could be prevented or mitigated, (2) failing to promptly pay third parties amounts owed to them when the law firm checks bounced, and (3) failing adequately to supervise his partner's conduct to be sure that he complied with the ethics rules. The court agreed with the grievance committee that the respondent "ignored multiple warning signs and blatantly apparent indicators of criminality which could have forestalled such a massive escrow fraud."

c. Attorney Grievance Commission v. Kimmel, 955 A.2d 269 (Md. 2008), examined the conduct of a managing partner of a well-known Pennsylvania law firm who opened a Maryland office to handle "Lemon Law" cases. The law firm staffed the office with an associate who was expected to file 15 cases a week and to settle a sufficient number of cases to generate $10,000 a week in legal fees. The office eventually had 500 files and 100 active cases, and the associate failed to log some of the new cases into the tickler system. Ultimately, the court dismissed 47 cases filed by the associate. In Maryland, the managing partner was suspended for 90 days for his failure to supervise the new office. A firm's "executive lawyers [must] design and implement supervisory procedures that anticipate the ethical demands specific to the practice they lead." On the same facts, the New York bar authorities imposed only a censure. Matter of Kimmel, 872 N.Y.S.2d 922 (N.Y.App.Div. 2009). The managing lawyers showed sincere remorse for the failure to supervise and took steps that it would not happen again.

d. Does the duty to supervise a lawyer extend to lawyers outside your own law firm? Whalen v. DeGraff, Foy, Conway, et al., 863 N.Y.S.2d 100 (N.Y.App.Div. 2008), found that a New York firm that had secured a $1.2 million judgment against a Florida defendant was responsible in malpractice for the conduct of the Florida law firm hired to obtain a satisfaction of the judgment. The New York law firm, not the client, hired the Florida law firm; thus, it was responsible for assuring that the Florida lawyers filed the appropriate claims to protect the judgment.

e. Would it be enough for Howe to show that the firm's orientation video contains a two-minute section in which Howe tells the new lawyers that the firm expects them to bill honestly? What more, if anything, should Model Rule 5.1(a) require? Would failure to put such a statement in the orientation program constitute a per se violation of Model Rule 5.1(a)?

4. Would Able's liability be different if overbilling was not his idea; he was just following orders?

a. Suppose Sarah Smart had said to Able, "That checklist that you took 40 hours to prepare lets you do complex real estate transactions in half the time it takes lawyers at other firms. There is no reason our current clients should pay less for our superior work; bill every client an extra 40 hours for preparation of the checklist as if we had prepared it just for them." Would following Smart's direction give Able a defense to discipline?

b. Is the answer given in Model Rule 5.2(a) completely clear? Does billing clients for valuable work, but work that the firm has previously done, raise an "arguable question of professional duty" under Model Rules 1.5 and 8.4 and make Able immune from discipline under Model Rule 5.2(b)?

c. ABA Formal Opinion 93–379 (Dec. 6, 1993) opines that billing for recycled work as if it had been done anew violates Model Rule 1.5. Should the disciplinary authorities assume that young associates know the substance of all ABA ethics opinions? Should the ethics rules require young associates to investigate the propriety of all directions by superiors, even if violating those directions could get them fired?

d. Texas Comm. on Prof'l Ethics, Opinion 523 (1997), examined the extent to which the partners have a duty to inform a former associate that they had complied with the ethics rules. An associate working on a client tax matter discovered that in a prior year a lawyer in the firm had negligently advised the client and this resulted in the filing of inaccurate tax returns. The associate resigned from the firm but asked the partners to inform him that they had told the client about the negligent advice. The partners refused and the associate filed a request for an ethics opinion. The Committee concluded that the associate had a right to receive written confirmation that the firm informed the client of the firm's negligent advice. "If the partners or shareholders refuse to give a written assurance, the former associate is obligated to inform the client about the negligent representation."

e. What is the principled basis for Model Rule 5.2(b), if any? Once a lawyer takes an oath to live up to professional standards, why should he or she be able to defend by saying "the devil made me do it"?

5. Regardless of individual discipline that the law may impose, should the Smart & Howe law firm be subject to professional discipline as a law firm for the conduct of Arnie Able?

a. Will Smart & Howe be liable if they are sued by clients who were overbilled? Wasn't the firm the principal beneficiary of Able's misconduct? If firms qua firms can be forced to bear civil liability, why don't we subject firms to professional discipline as well?

b. As you may remember from Problem 2, New York is the first jurisdiction to make a law firm itself subject to professional discipline. See N.Y. Rules of Prof'l Conduct, Rule 8.4. New York Rule 5.1(a) imposes a duty upon law firms "to ensure that other lawyers in the law firm conform to these Rules." What form should discipline of a law firm take in a case like this? Could the disciplinary authorities disbar a law firm, i.e., put it out of business, for example? Could the authorities publicly censure it?

6. In recent years, law firms have began to outsource legal work to law firms outside of the United States. What are a law firm's responsibilities with respect to supervising the employees of the outsourcing entity?

a. The perceived benefits of outsourcing include lower labor costs and the ability to work on client matters 24 hours a day given the time differences. Some law firms have formed subsidiaries often referred to as captive outsourcing centers that only work on one law firm's cases. But other law firms use outsourcing firms that perform work for many different law firms and in-house legal departments. At first, the outsourced work was a kind normally done by paralegals and other nonlawyers, such as document review. However, more recently, outsourcing firms are offering legal services directed at American lawyers.

b. Ass'n of the Bar of the City of New York, Committee on Professional and Judicial Ethics, Formal Opinion 2006–3 (Aug. 2006), says that outsourcing work to an Indian firm is fine as long as the New York law firm (1) assumes responsibility for the work and assures its quality, (2) supervises the Indian nonlawyers in "vigilant and creative" ways such as interviewing them and conducting reference checks, (3) sees that confidential information of the client is protected, (4) checks for conflicts the Indian firm might have, (5) bills only the direct cost to the client, and (6) obtains advance consent from the client to outsource, particularly if the role of the Indian firm is likely to be substantial.

c. ABA Formal Opinion 08–451 (Aug. 5, 2008) offers similar guidance. Lawyers who outsource legal work must "ensure that tasks delegated to individuals who are competent to perform them, and then to oversee the executive of the project adequately and appropriately." The opinion requires that lawyers perform background checks on the lawyers doing the work. If the outsourced work is of a sensitive nature, the lawyers should investigate the security of the entity performing the work. If confidential information is released to individuals outside of the law firm, the lawyers must obtain the clients' consent to the disclosure. But, the ABA opinion does not seem to require client consent in every outsourcing situation.

B.   The rights of a lawyer who refuses to violate the law

1. If a lawyer refuses a direction to do something illegal, does that lawyer have any protection against being fired for his or her courage?

a. The issue first arose in a setting involving an in-house corporate counsel who sued for wrongful discharge in Herbster v. North American Co. for Life and Health Insurance, 501 N.E.2d 343 (Ill.App.1986), cert. denied, 484 U.S. 850 (1987). The chief legal officer of North American Insurance alleged that the company had fired him for refusing to destroy or remove documents that tended to show the company's fraud in its sale of flexible annuities and that a federal court had ordered to be turned over. The Illinois court assumed this allegation was true but still held the lawyer had no recourse for his discharge. The court conceded that "at will" employees typically can sue for retaliatory discharge if the discharge contravenes a clearly mandated public policy, but it said that lawyers are different. "The attorney is placed in the unique position of maintaining a close relationship with a client where the attorney receives * * * information that otherwise would not be divulged to intimate friends," the court said. 501 N.E.2d at 346. Because of the sensitive nature of this relationship, a private client always has the right to change lawyers for any reason. The court was unwilling to create an exception to that principle, even where the client wanted the lawyer to violate the law.

b. In Balla v. Gambro, Inc., 584 N.E.2d 104 (Ill.1991), the Illinois Supreme Court extended this holding. The former house counsel, Balla, had threatened to reveal that his employer's kidney dialysis devices did not comply with FDA regulations and presented a danger to patients' lives. When the company fired him for his insubordination, the Illinois Supreme Court reached the same result as it had in *Herbster*. Its reasoning was ingenious. The ethics rules already *require* the lawyer to report the employer's wrongdoing, the court said. Thus, to say the employer could not fire him for doing so would discourage the employer from consulting the lawyer about the issue in the first place and impose the cost of ethical compliance on the client instead of the lawyer. "Since the relationship between the plaintiff and the defendant company required an atmosphere of continued mutual trust, the breakdown of that trust allowed the defendant to discharge the plaintiff without liability." 584 N.E.2d at 111.[1]

2. Do these results make sense to you? Should saying that a client may fire a lawyer for no reason be the same as saying that the client may fire the lawyer for a wrong reason, i.e., for a failure to violate the law?

a. Even if the lawyer's actions would rupture the trust relationship between the lawyer and the officers of the client, does it follow that the entity itself would not benefit from the lawyer's action? Would the relief for wrongful discharge have to be reinstatement? How about damages?

b. The California Supreme Court refused to follow the Illinois approach in General Dynamics Corp. v. Superior Court, 876 P.2d 487 (Cal. 1994). This time, the lawyer allegedly had given his employer advice it did not want to hear about violations of the Fair Labor Standards Act and the alleged bugging of the office of the chief of security. Although it reaffirmed

---

1. See also, Ausman v. Arthur Andersen, LLP, 810 N.E.2d 566 (Ill.App.2004). In-house counsel for an accounting firm sued the firm for retaliatory discharge and breach of contract, alleging that it fired her for insisting that proposed business transactions be subjected to independent review for compliance with SEC regulations. Following *Bal-la*, the court held that in-house counsel could not bring a retaliatory discharge claim, because allowing such a claim would have a "chilling effect" on the communications between the employer/client and the lawyer. The Illinois Supreme Court declined to review the case. 823 N.E.2d 962 (Ill.2004).

the general rule that a private client in a single case may fire its lawyer for any reason, the court believed that a lawyer working for a corporate employer was in a different position. The private lawyer with many clients can lose one without being unemployed; a fired in-house counsel, by contrast, loses everything. By "providing the employee with a remedy in tort damages for resisting socially damaging organizational conduct, the courts mitigate the otherwise considerable economic and cultural pressures on the individual employee to silently conform." 876 P.2d at 501. The court offered two qualifications. First, the values being protected by the lawyer must be grounded in the Rules of Professional Conduct or specific statutes. Second, "the in-house attorney who publicly exposes the client's secrets will usually find no sanctuary in the courts." 876 P.2d at 503.

c.   In Kachmar v. SunGard Data Systems, Inc., 109 F.3d 173 (3d Cir.1997), the lawyer had objected to the company's handling of Equal Employment Opportunity (EEO) matters and she alleged her dismissal was based on her "campaigning on women's issues." The Third Circuit reinstated her complaint, agreeing that the fact she was a lawyer did not cause her to lose the right to sue for retaliatory discharge. The company argued such a suit would require disclosure of confidential information beyond that permitted by Model Rule 1.6(b)(5). The court agreed that protection of material protected by the attorney-client privilege was an important consideration, but it left it up to the district judge to use protective orders, in camera review, and similar devices to protect such privileged material from public disclosure.

d.   In Fox Searchlight Pictures, Inc. v. Paladino, 106 Cal.Rptr.2d 906 (Cal.Ct.App.2001), the employer, Fox, sued Paladino, one of its former in-house attorneys, when it learned that she intended to file a wrongful discharge action. Paladino's lawyers had sent Fox a copy of Paladino's draft complaint for wrongful discharge and had asked Fox to let the lawyers know if it contained privileged information before they filed the complaint. Fox responded with this suit alleging that Paladino improperly disclosed confidential company information when she explained her concerns to her lawyers in the first place. Fox also tried to disqualify her lawyers on the grounds that she had exposed them to the confidential information. This court refused, because Fox's view would effectively bar any suit by an in-house counsel against a former employer even if the lawyer represented herself. The court said, quoting another case: "Where privileged information goes to the heart of the claim, fundamental fairness requires that it be disclosed for the litigation to proceed." The court reiterated, however, that Paladino may not disclose the confidential information any more publicly than the litigation requires.

e.   ABA Formal Opinion 01–424 (Sept. 22, 2001) affirms that the Model Rules do not prohibit in-house lawyers from filing a suit for retaliatory discharge if the lawyers were discharged for complying with ethical obligations. The opinion requires that in doing so, the lawyer not use information relating to the former representation that is protected by Model Rule 1.9(c) except as permitted by Model Rules 1.6(b)(5) and 3.3.

The opinion holds that a suit for retaliatory discharge is a "claim" within the meaning of Model Rule 1.6(b)(5), but it reminds lawyers that Comment 14 to Model Rule 1.6 requires that disclosures be "no greater than the lawyer reasonably believes necessary to accomplish the purpose" and that "appropriate protective orders or other arrangements should be sought by the lawyer to the fullest extent practicable."

3. The important question for most young lawyers is how all this should apply to an associate's discharge by a law firm for reporting an ethical violation. Is discharge by a law firm subject to the same principles as discharge by a corporate client?

a. The courts have not reached consensus on these issues. In Wieder v. Skala, 609 N.E.2d 105 (N.Y.1992), Weider had asked his own law firm to represent him in the purchase of an apartment. The associate the firm assigned to do the work did little or nothing, and when Weider inquired, he found that the firm knew that the associate was a "pathological liar" who had neglected several other clients' matters as well. Weider insisted that the associate be reported to the discipline commission, and for so insisting, Weider was fired. The New York Court of Appeals found that a law firm does not have the same freedom to dismiss a lawyer that a private client would have. "Associates are, to be sure, employees of the firm but they remain independent officers of the court responsible in a broader public sense for their professional obligations." The contract between an associate and the firm contains an implied term that the firm will not impair the associate's obligations to obey the "prevailing rules of conduct and ethical standards of the profession." Weider's suit for breach of contract was thus found to state a cause of action.

b. Yet other cases come out the other way. Jacobson v. Knepper & Moga, P.C., 706 N.E.2d 491 (Ill.1998), involved a lawyer who concluded that some of his firm's practices violated venue provisions of the Fair Debt Collection Agency Act. He pointed it out to one of the firm's principal partners who promised things would change. They did not, so he protested a second and third time, after which he was fired. The Illinois Supreme Court agreed that the conduct discovered by the lawyer violated duties under the Rules of Professional Conduct but it said the lawyer should have reported it to disciplinary authorities. Such a report would have adequately protected "the public policy established by the collection statutes," and the court found it unnecessary to create a tort of retaliatory discharge to protect that policy. Chief Justice Freeman dissented, saying the opinion sent a clear message that it was more "economically advantageous to a lawyer to keep quiet" than to try to get his law firm to conform to proper professional conduct.

c. Bohatch v. Butler & Binion, 977 S.W.2d 543 (Tex.1998), involved the discharge of a partner and held that she had no cause of action when the law firm expelled her from the partnership for, in good faith, accusing another partner of overbilling a major client. Such an accusation "may have a profound effect on the personal confidence and trust essential to the partner relationship," the court said. "Once such charges are made, partners may find it impossible to continue to work together to the * * * benefit of their clients." 977 S.W.2d at 546–47.

Justice Spector and Chief Justice Phillips dissented, saying that "retaliation against a partner who tries in good faith to correct or report perceived misconduct virtually assures that others will not take these appropriate steps in the future," and the result "sends an inappropriate signal to lawyers and to the public that the rules of professional responsibility are subordinate to a law firm's other interests." 977 S.W.2d at 561.

d.   Should a law firm be able to fire or expel a lawyer for insisting that the firm's lawyers comply with their professional obligations? Is there any good explanation for how well-informed courts would come out so differently on the question? Are the competing values too absolute to be treated in a nuanced way?

C.   Some other legal rights of lawyers as compared to employees generally

1.   Should all law firm partners have a right to be treated equally in terms of pay and responsibilities?

a.   Quite the opposite is true at most firms. Law firms are sometimes said to categorize lawyers as "finders," "minders" and "grinders"; that is, some lawyers primarily bring in clients, others manage and supervise cases, while still others do most of the detail work. Often, firms distinguish sharply among these groups in terms of pay, the "finders" typically commanding the highest share of firm profits. "Minders" or "grinders"— even those who are called "partners" today—sometimes work on a salary and have no equity interest in the firm.

b.   The question for law firms, then, is whether any of these realities should give rise to a cause of action for discrimination. What do you think?

2.   Should a law firm incur legal liability for failing to give a new associate the job assignment discussed in the interview that made the firm attractive to the associate?

a.   Stewart v. Jackson & Nash, 976 F.2d 86 (2d Cir.1992), upheld a cause of action for fraudulent inducement where a lawyer resigned from one firm and joined this one because the firm falsely asserted that it had a large environmental case and was building an environmental law department that the plaintiff would head. The firm's representations about its client base were "not future promises but representations of present fact," the court said. Even the promise to be promoted head of the department, if known to be false when made, would support a fraudulent inducement claim.

b.   Geary v. Hunton & Williams, 684 N.Y.S.2d 207 (N.Y.App.Div. 1999), however, said that a lawyer could not recover for the loss of his earning potential allegedly resulting from the firm's misrepresentations about the size of its banking litigation practice. Any damages from such a misrepresentation were "inherently speculative," the court said, because no one could know what the lawyer's experience would have been at another firm.

c. In Slate v. Saxon, Marquoit, Bertoni & Todd, 999 P.2d 1152 (Or.Ct.App.2000), the lawyer had worked for a firm while in law school and was allegedly promised a job by the firm as soon as he passed the Oregon bar examination. After he passed, the firm said it had no room for him. The court held that because a lawyer's employment with a firm is terminable at will, the lawyer can also be fired before he begins work. The offer could not have been a basis for reliance or substantial change of position by the lawyer. The dissent responded that the student performed his part of a unilateral contract and should be at least entitled to compensation for any opportunities foregone.

d. If you can answer without a conflict of interest, what do you think the rule in these cases should be? Should the law presume that Ted Truthful in our problem, and other lawyers such as yourself, can simply leave and practice somewhere else if they are unhappy? Is that easier for young lawyers to do than for older or retired ones? Indeed, in a tight employment market for lawyers, is the assumption of easy lawyer mobility open to question?

3. Should federal antidiscrimination laws apply to law firms? Are issues about hiring and promotion of lawyers inherently too complex to be second-guessed by a judge or jury?

a. A number of cases have held that hiring and promotion decisions of law firms can be reviewed under federal law. Lucido v. Cravath, Swaine & Moore, 425 F.Supp. 123 (S.D.N.Y.1977), for example, held that an associate may sue his law firm under Title VII of the Civil Rights Act of 1964 for discrimination on the basis of religion (Catholic) and national origin (Italian). Lucido alleged he was subjected to discrimination with respect to work assignments, training, rotation and outside work appointments, and that he was denied promotion to partner for the same unlawful reasons. Plaintiff alleged a valid cause of action.

b. In Hishon v. King & Spalding, 467 U.S. 69 (1984), a unanimous Supreme Court held that Title VII prohibits a law firm from discriminating on the basis of sex, race, religion, or national origin in deciding which associates to promote to partner. Even if elevation to partnership is a change in status from employee to employer, consideration for partnership is still a term, condition, or privilege of an associate's employment. Plaintiff's claim of sex discrimination stated a cause of action.[2]

c. Should a firm be permitted to fire a lawyer because he has AIDS? Doe v. Kohn Nast & Graf, P.C., 866 F.Supp. 190 (E.D.Pa.1994), held that a

---

2. There is a difference, of course, between alleging sex discrimination and proving it. In Ezold v. Wolf, Block, Schorr and Solis–Cohen, 983 F.2d 509 (3d Cir.1992), cert. denied, 510 U.S. 826 (1993), the plaintiff alleged that the firm denied her partnership because of her sex. The court examined in great detail both her evaluations and those of males who made partner, and reversed a judgment in her favor, apparently concluding that the law firm reasonably thought the plaintiff was not capable of handling complex litigation.

lawyer fired when he was discovered to be HIV positive has a cause of action under Section 12112 of the Americans with Disabilities Act.[3]

d. What do you think is likely to be the effect of these decisions? Would the existence of statutory grounds to resist termination tend to reduce the incidence of unfair treatment? Or, would law firms, fearing the consequences and cost of trying to terminate lawyers, keep lawyers on the job who really should be terminated?

e. Should a lawyer's violation of federal antidiscrimination law also constitute a basis for state professional discipline? California Rule 2–400 forbids lawyers from discriminating on the basis of race, sex, national origin, sexual orientation, religion, age or disability. D.C. Rule 9.1 forbids discrimination on all those bases plus color, marital status and family responsibility. The farthest the ABA has been willing to go is Model Rule 8.4, Comment 3. Do you think the ABA has gone far enough? Indeed, does Comment 3 reach the conduct raised in this problem at all?

4. May a partnership terminate partners when they are thought to be too old or insufficiently docile?

a. In EEOC v. Sidley Austin Brown & Wood, 315 F.3d 696 (7th Cir.2002), the EEOC tried to enforce a subpoena *duces tecum* issued to a law firm to investigate charges of age discrimination resulting from the firm's newly adopted retirement plan. The plan demoted 32 partners who were over the age of 40 to senior counsel status. Sidley responded that decisions of partnerships are outside the scope of EEOC review because everybody is an equal and no one is an employee. The EEOC responded that it was entitled to review independently whether Sidley was a partnership. The Seventh Circuit agreed that "[a]n individual who was classified as a partner-employer under state partnership law might be classified as an employee for * * * the purpose for which federal antidiscrimination law extends protection to employees but not employers." 315 F.3d at 702. The EEOC alleged that a powerful executive committee ran this firm, the court said; partners were not all equal, and the EEOC needed access to the requested information so as to evaluate the nature of the organization and the EEOC's authority over its employment decisions.

In 2007, Sidley paid $27.5 million to settle the case and, while not admitting past wrongdoing, agreed not to terminate its partners because of age. United States Equal Employment Opportunity Commission v. Sidley Austin LLP, 2007 WL 2915852 (N.D.Ill.2007).

b. Bane v. Ferguson, 890 F.2d 11 (7th Cir.1989), asked whether a retired law partner has a cause of action against his former law firm's management committee for allegedly negligent acts that caused the firm to dissolve, resulting in the termination of his retirement benefits. Judge Posner, for the Seventh Circuit, said no. A partner of a firm has a fiduciary

---

3. See also, Robert C. Ozer, P.C. v. Borquez, 940 P.2d 371 (Colo.1997) (no cause of action for lawyer dismissal because his companion had AIDS, but there is a cause of action for firm's invasion of privacy in giving unreasonable publicity to the lawyer's private life).

duty to his partners, the court wrote, but none to his former partners. Furthermore, firms collapse for many reasons and the managers are not liable to their partners for that collapse. Posner acknowledged that he was "sorry about the financial blow" to the plaintiff, who was 72 years old when he retired and, other than Social Security, apparently had no source of income other than the pension (now lost) of less than $28,000 per year. However, the former partner should have protected himself through contract; "people should be encouraged to protect themselves through voluntary transactions rather than to look to tort law to repair the consequences of their improvidence." 890 F.2d at 15. Perhaps the former partner thought he had protected himself by dealing with his former partners whom he thought had a duty not to act negligently.

c.   Should the law prefer senior lawyers over younger, or vice versa? How would you recommend that firms handle issues of productivity and compensation to protect all lawyers in a firm?

5.   Suppose that a client threatens to fire a law firm unless it engages in discriminatory conduct? Recall that courts usually hold that a client may terminate a lawyer for any reason.

a.   In Plessinger v. Castleman & Haskell, 838 F.Supp. 448 (N.D.Cal. 1993), a fired associate sued his firm for age discrimination and also sued the firm's client (Allstate Insurance) for tortious interference with business relations. The complaint alleged that Allstate had ordered the firm to fire him because it wanted younger lawyers working on its cases. Allstate asserted that it had an absolute right to counsel of its choice and thus that the court should dismiss the claim. The court disagreed, saying that state law would "not recognize a client's unlimited right to select among associates * * * where the selection criteria involves discrimination against a member of a protected class. To hold otherwise would allow * * * clients to demand that law firms not assign cases to women, racial minorities, or members of any other protected class * * *." Thus, it denied Allstate's motion to dismiss.

b.   Do you agree with this result? Does it leave the usual assumption that a client may freely terminate a lawyer open to doubt? Is the principle that clients may fire their lawyers for reasons that they could not use to fire an employee, for example, a principle worth defending today?

D.   DOUBTS ABOUT LIFE IN THE MODERN LARGE LAW FIRM

1.   Were you shocked to read that Smart & Howe requires its lawyers to bill 2,500 hours per year?

a.   Most firms for which you will work will require fewer hours, but some perspective on such requirements is useful. "Conventional wisdom just a few decades ago was that lawyers could not reasonably expect to charge for more than 1200 to 1500 hours per year."[4]

---

4. Patrick J. Schiltz, On Being a Happy, Healthy, and Ethical Member of an Un-   happy, Unhealthy, and Unethical Profession, 52 Vanderbilt L. Rev. 871, 891 (1999).

b.   Apart from a system of required billable hours, new graduates face the prospect of becoming one associate in a pyramid of associates chasing the prize of equity partnership. This model allows partners to bill clients for work done by first through third year associates and then edited by fourth through sixth year associates and assembled by junior partners for eventual client presentation by a senior partner. The associate partner pyramid produces the $30,000 memorandum for the client. In light of the recent financial crisis, it appears that few corporate clients will be willing to pay for legal services delivered in this manner. Will the pyramid-structured big law firm survive?

c.   Professor Deborah L. Rhode, Chair of the ABA Commission on Women and the Legal Profession, finds women particularly disadvantaged by current law firm expectations. "Women's opportunities are limited in three crucial ways," she says, "by traditional gender stereotypes; by inadequate access to mentors and informal networks of support; and by inflexible workplace structures."[5]

"Gender * * * characteristics traditionally associated with women are at odds with those traditionally associated with professional success, such as assertiveness, competitiveness, and business judgment. Some lawyers and clients still assume that women lack the aptitude for complex financial transactions or the combativeness for high-stakes litigation. Yet professional women also tend to be rated lower when they adopt 'masculine,' authoritative styles, particularly when the evaluators are men. * * * And what is assertive in a man often seems abrasive in a woman. * * *

" * * * Attorneys who assume that women with children are less committed or that women of color are less qualified will recall their errors more readily than their insights. They will note the times mothers leave early, not the times they stay late. * * *

"These assumptions can then become self-fulfilling prophecies. * * *

"[As for mentoring], [m]any men who endorse equal opportunity in principle fall short in practice; they end up supporting those who seem most similar in backgrounds, experiences, and values. * * * Even women who make real sacrifices to get a foot in the door find that a foot is all they get in. Working mothers short on time, interest, or innate ability have nonetheless learned to play golf, which makes it all the more aggravating when they still aren't invited to play. * * *

"The result is that many female lawyers remain out of the loop of career development. They are not given enough challenging, high visibility assignments, nor are they included in social events that yield professional opportunities. Problems of exclusion are greatest for those

---

5.   Deborah L. Rhode, Gender and the Profession: The No–Problem Problem, 30   Hofstra L. Rev. 1001, 1003–04 (2002).

who appear 'different' on other grounds as well as gender, such as race, ethnicity, disability, or sexual orientation. * * *

"A final obstacle involves workplace structures that fail to accommodate personal needs and commitments, particularly family responsibilities. * * *

"The most obvious ongoing failure is inhumane hours and a resistance to reduced or flexible schedules * * *. The problem is reinforced by the increasing pace and competition of legal life. Technological innovations have created expectations of instant responsiveness and total availability, while increasing billable hour quotas have pushed working hours to new and often excessive limits. Lawyers remain perpetually on call—tethered to the workplace through cell phones, emails, faxes, and beepers. 'Face time' is taken as a proxy for commitment, ambition, and reliability under pressure. The result is a 'rat race equilibrium' in which most lawyers feel that they would be better off with shorter or more flexible schedules, but find themselves within institutional structures that offer no such alternatives."[6]

d.   Do these concerns reflect your own perceptions about much in law practice today? Are the problems one sees in practice limited to large firm associates? Do women face these problems disproportionately? Are the perceptions and habits about which Professor Rhode writes unique to the legal profession? If so, does that make any of them matters of less appropriate concern?

2.   In our problem, Andy Howe has proposed that the law firm give associates the option of working 80% of a full-time job for 80% of the pay. Is Sarah Smart correct that not many lawyers would choose that option? Is Smart also right that the firm should be suspicious of the values of lawyers who would choose it?

a.   Professor Rhode observes: "Even in workplaces that in theory offer these options, a wide gap persists between formal policies and actual practices. Although over 90% of surveyed law firms report policies permitting part-time schedules, only about 3% of lawyers actually use them. Most women surveyed believe, with good reason, that any reduction in hours or availability will carry a permanent price."[7]

b.   Federal District Judge Patrick Schiltz offers another suggestion about why part-time work seems rarely chosen:

"If all such lawyers making $160,000 per year sat down and asked themselves, 'What will make me a happier and healthier person: another $40,000 in income (which, after taxes, will mean another $25,000 or so in the bank) or 600 hours to do whatever I enjoy most?,' it is hard to believe that many of them would take the money.

"But many of them do take the money. * * * And they do so merely to be able to make seven or eight times the national median

6.   30 Hofstra L. Rev. at 1004–08.

7.   30 Hofstra L. Rev. at 1008 (footnotes omitted).

income instead of five or six times the national median income. Why? Are lawyers just greedy?

"Well, some are, but it is more complicated than that. For one thing, lawyers * * * don't sit down and think logically about why they are leading the lives they are leading any more than buffalo sit down and think logically about why they are stampeding. * * *

"More importantly, though, the flaw in my analysis is that it assumes that the reason lawyers push themselves to make so much money is the money itself. * * * What you need to understand, though, is that * * * [t]hey are doing it for a different reason.

"Big firm lawyers are, on the whole, a remarkably insecure and competitive group of people. Many of them have spent almost their entire lives competing to win games that other people have set up for them. First they competed to get into a prestigious college. Then they competed for college grades. Then they competed for LSAT scores. Then they competed to get into a prestigious law school. Then they competed for law school grades. Then they competed to make the law review. Then they competed for clerkships. Then they competed to get hired by a big law firm.

"Now that they're in a big law firm, what's going to happen? Are they going to stop competing? Are they going to stop comparing themselves to others? Of course not. They're going to keep competing—competing to bill more hours, to attract more clients, to win more cases, to do more deals. They're playing a game. And money is how the score is kept in that game. * * *

" * * * If a lawyer's life is dominated by the game—and if his success in the game is measured by money—then his life is dominated by money. For many, many lawyers, it's that simple."[8]

c. Do you agree with Judge Schiltz's analysis of lawyer motivation? Is "the game" what is motivating you? Should we care about such psychological explanations for lawyer behavior? Does the motivation potentially manifest itself in behavior that can have a real impact on clients and third parties?

————

PROBLEM 34

LEAVING ONE LAW FIRM AND FORMING ANOTHER

Lawyers once pictured themselves as wedded to their law firms for life. In recent years, however, those bonds have weakened. Whether because of unhappiness with pay, work assignments, hours at the office, or insensitive

---

8. Patrick J. Schiltz, On Being a Happy, Healthy, and Ethical Member of an Unhappy, Unhealthy, and Unethical Profession, 52 Vanderbilt L. Rev. 871, 904–06 (1999).

treatment by superiors, lawyers are leaving one firm to move to another setting. When they go, they often like to take as much familiar work with them as they can. Doing so usually increases their financial rewards at a new firm and reduces their dependence upon cases assigned by that firm. In this problem, we look first at the law and ethics of departure from a law firm—what Professor Robert Hillman calls the "law and ethics of grabbing and leaving."[1] Second, we examine firms' efforts to limit such departures by restrictive agreements with their partners and associates. Third, we consider when lawyers handle a departure by actually buying all or part of a law practice. Finally, we ask whether lawyers should be able to agree, for a fixed fee, to deliver legal services to all members of a defined group.

FACTS

Several years ago, Bill Bright and Larry Learned started the firm of Bright & Learned. It prospered and has grown to 425 lawyers. The two female partners and eight female associates who make up Bright & Learned's estate planning group, however, view the firm as singularly unenlightened. None has been allowed to move into the litigation section of the firm, and many of the firm's partnership meetings are held in the all-male Thomas Jefferson Club. Although estate planning brings the firm substantial, steady revenue, the group believe they have not been paid as well as they would be in a firm of their own.

The group's lawyers believe that, if they leave together, they can bring with them most of the client families on whose estate plans they have worked during the past several years. Each lawyer will write a letter to the clients she knows best before she leaves Bright & Learned. The lawyers then plan to use these clients' expressions of willingness to follow them to the new firm as a basis for getting loans to finance the new firm's start-up costs.

Before she became a lawyer and one of the group's partners, Mary Cord had been an officer of the local electrician's union. She hopes to present the union with a proposal under which, for a premium of $100 per union member per year, the group's new firm will write wills and give periodic estate planning advice to persons in the immediate family of any of the union members.

When Bill Bright and Larry Learned came in one morning and found that their entire estate planning group had disappeared, they were hurt and angry. As part of an effort to avoid a lawsuit, however, Bright & Learned offered to sell its former estate planning practice to the departing lawyers for an amount equal to the group's prior two years' billings, payable in equal installments over the next five years.

---

1. Robert W. Hillman, Hillman on Lawyer Mobility: The Law and Ethics of Partner Withdrawals and Law Firm Breakups § 1.3 (1994).

QUESTIONS

A. THE LAW AND ETHICS OF DEPARTING FROM A LAW FIRM

1. What duties do law firm partners owe to each other? May some decide they would like to practice law somewhere else without violating their duties to the others?

a. Partners are traditionally said to owe each other the fiduciary duties of loyalty and care. Revised Uniform Partnership Act § 404. That includes the duty "to refrain from competing with the partnership and the other partners in the conduct of the partnership business before the dissolution of the partnership." Id. § 404(b)(3). The usual complaint of the original firm when partners leave with little warning is that the departing lawyers have breached their fiduciary duties.

b. How should courts approach that claim? Should partners be yoked together for life? Does the quoted prohibition imply that at all? Indeed, Revised Uniform Partnership Act § 601(1) recognizes that a partner becomes "dissociated" from the partnership upon "the partnership's having notice of the partner's express will to withdraw as a partner or on a later date specified by the partner." The critical issues on departure, then, are likely to be openness and fairness. After the desire to depart is known, the issues become payment of sums to which the departing partners are entitled and who will have ongoing relationship with the firm's clients.

c. In Dowd & Dowd, Ltd. v. Gleason, 693 N.E.2d 358 (Ill.1998), 58% of the firm's business was for a single client, a subsidiary of Allstate Insurance. The two departing lawyers contacted that client on December 31, the same day they notified the firm. That same day, the client sent a letter to the old firm requesting that its files be sent to the new one. The departing lawyers then hired others from the old firm to help work on the cases.

Lawyers who plan to leave a firm, the court recognizes, "face a dilemma, caught between the fiduciary obligations they owe the other members of their firm * * * and the duty of being able to adequately represent clients who choose to follow them to their new place of employment * * *." 693 N.E.2d at 364. As a way of accommodating these competing pressures, the court says, lawyers "may make arrangements, prior to their departure, to obtain new office space * * * and other materials necessary for the practice of law." 693 N.E.2d at 364. However, "pretermination solicitation of clients by members of an existing firm for the benefit of a new firm rises to a breach of fiduciary duty." 693 N.E.2d at 366. Determining both the actual facts and what fiduciary duties partners owe each other under those circumstances, however, is not the stuff of summary judgment motions, so the case was remanded for trial.

2. Who owns a law firm's clients? What rights do departing partners and associates have to persuade clients to follow them to their new firm?

a. Should clients properly be considered an "asset" of a law firm? Should it matter whether the clients originally came to Bright & Learned because of the firm's reputation, not that of the individual departing lawyers? Should it be relevant whether the clients now consider the individual women, not the firm, as their lawyers?

b. Koehler v. Wales, 556 P.2d 233 (Wash.App.1976), accepts the traditional view that a client's exercise of the power to hire or fire a lawyer at any time does not give rise to a cause of action by their lawyer. In this case, one lawyer had agreed to handle another's cases while the latter was out of the country; they based their fee division on work performed. When the absent lawyer returned, some of her clients left with the "interim" lawyer, but the court refused to allow the formerly-absent lawyer to sue for damages for business interference. "The attorney-client relationship is personal and confidential, and the client's choice of attorneys in civil cases is near absolute." 556 P.2d at 236. "[W]e decline to recognize that plaintiff had any proprietary interest in her former law practice." 556 P.2d at 238.

c. In Fred Siegel Co., L.P.A. v. Arter & Hadden, 707 N.E.2d 853 (Ohio 1999), KB had worked for Fred Siegel Co. for ten years when she resigned to join Arter & Hadden. Her expertise involved real estate property assessments. She told Arter & Hadden who Fred Siegel's clients were and that she thought several would follow her. When she left, she took the cards she had in her Rolodex, and wrote letters to Siegel clients notifying them of her new association and closing, "When you need assistance or have questions, please contact me." Siegel responded, and wrote to the same clients telling them that it was still fully capable of serving them. Then Siegel filed suit against Arter & Hadden, claiming tortious interference with business relationships, and against KB for breach of fiduciary duty. The court rejected the tortious interference claim, saying that the right of fair competition in Restatement of Torts § 768 trumps that theory when a contract is terminable at will. However, the court remanded the case to determine whether KB's use of the names in her Rolodex was an improper appropriation of the Siegel firm's trade secret.

d. In Meehan v. Shaughnessy, 535 N.E.2d 1255 (Mass.1989), two partners left to open a new office. They sued for fees due from their old partners, and the firm countersued for violation of fiduciary obligations and tortious interference with relations with clients. The two partners had decided in July to leave the firm at the end of December and had recruited four others to join them. During the summer and fall, they worked on getting office space and financing, and they kept up their caseload at the firm rather than letting people who would stay at the firm become familiar with the cases. During this period, they expressly denied plans to leave. They eventually gave the old firm 30 days' notice, immediately called clients, and were able to get 142 out of 350 active cases shifted to the new firm. The court began by reminding lawyers that law partners owe fiduciary obligations to each other. The departing partners "used speed and preemptive" tactics and abused "their position of trust and confidence" in the firm. Then the court remanded to let the old firm show its economic harm from the loss of clients, and it imposed on the departing lawyers the burden to prove that the clients would have come even if the lawyers had acted properly.

e. In all such cases, ultimately the court must accommodate the legitimate interests of the old firm, the departing lawyers, and freedom of choice of the clients that each would like to serve. Which course of action do you think best strikes that balance?

3. Should there be any limits on the departing lawyers' contacts with the old firm's clients in order to persuade them to follow the lawyers to the new firm? What may the old firm say to try to persuade its clients to stay?

a. Original ABA Canon of Ethics 7 provided that "Efforts, direct or indirect, in any way to encroach upon the business of another lawyer, are unworthy of those who should be brethren at the Bar; * * * ." Does that answer the question? Which lawyers' "business" do these clients represent?

b. Have the Model Rules rejected the old approach? Take another look at Model Rule 7.3(a). With which lawyers should the clients be said to have had a "prior professional relationship"? If a client asked the lawyer why she is leaving and where she may be reached, should the lawyer be permitted to give an honest and responsive answer?

c. In one well-known case, associates in a law office decided to form their own firm. After telling their firm they planned to leave, they told 400 clients on whose cases they were working of their plans. They mailed forms to the clients that they could use to terminate the present firm and retain the new one as their counsel. Clients with about 1,300 cases pending at the old firm moved the work to the new one. The old firm filed suit to enjoin the departing lawyers from "contacting and/or communicating with" persons who were its clients. If you were the trial court would you have entered the injunction?

The trial court enjoined the conduct, but the Superior Court reversed. Adler, Barish, Daniels, Levin & Creskoff v. Epstein, 382 A.2d 1226 (Pa.Super.1977). The communication was "not false, misleading or coercive," the court reasoned (citing Bates v. State Bar of Arizona, 433 U.S. 350 (1977), the lawyer advertising case discussed in Problem 31). Furthermore, while the first firm had expected additional fee-generating business from these clients, "[b]ecause the law permits a client to seek and re-seek counsel of his choice, any expectation that a client would remain constant * * * is unrealistic." 382 A.2d at 1232. The court believed the clients would be best served by permitting contacts from the associates. "Many of the clients have dealt personally [with the departing lawyers]. * * * Having one's file transferred to a new associate [as proposed by the existing firm] will undoubtedly engender additional cost and time to the client." Id. Balancing the interests at stake, the court held the associates' contacts are valuable to the clients, not a tort to enjoin.

However, the Pennsylvania Supreme Court disagreed, 393 A.2d 1175 (Pa.1978), cert. denied, 442 U.S. 907 (1979). Its first expressed concern was also for the clients. The departing lawyers were—

> "actively attempting to induce the clients to change law firms in the middle of their active cases. Appellees' concern for their line of credit and the success of their new law firm gave them an immediate, personally created financial interest in the clients' decisions. In this atmosphere, appellees' contacts posed too great a risk that clients would not have the opportunity to make a careful, informed decision." 393 A.2d at 1181.

The court's other concern was for the nature of relationships within law firms. The court reasoned that the lawyers' contacts—

> "were possible because Adler Barish partners trusted appellees with the high responsibility of developing its clients' cases. From this position of trust and responsibility, appellees were able to gain knowledge of the details, and status, of each case to which appellees had been assigned. In the atmosphere surrounding appellees' departure, appellees' contacts unduly suggested a course of action for Adler Barish clients and unfairly prejudiced Adler Barish. No public interest is served in condoning use of confidential information which has these effects. Clients too easily may suffer in the end." 393 A.2d at 1185.

It reinstated the injunction.

With which view do you agree? Which one is more nearly true to *Bates, Ohralik, Primus,* and *Shapero* that you saw in Problem 31? Does the analysis of client interests in those cases apply to departing lawyer situations as well?

d. Restatement Third, The Law Governing Lawyers § 9(3), summarizes the law of leaving a law firm as follows:

> "(3) Absent an agreement with the firm providing a more permissive rule, a lawyer leaving a law firm may solicit firm clients:
>
>> (a) prior to leaving the firm:
>>
>>> (i) only with respect to firm clients on whose matters the lawyer is actively and substantially working; and
>>>
>>> (ii) only after the lawyer has adequately and timely informed the firm of the lawyer's intent to contact firm clients for that purpose; and
>>
>> "(b) after ceasing employment in the firm, to the same extent as any other nonfirm lawyer."

Comment *i* to § 9(3) authorizes the lawyer who is planning a departure to "make such predeparture arrangements as leasing space, printing a new letterhead, and obtaining financing." The lawyer who has left the firm may "continue to represent former firm clients who choose such representation, so long as the lawyer has complied with the rules of Subsection (3)." As a general rule, the Restatement advises, a lawyer "may plan mutual or serial departures from their law firm" by other firm lawyers and employees.

e.   Attorney Grievance Comm'n of Maryland v. Potter, 844 A.2d 367 (Md.2004), involved Potter, a lawyer who shared offices with, and worked for, lawyer Weitzman. Potter brought in two cases and did most of the work on them. Potter believed that Weitzman had not paid him all that he was due, and he left and convinced the two clients to follow him. When he left, Potter took the two case files with him and deleted all material about the cases from the Weitzman firm's computers. The court ruled that intentionally deleting someone else's computer files is a crime in Maryland. Potter's removal of the paper files was also dishonest. The court made clear that it was not condemning Potter's efforts to get the two clients to follow him to his new practice. Unauthorized removal of files went too far, however, violated Rule 8.4(b), (c), and (d), and merited a 90–day suspension.

f.   In Reeves v. Hanlon, 95 P.3d 513 (Cal.2004), Hanlon and another attorney, Greene, were employees of Reeves' law firm. They decided to leave Reeves' firm to form their own practice. Before leaving, they took Reeves' client list, intentionally erased data from computer files, "intentionally fomented dissatisfaction" among Reeves' employees, and invited some of Reeves' key employees to join their new law firm. Reeves subsequently sued Hanlon and Greene for intentional interference with the at-will employment contracts of his former employees. The California Supreme Court held that interference with an at-will employment contract is actionable under the theory of interference with a prospective economic advantage. Plaintiff must prove that the defendant "engaged in an independently wrongful act in disrupting the relationship," however; merely extending a job offer to an employer's current employee is not actionable. The court found that in this case Hanlon and Greene had engaged in unlawful acts by improperly soliciting Reeves' then-clients and employees.

4.   How should lawyers proceed when leaving a law firm?

a.   In the wake of *Adler Barish*, ABA Informal Opinion 1457 (Apr. 29, 1980), attempted to give practical advice to lawyers. It authorized sending the following letter:

"Dear [Client]:

"Effective [date], I became the resident partner in this city of the *XYZ* law firm, having withdrawn from the *ABC* law firm. My decision should not be construed as adversely reflecting in any way on my former firm. It is simply one of those things that sometimes happens in business and professional life.

"I want to be sure that there is no disadvantage to you, as the client, from my move. The decision as to how the matters I have worked on for you are handled and who handles them in the future will be completely yours, and whatever you decide will be determinative."

The ABA Committee made clear that—

"This opinion is limited to the facts presented: (a) the notice is mailed; (b) the notice is sent only to persons with whom the lawyer had an active lawyer-client relationship immediately before the change in the lawyer's professional association; (c) the notice is clearly related to open and pending matters for which the lawyer had direct professional responsibility to the client immediately before the change; (d) the notice is sent promptly after the change; (e) the notice does not urge the client to sever relationship with the lawyer's former firm and does not recommend the lawyer's employment (although it indicates the lawyer's willingness to continue his responsibility for the matters); (f) the notice makes clear that the client has the right to decide who will complete or continue the matters; and (g) the notice is brief, dignified, and not disparaging of the lawyer's former firm."[2]

Should *all* of the elements noted by the ABA Committee have to be present for the communication to be proper? Which, if any, are unnecessary? Is part (g), the notice must not be "disparaging of the lawyer's former firm," a requirement that serves a public interest or only the interest of the original firm?

b. ABA Formal Opinion 99–414 (Sept. 8, 1999) declared that notice to affected clients is not only permissible, it is required. The departure of a lawyer who has played a significant role in the client's representation is information that may affect the "status" of a matter within the meaning of Model Rule 1.4(a)(3). Direct contact with the client does not violate Model Rule 7.3 unless the lawyer's work on a matter afforded little or no direct contact with that client. In any event, the departing lawyer "must not disparage the lawyer's former firm" and "should not urge the client to sever its relationship with the firm, but may indicate the lawyer's willingness and ability to continue her responsibility for the matters upon which she currently is working," while making "clear that the client has the ultimate right to decide who will complete or continue the matters." The departing lawyer may also respond to questions about billing rates and available resources at the new firm. The opinion, however, prefers that the lawyer and the old firm give *joint* notification.

c. Kentucky Bar Association v. An Unnamed Attorney, 205 S.W.3d 204 (Ky.2006), also holds that a lawyer has an *obligation*, not just a right, to contact former clients. In this case, the lawyer had accepted the representation of a client and seems not to have told his firm. Thus, when the lawyer left the firm (and the practice of law), no one was paying attention to the client's case. The Court accepted the ABA Formal Opinion 99–414 standard imposing the duty to inform on those "responsible" for the client's representation or those who "play a principal role in the law firm's delivery of legal services" in the matter. In this case, once the client inquired about the status of his matter, the firm was able to take charge

2. Excerpted from Recent Ethics Opinions, as updated 1981, copyright American   Bar Association.

and achieve the desired result. "[U]nder the facts of this case, the respondent was required to tell the man that he was leaving the firm, inform other attorneys in the firm about the status of the man's case, offer to refund the unearned fee, and offer the man the choice of allowing someone else in the firm to represent him or another attorney not associated with the firm to represent him." The court imposed a private reprimand on the lawyer for leaving the client at risk.

d.   "Ethical Obligations When a Lawyer Changes Firms," Joint Formal Opinion 2007–300 of the Pennsylvania Bar Association Committee on Legal Ethics and Professional Responsibility and the Philadelphia Bar Association Professional Guidance Committee (June 2007), is to the same effect. It requires client notification when a lawyer playing "a principal role" in a client's representation leaves the firm, advocates joint notice, and says that if joint notice is not possible, "in most cases client notice should not precede notice to the old firm."

e.   Do you think these opinions represent realistic solutions to the issues surrounding departure from a law firm? What problems can you see that the opinions do not address?

5.   How much may a departing lawyer tell the law firm to which the lawyer wants to move about the lawyer's present practice and clients?

a.   Up to now, our questions have assumed the departing lawyer is forming a new firm. At least as often, however, lawyers leave one firm to go to another, preexisting firm. In considering whether to make such a lateral hire, a firm is likely to want to know what experience the lawyer has and what clients want to come with him or her. As you can imagine, Model Rule 1.6(a) protects much of that information from disclosure.

b.   ABA Formal Opinion 09–455 (2009), examined the tension between the need for conflict of interest analysis when a lawyer moves to a new practice, and the requirement of client confidentiality. The Committee began by discussing lawyer mobility and the importance of conflicts screening prior to association to ensure that neither the clients of the moving lawyer nor those of the association the lawyer is moving to are harmed by conflicts of interest. However, Rule 1.6 does not obviously permit the disclosure of information necessary to conduct an adequate conflicts screening. Disclosure would not likely be permitted under the exception in Rule 1.6(a) for information "implicitly authorized to carry out the representation," because the disclosure would be more in the lawyer's personal interests than in the interests of the client's representation. Disclosure also would not fall under the exception in Rule 1.6(b)(6) that allows disclosure of information the lawyer believes is necessary "to comply with other law." "Other law" refers to external law and not the requirements of other ethical rules, and there is no external law requiring lawyer mobility. The Committee also found that getting all current and former clients' informed consent to disclosure for conflicts purposes would be impracticable, as the lawyer would need to get consent for every interview and any single client could, by withholding consent, prevent a lawyer from seeking a new association. The Committee concluded that a lawyer should be permitted to disclose the basic information necessary to conduct a conflicts analysis, which it listed as the persons and issues involved in a matter. It determined that the Model Rules were "rules of reason," and to read Rule 1.6 literally to prohibit disclosure of the information necessary for conflicts analysis would make it impossible for a lawyer to avoid conflicts of interest and comply with the requirements of Rules 1.7, 1.9, and 1.10. The Committee discussed other ABA rules that allow disclosure even though it is not "implicitly authorized" by the client, including Rule 1.6(b)(4) that permits a lawyer to seek legal advice concerning his or her compliance with the ethical rules.

The Committee then explained what it thought were the appropriate limitations on necessary disclosures. It stated that the disclosure should only include the information "reasonably necessary" to determine if a conflict of interest exists. This normally would include the persons and issues involved in matters that may pose a conflict. It noted that sometimes it may be readily apparent that a conflict might exist and even less disclosure would be necessary. These include situations where the lawyer and the new firm are adverse to each other in several matters, instances where the lawyer and new firm generally represent constituencies that are usually adverse to one another, or situations where a simple examination of client lists would reveal potential conflicts. It also explained that certain situations arise where disclosure of a client's identity or the subject matter of a representation may prejudice the client, and therefore informed consent would be required. It further stated that in some situations more information than the names and issues involved would be required for analysis, and consent also would be required there if the firm or lawyer could not find the relevant information from an alternate source. The Opinion also suggests that the lawyer and new firm might seek advice from an intermediate lawyer to whom they could disclose the conflict information. Finally, the Opinion addressed the issue of the timing of conflicts disclosures and determined that disclosures should not be made until it is "reasonably necessary." This means that substantial discussions, as opposed to mere initial contacts, have taken place concerning a new association. Does the rule of reason approach to this disclosure of confidentiality make sense? Should the ABA include this exception in the comments to Rule 1.6 or Rule 1.17?

c. Look at the first two sentences of Model Rule 1.17, Comment 7. Do they suggest a reasonable way to handle use of confidential information in doing conflicts checks? Would the need to get client consent to provide detail about clients' representation to a prospective employer undercut the lawyer's obligation to first tell the lawyer's current firm about the moving plans?

B. EFFORTS BY LAW FIRMS TO INHIBIT THEIR LAWYERS' ABILITY TO LEAVE

1. Rather than relying on a suit for breach of fiduciary duty to inhibit departures, should a law firm add a covenant not to

compete in its partnership and employment agreements to require its partners and associates not to practice law in competition with the firm for a period of three years after leaving the firm?

a. Look at Model Rule 5.6(a). Is it ambiguous about this point? Does Model Rule 5.6, Comment 1, persuade you that the rule makes sense?

b. In Cohen v. Lord, Day & Lord, 550 N.E.2d 410 (N.Y.1989), the head of Lord, Day's tax department left that firm and joined another New York City firm. The Lord, Day partnership agreement provided that departing partners were entitled to a share of future partnership profits representing unpaid or unbilled fees. If the lawyer went into competition with Lord, Day, however, the agreement said there was to be no such right. Cohen requested his share of profits, the firm interposed the competition exception, and Cohen asserted its invalidity under DR 2–108(A) of the New York Code of Professional Responsibility [Model Rule 5.6(a)]. The court agreed the provision was invalid and thus unenforceable. "While a law firm has a legitimate interest in its own survival and economic well-being and in maintaining its clients," the court said, "it cannot protect those interests by contracting for the forfeiture of earned revenues * * * [and thereby restrict] the choices of the clients to retain and continue the withdrawing member as counsel." 550 N.E.2d at 413. See also, Eisenstein v. David G. Conlin, P.C., 827 N.E.2d 686 (Mass.2005), which invalidated a partnership agreement providing that partners who left a firm and took clients must pay the old firm part of what they bill at the new firm for work done for those clients.

c. ABA Formal Opinion 94–381 (May 9, 1994) advised that a corporation may *not* require, and a lawyer may not accept, a term in an employment agreement that requires in-house lawyers who leave the corporation never to take a case against it, even if the case is unrelated to work the lawyer did for the corporation. Model Rule 1.9 provides sufficient protection to the client, the opinion says. Requiring any more protection would violate Model Rule 5.6(a). New Jersey Supreme Court Advisory Committee on Professional Ethics Opinion 708 (July 2006) is to the same effect.[3]

2. How broadly should the rule reach? Should firms be able to impose restrictions designed to protect reasonable investment expectations of the firm?

a. Denburg v. Parker Chapin Flattau & Klimpl, 624 N.E.2d 995 (N.Y.1993), involved a firm that had contracted for larger space and believed it would take five years to pay off the debt and lease obligations. The provision in question required that if a partner withdrew and practiced in the private sector, he or she had to pay the firm 12.5% of the profits

---

3. See also, People v. Wilson, 953 P.2d 1292 (Colo.1998) (en banc) (lawyer publicly censured for making his associates sign a "covenant not to steal" firm clients if they leave the firm and to pay over 75% of any fee earned on cases the clients choose to take to the departing lawyer); D.C. Bar Ethics Comm. Opinion 194 (Nov. 15, 1988) (contract providing that, if departing lawyer competes with the firm within a year of leaving the firm, lawyer loses rights to half of unearned fees improperly limits both client's right to choose counsel freely and lawyer's right to practice).

allocated to the partner in the preceding two years, or 12.5% of the billings to the firm's former clients who followed the lawyer to the new firm, whichever was greater. The lower courts had said the purpose of this requirement made it different from *Cohen*, but the Court of Appeals disagreed. Only lawyers who went into competition with the firm had to pay. Thus, it refused to enforce the agreement.

b.   In Howard v. Babcock, 863 P.2d 150 (Cal.1993), the partnership agreement provided that a partner who withdrew and engaged in the same kind of practice in the same county would be entitled to return of his capital interest in the firm but no share in the next 12 months' receipts of the firm to which he would have been entitled but for the competition. The court said that California has a public policy in favor of competition and that only "reasonable" noncompetition agreements will be upheld. But, it said, "[c]ommercial concerns are now openly recognized as important in the practice of law," and the decision to practice in competition with one's former partners does not have to be costless. An agreement like the one in this case is not a prohibition on competition. Rather, it can be seen as a "tax" or "liquidated damages" for the real costs the departure imposes on the partners who remain in the firm. Thus, it does not violate California's version of Model Rule 5.6(a) to put reasonable limits on the absolute freedom of lawyers to practice somewhere else.

c.   In Shuttleworth, Ruloff & Giordano, P.C. v. Nutter, 493 S.E.2d 364 (Va.1997), the firm leased new office space, required its partners and associates to sign personal guarantees of the lease and to pay their share of the rent for the eleven-year term of the lease if they remained in the practice of law. The court held the agreement did not improperly burden the lawyers' right to practice in competition with the firm. The purpose of the provision was not anticompetitive; it was needed to be sure the rent was paid. Also, the duty to pay applied whatever kind of practice the lawyer undertook, not just if he or she did competitive work.

d.   Fearnow v. Ridenour, Swenson, Cleere & Evans, P.C., 138 P.3d 723 (Ariz.2006), clearly comes down on the side of a law firm imposing financial penalties on a lawyer leaving the firm. Fearnow had a partnership share of $33,674 in his law firm. The partnership agreement said that if any partner left to join a firm competing with this one, that partnership share would be forfeited. The court clearly understood that other courts have interpreted Rule 5.6 quite restrictively, but it said that the forfeiture in this case did not forbid the lawyer's right to practice; it simply made it more costly to do so. Such an agreement should be interpreted consistent with the law of restrictive covenants applicable to nonlawyers; Rule 5.6 should not change the result.

e.   Is one effect of these decisions likely to be that partners will be less likely to withdraw because they are more likely to be held liable for some of their act's collateral consequences? Is that an effect that should concern the courts? Why or why not?

f.   Ariz. Ethics Opinion 09–01 (2009), concluded that a law firm may not include a provision in an employment contract with its associates that requires a departing lawyer to pay the firm $3500 for each situation in which the lawyer continues to represent the client after leaving the firm. The firm called the provision "reimbursement of an advertising expense" and granted an exception when the client had not been identified through firm marketing. The Opinion cited Arizona's version of Rule 5.6 and the general policy of client autonomy in choosing a law firm. "A client's right to choose counsel must have precedence over the lawyer's commercial interests."

3.   How should courts interpret the "concerning benefits upon retirement" provision of Model Rule 5.6(a)?

a.   In Neuman v. Akman, 715 A.2d 127 (D.C.1998), the firm's partner-ship agreement provided that lawyers who retired completely received their partnership share plus an "additional amount" out of the firm's future earnings based on their productivity over the years preceding retirement. Lawyers who went to work for another firm, however, received only a return of their partnership contribution. Lawyer Neuman argued that this distinction constituted a restriction on his right to practice law in violation of Rule 5.6(a), but the D.C. Court of Appeals disagreed. Nothing in the arrangement restricted Neuman's right to practice; it simply paid an additional amount to partners who really retired and earned no outside professional income. That made the payment a "benefit upon retirement" that was fully consistent with Rule 5.6.

b.   In Hoff v. Mayer, Brown & Platt, 772 N.E.2d 263 (Ill.App.2002), the firm's retirement plan would pay Hoff about $94,000 per year after his retirement at age 60 if he had ceased practicing law. Instead, he formed a new firm. The old firm returned his capital shares and fees earned before retirement, but refused to send him retirement checks. This opinion held that, while Model Rule 5.6(a) prohibits a law firm from financially penaliz-ing a lawyer for going into competition with the firm, it does not forbid the firm from withholding bona fide retirement payments from lawyers who do not really retire.

c.   Donnelly v. Brown, Winick, Graves, Gross, Baskerville, Schoene-baum & Walker, P.L.C., 599 N.W.2d 677 (Iowa 1999), upheld a plan that defined "retirement from practice of law" as meaning "a member elects to terminate his (her) private practice of law within the State of Iowa." This plan only provided retirement payments to lawyers over age 60 and paid them over a 10–year period. The lawyer was retirement age, but he had gone to work for another law firm, also in Iowa. He tried to distinguish the *Neuman* case by saying that, if the lawyer could practice in another state, the plan could not really relate to retirement. But the court said that the "retirement plan" exception to Rule 5.6(a) can apply even where the lawyer is not fully retired.

d.   ABA Formal Opinion 06–444 (Sept. 2006) expressly weighs in on restrictions that may be imposed on retiring lawyers. The key concept in Model Rule 5.6(a) is that the program qualify as a retirement plan. The opinion says that such a plan should require lawyers to satisfy a minimum age and years-of-service requirement, for example, although firms might create an early retirement program for younger lawyers with long service. A clear relationship between the retirement program and benefits such as Social Security would also help establish the bona fides of such a plan. Assuming the program qualifies as a retirement plan, most restrictions will be OK. Lawyers may be required to withdraw completely from the practice of law, but a plan could also to let them teach, serve as a judge, or do some other non-competitive work.

e. Do these results make sense to you? What factors distinguish these cases from cases like *Cohen* that found the limitations on future practice unduly restrictive?

4. Is the rule courts adopt as to lawyers' rights upon leaving a firm likely to affect how lawyers are treated while at the firm?

a. Professor Robert Hillman argues that a law firm would have an incentive to treat its lawyers more humanely to try to prevent their departures if the law did less to restrain partners who left firms and tried to take their clients with them:

> "That some lawyers prosper from grabbing [business and leaving] while others suffer is likely evidence of market forces at work. A significant factor underlying the growth of grabbing and leaving is the inability of many firms to develop a method of compensation acceptable to their more mobile partners. Because there is now a market for lawyers who can carry a substantial 'portfolio' of clients to another firm, these lawyers have something to auction. Viewed from this perspective, the solution to the problem of grabbing may lie more in the modification of business practices, particularly those pertaining to compensation, than in law reform.

> "A laissez faire approach to the machinations of law partners is not without its drawbacks, however. One of the more important problems is that a hands off attitude fails to address the interests and values advanced in a more stable environment for law firms. An atmosphere conducive to grabbing encourages the hoarding of clients by lawyers within the same firm. At least a modicum of cooperation is required to maximize the value of a firm to both its lawyers and clients. Furthermore, firms need some sense of confidence concerning the client base in order, as businesses, to engage in long-term planning and commitments in such areas as hiring and promotion of associates and support staff * * *.

> "It may be that another kind of market—a market for stable law firms—already exists and may develop further over time. * * * Those firms presently enjoying relative stability of membership are well positioned to capture gains in an environment of instability."[4]

---

4. Robert W. Hillman, Law Firm Breakups: The Law and Ethics of Grabbing and Leaving 143–45 (1990) (footnotes omitted). See also, Ronald J. Gilson & Robert H.

b.   Do you agree with Professor Hillman? Without the covenants not to compete that Model Rule 5.6(a) seeks to inhibit, is simple humanity likely to be insufficient to cause lawyers to turn down lucrative opportunities to take their clients and move elsewhere?

C.   BUYING A LAWYER'S OR LAW FIRM'S PRACTICE

1.   Would any ethical problem have been presented if the women associates had paid Bright & Learned for the estate planning portion of the law practice?

a.   Look at ABA Model Rule 1.17. What is the purpose of this rule? Does it seem incongruous to think of a lawyer selling her practice?

b.   ABA Formal Opinion 266 (June 2, 1945) asserts: "Clients are not merchandise. Lawyers are not tradesmen. They have nothing to sell but personal service. An attempt, therefore, to barter in clients, would appear to be inconsistent with the best concepts of our professional status." Does that end the matter? Can you come up with reasons other than "professional status" to criticize sale of a practice?

c.   When a partner in a law firm retires, the cases cited above allow the firm to pay that person retirement benefits. Is the sale of a practice the corresponding way for a solo practitioner to pay for her retirement? Does that make Rule 1.17 make more sense?

2.   What problems can you see associated with a sale of client files?

a.   Should a lawyer be permitted to sell case files to someone the clients have never met? Do the relevant confidentiality interests have anything to do with whether the practice is sold? Would the ethical problems be fewer if the retiring lawyer gave, not sold, the files to a new lawyer, for example? Are those concerns minimized in this problem because the members of the estate planning group have all been a part of the firm of Bright & Learned?

b.   How does Model Rule 1.17(c) address the problem of confidential client information? Does the Rule let the sale be completed before clients have had a right to decide whether they want the new lawyer to see their file? Do Model Rule 1.17, Comments 7 and 8, adequately explain how the steps in the sale process are to be handled?

c.   May a lawyer properly recommend that his or her clients retain the lawyer who has bought the practice? Model Rule 7.2(b)(3) certainly seems to imply that such a recommendation is permissible. Would the selling lawyer have a conflict of interest in making that recommendation? Is the selling lawyer required to reveal that conflict to the clients before they decide whether to let the purchaser take over their file?

d.   Think back to Model Rule 1.5(e). Remember that under that rule, the forwarding lawyer had to remain liable for the new lawyer's malprac-

Mnookin, Sharing Among the Human Capitalists: An Economic Inquiry into the Corporate Law Firm and How Partners Split Profits, 37 Stanford L. Rev. 313 (1985).

tice. Is there a corresponding requirement in Model Rule 1.17? Should there be?

3. Are the terms of Model Rule 1.17 in fact applicable to the facts of this problem?

a. Does Model Rule 1.17 only apply to sale of a firm to a stranger? Does Rule 1.17, Comment 5, answer that question adequately?

b. If Bright & Learned sold the estate planning portion of its practice, would that mean that no one at Bright & Learned may ever again engage in estate planning? What would be the justification for such a rule? Does it sound suspiciously inconsistent with Model Rule 5.6(a)?

c. Should Model Rule 1.17 apply when a firm sells part of its practice to departing partners, just as it does when a single lawyer retires and sells the entire practice to one or more other lawyers? Should we leave the law applicable to selling a practice to lawyers departing from a firm subject to principles outside the Model Rules?

4. Do the Model Rules treat the sale of a deceased lawyer's practice differently than sale of the practice of a lawyer who is retiring?

a. Look at Model Rule 5.4(a). Does it give you much guidance about how to handle such a situation? If you were the executor for a deceased solo practitioner, how would you go about realizing the most you could for the lawyer's heirs and beneficiaries?

b. ABA Formal Opinion 92–369 (Dec. 7, 1992) recommends that lawyers, particularly solo practitioners, have a plan as to who will take over their files if they should die unexpectedly. The opinion advises the successor lawyer to contact each client, and preserve each client's property and files until each client can decide whom to retain as a new lawyer. Do you agree?

c. In Sears, Roebuck & Co. v. Goldstone & Sudalter, P.C., 128 F.3d 10 (1st Cir.1997), the lawyer bought the practice of a deceased collection attorney. Some of the firm's assets included unbilled work and the new lawyer sent bills for that work to Sears, his largest client. After a while, Sears contested the bills and the lawyer had to admit he had no idea what work had actually been done by the former lawyer on the matters. This case held that the new lawyer's sending bills under such circumstances was both a breach of contract with the client and a violation of the state consumer protection statute. Does this seem to be an excessively harsh result?

D. ESTABLISHING A GROUP LEGAL SERVICES PLAN AS PART OF A LAW FIRM

1. What is a group legal services plan? Why would anyone want to receive legal services from a firm pursuant to such a plan?

a. Our problem says that the new firm wants to set up a plan for serving members of a local union, and that Mary Cord, one of the lawyers, was once a member of that union. The concept of group legal services began with efforts of other labor unions to assure their members that lawyers would be available to handle their cases against companies that typically were already the clients of prominent law firms in each city.

b. Brotherhood of R.R. Trainmen v. Virginia ex rel. Va. State Bar, 377 U.S. 1 (1964), was a suit to enjoin a railway union's recommendations of lawyers who would handle worker injury cases for its members. The district court had held that letting a lay organization like a labor union "channel" cases to particular lawyers was improper. The Supreme Court held it was protected by the First and Fourteenth Amendments. Justice Black wrote for the Court:

"It cannot be seriously doubted that the First Amendment's guarantees of free speech, petition and assembly give railroad workers the right to gather together for the lawful purpose of helping and advising one another in asserting the rights Congress gave them in the Safety Appliance Act and the Federal Employers' Liability Act, statutory rights which would be vain and futile if the workers could not talk together freely as to the best course to follow. The right of members to consult with each other in a fraternal organization necessarily includes the right to select a spokesman from their number who could be expected to give the wisest counsel. * * * And the right of the workers personally or through a special department of their Brotherhood to advise concerning the need for legal assistance—and, most importantly, what lawyer a member could confidently rely on—is an inseparable part of this constitutionally guaranteed right to assist and advise each other. * * *

"Only last Term we had occasion to consider an earlier attempt by Virginia to enjoin the National Association for the Advancement of Colored People from advising prospective litigants to seek the assistance of particular attorneys. In fact, in that case, unlike this one, the attorneys were actually employed by the association which recommended them, and recommendations were made even to nonmembers. NAACP v. Button [, 371 U.S. 415 (1963)]. We held that 'although the petitioner has amply shown that its activities fall within the First Amendment's protections, the State has failed to advance any substantial regulatory interest, in the form of substantive evils flowing from petitioner's activities, which can justify the broad prohibitions which it has imposed.' In the present case the State again has failed to show any appreciable public interest in preventing the Brotherhood from carrying out its plan to recommend the lawyers it selects to represent injured workers. The Brotherhood's activities fall just as clearly within the protection of the First Amendment. And the Constitution protects the associational rights of the members of the union precisely as it does those of the NAACP. * * * "377 U.S. at 5–8.

c. Dissenting Justices Clark and Harlan were chagrined by the Court's indifference to what they believed was a corrupt system:

"By its decision today the Court overthrows state regulation of the legal profession and relegates the practice of law to the level of a commercial enterprise. * * * Local officials of the union call on each member suffering an injury and seek to secure employment of these approved attorneys in the prosecution of claims for damages arising therefrom. Moreover the union, through its president, not only controls the appointment and dismissal of the approved attorney but also has considerable influence over his fees and often controls the disposition of cases. Furthermore, from 1930 to at least 1959, the union had required these approved attorneys to pay to it a portion of their fees, usually 25%. Such an arrangement may even now be in effect through the ruse of reimbursement for investigatory services rendered by the union. This state of affairs degrades the profession, proselytes the approved attorneys to certain required attitudes and contravenes both the accepted ethics of the profession and the statutory and judicial rules of acceptable conduct. * * * 377 U.S. at 9.[5]

d.   With which opinion do you agree?

2.   Why was there concern about such plans, the legal equivalent of Health Maintenance Organizations (HMOs)? Is it simply a fear of competition, i.e., unions steering a group of attractive clients to preferred lawyers and denying lawyers outside the plan a chance to get their business?

a.   One critic, Howard C. Sorenson, argued that:

"Under some proposals, groups of organizations such as labor unions, credit unions, farm organizations, corporations, banks and chambers of commerce could deliver legal services and benefits to their employees, members, or depositors. Unrestricted, these groups are placed in a position where they dominate the delivery, the rendition, and the exercise of judgment necessary to legal services. No longer is the attorney the dominant figure in upholding the rule of law. The lay intermediary becomes a significant factor, threatening the quality of service and the existence of the vast majority of small firms dependent upon middle income clientele.

"Quite possibly, the untoward effect will be the reduced availability of legal services to neighborhoods and country towns, which surveys show need legal services the most. * * * Change in our traditional

---

5.   Editors' note: Justice Stewart took no part in the disposition of this case. Following this case, in United Mine Workers of America, Dist. 12 v. Illinois State Bar Ass'n, 389 U.S. 217 (1967), the Court upheld as constitutionally protected the practice of the United Mine Workers in employing a licensed attorney on a salaried basis to represent any of its members who wished to prosecute workmen's compensation claims before the Illinois Industrial Commission. Next, in United Transportation Union v. State Bar of Michigan, 401 U.S. 576 (1971), the union recommended selected attorneys to its members and their families in connection with suits for damages under the Federal Employers' Liability Act; it secured a commitment from those attorneys that the maximum fee charged would not exceed 25% of the recovery, and it recommended Chicago lawyers to represent Michigan claimants. The Court reversed the state court, found the practice constitutionally protected, and concluded that the "common thread running through our decisions in *NAACP v. Button, Trainmen,* and *United Mine Workers* is that collective activity undertaken to obtain meaningful access to the courts is a fundamental right within the protection of the First Amendment." 401 U.S. at 585.

delivery system must not do violence to the basic tenets that the legal profession stands upon. It is in the public interest that we as a profession promote and preserve the integrity, competence, confidentiality, and independence of judgment within our ranks. * * * "[6]

b.   Do you share Mr. Sorenson's concern? Do clients participate in a group legal services plan every time they buy auto insurance? As we saw in Problem 13, under most policies, the insurance company promises to select and provide a lawyer to defend the insured and to pay any judgments within policy limits. Even ABA Model Code of Professional Responsibility DR 2–103(D)(4)(a) permitted insurance companies to do this. Why? Should it be important as a matter of legal ethics that in the insurance situation, the insurance company is obliged to pay the judgment?

3.   Do the risks that bothered Mr. Sorenson and Justices Clark and Harlan apply equally to the arrangement that the lawyers in this problem plan to make with the electricians' union? Is the proposed plan consistent with the Model Rules?

a.   Look at ABA Model Rule 7.3(d). Does the exception for an "organization not owned or directed by the lawyer" suggest a prohibition on our new law firm's organizing such a plan? Look at Model Rule 7.3, Comment 6. Doesn't it clearly speak of a "plan or arrangement which the * * * lawyer's firm is willing to offer"?

b.   Then what is the point of Model Rule 7.3(d)? Does it forbid lawyers in our new firm from talking with union members to help convince them the plan would be a good idea? Does Model Rule 7.3, Comment 8, convince you of the need for this limitation?

c.   Is Model Rule 7.2(b)(2) addressing the same issue? Does a group legal services plan have some of the characteristics of a lawyer referral service? From the standpoint of the law firm, for example, will the union with which the firm is working send clients to the firm?

4.   Will group legal services mean the end of the solo practitioner? Or, will the groups instead provide a flow of new clients to lawyers?

a.   For many years, there has been relatively slow growth in the number of union-sponsored prepaid legal plans. One development, however, has been the creation of "individual access" plans under which members pay a certain fee every month which usually grants them unlimited telephone consultation with "access" attorneys and then the right to deal with "referral" attorneys for more complex problems at a lower-than-normal hourly fee.

b.   Montgomery Ward (once a department store similar to Sears), for example, introduced an individual access plan in 1985. In 1989, a customer paying just $6.75 a month would receive unlimited telephone consultation with an attorney, "who will write letters and make phone calls on the

6. Howard C. Sorenson, Bar Ethics: Guardian of the Profession, Trial Magazine, Mar.–Apr. 1975, p. 15. The late Mr. Sorenson practiced law in Chicago.

client's behalf. The plan also offers a laundry list of free services, including a 'simple' will, document review of up to six pages and a 24–hour emergency bail service." For referral work, the plan provided discounted contingency fees and guaranteed maximum rates of $50 per hour.

c. Group legal services plans continue to operate. The American Prepaid Legal Services Institute lists fifteen providers of prepaid legal services on its plan list. Several plans are owned by insurance companies: Hyatt Legal Plans is operated by MetLife and the AARP Plan is operated by the Legal Services Network from Allstate. The Hyatt Legal Plans website boasts having over 5 million plan members from 1200 sponsoring employers. Over 115 of the Fortune 500 are customers of the Hyatt Legal Plans.

d. Should the creators of legal services plans be liable for the malpractice of lawyers whom they provide? In Gonzales v. American Express Credit Corp., 733 N.E.2d 345 (Ill.App.2000), plaintiff joined a legal services referral plan that American Express operated. After the plan attorney allegedly failed to provide the plaintiff with adequate representation, the plaintiff sued American Express for negligent referral, breach of contract, and breach of its duty to provide him with "competent legal representation." The court rejected plaintiff's claims. There was no breach of contract, because defendants kept their only promise, which was to provide a lawyer licensed in Illinois at a specified price. There was no case for negligent referral, because a referral service is not responsible for services provided by the referred attorney. American Express is not a licensed attorney and plaintiff did not retain it to perform legal services. Hence, the plaintiff had no cause of action against the plan provider.

e. Is it preferable for unions and other organizations to publish directories of lawyers with whom their members have sought help in the past? Or, is it asking for trouble if the directory reports information about experiences (some unflattering) the members have had with the lawyers?

In Flamm v. American Ass'n of University Women, 201 F.3d 144 (2d Cir.2000), the association published a directory to help women select counsel for sex discrimination cases. The directory said that "[a]t least one plaintiff has described lawyer [Flamm] as an 'ambulance chaser' with interest only in 'slam dunk cases.'" Flamm sued for defamation, and the court agreed that a jury should be able to decide whether the statement was defamatory. The statement was offered as more than an opinion, the court said, and Flamm was entitled to make this nonprofit organization defend its assertion.

5. Should a professionally proper plan be required to have an "opt-out" provision allowing a client to reject an attorney assigned by the plan?

a. Look at ABA Model Code of Professional Responsibility DR 2–103(D)(4)(e). For many years an ability to change lawyers was considered essential for such a plan. Why would plan advocates resist that feature? Is it enough to say that the union member can always hire his or her own attorney?

b.   Does an indigent criminal defendant have to be represented by the public defender if the latter has a genuine conflict of interest? What if the defendant has a personality conflict with the assigned lawyer? Should the need for an opt-out feature in a group legal services plan be judged by the same standard applied in the "right to counsel" settings that we saw in Problem 11?

––––––––

PROBLEM 35

THE DUTY TO WORK FOR NO COMPENSATION

Although earlier problems have introduced some issues about pro bono work, for the most part we have thus far assumed that lawyers provide legal services to people who agree to pay for them. In this problem, we acknowledge the obvious reality that many people in our society cannot afford the kinds of bills you will send your other clients. If such people are to get help on what are often significant matters to them, they will require that lawyers provide their services free, or at very reduced cost. This problem first explores whether lawyers have a moral obligation to provide such services. Next, it asks whether there is any basis for putting legal force behind the obligations. Third, it examines the appointment of lawyers as defense counsel in criminal cases and considers whether the legal obligation to serve should be so limited. Finally, it presents some more general efforts to fund delivery of legal services to the poor.

FACTS

The State Bar of Georgia, to which all the state's lawyers are required to belong,[1] has proposed a requirement that each lawyer in the state devote a minimum of 100 hours per year to uncompensated legal assistance in legal aid clinics to be established by the bar. The attorney's time would be scheduled insofar as possible to suit his or her convenience, and no attorney would be required to take an individual case in which there was a conflict of interest. An attorney could begin a case at the legal aid office but credit work done on the case in his or her own office against the 100 hours.

Not pursuant to any formal plan, the court appointed J.R. Wright to represent a defendant in a murder case after the defendant refused representation by the public defender. The statutory compensation in such a case is a maximum of $750.

–––

1. As described in this problem, the State Bar of Georgia is an "integrated" or "unified" bar. That concept, and limits on how such a bar may use income from member dues, are discussed in the introduction to Chapter II.

Wright believed his client was guilty, but the defendant protested his innocence and the case ultimately required 300 hours of the attorney's time. Wright sued the state for a fee of $30,000 based on his regular hourly fee of $100 per hour. The state's defense was, in part, that the work was part of the inherent duty of an attorney.

QUESTIONS

A. THE MORAL OBLIGATION TO PROVIDE PRO BONO LEGAL SERVICES

1. Do lawyers have any moral obligation to provide free or reduced-price legal services?

a. In 1958, the Joint Committee on Professional Responsibility of the ABA and the Association of American Law Schools (AALS) set out a rationale for pro bono services in clear tones:

> "The moral position of the advocate is here at stake. Partisan advocacy finds its justification in the contribution it makes to a sound and informed disposition of controversies. Where this contribution is lacking, the partisan position permitted to the advocate loses its reason for being. The legal profession has, therefore, a clear moral obligation to see to it that those already handicapped do not suffer the cumulative disadvantage of being without proper legal representation, for it is obvious that adjudication can neither be effective nor fair where only one side is represented by counsel.

> "In discharging this obligation, the legal profession can help to bring about a better understanding of the role of the advocate in our system of government. Popular misconceptions of the advocate's function disappear when the lawyer pleads without a fee, and the true value of his service to society is immediately perceived. The insight thus obtained by the public promotes a deeper understanding of the work of the legal profession as a whole.

> "The obligation to provide legal services for those actually caught up in litigation carries with it the obligation to make preventive legal advice accessible to all. It is among those unaccustomed to business affairs and fearful of the ways of the law that such advice is often most needed. If it is not received in time, the most valiant and skillful representation in court may come too late."[2]

b. Raymond Marks and colleagues at the American Bar Foundation articulated the source of such an obligation this way:

> "Given the function that the lawyer has to perform—structuring the conflicts of society so that they are capable of peaceful resolution—we feel that even without a monopoly grant of power the legal profession is a public utility. The law is a calling which by definition

---

2. 44 A.B.A.J. 1159, 1216 (1958).

deals with public interest, not self-interest. The monopoly grant simply makes the need for regulation by self or state more urgent.

"In many ways the legal profession is like that sensitive area of the field of radio and television in which licensees control access to public discussion. In the communications field, the announced public policy—the Communications Act—requires that a commitment be made when a license is granted, that the licensee affirmatively undertake to 'operate its license in the public interest.' * * *

" * * * The absence of controls over the lawyer with respect to what he turns away is socially dangerous. It is more dangerous than the risk involved in drafting or socializing a percentage of a lawyer's time."[3]

c.   Should the obligation to provide pro bono legal services fall on all lawyers, including those in government, law teaching, and the judiciary? Should the obligation vary based upon the income the lawyer receives from the practice of law? Is the likely inability to craft a fair allocation of the burden of pro bono services relevant to the issue of whether there should be an obligation in the first place?

2.   Are you persuaded by these arguments that members of the bar have a moral obligation to see that all have access to their services?

a.   Is the obligation, if any, derived from the lawyer's role as advocate? Is it based on the fact that only lawyers are authorized to provide legal services?

b.   Is there such a shortage of available legal help that part of it must be allocated to poor people as one might allocate food after a hurricane? Is Marks right that the number of lawyers is as limited as the number of broadcast licenses, for example?

c.   Is there a "market failure" in the provision of legal services? That is, while there are certainly some lawyers who serve poor people, do we see a commercial market to serve them analogous to the marketplace of doctors willing to serve Medicaid patients, for example? Does this kind of market failure require a response from lawyers or does it suggest the need for a publicly funded system such as the one adopted for medical care?

d.   Should lawyers see a moral obligation that flows from the number of persons who had to sacrifice to see that they obtained a legal education? Are any of us truly self-made? Are all members of the bar privileged to have a talent that others badly need and only some can pay for?

B.   EFFORTS TO TRANSLATE A MORAL OBLIGATION INTO A LEGAL REQUIREMENT

1.   Assuming that lawyers have some moral obligation to use their legally protected license to practice on behalf of those who

3. F. Raymond Marks, et al., The Lawyer, the Public and Professional Responsibili-   ty 288–92 (1972).

cannot afford to pay, do we see that obligation reflected anywhere in the Model Rules?

a. Does Model Rule 6.1 impose such a requirement? Why should a rule be specific—i.e., set a standard of 50 hours per year and prescribe how that standard should be met—if it is not to be made mandatory?

b. Some explanation—if not justification—for the voluntary rule we have comes from an ABA Report on the lawyer's public interest obligation that said in part:

> "In August, 1975, in Montreal, the American Bar Association House of Delegates confirmed 'the basic responsibility of each lawyer engaged in the practice of law to provide public interest legal services' without fee, or at a substantially reduced fee, in one or more of the following areas: poverty law, civil rights law, public rights law, charitable organization representation, and administration of justice. * * * We suggest * * * that the ABA encourage each state and local bar association to adopt *specific guidelines* for members of the bar who wish to budget their public interest legal service. * * *

> "In this connection, it is important to note that a practicing lawyer may spend from 1,000 to 2,000 hours or more each year on billable client matters (as distinguished from non-client matters such as law firm administration, continuing legal education, bar association activity, and professional writing and speaking). Without focusing on this wide range of legal practice, some commentators have urged every lawyer to budget a flat 5% of client-related time for public interest legal service, yielding 50 to 100 hours per year; others have called for 10% of a lawyer's time, or 100 to 200 hours per year. Still others have suggested that a more realistic and manageable approach would be for the bar to settle on a fixed minimum number of hours, without reference to the time a lawyer spends on fee-producing matters. * * * "[4]

c. To the argument that poverty law is largely its own specialty, unknown to most private practitioners, the committee responded:

> "In our committee's judgment, the professional responsibility to contribute public interest legal service is inherently an obligation to contribute one's time—one's abilities. Given the breadth of the 1975 definition, few lawyers, if any, can responsibly argue that they are unable to make a useful, personal contribution. * * *

Do you agree?

2. From what legal authority would a requirement to deliver free legal services be derived?

a. Is the duty to take cases without compensation "inherent" in being a lawyer? Is the same duty inherent in being a plumber, a funeral director,

---

4. A.B.A. Special Committee on Public Interest Practice, Implementing the Lawyer's Public Interest Obligation 1–7 (June 1977).

or some other licensed professional? Do we require landowners to devote their land to public uses without compensation? Do the moral arguments made in the earlier questions translate easily into legal duties?

b.   Schwarz v. Kogan, 132 F.3d 1387 (11th Cir.1998), was an action under 42 U.S.C.A. § 1983 challenging the Florida Bar rule that required its members to report the number of pro bono hours they worked each year. It encouraged them to donate at least 20 hours of such work each year or to pay $350 to a legal aid organization if they did not want to do the work themselves. In upholding the requirement, the Eleventh Circuit said that Florida "undoubtedly has a legitimate interest" in encouraging pro bono service and that "[d]ue to the unique and important role of the legal profession in this country, the free provision of legal services to the poor has long been recognized as an essential component of the practice of law." 132 F.3d at 1391. Indeed, the court said, "one of the traditions of the legal profession is that a lawyer, as an officer of the Court, is 'obligated to represent indigents for little or no compensation upon court order'." 132 F.3d at 1391. The Florida program was a rational way for the Florida Bar to know how much pro bono service was being done and where in the state more services may be needed. Only reporting, not service, was mandatory, but "even assuming that the reporting requirement may have some implicit coercive effect, and thereby motivates otherwise reluctant lawyers to honor their professional responsibility, this result justifiably furthers the Rule's legitimate purpose." 132 F.3d at 1392.

c.   Is *Kogan* precedent for upholding a requirement of providing free legal services to the poor? Does a reporting requirement raise quite different issues? Would you favor adoption of such a reporting requirement in your own state?

3.   Rule 6.1 is directed at individual lawyers. Should law firms as organizations profiting from the practice of law bear some burden in encouraging their lawyers to deliver pro bono legal services?

a.   In the thirty-five year period of law firm growth from 1970–2005, the competition for law students grew at a fierce pace. In 1971, the National Association of Legal Placement, NALP, was formed by 36 law school placement directors to help facilitate legal career counseling and planning. At some point, NALP began to ask law firms for information about their pro bono programs. This information included whether the firm had a commitment to pro bono, whether the firm counted pro bono hours as billable hours, and whether the firm had a pro bono coordinator. These questionnaires, along with the competition for law students, led many large firms to implement formal pro bono programs for their lawyers.

b.   Partners at big law firms have many motivations to embrace an organized pro bono program. Pro bono work: (1) gives junior attorneys control over cases, thus enhancing and diversifying their skills; (2) exemplifies noblesse oblige, (3) may arise from a major event such as Hurricane Katrina or 9/11, (4) gives firms points on external ranking systems, (5) can generate positive publicity, (6) may generate funds from attorneys' fees award to fund future pro bono work, and (7) may enable partners to advance political causes. See, e.g., Scott Cummings & Deborah Rhode, Managing Pro Bono: Doing Well by Doing Better, 78 Fordham L. Rev. 2357 (2010).

C.   THE TRADITION OF ACCEPTING COURT APPOINTMENT IN A CRIMINAL CASE

1.   What is the basis, if any, of the distinction between the "*should* [do pro bono service]" in Model Rule 6.1 and the "*shall* [accept court appointments]" in Model Rule 6.2? Do cases holding that defendants have a constitutional right to counsel necessarily imply that attorneys must bear the uncompensated burden of such representation?

a.   Some lawyers have not taken low pay in assigned cases without protest. Matter of Hunoval, 247 S.E.2d 230 (N.C.1977), for example, concerned an appointed attorney who had seen his client convicted and sentenced to death. The conviction was affirmed by the state supreme court, but it then granted a stay of execution for the attorney to seek certiorari in the U.S. Supreme Court. At that point, the attorney refused to file the petition for certiorari until the state court approved paying him more money, saying "I cannot justify working for * * * a rate less than that received by a garage mechanic." The court turned down the demand for money, and the lawyer failed to file the petition for certiorari on behalf of the condemned man. The court was not sympathetic. It suspended the attorney from practice in the state's appellate courts and barred him from receiving appointments in criminal cases for one year.[5]

b.   Some attorneys have had greater success protesting low pay in assigned cases. DeLisio v. Alaska Superior Court, 740 P.2d 437 (Alaska 1987), for example, reversed the contempt conviction of a lawyer who refused to accept a trial court's order to serve as appointed counsel. Quoting a case from 1854, the court said that a lawyer's "professional services are no more at the mercy of the public, as to remuneration, than are the goods of the merchant, or the crops of the farmer, or the wares of the mechanic." 740 P.2d at 440. The court reasoned that "requiring an attorney to represent an indigent criminal defendant for only nominal compensation unfairly burdens the attorney by disproportionately placing the cost of a program intended to benefit the public upon the attorney rather than upon the citizenry as a whole." 740 P.2d at 443. An attorney should receive "just compensation," the court said, defined as the rate reflecting compensation received by the average competent attorney operating in the open market.

5.   See also, State v. Richardson, 631 P.2d 221 (Kan.1981) (lawyer indefinitely suspended for failing to take steps to represent defendant for whom he was appointed counsel); Federal Trade Comm'n v. Superior Court Trial Lawyers Ass'n, 493 U.S. 411 (1990) (lawyers who were not employees of the same law firm or other entity and who regularly volunteered to take assigned cases held to have committed a per se violation of the antitrust laws when they agreed to withhold services until the D.C. government raised their rates of compensation).

c. Olive v. Maas, 811 So.2d 644 (Fla.2002), involved an attorney regularly appointed as counsel for death row inmates in postconviction proceedings. In one case, however, he refused to sign the usual engagement contract that contained a cap on the fee he could receive. By a 4 to 3 vote, the Florida Supreme Court agreed that a mandatory cap on an attorney's fee in postconviction review of a capital case interferes with the prisoner's right to counsel. Such a fee cap discourages an attorney from expending extra time and effort on the defendant's case, the court said, and risks reducing the effectiveness of a defendant's representation. Thus, attorneys may petition the court for additional compensation in appropriate capital cases.[6]

d. Are these results persuasive to you? The timing of the protest in *Hunoval* was clearly inexcusable, but do you agree that courts should listen sympathetically to a lawyer's complaint about being forced to work for little or no compensation? Look at Model Rule 6.2(b). Should the lawyer's right to payment be the principal focus of the court, or should the real question be the effect on the clients' representation?[7]

e. Should the right to reimbursement of expenses be seen as a separate issue or as part of the fee question? Compare State v. Lynch, 796 P.2d 1150 (Okla.1990) (lawyers for indigent defendants must be paid expenses, plus same hourly rate that state pays public defenders), with Williamson v. Vardeman, 674 F.2d 1211 (8th Cir.1982) (state may compel lawyer's services without compensation but may not deny reimbursement of litigation expenses).

2. Should appointed counsel in a criminal case be excused from acting where the defendant's conduct puts him in a difficult ethical position?

a. In Chaleff v. Superior Court, 138 Cal.Rptr. 735 (Cal.Ct.App.1977), the defendant was trying to represent himself and the court appointed a deputy public defender as "advisory counsel." This counsel asked to withdraw because the defendant's conduct allegedly put him in an "untenable ethical position." He said he could not explain further, but it later came out that the client's self-destructive urges caused him to reject the lawyer's suggestions of defenses and to seek imposition of the death penalty. Should the lawyer be relieved in such a case? The court said yes, citing California Rule 2–111 [comparable to Model Rule 1.16]. It noted that "while the attorney's duty is to his client, he cannot be placed in the position where discharging that duty impinges upon his ethical responsibilities as a member of the bar." 138 Cal.Rptr. at 737.

---

6. The dissenting justices' concerns went to the issue of declaratory relief and not necessarily to the merits of the court's result. See also, People ex rel. Conn v. Randolph, 219 N.E.2d 337 (Ill.1966) (reimbursement in excess of statutory maximum required where "extraordinary" time and financial burden is required to defend case).

7. See, e.g., Sheppard & White, P.A. v. City of Jacksonville, 827 So.2d 925 (Fla. 2002), saying rate of pay lawyer entitled to receive must be a rate "that ensures the provision of effective assistance to his client," not the rate lawyers earn for other kinds of work. 827 So.2d at 935.

b.   Should appointed counsel be excused if he can show he lacks the skill to represent the client competently? United States v. Wendy, 575 F.2d 1025 (2d Cir.1978), said that he should. The trial court had held a lawyer in contempt for refusing to accept an assignment to defend a felony tax case carrying a potential five-year prison term. The lawyer's expertise was in tax and accounting, but he had never tried a case "civil or criminal, state or federal." The Second Circuit reversed, saying that a lawyer cannot be required to do what he is incapable of doing.

c.   Zarabia v. Bradshaw, 912 P.2d 5 (Ariz.1996), held the entire Yuma County system for appointing counsel unconstitutional. When there were not enough experienced lawyers who wanted court appointments, the plan required appointments on a "rotational basis" from a pool that included lawyers with no experience in either criminal law or trial work. "Mentors" were available for consultation, but the assumption was that any lawyer who worked hard could become competent to conduct a defense once in a while. The court said it did "not share [the county's] optimism that an attorney * * *, who has no trial or criminal experience, can become reasonably competent to represent a defendant * * * charged with a very serious crime." The court held a county has a duty to appoint only competent counsel and then to pay them a reasonable fee.

d.   Do you agree with these results? Look at Model Rule 6.2(a) and Comment 2. Are courts too willing to accept an "ethics" rationale when a lawyer is unwilling to accept an assigned case? Don't we normally presume that every lawyer will become competent with sufficient study and preparation? Is it relevant that, if the lawyer does accept an assignment, the client can later sue him for malpractice? See Ferri v. Ackerman, 444 U.S. 193 (1979) (indigent defendant in a federal criminal trial may file malpractice suit against appointed counsel).

3.   Even though most appointments are made in criminal cases, should courts be able to appoint counsel to serve indigents in civil cases as well?

a.   In Ex parte Dibble, 310 S.E.2d 440 (S.C.Ct.App.1983), a prisoner brought civil actions complaining of conditions in the state penitentiary. The trial judge appointed two lawyers to represent the prisoners in those actions. The Court of Appeals recognized that this was not a criminal case and the defendant had no constitutional right to counsel, but it refused to hold that requiring representation without compensation was a violation of the lawyer's own constitutional rights. The court noted that lawyers are an "integral and necessary part" of the justice system and concluded that courts have "the inherent power" to appoint lawyers "to serve without compensation where it appears reasonably necessary for the court to do justice." Law is a profession, the court said, and "the chief end of a profession is public service." The case was remanded, however, for a determination by the trial court that (1) the clients in fact required free counsel, (2) no other lawyers were willing to take the case pro bono, and (3) such assignments would be distributed fairly among the bar rather than falling on a limited group of lawyers.

b. Yarbrough v. Superior Court of Napa County, 702 P.2d 583 (Cal. 1985), involved court appointment of a lawyer to defend a prisoner sued in a civil suit for the wrongful death of his murder victim. The facts were very close to the ones for which he had been originally convicted, and the question was whether the court could appoint the criminal defense lawyer to defend the defendant in this civil matter too. The court held that the trial court had the power to make such an appointment and such a decision should consider the inmate's indigency, whether an adverse judgment would affect the prisoner's present or future property rights (i.e., does the indigent have a reasonable likelihood of acquiring property subject to judgment), whether counsel would be helpful in the circumstances of the case before it, and whether the cause of action could be abated until the prisoner is released "and therefore better able to make his own arrangements." The court did not reach issues of what to do if the lawyer were unwilling to be appointed and whether the court can provide compensation to the lawyer.

Chief Justice Rose Bird dissented. "As with any other working person, lawyers should be properly compensated for their time and effort," she said. She criticized the majority for avoiding this issue and (quoting the Court of Appeals) went on: "No one would dare suggest courts have the authority to order a doctor, dentist or any other professional to provide free services, while at the same time telling them they must personally pay their own overhead charges for that time. No crystal ball is necessary to foresee the public outrage which would erupt if we ordered grocery store owners to give indigents two months of free groceries or automobile dealers to give them two months of free cars. Lawyers in our society are entitled to no greater privileges than the butcher, the baker and the candlestick maker; but they certainly are entitled to no less." 702 P.2d at 590.

With which opinion do you agree?

4. Are there different rules in federal court than in state court?

a. Federal statutory law provides authority for appointing counsel. For example, in a civil case the "court may *request* an attorney to represent any [person claiming *in forma pauperis* status] unable to employ counsel." 28 U.S.C. § 1915(e)(1).

In Mallard v. United States District Court for Southern Dist. of Iowa, 490 U.S. 296 (1989), the Court held (5 to 4) that what is now § 1915(e)(1), does *not* authorize federal courts to impose *compulsory* appointment of attorneys in civil cases, in this instance an action brought by inmates against prison guards under 42 U.S.C. § 1983. The statute only authorizes courts to "request", i.e., ask a lawyer to serve voluntarily as appointed counsel in a civil case. In a footnote, the Court said that it did "not reach the question whether the federal courts have inherent authority to order attorneys to represent litigants without pay * * *." 490 U.S. at 308, n.4. Justice Kennedy, concurring, stressed lawyers' duty to volunteer their services. Lawyers, he said, "like all those who practice a profession, have obligations to their calling which exceed their obligations to the State. [I]t is precisely because our duties go beyond what the law demands that ours remains a noble profession." 490 U.S. at 310–11.

Justices Stevens, Marshall, Blackmun, and O'Connor dissented. They believed the word "request" was another way of saying "respectfully command." They said the federal statute made a lawyer's professional obligation compulsory and part of the terms on which any lawyer accepts a law license.

b. Some lower courts seem impressed with the spirit of the dissent in *Mallard*. In Tabron v. Grace, 6 F.3d 147 (3d Cir.1993), for example, the district court had said that even a request to a lawyer to act as counsel for a prisoner in a 42 U.S.C. § 1983 action against prison officials for failing to protect him against assault by other prisoners required "exceptional circumstances." The Third Circuit found no authority for such a limit on the power to make requests of lawyers. It acknowledged that the number of cases greatly exceeds the number of available lawyers, and it acknowledged the discretion of a district judge to refuse to appoint counsel, but it urged lawyers to serve when asked.

c. Scott v. Tyson Foods, Inc., 943 F.2d 17 (8th Cir.1991), was an employment discrimination case in which the employee asked the court to appoint counsel for him. Citing *Mallard*, the trial court said that it lacked power to do so, but the Eighth Circuit disagreed. Title VII has a special provision for appointment of counsel, the court said, and the district court should appoint counsel for Mr. Scott.

d. In Bothwell v. Republic Tobacco Co., 912 F.Supp. 1221 (D.Neb. 1995), the court released the lawyer it had appointed to represent an indigent prisoner in a civil suit alleging that the prisoner became ill as a result of using tobacco that lacked an appropriate warning label when he made "roll-your-own" cigarettes. The court asserted that, in spite of *Mallard*, it had inherent authority to appoint counsel in civil cases. However, it declined to continue to exercise that authority in this case because the reason the plaintiff had not been able to get private counsel was not because of his indigence; it was because trying tobacco cases is expensive and unlikely to be successful.

e. Should judges have the power to appoint counsel in civil cases? Even if such appointments would be justified in some cases, should judges be cautious about using scarce lawyer resources in cases where there is no constitutional right to counsel at all?

D. OTHER SOURCES OF FUNDING FOR LEGAL SERVICES TO THE POOR

1. Should lawyers expect public funding to be the solution to the lack of adequate legal services for the poor?

a. Requiring individual lawyers to provide uncompensated legal services is, of course, only one possible way to provide assistance to the poor. The Legal Services Corporation (LSC), for example, is a federal agency that provides funding to over 175 local affiliates around the country that hire lawyers to provide a wide variety of legal services. Annual funding for LSC activities was as high as $400 million in 1994–95. It dropped to $278 million in 1996, but rose to $329 million in 2001.[8]

b.   Those who live by federal funding may find themselves handcuffed by it. Congress imposed statutory restrictions on the LSC's expenditure of funds in the agency's 1996 and 1997 appropriations acts. Congress forbade use of LSC funds to aid entities in lobbying, class actions, giving aid to certain aliens, supporting advocacy training, litigating on behalf of prisoners, and suing to reform welfare. The restrictions were imposed on non-federal funds raised by the LSC and its local entities as well.[9]

c.   Legal Services Corp. v. Velazquez, 531 U.S. 533 (2001), involved a challenge to the congressional prohibition on the use of LSC appropriations to seek to amend or otherwise challenge the existing welfare law. The Second Circuit held that was an unconstitutional content-based restriction on speech and the Supreme Court agreed (5 to 4). In an opinion by Justice Kennedy, the Court acknowledged that Congress has excluded several kinds of cases from LSC jurisdiction, e.g., most criminal cases. However, restricting the kinds of arguments LSC lawyers can make in cases they may take is another story. That "distorts the legal system by altering the traditional role of attorneys * * * [and] threatens severe impairment of the judicial function. * * * The statute is an attempt to draw lines around the LSC program to exclude from litigation those arguments and theories Congress finds unacceptable but which by their nature are within the province of the courts to consider." 531 U.S. at 544–46.

Justice Scalia, joined by Chief Justice Rehnquist and Justices O'Connor and Thomas, argued that the statute did not regulate speech; it defined the scope of a program. Congress routinely says that federal dollars may be used for some things but not others, they observed. Poor people are free to seek welfare reform; they simply may not use LSC dollars to do it.

Which opinion makes more sense to you? If the statute said that welfare cases in general, like most criminal cases, were off limits to LSC lawyers, would the statute have been proper? Is there any limit to the Court's logic? If Congress sets up a system for funding litigation on behalf of the poor, may it impose any limits on use of those funds without intruding on some argument that some lawyer would like to make on behalf of some client?

d.   ABA Formal Opinion 06–441 (May 13, 2006) focuses on the obligations of a public defender whose caseload is too heavy to be able to represent each client competently and diligently. The opinion notes that all lawyers have a duty to act competently, communicate with their clients, abide by certain client decisions and control their workload so as to be able to meet each of their obligations. The lawyer's primary responsibility is to existing clients, so a public defender must turn down new cases before withdrawing from current ones. The lawyer should seek help from a

---

8. This and other information about the LSC can be found at its website, www.lsc.gov.

9. Data on the LSC website suggests that those sums amount to another $250 million annually.

supervisor in managing the workload and supervisors have a duty to provide that help. Ultimately, supervisors have a duty to tell the court not to assign any more cases until adequate resources are provided.

e. Louisiana v. Tonguis, 898 So.2d 325 (La.2005), further bolstered the state's obligation to provide funding for indigent defense. The defendant in this case was charged with first degree murder. When the public defender pointed out his excessive case load, the court appointed a private lawyer who, in turn, filed a motion to assure there were funds to pay her. The parish said it had no obligation to divert funds designated to run the judicial system to provision of indigent defense, but the trial court found no other source of funds and ordered sufficient funds set aside for this purpose. On this appeal, the Court noted defendants' right to counsel and lawyers' duty to accept appointments, provided they are reimbursed for expenses and overhead. The state legislature, in turn, had expressly provided that parishes had no duty to provide those funds. The court recognized the state legislature had a duty to do so and had taken steps in that direction, but the funds were not yet available. Thus, the court declared that trial judges initially should appoint counsel even in the absence of funds, but if on further inquiry, funds do not seem to be available, the state should be barred from prosecuting defendants until funds for their defense become available.[10]

2. What is the role of charitable or educational legal clinics in meeting the legal needs of poor citizens?

a. Well before creation of the public Legal Services Corporation, charitable legal services agencies provided free services to the poor. In this country, legal aid is often traced back to 1876 and the formation of a legal aid society for German immigrants living in New York. By 1916, there were legal aid societies in 37 American cities.[11]

b. One common form of those agencies today are law school clinics. They, too, sometimes come under fire from those who oppose their activities on behalf of poor clients.

Southern Christian Leadership Conference v. Supreme Court of Louisiana, 252 F.3d 781 (5th Cir.2001), involved an effort by law professors, law students, and community organizations, to challenge an amendment to the student practice rules of the Louisiana Supreme Court adopting a more restrictive definition for the "indigence" of clients whom students could represent. Those who opposed this amendment argued that it was a response to the Tulane Law School clinic's environmental cases that angered business interests. The Fifth Circuit rejected all constitutional

---

10. See also, State v. Young, 172 P.3d 138 (N.M.2007) (state barred from seeking death penalty until additional funds appropriated to pay defense counsel). But see, Britt v. State, 653 S.E.2d 713 (Ga.2007) (contempt convictions upheld against lawyers who resisted proceeding with defense, contending that failure to provide them adequate compensation denied defendant in a capital case the effective assistance of counsel).

11. The most comprehensive treatments of this early period are Reginald Heber Smith, Justice and the Poor (1919), and Emery A. Brownell, Legal Aid in the United States (1951).

challenges to the new rule, concluding that the new legal requirement of detailed financial disclosures before clients could obtain representation did not deny equal protection: the wealth classification was rationally related to the purpose of the law to help poor people. Second, although the new rule effectively limited certain kinds of representation by student clinics, it did not implicate the constitutional right of free speech. Even *Velazquez* did not require a different result. A restriction based on client wealth was content-neutral, the court reasoned, unlike the restrictions in *Velazquez*.

Do you agree with the court? Should the political purpose behind legislation be relevant to its constitutionality if on its face the legislation is content-neutral? Do we want courts trying to discern whether legislators had appropriate motives when they voted for or against a law?

c. Does the existence of the Legal Services Corporation, and of charitable organizations serving the poor, reduce the moral obligation of lawyers generally to provide legal services to the poor? Is the duty to work without fee made more pressing by the relatively modest funding of such agencies?

3. Might the bar avoid the problems of pleasing outside funding sources by finding "free" money in IOLTA accounts? Should the rules require lawyers to deposit client trust funds that are small in amount or held only for a short time, in an interest-bearing account with the interest going to the bar and not the client?

a. IOLTA (Interest on Lawyer Trust Accounts) programs are in existence in most jurisdictions today, and even though the plans rarely require the lawyers to notify the client or seek client consent, the ABA has concluded that lawyers may properly participate in such programs. Formal Opinion 348 (July 23, 1982) accepts the long tradition that the ethics rules do *not* permit the lawyer to use interest earned on client funds even to defray the lawyer's own operating expenses unless the lawyer first secures the client's specific and informed consent. As you saw in Problem 6, interest on a client's funds normally belong to the client. However, Formal Opinion 348 said:

> " * * * [N]othing in the Model Code prohibits a lawyer from placing clients' funds in interest-bearing accounts * * *. [However, in] addition to expenses created by the notification, record keeping and accounting requirements of DR 9–102(B), lawyers may incur other costs in attempting to place clients' funds at interest. Income tax filings may be necessary to enable the client to report the interest earned on the funds, and bank handling fees may further reduce the potential return. It is evident, therefore, that in many—if not most— instances, the accounting and administrative costs, plus any bank charges, will more than offset the potential gains to the client. Thus, while no ethical rule proscribes placing client funds at interest for the benefit of an individual client, administrative costs and practical considerations often will make it self-defeating for the lawyer to attempt

to obtain interest on small sums or even on large amounts of clients' funds held for short periods of time. * * *

" * * * The Committee perceives no intention by the drafters of the Model Code to relax in any manner the long-standing restrictions on a lawyer's [own] use of client funds. * * *

"[However, s]uccessful programs using the interest on lawyers' trust accounts for law-related public service projects in Canadian provinces and several British Commonwealth countries have inspired bar groups in the United States to consider the creation of similar programs. Several recent developments have caused the use of this untapped resource to become desirable and feasible. The availability of public funds for law-related public service uses, such as legal services for the indigent, has been reduced. The Internal Revenue Service has ruled that income generated under the circumstances of one program is not taxable to the client. * * *

"The programs being implemented vary in detail but have certain elements in common. All strive to have the pooled funds generate income for remittance to tax-exempt organizations where it will be applied to underwrite law-related public service activities. * * * Prior client consent is not required. Notice to clients also is not required but is encouraged where practicable. The funds are placed in interest-bearing accounts in conventionally insured depository institutions and can be withdrawn on request. The banks are directed to remit earnings net of handling charges to a designated receiving entity, usually a bar foundation or similar tax-exempt organization, and to report account activity periodically to both the organization and the participating lawyer. The tax-exempt organizations generally segregate and strictly account for the funds, and apply them as directed by governing boards to law-related uses compatible with section 501(c)(3) of the Internal Revenue Code. * * *

" * * * In the opinion of the Committee, * * * the rationale for the ethical acceptability of these programs is the same as the premise for acceptability in constitutional law and tax law. The client has no right under the circumstances to require the payment of any interest on the funds to himself or herself because the amount of interest which the funds could earn is likely to be less than the appropriate charges for administering the earnings. The practical effect of implementing these programs is to shift a part of the economic benefit from depository institutions to tax-exempt organizations. There is no economic injury to any client. The program creates income where there was none before. For these reasons, the interest is not client funds in the ethical sense any more than the interest is client property in the constitutional sense or client income in the tax law sense." * * *

b.   Do you agree with this analysis? Have lawyers instead created a special exception for themselves from normal fiduciary standards so as to divert clients' money to fund services lawyers would otherwise be morally obliged to provide without compensation? That issue has been before the courts for several years.

c. Lawyers would probably not participate in such programs if their clients explicitly objected. However, because the costs of accounting for each client's share of the interest would exceed the interest earned, the courts said that clients have no expectation of receiving the interest and thus no "property" that was unconstitutionally "taken" without just compensation. See, e.g., Cone v. State Bar of Florida, 819 F.2d 1002 (11th Cir.1987), cert. denied, 484 U.S. 917 (1987) (upholding constitutionality of Florida's Interest on Trust Accounts program).[12]

4. Do you agree with ABA Formal Opinion 348 and *Cone*, supra, that no "takings" issue is presented by an IOLTA program?

a. In Webb's Fabulous Pharmacies, Inc. v. Beckwith, 449 U.S. 155 (1980), Justice Blackmun, for a unanimous Court, invalidated a Florida statute that provided that the county may take for itself the interest accruing on an interpleader fund deposited in the county court. The Court rejected the rationale that the funds deposited were considered to be "public money" from the date of deposit until they left the account: "[A] State, by *ipse dixit*, may not transform private property into public property without compensation, even for the limited duration of the deposit in court. This is the very kind of thing that the taking clause of the Fifth Amendment was meant to prevent." 449 U.S. at 164.

b. Phillips v. Washington Legal Foundation, 524 U.S. 156 (1998), brought the constitutionality of state IOLTA plans to the Supreme Court. The issue before the Court was very specific. The Court assumed that a lawyer was required to put funds into an IOLTA account only if the interest generated on the funds would not be sufficient to offset bank service charges and accounting for the interest. The issue thus was whether the interest was nevertheless "property" of the client so that the takings clause could apply.

Chief Justice Rehnquist, for the Court (5 to 4), held that even that little bit of interest on a client's funds in a lawyer's account is property of the client for purposes of the takings clause. The amount at stake is not the issue, the Court said. "[P]roperty is more than economic value; it also consists of 'the group of rights which the so-called owner exercises in his dominion of the physical thing.'" 524 U.S. at 170. Rental income would be the property of the owner of a building, for example, even if collecting the rent cost more than the tenant owed. Because other issues had not yet been decided below, the Court left for another day whether, given this view of property, the IOLTA program constituted an unconstitutional taking and what, if any, compensation might be due.

---

12. See also, Washington Legal Foundation v. Massachusetts Bar Foundation, 993 F.2d 962 (1st Cir.1993), reaching the same result, and IRS Revenue Ruling 87–2 saying that the sums on deposit in an IOLTA program are not taxable to the client or the lawyer.

In dissent, Justices Souter, Stevens, Ginsburg, and Breyer asserted that the Court had reached out unnecessarily to decide an abstract issue, and that it could only properly decide the property issue in light of the issues that were not before the Court. They also believed, however, that it was meaningless to talk of "taking" an asset or calling it "property" when it had no practical value to the client.

c. Washington Legal Foundation v. Texas Equal Access to Justice Foundation, 270 F.3d 180 (5th Cir.2001), was the remand of *Phillips*. A Fifth Circuit panel held (2 to 1) that the confiscation of the interest income was a taking of property, because it was not in exchange for any services performed by the state. In addition, the statutory scheme did not allow a client to withdraw any of the interest that his account generated. Thus, the program permanently appropriated the client's income, and use of the funds constituted a per se taking that was subject to injunction even if not a measurable damage award.

d. The Supreme Court rejected a later "just compensation" challenge to IOLTA programs in Brown v. Legal Foundation of Washington, 538 U.S. 216 (2003). When the Washington Supreme Court set up its IOLTA program it required that: (a) *all* client funds be deposited in interest-bearing trust accounts, (b) funds that cannot earn net interest for the client be deposited in an IOLTA account, (c) lawyers direct banks to pay the net interest on the IOLTA accounts to the Legal Foundation of Washington (Foundation), and (d) the Foundation use all such funds for tax-exempt, law-related charitable and educational purposes. Later, that court made its IOLTA Rules applicable to Limited Practice Officers (LPOs), i.e., nonlawyers who are licensed to act as escrowees in real estate closings. Petitioners, who had funds that were deposited by LPOs in IOLTA accounts, and others sought to enjoin state officials from continuing this requirement, alleging *inter alia* that taking the interest earned on their funds in IOLTA accounts violates the just compensation clause, and requiring that client funds be placed in these accounts is an illegal taking of the beneficial use of those funds.

The Court accepted that the petitioners' funds generated some interest that was paid to the foundation, but without IOLTA, they would have produced no interest net of bank charges. The Ninth Circuit ruled that there was no taking because petitioners had suffered neither an actual loss nor an interference with any investment-backed expectations, and that if there were such a taking, the just compensation due was zero. The Supreme Court (5 to 4) affirmed.

Justice Stevens, writing for the Court, agreed that a law requiring that the interest on IOLTA accounts be transferred to a different owner for a legitimate public use could be a per se taking requiring the payment of "just compensation" to the client. However, he viewed the amount of interest generated for any individual client-owner of the principle to be so small that the net benefits to the client-owner after paying the bank fees was, in essence, zero. Moreover, the use of this interest to benefit "millions of needy Americans'' satisfied the ''public use'' requirement of the just compensation clause.

The Court held that the requirement that the petitioners' funds be placed in an IOLTA account is merely a transfer of principal and therefore did not effect a confiscation of any interest. The Court assumed that petitioners retained the beneficial ownership of at least a portion of their escrow deposits until the funds were disbursed at closings, that those funds generated interest in the IOLTA accounts, and that the interest was taken for a public use when it was turned over to the foundation.

However, the Court concluded that the petitioners were not entitled to any compensation for the non-pecuniary consequences of the taking of the interest on deposited funds, and that any pecuniary compensation must be measured by the petitioners' net losses rather than the public's gain. The majority argued that petitioners' net loss was zero, because the amount of interest is so small for most clients that the owner's net benefit (after paying bank fees) is zero, so any compensation due would also be zero.

Justice Scalia, joined by Chief Justice Rehnquist and Justices Kennedy and Thomas, dissented, objecting that the Court ''creates a novel exception to our oft-repeated rule that the just compensation owed to former owners of confiscated property is the fair market value of the property taken.'' Justice Kennedy also filed a dissent raising First Amendment concerns: ''One constitutional violation (the taking of property) likely will lead to another (compelled speech). These matters may have to come before the Court in due course.'' The Washington Supreme Court had granted to itself ''a monopoly which might then be used for the forced support of certain viewpoints.'' Under these IOLTA programs, ''the true owner cannot even opt out of the State's monopoly.''[13]

    e. With which of these opinions do you agree?

PROBLEM 36

PROBLEMS IN CLASS ACTION REPRESENTATION

Class actions represent a quite different way of delivering legal services to people too poor to pay for them—or people whose individual injuries would not justify hiring lawyers for each. Where several individuals have suffered a similar injury, often whether or not many of them know it, a suit may be filed in the name of some of them but on behalf of all, and in many such cases, the court will require the defendants to pay the plaintiffs' lawyers. This problem considers some of the ethical issues raised in such class action cases. First, it considers the ethics of recruiting clients to serve

---

13. The case is discussed in Ronald D. Rotunda, Found Money: IOLTA, Brown v. Legal Foundation of Washington, and the Taking of Property without the Payment of Compensation, 2002–2003 Cato Supreme Court Rev. 245 (2003).

as representative plaintiffs, and then, whether the plaintiffs must be warned about the possible dangers of proceeding by class action. Third, it examines the usual rules against a lawyer's paying the expenses of litigation, and finally, it looks at the complex world of setting the fees paid to class action and civil rights lawyers for their services.

FACTS

You know that landlords' failure to pay interest on tenants' damage deposits has cost tenants, in the aggregate, large sums of money each year. You believe that this practice is unconscionable and illegal. You want to stop it by requiring the landlords to pay their tenants interest on the deposits at the average prime rate for the term of the lease. You have put an advertisement in the local newspaper asking any tenant who is interested in filing a suit against his landlord on this basis to come to you for free legal assistance. Three persons come to your office, and you pick the most attractive and articulate one.

You are thinking of filing a class action in the name of this individual and all other tenants similarly situated, but as of now you have not done so and have simply written to your client's landlord threatening suit. The landlord has shown no interest in settlement, and it has become clear that your lawsuit will require a large amount of professional survey work. The requirement of notice to the members of the class may also be expensive. Your named client has no funds with which to pay those expenses, and she has expressed her concern to you about how she can possibly pay your fee.

QUESTIONS

A.   THE USE OF PUBLICITY TO FIND CLIENTS FOR A CLASS ACTION SUIT

1. Should lawyers be allowed to advertise to find clients in whose names to bring class action cases?

a. An early concern for lawyers seeking to file a class action is to advise members of the putative class of their legal rights and to persuade them not to opt out of the class. That sounds a lot like the issues that arose in Problem 31 on lawyer marketing. Indeed, you will find a passing reference to the issue in Model Rule 7.2, Comment 4.

b. The courts have found authority to contact potential class members is implicit in Federal Rule of Civil Procedure 23, rather than the Constitution alone. See, e.g., Coles v. Marsh, 560 F.2d 186, 189 (3d Cir.1977), cert. denied, 434 U.S. 985 (1977): "We hold * * * that the district court lacked power to impose any restraint on communication for the purpose of preventing the recruitment of additional parties plaintiff or of the solicitation of financial or other support to maintain the action.''[1]

c. The Supreme Court quoted from *Coles* with approval in Gulf Oil Co. v. Bernard, 452 U.S. 89 (1981). Gulf Oil, pursuant to an agreement with the EEOC, sent notices to alleged victims of racial and gender discrimination offering back pay in exchange for signed releases of all claims based on discrimination. Respondents then filed a class action on behalf of all present and former employees who had been subject to discrimination. Gulf moved for an order limiting communications between the named class action plaintiffs and their counsel to prospective or actual class members. The district court granted the order but the en banc Fifth Circuit reversed. The Supreme Court agreed with the Fifth Circuit, holding that the order involved an abuse of discretion under Federal Rule 23 and potentially involved serious restraints on expression in violation of the First Amendment:

> "The order interfered with their [the class representatives'] efforts to inform potential class members of the existence of this lawsuit, and may have been particularly injurious * * * because the employees at that time were being pressed to decide whether to accept a back-pay offer from Gulf that required them to sign a full release of all liability for discriminatory acts. In addition, the order made it more difficult for respondents, as the class representatives, to obtain information about the merits of the case from the persons they sought to represent.

> "Because of these potential problems, an order limiting communications between parties and potential class members should be based on a clear record and specific findings that reflect a weighing of the need for a limitation and the potential interference with the rights of the parties. * * * In addition, such a weighing— identifying the potential abuses being addressed—should result in a carefully drawn order that limits speech as little as possible, consistent with the rights of the parties under the circumstances. * * * [T]he mere possibility of abuses does not justify routine adoption of a communications ban that interferes with the formation of a class or the prosecution of a class action in accordance with the Rules." 452 U.S. at 101–04.

d. Is this holding consistent with the Supreme Court's earlier decisions, In re Primus, 436 U.S. 412 (1978) (upholding solicitation of pro bono cases), and Shapero v. Kentucky Bar Ass'n, 486 U.S. 466 (1988) (upholding direct mail advertising/solicitation), both discussed in Problem 31?[2]

---

1. The indictment of the prominent class-action firm Milberg, Weiss, Bershad & Schulman, and two of its partners, for allegedly paying people to be named plaintiffs in class action and shareholder derivative suits shows the issue of recruiting named plaintiffs in painful detail. Some of the principals in the case have pled guilty to serious crimes, and the firm has closed its doors.

2. Devlin v. Scardelletti, 536 U.S. 1 (2002), held that non-named class members may appeal a settlement where it fixes their legal rights and obligations and where the non-named class members objected to settlement agreement at fairness hearing.

To the extent lawyers recruit clients to aid the lawyer's chances of being named to

2. Do the same free speech principles justify communication with class members by defense counsel seeking to persuade them to opt out of the class?

a. Resnick v. American Dental Ass'n, 95 F.R.D. 372, 376–78 (N.D.Ill. 1982), ordered *defense* counsel, in a class action charging employment discrimination, not to communicate with *plaintiff* class action members because of Model Code of Professional Responsibility DR 7–104(A)(1) (now Model Rule 4.2). *Gulf Oil* itself, in fact, stated in dictum that DR 7–104 is an example of a "properly impose[d]" restraint on communication. 452 U.S. at 104 n.21.

b. Kleiner v. First Nat'l Bank of Atlanta, 751 F.2d 1193 (11th Cir.1985), was a class action involving alleged violation of an agreement to give small borrowers the "prime rate." To try to limit its liability, the bank embarked on a program of calling potential class members to try to persuade them to opt out of the suit. One loan officer, who was also a lawyer, objected to the pressure tactics being used in the calls and was forced to resign for refusing to participate. The trial judge was incensed and imposed disqualification and a $50,000 fine on the defense lawyer. Although sending the case back for a hearing, the Eleventh Circuit relied on Ohralik v. Ohio State Bar, discussed in Problem 31, to say that sanctions would be appropriate. The defense effort to urge potential plaintiffs to opt out of the class was "inherently conducive to overreaching and duress" and thus not simply the exercise of free speech. 751 F.2d at 1206.

c. Do you think courts have been even-handed in their treatment of such contacts? Should potential class members be considered represented persons for purposes of Model Rule 4.2 even before they have decided whether to remain part of the class? Is treating them that way important to carrying out the purposes of Federal Rule 23 and the class action process?

d. ABA Formal Opinion 07–445 (Apr. 11, 2007) says that Model Rule 4.2 does not prohibit defense counsel's contacting potential class members before the class is certified, because at that point the boundaries of the class have not yet been set. Both plaintiff and defense counsel are bound, however, to deal with such persons as protected by Model Rule 4.3. Do you agree with this analysis? The ABA Standing Committee on Ethics and Professional Responsibility expressly does not use constitutional or other law to answer questions; it looks only to the Model Rules. Might that tend to make its answers less useful or even potentially misleading?

B. POSSIBLE CONFLICTS OF INTEREST IN CLASS ACTION CASES

1. Federal Rules of Civil Procedure, Rule 23(a)(4), requires a finding that "the representative parties will fairly and adequately protect the interests of the class." Is that merely a procedural rule

---

represent the class and collect the largest share of the fee award, use of competitive bidding to select class counsel might reduce some early communication. But see, e.g., Developments in the Law: The Paths of Civil Litigation, 113 Harvard L. Rev. 1827, 1842 (2000) (bidding rarely used); Third Circuit Task Force on the Selection of Class Counsel (2002) (criticizing the practice).

for the guidance of the court, or does it have a conflict of interest element as well?

a. Who is the "client" in a class action? Is it the named class representatives? Is it "the class"? In Bachman v. Pertschuk, 437 F.Supp. 973 (D.D.C.1977), a government lawyer tried to act as counsel for a class of employees of which he was also a member. The court found that such representation would violate what is now Model Rule 1.7(a)(2). Any class inevitably consists of people with some interests different from those of others in the class, the court said, concluding:

> "[The attorney] is a present employee seeking relief as a member of a class consisting of persons who are presently employed, were denied employment, or were discharged. Whenever an attorney's personal interest as a class member is limited to the interest of those persons presently employed, the possibility exists that he may favor a settlement which gives preference to the interests of such persons over those denied employment by or discharged from the FTC. Furthermore, he may devote a disproportionate amount of time preparing for trial on the issues relevant to the subgroup to which he belongs. Thus, the varying interests of the class represented coupled with the difficulty of viewing one's own limited interest in the context of the interests of the entire class require that [the attorney] be disqualified as attorney for the class because he may not adequately be able to 'protect the interests of the [entire] class.' Fed.R.Civ.P. 23(a)(4)." 437 F.Supp. at 977.

b. Amchem Products, Inc. v. Windsor, 521 U.S. 591 (1997), raised another kind of conflict. For many years, asbestos litigation has been a management nightmare for the federal courts. In 1991, the Multi–District Litigation (MDL) panel consolidated all pending asbestos cases in a single federal district. Settlement talks began but the specter of future liability to unknown victims made the defendants unwilling to commit to a figure for current cases. Thus, plaintiffs and defendants together tried to define a class that included everyone who has become ill as a result of asbestos exposure and everyone whose symptoms might develop in the future. The defendants were prepared to create a huge fund with which to pay all claims. Both sides agreed to a schedule for payments to be made depending on the severity of the illness, and they created an alternative dispute resolution process through which to make payments promptly. The district court certified the class for settlement purposes only and found the proposed settlement fair. Georgine v. Amchem Products, Inc., 878 F.Supp. 716 (E.D.Pa.1994). However, the Third Circuit reversed. 83 F.3d 610 (3d Cir.1996).

The Supreme Court agreed with the Third Circuit. The Court acknowledged the problem the district court faced. However, Rule 23 still requires that "common questions" of fact or law "predominate." A shared interest in getting compensation does not, by itself, satisfy the predominance requirement. In the proposed settlement class, issues of both liability and injury were so diverse as to make the class too "sprawling" to certify. The plaintiffs could not represent the class adequately because conflicts of interest within the class abounded. People sick today would want more of the settlement to go to them than to have it saved for future victims, for example. Indeed, the Court found it hard to imagine how future claimants could receive adequate notice and have a basis to decide whether to opt out of a class of people who did not know they had been injured.[3]

2. Assume that the class action is governed by Federal Rule 23(e), which provides that a class action "shall not be dismissed or compromised without the approval of the court. * * *" Must you warn your client that if you file as a class action, it will no longer be in his discretion when to settle out of court and on what terms?

a. What would you be required to do if you represented a number of similarly situated people other than in a class action, and if the defendant proposed an aggregate settlement—a single sum to cover the losses of all of them—so that an independently-tailored award for this client is not possible? See Model Rule 1.8(g).

b. Assume that the client you have picked—when told of the difficulties of a class action for damages—decides that he wants you to file suit only in his individual capacity. May you "fire" that client and pick another? Is a class action filed for the benefit of the named client, the lawyer, or the class? Does the rhetoric fit the reality in all cases?

c. Suppose the landlord whom you have chosen to sue is a major property owner in the community. He offers to settle the case for five times the actual damages of your client, a total of $125, if your client refrains from filing the class action. May you permit your client to settle on that basis? May you ethically refuse to do so? Note that since you have not yet filed the class action, Rule 23(e), quoted above, has not yet come into play.

3. Now assume that you have filed a class action on behalf of construction workers seeking to require the city to institute an affirmative action program for its construction work. City officials are anxious to settle but they do not like the named plaintiff. The city proposes to settle the class action and offers a reasonable affirmative action program for all construction workers, but informs you orally that it will never employ the named plaintiff. As counsel to the entire class, may you—must you—urge acceptance of the plan? What, if anything, should or must you tell the named plaintiff?

a. Parker v. Anderson, 667 F.2d 1204 (5th Cir.1982), alleged employment discrimination at Bell Helicopter. Class counsel negotiated a settle-

---

3. Justices Breyer and Stevens dissented, arguing that the interest in achieving some settlement of this intractable controversy was greater than the court acknowledged. Justice O'Connor did not participate in the decision.

The *Amchem* case has not completely ended the use of settlement classes, at least if they do not present the case management problems that *Amchem* involved. See, e.g., Hanlon v. Chrysler Corp., 150 F.3d 1011 (9th Cir.1998) (class of owners of minivans with defective latches; all death and personal injury victims' cases excluded from class to be sure issues common to all cases).

ment worth about $2.5 million, a sum the district court found fair. The named plaintiffs, however, demanded personal payments of up to $100,000 each, and objected when told the proposed settlement would give each much less. The Fifth Circuit affirmed approval of the settlement over the named plaintiffs' objections. "The courts have recognized that the duty owed by class counsel is to the entire class and is not dependent on the special desires of the named plaintiffs," the court said. " * * * [T]he named plaintiffs should not be permitted to hold the absentee class hostage by refusing to assent to an otherwise fair and adequate settlement in order to secure their individual demands." 667 F.2d at 1211.

b. In Blanchard v. EdgeMark Financial Corp., 175 F.R.D. 293 (N.D.Ill.1997), the named plaintiff retained a second lawyer to conduct settlement negotiations of his individual claims. Class counsel sat silent and then proposed to look for a new named plaintiff. The court found that the named plaintiff, by settling separately, violated his fiduciary obligation to the class. Once the court certifies the class, any settlement with the class representative, even if only of his individual claims, must be submitted to court for review and approval. The court also said that defense counsel violated Model Rule 4.2 by talking to the named plaintiff while he was still represented by class counsel. The court forced the named plaintiff to pay attorneys' fees and costs of the class created by the litigation because of what he had done.

4. Assume instead that, in order to avoid the need to follow the rules applicable to class actions, a lawyer files hundreds of identical cases on behalf of individual plaintiffs but then tries to get the defendant to settle them for a single aggregate sum. What must the lawyer do to get client consent to the settlement?

a. Look at Model Rule 1.8(g). Is there any doubt that, for consent to be informed, each plaintiff must know the total amount of the award and the amount every other plaintiff is getting? Is that rule practical in cases where the number of plaintiffs is large?

b. The Tax Authority v. Jackson Hewitt, Inc., 898 A.2d 512 (N.J. 2006), examined whether the multiple plaintiffs in such a non-class action aggregate settlement may agree that a weighted majority of the plaintiffs may approve a proposed settlement and bind those who dissent. Plaintiffs' lawyers argue that getting unanimity of plaintiffs creates an incentive for some to hold out for a larger share, so a system of majority voting looks attractive. In an opinion that does a good job of discussing the relevant authorities, however, the court approved the Model Rule 1.8(g) requirement and did not permit even super-majority voting.

c. Is Model Rule 1.8(g) a conflict of interest rule that should be subject to advance waiver? That is, should plaintiffs be able to bind themselves *now* in the engagement letters to accept majority voting in the *future*? For example, assume that 150 clients all sue the defendant for installing inadequate insulation in their houses. The 150 know that it will be easier to settle the cases with the defendant if they settle them as a group, but they recognize that under Rule 1.8(g), one or more hold-outs could torpedo a settlement. Thus, they agree that they will all be bound by any deal that at least 100 of them approve and that brings each of the plaintiffs at least $5,000 in damages. Assuming that all 150 give informed consent to this procedure initially, should Rule 1.8(g) permit it?

ABA Formal Opinion 06–438 (Feb. 10, 2006) said no. Rule 1.8(g) "empowers each client to withhold consent and thus prevent the lawyer from subordinating the interests of the client to those of another client or to those of the lawyer," the opinion said. "The informed consent required by the rule generally cannot be obtained in advance of the formulation of such an offer or demand."

Do you agree with Formal Opinion 06–438? Might it reflect an implicit suspicion that many plaintiffs will not in fact be sufficiently informed to give appropriate advance consent? Ass'n of the Bar of the City of New York, Comm. on Prof'l and Judicial Ethics, Formal Opinion 2009–6 (2009), arrived at the same answer as the ABA Opinion. It states that it is nearly impossible for a lawyer to possess enough information about the risks involved in a waiver prior to settlement negotiations, and therefore the lawyer could not provide adequate disclosure and permit the client to give truly informed consent. An aggregate settlement requires the informed consent of every client, and individual informed consent may not be waived.

C. LIMITATIONS ON ADVANCING FUNDS NEEDED TO MEET EXPENSES OF LITIGATION; NEW WAYS OF FINANCING LITIGATION

1. This problem says your lawsuit will require a large amount of professional survey work and your named client has no funds to pay for it. Should you be able to advance the funds necessary to do that work?

a. Look at ABA Model Rule 1.8(e). What could possibly be the rationale for forbidding your providing help to a client in need? Restatement Third, The Law Governing Lawyers § 36(2), Comment c, says that advancing funds to a client "gives the lawyer the conflicting role of a creditor and could induce the lawyer to conduct the litigation so as to protect the lawyer's interests rather than the client's." See also, Model Rule 1.8, Comment 10. Are you convinced?

b. Model Rule 1.8(e)(1) creates an exception for litigation expenses and court costs. Why don't those expenses make the lawyer a creditor of the client? In both cases, does the fact that repayment will be "contingent on the outcome of the matter" tend to encourage a lawyer to try to settle a case for a sum certain rather than taking the matter to trial where the client could recover more but the expenses advanced by the lawyer would be at risk?

c. If the suit is a class action, should a different rule apply? Rand v. Monsanto Co., 926 F.2d 596 (7th Cir.1991), was a securities class action. The district court denied class certification when the named plaintiff refused to be personally liable for all costs of litigation. The district court said letting the lawyer advance the expenses violated the local rule counterpart to Model Rule 1.8(e), but the Seventh Circuit reversed. Almost by definition, a class member has a small personal claim, Judge Easterbrook wrote. "A conscientious plaintiff is likely to be willing to make some financial commitment to the case. But no person need be willing to stake his entire fortune for the benefit of strangers." 926 F.2d at 599. DR 5-103(B), the predecessor to Model Rule 1.8(e), is "long in the tooth," he said, a "relic of the rules against champerty and barratry," and inconsistent with Federal Rule 23. Do you agree?

d. ABA Formal Opinion 04–432 (Jan. 14, 2004) considered an analogous issue and concluded that normally a lawyer may not post a bond, or arrange for its posting, to secure the release of a client whom the lawyer represents in the matter with respect to which the client has been detained. To do so, the opinion says, would "create a significant risk that [the lawyer's] representation of the client would be materially limited" in violation of Model Rule 1.7(a)(2). While Rule 1.7(b) permits continued representation even with a conflict between the personal interests of a lawyer and the interests of a client *if* the client gives informed consent, "in all but the rarest of circumstances" the unique conditions of incarceration mean that the client's acquiescence will not be sufficiently genuine and voluntary to qualify as "informed consent" under Rule 1.7(b). The opinion acknowledges that there may be "rare circumstances in which there is no significant risk that her representation of the client will be materially limited by her personal interest in recovering the amount advanced." Possible circumstances where posting a bond may be permissible include where (1) the amount involved is negligible, (2) the lawyer is a friend of the family of the client and can expect indemnification from the family, or (3) the representation is in something like a civil rights case where it is likely that no one else will post bond on behalf of the defendant.

2. Should you be permitted to you pay your client an allowance for living expenses during the pendency of a case?

a. The traditional answer has been no. In State of Oklahoma ex rel. Okla. Bar Ass'n v. Smolen, 17 P.3d 456 (Okla.2000), a lawyer loaned his worker's compensation client $1,200 for living expenses after the client's house burned down. The client agreed to pay the loan back at a rate of $100 per month out of the benefits received in the case. Because the court knew the lawyer had made similar loans to other clients, it was concerned that new clients might choose counsel based on "improper inducements" and suspended him from practice for six months.

b. Cleveland Bar Ass'n v. Nusbaum, 753 N.E.2d 183 (Ohio 2001), publicly censured a lawyer for advancing $26,000 in living expenses to a client who was also a friend. The client was out of work and undergoing twenty operations to deal with his injuries. Do you agree that such loans represent a decline in professional standards of the bar? Is it naive to suggest that such cases show that some lawyers retain human compassion?

c. The reporters for the Restatement Third, The Law Governing Lawyers originally suggested in § 36(2), Comment *c*, that the law should be understood to permit payment of living expenses, at least where the loan would permit the client "to withstand delay in litigation that otherwise might unjustly induce the client to settle or dismiss a case because of financial hardship rather than on the merits." The American Law Institute membership voted down that proposal, however, after an impassioned appeal that support would be offered by lawyers who were less than scrupulous, thus putting honorable lawyers at a competitive disadvantage. What do you think of such an argument?

d. The law may be becoming more flexible on this issue. Shade v. Great Lakes Dredge & Dock Co., 72 F.Supp.2d 518 (E.D.Pa.1999), was a Jones Act case where the defendant tried to disqualify plaintiff's counsel because counsel paid the plaintiff's apartment rent after the plaintiff lost his house and his job. His wife was also injured. After discussing what, if any, continuing justification Rule 1.8(e) might have, the court concluded that the payments would not have an improper effect on the litigation. Discipline, not disqualification, was the way to deal with any violation.

e. How would you recommend that the issue of loans to clients be handled? Would you require that a client must repay all such loans? If a lawyer may waive payment of fees even if the case is successfully resolved, should a lawyer also be permitted to waive repayment of expenses? Does Model Rule 1.8, Comment 10, persuade you that Model Rule 1.8(e) properly resolves these issues?

3. Are the same issues raised if the case also needs the aid of an expert witness and the clients are too poor to hire one? Should you be able to hire the expert witness and make his or her fee contingent on the outcome of the case?

a. Look at Model Rule 3.4(b). The prohibition of the payment of contingent fees to expert witnesses was attacked in Person v. Association of the Bar of the City of New York, 554 F.2d 534 (2d Cir.1977), cert. denied, 434 U.S. 924 (1977). The district court struck down the prohibition, but the Court of Appeals reversed, reasoning:

> "States have a compelling interest in regulating the conduct of professionals who practice within their borders. * * * Expert testimony, by its very nature, concerns areas of knowledge with which the ordinary juror and the court are unfamiliar, and perjured expert testimony is particularly difficult for a juror to detect. New York has adopted DR 7–109(C) to lessen the likelihood of false expert testimony. * * *

> "We hold that [the prohibition] has a sufficient rational basis to withstand a constitutional challenge under the equal protection and due process clauses of the Fourteenth Amendment." 554 F.2d at 538–39.

b. Is the policy behind the prohibition persuasive to you? Look at Model Rule 3.4, Comment 3.[4]

---

4. First National Bank of Springfield v. Malpractice Research, Inc., 688 N.E.2d 1179   (Ill.1997), makes a simple but important point. Just as a lawyer may not hire an

4. Suppose the law firm is not able to finance the cost of litigation. May the lawyers in the firm spread the risk to third parties such as litigation finance companies?

a. In recent years, litigation costs have risen at astonishing rates so that only the largest firms may have the resources to fund the costs of major complex litigation. Plaintiffs and law firms have not been able to obtain traditional bank financing for these expenses. These financial pressures have led to an emergence of a "litigation funding" or "third party financing" industry abroad and now in the United States.[5] Essentially, litigation funding companies provide plaintiffs with cash advances to fund the litigation expenses for a share of the litigation proceeds.

b. Before the codification of crimes into a Model Penal Code, three common law crimes prohibited third party involvement in litigation. (1) *Champerty* prohibited a third party from becoming an investor in another person's litigation. (2) *Maintenance* prohibited third party support for another person's lawsuit. (3) *Barratry* prohibited stirring up litigation. Although in most jurisdictions, these common law crimes do not exist in the criminal codes, courts and state bar organizations could still view such behavior as violating state public policy. One author concludes that 29 states, including Texas, prohibit some forms of champertous agreements.[6] Third party financing would need to take into account these restrictions, but why impose the restrictions at all?

c. In Rancman v. Interim Settlement Funding Corp., 789 N.E.2d 217 (Ohio 2003), Rancman had filed suit against her husband's insurance company for recovery of an uninsured motorist claim. While awaiting its resolution, Rancman entered into a contract with defendant Interim Settlement, which lent her $7,000 contingent on the outcome of her case. The contract stated that, in exchange for the $7,000, Rancman would pay Interim Settlement $19,600 if the case was resolved within 12 months, $25,000 if resolved within 18 months, $30,400 if resolved within 24 months, and nothing if the case was not resolved in her favor. After settling with the insurance company for $100,000, Rancman refused payment on the contract and instead returned the $7,000 plus interest at 8%. She then sued to have the contracts rescinded, alleging that Interim Settlement's practices were "unfair, deceptive, and unconscionable sales practices." Interim argued that its advances were investments, not loans. The Ohio Supreme

expert on a contingent fee basis, the lawyer may not pay a firm on a contingent basis to procure an expert either. The contingent payment would create an incentive to find an expert who could be "coached," which is why the courts have denied contingent fees to experts themselves.

5. "[I]n order to keep the courthouse doors open in legal systems where losers pay winners' legal costs and lawyers generally charge hourly rather than contingent fees, many countries including the UK, Australia, the Netherlands, Belgium, Germany, and South Africa have become more amenable to third parties financing lawsuits, typically on a contingency basis." Susan Lorde Martin, Litigation Financing: Another Subprime Industry that has a Place in the United States Market, 53 Villanova L. Rev. 83, 107–08 (2008).

6. Christy B. Bushnell, Champerty is Still No Excuse in Texas: Why Texas Courts (and the Legislature) Should Uphold Litigation Funding Agreements, 7 Houston Bus. & Tax J. 358, 369 (2007).

Court agreed with Rancman: "Except as otherwise permitted by legislative enactment or the Code of Professional Responsibility, a contract making the repayment of funds advanced to a party to a pending case contingent upon the outcome of that case is void as champerty and maintenance. Such an advance constitutes champerty and maintenance because it gives a nonparty an impermissible interest in a suit, impedes the settlement of the underlying case, and promotes speculation in lawsuits." 789 N.E.2d at 221.

d.   In Osprey v. Cabana Ltd. Partnership, 532 S.E.2d 269 (S.C.2000), when the plaintiff in a lender liability action was short on funds to pay legal bills, the Osprey company lent it $50,000 and bought "an interest in said lawsuit." Osprey was to get the first $150,000 of any judgment. The case settled for $650,000 and Osprey sought to enforce its claim. The borrower's defense was that the contract constituted common law champerty and thus was void. The court traced the history of champerty back to medieval times and concluded that it would abolish champerty as a defense in the state. Contracts such as the one in this case could be examined as to unconscionability, duress, and fair dealing, the court said, but there was no longer any reason to forbid such contracts per se.

e.   If the third party financing is structured as a loan without any contingency, the arrangement may violate state usury laws. The commentators have split on whether state usury laws should apply to such arrangements, but these laws present a significant potential impediment to third party financing in the United States.[7] Some state legislatures have enacted statutes to provide guidelines for "non-recourse civil litigation advance contracts." E.g., Ohio Rev. Code Ann. sec. 1349.55 (2009).

f.   Litigation financing by third parties raises other ethical issues. First, may a lawyer refer a client to a third party financing company? New Jersey Advisory Committee on Professional Ethics, Opinion 691 (2001) approved of referrals "provided the lawyer has no financial interest in the entity securing or providing the funding, the entity will not be funding any portion of the unrealized legal fees, and the lawyer will be independent of and will not profit from the business of the entity." Second, because third parties will not provide financing unless they can evaluate the strengths and weaknesses of the litigation, the client will need to authorize the lawyer to disclose confidential information to the third party. Before the client can consent to such disclosure, the lawyer needs to discuss the risks of revealing confidential information to a third person, including the possible loss of attorney-client privilege. See Connecticut Opinion 99–42 (1999). Finally, some litigation financing agreements may give the third party companies too much control and access to the client's litigation case and thus interfere with the lawyer's independent professional judgment to the client in violation of Model Rule 5.4(c).

---

7.   Compare Julie H. McLaughlin, Litigation Funding: Charting a Legal and Ethical Course, 31 Vt. L. Rev. 615, 635–39 (2007) (usury laws should apply) with Douglas R. Richmond, Litigation Funding: Investing, Lending, or Loan Sharking, 2005 Prof. Lawyer 17, 31–34 (2005) ("litigation funding agreements are not usurious"). See also Courtney R. Barksdale, All That Glitters Isn't Gold: Analyzing the Costs and Benefits of Litigation Finance, 26 Rev. Litigation 707 (2007).

g. Does third party financing help to increase plaintiff access to the litigation system or does it simply reduce lawyer risk in funding litigation? Could a lawyer assign part of her legal fees to a litigation funding company directly for a nonrecouse loan or would such an arrangement violate the prohibition of sharing legal fees with a nonlawyer? Do third party financing arrangements create unresolvable conflicts of interest? See Model Rule 1.7(a)(2). Will such arrangements lead to the filing of frivolous cases? And, should the American judicial system remain essentially a free public good with small filing costs if large companies can invest in the plaintiffs cases?

D. CALCULATING FEES FOR PREVAILING IN A CLASS ACTION OR CIVIL RIGHTS CASE

1. Who should bear attorneys' fees in class action and civil rights cases?

a. Most non-class action, non-civil rights cases in this country follow what is called the American Rule: all parties in litigation bear their own costs and attorneys' fees. However, courts have the power to award attorney fees in certain classes of cases.

(1) The "common fund doctrine" says that when the plaintiff's class action creates a fund of money to be distributed to members of the class, the court may allow court costs, other expenses, and counsel fees to be paid out of the fund on the theory that those who have benefitted from the fund should pay for the legal services rendered.

(2) Other times, Congress by statute may require the losing party to pay the winner's legal fees, for example, where the plaintiff is treated as a private attorney general vindicating public rights. The lawyer is said to have conferred a benefit upon the public, even if that benefit is not monetary.

(3) Congress has also authorized attorneys' fees in civil rights cases. 42 U.S.C. § 1988 provides that "the court, in its discretion, may allow the prevailing party, other than the United States, a reasonable attorney's fee as part of the costs" in "any action or proceeding" to enforce civil rights laws such as 42 U.S.C.A. §§ 1981–86, 20 U.S.C. § 1681 et seq., and 42 U.S.C.A. § 20004 et seq.

b. The fact that a nonprofit legal aid group represented plaintiff free of charge does not preclude the plaintiff from collecting attorneys' fees based on the rates charged by private counsel for the same kind of work. Blum v. Stenson, 465 U.S. 886 (1984). However, a lawyer may not recover attorneys' fees under § 1988 when the lawyer appears *pro se*. Kay v. Ehrler, 499 U.S. 432 (1991).

c. In Doe v. Board of Education, 165 F.3d 260 (4th Cir.1998), cert. denied, 526 U.S. 1159 (1999), a suit under the Individuals with Disabilities Education Act, the lawyer was the child's father. The court held that *Kay* controlled the result. Granting fees was not necessary to encourage a parent to fight for his child, the court said, and rather than encouraging inexperienced parents to bring cases in the hope of a fee award, the court denied these fees. See also Kooritzky v. Herman, 178 F.3d 1315 (D.C.Cir. 1999) (lawyer appearing *pro se* not entitled to claim "costs" for his own work as an "expert" in the case).[8]

d. Augustine v. Department of Veterans Affairs, 429 F.3d 1334 (Fed. Cir.2005), reviewed a decision of the United States Merit Systems Protection Board denying a prevailing party's request for attorneys' fees because her attorney was not licensed to practice in the state in which the services were rendered. Under the Board's rules, a nonlawyer may represent a litigant, but such a nonlawyer is not entitled to attorneys' fees. The board argued that because this lawyer was not licensed in California where the case was heard, in effect he was a nonlawyer. The Federal Circuit disagreed. State licensing requirements purporting to regulate appearances before a federal agency are invalid under the Supremacy Clause, the court held. California has no authority to regulate the award of fees for work before federal agencies, so whether or not the lawyer was licensed in California could not affect his entitlement to collect his fee.

2. What kind of relief should the court require before treating a person as a "prevailing party" for purposes of receiving an attorney's fee award?

a. Hensley v. Eckerhart, 461 U.S. 424, 433 (1983), embraced this definition of a prevailing party: "plaintiffs may be considered 'prevailing parties' for attorney's fees purposes if they succeed on any significant issue in litigation which achieves some of the benefit the parties sought in bringing suit." The Court described this as a "generous formulation." Id.

b. Buckhannon Board & Care Home v. West Virginia Dept. of Health and Human Resources, 532 U.S. 598 (2001), considered whether the term "prevailing party" applies to someone who did not secure a judgment on the merits but achieved a desired result by another means. Buckhannon sued the state health department claiming that its requirement that residents all be capable of "self-preservation" violated the Fair Housing Amendments Act (FHAA) of 1988. After discovery had begun, the state legislature eliminated the requirement and the case was dismissed as moot. Buckhannon then sought an attorney's fee as the "prevailing party" under the FHAA, arguing based on the "catalyst theory" that a plaintiff is a

---

8. However, Gilbert v. Master Washer & Stamping Co., Inc., 104 Cal.Rptr.2d 461 (Cal.Ct.App.2001), holds that under California law an attorney who is represented by his own law firm may collect reasonable attorneys' fees. If the lawyer had represented himself, he would not have been entitled to an attorney's fee at all, but because he was represented by others in his law firm, he got them. The court also said that the fees need not be limited to amounts actually paid by the lawyer; the trial court may assess the fees the firm would have charged an outside client.

Bond v. Blum, 317 F.3d 385 (4th Cir. 2003), also allowed attorneys' fees in a federal case where an entity (in this case, a law firm) represents itself through in-house counsel. In this case, plaintiff sued a law firm and lawyers within that firm represented it. The firm is a "legal entity represented by attorneys," albeit attorneys within the firm. *Kay v. Ehrler, supra*, in fact, said that "an organization is not comparable to a pro se litigant." The law firm is a business and professional entity distinct from its members, and the member representing the firm as an entity represents the firm's distinct interests.

prevailing party if it achieves a desired result through a voluntary change in the defendant's conduct. Several courts of appeals had adopted that theory, but the Supreme Court rejected it, saying that the catalyst theory would allow "an award where there is no judicially sanctioned change in the legal relationship of the parties." 532 U.S. at 605. Therefore, it is not a basis for the award of attorney's fees.[9]

c. The *Buckhannon* decision has rippled through the federal courts under a number of important federal statutes. Oil, Chemical and Atomic Workers International Union, AFL–CIO v. Department of Energy, 288 F.3d 452 (D.C.Cir.2002), for example, applied it to deny fees under the Freedom of Information Act where the government ultimately turned over the requested documents before a court ordered it to do so.

d. Brickwood Contractors, Inc. v. United States, 288 F.3d 1371 (Fed. Cir.2002), applied *Buckhannon* to the Equal Access to Justice Act and denied fees where the government withdrew a bid solicitation with the result that the plaintiff's bid protest was dismissed by the Court of Federal Claims without reaching the merits.[10]

e. What do you think of the *Buckhannon* approach to deciding who has prevailed in a matter? Will lawyers be as willing to bring cases if they know government officials can avoid paying them simply by changing the challenged policy shortly before entry of a decree? Is deterrence of such cases a good thing? Does the ability to have the other side pay the fees tend to create an excessive incentive to bring litigation?[11]

3. How should the amount of appropriate attorneys' fees be calculated?

a. In determining attorneys' fees under 42 U.S.C. § 1988, the Supreme Court said in Hensley v. Eckerhart, 461 U.S. 424, 433 (1983), that the "most useful starting point" is to take the "number of hours reasonably expended on the litigation multiplied by a reasonable hourly rate. This calculation provides an objective basis on which to make an initial estimate of the value of a lawyer's services." This figure is often called the lodestar.

b. Central States, Southeast & Southwest Areas Pension Fund v. Central Cartage Co., 76 F.3d 114 (7th Cir.1996), held that the appropriate value to be placed on legal services rendered by in-house counsel is the going rate in the market, regardless of where the client actually turned for

---

9. Justices Scalia and Thomas wrote a concurring opinion. Justice Ginsburg, in an opinion for herself and Justices Stevens, Souter and Breyer, dissented, saying that requiring a "document filed in court" before a plaintiff can be said to "prevail" is not required by the statutory language and will impair the enforcement of civil rights.

10. See also, Smyth v. Rivero, 282 F.3d 268 (4th Cir.2002) (getting preliminary injunction against policy doesn't make one a prevailing party under Aid to Families with Dependent Children statute where the gov-

ernment changed policy before a final judgment entered). But see Loggerhead Turtle v. County Council of Volusia County, 307 F.3d 1318 (11th Cir.2002) (*Buckhannon* does not limit grant of attorneys' fees under Endangered Species Act allowing award of fees "where appropriate").

11. In Sole v. Wyner, 551 U.S. 74 (2007), the Supreme Court held that litigants who lost the case on the merits were not prevailing parties even though they had obtained a preliminary and a permanent injunction in the lower court.

legal help. Raney v. Federal Bureau of Prisons, 222 F.3d 927 (Fed.Cir. 2000), similarly held that market rates were to be the basis for calculating fees when the litigant was represented by a union lawyer.[12]

c. The "going rate" for legal services can vary. Davis County Solid Waste Management and Energy Recovery Special Service District v. Environmental Protection Agency, 169 F.3d 755 (D.C.Cir.1999), was tried in the District of Columbia, but most of the work was done by Salt Lake City firms in Utah where legal fees are lower. The court said the Utah rates should be used because "it produces a result that better reflects the purpose of fee shifting statutes," i.e., to enable parties to get legal help. Davis County could hire lawyers at local rates, the court reasoned, so those lawyers should not be able to charge D.C. rates. Parties from markets with lawyer rates even higher than those in D.C. should similarly be able to collect at the higher rates.

d. Mathur v. Board of Trustees of Southern Illinois University, 317 F.3d 738 (7th Cir.2003), held that the proper rate to be used in calculating the lodestar amount for an award of fees was the attorneys' market rate ($225 per hour in Chicago), and not the local rate ($125) in the small town where the case was tried. A professor sued Southern Illinois University for employment discrimination and retaliation. He attempted to find a local attorney, but was unable to do so because many either had little experience with this issue or had conflicts of interests. The district court reduced the Chicago attorneys' hourly rates to Carbondale rates (the university's location) when it determined the award. The appellate court found that district courts should defer to an out-of-town attorney's rates unless local attorneys could do as good a job. A "good faith effort to find local counsel is all that is necessary, lest the meticulous generation of a comprehensive log of inquiries deter plaintiffs from bringing worthy discrimination suits, frustrating the rationale for statutes enabling private civil rights suits." Id. at 744.

e. Perdue v. Kenny A. ex rel. Winn, 559 U.S. ___, 130 S.Ct. 1662, 176 L.Ed.2d 494 (2010), asked whether calculation of an attorney's fee under a federal fee-shifting statute pursuant to a lodestar method may be increased based on superior performance and results. This case presented a long and complicated dispute over the treatment of a class of children in the Georgia foster care system. All of the issued were eventually resolved in a consent decree, except the attorneys fees to which plaintiffs' lawyers were entitled to under 42 U.S.C. § 1988. The district court ultimately awarded the lawyers about $10.5 million in fees, which included the lodestar calculation of approximately $6 million, plus a 75% enhancement. The district court stated that the lodestar calculation did not take into account factors such as that the lawyers had advanced a large amount of expenses with no on-going reimbursement, they were not being paid on an on-going basis, recovery of any attorney's fee was dependent upon success in the litigation,

---

12. In State of Wisconsin v. Hotline Indus., Inc., 236 F.3d 363 (7th Cir.2000), a statute only allowed payment of "actual" attorneys' fees and the state used salaried government attorneys. Because the statute limits fee awards to "actual outlays," not "reasonable" fees, the court said, the state was entitled only to a proportional share of the salaries of its attorneys plus related overhead costs.

and the district court said that it had not previously seen a plaintiff class achieve such a favorable result on such a scale. The 11th Circuit affirmed the district court's award, and the Supreme Court granted certiorari.

The Supreme Court agreed that attorneys' fees may be increased due to superior performance and results, but it said the instances will be rare, exceptional and require specific evidence that the lodestar fee was inadequate to attract competent counsel and failed already to account for good performance. The Court said enhancement would be appropriate where the method used to calculate the hourly rate did not accurately reflect an attorney's true market value, where the attorney's performance includes an extraordinary outlay of expenses, where the course of litigation is exceptionally protracted, or where there is exceptional delay in the payment of the attorney's fees. The Court explained that civil rights cases typically involve an understanding that attorneys will have to advance expenses and that payment of fees will be delayed until the successful resolution of the case, so it take a particularly extraordinary situation to warrant an enhancement.

The Court held that the district court did not provide sufficient justification for its 75% enhancement in this case. The amount of the enhancement appeared "essentially arbitrary." The district court had said that counsel had made extraordinary outlays for expenses and had to wait for delay in reimbursement, but it did not calculate the amount of the enhancement attributable to this factor. It said that counsel did not receive fees on an ongoing basis during the case, but it did not sufficiently link this to proof that the delay was outside the normal range expected by lawyers who rely on § 1998 for fees. It also did not calculate the cost to counsel of any extraordinary or unwarranted delay. The court did purport to compare counsel's performance in this case with that of lawyers in unnamed prior cases, but it did not employ a methodology that permitted meaningful appellate review. The Court thus reversed and remanded for further proceedings consistent with the opinion.

4. When might it be appropriate to calculate the fee as if it were a contingent fee, i.e., as a percentage of the sum recovered?

a. Swedish Hospital Corp. v. Shalala, 1 F.3d 1261 (D.C.Cir.1993) allowed fees to be set as a percentage of the "common fund" recovery instead of the lodestar method. The class action recovered $27.8 million for a group of hospitals. The court found a percentage fee appropriate; such a fee reduces the lawyer's incentive for inefficiency and "more accurately reflects the economics of litigation practice." The court approved setting the percentage at 20% but applied it only to the portion of the recovery that reflected the lawyers' efforts. Because that portion was $10 million (the government had conceded the rest), the fee was set at $2 million.

b. Welch & Forbes, Inc. v. Cendant Corp. (In re Cendant Corp. PRIDES Litigation), 243 F.3d 722 (3d Cir.2001), also found that a percentage fee arrangement would be more appropriate than the lodestar method. The court set out seven factors to consider in deciding what is a reasonable percentage fee award in common fund cases: (1) the complexity and duration of litigation; (2) the range of percentage awards in other cases, (3) the absolute size of other fee awards, (4) how much a percentage award would exceed a lodestar approach, (5) the presence or absence of substantial objections by members of the class to the settlement terms or fees requested by counsel, (6) the skill and efficiency of the attorneys involved, and (7) the amount of time that counsel devoted to the case. In this case, the Third Circuit found that the trial court abused its discretion when it awarded a fee (5.7% of the $341 million recovery) that was out of proportion to (i.e., seven times) what the lodestar approach would have yielded. The case was neither legally nor factually complex, and the entire duration of the case was only four months.

c. In Matter of Synthroid Marketing Litigation, 264 F.3d 712 (7th Cir.2001), a district court limited attorney's fees to 10% of the settlement amount, citing cases that said 10% represented the upper limit in cases with a "megafund" settlement greater than $75 million. The Seventh Circuit overturned the award, arguing that awards should simulate the market price for legal services. The court suggested several ways in which private parties could determine fees in advance, while preserving incentives for the attorneys to act in the best interest of their clients. They might set a declining marginal fee rate as the level of recovery increased. They might take account of the risk of non-payment. Some rates might be set in a competitive bidding process. The court argued that the flat 10% rate applied in this case for cases over $75 million would create illogical distinctions in the amount attorneys earned for settlements that were relatively close in value (e.g., a settlement of $74 million versus one of $76 million). Indeed, the rule would discourage counsel from obtaining settlements above the "megafund" threshold amount.[13]

d. Vizcaino v. Microsoft Corp., 290 F.3d 1043 (9th Cir.2002), expressly rejected the Seventh Circuit's effort to simulate what it claimed was a market-based determination of fees. In upholding an attorney's fee of 28% of the settlement, or over $27 million, the court noted that the case was "extremely risky" and the lawyers had achieved "exceptional results" for the class. The court also used a lodestar calculation as a cross-check of the reasonableness of the fee and found that at normal hourly rates, the fee would have come to less than $7.4 million. In this case, however, the court found a multiplier of 3.65 was justified.

e. How would you go about assessing an appropriate fee in such cases? Is there any wholly objective method for doing so? Which methods create greater incentives for lawyers to place their own interest in collecting a fee above the interest of the class in getting appropriate relief?

5. How should a lawyer respond when presented with a settlement where the defense has made a good offer to the class but an

---

13. On remand, the district court, 201 F.Supp.2d 861 (N.D.Ill.2002), awarded counsel for the consumer class about 15% of the amount recovered, calculated as 30% of the first $10 million, 25% of the second $10 million, etc., down to 10% of the remainder. This award was based on the range of bids in similar cases, the risk assumed (high) and the relative productivity of the lawyers (low).

offer of low or no attorneys' fees? Does that create a conflict of interest between the class and its counsel? What should a court do about that conflict?

a.   In Evans v. Jeff D., 475 U.S. 717 (1986), the Court held that a judge in a class action may approve a class settlement even if it is conditioned on the waiver of attorneys' fees authorized by statute. In *Jeff D.*, plaintiffs filed a class action to improve conditions of institutionalized handicapped children in Idaho. As part of the settlement agreement, the plaintiffs' lawyers (a public interest law firm) stipulated they would waive attorneys' fees, but only if the court approved. The Ninth Circuit recognized the strong principle in favor of settlements but said that the defendants could not force the plaintiffs to waive statutory attorneys' fees. The district court, said the Ninth Circuit, should have determined what reasonable fees should be in a case like this.

The Supreme Court reversed. In a 6 to 3 opinion, Justice Stevens for the Court, held that the question "derives ultimately from the Fees Act rather than from the strictures of professional ethics." The lawyer had said the tension between a good settlement for the class and a good fee for the public interest law firm put him in an "ethical dilemma." The Court reasoned, however, that the attorney "had no *ethical* obligation to seek a statutory fee award. His ethical duty was to serve his clients loyally and competently. Since the proposal to settle on the merits was more favorable than the probable outcome of the trial, [the attorney's] decision to recommend acceptance was consistent with the highest standards of our profession. The district court, therefore, correctly concluded that approval of the settlement involved no breach of ethics in this case." 475 U.S. at 728 (emphasis in original).

Justices Brennan, Marshall and Blackmun, dissented, concerned that the Court's result would likely lead to fewer civil rights actions being brought because lawyers would be uncertain about getting their fees. Do you agree?

b.   In Bernhardt v. County of Los Angeles, 279 F.3d 862 (9th Cir. 2002), the plaintiff complained that the defendant's policy of settling civil rights claims with a lump sum payment that included all attorneys' fees meant that she had not been able to find a lawyer. The Ninth Circuit acknowledged that *Evans v. Jeff D.* had upheld a settlement that required waiver of statutory attorneys' fees, but it noted that *Evans* specifically recognized that the parties could challenge a settlement agreement if 1) a government implemented a "statute, policy, or practice" of requiring waiver of attorneys' fees in settlement agreements, 2) the settling party required fee waivers as part of a "vindictive effort to deter attorneys from representing plaintiffs in civil rights suits," or 3) such settlement agreements had the overall effect of reducing the number of attorneys willing to accept civil rights claims. The Ninth Circuit held that Bernhardt had standing to press her claim. The court dismissed Bernhardt's claim for prospective relief, because it had already dismissed her underlying civil rights claim, but it observed that Bernhardt's possible entitlement to compensatory, punitive, or nominal damages prevented the entire case from being moot.

c. Johnson v. District of Columbia, 190 F.Supp.2d 34 (D.D.C.2002), refused to dismiss the complaint of a handicapped child and his mother suing the District of Columbia Public Schools (DCPS) under the Individuals with Disabilities Education Act (IDEA). The court found that the defendant's policy of only settling cases on the condition that the plaintiff waive attorneys' fees stated a cause of action for denial of the right to counsel.

d. Bar opinions have generally said that it is unethical for defense counsel to submit a settlement offer to the plaintiff conditioned on an agreement to waive or limit attorneys' fees, e.g., D.C. Bar Ethics Opinion 147 (Jan. 22, 1985); Committee on Professional and Judicial Ethics of the New York City Bar Association, Opinion 80–94 ("Defense Counsel * * * are in a uniquely favorable position when they condition settlement on the waiver of the statutory fee: they make a demand for a benefit which the plaintiff's lawyer cannot resist as a matter of ethics and which the plaintiff will not resist due to lack of interest."); Grievance Comm'n of Board of Overseers of the Bar of Maine Advisory Opinion 17 (1983).

But State Bar of California Comm. on Prof'l Responsibility and Conduct, Formal Opinion 2009–176 (2009), opined that lawyers are not ethically prohibited from making such a settlement offer. The purpose of statutory awards of attorney's fees is to allow the plaintiff the opportunity to assert and vindicate their rights through litigation, not to benefit his or her lawyer. The Committee acknowledged that permitting such settlements might shrink the pool of lawyers willing to take such cases, but it determined that there was not enough evidence as to the effects, and it was not clear how the balancing of burdens and benefits would work out in practice.

What role should such opinions have in cases like those cited? Do *Jeff D.* and the other cases address the ethical obligations of defense counsel at all?

6. Can counsel in class action and civil rights cases protect themselves against defense efforts like the ones just described?

a. *Jeff D.* acknowledged that the client's eligibility for fees from the losing party is a different question than the fee agreement between the lawyer and his or her client. In Blanchard v. Bergeron, 489 U.S. 87 (1989), the lawyer and client had negotiated a contingent fee of 40% of any recovery. The amount recovered was $10,000 so the contract fee was $4,000. The Supreme Court unanimously held that, under 42 U.S.C.A. § 1988, the contingent fee agreement does not define or impose a limit upon the amount that the defendant can be required to pay; that amount should instead be set by the lodestar method.

b. In Venegas v. Mitchell, 495 U.S. 82 (1990), plaintiff and attorney entered into a contingent fee contract that provided that the attorney would receive 40% of the gross amount of recovery. Any court-awarded fee would be applied, dollar for dollar, to offset the contingent fee. A unanimous Court held that § 1988 does not prevent a lawyer from collecting a reasonable contingent fee even if it *exceeds* the statutory fee award. "[N]either *Blanchard* nor any other of our cases has indicated that § 1988, by it own force, protects plaintiffs from having to pay what they have contracted to pay, even though their contractual liability is greater than the statutory award that they may collect from losing opponents." Section 1988 "controls what the losing defendant must pay, not what the prevailing plaintiff must pay his lawyer." 495 U.S. at 89–90.

c. In light of *Blanchard* and *Venegas,* should class action and civil rights lawyers arrange fees by contract and not rely exclusively on a later court award? If lawyers protected themselves in advance by such arrangements, would a settlement for a lump sum that includes attorneys' fees—or a sum that purports to deny such fees—be unfair or improper after all? Should lawyers feel awkward about negotiating such contracts with their clients in cases where fee shifting is supposed to be the rule?

e. Astrue v. Ratliff, 560 U.S. ___, 130 S.Ct. 2521, 177 L.Ed.2d 91 (2010), however, makes clear that an advance contract may not provide full protection. The Supreme Court reaffirmed that an award of attorney's fees under the Equal Access to Justice Act (EAJA) belongs to the client, not the lawyer. But before the United States cut a check, it realized that the claimant still owed a debt to the government in an unrelated matter. Under the Debt Collection Improvement Act of 1996 (DCIA), the Treasury may take what the U.S. owes as partial payment of such a debt. The Eighth Circuit said that allowing a fee award to go back to the government in this way was contrary to Congress' intent, but the Supreme Court unanimously agreed that Congress specified that the fee award belongs to the client and that the government's claim has priority over everyone else's.

PROBLEM 37

THE FUTURE OF THE PRACTICE OF LAW: UNAUTHORIZED PRACTICE, MULTIJURISDICTIONAL PRACTICE, AND ANCILLARY LEGAL SERVICES

Will law forever be practiced only by lawyers licensed in individual states and working in traditional law firms? We cannot be sure what the future will hold, but a formidable challenge to the present system began in Europe where lawyers may now practice across national borders and worldwide accounting firms may hold themselves out as providing clients with lawyers in addition to business advice and auditing services. Many of the issues raised by the new service providers, however, go to issues of delivering services to ordinary Americans, many of whom are underserved today. That is the context in which this problem introduces the issues. First, it looks at the concept of unauthorized practice, the principle that reserves legal work to lawyers. Next, it considers jurisdictional limits on a lawyer's practice. Third, it considers the prohibition of a corporation's delivering legal services, and finally, it examines how law firms themselves are offering nontraditional services that are said to be "ancillary" to their regular practice.

FACTS

Victor Dowd is an attorney who believes that persons of even relatively modest means should plan their estates better than they do. He also believes that many people are afraid of the expense of estate planning by current methods of private law practice.

Dowd knows that, even now, financial planners and insurance agents are counseling their clients about basic estate planning issues. He proposes to help them do so more effectively. As another step toward making estate planning available to persons with small estates, Dowd proposes to publish do-it-yourself kits both for planning and administration. He plans to sell these kits only in states for which they have been fully verified as to legal accuracy. The forms and instructions are to be carefully prepared and there is no reason to question the ability of an ordinarily intelligent person, perhaps assisted by a financial planner, to follow them step by step and handle a completely routine case.

A nationwide insurance company thinks Dowd is on to something and has offered to refer its customers to him for preparation of a basic will. Dowd agrees to draft a basic will and any other necessary simple documents for a fee of $225. The insurance agency will pay the fee directly to him as part of the $399 fee it charges for its own "complete financial planning services." The clients can come from any state in the country.

Now, Dowd proposes to create an estate planning subsidiary that will work out of his law offices, and employ financial planners and insurance agents. The subsidiary plans to offer a complete package service in ten states consisting of planning before death and estate administration after. Dowd is admitted to practice in only one of those states. All participants will bill at a single hourly rate, no matter which type of specialty is involved. They propose to advertise the service with television commercials that say, "We've all got to go sometime. We might as well do it right."

QUESTIONS

A. THE UNAUTHORIZED PRACTICE OF LAW

1. What is the practice of law?

a. Look at Model Rule 5.5, Comment 2: "The definition of the practice of law is established by law and varies from one jurisdiction to another." Not much help there!

b. Restatement Third, The Law Governing Lawyers § 4, Comment *c*, is not much better: "The definitions and tests employed by courts to delineate unauthorized practice by nonlawyers have been vague or conclusory, while jurisdictions have differed significantly in describing what constitutes unauthorized practice in particular areas."

c. Perhaps the closest thing to an authoritative definition was provided in ABA Model Code of Professional Responsibility, EC 3–5: "[T]he practice of law relates to the rendition of services for others that call for the professional judgment of the lawyer * * * [consisting of the lawyer's] educated ability to relate the general body and philosophy of law to a specific legal problem of the client."

d. A draft report of an ABA Task Force charged to refine the definition suggested that:

"A person is presumed to be practicing law when engaging in any of the following conduct on behalf of another:

"(1) Giving advice or counsel to persons as to their legal rights or responsibilities or to those of others;

"(2) Selecting, drafting, or completing legal documents or agreements that affect the legal rights of a person;

"(3) Representing a person before an adjudicative body, including but not limited to, preparing or filing documents or conducting discovery; or

"(4) Negotiating legal rights or responsibilities on behalf of a person."[1]

In 2003, the ABA Task Force chose not to adopt a national definition for the practice of law. Instead, it issued a report that listed a set of considerations and procedures that states should use in drafting their own definition. In other words, it left the definition to the individual states rather than to attempt to fashion a national standard. This decision reflects the judgment that a definition of the practice of law involves a consideration of history, current practices of lawyers and nonlawyers, whether conduct can fit within the protections of the first amendment, the market power of other professional groups such as accountants and real estate agents, and the efforts of the local bar to police unauthorized practice of law.

e. After reading these definitions, do you know much more than you did before about whether the financial planners and insurance agents in this problem will be engaged in the practice of law? Estate administration involves following prescribed procedures and filling out legal forms, for example, but are only lawyers capable of knowing how to do that?

2. Why does the definition of the practice of law matter?

a. Unauthorized practice usually arises in four distinct contexts: (1) lay persons and organizations that offer a services close to the practice of

---

1. ABA Task Force on the Model Definition of the Practice of Law, Draft Definition (Sept. 18, 2002).

law (e.g., immigration services or estate administration); (2) persons and organizations who offer a service or product outside of the practice of law (e.g., banking, real estate, or investment services), but who as they offer the nonlaw services or products also provide some legal service; (3) lawyers who unlawfully assist lay persons and organizations to engage in unauthorized practice under the first two categories (a violation of Model Rule 5.5(a)), and (4) lawyers who practice outside the jurisdiction in which they are licensed.

b. In many states, engaging in the unauthorized practice of law is a crime, typically a misdemeanor. In other states, unauthorized practice is a contempt of court, i.e., engaging in an activity that only a court may license. Under either approach, the usual sanctions are fines and injunctions against further violations.

c. Defining the practice of law may also affect what conduct will expose you to liability for malpractice. When you umpire a children's baseball game, for example, if you make an error in interpreting the rules, it will make the other parents upset but not expose you to a suit for malpractice. When a nonlawyer makes a mistake in work that is the practice of law, however, that nonlawyer is held to the standards of a licensed lawyer and the exposure to malpractice liability is real. Even the fact that you perform as competently as a licensed lawyer is not a complete defense.

In Preston v. University of Arkansas for Medical Sciences, 128 S.W.3d 430 (Ark.2003), plaintiffs filed a medical malpractice suit against several doctors associated with a medical school. The plaintiffs' lawyers were from Oklahoma and they had not applied for *pro hac vice* admission, so they clearly were engaged in the unauthorized practice of law. The Arkansas Supreme Court held that the complaint was therefore a nullity; the court did not even toll the statute of limitations, which had now run. Whom do you suppose will be the subject of the next malpractice complaint?[2]

d. Fee forfeitures also help to enforce the unauthorized practice rules, even if the provider of services performed competently. If a nonlawyer performs a service that is held to be the practice of law, the client often will be excused from paying the fees even if the nonlawyer performed the work with no legal error. Patton v. Scholl, 1999 WL 431095 (E.D.Pa.1999), for example, enjoined the work of a "non-attorney bankruptcy preparer" and ordered the return of fees charged for what had been the unauthorized practice of law.

e. On the other hand, the law does not enforce the unauthorized practice rules by denying the attorney-client evidentiary privilege to the client. If a person talks to someone that he or she reasonably believes is a lawyer, conversations with that person are privileged even though the

---

2. See also, Blackman v. District of Columbia and Clark v. District of Columbia, 355 F.Supp.2d 171 (D.D.C.2005), *sua sponte* striking a motion for preliminary injunction filed by a lawyer who was not admitted to the District of Columbia Bar, but who maintained a law office in the District.

nonlawyer is engaged in the unauthorized practice of law. See Restatement Third, The Law Governing Lawyers § 72, Comment *e*.

3.   A person may represent herself in court. She may act as her own lawyer in negotiating a contract. Why do we let people act *pro se* if unauthorized practice rules are so important?

a.   Restatement Third, The Law Governing Lawyers § 4, Comment *d*, says that "every jurisdiction recognizes the right of an individual to proceed 'pro se' * * * [b]ecause the appearance is personal only." Unauthorized practice, in short, involves assisting another with a legal matter, not handling a matter for one's self.

b.   Should it constitute the unauthorized practice of law for a family member who is an officer of a family corporation to represent the corporation in court? Should the answer turn on whether the corporation is large or small? Whether the amount in controversy is large or small? What policies are served by allowing a sole proprietor of an unincorporated business to appear *pro se* but denying the 100% owner of a corporation the same right to appear?

c.   Regardless of the policies served, corporations are usually forced to hire lawyers. See, e.g., Restatement Third, The Law Governing Lawyers § 4, Comment *e* (rule only applies in litigation; corporate officers may negotiate business deals); Merco Constr. Engineers, Inc. v. Municipal Ct., 581 P.2d 636 (Cal.1978) (statute designed to reverse rule in municipal courts held unconstitutional as invading the judicial power).

d.   Of particular importance to a lawyer's disciplinary exposure is Model Rule 5.5(a), which prohibits a lawyer from assisting a nonlawyer in the unauthorized practice of law. See also, Model Rule 5.4, which prohibits (a) sharing legal fees with a nonlawyer, and (b) forming a partnership with a nonlawyer where any of the firm's activities involve the practice of law.

In re Sledge, 859 So.2d 671 (La.2003), disbarred Sledge, a high-volume solo practitioner who nominally ran his office but in fact largely left the cases in the hands of law clerks and other nonlawyers who used a rubber stamp to put the lawyer's name on pleadings, discovery responses, and correspondence. In most cases, Sledge only went to court and attended depositions. Sometimes, he was not present in the office for months at a time while he attended Scientology retreats and wrote a novel. Meanwhile, his staff signed up clients, wrote letters and pleadings, and negotiated settlements. There were obviously several grounds on which the Louisiana Supreme Court could discipline Sledge, including utter neglect of cases, but it focused on his facilitation of the unauthorized practice of law by his staff and the complete delegation of "professional judgment to a non-lawyer."

4.   Does the insurance company program with which Dowd works involve him in assisting the unauthorized practice of law?

a.   Lawline v. American Bar Association, 956 F.2d 1378 (7th Cir.1992), involved a suit by a group of lawyers, paralegals, and lay people who had organized a service to answer legal questions to the public over the phone. Prior to the suit, they had already answered over 500,000 calls. The group also made referrals to legal aid and to lawyers who would charge reduced fees. Their suit alleged that what are now ABA Model Rules 5.4(b) and 5.5(a) were the product of an illegal conspiracy among lawyers to maintain traditional forms of practice and also were unconstitutional on their face. The Seventh Circuit affirmed dismissal of the action. The rules only had effect if state supreme courts adopted them and thus they were immune from antitrust challenge. Also, the rules rationally relate to the goal of "safeguard[ing] the public, maintain[ing] the integrity of the profession, and protect[ing] the administration of justice from reproach." 956 F.2d at 1385. Do you agree?

b.   In The Florida Bar v. Beach, 675 So.2d 106 (Fla.1996), attorney Beach had a contract with King and King Paralegals, a company that prepared and sold legal documents for consumers. For a flat fee of $75, Beach would review the documents King and King prepared and meet briefly with a King and King client, but clients agreed they had no lawyer-client relationship with Beach. In some cases, Beach met with King to discuss the client's matter but did not meet with the client at all. For assisting King and King Paralegals to do legal work, the court suspended Beach from the practice of law for ninety days.

c.   The lawyer in Cincinnati Bar Ass'n v. Kathman, 748 N.E.2d 1091 (Ohio 2001), worked as a "review attorney" for the Estate Preservation Group (EPG), a company that sold insurance and living trusts. EPG clients, with the assistance of a nonlawyer, filled out a financial workbook describing their assets and disposition directives. The lawyer would then call the client, explain who he was, and direct EPG to prepare the client's documents. The client sent the fee of $1,995 to the lawyer, who kept $200 and remitted the rest to EPG. The court found that the lawyer's actions were aiding the unauthorized practice of law by EPG. No client received the "carefully considered, independent advice" of a lawyer. The payment process constituted illegal feesharing with a nonlawyer. The court even held that the lawyer violated state rules against practicing under a trade name by including his name on the company's letterhead. The court suspended him from practice for six months.

5.   Should Dowd's proposed sale of do-it-yourself kits constitute the unauthorized practice of law?

a.   Are people likely to be misled by the kits into believing they have had all the legal advice that they need? Can a lay person tell whether he or she has a "completely routine case" for which the kit would be adequate?

b.   Books alone have traditionally not been deemed unauthorized practice. The leading case is New York County Lawyers' Ass'n v. Dacey, 283 N.Y.S.2d 984 (N.Y.App.Div.), rev'd, 234 N.E.2d 459 (N.Y.1967). Author Norman Dacey had been found guilty of criminal contempt for writing and selling "How to Avoid Probate," a book in which he advised people to put all their property into "living trusts." The book contained 310 pages of forms "perforated for easy removal from the book," and the book told readers the forms "will be suitable for use" to achieve the desired results. "The giving of legal advice * * * including instructions and advice as to the preparation and use of legal instruments, constitutes the practice of law which is forbidden * * * to all but duly licensed New York attorneys," the appellate division said. 283 N.Y.S.2d at 989. "It is immaterial that Dacey has no face-to-face dealings nor a confidential relationship with particular clients." 283 N.Y.S.2d at 991.

The Court of Appeals reversed, adopting the opinion of dissenting appellate justice Stevens who had said: "It cannot be claimed that the publication of a legal text which purports to say what the law is amounts to legal practice. And the mere fact that the principles or rules stated in the text may be accepted by a particular reader * * * does not affect this. * * * This is the essential of a legal practice—the representation and the advising of a particular person in a particular situation." 283 N.Y.S.2d at 997–98.

With which opinion do you agree?

6. Traditionally, if a lay advisor goes beyond writing books and starts giving personalized legal advice, unauthorized practice issues again arise. Should filling in the blanks on prepared forms constitute the practice of law?

a.   The leading case on this issue, State Bar of Arizona v. Arizona Land Title and Trust Co., 366 P.2d 1 (Ariz.1961), supplemented 371 P.2d 1020 (Ariz.1962), held that real estate agents were engaged in the unauthorized practice of law when they helped buyers and sellers fill in the blanks on preprinted forms for use in real estate transactions. Arizona citizens responded with a ballot initiative that amended the state constitution and reversed the decision. See Arizona Constitution, Art. 26, § 1.

b.   In Fifteenth Judicial Dist. Unified Bar Ass'n v. Glasgow, 1999 WL 1128847 (Tenn.App.1999), Glasgow was filling in the blanks on divorce forms for low-income clients who would then represent themselves in court. She charged them a fee of from $99 to $148 and suggested where and "approximately" when the papers should be filed. She even prepared some quitclaim deeds if they were necessary to divide real property. Ever vigilant, the Tennessee Bar sued to enjoin Glasgow's services, and the court complied. The applicable statute defines drafting "any paper, document or instrument affecting or relating to secular rights" as the practice of law that can be only performed by lawyers. The statute is constitutional because "the practice of law by untrained persons endangers the public's personal and property rights, as well as the orderly administration of the judicial system."

Suppose Glasgow offers fully competent legal services? Is the public entitled to have only high-quality legal services? Should we be concerned whether Glasgow's clients can afford superior services?

c.   Countrywide Home Loans, Inc. v. Kentucky Bar Ass'n, 113 S.W.3d 105 (Ky.2003), rejected a Kentucky Bar Association advisory opinion arguing that performance of a real estate closing by a lay closing agent is the unauthorized practice of law. The court concluded that laypersons may conduct real estate closings on behalf of other parties, but they may not answer legal questions that arise at the closing or offer any legal advice to the parties. The record showed that 95% of the documents in all closings are identical; largely for regulatory reasons, none are subject to negotiation or change. Other aspects of real estate work are different, e.g., preparation of a title commitment letter and the preparation of deeds and mortgages. The court held that a closing is largely ministerial and involves little or no legal judgment. A layperson may conduct it without violating the prohibition against the unauthorized practice of law.

d.   Charter One Mortgage Corp. v. Condra, 865 N.E.2d 602 (Ind.2007), was a class action seeking return of the fee charged by a mortgage company to have nonlawyer employees fill in the blanks on mortgage documents. The defendant alleged that it was a subsidiary of a national bank and thus not subject to state unauthorized practice rules, but the court found it unnecessary to reach the preemption issue. Acknowledging that some states have gone the other way, the Indiana Supreme Court found that because no legal advice was involved and because filling in the blanks was well within the skill set of the nonlawyers, the work did not involve unauthorized practice of law, whether or not a fee was charged for the service.

7.   Where do computer-assisted drafting programs fit into our unauthorized practice analysis?

a.   In Unauthorized Practice of Law Comm. v. Parsons Technology, Inc., 1999 WL 47235 (N.D.Tex.1999), a federal district court found the creators of Quicken Family Lawyer guilty of unauthorized practice. The "Family Lawyer" software package contains over 100 legal forms that are represented to be "valid in 49 states." The program asks questions about the user and, based on the responses, generates forms to deal with the user's problem in the user's jurisdiction, all the while expressly disclaiming providing "specific information for your exact situation." The court held that both the preparation of legal forms and the selection of which form to use constitute the practice of law in Texas. The court also argued that the state had a justifiable interest in not letting people who are not lawyers give legal advice harmful to Texas citizens. Thus, the court said, the prohibition in this case did not burden commercial speech more than was necessary, and it enjoined the sale of the software.

b.   Frankfort Digital Services v. Kistler, 477 F.3d 1117 (9th Cir.2007), was another test of the propriety of computer programs generating legal services. For a fee of $219, Frankfort would grant people a 60-day license to use its "expert system" that would elicit client information and generate bankruptcy forms completely filled-in. This was no mere word processor; it purported to take into consideration multiple facts about the client and select the best approach. It even provided clients with information about "loopholes" and "stealth techniques." The U.S. Bankruptcy Trustee challenged Frankfort's operation as the unauthorized practice of law. The court found first that Frankfort was a "bankruptcy petition preparer" and had failed to list itself as such on the prepared forms. It could prepare the forms because bankruptcy law acknowledges that role for a "preparer." But

Frankfort also offered "personalized—albeit automated—counsel" and that constituted the unauthorized practice of law.

Do you agree with the *Quicken* and *Frankfort* decisions? Were the courts defending client protection, lawyer protection, or both?

c.   Shortly after the *Quicken* decision, the Texas legislature enacted a law specifically providing that "the 'practice of law' does not include the design, creation, publication, distribution, display, or sale ... [of] computer software, or similar products if the products clearly and conspicuously state that the products are not a substitute for the advice of an attorney." The law was effective immediately. The Fifth Circuit then vacated the lower court injunction and judgment, 179 F.3d 956 (5th Cir.1999) (per curiam), and remanded in light of the statute.

Does the outcome tell you whom lay people tend to think unauthorized practice rules are protecting? Do you agree with their view? Why or why not?

B.   The multijurisdictional practice of law

1.   In what jurisdictions may a licensed lawyer regularly practice?

a.   To many people, the answer is obvious; admission to the bar of one state should guarantee admission to the bar of every other. Under traditional standards, however, that answer is incorrect. The Supreme Court has made clear that states' ability to condition admitting lawyers licensed in other states to practice in their own is not unlimited. Supreme Court of Virginia v. Friedman, 487 U.S. 59 (1988), for example, involved a Maryland resident who challenged a Virginia requirement that, in order to be admitted to the Virginia bar without taking the bar exam, a lawyer had to be a resident of Virginia. The state argued that because a nonresident could be admitted by passing the bar examination, there was no denial of her right to become a member of the Virginia bar. However, the Supreme Court held that making nonresidents take an additional test went to a matter of "fundamental concern" and violated the privileges and immunities clause.[3]

b.   As a practical matter, many states automatically admit experienced lawyers who are licensed in other states if the state of licensing will do the same for other states' lawyers. That tit-for-tat system is called "reciprocity." However, states typically require an examination of lawyers from states that do not grant reciprocity or grant it only on certain conditions. So far, the courts have rejected most challenges to the constitutionality of lawyer reciprocity requirements.[4]

---

3. See also, Barnard v. Thorstenn, 489 U.S. 546 (1989) (same result with respect to a one-year residency with an intent-to-remain rule imposed by the Virgin Islands bar). But see Scariano v. Justices of the Supreme Court of the State of Indiana, 38 F.3d 920 (7th Cir.1994), cert. denied, 515 U.S. 1144 (1995), upholding rule granting admission only to lawyers who have "practiced predominantly" in Indiana for five years under a conditional license; this rule relates to familiarity with Indiana law and is not a residency requirement per se.

4. However, in other contexts the Supreme Court, using the dormant commerce clause, has invalidated reciprocal barriers to

Schumacher v. Nix, 965 F.2d 1262 (3d Cir.1992), for example, upheld the Pennsylvania rule preventing California graduates of non-ABA accredited law schools from sitting for the Pennsylvania bar exam. California does not admit Pennsylvania lawyers without taking the California exam and thus it is not a "reciprocal state" under Pennsylvania law. The court agreed that it was hard to see any rational basis for the Pennsylvania rule, but it found one by saying that Pennsylvania may have hoped to "entice states to enter into reciprocal agreements with it and thereby promote its interest in securing similar treatment for its attorneys who are graduates of accredited law schools." 965 F.2d at 1272.

c. In Matter of Saretsky, 506 N.W.2d 151 (Wis.1993) (per curiam), Michigan required that lawyers maintain a local office; thus, Wisconsin, under its reciprocity rule, imposed the same requirement. The Wisconsin Supreme Court upheld this rule. Because the applicant planned to keep his office in Michigan, not maintain an office in Wisconsin, and only planned to practice in Wisconsin from time to time, he could not be admitted by reciprocity and had to take the Wisconsin bar exam. Justice Shirley Abrahamson concurred and dissented, because the Wisconsin rule produced "strange results. A Michigan lawyer seeking admission to the Wisconsin bar without examination must state that he or she intends in good faith to maintain an office in the state of Wisconsin for the practice of law. An Indiana lawyer, however, may be admitted without making this declaration. Any lawyer presently admitted to the Wisconsin bar on diploma privilege or on examination or on motion need not retain an office in Wisconsin in order to continue membership in the Wisconsin bar."

d. Do these cases make sense to you? Can they be justified as anything more than an effort by lawyers who already have licenses in a state to make it harder for out-of-state lawyers to become admitted to the bar?

2. Litigators' clients often get sued in states in which the lawyers are not licensed. Should there be a way for them to continue to represent their clients in those cases?

a. In general, if a litigator is not a member of the bar where the litigation is filed, she will file an appearance in court and ask to be admitted *pro hac vice*, i.e., for that particular case.[5] The lawyer so admitted

---

the transfer of goods and services across state lines. Great Atlantic & Pacific Tea Co., Inc. v. Cottrell, 424 U.S. 366 (1976), unanimously invalidated a Mississippi law providing that milk from another state may not be sold in Mississippi unless that other state accepts milk processed in Mississippi. If a state concludes that another state's rules on milk imports are unfair, the Court said, it should file a lawsuit, not impose a trade barrier. Mississippi could require that all milk (including milk imported from other states) meet its standards, but it could not exclude milk that met those standards simply because that oth-er state did not sign a reciprocal trade agreement with Mississippi.

5. As to whether concerns about the lawyer's possible "courtroom demeanor" permit denial of a *pro hac vice* appearance, compare In re Evans, 524 F.2d 1004 (5th Cir. 1975) (insufficiently specific charges and no opportunity for lawyer to defend himself), with In re Admission Pro Hac Vice of Lumumba, 526 F.Supp. 163 (S.D.N.Y.1981) (alleged terrorist denied *pro hac vice* admission and denied access to client at local jail).

sometimes must associate in that litigation with a lawyer in the state who is admitted in that state for all purposes.

b.   Some states try to limit the number of *pro hac vice* appearances to prevent lawyers from ignoring the obligation to become admitted to the bar. However, such limits can have significant adverse effects on the availability of counsel in civil rights cases, so Sanders v. Russell, 401 F.2d 241 (5th Cir.1968), struck down a district court rule limiting *pro hac vice* appearances by out-of-state lawyers to one case per year.

c.   Paciulan v. George, 229 F.3d 1226 (9th Cir.2000), challenged California's rule that permits nonresident lawyers to appear *pro hac vice*, but does not permit lawyers without California licenses who reside in California to so appear. The Ninth Circuit upheld the rule. A state has a significant interest in not letting its residents secure a license elsewhere, the court said, and then regularly practice in California. Granting nonresidents occasional *pro hac vice* status is not inconsistent with that interest. Do you agree?

3.   Should transactional lawyers, i.e., those doing deals or other kinds of commercial activity, have a similar way to follow their clients to other jurisdictions?

a.   For transactional lawyers giving advice to clients with interests around the country or around the world, the practical problems of state-by-state admission are different. There is no "proceeding" in which one can ask a court to be admitted for purposes of a particular negotiation or closing. Even in litigation, there are often prelitigation activities (such as interviewing witnesses and other investigation) that may occur before any litigation is filed. Or, matters may be resolved in alternative dispute resolution proceedings before a judge ever enters the picture.

b.   Birbrower, Montalbano, Condon & Frank, P.C. v. Superior Court, 949 P.2d 1 (Cal.1998), struck terror in the management committees of many "national" law firms. Birbrower, a New York law firm, represented ESQ, a California corporation, in claims it had against Tandem Computers, Inc., relating to a software and marketing contract. California law governed the contract and New York firm partners traveled to California on several occasions. The case was going to arbitration, but the parties ultimately settled the dispute. The firm asked for its fee, which was to be over a million dollars. At that point, the client refused to pay.

To the surprise of many, the court agreed with ESQ that it had no obligation to pay because the Birbrower firm had engaged in unauthorized practice. One traditional remedy for the unauthorized practice of law by nonlawyers is the denial of fees. While the Birbrower lawyers may be competent in New York, "[c]ompetence in one jurisdiction does not necessarily guarantee competence in another." 949 P.2d at 8. Nor was there an exception to the unauthorized practice prohibition for arbitration proceedings, even though there was no way to be admitted *pro hac vice* in such proceedings.

Ultimately, the California Supreme Court made two findings. First, the New York lawyers "practiced" in California. While the lawyers did much of their work in the New York office, they were physically present in California when they advised the California company about the arbitration held in California and governed by California law. Second, even nonphysical presence in California can constitute unauthorized practice of law. One may be said to practice in California "although not physically present here [such as] by advising a California client on California law in connection with a California legal dispute by telephone, fax, computer, or other modern technological means." 949 P.2d at 5–6. However, the court did "reject the notion that a person automatically practices law 'in California' whenever that person practices California law anywhere, or 'virtually' enters the state by telephone, fax, email, or satellite." Id. at 6. The court allowed the firm to collect payment for services rendered to the client in New York but only for those services that could be severed from the rest of the services performed in California.[6]

c. *Birbrower* is a landmark case on this subject, but it does not stand alone. Koscove v. Bolte, 30 P.3d 784 (Colo.Ct.App.2001), for example, involved a lawyer licensed in Wisconsin but not Colorado. Bolte agreed to pursue royalty payments due to Koscove from an oil company. After obtaining a significant recovery, aided in part by the work of a Colorado lawyer, Koscove moved to get back all fees she had paid to Bolte. The court agreed that, in spite of his efforts and success, Bolte could not collect a fee because he was not licensed to practice in the state. Analyzing the lease in question and giving opinions as to theories for recovery of damages in Colorado, the court found, was the unauthorized practice of law and Bolte could not collect fees based on illegal work.

d. In re Ferrey, 774 A.2d 62 (R.I.2001), involved a lawyer who had appeared several times before a state energy agency in Rhode Island even though he was only licensed to practice law in Massachusetts. The state agency had granted the respondent permission to appear before it, but the Rhode Island Supreme Court said the permission exceeded agency authority and was invalid. Thereafter, the court granted the respondent *pro hac vice* status to practice before the state agency, holding that he was justified in relying on the permission of the agency. However, on the key issue, the court declined to allow the respondent to obtain fees for any prior appearances because they constituted the unauthorized practice of law.

e. Not all cases have construed unauthorized practice rules this restrictively. Fought & Co., Inc. v. Steel Engineering and Erection, Inc., 951 P.2d 487 (Haw. 1998), for example, involved an Oregon firm acting as general counsel to an international client that built an airport on Maui. The client won a judgment against the state of Hawaii in a case handled by lawyers licensed there, but the Oregon firm sought a portion of the statutory attorneys' fees for work it did helping prepare for the litigation.

6. The California legislature reversed *Birbrower* as applied to arbitration cases for work *before* January 1, 2007. Code of Civil Procedure § 1282.4 and Rule 983.4 of the Rules of Court.

Many clients do work that is interstate and international, the court said. These clients, whether or not based in Hawaii, get important help from law firms who are familiar with their operations, wherever the firms are based. Making it impossible for firms to collect fees for work relating to Hawaii would make it hard for all clients to get high-quality, efficiently delivered legal services. Even applying the standards set forth in *Birbrower,* the court said, the Oregon firm had retained local counsel for work done in Hawaii. It could be seen as simply assisting the Hawaiian counsel and thus it was not barred from collecting a fee.

f.   In the Matter of Opinion 33 of the Comm. on Unauthorized Practice of Law, 733 A.2d 478 (N.J.1999), addressed whether out-of-state bond lawyers may advise public entities issuing state and municipal bonds. The unauthorized practice committee had said no; the bond issues raised only issues of New Jersey law. The state supreme court noted that a number of New Jersey firms now have the expertise to advise on bond issues, but ten to twenty out-of-state firms have greater national reputations in the field than any New Jersey firm. Unauthorized practice prohibitions are "not designed to give rise to a professional monopoly, but rather to serve the public right to protection against unlearned and unskilled advice." 733 A.2d at 484. Previously, the court had upheld the right of accountants to prepare inheritance tax returns and real estate brokers to close residential real estate transactions. The court held that here, too, the public interest required that New Jersey law firms be able to involve out-of-state lawyers in bond issues and, in complex cases, issuers could even hire out-of-state lawyers directly.

g.   Estate of Condon, 76 Cal.Rptr.2d 922 (Cal.Ct.App.1998), somewhat eased concerns about what California courts would do about fees payable to out-of-state lawyers. A Colorado firm had prepared the will of a woman who at the time of death lived in California. A Colorado lawyer in that firm was hired by a Colorado co-executor to help administer the estate, most of whose assets were in California. Much of the work of the executor was selling a California business, and the Colorado lawyer helped with that too. When the time came to award fees to executors' counsel, the California probate court refused to award any to the Colorado lawyer, but the Court of Appeals reversed. The lawyer had not set up an office in California to give legal advice, the court said. He represented a Colorado citizen and did most of his work in Colorado; the fact most of the estate was in California did not make his work there improper.

4.   If a transactional lawyer works exclusively on questions of federal law, should state definitions of the practice of law nevertheless be controlling?

a.   Sometimes federal rules govern not only when a federal court will allow *pro hac vice* admission, but also when the court will treat something as not the unauthorized practice of law.

The leading case is Sperry v. Florida Bar, 373 U.S. 379 (1963), where the Supreme Court held that Florida could not enjoin a nonlawyer registered to practice before the United States Patent Office from preparing and prosecuting patent applications in Florida, notwithstanding that such activity, under state law, constituted the "practice of law." The court noted that both a federal statute and patent office regulations specifically authorized practice before the patent office by nonlawyers. Thus, the supremacy clause overrode the state restriction because no state law "can hinder or obstruct the free use of a license granted under an act of Congress." 373 U.S. at 385.[7]

b. In re Desilets, 291 F.3d 925 (6th Cir.2002), is a modern application of the *Sperry* doctrine. A lawyer, Rittenhouse, was licensed in Texas, moved to Wisconsin and opened an office in Michigan to handle only bankruptcy cases. He was not admitted to practice in either Wisconsin or Michigan, but he was admitted in the federal court for the Western District of Michigan. The state bar of Michigan accused him of the unauthorized practice of law, and the federal bankruptcy court refused to award him fees because he was not an "attorney" where he practiced law. Rittenhouse relied on the fact he only practiced federal law and was admitted in the federal district court. Judge Boggs, speaking for the Sixth Circuit, agreed. Citing *Sperry*, the court held that states may not decide who may practice federal law in federal court. Dissenting, Judge Merritt said that federal court admission does not preclude separate state regulation of a lawyer who opens an office to practice in that state.[8]

c. Schindler v. Finnerty, 74 F.Supp.2d 253 (E.D.N.Y.1999), however, held that lawyers who did federal patent work were not exempt from jurisdiction of the New York lawyer discipline system when their clients complained of neglect and similar misconduct. The district court acknowledged *Sperry*, but it said that state law governs all lawyers to the extent state law does not hinder operation of the patent system. Keeping practitioners honest is consistent with federal objectives, so the lawyers had to respond to their clients' complaints in the discipline proceedings.

5. Can you derive any practical guidelines from these cases about when a lawyer may represent a client from a jurisdiction— or with respect to work in a jurisdiction—in which the lawyer is not admitted?

a. Restatement Third, The Law Governing Lawyers § 3, suggested that a lawyer may only act "to the extent the lawyer's activities in the matter arise out of or are otherwise reasonably related to the lawyer's practice" in the state in which the lawyer is licensed. Comment e explained

---

7. Note however, that federal courts often make a part of their own rules for admission to practice before them, a requirement that the lawyers also be admitted in the state where the federal court sits. See "Sample Federal Court Rules" in the Supplement.

8. Gallo v. United States Dist. Ct. for the Dist. of Arizona, 349 F.3d 1169 (9th Cir.2003), challenged an amendment to the rules of the local district court admitting to practice only lawyers who were also members of the Arizona state bar. This rule could be an attempt to avoid the backdoor admission problem suggested by *In re Desilets*. The court held that the rule change does not violate either substantive or procedural due process. An out-of-state lawyer simply must apply to be admitted *pro hac vice* to appear in the federal district court in Arizona.

that several factors are relevant to determining whether a matter is "reasonably related" to the lawyer's home state practice, including:

> "whether the lawyer's client is a regular client of the lawyer or, if a new client, is from the lawyer's home state, has extensive contacts with that state, or contacted the lawyer there; whether a multistate transaction has other significant connections with the lawyer's home state; whether significant aspects of the lawyer's activities are conducted in the lawyer's home state; whether a significant aspect of the matter involves the law of the lawyer's home state; and whether either the activities of the client involve multiple jurisdictions or the legal issues involved are primarily either multistate or federal in nature."

Is that helpful guidance? Does it seem to be consistent with the cases?

b.   The report of the American Bar Association Commission on Multi-jurisdictional Practice (Aug. 2002) proposed liberalizing the rules on who can practice in a state on a "temporary" basis. Its proposals were adopted by the ABA House of Delegates and the proposed circumstances under which a lawyer may practice in a jurisdiction other than one of the lawyer's admission are now described in Model Rule 5.5(c) and (d). Can you identify any cases that would not fit within at least one of those provisions?

c.   Remember that as a result of a parallel change in ABA Model Rule 8.5, a lawyer who travels to another jurisdiction in handling a matter will be subject to the disciplinary jurisdiction of the state to which she travels. See, e.g., In re Harper, 785 A.2d 311 (D.C.2001) (reciprocal discipline after D.C. lawyer who had never been licensed in Maryland was formally "disbarred" from practicing there in the future because of misconduct during his unauthorized practice).[9]

d.   The European Union has sought to remove obstacles to the free movement of capital, persons, and services among the member states. Under the Treaty, a qualified European Community (EC) lawyer may provide legal services in another member state either by visiting on an occasional basis or by setting up a permanent office. He or she may provide this legal service using the qualifications of his or her original home (home title), or by obtaining additional qualifications as an "integrated lawyer" from the place where he or she is setting up the permanent office. * * * A lawyer from one country in the European Community relying on his or her home title while practicing in another country in the EC may give legal advice, "including advice in local law." John Toulmin, Legal Practice in Europe, International Financial Law Review (Aug. 1989).

Look at ABA Model Rule 5.5(a). Do we have something to learn from the "United States of Europe"?[10]

---

9.   There may be other consequences of a lawyer's unauthorized practice. In re Jackman, 761 A.2d 1103 (N.J.2000), involved a Massachusetts lawyer who had practiced as a senior associate in New Jersey for seven years without a license to practice there. The court found that he had engaged in the unauthorized practice of law for those seven years and thus withheld his admission to the New Jersey bar for an unlimited period.

10.   The United States is slowly moving closer to the European model. In response to foreign pressure, and the pressure of Ameri-

6. May lawyers form a virtual law firm without physical offices and with a centralized referral system that sends work to lawyers who work out of their home to provide the clients with legal services?

a. One possible evolution of the traditional law firm may be towards a virtual law practice, a group of lawyers practicing together with modern technology. As you think about a number of lawyers who provide legal services to clients from physically separated locations, what ethics problems arise? Such practices promise the delivery of high quality legal services at low prices because of the low overhead costs. But can e-lawyers deliver quality legal services to clients without face to face meetings with clients or other lawyers? How can the owners of such firms supervise the delivery of legal services? What issues should the virtual law firm raise with clients before commencing the representation? Could a virtual law firm ever hire a first year associate? Should such practices offer document-based or unbundled legal services to clients who wish to save money?

b. North Carolina State Bar, 2005 Formal Ethics Opinion 10 (Jan. 20, 2006), addressed whether a lawyer may maintain an exclusively virtual law firm (VLF) that delivers legal services exclusively over the internet without face-to-face communication. The opinion approved such a practice—and even approved providing unbundled services to clients, subject to the requirements of Rule 1.2(c). However, it identified five pitfalls such a virtual practice must avoid. First, it must avoid unauthorized practice in jurisdictions in which the lawyers are not licensed, a problem that is endemic to virtual practice. Second, the firm must comply with local advertising rules, ironically including the requirement that the firm's website display a physical office address. Third, the firm must provide competent client representation in spite of the limited client contact. Fourth, it must not create lawyer-client relationships with people the firm does not mean to represent. And fifth, the firm must preserve client confidences.

C. PROHIBITION OF THE CORPORATE PRACTICE OF LAW

1. Should courts be concerned if Dowd, a licensed lawyer, does general estate planning work for the customers of an insurance company?

a. Traditionally, lawyer-client relationships have been imagined as personal relationships between one lawyer and one client. Consistent with that model, laws typically prohibit corporations from selling legal services. They clearly may have in-house legal departments to handle the company's own legal matters, but they may not let those lawyers represent customers or other third parties. This is the reason, for example, that a bank trust

can lawyers who want to open access to legal markets abroad, the New York Court of Appeals permits licensing foreign legal consultants. The rules allow foreign lawyers to form partnerships with New York lawyers. See Rules of the Court of Appeals for the Licensing of Legal Consultants, 22 N.Y.C.R.R. Part 521.

department ordinarily may not draft a will for a client of the bank, even if the trust officer is a lawyer.

b. Why doesn't the law allow a bank trust department to give legal advice to third parties? Does the arrangement create conflicts of interest or are conflicts simply inherent in such a situation? Can a lawyer be expected to give impartial advice on estate planning when his fee is coming from an insurance company? Take a look at Model Rule 5.4(d), for example, and the concern expressed in Model Rule 5.4, Comment 2. Do you agree that the concern is justified?

c. In spite of the concern and traditional prohibition, some cases have upheld the corporate delivery of legal services. Perkins v. CTX Mortgage Co., 969 P.2d 93 (Wash.1999), held that a mortgage company that prepared documents for loan closings was not engaged in the unauthorized practice of law. Only licensed lawyers selected the legal documents and only lawyers exercised legal judgment. Nonlawyers filled in some blanks, and the court held the company to the same standard of practice as a lawyer.

d. The lawyer in State ex rel. Oklahoma Bar Ass'n v. Israel, 25 P.3d 909 (Okla.2001), specialized in obtaining child support orders. He also created a corporation that helped clients collect court-ordered payments. He received 25% of each child support payment for his legal fees and his corporation received another 25% of each payment for its own work. The court held that the lawyer's involvement with the company was not an impermissible conflict of interest. The corporation's interest was aligned with the client's interest in collecting the money, and the respondent adequately disclosed his interest in the company through his oral statements to his client and in the fee stipulation in the client's contract.

e. Federal law may preempt state law on the issue of unauthorized practice. Congress, federal agencies, and federal courts may authorize individuals to practice before them regardless of the location of the person's place of work. Several prominent areas of federal practice come to mind, e.g., tax, patent filing and research, and pension planning, but dozens of other examples exist where states may not regulate the authority of an individual to provide legal or quasi legal services because of federal preemption. In Casey v. F.D.I.C., 583 F.3d 586 (8th Cir. 2009), plaintiffs argued that savings and loan institutions were engaged in unauthorized practice of law because they charged fees for the preparation of legal documents completed by nonlawyers. The court found that federal banking regulations preempted Missouri unauthorized practice of law rules.

f. Is the increasing liberality toward corporate legal services justified? Do these cases simply recognize that there is more to solving a client's problem than can justify an expenditure for expensive legal services? Or, are courts overlooking some protections the law previously thought were worth providing?

g. State ex rel. Indiana State Bar Ass'n v. United Financial Systems Corporation, 926 N.E.2d 8 (Ind. 2010), was less tolerant of corporate practice. The company targeted potential clients with mailings that included information on how to avoid probate. The company's sales representatives, who were not attorneys, would meet with those who responded to the mailings. During the meetings, the sales representatives obtained the clients' financial information and sold them estate planning services, including wills and trusts. The financial information was then forwarded to the company's in-house counsel, who sent the information to panel attorneys contracted by the company. The panel attorneys would call the client to discuss briefly the services they had purchased and then prepare the documentation; contact between the attorney and the client was generally limited to this one phone call. After the documents were prepared, non-lawyer sales representatives within the company took the documents to the clients, explained the nature of the documents and assisted the clients with their execution. They would also attempt to sell the clients insurance products and annuities.

The court found that the company's use of attorneys did not avoid illegality. It explained that under the company's business model the attorney's role was often marginalized in favor of producing sales and revenue. It also noted the discrepancy between commissions paid to sales representatives for the sale of the estate planning services, which ranged from $750 to $900 per sale, and fees paid to the panel attorneys, which amounted to $225 per client. The court also pointed out that, of all of the company's clients, only a small handful downgraded the package they purchased after consulting with the attorneys. The court believed that these facts, combined with the work of the sales representatives, indicated that the company focused on sales and revenue over independent legal advice. Thus, the court enjoined the company from continuing its style of practice.

2.   How should unauthorized practice of law principles apply to insurance companies who hire licensed lawyers as full-time employees to represent the company's policyholders as counsel of record in actions brought by third parties for incidents covered by the terms of the policy? Is that simply a more efficient way to pay the lawyers?

a.   Gardner v. North Carolina State Bar, 341 S.E.2d 517 (N.C.1986), was a relatively early case holding that insurance companies cannot employ its lawyer-employees to represent the insured. Nor may the attorney appear as counsel of record for the insured in the prosecution of a subrogation claim for property damage. "Since a corporation cannot practice law directly," the court said, "it cannot do so indirectly by employing lawyers to practice for it." 341 S.E.2d at 521.[11]

b.   In re Allstate Insurance Co., 722 S.W.2d 947 (Mo.1987) (en banc), specifically refused to follow *Gardner* and concluded that the insurance company may either hire independent lawyers or use its own employees instead. "An insurer has a very substantial interest in litigation involving its insured, and is entitled to retain counsel of its own choosing to protect its interest." 722 S.W.2d at 950. If an insurer can hire an independent

---

11. You may remember that we took up these insurance issues in a different context in Problem 13, *supra*.

contractor, it may act through its employee. Any danger of conflict of interest is minimized because the company uses its employee-lawyers "only when there is no question of coverage, and when the claim is within policy limits." 722 S.W.2d at 951.

c.   In Cincinnati Insurance Co. v. Wills, 717 N.E.2d 151 (Ind.1999), the insurance company provided the lawyers through a "captive" firm called "Berlon & Timmel" whose only practice was on behalf of policyholders of the insurer. The court agreed that Indiana corporations could not practice law; they could, however, hire lawyers to represent themselves, and the only question was whether they could hire lawyers to represent others. Conflicts could arise and be addressed, the court said, but a blanket prohibition was not required. However, the court found it misleading to use a traditional law firm name for a group of lawyers who do all their work for a single company. Change that and the practice may continue.

d.   Gafcon, Inc. v. Ponsor & Associates, 120 Cal.Rptr.2d 392 (Cal.Ct. App.2002), also upheld an insurance company's use of captive law firms to defend its insureds. A lawyer retained to defend an insured owes a fiduciary duty to both insurer and insured, the court said. A corporation may not practice law, but corporations frequently employ in-house counsel who may appear on their behalf. Where the insured's interest is congruent with the insurer's, and where the lawyers retain independence of professional judgment, counsel employed by an insurance company may also represent policyholders without violating the rule against the corporate practice of law.

e.   Insurance companies are trying to expand the use of in-house lawyers. With which of these cases do you agree? Is what the insurance companies are doing significantly different from the system of prepaid legal insurance discussed in Problem 34?

3.   How do these principles apply to the practice of accounting firms hiring lawyers full-time to give corporate and transactional advice to the firms' business clients?

a.   By far the most important issues of practice by nonlawyer organizations—as well as the most important multidisciplinary practice issues— are raised by the fact that the largest firms offering legal services in Europe at the turn of the millennium were American accounting firms. What Model Rules seem to impose the greatest barriers to these firms expanding their practice to the representation of clients in the United States?

b.   Does Model Rule 5.4 stand as a barrier to the delivery of "one-stop business services" by accounting firms? What interests of clients—as distinct from interests of lawyers in traditional law firms—can you see against the phenomenon?

4.   What should be the content of an ethics rule dealing with "one-stop business services" by accounting firms?

a.   Should the law make it clear that lawyers working for accounting firms remain subject to their state's lawyer rules of professional conduct? Should this new rule provide that nonlawyers may not direct the professional judgment of lawyers? Why or why not? Laypersons direct the professional judgment of in-house lawyers in a corporation (e.g., "I want you to waive the statute of limitations defense"). Should accounting firms that hire lawyers to represent third parties be permitted to exercise similar powers?

b. Should accounting firms be subject to the same conflict of interest rules that govern law firms? Should that include the requirement of imputation of all conflicts throughout the accounting firm? Given the small number of large accounting firms, that requirement would probably prohibit the provision of legal services by such firms.

c. Should the attorney-client privilege protect the client's communications with lawyers employed by accounting firms even though communications with accountants in those firms are not protected? Should the law treat accountants performing audits of clients to whom legal services are being delivered as knowing all confidential information disclosed by the clients to the lawyers in their firm?

d. An early draft of the Model Rules recommended that nonlawyers be permitted to form partnerships with lawyers if there would be no interference with the lawyers' independent professional judgment or with the lawyer-client relationship, client confidentiality would be maintained, and advising and fee arrangements did not violate the Rules governing lawyers. During the ABA floor debates an ABA delegate asked: "Does this rule mean Sears & Roebuck will be able to open a law office?" Professor Geoffrey C. Hazard, Jr., the Reporter for the Model Rules, answered "Yes." The proposal failed.[12]

e. The ABA Commission on Multidisciplinary Practice (MDP) issued a report in 1999 acknowledging the development of one-stop business services by accounting firms, and concluded that it inevitably represented a useful new way to deliver legal services to some clients. The MDP Commission proposed a new Model Rule 5.8 to regulate such firms. In February 2000, the ABA summarily rejected this report, but directed the ABA Ethics Committee to determine whether additional restrictions should be placed on "side-by-side" relationships between law firms and other service providers. In such relationships, the law firm would regularly send its clients to a single economic consulting firm, for example, while the economic consulting firm would regularly recommend the law firm to its clients.

In 2002, the major accounting firm of Arthur Andersen (one of the accounting firms most responsible for the MDP phenomenon) imploded as part of the Enron bankruptcy, and that series of events put the future of such organizations in the United States in some doubt.

f. New York, under the leadership of the late Steven Krane, advocated the delivery of law and non-law services to clients through joint cooperation agreements. In 2002, the ABA amended Model Rule 7.2 to authorize reciprocal referral agreements between lawyers and nonlawyer professionals. New York and the ABA viewed reciprocal referral agreements as an alternative to the prohibited integrated law and non-law entities sought by the advocates of the MDP movement. Rule 7.2(b)(4) permits such arrangements as long as they are not exclusive and the client is informed of their existence.

---

12. See Rita Henley Jensen, Ethics Row Looms on [Law Firm] Affiliates, National L. J., Feb. 20, 1989, at 1, 28.

g.   Wouters v. Algemene Raad van de Nederlandse Orde van Advocaten (C309/99), 2002 WL 29971, [2002] All E.R. (EC) 193, [2002] 4 C.M.L.R. 27, may have undercut the growth of multidisciplinary partnerships (MDPs) in Europe where the phenomenon began. This case held that, under European Union law, whether MDPs may include lawyers is a matter for national law. Arthur Andersen and other large accounting firms were providing legal services all over Europe, and the Netherlands Bar, a national entity, adopted rules prohibiting such partnerships from operating there. Plaintiffs challenged those rules as the product of a cartel, which the EU Treaty (Articles 81 and 82) prohibited, but the European Court of Justice found that those articles do not limit proper exercise of power by national authorities. The court believed that whether multidisciplinary partnerships would increase competition among legal service providers or lead to domination of the market by a few firms was far from clear, but it held that it was a matter properly resolved at a national level. The decision itself did not outlaw European MDPs, but it did deter their presence.

h.   Most importantly, in 2007, England enacted the Legal Services Act, which represents a significant transformation of the British legal services industry. First, the Act created a new regulatory structure for supervising the regulation and delivery of legal services in the United Kingdom. This included the creation of the Legal Services Board as the key policy and oversight regulatory agency and an Office for Legal Complaints to serve as the independent source for redress of consumer complaints. Second, the Act authorized lawyers in the United Kingdom to associate with nonlawyers (up to a limit of 25% ownership) for the purposes of delivering legal disciplinary practices (LDPs) to consumers. Such LDPs have been permitted to operate since March 2009. Finally, the Act expressly allows the creation of alternative business structures (ABS) to deliver legal and nonlegal services. The basic concept of an ABS is that the regulations will permit nonlawyers to practice together with lawyers to deliver legal and nonlegal services and such entities may have nonlawyer owners and managers. It is expected that law firms will be able to attract investment and capital from nonlawyers to operate an ABS. The British regulators have studied the challenges presented by ABSs since 2007 and have announced that they will authorize the first ABSs in October 2011. The most recent draft of the Solicitor's Regulation Authority on Preparing for Alternative Business Structures is available at http://www.sra.org.uk/solicitors/code-of-conduct/1883.article (Nov. 2010). These developments have the potential to have a profound impact on legal professions around the world.

5.   Is there a place for multidisciplinary organizations to deliver legal services to low-and middle-income clients?

a.   Think of an office serving clients like Mrs. Andrews, whom we met in Problem 17, for example. She was the woman in an abusive relationship who had lost custody of her children. Can you see circumstances in which she would be better served by a social services agency that had a lawyer on its staff than by a traditional private law firm?

b. New Jersey Supreme Court Advisory Committee on Professional Ethics, Opinion 711 (July 2007) considered a "center for divorce mediation," established by a lawyer, that referred parties to experienced accountants, therapists and mediators to try to achieve relatively noncontentious divorce settlements. The opinion found that the arrangement constituted the practice of law. Thus, the requirement that affiliated attorneys refer clients only to center-approved professionals violated Rule 5.4(c), the name of the center was not a permitted trade name under Rule 7.5, and Rule 5.4(b) prohibited the center from sharing its fees with the nonlawyer professionals. Do you think New Jersey citizens seeking divorces will be better served by contesting lawyers than by mediation services such as the center?

c. Should we let banks help their clients prepare wills and trusts? Dowd's organization is clearly nontraditional, but is it as crazy as it might have sounded when you first read about it? Until lawyers figure out a way to deliver legal services relatively noncontentiously and at a price most people can afford, do lawyers have the moral authority to stand in the way of people who can deliver such services?

D. LAW FIRM DELIVERY OF ANCILLARY, NOT-TRADITIONALLY-LEGAL SERVICES

1. Could Dowd eliminate all problems with his multidisciplinary organization if he simply ran it out of his law firm?

a. Subsidiaries or law firm "affiliates" are becoming more common today as law firms have gone into the publishing business, financial consulting, and even forms of investment banking. Are these positive developments or do they constitute a threat to the independence and professionalism of lawyers?[13] The debate as to whether law firms should be able to operate nonlaw entities has become more heated over the years.

b. Washington, D.C. firms initially founded many of the first wave of law firm affiliates. A partner in Arnold & Porter explained a typical reason for creating the subsidiary: the firm wished to hire a departing government official who was not a lawyer; this official would be hired to engage in lobbying activities for clients but "[w]e would have to call him or her a paralegal."

2. What advantages and problems can you see with such arrangements?

a. The arguments in favor of such affiliates seem to be fourfold. First, they make the law firm more convenient for the client. When the client has a problem that requires the services of several professionals, as is often the

---

13. There is clearly no ethical restriction on a lawyer's owning a business that is not ancillary to the practice of law. Two lawyers in a law partnership may buy a res-taurant, for example, and they presumably may take clients there to dine without the restaurant's becoming law-related.

case, it is beneficial and useful for the client be able to engage in one-stop shopping. Second, the law firm wishes to give the nonlawyer professionals the status and titles that they deserve. Third, these entities are perhaps not as constrained in the manner of calculating fees as lawyers may be. Fourth, having the affiliates may retain existing clients, bring in new clients, and thus offer new sources of revenue.

b.   The arguments against creating such affiliates are both ethical and pragmatic. Ethically, a lawyer who advises a client in dealings with the lawyer's affiliate may not have the independent judgment needed to give sound advice, such as the advice to fire the affiliate. Also, such arrangements inevitably involve the lawyer in business transactions with the client, raising separate problems under Rule 1.8(a).

c.   Pragmatically, law firms must be concerned, first, about the partners' being jointly and severally liable for the acts of the affiliates, ranging from simple negligence to dishonesty of the nonlawyers. When the affiliate is making large sums of money by brokering substantial transactions, the potential exposure to malpractice may look small by comparison, but liability can be enormous.

d.   Next, the affiliate may expand the number of situations disqualifying the law firm, e.g., the affiliate may work on behalf of a client who has an interest that conflicts with a different client of the law firm.

e.   To the extent that law firms become one-stop shopping centers instead of dispensers of a unique service, there is a danger that lawyers will lose their power of self-regulation and that the state supreme courts, which usually claim an inherent power to regulate the practice of law, will lose that claim of authority.

f.   If the law permits a law firm to set up a nonlawyer affiliate, there is the risk that the law will eventually allow a nonlawyer entity to set up a law firm subsidiary. The fear of becoming a Wal–Mart employee seems to haunt many lawyers.

3.   Take a look at Model Rule 5.7 and its Comments. The ABA adopted a similar rule in 1992, repealed it in 1993, and adopted the present version in 1994. What should constitute "law-related services" within the meaning of the rule?

a.   Is "financial planning" a law-related service, for example? Is the test whether a service is one that some lawyers might offer to some clients? By that definition, is every service performed by any lawyer potentially law-related?

b.   What is the significance of calling something "law-related"? Is a lawyer's title insurance business subject to different in-person solicitation rules than would govern sale of the usual insurance policy, for example? What is the rationale for holding lawyers to a more restrictive standard?

c.   Is there any reason not to call every service a lawyer provides a legal service? Should a lawyer's ancillary business be permitted to do environmental consulting for a customer that may disadvantage one of the lawyer's clients, for example, without the consent of that client?

d.   In Matter of Hear, 755 N.E.2d 579 (Ind.2001), a lawyer entered into a debt collection business with a nonlawyer. He allowed the nonlawyer to solicit clients and to administer and manage the cases that he solicited. He also authorized the nonlawyer to use letterhead captioned "Charles F. Hear, Attorney at Law" and to collect debtors' payments made out to the lawyer. At some point, the nonlawyer stole funds held for a client by writing checks to himself from the respondent's account. The court suspended the respondent from the practice of law for 100 days for failure to supervise the nonlawyer properly, failure to make reasonable efforts to ensure that the nonlawyer's conduct complied with the respondent's professional obligations, and for allowing the nonlawyer to solicit work on his behalf.

Do you agree with this result? Does it tend to confirm that if problems arise in the law-related activity, the lawyer will likely be held to traditional lawyer conduct standards?

4.   If the law allows law firms to provide nonlaw services, should law firms be able to admit nonlawyers as partners to perform those services?

a.   One jurisdiction permits nonlawyers to be partners of law firms. District of Columbia Court of Appeals Rule 5.4 provides:

(b) A lawyer may practice law in a partnership or other form of organization in which a financial interest is held or managerial authority is exercised by an individual nonlawyer who performs professional services which assist the organization in providing legal services to clients, but only if:

(1) The partnership or organization has as its sole purpose providing legal services to clients;

(2) All persons having such managerial authority or holding a financial interest undertake to abide by these rules of professional conduct;

(3) The lawyers who have a financial interest or managerial authority in the partnership or organization undertake to be responsible for the nonlawyer participants to the same extent as if nonlawyer participants were lawyers under Rule 5.1;

(4) The foregoing conditions are set forth in writing.

Comment 5 to this Rule explains that nonlawyer participants "ought not to be confused with nonlawyer assistants under Rule 5.3. Nonlawyer participants are persons having managerial authority or financial interests in organizations which provide legal services."

b.   Comment 8 adds that the D.C. Rule "does not permit an individual or entity to acquire all or any part of the ownership of a law practice organization for investment or other purposes" because "such an investor would not be an individual performing professional services within the law firm or other organization."

Why not? If a firm can pay a lawyer with a well-known name to meet with potential clients but do little else, why shouldn't the firm be able to pay a passive investor to provide the firm with operating capital?

In 2007, the Australian law firm Slater & Gordon raised several million dollars selling shares in itself on the Australian Stock Exchange. Are you shocked by this development? Do you see any reason not to permit the same practice in the United States?[14]

c. In an important opinion applicable beyond D.C., ABA Formal Opinion 01–423 (Sept. 22, 2001), advised that U.S. lawyers may form partnerships with lawyers not licensed in the United States, so long as the foreign lawyers are members of a recognized legal profession in a foreign jurisdiction and the arrangement is in compliance with the law of all jurisdictions where the firm practices. If the foreign nation's lawyers are not recognized as a legal profession, they would be deemed "nonlawyers" and making them partners would violate Rule 5.4. The purpose of Rule 5.4 is to protect a lawyer's independence in exercising professional judgment on the client's behalf, the opinion says. As long as a foreign lawyer is a member of a recognized legal profession this objective would be realized.[15]

In order to be deemed a member of a recognized legal profession, the opinion says, a person must be specially trained to give advice on the laws of the foreign jurisdiction and licensed to represent clients in its legal system. U.S. lawyers must take reasonable steps to ensure that foreign lawyers meet these requirements, that the arrangement is in compliance with the law of jurisdictions where the firm practices, and that matters in foreign jurisdiction are managed pursuant to all applicable Model Rules that apply to the firm's practice.

d. What kinds of legal delivery organizations do you see in your future? Is the prospect of using your legal skills to work for many different kinds of organizations a cause for celebration or a cause for apprehension?

---

14. One result of this prohibition is that it "can forestall attempts to form the capital structures necessary to make law practice a true consumer product for a mass market. It also prevents competition from banks, insurance companies, title insurance companies and other potential competitors. The prohibition presented a momentary embarrassment when, for tax reasons, it made economic sense for a lawyers to practice in the corporate form. That was gotten around by obtaining state legislation permitting lawyers to form 'professional corporations.'" Charles W. Wolfram, Modern Legal Ethics 840 (1986).

15. New York law has been to this effect for several years. See Rules of the Court of Appeals for the Licensing of Legal Consultants, 22 N.Y.C.R.R. Part 521.

CHAPTER VIII

ETHICAL CONDUCT OF JUDGES

Not all lawyers will be judges, but almost all lawyers will appear before them. And public and professional confidence in the integrity of the judiciary is close to the heart of the respect for law. Thus, judicial ethics is of central importance to any lawyer, whether or not he or she aspires to be on the bench.

Judges are usually lawyers and continue to be governed by their state version of the ABA Model Rules of Professional Conduct, particularly Rule 8.4. The conduct of lawyers who deal with judges—or who want to become judges—is also the concern of the Model Rules.

However, for the issues in this chapter, judicial conduct is regulated by state or federal versions of the ABA Model Code of Judicial Conduct. By this time, it should be clear to you that ethical standards do not draw simple lines between honest persons and crooks. The Model Code of Judicial Conduct is no exception.[1]

As you work through these materials, ask yourself questions such as:

a. Which of the principles of judicial ethics are designed to help assure "correct" or at least disinterested decisions?

b. Which principles are primarily designed to prevent judges from abusing the unusual influence they have over lawyers and in the community?

c. How do issues of judicial misconduct reach official attention and what is the role of lawyers in that process?

d. To what extent would the Model Code of Judicial Conduct be unnecessary if judges were appointed and not elected?

e. Are any aspects of the Model Code unnecessarily restrictive on judges? Do any ethics rules tend to discourage able people from seeking judicial office?

f. Rule 1.2 of the 2007 Model Code requires judges to avoid "the appearance of impropriety." Is that standard too vague to use as a basis for judicial discipline?

---

1. In February 2007, the ABA approved a new Model Code of Judicial Conduct that changed the format of the 1990 Model Code and substantially reorganized the standards. Unless described otherwise, all references in this chapter are to the 2007 Model Code.

PROBLEM 38

JUDGES' DISQUALIFYING CONFLICTS OF INTEREST

Grounds for disqualifying judges are probably the judicial ethics issues of most interest to practicing litigators. Judges, like everyone else, have financial dealings. They get a mortgage to buy a house, borrow money to purchase a car, and try to take advantage of investment opportunities. Their family members lead their own lives and have their own financial relationships and careers, but the judge is not likely to be indifferent to their welfare. Judges also often have strongly held views on public questions, some of which may come before their court. This problem first asks what financial relationships create a conflict of interest that requires the judge's disqualification. Next, it asks when interests of the judge's family may create similar problems for the judge. It then examines whether views about policy issues constitute a similarly disqualifying bias, and it closes by exploring when and how a judge's conflict of interest may be waived.

FACTS

Harold Baxter and Martha Anderson met in law school and have been good friends ever since. Baxter has now become a state trial judge and Anderson practices in the same city. Recently, Baxter sought to buy a new house, but the required down payment was higher than he had expected. Anderson, who was an attorney for the bank from which Baxter planned to borrow, personally lent Baxter $25,000, evidenced by a demand note that Anderson assured Baxter would not be "called under any conditions I can foresee." Judge Baxter then got his mortgage from the bank.

Anderson is now representing the same bank, which is the plaintiff in a case assigned to Judge Baxter. The case involves a close question of lien priorities and both sides expect the case to go to the state supreme court. Judge Baxter orally informed defense counsel about the loans in an early pretrial conference and asked, "Do you have any problems with my presiding in this case?" Both Anderson and the defense counsel, who frequently appears before Judge Baxter, replied, "No, sir."

Judge Baxter's niece is 19 and lives with the Baxters while going to college. She has some money of her own that she has invested. She owns ten shares, a 1/100,000 interest, in the insurance company that is defendant in the lien priorities case before Judge Baxter. The judge does not know of her interest. "I don't ask my relatives about their business dealings nor tell them about mine," he says.

Before going on the bench, Judge Baxter had been local chair of the "Committee for Responsible Assessment Policy," a committee of citizens who favored correction of what they saw as an inequitable method of making local tax assessments. He is no longer a member of that committee. Cases are randomly assigned to judges in this district, and Judge Baxter has been assigned to hear a case in which a local taxpayer is challenging the validity of her own assessment. Judge Baxter has taken no steps either to recuse himself from the matter or to determine whether either party believes he should do so.

QUESTIONS

A.   FINANCIAL INTERESTS THAT MAY CREATE DISQUALIFYING BIAS

1. Was it improper for Anderson to lend money to Judge Baxter to help him buy a house, or for Judge Baxter to accept the loan?

a.   Look at Model Rules 3.5(a) and 8.4(f). Do they tell you that Martha Anderson has to take a good look at the Model Code of Judicial Conduct to know the status of her own conduct under the Model Rules of Professional Conduct?

b.   What will Anderson find when she turns to the Code of Judicial Conduct? Does Rule 3.11(C)(3) provide an unambiguous answer to the propriety of the loan? Does Rule 3.13(C)(3) give Anderson and Judge Baxter a better sense of the answer to their question? Does Rule 3.15 require Judge Baxter to publicly report the loan? Does the loan require automatic disqualification under Rule 2.11? Was Judge Baxter required to disclose the loan to opposing counsel as the problem says he did?

c.   In re Corboy, 528 N.E.2d 694 (Ill.1988) (per curiam), involved lawyers who gave checks for $1,000 each to a state judge. Each of the lawyers testified that they considered the checks to be a gift or loan to the judge's mother to pay the mother's hospital bills so that she could come home for Christmas. The checks were deposited in the judge's own checking account. The funds were not used to pay the hospital bills, which were covered by insurance. The court rejected the argument that gifts to judges are only proscribed if they are motivated by a subjective intent to bribe the judge; such gifts are too subject to abuse to make their propriety turn on later testimony about intent. Similarly, the money given to the judge was not "ordinary social hospitality" under what is now Rule 3.13(B)(3) of the ABA Model Code of Judicial Conduct. The transactions were "a far cry from the social dinners, gratuitous rides, birthday recognitions and gifts of books or flowers, which might be genuine instances of social hospitality * * *." 528 N.E.2d at 700. The court refused to censure any of the attorneys (including prominent lawyers such as Philip Corboy and William James Harte) because "They acted without the guidance of precedent or settled opinion, and there was, apparently, considerable belief among members of the bar that they acted properly." 528 N.E.2d at 701. Do you agree that reasonable lawyers should have been confused about the propriety of such gifts?[1]

---

1. But see, In re Alexander, 585 N.E.2d 70 (Ill.1991) (accepting a guardian ad litem appointment from a judge to whom the lawyer had loaned $11,000 reflected a lack of

d. In Lisi v. Several Attorneys, 596 A.2d 313 (R.I.1991), a judge had called twenty-one lawyers at various times, pleading that he desperately needed money to cover some urgent needs. Some of the lawyers had appeared before the judge in family court but several had known him in other settings. Each lent him the money he requested, not knowing others were doing so as well. There was no reported quid pro quo treatment, but some lawyers did have matters pending before the judge while the loans were outstanding. The judge resigned; the court suspended four of the lawyers for a year and imposed public reprimands on seventeen others.

e. Operation Wrinkled Robe was a federal investigation that video-taped Judge Alan Green soliciting and accepting a campaign contribution for his niece who was running for the Louisiana House of Representatives. One lawyer making a donation had just won a large verdict before Judge Green. For his conduct, Judge Green was convicted by a federal jury of mail fraud and sentenced to 51 months in prison. He also resigned as a judge and was permanently disbarred. In re Green, 913 So.2d 113 (La.2005) and 920 So.2d 861 (La.2006). The lawyer who made the contribution was suspended from practice for a year and a day. In re LeBlanc, 972 So.2d 315 (La.2007).

2. Was it improper for Judge Baxter to finance his home mortgage with a bank that regularly brought cases before him?

a. Look generally at Rule 3.13 of the ABA Model Code of Judicial Conduct, and particularly at Rule 3.13(B)(4) & Comment 3. Do you agree that borrowing from a bank—even a litigious bank—should be treated differently from borrowing from the bank's attorney? Why?

b. In Ausherman v. Bank of America, 216 F.Supp.2d 530 (D.Md. 2002), the plaintiffs claimed that a bank had improperly accessed their credit reports. They sought to disqualify the federal magistrate judge because the defendant bank held his home mortgage, but the judge refused to step down. Citing 28 U.S.C. § 455,[2] the federal law counterpart to Rule 2.11 of the Model Code of Judicial Conduct, the judge observed, "A loss for the bank, even if ruinous, would not extinguish or reduce the obligation of the mortgagor to repay * * *. Similarly, a victory for the bank, regardless of how substantial, affords no possible benefit to the mortgagor." 216 F.Supp.2d at 533–34. Do you agree that the issue of how having the loan might influence the judge is that simple?

c. In re United States, 158 F.3d 26 (1st Cir.1998), involved a government motion to recuse a federal judge in a criminal trial of officials of a bank where the judge and her husband had an overdrawn account and a delinquent commercial loan during the period when the defendants were bank officers. The trial judge refused to recuse herself, the government

"common sense and sound judgment" that required suspending the lawyer from practice for six months). Arguably, the Illinois court was belatedly closing the door that it had appeared to open in *Corboy*.

2. The text of 28 U.S.C. § 455 can be found among the federal statutory materials in the Standards Supplement to this book.

filed a mandamus action, and the First Circuit held that the judge's decision not to recuse herself was not an abuse of discretion. The government had not shown that the officials on trial had anything to do with the bank's decision to grant the judge's loan or that the bank had treated the judge differently from other borrowers.

3. How large must the judge's financial interest be before there is a disqualifying financial interest in the subject matter of litigation over which the judge is presiding?

a. Look at Rule 2.11(A)(3), and the definition of "economic interest" in the Terminology section of the ABA Model Code of Judicial Conduct.[3] What makes an interest "more than de minimis"? The 1972 version of the ABA Model Code of Judicial Conduct defined "financial interest" as any interest "however small."

b. Should a judge be disqualified from hearing a case involving IBM if he or she owns ten shares of IBM stock? Does the process for determining when an interest is "de minimis" intrude on the privacy of the judge? After all, what may seem like a large amount to a judge of modest means may be de minimis to a very rich judge, and thus litigants might have to inquire into the judge's overall financial position in order to determine whether the interest is de minimis. The Reporter's Notes to the 1972 Judicial Code explain that, to avoid such inquiries, the 1972 Code adopted an absolute prohibition that was mitigated by the fact that the parties could implement the waiver provisions of Rule 2.11(C), discussed below.

Was the 1972 approach preferable to the current provision? Did that approach give parties too much opportunity to disqualify a judge they did not like for reasons unrelated to the issue of financial interest?

c. Virginia Electric & Power Co. v. Sun Shipbuilding & Dry Dock Co., 539 F.2d 357 (4th Cir.1976), extensively analyzed both 28 U.S.C. § 455 and what is now Rule 2.11. The electric utility sued for damages caused by the defendant's fabrication of pump supports. At least in principle, if the utility won the case, the state regulatory commission could require it to lower the electric bills of everyone in Virginia, including the trial judge's bills. The total reduction could have been $100, payable in small amounts over 40 years. The Fourth Circuit held that the trial judge should not be disqualified because he had no "financial" interest in the outcome of the case, because any rate relief was speculative and wholly within the discretion of the Virginia Corporation Commission that sets utility rates. That possibility did constitute an "other interest" that is a basis for disqualification within the meaning of that section, but the interest was too speculative and remote to require the judge's recusal.

d. Matter of Fuchsberg, 426 N.Y.S.2d 639 (Ct.Jud.1978) (per curiam), involved a judge of the New York Court of Appeals who engaged in

---

3. The Terminology section of the 2007 Model Code adds several terms that were not in the 1990 Code (such as, "domestic partner," and "impending matter"). And it removes some definitions as unnecessary. Other than that, definitions in the 1990 Model Code are the same as the 2007 Model Code. The Reporter's Explanation of Changes explains that "any differences are intended to be purely stylistic."

transactions in New York City bonds while cases affecting the value of those bonds were before the New York courts, including his own court. On the day the judge took office, he owned $3.4 million in par value in city notes. He redeemed some notes and bought others thereafter. One issue before his court was the constitutionality of a state law that imposed a three-year freeze on some of these notes. In one of the cases the judge voted against his apparent financial interest and in two others he did not participate. The Court on the Judiciary held that the judge's ownership, purchase and sale of municipal and state securities and his participation in cases affecting the value of those holdings violated the "spirit" of the judicial canons that correspond to Rule 1.1, Rule 1.2, and Rule 3.11(C)(2). The court also noted: "Respondent's failure either to disqualify himself from this case or utilize this [waiver] procedure constituted a violation of" the judicial canons. But, the majority concluded, his conduct did not warrant removing him from office. "The record establishes his inattentiveness to and, at times, a cavalier disregard for the necessity of avoiding the appearance of impropriety," the court said, "yet the same record does not show deliberately fraudulent conduct, willful violations of Rules and Canons, or corrupt actions inspired by financial interest." 426 N.Y.S.2d at 649. Do you agree with the court's disposition of the matter?

e.   Should placing the judge's assets into a blind trust satisfy the Code of Judicial Conduct? Why or why not? Does a blind trust satisfy the requirements of Rule 2.11(B)? Is a judge who puts property into a blind trust keeping informed about his or her financial holdings?

4.   Is a judge disqualified from ruling on a court challenge to the judge's own pay, or does the "Rule of Necessity" allow the judge to hear the case? Should it matter that the reason for disqualifying this judge extends to all judges, so that no one could decide the case in a wholly impartial manner?

a.   In 1976, 140 federal judges filed a lawsuit arguing that since their last pay increase, inflation had reduced the purchasing power of their salaries by over 34%. The failure to grant them cost-of-living pay increases, they said, constituted an unconstitutional reduction of their salaries. Then, as now, 28 U.S.C. § 455(e) said that federal judges could not accept a waiver of recusal in a case involving the judge's personal financial interest. The Court of Claims applied the "rule of necessity" and held that, under that rule, its judges could hear the case. Otherwise, some important legal questions could never be decided. The court then turned to the judges' substantive claim and denied it. Atkins v. United States, 556 F.2d 1028 (Ct.Cl.1977) (per curiam), cert. denied, 434 U.S. 1009 (1978).

b.   Despite failing to win *Atkins*, 13 judges filed new suits in a federal district court. The Supreme Court heard their appeal and decided that the rule of necessity allowed both the lower courts and the Supreme Court to hear the case, notwithstanding 28 U.S.C.A. § 455. United States v. Will, 449 U.S. 200 (1980). The *Will* Court explained: "The Rule of Necessity had its genesis at least five-and-a-half centuries ago. Its earliest recorded invocation was in 1430, when it was held that the Chancellor of Oxford could act as judge of a case in which he was a party when there was no provision for appointment of another judge." 449 U.S. at 213. The rule of necessity is a "well-settled principle at common law that, as Pollack put it, 'although a judge had better not, if it can be avoided, take part in the decision of a case in which he has any personal interest, yet he not only may but must do so if the case cannot be heard otherwise.' F. Pollack, A First Book of Jurisprudence 270 (6th ed. 1929)." Id. *Will* concluded that Congress did not intend § 455 to change the rule of necessity, "a doctrine that had not been questioned under prior judicial disqualification statutes." Id. at 481. *Will* then held that Congress had unconstitutionally diminished salaries of Article III judges and justices for two of the four years in dispute.

c.   Does this exception to required recusal make sense to you? Note that Model Code of Judicial Conduct, Rule 2.11, Comment 3, acknowledges the "rule of necessity."

5.   What other "personal interests" might bias a judge?

a.   Should a Supreme Court justice be considered biased in favor of the incumbent administration because the Vice President invites the justice to go hunting? That issue arose in 2004 when Justice Scalia and Vice President Cheney, who had known each other for many years, were among a group of nine that hunted together in Louisiana. At the time of the trip, the Supreme Court had granted certiorari in a case involving the Vice President's handling of an energy task force. Justice Scalia refused to recuse himself from the pending case, saying that informal relationships between government officers are common and do not normally affect the exercise of their official duties. Cheney v. U.S. District Court for the District of Columbia, 541 U.S. 913 (2004). Are you comfortable about such associations? Should it matter that the Vice President was being sued only in his official capacity?

b.   Is a judge biased in one case because he took a bribe in a completely different case? Bracy v. Gramley, 520 U.S. 899 (1997), a habeas corpus case, allowed discovery to show judicial bias during habeas review after a judge sentenced the defendant to death. The defendant wanted to show that the judge at his state court trial, Judge Thomas J. Maloney, had accepted bribes in other murder cases and had a compensatory bias against defendants who did not bribe him so as to avoid appearing "soft" on criminal defendants. A unanimous Court concluded that the defendant should be permitted to try to prove his point. Defendant did more than charge a judge's bias in general; he specifically alleged that he did not get a fair trial. The Court remanded the case for further discovery.

c.   Should a judge be considered biased against a defendant because the defendant had threatened to kill the judge? Should we be worried that a defendant might engage in judge shopping by threatening to kill each judge assigned to his case? Does the risk of criminal prosecution for uttering such threats prevent that? In United States v. Greenspan, 26 F.3d 1001 (10th Cir.1994), the FBI reported that the defendant had taken steps to hire a hit man to kill the trial judge and his family. The trial judge knew of the threats and expedited the sentencing hearing to get the defendant off the streets "immediately." The Court of Appeals held that a defendant may not require a judge's recusal simply by uttering a threat, but in this case—where the facts suggested this was more than a ruse to disqualify the judge—a reasonable person would think the judge's impartiality would be affected. The court held that § 455(a) required that another judge impose the defendant's sentence.

B. FINANCIAL INTERESTS OF THE JUDGE'S FAMILY

1. What obligation does Judge Baxter have to know his niece's financial holdings?

a. Should a judge be able to take an "I don't ask" attitude about his or her relatives' financial affairs? Look carefully at Rules 2.11(A)(2) & (3) and Rule 2.11(B). Is Judge Baxter's 19–year–old niece a "member of the judge's family residing in the judge's household"? Is she a minor child? Is she "within the third degree of relationship" to Judge Baxter? The 2007 Model Code defines the "third degree of relationship" in its Terminology section.

b. If Judge Baxter had known of the niece's holdings, would he have been obliged to recuse himself in this case? Would his "don't ask, don't tell" approach to others' financial interests subject him to discipline no matter what appropriate inquiry would have revealed?[4]

c. Should a judge be able to "cure" a financial conflict of a relative by having the relative sell the stock? During the discovery period in Union Carbide Corporation v. United States Cutting Service, Inc., 782 F.2d 710 (7th Cir.1986), an antitrust class action, Judge Susan Getzendanner got married. Her husband had a self-managed retirement account that contained stock in IBM and Kodak. At the time, there was no list of class members. When the judge disclosed her husband's holdings in her annual financial disclosure statements, the defendant moved to disqualify her because it knew that IBM and Kodak had bought products from the defendant. Instead, the judge immediately ceased ruling on motions in the case while her husband sold his interest in the two companies. The Court of Appeals upheld that procedure. After the sale, the husband no longer had an interest in the stock, the court reasoned. The majority said "we do not mean to endorse sale as a cure for disqualification in all cases," but in this

---

4. You can find out the financial holdings of a federal judge and his or her close relatives. See P.L. 95–521, Title III, Judicial Personnel Financial Disclosure Requirements § 305, in the Standards Supplement. The Fifth Circuit summarily rejected a challenge to these disclosure requirements. Duplantier v. United States, 606 F.2d 654 (5th Cir.1979), cert. denied, 449 U.S. 1076 (1981).

Federal judges do not always disqualify themselves when their ethics rules require them to do so. "A number of federal appellate judges have ruled on cases involving companies in which they own stock, despite a federal law designed to prevent judges from taking part in any case in which they have a financial interest." When interviewed, the judges, "who include some of the nation's best-known jurists, attributed their participation in the cases to innocent mistakes or memory lapses about their financial portfolios." As one judge remarked, "It's embarrassing." See Joe Stephens, Taking Stock On the Bench: Federal Appeals Court Judges With Conflicts of Interest, Washington Post, Sept. 13, 1999, at p. A1.

case there was no basis for saying the judge's impartiality could reasonably be questioned.

Judge Flaum's dissent argued that nothing in 28 U.S.C. § 455(b)(4)—which corresponds to Rule 2.11(A)(3)—permits a judge to "cure" a disqualifying situation in this way. "Congress desired to rid the statute of flexibility where financial interests are concerned." After the case, Congress added 28 U.S.C.A. § 455(f), which largely codified the Seventh Circuit ruling.

2. If Judge Baxter has a daughter who practices federal tax law in a local firm, must he recuse himself whenever his daughter's firm enters an appearance in a case?

a. Does Rule 2.11(A)(2)(b) provide the answer? The daughter's direct involvement in the case would disqualify Judge Baxter; do the 2007 Rules also require disqualification whenever any member of the daughter's law firm is before him? Does Rule 2.11, Comment 4, provide a clear answer? Should the answer to the question be the same in a large city with many available judges as in a small town with no other available judges within 50 miles?

b. In Bernard v. Coyne, 31 F.3d 842 (9th Cir.1994), Judge Kozinski had to decide when he must disqualify himself in bankruptcy cases arising out of the district in which his wife was the United States bankruptcy trustee. Most of the trustee's actual duties are administrative, but she has the right to become involved in any case and some of the cases establish precedents that are important to her office. Judge Kozinski had referred the issue to the Judicial Conference's Committee on the Code of Conduct, which had concluded that, unless a case involved the trustee as a party or was of such high profile that her career would be affected, no recusal was required. He took that advice and decided that he could hear this case.

c. If there is any question about the issue, how should Judge Baxter determine whether his daughter has "more than a de minimis interest" that will be "substantially affected" by the outcome of a case? May he call his daughter on the telephone and ask her how her firm divides income from such cases? Must the parties be permitted to contact the relative to make a similar inquiry? Must the judge hold a public hearing?[5]

d. Should it matter whether the firm has taken the case on a contingent fee so that its fee is may be directly affected by the outcome of the proceedings? Suppose the daughter were "of counsel" to the firm, i.e., she did not automatically share all fees?

e. Might Rule 2.11(A)(2)(b) encourage litigants to use its limitations as a way of disqualifying judges or justices? Several justices of the U.S. Supreme Court have spouses, children, or other relatives who practice law and whose law firms may work on matters that will come before the Court. On November 1, 1993, seven justices[6] announced that, absent "some special

---

5. One federal case that seems to read 28 U.S.C.A. § 455(a) and (b)(5) to disqualify the judge when anyone in his brother's firm appeared before him was SCA Services, Inc. v. Morgan, 557 F.2d 110 (7th Cir.1977).

6. Justice Blackmun, who was about to retire, and Justice Souter, a bachelor, did not sign the statement. 112 S.Ct. at CIX (1993).

factor," they would not recuse themselves solely because a relative of theirs had personally worked on a matter at an earlier stage before it reached the Supreme Court. One "special factor" would be that the relative was "lead counsel below," because then the outcome of the case "might reasonably be thought capable of enhancing or damaging his or her professional reputation." 112 S.Ct. at *CX* (Dec. 1, 1993) (unbound). See also, 80 A.B.A.J. 18 (Feb. 1994). If the relative is a law firm partner, the rule mandates recusal unless the relative's firm gives "written assurance that income from Supreme Court litigation is, on a permanent basis, excluded from our relative's partnership shares." 112 S.Ct. at *CXI*.

Have the justices appropriately balanced the competing interests in establishing these standards? Were they properly concerned that recusing themselves in any more cases would create opportunities for " 'strategizing' recusals, that is, selecting law firms with an eye to producing the recusal of particular Justices." Id. at *CX*.[7]

3. Should a judge be disqualified when someone from the judge's former firm (or the judge's former law clerk) appears before the judge?

a.   In National Auto Brokers Corp. v. General Motors Corp., 572 F.2d 953 (2d Cir.1978), four years into an antitrust case, the plaintiffs moved to recuse the judge because the judge's former law firm represented the defendant. The Second Circuit held that, while the defendant was a client of the firm while the judge was there, he had never represented the defendant and the specific case did not come to the firm until after the judge had left. Would the case come out the same under Rule 2.11(A)(6)(a)?

b.   Is the judge–clerk relationship likely to have been more close or less than the judge's relationship with his or her law partners? Should a judge's former law clerk be barred from appearing before the judge?

Monument Builders of Pennsylvania, Inc. v. Catholic Cemeteries Association, Inc., 190 F.R.D. 164 (E.D.Pa.1999), involved a lawyer who had been the judge's clerk in 1984 when the federal district court considered a class action against various cemetery associations. Indeed, she had been the judge's clerk until his retirement in 1998. The parties brought a new case in 1999 to enforce a settlement agreement that the parties had entered into with the judge's approval in 1989. The former clerk was with the firm representing the plaintiff and had been involved in working on the enforcement action. The court held that the enforcement action was the same matter as the case that began in 1984 so it disqualified the lawyer pursuant to Rule 1.12 of the ABA Model Rules of Professional Conduct and Canon 2 of the federal Code of Conduct for Law Clerks. However, the court did not disqualify her law firm because she telecommuted and the firm could easily screen her from further involvement in the matter.

---

7. See Ronald D. Rotunda, Rubbish   at A26.
About Recusal, Wall Street J., Dec. 13, 2000,

c. In Bradley v. State of Alaska, 16 P.3d 187 (Alaska App.2001), the state moved to allow a former appellate court law clerk to represent the state in the appeal. The proposed lawyer had been a clerk while the appeal was pending, but by the time the appeal had been assigned to a judge within the court, the clerk had finished his clerkship and begun working for the state. The state appellate rule seemed to impose an inflexible ban on participation in a case that had been pending in the court during the period in which he served as a law clerk. The court turned to the state's later adoption of Model Rule of Professional Conduct 1.12(a), allowing a law clerk to participate in a case that was previously pending in the court in which the clerk served unless he "participated personally and substantially" in the matter during his time as a clerk. The court held that Rule 1.12(a) is "inconsistent" with the earlier rule, and that Rule 1.12(a) is now the law. The former clerk submitted an affidavit declaring that he had no contact with any of the pleadings in this appeal and that he did not discuss any aspect of this case with any judge, secretary, law clerk, or other court system employee. Thus, the court granted the state's motion to let him handle the appeal.

d. Should we suspect bias if the judge's personal lawyer appears before her in an matter? ABA Formal Opinion 07–449 (Aug. 9, 2007) said such a situation presents a conflict for the lawyer under Model Rule 1.7(a)(2). Only if the lawyer concludes he can provide competent and diligent representation to both the judge and to the client before the judge, and only with the informed consent of each confirmed in writing, may the lawyer handle both cases. If the judge, in turn, would have a personal bias for or against the lawyer or the lawyer's firm as a result of the representation the judge has received, the judge would be required to disqualify herself under Code of Judicial Conduct Rule 2.11(A) and may not seek a waiver under Rule 2.11(C). Such bias is not inevitable, however, and where the judge concludes she has no bias, she may put the issue of waiver before the parties and accept a Rule 2.11(C) waiver.

In a situation where the judge refuses to recuse herself or seek a waiver, the opinion says, the lawyer is required to withdraw under Model Rule 1.16(a) from one or both representations. Otherwise, the opinion concludes that the lawyer would be in violation of Model Rule 8.4(f), i.e., assisting the judge to violate the CJC. To try to avoid the need for withdrawal, the opinion says the lawyer may talk to the judge about her obligations without violating the Model Rule 3.5 or the CJC Rule 2.9(A) prohibitions of ex parte contact.

C. BIAS ARISING FROM PERSONAL VIEWS RATHER THAN FINANCIAL INTEREST

1. Does Judge Baxter's prior involvement in the Committee for Responsible Assessment Policy require his recusal from the case challenging the plaintiff's assessment?

a. Do Rule 1.2 and Rule 2.11(A) provide an answer or only suggest more questions? Look at the definitions of "impartiality" and "impropriety" in 2007 Model Code, Terminology. The 1990 Model Code did not define these terms. Do the new definitions help? Look at Rule 1.2, Comment 5, which elaborates on the prohibition against an "appearance of impropriety." Does 2007 Model Code give any examples of something that is not an impropriety but *appears* to be an impropriety to "reasonable minds"? Can you think of any?[8]

b.   Chief Justice Rehnquist weighed in on the question of issue bias shortly after he joined the Supreme Court:

"Though the Canons of Ethics are extraordinarily detailed and specific about what shall constitute a 'financial interest,' they have virtually nothing to say about what constitutes 'bias.' The Canons state that: 'A judge should disqualify himself in a proceeding in which his impartiality might reasonably be questioned * * *.' [Webster's Dictionary defines 'impartiality' as] 'freedom from bias or favoritism'; one of the definitions of 'bias' in that same volume is 'an inclination of temperament or outlook.' In that broad definition of 'bias,' one can scarcely escape the conclusion that all judges, to a greater or lesser extent, are biased. * * * The late Justice Black was, in this sense of the word, 'biased' in favor of a literal construction of the First Amendment to the United States Constitution, and made no bones about saying so. But it cannot be this sort of 'bias' which would disqualify a judge, else it would be the rare case in which a quorum of a court could be mustered for decision.

"[The] true distinction is between the concept of attitude or outlook, which is not disqualifying, and the concept of 'favoritism,' which is disqualifying. Favoritism to me means a tendency or inclination to treat a particular litigant more or less generously than a different litigant raising the identical legal issue.

" * * * It is apparently thought by some that if a judge has spoken publicly on an issue which later comes before him as a judge, he ought to disqualify himself from sitting in the case. * * * If what is sought to be avoided is any publicly expressed notion of how the judge might vote on a particular issue, the best evidence of his propensities would presumably be previous opinions on the same question or a related question which he has either authored or concurred in as a judge; and yet no one has ever advanced this as a ground for disqualification. Even if the concept be limited to statements made prior to assuming the bench, enforcement of such a rule would scarcely guarantee that the judge's mind would be a *tabula rasa*, even if such were thought desirable; it would merely separate those who might have advanced

---

8.   For criticism of the ABA's decision to elevate "appearance of impropriety" to a standard of discipline, see, e.g., Ronald D. Rotunda, Judicial Ethics, the Appearance of Impropriety, and the Proposed New ABA Judicial Code, 34 Hofstra L. Rev. 1337 (2006). The ABA Commission that drafted the 2007 Model Code of Judicial Conduct was concerned that "a duty to avoid the appearance of impropriety was too vague to be independently enforceable," but lobbying "from legal organizations and the judiciary led the Commission to accept an amendment, during debate in the House of Delegates, that reinstated the obligation of a judge to avoid impropriety and the appearance of impropriety as black letter Rule 1.2." 2007 Model Code, Reporter's Explanations of Changes, at 8.

professional opinions publicly from those who advanced them privately.
* * *

"Even more far afield from any established norm of judicial disqualification is the notion that a sitting judge may not properly engage in private conversations at a social event about matters of general interest, even those with legal overtones, without fear of some sort of professional damnation or the prospect of having to disqualify himself if a case involving some aspect of this general issue should ever come before him. I was sitting with a group of people whom I didn't know very well at a dinner party in Washington this summer, during the time the Watergate hearings were being televised daily. Not long after we sat down, the subject turned, as it doubtless did at most other dinner parties in Washington that evening, to the subject of Watergate and what the various diners thought of the various witnesses. In the midst of the discussion, one of the speakers turned to me and said: 'Wait a minute. We probably shouldn't be talking about this in front of you, because it will probably come to the Supreme Court eventually.'

"I thanked him for his consideration, but added that if listening to this conversation were to render me damaged goods for the purpose of adjudication, it was at most harmless error in view of the damage I had already sustained by being exposed to the daily newspapers and television news programs.

"[Some people] treat judicial disqualification for interest or bias as a matter of personal honor, such that the more ready a judge is to disqualify himself, the higher shall be his standing on the list compiled by that descendant of Abou Ben Adhem who specializes in judges. Once we depart from the area of corruption, or reasonable grounds to suspect corruption, * * * the decision as to disqualification in a particular instance ought, like so many other questions, to be decided by weighing the relevant factors on the appropriate legal scale. The factors favoring disqualification are familiar to us all; the factors which weigh against disqualification are less well advertised.

"Judicial disqualification at the trial court level, and often at the appellate court level where the appellate court does not sit *en banc* can result in docketing and scheduling problems which, while no one would say they outweigh a moral imperative on the other side, ought not to be lightly disregarded. Judicial disqualification at the appellate level has the added disadvantage of causing the decision of the case to be made by less than a full complement of the court charged with responsibility for the decision. [The] standards, both of the statute and of the Canons, pertaining to disqualification for interest and for bias are themselves based on the desire to avoid the appearance of impropriety on the part of a judge, there is no need to throw into the scales, as an additional standard over and above those addressed to disqualification, a desire to 'avoid the appearance of impropriety.'

"During my sixteen years of the private practice of law, the judge who was the most 'sensitive' to the 'appearance of impropriety' of any

I knew sat in a court of general jurisdiction in the state where I practiced. He was so 'sensitive' to the appearance of impropriety that if he had so much as shaken hands at a large political gathering with one of the litigants who appeared before him, he would summarily disqualify himself. The principal result of this 'sensitivity' on his part, so far as I could see, was that at least one working day a week he was able to reach the first tee of the golf course before eleven o'clock in the morning, or else get home and do some of those odd jobs which escape the attention of all of us on the weekends. * * * ''[9]

b. Do you agree with Chief Justice Rehnquist's approach to policy bias? Will his attempt to distinguish "bias" from "favoritism" help Judge Baxter know what he should do? Is any thoughtful person old enough to become a judge likely to have well-formed views on many questions of public policy?

2. Should it be harder to disqualify a judge for a bias based on policy preferences than for bias based on financial or other personal grounds?

a. Sometimes the line between financial grounds for disqualification and the judge's policy preferences grounds is less clear than one might expect.

In Aetna Life Insurance Co. v. Lavoie, 475 U.S. 813 (1986), appellees had submitted a health insurance claim to Aetna, which had paid about half of the amount requested. It had failed to pay the rest, about $1,375, on the ground that the length of the hospitalization was unnecessary. Appellant sought punitive damages for the alleged bad faith refusal to pay the claim and the jury awarded $3.5 million in punitive damages. The Alabama Supreme Court affirmed (5 to 4) in an opinion written by Justice Embry. While the case was pending before the Alabama Supreme Court, Justice Embry had himself filed two actions against other insurance companies making similar allegations and seeking punitive damages. The U.S. Supreme Court held that "only in the most extreme of cases would disqualification [for bias or prejudice] be constitutionally required, and appellant's arguments [based on the judge's general hostility toward insurance companies] here fall well below that level." However, the Court held, much more than Justice Embry's general hostility was at stake. This was the first case in which the Alabama Supreme Court clearly established the right of action upon which Justice Embry was seeking to rely in his own simultaneous litigation. The Supreme Court held that a decision rendered under these circumstances violated due process. "Justice Embry's opinion for the Alabama Supreme Court had the clear and immediate effect of enhancing both the legal status and the settlement value of his own case," it said. "We hold simply that when Justice Embry made that judgment, he acted as 'a judge in his own case.'" 475 U.S. at 824. Three justices concurred but made the point that they would have found Justice Embry's participation improper

---

9. William H. Rehnquist, Sense and Nonsense About Judicial Ethics, 28 Record of Assoc. of the Bar of the City of New York 694, 708–13 (1973).

even if his had not been the deciding vote in the case and even if he had not written the majority opinion.

b. Interests the judge may have forgotten may still constitute an impermissible "bias" in a judge.

In Liljeberg v. Health Services Acquisition Corp., 486 U.S. 847 (1988), after a bench trial about who owned a hospital corporation, the loser learned that the trial judge was a trustee of Loyola University. During the time the case was pending, the ultimate winner, Liljeberg, was negotiating with Loyola to buy some land for a hospital and prevailing in the litigation was central to Liljeberg's ability to buy Loyola's land. The judge had ruled for Liljeberg, which thereby benefitted Loyola. Health Services thus moved to vacate the judgment, alleging that the trial judge should have disqualified himself under § 455(a). At a hearing to determine what the trial judge knew, he testified that he knew about the land dealings before the case was filed, but that he had forgotten all about them during the pendency of the matter. He learned again of Loyola's interest after his decision, but before the expiration of the ten days in which the loser could move for a new trial. Even then, the judge did not recuse himself or tell the parties what he knew.

The Court of Appeals reversed the judgment in favor of Liljeberg in the underlying case and the Supreme Court affirmed by a 5 to 4 vote. The Court held that "[s]cienter is not an element of a violation of § 455(a)." While the trial judge could not have disqualified himself over something about which he was unaware, he was "called upon to rectify an oversight and to take the steps necessary to maintain public confidence in the impartiality of the judiciary." Moreover, while § 455 does not, on its own, authorize the reopening of closed litigation, "Congress has wisely delegated to the judiciary the task of fashioning the remedies that will best serve the purpose of the litigation." The Court recognized that while harmless error could justify failing to reverse a judgment in some cases, in this instance the appearance of impropriety required reversal of the judgment because there was "ample basis in the record for concluding that an objective observer would have questioned" the trial judge's impartiality. Moreover, the trial judge's failure to stay informed of his fiduciary interest in Loyola University "may well constitute a separate violation of § 455. See § 455(c)." Chief Justice Rehnquist, joined by Justices White and Scalia, dissented, saying that § 455(a) required an "actual knowledge" standard. Justice O'Connor agreed and would have remanded as well to determine whether "extraordinary circumstances" justified a reversal of the underlying case. With which of these opinions do you agree?

c. Might a judge's religious beliefs constitute "bias" under Rule 2.11(A)(1) or 28 U.S.C. § 455? Look at the definitions of "impartiality" and "independence" in the Terminology section of the 2007 Model Code.

Idaho v. Freeman, 507 F.Supp. 706 (D.Idaho 1981), involved a judge hearing a case concerning the constitutionality of Congress' extension of the deadline for ratification of the equal rights amendment (ERA). The principal leaders of the Church of Jesus Christ of Latter-day Saints (popularly called the "Mormons") had publicly opposed both the ERA and extension of the deadline. The judge was a Mormon; indeed he was a lay regional representative of that church. However, the church was not a party to the case, the judge was neither required nor requested to promote the church's position as a judge, and his duties as a church officer did not relate to the ERA. The judge concluded that his religious affiliation did not require him to disqualify himself. Do you agree with the judge's conclusion? Does the "appearance of bias" standard have to be subject to reasonable limits? Would a conclusion that religious beliefs did constitute impermissible bias lead to consequences worse than having the judge hear the case? For example, if recusal were required in this case, could a judge who believed in God hear a case brought by an atheist objecting to a city display of a Christmas tree? If the judge who believed in God were disqualified, would an atheist be similarly disqualified? The general rule is, then, that religious beliefs (or lack of them) do not mandate disqualification.

3. Should it matter whether the judge formed her views based on information learned in the courtroom rather than information learned in other settings?

a. The "extrajudicial source doctrine," that views formed in the course of trying a case should not normally be disqualifying, is usually traced to United States v. Grinnell Corp., 384 U.S. 563 (1966): "The alleged bias and prejudice to be disqualifying must stem from an extrajudicial source." The challenge for later courts has been defining when that doctrine should apply and when it should not.

b. In Liteky v. United States, 510 U.S. 540 (1994), for example, the government charged three defendants with spilling human blood on walls and objects at Fort Benning, GA. The judge assigned to preside at their trial had tried and convicted one of the defendants, Father Bourgeois, for similar conduct eight years earlier. During that first trial, the judge had repeatedly admonished the defense to limit its evidence and argument to the issues in the case, not the motivations for the protest. On the basis of those admonitions, defendants alleged that the judge's "impartiality might reasonably be questioned" and that 28 U.S.C.A. § 455(a) required his recusal. The judge refused to recuse himself, and the defendants were convicted.

Justice Scalia, writing for the Court, observed that a "judge who presides at a trial may, upon completion of the evidence, be exceedingly ill disposed towards the defendant, who has been shown to be a thoroughly reprehensible person. But the judge is not thereby recusable for bias or prejudice, since his knowledge and the opinion it produced were properly and necessarily acquired in the course of the proceedings, and are indeed sometimes (as in a bench trial) necessary to completion of the judge's task." 510 U.S. at 550–51.

However, extrajudicial sources are "not the *exclusive* reason a predisposition can be wrongful or inappropriate." A point of view can also constitute "bias or prejudice" even if it comes from a judicial source, if "it is so extreme as to display clear inability to render fair judgment." 510 U.S.

at 550–51 The Court concluded that judicial rulings alone almost never constitute valid basis for a disqualification motion; "they are proper grounds for appeal, not recusal." And, "opinions formed by the judge on the basis of facts introduced or events occurring in the course of the current proceedings, or of prior proceedings, do not constitute a basis for a bias or partiality motion unless they display a deep–seated favoritism or antagonism that would make a fair judgment impossible." Clearly, "expressions of impatience, dissatisfaction, annoyance, and even anger" such as shown by this judge at the first trial, do not constitute bias. 510 U.S. at 555–56.

Justice Kennedy, concurring in the judgment joined by Justices Blackmun, Stevens and Souter, found the Court's "impossibility of fair judgment" standard objectively different from the "impartiality might reasonably be questioned" standard of 28 U.S.C. § 455(a). These justices believed that the first test may be a fair reading of § 455(b)(1), but that Congress intended § 455(a) to reach any case where "an objective observer [would] conclude that a fair and impartial hearing is unlikely." In this case, however, they concluded that the judge's prior conduct did not require recusal under either standard. 510 U.S. at 564.

c. Just two years before *Liteky*, Haines v. Liggett Group, 975 F.2d 81 (3d Cir.1992), ordered a change in trial judges. Judge Lee Sarokin had conducted the trial of, and was assigned to retry, the nation's major cigarette companies who stood accused of producing a product that caused cancer. In a ruling applying the crime-fraud exception to allegedly privileged documents, he said: "Who are these persons who knowingly and secretly decide to put the buying public at risk solely for the purpose of making profits and who believe that illness and death of consumers is an appropriate cost of their own prosperity! * * * [T]he tobacco industry may be the king of concealment and disinformation." 975 F.2d at 97. The Court of Appeals acknowledged that they believed Judge Sarokin could try the case "free from bias or prejudice," but "that is not the test." Instead, the "polestar is 'impartiality and the appearance of impartiality.' " 975 F.2d at 98. The court ordered a change of judge.

Should a court reach the same result on these facts after *Liteky*? Was this factual scenario what Justice Scalia had in mind in leaving open the possibility that some statements made in the course of judicial proceedings would show that a judge's "fair judgment [is] impossible"?[10]

d. Los Angeles County Bar Association, Professional Responsibility and Ethics Committee Formal Opinion No. 514 (Aug. 19, 2005) advised judges of the risks when they participate in listservs that might include communications about issues that could come before them. "[M]embers of

10. Compare United States v. Microsoft Corporation, 253 F.3d 34, 116 (D.C.Cir.2001) (district judge disqualified as to future proceedings in the case). See also, In re International Business Machines Corp., 45 F.3d 641 (2d Cir.1995) (mandamus issued to recuse judge who was critical of government decision to dismiss case); United States v. Microsoft Corp., 56 F.3d 1448 (D.C.Cir.1995) (new judge required to hear remand of case in which judge had set aside consent decree agreed to by the Antitrust Division); Hathcock v. Navistar International, 53 F.3d 36 (4th Cir.1995) (judge showed bias against tort defendants in speech before Trial Lawyers' Association).

the bench do not foreswear participating in society when they become judges," the opinion observes. But judges should not participate in a "litigation advocacy" listserv, for example, if the people and subjects discussed on it might be at issue in cases before the judge's court.

e.   If you were Judge Baxter, would these authorities tell you whether you should sit when issues concerning real estate assessments were before the court? Would you be more confused than ever? What would you do?

D.   WAIVING JUDICIAL DISQUALIFICATION

1.   Are all circumstances requiring a judge's disqualification subject to waiver by the parties? How about all of the issues raised by this problem?

a.   May the parties waive the conflict created by Martha Anderson's loan to Judge Baxter? Look at Model Code of Judicial Conduct, Rule 2.11(C). Compare 28 U.S.C. § 455(e). Why does the federal statute allow the parties to waive fewer conflicts than the Judicial Code does?

b.   Would conflicts created by financial interests of the judge's relatives be subject to waiver by the parties? Is there any justification for treating state and federal judges differently as to this issue?

c.   If Judge Baxter's possible bias against current assessment practices is deemed disqualifying, is it subject to waiver? Would his views constitute "personal bias or prejudice concerning a party"? If so, would his recusal be subject to waiver in either the state or federal system?

2.   How should the judge secure a valid waiver?

a.   Compare Model Code of Judicial Conduct, Rule 2.11(C), with 28 U.S.C. § 455(e). What must the judge "disclose" about the grounds for required recusal? Must consent to waive a judge's recusal be as "informed" as consent to waive a lawyer's conflict of interest? See Model Rule of Professional Conduct 1.0(e).

b.   May counsel make the waiver orally on the record in the manner defense counsel did in this problem? Look at Rule 2.11(C). Is there any comparable requirement in § 455(e)? Should lawyers be permitted to waive a disqualifying circumstance on behalf of their clients?

c.   Are you satisfied that the procedure specified in the Code of Judicial Conduct will guarantee anonymity to an objector? Is this anonymity important in a setting where the parties and their counsel may have to appear again before the judge in the future?

———

PROBLEM 39

THE JUDGE AS A POLITICAL CANDIDATE AND PUBLIC FIGURE

Many states choose their judges by popular election. Judges who run for office have to raise campaign funds, engage in political speeches and participate in other forms of political campaigns, and the rules relating to political activity have been among the most controversial aspects of judicial ethics. Some people think that it is unseemly for judges to campaign for office; others support election of judges but believe that ethical rules should limit what a judge can say or do in a political campaign. Further, if judges are limited in what they can say about themselves, then arguably others should also be limited in what they may say about judges. This problem first looks at what judges may say and do in a political campaign. Next, it examines how a judge may raise the funds necessary to participate in electoral politics. Third, it asks what limits lawyers face in making critical comments about a judge. Fourth, it considers what limits are imposed on what a judge may say about others.

FACTS

J.R. Kraft, a local lawyer, was a declared candidate for a vacancy on the trial court at a recent election. Shortly before the primary, the following advertisement appeared in the newspaper in his judicial district:

J. R. KRAFT

(A Working Man's Son)

— The Next Best Thing to Being a Judge Yourself —

I, J. R. Kraft, am a local boy. My Dad died when I was eight, and I worked in a foundry for ten years to earn enough money to go to law school. I have never lost a jury trial in all my time in practice and I have never been a member of a political party. If elected, I will do my best to stop inflation, give the benefit of the doubt to any working man who comes before me, and throw the book at every weirdo and pervert I can find.

Permissiveness is the issue in this campaign. My opponent stupidly gave bail to a 45-year-old low-life who everybody knew had raped a 12-year-old child, but then he slapped a $500 fine on a working man who had been laid off. You can count on me never to do those things!

VOTE FOR J. R. KRAFT

[C2592]

To most people's surprise, Kraft won the primary. To everyone's surprise, the "nonpolitician" became a party stalwart. He made the rounds of political meetings and gave a five-minute speech at each about how good it was for a working man's son to be on the ticket with the likes of Governor Ford, Senator Barker, and Mayor Black. He called upon "all working people" to support the entire ticket "from the top down to little me at the bottom."

At several meetings, listeners called him aside and pressed $1, $5, $10, or even $20 into his hand to help him meet his campaign expenses. He turned most of the money over to his campaign committee, but he used $389.95 of it to buy a second suit.

Kraft's style appealed to the voters. He won the general election as well and became a judge. He still had some campaign expenses left unpaid, so two weeks after the election he asked his campaign committee to solicit members of the bar to make up the deficit.

After Kraft was on the bench for less than a year, he presided over a major murder trial, which the defense won after Kraft approved unusual jury instructions. Ellen Embers, the state's attorney, was quite upset. She had no right of appeal, of course, so she called a press conference and said: "Judge Kraft is the most biased, incompetent judge that I have ever seen. He ruled against the people throughout the recent murder trial, and he alone is responsible for letting a maniacal killer out to prey on the citizens of this county."

Two weeks later, state's attorney Embers issued a statement from her office. "The rumors around the court house have been intense the past several weeks that Judge Kraft tilts his decisions toward Anthony Roberts, the city's leading slum landlord and a regular litigant before Judge Kraft, because Roberts was a major contributor to Kraft's election campaign. I have filed a grievance with the Judicial Inquiry Board to have Judge Kraft investigated and, if the rumors are true, to have him removed from the bench."

In the meantime, one of Kraft's close friends, who was also a major contributor to Kraft's campaign, is now on trial for perjury and bribery in connection with allegedly corrupt labor practices. His defense is that he engaged in an innocent, if careless, oversight. He has asked Judge Kraft to be a character witness. Kraft, who would disqualify himself anyway if the case came before him, said: "Of course, but it would be better if you would subpoena me."

QUESTIONS

A.   THE CONTENT OF JUDICIAL CAMPAIGN SPEECH AND ACTIVITIES

1. What does the Model Code of Judicial Conduct say about Kraft's advertisement in his campaign to become a state judge?

a.   Should it matter that Kraft was not yet a judge at the time the advertisement was run? Look at ABA Model Rules of Professional Conduct, Rule 8.2(b). Is such a rule required to assure that no candidate can impair the dignity of a judicial campaign? Does it necessarily favor incumbent judges by making it harder for newcomers to unseat them?

b.   Under the 2007 ABA Model Code of Judicial Conduct, does the content of Kraft's advertisement subject him to discipline? Look at Rule 4.1(A)(13) and Rule 4.1, Comments 11–15. Consider also Rule 4.2(A)(1). If Kraft's advertisement had extolled his credentials for sheriff, would it violate ethical standards for him to make these charges and promises? Why is the standard different when a lawyer is running for judge? See Rule 4.1, Comment 11.

c.   In re Judicial Campaign Complaint Against Burick, 705 N.E.2d 422 (Ohio Commission of Judges 1999), found that a judicial candidate had: (1) said that "political bosses" had appointed the incumbent judge the previous year, (2) said that she (the candidate) "supports the death penalty and isn't afraid to use it," and (3) accused the incumbent judge of giving a lenient sentence to a convicted rapist when in fact the judge gave the defendant the maximum sentence for a lesser offense to which the defendant had pled guilty. The special commission appointed to hear the case held that a judicial candidate could only say things about the appointment process that would "further, not obscure, the public's understanding of the law and legal system." It then found that the governor, not political bosses, had appointed the incumbent judge. Further, while a nonjudicial candidate could express views about the death penalty, a judicial candidate must refrain from making statements "that adversely reflect on their impartiality." It concluded that the comment about the alleged rape sentence was improper because the case was still pending on appeal. Then, it publicly reprimanded the candidate, fined her $7,500, and ordered her to pay the complainant $5,000 for attorneys' fees and expenses. Do you agree that the candidate's statements justified this result?

2.   Is J. R. Kraft's campaign speech constitutionally protected even if it violated the Model Code of Judicial Conduct?

a.   Courts are looking more carefully at restrictions imposed on judicial campaign speech. In Republican Party of Minnesota v. White, 536 U.S. 765 (2002), the U.S. Supreme Court held that state ethics rules that unduly restrict political campaign speech of judicial candidates violate the First Amendment. The parties did not challenge the Minnesota rule that prohibits a judicial candidate or judge from making "pledges or promises" as to how he or she will rule in a particular case. However, the Court declared unconstitutional the rule prohibiting a candidate for judicial office from "announcing" a view on a "disputed legal or political" issue, even as interpreted to apply only to matters likely to come before the candidate's court.

Speaking through Justice Scalia, the five-person majority said that the announce clause must not "unnecessarily circumscrib[e] protected expression," and the Minnesota rule failed this test. One common view of "impartiality" is an absence of bias toward any party to the proceeding, the Court said, but the announce clause is not tailored to serve that interest because "it does not restrict speech for or against particular parties, but rather speech for or against particular issues." A lack of preconception for or against a particular legal view is not a compelling state interest,"since it is virtually impossible, and hardly desirable, to find a judge who does not have preconceptions about the law."[1] 536 U.S. at 777.

Nor does the prohibition promote impartiality in the sense of "open-mindedness" because the announce clause is "woefully underinclusive." For example, a judge may confront a legal issue on which he has expressed an opinion, whether on or off the bench. "Judges often state their views on disputed legal issues outside the context of adjudication, in classes that they conduct, and in books and speeches." 536 U.S. at 779. The Minnesota rule allows a judicial candidate to say, "I think it is constitutional for the legislature to prohibit same-sex marriage" up until "the very day before he declares himself a candidate, and [he] may say it repeatedly (until litigation is pending) after he is elected. As a means of pursuing the objective of open-mindedness that respondents now articulate, the announce clause is so woefully underinclusive as to render belief in that purpose a challenge to the credulous." 536 U.S. at 780.[2]

Justice Kennedy, concurring, added: "Minnesota may not * * * censor what the people hear as they undertake to decide for themselves which candidate is most likely to be an exemplary judicial officer. Deciding the relevance of candidate speech is the right of the voters, not the State." 536 U.S. at 784.

Justices Stevens and Ginsburg filed dissenting opinions joined by Justices Souter and Breyer. They argued that the office of judge is significantly different from a legislative or executive office. Judges, they argued, should be elected because they have integrity, not because their views are popular. Thus, they argued, the government can restrict the speech of judges, and those seeking to be judges, in ways it cannot regulate the speech of others.

With which of these positions do you agree? Given the logic of these cases, do you believe that other provisions of Rule 4.1 and Rule 4.2 of the ABA Model Code of Judicial Conduct are likely to be similarly at risk of being successfully challenged?

b. In response to Republican Party of Minnesota v. White, there is pressure to ban judges from answering questions that political interest

---

1. The Court acknowledged the views of then-Justice Rehnquist described in Problem 38, supra. See Ronald D. Rotunda, Judicial Campaigns in the Shadow of Republican Party v. White, 14 The Professional Lawyer 2 (2002); Ronald D. Rotunda, A Preliminary Empirical Inquiry into the Connection between Judicial Decision Making and Campaign Contributions to Judicial Candidates, 14 The Professional Lawyer 16 (2003).

2. Compare 2007 Model Code, Rule 2.2, Comment 1. The Reporters' Explanation of Changes to the 2007 Model Rules says: "This new Comment defines impartiality with reference to the two definitions of impartiality accepted by the Supreme Court in Republican Party of Minnesota v. White, lack of bias toward a participant in the judicial process, and open-mindedness."

groups (e.g., organizations that favor or oppose abortion rules) may pose to them. Does the Code of Judicial Conduct prohibit judges from responding to such questionnaires? Look at Rule 4.1, Comment 15. Should it do so? Would it be constitutional, in light of *White*, for state judicial authorities to forbid judges from answering?

3. How misleading or inaccurate should judicial advertising have to be before it subjects the judge to discipline? Should the judge be subject to discipline because he makes a statement that his opponents think is incomplete? Should we leave it to the judge's opponents to point that out in the campaign?

a. In an Illinois judicial election, the Chicago Council of Lawyers—a group representing an important segment of the bar—wrote:

"Judge Elward * * * is *a person of substantial intellectual ability who works hard,* but reports from many lawyers also indicate clearly that he has a terrible judicial temperament characterized by extreme rigidity, unreasonable demands and positions, and closed-mindedness. His efforts *to achieve worthy objectives—such as avoiding delays in the court process* attributable to dilatory lawyers—have in several cases been vitiated by the rigidity and excessive zeal with which he has attempted to pursue them. Because of his clear lack of judicial temperament, the Council concludes that he should not be retained as a judge." (emphasis added).

With the judge's approval, a "citizens committee" published an advertisement before the election in certain suburban newspapers and the *Chicago Sun Times*. The advertisements quoted from an editorial that had appeared in the *Chicago Tribune*, a statement by a former president of the Chicago Bar Association, and continued:

" * * * a person of substantial intellectual ability who works hard * * * to achieve worthy objectives—such as avoiding delays in the court process. Chicago Council of Lawyers."

Judge Elward was retained in office and he then faced a complaint for publishing an advertisement that was "materially misleading." The Courts Commission, a panel of judges established to consider judicial discipline, disagreed:

"We find analogous the test which has been applied in determining whether in the light of the circumstances under which they were made, omissions to state a material fact in a registration statement, filed with the Securities and Exchange Commission, were misleading. The rule applied is that 'the adequacy of disclosure of material information must be evaluated by a consideration of the "total mix" of all information conveyed or available to the investors [voters].' "

The Commission found that several unrelated news stories and editorials had appeared that were critical of Judge Elward and that several had accurately reported the Chicago Council of Lawyers evaluation. The Commission concluded:

"Measured against this 'total mix,' we conclude that the respondent, in the use of excerpts from the Council's statements, did not create the false impression that the Council had recommended him for retention or that he had significant Bar Association support.

" * * * The Complaint is, accordingly, dismissed."

In re Circuit Judge Paul F. Elward, Case No. 77, Illinois Courts Commission 1 (1977).

b. Do you agree with this result? Is the right issue whether Judge Elward's advertisement was misleading? Whether or not it was misleading, did its use show Judge Elward to be dishonest or otherwise unfit?

c. Is the SEC analogy apt? Would a person charged with misstatements in a registration statement be heard to defend that the investor could have put together the true picture from stories in the *Wall Street Journal*?[3]

d. Look at Rule 4.1, Comment 7. Does it obligate the judge to refrain from omitting facts "necessary to make the communication considered as a whole not materially misleading"? Assume that a trial judge, running against another trial judge for an appellate position says, "My opponent gave the minimum sentence to four convicted rapists, and that was wrong." Is that judge subject to discipline if that statement is correct, but the judge did not disclose that the prosecutor agreed with the sentencing judge in two of those cases? Or all four? Or in one?

4. What other limits are there on other political activities in which a judge may engage?

a. May he or she make speeches on behalf of candidates for nonjudicial public office? Look at 2007 ABA Model Code of Judicial Conduct, Rule 4.1(A)(2) & (3) & Comment 4. How about contributing money to a political party or to other candidates? Compare Rules 4.1(A)(4) & (5), with Rule 4.2(B)(4) & (6).

b. May a judicial candidate run as part of a party team? See Rule 4.2(B)(5) & (6), Rule 4.2(C) & Rule 4.2, Comment 7. In Republican Party of Minnesota v. White, 416 F.3d 738 (8th Cir.2005) (en banc), cert. denied sub. nom. Dimick v. Republican Party of Minnesota, 546 U.S. 1157 (2006), the court examined the constitutionality of restrictions on partisan activities in light of the Supreme Court's decision discussed above. The state defended the restrictions by saying that identification with a party label is "nothing more than shorthand for the views a judicial candidate holds." 416 F.3d at 754. In light of the Supreme Court's analysis of the "announce" clause, however, the court said that requiring judges to conceal

---

3. Compare Rubin G. Cohn, Judicial Discipline in Illinois—a Commentary on the Judge Elward Decision, 59 Chi. Bar Rec. 200 (1978), with Donald H. Reuben and Leonard M. Ring, Judges Have Rights Too, 59 Chi. Bar Rec. 220 (1978).

their party affiliation during the course of a judicial campaign "can hardly be expected to open the mind of a candidate who has engaged in years of prior political activity." 416 F.3d at 758. The court held the restrictions unconstitutionally violated judges' rights of free association.

c. Siefert v. Alexander, 608 F.3d 974 (7th Cir. 2010), challenged the Wisconsin Code of Judicial Conduct rules prohibiting judges and judicial candidates from asserting their membership in a political party, endorsing partisan candidates for office, and personally soliciting campaign contributions. The plaintiff had been an active Democrat before becoming a judge; he wanted to again join the party and be able to endorse President Obama. The district court declared the rules prohibiting such conduct unconstitutional. The Seventh Circuit agreed that the ban on joining a political party was unconstitutional, citing *Republican Party v. White*. The policy behind such a ban was to avoid indicating the judge's possible views on policy issues, but "that is the purported compelling state interest that *White* squarely rejected." If party membership were somehow relevant to issues in a particular case, the court believed, recusal could solve the problem.

The court held that endorsement of political candidates, on the other hand, was subject to a balancing analysis, not strict scrutiny. Persons the judge has endorsed might appear in the judge's court, and a judge might trade his or her endorsement of political figures for reciprocal support by the officials. Further, because the prohibition against endorsements does not "inform the electorate of [the judge's] qualifications and beliefs," the public interest in allowing judges unregulated speech is less.

d. May the law regulate how a political party selects its judicial candidates? In New York State Board of Elections v. Lopez Torres, 552 U.S. 196 (2008), candidates for judge of the New York Supreme Court (the state's principal trial court) challenged a state law requiring that judges for that court seeking to be nominated by a political party, be nominated by a convention, not a primary election. The lower courts had held that the system preserved "one-party rule" and thus unconstitutionally denied plaintiffs the right to run for judge. The Supreme Court disagreed. Judicial candidates could get on the ballot by petition, the Court said, and one-party rule may simply reflect voter approval of that party's nominees. In any event, federal courts have no authority to open up the process. In a concurring opinion, Justice Stevens quoted Justice Marshall as often remarking: "The Constitution does not prohibit legislatures from enacting stupid laws."

e. If Judge Kraft entered a race for Congress, would he be required to resign from the bench? Look at Rule 4.5(A). If a state senator ran for Congress, would he or she similarly be required to resign the old office before running for the new one? Why do we treat judges differently? See Rule 4.5, Comment 1 and Rule 4.1, Comment 11.

f. Should the rules be different if the judicial candidate is campaigning in a nonpartisan election? The 1990 Judicial Code did not distinguish between these different types of elections, and allowed judicial candidates to solicit endorsements—"publicly stated support"—through campaign committees. Rule 4.2(B)(5) of the 2007 Model Code, by contrast, permits candidates in a non-partisan election to solicit such support on their own from persons or organizations, but not from partisan political organizations. Are the rules wise to make such a distinction?

B. JUDGES SOLICITING AND RECEIVING CAMPAIGN CONTRIBUTIONS

1. Are you troubled by the fact that judges receive endorsements and campaign contributions from the lawyers who appear before them?

a. Think back to Problem 38 and the cases condemning lawyers' payments to judges. Why should campaign contributions be distinguished from any other gifts made to a judge?

b. The multibillion dollar Pennzoil v. Texaco litigation was conducted primarily in the Texas state courts. The trial judge received a $10,000 campaign contribution from Pennzoil's chief trial lawyer "[w]ithin days of being assigned the Pennzoil case," a sum the trial judge described as "princely." Wall Street J., Nov. 4, 1987, at 1, 20, col. 2. In the three-and-one-half years prior to their decision in *Pennzoil*, all nine members of the Texas Supreme Court, consistent with Texas law, "openly accepted campaign contributions from lawyers with cases pending before them." Forbes, Sept. 7, 1987, at 8.

c. If lawyers may make contributions to judges deciding their clients' cases, do the lawyers have any choice but to make those contributions? Do you think that large campaign contributions from a litigant or lawyer could be a basis for questioning the judge's impartiality? See Rule 4.4 & Comment 3.

2. In this problem, J.R. Kraft accepted campaign contributions pressed into his hand. Was it proper for him to do so?

a. Look at Rule 4.1(A)(8). Is there any doubt that J.R. Kraft has violated the 2007 ABA Model Code of Judicial Conduct?

b. The 2007 Model Code prescribes the proper method of handling campaign contributions in Rules 4.2(B) and 4.4. Do you think establishment of a campaign committee will prevent the judge from learning which lawyers support his or her candidacy and the generosity of that support? Are there other reasons to require creating such a committee?

c. Does the requirement of a campaign committee impair free speech? Weaver v. Bonner, 309 F.3d 1312 (11th Cir.2002), held Georgia's version of it unconstitutional, saying:

"[E]ven if there is a risk that judges will be tempted to rule a particular way because of contributions or endorsements, this risk is not significantly reduced by allowing the candidate's agent to seek these contributions and endorsements on the candidate's behalf rather than the candidate seeking them himself. Successful candidates will feel beholden to the people who helped them get elected regardless of who did the soliciting of support. Canon [5C(2); Rule 4.1(A)(8) &

Terminology 21] thus fails strict scrutiny because it completely chills a candidate's speech on these topics while hardly advancing the state's interest in judicial impartiality at all." 309 F.3d at 1322–23.

Do you agree with the court's analysis? Whose free speech is limited by requiring that an intermediary be placed between the judge and those who want to give the judge money?[4]

3. May a judge's campaign committee solicit funds from lawyers *after* the election when the winner is known?

a. Look at Rule 4.4(B)(2). Do you agree that a judicial campaign committee should be permitted to solicit campaign contributions until an "[insert number]" of days after the election?

b. What arguments support this position? Do we want to avoid having judges start out a new term of judicial service in substantial debt because of the campaign? Might that put them under financial pressures that others could later exploit?

c. Commentary 2 following Canon 5C(2) of the 1990 Model Code advised that campaign committees "should manage campaign finances responsibly avoiding deficits that might necessitate post-election fund-raising, to the extent possible." That provision was not included in the 2007 Model Code of Judicial Conduct. Did the provision have any teeth? Was its suggestion of good budgeting and self-restraint just a way to assuage our collective embarrassment at permitting the practice of post-election fund raising?

4. Should we be concerned when a third party expends funds to praise the judge publicly or to criticize the judge's opponent?

a. In Caperton v. A.T. Massey Coal Co., 556 U.S. ___, 129 S.Ct. 2252, 173 L.Ed.2d 1208 (2009), a state jury found the Massey company liable for $50 million. The case was appealed to the West Virginia supreme court, and Don Blankenship, Massey's chairman and principal officer, supported candidate Brent Benjamin rather than the incumbent justice seeking reelection. Blankenship gave $1,000—the statutory maximum—to Benjamin's campaign committee. That contribution raised no issue of bias. Blankenship also donated $3 million of his own money, however, to an organization that made independent expenditures to oppose the incumbent judge against whom Benjamin was running. Benjamin won the election and when the *Massey* case came before the court, Benjamin refused to disqualify himself and cast the deciding vote to reverse the judgment against Massey. The U.S. Supreme Court held (5 to 4) that the due process clause required Justice Benjamin not to participate in the decision of a case after having

---

4. The Eighth Circuit joined the Eleventh Circuit in Republican Party of Minnesota v. White, 416 F.3d 738 (8th Cir.2005), in upholding the ban on personal solicitation of campaign funds as a way of limiting corruption, citing Buckley v. Valeo, 424 U.S. 1 (1976). "A direct solicitation closely links the quid—avoiding the judge's future disfavor—to the quo—the contribution." While the ban was not perfectly tailored—judges could serve on their own finance committees and know who had contributed, for example—it was sufficient to be constitutional.

received the benefit of such a large campaign expenditure by an individual interested in the result.

Do you think this case will be seen as unique or will it lead to routine motions seeking to disqualify judges because of what the Court called a "debt of gratitude" to their donors. In this case, Justice Benjamin did not know Blankenship and Blankenship owned less than 0.5% of Massey, the company that prevailed in the case. But the Court said that a party seeking recusal need not prove actual bias. Instead, the Court cited the need for an "objective standard," i.e., "whether, under a realistic appraisal of psychological tendencies and human weaknesses, the interest poses such a risk of actual bias or prejudgment that the practice must be forbidden if the guarantee of due process is to be adequately implemented." Do you think that is an objective standard? The dissents predicted that a "flood of recusal motions" would follow this decision. Chief Justice Roberts, for example, listed 40 open questions including how a court is to tell when a contributor's influence in putting the judge on the bench was "disproportionate."[5]

b.   The issues raised in *Caperton* are made even more interesting after the Court's decision in Citizens United v. Federal Election Commission, 558 U.S. ___, 130 S.Ct. 876, 175 L.Ed.2d 753 (2010). *Citizens United* held that entities such as corporations or unions have a constitutional right to make independent expenditures to favor or oppose candidates for elective office. Facing the requirement imposed by *Caperton*, must a judge recuse herself if one of the parties spent money to support the judge or her opponent without the judge's consent? How is the judge to know which parties made independent expenditures to support particular judicial candidates? May the judge leave the detective work to the parties? May the judge simply assume that if anyone thinks there may be a problem, they will call it to the judge's attention?

5.   Would a "merit system" of judicial selection—i.e., appointing judges as in the federal system—remove ethical issues from the selection process?

a.   If all judges were appointed, would "political activity" take other forms? Should it be proper for an attorney to work in a senator's election campaign, for example, in the hope of being rewarded with a federal judicial appointment? Look at Rule 4.3.

b.   Would it be proper for a governor's aide to question a prospective judge about his or her attitudes on bail for "low-lifes"? Look at Rule 4.3 & Comment 1.

---

5. See Ronald D. Rotunda, Judicial Disqualification in the Aftermath of Caperton v. A.T. Massey Coal Co., 60 Syracuse L. Rev. 247 (2009). The *Caperton* case was remanded to the West Virginia Supreme Court and a retired justice was appointed to join the court to hear the case in the absence of Justice Benjamin. The court reached the same result it had reached the first time. Caperton v. A.T. Massey Coal Co., 690 S.E.2d 322 (2009). See also, Ronald D. Rotunda, Codifying Caperton v. A.T. Massey Coal Co., 42 McGeorge L. Rev. 95 (2010).

C. LAWYER CRITICISM OF JUDGES

1. Should Ellen Embers, the state's attorney in this problem, be subject to discipline for making critical remarks about Judge Kraft at her press conference?

a. In Justices of Appellate Division v. Erdmann, 301 N.E.2d 426 (N.Y.1973) (per curiam), the Appellate Division had censured the lawyer for his criticism of judges, but the Court of Appeals, in a brief opinion reversed, imposed no discipline, and concluded:

> "Without more, isolated instances of disrespect for the law, Judges and courts expressed by vulgar and insulting words or other incivility, uttered, written, or committed outside the precincts of a court are not subject to professional discipline. * * * Perhaps persistent or general courses of conduct, even if parading as criticism, which are degrading to the law, the Bar, and the courts, and are irrelevant or grossly excessive, would present a different issue. No such issue is presented now."

The dissenting justices, in contrast, wanted to censure the lawyer. First, they had to explain the facts:

> "The charge was based on [Erdmann's] statements and language used in an article entitled 'I Have Nothing To Do With Justice', which appeared in the March 12, 1971 issue of Life magazine. Lawyer Erdmann said of and concerning the courts within the First Judicial Department: 'There are so few trial judges who just judge, who rule on questions of law, and leave guilt or innocence to the jury. And Appellate Division judges aren't any better. They're the whores who became madams. I would like to [be a judge] just to see if I could be the kind of judge I think a judge should be. But the only way you can get it is to be in politics or buy it—and I don't even know the going price.' * * * To play the game well, a lawyer must be ruthless. He is working within, but against a system that has been battered to its knees. He must not hesitate to kick it when it's down, and to take advantage of its weakness. * * * The exultation of winning dampens any moral feelings you have." 301 N.E.2d at 427 (dissenting opinion).

Judge Burke, dissenting from the failure to censure, argued:

> "The article, as well as the remarks, violate restrictions placed on attorneys which they impliedly assume when they accept admission to the Bar. * * * To require civility of a lawyer is not arbitrary or a violation of his constitutional rights. Children are repeatedly reprimanded for incivility. Does this amount to an abrogation of Federally protected rights?"

Judge Gabrielli, also dissenting, added:

> "[I]t matters not whether the instances of disrespect for the administration of justice by the use of vulgar and insulting words or other acts of incivility, are uttered or committed outside the

courtroom. The standard of conduct must remain unchanged even when the lawyer departs from the courtroom."

Would you have imposed discipline on lawyer Erdmann? Why or why not?

b.   In re Holtzman, 577 N.E.2d 30 (N.Y.1991) (per curiam), upheld a letter of reprimand that the Grievance Committee issued to a district attorney who had publicly released a letter charging a trial judge with misconduct. Someone erroneously told the district attorney that the judge in a sexual assault trial had made the complainant get down on the floor and in effect reenact the crime before the judge and counsel. The district attorney repeated these charges in her letter, which also said that the incident made the complainant feel degraded and humiliated. The district attorney made no effort to speak with court officers, the court reporter, defense counsel or any other person present during the alleged misconduct. A later investigation determined the charge was false.

New York Times v. Sullivan, 376 U.S. 254 (1964), held that a public official cannot recover damages for a defamatory falsehood relating to his official conduct unless he proves that the defendant made the statement with "actual malice," which the Court defined as *scienter*; that is, that the statement was made "with knowledge that it was false or with reckless disregard of whether it was false or not." The N.Y Court of Appeals, however, refused to apply the *Sullivan* standard to lawyer discipline cases. To do so, it said, "would immunize all accusations, however reckless or irresponsible, from censure as long as the attorney uttering them did not actually entertain serious doubts as to their truth. * * * It is the reasonableness of the belief, not the state of mind of the attorney, that is determinative" 577 N.E.2d at 31.

c.   Should a court applying Model Rule 8.2(a) reach the same result? United States District Court v. Sandlin, 12 F.3d 861 (9th Cir.1993), affirmed a lawyer's six-month suspension from practice before the district court for falsely charging that the district judge had ordered important passages deleted from the transcript of a recusal hearing. The lawyer made the statements in a hearing on the lawyer's charges and also in a statement to an assistant U.S. attorney. That, in turn, led to FBI scientific tests and a grand jury investigation that cleared the judge. The court agreed that Rule 8.2(a) does not prohibit all criticism of judges, but it refused to read an "actual malice" standard into the "reckless disregard as to its truth or falsity" language of the rule. The test should be "what the reasonable attorney, considered in light of all his professional functions, would do in the same or similar circumstances." 12 F.3d at 867.

Do you agree with this reading of Model Rule 8.2(a)? See Restatement Third, The Law Governing Lawyers § 114, Comment *b* (*New York Times* rule should apply to charges by lawyers about conduct of judges).

d.   Standing Committee on Discipline of the United States District Court v. Yagman, 55 F.3d 1430 (9th Cir.1995), provides an interesting contrast to the result in *Sandlin*. Yagman, the lawyer, had tried to disqualify Judge Real from hearing a case. Judge Keller heard and rejected the disqualification motion and also imposed sanctions. Then, Yagman went after Judge Keller as well. He told the *L.A. Daily Journal*, a legal newspaper, that Judge Keller was "anti-Semitic," has "a penchant for sanctioning Jewish lawyers," and was "drunk on the bench." The district court concluded, after hearing testimony, that Yagman told another lawyer that by conducting this campaign against Judge Keller, he hoped to be able to disqualify Judge Keller from hearing any future cases he filed.

Relying on *Sandlin*, the disciplinary committee suspended Yagman from practicing in the Central District of California for two years, but the Ninth Circuit reversed. The disciplinary standard—conduct that "impugns the integrity of the Court"—was overbroad. The lawyer's statements were mere opinion and "rhetorical hyperbole," the court said, and it placed the burden on the court to prove them false. "[R]espect for the judiciary [cannot] be won by shielding judges from published criticism." However, the court then went on to impose perhaps the ultimate sanction. It expressly said that Judge Keller was not required to recuse himself from hearing future cases in which Yagman appeared as counsel.[6]

e. But in Board of Professional Responsibility v. Davidson, 205 P.3d 1008 (Wyo. 2009), the lawyer failed to investigate an accusation against a judge before including it in a pleading. The lawyer's client in a domestic relations case directed her lawyer to "do what you have to do" to get the case assigned to someone other than Judge Arnold. The lawyer filed a motion accusing Judge Arnold of engaging in prohibited ex parte contact with opposing counsel and of being "rumored" to favor opposing counsel's firm. The lawyer had not investigated her charges and indeed they proved false. The court held that the Rule 8.2 standard requires more of lawyers than simply not violating the standard of *N.Y. Times v. Sullivan*, and it suspended lawyer Davidson for two months.

See also, In re Evergreen Security, Ltd., 570 F.3d 1257 (11th Cir. 2009) (upholds large sanction for filing recusal motion with no credible evidence supporting charges that judge had engaged in ex parte contact with other side); Fieger v. Michigan Supreme Court, 553 F.3d 955 (6th Cir. 2009) (Michigan requirements of lawyer civility upheld).

f. Should questions regarding criticism of judges be affected by whether or not judges are elected in your state? Consider Model Rule 8.2, Comment 1. Does the public have an interest in knowing about the characteristics of the judges who stand for election? Would it matter how long it was until these judges next had to face the voters? On the other hand, are elected judges particularly exposed to unjust vilification and unusually limited in the propriety of their responding to criticism? Should it be the judges with life tenure whom lawyers are most free to criticize?

2. If another judge believed that Embers' charges against Judge Kraft were true, would that judge have an obligation to report Judge Kraft?

---

6. See, e.g., Ronald D. Rotunda, Judicial Transparency, Judicial Ethics, and a Ju-dicial Solution: An Inspector General for the Courts, 41 Loyola U. Chicago L.J. 301 (2009).

a. Look at Model Code of Judicial Conduct, Rule 2.15(A). Does Rule 8.3(b) of the Model Rules of Professional Conduct also give state's attorney Embers an obligation to file a disciplinary complaint against Judge Kraft?

b. Should a lawyer be more limited in publicly announcing the filing of charges against a judge than if the charges had been filed against another public official? Is there a public interest in preserving confidence in the judiciary that may distinguish these from ordinary cases? Does the argument cut the other way, i.e., that public confidence in judges is instilled by making it known that the system aggressively roots out corruption?

c. If a judge were reckless in her comments accusing a fellow judge of misconduct, could the judge be civilly liable for making the comments? The 1990 Model Code of Judicial Conduct, Canon 3D(3), said that a judge is "absolutely privileged" for filing a disciplinary charge against another judge or lawyer, "and no civil action predicated thereon may be instituted against the judge." The 2007 Model Code deleted this provision. The Reporters' Explanation said that neither "the ABA nor any adopting court is in the position to grant or deny immunity in the context of judicial conduct standards."

d. Would it be proper for a judge to punish a lawyer who filed a disciplinary charge against the judge, such as by denying the lawyer a routine continuance? Look at Rule 2.16(b), which forbids retaliation, "directly or indirectly." This Rule also had no counterpart in the 1990 Model Code.

3. Should judicial discipline proceedings be confidential or open to the public?

a. Some states require that judicial discipline proceedings take place behind closed doors. In Illinois, for example, the state constitution provides that "All proceedings of the [Judicial Inquiry] Board shall be confidential except the filing of a complaint with the Courts Commission." Art. 6, sec. 15(c). Should any proceedings against Judge Kraft be closed to the public? Why or why not?

b. The American Bar Foundation published a study of judicial discipline by William T. Braithwaite that argued in favor of confidentiality:

> "Although it is sometimes necessary (and sometimes unavoidable) that a trial of misconduct charges be public—for example, when the charges have been publicly made and are apparently well founded—there is in most cases nothing to be gained, and respect for the judiciary to be lost, by having a public proceeding. It is reasonable to assume that once the charges and evidence are privately made known to them, most judges who are accused of misconduct serious enough to warrant initiating a proceeding to remove them will prefer to resign or retire. After the charges become public, the judge has less to lose by contesting them to the finish. [Our research found that] in most cases where the sanction imposed is

discipline rather than removal, it is done confidentially (and often informally) rather than publicly.

"The argument for confidentiality is even stronger in the case of disability. We learned * * * that the legal community finds it unacceptable to deal with the problem of disability by means of formal, public, adversary proceedings. * * *

"Maintaining confidentiality, at least in preliminary proceedings, serves several purposes. First, in those cases where termination of service is warranted, it allows the judge to avoid the time, expense, and spectacle of a public trial by resigning or retiring, a convenient and desirable disposition from the agency's point of view also. * * * Publicizing incidents of minor misconduct serves no purpose in most cases, and contrition and cooperation from the judge are more likely if he is not made needlessly to suffer a public recitation of his professional or personal failings.

"Confidentiality also protects judges from groundless accusations. * * * Many complaints come from losing litigants and jailhouse lawyers. A removal-retirement agency may arguably be serving a therapeutic function by providing these people a means to express their dissatisfaction with the court system. It need not also provide a means for them to defame honest judges.

"Finally, confidentiality may also help protect lawyer-complainants. This research found that some lawyers who appear in court frequently, while they are in a good position to know firsthand about disability and some kinds of misconduct, are reluctant to report it because they believe (whether justifiably is not the point) that if they do, their clients' interests will suffer. A practice of keeping complainants' identity confidential can help allay this anxiety, although there will of course be cases where confidentiality is impossible to maintain, such as a case eventuating in a formal hearing at which the complainant must be called as witness.[7]

What do you think? People may file frivolous complaints against judges, but people also file frivolous lawsuits against lawyers and others. Those lawsuits are never kept secret. Is making the hearing public a part of the sanction for judges who deserve discipline?

c. Kamasinski v. Judicial Review Council, 44 F.3d 106 (2d Cir.1994), was a challenge to a Connecticut rule against disclosing the filing of a complaint against a judge. The court found the rule to be a content-based regulation of speech and applied strict scrutiny review. The court concluded that until the Judicial Review Council makes a finding of probable cause the state has a compelling interest in not having judges harassed that justifies keeping confidential both the filing and the fact of testifying before

7. William T. Braithwaite, Who Judges the Judges? 161–65 (1971).

the council. However, once there is a finding of probable cause, no state interest is compelling enough to prohibit public discussion of the case. But see, Doe v. Florida Judicial Qualifications Commission, 748 F.Supp. 1520 (S.D.Fla.1990) (unconstitutional to forbid disclosure of fact complaint filed even if finding of probable cause never issued).

4. Would state's attorney Embers be subject to any different form of discipline if she made her remarks about Judge Kraft to the judge's face or in a letter to the judge?

a. In re Snyder, 472 U.S. 634 (1985), involved a lawyer appointed to handle a case under the Criminal Justice Act. He submitted a claim for fees but that was returned with a request for additional information. Because the lawyer had technical problems with his computer software, he did not provide the information in the form that the chief judge requested. The lawyer did provide a supplemental application, which the secretary to the chief judge also returned. The lawyer then wrote the judge's secretary complaining of the "extreme gymnastics" required of him to get paid "puny amounts," which he said did not even cover overhead. He added that he was "extremely disgusted" by the Eighth Circuit's treatment and asked to be taken off the list of counsel willing to accept appointment. For these "disrespectful remarks," and because he refused to apologize "for what I consider to be telling the truth, albeit in harsh terms," the court suspended the lawyer from practice before federal courts for six months, 734 F.2d 334 (8th Cir.1984).

A unanimous Supreme Court reversed. One intemperate letter does not justify such a sanction, the Court said. The Court did not reach the First Amendment issue but rather relied on its interpretation of Federal Rule of Appellate Procedure 46, which authorizes a court to suspend or disbar an attorney "guilty of conduct unbecoming a member of the bar of the court * * *." The Supreme Court noted that the lawyer's criticisms of the administration of the Criminal Justice Act had merit (a point the Eighth Circuit had conceded) and that such criticism cannot be a cause for discipline or suspension. The Court of Appeals' testy opinion on remand is at 770 F.2d 743 (8th Cir.1985).

b. Williams v. Williams, 721 A.2d 1072 (Pa.1998), involved a lawyer frustrated with a judge's conduct who, after an unfavorable ruling on an objection to a question, said under his breath, "He's such a [f—a—]." The opposing lawyer, always concerned about protecting the court's dignity, repeated the remark in a much louder voice to get it on the record. The Pennsylvania Supreme Court said the remark was ill-mannered but caused no significant disruption in the proceeding and therefore did not rise to the level of criminal contempt.

c. Contrast, Morrissey v. Commonwealth, 428 S.E.2d 503 (Va.App. 1993). A prosecutor sought to protect his assistants against what he considered to be a judge's high-handed conduct. After the judge had refused to approve a plea agreement and had publicly called the prosecutor's office "lazy," the Commonwealth attorney wrote to the judge, saying: "In the future, should you have any criticism of this Office or [one of my assistants], you are directed to set up an appointment with [my deputy] so that you can voice your complaints in a more professional manner. * * * [I]f that behavior ever, ever happens again, I will not be so kind as to merely draft you a letter of indignation." 428 S.E.2d at 504–05.

The Virginia Court of Appeals affirmed the prosecutor's conviction for contempt of court. Even if the letter were not threatening violence but were only threatening to report the judge to the disciplinary commission, the letter was intimidating and thus "calculated to embarrass, hinder or obstruct the court in the administration of justice." Do you agree?

d. In the *Yagman* case, supra, the Court of Appeals expressly allowed the trial judge to hear cases brought by a lawyer who had publicly criticized the judge. However, other courts have sometimes required recusal of the judge in later cases involving lawyers whose criticism has seemed more justified. In United States v. Anderson, 160 F.3d 231 (5th Cir.1998), for example, the court vacated the sentence handed down by a judge against whom defense counsel had testified before the Fifth Circuit Judicial Council. See also, United States v. Avilez–Reyes, 160 F.3d 258 (5th Cir.1998) (same result and same judge). Cf. United States v. Vadner, 160 F.3d 263 (5th Cir.1998) (no recusal required where lawyer had not testified but others in his federal defender office had).

e. In MacDraw, Inc. v. CIT Group Equipment Financing, Inc., 138 F.3d 33 (2d Cir.1998), counsel wrote a letter to the judge asking whether the judge had any dealings with John Huang, an Asian businessman accused of illegal campaign contributions to President Clinton. The lawyers, who were appearing in a bench trial before the judge, were challenging Clinton administration policy in another matter. The judge, a Clinton appointee, was Asian–American, and took the inquiry as a challenge to his integrity based on his race. He revoked the lawyers' *pro hac vice* status and ordered them to show his order to any other judge in the district to whom they might apply for such status. The Second Circuit upheld the order. It said that no one should "charge that a judge is not impartial solely because an attorney is embroiled in a controversy with the administration that appointed the judge" or "because of membership in a particular racial or ethnic group." The attorneys' letter was "discourteous," "insulting," and also "smacked of intimidation," so "Judge Chin was in no way required to tolerate it." Do you agree? Should the Second Circuit's answer be the same if there were any indication that John Huang had something to do with the case before the court?

D. THE JUDGE REWARDING HIS FRIENDS

1. May Judge Kraft testify as a character witness on behalf of his friend?

a. Judges often have friends. Some of those friends are in politics. The politicians may wish to have the judge vouch for them. What is the point of Model Code of Judicial Conduct, Rule 3.3? When Kraft said "it would be better if you would subpoena me," did he satisfy his obligation not to testify "voluntarily"?

b. One state bar committee proposed that what is now Rule 3.3 should read:

> "He should not appear as a character witness unless he appears pursuant to compulsory process of law * * * and unless the judge or other official presiding in the proceeding determines that his testimony is needed to protect the constitutional rights of a party or to provide a fair hearing."[8]

Do you see the reason for the different language? Would such an approach make the subpoena more than a formality? Do you agree with the proposed change? How would you have a court make the determination of which witnesses a "fair hearing" requires?

c. May a judge offer comments in support of a friend's nomination to a public position? In re Honorable Nathan Hecht, 213 S.W.3d 547 (Tex. Spec.Ct.Rev.2006), asked whether it was improper for a Texas Supreme Court justice and close personal friend of Harriet Miers to tell the U.S. Senate Judiciary Committee and several reporters that she would make a wonderful U.S. Supreme Court justice. After Miers' nomination was announced by President Bush, Hecht was apparently asked by Karl Rove to talk to Christian leaders to tell them that he knew Miers to be a born-again Christian and solid conservative. Hecht had known Miers for many years and welcomed the chance to help his friend in this way. Critics charged that Hecht's statements violated the Texas equivalent of ABA Model Code of Judicial Conduct Rule 4.1(A)(3), saying a judge may not "publicly endorse a candidate for public office," and Rule 1.3, providing that a judge shall not lend the prestige of judicial office to advance the private interests of the judge or others.

This special court of review rejected those contentions: "we interpret 'endorsing' under the circumstances of this case to mean more than support, that is, more than spoken praise." The Senate Judiciary Committee said it would have subpoenaed Hecht to testify had Miers not withdrawn her name, the court reasoned, and what Hecht told the reporters and others were things he certainly could have told the committee. Judge McClure, concurring, believed that Hecht's conduct was not consistent with the cited rules; she would simply have declared those rules unconstitutional.

2. Should there be any restrictions on a judge appointing friends to a position that is within the power of the judge to fill, for example, naming a friend as a special master?

a. Look at ABA Model Rules of Professional Conduct, Rule 7.6. What is that Rule trying to regulate? Does it apply to seeking a senator's recommendation for a judgeship? Does Rule 7.6 relate to being appointed to a position that a judge may fill?

---

8. Report and Recommendations of the Joint Illinois State Bar Association–Chicago Bar Association Committee on Rules of Judicial Conduct, Apr. 1974, at 5.

b. Suppose lawyer Mary has contributed substantial amounts to Kraft's campaign because she and Kraft went to high school together and she wanted her old friend to win the election. May Judge Kraft appoint Mary as a special master in a case in which the fee would be substantial? Mary if asked, could truthfully say that she did not contribute any money "for the purpose of obtaining or being considered" for that appointment by Judge Kraft. May Mary accept the appointment from Judge Kraft under Model Rule 7.6 of the ABA Model Rules of Professional Conduct? May Judge Kraft appoint Mary if Mary has contributed more than the amount the state inserts into its version of Rule 2.13(B)?

c. Lawyer Harry has given no money to Judge Kraft's campaign, but he has contributed substantial amounts of time. He distributed leaflets, visited various newspapers and urged the editorial departments to endorse Kraft for election as judge. Now, Judge Kraft would like to appoint Harry to become an associate judge of the court. Does Model Rule 7.6 limit Harry's ability to accept this appointment? Look particularly at Comment 2. Why should the rule distinguish between cash and in-kind contributions to the judge?

PROBLEM 40

THE ACTIVE FEDERAL JUDGE

Judges are people too. Some have a background in litigation and are tempted to involve themselves in a trial, particularly when it appears that one lawyer is not as effective as the other. Even when judges act more like umpires, they may affect what the jury thinks of the case by the way they treat the litigants and their counsel. Judges often have achieved distinction in fields other than law and may want to write books or participate in civic and educational programs. Unfortunately, still others become most visible when others discover their indiscretions. This problem looks first at the issues surrounding how a judge manages the courtroom and judicial proceedings. It then asks what extrajudicial activities are proper for a judge. Third, it tries to give content to the idea that a judge should act honorably. Finally, it looks at special problems enforcing these rules in the case of federal judges, who have lifetime appointments.

FACTS

L.M. Richardson, chief judge of the Federal District Court for the District of Massachusetts, is known behind his back as "Loud Mouth" because of the way he interjects himself into trials. His long experience on the bench has given him what he believes to be an unfailing sense of who is telling the truth. If a witness appears to be lying, Richardson will interrupt to question the witness himself. If a skilled attorney is making an apparently honest witness look bad, Richardson will call a recess.

Judge Richardson can be particularly insensitive in dealing with female lawyers. He typically uses the title "Mr." when addressing male lawyers, while he usually calls female lawyers by their first name. He told one female lawyer who appeared before him: "With a pretty young lady like you in the courtroom, I wonder if the jury will pay any attention to me."

On the other hand, Judge Richardson has had a longtime concern about the homeless. He is an officer of a local organization that runs a homeless shelter, and he has testified before the state legislature that more funds should be appropriated to fund services for the homeless. The organization also tries to raise such funds from local businesses.

Because of his experience and judicial prominence, a Boston-area law school has invited him to teach classes in federal jurisdiction. In class, he tries out new theories he hopes to introduce in upcoming opinions. In substantive fields with which he is less familiar, he plans to ask some of his friends on the faculty to write drafts of opinions in cases he has before him.

Judge Richardson is 65 years of age. Recently he was stopped by local police for traveling 70 miles per hour in a residential zone. He was incoherent and chemical tests showed him to be intoxicated. His companion, a 28 year–old dancer in a local "nude review," attempted to flee when the car was stopped. The story has received front-page newspaper coverage in the Boston area and the dancer has appeared on several television programs to detail her experiences with Judge Richardson. She explained that she met Judge Richardson through a mutual friend at a dinner at the Owl Club, an athletic club to which the Judge belongs. Owl Club membership is open only to white males. The judge and his wife of 42 years have been unavailable for comment.

QUESTIONS

A. A JUDGE'S PERFORMANCE OF OFFICIAL DUTIES

1. How much should Judge Richardson insert himself into a trial?

a. Judge Charles Wyzanski once contended that the judge's role should depend on the nature of the case, with the judge generally passive in tort cases, more active in commercial cases (because he is more likely to have a specialized knowledge) and passive in criminal cases until the point of sentencing.[1] Later, Judge Wyzanski had changed his view. As reported

---

1. Charles Wyzanski, A Trial Judge's Freedom and Responsibility, 65 Harvard L. Rev. 1281, 1283–93 (1952).

by Judge Marvin Frankel, Wyzanski became "confessedly more activist today than [he] was a quarter of a century ago."[2] Frankel himself has admitted:

> "Introspecting, I think I have usually put my penetrating questions to witnesses I thought were lying, exaggerating, or obscuring the facts. Less frequently, I have intruded to rescue a witness from questions that seemed unfairly to put the testimony in a bad light or to confuse its import. * * * [But within] the confines of the adversary framework, the trial judge probably serves best as relatively passive moderator."[3]

b. What limits does Canon 2 of the 2007 ABA Model Code of Judicial Conduct place on the judge's conduct in his courtroom? Does Judge Richardson seem to comply with those requirements? Is the proper level of judicial involvement in a trial something that is very hard to capture in regulatory standards?

c. Matter of Ross, 428 A.2d 858 (Me.1981) (per curiam), showed that a judge's use of abusive language against persons appearing before the court can subject the judge to professional discipline. In one case, the judge told a defendant who, while outside the courtroom, had criticized the fine he had received, that "the fine was no longer $50 but rather $200, and he had a choice to pay his fine or serve it at $5 per day." That fine exceeded the court's authority, and to make his displeasure even clearer, the judge used a vulgar term and added, "Young man, you will remember that the likes of you I chew up and spit out before breakfast, and I never have breakfast until 8:00 o'clock at night." The Maine Supreme Court acknowledged that "[d]ifferences in style and personality do not of themselves suggest misconduct." However, while "[i]ntemperate language is on occasion understandable, * * * vile and abusive language is inexcusable." The court suspended the judge for 90 days.

d. Is it proper for the judge to strongly encourage the parties to settle? For example, what if Judge Richardson said to one of the parties, "I think the other side has made a reasonable offer. If you do not accept it—well, there are a lot of things I can do that no appellate court will ever reverse me on because of the judge's broad discretion." Look at Rule 2.6(B). During discussion of the 2007 Model Rules, some people proposed prohibiting judges from presiding at trial over cases if they had previously conducted unsuccessful settlement negotiations. Several members of the drafting commission agreed that, as a general matter, it was the better practice for judges not to try cases they had attempted to settle, because statements the judge made during settlement negotiations might later be construed as lack of impartiality. Should the Rules have included the prohibition?

2. Are Judge Richardson's sexist remarks a particular cause for concern?

---

2. Marvin Frankel, The Search for Truth: An Umpireal View, 123 U. Pennsylvania L. Rev. 1031, 1045 (1975).

3. 123 U. Pennsylvania L. Rev. at 1043.

a. The ABA Journal reports that several years ago, a 27 year–old female lawyer from a large, prestigious Chicago law firm, appeared before an Illinois Circuit Court Judge for a pretrial conference. The judge said: "I am going to hear the young lady's case first. They say I'm a male chauvinist. I don't think that ladies should be lawyers. I believe that you belong at home raising a family. Ladies do not belong down here. Are you married?" "Yes," she replied. "What does your husband think about you working here?" The lawyer was concerned because she feared judicial reprisal against her client's interests. The judge later said, in defense of his actions: "I don't think I did anything wrong." He said: "I have a way of kidding around but some women take on the status of prima donnas and misconstrue what is being done. She said I should call her counsel, not young lady. It's nonsense. If she were 10 or 12 years older, she'd like to be called young lady."[4]

Should the judge be disciplined for his comments to the lawyer? How should Judge Richardson address attorneys who appear before him? Look especially at Rule 2.3.

b. In Disciplinary Counsel v. Campbell, 623 N.E.2d 24 (Ohio 1993), a judge told one female prosecutor, twice, that her success in cases before him would depend on whether she became his lover! When another female prosecutor said at the start of the day's docket that she was "ready to go," the judge made an overtly sexual response. The Ohio Supreme Court observed that conduct that would be reprehensible in any context is even more so when engaged in by someone with the authority of a judge. The respondent resigned as a judge, and in this case, the court also suspended him from the practice of law for a year.[5]

c. In re Rome, 542 P.2d 676 (Kan.1975), involved a magistrate judge who granted a convicted prostitute two years' probation. The judge wrote his decision in humorous poetic verse. The local newspaper reprinted the decision, and a local group alleged that the judge had held the defendant up to public ridicule. The Kansas Supreme Court upheld a censure of the judge. Pointing to the state version of Rule 2.8(B), the court said a judge must be "dignified and courteous" to litigants. It agreed that judges may write opinions in verse, but in this case, the defendant was portrayed in a "ludicrous or comical situation" and her "integrity as an individual, convicted of a crime though she was, was disregarded." 542 P.2d at 685. A judge, of course, has First Amendment rights, but the court believed the Code of Judicial Conduct properly limits a judge's right to free speech. Do you agree?

d. If a lawyer in Judge Richardson's court refers to a female lawyer as "the little lady," should the judge do anything? Take a look at Rule 2.3(C) and Rule 2.15(B). Should judges have an affirmative duty to see that their staff and lawyers appearing before them do not manifest bias or prejudice

4. See Nancy Blodgett, "I Don't Think That Ladies Should be Lawyers," 72 ABA J. (Dec. 1986), at 48.

5. The court approved his reinstatement as a lawyer in Disciplinary Counsel v. Campbell, 644 N.E.2d 1024 (Ohio 1995).

based on race, sex, religion, national origin, disability, age, sexual orientation or socioeconomic status? See Rules 2.3(B) and 2.12(A).

e. The ABA House of Delegates has recommended that judicial education programs for state and federal judges include "a separate course on the role of the judge in keeping a courtroom free from sex and race bias, and that relevant courses include a discussion of sexual and racial stereotypes that may affect judicial decisions."[6] Do you agree that some judges need education about these issues?

3. May Judge Richardson speak to the press about a newsworthy case?

a. In United States v. Microsoft Corp., 253 F.3d 34 (D.C.Cir.2001), the trial judge had given interviews to the press while the highly publicized case was pending in his court. He was apparently making an historical record, because the interviews were not to be publicly released until after he issued his decision in the case. Would such interviews violate the ABA Model Code of Judicial Conduct? Look at Rule 2.10(A), (C), and (D).

The D.C. Circuit said that the conduct required the judge's disqualification on remand. The court relied on 28 U.S.C. § 455(a) and acknowledged that ordinarily what a judge learns in his judicial capacity cannot be used to force his later recusal. However, it said that in this case the trial judge's—

> "crude characterizations of Microsoft, his frequent denigrations of Bill Gates, his mule trainer analogy as a reason for his remedy—all of these remarks and others might not have given rise to a violation of the Canons or of § 455(a) had he uttered them from the bench. But then Microsoft would have had an opportunity to object, perhaps even to persuade, and the Judge would have made a record for review on appeal. It is an altogether different matter when the statements are made outside the courtroom, in private meetings unknown to the parties, in anticipation that ultimately the Judge's remarks would be reported. Rather than manifesting neutrality and impartiality, the reports of the interviews with the District Judge convey the impression of a judge posturing for posterity, trying to please the reporters with colorful analogies and observations bound to wind up in the stories they write. Members of the public may reasonably question whether the District Judge's desire for press coverage influenced his judgments, indeed whether a publicity-seeking judge might consciously or subconsciously seek the publicity-maximizing outcome. We believe, therefore, that the District Judge's interviews with reporters created an appearance that he was not acting impartially as the Code of Conduct and § 455(a) require." 253 F.3d at 115.

b. Do you agree with the Court of Appeal's analysis? Consider one observer's comments about a hypothetical Judge Loquacious:

---

6. ABA J., Dec. 1986, at 49.

"[If Judge Loqacious] discussed his deliberative processes, or his thought-process, or his evaluation of the evidence with a reporter, those statements are part of the published newspaper interview, but are not part of the record. Should a party be able, on appeal, to argue that the judge's factual assumption was wrong, or the party should have a right to * * * counter the judge's evaluation of the evidence, as reported in the newspaper interview? If so, should the other party be able to show (by cross-examining the judge or the reporter) that the judge never really relied on that thought-process or evaluation to the extent or in the way that the reporter believed? * * * Judge Loquacious will be communicating with reporters, and these reporters, unlike the jurors, will have been exposed to information that is outside the record. The problem is not simply that the judge is talking to reporters; it is that reporters are talking to the judge. If Judge Loquacious engages in conversations with reporters about the pending case, the very nature of a 'conversation' is that there is give and take. The judge will not only be communicating information to the reporters, they will be communicating information to him. A conversation is a dialogue, a spoken exchange."[7]

c.   May a judge comment publicly about a case over which he or she has not presided? In re Inquiry of Broadbelt, 683 A.2d 543 (N.J.1996), cert. denied, 520 U.S. 1118 (1997), reviewed the acts of a municipal court judge in appearing as an uncompensated guest commentator on Court TV and CNBC to discuss the murder prosecution of former football star O.J. Simpson. The New Jersey Supreme Court found that the judge's conduct violated what is now Rule 2.10(A) of the ABA Model Code of Judicial Conduct even though the case could not possibly ever come before him. "We find the Canon to be clear and unambiguous: a judge should not comment on pending cases in any court." In particular, his appearance on " 'Geraldo Live' was inappropriate and had the potential to compromise the integrity of the judiciary in New Jersey." 683 A.2d at 548. In addition, the court said, the conduct violated what is now Rule 1.3 in that the regular appearances caused the judge to become identified with the programs and used the prestige of his judicial office to further the interests of the television producers. The fact that his appearances were educational and consistent with what is now Canon 3 of the 2007 ABA Model Code of Judicial Conduct did not, in the court's view, excuse the violations. Do you agree with the court's analysis?

d.   If a newspaper criticizes a judge for his actions in a judicial proceeding, may the judge respond directly to the newspaper? Note that Rule 2.10(E) & Comment 3 authorize a judge to respond, either directly or through a third party. This Rule had no counterpart in the 1990 Model Code. Should a judge take advantage of this newly created freedom to strike back?

7.   Ronald D. Rotunda, Judicial Comments on Pending Cases: The Ethical Restrictions and the Sanctions—A Case Study of the Microsoft Litigation, 2001 U. Illinois L. Rev. 611, 612 (2001).

B.   A JUDGE'S PARTICIPATION IN NON-JUDICIAL ACTIVITIES

1.   Is it proper for Judge Richardson to be an officer of a civic organization that serves the homeless in his community?

a.   In what kinds of nonjudicial groups may a judge participate? Is the organization "concerned with the law, the legal system, or the administration of justice," within the meaning of Rule 3.7(A)?[8] Is it a "civic organization" not conducted for profit? If it is not an organization described in Rule 3.7, may the judge still remain a member?

b.   Should it be important whether the organization is frequently involved in litigation that may come before the federal district court? Look at Rule 3.7(A)(6). If it does file such litigation, must Judge Richardson withdraw from membership in the organization? If so, does that mean that no judge may be a member of the ACLU, because it is frequently involved in litigation? May the judge be an officer of the NAACP if a separate organization (the NAACP Legal Defense Fund) is the party in litigation?

c.   May the judge hear a case filed by an organization of which the judge is a member? Remember Rule 2.11(A)(1).

d.   If the governor appoints Judge Richardson to a new commission to examine problems of the homeless, may the judge accept that appointment? Look at Rule 3.4. Is there any way to read that Rule to permit Judge Richardson to serve? Does it make sense that such commissions should not have judicial participation?

e.   May the governor appoint the judge a trustee of State Law School? Does the answer change if the governor appoints the judge a trustee of State Medical School or State University? Do such distinctions make any sense to you?

2.   May Judge Richardson seek to raise money to help the homeless?

a.   May he testify before a public body about the need for more public funds to provide homeless shelters around the state? Look at Rule 3.2. Are you persuaded by Rule 3.1, Comment 4? Would Judge Richardson be put in an awkward position if someone asked him whether homeless persons have a legal right to shelter? Would legislators be put in an awkward position if Judge Richardson often rules on the constitutionality of state legislation? May Judge Richardson testify in favor of proposed laws that he believes will help the homeless? Is there any reason to treat such testimony as less problematic?

b.   May a judge, either alone or with others, ask local businesses to donate money to help the homeless? Look at Rule 3.7(A)(2) and Comments 2 & 3. ABA Formal Opinion 08–452 (Oct. 17, 2008) examined whether judges may participate in fundraising for specialized "problem-solving

---

8.   1990 Model Code, Canon 4C(3), referred to an organization that was devoted to an "improvement of the law," but the 2007 Model Code changes that language because "because what constitutes an 'improvement' is almost always debatable." Reporters' Explanation of Changes in the 2007 Judicial Code.

courts" such as those dealing with drug abuse, mental health issues, and domestic violence. The opinion recognized that the courts are "concerned with the law, the legal system or the administration of justice" but it acknowledged that it is awkward to have judges solicit lawyers for funds. It is fine for judges to advocate and work for the creation of such courts, the opinion says, but their activities must be limited to those permitted by Model Code of Judicial Conduct, Rule 3.7(A).

c.   May the judge encourage the lawyers who appear before him to represent the homeless in pro bono litigation? See Rule 3.7(B) & Comment 5.

3.   May Judge Richardson work as a part-time law professor?

a.   Is there any problem with the propriety of part-time law teaching? Look at Rule 3.1 & Comment 1,[9] which "encourage[s]" judges to "engage in educational, religious, charitable, fraternal or civic extrajudicial activities not conducted for profit, even when the activities do not involve the law."

b.   Rule 3.10, on the other hand, provides that (subject to a few exceptions) a "judge shall not practice law." Why distinguish between the two activities?

c.   Should a judge be obliged not to take positions in class on unsettled questions of law? Look at Rule 3.1. Could opinions expressed in class be a basis for disqualifying the judge in later cases? Would you as an advocate before the judge believe you should know the opinions he or she has expressed?

d.   May the judge write articles on issues that may come before him? Is it better or worse to encourage students to write the articles? Is the degree of intellectual independence of the law review editors relevant to your answer? Could an ethical rule be made to turn on something that variable?[10]

9. The 2007 Model Code removed 1990 Model Code, Canon 4B. The Reporters' Explanation of changes, said: "Specific examples in the 1990 Code, both in black letter (avocational activities such as speaking and writing) and in the Commentary, * * * were removed as unnecessarily restrictive or of insufficiently general application." Reporters' Explanation, at Rule 3.1, Explanation of Comments.

10. Cf. Bruce Alan Murphy, The Brandeis/Frankfurter Connection: The Secret Political Activities of Two Supreme Court Justices (1982), documenting how Frankfurter and Brandeis "found it impossible to curb their political zeal after their appointment to the bench." While Frankfurter was a law professor, Justice Brandeis enlisted him "as his paid political lobbyist and lieutenant." They "placed a network of disciples in positions of influence and labored diligently for the enactment of their desired programs." The "adroit use of the politically skillful

Frankfurter as an intermediary enabled Brandeis to keep his considerable political endeavors hidden from the public." Frankfurter became the clearinghouse through which the justice's ideas were passed on to a variety of liberal publications, particularly the *New Republic*. "Frankfurter was instructed by Brandeis to propose those ideas that he liked under his own name at future meetings of *The New Republic*'s board of editors." Thus "Brandeis began to prepare the climate of public opinion for his reform programs [by educating] the editorial board on his views so that the whole slant of the journal would favor his philosophy." Brandeis' letters to Frankfurter were redrafted and published in *The New Republic* as unsigned articles and covered such issues as the 1924 Immigration Act, the McNary–Haugen bill on agriculture surplus, and Coolidge's silence on Teapot Dome. Id. at 9–10, 89–91.

4. What do you think of Judge Richardson's plan to ask outside experts to write drafts of his opinions?

a. Look at Rule 2.9(A)(2) & Comment 3. Are you surprised that a judge may ask an expert on an area of law to suggest how cases should be decided? Does permitting such a practice make sense to you? Is such a practice different from having law clerks write the opinions? See Rule 2.9(A)(3) & Comment 5. Does the fact that the judge is required to disclose which expert was consulted and what he or she said enough to make the advice little more than an amicus curiae brief?

b. In Matter of Fuchsberg, 426 N.Y.S.2d 639 (Ct.Jud.1978), the evidence showed that a judge of the New York Court of Appeals had consulted with law professors in at least 12 cases. In some, telephone conversations were held about developments in particular areas of the law. In others, the judge sent the briefs to a professor and asked for a draft opinion, substantial portions of which he used in his own opinion. In at least one case the judge sent a draft opinion from another judge to a professor for comments. Do any of these acts violate Rule 2.9(A)(2),(3)? Do they violate Rule 1.2 and Rule 2.4(C) as well? Is it revealing that neither the judge nor any of the professors said that they knew the content of these Rules? The court's opinion concludes that his behavior "properly subjects [Judge Fuchsberg] to censure and disapproval" but not to removal from office.

c. Edgar v. K.L., 93 F.3d 256 (7th Cir.), cert. denied sub nom. Duff v. Governor of Illinois, 519 U.S. 1111 (1997), was a challenge to the constitutionality of the Illinois mental health system. The trial judge, Brian Duff, had appointed a panel of three experts to investigate the system. The judge and parties had authorized the experts to conduct interviews out of the presence of counsel to get more reliable answers, but then the judge unilaterally decided to meet ex parte with the experts. These meetings became lengthy and substantive, and the judge claimed a "judicial privilege" prevented the parties from learning their substance. The Seventh Circuit put an end to the trial judge's approach. ABA Rule 2.9 of the Model Rules of Judicial Conduct prohibits a judge from initiating or considering ex parte information, the court said, and 28 U.S.C. § 455(b) requires disqualification if the judge has "personal knowledge of disputed evidentiary facts." Judge Duff violated both provisions, so the court issued a writ of mandamus removing him from the case.

C. A JUDGE'S OBLIGATION TO ENGAGE IN PROPER OFF-BENCH BEHAVIOR

1. Is it proper for Judge Richardson to belong to a private club that only admits white males to membership?

a. Look at Rule 3.6 and the accompanying Comments. Do you agree that parties are likely to be concerned about the clubs to which a judge belongs? There is presently nothing in the Model Rules or Model Code that restricts *lawyers* from joining clubs which exclude persons from membership because of race, religion, or sex. Should judges be subject to different standards?

b. If the judge is a member of a discriminatory organization, the judge must resign immediately. Rule 3.6, Comment 3. Previously, the Canons gave the judge up to one year before the forced resignation. 1990 Model Code, Canon 2C, Commentary 3. If a friend invites the judge and his family to a wedding reception at the discriminatory club, may the judge attend? Rule 3.6(B).

c. In August 1990, the U.S. Senate Judiciary Committee passed a nonbinding resolution declaring that it is "inappropriate" for nominees to the federal bench or to posts in the Justice Department to belong to clubs that discriminate on the basis of race, color, religion, sex, disability, or national origin. The resolution provided that senators should consider such continued membership "an important factor" in evaluating nominees, but nominees are excused from this requirement if they "are actively engaged in bona fide efforts to eliminate the discriminatory practices" in the clubs to which they belong. The resolution also states: "So as to promote a consistent policy on this issue, any Senator belonging to such a club should resign." Do you think this resolution appropriately deals with the relevant issues? Does it create a standard that is more than window dressing?

2. Should Judge Richardson's arrest for drunk driving and the fact a young dancer was in the car at the time be considered bases for judicial discipline?

a. What operational content should be given to Model Code of Judicial Conduct Rules 1.1 and 1.2? Other than providing that judges should obey the law (Rule 1.1) are the provisions too vague to be enforced? Are they more than sanctimonious hyperbole?

b. Judges, obviously, should obey the law. But should judges be disciplined for every violation of law (e.g., parking tickets) or only some laws? Is there any basis for believing Judge Richardson's effectiveness as a federal judge will be impaired by one incident of drunk driving? Is the answer different if Judge Richardson were an alcoholic?

c. Would the case be different if the judge sought to avoid the ticket by showing the officer his judicial identification card? See Rule 1.3 & Comment 1.

d. Is Judge Richardson's affair with the young woman who was in his car a personal matter or a professional offense? Is a judge's open and notorious adulterous relationship a basis for disciplinary action? In Matter of Dalessandro, 397 A.2d 743 (Pa.1979), the Pennsylvania Supreme Court said no disciplinary action could be taken. Rules 1.1 & 1.2, the court said, "are concerned with the conduct of a judge in his official capacity and not with his conduct in his private life. * * * Conduct of a judge * * * which may be offensive to the personal sensibilities of a segment of the society is properly judged in the privacy of the ballot box." 397 A.2d at 757. One dissenter maintained, however, that "to read these rules of conduct as restricted to activities while a judge is clothed in a robe * * * is pure sophistry."

With which of these positions do you agree? Should it matter that Judge Richardson does not have to face the voters and the discipline of the ballot box? Do the Comments following Rule 1.2 support the view of the majority or the dissent?[11]

e. Should someone like Judge Richardson try to avoid the public eye? A clothing store in the small town where a trial judge lived had a wall on which hung pictures of famous local citizens who wore neckties sold at the store. The judge agreed to have his picture hung on the wall of the store as well, and for doing so, the store gave him a free necktie. Citing what are now Rules 1.3 and 2.4(C), Ohio Supreme Court Opinion 87–42 (1987) held that it is unseemly for a judge to further a private business in this way. Do you agree? Presumably, now the judge either will pay for his neckties or wear open-neck shirts under his robe.

D.   SPECIAL ISSUES INVOLVING FEDERAL JUDGES

1.   What methods exist by which to sanction or discipline a federal judge?

a. As the cases cited in this chapter reveal, states have various processes to remove their judges. In addition to impeachment and removal by the state legislature, in many states a judicial conduct commission can hear complaints against judges and provide for suitable discipline, ranging from private censure to suspension to removal from office.

b. It is much harder to discipline a federal judge who has a constitutional guarantee of life tenure and salary protection. Could Congress constitutionally create a panel of federal judges to impose discipline on other federal judges? Should a constitutional amendment be adopted to provide for a fixed term of office for federal judges? Periodic reconfirmation by the Senate?

c. An ABA committee to study professional discipline of federal judges concluded:

> "The federal judicial system should have an appropriate structure for the discipline of federal judges. This can be accomplished through: (1) limited inherent power of the United States Supreme Court; (2) a constitutional amendment; or (3) a congressional act.

> "With regard to the first alternative, the United States Supreme Court does not have any constitutional authority to remove a judge from office but it may by administrative order provide procedures for the investigation and the discipline by reprimand and declination to assign cases. This authority is derived from the court's inherent power. The United States Supreme Court also after investigation and due process may recommend impeachment of a judge to the Congress of the United States. It is, however,

11. The Pennsylvania Supreme Court later modified its earlier position. In Matter of Larsen, 616 A.2d 529, 582 (Pa.1992), the court said: "We reject the implication in [*Dalessandro*] that matters in one's personal life which legitimately reflect upon the jurists' professional integrity are immune from censure."

doubtful the court would ever take this action. The view that the United States Supreme Court has the inherent power to discipline the federal judiciary is not widely accepted * * *. Justices Douglas and Black, in a dissent, reflected what may well be a majority opinion of the United States Supreme Court when they stated:

> "An independent judiciary is one of this nation's outstanding characteristics. Once a federal judge is confirmed by the Senate and takes his oath, he is independent of every other judge. He commonly works with other federal judges who are likewise sovereign. But neither one alone nor any number banded together can act as censor and place sanctions on him. Under the Constitution the only leverage that can be asserted against him is impeachment * * *.

> 'It is time that an end be put to these efforts of federal judges to ride herd on other federal judges. This is a form of "hazing" having no place under the Constitution. Federal judges are entitled, like other people, to the full freedom of the First Amendment. If they break a law, they can be prosecuted. If they become corrupt or sit in cases in which they have a personal or family stake, they can be impeached by Congress. But I search the Constitution in vain for any power of surveillance that other federal judges have over those aberrations * * *. Chandler v. Judicial Council of Tenth Circuit of the United States (Douglas dissenting), 398 U.S. 74, 136–37, 140 (1970), rehearing denied 399 U.S. 937.'[12]

"The court, however, has stated in a matter involving the discipline of an attorney:

> '[T]he courts ought not to hesitate * * * to protect themselves from scandal and contempt and the public from prejudice, by removing grossly improper persons from participation in the administration of the law. Ex Parte Wall, 107 U.S. (17 Otto) 265 (1883).'

"Some writers have gone further and stated that the United States Supreme Court, as part of its implied and inherent powers, has the right to discipline as well as remove federal judges. * * *

ABA Standards Relating to Judicial Discipline and Disability Retirement, Part 10 (1977).

    d. Congress has enacted a law creating the Judicial Council of each circuit as the body to hear complaints against federal judges. See 28

---

12. Ed. Note: In *Chandler* the Tenth Circuit Judicial Council refused to assign any cases to a federal judge because of its belief that Judge Chandler was "unable, or unwilling, to discharge his duties efficiently" and the Supreme Court, for procedural reasons, did not reverse the Tenth Circuit order.

U.S.C.A. § 372.[13] And although Federal judges are not subject to the ABA Model Code of Judicial Conduct, in March 2009, the Judicial Conference of the United States adopted a new Code of Conduct for Federal Judges. The new federal code borrows many concepts from the ABA Model Code of Judicial Conduct (2007), but rather than adopting the detailed rule-based approach of the ABA Code, the drafters chose to retain the canon-based approach of the 1972 and 1990 ABA codes of judicial conduct.[14]

e. New substantive issues are few in the 2009 Code of Conduct for Federal Judges, but one of the most interesting is the attempt to define "appearance of impropriety" in Canon 2A: "An appearance of impropriety occurs when reasonable minds, with knowledge of all the relevant circumstances disclosed by a reasonable inquiry, would conclude that the judge's honesty, integrity, impartiality, temperament, or fitness to serve as a judge is impaired."

2. What kinds of circumstances make discipline of a federal judge appropriate?

a. *Gardiner v. A.H. Robins Co., Inc.,* 747 F.2d 1180 (8th Cir.1984), involved an effort to control the allegedly intemperate statements of a federal judge. Judge Miles Lord of Minnesota, in approving a settlement of some tort actions arising out of the use of the Dalkon Shield, had read a "speech" to officers of the defendant condemning them for violating "every ethical precept to which every doctor under your supervision must pledge." Later, he read to the defendants from a speech he had written about sin and accused them of conduct for which they should "confess" and "beg forgiveness." The Eighth Circuit struck the prejudicial statements from the record, but imposed no formal discipline. Shortly thereafter, Judge Lord retired. Do you think this conduct merited discipline? Was the Eighth Circuit's approach probably a discrete and humane way to end the matter?

b. In October of 1986, Federal District Judge Harry Claiborne of Nevada became the first judge in approximately a half century to be impeached by the House and removed by the Senate after he was convicted in federal court of income tax evasion. Since then, Congress has impeached several other judges, including Judge Walter Nixon, who was convicted of perjury but refused to resign and sought review of the manner of his impeachment in the Supreme Court. *Nixon v. United States,* 506 U.S. 224 (1993) (conducting impeachment trial before a committee of senators is a matter for the Senate and not subject to judicial review).

---

13. In addition, in September 2006, the Judicial Conference of the United States adopted two new provisions governing federal judges. The first requires use of conflict checking software to identify cases in which the judge may have disqualifying personal interest. The second requires many nongovernmental providers of educational programs attended by federal judges to register with the Administrative Office of U.S. Courts and reveal sources of their funding. This latter rule had been sought by critics of law-and-economics programs for federal judges. See www.uscourts.gov/Press_Releases/judicial conference091906.html.

14. See http://www.uscourts.gov/li brary/codeOfConduct/Revised_Code_Effec tive_July-01-09.pdf.

c. Hastings v. Judicial Conference of the United States, 829 F.2d 91 (D.C.Cir.1987), upheld the constitutionality of the federal judicial discipline system in the context of the Judicial Council of the Eleventh Circuit's investigation of Judge Alcee Hastings of Florida.[15] The Council investigated allegations of several violations of the Code of Judicial Conduct, including a charge that Judge Hastings conspired to obtain a bribe. The court upheld the propriety of referring the Hastings matter to the House of Representatives for possible impeachment even though a jury had acquitted Hastings of accepting the alleged bribe. Judge Hastings claimed that the charges levied against him were false and racially motivated, but the House voted to impeach and the Senate voted to remove him from office. In October 1989, Hastings became the first judge impeached and removed from office on the basis of charges for which he had earlier been acquitted. In November 1992, he was elected a member of the House of Representatives that had impeached him.

d. McBryde v. Committee to Review Circuit Council Conduct, 264 F.3d 52 (D.C.Cir.2001), involved conduct having some of the elements of this problem. The Fifth Circuit Judicial Council reprimanded Judge McBryde and barred him from hearing cases involving lawyers who had complained of his "pattern of abusive behavior" toward lawyers who appeared before him. In one case, for example, a lawyer had failed to bring one of the parties to a court-ordered mediation in violation of the court's rules. Judge McBryde required the lawyer to attend a reading comprehension course. When she did so, he then required her to list each day that she attended and the name of every person who could verify her attendance. Judge McBryde challenged the authority of anyone to criticize the exercise of what he considered to be his right to run his court as he pleased. The D.C. Circuit rejected that challenge. Quoting the *Chandler* case cited above, the court said: "There can, of course, be no disagreement among us as to the imperative need for total and absolute independence of judges in deciding cases or in any phase of the decisional function. But it is quite another matter to say that each judge in a complex system shall be the absolute ruler of his manner of conducting judicial business."[16]

e. If you were Judge Richardson in this problem, would you conclude that—even as a federal judge—you had better change some of your ways?

15. Matter of Certain Complaints Under Investigation, 783 F.2d 1488 (11th Cir. 1986).

16. Discipline of federal judges is exhaustively addressed in a Sept. 2006 report of a committee chaired by Justice Breyer, Implementation of the Judicial Conduct and Disability Act of 1980, found at www.supremecourt.gov/publicinfo/breyercommittee report.pdf. The Committee and its staff examined almost 600 charges against federal judges over the last quarter-century and found the handling of only 25 raised any issues about proper disposition.

INDEX

References are to pages.

†